AMERICAN
CONSERVATISM

An Encyclopedia

AMERICAN CONSERVATISM

An Encyclopedia

EDITED BY

Bruce Frohnen, Jeremy Beer,
and Jeffrey O. Nelson

ISI BOOKS
WILMINGTON, DELAWARE
2006

Copyright © 2006 ISI Books

Cataloging-in-Publication Data

American conservatism : an encyclopedia / edited by Bruce P.
Frohnen, Jeremy Beer, and Jeffrey O. Nelson. — 1st ed. —
Wilmington, Del. : ISI Books, 2006.

    p. ; cm.
    ISBN-13: 978-1-932236-43-9
    978-1-932236-44-6 (pbk.)
    ISBN-10: 1-932236-43-0
    1-932236-44-9 (pbk.)
    Includes bibliographical references and indexes.

    1. Conservatism—United States—Encyclopedias. 2. United
States—Politics and government—1945-1989—Encyclopedias.
3. United States—Politics and government—1989- — Encyclopedias.
I. Frohnen, Bruce P. II. Beer, Jeremy. III. Nelson, Jeffrey O.

E743 .A44 2006   2005921373
320.52/0973/0904—dc22   0206

Published in the United States by:
ISI Books
Post Office Box 4431
Wilmington, DE 19807-0431

Interior design by Sam Torode
Manufactured in the United States

CONTENTS

ACKNOWLEDGMENTS

No encyclopedia of the size and scope of this one is the work of even a dozen people, let alone three. Since taking over this project in 2000, the editors—all at work at their full-time jobs and on numerous other side projects—have been necessarily and ably assisted by numerous interns, editorial assistants, designers, proofreaders, and others, not to mention the 250-plus contributors to the volume, many of whom gladly took on multiple entries in exchange for little or no pay.

We must first thank Gregory Wolfe for getting this volume up and running in the early 1990s and for continuing to assist in its completion after it was formally handed off to ISI. Indeed, this volume is no exception to the rule that everything has its history. Greg conceived of this work and was initially commissioned by Garland Publishers to edit an "encyclopedia of the American Right," which was to be an explicit companion to the instructive and professionally compiled *Encyclopedia of the American Left* (1990, rev. ed. 1992). The scope of the project, however, proved overwhelming for one individual with no institutional support, and so Greg asked Jeff Nelson if he and ISI would be willing to take the project over. Believing ISI was the perfect home for such a work—and encouraged to undertake it by ISI's president, T. Kenneth Cribb Jr., senior vice president H. Spencer Masloff, and ISI's late executive vice president, John F. Lulves Jr.—the editors began working on it in earnest at the turn of the new millennium. Needless to say, every entry already penned had to be revisited and most of them revised. In addition, the new editors undertook to adjust the conception of the project from an encyclopedia of the American Right to a reference work on "American conservatism." At least two-thirds of the entries in the present volume were added, some previous ones deleted, and after much hard work the encyclopedia took its present form.

Besides Greg, perhaps no one worked harder on the myriad day-to-day tasks associated with pulling such a large project together than did Anne Krulikowski, who worked on the project at ISI from 2001 to 2003. Our colleagues Mark Henrie and John Zmirak took on difficult writing assignments and provided wise counsel on the shape of the volume, while various others—including interns Laura Barrosse-Antle and Alexandria Chiasson, former ISI Books managing editor Xandy Gilman, June Weaver, and Megan Muncy—also played key roles in bringing this encyclopedia to fruition. Sam Torode, with help from John Vella, provided the book with its elegant layout and photo illustrations, and Jennifer Connolly helped shepherd this volume through the printing process. We also thank the distinguished members of our editorial advisory board for their advice on entries, balance, and other matters.

For their crucial financial support of this volume, we thank Earhart Foundation and the Historical Research Foundation. Finally, we are grateful to all of the contributors for their good work and especially their patience—a virtue sorely tried at times, we know. James Person, Rob Waters, Max Schulz, and the late John Attarian deserve special thanks for diving in time and time again to the sizeable pool of work that lay before us back in 2001. This encyclopedia certainly would never have appeared without their efforts.

This volume is dedicated to Henry Regnery, ISI's longest serving chairman; E. Victor Milione, ISI's longest serving president; Charles H. Hoeflich, founding trustee and ISI's longest serving treasurer, and John F. Lulves Jr., ISI's longest serving executive vice president: stewards of the Word, custodians of our heritage, and teachers who have shaped the lives of thousands of students in the knowledge and hope that each generation is a new people.

EDITORS' INTRODUCTION

SINCE it emerged in the years following World War II, conservatism in America has been declared intellectually and politically victorious— and dead—many times over. As a new, self-conscious intellectual movement, postwar conservatism was launched through the publication of groundbreaking books, including Friedrich Hayek's *Road to Serfdom* (1944), Richard Weaver's *Ideas Have Consequences* (1948), and Russell Kirk's *Conservative Mind* (1953); the establishment of new, opinion-shaping periodicals, such as *Human Events* (1944) and William F. Buckley Jr.'s *National Review* (1955); and the formation of organizations such as the Foundation for Economic Education (1946) and the Young Americans for Freedom (1960). Nevertheless, conservatism in America still has been defined, for many, by its political rather than its intellectual fortunes: Barry Goldwater's dramatically unsuccessful 1964 presidential bid and Ronald Reagan's equally dramatic but successful 1980 run for the presidency are usually portrayed as defining moments for American conservatism, with the first ironically paving the way for the second. Since the election of Reagan, the political ups and downs of the conservative movement in America have continued: the so-called "Republican Revolution" of 1994, for example, has left in its wake an ambiguous legacy, including the impeachment of a Democratic president, growing deficits, a war fought overseas in the name of democracy, and a splintering of the conservative movement.

Conservatism's mixed political fortunes, along with the often acrimonious debates that have persisted among the critics of postwar American society, including neoconservatives, paleoconservatives, traditionalists, libertarians, and those who simply call themselves "conservatives," reveal a continuing crisis of identity among Americans on the political right. One reason for this crisis may be a lack of historical knowledge and perspective. Unfortunately, the most interesting intellectual debates in the last fifty years have arguably taken place not between conservatives and liberals but between adherents of different positions within the conservative camp. George Nash's *Conservative Intellectual Movement in America since 1945* (revised ed., 1996) provides a masterful narrative history of conservatism, but there has as yet been no comprehensive treatment of the different elements of conservatism in all their conflicting and complementary variety. As Pepperdine University political theorist Ted V. McAlister has poinetd out, "The historiography of American conservatism . . . remains immature. For decades, the academic historical establishment largely ignored American conservatives or dealt with them as a sort of fringe group. Only after the surprising and enduring appeal of Ronald Reagan did most historians begin to take serious scholarly notice of self-proclaimed conservatives. Slowly, the historical literature is growing richer. But for now, the story of conservatism in America, as told by the academics, is fractured and inconclusive." This volume is intended to contribute to the ongoing effort to understand what it has meant—and still means—to be a conservative in America.

THE editors do not see in the history of conservatism the inevitable development of an increasingly powerful and coherent ideology of any kind, nor do they believe in the inevitable triumph of any particular set of policy positions. This eschewal of ideological clarity may leave some readers of this encyclopedia dissatisfied. Indeed, the reader will not get very far in this volume before beginning to notice the tensions and outright contradictions that exist and have ever existed among conservatives—on matters of principle no less than on matters of policy. If it has been marked by anything, conservatism in America has clearly been marked by diversity. How is it, then, that such a range of views came to be associated with a single social-political philosophy?

The full answer to that question is complex. It is true, as has been often stated, that from 1945 to 1991 conservatism, as a political movement, was held together primarily by the glue of anticommunism. But then there also were many staunch liberal anticommunists (e.g., Lionel Trilling) and even some staunch radical anticommunists (e.g., George Orwell). Furthermore, there were even anti-anticommunists among conservatives and their fellow travelers (e.g., John Lukacs). So, while anticommunism provided a center of gravity for the conservative intellectual movement, there must be more to the story.

The realities of coalition politics in a vast, diverse country like the United States provide part of the answer. For with the effort to elect Barry Goldwater, American postwar conservatism became a political movement as much as a political philosophy. And practical political movements are founded on compromise. Of course, such compromises are susceptible to explanation. Thus Frank Meyer's well known "fusionism" served for decades as a kind of justification for conservatism as a political coalition. Through "fusionism," Meyer and those who followed him argued that the great goals of life are freedom and virtue, and that in order for virtue, the special concern of traditionalists, to be authentic, it must be attained in a context of maximal individual freedom, the special concern of libertarians. In turn, argued Meyer, freedom may only claim our moral allegiance insofar as its ultimate purpose is to allow men and women to attain virtue. Thought of in this way, libertarians and traditionalists could be understood to pursue much the same practical ends for human beings.

This fusionist philosophy has in fact played a large role in uniting conservatives at the level of public policy debate and practice. Rapidly embraced by *National Review* and other movement-shaping organs, fusionism is today the implicit background philosophy of most conservative institutions, politicians, journalists, and activists. And why not? As an inclusive doctrine it has inestimable practical advantages. But at the level of theory fusionism has always remained controversial. Indeed, with the exception of the nuanced treatment it has received at the hands of M. Stanton Evans, it has remained largely unelaborated. Traditionalists, for their part, argue that it is a *tradition* of *ordered* liberty that they defend, and not just virtue, which often flourishes under the worst, most brutal and unfree circumstances; saints may be found in concentration camps, even as good people may be led astray by libertines. Then, too, there is the problem that thoroughgoing libertarians have often remained agnostic as to whether the end of freedom is really virtue, as Meyer claimed; for former *Reason* editor Virginia Postrel, for example, freedom is an end in itself, and if individuals decide to use it to attain virtue, that is their business.

Thus, while Meyer's fusionism may be largely responsible for providing a practical foundation for the conservative political coalition, it has not succeeded in providing a unifying theoretical basis for the conservative intellectual movement. Does, then, such a basis exist?

Perhaps the suggestive analysis of sociologist Philip Rieff offers one possible approach to this question of what might unite conservatives at the level of theory. In Rieff's typology of the succession of ideal character types in the history of the West, the political man of the Greeks was replaced by the religious man of the Hebrews and Christians and finally by the short-lived, transitional character of the economic man of the Enlightenment. Economic man was short-lived because a new type, psychological man, displaced him near the beginning of the twentieth century. And, as Rieff argues, this new man was quite different from the preceding three, in that he no longer recognized the existence of a hierarchy of impulses in man's nature. In other words, psychological man is similar to the "mass man" whose advent Ortega described and conservatives of all stripes have feared. Accepting no hierarchy "imposed" from a source outside the sovereign self, mass man is too easily manipulated by the state—with its twin promises of security and freedom—into detaching himself from those mediating institutions which not only present obstacles to the state's consolidation of power, but also provide the self with its ethical education. The abstractions of ideology fuel the engine of this manipulation by bringing the atomized individual into conformance with the needs of the new therapeutic social and political order.

Although they do not typically think of the matter in this way, it could be argued that different sorts of conservatives have held, and continue to hold, different beliefs as to which of the character types described by Rieff represents a superior human ideal. For many of the followers of Leo Strauss and some neoconservatives, it is political man; for most traditional Jews and Christians, it is religious man; for libertarians and other neoconservatives, economic man represents an authentic characterological advance. Probably most theorists regarded as essentially conservative would regard a hybrid of two or three of these types as the best option of all (leave aside for now whether such a hybrid is really possible). But if Rieff is correct that psychological or mass man became the characteristic American type in the twentieth century, opposition to his elevation as the human ideal—and the concomitant rejection of any notion of an ethical or moral hierarchy in human desire and action—may be the most important thing that has united American conservatives.

Indeed, it might be said that conservatives of all stripes have regarded acquiescence in the advent of mass man to form the core of what they have opposed and often labeled as "liberalism." Their common opposition to the enthronement of mass man and all that his ascension entails provides, perhaps, enough shared philosophical ground that the postwar conservative intellectual movement has not been *simply* a convenient political arrangement.

Whether this shared revolt against the masses is sufficient to maintain conservatism's viability as a movement remains open to question. New, fundamental questions about man and society must now engage the conservative imagination, including Islamic terrorism, the economic and political rise of China, the advancing frontier of biotechnology, the emergence of transnational bureaucracies and the corresponding deemphasis of nation-states, the ongoing erosion of our constitutional order, challenges to the traditional understanding of marriage and family, increasing ecological concerns, and the deterioration of

American community life. In other words, history is living—but so is the conservative tradition. We hope that in the face of these challenges, this encyclopedia will serve as a touchstone for those seeking resources in conservatism's American past.

American Conservatism: An Encyclopedia seeks not to establish any orthodox definition of conservatism but rather to offer information and insight on the persons, schools, concepts, organizations, events, publications, and other topics of major importance to the nature and development of the conservative intellectual movement in America since World War II. Its 626 entries—ranging, in the main, from 250 to 2,500 words in length—cover social issues from abortion to welfare, thinkers from Lord Acton to Donald Atwell Zoll, politicians from John Adams to John Witherspoon, magazines from the *American Mercury* to the *Weekly Standard*, books from *The Conscience of a Conservative* to *Witness*, historical events from the American Revolution to the Vietnam War, social-political philosophies from agrarianism to totalitarianism, concepts from academic freedom to tradition, organizations from the America First Committee to the Young Americans for Freedom—and much else. The most comprehensive encyclopedia of American conservatism yet compiled, it is the editors' hope and belief that the volume will be of value to all students, journalists, academics, and lay readers interested in what has probably been the most important intellectual movement of the last fifty years.

The criterion for an entry's inclusion in this encyclopedia was deceptively simple: the topic under consideration must have been of substantial importance to the shaping of postwar American conservatism considered primarily in its *intellectual* (rather than simply its political or social) aspect. This means that there is (a) a prejudice against conservative politicians and pundits who have not clearly had a deep and lasting influence on conservatism, (b) a prejudice against foreign figures, unless they had a major impact on postwar American conservative thought (the only non-American politician included here, besides Edmund Burke, is Margaret Thatcher), and (c) a pronounced bias towards the years since 1945. Publications, persons, and events prior to 1945 were included only if they had a significant bearing on conservatism in America since the end of World War II. Furthermore, in order to limit the scope of the project, the editors decided that, with very few exceptions (most of which pertain to the founders and earlier American figures), only books, persons, events, etc., to have emerged since the Constitution was ratified in 1789 would be included. Thus, there are no entries on such figures as Plato, Aquinas, Locke, or Hume, and none on such events as the Renaissance, Reformation, Counter-Reformation, or Glorious Revolution of 1688.

As we have already intimated, there is today—and always has been—much debate as to what is and is not authentic conservatism. It is not the intent of this encyclopedia to adjudicate this debate; a rather broad meaning of conservatism is here taken for granted. The intent of this volume is to provide coverage of those matters of importance to each of the major schools of postwar conservative thought and to do so as evenhandedly as possible.

This is not to say that in the entries included here the reader will not encounter specific points of view. Far from it. The editors understand that some articles are more neutral in tone than others. In fact, they relish the strong opinions that often are on display, which they believe has made for a more interesting volume than would have been the case had contributors been forced into the iron cage of a supposed neutrality. To the editors' minds, at least, it is more important that a variety of points of view are present and accounted for: anarchist, classical-liberal, secular, religious, populist, aristocratic, Straussian, Voegelinian, Reaganite, antiinterventionist, interventionist, modernist, antimodernist, fusionist, agrarian, industrialist, southern, northern, and so on. But they have striven to see that each article is, so far as it goes, accurate and fair in its treatment of its subject, even if the subject is approached from a perspective with which not all conservatives would agree. Only views that seemed to be clearly beyond the pale of mainstream conservative thought have been intentionally excluded. In other words, the editors have resisted allowing the volume, taken as a whole, to present the story of American conservatism as an unwaveringly straight line from Goldwater to Reagan to George W. Bush, or from the founding of *National Review* to, say, the advent of Rush Limbaugh. The story is more complicated than that . . . and more interesting.

THE reader will find at the end of almost every entry in this encyclopedia a list of articles and books for further reading. The reader should note that, in the interest of conserving space, these "further reading" sections do not include references mentioned in the entries themselves. The reader will also find after each entry a list of other entries to consult that touch on the topic at hand.

The bulk of this volume notwithstanding, we are acutely aware that there are dozens of important persons, concepts, and publications not profiled here that might well have been included. In order to keep the size of the project manageable, the editors decided to employ a strong bias toward including only those living men and women whose careers were sufficiently advanced to allow for an adequate assessment of their contributions. Similarly, in the last quarter-century there has been such a proliferation of conservative institutes, centers, publications, and now blogs that it became impossible to include all of them in this volume. Thus, the editors have chosen to focus principally on more venerable institutions and publications, those which seem already to have reached a kind of "canonical" place in the bibliography of conservatism. We welcome the reactions and suggestions of readers, which will be gratefully considered as we plan a projected, and clearly necessary, second volume.

ALPHABETICAL LISTING
OF ENTRIES

abortion

Abortion may be defined as the "deliberately procured (or induced) termination of a pregnancy . . . at any stage after conception," the "immediate purpose" of which is the destruction of the "human fetus." For conservatives it involves profound moral and legal questions. The flash point for the abortion debate in the United States occurred on January 22, 1973, when, in a couplet of cases titled *Roe v. Wade* and *Doe v. Bolton*, the Supreme Court discovered a right to abortion in the United States Constitution.

Eight years earlier, in *Griswold v. Connecticut*, the Supreme Court found unconstitutional as applied to married persons Connecticut's law banning the use of contraceptives. The Court held that the Constitution protected a right of privacy and that the marital use of contraception lay within this zone of privacy. In 1972, in *Eisenstadt v. Baird*, this right was, for all intents and purposes, extended to the use of contraceptives by unmarried persons. These cases set the stage for *Roe*.

In *Roe*, the Court held that the Texas criminal abortion statute violated the Constitution. Justice Harry Blackmun, writing for the seven-person majority, rooted the right to abortion in the privacy right found in *Griswold*. The Court failed to give any account of where within the Constitution this right to privacy resides. But whether this privacy right was located in the "Fourteenth Amendment's concept of personal liberty" or in the "Ninth Amendment's reservation of rights to the people," the Court was quite certain that it was a right "broad enough to encompass a woman's decision whether or not to terminate her pregnancy." The Court also dismissed the argument that the fetus had rights as a person under the Equal Protection Clause of the Fourteenth Amendment.

The Court set out the requirements of this new right to abortion with legislative specificity. A state could from the end of the first trimester "regulate the abortion procedure," but only to protect "maternal health." Before the second trimester, the state could mandate only that an abortion be performed by a licensed physician. At the point of viability a state could go "so far as to proscribe abortion . . . except when necessary to preserve the life or health of the mother." Though this seemed to give a state much latitude to prohibit abortion, it was in practice feckless. For in *Doe*, the Court had defined health in the most expansive way possible to include "all factors—physical, emotional, psychological, familial, and the woman's age—relevant to [her] well-being." Practically, then, a state could prohibit no abortion.

For conservatives, *Roe* raised interrelated questions about the proper role of judges and the proper manner of interpreting the Constitution. At the heart of the American republic are the principles of self-government and the intrinsic dignity of each individual. A free people have the right to rule themselves so long as their laws do not infringe on the basic and civil human rights specifically enunciated in the Bill of Rights.

The judge's role within this framework is restrained by the limited scope of the constitutional charter. A law must stand unless some provision of the Constitution is violated by the law. Where a judge departs from his limited role and imposes his will upon the law—rather than abiding by the actual text of the Constitution—he does a real injustice to those subject to his judicial decrees, even where the end effected is morally laudable.

In finding a right to abortion in the Constitution—a right clearly not present under any reasonable reading of the Constitution—the Court removed an issue that almost certainly was intended to be left to the people's discretion. Conservatives have argued for more than three decades that gleaning a right to abortion from the alleged right to privacy was nothing more than an act of constitutional amendment by seven unelected men. For the Court to create such a right and then enforce it universally against the people subverted the meaning of the Constitution. Furthermore, even assuming that a right to abortion exists, there is nothing private about abortion. It involves a doctor, a father, and, arguably, the life of another human being, the unborn child. Even on its own legal terms, *Roe* failed.

For most conservatives the wrongness of *Roe* is compounded by its moral consequences. They challenge the central and fundamental principle animating *Roe* by contending that the fetus does not merely represent *potential* human life but rather is *actual* human life. We know this, they argue, not because of a dictate of faith but because of textbook biology.

Furthermore, conservatives argue that one may never intentionally kill innocent persons because of each person's intrinsic dignity, regardless of mitigating circumstances. Thus, because the being present at conception is human, the moral principle governing abortion is clear, if difficult to

accept: one can never justify abortion—by definition the intentional destruction of an innocent human being. The human life present from conception is entitled to the equal protection of law.

For some conservatives, albeit a small minority, *Roe*'s wrongness is multiplied by the fact that they believes the Fourteenth Amendment proscribes laws allowing abortion. Professor Robert P. George, while not endorsing this reading, has stated that a "genuinely principled argument . . . can be made that the American people have, by ratifying the Fourteenth Amendment's guarantee of equal protection, committed themselves to a proposition which is inconsistent with the regime of abortion-on-demand." Thus, for some conservatives *Roe* is wrong because it explicitly contradicts the mandate of the Constitution to give persons the equal protection of the law.

Unfortunately *Roe* did not signal the worst from the Court on abortion. Nearly twenty years later, in the 1992 case of *Planned Parenthood v. Casey*, the Court heard argument concerning abortion regulations instituted by the state of Pennsylvania. Changes in the composition of the Court and decisions seemingly curtailing *Roe* had led to uncertainty concerning the status of *Roe*. The stage was set for its reconsideration.

Unfortunately, in *Casey* the controlling, joint opinion of Justices Kennedy, O'Connor, and Souter concluded that "the essential holding of *Roe v. Wade* should be retained and once again reaffirmed." The majority came to this conclusion, it claimed, because of the demands of constitutional liberty and *stare decisis*—the legal principle that earlier decisions should be followed or "adhere[d] to" by a court in later decisions so as to give stability and continuity to the law.

The Court stated that the Constitution promises that the government cannot enter a "realm of personal liberty." The constitutional liberty implicated in the abortion question is the liberty related to those "personal decisions" concerning "marriage, procreation, contraception, family relationships, child rearing and education." Such personal decisions are constitutionally protected because "[a]t the heart of liberty is the right to define one's own concept of existence, of meaning, of the universe, and of the mystery of human life. Beliefs about these matters could not define the attributes of personhood were they formed under compulsion of the State." This passage, referred to subsequently as the "Mystery Passage," has been the source of much derision. Abortion was to be permitted because the "destiny of the woman must be shaped to large extent on her own conception of her spiritual imperatives and her place in society." Because of the vague and seemingly all-encompassing right to define one's universe, a state is not "entitled to proscribe" abortion in "all instances."

Stare decisis required upholding *Roe* in large part because the Court believed that *Roe* had formed the fabric of numerous social interactions; women and men had ordered their lives assuming the right to abortion guaranteed by *Roe*. Second, the Court believed that to overrule *Roe* would exact a heavy toll on the Court's legitimacy. This argument amounts to the principle that even where the Court is wrong in a previous decision it should be extremely reluctant to overturn that decision lest in doing so it confirm in the minds of the people its own error.

The Court also set out a new legal standard—the undue burden standard—to govern abortion regulations before viability. After viability the Court adopted *Roe*'s formulation that the state could proscribe abortion except when necessary for the life or health of the mother.

Conservatives' criticisms of *Casey* are numerous. First, they argue, the Court once again overstepped its authority and ruled on an issue about which the Constitution is, at best, silent. Worse, presented with an opportunity to correct the errors of the past, the Court instead repeated them. The utter intellectual bankruptcy of the Court's opinion was demonstrated by the fact that the Court could no better explain where the right to abortion was lodged in the Constitution than had Justice Blackmun in *Roe*.

Second, the conception of liberty that animates the joint opinion in the Mystery Passage is both legally and philosophically nonsensical. As a legal matter, the Court could not have meant what it said. Every time it rules the Supreme Court upholds laws that limit a person's ability to define the "concept of existence, of meaning, of the universe, and of the mystery of human life." Furthermore, conservatives understand that at the heart of liberty is the freedom to pursue the good and human flourishing. The Mystery Passage's vision of human freedom posits a radical personal autonomy that trumps any considerations of truth and the good life.

Third, the Court's affirmation of *Roe* arose in large part because of the hubris that animated the Court's view of itself. The Court saw itself as an indispensable—perhaps *the* indispensable—body helping the American people actualize their vision of themselves as a people of the rule of law. And it believed that self-understanding would be shaken to the core if it overruled *Roe*. The Court seemed oblivious to the fact that if *Roe* was wrongly decided then its legitimacy was already in question.

Fourth, conservatives notes that *Casey*, like *Roe* before it, turns on the assumption that the fetus is, at most, potential human life. But this assumption is factually wrong. Finally, *Casey*, like *Roe*, never once discusses the right it is guaranteeing, never describes what is involved in abortion, what occurs, what the necessary means to achieve the goal of ending a pregnancy are. *Casey* and *Roe* simply elide any such description.

In the years after *Casey*, the Court has

not become the focal point for much abortion litigation. With the addition of two Democratic appointees the Court's philosophic makeup changed little. The undue burden test does allow states to place more meaningful restrictions on the abortion license. Yet, in the only Supreme Court abortion case of import in subsequent years, *Stenberg v. Carhart* (2000), the seemingly limitless right to liberty in *Casey* led the Supreme Court to strike down Nebraska's ban of the barbaric practice of partial-birth abortion.

Thus, the abortion controversy remains. With the controversy come continuing questions regarding the Supreme Court's legitimacy and the realization on the part of many conservatives that no democratic republic that allows her most vulnerable citizens to be exposed to the whims of the strong can be called healthy. *Roe*, reaffirmed by *Casey*, was the legally illegitimate act that ushered in this age of abortion. For most conservatives, abortion, like slavery, is an aberration—an example of where the Republic has turned against her deepest principles.

—CHARLES DENISON

Further Reading

Arkes, Hadley. *Natural Law and the Right to Choose*. Cambridge: Cambridge University Press, 2002.

Bork, Robert H. *The Tempting of America: The Political Seduction of the Law*. New York: Free Press, 1990.

Ely, John Hart. "The Wages of Crying Wolf: A Comment on *Roe v. Wade*." *Yale Law Journal* 82 (1973): 920–49.

George, Robert P. *The Clash of Orthodoxies: Law, Religion, and Morality in Crisis*. Wilmington, Del.: ISI Books, 2001.

Muncy, Mitchell S., ed. *The End of Democracy: The Celebrated* First Things *Debate with Arguments Pro and Con and "The Anatomy of a Controversy."* Dallas: Spence Publishing, 1997.

Paulsen, Michael Stokes. "The Worst Constitutional Decision of All Time," *University of Notre Dame Law Review* 78 (2003): 995–1043.

Schlueter, Nathan, and Robert H. Bork. "Constitutional Persons: An Exchange." *First Things* 129 (2003): 28–36.

See also: Supreme Court; Constitution, interpretations of; culture wars; family; Human Life Review; *Hyde, Henry; incorporation doctrine; judicial activism*

academic freedom

The engagement of twentieth-century American conservatism with academic freedom is an ironic one. In 1951, William F. Buckley's *God and Man at Yale: The Superstitions of "Academic Freedom,"* one of the seminal books of the American Right, attacked the reigning conception of academic freedom for allowing agnostic and collectivist professors to undermine the religious and individualist foundations of Yale. The beginning of the twenty-first century finds conservative professors and students appealing to academic freedom as a defense against contemporary ideologies that they believe threaten an entire generation with intellectual conformity.

Academic freedom has both institutional and individual components. The institutional component, in a famous summary by Justice Felix Frankfurter, comprises "the four essential freedoms of a university—to determine for itself on academic grounds who may teach, what may be taught, how it shall be taught, and who may be admitted to study" (*Sweezy* v. *New Hampshire*, 1957). The individual component comprises the freedom of the teacher and (to a lesser extent) the student. The *1940 Statement on Academic Freedom and Tenure* of the American Association of University Professors, perhaps the most important single statement on the subject, states that "[t]eachers are entitled to full freedom in research and in the publication of the results," and "to freedom in the classroom in discussing their subjects, but they should be careful not to introduce into their teaching controversial matter which has no relation to their subjects." During the 1950s, the institutional and individual components were usually in harmony, as institutions frequently appealed to academic freedom in defense of leftist professors such as those attacked by Buckley. (Many of those same institutions, however, refused to defend the academic freedom of Communist Party members, on the grounds that they were obliged to use their positions to indoctrinate rather than teach.) To date, no case concerning a direct clash of the institutional and individual components has reached the Supreme Court. The Eleventh Circuit Court of Appeals, however, has ruled on such a case, in favor of the University of Alabama, which restrained a tenured professor from making occasional classroom comments or holding voluntary after-class sessions on the Christian implications of health physiology (*Bishop v. Aronov*, 1991). While the professor appealed for protection of his individual academic freedom, the university appealed for the government to refrain from interfering in its institutional academic freedom.

Most American discussions of this subject begin with the brief *1940 Statement* and its much longer predecessor, the AAUP's *1915 Declaration of Principles*. There is much in the *1915 Declaration* for conservatives to admire, particularly the way in which it relates the concept of academic freedom to the public trust that educational institutions carry, as well as to the role of an academic institution in promoting inquiry, advancing knowledge, and providing instruction, among other goals. Unlike the 1940 document and more recent discussions, the *1915 Declaration* frames academic freedom in fundamentally communitarian and teleological terms. Many conservatives would nevertheless dissent from the *1915 Declaration*—and from most recent discussions of the subject—in its presupposition that free inquiry is hindered by

an institutional commitment to religion. The purpose of religious schools, says the *Declaration*, "is not to advance knowledge by the unrestricted research and unfettered discussion of impartial investigators, but rather to subsidize the promotion of opinions held by the persons . . . who provide the funds for their maintenance." This secular and ahistorical understanding of academic freedom was challenged by Russell Kirk in *Academic Freedom* (1955): "[I]n the Middle Ages . . . the academy possessed freedom unknown to other bodies and persons because the philosopher, the scholar, and the student were looked upon as men consecrated to the service of Truth. . . . [Their] freedom was sanctioned by an authority more than human." In more recent years, Pope John Paul II, in *Ex Corde Ecclesiae* (1990), pointed out that the Catholic tradition, in which the Western concept of the university first developed, regards the search for truth as a matter of faith working together harmoniously with reason. Nevertheless, in 1970 the AAUP issued "Interpretive Comments" on its *1940 Statement* that warned church-related institutions against departing from the AAUP's own understanding of academic freedom.

One presupposition of the AAUP documents and their defenders is that there is a valid distinction between teaching and proselytizing, between learning and propaganda. "Every social scientist who is worthy of the name," wrote Robert MacIver in response to *God and Man at Yale*, "seeks to learn and to enlighten, not to propagandize." That distinction is now a questionable one for practitioners of certain academic methodologies, such as some types of feminism, who see their scholarship as an extension of their political activism. The academic freedom of their ideological opponents, and especially their students, is therefore a matter of concern.

Academic freedom develops in response to historical events, and the events of most concern to conservatives have been the increasing demands that the extracurricular activities, course offerings, syllabi, lectures, even professors' choices of words reflect the demands of feminism and "multiculturalism," regardless of the judgment of the professors themselves. Disruptions of classrooms, suppression of conservative student newspapers, and threats against conservative organizations (such as the National Association of Scholars) have reminded some of the deterioration of academic freedom experienced in Weimar Germany. The sexual and racial harassment codes adopted during the last ten or twenty years, moreover, usually proscribe certain forms of speech if they create (in the mind of the offended party) a hostile or intimidating environment. The AAUP has reported that sexual harassment charges are now the most frequent cause of stripping professors of tenure and forcing them to resign without formal review procedures or due process. In the winter 1990–91 issue of *Academic Questions,* Professor Stephen Thernstrom of Harvard recounted his (and others') experience of being charged with "racial insensitivity" for such offenses as using the term "American Indian" rather than "Native American." As Thernstrom pointed out, these attacks on academic freedom differ markedly from those of the McCarthy era because the attackers now have substantial backing within the academy itself. Public aversion to this sort of attempted political conformity, however, may temporarily postpone a showdown over the coherence of the purely secular conception of academic freedom.

Ultimately, most conservatives see the shape of academic freedom as determined by the role of knowledge in fulfilling the social nature of man. Conservatives are therefore likely to continue to press for a pluralism of approaches to the pursuit of knowledge and for the valid distinction between teaching and propagandizing. A contemporary periodical of special interest to the Right concerning issues of academic freedom is *Academic Questions,* published by the National Association of Scholars.

—DANIEL E. RITCHIE

Further Reading

Baade, Hans W., ed. *Academic Freedom.* Dobbs Ferry, N.Y.: Oceana, 1964.

Hofstadter, Richard and Walter P. Metzger. *The Development of Academic Freedom in the United States.* New York: Columbia University Press, 1955.

Pincoffs, Edmund, ed. *The Concept of Academic Freedom.* Austin, Tex.: University of Texas, 1972.

Van Alstyne, William W., ed. "Freedom and Tenure in the Academy: The Fiftieth Anniversary of the 1940 Statement of Principles." *Law and Contemporary Problems* 53, no. 3 (Summer 1990): 1–418.

See also: education, higher; God and Man at Yale; *Kors, Alan C.; National Association of Scholars*

Acton, Lord (1834–1902)

In the 1920s and 1930s, Lord John Emerich Edward Dalberg Acton's reputation had become obscured. But the succeeding age of totalitarianism and socialism brought a new appreciation for Acton and his never-failing love of liberty by the few who still read and studied him. A wider and more appreciative audience for the message of Acton came after the publication of Friedrich A. Hayek's *Road to Serfdom* (1944), in which Acton shares with Tocqueville the roles of prophetic critic of socialism and tyranny and apostle of liberty. The rediscovery and growing appreciation of Acton was further stimulated by the subsequent publication of Gertrude Himmelfarb's *Lord Acton: A Study of Conscience and Politics* (1952) and a number of articles by other scholars in journals of political science and history.

Lord Acton was born on January 10, 1834, in Naples, the descendant of a long line of Shropshire baronets and the Dalbergs, one of the most honored families in the imperial aristocracy of the Holy Roman Empire. He was more continental than English, as aristocratic and traditional in politics as he was Roman Catholic in religion. His Whiggery was the Whiggery of Edmund Burke. Because he was Catholic he was unable to study at either Oxford or Cambridge and was educated on the Continent: in Paris at the school run by Feliz Dupauloup, later Bishop of Orleans, and in Munich where he spent six years in the home of Ignaz von Döllinger while he studied at the University. Döllinger was German Catholicism's leading historian and historical theologian.

Lord Acton

The essential pivot in Acton's life was religious and moral. He believed that only the conscience acting in liberty could perform a moral action. He believed that "Christ was risen on the world" and that the consequences of the Incarnation were liberty and the amelioration of the human condition. He believed that God so loved liberty that he permitted even sin. He believed, moreover, that free inquiry would result in the establishment of God's truth. When the young Acton returned to England from Germany in 1857 he cooperated with John Henry Newman in the publication of liberal Catholic journals that he hoped would demonstrate the dedication to free inquiry within the Catholic Church and the compatibility of political liberty and the indispensable need for liberty of conscience in the moral Catholic life. These journals met with Ultra-montane opposition and condemnation by the Church.

Acton believed that political liberty had grown up in the no-man's-land of conflicts between church and state. Modern liberty in England and America, Acton asserted, resulted from the claims of persecuted religious sectarians to liberty of conscience and their insistence upon an obedience to a higher law.

Acton's philosophy of history and love of liberty involved him in a bitter conflict with Ultramontane theology. He resisted to the fullest the definition of papal infallibility by the first Vatican Council, though after the definition he remained a pious, loyal, and conforming Catholic.

Acton projected but never finished a great *History of Liberty*. The rudimentary outlines may be traced in his essays, lectures, and in his massive manuscript notes. The best and fullest presentation of his work is presented in J. Rufus Fears's edited compilation, *Selected Writings of Lord Acton* (1985-88). The exchange of letters between Acton and his mentor, Ignaz von Döllinger, is essential to a full understanding of his motives. The definitive biography, Roland Hill's *Lord Acton* (2000), is also indispensable.

Acton was increasingly fearful as the nineteenth century wore on. He believed that the French Revolution threatened to destroy liberty. Democracy and nationalism were the great threats to freedom and civilization. He equated socialism with slavery. When he was appointed Regius Professor of Modern History at Cambridge University by the Queen, it was generally agreed that he was the most erudite and astute student of history in England. As a consequence, he became the first editor of *The Cambridge Modern History* (1902–10).

Acton's high appeal to conscience, dedication to liberty, defense of Catholicism, and transforming influence on the study of history in England make him one of the most important figures in European thought in the nineteenth century and one of the most influential in the twentieth century.

—STEPHEN J. TONSOR

Further Reading

Acton, John Emerich Edward Dalberg. *Lectures on the French Revolution.* Edited by John Neville Figgis and Reginald Vere Laurence. Indianapolis, Ind.: Liberty Fund, 2000.

———. *Essays on Church and State.* New York: Crowell, 1968.

———. *Essays in the Liberal Interpretation of History: Selected Papers.* Edited by William H. McNeill. Chicago: University of Chicago Press, 1967.

Butterfield, Herbert. *The Whig Interpretation of History.* London: Bell, 1931.

See also: Acton Institute; classical liberalism; liberty; Road to Serfdom, The

Acton Institute

Founded in April 1990 by Rev. Robert Sirico and Kris Alan Mauren, the Acton Institute for the Study of Religion and Liberty is a nonprofit educational institution located in Grand Rapids, Michigan. Taking both its name and the basis of its mission from the writings and teachings of the great Cambridge historian and moralist Lord John Emerich Edward Dalberg Acton, the institute holds seminars, conducts research, and publishes books, papers, and periodicals that explore the religious underpinnings of a free market and free society. To that end, the institute seeks to stimulate dialogue between religious, business, and scholarly communities and to familiarize those communities (particularly students and seminarians) with the ethical and Christian foundations of political liberty and free-market economics. The Acton Institute also tries to serve as a clearinghouse of ideas for entrepreneurs interested in the ethical dimensions of their commercial activities.

Within the larger context of the conservative intellectual movement, the Acton Institute is usually thought of as classically liberal or libertarian in orientation. Of the two labels, the institute prefers to identify itself with the first, especially in its advancement of "economic personalism." The institute defines economic personalism as an approach to the social order "inspired by the centuries-old tradition of Christian reflection on the ethical character of social, political, and economic life." In this regard, economic personalism seeks to complement the classical liberal tradition with a distinctly Christian anthropology that draws upon the resources of faith and right reason. It recognizes the natural law tradition as one way of communicating these insights within pluralist societies, which are often characterized by significant differences in foundational belief. Among the institute's more prominent programs is the Center for Economic Personalism, which publishes the semiannual academic journal *Markets and Morality,* edited by the center's director, Samuel Gregg, a moral philosopher who took his doctorate from the University of Oxford under the prominent natural law scholar John Finnis.

—CORY ANDREWS

See also: Acton, Lord; liberalism, classical; libertarianism

Adams, Brooks (1848–1927)

Brooks Adams was the son of Charles Francis Adams and Abigail Brown Brooks. His father was ambassador to the Court of St. James during the American Civil War and did as much as anyone to save the Union by persuading Britain not to intervene on the side of the Confederacy. His grandfather, John Quincy Adams, was an ambassador, president, and member of the House of Representatives, and his great-grandfather, John Adams, was a founding father, ambassador, and second president of the United States. Brooks Adams was christened Peter Chadron Brooks Adams in honor of his maternal grandfather, Peter Chadron Brooks, Boston's first multimillionaire.

In background and temperament Brooks Adams was a conservative. Like his ancestors he mistrusted political change and anticipated the early demise of the republic. Like them he feared the power of the moneyed interest and speculative enterprise, or what he and his brother Henry called the power of the "Gold Bugs." These intellectual tendencies were never articulated into an integrated conservative philosophy. Brooks Adams became a "man of the Right" rather than a conservative. He was much influenced by European ideas of *fin de siècle* pessimism and decadence. And he was an intellectual eccentric. In fact, it is not short of the mark to describe many of his ideas as half-baked. His thought was not, however, "proto-fascist," as his biographer Arthur F. Beringause suggests.

Brooks Adams lived in the intellectual shadow of his brother Henry, who was ten years his senior. Even though he never achieved the acclaim and distinction of his brother, Brooks, as Charles A. Beard was the first to demonstrate in his introduction to *The Law of Civilization and Decay* (1895), exerted a profound influence on Henry's historical theories. It was Brooks who edited and provided a long introduction to Henry's collected essays on the theory of history, *The Degradation of the Democratic Dogma* (1919). Through Henry, the spread and influence of

Brooks's thought was greatly facilitated. Though Brooks wrote and published throughout his lifetime, his *Law of Civilization and Decay,* first published in 1895, was his most important contribution to the development of conservative thought.

Darwin and the methodology of natural science were decisive influences on Brooks's historical thought. Throughout his life he was preoccupied with the problem of the nature and meaning of historical experience. His pessimism was rooted in his inability, try as he might, to accept religious belief. He believed that the course of history was governed by causal law, that history was determined, and that free will and human choice had little or no impact on the turn of events. Darwinism provided the basis for his antidemocratic views. He was the first American to attempt a developmental explanation of the whole of human history. He saw the pattern of history as cyclical and oscillating "between barbarism and civilization," or moving "from a condition of physical dispersion to one of concentration." The resulting law of force and energy as a phase of cosmic dynamics has universal application. The early stages of concentration (civilization) produce mental types embodied in religious, military, and artistic men. However, "fear yields to greed and the economic organization tends to supersede the emotional and the martial." When economic man becomes dominant, the course of decline is already well under way. The decline of Rome provides the great example. The capitalist and the "suction of the usurer" bring about the destruction of civilization. In many respects, *The Law of Civilization and Decay* should be seen as a belated partisan tract in the campaign against gold.

—STEPHEN J. TONSOR

Further Reading
Adams, Brooks. *The New Empire.* New York: Macmillan, 1902.

———. *The Theory of Social Revolutions.* New York: Macmillan, 1913.

Beringause, Arthur F. *Brooks Adams: A Biography.* New York: Alfred A. Knopf, 1955.

See also: Adams, Henry; Adams, John

Adams, Henry (1838–1918)

If continuity in tradition and fidelity to type are among the marks of conservatism, the first four generations of the Adams family must constitute the most distinguished succession of conservative achievement and aristocratic talent in American history. Henry Adams's great-grandfather was President John Adams; his grandfather was President John Quincy Adams; his father Charles Francis Adams was appointed by President Lincoln as ambassador to the Court of St. James during the American Civil War. Young Henry served as secretary to Charles Francis, who was in large measure responsible for keeping Great Britain out of the Civil War as a Confederate States ally. The Adams family lived simply and served greatly for three generations. Compared to Jefferson's Monticello, Washington's Mt. Vernon, or Madison's Georgian Mansion, the Adams family's "Old House" at Quincy, Massachusetts, was a rambling, drafty farmhouse with small rooms and few conveniences. Until the third generation and the marriage of Charles Francis Adams to a woman of wealth, Abigail Brooks (1808–89), the modest means of the Adams family were barely sufficient to cover their needs and the demands incurred by public service. They were a family who did not simply collect books but read and studied them. They knew Greek and Latin well and, unusual in America, were well versed in the modern European languages. Three generations of greatness in the past brought both a challenge and a realization to its members that the fourth generation was unlikely to live up to the high achievements of the earlier Adamses.

Henry Adams

There had been a slow and steady decay of religious belief in the Adams family. Henry recalls in his autobiography that religion was never mentioned in the family. Both Henry and his brother Brooks hungered for religion; both were unable finally to accept its assurances. Both of them were inclined to Catholicism because of its beauty and the historical fact that in the medieval period Catholicism had, through the reconciliation of faith and reason, provided an ordering system that had given total meaning to human experience. Both died in an invincible agnosticism. It is this note of a life devoid of meaning, without great or noble purposes and empty of a grand design, which haunts us in the prose of Henry Adams.

Harvard, from which Henry graduated in 1858, was not the place to imbibe the spirit of religion. He half-heartedly studied civil law at Berlin and Dresden from 1859 to 1860. From 1861 to 1868 he served in London as his father's secretary at the Court of St. James.

At the instigation of Charles W. Eliot, the new president of Harvard College, Henry Adams was offered a professorship in medieval history in 1870. It is likely that he was unprepared for the task, but he was nevertheless a brilliant teacher, introducing the seminar system and training a number of distinguished students.

Washington had always served as a pole of attraction for the Adams men. In 1877 Henry gave up teaching at Harvard and moved to the nation's capital. Henry was an aristocrat and an elitist. He thought the democratic process was essentially corrupting. He took a dim view of the materialism and emptiness, the triviality and vulgarity of American life. He and John Hay built an extravagant and beautiful house on the spot in Washington now occupied by the Hay-Adams Hotel. There Henry and his wife gathered about them a distinguished circle that included John Hay, Clarence King, and John LaFarge. Adams observed political life at first hand—and with contempt. His satirical novel, *Democracy* (1880), which he published anonymously, makes his disdain for democracy clear. From John Adams to Henry Adams the Adamses always believed and said that the American experiment was on the point of failure; that it might not last another presidential term. Henry Adams was predisposed to a sense of cosmic failure, a belief that the universe was running down, that indeed decadence was upon the world. The Adams family, as no other American family, was attuned to Europe. In each generation they spent a considerable portion of their lives abroad. Henry was attuned to the patterns of European intellectuality and was aware of what European, particularly French, writers and painters of decadence were doing. He reflected, in his way, their vision of the world.

Henry Adams was a historian by training, inclination, and talent. His magisterial work, *History of the United States during the Administrations of Jefferson and Madison* (9 vols., 1889-91) is perhaps the greatest piece of historical writing by any American. *Mont-Saint-Michel and Chartres* (1904) is more revealing of his philosophy of history and the remarkable *jeu d'esprit* of his personality. His later historical-philosophical speculations are tangled in pseudoscience (*A Letter to American Teachers of History*, 1910). *Documents Relating to New England Federalism* (1877) and the *Life of Albert Gallatin* (1879) illustrate the depth and quality of his historical research. His charming, profound, and idiosyncratic autobiography, *The Education of Henry Adams* (1918), is both illuminating and puzzling.

—STEPHEN J. TONSOR

Further Reading

O'Toole, Patricia. *The Five of Hearts: An Intimate Portrait of Henry Adams and His Friends, 1880-1918*. New York: Crown, 1990.

Samuels, Ernest. *The Young Henry Adams*. Cambridge, Mass.: Harvard University Press, 1948.

———. *Henry Adams: The Middle Years*. Cambridge, Mass.: Harvard University Press, 1958.

———. *Henry Adams: The Major Phase*. Cambridge, Mass.: Harvard University Press, 1964.

See also: Adams, Brooks; Adams, John; anarchism

Adams, John (1735–1826)

A member of the fourth generation of the Adams family, second president of the United States and major American author of political theory and political history, John Adams sought to preserve America's heritage of English-ordered freedom. He was a powerful advocate of separation from Britain, but (when president) sternly opposed the French Revolution. His courage, honesty, and strength of intellect were more widely recognized by historians and biographers in the latter half of the twentieth century than in the nineteenth century. Some writers regard him as America's most important conservative public man.

Born in Braintree, Massachusetts, where the family mansion still stands, Adams graduated from Harvard College in 1755. He taught for a time and thought of taking up ministry, but drawing back from the rigorous doctrines of Calvinism, he turned instead to law and was admitted to the Boston bar in 1758. In 1764, he married a young woman of high talents, Abigail Smith. In 1765, he published essays on canon and feudal law.

Parliament's passing of the Sugar Act in 1764 and the Stamp Act in 1765 roused vehement opposition in Massachusetts. Although conservative by nature, Adams was drawn into the protest and condemned taxation without representation as unconstitutional. As a man of law, however, Adams opposed revolutionary violence and sought instead to obtain redress through resolutions of protest. And while he defended Patriots in the courts, he also defended Captain Preston, commander of British troops at the "Boston Massacre."

The Tea Act of 1773 led to the Boston Tea Party that same year. Adams condemned the resulting Boston Port Act but, at the time, still opposed independence from Britain. In June, 1774, Massachusetts sent him as a delegate to the First Continental Congress. After the Congress adjourned, Adams served in the provincial congress of Massachusetts. Events moved rapidly in 1775 after the battle of Lexington. By July, Adams declared that Massachusetts and the other colonies must establish a new government, banding together indissolubly. He also offered advice to the several colonies applying to the Congress for counsel as to how they should govern themselves.

Opposed to the radical politics of Thomas Paine's new book, *Common Sense* (1776), Adams published *Thoughts on Government* (early 1776), advocating the politics of prudence. By May 1776, Adams was recommending independence for America. Congress appointed him to the small committee that drew up the Declaration of Independence, and he was its ablest advocate on the floor. For a year after the Declaration was adopted,

Adams was exhaustingly occupied as a member of important committees and boards, and in diplomacy.

In November 1777, Adams was named a commissioner to France. In Paris, he shared a house with Benjamin Franklin. When Franklin was appointed sole commissioner (France having meanwhile extended diplomatic recognition to the United States), Adams returned to America, landing in Boston on August 2, 1779. Back in Massachusetts, he did much to frame a constitution for his state.

Adams returned to France in December, on behalf of Congress, to negotiate an end to the war in America. He was engaged in complex diplomacy in France and the Netherlands (arranging a loan from the Netherlands to the United States) until February 1785, when he was appointed American envoy to Britain. There, he conducted negotiations to implement provisions of the peace treaty that had been signed in 1783.

In London for nearly three years, Adams could take no direct part in the framing of the United States Constitution. However, because he was eager to secure the adoption of a national constitution that would reject the direct democracy advocated by Rousseau and the radicalism of Thomas Paine, Richard Price, the French financier Turgot, and other Europeans, Adams commenced writing a long, learned disquisition of government, *Defense of the Constitutions of Government of the United States of America* (1787–88). The first volume of this three-volume work was published while the Constitutional Convention was deliberating at Philadelphia in 1787. To date, Adams's work is the most thorough examination of political institutions produced by an American writer.

Turgot had declared, in a letter to Richard Price in 1778, that the Americans should collect "all authority into one centre, the nation." Adams argued for federal, as opposed to central, government and for elaborate devices to achieve political balance and stability. Turgot, Adams wrote, was blind to the truth that Liberty, practically speaking, is made up of particular and personal liberties. Turgot was ignorant of the great prerequisite for just government, which is the recognition of local rights, interests, and diversities. Adams's huge treatise, buttressed by ancient and modern historical examples, was much discussed between 1787 and 1791.

Early in 1788, Adams returned from England to the new Republic, where soon he was elected the first vice president (an office for which he expressed contempt) of the United States. Alexander Hamilton fought Adams's election, and his hostility caused Adams to receive only a plurality, not a majority, of the vote in the Electoral College. On the numerous occasions when, as presiding officer of the Senate, Adams voted to break a tie, he voted on the Federalist side. He was, however, no strict party man. Hamilton's faction of the Federalists often endeavored to undermine Adams and at last succeeded to the ruin of their party in 1800. Sometimes Adams found the Anti-Federalists—Thomas Jefferson and his Republicans—less hostile than Hamilton and his followers.

While Adams presided over the Senate from 1789 to 1797, the French Revolution convulsed Europe. Vice President Adams exposed the political fallacies of the revolutionaries in his *Discourses on Davila* (1805). During George Washington's first administration, marked hostility continued between Adams and Alexander Hamilton, secretary of the treasury. This rivalry grew fiercer still during Washington's second administration,

John Adams

in which Adams remained vice president despite Hamilton's attempt to exclude him from office. Against Adams's candidacy for the presidency in 1796, Hamilton supported Thomas Pinckney. Nevertheless, Adams won and Thomas Jefferson was elected his vice president.

As president of the United States, Adams soon found himself in difficulties with both Jefferson's Republicans and Hamilton's Federalists, in particular over the question of relations with France. The Paris Directory treated America's emissaries with contempt, and French military and naval action against the United States became a real threat. Adams's preparations for defense, and his negotiations with France, were courageous and intelligent. But the Alien and Sedition Acts, with which Adams's administration had been saddled by the extreme Federalists, made Adams unpopular. However, he succeeded in reorganizing the federal judiciary (appointing John Marshall, who had been in his cabinet, chief justice of the Supreme Court), and in other ways was an able political administrator.

Defeated by Thomas Jefferson in the presidential election of 1800, Adams retired to Quincy, Massachusetts, concluding more than thirty-five years of political leadership. Upon him in 1800—so he wrote to Jefferson near the end of his life—unpopularity had fallen "like the tower of Siloam." Stoutly conservative in his convictions, he wrote to Josiah Quincy in 1811, "Should I let loose my imagination into futurity, I could imagine that I foresee changes and revolutions such as eye hath not seen nor ear heard. . . . I cannot see any better principle at present than to make as little innovation as possible; keep things going as well as we can in the present train."

For intellectual power, no other president has surpassed Adams. His honesty and strength of character were acknowledged and praised by such opponents as Jefferson. In recent decades, biographers and historians have also recognized his great worth. Books about Adams that are worth mentioning include Gilbert Chinard's *Honest John Adams* (1933); Zoltan Haraszti's *John Adams and the Prophets of Progress* (1952); Anne Husted Burleigh's *John Adams* (1969); Page Smith's *John Adams* (two volumes, 1962-63); Peter Shaw's *The Character of John Adams* (1976); Stephen G. Kurtz's *The Presidency of John Adams* (1957); and Manning J. Dauer's *The Adams Federalists* (1953).

—Russell Kirk

Further Reading

Brookhiser, Richard. *America's First Dynasty: The Adamses, 1735–1918*. New York: Free Press, 2002.

Diggins, John Patrick. *John Adams* (The American Presidents Series). New York: Times Books, 2003.

McCullough, David. *John Adams*. New York: Simon & Schuster, 2001.

See also: Federalist Party; French Revolution; Hamilton, Alexander; Jefferson, Thomas

affirmative action

The expression *affirmative action* was used in 1965 by President Lyndon Johnson in Executive Order No. 11246. That executive order was intended to implement the Civil Rights Act of 1964, and the order specifically mentions "minorities." Executive Order No. 11375 of 1967 extended affirmative action to women. The expression did not appear in the

Civil Rights Act of 1964, nor was the concept defined in the executive order. The meaning and application of the concept emerged within the federal executive bureaucracy (specifically the Department of Health, Education and Welfare, as well as the Equal Employment Opportunity Commission). As a consequence of the Department of Labor Order No. 4, issued in May 1968, proponents of affirmative action within the bureaucracy understood the policy to mean that the work force should mirror the population as a whole, where the population as a whole is categorized by race, sex, and certain selected national origins. If the work force fails to do so, then this is taken to be *prima facie* evidence that an employer or an institution has practiced discrimination. Any employment policy, including quality controls, that inhibits proportional representation in hiring, retention, and promotion is said to be discriminatory. Rather than an employee or prospective employee having to establish in a court of law that a deliberate policy of exclusion was responsible, the employer is required to establish that no such policy was used. For an employer to avoid litigation or gain access to federal funds, all that is required is that the work force be statistically representative. Although affirmative action's advocates eschew the term quota, in practice an employer can avoid litigation by using quotas. Affirmative action thus consists of any policy used by employers to rectify statistical racial, gender, or ethnic imbalances in the work force.

There are five popular definitions of affirmative action: (1) Affirmative action consists of those policies designed to advertise all openings as widely as possible and to monitor appointments and promotions processes in order to ensure that the process is open, nondiscriminatory, and promotes excellence (the meritocratic definition). (2) Affirmative action consists of any policy, private or public, ordered by the court to redress proven cases of individual discrimination; the remedy may involve a numerical objective, but the numerical objective is limited to a specific time and place (the punitive definition). (3) Affirmative action refers to congressionally mandated rules concerning federal contracts and involves a specific percentage of contracts to be set aside for minority contractors (the minority set-asides definition). (4) Affirmative action consists of policies designed to redress alleged cases of discrimination against a group by placing members of the group in the positions they would have allegedly held if the alleged discrimination had not taken place. This is a contrary-to-fact conditional: it claims to identify what would have happened if something else had not happened (the backward-compensation definition). (5) Affirmative action designates any policy in social planning, independent of any causal claim of what would have been, designed to produce a society or institution which reflects some stated goal and invokes quotas of group representation (the forward-preferential definition).

The executive policy of affirmative action has been challenged in court. The first important case was *Bakke v. California Regents* (1978), in which the Supreme Court ruled 5 to 4 that the University of California at Davis Medical School had unlawfully discriminated against Bakke, a white applicant, in denying him admission; some of the justices cited Titles VI and VII of the Civil Rights Act of 1964 as unequivocally outlawing U.C.-Davis's preference's (definition 5). The Legislative Record (speeches by the bill's supporters including Hubert Humphrey and Emanuel Cellar, among others) supports this reading. In a separate opinion, Justice Lewis Powell specifically attacked and rejected the backward-looking argument for compensation (definition 4).

Another important affirmative action case is *Adarand Constructors, Inc. v. Pena* (1995). Congress had, in the Minority Business Enterprise provision of the Public Works Employment Act of 1977, required that 10 percent of federal funds allocated to state and local governments for public works projects be used to purchase goods and services from minority-owned businesses even if non-minority-owned firms offered a lower bid. Speaking on behalf of the majority, Justice O'Connor stated that "all racial classifications . . . must be analyzed by a reviewing court under strict scrutiny. In other words, such classifications are constitutional only if they are narrowly tailored measures that further compelling governmental interests." Thus, in effect, affirmative action as a minority set-aside (definition 3) must establish prior discrimination

One of the areas in which the use of affirmative action has been most pervasive, visible and hence controversial has been university admissions. Often defended as only one factor considered in the admissions process and as a proxy for selecting students of different backgrounds and opinions so that "diversity" is promoted, university-formulated affirmative action policies have led to a significant decline in academic requirements. Citizens in Texas and California have responded in part by voting to ban the practice. But in both instances state governments have reinstituted affirmative action. Moreover, Supreme Court decisions during the 1990s that seemed to be trending against affirmative action in university admissions abruptly shifted in a significantly pro–affirmative action direction with the Court's decision in *Grutter v. Bollinger* (2003). In that case the Court declared that, while racial classifications would be subjected to strict scrutiny, (a) "diversity" would be deemed to constitute a compelling state interest, and (b) the Court would accept, with little actual scrutiny, claims that the university was providing individualized review to applications within its affirmative action plan. Thus, racial quotas, provided they are accompanied by an administrative apparatus that theoretically allows for individualized review, are now deemed constitutional.

Affirmative action continues to be a widely debated policy. Although it is claimed by proponents to apply to a number of allegedly disadvantaged groups, including women, in practice it seems to be focused on race. Proponents of affirmative action believe that racism, discrimination, and all of the social problems associated with them are rooted in history and social forces beyond the control of private individuals, other public institutions, or market forces. Hence, there is need for governmental agencies to rectify injustice. Opponents of affirmative action retort that such policies are illegal, immoral in that they violate fundamental American values (substituting equality of result for equality of opportunity), impractical, incoherent (i.e., they lead to reverse discrimination), and dangerously divisive.

—NICHOLAS CAPALDI

Further Reading

Capaldi, Nicholas. *Out of Order: Affirmative Action and the Crisis of Doctrinaire Liberalism.* Buffalo, N.Y.: Prometheus, 1985.

Curry, George E. and Cornell West, eds. *The Affirmative Action Debate.* Reading, Mass.: Perseus Press, 1998.

D'Souza, Dinesh. *The End of Racism.* New York: Free Press, 1995.

Mosley, Albert G., and Nicholas Capaldi. *Affirmative Action: Social Justice or Unfair Preference?* New York: Rowman & Littlefield, 1996.

Sowell, Thomas. *Affirmative Action around the World: An Empirical Study.* New Haven, Conn.: Yale University Press, 2004.

See also: Brown v. Board of Education; *civil rights; diversity; Jewish conservatives; quotas; Sowell, Thomas; Thernstrom, Abigail*

Agar, Herbert (1897–1980)

One of America's leading conservative intellectuals of the 1930s, Agar was born in New Rochelle, New York, served in the Navy during World War I, and graduated from Columbia University in 1919. After receiving a Ph.D. in English from Princeton in 1922, he taught English and history for the next six years at the Hun School in Princeton, New Jersey. In 1929 he moved to England. There he served as London correspondent for the *Louisville Courier-Journal*, press attaché to Robert Bingham, American ambassador to Great Britain, and literary editor of Douglas Jerrold's *English Review*. He also worked for G. K. Chesterton's *G.K.'s Weekly*. He returned to the United States in 1935.

In 1935, Agar joined the editorial staff of Bingham's *Louisville Courier-Journal* and commenced writing his syndicated newspaper column, "Tide and Tide." Between 1940 and 1942 he was editor of the *Louisville Courier-Journal*. In 1942, while a lieutenant commander in the United States Navy, he was appointed special assistant to John G. Winant, the American ambassador to Great Britain. During World War II, Agar was also director of the British division of the Office of War Information. He settled in England after the war and died in Sussex on November 24, 1980.

The most formative period in Agar's intellectual development was the time he spent in England from 1929 to 1935. It was then that he was influenced by the English distributist movement of Hilaire Belloc, Douglas Jerrold, and G. K. Chesterton, and he became Chesterton's most important American political disciple. The English distributists' major assumptions—that the ultimate basis of democracy was the widespread distribution of property, that plutocracy was the greatest threat to a propertied society, and that socialism and communism were inevitable byproducts of the economic centralization of modern capitalism—shaped Agar's copious political and historical writings of the 1930s.

In 1934, Agar won the Pulitzer Prize for history for *The People's Choice, From Washington to Harding: A Study in Politics* (1933), a caustic chronicle of American presidential elections written from a Jeffersonian perspective. *The People's Choice* argued that American democracy had degenerated into a "democracy of massed city populations, ignorant foreign labor, graft and 'machine politics'—the democracy . . . that was really plutocracy." If Americans wished to destroy oligarchy and avoid political collectivism, Agar said in *The People's Choice*, they would have to restore the widespread distribution of property.

In 1935, Agar published *Land of the Free*, a book that cemented his reputation as America's most articulate proponent of a propertied society. Agar described himself here as a Jeffersonian conservative and asserted that America could again become "a nation with a majority of small proprietors, with no all powerful plutocracy at the top and no large proletarian class at the bottom." He predicted that the American population would respond enthusiastically to any politician who espoused such a program.

After returning to the United States, Agar hoped to participate in and shape a movement of agrarians, distributists, and other decentralists to restore widespread property ownership. He believed that America stood at a political crossroads. It could attempt to solve the problems brought on by the depression through centralized economic and political planning that would leave economic bigness untouched. This, however, would merely ameliorate the most egregious failings of modern capitalism. Or America could attack the economic centralization and dispossession that lay at the root of her social and economic ills. Unfortunately for Agar, no major American political movement emphasizing proprietorship and the restoration of the widespread distribution of property appeared during the 1930s.

Agar's assaults on economic centralization and his defense of property brought him to the attention of like-minded intellectuals, particularly the Southern Agrarians. Allen Tate, one of the contributors to the Agrarian symposium *I'll Take My Stand: The South and the Agrarian Tradition* (1930), proposed that Agar ally with the Agrarians to oppose "the pseudo-metaphysical dogma of capitalist-communist philosophy." This overture led to the publication of *Who Owns America? A New Declaration of Independence* (1936), a collection of essays edited by Tate and Agar. *Who Owns America?* was the most important defense of economic and political decentralization and the widespread distribution of property published in the United States during the 1930s. It contains essays by eight of the twelve Agrarians, as well as essays by six southern supporters of the Agrarians, essays by Belloc and Jerrold, and pieces by several others sympathetic to the agrarian-distributist message. But *Who Owns America?* did not fulfill Agar and Tate's hopes of pushing the New Deal in an agrarian-distributist direction, nor did it elevate the Agrarians and distributists to a position as philosophers of a reformed New Deal.

Agar was also instrumental in the founding in 1937 of *Free America*, the only periodical of the 1930s devoted exclusively to disseminating the message of economic decentralization and the restoration of property. Agar hoped *Free America* could become an alternative to collectivist weeklies like the *New Republic* and the *Nation*. But *Free America* never attained a large circulation, and it was unable to fulfill Agar's grandiose expectations. During the war it degenerated into an eclectic journal encouraging home gardening, consumer cooperatives, and domestic manufacturing. It ended publication in 1947.

By the late 1930s, Agar's major interest was no longer the restoration of the widespread distribution of property but defending Western civilization from the threat posed by fascism. He was one of the earliest advocates of American entry into World War II on the side of Great Britain. In 1941, he helped found and was the first president of Freedom House, Inc., which was established to encourage international cooperation and peace and to oppose totalitarianism. Agar defended Western democracy in *Beyond German Victory* (1940) and *A Time for Greatness* (1942). His books also include *The Saving Remnant: An Account of Jewish Survival* (1960) and *The Darkest Year: Britain Alone, June 1940–June 1941* (1973).

—EDWARD S. SHAPIRO

Further Reading

Carlson, Allan. *The New Agrarian Mind: The Movement toward Decentralist Thought in Twentieth-Century America.* New Brunswick, N.J.: Transaction, 2000.

Leverette, William E. Jr. and David E. Shi. "Herbert Agar and *Free America*: A Jeffersonian Alternative to the New Deal." *Journal of American Studies* 16 (1982): 189-206.

Lubick, George M. "Restoring the American Dream: The Agrarian Decentralist Movement, 1930-1946." *South Atlantic Quarterly* 84 (1985): 63-80.

Shapiro, Edward S. "Decentralist Intellectuals and the New Deal." *Journal of American History* 58 (1972): 938-57.

———. "American Conservative Intellectuals, the 1930's, and the Crisis of Ideology." *Modern Age* 23 (1979): 370-80.

See also: agrarianism; Belloc, Hilaire; Chesterton, G. K.; distributism; Southern Agrarians

agrarianism

Agrarianism posits that the practices associated with the agricultural life are particularly—and in some cases uniquely—well suited to yield important personal, social, and political goods. The precise character of these goods—and the respective roles of government, society, and individuals in procuring them—varies according to which school of agrarian thought one wishes to consider. The first school important to postwar conservatives is that promoted, in various degrees, by the "Old Whig," Anti-Federalist American founders. The second strand of agrarianism with particular importance for conservatives is that found running through the work of various antimodern thinkers of the twentieth and twenty-first centuries.

John Taylor of Caroline, Thomas Jefferson, and their fellow Old Whigs, such as Edmund Ruffin, self-consciously sought to retrieve the classical agrarian tradition represented by Hesiod, Cato the Elder, Varro, and Vergil, who like them were concerned about the relationship between politics and farming. These ancient thinkers celebrated the personal and civic virtues associated with farming—economic independence, willingness to engage in hard work, rural sturdiness, hatred of tyranny—that the old Whig founders saw themselves as protecting through the Revolution.

Thomas Jefferson's agrarian observations are scattered throughout his letters and other documents. "Those who labour in the earth are the chosen people of God, if ever he had a chosen people, whose breasts he has made his peculiar deposit for substantial and genuine virtue. . . ." he declaims in Query XIX of *Notes on the State of Virginia* (1781-82). "Corruption of morals in the mass of cultivators is a phenomenon of which no age nor nation has furnished an example." Jefferson and the other Anti-Federalists believed that yeoman farming nurtured a spirit of self-reliance that made economic—and therefore genuine political—independence possible. In that fact lay farming's principle value.

Jefferson was a reliable spokesman for republican agrarianism, but John Taylor of

Caroline was its most dogged and insightful defender. His *Arator,* first published as a series of newspaper articles in 1803, consists of Taylor's practical suggestions, based on his own analysis, observation, and experiments, for improving American agriculture, the condition of which he lamented. Taylor's defense of republican agrarianism rests on much the same ground as Jefferson's. Political independence, Taylor agrees with Jefferson, cannot be secured by "bankers and capitalists." But not only does Taylor place more emphasis than does Jefferson on the role of agriculture as "the mother of wealth" as well as "the guardian of liberty," he also goes further in articulating the personal benefits afforded by life on the land. Farming, he maintains, brings more pleasure than other modes of employment. It provides continual novelty and challenges to the mind. It meets the physical needs of the body. It promotes the virtue of liberality and rewards almost every other virtue. It is an aid in the quest for eternal life, for it feeds the hungry, clothes the naked, and gives drink to the thirsty. And because it is a vocation inevitably more concerned with practical affairs than abstract speculations, it is the "best architect of a complete man." Virtually every claim for the farming life to be made by American agrarians in the following centuries is anticipated here.

Republican agrarianism permeated American politics and literature for many years—indeed, it continues to find resonance in recent works such as Victor Davis Hanson's influential *The Other Greeks: The Family Farm and the Agrarian Roots of Western Civilization* (1995). But in the mid- to late 1800s defenses of agrarian ways became entangled with populist politics. During this period, agrarian arguments were less explicitly focused on the goods of the farming life per se than on the economic interests of farmers. However, with the closing of the frontier at the end of the nineteenth century,

and with the concomitant slow but steady decline in the proportion of Americans living on farms, a new generation of self-consciously agrarian thinkers began to emerge. These included economist Ralph Borsodi, the Iowa priest and Catholic Rural Life activist Luigi Ligutti, and Harvard sociologist Carle Zimmerman, all of whom—along with several others—are profiled in Allan Carlson's indispensable history, *The New Agrarian Mind: The Movement toward Decentralist Thought in Twentieth-Century America* (2000).

As Carlson shows, this group heralds the advent of a new and distinct type of agrarianism. Although its proponents' political affiliations varied widely, they all shared a deep dissatisfaction with many aspects of modern economic, political, social, and religious structures. The urbanized, mass consumerism of industrial society had come into focus for them as a characteristic feature of modernity in a way that it could not have for the earlier republican agrarians. Some form of resistance to modernity, some alternative, was therefore needed. Several antimodern agrarians, among them John Crowe Ransom and Allen Tate, also developed an epistemological critique of Enlightenment scientific rationality, a critique that has been carried forward today by Wendell Berry. Much like Tate, Berry's ethical critique of modern society rests, like his epistemological critique, on the argument that mass technological industrialism collaborates with science to enshrine a view of human beings and the natural world that treats objects and people as essentially interchangeable. Such arguments can be found throughout Berry's corpus, but they are brought together most systematically in his *Life Is a Miracle: An Essay against Superstition* (2000).

For conservatives, the Southern Agrarians have been the most influential of the antimodern agrarians. Their manifesto, *I'll Take My Stand,* was published in 1930 and is usually regarded as a classic of conservative cultural criticism. An oft-overlooked sequel, *Who Owns America?* appeared six years later. The leaders of the Southern Agrarians—Ransom, Tate, Donald Davidson, and Andrew Nelson Lytle—would continue to develop agrarian themes and arguments for some years, although Ransom bowed out of the struggle earlier than the others. While they shared the republican concerns of their southern forebears Jefferson and Taylor, they also charged modern industrialism with promoting irreligion, extinguishing great art and high culture, degrading the quality of human relations, and, not least, destroying the older rural, aristocratic culture—all of which were to become central concerns for later traditionalist conservatives.

The Southern Agrarians failed to spark the agrarian renaissance for which they had hoped, even in the South, but they did leave behind some intellectual successors, most notably Richard Weaver, M. E. Bradford, and the self-proclaimed "Northern Agrarian" Russell Kirk. Still, except for its occasional championing by writers like these, agrarianism has persisted at the margins of mainstream postwar conservative thought. Many conservatives have regarded agrarianism as romantic, reactionary, illiberal, impractical, and insufficiently appreciative of the manifold material and physical blessings that are the fruit of modern industrial society. Thus, agrarianism is a wedge that highlights the deep philosophical differences concerning the social, political, and cultural conditions that promote human flourishing which run like a fault line through the conservative movement.

By far the most influential agrarian today is Berry, a novelist, essayist, poet, and critic who lives and farms in Kentucky. Although Berry does not call himself a conservative, his stories and essays are profoundly subversive of liberal modernity and share many affinities with traditionalist or agrarian conservatism. His essays are character-ized by humility toward nature and the cosmos, unwavering skepticism toward modern notions of progress, and a practical and epistemological critique of technology. Berry's agrarian economics attempts to call attention to the ways in which the contemporary global economy undermines traditional cultures and stable communities, divorces economics from ethics, supports and is supported by big, distant, bureaucratic government (and is thus antidemocratic), and threatens ecological health. In his fiction Berry attempts to evoke the traditional agrarian world of midcentury Kentucky, with all its vices and virtues, in an attempt to preserve in a modern audience some memory of the good that existed in such a world, a type of good that he fears has now been, or is being, lost. Berry has found a sizable audience among traditionalists and social conservatives.

In the 1990s, magazines like the Anabaptist *Plain* and the Catholic *Caelum et Terra* (1991–96) emerged as loci of a new grassroots agrarian movement, attracting readers from across the political spectrum, though virtually all could in some sense be called culturally conservative. And in the last decade, Hanson, until recently professor of classics at Fresno State University, and Carlson, president of the Howard Center for Family, Religion, and Society, have also emerged as leading scholars and conservative defenders of the agrarian vision. Their different approaches reflect the bifurcation of the conservative agrarian tradition: Hanson the republican agrarian focuses on the role the farming life has played in inculcating the rougher democratic and masculine virtues, while Carlson the antimodern agrarian emphasizes the family-friendly, traditional culture that agrarianism tends to nurture.

—Jeremy Beer

Further Reading

Berry, Wendell. *The Art of the Commonplace: The Agrarian Essays of Wendell Berry.* Edited by Norman Wirzba. Washington, D.C.: Counterpoint, 2002.

Freyfogle, Eric T., ed. *The New Agrarianism: Land, Culture, and the Community of Life.* Washington, D.C.: Island Press, 2001.

Malvasi, Mark G. *The Unregenerate South: The Agrarian Thought of John Crowe Ransom, Allen Tate, and Donald Davidson.* Baton Rouge, La.: Louisiana State University Press, 1997.

Taylor, John. *Arator: Being a Series of Agricultural Essays, Practical and Political: In Sixty-Four Numbers.* Indianapolis, Ind.: Liberty Fund, 1977.

See also: Agar, Herbert; Berry, Wendell; Bradford, M. E.; Carlson, Allan; Davidson, Donald G.; distributism; I'll Take My Stand; Jefferson, Thomas; Lytle, Andrew Nelson; Owsley, Frank; Ransom, John Crowe; Southern Agrarians; Southern conservatism; Tate, Allen; Taylor, John (of Caroline); Wade, John Donald; Weaver, Richard M., Jr.

Allen, Richard V. (1936–)

Raised in Collingswood, New Jersey, Richard V. Allen attended the University of Notre Dame, where, working under the direction of Gerhart Niemeyer, he received both B.A. and M.A. degrees in international relations before working towards a doctorate at the Universities of Freiburg and Munich. An expert on international security, Allen was a member of the Intercollegiate Society of Individualists and Young Americans for Freedom and an assistant professor of international studies at Georgia Tech from 1961 to 1962. He also founded the Georgetown University Center for Strategic and International Studies.

Allen advised Richard Nixon's presidential campaign in 1968 and served in the administration as assistant to National Security Advisor Henry Kissinger. He left the Nixon White House in 1969 and was appointed a senior fellow at the Hoover Institution at Stanford University, a position he still holds. He advised Ronald Reagan during his 1976 and 1980 presidential campaigns and was named National Security Advisor to President Reagan, serving from January 1981 until January 1982. Allen resigned after being charged with allegations that he had inappropriately accepted a $1,000 check given by Japanese journalists to Nancy Reagan, but was cleared of any wrongdoing by the Justice Department.

Allen helped shape Reagan's foreign policy. He advised candidate Reagan to join the Committee on the Present Danger and initiated meetings between Reagan and prominent "neoconservatives" like Jeane Kirkpatrick. While National Security Advisor, Allen took a hard line approach towards the Soviet Union, often conflicting with Secretary of State Alexander Haig's more pragmatic approach.

—GREGORY L. SCHNEIDER

Further Reading

Anderson, Martin. *Revolution.* San Diego: Harcourt Brace Jovanovich, 1988.

Edwards, Lee. *Educating for Liberty: The First Half-Century of the Intercollegiate Studies Institute.* Washington, D.C.: Regnery, 2003.

See also: Reagan Doctrine

America First Committee

When World War II broke out in 1939, anti-interventionist sentiment was diffuse and unorganized. Only in the summer of 1940, after France had fallen and interventionists had established well organized and well-financed pressure groups, did foes of Franklin D. Roosevelt's foreign policy undertake a concerted opposition, which centered on the America First Committee (AFC). The committee, formally organized that September, coordinated all efforts to oppose Roosevelt's proposals for providing Lend-Lease assistance, arming merchant ships, and escorting war supplies to Allied ports. The AFC also criticized other administration moves, such as the occupation of Iceland, the drafting of the Atlantic Charter, and the placing of economic pressures on Japan. By the time the Japanese bombed Pearl Harbor on December 7, 1941, the AFC had 450 units and at least a quarter of a million members. It held massive rallies, distributed tons of literature, sponsored national radio speakers, and supplied research data to members of Congress. It remained in existence until Germany declared war on the United States, at which time it formally disbanded.

Late in the spring of 1940, Yale law student R. Douglas Stuart and four of his colleagues launched a petition aimed at organizing college students into a nationwide anti-interventionist organization. Their efforts centered on enforcing key provisions of the Neutrality Act of 1939: banning loans to belligerents and blocking the shipment of war goods abroad. Insisting on cash and carry, the students said, "We demand that Congress refrain from war, even if England is on the verge of defeat."

The law students soon enlarged their focus, seeking supporters not only among college graduates but in all areas of national leadership. General Robert E. Wood, sixty-one-year-old board chairman of Sears, Roebuck, volunteered to lead a national organization, becoming acting chairman. By mid-1940, other prominent supporters included aviator Charles A. Lindbergh, textile manufacturer William H. Regnery, retired diplomat William R. Castle, columnist and reserve general Hugh Johnson, attorney Clay Judson, investor Sterling Morton, and columnist John T. Flynn. Two men who later became presidents, Gerald R. Ford and John F. Kennedy, contributed to the organization, Kennedy saying, "What you are doing is vital."

Although it included adherents to the domestic New Deal as well as its foes, and although its research division was staffed by liberals, socialists, and pacifists, politically the AFC had an anti–New Deal cast. Officially neutral on the matter of party politics, it contained far more Republicans than Democrats. Moreover, as noted by historian Wayne S. Cole, many speakers at AFC rallies attacked both the president and his domestic politics. Certainly the AFC executive committee—composed of leaders of the Chicago business community—could be seen as representative of conservatism, and major parts of the midwestern business establishment bankrolled the AFC.

The war, said the AFC, was simply "another chapter in the series of conflicts between European states that have been going on in war and peace for hundreds of years." A new German empire was attempting to compete with well-established ones, and when Britain learned that Germany would be expanding at Britain's expense, instead of the Soviet Union's, it declared war on the Third Reich. Fortunately, if the United States preserved its democracy, it could insulate itself from National Socialism. Even if Britain were victorious, it would be unable to restore the governments destroyed by Germany. Moreover, any restored states would be too small to defend themselves, and the unstable political order created by the Versailles peace would simply continue. One thing remained clear: neither the survival of democracy nor the preservation of the global balance of power was at stake.

On one level, the AFC was a failure. Congress passed every bill the committee opposed, and public opinion polls seldom comforted the foes of intervention. More importantly, the United States entered a war the AFC saw as destructive to the nation's security and ruinous to its republican form of government. Anti-interventionism as a political posture was discredited ever after.

Yet the America First Committee cannot be lightly dismissed. It helped generate a public sentiment that forced Roosevelt to be circumspect in some of his demands on Congress, such as draft renewal, and secretive about such warlike moves as escorting British vessels. The AFC took credit for a number of things: a Lend-Lease amendment preventing actual delivery of war goods to Britain; Roosevelt's failure to announce convoys in his "national emergency" address of late May 1941; and elimination of an administration-sponsored clause in the original draft renewal bill explicitly permitting American troops to be stationed outside the hemisphere. It is hard to trace specific influence, but obviously the committee had enough public support to make Roosevelt more cautious. In addition, as Wayne Cole notes, anti-interventionist strength in Congress increased throughout 1941 in large part because of AFC efforts. If the Pearl Harbor attack had not taken place, and if Hitler had exercised restraint in the Atlantic, the America First Committee might have won its campaign.

—JUSTUS D. DOENECKE

Further Reading

Cole, Wayne S. *Roosevelt and the Isolationists, 1932–1945.* Lincoln, Neb.: University of Nebraska Press, 1983.

Doenecke, Justus D. *Storm on the Horizon: The Challenge to American Intervention, 1939–1941.* Lanham, Md.: Rowman & Littlefield, 2000.

Schneider, James C. *Should America Go to War? The Debate over Foreign Policy in Chicago, 1939–1941.* Chapel Hill, N.C.: University of North Carolina Press, 1989.

Stenehjem, Michele Flynn. *An American First: John T. Flynn and the America First Committee.* New Rochelle, N.Y.: Arlington House, 1976.

See also: Fish, Hamilton, III; Flynn, John T.; isolationism; Lindbergh, Charles A.; Old Right; Regnery, Henry; Villard, Oswald Garrison

American Conservative

Founded by columnist and sometime presidential candidate Pat Buchanan, shipping magnate Taki Theodoracopulos, and former *New York Post* editorial page editor Scott McConnell in 2002, the biweekly *American Conservative* was conceived as a thoroughly conservative alternative to the neoconservative internationalism regnant in the pages of the *Weekly Standard, National Review, Commentary,* and the *American Enterprise,* among other periodicals of the right. In look and design, the magazine was purposely modeled along the lines of the *Nation.*

Until early 2005, Taki and Buchanan served as the magazine's editors, with McConnell as executive editor. From the beginning, the magazine was dubbed as "paleoconservative" by the press, and it certainly has been Buchananite in that it has savagely opposed the Iraq War while adopting a critical stance toward global free trade and current immigration policies. It has also been vehemently critical of the Bush administration; in November 2004, the magazine published separate editorial endorsements of Ralph Nader, Howard Peroutka, Michael Badnarik, even John Kerry (McConnell's choice) for president over Bush, while only Buchanan, ironically, favored the incumbent.

In truth the *American Conservative* is not necessarily paleoconservative in its fundamental intellectual orientation or preoccupations. It is probably better described as traditionalist, decentralist, or populist, but in any case it is not overly concerned about its place within the mainstream conservative movement. As the editors put it in their opening editorial of October 7, 2002, they sought "to ignite the conversation that conservatives ought to have engaged in since the end of the Cold War, but didn't." "So much of what passes for contemporary conservatism," they charged, "is wedded to a kind of radicalism—fantasies of global hegemony, the hubristic notion of America as a universal nation for all the world's peoples, a hyperglobal economy." The magazine has not hesitated to question mainstream conservative doctrine on certain issues, such as the Israeli-Palestinian conflict or the need for a constitutional amendment to prevent same-sex marriage. It has also occasionally brought authentically conservative reflection to bear on topics often ignored on the cultural-political right, such as the treatment of animals in factory farms.

As had been planned all along, Taki withdrew from his role as publisher in 2005. Buchanan is now editor emeritus, while McConnell, who holds a doctorate in history from Columbia, serves as editor and publisher.

—JEREMY BEER

Further Reading

Buchanan, Patrick J. *Where the Right Went Wrong: How Neoconservatives Subverted the Reagan Revolution and Hijacked the Bush Presidency.* New York: Thomas Dunne Books, 2004.

See also: Buchanan, Patrick J.; isolationism; paleoconservatism

American Conservative Union

One of the nation's premier conservative activist groups since its inception in 1964, the ACU was formed in the wake of the Barry Goldwater electoral debacle. Like the conservative movement itself, the organization has had its ups and downs, but it is now fairly entrenched as a heavyweight of conservative political activism. Throughout the years its board of directors has been a veritable Who's Who of the conservative movement, featuring everyone from M. Stanton Evans and John Chamberlain to Jesse Helms.

ACU boasts two signature annual events—its comprehensive ratings of members of Congress and the Conservative Political Action Conference (CPAC). While it has become customary for interest groups to release ratings examining House and Senate members' voting records on the issues they follow, it was the ACU that pioneered the practice, and since 1971 the ACU ratings have been the most important quantitative scorecard used to gauge members' conservatism. The ACU looks at important votes on economic, social, regulatory, and foreign policy issues, as well as Senate votes on important nominations and treaties. Jesse Helms has a 99 percent lifetime ACU rating; Ted Kennedy scores at 2 percent.

Those ratings indicate the extent of the ACU's commitment to the entire body of conservative principles. Indeed, the ACU first made its mark during the 1970s when it criticized the Nixon Administration for not being conservative enough. It even backed John Ashbrook in the 1972 Republican presidential primary.

ACU started its Conservative Political Action Conference in 1971. The annual event held in the Washington, D.C., area is the largest regular gathering of conservative activists and leaders in the country, usually drawing a crowd of nearly 3,000 attendees. CPAC assembles an impressive lineup of speakers culled from the Republican leadership in Congress and, when a Republican is in the White House, the administration. It also features guest speakers from the ranks of conservative columnists and commentators as well as think tanks. For nearly two decades the conference's highlight has been the regular debate between conservative reporter and television commentator Robert Novak and liberal ABC newsman Sam Donaldson.

The presidency of David Keene has been a critical factor in the organization's waxing fortunes in the last two decades. Under Keene's leadership the ACU has become a leader in the conservative political movement inside the Beltway. Upon his arrival in

1984, Keene instituted aggressive direct mail campaigns and other fundraising efforts that pulled the organization out of a financial quagmire. As a result, the ACU's visibility and influence increased throughout the 1990s, as evidenced by the renewed interest in CPAC.

—MAX SCHULZ

See also: Conservative Party of New York; political action committees

American Enterprise Institute

The American Enterprise Institute, a public policy research organization, began in 1943 as the American Enterprise Association. AEA was organized in 1938 in New York City, but was officially incorporated in Washington in 1943. The name was changed to AEI in 1962. The organization is "dedicated to the preservation of the American free enterprise system" and its purpose is to "bring about a clearer understanding of our system of free enterprise and its relationship to America's social and political institutions."

Lewis Brown (1894–1951), the chairman of the Johns Manville Corporation, conceived of the idea for AEA. A visionary businessman, he instituted collective bargaining and an eight-hour workday before they were required by law, surveyed employee attitudes regularly, and had regional meetings to discuss his company's performance. Brown also performed extensive government service, including drawing up a blueprint for postwar European economic recovery. In part because of his concerns about the growth of governmental regulation and bureaucracy during the New Deal and World War II, Brown wanted to found an organization that would expound the benefits of a system of limited government while providing impartial and nonpolitical studies of current problems. The growth of centralized government power in the war years convinced Brown and the

other business leaders who founded AEA that Washington should be the locus of their activities. So concerned were they about the future of private business and industry, that an early publication warned, "[U]nless the public and our public officials reawaken to an understanding of the principles which underlie the system of private enterprise, that system may come to be numbered among the economic casualties of the war—not merely wounded, but dead."

In its early years, AEA published analyses of individual pieces of legislation prepared by outside experts. The first such publication was an analysis of a bill introduced in 1943 to establish an Office of War Mobilization with sweeping powers over economic activity. The association also published special studies, precursors to the scholarly studies AEI publishes today, and digests of books, speeches, and magazine articles. By 1950, nearly 500 publications bore the AEA name.

After Brown's death in 1951, AEA languished. In 1954, the board hired William J. Baroody as executive vice president. Baroody had come to Washington after World War II to join the Veterans Administration and had later moved to the Chamber of Commerce. He improved the association's publications and added intellectual heft by convincing economists Milton Friedman, Paul McCracken, and Gottfried Haberler to serve on the advisory board. Most significantly, Baroody instituted a resident scholars program, which would change the character of AEI and propel it to the first rank of research institutes. During the 1970s, he brought to AEI a host of intellectual heavyweights: former president Gerald Ford; constitutional scholars Walter Berns and Robert Goldwin; conservative jurists Robert Bork and Antonin Scalia; Federal Reserve Chairman Arthur Burns; economists Herbert Stein, William Fellner, Murray Weidenbaum and Gottfried Haberler; political scientist Jeane Kirkpatrick; leading neoconservative thinker

Irving Kristol; Defense Secretary Melvin Laird; sociologist Robert Nisbet; theologian Michael Novak; and writer Ben Wattenberg. Of diverse political affiliations, most AEI scholars nevertheless staunchly opposed communism and embraced free markets. Although the institute was best known for its economic analysis, Baroody's interest in foreign affairs, and especially Middle East policy, led him to enlist scholars who examined a wide range of foreign policy and defense issues. When Baroody came to AEA in 1954, the organization had a staff of five and its budget was around $80,000. When he left AEI twenty-four years later, the staff numbered about 125, and the budget was approximately $8 million.

After Baroody retired in 1978, his son William J. Baroody Jr. became president. But the expansion of AEI's budget and activities, increased competition in the think tank world, changing philanthropic giving patterns, and the strains of too-rapid growth in too many new directions precipitated a severe financial crisis. Baroody resigned as AEI's president in June 1986. In December 1986, the board announced the selection of Christopher C. DeMuth as AEI's new president. DeMuth was no stranger to AEI activities, especially those involving economic policy. A lawyer by training, DeMuth had served as executive director of President Reagan's Presidential Task Force on Regulatory Relief and had directed the Washington office of an economic consulting firm, Lexecon Inc.

DeMuth refocused institute research and scholarship in the core areas of economic studies, foreign policy, and political and social analysis. His first priority was to get the institute back on a sound financial footing, a task he accomplished in a very short time. Today the institute has fifty resident scholars and fellows, and more than one hundred nonresident adjunct scholars. The work of the institute and its scholars is cited more

often than that of any other think tank in America. Many of the scholars William J. Baroody brought to AEI in the 1970s remain at the institute, and DeMuth has attracted others likely to serve as their intellectual successors. The institute's bimonthly publication, the *American Enterprise*, a national magazine of politics, business, and culture, has some 30,000 readers, and the institute maintains a lively publishing imprint, AEI Press.
—CARLIN BOWMAN

Further Reading

Donnelly, Thomas. *The Military We Need: The Defense Requirements of the Bush Doctrine*. Washington, D.C.: AEI Press, 2005.

Maddison, Angus. *Growth and Interaction in the World Economy: The Roots of Modernity*. Washington, D.C.: AEI Press, 2005.

See also: Baroody, William J.; DeMuth, Christopher; think tanks, conservative

American Liberty League

The American Liberty League (1934–40) coalesced as the largest organized political opposition to the New Deal, particularly during Franklin Roosevelt's first term. Stepping into the role abandoned by a Republican Party under reconstruction, the league oversaw mass media educational programs to rally mainstream conservatives against Roosevelt's administration but failed to achieve the support critical to popular success.

Much of the impetus for the league came from Democratic Party leaders and financiers who, though one-time supporters of the New Deal, had become disillusioned with its lengthening raids on the private economy. The organization's founders included John J. Raskob, a DuPont executive and former Democratic National Committee chairman; Jouett Shouse, a Raskob ally and ex-president of the league's predecessor organization, the Association Against the Prohibition Amendment; former Democratic presidential nominees Alfred E. Smith (1928) and John W. Davis (1924); steel magnate Ernest T. Weir; and General Motors president Alfred P. Sloan Jr. Initial Republican supporters included former New York governor Nathan Miller and former senator James W. Wadsworth Jr. Lammot, Pierre, and especially Irénée du Pont constituted the bond that united many of these men; ties to du Pont business (Raskob), money (Sloan), or political adventures (Smith and Shouse) helped create a common outlook. Not surprisingly, the du Ponts were the largest source of league funding during its existence.

The league positioned itself as a defender of American traditions, including the Constitution, the Bill of Rights, laissez-faire capitalism, private property, low taxation, and reduced executive power, and as the enemy of communistic (or sometimes fascistic) change. Though officially nonpartisan, the league flooded the press with anti–New Deal pamphlets, newspaper columns, speeches, and radio talks. Even its positive program, as represented by the 1936 "Program to Congress," consisted largely of demolishing the alphabet agencies of the New Deal.

With a maximum membership of just 125,000, the league never developed into a mass organization and was ineffective, after its early publicity blitz, as a counterweight to the New Deal. Master campaigner Roosevelt fashioned Al Smith's January 1936 Mayflower Hotel speech to wealthy "economic royalists," which the league planned as the opening salvo of its effort to deny the President a second term, into class-warfare ballast that dragged first the league and then Republican candidate Alfred M. Landon down to defeat in the November election. The league was also touched by several scandals, including the Pierre du Pont/John Raskob stock-swap tax imbroglio and the

financial contributions made by careless members to the racist Southern Committee to Uphold the Constitution.

The 1936 election debilitated the league, though it continued in a truncated form until 1940. Despite spending $1.2 million in six years, and having at one point a staff larger than that of the National Republican Party, the league was a poor investment for conservatives. (In Shouse's opinion, the league's chief accomplishment was applying the brakes to Roosevelt at a time when he had begun to openly flirt with the Left.) How then does one explain the league's failure, given that it was the creation of wealthy, successful, and sophisticated men?

The standard analysis has been that the du Ponts and their cohorts, insulated by money, misjudged the mood of the American public, which supported the New Deal's political attempts to bring to heel a traitorous economic system. In recent years, a second interpretation has gained currency among both pro- and antimarket revisionists. The founding of the American Liberty League represented a squabble among elites in which both sides favored state intervention in the private sector, differing only on the degree of intervention they wanted. (It is interesting to note, in this context, the marriage of Roosevelt's son, Franklin Jr., to Ethel du Pont in 1937.)

Regardless of which interpretation one prefers, it is difficult to believe, as has been argued by at least one scholar, that the league presented the most determined defense of individualism in American history. More consistent proponents of the old liberal order—including Albert Jay Nock, H. L. Mencken, and Rose Wilder Lane—were conspicuous in their absence from league activities, as Sheldon Richman has noted. The American Liberty League was a conservatism of compromise with the modern era.

—DAVID A. HOEFER

Further Reading

Carr, William H. A. *The Du Ponts of Delaware.* New York: Dodd, Mead, 1964.

Ekirch, Arthur, A. Jr. *The Decline of American Liberalism.* New York: Atheneum, 1980.

Johnson, Hugh S. *The Blue Eagle from Egg to Earth.* Garden City, N.Y.: Doubleday, Doran & Co., 1935.

Wolfskill, George. *The Revolt of the Conservatives: A History of the American Liberty League, 1934–1940.* Boston: Houghton Mifflin, 1962.

Zilg, Gerard Colby. *Du Pont: Behind the Nylon Curtain.* Englewood Cliffs, N.J.: Prentice-Hall, 1974.

See also: New Deal

American Mercury

Founded in 1924 by H. L. Mencken and George Jean Nathan, the *American Mercury* was, during its first ten years of existence, one of the most influential and distinguished monthly periodicals to appear in an era of irreverence and sardonic fun. During those ten years—from January 1924 until December 1933—it largely reflected the libertarian and anticlerical thought of Mencken, who scandalized polite society by ruthlessly mocking Christianity, rural folk, patriotism, lodge-joiners, politicians of every stripe, business, virginity, Prohibition advocates, purveyors of moral uplift in any form, statist liberalism, writers of sentimental fiction, pretentious aesthetes in arts and letters, and anyone else who stood opposed to his own view of the autonomous individual, the "thinking minority." In an article published in the *Nation* less than a month before the first issue of the *Mercury* appeared, Mencken declared his credo as a critic and editor, stating, "I believe in liberty. And when I say liberty I mean the thing in its widest imaginable sense—liberty up to the extreme limits of the feasible and tolerable." He later wrote that "the *American*

Mercury is wholly without moral purpose or what is called public spirit. It harbors no yearning to make the world better, and least of all the American world. It rejoices in this great Republic as something rich and racy, and strives only to depict its life realistically and in good humor."

Mencken and Nathan had earlier honed their craft as reviewers (and, in time, editors) at the *Smart Set*, a literary magazine that had about it an air of strained, self-conscious cleverness reminiscent of the 1890s. They resigned from the *Smart Set* at the end of 1923, having made an arrangement with publisher Alfred A. Knopf to bring out a magazine not only literary in content, but also offering historical revisionism and social criticism, examining all aspects of American culture with a sardonic eye. Unlike their situation at the *Smart Set*, the co-editors were to have total editorial control over the periodical's content. Within a short time after the magazine's founding, however, it became apparent that although Nathan was listed as co-editor, the *American Mercury* was really Mencken's vehicle (after being quickly reduced to a lesser role at the *Mercury*, within a few years Nathan left completely). From the beginning, the magazine specialized in articles debunking past and then-current American myths, puncturing the reputations of Abraham Lincoln and abolitionist John Brown, mocking the self-regarding *artistes* of Greenwich Village, and assailing the treasured American belief in small-town decency and the inherent goodness of the common people. One of Mencken's favorite targets was the concept and practice of pure democracy: the leveler's belief that the opinions of any person, no matter how abysmally stupid or herd-driven, are of equal worth to those of the prudent and thinking individual. Mencken wrote, "Democracy is the theory that the plain people know what they want and deserve to get it good and hard." While he was a scandal to the generally conservative American middle class, Mencken (and, by extension, the *Mercury*) was by temperament a political Tory who scoffed raucously at the books and ideas of Upton Sinclair, Emma Goldman, and other "utopians." Under Mencken, the *Mercury* became one of the most widely quoted (and, in certain quarters, widely hated) magazines in the United States, with the anticipated arrival of each monthly issue becoming something of an event, especially among college students.

But by the end of 1933, with the United States in the depths of the Great Depression, the *Mercury*'s jabs at American stupidity, the foibles of what Mencken called "the *booboisie*," had ceased to amuse many readers. In addition, Mencken may have become a victim of his own success: after years

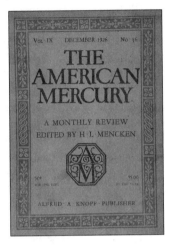

of ridiculing America's cultural follies, the shine had worn off the magazine's original luster. The number of readers of the *Mercury* had been declining since 1928, when it had attained a peak circulation of 84,000 readers; and now, with the numbers continuing to fall, along with his own popularity, Mencken stepped down as editor, turning over the reins to another libertarian, Henry Hazlitt, formerly the book-review editor at the *Nation*. Hazlitt struggled to retain the old fire that had once driven the *Mercury*, but he left after editing only four issues. He was succeeded by Mencken's former assistant, Charles Angoff, who steered the *Mercury* to the political Left during his year-long service as editor.

In December 1934, one year after Mencken's departure, Knopf sold the *American Mercury* to Paul Palmer of the Baltimore Sun papers. Despite the best efforts of Angoff and Palmer, the *Mercury* entered a

gradual downward spiral in editorial quality and outlook that continued at an inconsistent rate for the rest of its existence. As the Depression lingered and the magazine continued to lose readers, its opposition to "the common herd" took on a somewhat shrill tone, with contributors training their sights not so much on American culture in general but on the federal government and its motives. In 1939 Palmer sold the *Mercury* to Lawrence A. Spivak, the third in a succession of many owners of the magazine during the remainder of its existence.

During the late 1940s and into the 1950s, the magazine enjoyed a brief renaissance, boasting a number of distinguished contributors and editors, including Max Eastman, William F. Buckley Jr., and Frank Meyer, libertarians all. Their writings in the *Mercury* and elsewhere helped launch the post–World War II conservative movement in the United States. But the ownership and personnel of the *American Mercury* changed frequently; and with each new owner and each new change of editorial headquarters—the *Mercury*'s offices moved from New York to Oklahoma City to Texas to Torrence, California—the magazine's editorial stance became increasingly indefensible, especially in regard to racial matters. Where Mencken had opened the *Mercury*'s pages to people of all ethnic and racial backgrounds, his only editorial criterion being the quality of the work, the aging journal's editorials and articles increasingly focused on the defense of white supremacy, the inferiority of nonwhite races, the inherent evil of blacks and Jews, the danger of miscegenation, and the omnipresence of communists in America. In time, long after the departure of Buckley and the other founders of modern conservatism, the *Mer-*

cury offered defenses of Nazism and depicted Adolf Hitler as a badly misunderstood hero.

In its final years, novelist Taylor Caldwell, author of *Captains and the Kings* (1972) among other works, was the only writer of national repute who still contributed to the magazine. In 1980, on the one-hundredth anniversary of Mencken's birth, the *Mercury* published a special issue celebrating the America of its imagination that had been swept away, a country where people had lived free from the egalitarian demands of feminists and nonwhites. In this same issue, readers were asked to contribute to a fund for the creation of a mammoth computer database to track the activities of America's 15,000 most dangerous left-wing radicals. Nothing serious came of this crackpot appeal to the magazine's dwindling readership; and with the first issue of 1981, in its fifty-seventh year, the *American Mercury* finally ceased publication.

—JAMES E. PERSON JR.

Further Reading

Knopf, Alfred A. "H. L. Mencken, George Jean Nathan, and the *American Mercury* Venture." *Menckeniana* 78 (1981): 1–10.

Mencken, H. L. *A Second Mencken Chrestomathy.* Edited by Terry Teachout. New York: Alfred A. Knopf, 1994.

Mott, Frank Luther. *Sketches of 21 Magazines, 1905– 1930.* Vol. 5 of *A History of American Magazines.* Cambridge, Mass.: Harvard University Press, 1968.

Russell, Richard K. Introduction to *The American Mercury: Facsimile Edition of Volume I.* Blauvelt, N.Y.: Freedeeds Books, 1984.

Singleton, M. K. *H. L. Mencken and the American Mercury Adventure.* Durham: N.C.: Duke University Press, 1962.

See also: Hazlitt, Henry; fascism; Mencken, H. L.

American Review

Edited by Seward Collins and published from 1933 to 1937, the *American Review* was a significant journal of antimodern conservatism. Although it did not have a wide readership or influence public policy, it was the major forum for intellectual currents in the United States that resisted political liberalism, industrial capitalism, and cultural modernism. Its sympathies ranged from traditional Christianity to contemporary fascism.

Seward Collins, a man of independent wealth, had been editor of the *Bookman*, which he had purchased in 1927. A follower of Irving Babbitt and the New Humanists, Collins made the *Bookman* a voice of conservative literary opinion, opening its pages to Babbitt, Paul Elmer More, and many of the younger New Humanists. But Collins's interests became more emphatically political and economic in succeeding years, and in 1931 he transformed the *Bookman* into the *American Review.* His wife, the former Dorothea Brand, became its literary editor. Collins himself, formerly a political leftist, now embraced the ideology of Italian fascism and welcomed the economic agenda of Benito Mussolini. Collins believed that industrial capitalism was in a state of near collapse and must be reformed. In this conviction he was influenced by the distributist ideas of G. K. Chesterton and Hilaire Belloc. Without a reformist program, Collins could see only the eventual triumph of communism.

Among American intellectual movements, the Southern Agrarians, although their members had little to no sympathy for fascism, had the largest representation in the *American Review.* Their case against the ascendancy of industrialism in the northern states and the culture of materialism and consumerism it fostered had been familiar since the publication of their 1930 manifesto *I'll Take My Stand: The South and the Agrarian Tradition.* Now, in the *American Review,*

Herbert Agar denounced the cash nexus that had destroyed communal and personal relations in the United States; Donald Davidson repeated his plea for the more genuinely human and organic life of the rural South; and Frank L. Owsley outlined his program to dismantle corporations, holding companies, and farms under absentee ownership and to restructure them in small units. Cleanth Brooks gave voice to a common Agrarian intellectual theme in criticizing liberal Protestantism for its accommodation to science and for its alliance with liberal-progressive reform programs in politics. Other Agrarian contributors to the *American Review* included John Crowe Ransom, Allen Tate, Robert Penn Warren, and John Gould Fletcher.

Medievalism was another cultural motif of the *American Review*. This often assumed the form of a High Catholicism, as advanced by Christopher Dawson; at other times it appeared as part of a sustained critique of modern society, as in the essays written for the magazine by Ralph Adams Cram. Cram, a noted architect and apologist of the Gothic tradition, contributed pieces to the *American Review* that argued for an aesthetic retreat from modernism, to which many of his fellow contributors were sympathetic. Cram's medievalism undergirded his excoriation of the modern economic system—banking and usury, state centralization, factories—and his disdain for mass democracy. Cram, like other *American Review* writers, believed that he was speaking for "the forgotten classes," all those people who were the victims of industrial capitalism—farmers, small shopkeepers, craftsmen and artisans, intellectuals and artists, and nonunionized laborers.

The *American Review* ceased publication in 1937. Its conservatism was often romantic and sometimes even utopian. But undercurrents of dissent from the entire program of modernity, in all its social and cultural manifestations, were widespread in the American intellectual community in the years following the great crash of 1929. The *American Review* tapped those feelings and gave them vigorous and challenging presentations.

—J. David Hoeveler Jr.

Further Reading

Hoeveler, J. David, Jr. "The *American Review*." In *The Conservative Press in Twentieth-Century America*, edited by Ronald Lora and William Longton. Westport, Conn.: Greenwood, 1999.

Stone, Albert E., Jr. "Seward Collins and the *American Review*: Experiment in Pro-Fascism, 1933-1937." *American Quarterly* 12 (1960): 3-19.

See also: Collins, Seward; distributism; New Humanism; Southern Agrarians

American Revolution

The war by which the American colonies seceded from the British Empire is the subject of significant debate within the conservative movement. What one thinks of the nature of this war says much about what one thinks of America and of conservatism as a philosophy and way of life. Many within the conservative movement accept the notion that the American Revolution created a new America, radically separated from the institutions and habits of the old world. As a "new" nation, America, in this view, is held together only by its people's ideological commitment to freedom and progress. However, traditional conservatives argue that this is a fundamentally liberal reading of America and its beginnings; it ignores the role of history—in this case the 256 years between the landing at Plymouth Rock and the Declaration of Independence, during which Americans lived and ruled themselves in their own communities, facing new circumstances through their accustomed (highly British) means of constitution- and law-writing, local political control, and deep integration of religious and social life. To see the United States as a "new" nation is thus to ignore the historical roots of the rights we enjoy, of the customs and traditions that surround and protect those rights, and of the local institutions central to our way of life.

Most conservatives, wanting to preserve a common memory of our historical moorings, prefer to see the American Revolution itself in historical context; they view it as the last battle of American colonists with an overbearing King and Parliament seeking to deny them the rights enjoyed by their forebears. Indeed, many conservatives often refer to the American Revolution as the War for Independence in order to emphasize their view that the American colonists' break with Great Britain did not usher in the kind of radical innovations in political, social and religious life that marked the French Revolution of 1789. This terminological preference may raise eyebrows, since so many Americans during the founding and subsequent eras have referred to the break with Britain as a revolution. But more recent studies of the term "revolution," particularly those undertaken by scholars of the classical republican school, have shown how one can see the war of 1776 as both a revolution and a conservative event. In classical and early modern times it was thought that societies, and free republican societies in particular, periodically had to be brought back to their original principles in order to cleanse them of corruption and selfishness. Thus a "revolution" consisted of bringing a society's institutions, beliefs, and practices back to their more pure and public-spirited beginnings. It is in this sense that the American War for Independence may be seen as revolutionary, for it renewed American commitment to the principles and practices of ordered liberty that had been brought over from Great Britain and modified to fit the circumstances in the new world.

This is not to say that there were no truly radical ideologues active during the revolutionary era. Tom Paine in particular was a highly effective orator in support of the split with Britain and would later go on to champion the radical, anticlerical, leveling policies of the French Revolution. But Paine was one of a small group of radicals and, while his rhetoric was highly effective during the heat of war, he soon lost popularity during the ensuing peace and was unable to find employment in the United States. The main current of political thought in revolutionary America was similar to that of New York's agent in the British Parliament, Edmund Burke: Old Whig. That is, it was tied to the principles and institutions behind the Glorious Revolution of 1689 in Britain. In that Revolution, James II was chased from the throne for acting as a legislator without consent of his Parliament, for raising a standing army to threaten his people, for revoking the charters of Britain's local townships, and for outraging his people's religious convictions through his support of Catholics, whom the British deemed servants of foreign powers, including both the papacy and the much more physically threatening French monarchy. At root, James was dethroned because he sought to undermine the tradition of ordered liberty embodied in traditions and charters of rights going back at least as far as the thirteenth-century Magna Carta, which itself declared the king's responsibility to govern according to the preexisting law of the land and the rights recognized therein.

The Whig establishment, which engineered James's ouster, saw itself as protecting the inherited, chartered rights of Englishmen to trial by jury, local political autonomy, consent to taxation, and so on. And it was these same rights, embodied in their own colonial charters, that the American colonists sought to defend, first by opposing new taxes imposed by the English Parliament, and then, when that failed, by seeking independence. Thus, for conservatives, the American Revolution does not mark an abrupt break with the politics of Britain or with an "old world" of superstition and oppression. Rather, in the face of would-be oppressors and in direct contrast with the French Revolution, in which the desire for change ran riot, the American Revolution marked the successful conservation of inherited rights by the American people.

In seeking to understand why conservatives conceive of the War for Independence as a successful conservative reaction in America, one must look to the significant number of men of high talent and character called upon (some might say at least in part created) by revolutionary events. These founders—from Washington to Madison, Jefferson to Adams and Hamilton—led the colonies to independence without overthrowing their basic, preexisting institutions, including common law rights, the court systems themselves, social and political hierarchies, and church establishments protecting the role of religion in public and private life. While conservatives tend to be leery of Great Men, or of crediting particular individuals with the power to make and break history, it is clear that the education, training, and upbringing provided the upper classes in America in the mid- to late-eighteenth century instilled a public virtue, commitment to stability, insistence on reasoned discourse, and attachment to historically rooted institutions that helped prevent the advent of any radical revolution.

From the conservative viewpoint, the American Revolution "produced" some radical rhetoric, but it mainly preserved the continuation of local life governed through town and state institutions, with only derivative powers being exercised at any higher, more centralized level. Those derivative powers were transferred from King and Parliament to the American Confederacy, then to a more powerful Constitutional government, even-

tually situated in Washington, D.C. But this change of venue, and even of form and content, did not alter the basic nature of American life, its local character, and its emphasis on the importance of local autonomy.

—Bruce Frohnen

Further Reading

Kendall, Willmoore, and George W. Carey. *The Basic Symbols of the American Political Tradition.* Washington, D.C.: Catholic University of America Press, 1995.

Kirk, Russell. *The Roots of American Order.* La Salle, Ill.: Open Court, 1974.

Shain, Barry Alan. *The Myth of American Individualism.* Princeton, N.J.: Princeton University Press, 1996.

See also: Bradford, M. E.; Declaration of Independence; Henry, Patrick; Jaffa, Harry V.; Tories, American (Loyalists); tradition; Washington, George

American Spectator

The *American Spectator* inaugurated a movement in conservative campus journalism. Born amid the student leftist movement of the late 1960s, it moved from its birthplace on the Indiana University campus into national, commercial circulation, eventually attaining in 1995 a circulation of 309,000, making it for a time the most widely circulated conservative periodical in America. Its founder and editor, R. Emmett Tyrrell Jr., became a nationally renowned conservative pundit.

Tyrrell, a product of Chicago, was an undergraduate and graduate student in history at Indiana University when he teamed with John "Barron" Von Kannon and Ronald Burr to launch *The Alternative: An American Spectator* in 1967. They first used the summer cottage of a friend, which they called "The Establishment," to prepare and print the journal, later moving to quarters in downtown Bloomington. Their intention was to issue a publication that challenged the reigning political leftism on campus. Their efforts drew attention from prominent conservatives like William F. Buckley Jr., and Tyrrell began to think big. After changing the magazine's name to the *American Spectator,* he eventually moved the *Spectator*'s offices to Washington, D.C.

Tyrrell was a self-conscious disciple of H. L. Mencken and the *Spectator* was partially successful in emulating Mencken's own journal, the *American Mercury*. Tyrrell believed that much of the New Left represented a resurgence of Puritanism in America, a spirit that Mencken had called the bane of life in the United States. On issues ranging from feminism to the antibusiness crusading of Ralph Nader, Tyrrell used the *Spectator* to launch a counterattack. The spirit of the magazine was libertarian, although it did not adhere consistently to libertarian ideology. A popular section of the *Spectator* was its "Great American Saloon Series," in which veterans of historic pubs and taverns celebrated, almost nostalgically, an era before Muzak, disco, female bartenders, and Perrier water became fashionable.

Although the *Spectator* carried weighty articles on serious political issues, some of which won national attention, its appeal seemed to derive from its iconoclastic style. Tyrrell wanted to destroy what he called the "New Age" culture. In the tradition of his mentor Mencken, Tyrell used ridicule and sarcasm to expose the inanities of feminism, environmentalism, pacifism, vegetarianism, and other causes promoted by liberals. The *Spectator* liked to expose the extremes of these movements. Its opening column, "The Continuing Crisis," recounted stories from around the United States that documented the follies of American life, much as Mencken's "Americana" section had done in the *Mercury*. And the back section, "Current Wisdom," quoted from magazines such as *Ms.*, the *Progressive*, and *Vegetarian Times* in a manner that made their ideas seem absurd. Tyrrell quite seriously believed that the horselaugh was a better tactic than serious discourse in refuting the ideas of his rivals. To that extent the magazine functioned as a kind of cultural exorcist.

Tyrrell and the *Spectator* differed from Mencken in one important respect. Like much of the intellectual conservatism of the 1970s and 1980s, the *Spectator* reflected an anti-intellectual bias and tended toward a populist position. Whereas Mencken had few kind words for American intellectual leadership, he was even more disdainful of the average citizen in the United States, whom he was likely to dismiss for his simplistic Rotarian mentality. Tyrrell and the *Spectator,* however, were inclined to find in the norms of American life a healthy retreat from the feverish reformist programs of liberalism and the zealous aspirations of the counterculture. The *Spectator* preferred the barbershop pieties of Main Street to the refined wisdom of academia.

The *Spectator* looked for a world free from the constraints of the state, but it was not a journal of consistent ideological libertarianism. What made its program fall short of such consistency was libertarianism's dangerous proximity to New Age culture—its experimentation with drugs, sexual freedom, and other concessions to individual discretion. Nor did the *Spectator* welcome the homosexual movement. The journal defended basic constitutional freedoms but did not embrace the new lifestyles that emerged from the 1960s. When new causes and crusades emerged, the *Spectator* generally retreated to a rule of reason or appealed to the common-sense wisdom of the majority of Americans.

The Clinton era saw the *Spectator's* readership skyrocket, as the editors made the most of every lie, liaison, and scandal—often digging up much of the dirt themselves Alas, their business judgment failed them as rising salaries, expensive investigations into Clinton's background, and defectors (particularly David Brock, who had written headline- and readership-grabbing stories on Anita Hill before turning to the Left) cost the magazine more money than their near-obsessive anti-Clinton focus brought in. By the end of the '90s, the magazine had lost a large proportion of its readership and was in serious financial trouble. In 2000, George Gilder stepped in, adding the magazine to his media empire while refocusing much of its content on technology and business news. But this attempt at radical transformation failed. Gilder sold the magazine in 2003. Tyrrell, who had been ousted from his editorial post in the Gilder regime, now returned, while the magazine was bought in 2004 by Alfred S. Regnery. The magazine, though weakened, still has a circulation of about 50,000 and seems to be gaining strength once again.

—J. David Hoeveler Jr.

Further Reading

Hoeveler, J. David, Jr. *"The American Spectator."* In *The Conservative Press in Twentieth-Century America*, edited by Ronald Lora and William Longton. Westport, Conn.: Greenwood, 1999.

———. *Watch on the Right: Conservative Intellectuals in the Reagan Era.* Madison, Wis.: University of Wisconsin Press, 1991.

York, Byron. "The Life and Death of *The American Spectator.*" *Atlantic Monthly,* November 2001, 91–105.

See also: American Mercury; Clinton, William Jefferson, impeachment of; Mencken, H. L.; Tyrrell, R. Emmett, Jr.

anarchism

Perhaps no political term is quite so misunderstood as "anarchy." In the popular press, it is a synonym for disorder and chaos, not to mention looting and pillage: countries like Haiti are always being "plunged into anarchy." The anarchist, meanwhile, is frozen into a late-nineteenth-century caricature: he is furtive, hirsute, beady-eyed, given to gesticulation, gibberish, and, most of all, pointless acts of violence. Yet anarchy, according to most of its proponents through the years, is peaceable, wholly voluntary, and perhaps a bit utopian. The word means "without a ruler"; anarchy is defined as the absence of a state and its attendant coercive powers. It implies nothing about social arrangements, family and sexual life, or religion; and in fact the most persuasive anarchists, from Russian novelist Leo Tolstoy to Catholic Worker founder Dorothy Day, have been Christians.

Under anarchy, wrote its advocate Prince Peter Kropotkin in the *Encyclopedia Britannica* (1910), "the voluntary associations which already now begin to cover all the fields of human activity would take a still greater extension so as to substitute themselves for the state in all its functions." From alms to arms, "an anarchist is a voluntarist," explained Karl Hess, the speechwriter for Barry Goldwater who chucked it all to live as a husband, neighbor, and welder in rural West Virginia. Anarchists would separate state from church, state from education, state from welfare, even state from justice. (Murray N. Rothbard and David Friedman, among others, have explored how courts and policing might work in a stateless society.)

The word anarchism was not popularized until 1840 (by Pierre-Joseph Proudhon), but its practice predates its philosophical defenders. In many ways, the American settlers and citizens of the early republic were, in their daily deeds, living anarchism. As Ralph Waldo Emerson explained, "Massachusetts, in its heroic day, had no government—was an anarchy. Every man stood on his own feet, was his own governor; and there was no breach of peace from Cape Cod to Mount Hoosac." "The new race is stiff, heady, and rebellious" said Emerson of his confreres in the 1830s, the heyday of American anarchism. "They are fanatics in freedom; they hate tolls, taxes, turnpikes, banks, hierarchies, governors, yea, almost laws." Emerson's handyman, Henry David Thoreau, expressed his anarchism aphoristically, altering the maxim of Thomas Jefferson to read "that government is best which governs not at all."

The abolitionist ranks included a number of anarchists, among them the wealthy New York Congressman Gerrit Smith, who made an exception to his antistatism by advocating the prohibition of alcohol. Smith might appear a hypocrite, but with a nod to Emerson's counsel about hobgoblins and little minds, the inconsistency of American anarchists has been one of their charms. Systematic anarchists weaving their elaborate schemes have usually been bores, men just as trapped in webs of abstraction as the statists against whom they rail. Their influence within the broader culture has been nil. American anarchism has been more a tendency than a philosophy; the most appealing anarchists have been literary men deeply dyed in the American grain.

Anarchists acquired the twin taints of violence and alienness in the late nineteenth century. Although a handful of "individualist anarchists," most prominently Benjamin Tucker, editor of the publication *Liberty,* have attracted scholarly attention, the "anarchist-communists" of the era were far more visible, vocal, and execrated. While most American anarchists have agreed with Dorothy Day that "property is proper to man," the anarchist-communists generally sought collective ownership of property, including land. As the Russian-born Emma Goldman, America's most noted anarchist-communist, explained her ideal: "Voluntary economic cooperation

of all toward the needs of each." (Despite her collectivism, Goldman was a fierce critic of the Soviet Union's denial of individual liberties.) The anarchist-communists, largely foreign-born, acting outside any local or even identifiably American context, were persecuted by the Wilson administration for their opposition to the First World War and disappeared, leaving few traces.

Yet echoes of native anarchism may be heard throughout American history: in the warnings of the Anti-Federalists about the centralizing thrust of the new Constitution; in the Garrisonian abolitionists who reviled any government that countenanced slavery; in the Populists of the 1890s, with their attacks on chartered corporations and paper wealth; in the Old Right of the 1930s, which saw the New Deal as potentially totalitarian; in the New Left of the 1960s, which denounced the military, the university, and the corporation as dehumanizing; and among contemporary libertarians, especially those influenced by the economist and anti-imperialist Murray N. Rothbard. But except for the anarchist-tinged Industrial Workers of the World, the radical labor union that reached its zenith in the early twentieth century, anarchists have never been adept organizers. For the most part anarchy in the United States has been a literary-political tendency. A very partial list of American men and women of letters who have described themselves as anarchists includes Henry Adams (a "conservative Christian anarchist"), Paul Goodman, Norman Mailer, Robinson Jeffers, e. e. cummings, Lawrence Ferlinghetti, Ursula Le Guin, William Saroyan, Dwight Macdonald, and Edward Abbey. Abbey's novels, especially *The Brave Cowboy* (1956), *The Monkeywrench Gang* (1975), and *The Fool's Progress* (1988), feature merry anarchist heroes who live by Abbey's anarchist creed: "Be loyal to your family, your clan, your friends, and your community. Let the nation-state go hang itself."

Literary anarchists often display an intense localism, reflecting Ernest Hemingway's belief that "No larger unit than the village can exist without things being impossible." They are antipolitical in that they deny that politics, or the demands of state, have any claim to our time, our families, our lives. In *Notes of a Neolithic Conservative* (1970), Paul Goodman, sometime guru of the New Left, wrote, "As a conservative anarchist, I believe that to seek for Power is otiose, yet I want to derange as little as possible the powers that be; I am eager to sign off as soon as conditions are tolerable, so people can go back to the things that matter, their professions, their sports, and friendships."

Ernest Crosby, who succeeded Theodore Roosevelt in the New York State Assembly in 1887, was a fervent admirer of Tolstoy and something of an anarchist himself. Crosby is remembered for *Captain Jinks: Hero* (1902), his satirical novel of American imperialism, but his poem, "The State," might serve as a stark summation of the anarchist view:

> They talked much of the State—the State.
>
> I had never seen the State, and I asked them to picture it to me, as my gross mind could not follow their subtle language when they spake of it.
>
> Then they told me to think of it as of a beautiful goddess, enthroned and sceptred, benignly caring for her children.
>
> But for some reason I was not satisfied.
>
> And once upon a time, as I was lying awake at night and thinking, I had as it were a vision,
>
> And I seemed to see a barren ridge of sand beneath a lurid sky;
>
> And lo, against the sky stood out in bold relief a black scaffold and gallows-tree, and from the end of its gaunt arm

> hung, limp and motionless, a shadowy, empty noose.
>
> And a Voice whispered in my ear, "Behold the State incarnate!"
>
> —BILL KAUFFMAN

Further Reading

Madison, Charles A. "Anarchism in the United States." *Journal of the History of Ideas* 6, no. 1 (January 1945): 46–66.

Martin, James J. *Men Against the State: The Expositors of Individualist Anarchism in America, 1827–1908.* Colorado Springs, Colo.: Ralph Myles Publisher, 1970.

Reichert, William O. *Partisans of Freedom: A Study in American Anarchism.* Bowling Green, Ohio: Bowling Green University Popular Press, 1976.

Schuster, Eunice Minette. "Native American Anarchism." *Smith College Studies in History* 17, nos. 1–4 (October 1931–July 1932): 1–202.

See also: Adams, Henry; Anti-Federalists; Jeffers, Robinson; Old Right; Rothbard, Murray

Anderson, Martin (1936–)

A free-market economist prominent in Republican politics, Martin Anderson received his Ph.D. in industrial management from the Massachusetts Institute of Technology in 1962. After serving as a research fellow for the MIT–Harvard University Joint Center for Urban Studies, Anderson taught at Columbia University's Graduate School of Business. He has been a Senior Fellow at the Hoover Institute on War, Revolution and Peace since 1971.

Anderson's carefully researched examination of federal urban renewal, *The Federal Bulldozer* (1964), argued that urban renewal was costly, destructive of property rights, and incapable of providing decent housing and a suitable living environment; he recommended its repeal. An intellectually respectable debunking of a prominent liberal endeavor in social engineering, *The Federal Bull-dozer* was much acclaimed by conservatives.

Anderson directed research for Richard Nixon's 1968 presidential campaign and was a policy advisor for candidates Ronald Reagan (1976 and 1980), Robert Dole (1996), and George W. Bush (1998). President Richard Nixon employed him as a special assistant and a special consultant for systems analysis. He served President Reagan as an assistant for policy development and was also on the President's Economic Advisory Board, Foreign Intelligence Advisory Board, and General Advisory Committee on Arms Control and Disarmament.

Active in the push to replace the draft with an all-volunteer military, Anderson also helped defeat a 1970s proposal to replace welfare with a guaranteed income. His books include *Welfare* (1978), a study of welfare reform; *Revolution* (1988), an account of his role in the Reagan administration; and *Impostors in the Temple* (1992), a critique of higher education.
—JOHN ATTARIAN

Further Reading

Anderson, Martin, ed. *Conscription: A Select and Annotated Bibliography.* Stanford, Calif.: Hoover Institution Press, 1976.

Reagan, Ronald. *Reagan: A Life in Letters.* Edited by Kiron K. Skinner, Annelise Anderson, and Martin Anderson. New York: Free Press, 2003.

See also: education, higher; welfare policy

anticommunism

When Vladimir Lenin and his Bolshevik Party overthrew Russia's democratic government in November 1917 to create the Soviet Union, few in the West understood the potential long-term significance of the act. The most eloquent observer was Winston Churchill, who said of the Communist government, "Of all tyrannies in history, the Bolshevik tyranny is the worst, the most destructive, and the most degrading." Churchill called on the world's governments "to strangle the infant bolshevism in its cradle." A half-hearted effort by the West failed, and the Soviet Union survived. Leading a millenarian movement that sought to communize the world, Lenin followed traditional state-to-state foreign policy but also set up an underground foreign policy by creating national communist parties around the globe, all of which were under Soviet control through the Communist International (Comintern). The American Communist Party was one of those communist parties.

The American Communist Party was a criminal enterprise from start to finish, loyal to the Soviet Union instead of the United States, directed by Moscow, and involved in espionage against the government of the United States for the Soviets. Many in the West were enamored of the communist experiment, particularly intellectuals, whom the Soviets targeted because of their influence. Soviet agents recognized that intellectuals were more susceptible to recruitment than the average person because communism's pseudoscientific ideology appealed to their rationality, and the vanguard role communism offered them appealed to their vanity. Many intellectuals visited the Soviet Union to see utopia. Most believed they had found it. Only a few who paid the USSR a visit, such as Bertrand Russell, Malcom Muggeridge, and Eugene Lyons, were horrified by what they saw. After meeting with Lenin, Russell explained why he turned against communism: "His guffaw at the thought of those massacred made my blood run cold."

For most Americans, anticommunism was a natural response to a totalitarian system that sought to obliterate what they believed were the very pillars of American freedom: democracy, religion, and individual free enterprise. In the face of Lenin's calls for revolution, a series of massive leftist-led strikes and a series of bombings of politicians and business leaders led to a government crackdown that focused on deporting leftist aliens, particularly communists. These tactics, called the "Red Scare" by their opponents and under the direction of Attorney General A. Mitchell Palmer, who had been targeted by the bombers, were stopped through the efforts of civil liberties groups and most of those rounded up were subsequently freed. Civil libertarians claimed that the anticommunists' real purpose was the destruction of all Americans' civil liberties, a theme that arose each time the government acted against domestic communism. But President Hoover and other anticommunists truly believed that the communists constituted a clear and present danger. One lasting effect of the "Red Scare" was the appointment of twenty-four-year-old J. Edgar Hoover to head up the "Radical Division" of the Justice Department, which became the Federal Bureau of Investigation.

The Great Depression and the rise of fascism in Europe gave communism new respectability among a wider public during the 1930s. Capitalism in the West seemed to have created an economic crisis the like of which the world had never seen, while communism appeared to have transformed the Soviet Union from a backwater into a mighty and egalitarian power. Great Britain and France, terrified of sparking World War II, appeased Adolf Hitler's every territorial whim, while only the Soviet Union, under Lenin's successor, Joseph Stalin, stood up to Hitler. Thousands of Americans became communists and hundreds of thousands more joined the "Popular Front" of the Left and became "fellow travelers" who parroted the Soviet line without actually becoming communists. Some American conservatives, especially those on the House Committee on Un-American Activities (HUAC), equated the Soviet Union with Nazi Germany and called

for investigation of subversion by supporters of both regimes, but most Americans focused squarely on the Nazi threat.

World War II changed most Americans' opinions about communism, despite Stalin's treaty with Hitler that divided Europe among them and allowed Hitler to start the war. Following Hitler's invasion of the Soviet Union and U.S. entry into the war, favorable portrayals by the American government and press combined with the Russians' heroic struggle against the Nazis combined to create a reservoir of goodwill toward communism. President Franklin Roosevelt was convinced that he could work with the Soviet dictator, Stalin, and frequently sided with him against British Prime Minister Winston Churchill, whose support for colonialism Roosevelt found more destabilizing than communism. In the weeks before he died, Roosevelt seemed to have begun to take a harder line toward Stalin, but Vice President Harry Truman, whom Roosevelt had neither consulted nor briefed on the situation, needed almost another year following his accession to the presidency to realize that he could not work with "Uncle Joe."

Once they understood the Soviet threat for what it was, liberal anticommunist internationalists fought against the Popular Front liberals—led by former vice president Henry Wallace, who believed that the United States and Soviet Union could continue to work together as they had during World War II—for the mantle of successors to Roosevelt's New Deal. The anticommunists won the electoral battle when Truman overwhelmingly defeated Wallace in the 1948 election, and they scored an important success within the labor movement when the Communists were expelled from the Congress of Industrial Organizations (CIO). Despite these victories, the Truman administration tried to ignore past communist infiltration into the Roosevelt administration, including the strong and often overwhelming evidence that such important figures as Alger Hiss, Harry Dexter White, and Laurence Duggan were communist spies. The most famous example of this intentional blindness came when Secretary of State Dean Acheson said "I will not turn my back on Alger Hiss" following Hiss's conviction for perjury after denying under oath that he was a communist. Hiss's accuser, Whittaker Chambers, brilliantly and almost apocalyptically described his decision to break with communism in *Witness* (1952). The book so impressed Ronald Reagan that he made a point to re-read it every year and awarded the Presidential Medal of Freedom to Chambers despite tremendous protests from liberals.

Although it ignored past treason, the Truman administration tried to prevent future subversion by instituting "loyalty oaths" for positions within the federal government, successfully prosecuting leaders of the Communist Party for belonging to an organization that called for the forcible overthrow of the United States government, and calling on the American people to be vigilant against communists where they worked. Despite the fact that many communists or fellow travelers already in government were left untouched, Truman's anticommunist tactics led leftist historians such as Athan Theoharis and Ellen Schrecker to charge Truman with starting another "Red Scare," which they considered to have been more dangerous to American liberties than communism itself. (The crimes referred to in Schrecker's *Many are the Crimes* (1998) are those of the anticommunists, not the Stalinists.)

Liberal anticommunist historians like Arthur Schlesinger Jr. and Theodore Draper disagreed with the New Left's interpretation of postwar anticommunism. They blamed conservative Republicans for the "Red Scare," which they called "McCarthyism" after Wisconsin senator Joseph McCarthy. McCarthy and other Republicans attacked the Truman administration for its failure to expose or speak out against treason. While conservatives generally supported Truman's anticommunist policy in Western Europe, they bitterly opposed his Far Eastern policy, which they believed led to the loss of China because of the purposely erroneous advice of communists and fellow travelers working within the State Department. McCarthy named names and revealed shoddy security measures throughout the national security sector of the government, but he often went beyond the evidence, demagogically bullying and smearing the innocent and frequently using anticommunism as a partisan political bludgeon. For many Americans, anticommunism became a disreputable cause, identified as it was with McCarthy's sometimes unsavory tactics. Following McCarthy's censure by the Senate, anticommunism came to be considered unsophisticated, lacking in nuance, and anti-anticommunism became the more respectable position among much of the nation's cultural elites.

Western liberal anticommunist intellectuals and labor unions also stood up to the Soviets and to the many communists and fellow travelers among Western leftist intellectuals. Following a series of massive Soviet-staged rallies for the arts and culture, they formed the Congress for Cultural Freedom in 1950, a moderately leftist, anticommunist, anti-McCarthyite group. The Congress's goal was to expose the lies of Soviet propaganda and show the reality of Soviet totalitarianism. It organized international protests against the oppression of intellectuals in authoritarian and totalitarian dictatorships, organized festivals of the arts patterned after the Soviets' festivals, assisted refugee writers, and financed magazines around the world that published many of the period's finest anticommunist thinkers. The excitement that the Congress generated at its first meeting was evident in the words of Arthur Koestler, one of the group's founders, before a crowd of 15,000 in West Berlin: "Friends, freedom has seized the offensive!" Organized labor also stood up to the communists. The American Federation of Labor (AFL) funded anticommunist unions around the world and thereby played a significant role in preventing France and Italy from succumbing to communism.

This liberal anticommunist offensive was funded by the CIA through a series of dummy foundations. The outlays were heavy but the results impressive: no longer could the Soviets dominate the international intellectual discourse despite their far greater expenditures, and no longer could they claim to be the solitary voice of the working man. While labor continued steadfast in its anticommunism, the Vietnam War eroded the Congress's influence because it drove many anticommunists into the anti-anticommunist New Left camp. The 1967 exposure of the CIA's role in both ventures doomed the Congress, but labor's anticommunist efforts were less damaged because of its independent funding through membership dues (although many liberals accused the AFL-CIO of being more interested in fighting communism than in assisting labor, especially in the underdeveloped world).

Vietnam destroyed liberal anticommunism. Many liberal anticommunists abandoned the field and joined the anti-anticommunist Left while others joined the conservative anticommunist Right. By the time of Jimmy Carter's presidency, the containment doctrine was in disrepute with the Left, while the president himself said that the United States must move on from its "inordinate fear of communism." Ronald Reagan's presidency solidified the new division. Reagan was probably the first president who saw the Cold War as something more than an effort to contain an aggressive but conventional great power. Reagan believed that the Soviet Union was the product of an implacable millenarian ideology that sought world domination. For Reagan, the only thing that

would destroy the communist Soviet Union was the concerted and sustained effort of Western civilization to battle against it. Anti-anticommunists were terrified by his rhetoric, weapons build-up, strategic defense plan, assistance to those countries threatened by communism, and assistance to anticommunist rebels, all of which they believed moved the world closer to a nuclear abyss. Following the Soviet Union's collapse and the fall of communism as an ideology, some of the former liberal anti-anticommunists recast themselves as anticommunists. Even news stories in the *New York Times* referred without irony to the former Soviet Union as an "evil empire," even though during the '80s it had mercilessly and repeatedly attacked Reagan for having used the phrase.

—ROBERT WATERS

Further Reading

Coleman, Peter. *The Liberal Conspiracy: The Congress for Cultural Freedom and the Struggle for the Mind of Postwar Europe.* New York: Free Press, 1989.

Furet, François. *The Passing of an Illusion: The Idea of Communism in the Twentieth Century.* Translated by Deborah Furet. Chicago: University of Chicago Press, 1999.

Griffith, Robert and Athan Theoharis, eds. *The Specter: Original Essays on the Cold War and the Origins of McCarthyism.* New York: New Viewpoints, 1974.

Herman, Arthur. *Joseph McCarthy: Reexamining the Life and Legacy of America's Most Hated Senator.* New York: Free Press, 2000.

Powers, Richard Gid. *Not without Honor: The History of American Anticommunism.* New York: Free Press, 1995.

See also: Burnham, James; Cold War; containment; fusionism; God That Failed, The; *Hiss-Chambers trial; Hook, Sidney; Lukacs, John; McCarthyism; Nixon, Richard M.; paleoconservatism; Radio Free Europe; Reagan Doctrine; Red Scare; Solzhenitsyn, Aleksandr; Vietnam War;* Witness

Anti-Federalists

In eighteenth-century usage, a federation was a league between sovereign states. The federal government could relate only to the state governments; it could not deal directly with the individual citizens of those states. This arrangement characterized the Articles of Confederation. Hence, Congress could not impose taxes on individuals directly but had to petition the states for money. In February 1787 Congress called a convention "for the sole and express purpose of revising the Articles of Confederation." What emerged from this convention was not a revision of the Articles, but a proposal for a new form of government—one that rejected the federal principle and created instead a national government that could directly govern individual citizens.

A period of intense debate followed, as individual state conventions met to consider whether to ratify the new constitution. The Anti-Federalists opposed ratification. In one of the more notable ironies of American history, those who wanted to maintain the federal principle were called Anti-Federalists, while those who wanted to create a national government were called Federalists. In the June 1788 debate in the New York convention over ratification, Melancton Smith, in rebutting Alexander Hamilton's advocacy of the new constitution, remarked that he "hoped the gentleman [Hamilton] would be complaisant enough to exchange names with those who disliked the Constitution, as it appeared from his own concession that they were Federalists, and those who advocated it Anti-Federalists."

Anti-Federalists and Federalists agreed on the essential aims and ends of government. Brutus's statement that "common good . . . is the end of civil government, and common consent, the foundation on which it is established" would have found no demurral among the Constitution's support-

ers. Both sides also agreed that self-interest was predominant in all human activity, in government as well as in commerce. The justification for government resided in the need to control the darker side of self-interest. Yet fulfillment of this justification is no easy task in light of Brutus's assertion, which the authors of the *Federalist* would have seconded, that "rulers have the same propensities as other men; they are as likely to use the power with which they are vested for private purposes, and to the injury and oppression of those over whom they are placed, as individuals in a state of nature are to injure and oppress one another."

The problem of constitutional design was one of how to control the operation of self-interest within government while allowing government the ability to perform those tasks that its justification requires. Anti-Federalists and Federalists alike saw government as a Faustian bargain: an instrument of evil—granting power to some over others—was to be employed because of the good it might do, while evil would also result. Making the bargain worthwhile, both sides thought, was a matter of proper constitutional construction. While they differed in how that construction ought to proceed, these differences were largely a product of their different prudential judgments about such matters as the likelihood of foreign aggression and the comparative benefits of small vs. large republics.

Anti-Federalists and Federalists alike generally desired to strengthen the federal government. They were concerned, for instance, in forestalling conflicts between the states that might arise over the looming settlement of western territories. They also wanted to deter aggression by European powers. The Anti-Federalists thought the federal government could be strengthened while adhering to the federal principle. The Federalists disagreed.

Federalist John Jay and Anti-Federalist Brutus operated from the same assumptions about human nature and the Faustian character of government. Yet they reached different conclusions about how to deal with the threat of foreign aggression. Jay put the matter thusly in *Federalist* 4:

> Leave America divided into thirteen . . . independent governments—what armies could they raise and pay—what fleets could they ever hope to have? If one was attacked, would the others fly to its succor and spend their blood and money in its defense? Would there be no danger of their being flattered into neutrality by specious promises, or seduced by a too great fondness for peace to decline hazarding their tranquility and present safety for the sake of neighbors, of whom perhaps they have been jealous, and whose importance they are content to see diminished.

Brutus thought the likelihood that Jay's fears would be realized was low: "We have no powerful nation in our neighborhood. . . . Some of the European nations, it is true, have provinces bordering upon us, but from these . . . we have nothing to apprehend; if any of them should attack us, they will have to transport their armies across the Atlantic, at immense expense, while we should defend ourselves in our own country, which abounds with every necessary of life."

The Anti-Federalists also thought the Federalists exaggerated the difficulty of financing the federal government. The (Anti-Federalist) Federal Farmer noted that the states had paid $24 million of the $36 million in requisitions over the preceding decade and then asked "whether that delinquency is to be imputed solely to the nature of requisitions" or whether it should "be imputed to two other causes[:] . . . first, an

opinion . . . that the requisitions for domestic interest have not been founded on just principles; and secondly, . . . that the government itself . . . has departed from the constitutional system." He went on to note that although the Articles of Confederation were in some ways weak and inconvenient, these disadvantages were "but as a feather in the balance against a mountain" when compared with the loss of liberty that would result under the proposed constitution.

The Anti-Federalists saw the primary task of government as securing individual liberty. They also recognized that the cultivation of republican virtues was necessary for liberty, and believed that such cultivation would fare better in a small, homogeneous republic. Agrippa asserted that "no extensive empire can be governed upon republican principles, and such a government will degenerate into a despotism unless it be made up of a confederacy of smaller states. . . ." Brutus argued that only in a small republic could representation be meaningful: "The very term, representative, implies, that the person or body chosen for this purpose, should resemble those who appoint them. . . . One man, or a few men, cannot possibly represent the feelings, opinions, and characters of a great multitude." Some Anti-Federalists even acknowledged that states could become so large as to lose their republican character, and in such cases should be divided into smaller units.

Furthermore, within a small, relatively homogeneous republic, items presented for public discussion would generally be of concern to all. People would be connected with one another and could participate meaningfully in civic life. No divide would separate governing officials from those they governed. The Anti-Federalists believed that active participation in civic life would help weave the bonds of affection and support that would sustain a regime of responsible liberty. In this regard, it is worth noting that the thirteen states contained nearly four million people in 1790. Present-day Switzerland, with a population of less than seven million organized into twenty-six cantons, has roughly the same governmental scale as America possessed two centuries ago.

As the Anti-Federalists feared, with a large republic comes anonymity and oligarchy. As the republic becomes larger, each individual becomes less significant and incentives to participate in governmental processes wane. The moral quality of human conduct likewise declines when personal relationships are replaced by impersonal and formal relationships.

The Federalists, however, doubted that small republics could be as supportive of liberty as could extended or compound republics, whereby a majority that might infringe upon a minority's rights in one republic could be negated by its lack of influence in the more extensive, compound republic. Thus, the debate between the Federalists and Anti-Federalists revolved around both sides' legitimate concerns about the probable consequences of different patterns of governmental organization.

—RICHARD E. WAGNER

Further Reading

Benson, G. C. S., ed. *Essays in Federalism.* Claremont, Calif.: Claremont Men's College, 1961.

Goldwin, Robert A., and William A. Schambra, eds. *How Federal is the Constitution?* Washington, D.C.: American Enterprise Institute, 1987.

Ostrom, Vincent. *The Political Theory of a Compound Republic.* 2nd ed. Lincoln, Neb.: University of Nebraska Press, 1987.

Storing, Herbert J. *What the Anti-Federalists Were For.* Chicago: University of Chicago Press, 1981.

Walker, Graham. *Moral Foundations of Constitutional Thought: Current Problems, Augustinian Prospects.* Princeton, N.J.: Princeton University Press, 1990.

See also: agrarianism; Constitution, interpretations of; federalism; Federalist, The; Federalist Party; Storing, Herbert J.

Arkes, Hadley (1940–)

A professor of jurisprudence at Amherst College, Arkes is a prominent American legal scholar and commentator upon legal matters and their relation to ethics. He is a frequent contributor to *First Things* and similar periodicals, in which he often writes on such topics as constitutional law, humanistic culture, and abortion. Indeed, Arkes often unites his scholarship on natural law and natural right with his concern for the rights of the unborn.

Arkes is the author of numerous books, notably *First Things: An Inquiry into the First Principles of Morals and Justice* (1986), *The Return of George Sutherland: Restoring a Jurisprudence of Natural Rights* (1994), and *Natural Rights and the Right to Choose* (2002). Reviewing the earlier volume, Joseph Sobran wrote "Arkes tries to show that moral truth is as truly true as mathematical truth." Sobran described this work as one in which Arkes discusses "the nature of man, the nature of legitimate government, the fact/value dichotomy, conscientious objection, Vietnam, the welfare state, and abortion, in effect constructing a post-Kantian version of natural law," adding that "the answers he reaches are evidently true." In *The Return of George Sutherland*, Arkes examined the legal thought of one of the so-called "Four Horsemen" of the U. S. Supreme Court who overturned major portions of President Franklin Roosevelt's New Deal agenda during the Great Depression. Despised by liberal pundits and legal scholars ever since, Sutherland's judicial theory would provide, Arkes argued, "the moral ground that is missing in the jurisprudence of both liberals and conservatives in our own time." These words allude to the fact that one of Arkes' major concerns has been to combat legal positivism, which has led him to critique conservative jurists such as Robert Bork and Supreme Court Justice Antonin Scalia.

In addition to his work in academe and as a writer, Arkes is active in conservative politics: he has helped to draft several legislative bills, including The Defense of Marriage Act (1996).

—JAMES E. PERSON JR.

Further Reading

Arkes, Hadley. *Beyond the Constitution*. Princeton, N.J.: Princeton University Press, 1990.

———. *The Philosopher in the City: The Moral Dimensions of Urban Politics*. Princeton, N.J.: Princeton University Press, 1981.

See also: judicial activism; natural law theory, new

arms control

Arms control has long been a national concern. But since the end of the Second World War and beginning of the Cold War, arms control has been intimately linked to broader issues of U.S. national security. So just what does arms control mean to modern conservatives?

Academics, including political scientists, foreign affairs analysts, and the technical staff of major governmental institutions, have long and readily differentiated the activities associated with disarmament from those related to arms control. Disarmament is the label commonly used to identify policies and actions that aim to deliberately remove designated weapons (or somewhat more broadly, a portion of defensive or offensive capability) from a country's inventory and positively reduce the numbers and/or types of weapons available to military forces. The declaration and implementation of such policies may be undertaken unilaterally (a rare but not unknown event) or in accordance with international agreements negotiated with other states. One example of such a disarmament agreement is the 1987 INF Treaty between the United States and the Soviet Union (covering intermediate- and short-range nuclear forces in Europe), which wholly eliminated an entire class of weapon—nuclear-tipped missiles with ranges of 500 to 5000 kilometers.

Arms control, on the other hand, is a label with both a narrower and a broader connotation. More broadly, it connotes those policies and actions that plainly affect the level or availability of armaments for, or comprehensive management of, a country's forces. On this construal of the term, disarmament denotes a type of arms control, but arms control as the umbrella category also covers any other policies and actions that have an impact on force postures (e.g., defense department budgetary agreements limiting weapons research or deployment, and unilateral or coordinated bans on weapons testing). Common examples include so-called confidence- and security-building measures (CSBMs), such as agreements to provide prior notification before undertaking major troop movements in sensitive regions or testing launches of ballistic missiles. Agreements concerning the spread of weapons capabilities, such as the formally negotiated Nuclear Nonproliferation Treaty (NPT) and the informally agreed and administered Missile Technology Control Regime (MTCR), similarly fall into this broader usage.

More narrowly, and more commonly, arms control is the label used to identify those policies and actions associated with bilateral or multilateral agreements negotiated between countries that seek directly to *control* weapons inventories. However, this control can be technologically or politically motivated rather than numbers-oriented and thus such control agreements may actually lead to higher numbers and more technologically sophisticated weapons than are currently in a nation's inventory. In brief, control does not equal reduction, and the best controls may be judged to require real increases. In this sense, arms control is the opposite of disarmament, even though the goal of a more peaceful world (or at least, producing a less likely chance of the use of military force) may be shared by each party to the control agreement. Contemporary examples of such control agreements and their impact on force levels are SALT I and II (the Strategic Arms Limitation Talks between the United States and the Soviet Union during the 1970s), which permitted increases in strategic forces overall but set limits on the use of newer technological developments. In fact, the overall number of strategic nuclear warheads increased during this arms control period, with the result that the number of Soviet warheads went from 4,500 in 1967 to 13,000 in 1989, while American warheads during the same period went from 1,000 to 11,500.

For all that, in common parlance the terms "arms control" and "disarmament" are widely understood to be synonyms. In fact, U.S. legislation deliberately conflates them. It is no coincidence that we once had an Arms Control and Disarmament Agency (ACDA) and that the legislation establishing the agency defined the scope of its work by defining arms control and disarmament as equivalent terms. (ACDA folded into the State Department in 1999.)

In this regard, it is sometimes difficult to distinguish between conservative and liberal approaches in the arms control and disarmament policies and activities of various U.S. administrations. This is not to say that there have existed no differences of opinion about these issues over the years, but the actual agreements and policies to which various U.S. presidents have committed the country since the World War II are quite similar in structure and concern in that perceptions of national security requirements have trumped ideological or partisan commitments. Thus, while so-called defense budget–cutting liberal Democrats oversaw arms control policies that moved the United States to higher numbers of more sophisticated weapons, defense budget–increasing conservative Republicans found themselves shepherding disarmament commitments through the Senate for ratification.

While arms control during the Cold War period focused almost exclusively on the adversarial relationship between the Soviet Union and the United States and their nuclear weapons inventories, arms control in the post–Cold War period has shifted towards more global concerns over the proliferation of weapons of mass destruction (which include not only nuclear but also chemical and biological weapons, as well as the technology to accurately deliver these weapons over long distances with advanced missiles). It has also started to focus on the significant increases in conventional weapons capabilities of various international actors. More attention is also being given the armaments and capabilities of pariah states such as Iran and North Korea. Future arms control negotiations will likely involve attempts to settle regional conflicts and concerns over balances of power (such as in the Middle East, South Asia, and the Balkans) with the cooperation of major international organizations like NATO and the United Nations.

—DANIEL W. SKUBIK

Further Reading

Glynn, Patrick. *Closing Pandora's Box: Arms Races, Arms Control, and the History of the Cold War.* New York: Basic Books, 1992.

Sawyer, Kem Knapp. *The U.S. Arms Control and Disarmament Agency.* New York: Chelsea House Publishers, 1990.

See also: Cold War

Ashbrook Center

The Ashbrook Center, named for former Ohio congressman John Ashbrook, was established in 1983 to provide a forum for studying the United States Constitution, constitutional government, and American politics. To this end, the Ashbrook Center hosts conferences and lectures focusing on individual liberty, limited government and civic morality, and publishes books and periodicals which address similar themes. It regularly offers seminars for high school history teachers, aiming to broaden the teachers' understanding of American history and public affairs; past topics have dealt with the Civil War and Reconstruction, American foreign policy, and the American Revolution. The center also recently announced a new master's degree program in American history and government that aims to remedy "America's crisis in civic illiteracy."

The center's Ashbrook Scholar program invites college students to study public affairs and American politics by reading primary sources and then participating in private seminars with prominent figures, whose ranks in past years have included Margaret Thatcher, Clarence Thomas, and Henry Kissinger.

In addition to these programs, the center houses the congressional papers of John Ashbrook, to whose political vision the center is dedicated. During his twenty-two years in Congress, Ashbrook worked for limited government and to reduce government spending, running against Richard Nixon in the Republican state primaries in 1971 in protest of the latter's more liberal policies. Research at the center concentrates on the Ashbrook papers and related political material.

The center is currently directed by Peter W. Schramm, professor of political science at Ashland University and former director of the Center for International Education under President Reagan. Schramm writes regularly for the center's publications, which include *On Principle, Dialogues,* and *Res Publica,* and has edited several of the books distributed by the center.

The Ashbrook Center is located at Ashland University, a private regional teaching university in Ashland, Ohio.

—ALEXANDRA GILMAN

Further Reading

Schramm, Peter W., and Bradford P. Wilson, eds. *American Political Parties and Constitutional Politics.* Lanham, Md.: Rowman & Littlefield, 1993.

Wilson, Bradford P., and Peter W. Schramm, eds. *Separation of Powers and Good Government.* Lanham, Md.: Rowman & Littlefield, 1994.

Atkinson, Edward (1827–1905)

In the forty years after the Civil War, Edward Atkinson was a leading writer on economic issues. Active in the commercial cotton business and treasurer of the Boston Manufacturers' Fire Insurance Company, Atkinson understood economics to be a body of natural law, drawing from Adam Smith, Jean-Baptiste Say, John Stuart Mill, and, in particular, the natural harmony analysis of Frederic Bastiat.

Like E. L. Godkin and Henry Villard, Atkinson belonged to the American Social Science Association. He was a vice president of the American Association for the Advancement of Science.

Atkinson opposed tariffs and attacked the immorality of fiat money, arguing instead for the morality of the gold standard. After the U.S. acquisition of the Philippines, Atkinson joined Andrew Carnegie, Grover Cleveland, William Graham Sumner, Carl Schurz, and E. L. Godkin in the formation of the Anti-Imperialist League, of which Atkinson was vice president. A pamphlet he wrote favoring the independence of the Philippines was mailed to U.S. military officers in the Philippines and seized. Rumors of charges against Atkinson and the other laissez-faire Republicans involved with the Anti-Imperialist League led to the increased circulation of their writings.

—LEONARD LIGGIO

Further Reading

Williamson, Harold F. *Edward Atkinson: The Biography of an American Liberal, 1827–1905.* Boston: Old Corner Books Store, 1934.

Tompkins, E. Berkeley. *Anti-Imperialism in the United States: The Great Debate, 1890–1920.* Philadelphia: University of Pennsylvania Press, 1970.

Atlas Economic Research Foundation

The Atlas Economic Research Foundation was established in 1981 by Sir Antony Fisher, a British Royal Air Force pilot in World War II and businessman, to advance a vision of a society of free and responsible individuals based upon private property rights, limited government under the rule of law, and the market order. It cooperates with and coordinates the efforts of more than 150 independent research institutes, think tanks, and individuals around the world that share its commitment to liberty.

The Atlas story began in 1947 when Fisher met with the economist Friedrich Hayek, who had recently authored *The Road to Serfdom* (1944). Hayek's work resonated with Fisher, who was alarmed by the growing public acceptance of intrusive government in Western democracies. Fisher was inclined to enter politics to defend individual liberty against creeping socialism, but Hayek cautioned that positive reform would be impossible without first effecting a change in the climate of ideas. To accomplish this,

Fisher began establishing independent research institutes in Great Britain, the United States, and Canada that would bring innovative, market-based perspectives to issues of public policy. The first of these, the Institute of Economic Affairs, was established in London in 1955. By founding Atlas, Fisher institutionalized this process.

Sir Antony Fisher died in 1988. Atlas's president since 1991 has been Alejandro Antonio Chafuen. Leonard Liggio has been the organization's executive vice president since 1994.

—INGRID GREGG

See also: Hayek, Friedrich A. von; Liggio, Leonard; Road to Serfdom, The

Austrian school of economics

Named for the nationality of its founders, the Austrian school of economics played a uniquely influential role in the development of twentieth-century economic doctrine and in the advancement of free-market economics within postwar American conservatism. Among the school's most important scientific contributions are its demonstrations of the market-based origins of money, the impossibility of socialist economic calculation, the origin of interest in the scarcity of time, the central place of opportunity cost in human choice, the critical importance of the process of competition, the subjectivist/ordinalist approach to microeconomics, the futility of Keynesian macro-management, the monetary origins of the business cycle, and the essential role of logical deduction in the methodology of the social sciences.

On matters of policy, the Austrian school is principally known for making the most consistent case for the freeing of markets from all government interventions. The Austrian school takes a negative view of government ownership, taxation, regulation, bureaucracy, trade barriers, wage and price restrictions, antitrust laws, central banking, and government spending, especially deficit spending. It takes a positive view of private property, sound money, free markets, entrepreneurship, freedom of association, and the rule of law.

The two best-known economists in the Austrian school tradition are Ludwig von Mises and Friedrich A. Hayek. Other notable figures include Carl Menger, Eugen von Böhm-Bawerk, Richard von Strigl, Wilhelm Röpke, Frank Fetter, Ludwig Erhard, Henry Hazlitt, Murray N. Rothbard, and Israel Kirzner. The number of academic economists who count themselves as part of the Austrian school is substantial and growing, although such economists remain a minority in the profession. Although its roots are in late scholasticism, the tradition of the Austrian school began with the publication of Carl Menger's *Principles of Economics* (1871), which contributed to the "marginalist revolution" in economics. In that text, Menger opposed the classical doctrine of economic value and price, which held that economic value is intrinsic to the good or service and that price is determined by the labor inputs required for its production. Karl Marx used this Smithian doctrine to advance his own version of the labor theory of value and the exploitation theory of wages. Menger argued, in contrast, that economic value resided not in the good itself, but in the minds of individuals acting in the market. Although Menger's view had been anticipated by the late-scholastic economists, it had been lost with the ascendancy of the British or classical school of political economy.

Menger also demonstrated that the institution of money is a product of the market itself, not of social compact or government edict. The most liquid good, money is desired not only for its direct value as a commodity, but also as a means of acquiring other goods and services. Menger saw no rea-

son for government to manage the currency as long as it was defined in terms of a market commodity like gold, then the most common form of currency, and chosen for its durability, divisibility, and homogeneity. As for methodology, Menger argued for the necessity and realism of economic theorizing against the claims of the German historical school, which held that economic science only advanced through the collection of empirical data. His methodological treatise appeared in 1883 and entered the fray of a bitter *methodenstreit* among economists, with the Mengerians ultimately winning. One notable aspect of Menger's work in both economics and methodology was his omission of mathematics. The Austrian notions of utility, preference, value, and pricing stressed the subjective nature of valuation, an emphasis that shunned mathematical constructs in favor of logical deduction from the first principles of individual action.

The second important figure in Austrian economics was Eugen von Böhm-Bawerk, professor of economics at the University of Vienna and finance minister of the imperial government. In 1884, he published a massive volume on the role of time and capital in economics, arguing for the "time-preference" theory of interest rates. His subjectivist view argued that the interest rate charged on the market solely reflects the tendency of individuals to prefer goods sooner rather than later. The higher the interest rate, all else remaining equal, the more people prefer goods sooner rather than later, or the higher their time preference. The reverse is also true.

In addition, Böhm-Bawerk argued for the importance of time in the production process. In his theory, the price of factory goods was determined by the value consumers placed on final goods. Thus, the price of goods and services was not determined by the costs of production, as the Marxists and classicists had thought, but by the valuation of the "sovereign" consumer. He further demonstrated the superior productivity of more "roundabout" production methods; that is, those that require more stages, more capital inputs, and more time to complete. In 1896, Böhm-Bawerk wrote a devastating analysis of the Marxian doctrine of exploitation. His critique established the Austrians as the most relentless critics of Marxian and socialist economics, creating deep frictions that continued until the collapse of communism in 1989.

Böhm-Bawerk's economic seminar attracted younger scholars, including Josef A. Schumpeter and Ludwig von Mises. Mises' 1912 book, *The Theory of Money and Credit*, which planted the first seeds of the Austrian theory of the business cycle, was hotly debated in this seminar. After Böhm-Bawerk's death, Mises carried on the seminar tradition. While holding a prestigious but unsalaried post at the University of Vienna, Mises conducted seminars in his offices at the Austrian Chamber of Commerce, where he was chief economist. Gottfried Haberler, Hayek, Felix Kaufmann, Fritz Machlup, Oskar Morgenstern, Alfred Schutz, Richard von Strigl, and Eric Voegelin were among those who regularly attended.

Mises' 1922 book *Socialism* carried the Austrian tradition to new heights. A continent-wide debate, a debate that affected American academics to a much lesser extent, ensued over Mises' view that socialism made rational economic calculation impossible. Without private property in the means of production, there could be no prices, which could only result in economic chaos. (In 1944, Mises used the same point to attack bureaucracies under mixed-economy systems.) He challenged socialists to explain exactly how their utopian economics would work in the real world. The most famous response came in the 1930s from Polish economist Oskar Lange, who conceded the need for prices in calculation but thought they need not be market-generated; they could be set by so-

cialist managers. This position is today known as "market socialism." Mises countered that the private investor-entrepreneur—in his incentives, risk exposure, and access to information—is entirely different from the government manager, who merely "plays market." Their roles are not interchangeable.

Hayek took Mises' calculation argument in a new direction by emphasizing the role of the price system in eliciting and transmitting "knowledge" to economic actors, knowledge that would be inaccessible to any single mind (i.e., the central planner). In the market process, Hayek argued, the price system facilitates the discovery and assembling of dispersed information for decision making. Hayek's theory became prominent after he received the Nobel Prize in 1974, in part for the Mises-Hayek business cycle theory he had elaborated.

The Misesian theory of the business cycle contends that the boom phase is caused by an expansion of credit by the central bank, leading to an artificial lowering of interest rates and overproduction in the capital goods sector. When this "malinvestment" corrects itself, the bust phase sets in. Hayek, who had himself been converted from socialism by Mises, carried Mises' business cycle theory to the London School of Economics. There, at the encouragement of Lionel Robbins, Hayek wrote several books on business cycle theory that were eventually to earn him the Nobel Prize.

The Austrian doctrine is distinct from the monetarist view of Milton Friedman and others, because it regards any artificial increase in the supply of money and credit, not only those increases that lead to an increase in prices, as destructive of economic coordination. The Austrian school recommends free-market money and banking, with the monetary unit defined in terms of gold or another market-chosen commodity. Not only would this prevent the artificial expansion of credit that sets off the business cycle, it would also prevent the monetization of government debt and limit the government's propensity to spend.

The Austrian theory of the business cycle was for decades the only real challenge to the Keynesian view (which stressed lack of coordination by markets). In the 1930s, while the Austrians were arguing that the Great Depression was caused by central bank manipulation of money and interest rates, the Keynesians were calling for government intervention in all areas to re-coordinate the economy. Eventually, the Keynesian view swept the profession, taking with it some Austrians (for example, and to varying degrees, Morgenstern, Machlup, Robbins, and Haberler).

Mises having emigrated to the United States, the center of Austrian thought shifted to America after World War II. The universities were largely shut to all but socialists and Keynesians, so work in the Austrian school flourished mainly outside the academy. It was largely the conservative intellectual movement—in its institutions, conferences, publishers, and magazines—that made continued work in Austrian economics possible, even when government planning seemed to have won the academic debate.

During this time Mises published his tremendously important treatise in economics, *Human Action* (1949), which brought to a select audience of conservatives and libertarians a thorough and scientific defense of the free market. For the next two decades, the Austrian school was the dominant economic doctrine on the American Right; it resonated with the American Jeffersonian tradition of property-rights protection and political decentralism, and Mises and the other Austrians uniquely combined a radical anti-statism with a socially conservative cultural outlook. Mises also recreated his Vienna seminar in New York City, where it attracted conservative and libertarian academics, journalists, and businessmen from all over the country.

One important student was journalist Henry Hazlitt, author of *Economics in One Lesson* (1946), who transmitted Austrian theory to the American conservative political movement and beyond through his many books, articles, and columns in *Newsweek*.

Murray N. Rothbard was Mises' most prominent student during this period. Rothbard initially identified politically with the Old Right of the prewar period, extended the anti-statism of Albert Jay Nock and H. L. Mencken and became a consistent Right-libertarian theorist. Rothbard completed his economic treatise *Man, Economy, and State* in 1962, elaborating on Mises' contributions to economics and adding a consistent view of monopoly pricing and antitrust, as well as a taxonomy of interventionism. In addition, Rothbard distinguished himself by incorporating Austrian economics into a more general theory of human liberty, emphasizing individual and property rights. His final contribution was a massive history of economic thought that demonstrated the late-medieval origins of the Austrian strain in economic theory. Another prominent student of Mises', Israel Kirzner, enlarged on the critical role of entrepreneurship in innovation and equilibration in a market economy.

The Austrian school's dominance of the American Right went unchallenged until the monetarist, public choice, and rational expectations doctrines came into their own in the late 1960s. The 1970s stagnation (which the Keynesian paradigm had ruled impossible) brought a resurgence in Austrian thought. When Hayek won the Nobel Prize in 1974, Austrian economics once again received attention in the academic world and within conservative circles. Since the events of 1989 in Eastern Europe, interest in the Austrian school has expanded worldwide.

Austrian doctrine played a role in the privatizing of formerly socialist economies, in part because of renewed attention given to Ludwig Erhard, the German finance minister who transformed a National Socialist economy into a relatively free market under the influence of the Misesian-Austrian tradition. On the American Right, from traditionalists to radical libertarians, Austrian economics continues to be widely revered.

—LLEWELLYN H. ROCKWELL JR.

Further Reading

Grassl, Wolfgang, and Barry Smith, eds. *Austrian Economics: Historical and Philosophical Background*. New York: New York University Press, 1986.

Hayek, F. A., ed. *Collectivist Economic Planning: Critical Studies on the Possibilities of Socialism*. Clifton, N.J.: Augustus M. Kelley, 1975.

Holcombe, Randall. *Fifteen Great Austrian Economists*. Auburn, Ala.: The Mises Institute, 2000.

Kirzner, Israel M. *Competition and Entrepreneurship*. Chicago: University of Chicago Press, 1973.

See also: fusionism; Haberler, Gottfried; Hayek, Friedrich A. von; Hazlitt, Henry; Hutt, William H.; Institute for Humane Studies; Mises, Ludwig von; Mises, Ludwig von, Institute; Röpke, Wilhelm; Rothbard, Murray

authority

The term "authority" has had an expanding range of associations since ancient times, and it may be useful to examine its classical meanings in order to grasp its conceptual evolution. The Greek words that come closest to "authority" are *ekzousia* and *timē,* one term referring to power and the other to honor. Although in both Thucydides and Xenophon *ekzousia* generally designates the exercise of brute force, in Aristotle's *Nicomachean Ethics* this quality becomes linked to honor as well. Thus (see 1163b) while a son or debtor has no claim to *ekzousia* (precedence and power) in relation to his father or creditor, the latter two possess this attribute in dealing with those who are under their command. We are also told that *ekzousia* (1161a) is necessarily weak in a democracy, a form of government that resembles a household without a master (*en tais adespotois tōn oikeseōn*). Where all are equal, the magistrate's sphere of control is accordingly limited.

In the New Testament (Romans 13) St. Paul links *ekzousia* to the divine will. The magistrate when he restrains the wicked is exercising what according to the Vulgate is "auctoritas," a quality of leadership that goes beyond mere might. The Pauline magistrate, whether a Christian or not, is given the sword for the purpose of maintaining a divinely established order. By Roman times *ekzousia* and *timē* were becoming fused in the notion of *auctoritas,* which in Cicero and in later Roman authors suggests moral dignity. Roman *auctoritas* moves conceptually from authorization, as in the formula *"senatus consulti auctoritas,"* to a second and more lasting association with ethical value. Thus one finds Cicero declaiming in his invective against the corrupt Sicilian proconsul Gaius Verres *"aequitate causae et auctoritate sua commovere,"* by which he stresses the moral urgency of the plea for justice that he is making.

The dual understanding of authority, as power combined with dignity, guided Christian theologians from Augustine through Aquinas to the Protestant Reformers. All of them argue for the need for "Christian magistrates" who avoid tyranny and govern with prudence, according to divine precepts and established customs. While for Augustine and Luther it was enough that princes avoid evil and be well disposed toward the Christian religion, for Aquinas (*De regimine principium*) political authority is raised to an almost pagan centrality. For him, political authority would supposedly be present to perfect man's nature, in conformity with the "light of reason," even if Adam had not fallen. Aquinas dwells on the fortune of those who live under "good kings" who diligently tend to their subjects' welfare, and he notes "that it would require particularly strong malice for those who are thus blessed to repay their benefactors with hate."

From early modern times on, the concept of authority would wander among varying reference points, from Thomas Hobbes's "sovereign" who maintains civil order against all challengers to communal structures of command to papal and monarchical dispensations among nineteenth-century counterrevolutionary theorists. The rise of the modern state, the breakdown of ecclesiastical unity, and the growth in prestige of scientific methods all contributed to the growing difficulty of finding a single source or definition of authority. The German legal theorist Carl Schmitt called attention to a critical distinction in trying to understand the essence of authority when he uncoupled "legitimacy" from "legality." Unlike the mere acceptance of what is legislated or decreed, what is "legitimate" is presumed to enjoy moral force, which is derived from its point of origin (*auctor*). When those who rule elicit respect and natural obedience, what they command will evoke the same. In modern constitutional regimes, in which traditional leadership no longer exists or has grown weak, legality, according to Schmitt, must create its own legitimacy; that is, authority must be vested in laws rather than be attached to any hereditary ruling class.

Even more significant than this distinction, however, is the one between a type of constitutional government that permits a flourishing communal and family life, and a regime that is committed to looking after and, if possible, creating autonomous individuals. This second development has become for Western traditionalists and classical liberals the key political problem, one that continues to becloud our conceptions of both state and authority. Robert Nisbet, Bertrand de Jouvenel, Michael Oakeshott, Eric von Kühnelt-Leddhin und Wilhelm Röpke have all tried to distinguish tradi-

tional sources of command and socialization from the power wielded by the modern administrative state. Such traditionalists or quasi-traditionalists have challenged the age-old relation between power and moral rank and have usually treated the second but not the first as worthy of deference. They have focused their efforts on shoring up intermediate institutions between the isolated individual and the ruling bureaucracy and on defending the frequently battered remnants of older, more traditional societies.

Celebrity has also taken the place of politically situated authority. Celebrity, a creation of entertainers and journalists, has had the effect of riveting public attention and moral approval on TV and movie personalities. Political careers can assist the rise to celebrity status, but such success depends on expressing the ideological preferences of the celebrity-creators and on being photogenic—or at least on having a glamorous appearance. What the cult of celebrity illustrates, beside obvious cultural decadence, is another phase in the depoliticization of authority. Those who hold public office can only succeed by becoming movie stars or else by imitating them.

—Paul Gottfried

Further Reading

Gottfried, Paul. *After Liberalism: Mass Democracy in the Administrative State.* Princeton, N.J.: Princeton University Press, 1999.

Jouvenel, Bertrand de. *On Power: The Natural History of Its Growth.* Indianapolis: Liberty Fund, 1993.

Nisbet, Robert. *The Quest for Community.* San Francisco: ICS Press, 1990.

Oakeshott, Michael. *Rationalism in Politics.* Indianapolis, Ind.: Liberty Fund, 1991.

See also: centralization; democracy; equality; historicism; Jewish conservatives; liberalism, classical neoconservatism; Nisbet, Robert A.; Oakeshott, Michael; paleoconservatism; populism; prescription; traditionalism

B

Babbitt, Irving (1865–1933)

Irving Babbitt was the intellectual leader of the New Humanists. In a series of essays and books, including *Literature and the American College* (1908), *Rousseau and Romanticism* (1919), and *Democracy and Leadership* (1924), Babbitt applied his humanist philosophy to a variety of subjects—literature, higher education, politics, and religion. He influenced the other leaders of the movement—Paul Elmer More, Stuart Sherman, and Norman Foerster—as well as younger disciples who made the New Humanism a controversial movement by the end of the 1920s.

Babbitt was born in Dayton, Ohio. His father was a physician of eclectic intellectual interests, spiritualism among them, and would later represent to his son an example of the indiscriminate and facile sentimentalism that marked the modern age. The family moved frequently before Babbitt began his undergraduate career at Harvard University in 1885. There he met Paul Elmer More, the two being the only enrollees in a Sanskrit class. After travel in Europe, Babbitt began a teaching career at Harvard as professor of romance languages. He was an immensely popular teacher, known for his repertoire of ready quotations from great writers and thinkers. His students included Walter Lippmann,

Irving Babbitt

T. S. Eliot, Van Wyck Brooks, Foerster, and Sherman. Babbitt was generally unappreciated by his colleagues at the university, however. His defense of neoclassical standards in literature set him against more fashionable directions in literary criticism.

In the 1920s Babbitt's influence grew steadily, and the New Humanist movement won a significant following, mostly in academic circles. In 1930, at the height of its influence, Norman Foerster published a collection of essays titled *Humanism and America*, to which Babbitt and others contributed and which became an intellectual manifesto of the movement. In the same year, C. Hartley Grattan summoned opponents of New Humanism to organize a counterattack called *The Critique of Humanism*.

Babbitt's humanism defended a dualistic view of human nature, locating in it two opposing forces. On the one hand, human nature possesses an inherently expansionist instinct that seeks release from all constraints and pursues an indefinite liberation of will and imagination. But it also possesses a principle of control, a force for discipline and moderation. As paragon of the undisciplined romantic spirit, the French romantic Jean-Jacques Rousseau was, Babbitt believed, the major corrupting influence on modern culture. Babbitt always associated romanticism with the celebration of idiosyncrasy and the uniqueness of personality at the expense of a common human nature, especially as depicted in classical literature and its later emulations. Babbitt believed that romanticism had become endemic in modern life and culture, and he saw it reflected in the mindless cult of individuality that had deprived literature of any meaningful wholeness.

Babbitt also criticized the more recent influence of naturalism. Depicting man as the reflex agent of natural forces, this mode of understanding human nature, he believed, dissolved the principle of control and explained human behavior by reference to his race and environment. Romanticism and naturalism thus had reinforcing tendencies, depriving human experience of any center or universality. Babbitt further believed that these reinforcing effects were especially acute in the United States of his time. America, Babbitt said, had produced a culture that was both mechanistic, worshipping power and force, and at the same time sentimentalist and emotionally indulgent, as witnessed by the popularity of Hollywood movies and frivolous, romantic novels among the general public.

Over the course of his writing career, Babbitt artfully applied his dualism to a number of categories. *The Masters of Modern French Criticism* (1912) most fully outlines his literary theory, offering essays on Charles-Augustin Saint-Beuve, Joseph Joubert, and others. While he did not himself enter the "battle of the books" that raged after World War I (his followers, especially Sherman, took on the enemies of New Humanism, H. L. Mencken in particular), Babbitt opposed the new currents of impressionist criticism, with its emphasis on successful expression as the end of art, and historical criticism, with its efforts to explain art in terms of time, place, and environment. Both schools, he believed, made reductionist errors that deprived criticism of useful standards of judgment.

On the subject of education, Babbitt became an outspoken conservative critic of the elective system instituted by Charles William Eliot of Harvard in 1869. The issue symbolized the division between those who championed a broader curriculum in American colleges and those who wanted individual choice to weigh more heavily in students' academic programs. Babbitt saw this direction as representative of the indulgent individualism of American culture and remarked that the modern college permitted unlearned youth to ignore the accumulated wisdom of the past in passing through an undergraduate program determined by individual whim.

In his views on society and politics, Babbitt was a conscious follower of Edmund Burke. He believed that modern politics had become essentially a contest between the "idyllic imagination" of Rousseau, which fostered utopian and egalitarian schemes of social salvation, and the "moral imagination" of Burke. For any society, the primary challenge was to grasp by imagination and symbol the enduring tradition joining past to present. Against the democratic tendencies by which people meet at a low commonality, Babbitt urged that individuals discover their common higher selves as defined by historical memory and tradition. Babbitt criticized the excesses of democracy, deplored socialistic reforms, and championed the rights of property. But he argued also that American society could not find its necessary leadership class among the reigning, vulgar plutocracy.

The New Humanists disagreed on the subject of religion. Some adhered to principles founded in divine inspiration or supernatural authority; others called for an empirical humanism. Babbitt liked to say that he wanted to meet the moderns on their own grounds. His defense of humanism's "first principles" was made without appeal to supernatural sanctions. He defined humanism and religion as natural allies and even acknowledged a certain dependency of humanism on religious insight, but in an age of materialism and secularism a humanistic recovery, he believed, could be secured only by a strict account of human experience itself.

Babbitt was a major American voice of classic conservatism in the tradition of Burke. His dualistic philosophy was simple in outline but gained richness of insight and application in Babbitt's more mature works. In the years after his death, Babbitt's following grew and included some significant conservative thinkers, among them Russell Kirk, Peter Viereck, and George Will.

—J. DAVID HOEVELER JR.

Further Reading

Hoeveler, J. David, Jr. *The New Humanism: A Critique of Modern America, 1900–1940.* Charlottesville, Va.: University Press of Virginia, 1977.

Manchester, Frederick, and Odell Shepard, eds. *Irving Babbitt: Man and Teacher.* New York: G. P. Putnam's Sons, 1941.

Nevin, Thomas R. *Irving Babbitt: An Intellectual Study.* Chapel Hill, N.C.: University of North Carolina Press, 1984.

Panichas, George A. *The Critical Legacy of Irving Babbitt: An Appreciation.* Wilmington, Del.: ISI Books, 1999.

Panichas, George A., and Claes G. Ryn, eds. *Irving Babbitt in Our Time.* Washington, D.C.: Catholic University of America Press, 1986.

Ryn, Claes G. *Will, Imagination and Reason: Irving Babbitt and the Problem of Reality.* Chicago: Regnery, 1986.

See also: Bookman; *Eliot, T. S.; moral imagination; More, Paul Elmer; New Humanism; Ryn, Claes G.; Viereck, Peter*

Ball, William Bentley (1916–99)

William Bentley Ball—"God's Litigator"—received his law degree from the University of Notre Dame in 1948. After five years as a professor at Villanova University, he served as General Counsel to the Pennsylvania Catholic Conference, during which time he founded his own law firm. Over the course of his life, he argued before the Supreme Court more than twenty times, most frequently in defense of the freedom of religion.

As leading counsel in *Lemon v. Kurtzman* (1971), *Wisconsin v. Yoder* (1972), and *Zobrest v. Catalina Foothills School District* (1993), Ball attempted to secure the freedom of religious parents to educate their children in a manner consistent with their beliefs. He lamented that the First Amendment prohibition of state-established religion was frequently interpreted as a prohibition of religion, stating that "the means (no establishment) [was] turned into the end, and the end (free exercise) [was] viewed as a terrible nuisance." As a result of this oversimplification and, as Ball saw it, deep-seated resentment of Christianity, parents were financially penalized for sending their children to religious schools. He posited that both economic freedom and freedom from undue governmental regulation are necessary to allow religious schools to continue and parental authority to flourish.

Ball believed that parents are ultimately responsible for the type of education that their children receive. Refusing to see children as "mere creatures of the state," he repeatedly defended the rights of parents to oversee their children's formation and decried the "the organized, highly financed drive to organize civilization without God."

—LAURA BARROSSE-ANTLE

Further Reading

Kmiec, Douglas W. "God's Litigator Rests: In Memory of William Bentley Ball." *University Bookman* 38 (Winter 1998): 33–44.

Neuhaus, Richard. "William Bentley Ball." *First Things* (April 1999): 77.

Ball, William Bentley. *Mere Creatures of the State? Education, Religion, and the Courts.* Notre Dame, Ind.: Crisis Books, 1994.

See also: Constitution, interpretations of; church and state; homeschooling; Supreme Court

Banfield, Edward C. (1916–99)

Best known for his study *The Unheavenly City: The Nature and Future of Our Urban Crisis* (1970), Edward Christie Banfield was a political analyst and essayist whose works challenge liberal assumptions favoring government intervention in the shaping of communities and cities. Writing at a time when the motives and effects of Lyndon Johnson's "War on Poverty" initiatives were widely considered beyond cavil, Banfield's masterwork demonstrated that the problems affecting urban life in general and the urban poor in particular—joblessness, crime, lack of decent housing, and other issues—were in fact exacerbated by political solutions. The author of *The Unheavenly City* saw the core problem not as one of poverty, but of class; not of race, but of resolve. "If ever there was an iconoclastic book, this was it," wrote historian George H. Nash.

Born the son of a machinist and factory foreman in Connecticut, Banfield received his A.B. from the University of Connecticut in 1938, the year he married, and served for a brief time as a journalist. From newspaper work he went on to hold a series of minor government positions related to agricultural policy while pursuing an advanced degree in political science at the University of Chicago. At Chicago, Banfield studied under Rexford G. Tugwell, a key member of President Franklin Roosevelt's "brain trust," while pursuing answers to the question of why the federal agricultural programs instituted during the New Deal era had failed so miserably. The answer, posited and developed over the rest of his career, lay in the fact that while the programs had been implemented in good faith, the assumptions behind them had been fatally flawed. That is to say, the "Brain Trust" had based their hopes for success on mathematical calculations and an elevated vision of human nature, thus failing to factor in the unintended consequences of human corruption and nonrational action.

After receiving his doctorate in 1951, Banfield worked as a political science professor for more than two decades at the University of Chicago, the University of Pennsylvania, and Harvard University. During this time, he published or contributed significantly to some seventeen books, of which the most significant (other than *The Unheavenly City*) is *The Moral Basis of a Backward Society* (1958), which he co-wrote with his wife, Laura. This work, based on research conducted in a small Italian village, examines the villagers' inability to "act together for their common good or, indeed, for any end transcending the immediate, material interest of the nuclear family." On the basis of their firsthand observation and interviews, the Banfields developed and discussed in their book a concept they termed "amoral familism," a state of affairs in which each family unit is basically a closed corporate system. The effect of this "amoral familism," claimed the authors, was that the villagers remained fatalists rather than active citizens, and that the village itself was a collection of mutually suspicious enclaves rather than a community.

Ten years after this signal work appeared, Banfield was tapped by President Richard M. Nixon to serve as chairman of a preinauguration task force on urban affairs and to head a study group to evaluate the state of America's cities. *The Unheavenly City* emerged from Banfield's work for these organizations. Banfield's thesis was that the problems of America's cities were not the result of white racism, but were instead expressions of lower-class culture. He further argued that the various programs designed to help the urban poor in fact made their plight worse, and that a hands-off policy by the federal government—"benign neglect," as Senator Daniel Patrick Moynihan approvingly termed it—would go much further to help urban-dwellers than the administration of programs, the unintended effect of which was to encourage dependency and resentment. As George Nash has written, upon its appearance *The Unheavenly City* achieved a *succès de scandale*, selling over 100,000 copies in three years.

Banfield's final work of significance was *The Democratic Muse: Visual Arts and the Public Interest* (1984). In this work, he tackled the issue of how and why, via the National Endowment for the Arts and the National Endowment for the Humanities, the federal government had become involved in funding the arts, ultimately concluding that only a circumstantial case could be made for the endowments.

As a political scientist, Banfield was an earnest, methodical gadfly who insisted on asking discomfiting questions and who consistently challenged the entrenched institutions of the American welfare state.

—JAMES E. PERSON JR.

Further Reading

Banfield, Edward C. *Political Influence.* New Brunswick, N.J.: Transaction, 2003.

———. *Unheavenly City Revisited.* Boston: Little, Brown, 1974.

Kesler, Charles R. "Edward C. Banfield, R.I.P." *National Review,* November 8, 1999.

See also: welfare policy; welfare state

Baroody, William J. (1916–80)

A leading public-policy analyst and think tank executive, William J. Baroody created the American Enterprise Institute, one of the world's most important research institutes. A staunch anticommunist and free-marketeer, Baroody joined the American Enterprise Association in 1954 and became its president in 1962. That same year, under his leadership the association's name was changed to the American Enterprise Institute for Public Policy Research. As head of AEI, Baroody helped to bring conservative ideas into the fore of national public-policy debates and fought to attain a new level of acceptance for views that had not previously been taken seriously by either government or media elites.

A first-generation American, Baroody was born in 1916 in Manchester, New Hampshire, to immigrant Lebanese stonecutter Joseph Baroody and his wife Helen. After attending local Catholic schools and graduating as valedictorian of his high school class, Baroody attended St. Anselm's College, receiving his B.A. in 1936. He enlisted in the Naval Reserve during World War II and served as a lieutenant on the escort carrier *Mission Bay*. After the war, Baroody made his way to the Veterans Administration in Washington. In 1950, he joined the U.S. Chamber of Commerce, where he spent three years as executive secretary of the committee on economic security and associate editor of *American Economic Security*.

In 1954, when he arrived at AEA's modest offices after the death of the organization's founder, Lewis Brown, Baroody saw an opportunity to transform the foundering organization into a significant research institute. He improved the quality of the association's publications and invigorated the institute's scholarly programs and publications, while preserving AEI's reputation for impartial scholarship. Early in his tenure, Baroody enlisted prominent economists

Milton Friedman, Paul McCracken, and Gottfried Haberler to serve on the organization's advisory board. And in 1971 he instituted a resident scholars program that propelled AEI to the first rank of research institutes. Baroody also understood the importance of the culture wars before the term became widely used, allocating institute resources to the study of culture and religion.

For Baroody, impartiality in scholarship did not preclude active participation in public life. In 1964, he led Barry Goldwater's "brain trust" and made available the intellectual resources of AEI to the Republican nominee's campaign. Because of AEI's tax-exempt status, Baroody's intimate involvement in the Goldwater campaign precipitated a congressional inquiry into AEI's activities. The institute was cleared of any wrongdoing, but the investigation reinforced Baroody's commitment to the competition of ideas as a fundamental requisite for a free society.

Baroody was also a founder of Georgetown University's Center for Strategic and International Studies, a member of the board of overseers at the Hoover Institution for twenty years, and chairman of the board of the Woodrow Wilson International Center for Scholars from 1972 to 1979. In 1978, his son William Baroody Jr. became AEI's president and the elder Baroody became chairman of AEI's development committee, a position he retained until his death in 1980.

—CORY ANDREWS

Further Reading

Baroody, William J. *The Critical Choices We Face.* Washington, D.C.: American Enterprise Institute, 1978.

———. *Education: More than Mere Knowledge.* Washington, D.C.: American Enterprise Institute, 1980.

See also: American Enterprise Institute; think tanks, conservative

Bartley, Robert L. (1937–2003)

Until he passed the reins to Paul Gigot in late 2001, Robert L. Bartley was the longtime and legendary editor of the *Wall Street Journal*. The title was something of a misnomer, since he didn't guide the paper's news coverage, but only its editorial pages. Still, what Bartley did with the *Journal*'s editorials was enough to make him one of the most important and influential journalists of the last quarter century.

Bartley graduated from Iowa State University with a degree in journalism and received a master's degree in political science from the University of Wisconsin. He joined the *Wall Street Journal* as a reporter in 1962 and moved to the editorial page two years later. He took over the page in 1972 and assumed the title of *Journal* editor in 1979. One year later, his editorials won a Pulitzer Prize.

Under Bartley's direction, the *Journal* advocated innovative pro-growth economic policies. In the 1970s, Bartley, along with Jack Kemp, Jude Wanniski, and Arthur Laffer, advocated slashing tax rates and simplifying the tax code, while stabilizing a monetary supply ravaged by cancerous inflation. These ideas formed the core of Ronald Reagan's economic policy and represented a repudiation of more than a half-century of accepted Keynesian wisdom. The resulting economic boom saw the United States increase its GDP by more than a third in just "seven fat years." This was the equivalent, Bartley would boast, of creating a whole new West Germany.

Bartley's first-hand report of the Reagan economic revolution, *The Seven Fat Years: And How to Do It Again,* was published in 1992. It remains the definitive account of the United States' economic renaissance, despite the fact that it came out halfway through the nearly two-decade boom.

—MAX SCHULZ

See also: supply-side economics; Wall Street Journal

Becker, Gary S. (1930–)

A Nobel Prize–winning economist at the University of Chicago, and the contemporary leader of the so-called Chicago school of economics, Gary Becker has distinguished himself by extending economic analysis to new areas. He earned his Ph.D. at Chicago in 1955 and began his career at Columbia University.

To Becker, economics is not about wealth in the narrow sense, but about how people choose between scarce alternatives generally. For example, Becker focuses on how people use time in activities that they value. Becker has analyzed how people allocate their time between production at work for wages and "household production" of goods for their own consumption. And he has inquired into competition in "marriage markets," asking how people shop for spouses, invest in children and their education, and decide to divorce.

Becker also has employed the logic of economics in his analyses of discrimination and crime. In order for businesses to maximize their profits, they must hire the most productive employees and court the best customers. If businesses turn away employees or customers on some basis other than profit, they give up some profit in the process. Thus, Becker concludes that capitalism punishes discrimination.

Becker also contends that criminals commit crime in pursuit of personal profit, given relevant costs. From this proposition he has derived some commonsense conclusions. Since criminals worry about the likely costs of punishment, we can best deal with crime by punishing criminals according to the probability that they will be caught and convicted. If there is a 10 percent chance of being punished for theft and we set the penalty at ten times the amount of the theft, then there is no rational reason for anyone to steal. Becker's insights in these areas might appear to be common sense to many.

However, he has challenged many deeply held beliefs in academia—particularly those of Marxists who insist that capitalism promotes racism.

The concept of human capital is central to Becker's work. Human capital is the skill that people use in any kind of purposeful activity. Obviously, human capital relates to Becker's work on household decisions to invest in education. However, Becker sees deeper implications here. According to Becker, underlying consumer preferences never change. Variations in consumer demand derive from changes in prices, knowledge about products, and human capital, but not from preference changes. In his view, one will want to ski more if the price of lift tickets falls, or if one becomes better at it (by developing, in his terms, one's human capital), but not because one comes to like it more. In this way, Becker argues against those who contend that businesses use advertising to manipulate consumer preferences.

Becker has a reputation for promoting free markets. But he also argues that the political process is efficient. Becker contends that competition between special interests minimizes government waste. Becker does not deny that government policies are often misguided, but he maintains that since the interests that get harmed can fight back, the costs of bad policies tend to get minimized.

The general public knows Becker best through his column in *Business Week* and his book *The Economics of Life* (1996). While his work is often controversial, Becker has had an enormous impact on the economics profession through his steady application of economic concepts to social phenomena.

—Doug MacKenzie

Further Reading

Becker, Gary S. *A Treatise on The Family*. Cambridge, Mass.: Harvard University Press, 1981.

———. "Crime and Punishment: An Economic Approach." *Journal of Political Economy* 76 (1968): 169–217.

———. *Human Capital.* Chicago: University of Chicago Press, 1975.

———. *The Economics of Discrimination.* Chicago: University of Chicago Press, 1971.

See also: Friedman, Milton; Knight, Frank H.; Stigler, George J.

Bell, Bernard Iddings (1886–1958)

Bernard Iddings Bell, an Episcopal clergyman, wrote more than twenty books examining the American way of life from the point of view of Christian orthodoxy. Among his principal works are *Right and Wrong after the War* (1918), *Beyond Agnosticism* (1929), *In the City of Confusion* (1938), *God Is Not Dead* (1945), *Crisis in Education* (1949), and *Crowd Culture* (1952). In all these works, he argued that Americans were mistakenly pursuing comfort as the end of life and beginning to believe that "one may eat one's cake and have it too, that there can be reward without quest, wages without work, a master's prestige without a master's skill, marriage without fidelity, national security without sacrifice."

Bell maintained that American culture was in serious trouble. He insisted that parents and educators were largely to blame because, in failing to provide the young with a coherent, time-tested moral framework for thinking and behaving, they were failing to furnish America with the kind of leaders it needed. He thought the church, in practicing tolerance to a fault and trying to appear "up-to-date," had become as ineffectual as families and public schools in making Americans wise and reasonable. He cautioned that churches of all denominations were paying too high a price for preferring popularity to prophecy, a price amounting to their becoming laughable as well as powerless. Bell concluded that America was doomed to wander in a state of intellectual and spiritual aimlessness until an aristocracy of character, well catechized and deliberately educated in the humane tradition, arose to guide the populace into a more meaningful existence.

When first published Bell's books attracted considerable attention. Notable conservatives of the time read and praised them, men such as Albert J. Nock, T. S. Eliot, and Richard M. Weaver. Few theologians have reached as wide and diverse a public as Bell did during the first half of the twentieth century. His audience extended to England and Canada, where he frequently lectured and gave sermons. His writings had a lasting influence on the father of modern American conservatism, Russell Kirk, who called Bell "an Isaiah preaching to the Remnant," a "High Churchman" who conceded nothing "to the social gospellers, liberals, latitudinarians, modernists, humanitarians, or public-relations experts."

Bell was born in Dayton, Ohio. He received a B.A. in 1907 from the University of Chicago, where he majored in social history. He studied religion at Western Theological Seminary, from which he graduated in 1912 with a bachelor's degree in sacred theology. In 1919, after serving as vicar and dean of St. Paul's Church in Fond du Lac, Wisconsin, Bell accepted an offer to preside as warden at St. Stephen's College (now Bard College) in New York, a position he held until 1933. While at St. Stephen's he taught religion at Columbia University. As canon of St. John's Cathedral in Providence, Rhode Island, as canon of the Cathedral of Saints Peter and Paul in Chicago, Illinois, and as William Vaughn Moody Lecturer at the University of Chicago, Bell dedicated his later years to the religious training of adults and his work in the classroom.

—Cicero Bruce

Further Reading

Bruce, Cicero. "Bernard Iddings Bell, Rebel Rouser." *Modern Age* 41 (1999): 252–61.

———. Introduction to *Crowd Culture: An Examination of the American Way of Life*, by Bernard Iddings Bell. Wilmington, Del.: ISI Books, 2001.

See also: Nock, Albert Jay

Belloc, Hilaire (1870–1953)

An important figure in the defense of traditional Western religion and culture against the modern threat of atheistic materialism, Hilaire Belloc was born in France, but after the death of his father his English mother took him to England. He was educated at Cardinal Newman's Oratory School and at Oxford, where he garnered first class honors in modern history. He worked in journalism and for a term sat in Parliament as a Liberal, but quickly became disillusioned with British politics.

Hilaire Belloc

Belloc was a prolific writer, publishing more than one hundred books, including volumes of verse, fiction, travel writing, biography, history, and social, political, and economic thought. His influence on the outlook of his friend G. K. Chesterton was considerable, and together they expounded and advocated the economic theory known as distributism, which arose out of Belloc's hostile critique of industrial capitalism and the Whig interpretation of history. It is as a Catholic apologist and controversialist, revising European and especially English history from a pugnacious Catholic standpoint, that he is best known today.

Belloc's attack on the Whig interpretation of history was more personally committed than a mere philosophical skepticism of the idea of progress. He believed English history was written from the viewpoint of Protestant victors at the Reformation and that the Whig interpretation in effect legitimized the new social order erected on the plunder of the monasteries and dispossession of the peasantry that began with the break with Rome. According to Belloc, the enclosure movement drove the peasantry from the land, thus depriving them of a sure measure of independent self-support, and herded them into the towns, where they were proletarianized by the advance of industrial capitalism. The people were dispossessed of property and the spiritual and material comforts of the Church, in the process becoming reduced to the effective condition of pagan slaves.

Belloc's proposed social and economic remedies arose directly from this historical analysis and were influenced by Cardinal Henry Manning and by the Catholic Church's hostility to industrial capitalism, socialism, and communism, especially as that position was crystallized in the papal encyclical *Rerum Novarum*. Collectivism substituted one monopoly of property for another, that of the state for that of a few rich men. In contrast, Belloc argued for a return to preindustrial models, including the medieval guild system and the restriction of usury, and a wider distribution of property that reinforced the freedom of individuals and families. *The Servile State* (1912) and *Europe and the Faith* (1920) are representative of his historical and social analysis.

Belloc's radical critique treated Europe, Christendom, and Catholicism as essentially the same entity. As a political commentator he opposed "Prussianism" and perceived the Nazis as a pagan form of typically baleful

German influence. However, he strongly supported the Nationalists in Spain, seeing them as defenders of Christendom against the mortal threat of Bolshevism, and he viewed Mussolini in a similar light, believing that a strong form of Christian "monarchy" (as also in the American presidency) lifted the executive above bribery and bullying. His health collapsed in 1942, after which he wrote little.

—ANDRÉ GUSHURST-MOORE

Further Reading

McCarthy, John P. *Hilaire Belloc: Edwardian Radical.* Indianapolis, Ind.: Liberty Fund, 1979.

Speaight, Robert. *The Life of Hilaire Belloc.* New York: Farrar, Straus and Cudahy, 1957.

Wilhelmsen, Frederick D. *Hilaire Belloc: No Alienated Man: A Study in Christian Integration.* New York: Sheed and Ward, 1953.

See also: Agar, Herbert; Catholic social teaching; Chesterton, G. K.; distributism; Road to Serfdom, The

Bennett, William J. (1943–)

A Reagan-era cabinet member and bestselling author, William J. Bennett has made frequent appearances on television talk shows discussing everything from President Clinton's sexual escapades to tax policy to stem cell research, becoming one of the nation's foremost pundits on moral and ethical issues affecting the family and society.

Bennett, whose father left the family when he was young, attended a Jesuit high school, then Williams College. He earned a Ph.D. in philosophy from the University of Texas and a law degree from Harvard. Though at the center of the turbulence on college campuses during the 1960s, Bennett did not indulge in left-wing activism. (He *did* show some youthful interest in Students for a Democratic Society, but never joined.) Bennett was introduced firsthand to the rough and tumble of controversial issues when he took a job teaching at the University of Southern Mississippi. He ruffled feathers with his calls for racial and political equality. "If you believed in equality of the races in the 1960s, you were called a liberal," he has said. "If you believe in it in the 1990s, they call you a conservative."

Bennett was named chairman of the National Endowment for the Humanities in 1982 and so impressed the Reagan administration that President Reagan named him Secretary of Education in 1985. Just five days after being sworn in, Bennett launched an assault on the federal student loan program and continued throughout his tenure to support unpopular causes and to risk the wrath of the education and media establishment. For example, he often locked horns with the teachers' unions, declaring them the enemies of American children. In 1989, President Bush named Bennett to be the first director of the Office of National Drug Control Policy, an office with moral stature if limited authority.

Bennett joined with Jack Kemp and Jeane Kirkpatrick in 1993 to start the issue advocacy group Empower America. Bennett has used Empower America as a base from which to write and comment on a host of issues (he has written or edited fourteen books). His *Book of Virtues* (1993), a collection of fables and morality tales, occupied the *New York Times* bestseller list for eighty-eight weeks. A number of spinoff projects (*Children's Book of Virtues* [1995], *Book of Virtues for Young People* [1996], a cartoon series, etc.) have capitalized on the book's success.

The Death of Outrage (1998), Bennett's book about the Clinton scandals, topped the bestseller lists in 1999 and early 2000. (Ironically, Bennett's older brother served as Clinton's personal attorney in the Paula Jones affair.) In 1999, Bennett launched another high-profile venture, K12, a for-profit traditional education program available over the Internet. The company received much favorable attention in the months after the September 11 attacks when it offered its online lessons on patriotism free of charge. This move coincided with a renewed public emphasis by Bennett on matters of citizenship and patriotism, including another book, *Why We Fight: Moral Clarity and the War on Terrorism* (2002).

Bennett's status as a public proponent of traditional virtues was called into question in 2003 when the *Washington Monthly* revealed that over the previous decade he had lost more than $8 million at Atlantic City casinos and elsewhere, including several one-time losses of several hundred thousand dollars or more. Although such gambling was legal, Bennettt was severely chided by many—including some conservatives—for the questionable prudence and exercise of stewardship he displayed by engaging in obscenely high-stakes betting. Bennett soon announced that his "gambling days were over." Since that controversy, Bennett has continued his work with Empower America, which merged with Citizens for a Sound Economy in July 2004 to form the think tank Freedom Works, where Bennett serves as a senior fellow. He also hosts a three-hour daily radio show, "Bill Bennett's Morning in America," which is presented on radio stations throughout the country.

—MAX SCHULZ

Further Reading

Bennett, William J. *The Broken Hearth: Reversing the Moral Collapse of the American Family.* New York: Doubleday, 2001.

———. *The Index of Leading Cultural Indicators: American Society at the End of the Twentieth Century.* Updated and expanded ed. New York: Broadway Books, 1999.

See also: education, public

Benthamism

Englishman Jeremy Bentham (1748–1832) was one of the founders of modern liberal thought and developed a political philosophy known variously as utilitarianism, philosophical radicalism, or Benthamism. His influence on both sides of the Atlantic, especially during the nineteenth century, is evident in the fact that Benthamism is one of the few creeds in the English-speaking world named after an individual. Its most renowned principle is that of "utility, or the greatest happiness of the greatest number" (a principle, by the way, which was not original with Bentham but was suggested to him by the English radical Joseph Priestley). According to the principle of utility, the rightness or goodness of an act is assessed not by motive or intention, but by consequences: the more people that are made happy by an act, the better that act is.

The opening lines of Bentham's most famous book, *Introduction to the Principles of Morals and Legislation* (1789), summarize the altruistic hedonism that underlies the principle of utility: "Nature has placed mankind under the governance of two sovereign masters, pain and pleasure. It is for them alone to point out what we ought to do, as well as to determine what we shall do." Thus, the rightness and goodness of an action, law, institution, or social arrangement are determined by the extent to which it "produces benefit, advantage, pleasure, good, or happiness" in the individuals concerned. "Benthamism," summarizes Gertrude Himmelfarb, "prided itself on its ability to reduce the entire range of human behavior, individual as well as social behavior, to the single principle of happiness, a calculus of pleasure and pain." John Stuart Mill, an early student of Benthamism and eventually its most famous critic, came to reject this reductionist view of human nature: human behavior, Mill concluded, was motivated by more than a calculus of pleasure and pain.

Bentham sought extensive reforms in British law and politics, education and society. A child of the Enlightenment, Bentham shared the reformer's faith that man's personality and behavior are not imprisoned in a static nature but can be changed through good legislation and education. Accordingly, Benthamism calls for subjecting every political and social institution to the test of utility. Benthamists believe in the common people, pure democracy, and an empirical approach to social problems; they dismiss fictitious social contract theories, the need for checks and balances, and many of the truth claims of religion, metaphysics, and natural law (which Bentham called "nonsense on stilts").

Bentham's first book, *Fragment on Government*, was published in 1776, the same year the *Declaration of Independence* was written. It is sometimes suggested that many of America's founding fathers were de facto utilitarians because they believed that "the pursuit of happiness" is a self-evident and unalienable right (Jefferson) and "that the happiness of society is the end of government" (Adams). Yet, as Morton White shows, this claim ignores the fact that the founding fathers usually couched such ideas within the framework of natural law. When Bentham (who had never visited the United States) wrote to President Madison and to several state governors, offering to draw up a perfect new code of laws based on the principle of utility, he was politely turned down.

Benthamism's relationship with the American Right is a complex one. On the one hand Bentham himself was a vigorous advocate of the free market, and the principle of utility, combined with Adam Smith's ideas, inform his *Defense of Usury* (1818). Not surprisingly, the idea of utility can be discerned in various free-market studies—witness public choice economics. On the other hand, because Bentham dismissed Edmund Burke's regard for political, social, and religious traditions, many conservatives tend to be highly critical of Benthamism. It has not escaped their notice that in August 1792 French revolutionaries in the National Assembly conferred upon Bentham the title of Citizen of France. Russell Kirk maintained that Bentham did more to legitimate egalitarianism than most other radical reformers in the early 1800s.

Neoconservatives like Irving Kristol voice skepticism that an individuals' mere "utility schedules" will necessarily usher in a better society, especially under modern conditions. Indeed, many conservatives detect a subtle strain of nihilism in the Benthamist's assertion that society can be sustained without the support of religious beliefs or institutions. As James Crimmins points out, Bentham in later life was a zealous atheist and "pondered the vision of a world without religion."

—GLEAVES WHITNEY

Further Reading:

Crimmins, James E. *Secular Utilitarianism: Social Science and the Critique of Religion in the Thought of Jeremy Bentham*. Oxford: Oxford University Press, 1990.

Himmelfarb, Gertrude. *On Liberty and Liberalism*. New York: Knopf, 1974.

Mill, John Stuart. *Essays on Politics and Culture*. Gloucester, Mass.: Peter Smith, 1973.

———. *Utilitarianism*. Edited by Mary Warnock. New York: New American Library, 1974.

White, Morton. *The Philosophy of the American Revolution*. Oxford: Oxford University Press, 1978.

See also: community; Conservative Mind, The; mediating structures; progressivism; Smith, Adam

Berger, Peter L. (1929–)

Prominent sociologist, lay theologian, and author Peter Ludwig Berger was born in Austria in 1929. He became a citizen of the United States in 1952 and received his Ph.D. from the New School for Social Research in 1954. He is currently director of the Institute for the Study of Economic Culture and professor emeritus of religion, sociology, and theology at Boston University.

Berger's most famous books are probably *The Social Construction of Reality* (1966) and *The Sacred Canopy* (1967). The former, highly influential volume put forth the epistemological view that reality is socially constructed. Among conservatives it drew, and has continued to draw, a mixed response because of its arguably relativist implications. In *The Sacred Canopy* Berger argued that when pluralism shatters society's religious consensus, religion's plausibility is questioned, creating a crisis of faith. Though he correlated modernism with secularization as a writer in the 1960s, he now rejects that view, instead focusing on the "New Class" of secular elites.

In *The Capitalist Revolution* (1986) Berger asserted that no democracy is possible without a capitalist or market economy, although a market economy could exist outside democracy. The modern state, already ultrapowerful, tends toward dictatorship if it possesses socialist economic control.

A longtime collaborator with fellow neoconservative Fr. Richard John Neuhaus (they have worked together on several volumes, including *Against the World for the World*, 1976), Berger broke with Neuhaus's *First Things* magazine in 1996 for its questioning of the legitimacy of the American political regime. Berger later identified the editors' rigorism over abortion as the root of his *First Things* dissent.

A self-described liberal Protestant, Berger claims a theological middle ground between relativism and orthodoxy. He espouses "modest" belief that disclaims absolute certainty about values, instead buttressing faith with "signals of transcen-

dence" in ordinary life that point to the eternal.

—MATTHEW BOWMAN

Further Reading

Berger, Peter L. "Epistemological Modesty: An Interview with Peter Berger." *Christian Century*, October 29, 1997, 972–78.

———. *Facing Up to Modernity: Excursions in Society, Politics, and Religion.* New York: Basic Books, 1977.

———. *Questions of Faith: A Skeptical Affirmation of Christianity.* Malden, Mass.: Blackwell, 2004.

Berger, Peter L., Brigitte Berger, and Hansfried Kellner. *The Homeless Mind: Modernization and Consciousness.* New York: Random House, 1973.

See also: mediating structures; Neuhaus, Richard John

Berger, Raoul (1901–2000)

The body of Raoul Berger's historical work is animated throughout by the relentless application of accepted professional methodology in pursuit of legislative intent. Whether relying on the vast record supplied by the Great Convention, the Ratification Debates, or the history surrounding any given piece of legislation, Berger proceeded in accord with the accepted canons of interpretation upon which the intelligibility and practice of law rest outside of "advocacy history."

Berger began his career as a symphonic violinist, working his way through the University of Cincinnati. He received a J.D. at Northwestern in 1935 and an L.L.M. from Harvard in 1938. Following distinguished service as a government attorney and in private practice, Berger became a Charles Warren Senior Fellow in American Legal History at Harvard University in 1976. Several of his seminal articles were collected in *Selected Writings on the Constitution* (1987).

In his first book, *Congress v. the Supreme*

Court (1969), Berger considered the competing paradigms of judicial preeminence (as embodied by Lord Coke) in opposition to legislative supremacy (as embodied by the Blackstonian tradition). The framers feared the geographically remote power of Congress, just as they feared the British empire. Against this suspicion, the Supreme Court was designed to stand as the final arbiter of constitutionality with respect to legislative, administrative, and judicial conduct. Berger argued that the investment of the Supreme Court with this power was not only intended to meet the obvious practical need for a "final word" in resolving questions of constitutional interpretation, but also designed to check the growth of federal power beyond carefully enumerated boundaries. Judicial review was openly debated and clearly intended by both the Convention and the Ratifiers.

In *Impeachment: The Constitutional Problems* (1973), Berger (following Bernard Bailyn) emphasized the framers' reliance on the example provided by seventeenth-century England, when a succession of the king's favorites were toppled from power. "High crimes and misdemeanors" as grounds for impeachment are explained as terms of art with a rich history embracing political crimes beyond the reach of ordinary criminal redress, as opposed to any literalist statutory definition. This understanding contrasts with the investigative parliamentary tradition of the "grand inquest" adopted by the framers, which urges even the minority into the role of fact-finding and the oversight of domestic, foreign, and military affairs. In *Executive Privilege: A Constitutional Myth* (1974), Berger noted the unwarranted expansion of modern claims for executive privilege. Extension of the privilege to ever-lower levels of the bureaucracy is analyzed as an unanticipated expansion of Eisenhower's attempt to protect cabinet-level discourse against the excesses of the McCarthy era.

In *Death Penalties: The Supreme Court's Obstacle Course* (1982), Berger again relied on British precedent to decimate a revisionist contemporary argument urging that capital punishment is "cruel and unusual." Used as a term of art in the Eighth Amendment, the historical definition of the phrase in the English tradition was sufficiently broad to include "drawing and quartering," which remained on the books until 1814 in England. The Fifth Amendment, he further argued, clearly envisions the possibility of capital punishment, stating, "No person shall be held to answer for a capital [punishable by death] . . . crime, unless on a presentment or indictment," or "be twice put in jeopardy of life" for the same offense, or "be deprived of life . . . without due process of law."

In *Government by Judiciary: The Transformation of the Fourteenth Amendment* (1977) and in *The Fourteenth Amendment and the Bill of Rights* (1989), the current role of the Fourteenth Amendment was revealed by Berger to be a startling departure from its authors' intentions. The modern doctrine of "incorporation" maintains that the entire Bill of Rights was intended to be enforced against the power of state governments. In reality, the Bill of Rights was added to the Constitution as an absolute barrier against the central government's intrusion in any of the areas specified by it, mollifying those fearful of a strong central government.

The erosion of the autonomous authority of the several states as the regulators of health, safety, and commerce under local police powers, in conjunction with the shift to a federally guaranteed set of personal rights, has resulted in the reduction of state governments to mere shadows of what the framers envisioned as the natural loci of virtually all legislation. In *Federalism: The Founders' Design* (1987), Berger continued his exploration of the erosion of states' rights, emphasizing the impossibility of a narrowly won ratification in 1788–1789 if anything remotely approaching the modern version of federalism had been anticipated.

Fame follows a justice on the basis of his enlargement of federal power, as opposed to his or her reliance on the narrow procedural and jurisdictional limitations present in the framers' Constitution. Against this temptation stand the works of Berger, calling for a return to a Constitution informed by the accessible and intelligible intent of those who made it.

—Douglas E. Bradford

Further Reading

Fisher, Louis. "Raoul Berger on Public Law." *Political Science Reviewer* 8 (Fall 1978): 174–99.

See also: capital punishment; equal protection; incorporation doctrine; Supreme Court

Berns, Walter (1919–)

Walter Berns, a political scientist, specializes in modern political philosophy, the political theory of the American founding, and U.S. Supreme Court adjudication, especially of the First Amendment to the U.S. Constitution. A student of political philosopher Leo Strauss at the University of Chicago, where he received his doctorate in 1953, Berns has taught at Yale, Cornell, the University of Toronto, and other institutions. He has published widely in both professional and popular journals and has written several books. Until recently he was John M. Olin University Professor at Georgetown University. He is now an adjunct scholar at the American Enterprise Institute in Washington, D.C.

Berns is best known for his analysis of First Amendment adjudication—especially concerning the so-called "religion clauses"—and for his more general interpretation of the role of religion in the American Founding. America is essentially informed by the philosophy of Hobbes and Locke and secu-

lar in nature, Berns argues. The individual "natural rights" upon which both the Declaration of Independence and Constitution are based explicitly contradict the Christian understanding of man and his duties to God and fellow man, and were known by the founders to do so. Thus, the American founding merely *tolerates* religion, and then only when it does not disturb civil peace. Moreover, the Constitution permits generally applicable laws that might incidentally inhibit religious practice, as long as they are not religiously specific; constitutional commitment to philosophical liberalism always has precedence.

Similarly, writes Berns, the speech that the First Amendment protects is *political* speech. So-called "speech" represented by, say, flag-burning or pornographic art, while not necessarily forbidden, does not enjoy constitutional immunity. The purpose of the speech clauses is to protect political discourse for the sake of furthering and strengthening democracy. Speech or actions that actually threaten to undermine the very Constitution to which they appeal for protection may properly be suppressed or at least positively discouraged by the state.

This position reflects Berns's view that we should take seriously the Constitution and the political philosophy that informs it. One of the chief principles of this philosophy is that private judgment ought to have no place in politics and government. Whether the pious opinion of minority religious adherents, or the radical egalitarian views of a Supreme Court justice, private judgment cannot have precedence over constitutionally established political procedure. Since all men are equal, all men's opinions are equal. Only a *union* of opinions may be translated into law, and no individual opinion may prevail over the general one. Individual opinion, while protected, has no standing in constitutional government.

Thus, Berns believes in a conservative—

"originalist," in the words of Robert Bork—role of the Supreme Court. Justices are not granted the prerogative of interpreting the Constitution according to an unwritten "natural law" (which is law merely in the opinion of the particular justice), but only according to the intention of the framers, as actually written in the Constitution. Private judgment—even judgment that Berns himself might find compelling or true—has no proper role in constitutional adjudication.

—KENNETH R. CRAYCRAFT JR.

Further Reading

Berns, Walter. *The First Amendment and the Future of American Democracy.* New York: Basic Books, 1976.

———. *Freedom, Virtue, and the First Amendment.* Chicago: Regnery, 1965.

———. *Taking the Constitution Seriously.* New York: Simon & Schuster, 1987.

See also: church and state; Constitution, interpretations of; speech, freedom of

Berry, Wendell (1934–)

A working farmer, conservationist, and man of letters, Wendell Berry is respected by members of both the American Right and Left for his accomplishment in promoting the recurrent themes of his written work: the timelessness and practicality of recognizing and living out the interconnectedness between faith, family, the small community, and the land. As a localist and believer in small-scale sustainable economies, he is a humanistic writer working firmly in the tradition of the Agrarians; but where the original Agrarians of the early 1930s—with the exception of Andrew Lytle—merely *wrote* about the importance of sustaining agricultural life in the American South, Berry actually *lives* the agrarian life, farming ancestral land near Port Royal, Kentucky. Recognizing the land itself as a trust linking the dead, the living, and those yet unborn, he perceives his life's work as that of being a responsible steward of the soil and a responsible member of the small community of souls of which he is a part.

Berry holds that while the subsistence farmer in general is down-to-earth and practical, he is no materialist; he is a nurturer of the soil (and, by extension, the soul), not an exploiter who takes what he can from the land in terms of lumber, crops, and soil quality, and then sells his depleted property to the highest bidder—perhaps to be transformed into a new housing development. Berry thus stands at odds with those conservatives who view the acquisition of wealth, often through unceasing land development, as the end of life. (At the same time, his agrarian philosophy sits uncomfortably with some leftists/liberals, who are suspicious of Berry's emphasis on the importance of faith in God, the strong need for rootedness and place, and community reliance, as opposed to government regulations and scientist solutions to life's challenges.) Berry's farming methods are as radical as his cultural criticism: he uses mule-power and other natural methods in farming, eschewing computers, chemical fertilizers, expensive machinery, and the other accoutrements of contemporary "agribusiness," which he detests. In choosing such a course, Berry believes that he better preserves the dance-like rhythm of the seasons and weather: the annual birth, ascent, decline, death, and rebirth of creation.

During the few hours every day when he is not working the land, Berry writes. As a craftsman of novels, short stories, poetry, and essays, he enjoys a growing and passionately enthusiastic following. Such nonfiction works as *The Unsettling of America: Culture and Agriculture* (1977), *What Are People For?* (1990), and *Sex, Economy, Freedom, and Community: Eight Essays* (1993), as well as such novels as *Nathan Coulter* (1960) and *Jayber Crow* (2000), make it clear that Berry is not only contemporary America's most important agrarian thinker but also a serious proponent of an alternative vision of cultural conservatism.

—JAMES E. PERSON JR.

Further Reading:

Angyal, Andrew J. *Wendell Berry*. Boston: Twayne Publishers, 1995.

Berry, Wendell. *The Art of the Commonplace: The Agrarian Essays of Wendell Berry,* Edited by Norman Wirzba. Washington, D.C.: Counterpoint, 2002.

Carlson, Allan. *The New Agrarian Mind: The Movement toward Decentralist Thought in Twentieth-Century America.* New Brunswick, N.J.: Transaction, 2000.

Cornell, Daniel. "The Country of Marriage: Wendell Berry's Personal Political Vision." *Southern Literary Journal* 16, no. 1 (1983): 59–70.

Smith, Kimberly K. *Wendell Berry and the Agrarian Tradition: A Common Grace.* Lawrence, Kan.: University Press of Kansas, 2003.

See also: agrarianism; community; localism; technology

Bill of Rights

The Bill of Rights refers to the first ten amendments to the U.S. Constitution. The first Congress that convened under the new Constitution passed these amendments in 1789, and they were quickly ratified by the states and added to the Constitution in 1791. They were generally regarded as clarifying, emphasizing and reinforcing the terms of the original Constitution, unlike the later amendments to the Constitution that have either altered the original Constitution or "overturned" Supreme Court interpretations of the Constitution. The Bill of Rights is an important manifestation of the American commitment to limited and decentralized government and individual rights.

Bills or declarations of rights have a long and rich history in Britain and the United States. Such documents as the *Magna Carta* (1215) and the *Declaration of Rights* (1689) enshrined the rights of individuals and important groups against the king in Britain. Many of the specific rights contained in those declarations were incorporated into the English common law (the judge-made law governing the English legal process) and accepted as the common and fundamental rights of Englishmen. As such, they were carried to the British colonies in North America and elsewhere and absorbed into American colonial law and documents such as the *Massachusetts Body of Liberties* (1641). When many of the states drafted new constitutions during the American Revolution, they often included bills of rights enumerating liberties to be protected under the new state governments.

The original Constitution drafted in the Philadelphia Convention of 1787 and ratified by the states did not include a separate bill of rights. Some specific rights and limits on government power were written directly into the main body of the constitutional text, such as a prohibition on ex post facto laws (retroactive criminal legislation) or bills of attainder (laws imposing punishment on individuals). Many other commonly recognized rights were not specifically protected by the Constitution, however. Near the end of the Philadelphia Convention, George Mason and Elbridge Gerry suggested the inclusion of a bill of rights, but their proposal was not accepted. They refused to sign the completed Constitution and eventually joined the Anti-Federalist opponents to the ratification of the Constitution largely because of the absence of a bill of rights.

Even after the Constitution was ratified, many of its defenders and critics remained troubled by the lack of a national bill of rights to accompany the strengthening of the national government, and many states immediately proposed constitutional amendments to recognize more rights. Serving in the first House of Representatives, James Madison, who had initially opposed such a bill, drafted the amendments that would become the Bill of Rights. Congress passed Madison's proposals as twelve constitutional amendments, and ten were quickly ratified by the states. An eleventh, relating to congressional pay, was finally ratified in 1992 and became the Twenty-seventh Amendment.

The Federalist defenders of the Constitution offered various reasons for not including a bill of rights. The most common defense, argued by Alexander Hamilton in the *Federalist* (1787), contended that a separate bill of rights was unnecessary. Unlike the British or American state governments, the proposed federal government was one of enumerated powers. The federal government was only to exercise the powers specifically granted to it in the U.S. Constitution. A bill of rights, it was argued, was only needed to carve out exceptions to powers that the government was already presumed to have. The careful enumeration of federal powers should make it unnecessary to create a separate list of specifically protected rights. The Federalists also argued that a bill of rights could be dangerous, since it might imply that the federal government could do anything not specifically prohibited by the bill of rights. In private, Madison also doubted whether a bill of rights could be effective in a democratic government. A bill of rights could not be expected to protect the people from the government when the people themselves were the government. He thought the state declarations of rights had proven to be mere "parchment barriers." Madison preferred other methods of controlling the government, such as elections and the separation of powers. He also worried that some important liberties would be left out or curtailed in the process of creating a specific bill of rights. Thomas Jefferson helped persuade Madison that "half a loaf is better than no

bread" and that a federal bill of rights could be useful for protecting liberty, in part by empowering the judiciary. The strong political support for a federal bill of rights, including in his home state of Virginia, led Madison to sponsor the amendments as necessary to secure full public support for the new Constitution.

The Bill of Rights reflects many of the traditional liberties found in the common law and the earlier British and American constitutional documents. Thus, the Bill of Rights primarily attempted to preserve the liberties that the new Americans thought they already possessed and on which they largely agreed, but that historically had come under threat from abusive governments. Many of the protections in the Bill of Rights relate to the legal and judicial process. Their inclusion in the Bill of Rights reflects their centrality to the British constitutional and legal tradition, as well as concerns raised by the prospect of a new and relatively distant federal judiciary. Thus, the Fourth through Eighth Amendments largely address the circumstances, procedures, and limits of trials. Those amendments secure such things as the right to a speedy, fair, and public trial, reasonable bail for those accused of crimes, protection from cruel punishments and double jeopardy, and security from unreasonable searches and uncompensated seizure of property. The Third Amendment prohibition on the quartering of troops in private homes reflects both the colonial and British experiences with occupation armies. The Second Amendment protection of the right to bear arms likewise reflects the value put on an armed citizenry in the British and American legal and political tradition. The First Amendment reflects a growing commitment to religious freedom and toleration and public participation in politics through debate and petition.

The Bill of Rights also reflects some particular features of the U.S. Constitution.

The Ninth Amendment is unusual in simply noting that "the enumeration in the Constitution of certain rights shall not be construed to deny or disparage others retained by the people." The Ninth Amendment thus responds to the Federalist skepticism voiced by Hamilton that some valuable rights would be left unprotected. The Ninth Amendment also helps create a constitutional presumption in favor of individual rights and points toward an extended universe of natural and common law rights. The Bill of Rights also embodies a respect for federalism and the importance of state and local governments. The Tenth Amendment is the most explicit on this point, emphasizing that the "powers not delegated to the United States by the Constitution, nor prohibited by it to the States, are reserved to the States respectively, or to the people." The revolutionary distrust of a distant and centralized government is evident in other parts of the Bill of Rights as well. The First Amendment, for example, specifically prohibits Congress from making any law "respecting" the establishment of religion. In doing so, it not only forbids a national established religion, but also protected from national interference the already-established religions in several of the states. Similarly, the Second Amendment helps protect the state militias from national interference.

The Bill of Rights was designed as a constraint on the national government. But in the twentieth century, it has also been applied to the state governments. This new application of the Bill of Rights was the result of the adoption of the Fourteenth Amendment after the Civil War, which gave federal protection to individual rights *against* the interference of state governments. A key clause of the Fourteenth Amendment prohibits the states from depriving "any person of life, liberty, or property, without due process of law." Although this clause repeats language from the Fifth Amendment, the Supreme Court has read the due process clause as requiring the states to meet many of the same constitutional requirements as the federal government, thus "incorporating" the Bill of Rights, and the Court's interpretations of it, into the Fourteenth Amendment. At various times in its history, the Court has also embraced notions of "substantive due process" or "unenumerated rights," whereby the due process clause is interpreted to include a variety of individual rights not specifically written anywhere in the Constitution, such as a broad "right to privacy." Since the states still have the most direct impact on ordinary citizens (through law enforcement, for example), this interpretation of the Fourteenth Amendment has had dramatic political and legal consequences, especially when combined with the Court's new interpretations of those basic liberties. The Court's decisions on obscenity and school prayer, the exclusionary rule and the death penalty, birth control and abortion have their greatest effect and relevance because of the application of the Bill of Rights to the states and the nationalization of the definition and protection of individual liberties.

For many conservatives, these decisions in particular have led to complaints of "government by judiciary" as judges "invent" new rights and oversee a vast number of state and federal political decisions. For some libertarians, however, this activist interpretation of constitutional rights holds the potential for sharply limiting government by emphasizing the constitutional constraints on political power even when exercised by democratic majorities.

—KEITH E. WHITTINGTON

Further Reading

Amar, Akhil R. *The Bill of Rights: Creation and Reconstruction*. New Haven, Conn.: Yale University Press, 1998.

Hickok, Eugene W. *The Bill of Rights: Original Meaning and Current Understanding.* Charlottesville:,

Va.: University Press of Virginia, 1991.

Levy, Leonard W. *Origins of the Bill of Rights.* New Haven, Conn.: Yale University Press, 1999.

Rakove, Jack N. *Declaring Rights: A Brief History with Documents.* Boston: Bedford Books, 1998.

Schwartz, Bernard. *Roots of the Bill of Rights.* New York: Chelsea House, 1980.

See also: church and state; due process; incorporation doctrine; speech, freedom of; states' rights

Blackwell, Morton (1939–)

Born in Colorado and raised in Louisiana, Morton Blackwell attended Louisiana State University, where he studied chemical engineering, never completing the degree. At age 23, he was the youngest delegate to the 1964 Republican convention. A lifelong political aficionado, Blackwell was a member of Young Americans for Freedom and executive director of the College Young Republicans from 1965 to 1970. He was an account executive with the Viguerie Company from 1972 to 1979, also editing the *New Right Report* and serving as a contributing editor to *Conservative Digest.* A founding member of the New Right, in 1978–79 Blackwell was policy director for Senator Gordon Humphrey (R-N.H.) before becoming the Director of Youth for Ronald Reagan in 1980. In 1981 he was appointed Special Assistant for Public Liaison to Reagan, a position he held until 1984, co-authoring Reagan's Voluntary Prayer Amendment. He has appeared on numerous radio and TV programs and has contributed articles to *Human Events*, the *Washington Times* and the *Washington Post,* among other periodicals.

Labeled "the eyes and ears of the New Right" by *Human Events*, and the "Johnny Appleseed of American politics" by activist Grover Norquist, Blackwell's major contribution to conservatism has been his mentoring of young conservatives. In 1979

Blackwell founded the Leadership Institute "to increase the number and effectiveness of conservative public policy leaders." The institute has trained tens of thousands of young people for careers as conservatives in think tanks, legislative offices, politics, and the media.

—Gregory L. Schneider

Further Reading

Martin, William. *With God on Our Side: The Rise of the Religious Right in America.* (New York: Broadway Books, 1996).

Viguerie, Richard. *The New Right: We're Ready to Lead* (Falls Church, Va.: The Viguerie Co,: 1981).

See also: New Right

Bledsoe, Albert Taylor (1809–77)

A highly educated, widely respected Southern writer and editor whose life spanned much of the nineteenth century, Albert Taylor Bledsoe was one of the preeminent defenders of states' rights both before and after the War Between the States. In several books and numerous essays and reviews he articulated the right of states to secede from the Union and upheld slavery as an institution beneficial to Southern society at large.

Born and privately educated in Kentucky, Bledsoe attended West Point, where he was recognized as a tenacious scholar, and in 1830 he graduated sixteenth in a class of forty-two. While at West Point he converted to Christianity and became acquainted with two men whose paths were to cross his own many years later, Robert E. Lee and Jefferson Davis. In the years that followed, Bledsoe exemplified the life of a man easily bored by routine, pursuing numerous jobs—soldier, lawyer, Christian minister, educator, writer— and settling for short times in cities and towns throughout Ohio, Illinois, and Mississippi. In 1845 he published his first book, *An Examination of President Edwards' Inquiry into the Freedom of the Will*, a lengthy refutation of Jonathan Edwards's Calvinist theories of predestination and doctrine of the elect. A later book, *An Essay on Liberty and Slavery* (1856), defended slavery as a positive good, with Bledsoe arguing that the black African race is inferior to the Caucasian race and that the "peculiar institution" made for a well-ordered society by delivering slaves from indolence and compelling them to serve their masters and the Southern economy.

With the outbreak of hostilities in 1861, Bledsoe, at the time a professor of mathematics at the University of Virginia, became head of the War Bureau in the Confederate States government. He left this position after a year and sailed to London to write articles stating the case for the Confederate cause. After the war, Bledsoe returned to America and took the required oath of allegiance to the United States. Ironically, he then wrote a defense of the South published as *Is Davis a Traitor; or, Was Secession a Constitutional Right Previous to the War of 1861?* (1866), allegedly upon the strong advice of Lee. Harking back to the doctrine of states' rights articulated by James Madison and other framers of the Constitution, he argued that the union of states was from the beginning voluntary, not compulsory, and that the Southern states were entirely within their rights to withdraw from the Union. In 1867 Bledsoe founded the *Southern Review* in Baltimore. As the editor of and primary contributor to that journal, he continued until the end of his life to promote the political philosophy of the "Lost Cause" in a manner described by Paula Cozort Renfro in the *Dictionary of Literary Biography* (1989) as "vigorous, passionate, erudite, earnest, sometimes profound, and almost always opinionated."

—JAMES E. PERSON JR.

Further Reading

Bennett, John B. "Albert Taylor Bledsoe: Transitional Philosopher of the Old South." *Methodist History* 11 (1972): 3–14.

Cooke, J. W. "Albert Taylor Bledsoe: An American Philosopher and Theologian of Liberty." *Southern Humanities Review* 8 (1974): 215–228.

Riley, Sam G. American Magazine Journalists, *1850–1900. Vol. 79 of Dictionary of Literary Biography*. Detroit: Gale Research, 1989.

Weaver, Richard M. "Albert Taylor Bledsoe." *Sewanee Review* 52 (1944): 34–45.

See also: Southern conservatism; states' rights

Bloom, Allan (1930–92)

Student of Leo Strauss, professor of political philosophy at the University of Chicago, passionate defender of the "old Great Books conviction," Allan Bloom was born and raised in Indianapolis and educated at the University of Chicago, taking his B.A., M.A., and Ph.D. there, the last received from the committee on social thought in 1955. The author or editor of several highly regarded books, including *Love and Friendship* (1993), and the translator of a widely used edition of Plato's *Republic* (1968), Bloom was catapulted into the so-called culture wars with the success of his book *The Closing of the American Mind* (1987), which brilliantly documented the decline of the American university over the previous thirty years. Bloom was perfectly situated to observe this collapse as a young professor at Cornell in the late 1960s, when armed student uprisings, abetted by weak-willed administrators and faculty eager to seem "with it," demanded the jettisoning of the college's core curriculum under the pretense that it was sexist, Eurocentric, and elitist. The result of this movement, mirrored in campuses across the country, has been an unmitigated crisis for higher education in America.

In Bloom's account, among students (and Americans in general), openness to discovery, or the passionate pursuit of new and foreign ideas and ways of life for the purpose of rationally testing them as true—the hallmark of the West since its birth in Greek philosophy—had given way to an "openness of indifference." Since all books and teachers are equal, they are useless as guides to truth. The contemporary student therefore decides that the so-called higher ideals are not worth arguing or fighting over, and goes about preparing himself for a life of meaningless consumerism and recreation, the satisfaction of his animal nature. Our eagerness to root out discrimination and achieve absolute equality has resulted in our "unwillingness or incapacity to make claims of superiority" in art, religion, and philosophy, wrote Bloom. Meanwhile, the student's soul has atrophied, his highest potential denied fruition, perhaps permanently.

Bloom had little time for "realistic" conservatives who urged contentment with such a life on the grounds that "utopianism" or "idealism" is dangerous. For Bloom, the essential quality of man is *eros*, longing for perfection. This yearning is native to all, particularly the young, but must be properly stimulated and guided through friendship with good teachers and the best books. Free love, exacerbated by easy divorce and the false eroticism of popular music, prematurely satiates the soul's longing and unfits it for pursuing the permanent questions and alternative ways of life addressed by the finest minds of the past. Nor are such minds necessarily conservative in the contemporary sense. Bloom himself, in a lecture at Harvard titled "Western Civ," expressed some surprise at being reckoned as such: "My teachers—Socrates, Machiavelli, Rousseau, and Nietzsche—could hardly be called conservatives."

In some ways Bloom was a disciple of Lockean classical liberalism, in that he believed that a rejection of the rationality of human rights and equality lay at the heart of the university's crisis. For Bloom, the pernicious influence in America of those strands of German philosophy which argued against reason's universalism and in favor of the notion that man was found his completion and happiness in a community grounded in its unique history and culture was the source of the New Left's affirmation of all cultural "roots" (except its own). A similar argument could be deployed against traditionalists and many religious conservatives as well. Bloom was thus a conservative only to the extent that contemporary conservatism is in fact the old liberalism of the founders, which affirms reason over roots and thus the equality of all men as reasoning beings. Thus, Bloom sometimes argued that the American Lockean regime was the proper home of reason and therefore intrinsically oriented toward the greatest minds in its midst and in its past: "A society based on reason needs those who reason best." But he sometimes implied that the Lockean regime was based not on reason itself, which would mean affirming those who reason best, but on an assertion of the equality of men's reasoning. This analysis revealed the fatal flaw in the new liberalism.

—Joshua Vandiver

Further Reading

Bellow, Saul. *Ravelstein*. New York: Viking Penguin, 2000.

Bloom, Allan. *Giants and Dwarfs: Essays 1960–1990*. New York: Simon & Schuster, 1990.

———, and Harry V. Jaffa. *Shakespeare's Politics*. New York: Basic Books, 1964.

Rousseau, Jean-Jacques. *Emile or On Education*. Edited and translated by Allan Bloom. New York: Basic Books, 1979.

See also: *culture wars; liberalism, classical; nihilism; relativism*

Bookman

In 1927 the *Bookman* became a major literary expression of the New Humanist movement. Purchased that year by Seward Collins, a recent Princeton University graduate and man of independent means, the *Bookman* entered the raging "battle of the books" on the side of traditional humanism and against the newer currents in literature. The *Bookman*'s entrance into this fray signaled the growing influence of Irving Babbitt and Paul Elmer More, the dominant voices of the New Humanists.

The *Bookman* came into existence in 1887. It was founded by Frank Howard Dodd, president of Dodd, Mead, and Co. of New York City. Under a succession of editors, the *Bookman* tried to be a window to the publishing world, offering reviews, essays, bestseller lists, and lively literary portraits of writers familiar and new. It surveyed its field without championing any particular cause. But Collins wanted to enter the philosophical arguments of the day. He seized editorial control from Burton Rascoe, an acerbic critic of the New Humanists and a champion of Theodore Dreiser, James Branch Cabell, and e. e. Cummings. In 1928, Collins restored the "Chronicle and Comment" section that had once been a staple of the *Bookman* and made it a pulpit for his conservative views. He denounced the "insurrectionist" tendencies in literature and criticism and called for a return to traditional standards.

The *Bookman* played several roles. First, it was an outlet for the major humanist writers. Collins published essays by Babbitt and More that summarized for a general readership their long-standing criticism of romanticism and naturalism. The journal offered important essays by Babbitt on William Wordsworth and James Joyce as well as Babbitt's key critical formulation, "On Being Creative." The *Bookman* also carried some major contributions to the New Humanism

by Norman Foerster, who advanced the movement's plea for a literature that captured the universal human spirit and transcended the particulars of time and place.

Second, the *Bookman* opened its pages to a second generation of humanist scholars, most of them disciples of Babbitt. They included Alan Reynolds Thompson, G. R. Elliott, Gorham Munson, and Robert Shafer. The latter offered a series of essays that summarized the New Humanist critique of American higher education, especially its dissent from the elective system and the vocational emphasis in American universities.

Third, the *Bookman* gave voice to other expressions of conservative antimodernism besides the New Humanism. Here especially it echoed the sentiments of Collins. Thus, A. J. Nock, T. S. Eliot, G. K. Chesterton, and the Southern Agrarians made appearances in its pages. Whether as disciples of Babbitt or as conservatives with different emphases, the *Bookman*'s writers generally recoiled from the disorderly forces of modern life. Their preferences were for self-control, tradition, and beauty as countervailing forces to what they considered to be the ugliness and primitivism of modernity. The *Bookman* writers never answered the call for literature to reflect "real life." They generally adhered to the aesthetic standards of the genteel tradition.

Nonetheless, the *Bookman* did not forsake its history as a news journal of literature. It offered some lively debates about new writers, and some of its contributors welcomed William Faulkner and Glenway Wescott among them. And it published clearly dissenting views. The Marxist V. F. Calverton was a contributor, as was C. Hartley Grattan, an avowed anti–New Humanist.

The *Bookman* died in 1933. Collins was becoming increasingly convinced that economics, more than culture, was the decisive battleground for the modern world, and he wanted a journal that reflected that fact. His antimodernism made him a supporter of Benito Mussolini's fascism and he now envisioned a new journal to bring together critics of industrial capitalism and mass democracy. Collins published the last issue of the *Bookman* in March 1933. The next month there appeared its successor, the *American Review*.

—J. DAVID HOEVELER JR.

Further Reading

Hoeveler, J. David, Jr. *"The Bookman."* In *The Conservative Press in Twentieth-Century America*, edited by Ronald Lora and William Longton. Westport, Conn.: Greenwood, 1999.

Mott, Frank Luther. *A History of American Magazines*. Cambridge, Mass.: Harvard University Press, 1930.

See also: American Review; *Collins, Seward; New Humanism; Southern Agrarians*

Books & Culture

Books & Culture: A Christian Review is the leading journal of evangelical Protestant engagement with the scholarly disciplines and the arts. A tabloid-style bimonthly loosely modeled on the *New York Review of Books, Books & Culture* was launched in 1995 by Christianity Today International with funding from the Pew Charitable Trusts.

The journal was conceived as a response to historian Mark Noll's 1994 book *The Scandal of the Evangelical Mind*, which lamented the lack of intellectual development within American evangelical Protestantism—a movement hampered, in Noll's view, by Fundamentalist populism and a preoccupation with creationism and the Rapture.

Books & Culture's editorial board is cochaired by Noll and popular lay-theologian Phillip Yancey. In its fifth anniversary issue, Noll wrote that *Books & Culture* "exists because of a growing willingness among at least some evangelical Christians to consider seriously—as part of their Christian vocation—the domains of science, art, psychology, history, world affairs, social forces, literature, politics, and more." John Wilson has edited the journal since its inception. In his online commentaries and editorial column, "Stranger in a Strange Land," Wilson lightly showcases his broad reading and interests, ranging from evolutionary science to the science fiction of Philip K. Dick.

Books & Culture is distinguished from the other publications of Christianity Today International (such as *Christianity Today* and *Today's Christian Woman*) by its focus on the wider culture—it reviews, for example, far more books from mainstream university presses than evangelical publishers—and by its broad range of contributors, including Catholic, Orthodox, and even non-Christian scholars.

While not an organ of political conservatism (Noll, Yancey, and Wilson would reject any connection to the Religious Right) *Books & Culture* publishes reviews from conservative-minded writers such as Jean Bethke Elshtain, Elizabeth Fox-Genovese, Eugene Genovese, Frederica Mathewes-Green, Vigen Guroian, Phillip E. Johnson, J. Bottom, Robert Royal, and Stephen Carter. It has also featured interviews with John Lukacs, Christina Hoff Sommers, and Francis Fukuyama.

—SAM TORODE

Further Reading

Wolfe, Alan. "The Opening of the Evangelical Mind." *Atlantic Monthly,* October 2000.

See also: Protestantism, evangelical

Boorstin, Daniel J. (1914–2003)

An eloquent and prolific historian, Daniel Boorstin narrated the past with an eye for curious details and an optimistic vision of

America's ability to develop indigenous traditions peacefully. Boorstin was one of the chief proponents of consensus history. The so-called consensus school of American historiography, with its quest for an underlying unity in ideas, traditions, or experiences in American society, reflected America's search for stability during the early years of the Cold War. Boorstin stood as a more right-leaning representative of this largely liberal school, in contrast to its "founders" Richard Hofstadter and Louis Hartz. Hofstadter and others emphasized political theory, or ideology, and pointed toward an enduring liberal tradition of revolution and radical reform. Boorstin, in contrast, focused on the common, concrete, and almost hidden experiences that could be found in the details of everyday life, such as whaling narratives, balloon frame homes, and refrigeration.

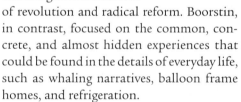

Within two years of his birth in 1914, Boorstin's family moved from Atlanta to Tulsa. Son of Russian Jews, the young Boorstin observed first hand the effects of racial and religious separatism that characterized an American frontier town. At fifteen he entered Harvard where, influenced by the writing of Edward Gibbon, he aspired to become an amateur historian—despite the omnipresence of the progressive school of historiography, with its emphasis on social realism and economic models of conflict. Professionally, Boorstin gravitated towards the law. As a Rhodes Scholar at Balliol College, Oxford (1934–37), Boorstin took a "double first" in jurisprudence and civil law and, for a time, associated with avant-garde political circles. Returning to Yale, however, Boorstin grew increasingly conservative.

At Yale he earned a doctorate in law. A revision of his dissertation became *The Mys-*

terious Science of the Law (1941), a study of Blackstone. Both here and in *The Lost World of Thomas Jefferson* (1948) Boorstin reconstructed the intellectual world of the eighteenth century as one in which calm public figures like Blackstone and many of the founders made prudent decisions based on the observation of experience over theory. He devoted little room to philosophical principles, and the dominant Jeffersonian (and Boorstinian) view of political science presented was one that developed from a pragmatic analysis of man's immediate relationship to nature and the rights contained therein; these rights limited the influence that institutions should have on individuals.

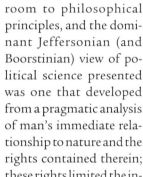
Daniel J. Boorstin

Working from such observations, Boorstin fashioned the controlling principle of later works. In *The Genius of American Politics* (1953) he argued that the American character and American institutions were formed not from the application of preconceived theories, but from unique experiences and facts "given" to America from its own past. Long periods of prosperity, Boorstin maintained, ensured the exclusion of divisive ideology and established a proclivity for compromise and consensus among Americans, a tradition that obviated the need for an intrusive centralized government. By their very nature such factors were organic and contingent, they could not be created by a government. Unlike Europeans, Americans reaped widespread economic wealth and political stability because they did not apply preconceived philosophies to the challenges they faced. The evidence for his thesis appeared over the next several decades in his trilogy, *The Americans* (1958–1973), in many ways a case study in Boorstinian axioms.

With the increasing domestic discord of

the 1960s the popularity and credibility of consensus historiography ebbed. *The Decline of Radicalism* (1969) marked Boorstin's turn towards social criticism. The thesis of the work was evident in the title: radicalism was—contrary to appearances—fading in political life. Critics of this phase wondered how Boorstin could speak of "decline," when in his previous works he had vehemently denied radicalism a significant place in American society. Nor was it clear why Boorstin criticized the agitators of the 1960s for not having a guiding philosophy, when he previously considered antimetaphysical pragmatism an element of the American genius.

Boorstin continued into the 1970s with essays on technology and popular culture, displaying a concern for the way in which community experiences were now being manufactured. He warned of the rise of "pseudo-events"—media-planned "significance"—and called for a prudent, but sanguine, approach to technological change. He counseled that a rash embrace of new forms of media or technology would sap Americans of historical understanding.

Appointed by President Ford, Boorstin directed the Library of Congress from 1975 to 1987, a post that fostered his literary productivity, as *The Discoverers* (1983) and *The Creators* (1992) evinced. Boorstin held many prestigious teaching positions in the United States and Europe, the longest post being twenty-five years of service at the University of Chicago, where he edited the thirty-volume Chicago History of American Civilization.

Elements of Boorstin's thought have met with criticism from both conservatives and liberals, who charge that he paid too little attention to periods of critical conflict or change, notably the Civil War; showered too much attention on apparent success, to the obscurity of defeated and marginalized sections of American society, such as the South; had too great a suspicion of dogmatism, which turned his attention away from a serious consideration of ideology and political principles; and had too great a preoccupation with American technical innovation, which hampered his assessment of artistic and intellectual endeavors. Boorstin's apotheosis of laissez faire capitalism seemed to prepare the way for a narrow neoconservative ideology and foreign policy. Yet Boorstin himself consistently argued against attempts to transplant American culture abroad and warned of foreign entanglements. His contention that American institutions grew organically out of local communities; that American democracy is peculiar to American soil; that the American founding was a revolution averted, gave ballast to conservative intellectuals in the 1950s and early 1960s. In this respect his thought parallels, to a degree, that of Russell Kirk and John Courtney Murray. Yet whereas Boorstin looked to Europe as a foil for American traditions, Kirk and Murray saw it as the source. Furthermore, Boorstin's suspicion of dogmatism led him to hold that venerable European institutions are to be transcended and that frontiers, the "unknown," are always to be crossed. In this respect, Boorstin's thought shows greater affinity with the style of conservatism promoted by men like Clinton Rossiter and Michael Novak.

—WILLIAM FAHEY

Further Reading

Boorstin, Daniel J. *America and the Image of Europe: Reflections on American Thought.* New York: World Publications, 1960.

———. *The Daniel J. Boorstin Reader.* New York: Modern Library, 1995.

Leonard, A. M., ed. and comp. *Daniel J. Boorstin: A Comprehensive and Selectively Annotated Bibliography.* Westport, Conn.: Greenwood Press, 2000.

See also: Kirk, Russell; Murray, John Courtney; Novak, Michael

Bork, Robert H. (1927–)

Robert Heron Bork is one of the most influential constitutional scholars of his time. He made his early reputation in the field of antitrust legislation, publishing many articles and a seminal book on the subject, in which he argued that twentieth-century American antitrust policy is fundamentally incoherent. Bork is best known, however, as a leading proponent of an "original understanding" approach to interpreting the U.S. Constitution, a position that led him to be denied a seat on the U.S. Supreme Court in 1987.

A graduate of the University of Chicago Law School (1953), after spending seven years in private practice Bork joined the faculty of the Yale Law School in 1962, where he taught in various capacities until 1981. He left Yale from 1973 to 1977 to serve as acting U.S. Attorney General (1973–1974) and U.S. Solicitor General (1973–1977). While serving as Circuit Judge for the U.S. Court of Appeals for the District of Columbia (1982–1988) Bork was nominated for Associate Justice of the U.S. Supreme Court by President Ronald Reagan in 1987. After some of the most controversial Supreme Court nomination hearings in U.S. history, Bork was denied confirmation by the U.S. Senate on October 23, 1987. In 1988 he left the Court of Appeals to become John M. Olin Resident Scholar in Legal Studies at the American Enterprise Institute.

During his Supreme Court confirmation hearings, Bork was the victim of an unprecedented media barrage against his personal character by various left-wing individuals and interest groups, and he was the target of virulent opposition from some U.S. Senators, most notably Edward Kennedy of Massachusetts. The opposition centered around Bork's many articles and essays in which he had outlined his theory of constitutional interpretation and its implications for jurisprudence, especially in the areas of civil rights legislation, due process, and free-speech issues.

Bork's theory of "original understanding" was presented most completely in his 1990 book, *The Tempting of America*. There he argued that the role of the judge is to determine the meaning of a law *at the time of its enactment* and to apply this meaning to future cases. As one person applying the law, the judge must not allow potential social consequences to affect his decision, nor may he inject his own opinion of the legitimacy of the law under consideration. If the application of the original meaning of a law produces undesirable results, this must be remedied by legislation, not judicial fiat.

Ironically, after his resignation from the Circuit Court, Bork joined in public debate with other conservatives who questioned his legal positivism and moral skepticism. Bork's contention that no transcendent moral principles may guide the judge in applying a particular positive law, and his agnosticism about the existence of such principles, precipitated a lively debate over the use of "natural law" in American jurisprudence. Bork has argued forcefully that the U.S. Constitution does not assume a natural law, and thus neither should the judge who interprets the Constitution or other laws in light of the Constitution.

—Kenneth R. Craycraft Jr.

Further Reading

Arkes, Hadley, Russell Hittinger, William Bentley Ball, and Robert H. Bork. "Natural Law and the Law: An Exchange." *First Things* 23 (1992): 45–54.

Bork, Robert. *Slouching Towards Gomorrah: Modern Liberalism and American Decline.* New York: HarperCollins, 1997.

———. *Coercing Virtue: The Worldwide Rule of Judges.* Toronto: Vintage Canada, 2002.

Bronner, Ethan. *Battle for Justice: How the Bork Nomination Shook America.* New York: Norton, 1989.

See also: Constitution, interpretations of; judicial activism; natural law; rule of law

Borsodi, Ralph (1888–1977)

During the 1930s and '40s, an era of tremendous growth in the public sector within the United States, Ralph Borsodi was an advocate of decentralization, self-sufficiency, and political economy on a humane scale. He wrote several books on these themes, notably *This Ugly Civilization* (1929) and *Flight from the City: The Story of a New Way to Family Security* (1933). An activist for his cause, Borsodi founded the School of Living community in Suffern, New York, the first of several such short-lived experiments in cooperative living, and promoted programs elsewhere in the nation to encourage people living in depressed areas to better their lot through home study. Historians have likened Borsodi's theories to G. K. Chesterton and Hilaire Belloc's distributist ideas and the "small is beautiful" philosophy of E. F. Schumacher.

Ralph Borsodi

An economist by vocation, Borsodi came to widespread attention with *This Ugly Civilization*, in which he identified the factory as the greatest contributor to the ugliness of modern Western civilization, not only for its hulking, smoke-belching appearance, but for its contribution to a culture in which people are separated from the earth. The industrial world, he wrote, promotes getting and spending as the highest values in life through deceptive advertising and the production of needless gadgets and luxuries. In his best-known work, *Flight from the City*, Borsodi called for a return to the land and a closed-corporate form of living which would emphasize independence and self-reliance, including the growing of community members' own food.

In 1935 Borsodi took direct action toward putting his theories into practice. That year, he and a group of like-minded individuals formed the Independence Foundation, purchasing forty acres of land in Suffern, New York, and then dividing this large plot into one- and two-acre parcels for homesteading and small-scale farming. The entire 40-acre plot was held in common tenure by the incorporated homesteaders, and when assessments to the Independence Foundation were completed, they received free and clear title to the land. Through careful planning, skilled tradesmen who lived and worked in the community were kept employed year-round, avoiding the typical annual cycle of boom or bust in terms of actual work. Moderately successful for several years, the Suffern School of Living inspired the building of several other communities on a similar plan. "With Borsodi and the cooperative movement showing the way, the decentralist, or distributist, movement in the United States gives promise of a vitality which it never had in the years when the Tennessee Agrarians were taking a literary stand in favor of small ownership," wrote John Chamberlain, hopefully, in 1940. However, the exigencies of World War II, including the departure of draft-age men and the resulting increase of wages at home, put a quiet end to the communities. After the demise of these cooperative ventures, Borsodi wrote several other books that were not widely noticed, and he spent the final thirty years of his life in obscurity.

—JAMES E. PERSON JR.

Further Reading

Carlson, Allan. *The New Agrarian Mind: The Movement toward Decentralist Thought in Twentieth-Century America.* New Brunswick, N.J.: Transaction, 2000.

Hicks, George L. *Experimental Americans: Celo and Utopian Community in the Twentieth Century.* Urbana, Ill.: University of Illinois Press, 2001.

Weller, George. "Decentralized City Homesteads." *Commonweal* 28 (July 22, 1938): 341–44.

See also: agrarianism; distributism; homeschooling

Bozell, L. Brent (1926–97)

Speechwriter, journalist, and debater, senior editor at *National Review*, ghostwriter of Barry Goldwater's bestselling *Conscience of a Conservative* (1960), and precocious critic of the judicial usurpation of politics (*The Warren Revolution*, 1966), L. Brent Bozell was an especially intelligent and articulate spokesman for the burgeoning postwar conservative movement's traditionalist Catholic wing until he broke with the movement in the mid-1960s.

Bozell's public career started as an undergraduate at Yale in the late '40s, where, with his close friend William F. Buckley Jr., the tall, skinny, redheaded Catholic convert from Nebraska dazzled audiences at the Yale Political Union, which he presided over as president, with his rhetorical abilities. While in law school at Yale, he joined with Buckley to coauthor *McCarthy and His Enemies* (1954), a defense of Senator Joseph McCarthy's congressional investigations.

Bozell married Buckley's sister Patricia in 1949, but intellectual cleavages between the brothers-in-law deepened as the years passed. Buckley preferred a rather big-tent notion of conservatism and did not see any necessary contradiction between his unique synthesis of libertarian and conservative ideas and his Catholic faith. Bozell, on the other hand, believed that orthodox Catholicism was opposed to the absolutizing of individual freedom displayed by prominent conservative writers. Foremost among such writers was Frank Meyer, *NR*'s literary editor and Bozell's bosom friend.

Thus, in 1962, while living in Spain, Bozell sent to *National Review* an article titled "Freedom or Virtue?" a brilliant polemical essay, aimed primarily at Meyer's "fusionism," which sparked much controversy and debate. In the article, Bozell attempted to show that, *pace* Meyer, nineteenth-century classical liberalism, with its emphasis on individual emancipation, was intrinsically linked to the totalitarian horrors of the twentieth century. Man's end is not freedom but virtue, and it is the duty of the state (among other institutions) to help provide an environment in which men can attain this end. Whether individual freedom must be curtailed for this purpose is simply, and legitimately, a matter of prudential judgment—not ideological doctrine—in which the principle of subsidiarity, the dangers of concentrated power, and other relevant factors must be considered. In short, "Freedom or Virtue?" bespoke the growing importance of the Catholic moral and political tradition for Bozell's work.

Soon thereafter, Bozell decided that political conservatism had trumped the genuine Catholic tradition. Thus, in 1965 he founded, with his wife Trish, Michael Lawrence, and several others, *Triumph* magazine, a monthly that would continue publishing for ten years. The mainstream conservative movement marginalized *Triumph*; even Old Right scholars like historian Stephen Tonsor dismissed it as too theocratic, too anti-American. *Triumph* was indeed rather unconcerned about the political viability of its stances; in its pages Bozell and other contributors charged, for example, that America had been from the very beginning an experiment in secularist individualism, and that therefore conservatives' call for a return to the founders' understanding of the American order was misguided. But despite (or perhaps because of) its radicalism, *Triumph* and the educational programs run by Bozell in El Escorial, Spain, were influential; many Catholics, especially younger ones, resonated to Bozell's cultural criticism, including theologian and *Communio* editor David Schindler and the founding president of Christendom College, Warren Carroll.

Bozell began to suffer from bipolar disorder in the mid-seventies, a condition that often made the publication of *Triumph*, in its late months, a chaotic and uncertain affair. This disorder plagued Bozell for the rest of his life. His highs were legendary (he reported that he once wrote an entire book while in a Northern Ireland prison, only to have it thrown away by the British guards) and extremely disruptive. In his later years he founded Misión Guadalupe, an organization dedicated to serving the physical and spiritual needs of Hispanic immigrants. He died in 1997.

—JEREMY BEER

Further Reading

Bozell, L. Brent. *Mustard Seeds: A Conservative Becomes a Catholic: Collected Essays*. Front Royal, Va.: Christendom Press, 2001.

Lawrence, E. Michael, ed. *The Best of Triumph*. Front Royal, Va.: Christendom Press, 2001.

See also: Buckley, William F., Jr.; Conscience of a Conservative, The; McCarthyism; Meyer, Frank S.; Roman Catholicism; Triumph

Bradford, M. E. (1934–93)

An Old Right conservative, traditionalist, and follower of Edmund Burke, the Anti-Federalists, and the Southern Agrarians, Melvin E. Bradford was born and reared in Fort Worth, Texas. He received his B.A. and M.A. in English from the University of Oklahoma and his Ph.D. from Vanderbilt University. He then taught English at the United States Naval Academy, Vanderbilt, Hardin-Simmons University, Northwestern State University of Louisiana, and—from 1967 until his untimely death in 1993—the University of Dallas. Though formally trained in literature, Bradford is primarily known among conservatives (as well as intellectuals on the Left) for his contributions to discussions of the ideas, men, and documents associated with the American Revolution. He is less known for his insightful literary studies (largely of Southern writers such as William Faulkner, Eudora Welty, and the leading Fugitives and Agrarians—Donald Davidson, Allen Tate, Andrew Lytle, Robert Penn Warren, Frank Owsley, and John Crowe Ransom) and for his writings on American culture and politics.

Bradford studied with Davidson, Randall Stewart, and others at Vanderbilt (1959–1962), enjoying the essentially conservative and intellectually stimulating atmosphere of the English department at the university. Instinctively drawn to tradition, Bradford defined and articulated his conservative views through reading and associating with other literate conservatives. His writings on the American Revolution remain his major contribution to conservative thought. The fruits of his study of the Revolution appear in *A Better Guide Than Reason* (1979); *A Worthy Company: Brief Lives of the Framers of the United States Constitution* (1982); a revised edition titled *Founding Fathers* (1994); and *Original Intentions: On the Making and Ratification of the United States Constitution* (1993). He also edited *Arator* (1977) by John Taylor of Caroline and coedited (with James McClellan) *Jonathan Elliot's Debates in the Several State Conventions on the Adoption of the Federal Constitution* (1989).

In his many writings on the Revolution, Bradford argues that the Declaration and the

Constitution are conservative documents and that the American Revolution itself was a conservative event. His scholarly labors were intended to enable Americans to recover their inheritance and to understand the American Revolution and the federal Constitution as they were understood by the founding fathers. "A Teaching for Republicans: Roman History and the Nation's First Identity" (in *A Better Guide Than Reason*) epitomizes Bradford's "teaching" on the Revolution. His close reading of Roman history and the writings of America's founding fathers reveals the Roman roots of American political order. With compelling illustrations, Bradford shows that George Washington, Patrick Henry, John Dickinson, John Adams, and others turned to Rome for a model of republican government. Like the Romans, they were committed to "blood, place, and history," to custom, to "prescribed rights and ordinances," not to *a priori* political formulas or to teleological, ameliorative visions of a blessed city on the hill. Like America's founding fathers, Bradford himself urged Americans to turn to the "laboratory of antiquity" and "the lamp of experience" for political guidance, not to an energetic, progressive government charmed by abstract doctrines and theories concerning liberty, egalitarianism, and natural rights.

Bradford also wrote with distinction and conviction about literature, usually on Southern writers and their works. His "literary" studies illustrate that literature has more than aesthetic significance because of its social, cultural, and political implications. Bradford's major essays on Southern literature appear in *Generations of the Faithful Heart* (1983), *Remembering Who We Are* (1985), and

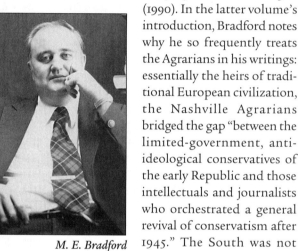

M. E. Bradford

The Reactionary Imperative (1990). Taken from the last line of Davidson's "Lee in the Mountains," the title of *Generations of the Faithful Heart* indicates Bradford's interest in Davidson and the other Agrarians—those poets, critics, and fiction writers who defended traditional Southern values and customs in the 1930s. Bradford edited two books concerned with Andrew Lytle: *The Form Discovered: Essays on the Achievement of Andrew Lytle* (1973) and *From Eden to Babylon: The Social and Political Essays of Andrew Nelson Lytle* (1990). In the latter volume's introduction, Bradford notes why he so frequently treats the Agrarians in his writings: essentially the heirs of traditional European civilization, the Nashville Agrarians bridged the gap "between the limited-government, anti-ideological conservatives of the early Republic and those intellectuals and journalists who orchestrated a general revival of conservatism after 1945." The South was not merely Bradford's home: it was the unifying subject and theme of his teaching and writing.

Bradford's work attracted detractors, notably the "Straussian" followers of political scientist Harry Jaffa—and Jaffa himself. In more than 250 essays and reviews, Bradford and his opponents engaged in lively intellectual fisticuffs about the meaning and significance of the War Between the States, the Declaration of Independence, abstract natural rights, and Abraham Lincoln. These debates were not without personal significance for the parties involved. In a nasty fight, Bradford's neoconservative opponents helped persuade Ronald Reagan not to nominate him as head of the National Endowment for the Humanities in the early '80s, a position that went to William J.

Bennett instead. The resulting rancor led directly to the public split between the neo- and paleoconservatives.

Bradford campaigned for Goldwater in 1964, for Wallace in 1972, for Reagan in 1976 and 1980, and for Buchanan in 1992. He served as president of the Philadelphia Society in 1985 and 1986. His labors as teacher-scholar and citizen earned him a prominent place in the post–World War II conservative movement. He opposed all ideologies (political and literary) and consistently championed traditional conservatism. With his untimely death at the age of 58, the American Right lost one of its most distinctive voices.

—MICHAEL JORDAN

Further Reading

Wilson, Clyde N., ed. *A Defender of Southern Conservatism: M. E. Bradford and His Achievements.* Columbia, Mo.: University of Missouri Press, 1999.

See also: agrarianism; American Revolution; Declaration of Independence; Jaffa, Harry V.; Philadelphia Society; Southern Agrarians; Southern conservatism; tradition

Bradley Foundation, Lynde and Harry

Formed in 1942, the Allen-Bradley Foundation was renamed the Lynde and Harry Bradley Foundation in 1985 after tremendously increasing its assets with the sale of the Allen-Bradley Company, a Milwaukee business started in 1903 by two brothers, Lynde and Harry Bradley. During his life Harry Bradley had supported conservative endeavors, including *National Review*; beginning in 1985, the foundation began to heavily fund conservative and free-market groups. At the beginning of 2002 the foundation held net assets of approximately $580 million (down from $720 million in 2000) and awarded about $36 million in grants.

The Bradley Foundation describes itself as committed to preserving "free representative government and private enterprise" in America, along with "democratic capitalism, . . . limited, competent government, . . . and academic achievement." The foundation also contributes significant funding to groups promoting improvements in "the quality of life in the Milwaukee metropolitan area."

Bradley has provided substantial support to a veritable "who's who" of conservative think tanks, policy institutes, and publishing organizations. Major recipients have included the American Enterprise Institute, Heritage Foundation, Institute for Justice, Federalist Society, the *American Spectator*, and *Crisis* magazine. The foundation also sponsors the "Bradley Graduate and Post Graduate Fellowship Program" at such schools as Boston University, Catholic University, Columbia, Georgetown, Harvard, Notre Dame, the University of Chicago, and the University of Virginia. The foundation provides broad assistance to various community projects in the greater Milwaukee area. In recent years it has put increasing emphasis on funding these local efforts.

Michael W. Grebe, the current president and CEO of the foundation, is a long-time Republican who has served in state and national party roles. Board members have included fifteen-year foundation president Michael S. Joyce, who retired in 2001 to head a private organization promoting President George W. Bush's "Faith-Based Initiatives" program, and William Bennett, former Secretary of Education under President Ronald Reagan. Michael M. Uhlmann, a former adjunct professor at Claremont McKenna College, left the Ethics and Public Policy Center in 1998 to serve as vice president for public policy at the foundation.

The foundation's political adversaries have criticized its promotion of welfare reform, school vouchers, and measures aimed at ending affirmative action and other quota programs. The foundation came under fire for grants given to Charles Murray for his 1994 book (coauthored with the late Richard J. Hernstein) *The Bell Curve*. Bradley has also been lambasted for financing PAVE (Partners Advancing Values in Education), which is dedicated to offering low-interest loans to charter and private schools in Milwaukee. The foundation, however, does not take a uniformly conservative line in its giving; in 2001, it gave a $60,000 grant to the Medical College of Wisconsin's Center for the Study of Bioethics, whose director, Robyn Shapiro, has testified before the U.S. House of Representatives in favor of human cloning.

—MATTHEW BOWMAN

Further Reading

Gurda, John. *The Bradley Legacy: Lynde and Harry Bradley, Their Company, and Their Foundation*. Milwaukee: Lynde and Harry Bradley Foundation, 1992.

See also: foundations, conservative; Heritage Foundation; Institute for Contemporary Studies

Bredvold, Louis I. (1888–1977)

Long associated with the University of Michigan's Department of English, Louis Bredvold was an authority on Edmund Burke and John Dryden. His monograph *The Intellectual Milieu of John Dryden* (1934) is considered a touchstone in the realm of Dryden scholarship. Aside from his interest in Dryden and Burke, Bredvold published learned essays and books on John Donne's religious thought, Samuel Taylor Coleridge's views of the seventeenth century, the Enlightenment, the poetry of Alexander Pope and Lord Byron, and numerous other topics. Several of his major full-length works were published by the University of Michigan Press, upon which Bredvold exercised a respected influence, recommending the publication of Peter J. Stanlis's first book on Burke, *Edmund Burke and the Natural Law* (1958), and other books by conservative scholars.

Bredvold was born in Springfield, Minnesota, and educated at Luther College, the Universities of Minnesota and Chicago, and the University of Illinois, from which he received his doctorate in 1921. That same year, he commenced a thirty-seven-year association with the University of Michigan. As an academic, Bredvold established his reputation in 1934 with the publication of *The Intellectual Milieu of John Dryden: Studies in Some Aspects of Seventeenth-Century Thought*, an essay collection that received a widely favorable critical reception. According to William Frost, "Dryden was for Bredvold a sincere, learned, and thoughtful poet led logically and inevitably into Toryism, royalism, and Catholicism by the sort of pyrrhonist distrust of human reason . . . that Bredvold found permeating every department of Renaissance and seventeenth century thought from Montaigne to Dryden's time."

The other large work for which Bredvold is renowned is *The Brave New World of the Enlightenment* (1961), a trenchant discourse upon the Enlightenment that drew praise from Russell Kirk. Bredvold also published two works on Burke, serving as editor of *The Philosophy of Edmund Burke* (1960) and contributing an essay to a scholarly collection titled *The Relevance of Edmund Burke* (1964).

—JAMES E. PERSON JR.

Further Reading

Kirk, Russell. "Ideologues' Folly." *Sewanee Review* 71 (1963): 332–42.

Stead, William Force. "Dryden's Conversion: The Struggle for Faith." *Times Literary Supplement*, no. 1837 (April 17, 1937): 281–82.

See also: Burke, Edmund; Enlightenment

Brooks, Cleanth (1906–94)

Brooks was a distinguished teacher and critic whose work was important in establishing the New Criticism, which stressed the close reading of literature, the integrity of the text, and the undesirability of biographical interpretation. The son of a Methodist minister, Brooks was raised in rural towns throughout western Tennessee. He studied Greek and Latin in high school and arrived at Vanderbilt University in 1924. At Vanderbilt, Brooks met and was decisively influenced by the Fugitives, a group of poets and critics that included John Crowe Ransom, Donald Davidson, Allen Tate, Robert Penn Warren, and Andrew Lytle.

Brooks earned a masters degree at Tulane and then studied at Oxford as a Rhodes scholar before returning in 1932 to teach at Louisiana State University. From 1935 to 1942 he edited with Robert Penn Warren the *Southern Review*, in which Brooks and Warren advanced the New Criticism and published the works of a new generation of Southern writers.

Cleanth Brooks

Brooks was in sympathy with the Southern Agrarians' volume *I'll Take My Stand* (1930), a pastoral rebuke of the dehumanizing effects of mass society. He contributed an essay to the Agrarian-distributist sequel *Who Owns America?* (1936) that was critical of trends within liberal Protestantism. Brooks was a devout Episcopalian and an advocate of the traditional *Book of Common Prayer*. In his approach to social matters, he was quick to acknowledge the remarkable benefits provided by advances in science and engineering, but he deplored the modern tendency to focus on *means* to the neglect of the *ends* of human activity.

Brooks was deeply impressed by the cultivation and wide learning of Eric Voegelin, the political scientist who joined Brooks on the LSU faculty in the 1940s. Both thinkers were tough-minded realists who made some accommodation to modernity but remained skeptical of the ability of science to provide complete answers to political and social questions.

Acutely aware of the shortcomings of the American South, Brooks was nonetheless quick to defend it against the indictments of those who did not know it intimately. In Brooks's view, the South had inherited characteristics of the classical civilizations and of Europe that were absent in the Puritan and industrialized North. Considering it to be the home of big-business interests and a force for homogenization, Brooks was never fond of the Republican Party.

Brooks's works of literary criticism include *Modern Poetry and the Tradition* (1939) and *The Well Wrought Urn* (1947). Brooks collaborated with others to produce several authoritative college texts: *Understanding Poetry* (1938) and *Understanding Fiction* (1943), written with Warren, and *Understanding Drama* (1948), with Robert Heilman. These books focused the teaching and reading of literature on the actual text under consideration rather than extraneous considerations. This focus of the New Criticism on the individual work as an independent unit of meaning has been interpreted by some to open the way to ahistorical relativism and deconstruction. But while Brooks and his fellow new critics emphasized the ambiguity of meaning in literary texts, they adhered to a firm moral conception of value. Furthermore, Brooks never denied the importance of historical and biographical data. His directly historical works included *The Relation of the Alabama-*

Georgia Dialect to the Provincial Dialects of Great Britain (1935) and *Historical Evidence and the Reading of Seventeenth-Century Poetry* (1991).

Brooks taught at Yale University from 1947 to 1975 and was also a Library of Congress fellow (1951–62) and cultural attaché at the U.S. embassy in London (1964–66). Brooks's later works include *Literary Criticism: A Short History* (1957, cowritten with William K. Wimsatt); *A Shaping Joy: Studies in the Writer's Craft* (1971); *The Language of the American South* (1985); and several books on William Faulkner, including *On the Prejudices, Predilections, and Firm Beliefs of William Faulkner* (1987).

Brooks's responses and challenges to the deconstructionists and other newer critical theoreticians are included in *Community, Religion, and Literature* (1995).

—GEORGE MICHOS

Further Reading

Winchell, Mark Royden. *Cleanth Brooks and the Rise of Modern Criticism.* Charlottesville, Va. University Press of Virginia, 1996.

Walsh, John Michael. *Cleanth Brooks: An Annotated Bibliography.* New York: Garland, 1990.

See also: literary criticism; New Criticism; Southern Agrarians; Southern Review

Brooks, David (1961–)

David Brooks went to the University of Chicago, where, as a senior, he wrote a parody of William F. Buckley Jr. that brought him to the attention of the father of modern conservatism. Brooks was not a conservative. Indeed, when later that year Buckley arrived on campus and inquired at his lecture if Brooks was present (Buckley wanted to offer him a job), Brooks was in California preparing to debate Milton Friedman from a socialist perspective. Brooks was devastated in the debate, and soon the slow process of

political transformation would move him toward the right. He became a reporter for the *Wall Street Journal* before helping found the *Weekly Standard* in 1995. In 2004 he became a columnist for the *New York Times*.

Brooks won renown for his sharp observations of the mores of what he called Bobos (bourgeois bohemians) in *Bobos in Paradise* (2000). There, Brooks described the new upper class of the educated elite. Bobos mix the ethic of meritocracy with a tamed bohemianism. The result is a ruling class that holds status to be determined by consumption, is uncomfortable with the concept of sin and traditional moral understandings and thus prefers therapeutic discourse and solutions, favors pharmacological remedies to straighten out the unwanted irregularities of life, fetishizes health concerns and ignores eternal salvation, and in general promotes a spiritually vapid, ever-hip consumerism. Bobos are Nietzsche's "last man" in nice khakis.

Bobos have been replicating themselves, Brooks has argued, and their offspring is the "organization kid." Ceaselessly ushered from one skill-enhancing activity to the next while in primary and secondary school, the organization kid goes to Harvard, Princeton, Yale or some similarly prestigious university. Organization kids are not rebels, but the happy products of the system who want to ascend the meritocratic ladder they see before them. So organization kids are content to defer to authority, work incredibly hard, be cheerful and earnest, and make it as far as their skills will take them.

While Brooks's first book was well received, his second, *On Paradise Drive* (2004) was greeted with less enthusiasm. Brooks set out to map the contours of classes and subcultures beyond the new elite and what he found was that Americans try to realize "grand and utopian ideals through material things." In other words, he stumbled onto Tocqueville's critique of the American character.

—TIMOTHY WEBSTER

Further Reading

Brooks, David, ed. *Backward and Upward: The New Conservative Writing.* New York: Vintage, 1996.

———. "The Organization Kid." *Atlantic Monthly,* April 2001, 40-53.

Brown v. Board of Education

Brown v. Board of Education (1954) is the Supreme Court decision that employed the equal protection clause of the Fourteenth Amendment to declare racially based segregation in primary and secondary public schools unconstitutional. The Court's decision was unanimous, and all the justices joined in the opinion of the Court by Chief Justice Earl Warren. Many conservatives opposed the Court's decision at the time, and still more objected to the argument given by the Court in its opinion. Conservatives generally oppose judicial activism, and this decision was certainly that. Conservatives also tend to be partisans of federalism or states' rights, and this decision did constrain state governments in unprecedented ways. Some conservatives, in fact, regret the existence of the Fourteenth Amendment; a few even believe it unconstitutional. Another conservative argument against *Brown* might be called democratic. The initiation of a successful social revolution by judges turned out to set a terrible precedent, leading to subsequent, much less justifiable judicial revolutions, such as the one inaugurated by *Roe v. Wade* (1973).

Today, however, there is a broad conservative consensus that the Court's decision—but not its opinion—in *Brown* was constitutional, and that America is better off without the burden of racial distinctions in the law. The conservative constitutional argu-

ment today is that all such distinctions are unconstitutional, and they use it to fight against the racial preferences granted by various affirmative action schemes. Thus, many conservatives now applaud judicial activism when it is directed against race-based preferences in employment and higher education. The two most able conservative members of the Supreme Court—Justices Antonin Scalia and Clarence Thomas—both view our Constitution and the law as colorblind.

From one viewpoint, the Supreme Court erred in its *Brown* opinion by being too conservative, too unwilling to overrule the reigning precedent in constitutional interpretation. In *Plessy v. Ferguson* (1896), a case concerning railroad transportation, the Court held that Louisiana law could require the separation of passengers by race as long as equal treatment was given to all. The view now held by Scalia and Thomas, but never affirmed by a majority of members of the Court, was put forward in a lone dissent by Justice John Marshall Harlan. The Court, in *Brown*, did not really reverse *Plessy*, much less affirm Harlan's view that American law should never take race into account.

The Court in *Brown* dealt first with evidence that the Congress that passed the Fourteenth Amendment failed to apply its principles against segregation in public education. The Court's response was that the intention of the amendment was protecting the rights of citizens. In 1868, public education was plausibly not such a right, given that the states did not offer compulsory public education and that service in the armed forces—the most basic duty of a citizen—could be performed by illiterates. In 1954, the provision of compulsory public education was "perhaps the most important function of state and local governments" and was widely regarded as "the very foundation of good citizenship." It now was required for military service. Principles remain the same, the Court explained, but circumstances change.

The Court then had to explain why separate educational facilities for the two races were "inherently unequal." It relied on recent precedents that claimed equality in education encompassed not only "tangible" facilities but also "intangible considerations" such as a school's reputation for greatness and a student's ability to interact with fellow students. In elementary and high school education, the Court argued, the relevant intangible or psychological consideration is that separating children "from others of similar age and qualification solely because of their race generates a feeling of inferiority as to their status in the community that may affect their hearts and minds in a way unlikely to be undone."

For evidence of both this feeling and its connection with educational equality the Court added a footnote full of social scientific studies. The first and most important of these "modern studies," by social psychologist Kenneth Clark, has been thoroughly discredited, and even Clark himself later acknowledged that he had not shown any connection between racially based feelings of inferiority and legally based educational segregation. The Court implied that the only thing wrong with *Plessy* was the 1896 Court's unavoidable ignorance of modern social science. But in truth, by 1954 social scientists had discovered nothing that would justify a reversal of *Plessy*. *Plessy* had to do with transportation, not education; passengers lacking in self-esteem do not keep the train from getting to the station on time. The Court did not really show that there was anything wrong with *Plessy*. Its intention was to seem to reverse *Plessy* without actually doing so. *Brown* does not even attempt to show why segregation, in general, is unconstitutional.

The resisting South's main argument against *Brown* was that it was based on bad applied social science rather than on sound principles of law, and the hope in some quarters was that if the studies were discredited segregation could return. This hope was unreasonable. Within a year, the Court, citing *Brown* as a precedent, struck down laws segregating recreational facilities and within two years, transportation itself. The Court made it clear enough that the social science was window dressing, but at the cost of great confusion, for it gave no other argument for the inherent unconstitutionality of racial distinctions in the law. It was, strictly speaking, ridiculous for the Court to say that *Brown* could provide any guidance concerning the constitutionality of segregated golf courses. Without an argument justifying its action, the Court rightly stands accused of judicial imperialism. But that does not mean that *Brown* was wrongly decided.

In retrospect, the Court clearly should have been bold enough actually to reverse *Plessy* by affirming Harlan's view of the colorblind intention of the Fourteenth Amendment. The confusion created by *Brown* was largely responsible for some of the worst moments in recent U.S. history, including the South's "massive resistance" and the chaos and resentment caused by court-ordered busing. Americans needed and still need to be taught why segregation is wrong, and they need to understand that affirmative action is wrong because it is too much like segregation. Racial distinctions, in both cases, are allegedly being used for the public good, but with both segregation and affirmative action the race that was monstrously degraded by slavery is again being stigmatized. The contemporary Supreme Court now regards all references to race in the law with strict scrutiny, and conservative justices have been doing well in explaining why. *Brown* is, of course, not going to be reversed, but its opinion has very little value as a precedent for today's Court.

The Court waited a year before deciding how to implement its *Brown* decision. In its second *Brown* decision, the Court refused to grant immediate relief to the individuals whose rights it had decided had been violated. Implementation was remanded, with very little guidance, to the federal district courts. The local courts were to require that admission to public schools "on a racially nondiscriminatory basis" be achieved "with all deliberate speed." The vagueness of that mandate placed local judges faced with hostile public opinion in an untenable position, which fact can be traced in part to the Court's failure in *Brown* to articulate a principled argument against segregation. Instead of giving relief to individuals whose constitutional rights were violated, the remedy was given only in some indefinite point in the future. There was no guarantee at all that the plaintiffs—the children—who brought suit in *Brown* would ever get to go to a desegregated school. The subtle but real racism of the remedy of *Brown* II ended up paving the way for the busing ordered in *Swann v. Charlotte-Mecklenburg Board of Education* (1971). In both cases, expediency justified significant and damaging deviation from sound constitutional principle.

The most intriguing recent conservative criticism of *Brown* is found in Justice Thomas's concurring opinion in *Missouri v. Jenkins* (1995). There he writes that "*Brown* I itself did not need to rely upon psychological or social science research in order to announce the simple, yet fundamental truth that the Government cannot discriminate among its citizens according to race." That is because the principle of the equal protection clause of the Fourteenth Amendment is "that the Government must treat citizens as individuals, and not as members of racial, ethnic or religious groups." Thomas's is a noble but perhaps too transparent effort to say what the Court should have said, an effort to find principle in the *Brown* opinion—principle that just isn't there.

—Peter Augustine Lawler

Further Reading

Berger, Raoul. *Government by Judiciary: The Transformation of the Fourteenth Amendment.* Cambridge, Mass.: Harvard University Press, 1977.

Graglia, Lino. *Disaster by Decree: The Supreme Court Decisions on Race and the Schools.* Ithaca, N.Y.: Cornell University Press, 1976.

McDowell, Gary L. *Equity and the Constitution.* Chicago: University of Chicago Press, 1982.

Thernstrom, Stephan and Abigail Thernstrom. *America in Black and White: One Nation, Indivisible.* New York: Simon & Schuster, 1997.

Wolters, Raymond. *The Burden of Brown.* Knoxville, Tenn.: University of Tennessee Press, 1984.

See also: civil rights; education, public; equal protection; judicial activism; Supreme Court

Brownson, Orestes A. (1803–76)

Prolific American essayist, philosopher, and literary critic, Orestes Augustus Brownson was a well-known figure in the New England Transcendentalist movement. As a young man Brownson had a strong interest in religious and philosophical subjects, and by the age of twenty-two he was ordained as a Universalist minister. His literary career began with a series of essays in *The Gospel Advocate and Impartial Investigator*. Espousing a form of religious naturalism, these early essays were critical of the "otherworldliness" of orthodox Christianity. For this reason Brownson soon developed a strong interest in utopian political thought; Robert Owen, Francis Wright, William Ellery Channing, William Godwin, and Comte de Saint-Simon were influences. Saint-Simon in particular inspired Brownson with a brand of neo-Gnostic socialism reflected in Brownson's 1836 book *New Views of Christianity, Society, and the Church*. In this work, Brownson expressed his faith in the progressive unfolding of a perfected civilization that would be free of all manner of political and social antagonisms. Similar visions of revolutionary transformation, together with their totalitarian implications, can be found in the proto-Marxist "Essay on the Laboring Classes" (1840) and "Church of the Future" (1842).

During the early 1840s, however, Brownson began a serious reexamination of his radical views. This process would eventually produce one of the most intriguing American conservative minds of the nineteenth century. A significant turning point was Brownson's encounter with the humanitarian socialist Theodore Parker. Upon studying Parker's work, Brownson was struck by the realization that the form of revolutionary socialism they shared was built upon a philosophically suspect moral and ethical foundation. As indicated in his autobiography *The Convert* (1857), Brownson sensed that his commitment to the "religion of humanity" would lead not to utopia but, in effect, to the death of God. In a manner reminiscent of later critics of modernity, Brownson became repulsed by the nihilistic tendencies of those whose secret wish is "to be as gods" and recreate the world. The search for meaning must focus upon the divine transcendent as the source of all progress. Particularly influential in this regard was Brownson's study of Pierre Leroux's philosophy of participatory consciousness, and the correlative doctrine of divine-human communion.

Brownson's acceptance of the notion that the human race is elevated by supernatural communion proved to be his "greatest step yet taken"(*The Convert*). This conclusion meant that revolutionary socialism lost all appeal, for God's creation contained within it all that was necessary for fulfilling the deepest human aspirations. For Brownson

Orestes Brownson

this meant a return to Christianity, for the figure of Christ struck him as the perfect manifestation of the communion principle ("The Mediatorial Life of Jesus," 1842). But, given the historical and sociological fact of the Reformation, how was one to obtain a reliable, authoritative understanding of Christian teaching? Brownson was convinced that only Catholicism would suffice, for he saw the spiritual and doctrinal individualism at the heart of all Protestant denominations as too closely bound up with the subjective nihilism of modernity ("Protestantism Ends in Transcendentalism," 1846).

In a dramatic turnaround from his early career, Brownson formally entered the Catholic Church in 1844.

Following his conversion Brownson became something of a pariah in New England intellectual circles. Nonetheless, he continued his writing career by filling the pages of his own journal, *Brownson's Quarterly Review*. Of concern throughout his later work was the familiar charge that a democratic regime is incompatible with Catholicism. In response, Brownson argued that only a conservative Catholic presence in society could supply the necessary moral foundation for democracy. The success of America's experiment in freedom depended upon the cultural vitality of Catholic moral teaching regarding the inherent worth and dignity of all persons. Moreover, he argued, the American constitutional order is ideally suited to the task of cultivating this presence because of the freedom guaranteed to Catholics by the constitutional principle of toleration. In no other society does the Church find so little resistance to the full exercise of its civilizational mission. This argument is developed in Brownson's best-known postconversion work, *The American Republic: Its Constitution, Tendencies, and Destiny* (1865).

—GREGORY S. BUTLER

Further Reading

Brownson, Henry F., ed. *Brownson's Works*. 20 vols. Detroit: Thorndike Nourse, 1882–87.

Butler, Gregory S. *In Search of the American Spirit: The Political Thought of Orestes Brownson.* Carbondale, Ill.: Southern Illinois University Press, 1992.

Lawler, Peter Augustine. Introduction to *The American Republic: Its Constitution, Tendencies, and Destiny.* Wilmington, Del.: ISI Books, 2003.

Ryan, Thomas R. *Orestes A. Brownson: A Definitive Biography.* Huntington, Ind.: Our Sunday Visitor, 1976.

See also: Parry, Stanley J.; Roman Catholicism

Bryan, William Jennings (1860–1925)

Known as "The Great Commoner," this American orator, politician, and Presbyterian leader was for some thirty-five years a notable figure on the national scene and enjoyed a worldwide reputation. William Jennings Bryan was a progressive in politics, a conservative in religion, and a crusader for a plethora of principles and policies, many of which have become law and are no longer considered by most Americans to be radical and dangerous but rather rudimentary and desirable. He served two terms as a congressional representative from Nebraska (1891–95), was secretary of state (1913–15), ran for the Senate (1892 and 1894) and for president (1896, 1900, and 1908), led the Democratic Party, published numerous articles and books, and spoke at countless political, religious, and social gatherings.

Bryan was born in Salem, Illinois, in 1860 and moved in 1887 to Lincoln, Nebraska, where he began his political career as a pro-

gressive Democrat who was successful in establishing a coalition with the Populists. A shrewd political strategist who fought hard but fair, researched the issues, and appealed to diverse groups, Bryan consistently built his platform on a foundation of high moral principle and presented his arguments in memorable speeches. Called "The Silver-Tongued Orator" because of his scintillating sincerity, simplicity, and substance, he ranks among America's greatest orators.

When he was thirty-six, aided by adroit organizational tactics and the forceful delivery of his famous "Cross of Gold" address at the 1896 Chicago Democratic Convention, Bryan won the presidential nomination. In a bitter contest against the eastern industrial and creditor establishment and Republican candidate William McKinley's gold-standard platform, Bryan became the voice of the western and southern farmers and debtor common people by espousing such reforms as silver coinage. Despite what a number of experts have deemed fraudulent Republican tactics that stole six states and consequently the presidency, and despite facing a campaign fund that was some twenty-five times larger than his, Bryan received 47 percent of the popular vote.

In 1900 Bryan again ran unsuccessfully against McKinley, this time on an anti-imperialist, antitrust platform that also focused on various labor issues. Bryan kept his principles and programs before the public from 1901 to 1923 by publishing the *Commoner*, a weekly/monthly newspaper that had an impressive circulation of 285,000. In the 1908 election, Bryan lost to William Howard Taft, but in 1912 Bryan's efforts helped Woodrow Wilson become president.

Appointed in 1913 as Wilson's secretary of state, Bryan negotiated peace treaties with thirty nations and piloted through Congress Wilson's New Freedom program, which contained reforms that Bryan had promoted for years, such as the Federal Reserve Act. He helped apply the Sixteenth Amendment (graduated income tax) and worked for the Seventeenth Amendment (popular election of senators). After World War I began in 1914, Bryan labored for peaceful arbitration and resigned in 1915 when Wilson ignored his counsel. But in 1916, Bryan campaigned successfully for Wilson's reelection and, when war was declared by Congress in 1917, Bryan supported the cause as the shortest path to peace. He won battles against liquor and for women's rights when the Eighteenth Amendment (prohibition) was passed in 1919 and the Nineteenth (women's suffrage) became law in 1920.

Bryan earned the epithet "The Defender of the Faith" by crusading for moral and spiritual concerns. In his adopted home of Miami, he taught a Bible class of five thousand people. His Bible lessons appeared in more than one hundred newspapers with a total readership of four million. In the 1920s he was often allied with the Fundamentalists as he lectured against Darwinism, considering the evidence insufficient for the theory of human evolution to be taught as scientific fact in a one-sided context that excluded the biblical account. But chiefly Bryan was concerned about social Darwinism, with its application of the survival-of-the-fittest doctrine in personal, business, and governmental relationships. When Tennessee passed an anti-evolution law in 1925 and the New York headquarters of the ACLU advertised for a test case, civic leaders in Dayton persuaded John Thomas Scopes to become the defendant and then, along with Fundamentalist leaders, invited Bryan to assist the prosecution. He came at his own expense and conducted himself ably as a guest counsel, but five days after help-

William Jennings Bryan

ing to win the case he died and was buried in Arlington National Cemetery under the inscription, "He kept the faith."

No traditional conservative, Bryan nonetheless left a lasting mark on American conservatism by espousing policies aimed at protecting religious life and the common man from the predations of big business. Moreover, his politics were firmly rooted in traditional Protestant biblical beliefs, which he consistently practiced and applied to political and social issues with a unique balance of progressivism and conservatism. Not only did he express his views with clear and quotable language, he also contended energetically for such fundamental principles as majority rule, international peace, human rights, fair business competition, good citizenship, and living in "harmony with the law of God."

—RICHARD CORNELIUS

Further Reading

Bryan, William Jennings. *Selected Orations of Willliam Jennings Bryan.* Edited by R. M. Cornelius. Dayton, Tenn.: Bryan College, 2000.

Cherny, Robert W. *A Righteous Cause: The Life of William Jennings Bryan.* Norman, Okla.: University of Oklahoma Press, 1994.

Coletta, Paolo E. *William Jennings Bryan.* 3 vols. Lincoln, Neb.: University of Nebraska Press, 1964-1969.

Hilleary, William et al., eds. *The World's Most Famous Court Trial: Tennessee Evolution Case.* 1925. Reprint, Dayton, Tenn.: Bryan College, 1990.

Larson, Edward J. *Summer for the Gods: The Scopes Trial and America's Continuing Debate over Science and Religion.* Cambridge, Mass.: Harvard University Press, 1997.

Levine, Lawrence, W. *Defender of the Faith: William Jennings Bryan, The Last Decade, 1915–1925.* New York: Oxford University Press, 1965.

See also: creationism; populism; Protestantism, evangelical; Scopes trial

Buchanan, James M. (1919–)

Professor of economics at George Mason University, 1986 Nobel Prize winner in economics, founder of the Center for the Study of Public Choice (now located at George Mason University), James Buchanan took his Ph.D. from the University of Chicago in 1948. Often referred to as the "father of public choice theory," he is best known for his analysis of how the political process works and how political institutions influence the operation of an economy.

Beginning in the early 1960s, Buchanan challenged the dominant social science perception of government as a supra-individual representing the public interest. In his development of public choice theory, he analyzed the interaction of voters, politicians, and bureaucrats as motivated by the same self-interest that is assumed to be operant for other economic decision-makers. His analysis indicated that political intervention into economic affairs would often waste resources and lead to policies favored by well-organized interest groups. Thus, if unconstrained by constitutional rules, even democratic governments based on majority rule could be expected to follow policies that were inconsistent with the efficient use of resources.

Buchanan is a constitutional conservative in the tradition of James Madison. *The Calculus of Consent: Logical Foundations of Constitutional Democracy* (1962), coauthored with Gordon Tullock, provides the most extensive presentation of his views on politics and the need for constitutional restraints. In this work, Buchanan and Tullock stress the importance of constitutional constraints and political rules. They argue that the efficient use of resources will result only if government activity is constrained (for example, restricted to the protection of individual rights and the production of public goods like national defense) and if steps are taken to bring the private interests of political decision-makers into harmony with the broader public interest. The reader should consult *Explorations into Constitutional Economics* (1989) for additional detail on Buchanan's view of constitutional economics.

Buchanan has also been one of the most persistent critics of Keynesian economics. His views in this area reflect the public choice approach. Rather than focusing on its effectiveness, Buchanan has long argued that Keynesian budgetary policy is politically naïve. Politicians have a preference for spending (in order to provide constituents with visible benefits) rather than taxes (which impose visible costs on voters). Therefore, releasing politicians from a balanced-budget requirement will result in continuous deficits and the use of budgetary policy for electoral gain, rather than the Keynesian prediction of deficits during recessions and surpluses during prosperous times. Thus, Buchanan argues that Keynesian stabilization policy is doomed to failure. *Democracy in Deficit: The Political Legacy of Lord Keynes* (1977), coauthored with Richard E. Wagner, provides an extensive presentation of Buchanan's views on Keynesian economics.

During the 1960–90 period Buchanan contributed substantially to the change in the way economists think about government. Most social scientists now recognize that government is an alternative form of social organization with important deficiencies rather than a public-minded corrective device. In turn, the recognition of these deficiencies has led to a renewal of interest in constitutional rules, an area of political economy that was largely ignored by social scientists prior to the work of Buchanan.

—JAMES GWARTNEY
AND ROBERT LAWSON

Further Reading

Buchanan, James M. *The Limits of Liberty: Between Anarchy and Leviathan.* Indianapolis, Ind.: Liberty Fund, 2001.

Brennan, Geoffrey, Hartmut Kliemt, and Robert D. Tollison, eds. *Method and Morals in Constitutional Economics: Essays in Honor of James M. Buchanan.* New York: Springer, 2001.

See also: public choice economics

Buchanan, Patrick J. (1938–)

Conservative journalist, politician, political commentator, and cultural critic, Patrick J. Buchanan was educated in Washington's Catholic parochial schools and later graduated third in his class *cum laude* from Georgetown University in 1961 (despite a one-year suspension for a donnybrook in which he hospitalized two policemen). Buchanan then studied at the Columbia University School of Journalism (M.S., 1962) and worked as editorial writer for the conservative *St. Louis Globe-Democrat* (1962–66).

Buchanan left the *Globe-Democrat* to work as executive assistant to former vice president Richard M. Nixon (1966–69), helping Nixon run for the White House in 1968. After Nixon's inauguration, Buchanan served as speechwriter and senior advisor, participating in historic summits—including Nixon's first visit to China—and contributing to important speeches for Nixon ("The Great Silent Majority") as well as Vice President Spiro Agnew's lively attacks on TV and in the print media. Buchanan left the White House several months after Nixon's resignation (1974). He wrote *Conservative Votes, Liberal Victories* (1975) and a successful syndi-cated newspaper column until he returned to the White House as President Reagan's director of communications, 1985–87.

In 1987 he returned to his column and became cohost of CNN's popular *Crossfire* political talk show (1987–99, when not campaigning). In 1988 he wrote a bestselling autobiography, *Right from the Beginning* (1988). He was a founding member of two other talk shows, *The Capitol Gang* (CNN) and *The McLaughlin Group* (NBC). Influenced by the Rockford Institute's flagship publication, *Chronicles,* Buchanan came to reject interventionism in foreign affairs and global free trade in economics, putting himself at odds with the George H.W. Bush administration. In 1991 Buchanan left his financially successful writing and television career to oppose Bush in the Republican primaries. His strong second-place showing in the New Hampshire primary (37 percent) evoked attacks from the media. (*National Review* and *Chronicles* supported him.) Although he won no primaries, he was invited to address the 1992 Republican convention. His speech, the most powerful since Everett Dirksen's attack on Thomas Dewey at the 1952 convention, warned of a leftist "culture war" being waged against traditional American values and ideals. The thunderous applause of the delegates left no doubt that they agreed with his message, which was nonetheless immediately repudiated by the Republican candidates, Bush and Quayle.

In 1996 Buchanan won early Republican contests in Alaska and Louisiana. His victory in the New Hampshire primary provoked a massive media assault. He came in second in Iowa and third in Arizona, the latter because of absentee ballots. After he lost the South Carolina primary, where the establishment Christian Right supported Robert Dole, Buchanan's candidacy lost momentum. Despite his primary victories, Buchanan was not allowed to address the convention. In 1999 Buchanan announced his defection to Ross Perot's Reform Party. Buchanan was popular with the Reform Party rank and file, but Perot, who had initially welcomed Buchanan, worked against him behind the scenes. At the Reform Party convention Buchanan decisively defeated Perot's forces and received the nomination. His acceptance speech advocated the protection of American industry and values and opposed abortion, global free trade, and interventionism. The last two positions were shared by Green Party candidate Ralph Nader, who garnered most of the protest vote in the historically close 2000 election won eventually by Republican George W. Bush.

The failure of Buchanan's candidacies was matched by the success of his books, despite negative reviews from all sides. *National Review*, for instance, soon came to officially oppose Buchanan, as did most other organs of conservative opinion. In *The Great Betrayal* (1998), Buchanan defended protectionism, which he called "economic nationalism." *A Republic, Not an Empire* (1999) told the story of America's isolationist foreign policy and its replacement by interventionism. Buchanan's resurrection of conservative opposition to American entry into the Second World War evoked protests from neoconservatives and others to Buchanan's left, and his occasionally intemperate remarks about American policy with regard to Israel have provoked charges that he is anti-Semitic, most of which seem groundless. In *The Death of the West* (2002), an instant bestseller, Buchanan argued that declining birth rates and massive immigration in Europe and America imperil Western civilization, which will disappear without a return to its historic Christian faith. These books reconstructed in a popular form the conservative positions on economics, politics, and culture of the Republican Party during its first century and may represent Buchanan's most enduring legacy.

—E. CHRISTIAN KOPFF

Further Reading

Buchanan, Patrick J. *Where the Right Went Wrong: How Neoconservatives Subverted the Reagan Revolution and Hijacked the Bush Presidency.* New York: Thomas Dunne Books, 2004.

See also: American Conservative; Chronicles; *isolationism; paleoconservatism*

Buckley, William F., Jr. (1925–)

Since the early 1950s, William F. Buckley Jr. has been one of the most visible and outspoken conservative intellectuals in the United States. By founding *National Review* magazine in the mid-1950s and thus providing conservative writers with a common organ of opinion, he brought a measure of cohesiveness to a disparate group of dissenters from the liberalism that dominated the American intellectual community. Buckley also hosted *Firing Line*, the Public Broadcasting System's longest-running program, where he engaged individuals of all political persuasions on a variety of issues and presented his conservative perspective to a large audience.

Buckley was born to staunchly Catholic parents, William Frank Buckley and Aloise Steiner Buckley. His father was a millionaire Texas oilman often embroiled in Mexican politics, frank in his racial prejudices, and politically allied with Southern Democrats. His mother was a pious and gentle southerner.

Even in the years when he attended Millbrook Academy in upstate New York and Yale University, Buckley was known for his spunk and often exhibited an outlaw independence when it came to rules and conventions. At Yale, he bristled under what he saw as the reigning liberal ideology of the institution. His defiance emerged forcefully in his book *God and Man at Yale* (1951), which won him national attention. In it, Buckley marshaled evidence to show that Yale had abandoned its allegiance to Christianity and free-market economics. Typical of his style, Buckley named names and described a conspiracy against these threatened American orthodoxies.

Buckley's early conservatism derived from several sources, including his father and one of his father's close friends, the aristocratically oriented libertarian Albert Jay Nock. At Yale, his irrepressible teacher, Willmoore Kendall, a noted constitutional theorist, influenced Buckley with his portrayal of America as a political battleground that pitted partisans of the "open society"—liberals with a program of relativism and individualism—against partisans of democratic majoritarianism, who defended the right of the community to preserve its traditional values. But Whittaker Chambers was probably the most important influence on Buckley. Chambers's autobiography, *Witness* (1952), dramatized for Buckley the great spiritual conflict that Chambers believed defined the Cold War between the United States and the Soviet Union. Chambers's spirited writing outlined a great contest between the religious and intellectual values of the West and the promise of a new global, secular society offered by communism. Chambers helped Buckley see the Cold War as a transcendent struggle, a view that Buckley would never wholly abandon.

By the time Buckley launched *National Review* in 1955, his particular style of conservatism had become evident. His was a conservatism of loyalties to the provincial and familial ways of the group and the nation at large. Thus, his book *McCarthy and His Enemies* (1954), coauthored by his brother-in-law L. Brent Bozell, heavily emphasized the right

William F. Buckley Jr.

of society to defend its folkways, and he gave priority to these interests over the civil liberties claimed by dissenters from majority opinion. Buckley viewed such dissenters as alien and subversive, enemies of traditional mores. Likewise, in *Up from Liberalism* (1959) Buckley spoke for the interests of the dominant white South as the civil rights movement intensified in that part of the country.

National Review itself was representative of Buckley's perspective. It saw the conservative movement, and especially its leading intellectual voices, as an embattled clan fighting to reclaim for the country a heritage of freedom and morality weakened and corroded by liberalism. A wide range of conservatives were given voice in *National Review*—anticommunists, libertarians, traditionalists, religious conservatives. The prominence of many former leftists also reflected an important component of the conservative community. Buckley's own Roman Catholicism was also reflected in the journal, but that fact often caused problems. Max Eastman and Ayn Rand parted company with Buckley largely because he took his religion seriously.

From the 1960s on, Buckley was one of the most widely syndicated columnists in the country. The versatile essayist wrote on subjects ranging from American foreign policy to peanut butter. His pieces were reprinted in *National Review* and from time to time anthologized into various collections. *The Jeweler's Eye* (1968) contains Buckley's essay on *Playboy* magazine, revealing how, on questions of sexual mores and some other issues, he moderated his libertarian ethos. At one point, Buckley endorsed the legalization of marijuana, but this essay shows that he was not at all inclined to accept Hugh Hefner's call for a new morality. *The Governor Listeth* (1970) contains Buckley's writings on the Vietnam War. *Inveighing We Will Go* (1972) has a lengthy interview with *Playboy* that is one of the most succinct summaries of Buckley's general outlook. Asked at the beginning of the interview what he thought was the most important development in the 1960s, Buckley replied: the philosophical acceptance of coexistence with the Soviet Union by the West. Asked at another point what he thought could be done to stop sexual promiscuity, he replied: get people to stop reading *Playboy*.

In *A Hymnal* (1978), Buckley offered an essay on Soviet writer Aleksandr Solzhenitsyn, one of his most powerful pieces. The essay revealed how Buckley, in the era of détente and accommodation with the Soviet Union, still saw the Cold War in spiritual terms and how he used Solzhenitsyn's graphic writings to help keep alive the recognition of communism's evils. *Right Reason* (1985) gathers Buckley's reflections on such events as the revolution in Iran, the downing of a Korean airplane by the Soviets, and the American intervention in Granada.

Buckley also wrote personal memoirs. In 1965, he ran for mayor of New York against a prominent Republican liberal, John Lindsay. He chronicled the issues and anecdotes of that campaign in *The Unmaking of a Mayor* (1966). A very personal account of his spiritual life appeared in *Nearer, My God* (1997); his autobiography, *Miles Gone By* (2004), recounts more particulars of his life and career.

In 1976, Buckley launched a new series of books that captivated his large audience. An avid sailor, Buckley began to recount his adventure on the brine with the publication of *Airborne* (1976). *Atlantic High* (1982) and *Racing Through Paradise* (1987) followed. The latter describes Buckley's enrapture with the Trimble Loran-C, a high-tech navigation calculator. Indeed, Buckley's enthusiasms for

such gadgetry and personal computers have revealed him to be a conservative quite at home in the modern world. That temperament has led at least one critic to question whether Buckley has a truly conservative mind, one enamored of antiquity and place, permanence and continuity. Buckley seemed too much a jet-age conservative, a contradiction. Indeed, Buckley is at home with cultural modernism, however much he prefers Bach to modern composers. A bathtub in one of the Buckley residences was painted in modernist style by the artist Robert Goodnough.

In 1976, Buckley ventured into fiction writing, specializing in the genre of Cold War political intrigue. His series introduced the hero Blackford Oakes—Ivy Leaguer, adventurer, romantic. In such books as *Saving the Queen* (1976), *Stained Glass* (1978), *Who's On First* (1980), and *High Jinx* (1986), Buckley, as he once said, vicariously relived the Cold War. He believed its existence needed to be restored to public memory. Buckley continued to set his novels during that period even after the fall of the Soviet Union, publishing his eleventh Blackford Oakes novel in 2005.

Buckley retired as editor of *National Review* in 1990, still maintaining a strong presence at the magazine even after he relinquished his controlling shares in 2004. In 2000, he aired his last *Firing Line*. As befitted a prominent and highly literate conservative, he continued to write prolifically for *National Review* and other periodicals even as he scaled back his public speaking and some of his more taxing hobbies. His outstanding achievements in a plethora of fields were rewarded in 1991 with the Presidential Medal of Freedom and again in 2003 with the Charles H. Hoeflich Lifetime Achievement Award.

Buckley's immense oeuvre has not amounted to a coherent and consistent conservative philosophy: to be fair, he never intended it to. Depending on the issue in question, Buckley has expressed both libertarian and traditionalist views, and sometimes rather extreme ones. It is fair to say, then, that there has been an ad hoc quality to Buckley's conservatism. Nonetheless, his writings constitute an immense, important, and highly influential catalogue of more than fifty years of conservative opinion.

—J. DAVID HOEVELER JR.

Further Reading

Hoeveler, J. David, Jr. *Watch on the Right: Conservative Intellectuals in the Reagan Era.* Madison, Wis.: University of Wisconsin Press, 1991.

Judis, John B. *William F. Buckley, Jr.: Patron Saint of the Conservatives.* New York: Simon & Schuster, 1988.

Meehan, William F., III. *William F. Buckley Jr.: A Bibliography.* Wilmington, Del.: ISI Books, 2001.

Nash, George H. *The Conservative Intellectual Movement in America since 1945.* New York: Basic Books, 1976.

Winchell, Mark Royden. *William F. Buckley Jr.* Boston: Twayne Publishers, 1984.

See also: academic freedom; Conservative Party of New York; God and Man at Yale; *McCarthyism; media, conservative;* National Review; *New Right; Young Americans for Freedom*

Burckhardt, Jacob (1818–97)

In 1860, Jacob Burckhardt published *The Civilization of the Renaissance in Italy*, which helped to invent—some would say created—the Renaissance as a historical period. Until the years following World War II Burckhardt's fame in the German and Anglo-Saxon worlds was largely the consequence of this book. The reexamination of the European and especially the German past led to a new interest in and a reevaluation of the role of Burckhardt as a liberal-conservative thinker, historical innovator, teacher, prophet, and philosopher of history.

Jacob Burckhardt was born in 1818 in Basel, Switzerland, and died in that same city in 1897. His family was patrician rather than bourgeois and had long been involved in the economic, political, and cultural life of Basel. Because of the location and culture of Basel, Burckhardt was as European in outlook as he was Swiss-German. He was educated at the University of Berlin, where he was von Ranke's student, and at the University of Bonn, where he and Carl Schurtz were both members of the circle of Professor Gottfried Kinkel. Early in 1845, he became editor of the important conservative newspaper *Basler Zeitung*, a post in which he served for eighteen months. In 1844, he was given the honorary title of professor at the tiny University of Basel, a post he held for virtually the remainder of his life (until 1895). When von Ranke retired from his post at the University of Berlin, Burckhardt was chosen as his successor. Burckhardt declined the appointment, no doubt because Prussia had become the epitome of everything in the modern world that Burckhardt detested: centralization, growing democratization, the commercial spirit, militarism, and a crass and vulgar smartness. He preferred culture to conquest. Besides, his colleagues at the University of Basel, Johann Bachofen and the young Friedrich Nietzsche, made the university one of the greatest constellations of genius in nineteenth-century Europe.

Burckhardt's lifestyle was one of ascetic dedication. He saw his mission as the instruction of his fellow citizens of Basel. He never married and, although he possessed independent means, lived in great simplicity. He never lectured at universities other than Basel and traveled to London, Paris, and Italy only in order to study the great art and architecture of the past.

Burckhardt viewed history as an act of contemplation and the creation of culture and its study the highest adventure of the human spirit. Cultural creativity, he believed, was possible only in the city-state: the Greek polis, the medieval cities, and the Renaissance cities of Italy. The enemies of culture were democracy, centralization, materialism, and the geographically extended state. He scorned specialization in historical writing and avoided meetings of professional historians, which he observed were attended by historians "in order to sniff each other like dogs."

Burckhardt was unabashedly elitist and aristocratic in his values. The Renaissance he viewed as an elite culture. While skeptical of the claims of orthodox Christianity, he was a Christian in ethical practice and hoped that a religious rebirth would rescue Europe from decadence and disaster. Both socialism and materialism he held to be evidences of cultural decline. He detested militarism and the pursuit of power. He believed that the world of the nineteenth century was moving inexorably toward a socialist tyranny. He saw the French Revolution and the Paris Commune as the beginning of this tragic development.

The rediscovery of Burckhardt in the Anglo-Saxon world immediately following World War II had a marked influence on the revival of conservative thought. The publication of *Force and Freedom* (1943), with its brilliant and trenchant introduction by James Hastings Nichols, was of decisive importance. Alexander Dru's selection, translation, and editing of Burckhardt's letters (1955), and his long and appreciative introduction, were also very important. Werner Kaegi's scholarly editions of Burckhardt's works, together with his biography (*Burckhardt, eine Biographie*, 1947–82), were essential to Burckhardt scholarship. The translation by Moses Hadas of Burckhardt's *Age of Constantine the Great* (1949) and Harry Zohn's translation of *Judgments on History and Historians* completed the sources of influence.
— STEPHEN J. TONSOR

Further Reading

Howard, Thomas Albert. *Religion and the Rise of Historicism: W. M. L. de Wette, Jacob Burkhardt, and the Theological Origins of Nineteenth-Century Historical Consciousness.* Cambridge: Cambridge University Press, 1999.

Hinde, John Roderick. *Jacob Burckhardt and the Crisis of Modernity.* Montreal: McGill-Queen's University Press, 2000.

Sigurdson, Richard. *Jacob Burckhardt's Social and Political Thought.* Toronto: University of Toronto Press, 2004.

bureaucracy

Government bureaus are responsible for a vast array of activities, ranging from law and order to welfare programs. About 20 percent of the labor force in the United States is employed by some level of government. Decision-makers in government agencies face problems unlike those faced by private entrepreneurs because of information and incentive problems that prevent them from coordinating economic activity as effectively as do market prices in the decentralized entrepreneurial market process—an essential requisite of conservatism.

Nobel Laureate F. A. Hayek stresses that information problems are endemic in government agencies because of the separation of power and knowledge. Consequently, bureau officials cannot obtain information on consumer preferences, resource availability, and production opportunities that would enable them to act in ways that are broadly beneficial. In short, decision-makers in government bureaus cannot efficiently determine actions that would be in the public interest.

However, even if bureaucrats could obtain the information to act in ways that promote the interests of the public at large, the incentive system is not conducive to their doing so. Incentive problems arise in bureaucracy because of the separation of power and responsibility. The fundamental problem is that there is no residual claimant in a governmental agency. In a free enterprise system, prices coordinate and transmit information to market participants and those firms survive that best anticipate market conditions. However, there is nothing in bureaucratic decision-making that corresponds to the profits and losses that influence entrepreneurial decisions in a private property system. In the absence of such signals, decision-makers in government agencies are likely to focus on other goals such as staying in office and agency growth. Moreover, there are a number of things they can do to further these goals.

First, maximizing the bureau's budget is likely to be emphasized because the size of the budget positively affects the bureaucrats' salaries, perquisites, public reputation, and patronage. There are two ways to increase the quantity demanded of a governmental service—through advertising and by reducing the price of the service provided. Therefore, it is not surprising that most governmental agencies have a public relations department to publicize the bureau's activities. And it is no accident that most governmental services are priced below the cost of providing the services.

The bureau's budget is also protected in times of financial austerity by following the "Washington Monument Syndrome." When the National Park Service was threatened with a budget cut, the agency responded by threatening to close down the Washington Monument, the most popular tourist attraction in Washington, D.C.

Second, bureaucrats can contribute to the goal of agency growth by making sure that their bureau's budget is exhausted by the end of the fiscal year. A government budget tends to be treated as a common pool resource—a resource no one owns but many people use. In the political process, the bu-

reau official who attempts to economize is not likely significantly to affect the total amount of government spending but will merely decrease the growth of his own agency. Thus, it is predictable that there will be a mad scramble by decision-makers in government agencies near the end of the fiscal year to make sure that all available funds are spent. It is not unusual to observe bureau officials remodeling offices, adding new carpeting, new furniture, and so on, even during a budget crunch.

Third, agency growth can be enhanced by expanding the bureau's jurisdiction. The "law of bureaucratic inertia" states that a government program set in motion tends to stay in motion. For example, the Rural Electrification Administration, a U.S. Department of Agriculture agency, was set up during the Great Depression to bring electricity to rural areas of the United States. However, now that the original mission is largely complete, USDA subsidized lending programs have been expanded to high-income urban and suburban areas throughout the United States, including such exclusive recreation areas as Aspen, Colorado, and Hilton Head, South Carolina.

Fourth, it is in the bureaucrat's interest to avoid risky activities because government officials do not stand to reap the benefits from risky activity, unlike decision-makers in the private sphere. If a new venture is successful, a government official may receive a plaque or some extra compensation but will be affected relatively little compared to the risk-taker (entrepreneur) in a free enterprise system. However, if the venture fails, the agency decision-maker may lose his or her job. Consequently, there is a natural tendency on the part of bureaucrats to avoid those risky activities that are inherent in economic progress. Indeed, the lack of incentive to provide for economic change and progress is a major defect of bureaucratic decision-making.

In short, decision-making in bureaucracy is constrained by information and incentive problems. Even if bureaucrats were completely dedicated to promoting the public weal, they could not obtain the information necessary to do so. Conversely, even an omniscient bureaucrat would be unlikely to act to promote the interest of the public at large because of incentive problems. Recognition of this problem has been a major element of the conservative critique of the massive growth of government bureaucracy in the last hundred years.

If we acknowledge that information and incentive problems are endemic in collective choice, how can more conservative policies be achieved through the political process? There are two possibilities—selecting better people and improving the rules of the political process. The incentive structure of the collective choice process may be compared to the law of gravity. Just as people always fall at thirty-two feet per second, so do individuals tend to respond predictably when confronted with the political incentive structure. This analysis suggests that conservative policies are more likely to be achieved through changes in the political and institutional framework than by appointing "better people" to positions of political power.

—E. C. PASOUR JR.

Further Reading

Buchanan, James M. *Explorations into Constitutional Economics*. College Station, Tex.: Texas A&M University Press, 1989.

Hayek, F.A. *Individualism and Economic Order*. Chicago: University of Chicago Press, 1948.

Mises, Ludwig von. *Bureaucracy*. New Rochelle, N.Y.: Arlington House, 1969.

Niskanen, William A., Jr. *Bureaucracy and Representative Government*. Chicago: Aldine, Atherton, 1971.

Tullock, Gordon. "Bureaucracy and the Growth of Government." In *The Taming of Government*. London: Institute of Economic Affairs, 1979.

See also: Hayek, Friedrich A. von; Mises, Ludwig von; public choice economics

Burke, Edmund (1729–97)

Edmund Burke was born in Dublin, Ireland, in 1729 and died in 1797 at his home in Beaconsfield, England, where he is buried. After graduating from Trinity College, Dublin, he went to London to study law but soon became active in literature and politics. In 1758 Burke contracted with the publisher Robert Dodsley to "write, collect, and compile" an *Annual Register*, reviewing the political and cultural events of Europe during the previous year. Burke wrote and edited the *Annual Register* from its first appearance in May 1759 until at least 1765–66, after which he retained supervisory control over it for about thirty years. This highly successful journal, which has continued throughout the nineteenth and twentieth centuries, was a valuable vehicle through which Burke was able to reach the British and American public with his views on political and cultural events.

On July 10, 1765, the Marquis of Rockingham became prime minister; the next day he appointed Burke as his private secretary. Burke's identification with the Rockingham Whigs was the most important personal political decision he ever made. It led directly to his election to the House of Commons in December 1765 and to a career in Parliament for twenty-nine years. For seventeen years, until Rockingham's death in 1782, Burke was the party whip and a major figure in British politics. Yet he never attained ministerial rank.

In the House of Commons Burke's great literary and political talents found expression on the broad stage of national and world politics, including the affairs of Britain's American colonies, Ireland, English domestic affairs, India, and France. Most of his political career was spent in opposition to the ministries of King George III on behalf of unpopular causes that almost always—at least at the time—went down to defeat. Through Burke the Rockingham Whigs were distinguished from all other political groups as the advocates of party government. Political parties in any modern sense did not exist in Burke's time, but in *Thoughts on the Cause of the Present Discontents* (1770) he may be said to have originated the idea of "his majesty's loyal opposition."

Burke's electrifying maiden speech in Parliament, which was given in January 1766 and urged repeal of the Stamp Act, catapulted him to national fame and established him as an expert on the American colonies. From May 1771 until military hostilities began, Burke was the agent in Parliament for the New York Colonial Assembly, a position that gave him valuable knowledge and understanding of the colonies. From beginning to end, Burke's main purpose regarding Britain's colonies was to preserve and harmonize American liberty and British sovereignty.

He was convinced that the conflict between Britain and America resulted from imprudent actions by the British government, including taxing the colonies without their consent and passing a series of repressive laws, which the colonists resisted through petitions of grievances, boycotts, and other means, and finally through military action that led ultimately to independence. Burke's *Speech on American Taxation* (1774), *Speech on Conciliation* (1775), and *A Letter to the Sheriffs of Bristol* (1777) were all unsuccessful attempts to persuade the king, his ministers, the majority in Parliament, and

Edmund Burke

the British public of the folly of England's policy toward the colonies and the great danger in attempting to coerce the Americans into obedience.

Burke never believed that the colonies sought independence on speculative or ideological theories of abstract "rights," but rather that they rebelled as disaffected subjects of Britain who wished to preserve their constitutional rights. Burke never referred to the conflict as the American Revolution, but as the American war, a civil war within the British Empire, in which America "was purely on the defensive." As the war of rebellion continued, Burke became convinced that the colonies were lost to Britain, and he was among the first to willingly grant independence to the colonies.

Burke's devotion to the cause of constitutional liberty for America and his inveterate enmity against the French Revolution have commanded so much attention by historians that his lifelong concern with Irish affairs has been unduly neglected. Yet the first political work of his public life was his *Tract Relative to the Laws against Popery in Ireland* (1765), and his last published work was also on Ireland.

Burke knew that under English rule Ireland's Catholic majority had suffered "penalties, incapacities, and proscriptions from generation to generation" and was "under a deprivation of all the rights of human nature." He summarized the "vicious perfection" of the laws against popery:

> It was a complete system full of coherence and consistency; well digested and well composed in all its parts. It was a machine of wise and elaborate contriv-

ance; and as well fitted for the oppression, impoverishment, and degradation of a people, and the debasement in them of human nature itself, as ever proceeded from the perverted ingenuity of man.

Burke perceived that the best means of depriving the Irish people of their natural and civil rights was to exclude them from the benefits of the English constitution, particularly in economics and religion.

Burke's method in seeking redress for Ireland was cautious, subdued, and prudent, partly because Ireland's subjection in religion, economics, and politics had deep historical roots, and also because anti-Catholic feeling in England, and among Irish Protestants, was so intense that every attempt to eliminate a few civil disabilities always provoked fanatical resistance. Three elements combined to make Burke's efforts to help Ireland very complex factors in his politics: his favorable view of the British Empire; his great sympathy with the plight of Irish Roman Catholics; and his general hatred of political tyranny. Yet during the 1770s, when Britain was increasingly involved in American affairs, Burke and his colleagues in Parliament succeeded in partially rescinding some of the anti-Catholic penal laws. In 1778 and 1782 Burke worked to eliminate restraints on Irish trade and to secure relief for Catholics. Although Irish Catholics complained that he did too little for them, Burke lost his Bristol constituency because his political enemies charged him with doing too much for them. In 1793 Burke helped to win the franchise for Irish Catholics. Most of Burke's policies for Ireland were fulfilled during the nineteenth and early twentieth centuries.

Historians have also largely ignored Burke's politics regarding India. Yet Burke considered his work on behalf of the "undone millions" of India as his most important achievement. The affairs of India occupied his attention for twenty-seven years, from 1767 until his retirement in 1794, but most actively during his last fourteen years in Parliament.

Burke's main objective was to secure a just government for India within the British Empire. To achieve this goal he sought to establish in practice the undoubted legal right of the British government to regulate the internal policies and public actions of the East India Company. He described the East India Company as "a state in the disguise of a merchant," and he was aware that, under Governor General Hastings, the agents of the company were the real rulers of India.

Between 1773 and 1783, Burke came to realize the nature and extent of British misrule in India and therefore abandoned his initial support of the East India Company against the encroachments of the Crown to become its most severe critic. In 1781, Burke became a member of the Select Committee of the House of Commons on the affairs of India, writing many of the reports it submitted to Parliament. In an attempt to provide India with its Magna Carta of liberty, Burke probably wrote most of Fox's East India Bill (1783). The bill was defeated in the House of Lords, and Burke became convinced that the East India Company was unwilling to reform itself. After much evidence of serious, systematic, and repeated abuses of power under Hastings, in 1786, with the help of Sir Philip Francis and others, Burke drew up the proceedings for Hastings's impeachment trial. Burke managed the trial before the House of Lords. The trial lasted eight years because of the legal impediments and delays thrown up by Hastings's lawyers, and ended in Hastings's acquittal. Many of Burke's efforts on behalf of India were realized through reforms enacted by Britain in the nineteenth century.

In 1769, long before the French Revolution burst upon Europe, Burke had predicted that France was heading toward "some extraordinary convulsion" because of its serious financial problems. A visit to France early in 1773 made him acutely aware of the militant atheism among some of the philosophes, and on his return to England, in his first speech in Parliament on March 17, 1773, he noted that "under the systematic attacks of these people, I see some of the props of good government already begin to fail. . . ." Burke believed that the chronic financial crisis of France, and the radical ideology among its "intellectuals," combined with economic and other causes, prepared the way for the great upheaval in 1789.

Burke's immediate response to the French Revolution was not hostile. For almost a year he allowed events to determine the position he would assume toward France. He noted that when Louis XVI recognized a unicameral National Assembly on June 27, 1789, in which the corporate orders of nobility and clergy were obliterated in favor of a numerical body dominated by the Third Estate, France was thereby committed to a new and revolutionary political and social order. Mob violence spread throughout France from the time the Paris populace stormed the Bastille on July 14 until the end of 1789. In October more than 300 of the more moderate deputies to the National Assembly fled France; the Jacobins assumed control, and proceeded by edicts to demolish the entire traditional legal, political, social, and religious order of France. By then Burke was convinced that the revolution was an evil force, aimed not at reforming economic and political inequities but at destroying the inherited civilization of France and all Europe. Yet not until January 1790, when English radicals expressed strong approval of events in France and held up the National Assembly as a model for England, did Burke enter the public arena to do battle with the French Revolution.

Burke's speeches in Parliament from February to June 1790 were a prelude to his *Reflections on the Revolution in France* (published later that year). Until his death in 1797, he continued his unrelenting attacks on the revolution in such works as *A Letter to a Member of the National Assembly* (1791), *An Appeal from the New to the Old Whigs* (1791), *Thoughts on French Affairs* (1791), *Remarks on the Policy of the Allies* (1793), *A Letter to a Noble Lord* (1796), and *Letters on a Regicide Peace* (1796). Burke's *Reflections* provoked the greatest political controversy ever conducted in English on the social nature of man, on reform and revolution, and on the origins, foundations, nature, and objectives of government and civil society. More than 225 books and pamphlets were written in "reply" to his *Reflections*, and more than 400 works attacking or defending Burke's writings on the revolution appeared before his death.

The most frequent charge of Burke's critics has been that after decades of defending the oppressed—in America, Ireland, India, and England—he betrayed his love of liberty and justice by defending the old regime in France, and in so doing was inconsistent with the political principles he had always professed. This charge shows ignorance of Burke, the French Revolution, or both. John Morley disposed of the charge of inconsistency by noting that there was no difference in principles between Burke's defense of the American colonies and his attacks on the French Jacobin revolutionaries. As Morley stated, Burke changed his front but never changed his ground. His consistency is most evident in his constant adherence to moral natural law and prudence as the ethical and legal standards and strategies for redress against political tyranny and injustice, whether that of kings or democrats.

—Peter J. Stanlis

Further Reading

Gandy, Clara, and Peter Stanlis. *Edmund Burke: A Bibliography of Secondary Studies to 1982.* New York: Garland Publishing, Inc., 1983.

Canavan, Francis. *Edmund Burke: Prescription and Providence.* Durham, N.C.: Carolina Academic Press, 1987.

Fennessy, R. R. *Burke, Paine and the Rights of Man.* The Hague: Martinus Nijhoff, 1963.

MacCunn, John. *The Political Philosophy of Burke.* London: Edward Arnold, 1913.

Stanlis, Peter J., ed. *Edmund Burke, the Enlightenment and the Modern World.* Detroit: University of Detroit Press, 1967.

See also: Burkean conservatism; Canavan, Francis, S.J.; centralization; conservatism; Conservative Mind, The; *custom; Enlightenment; French Revolution; historicism; Kirk, Russell; localism; Mansfield, Harvey C.; mediating structures; moral imagination; prejudice; prescription; relativism; Stanlis, Peter J.; Strauss, Leo; tradition*

Burkean conservatism

During the past two centuries Burke's political philosophy has been claimed by utilitarians, positivists, liberals, conservatives, Rousseauists, and even by neo-Marxists. Only since the middle of the twentieth century have his basic philosophical principles been so clearly identified as to justly categorize him as a political conservative.

Burke's statement that "the principles of true politics are those of morality enlarged" makes his politics a branch of ethics and thus separates him completely from Machiavelli and the whole modern political tradition that makes power supreme. His basic political principles are based on the ancient classical and Christian moral natural law, derived from God and perceived by all uncorrupted men through "right reason." The moral natural law provided Burke with the normative principles by which to judge whether or not rulers used their power to fulfill or to violate the great ends of civil society—the protection of life, liberty, and property—which Burke regarded as the nec-essary means of achieving temporal happiness. Through legal prescription, which derived from natural law, Burke defended private and corporate property as the necessary condition of the maintenance of freedom in society.

The natural law furnished the moral basis for Burke's other important political principles: his conception of international, constitutional, prescriptive, and statutory law; his view of human nature; the role of history in human affairs; his theory of the social contract; and the cardinal importance of moral prudence in practical politics. Burke believed that no moral problems are ever abstract matters, but are rather always embodied in concrete human conditions. Therefore, it was not necessary to appeal to the moral norms of natural law in every political conflict, since its principles were incorporated in the legal constitution of every justly organized society, which defined the legitimate powers and restrictions on power of sovereign rulers: "Power to be legitimate must be according to that eternal, immutable law, in which will and reason are the same." This view implied that all power was given as a trust and that rulers were to be held strictly accountable for their actions—to God under natural law and to their subjects under both natural and constitutional law. Appeals to natural law were reserved by Burke for extraordinary violations of the moral law, as in British misrule in Ireland and India and in the Jacobin tyranny expressed during the French Revolution.

Like Aristotle, Burke believed that man is by nature a social animal. Therefore, he rejected every political theory of the origins of society based on the *a priori* assumption of a primitive or pre-civil "state of nature," such as those propounded by Thomas Hobbes, John Locke, and Jean-Jacques Rousseau. He refuted them with the aphorism, "Art is man's nature." Theories based upon a supposed "state of nature" were to

Burke "the fairy land of philosophy." They were highly dangerous because they ignored history and opened the door to ideological, abstract speculations that substituted for the facts of history fictions that were then taken for reality in practical politics. Social contract theories invariably conceived of society as consisting of so many isolated and self-sufficient individuals rather than corporate human beings living in organized communities. Burke was aware that for the corporate conception of man Hobbes had substituted monarchical will, Locke majority will, and Rousseau collective will, and that all of them ended by replacing community with some form of collectivism.

Underlying Burke's view of civil society is his faith in a divinely ordained universe and a providential conception of history. Within history human nature, by virtue of reason and free will, provided the practical instrumental means of fulfilling its spiritual and temporal destiny through basic and necessary institutions, such as the family, church, and state. Burke's moral values, derived from the religious traditions of Christianity and natural law, are realized in the historical process by their embodiment in the church and in all the civil institutions of society, and are thus transmitted from generation to generation. That is why history, conceived as providential development and empirical experience, is an important part of Burke's political philosophy. In its unfolding, history reveals the divine purposes for man in the temporal order. This view does not mean, as some scholars have supposed, that Burke was a determinist or "historicist" who accepted whatever happened in history as good, including tyrannical regimes. Rather, it means that historical experience was an important source of knowledge and prudential wisdom. Burke defines history as "the known march of the ordinary providence of God"; it is to him a secondary form of revelation, supplementing in concrete

form religious revelation and natural law. To Burke, history was "a preceptor of prudence," not a depository of principles. A high regard for historical experience was one of Burke's cardinal principles in politics because historical experience taught governors the cardinal virtue of temperance and directed them to put restraints upon their use of power. Finally, history provided warnings against seeking violent change through ideological revolution.

Burke believed that "society is indeed a contract," but unlike Hobbes, Locke, and Rousseau, he believed that it was a contract between God and man and between all the generations of men within history—the past, present, and unborn generations.

Burke defined the politician as "the philosopher in action." As a philosopher, the politician should adhere to moral natural law; as a man of action, he ought to be guided by prudence in practical affairs. Burke regarded prudence in all things a virtue, but in politics it was the first of virtues. Prudence provides the practical means by which moral natural law and constitutional law are fulfilled in the various concrete circumstances of man's life in society. Prudence, which made politics an art, not a science, taught statesmen that "the situation of man is the preceptor of his duty." This meant that "a statesman, never losing sight of principles, is to be guided by circumstances; and judging contrary to the exigencies of the moment he may ruin his country forever."

Burke believed that although justice must always be observed, the determination of what is just in each particular instance, under all the different conditions and institutions of mankind, must vary. Prudence is the principle by which moral discretion informs statesmen when they should abate their demands for justice in favor of moderation in resolving social problems. Burke's ability to combine natural law and constitutional law with practical prudence make his political philosophy thoroughly consistent but almost wholly unsystematic.

—PETER J. STANLIS

Further Reading

Canavan, Francis. *The Political Reason of Edmund Burke.* Durham, N.C.: Duke University Press, 1960.

Cone, Carl B. *Burke and the Nature of Politics: The Age of the American Revolution.* Lexington, Ky.: University of Kentucky Press, 1957.

———. *Burke and the Nature of Politics: The Age of the French Revolution.* Lexington, Ky.: University of Kentucky Press, 1964.

Parkin, Charles. *The Moral Basis of Burke's Political Thought.* Cambridge: Cambridge University Press, 1956.

Stanlis, Peter J. *Edmund Burke and the Natural Law.* Ann Arbor, Mich.: University of Michigan Press, 1958.

See also: Burke, Edmund; centralization; conservatism; Conservative Mind, The; *custom; historicism; Kirk, Russell; localism; mediating structures; moral imagination; prejudice; prescription; relativism; tradition*

Burnham, James (1905–87)

American conservative political thinker, editor, and anticommunist theorist, James Burnham was part of the ex-communist Right that played a major role in defining American conservatism after World War II and for a generation afterwards. In this respect, he belongs in the same category as Whittaker Chambers, Frank S. Meyer, Max Eastman, Will Herberg, and others. As a senior editor of *National Review* from the time of its founding, and as the magazine's chief writer on foreign affairs, Burnham was instrumental in moving conservatives away from "isolationism" and toward an internationalist (though not globalist) foreign policy centered on anticommunism. Yet Burnham was also a major political thinker

apart from his writings on communism and foreign affairs. While the latter were probably the basis of his reputation during his lifetime, it is likely that his posthumous influence will increasingly reflect the importance of his "theory of the managerial revolution" and his "neo-Machiavellian" analysis of political and social affairs.

Burnham was born in Chicago, Illinois, on November 22, 1905, the son of Claude George Burnham, an English Catholic immigrant who died in 1928 as the wealthy vice president of the Burlington Railroad. Burnham attended Princeton University, where he was an editor of the *Princeton Tiger* and the *Nassau Literary Review,* and he graduated in 1927 with the highest academic average in his class. He studied at Balliol College, Oxford University, where he read English literature and took a B.A. with second class honors in 1929 and an M.A. in 1932. In 1934, he married Marcia Lightner, by whom he was the father of two sons and a daughter.

Burnham's early interests were literary and philosophical. He joined the faculty of New York University's Washington Square College in 1929 and taught philosophy there and at NYU until 1953. In 1932, Burnham and Philip Wheelwright published a textbook of philosophy, *An Introduction to Philosophical Analysis,* a highly skeptical treatment of both premodern and modern philosophical systems. From 1930 to 1933, he and Wheelwright edited a literary and philosophical journal, the *Symposium.* Burnham was one of the first literary critics to appreciate the genius of the young William Faulkner.

Burnham acquired an interest in politics during the Depression, and although he was at first highly critical of Marxism he became increasingly radical, influenced by Leon Trotsky's *History of the Russian Revolution* (English translation, 1932) and by a trip across the United States in 1933 that showed him the misery created by the Depression. In that year he formed the American Workers Party (AWP) with A. J. Muste, and in 1934, Burnham and the AWP emerged with the American adherents of Trotsky in the Workers Party (which became in 1937 the Socialist Workers Party), with which Burnham was affiliated until 1940. He and Max Schachtman became editors of the party's theoretical journal, the *New International*.

Burnham was a leading American disciple of Trotsky but broke with him because of Trotsky's defense of the Soviet Union as a "deformed" workers' state, even after Stalin's invasion of Finland. After an extended literary controversy with Trotsky, he resigned from the SWP in 1940. In the following year Burnham published *The Managerial Revolution*, which grew out of his disenchantment with Marxism and became the foundation of all of Burnham's later political thought.

During World War II, Burnham worked for the Office of Strategic Services (OSS), the parent of the Central Intelligence Agency, for which he also worked for some years, helping to plan the covert U.S. subversion of Mohammed Mossadegh in Iran and the installation of Shah Reza Pahlavi. He also was a founder and active leader of the American Committee for Cultural Freedom, the U.S. affiliate of the Congress for Cultural Freedom, which received funds from the CIA, and a contributor to the *Freeman,* the *American Mercury,* and *Partisan Review*, a leading New York literary review that published many of the ex-communist intellectuals of the 1940s and 1950s.

Burnham's increasingly outspoken anticommunism, his criticisms of fellow intellectuals for their communist sympathies or appeasement proposals, and his refusal to denounce Senator Joseph McCarthy caused

him to be increasingly isolated. In 1953, he resigned from the editorial board of *Partisan Review* and the faculty of NYU, and in 1955 he became associate (later senior) editor of *National Review*, with which he was affiliated for the remainder of his life. Burnham wrote a regular column, "The Third World War" (from 1970 titled "The Protracted Conflict"), as well as articles, book reviews, and editorials from 1955 until 1978, when a stroke impaired his memory and forced his retirement. In 1983, he was awarded the Ingersoll Prize

James Burnham

for Scholarly Letters as well as the Presidential Medal of Freedom from President Ronald Reagan. He died of cancer on July 28, 1987, at his home in Kent, Connecticut, converting to Roman Catholicism on his deathbed after a life of agnosticism.

The major theme of Burnham's political thought after 1940 was his emphasis on the emergence of a new ruling elite, the managerial class, and its implications for Western society. This new class, which he saw as replacing the old capitalist elite, rules through its control of the technical functions of economic production and political administration. Its aspiration is to consolidate total power through economic and social regimentation, exploitation of the masses against the capitalist or bourgeois elite, and global integration. Although Burnham's original analysis of the managerial class was largely Marxist, his second book (and most important theoretical statement), *The Machiavellians: Defenders of Freedom* (1943), abandoned Marxism and recast the theory. "The Machiavellians" included Niccolo Machiavelli himself and four modern social and political theorists: Vilfredo Pareto, Gaetano Mosca, Roberto Michels, and Georges Sorel. The common bond of these writers was their belief that the rule of elites or dominant minorities is inevitable in human society and that therefore anything like "democracy," egalitarianism, or real socialism is impossible. Another theme was that ideologies and governmental forms are in fact "myths," "political formulas," or "derivations" that disguise the real goals of the ruling classes and social groups that use them to justify their own power and interests. While democracy is not literally possible, Burnham and the Machiavellians argued, it is possible to establish a balance of powers within a ruling class to ensure that civil liberties, national independence, and cultural vitality flourish. It is these real social conflicts, not social harmony, that make civilized and free political life possible, but their existence is rare in human history, and the rise of managerial totalitarianism meant that their survival was unlikely.

Burnham's view of communism was closely related to the theory of the managerial revolution. The Soviet Union was the most advanced managerial regime, and its new ruling class was seeking global power through subversion, aggression, and intimidation. Burnham wrote a tetralogy—*The Struggle for the World* (1947), *The Coming Defeat of Communism* (1950), *Containment or Liberation?* (1952), and *The Web of Subversion* (1954)—to analyze the global strategy of the Soviets, their penetration of the U.S. government, and the response of the West in countering the Soviet drive for power. His strategy was essentially that the United States, as the leading Western managerial power, should seek to establish its own global hegemony and the destruction of the communist regime in the Soviet Union. In addition to the Machiavellian theorists, Burnham also relied on the first six volumes of Arnold J. Toynbee's *Study of History* (1934) and on the geopolitical theories of British geographer and strategist Sir Halford Mackinder to provide a conceptual framework for his anticommunist thought.

Burnham was originally almost brutally dispassionate in his own attitude toward the rise of a managerial regime in the United States, but he hoped that it would allow some degree of freedom to survive and would display more dynamism than the old capitalist (conservative) elite. But by the mid-1950s, he was skeptical of the managers' ability to rule and to resist the communist challenge forcefully. In *Congress and the American Tradition* (1959), he analyzed the decline of congressional government and the rise of a powerful presidency as part of the managerial revolution in American government. Burnham argued that freedom could not survive if the managerial presidency became the chief locus of political power, and he defended the rights and powers of Congress against the enlarged executive branch. In his last book, *Suicide of the West* (1964), Burnham argued subtly that the managerial class had adopted an ideology of liberalism as its chief political formula and that the psychic and social dynamics of liberalism reflected the decline of the West. The new managerial class had failed to take up the challenge of external and internal leadership.

Burnham's ideas have had a major influence on social and political thought. Peter Drucker, Milovan Djilas, Jacques Ellul, John Kenneth Galbraith, and Karl Wittfogel all acknowledged his influence on their own thought, and it is likely the theory of the managerial revolution influenced both C. Wright Mills's "power elite" theory and Daniel Bell's "post-industrial society" thesis. George Orwell's *Nineteen Eighty-Four* (1949) was intended in part as a fictional projection of the kind of managerial regime Burnham described in *The Managerial Revolution*. Burnham's importance as a thinker lies largely in four features of his thought: (1) his view of conflict and power as central in human society and determining the course of history—as opposed to ideas, moral values, religion, and other "spiritual" forces; (2) his secularist, historicist, pessimistic, and modernist vision of conservatism, as distinct from the antimodernist thought of most nonlibertarian theorists of the Right; (3) his formulation of a realistic anticommunist foreign policy that accepts the inevitability of international activism by the United States but firmly rejects a universalistic, antinational, and moralistic globalism; and (4) the theory of the managerial revolution itself, which offers the framework for a comprehensive interpretation of twentieth-century history from an antiliberal and anti-Marxist perspective.

—SAMUEL T. FRANCIS

Further Reading

Diggins, John P. *Up from Communism: Conservative Odysseys in American Intellectual History.* New York: Harper & Row, 1975.

Francis, Samuel T. *Power and History: The Political Thought of James Burnham.* Lanham, Md.: University Press of America, 1984.

Kelly, Daniel. *James Burnham and the Struggle for the World: A Life.* Wilmington, Del.: ISI Books, 2002.

See also: anticommunism; managerial revolution; National Review; *Orwell, George*

Bush, George W. (1946–)

Born in New Haven, Connecticut, into a patrician family with a commitment to public service, George Walker Bush was the first child born to George Herbert Walker and Barbara Pierce Bush. Shortly after his birth, his father moved the family to Texas to become involved in the oil industry. George Bush grew up primarily in the Houston and Midland areas until he moved to Massachusetts to attend Phillips Academy Andover and then to New Haven, where he enrolled at Yale University. He received a bachelor's degree from Yale in 1968 and served in the Texas Air National Guard as a fighter pilot during the Vietnam War.

After receiving an M.B.A. from Harvard University in 1975, Bush moved back to Texas to work in the oil industry. In 1977 he met a local librarian named Laura Welch. They married in November of that year. After running unsuccessfully for the United States House of Representatives in 1978, in 1981 he and Laura became parents of twin girls. In 1989, he convinced a group of business associates to acquire the Texas Rangers baseball team. Bush served as general managing partner of the team until 1994 when he pulled off a stunning defeat of the incumbent Texas governor, Ann Richards. When Bush was reelected in 1998, he became the first governor in Texas history to be elected to consecutive four-year terms.

Son of a former president and himself a popular governor of a major state, it naturally did not take long for Republican Party leaders to begin to view Bush as a possible presidential candidate. But his father's legacy as a one-term president and half-hearted conservative also worked against him. Thus, preceding his entry into the 2000 race for the Republican nomination, Bush courted conservative leaders who had felt betrayed by his father's lack of commitment to their values and goals. He amassed a massive war chest dwarfing that all other candidates and successfully mobilized the Republican leadership to fend off U.S. Senator John McCain, who emerged as his closet rival. In the fall campaign, Bush defeated incumbent vice president Albert Gore in one of the closest elections in American history. Though Gore drew approximately a half-million more votes than Bush, the Supreme Court eventually intervened to stop a controversial recount in Florida, whose electoral votes gave Bush the victory thirty-five days after the election.

With five fewer weeks to prepare for office, Bush still managed to put together one of the most talented and disciplined administrations in modern memory. His top priorities met with mixed success during his first few months in office. He successfully lobbied Congress to pass a massive cut in income taxes, a move cheered by conservatives, but he also worked with liberal Democrat icon Senator Ted Kennedy to pass his signature "No Child Left Behind Act," which met with mixed reviews among those conservatives who still believed education to be an issue for state and local governments. His efforts to allow federal programs to fund faith-based social-service providers did not gain much traction in Congress.

The Bush presidency took a major turn on September 11, 2001, when Islamic terrorists launched the most massive and successful terrorist attack in American history. The president's popularity soared following his tough and decisive leadership during this crisis. Indeed, in the weeks that followed 9/11 he became perhaps the most popular president in American history. Bush launched a successful invasion of Afghanistan that overthrew the Taliban regime and sent the terrorist leaders of al-Qaeda into hiding in the mountains between Afghanistan and Pakistan.

As part of America's reaction to the attacks of 9/11, Bush announced a new foreign policy doctrine of military preemption against nations who harbored terrorists or who might produce weapons of mass destruction that could threaten America. Faulty intelligence about Saddam Hussein's weapons program led Bush into a year-long campaign to build support for an invasion of Iraq. The initial invasion, launched on March 19, 2003, was massively successful in destroying Iraq's military and dethroning its government. Thereafter, a strong and organized insurgency developed, taking the lives of hundreds of American soldiers and thousands of Iraqis. The once popular invasion split the country and the conservative move-

ment. Neoconservatives backed Bush's aggressive foreign policy and his dedication to spreading freedom and democracy in the Middle East, but many traditionalists considered his foreign policy as owing more to Woodrow Wilson than to Robert Taft or Ronald Reagan.

In 2004 Bush was challenged by U.S. Senator John Kerry (D-Mass.) for the presidency. Bush's signing of a campaign finance reform bill in his first term opened the door for a massive influx of campaign contributions into the process as well as the introduction of outside organizations that spent heavily in an effort to defeat him. In the end, Bush won reelection by more than three million popular votes, despite being outspent by the Democrats and their supporters. The election results confirmed the electoral dynamics first seen in the 2000 race, with Bush's votes coming primarily from those who lived in rural areas and suburbs and from those who attended church regularly.

The presidency of George W. Bush has proved problematic for conservatives and the conservative movement. His evangelical background and willingness to express his personal faith appealed to many traditionalists and Christians. His opposition to stem-cell research, gay marriage, and abortion further solidified his popularity among his religious base. And his emphasis on tax cuts and reducing government regulation appealed to business interests. But his support for campaign finance reform, his seeming inability or unwillingness to control a massive budget deficit, and his support for federal programs such as the new prescription-drug benefit for Medicaid and the federal testing of local schools were anathema to many conservatives. His war in Iraq and the aggressive foreign policy goals outlined in his second inaugural address were hailed by neoconservatives but alienated many traditionalists. In the end, Bush's presidency revealed starkly the philosophical cleavages in the conservative movement as much as it also helped redefine political conservatism in the public mind.

—GARY L. GREGG II
AND N. SUSAN GAINES

Further Reading

Buchanan, Patrick J. *Where the Right Went Wrong: How Neoconservatives Subverted the Reagan Revolution and Hijacked the Bush Presidency.* New York: Thomas Dunne Books, 2004.

Frum, David. *The Right Man: The Surprise Presidency of George W. Bush.* New York: Random House, 2003.

Gregg II, Gary L., and Mark J. Rozell, eds. *Considering the Bush Presidency.* New York: Oxford University Press, 2004.

Kengor, Paul. *God and George W. Bush: A Spiritual Life.* New York: Regan Books, 2004.

See also: culture wars; education, public; Iraq War; Missile Defense, National; Republican Party; Terror, War on; West, American

Bushnell, Horace (1802–76)

Congregational pastor, social conservative, and organic nationalist, Horace Bushnell was one of the most significant theologians in nineteenth-century America. Raised in rural New Preston, Connecticut, Bushnell entered Yale in 1823, graduating in 1827. In 1831 he experienced a religious conversion and entered Yale Divinity School, where he studied under Nathaniel W. Taylor, the last of the New Divinity theologians in the Jonathan Edwards tradition. Despite Taylor's efforts to soften Calvinism, Bushnell rejected his and all other systematic approaches to faith. Other than the Bible, Bushnell was most deeply affected by the

Horace Bushnell

English romantic Samuel Taylor Coleridge's *Aids to Reflection* (1825). After graduating in 1833 he accepted a call to North Congregational Church in Hartford. The church was doctrinally divided, but Bushnell appealed to rival factions by seeking the truth found on both sides ("comprehensiveness") and emphasizing "a living faith" rather than metaphysical concepts. Despite occasional accusations of heresy by ecclesiastical opponents, he was always strongly supported by his parishioners. Although poor health forced his resignation in 1859, he continued his writing and involvement in community affairs until his death in 1876.

Bushnell is best known for his theological writings. *Christian Nurture* (1847), his most widely read book, stressed the organic nature of family and church and encouraged the Christian education of children to build up the church rather than relying on revivals, which he found unduly individualistic, nontraditional, and contrary to Scripture. Following a vision in which he "saw the Gospel," he wrote *God in Christ* (1849), in which he discussed the symbolic nature of language and an "instrumental Trinity" known through experience rather than theological doctrine. When accused of heresy by Calvinist clerics, he reaffirmed his Nicene orthodoxy with *Christ in Theology* (1851). Responding to the increasing challenge of science and materialism, he argued in *Nature and the Supernatural* (1858) that neither the Incarnation nor other miracles violated natural law, properly understood. In his last major work, *Forgiveness and Law* (1874), Bushnell presented a modified Calvinism that, in a final effort at "comprehensiveness," attempted to pull together the natural and supernatural, faith and reason, and other polarities.

Bushnell's social and political writings consistently revealed his social conservatism and Protestant nationalism. He despised Thomas Jefferson, whose "foreign" social compact theory and extreme individualism, he believed, undermined the moral basis of the state. In *Crisis of the Church* (1835), his first publication, he emphasized the symbiotic relationship between the republic and Protestantism. Concerned that civilization was breaking down on the frontier, he urged in *Barbarism: The First Danger* (1847) an extensive home missionary campaign to combat Mormonism, Catholicism, and slavery. At election times Bushnell frequently attacked the self-interested nature of American politics and politicians. By way of contrast he idealized the virtuous gentry- and clergy-dominated world of his rural Federalist boyhood in *Work and Play* (1864). Since the virtue of the republic was also intertwined with the stability of the family, he opposed votes for women in *Women's Suffrage: A Reform against Nature* (1869). He often criticized slavery and opposed the Fugitive Slave Act of 1850, but he was not an abolitionist. During the Civil War he strongly backed all efforts to save the Union so that it might continue its divine-historic mission.

Bushnell has been called the "father of American religious liberalism," but that label is misleading. His thinking, especially about language and nature, did prove useful to later modernists, but Bushnell himself rejected Darwin and believed his own radical theological forays had invariably brought him back to orthodoxy. Bushnell's penchant for seeking truth in paradox and his refusal to use accepted "metaphysical" terminology resulted in frequent misunderstanding. But socially and politically Bushnell was far less ambiguous: he was a social conservative and organic nationalist, ever sensitive to perceived threats to Protestant American civilization.

—P. BRADLEY NUTTING

Further Reading

Barnes, Howard. *Horace Bushnell and the Virtuous Republic*. Metuchen, N.J.: Scarecrow Press, 1991.

Cheney, Mary B., ed. *The Spirit of Man*. New York: Scribner, 1903.

———. *Life and Letters of Horace Bushnell*. New York: Harper, 1880.

Mullin, Robert Bruce. *The Puritan as Yankee: A Life of Horace Bushnell*. Grand Rapids, Mich.: W. B. Eerdmans, 2002.

Munger, Theodore. *Horace Bushnell: Preacher and Theologian*. Boston: Houghton Mifflin, 1899.

See also: Protestantism, evangelical

Butler, Nicholas Murray (1862–1947)

President of Columbia University (1902–45), Republican vice presidential candidate (1912), Nobel Peace Prize winner (1931), and founder and editor of *Educational Review* (1891–1919), Nicholas Murray Butler was an influential educational reformer, Republican Party leader, and an advisor to all Republican presidents from Harrison to Hoover.

The New Jersey-born Butler supported himself while earning his B.A., M.A., and Ph.D. in philosophy from Columbia College and then studied philosophy at Berlin. Butler taught briefly at Columbia, but found that his real talent and interests lay in administration. During his long tenure as president, Butler led the transformation of Columbia into a university. Butler believed the function of an American university was to train the nation's future leaders ("an aristocracy of intellect and service") while upholding American Constitutional principles and preserving a "reverence for that which lasts, . . . for that which bears the mark of excellence."

At first glance, Butler's activities can appear to be situated within the Progressive tradition. Butler created the Columbia Teachers' College because he supported professional training and certification of teachers. As a member of the New Jersey State Board of Education (1887–95) and as a supporter of New York's Unification Act of 1904, Butler worked for state control of public schools. Butler's goal, however, was to maintain intellectual standards; he had no sympathy for the child-centered approach of most Progressive reformers.

Active in the American peace movement, Butler helped establish the Carnegie Endowment for International Peace, serving as president from 1925–45. Butler looked to legal institutions and individual countries to uphold international law; with no contradiction he publicly supported United States intervention in World War I. For his support of the Kellogg-Briand Treaty (1928), Butler was co-winner of the 1931 Nobel Peace Prize, ironically sharing it with pacifist Jane Addams.

Nicholas Murray Butler

Regarding political reforms, there can be no mistaking Butler for a Progressive. Addams and other leading Progressives substituted for God a utopian vision they called democracy and worked to cleanse the political system of corruption through procedural reforms like the referendum, direct primary, and recall. Butler opposed direct democracy and often quoted Edmund Burke and James Madison (*Federalist* 48) on representative government. Butler believed that the initiative and referendum would make elected representatives less responsive to their constituents and thus would weaken the representative system. Butler argued that naïve reformers introduced the means for even greater political corruption: direct primaries, for instance, would increase the amount of money spent on political campaigns. Ultimately, Butler saw that corruption in politics reflected the corruption in the human soul, a condition that no election procedures could alter.

Butler preferred to wield influence, not power. He declined the opportunity to run for important offices and turned down numerous appointments. A longtime leader within the Republican Party, Butler was a delegate to Republican conventions in 1888 and from 1904–32. Theodore Roosevelt considered his friend a crucial advisor, but in 1912 Butler supported William Howard Taft. When Taft's running mate died during the campaign, Butler agreed to step in. In the 1920s, Butler was the leading Republican opponent of Prohibition, but soon found more to oppose in Franklin Roosevelt's New Deal.

Butler described himself as a "true liberal": throughout his life he opposed the "so-called liberalism" that espoused a "doctrine which makes for uniformity and conformity."

For many decades Butler was much in demand as a public speaker and most of his twenty books are compilations of his speeches.

—ANNE KRULIKOWSKI

Further Reading

Butler, Nicholas Murray. *Across the Busy Years.* 2 vols. New York: Charles Scribner's Sons, 1939–40.

———. *The Faith of a Liberal.* New York: Charles Scribner's Sons, 1924.

———. *The Meaning of Education.* New York: The Macmillan Company, 1898.

———. *True and False Democracy.* New York: Charles Scribner's Sons, 1940.

Herman, Sondra R. *Eleven against War: Studies in American Internationalist Thought, 1898–1921.* Stanford, Calif.: Hoover Institution Press, 1969.

Marrin, Albert. *Nicholas Murray Butler.* Boston: Twayne Publishers, 1975.

Southwick, Leslie H., comp. "Nicholas M. Butler," in *Presidential Also-Rans and Running Mates, 1788 through 1996.* 2nd ed. Jefferson, N.C.: McFarland & Company, 1998.

See also: education, higher; progressivism

C

Calhoun, John C. (1782–1850)

South Carolina planter and agriculturist, lawyer, constitutional theorist, state legislator, United States representative and senator, secretary of defense, vice president, secretary of state, member of Phi Beta Kappa, and presidential candidate, John Caldwell Calhoun was a major figure among the second generation of political leaders who shaped public policy in response to the new problems and issues that arose in the years after the momentous War of 1812: the admission of new states, foreign relations with Europe and the South American republics, internal improvements, Indian lands and treaties, the role of the military, fiscal policy and the tariff, the balance of power in a federal system of government, and, above all, the problem of slavery. To his credit, Calhoun addressed these problems forthrightly (often at the expense of popularity) and in so doing did his best to promote the public welfare and preserve the republic. At his death in 1850, not only had the nation been enlarged, but the union and the Constitution had been maintained in keeping with the original principles of 1776 and 1787.

A child of the War of Independence, Calhoun grew to manhood in a frontier environment of republican simplicity. Despite his crude surroundings, Calhoun received a classical education at Moses Waddell's Academy and with the help of his brothers was able to enter Yale College in 1802. After graduation in 1804, Calhoun studied law under the renowned Judge Tapping Reeve at his famous school in Litchfield, Connecticut. In 1807, Calhoun returned to Abbeville to practice law and begin his career as a farmer and politician, eventually serving two terms in the South Carolina General Assembly. As tensions increased between Great Britain and the United States following the Leopard affair, Calhoun offered himself as a candidate for Congress in 1810. Successfully elected for three consecutive terms, Calhoun followed a policy of protecting American rights even if that meant war. ("The honor of a nation," he declared, "is its life.") As one of the young "War Hawks," a group that included Calhoun's future adversary Henry Clay, Calhoun devoted himself to a vigorous prosecution of the war with Great Britain. This near-disastrous war, which the United States barely won, propelled the young South Carolinian to a new stage in his political career as an advocate of national measures aimed at strengthening the nation militarily and economically, including a second Bank of the United States, a national system of roads and canals, and a hike in tariff duties. Persuaded by Calhoun and Clay among others, Congress in 1816 passed legislation authorizing all three components of this enlarged national policy: a new bank, a new tariff, and a program of internal improvements (the last, however, was vetoed by President Madison).

As James Monroe's secretary of war, Calhoun rendered outstanding but not uncontroversial service to the nation from 1817 to 1824. He streamlined the War Department's internal procedures, had new fortifications and arsenals built, reorganized the army supply system, enlarged the Corps of Engineers, improved and clarified the command structure, increased militia training, and reinvigorated the Military Academy at West Point. Surveying parties of engineers were sent out, and their work contributed to an improved understanding of the nation's geography and resources. Equally important was the establishment of what would become the Bureau of Indian Tribes of the Northeast, West, and Southeast. Moreover, Calhoun's anti-British stance was influential in the shaping of the Monroe Doctrine of 1823.

Often accused of unscrupulously changing constitutional principles in an attempt to defend slavery, Calhoun in fact clung tightly to American constitutional tradition. He viewed states' rights and its corollary of strict construction as part and parcel of America's republican heritage and essential devices to prevent the abuse of power by keeping the government within prescribed bounds. Since their citizens had created the Constitution and the government, the states were sovereign and possessed the ultimate authority to change or abolish the federal compact. Slavery was a fact—albeit an unpleasant one—of American life and was protected by the Constitution. Calhoun maintained consistently throughout the controversy over slavery in the territories that slavery was strictly a matter for the states. A territorial government was a lesser creation and for Congress to recognize it was to "establish a direct relation between . . . individual citizens and the General Government, in utter subversion of [its] federal character. . . ."

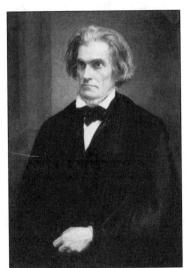

John C. Calhoun

The doctrine most closely associated with Calhoun, nullification, was actually not his discovery but rather Jefferson and Madison's. Calhoun's later forays into constitutional theorizing, *Disquisition on Government* and *Discourse on the Constitution and Government of the United States* (1851), were in large part extended glosses on the Constitution's delegated and reserved powers. The principle of concurrent majority was, he believed, built into the Constitution itself and was designed to prevent majority tyranny. Calhoun believed that a constitution was designed above all "to protect the subject against the Government. . . ." He recognized, with the founding fathers, that political power was so likely to be abused (given the selfish nature of men) that it had to be controlled to make responsible government possible.

For this reason, Calhoun argued, the framers of the Constitution created a limited government composed of powers divided between the states and the national government. Not only was power thus federalized, but it was also divided between the various departments of government—executive, legislative, and judicial. To Calhoun, this "division of power into two parts, with distinct and independent governments, regularly organized into departments . . . constitutes the great, striking and peculiar character of our system." Indeed, "the very essence of liberty was that . . . power should be divided, distributed, and organized, that one interest may check the other," a truth that "was fully understood at the time of the formation of [the] constitution."

But in Calhoun's view, after 1816 the

American system of government had become characterized by a sectional policy of plunder that benefited the industrializing North at the expense of the agricultural South. Economics and politics had merged to create a sectional rift that divided the nation and disrupted the old party system. To Calhoun, as well as to Jefferson and Madison, this new geographical alignment, not slavery, was the real "fire-bell in the night."

The remedy for this novel and dangerous situation, announced anonymously by Calhoun in the "South Carolina Exposition and Protest" of 1828 and publicly in his Fort Hill letter of 1831, was for a single state to interpose itself between the general government and the other states to arrest an unwarranted assumption of powers. Calhoun believed that this right of interposition belonged to a state as one of its reserved powers under the Tenth Amendment. In the case of the protective tariff, the national government had assumed an undelegated power, since the Constitution prescribed a tariff for revenue only.

By invoking interposition (available as a remedy in this specific instance only), a state was in Calhoun's mind doing nothing more than appealing to the sovereign power of the union itself. If enough states agreed with the one engaged in nullification to prevent a three-fourths or concurring majority from forming, then the contested power would have to be abandoned by the national government.

The crisis of 1832–33 that followed South Carolina's nullification action has been rightly portrayed as a prelude to civil war. In contrast to Calhoun, Andrew Jackson and those who agreed with him argued that (1) the union was older than the Constitution and the states and hence indestructible and (2) the operative principle of American democracy was simple majority rule. Although war was avoided for the next quarter-century or more by a states' rights revival led by

Calhoun, the Jacksonian position, and the Jacksonian assessment of Calhoun and his supporters—that they were antidemocratic, disunionists, and un-American—eventually prevailed. Only with the rediscovery of republicanism in recent years has it been possible to gain for Calhoun's political philosophy a renewed hearing.

—W. Kirk Wood

Further Reading

Calhoun, John C. *The Essential Calhoun: Selections from Writings, Speeches, and Letters.* Edited and introduced by Clyde N. Wilson. New Brunswick, N.J.: Transaction, 1992.

Cheek, H. Lee, Jr. *Calhoun and Popular Rule: The Political Theory of the Disquisition and Discourse.* Columbia, Mo. University of Missouri Press, 2001.

Ellis, Richard E. *The Union at Risk: Jacksonian Democracy, States' Rights, and the Nullification Crisis.* New York: Oxford University Press, 1987.

Lence, Ross M. *Union and Liberty: The Political Philosophy of John C. Calhoun.* Indianapolis, Ind.: Liberty Press, 1992.

Wilson, Clyde N. *John C. Calhoun: A Bibliography.* Westport, Conn.: Meckler, 1990.

See also: Southern conservatism; states' rights; Webster, Daniel

Campaigne, Jameson, Jr. (1940–)

Son of the conservative editor of the *Indianapolis Star,* Campaigne is a "cradle conservative." While growing up in Indianapolis, Indiana, Campaigne made connections with conservatives like Henry Regnery and M. Stanton Evans. He attended Williams College, graduating in 1962 with a degree in philosophy. At Williams he helped found a conservative club that invited speakers like William F. Buckley Jr. to campus and distributed conservative reading lists that challenged the views of liberal professors. He was a founding member of Young Americans for Freedom and served on the YAF national board from 1963 to 1975, the longest tenure of any board member. He was managing editor of Henry Regnery Publishing from 1962 to 1964 before joining Barry Goldwater's presidential campaign as a press aide in New York. In the fall of 1965 he joined with allies to take control of the Calumet Newspapers, a south-side Chicago newspaper chain, and in 1966 he became a member of the Mont Pelerin Society. In 1973 he joined Open Court Publishing Company as manager of their scholarly book division before forming his own publishing company, Green Hill Publishers (now Jameson Books) in 1976. A founding member of the Philadelphia Society, which he has served as a trustee, and a secretary of the American Conservative Union, Campaigne has also been a political activist, serving on the four-person steering committee that helped elect Philip Crane to Congress in 1969 and later on the Illinois Reagan-for-President campaign board.

While at Regnery and then through his own companies, Campaigne has published dozens of books that would not otherwise have reached an audience. An idea broker and an activist, Campaigne has served the conservative movement through his publishing activities and by fighting for conservative ideas through his political activism.

—GREGORY L. SCHNEIDER

See also: Philadelphia Society; Young Americans for Freedom

Canavan, Francis, S.J. (1917–)

A prominent Catholic intellectual and political theorist, Francis Canavan was born in New York City in 1917, joined the Society of Jesus in 1939, and was ordained in 1950. After receiving his doctorate from Duke University in political science in 1957 (where he studied under John H. Hallowell), Canavan taught at St. Peter's College and served as associate editor of *America* before joining the faculty of Fordham University, where he taught from 1966 until his retirement in 1988.

Best known as one of the world's preeminent Burke scholars, Canavan is the author of three books exploring various aspects of Burke's thought: *The Political Reason of Edmund Burke* (1960), *Edmund Burke: Providence and Prescription* (1987), and *The Political Economy of Edmund Burke* (1995). In these volumes and his other writings on Burke, Canavan has sought to restore Burke to his rightful place among the pantheon of Christian natural law thinkers by showing that Burke's thought had a fundamentally Thomistic character.

Canavan has also written on the political theory of freedom of speech (*Freedom of Expression: Purpose as Limit*, 1984), as well as on Catholicism and American culture and contemporary America's search for a public philosophy. Some of his most important writings on the latter subjects are collected in *Pins in the Liberal Balloon* (1990) and *The Pluralist Game: Pluralism, Liberalism, and the Moral Conscience* (1995). At the heart of these writings is a far-ranging critique of the liberal individualist intellectual tradition. Understanding liberal political theory to be shaped in important ways by the liberal tradition's philosophical commitments (in particular, by its embrace of a nominalist metaphysics), Canavan argues that the liberal model of man and society is flawed because it is incompatible with the Christian understanding of the nature and destiny of the human person and corrosive of the matrix of institutions, convictions, and virtues on which a democratic society depends for its vitality and ultimately its very viability. He further argues that the claim of liberalism to be "neutral" on the whole question of the human good is specious and turns politics into "a shell game" in which, in the name of neutrality, social life is reorganized in accordance with liberalism's distinctive and highly controversial vision of the human good.

—Kenneth Grasso

Further Reading

Grasso, Kenneth, and Robert Hunt, eds. *A Moral Enterprise: Politics, Reason, and the Human Good.* Wilmington, Del.: ISI Books, 2002.

See also: *Burke, Edmund; Burkean conservatism; Hallowell, John; speech, freedom of*

capital punishment

Controversies over capital punishment involve two primary lines of contention. One emphasizes morality and asks whether execution of the murderer is a justifiable response to the murder. The other emphasizes effectiveness in deterring murder and asks whether the execution of murderers reduces the number of murders committed. Whereas opponents claim that capital punishment is immoral, proponents argue that it is a valuable source of moral instruction. And while proponents claim that capital punishment is effective in reducing future murders, opponents deny any deterrent effect. Matters have been further complicated, for Catholic conservatives in particular, by the late Pope John Paul II's position that modern states rarely if ever need to resort to capital punishment. Because the pope's statement was not made as an official position of the Church, it is not binding on all Catholics. And although for Catholics a pope's authority in moral matters still carries great weight, there remains a rather strong consensus among American conservatives in favor of the death penalty.

There is no doubt that capital punishment satisfies a desire for retribution and for putting right wrongful acts. Retribution, however, speaks only for the victim and his family. Are retributive sentiments capable of being put to good civil use, or are they the barbaric remnants opponents of capital punishment claim them to be? Any effort to address this question must consider the contribution of punishment, including capital punishment, to moral education. Punishment is part of an educational process of producing conscience and good conduct. When this process succeeds, for each person who is deterred from some offense through a fear of punishment, there are many more who are restrained by conscience or by a fear of disapproval of friends and neighbors.

The concern with moral education would ask whether capital punishment generates more respect for the equal rights to life of others than does life imprisonment. This is perhaps particularly true for life imprisonment as currently practiced, which often means eventual parole, sometimes after only several years. Execution is ugly, but so is murder. For proponents of capital punishment, to forego executing a murderer seems to give more regard to the criminal than to the victim and thus to compromise the principle of equal rights to life.

Opponents of capital punishment sometimes join administrative-type arguments to their moral claims. One of these is that capital punishment is applied unevenly or arbitrarily, as illustrated by the evidence that rich murderers are less likely to be executed than poor murderers. Another is that capital punishment can be applied mistakenly. There is no way to know exactly how likely this prospect is. One study uncovered 74 cases since 1893 of alleged wrongful convictions in the United States, for which 31 death sentences were given and eight executions carried out. And in recent years, DNA testing has revealed that mistaken convictions for murder are not entirely infrequent, resulting in the release of dozens of those who had been condemned to death. The accuracy of judicial determination is certainly a relevant consideration in any effort to assess capital punishment's legitimacy, but these arguments do not so much attack the principle of capital punishment as raise issues concerning the administration of justice.

Focusing on deterrence allows one to look beyond a particular murder that has already been committed to ask whether execution of the murderer will help to reduce the number of murders committed in the future. The claim that capital punishment deters murder has a simple logic: the death penalty is more fearsome than life imprisonment, so there will be some people who might have committed murder had life imprisonment been the penalty who will not do so if death is the penalty. The great effort that most convicted murderers make to avoid execution is surely strong testimony that death is more feared than life imprisonment. Perhaps the most widely cited, and highly disputed, estimate in this literature is that each execution prevents somewhere between eight and twenty-four murders.

If the death penalty is a genuine deterrent, opposition to it on moral grounds loses a good deal of its force, for in that case it is no longer possible to occupy a moral position that refuses to follow one killing with another. In the presence of deterrence, a failure to execute murderers is to condemn other people to be murdered. A choice not to execute a murderer forces innocent people to participate in a lottery where losers get murdered. The relevant option thus becomes either to kill the murderer or to allow additional innocent people to be murdered.

It is easy to see why so much controversy has arisen over the deterrent effect of capital punishment. A good deal of opposition to the claim of deterrence has been based on the argument that murder is an irrational act that is therefore not subject to deterrence. This is a misunderstanding of the principle of deterrence, which holds only that an increase in the penalty will deter some people even if it does not deter everyone. Moreover, the existing deterrent effect of capital punishment is undoubtedly understated due to the way the death penalty is currently administered. The convicted murderer executed this year probably committed his offense fifteen or more years in the past. In light of the long delays and low probability that a death sentence will actually be carried out, the death penalty as presently administered may have little added deterrence over imprisonment. A swifter, more certain death penalty would surely have a greater deterrent effect.

The assessment of deterrence is also rendered more complicated by some subtleties in the logic of deterrence. That logic applies straightforwardly to people who commit a single murder, but it cannot be applied directly to people who commit multiple murders. If the penalty for murder is execution, additional murders beyond the first one have no penalty, save to the extent that multiple murders increase the likelihood that the murderer will be detected and convicted. People pay the same penalty, their life, whether they kill one person or ten.

Moreover, it should be noted that capital punishment has two distinct kinds of deterrent effect. One is the direct effect in deterring people who would have murdered had the penalty been lower. This effect has been the object of the controversy over the deterrent effect of capital punishment. The other is the indirect effect, which operates through moral education and its impact on the conscience. If the claims on behalf of moral education are correct, the indirect effect would doubtlessly be of far greater significance than the direct effect.

—RICHARD E. WAGNER

Further Reading
Bedau, Hugo Adam, ed. *The Death Penalty in America: Current Controversies.* New York: Oxford University Press, 1997.

Berns, Walter. *For Capital Punishment: Crime and the Morality of the Death Penalty.* New York: Basic Books, 1979.

Pojman, Louis P., and Jeffrey Reiman. *The Death Penalty: For and Against.* Lanham, Md.: Rowman & Littlefield, 1998.

Van Den Haag, Ernest, and Conrad, John P. *The Death Penalty: A Debate.* New York: Plenum Press, 1983.

See also: Berger, Raoul; van den Haag, Ernest

capitalism

Capitalism is the name applied to an economic system in which relationships among people are organized on the basis of individual liberty and private property. Capitalism is thus opposed to socialism, a system in which property is held in common and economic relationships are based on the politically organized compulsion that such common or collective ownership requires. To be sure, the term "capitalism" was coined by Marxists in the latter part of the nineteenth century and was used as a slur word to represent the idea that a capitalist economic system was run by and for capitalists. Such other terms as "market economy" and "free enterprise system" have also been used. But "capitalism" is the predominant term, and it does serve to focus attention on how the development of new ideas and their embodiment in capital goods is the source of material progress.

As a theory, capitalism is based on the conviction that we are social creatures and that it is through an elaborate network of cooperative relations that we are able to achieve the standards of living we take for granted. This complex of cooperative relationships is made possible because of certain institutions that have evolved over the ages. Primacy among these goes to private property, along with the related principle of freedom of contract and association. When people relate to one another within an institutional framework characterized by private property and freedom of contract and association, the result is a coherent, coordinated pattern of economic activity, even though it would be beyond the ability of any person or agency actually to plan that coordination. Economic life proceeds as an unconducted, self-orchestrated symphony. Adam Smith referred to this self-coordination as if it were the result of guidance from an invisible hand.

Through social cooperation it is possible to multiply the common level of material well-being beyond what it would be without that cooperation. Yet how can that cooperation be achieved? The Marxist vision is to achieve such cooperation without market competition. But market theorists argue that this is impossible. As Ludwig von Mises noted: "Even angels, if they were endowed only with human reason, could not form a socialistic community." The beauty of the market system is that it is not necessary to give the detailed instructions to billions of people that would otherwise be necessary to achieve the degree of social cooperation we actually observe all around us.

The fundamental paradox that economics seeks to explain is how it is that competition, within a framework of private property and freedom of contract and association, is the most effective process ever discovered for organizing social cooperation on a large scale. If each of us were to make up our wish lists of what we would like to have, the aggregation of those lists would exceed many times over our capacity to produce. Some wants will be fulfilled, others will not. Competition among us is inescapable. But competition within a legal and moral framework characterized by private property and freedom of contract and association fulfills those wants more fully than any other form of social organization because it harnesses individual interest to the service of social cooperation.

A market economy is a competitive process for organizing social cooperation. While there are many examples of real, organized markets, for the most part economists use "market" as an abstract noun to represent the network of exchange relationships that form within a society. To refer to the market for oranges is not to refer to some specific place, but simply to the idea that there are some people who grow and sell oranges and others who would like to eat oranges. The market for oranges is simply a representation of the complex network of exchange relationships through which the myriad choices and trades are made that result in oranges being grown, picked, delivered, sold, and eaten.

Market prices play a pivotal role in organizing this cooperative network of exchange relationships. If growers do not produce as many oranges as people would like to buy, prices and profits rise. This encourages existing growers to expand production, while it encourages others to start growing oranges, perhaps partly through shifting out of producing less profitable fruits. Areas of production in which profits are expanding attract new investment, while a contraction of profits discourages investment. Furthermore, a capitalist system encourages the invention and development of new products as part of the same quest to locate and exploit mutual gains from trade. Thus, the washing machine replaced the scrub board, the self-cleaning oven replaced scouring pads, and the bread machine replaced the need to roll and knead dough.

While it is generally granted that capitalism is splendid in encouraging production and the creation of wealth, critics claim that it suffers on moral grounds because of the acquisitive spirit it unleashes. Individual values are stressed to the detriment of communal well-being. Capitalism may enrich people economically but it impoverishes them spiritually. Images of Ebenezer Scrooge abound

as the archetypical representative of capitalism. The defenders of capitalism argue that such images are contrary both to reason and to experience. The examples of the communist and socialist nations of the twentieth century have not, to say the least, provided evidence that noncapitalist societies are necessarily more virtuous ones.

In fact, the ethical character of capitalism has both local and global dimensions. Locally, it constitutes a very concrete morality. The legal framework of capitalism incorporates the principles of property, contract, and tort law. These legal principles in turn involve moral content of a very concrete, personally manageable form. The principle of property law can be stated equivalently as the moral injunction not to take what's not yours. Contract law can be expressed in moral terms as a requirement to keep your promises. Tort law can be represented morally as an obligation to make good on the noncontractual wrongs you inflict on others. The legal institutions of capitalism clearly involve strong moral content of a highly practical character, especially as compared with such philosophically abstract and remote notions as acting as if you were choosing behind a veil of ignorance.

Globally, the ethical character of capitalism does not require people to do what is beyond their power to do. It does not, for instance, require that people should act to save the world, so to speak, for this is as much an impossibility as is a centrally planned economy. Rather, it says that if people conduct themselves in accordance with the legal and moral principles noted above, they will contribute to the well-being of all.

Care should be taken to distinguish between capitalism as an idealized system of social cooperation and the present-day economic system that we also describe as capitalist. Our actual system incorporates numerous noncapitalist features that often impede the processes of social cooperation that would otherwise assert themselves. There is a tenuous balance between capitalism or liberalism on the one hand and democracy on the other, as America's founders recognized.

A system of economic organization based on private property will require some measure of government activity, if for no other reason than to protect people's rights of person and property. Liberalism and capitalism are grounded in individual freedom and private property. In this scheme, government itself is simply a reflection of people's use of their rights of person and property and is not a source of those rights. Governmental authority is limited to securing individual rights.

Though there may be general agreement about the proper principles of governmental activity, that agreement often dissolves in the specifics of implementation. It would doubtlessly be agreed that someone who piped his car exhaust into his neighbor's house would have violated his neighbor's rights of property. Government action to prevent this violation would be consistent with capitalism. But what about the effect of millions of drivers doing the same thing to each other—just as surely even if not so directly and dramatically? Government efforts to counter air pollution would seem clearly to be consistent with the principles of private property and the protection of individual rights. Yet government action often follows perverse patterns. In large measure, common-law remedies have proved superior to regulation by the Environmental Protection Agency in protecting the quality of air and water. Increased regulation is usually more a testimony to the power of political muscle than it is to authentic attempts to achieve cleaner air through the securing of individual rights.

Finally, there is no doubt that capitalism is often distorted through the use of political power. In a genuinely capitalist

economy, perpetual diligence is the price of wealth. Those who rest on their past wealth will find it melting away as they rest, due to the presence of others who are not resting but instead are developing superior consumer offerings. Government power, however, may secure economic havens that could not be secured under capitalism. During its lifetime the Civil Aeronautics Board prevented any new trunk airline from entering the business, thereby protecting the wealth of established airlines against erosion through new competition. Similarly, a wide variety of occupational licensing restrictions have been used to prevent entry into the professions, thereby fortifying the wealth positions of existing practitioners. These are not inherent features of capitalism but represent rather the injection of noncapitalist elements into economic life.

—RICHARD E. WAGNER

Further Reading

Epstein, Richard A. *Simple Rules for a Complex World*. Cambridge, Mass.: Harvard University Press, 1995.

Friedman, Milton. *Capitalism and Freedom*. Chicago: University of Chicago Press, 1962.

Hazlitt, Henry. *The Foundations of Morality*. Princeton, N.J.: D. Van Nostrand, 1964.

Mises, Ludwig von. *Liberalism in the Classical Tradition*. 3rd ed. San Francisco: Cobden Press, 1985.

Reisman, George. *Capitalism*. Ottawa, Ill.: Jameson Books, 1996.

Sowell, Thomas. *Knowledge and Decisions*. New York: Basic Books, 1980.

See also: anticommunism; Becker, Gary S.; Catholic social teaching; conservatism; distributism; Friedman, Milton; law and economics; liberation theology; libertarianism; Marxism; Mises, Ludwig von; Novak, Michael; property rights, private; Schumpeter, Joseph A.; Smith, Adam; socialism; Sokolsky, George

Carey, George W. (1933–)

George W. Carey, professor of government at Georgetown University and author or co-author of several books and many articles, has been one of the foremost conservative interpreters of the American political tradition from the time his first publications began to appear in the early 1960s. A traditional conservative, Carey's primary concern has been to defend the American constitutional order bequeathed by the founding fathers from those he saw as bent on its destruction.

In the 1960s, Carey collaborated with Willmoore Kendall on a number of articles published in prestigious political science journals such as the *American Political Science Review*. This collaborative enterprise resulted eventually in the publication of *The Basic Symbols of the American Political Tradition* (1970), which Carey finished after Kendall's death in 1967. In *Basic Symbols*, Carey and Kendall made use of Eric Voegelin's conception of symbolic representation to understand the central documents of American political history. The work was a major contribution to what had been the much-neglected study of American political thought.

Over the years, Carey has published numerous articles on the American political tradition in such journals as *Modern Age* and the *Intercollegiate Review*. In 1989, the Center for Judicial Studies published *In Defense of the Constitution*, a collection of Carey's previously published essays on the Constitution and *The Federalist*. In the same year, Carey published *The Federalist: Design for a Constitutional Republic*, which marked him as one of the nation's foremost authorities on the essays of Madison, Hamilton, and Jay.

George W. Carey

Carey is also an important critic of the discipline of political science. Against both the positivistic behaviorism that dominated the discipline from the mid-twentieth century and the leftist Caucus for a New Political Science of the late 1960s, Carey defended a traditional approach to the discipline. As a counter to the Caucus, he founded and became the director of the short-lived Conference for Democratic Politics (CDP) and organized several official panels at the American Political Science Association meetings in the late 1960s and early 1970s. Around the same time he also contributed to and edited with George Graham *The Post-behavioral Era: Perspectives on Political Science* (1972), which brought together some of the leading lights of the discipline to reflect on its future. In perhaps his most direct impact on political science, Carey and James McClellan founded the *Political Science Reviewer*, a journal dedicated to a nonbehavioral, nonquantitative political science that first appeared in 1970. Carey later became editor of that journal. During the 1980s Carey contributed to several volumes published under the auspices of the Intercollegiate Studies Institute and served as a Reagan appointee on the Council of the National Endowment for Humanities.

Believing that any authentic American conservatism must be based on the principles of the American political tradition best expressed in the thought of the founding fathers, Carey's major contribution has been to remind conservatives of the imperative need to defend the Constitution and the political order it established. To that end, he has remained vigilant against those on both the Left and Right who he has thought more interested in political or ideological results than proper constitutional means. It is not surprising, then, that he has been a powerful critic of the activist federal judiciary and its apologists.

—GARY L. GREGG II

Further Reading

Carey, George W., ed. *Freedom and Virtue: The Conservative/Libertarian Debate.* Lanham, Md.: University Press of America and the Intercollegiate Studies Institute, 1984.

Hyneman, Charles S., and George W. Carey. *A Second Federalist: Congress Creates a Government.* New York: Appleton-Century-Crofts, 1967.

Schall, James V., and George W. Carey, eds. *Christianity and Political Philosophy.* Lanham, Md.: University Press of America and the Intercollegiate Studies Institute, 1984.

See also: judicial activism; Political Science Reviewer; *Supreme Court; tradition; traditionalism*

Carlson, Allan (1949–)

Born in Des Moines, Iowa, in 1949, Allan Carlson is an influential social historian and pro-family activist. Three years after taking his doctorate in modern European history from Ohio University in 1978, Carlson became executive vice president of the Rockford Institute in Illinois, where he became associated with the nascent paleoconservative movement. Having served as president since 1986, Carlson left the Rockford Institute in 1997 to found and become the president of the Howard Center for Family, Religion & Society, also located in Rockford.

Carlson's most important historical scholarship has been distilled in several books, including *Family Questions: Reflections on the American Social Crisis* (1988), *The Swedish Experiment in Family Politics* (1990), *From Cottage to Work Station: The Family's Search for Social Harmony in the Industrial Age* (1993), and *The New Agrarian Mind: The Movement Toward Decentralist Thought in the Twentieth Century* (2000). In these volumes and in his articles, Carlson's constant themes have been the impact of the modern economy and state on the family's well-being and the cultural illness indicated by modern societies' failures to reproduce at replacement fertility levels. He has recently become increasingly drawn toward the history of American agrarianism and has emerged as one of the nation's most prominent pro-agrarian voices.

Carlson's family activism has been perhaps most fruitful in his instrumental work in helping to convene The World Congress of Families, which has resulted in two large international gatherings that have flowered into a locus for international pro-family scholarship and activism.

—JEREMY BEER

Further Reading

Carlson, Allan. *The "American Way": Family and Community in the Shaping of the American Identity.* Wilmington, Del.: ISI Books, 2003.

See also: agrarianism; family; paleoconservatism; Rockford Institute

Carnegie, Andrew (1835–1919)

Andrew Carnegie rose from poverty to become an industrial magnate as well as a prolific and influential writer. His writings celebrated individualism, competition, economic growth, and democracy, and they challenged the wealthy to practice a philanthropy that would elevate mankind.

When Carnegie emigrated from Scotland at age thirteen, poverty compelled him to work as a bobbin boy. Making opportunities for himself, working hard, and learning fast, by age twenty-four he rose to become superintendent of the Pennsylvania Railroad's western division. Desiring greater autonomy, Carnegie left the railroad in 1865 to run his own enterprises. By the end of his career the vertically integrated Carnegie Steel Company was the world's largest steel producer. In 1901 he sold his interests to J. P. Morgan's syndicate for $300 million, making him one of the world's richest men. Thereafter he turned his attention to distributing his wealth and promoting international peace.

As much as he wanted to make money and outdo business rivals, Carnegie had a desire to influence public opinion, publishing numerous magazine articles and books. Carnegie's thesis was that America's democratic institutions and the economic and social freedoms they encouraged were responsible for its ascendance over monarchical Europe. His message and style are exemplified in *Triumphant Democracy* (1886), which begins: "The old nations of the earth creep on at a snail's pace; the Republic thunders past with the rush of the express." In language borrowed from Chartist radicals ("Down, privilege, down"), Carnegie stood for a meritocracy in which, with integrity, thrift, self-reliance, optimism, and hard work, any man and his family could ascend the economic ladder.

A friend and disciple of Herbert Spencer, he defended the era's relatively laissez-faire economic policies and championed the law of competition, "for it is to this law that we owe our wonderful material development, which brings improved conditions in its train. . . . [N]o substitutes for it have been found; and while the law may be sometimes hard for the individual, it is best for the race, because it insures the survival of the fittest in every department. To those who propose to substitute Communism for this intense Individualism, the answer therefore is: The race has tried that. All progress from that

barbarous day to the present time has resulted from its displacement."

While vast income inequalities were "inevitable," Carnegie did not glorify greed and opulence. Instead, he argued in *The Gospel of Wealth* (1900), that "the man who dies rich dies disgraced," because the wealthy man should "consider all surplus revenues which come to him simply as trust funds, which he is called upon to administer." Carnegie believed that wealth should not be given to "charity," but to libraries, schools, museums, and other projects that helped those who would help themselves.

—ROBERT WHAPLES

Andrew Carnegie

Further Reading

Carnegie, Andrew. *Autobiography of Andrew Carnegie*. Boston: Houghton Mifflin, 1920.

Livesay, Harold. *Andrew Carnegie and the Rise of Big Business*. Boston: Houghton Mifflin, 1975.

Wall, Joseph, ed. *The Andrew Carnegie Reader*. Pittsburgh, Pa.: University of Pittsburgh Press, 1992.

See also: foundations, conservative; robber barons

Casey, William J. (1913–87)

Archconservative Catholic Republican and quintessential anticommunist cold warrior, William Joseph Casey served as Ronald Reagan's 1980 presidential campaign manager and director of central intelligence (DCI). He was the wealthiest and oldest man (sixty-seven) ever appointed DCI and the first to be given cabinet rank. As coarchitect of the Reagan Doctrine, William Casey used the Central Intelligence Agency to combat the Soviets and support anticommunist resistance movements throughout the world.

Probably no other DCI exerted as much influence over the shaping of American foreign policy as the man whose mumbled speech President Reagan had difficulty comprehending at cabinet meetings.

Born in Queens, New York, of lower-middle-class Irish and French-Canadian parents, Casey attended a Jesuit school and served as an altar boy. After receiving a B.S. from Fordham and studying social work at Catholic University, he worked his way through law school at St. John's in just two years. Casey enjoyed a highly successful law practice, authored business, real estate, and tax guides, and served as chairman of the board of editors of the Research Institute of America.

During the Second World War, Casey served as the Office of Strategic Services' Chief of Secret Intelligence for the European Theater of Operations. From his London headquarters, he masterminded 102 mostly successful covert operations against Nazi Germany. Casey's efforts won him a Bronze Star and a lasting appreciation for a permanent central intelligence gathering and covert action agency. In his autobiographical *Secret War Against Hitler* (1987), Casey described his OSS exploits as "the greatest experience of my life."

After the war, Casey practiced law, continued writing and editing, ran unsuccessfully for Congress, and served as Associate General Counsel of the Marshall Plan, chairman of the Securities and Exchange Commission, Undersecretary of State for Economic Affairs, president and chairman of the Export-Import Bank, and member of the President's Foreign Intelligence Advisory Board.

Following Reagan's election to the presidency in 1980, Casey inherited a CIA demoralized by the congressional investigations and budget and personnel cuts of the 1970s. Determined to restore its morale, effectiveness, and standing, he tripled the agency's budget, revived the Clandestine Service, and reorganized the Directorate of Intelligence.

Convinced that the Soviets were the chief sponsors of international terrorism, Casey strengthened the agency's counterterrorism capability.

Its improved status notwithstanding, the CIA suffered its share of embarrassments during Casey's tenure. It was caught napping during the terrorist attack on Marine barracks in Beirut in 1983 and failed to predict the succession of Konstantin Chernenko to power in the Kremlin. The CIA's reputation was further undermined by Karl Koechner's betrayal of agency assets in Czechoslovakia, the redefection of KGB Colonel Vitali Yurchenko, the arrest of retired analyst Larry Wu-tai Chin (who spied for China), the first defection of a CIA employee (Edward Howard) to the Soviet Union, and the Walker spy ring's sale of top-secret submarine information to Moscow.

The worst crisis for Casey came in 1984–85 during the Iran-Contra affair, when Hezballah, a pro-Iranian Shiite terrorist group, kidnapped and murdered William Buckley, the agency's Beirut station chief. While Casey fully supported the secret arms-for-hostages deal with Iran and tried to conceal it from Congress, the CIA itself played only a minor role. Casey's support for the Nicaraguan Contras struggle against the communist-backed Sandinista regime included the controversial mining of Nicaraguan harbors, about which he failed to fully inform an angry Congress. It is, however, improbable that Casey knew of the diversion of funds from the arms sales to the Contras.

Paradoxically, Casey's role in the Iran-Contra affair undermined his efforts to restore the reputation and standing of the CIA. The damage of the scandal notwithstanding, the agency did not retreat back into its pre-1980 shell. It remained an active, essential component of American foreign policy thanks to an old OSS veteran who believed in the inevitable demise of the Soviet "evil empire."

—RORIN M. PLATT

Further Reading

Gates, Robert M. *From the Shadows: The Ultimate Insider's Story of Five Presidents and How They Won the Cold War*. New York: Simon & Schuster, 1996.

Jeffreys-Jones, Rhodri. *The CIA and American Democracy*. New Haven, Conn.: Yale University Press, 1989.

Kessler, Ronald. *Inside the CIA: Revealing the Secrets of the World's Most Powerful Spy Agency*. New York: Simon & Schuster, 1992.

Persico, Joseph E. *Casey: From the OSS to the CIA*. New York: Viking Penguin, 1990.

See also: anticommunism; Reagan doctrine

Catholic social teaching

The term "Catholic social teaching" usually refers to the official teaching of the Roman Catholic Church on matters of economic, political, and social justice. While the teaching of the church on these issues is clearly rooted in the Hebrew and Christian scriptures and in traditional Christian philosophy and theology, its modern articulation is embodied in a series of papal, conciliar, and other official documents issued by the church since the late nineteenth century.

Rerum Novarum, an encyclical promulgated in 1891 by Pope Leo XIII, represents the earliest official articulation of the major tenets of modern Catholic social teaching. Pope Leo's letter addresses the plight of industrial society and sets for itself the task of defining "the relative rights and mutual duties of the rich and of the poor, of capital and of labor." While Pope Leo clearly recognized the need for social change to support exploited workers, he was sharply critical of attempts by socialists and Marxists to effect such change by abolishing private property or by encouraging class struggle.

Rerum Novarum then goes on to articulate the central principles of the church's teaching on social matters. At the heart of this teaching is the idea that justice demands certain virtuous forms of life from all members of society. Workers are to carry out their jobs honestly and effectively; employers are to respect the dignity of their workers by paying them sufficiently and by providing appropriate working conditions; the rich are to recognize that excess wealth should be given to those in need; and the poor ought not look on their material poverty, which is indeed a great misfortune, as a disgrace. Pope Leo argued that Christian spirituality and the teachings of the church must be at the heart of any social renewal: "if human society is to be healed now, in no other way can it be healed save by a return to Christian life and Christian institutions."

Importantly, *Rerum Novarum* and the other major social encyclicals stress that the state has a role to play in furthering social justice and intervening in situations where the opportunities to live virtuously are seriously threatened. Leo argued for the importance of appropriately organized workers' unions, he claimed that the state has a duty to ensure that workers are paid what has come to be called a "living wage," and he noted that the essentially vulnerable condition of the poor gives them a claim to especial consideration in the eyes of the state. While he took care to note that "the law must not undertake more, nor proceed further, than is required for the remedy of the evil or the removal of the mischief," and to note the injustice of "excessive taxation," it is nevertheless clear that *Rerum Novarum* and the other official documents that follow in its path maintain that the state must play an essential part in helping the church carry out her mission to heal human society.

Pope Pius XI's 1931 encyclical *Quadragesimo Anno* ("On Reconstruction of the Social Order") emphasizes the importance of avoiding the errors of both "individualism" and "collectivism." Individualism, wrote

Pius, ignores the "social and public character" of the right to property, while collectivism fails to recognize property's "private and individual character." Pius emphasized that the public authority, under the guidance of divine and natural law, ought to consider the common good in determining what owners are and are not permitted to do with their property. What is perhaps most remarkable about *Quadragesimo Anno* is that while Leo had clearly singled out socialism as his primary target, Pius focused his criticisms more squarely on liberalism and capitalism. He argued that "free competition, while justified and certainly useful provided it is kept within certain limits, clearly cannot direct economic life," and he claimed that the deep economic disparities present in capitalist societies are evidence of grave injustice within liberal capitalist regimes. Importantly, Pius also articulated what has come to be known as the "principle of subsidiarity," which holds that "[t]he supreme authority of the State ought . . . to let subordinate groups handle matters and concerns of lesser importance."

Centesimus Annus, issued by the late Pope John Paul II in 1991, is the most recent official articulation of the principles of Catholic social teaching. In the course of offering a "re-reading" of *Rerum Novarum*, John Paul reaffirmed many of its core tenets, noting especially its teaching that "the more that individuals are defenseless within a given society, the more they require the care and concern of others, and in particular the intervention of governmental authority." Writing just after the fall of the Soviet Union in 1989, John Paul praised Leo's prescient critique of socialist political systems. He further contended that the root problem of socialism is its view of "the individual person simply as an element, a molecule within the social organism, so that the good of the individual is completely subordinated to the functioning of the socioeconomic mechanism."

John Paul indicated that the church prefers a political arrangement within which society and the state work together to protect the dignity of workers and ensure that they can find work at living wages and under acceptable working conditions. He argued that the fundamental problem identified by Leo is "an understanding of human freedom which detaches it from obedience to the truth, and consequently from the duty to respect the rights of others." Thus, he contended that opposing Marxism by setting up free-market economies is appropriate only so long as such economies do not undermine authentic human values or regard the human good purely in terms of material satisfaction. He emphasized, therefore, that we ought to approach the development of poorer countries "in a way that is fully human," by "concretely enhancing every individual's dignity and creativity, as well as his capacity to respond to his personal vocation, and thus to God's call." Indeed, Pope John Paul claimed that such development does not reach its pinnacle until the members of society turn to God in order to "know him and to live in accordance with that knowledge."

Hence, like his predecessors, John Paul stressed that while there are positive aspects of the modern "business economy," one must also bear in mind certain connected risks and problems. While he noted that modern societies have changed in many ways since *Rerum Novarum*, he reminded us also that "the human inadequacies of capitalism and the resulting domination of things over people are far from disappearing." He offered an extensive criticism of the "phenomenon of consumerism" in advanced economies and of the tendency in industrialized economies toward ecological irresponsibility, and he cautioned against what he called the "idolatry of the market." While the free market can effectively encourage social renewal in many ways, he noted that "there are many human needs which find no place on the market. It is a strict duty of justice and truth not to allow fundamental human needs to remain unsatisfied . . . . It is also necessary to help these needy people . . . develop their skills in order to make the best use of their capacities and resources." Still, he offered heavy criticism of what he called the "Social Assistance State," a form of political order that violates the principle of subsidiarity and in which bureaucratic state action interferes with the effective authority and rightful autonomy of lower-level associations.

In sum, John Paul responded to the question of whether capitalism ought to serve as the economic model for developing countries with a heavily qualified answer: insofar as "capitalism" is understood to refer to an economic system that recognizes the key role of a free market and true human creativity in a productive economy, the answer is affirmative; but insofar as it suggests "a system in which freedom in the economic sector is not circumscribed within a strong juridical framework which places it at the service of human freedom in its [ethical and religious] totality," then the answer must be in the negative. True liberation requires freedom from all forms of sin, and any socioeconomic arrangement that fails to so liberate its members is ipso facto unjust.

It should be noted that some commentators have argued that the Catholic Church's failure to more fully embrace liberal capitalism is the consequence of the church's earlier antimodern prejudices, which more recent church teachings have gradually abandoned. But a close reading of the relevant documents reveals very little of the sort of doctrinal "development" that such scholars claim to have found. Hence Catholic writer Michael Novak's claim in *The Spirit of Democratic Capitalism* that the democratic capitalist order "calls forward not only a new theology but a new type of religion" seems approximately correct; the problem, however, is that the theology and religion he advocates do not seem to be those of the Catholic Church.

It is perhaps unsurprising, then, that the relationship of postwar American conservatives to Catholic social teaching has been an uneasy one. While conservatives have been strongly opposed to communism and socialism, they have generally also allied themselves with liberal political systems and capitalist economic institutions in ways that are in deep tension with many of the church's core social doctrines. Less prominent strains within modern conservatism, however, seem more compatible with these teachings. Writers like Russell Kirk, Eric Voegelin, and Richard Weaver, for example, expressed a healthy distrust of modernity. Others, such as Irving Kristol, Robert Nisbet, and Wilhelm Röpke, have also concerned themselves with the justice of robustly capitalistic social orders.

It might be argued that the uneasy relationship between postwar conservatism and Catholic social teaching is best understood as a reflection of the breadth of, and internal tensions within, each of these traditions. Here it is important to recall Pope John Paul II's claim, in *Centesimus Annus*, that "[t]he Church has no [political or economic] models to present; models that are real and truly effective can only arise within the framework of different historical situations, through the efforts of all those who responsibly confront concrete problems in all their social, economic, political and cultural aspects." To the extent that conservatives view political systems in this way—as means to a transcendental end infinitely exceeding the importance of material goods, and as subject to criticism and in need of change insofar as they fail to steer their members toward this true end—there seems to be no good reason why conservatives cannot be allied with the Catholic Church toward the perpetual renewal of the political and social order.

—John Wheldon

Further Reading

Hauerwas, Stanley. *A Community of Character: Toward a Constructive Christian Social Ethic*. Notre Dame, Ind.: University of Notre Dame Press, 1981.

MacIntyre, Alasdair. *Dependent Rational Animals: Why Human Beings Need the Virtues*. La Salle, Ill.: Open Court, 1999.

O'Brien, David J., and Thomas A. Shannon, eds. *Catholic Social Thought: The Documentary Heritage*. Maryknoll, N.Y.: Orbis Books, 1992.

Schindler, David L. *Heart of the World, Center of the Church:* Communio *Ecclesiology, Liberalism, and Liberation*. Grand Rapids, Mich.: Wm. B. Eerdmans Publishing Co., 1996.

See also: distributism; John Paul II, Pope; liberation theology; Novak, Michael; Roman Catholicism; Schindler, David L.; Weigel, George

Cato Institute

The Cato Institute was originally called the "Libertarian Society" by cofounders Edward H. Crane III and oil business leader Charles Koch, but it was later renamed by libertarian scholar and cofounder Murray Rothbard for the eighteenth-century pamphlets, *Cato's Letters*, which laid the ideological foundations of the American Revolution. Cato was originally organized in San Francisco to be a libertarian research and educational organization by then–Libertarian Party (LP) national chairman Crane. With Koch providing multimillion-dollar funding, Cato has since become one of the most influential and active policy organizations in Washington, D.C.

Today, Cato pursues a program of publications and conferences, including the quarterly *Cato Journal*, bimonthly *Regulation* magazine (formerly published by the American Enterprise Institute), and *Cato Policy Report*. Its annual monetary conference has advanced free-market banking policy, especially during the course of the savings and loan crisis, and its conferences have triggered significant interest in free-market alternatives to socialism in developing countries. After the 2001 terrorist attacks, Cato was at the forefront of the debate to preserve civil liberties amidst the threat of more terrorist activities. Many articles opposing the war in Iraq—and pushing for an exit from the war—have come from the Cato Institute.

Seldom afraid of controversy, Cato was the target of major attacks by *National Review* and other conservative publications in 1979 out of fear that the Libertarian Party might threaten the Reagan-for-President campaign, and because Cato's anti-interventionist views on U.S. foreign policy—as voiced in its iconoclastic, biweekly magazine, *Inquiry*—opposed those of the conservative mainstream. Consuming the bulk of Cato's funding at the time, *Inquiry* was an attempt by Crane to attract a constituency of antiwar, pro–civil liberties young professionals (Crane's later term: "market liberals") who could also be attracted to free-market ideas. When it was later disbanded, this effort was redirected into an expanded research and publishing program that produced influential books (including *Beyond Liberal and Conservative*, 1984, and *Left, Right and Babyboom*, 1986) and publications. In the late 1970s and early 1980s Cato also began to organize many scholarly lectures and seminars, annual weekend seminars for business leaders (*Benefactor Summits*), and the week-long *Summer Seminars in Political Economy*, which later became the "Cato University" seminar program. The groundwork was also laid for the *Cato Journal*, which subsequently became the flagship publication for the institute. Cato's first major policy book, *Social Security: The Inherent Contradiction* (1980), by Peter Ferrara, successfully made private IRA accounts a serious alternative to compulsory Social Security in the public debate.

Cato moved its operations to Washington, D.C., in 1981, where its focus shifted from scholarly research to policy-oriented research. The new strategy was to focus Cato's analyses on those libertarian policies perceived as resting on the edge (but not over the edge) of what was considered politically acceptable inside the beltway. The focus of *Inquiry* was hence largely shifted from foreign policy and civil liberties to market-oriented economic issues.

In Washington, however, Cato did not achieve real respectability and intellectual influence until Crane persuaded William Niskanen to join as chairman in 1985. As a departing member of Reagan's Council of Economic Advisors, Niskanen brought to Cato a scholarly dimension that had been missing for several years, in addition to mainstream respectability. Furthermore, Niskanen's reputation attracted significant conservative funding, as well as the support of such luminaries as Nobel Laureate economist Milton Friedman.

Since that time, Cato has grown in stature, influence, and funding. The institute has continued to take strong anti-interventionist positions, as shown in its strong opposition to the 1991 Gulf War and the recent war in Iraq, refusing to blandly accept the conservative consensus on such matters and thus remaining true to its libertarian roots.

—DAVID J. THEROUX

Further Reading

Barnett, Randy E. *Restoring the Lost Constitution.* Washington, D.C.: Cato Institute, 2004.

Easterbrook, Gregg. "Ideas Move Nations." *Atlantic Monthly,* January 1986, 66–80.

Gottfried, Paul. *The Conservative Movement.* Boston: G. K. Hall, 1992.

Norberg, Johan. *In Defense of Global Capitalism.* Washington, D.C.: Cato Institute, 2003.

See also: Koch, Charles G., Charitable Foundation; Libertarian Party; libertarianism; think tanks, conservative

centralization

In a political context, "centralization" refers to the growth in power and authority of the modern state that comes at the expense of localisms such as kin, town, religious community, and custom. It represents the application of a detailed set of laws over the daily lives of persons and organic institutions in distinct localities. Conservatives see the contest between the central state and particularistic, customary institutions as lying at the core of modern politics, with their sympathies usually favoring localism.

Roman law from the period of empire provided a rough theoretical framework for centralization. It countenanced the atomization of rival mediating bodies and emphasized the superiority of the emperor to all other forms of authority. The great early modern theorist of centralization was Thomas Hobbes, who argued that no other institution should stand between the isolated individual and the absolute state. Multiplicity, plurality, family, and heritage had no place in Hobbes's vision of political order. Before the advent of the central state, the life of men was "solitary, poor, nasty, brutish, and short." Rival associations within the state were as "worms in the entrayles of a naturall man." All property rights derived from the sovereign as well. Human society would be built through contract and protected by the authoritarian ruler. Even the family itself had no inherent rights; rather, a parent gained legitimate dominion only "from the Child's consent."

Jean-Jacques Rousseau carried this vision forward, recognizing only two entities: the isolated individual, and the absolute state. There was no such thing as "society" composed of numerous intermediate bodies. Rather, Rousseau described the just order as one where "each citizen would . . . be completely independent of his fellow men, and absolutely dependent upon the state."

This would "free" the individual from spontaneous, stultifying society, thereby allowing him to find meaning in a "general will" divined by the sovereign.

Nineteenth-century theorists built on this foundation. Jeremy Bentham's utilitarianism advocated the centralization of administration at the expense of custom and tradition as a necessary measure of efficiency. Behind the rhetoric of "the withering of the state," Marx and Engels's *Communist Manifesto* (1848) urged the "centrali[zation of] all instruments of production in the hands of the state. . . . Centralization of credit . . . [c]entralization of the means of communication [etc.]." Nation-builders such as Otto von Bismarck in Germany and Guiseppe Garibaldi in Italy saw political centralization as a necessary step in ending the crippling divisions of provincialism.

Social reformers of the early twentieth century viewed the centralizing state as a way to overcome the "confusion and conflict" of premodern, feudal times, bringing instead reason and personal liberation. V. I. Lenin mocked "the flabbiness of the village" and crafted the revolutionary state resting on the dictatorship of the proletariat. Scandinavian social democracy rested on the displacement of true civil society by the mechanisms of the welfare state. In fulfillment of Rousseau's vision, wives would no longer be dependent on husbands, nor husbands on wives, nor children on parents, nor aged parents on grown children: all would be equally dependent on the central state.

A distinctive conservative critique of centralization began with Edmund Burke. In his *Reflections on the Revolution in France* (1790), Burke contrasted the growing "superiority of the city of Paris" with "the destruction of all the old bounds of provinces and jurisdictions, ecclesiastical and secular, and the dissolution of all ancient combinations of things." The power of the city of Paris served as the "one great spring" of revolutionary politics. He urged that we "love the little platoons we belong to in society," the "germ" as it were "of public affection." Alexis de Tocqueville gave considerable attention to centralization in *Democracy in America* (1835), emphasizing its close linkage to the pursuit of equality within a democratic polity. "Every central power which follows its natural instincts loves equality and favors it," he wrote. "For equality singularly facilitates, extends, and secures its influence." Democracy despised privilege and loved uniformity; equality destroyed the former and created the latter. Every citizen became "lost in the crowd, and nothing stands out conspicuously but the great and imposing image of the people itself."

Other critics followed. In the 1830s, the Bishop of Exeter called centralization "the vice of modern legislation," one alien to the true English constitution. Randolph Bourne identified modern war "as the health of the state," an engine for radical change. Writing for the Southern Agrarians in *I'll Take My Stand* (1936), Frank Owsley cast the American Civil War as a conflict between the "extreme centralization" of the commercialized Hamiltonian North and the "extreme decentralization" of the agricultural Jeffersonian South. He emphasized that the greatest growth of centralized power in America came only in the wake of the Southern defeat. Robert Nisbet's *Quest for Community* (1953) and *Twilight of Authority* (1975) dissected the origins of centralization, finding its roots in a monism blending "social nihilism and political affirmation." He urged that real power be restored to intermediate institutions such as family, neighborhood, and church, entities that both conferred and protected true liberty. Finally, Russell Kirk argued that the "worst thing about excessive concentration of power . . . is that in the long run such Behemoth centralization fails . . . and then the whole structure falls apart." He pointed to the collapse of Soviet Russia as an example.

Conservatives have differed, however, on how or whether to arraign capitalism and the modern joint-stock, limited liability corporation as contributing to centralization in a detrimental way. Some, such as Michael Novak and his allied neoconservatives, have regarded modern corporations as mediating institutions themselves, sheltering individuals from state authority in a manner similar to that of families. Others, such as Nisbet and the Agrarians, have seen the rise of the modern corporation as a key factor in the construction and growth of the centralizing state. In this view, mercantilism and then capitalism have been used by kings and democratic rulers alike as tools with which to destroy the "particularism of local and intermunicipal trading" (Karl Polanyi, *The Great Transformation,* 1944). This latter, more consistently decentralist brand of conservatism has argued, on both historical and theoretical grounds, that economic and political centralization is mutually self-sustaining.

—ALLAN CARLSON

Further Reading

Agar, Herbert, and Allen Tate, eds. *Who Owns America? A New Declaration of Independence.* New York: Houghton Mifflin, 1936.

Carlson, Allan. *The New Agrarian Mind: The Movement toward Decentralist Thought in Twentieth-Century America.* New Brunswick, N.J.: Transaction, 2000.

Kirk, Russell. *The Politics of Prudence.* Wilmington, Del.: Intercollegiate Studies Institute, 1993.

See also: Agar, Herbert; community; Davidson, Donald G.; due process; individualism; localism; mediating structures; states' rights

Chamberlain, John (1903–95)

John Chamberlain was one of the most prolific and respected conservative writers of the twentieth century. In a writing career spanning more than six decades, Chamberlain published more than 20,000 essays and reviews in such leading magazines as *Life, Fortune,* and *Harper's.* He was the first daily book reviewer for the *New York Times* (1932–36) and was an editorial page writer for the *Wall Street Journal* (1950–60). For a quarter of a century (1960–85) Chamberlain wrote an oft-quoted syndicated newspaper column for King Features on political, economic, and social issues.

His eight books include *The Roots of Capitalism* (1959), which explains how economic freedom increases the well-being of everyone, and *The Enterprising Americans* (1963), which profiles Samuel Colt, Eli Whitney, Alexander Graham Bell, and others who forged American capitalism. Chamberlain also worked with General Charles Willoughby to produce a highly praised history of General MacArthur's military leadership in the Pacific and later as pro-consul in Japan. He also helped General Albert Wedemeyer write his best-selling memoir, *Wedemeyer Reports!* (1958).

A graduate of Yale University, Chamberlain was an ardent socialist in the 1920s. But he turned anticommunist and then conservative (he preferred the Tocquevillian term "voluntarist") after witnessing "Leninist and Stalinist statism murder its millions in Soviet Russia." In the 1950s, as a senior editor of the *Freeman* and then *National Review,* Chamberlain participated in what he described in his autobiography, *A Life with the Printed Word* (1982), as a "fundamental assault on the regnant liberalism."

Chamberlain singled out his experience at *National Review* as the high point of his professional life. William F. Buckley Jr., he once wrote, "more than any other figure, has made conservatism a respectable force in American life."

The indefatigable Chamberlain served for a time as a professor at Columbia's graduate school of journalism and then as dean of journalism at Troy State University in Alabama. A believer in right reason, John Chamberlain was a quiet optimist who, having seen the decline and fall of the many deadly isms of the twentieth century—communism, fascism, socialism—ended his autobiography with these words, "We did not unsettle the Old World merely to reestablish its repressive ways in the New."

—LEE EDWARDS

Further Reading

Chamberlain, John. *Farewell to Reform: The Rise, Life, and Decay of the Progressive Mind in America.* Chicago: Quadrangle Books, 1965.

———. *The Turnabout Years: America's Cultural Life, 1900–1950.* Ottawa, Ill.: Jameson Books, 1991.

See also: Freeman

Chamberlin, William H. (1897–1969)

A leading conservative historian and journalist, William Henry Chamberlin was a prominent critic of communist ideology and the Soviet system. Born in Brooklyn in 1897, by the time Chamberlin graduated from Haverford College in 1917 he was an anarchist. After working as assistant managing editor at the *Philadelphia Press,* he served in the United States Army and, after the war, wrote book reviews for the *New York Tribune.* Chamberlin then joined the *Christian Science Monitor,* which appointed him as its Moscow correspondent in 1922. While in Moscow, he became Russian correspondent for the *Manchester Guardian* as well. He also wrote a series of books on Soviet life and politics, including a history (*The Russian Revolution,* 1935) that has remained a classic for its brevity and balance.

Chamberlin's Russian sojourn cooled his enthusiasm for the Soviet "experiment." In *Collectivism: A False Utopia* (1937),

Chamberlin offered his critique of Marxism, expressing skepticism toward the idea of a planned economy. He also offered tentative support of New Deal experimentation and endorsed the Munich agreement, declaring before the war broke out that it had been wise to renounce "interference" in Eastern Europe.

From 1935 to 1940, Chamberlin served as a correspondent in the Far East, a post that resulted in his book *Japan Over Asia* (1937). In *The World's Iron Age* (1941), based partly on his personal observations of the fall of France, Chamberlin combined a description of totalitarian rule in Europe and Asia with a plea for a negotiated peace and American isolation. He indicted Britain and France for permitting Hitler to remilitarize the Rhineland, for offering an unenforceable guarantee of Poland, and for waging war halfheartedly.

From 1940 on, Chamberlin held editorial posts at such diverse publications as the conservative *Human Events* and the socialist *New Leader.* As editorial contributor to the *Wall Street Journal,* he frequently reviewed books on history and politics. He also continued writing books criticizing the Soviet Union along with the Roosevelt administration's conduct leading up to war with Japan.

Unlike many conservatives who opposed Roosevelt's interventionism before Pearl Harbor, Chamberlin endorsed Truman's Cold War measures. His edition of official Comintern documents was published under the title *Blueprint for World Conquest* (1946); in his introduction he claimed that such sources proved that the Soviets intended to conquer the world. *The European Cockpit* (1947), based on a four-month trip to the continent, found in almost every country an arena of struggle between Soviet and Western influences.

When Truman announced his famous doctrine in March 1947, Chamberlin called it "the right note at last." Though he generally supported strong American commitments to the North Atlantic Treaty Organization, he wrote in January 1951 that Truman should not send troops to Europe before securing congressional approval. In a book titled *Beyond Containment* (1953), he called for programs that would start "the Soviet empire, the greatest threat to our Western civilization, on the road to decline and fall."

In 1947, alarmed by what he called "the Soviet pattern for Asia," Chamberlin warned against over-commitment to Chiang's forces. In January 1948, he argued for the Asian Marshall Plan for China and the Philippines. In May 1949, while Nationalist China was falling, he admitted that Chiang's forces were "not a strong, effective or reliable ally." In July 1950, within a month after the United States entered the Korean War, Chamberlin warned that communist occupation of Formosa would strengthen Philippine insurgents and imperil a major source of Japan's food supply. When in October it appeared the United Nations forces might be able to unite all Korea, Chamberlin praised America's firmness and courage: "Korea must set the pattern," he wrote. Yet in June 1951, Chamberlin endorsed Truman's truce efforts: "Half a loaf is better than none."

Chamberlin also became a conservative in domestic policy. In such works as *The Confessions of an Individualist* (1940), which contains much autobiography, and *The Evolution of a Conservative* (1959), he expressed his allegiance to classical liberalism, with its "rejection of state interference with the political, social, and economic freedom of the individual." He once said that "[c]onservatism at all times and in all countries has stood for religion, patriotism, the integrity of the family and respect for private property as the four pillars of a sound and healthy economy."

—JUSTUS D. DOENECKE

Further Reading

Doenecke, Justus D. *Not to the Swift: The Old Isolationists in the Cold War Era.* Lewisburg, Pa.: Bucknell University Press, 1979.

Muresianu, John W. "War of Ideas: American Intellectuals and the World Crisis, 1938–45." Ph.D. diss., Harvard University, 1982.

See also: Human Events

Chambers, Whittaker (1901–61)

Whittaker Chambers is best known for his role as the chief witness against Alger Hiss beginning in 1948. A former Communist Party journalist and agent in the communist underground espionage network in the 1930s, Chambers broke with communism, led a distinguished career as a journalist with Time Inc. in the 1940s, and was the author of *Witness* (1952), one of the architectonic texts of the postwar conservative movement. Conservatives remember Chambers for his brooding, portentous writings about the meaning of communism and "the crisis of the West."

Following an unhappy, tragedy-filled childhood and an abbreviated academic career at Columbia University, Chambers joined the Communist Party and turned his literary talents to account for the Communist Party journals, the *Daily Worker* and the *New Masses.* In the mid-1930s, Chambers discontinued his writing and joined the communist underground, working chiefly as a courier for an espionage ring that included Alger Hiss. Chambers broke from the Communist Party in 1938 and soon joined the staff of *Time* magazine as a book reviewer. At *Time* he rose eventually to the position of senior editor before testifying about Hiss before the House Committee on Un-American Activities in 1948.

Chambers explained at length in his autobiographical book *Witness* the motivations and philosophical outlook that led him first to embrace, and later to reject, communism. His gradual realization of the immorality of communist ideology led Chambers to find faith in God and to abandon communism. Chambers expressed his judgments about the crisis of the West in sweeping phrases that, along with his demeanor, led friends and associates to compare him with Dostoyevsky. At the core of modernity, Chambers thought, was an inadequate rationalistic materialism that led inevitably to a spiritual vacuum, a vacuum communism had rushed to fill. To Chambers, communism was a secular faith equivalent in its salvific promises to Christianity. This is the main theme of *Witness* and indeed most of Chambers's writing. Communism, Chambers wrote in *Witness*, is a form of man's rebellion against God.

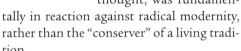

Whittaker Chambers

Following the tumultuous years of the Hiss case from 1948 to 1952, during which time Chambers severed his ties with Henry Luce and Time Inc., Chambers retired to his Maryland farm to write *Witness*. Following the success of that book, Chambers set out to write a sequel, a "big book" that would set out more fully his views about the crisis of the West. But Chambers produced only fragments of that projected volume, several of which were published in a posthumous volume titled *Cold Friday* (1964).

In 1957 Chambers joined the staff of *National Review*, then in its second year of publication. Chambers contributed regular columns, chiefly on foreign policy and communism behind the Iron Curtain. His most noted—and controversial—*National Review* article was his review of Ayn Rand's *Atlas Shrugged*, which was titled "Big Sister Is Watching You." Chambers objected to Rand's atheism and "forthright philosophical materialism." "From almost any page of *Atlas Shrugged*," Chambers wrote in one of his most memorable lines, "a voice can be heard, from painful necessity, commanding: 'To a gas chamber—go!'" This review, in the judgment of Buckley, "read Miss Rand right out of the conservative movement."

However, Chambers did not consider even himself a member of the conservative movement, drawing a distinction between being a conservative and a "man of the Right," in which latter category he placed himself. A man of the Right, Chambers thought, was fundamentally in reaction against radical modernity, rather than the "conserver" of a living tradition.

Chambers died on July 9, 1961, just a few weeks before the Berlin Wall was built. Arthur Koestler wrote, "I always thought Whittaker was the most misunderstood person of our time. . . . The witness is gone, the testimony will stand." Chambers himself felt misunderstood: "I never really hoped to do more in the Hiss Case than give the children of men a slightly better, only slightly better, chance to fight a battle already largely foredoomed. . . . How odd that most of the world seems to have missed the point in *Witness*; that it seems to suppose that I said: 'Destroy Communism and you can go back to business as usual.' Of course, what I really said was: 'This struggle is universal and mortal, and only *by means of it*, on condition that you are willing to die that your faith may live, can you conceivably recover the greatness which is in the souls of men.'"

—STEPHEN HAYWARD

Further Reading

Chambers, Whittaker. *Odyssey of a Friend: Letters to William F. Buckley, Jr., 1954–1961.* New York: Putnam, 1969.

Swan, Patrick, ed. *Alger Hiss, Whittaker Chambers, and the Schism in the American Soul.* Wilmington, Del.: ISI Books, 2003.

Tanenhaus, Sam. *Whittaker Chambers: A Biography.* New York: Random House, 1997.

Teachout, Terry, ed. *Ghosts on the Roof: Selected Journalism of Whittaker Chambers, 1931–1959.* Chicago: Regnery, 1989.

See also: *anticommunism; Buckley, William F., Jr.; fusionism; Hiss-Chambers trial; Toledano, Ralph de; Witness*

Chesterton, G. K. (Gilbert Keith) (1874–1936)

Born in London and educated at St. Paul's School, G. K. Chesterton attended, for a time, the Slade School of Fine Art and University College, London, where he read English literature. He worked as a journalist throughout his life. Chesterton's reception into the Catholic Church in 1922 marked the culmination of a spiritual journey from a home background of liberal, non-churchgoing, bourgeois decency, a psychological crisis associated with decadent aestheticism, through an Anglo-Catholic discovery of "the romance of orthodoxy." Although he always resisted the word "conservative," which he associated with the defense of the status quo and economic interests at variance with Christian norms, he also became disillusioned with the Liberal Party to which he was attached by upbringing. He nevertheless continued to see himself in the liberal, democratic political tradition of radical reform. But because of his championing and elucidation of Catholicism, the medieval inheritance, tradition, custom, and orthodoxy, he is usually seen today as a culturally conservative thinker.

Like his friend Hilaire Belloc, Chesterton was a prolific writer, producing well over a hundred books, including volumes of essays, verse, novels, travel books, biography, literary criticism, and religious, social, and political thought. He is widely known for his *Father Brown* detective stories and his novels, such as *The Napoleon of Notting Hill* (1904) and *The Man Who Was Thursday* (1908), which exemplify themes of conflict, order, and anarchy in original and allusive literary forms. His long poems *The Ballad of the White Horse* (1911) and *Lepanto* (1911) dramatize the conflict between Christendom and paganism and reveal Chesterton's penetrating historical, religious, and political imagination. He is at his most characteristic when combining powerful insight, a playful love of paradox, and clear-headed argument into an essentially comic and integrated vision of human life, wherein conflict is resolved in the joy and wonder of creation. The distinctive Chestertonian voice is heard whatever his ostensible subject or genre in which he is writing.

G. K. Chesterton

Much of Chesterton's writing involves an attack on the consequences of rationalism, materialism, and scientism, particularly for the religious idea of man. In contrast to the rationalism of writers such as George Bernard Shaw and H. G. Wells, who thought human salvation should be sought in a utopian socialist state, Chesterton showed how the mechanistic view of man and society struck at the roots of freedom and the human potential for happiness and fulfillment. In *Orthodoxy* (1909), Chesterton proposed, against the spirit of the age, "the desirability of an active and imaginative life, picturesque and full of a poetical curiosity, a life such as Western man at any rate always seems to have desired." A good life for Chesterton is a romance rooted in Rome, in Catholicism, and in the cultural inheritance of Christendom. Thus, history and tradition form the indispensable context of true democracy: "Tradition may be defined as an extension of the franchise. Tradition means giving votes to the most obscure of all classes, our ancestors. It is the democracy of the dead. Tradition refuses to submit to the small and arrogant oligarchy of those who merely happen to be walking about."

A frequent theme in Chesterton is that sanity, like orthodoxy, consists in balance: "The madman is not the man who has lost his reason. The madman is the man who has lost everything except his reason." This principle holds both for the person and for the community. Chesterton's writings on society closely identify Christianity and Christendom, and the economic problems of industrial capitalism are addressed via the moral norms governing Christian economic life from the Middle Ages onwards. Modern corporate monopoly is contrasted by Chesterton with the medieval guild system, and he advocates a wide distribution of property so that freedom can subsist in the family, the household, and the workplace. These economic ideas came to be known as distributism. Chesterton's social thought is well presented in *The Outline of Sanity* (1926). In politics, he emphasized subsidiarity, especially the importance of local patriotism and national self-determination.

Chesterton may be seen as writing within a conservative tradition that affirms the common nature of man and his common inheritance (in the West) of what is left of Christendom. What makes life worth living, for Chesterton, is that which is built on the normal, the sane, the balanced, and the integrated. There are close affinities between the thought of Chesterton and that of Aquinas, of whom Chesterton wrote a particularly accessible intellectual biography. *St. Thomas Aquinas* (1933) and *The Everlasting Man* (1925), a defense of the religious idea of man against the relativizing drift of cultural anthropology and Darwinism, are often considered his major literary achievements.

—ANDRÉ GUSHURST-MOORE

Further Reading

Chesterton, G. K. *Autobiography.* New York: Sheed & Ward, 1936.

Hollis, Christopher. *G. K. Chesterton.* London: Longmans, Green, 1950.

Pearce, Joseph. *Wisdom and Innocence: A Life of G. K. Chesterton.* San Francisco: Ignatius Press, 1997.

See also: Agar, Herbert; Belloc, Hilaire; Chesterton Review; *distributism; Eliot, T. S.; free trade*

Chesterton Review

The *Chesterton Review* is the quarterly journal of the International Chesterton Society. Founded on May 26, 1974, it is dedicated to the exploration of the life and works of G. K. Chesterton and other writers who share a commitment to Chestertonian principles, including his distributism and appreciation of the moral imagination. Over the years, the journal has dedicated issues to the legacies of such figures as C. S. Lewis, Christopher Dawson, Georges Bernanos, Vincent Mc-Nabb, Charles Dickens, and George Grant, as well as the Harry Potter phenomenon and fantasy literature. Lovingly and beautifully produced, each 150-plus-page issue includes reprints of Chesterton articles, original essays, book and film reviews, photos and illustrations, and comments on recent news.

The *Chesterton Review* was founded and is still edited by the Canadian Rev. Ian Boyd, C.S.B., at Seton Hall University in 1974 and is still based there and edited by him. For most of its history, the journal was produced out of St. Thomas More College in Saskatoon. However, in 2000 the college lost interest in the *Review* and Boyd was recruited to Seton Hall University by its president, Msgr. Robert Sheerhan. There, the *Review* spawned the Chesterton Institute for the Study of Faith and Culture, which Boyd created with fellow Basilian priest Rev. Daniel Callam, historian Dermot Quinn, attorney Hugh Mackinnon, economist John Mueller, editor and author Stratfod Caldecott, and ISI vice president Jeffrey Nelson. The institute and its programs, as well as the *Review,* are part of Seton Hall's Center for Catholic Studies.

—Alexandra Gilman

See also: Chesterton, G. K.; distributism

Chicago Tribune

Founded in 1847, the *Chicago Tribune* rose from humble beginnings as a four-page daily newspaper to become the most powerful media outlet in the American Midwest and the flagship of a large and influential media conglomerate. Under the ownership of Colonel Robert McCormick, the *Tribune* also became the single most conservative major newspaper in the United States during the middle decades of the twentieth century.

The *Tribune* began as a fairly liberal organ, taking a progressive stance on many nineteenth-century social issues, notably the antislavery movement. It backed Abraham Lincoln (the paper's most famous subscriber) during the Civil War and survived the Great Chicago Fire of 1871, which destroyed its offices. By the early twentieth century, it was merely one newspaper among many in Chicago, a state of affairs that changed when

McCormick—scion of a wealthy family descended from famed inventor Cyrus McCormick—assumed control in 1914. Under the flamboyant McCormick, the *Tribune* expanded into local radio and television, introduced the "Dick Tracy" comic strip (one of the most-read comics in America for many years), and printed the first-ever four-color news photographs. During the Great Depression, McCormick's *Tribune* was a thorn in the side of President Franklin Roosevelt, adamantly opposing the many social-relief programs of the New Deal and taking a staunch isolationist position in the years leading up to World War II. The newspaper firmly supported the war effort after the outbreak of hostilities, but pressed for a nationalist (rather than an internationalist) agenda and continued to pick its openings for criticism of Roosevelt, on one occasion leaking the contents of War Department documents which revealed FDR's prewar claims of American neutrality as a sham. (Ironically, the *Tribune* printed its most embarrassing headline on McCormick's watch: the famous 1948 headline on the national presidential race, "Dewey Defeats Truman.") After McCormick's death in 1955, the *Tribune* continued its policy of editorial conservatism into the 1970s. Although the newspaper's subsequent editorial leadership has sought to distance itself from McCormick—described by Joseph Epstein as "a figure about whom no one could be neutral"—his successes laid the groundwork for even greater corporate acquisitions by the paper's parent Tribune Company, such as the purchase of the Chicago Cubs baseball team and the Times Mirror Company.

—James E. Person Jr.

Further Reading

Gies, Joseph. *The Colonel of Chicago.* New York: Dutton, 1979.

Kinsley, Philip. *The Chicago Tribune: Its First Hundred Years.* New York: Knopf, 1943.

Smith, Richard Norton. *The Colonel: The Life and Legend of Robert R. McCormick.* Boston: Houghton Mifflin, 1997.

Wendt, Lloyd. *The Chicago Tribune: The Rise of a Great American Newspaper.* Chicago: Rand McNally, 1979.

See also: McCormick, Robert R.; Wall Street Journal

China Lobby

An informal group of congressmen and private individuals who supported the Nationalist government of Chiang Kai-shek (Jiang Jieshi) as China's legitimate government even after its exile to Taiwan (Formosa), the China Lobby played a key role in forcing the United States government to support Taiwan with military and economic assistance, thus preventing invasion by the communist Chinese government and allowing Taiwan ultimately to become a democracy and an economic colossus. Among the group's most important figures were Senators Henry Styles Bridges, William Knowland, and Barry Goldwater, Congressman Walter Judd, *Time* magazine's Henry Luce, and Gen. Claire Chennault—the "Flying Tiger"—and his wife Anne.

The China Lobby's origins lay in the mid-nineteenth century, when evangelical Protestant churches began sending thousands of missionaries to China. Together with businessmen who wanted equal access to China's markets at the time of European colonization, the churches were instrumental in the decision of the United States government to issue its "Open Door Policy" at the turn of the twentieth century, which called for the maintenance of Chinese territorial integrity. During the 1930s, these policies were directed at Japan and its rapacity against China, culminating in a U.S. embargo in the months before Pearl Harbor.

World War II saw Chiang's U.S. supporters pushing Presidents Franklin Roosevelt and Harry Truman for greater assistance to China, while the United States government pushed Chiang to focus on fighting the Japanese in coalition with the communist Mao Tse-tung (Mao Zedong) rather than fighting both simultaneously. At war's end, Chiang launched an all-out offensive against the communists in their Manchurian stronghold. On the verge of victory, Chiang broke off the attack under intense pressure from the Truman administration to form a coalition with the communists. The coalition failed and the communists used the respite to prepare for and launch a counteroffensive.

The China Lobby coalesced during the post–World War II period of the Chinese Civil War. Truman and his advisers were shocked by the everyday corruption and inefficiencies of Chinese life and concluded that Chiang was an arrogant and corrupt schemer without concern for his own people and thus unworthy of U.S. support. At the same time, State Department officials concluded that the communists were "agrarian reformers" rather than totalitarians. As Chiang's military and economic situation worsened, Truman decided to choke off his support. Mao defeated Chiang and drove his Nationalist forces off the mainland to Taiwan by May 1950, after which the Truman administration announced that its containment policy did not apply to Taiwan. The China Lobby charged Truman with having "lost China," an accusation made more telling in late November 1950 when at least 300,000 Chinese "volunteers" attacked U.S. forces fighting in North Korea. Although the China Lobby called on Truman and his successor, Dwight Eisenhower, to "unleash" Chiang Kai-shek against the communists, this option was never seriously considered at the presidential level.

Thereafter, as hope for the mainland's liberation dwindled, the China Lobby successfully worked to ensure Taiwan's defense from possible communist invasion when Eisenhower concluded a mutual defense treaty with Chiang in 1954 and prevented communist China from taking China's seat at the United Nations until 1971. Senator Barry Goldwater in particular carried on the struggle, protesting President Richard Nixon's 1972 visit to China and later going to court in an unsuccessful effort to stop President Jimmy Carter from withdrawing recognition from Taiwan, recognizing communist China, and abrogating the mutual defense treaty, actions Goldwater described as the "betrayal" of a loyal friend.

—Robert Waters

Further Reading

Koen, Ross Y. *The China Lobby in American Politics.* Edited by Richard C. Kagan. New York: Harper & Row, 1974.

Bachrack, Stanley D. *The Committee of One Million: "China Lobby" Politics, 1953–1971.* New York: Columbia University Press, 1976.

See also: Goldwater, Barry M.; Judd, Walter H.

Chodorov, Frank (1887–1966)

Son of Jewish immigrants, Frank Chodorov was born in New York City. Like his friend Albert Jay Nock, Chodorov was an individualist and an opponent of war and big government. Chodorov played a key role in the conservative movement by representing the "Old American Right," which believed in individual liberty and opposed governmental collectivism as well as foreign intervention.

In 1944 Chodorov started the journal *Analysis*, which in 1951 merged with *Human Events*, a leading conservative magazine, with Chodorov an associate editor. He later became an editor of the revived *Freeman* (now called *Ideas on Liberty*). Chodorov next joined the staff of *National Review*.

Besides numerous articles, Chodorov wrote several books, including *The Economics of Society, Government and State* (1946), *One is a Crowd* (1952), *The Income Tax: Root of All Evil* (1954), and *Out of Step: The Autobiography of an Individualist* (1962). Many of his articles are collected in *Fugitive Essays* (1980).

While living in Chicago, Chodorov read Henry George's *Progress and Poverty* (1879), which provided the economic underpinning of Chorodov's political philosophy of liberty. In 1937, he became the director of the Henry George School of Social Science in New York City, serving until 1942, when Chodorov's criticism of the war and its effects led to his dismissal. While directing the school, Chodorov edited the *Freeman*, a school periodical with the same name as the journal edited during the 1920s by Albert Jay Nock, which was to be revived later. The school's *Freeman* featured articles on land, Georgism, taxation, and intervention.

Chodorov's individualism was grounded in the philosophy of natural rights as authored by God. In a 1954 editorial in the *Freeman*, he wrote that a person's right to his life implied a right to the things he produces. Hence, any taxation of wages and goods is a violation of liberty and natural rights. Instead of taxing income and sales, Chodorov proposed the Henry George alternative of obtaining public revenue from land rent. This, he said, is not a tax in substance, but a market-based payment for the exclusive use of locational values created by the surrounding community and by natural resources.

Taxation was a frequent topic of Chodorov's essays. In the essay "Socialism via Taxation," published in *Analysis* (1946, reprinted in *Fugitive Essays*), Chodorov said that the taxation of productive activity is "highwaymanry made respectable by custom, thievery made moral by law." He regarded the income tax especially as a direct attack on private property because it liquidated the Jeffersonian ideal of inalienable rights and substituted the Marxist notion of state supremacy.

Chodorov's method of promoting individualism was via education rather than political action. As a teacher at the Henry George School, his emphasis was on teaching about liberty. Later, in his *Analysis* office, he taught classes for the Society of Individualists. From 1957 to 1961, Frank Chodorov taught at the Freedom School in Colorado. Chodorov was regarded as a great Socratic teacher.

In 1950, he wrote a pamphlet titled "A Fifty-Year Project" on the "transmutation of the American character from individualist to collectivist." Socialist organizations such as the Intercollegiate Socialist Society were promoting collectivism, and to counter this an individualist freedom organization for students was needed.

Chodorov rewrote the aforementioned pamphlet as an article for *Human Events* under the title "For Our Children's Children." This article attracted both attention and funding, leading directly to the founding of the Intercollegiate Society of Individualists, later renamed the Intercollegiate Studies Institute, which specialized in the distribution of free-market literature to interested students and the sponsorship of lectures by libertarian and conservative speakers on college campuses.

In his introduction to *Fugitive Essays,* Charles Hamilton states that ISI was the "high point" of "Chodorov's care of the Remnant," a biblical term that was a favorite of Nock's. After Chodorov suffered a stroke in 1961, some of his Georgist-libertarian friends founded the periodical *Fragments,* which carried on Chorodov's individualist philosophy under the editorship of Jack

Frank Chodorov

Schwartzman. William F. Buckley's eulogy of Chodorov, "Death of a Teacher," delivered at his funeral on December 31, 1966, was reprinted in the October–December 1966 issue of that magazine.

—FRED FOLDVARY

Further Reading

Edwards, Lee. *Educating for Liberty: The First Half-Century of the Intercollegiate Studies Institute.* Washington, D.C.: Regnery, 2003.

See also: Freeman; Human Events; *Intercollegiate Studies Institute; Jewish conservatives; think tanks, conservative*

Christian Reconstruction

Christian Reconstruction is the name originally given to a program of the Chalcedon Foundation to promote a restoration of Christian faith in every area of life and thought. As curently used, this designation embraces a number of separate but interlocking circles of Calvinist scholars, ministers, and journalists who share Chalcedon's hope, in the foundation's words, in "the earthly victory of Christian principles and Christian institutions" based on "God's revealed system of external law."

Organized in 1965 by the Rev. Rousas John Rushdoony, a Presbyterian minister and missionary, and named after the great ecclesiastical council of AD 451, Chalcedon [kalSEEdon] currently publishes two periodicals, *Chalcedon Report* and *Journal of Christian Reconstruction,* and two audiotape series. Ross House Books is Chalcedon's book publishing arm.

The central tenets of Christian Reconstruction are theological in description but held to be universal in application: presuppositionalism, theonomy, and postmillennialism.

Presuppositionalism refers to the apologetic system of the late Cornelius Van Til, a theologian at Westminster Seminary who taught that revelation is the beginning of all understanding and the promise of God its end. Reconstructionists believe that unstated presuppositions about the character of God and man underlie the problem of authority in modern society. Being religious in character this problem cannot be addressed by reason alone. Reality is defined authoritatively by the sovereign God rather than independently ascertained by autonomous men. Human reasoning, which depends on God's grace, is inescapably circular since it is circumscribed within the framework of God's creation.

Theonomy designates the system of biblical law that undergirds Western civilization and provides a universal standard of justice. Reconstructionists believe that, while Christ died for us sinners, he did not free us from our obligation to follow biblical law in all its detail. Thus, they hold that Old Testament law should be the basis for modern legislation.

Postmillennialism is a theological position regarding the coming fulfillment of God's plans in history. The postmillennial premise, as described by Rushdoony, is that the kingdom of God will grow until it fills the world: "People out of every tongue, tribe, and nation shall be converted, and the word of God shall prevail and rule in every part of the earth. There is therefore a necessity for action, and an assurance of victory."

Leading Reconstructionists have long attracted a conservative audience. Yet from its inception Chalcedon has taken a highly critical view of the conservative movement and does not promote a political program. Several prominent conservatives such as M. Stanton Evans, Phillip M. Crane, and Howard Phillips have been associated or involved with Chalcedon at one time or another. Several early Reconstructionists, such as Gary North, Greg Bahnsen, and David Chilton, were influential within Reconstructionist circles. Many of their works, including book-length replies to critics, have been published by Gary North's Institute for Christian Economics.

—STEVEN ALAN SAMSON

Further Reading

Bahnsen, Greg L. *No Other Standard: Theonomy and Its Critics*. Tyler, Tex.: Institute for Christian Economics, 1991.

Gentry, Kenneth L., Jr. *God's Law in the Modern World: The Continuing Relevance of Old Testament Law*. Phillipsburg, N.J.: P&R Publishing, 1993.

North, Gary, and Gary DeMar. *Christian Reconstruction: What It Is, What It Isn't*. Tyler, Tex.: Institute for Christian Economics, 1991.

Rushdoony, Rousas John. *The Roots of Reconstruction*. Vallecito, Calif.: Ross House, 1991.

See also: *Davenport, John; Rushdoony, Rousas John; Van Til, Cornelius*

Chronicles

Published as *Chronicles of Culture* from September 1977 to February 1986, *Chronicles* is the primary organ of opinion for the paleoconservative movement.

In 1977 John A. Howard retired as president of Rockford College (Rockford, Illinois) but remained president of the Rockford College Institute (founded in 1976, it became the Rockford Institute in 1981). The institute then began to publish *Chronicles of Culture*, edited by Leopold Tyrmand (1920–85), nom de plume of Jan Andrzej Stanisław Kowalski. Tyrmand, a Polish novelist and editor, had emigrated in 1966 and written for the prestigious *New Yorker* (1967–71), but his outspoken anticommunism stood in the way of a literary career in New York. Tyrmand and Howard envisioned *Chronicles of Culture* as faithful to conventional conservative positions on free trade and anticommunism but with an emphasis on literature, art, and music, which they saw as dominated by the Left. "*Chronicles of Culture* originated in a protest against the perversion of American culture by something we call the Liberal Culture," Tyrmand wrote in September 1982.

In its first decade the new magazine grew to some 5,000 subscribers. Part of its influence came from the Ingersoll Awards (funded by the Ingersoll Milling Machine Company of Rockford) it administers. The T. S. Eliot Award for Creative Writing and the Richard Weaver Award for Scholarly Letters are intended to honor important writers and thinkers denied the recognition they deserve because of their right-wing politics. The Weaver Award has gone to movement conservatives, such as James Burnham (1983) and Russell Kirk (1984), but also to philosopher Josef Pieper (1987), sociobiologist E. O. Wilson (1989), and historian Shelby Foote (1997). The more prestigious Eliot Award, a sort of right-wing Nobel Prize, has gone to writers such as Jorge Luis Borges (1983), Eugene Ionesco (1985) and Jean Raspail (1997). Eliot Award–winners V. S. Naipaul (1986) and Octavio Paz (1987) later became Noble laureates. The Eliot Award often has been given to Southerners, including Walker Percy (1988), George Garrett (1989), Fred Chappell (1993), and Madison Jones (1998).

The magazine, originally published six times a year, became a monthly in August 1982. Looking for a colleague, Tyrmand lured a Southern writer, James J. Thompson Jr., from William and Mary College to become his assistant editor. Thompson left in 1982, but not before publishing writers connected with the *Southern Partisan*, an intellectual conservative revue with a Southern perspective. In 1984 Tyrmand hired as managing editor Thomas Fleming, the founder of the *Southern Partisan*. When Tyrmand died suddenly while on vacation in 1985, Howard considered closing down the magazine but was persuaded to let Fleming try his hand as editor.

The next years saw remarkable growth in readership and influence. By 1989 the subscription list had grown to nearly 15,000. Fleming published a distinctive group of writers, including Samuel Francis, Clyde N. Wilson, Paul Gottfried, and Chilton Williamson. Gottfried first called the group paleoconservatives in opposition to the neoconservatives, the "mugged liberals" who had become increasingly influential during the 1980s.

Renamed *Chronicles* in March 1986, the magazine argued for an American nationalism rooted in the classical tradition and the historic Christian faith, defended by economic protectionism and restrictions on immigration, expressed politically by the federalism of the founders, and reflected in literature in the work of the conservative modernists and important Southern novelists, poets, and critics. Fleming's friendship with libertarian Murray Rothbard led to the founding of the John Randolph Club (1990) and the publication of libertarians in *Chronicles*.

The magazine's political influence reached its zenith in 1992 when prominent conservative Patrick J. Buchanan ran against incumbent Republican President George Bush. Buchanan was explicit about his intellectual debt to *Chronicles* and his speech on the "culture war" in American society, delivered from the podium at the 1992 Republican National Convention, clearly echoed *Chronicles'* themes. Buchanan's failed presidential candidacies in 1996 and 2000 paralleled *Chronicles'* own drop in subscribers in the 1990s from nearly 15,000 to about 6,000.

Neoconservatives and libertarians provided triumphalist explanations for this decline: *Chronicles* devoted much space to the editor's positions in favor of the neosecessionist League of the South and against the Clinton administration's bombing of Serbia. In addition, attacks on Protestantism after Fleming's conversion to the Church of Rome may have driven away Protestants, who constitute about two-thirds of American conservatives.

Howard stepped down as president of the Rockford Institute in 1986 but remained president of the Ingersoll Foundation and continued to participate in fundraising and other activities. In 1997 Howard and his successor, Allan C. Carlson, formed The Howard Center for Family, Religion, and Society. Fleming became president of the Rockford Institute but remained the editor of *Chronicles,* which continues to be a distinctive dissident voice on American culture and politics.

—E. CHRISTIAN KOPFF

Further Reading

Fleming, Thomas, ed. *Immigration and the American Identity*. Rockford, Ill,: Rockford Institute, 1995.

Gottfried, Paul. *The Conservative Movement*. Rev. ed. New York: Twayne, 1993.

See also: Buchanan, Patrick J.; Fleming, Thomas; Howard, John A.; paleoconservatism; Rockford Institute

church and state

Thomas Jefferson's famous remark about "a wall of separation between church and State," which has been embraced by the Supreme Court, has replaced in the public mind the meaning of the words in the First Amendment's religion clauses. As then-Justice (later Chief Justice) Rehnquist wrote, however, "[t]here is simply no historical foundation for the proposition that the Framers intended to build the 'wall of separation' that was constitutionalized in *Everson v. Board of Education* (in 1947)." The religion provisions of the First Amendment, consisting of the establishment clause and the free exercise clause, read as follows: "Congress shall make no law respecting an establishment of religion, or prohibiting the free exercise thereof."

The Rehnquist opinion observes that Jefferson is "a less than ideal source of contemporary history as to the meaning of the Religion Clauses of the First Amendment." Absent from the country when the Bill of Rights was written, Jefferson was simply not involved in the legislative drafting of the First Amendment. Jefferson had earlier figured prominently, along with James Madison, in the struggle over religious liberty in Virginia. It was Madison, however, who introduced the original draft of and promoted the adoption of the amendments that became the Bill of Rights. Madison and Jefferson shared similar views on many matters and cooperated during the struggle over religious liberty in Virginia. Nevertheless, in considering Madison's actions in the Congress, as the Rehnquist opinion states, it "is totally incorrect [to] suggest that Madison carried these views onto the floor of the United States House of Representatives when he proposed the language which would ultimately become the Bill of Rights."

The Bill of Rights was proposed and passed as a restraint only against the federal government. At least before the Civil War, the Bill of Rights had no application to the states. Indeed, Jefferson insisted on the primacy of state law in most matters, including religion. Although he read his own views on "separation" into the religion clauses, Jefferson agreed that the federal law had no effect on state laws respecting religion. Thus, in his second inaugural address as president, Jefferson stated that religion "must then rest with States, as far as it can be in any human authority."

When *Everson* invoked the "wall of separation" metaphor, the Supreme Court did something that Jefferson would never have agreed to; it applied the establishment clause for the first time to the states. Thus, even if one agrees with Jefferson's misconstruction of the religion clauses, the Supreme Court's application of the religion clauses represents something very different. The Court's justification for reconstructing the religion clauses has been the claim that the "due process" clause of the Fourteenth Amendment made some or all of the Bill of Rights applicable to the states. As a result, almost all of the federal cases imposing "separation of church and state" have been against state laws. Thus, current constitutional jurisprudence contradicts the original meaning of the religion clauses not only insofar as it insists on a "wall of separation," but also by intruding on matters left to the states.

The great accomplishment of the religion clauses was multifaceted. It not only protected religious liberty at the federal level by guaranteeing free exercise of religion, it freed the federal government from control by a religious group because Congress could not legislate one way or the other on an "establishment" of religion. That prohibited Congress not only from establishing a national religion, but also from affecting the establishments of religion that still existed in some of the states. Thus, the states could and did prefer one religious group over another, while Congress could not. However, that did not mean that the Constitution required neutrality towards religion itself. As evident from the government's practices after adoption of the religion clauses, the framers expected that religion and religious groups would and should play an important role in the life of the nation.

There are many pieces of evidence discussed in the Rehnquist opinion that contradict the "wall of separation" metaphor,

including Thanksgiving proclamations and other actions by presidents and the Congress. In particular, "[t]he actions of the First Congress, which reenacted the Northwest Ordinance for the governance of the Northwest Territory in 1789, confirm the view that Congress did not mean that the Government should be neutral between religion and irreligion." The Northwest Ordinance, which Congress took up on the same day the Bill of Rights was introduced, provides that "[r]eligion, morality, and knowledge, being necessary to good government and the happiness of mankind, schools and the means of education shall forever be encouraged." The Northwest Ordinance is generally known for providing land grants for public schools in the new states and territories, but it also allowed grants for religious schools until Congress limited grants to nonsectarian institutions in 1845. The Northwest Ordinance is significant because, as Jefferson Berkhofer notes, it represented a "consensus upon basic republican goals and principles" and it holds a place in history greater than that of an ordinary piece of legislation.

The original understanding of the religion clauses was most clearly explained by Justice Joseph Story in his legal treatise, *Commentaries on the Constitution* (1833), which states the following:

> The real object of the amendment was, not to countenance, much less to advance Mahometanism, or Judaism, or infidelity, by prostrating Christianity; but to exclude all rivalry among Christian sects, and to prevent any national ecclesiastical establishment, which should give to a hierarchy the exclusive patronage of the national government.

Story observed that this allows "the Catholic and the Protestant, the Calvinist and the Arminian, the Jew and the Infidel [to] sit down at the common table of the national councils, without any inquisition into their faith, or mode of worship."

Justice Story's writings on the Constitution carried great authority. Appointed by President Madison, whose views have been considered so important on the religion clauses, Justice Story relied heavily in his interpretations of the Constitution on the *Federalist Papers,* written by Madison, Hamilton and Jay. Sitting on the Supreme Court for thirty-four years, he spent twenty-four years in close collaboration with Chief Justice Marshall, who himself played a part in Virginia's struggle over religious liberty. Finally, he was the first to write for the Court on the issues of church-state relationships.

Story's explanation reflected the consistency between the religion clauses and the Northwest Ordinance. The Northwest Ordinance was largely the work of Nathan Dane, who like Story was from Massachusetts, and whose endowment at Harvard funded Story's writing. Story praised the ordinance "for its masterly display of the fundamentals of civil and religious liberty," and noted that "the third [section] provides for *the encouragement of religion,* and education, and schools... (emphasis added)." As both Story and Dane understood, on matters of education and religion, the Northwest Ordinance was modeled on the Massachusetts Constitution of 1780, not on the law of Virginia.

In *Terrett v. Taylor* (1815) a unanimous Supreme Court specifically addressed the Virginia law and its Declaration of Rights. The Court ruled that the legislature of the state of Virginia lacked the authority to expropriate land formerly granted to the Church of England. Jefferson had carried the logic of strict separation to the point of influencing the Virginia legislature to pass a statute in 1801 that, asserting its right to all the property of the Episcopal churches in the state, had directed that the churches' property be sold and the proceeds given to the poor. Justice Story spoke for the Court:

... [A]lthough it may be true that "religion can be directed only by reason and conviction, not by force or violence," and that "all men are equally entitled to the free exercise of religion according to the dictates of conscience," as the bill of rights of Virginia declares, yet *it is difficult to perceive how it follows as a consequence that the legislature may not enact laws more effectively to enable all sects to* of their [own] *accomplish the great objects of religion* by giving them corporate rights for the management [of] property, and the regulation of their temporal as well as spiritual concerns. Consistent with the constitution of Virginia the legislature could not create or continue a religious establishment which should have exclusive rights and prerogatives, or compel the citizens to worship under a stipulated form or discipline, or to pay taxes to those whose creed they could not conscientiously believe. But *the free exercise of religion cannot be justly deemed to be restrained by aiding with equal attention the votaries of every sect to perform their own religious duties,* or by establishing funds for the support of ministers, for public charities, for the endowment of churches, or for the sepulture of the dead (emphasis added)."

Even after adopting the "separationist" view in 1947, the Supreme Court's decisions have not always in fact enforced such separation. Indeed, the logic of strict separation is at odds with much of the case law under the religion clauses. In *Sherbert v. Verner* (1963) the Court held that the free exercise clause *required* certain accommodations for religious exercise. Later, in *Employment Division v. Smith* (1988) the Court held that the free exercise clause does not require religious exemptions from laws of general application. In the same case, however, the Court confirmed that government may make certain religious exemptions, even though it is not required to do so. Thus the establishment clause has permitted a number of accommodations not required by the free exercise clause, including: tuition tax credits, exemption of church operated–school employees from unemployment taxes, implied exemption of church operated–school employees from Labor Board jurisdiction, exemption of religious objectors from compulsory military service, property tax exemptions for religious organizations, off-premises public-school release-time programs; and use of Indian trust monies for sectarian education.

The free exercise and establishment clauses, as Justice Goldberg stated in *Abington School District v. Schempp* (1963), "are to be read together, and in light of [their] tolerance for all and to nurture the conditions which secure the best hope of attainment of that end." The failure to read the clauses together has at times created unnecessary tension. Reading the establishment clause in isolation from the free exercise clause has been the basis for promoting the separationist view. As the Court pointed out in *Lynch v. Donnelly* (1984), reading the two together as a single standard, the religion clause "affirmatively mandates accommodation, not merely tolerance, of all religions, and forbids hostility toward any." The purpose of the clauses is to promote and assure the fullest possible scope of religious liberty and tolerance.

—JOHN BAKER

Further Reading

Berkhofer, Jefferson. "The Ordinance of 1784 and the Principle of Territorial Evolution." In *The American Territorial System*, edited by John P. Bloom. Athens, Ohio: Ohio University Press, 1973.

Cobb, Sanford Hoadley. *The Rise of Religious Liberty in America*. New York: Johnson Reprint Corp., 1970.

McClellan, James. "Christianity and the Common Law." In *Joseph Story and the American Constitution*, edited by James McClellan. Norman, Okla.: University of Oklahoma Press, 1990.

See also: Ball, William Bentley; Bill of Rights; due process; Jefferson, Thomas; Neuhaus, Richard John; Rehnquist, William H.; Supreme Court

City Journal

The flagship publication of the Manhattan Institute, the New York City-based think tank dedicated to exploring urban policies from a free-market perspective, *City Journal*'s profile was raised considerably during the eight years of Rudolph Giuliani's tenure as mayor of New York. Giuliani made it very clear he looked to *City Journal* and the Manhattan Institute for novel solutions to urban problems exacerbated by more than a quarter-century of liberal social policy. The successes Giuliani enjoyed in turning around his city are very much *City Journal*'s as well, a point hammered home by Irwin Stelzer in an article in the *Public Interest*, which called *City Journal* "the magazine that saved the city."

The quarterly publication is edited by Myron Magnet, a former Columbia University professor and *Fortune* magazine writer whose works have helped shape President Bush's philosophy of "compassionate conservatism." Indeed, Bush has stated that after the Bible, Magnet's 1993 book *The Dream and the Nightmare: The Sixties' Legacy to the Underclass* is the most important book he's ever read. In *City Journal*, Magnet, senior editor Brian C. Anderson, and a host of prominent contributors regularly examine topics ranging from crime and welfare to race relations and school vouchers. Longtime contributor Heather Mac Donald, in particular, has earned praise for her groundbreaking articles on housing, homelessness, and racial profiling.

City Journal articles routinely offer a mixture of political theory and practical policy analysis, with application far outside the borders of New York City. Oakland's Jerry Brown, Milwaukee's John Norquist, and Indianapolis's Steven Goldsmith are just some of the nation's prominent urban leaders who have relied upon *City Journal* for innovative policy ideas.

—MAX SCHULZ

Further Reading

Magnet, Myron, ed. *The Millennial City: A New Urban Paradigm for Twenty-First-Century America*. Chicago: Ivan R. Dee, 2000.

See also: Magnet, Myron; Manhattan Institute

civil rights

In general, the term *civil rights* refers to rights created and protected by law, including such fundamentals as property and contract rights and the right to use the courts. In modern times, however, the term has come primarily to refer to prohibitions against certain types of discrimination, particularly discrimination on the basis of race. Conservatives strongly support and indeed insist upon a government prohibition of all forms of racial discrimination by government agencies. They are therefore sharply opposed to so-called affirmative action programs insofar as they use racial quotas or any form of racial preferences. Many liberals support such preferences today, however, and do so, paradoxically, in the name of civil rights.

By far our most important civil rights statute is the Civil Rights Act of 1964. Congress understood the Supreme Court's famous 1954 decision in *Brown v. Board of Education*, prohibiting school racial segregation, to establish a constitutional principle prohibiting all racial discrimination by government. By enacting the 1964 measure, Congress meant to ratify, extend, and make effective that principle. This act made the principle applicable to racial discrimination not only by government agencies but also by privately owned public accommodations, such as hotels and restaurants, private employment, and private activities or institutions that receive federal funds. It was quickly followed by the 1965 Voting Rights Act, which imposed drastic but effective methods to end racial discrimination against blacks in voting by disallowing literacy and other tests and by using federal officials to register voters. Finally, the Civil Rights Act of 1968 prohibited racial discrimination in the sale and rental of housing. The result of the these important statutes, it seemed, was that the day of racial discrimination by government was finally over and that the full weight of the federal government was now brought to bear to end such discrimination.

The story of civil rights since the 1964 act, however, has been the remarkable one of administrative agencies and courts effectively standing the act on its head by converting its prohibitions of official racial discrimination into requirements of or permission for such discrimination. The act defines school "desegregation," for example, as the assignment of students to public schools "without regard to their race." The Supreme Court has held, however, that it is consistent with the act for a court to require that students be assigned and transported to distant schools on the basis of race in order to increase school racial integration.

Similarly, the Supreme Court has held that the act's prohibition of racial discrimination by institutions receiving federal funds was not violated by a federally funded university's preferring blacks over whites in granting admissions. The Court has also held that the act's prohibition of racial discrimination in employment was not violated by an employer's preferring blacks over whites in granting promotions. Further, the Court has held that employers may not use such racially neutral ordinary employment criteria as literacy or education level if the effect is to disproportionally exclude blacks, unless the employers can show a "business necessity" for using such criteria. The effect has been to change the act's prohibition of considering race in making employment decisions into a requirement that race be considered.

Conservatives believe that these decisions are incorrect as a matter of law and mistaken as a matter of policy. The busing decisions, for example, have caused an exodus of the mostly white middle class from the nation's public schools, leaving them not more but less integrated, precisely the opposite of the intended result. The disallowing of valid racially neutral employment criteria that disproportionately disqualify blacks has required employers to favor less over more qualified employees. Racially preferential university admissions has meant the creation of a separate body of students, identifiable by race, that is clearly less qualified than regularly admitted students, a situation clearly detrimental to self-esteem, interracial respect and harmony, and academic achievement.

Conservatives believe that a government policy of advantaging some individuals and thereby disadvantaging others on the basis of race is a prescription for racial resentment and conflict inconsistent with the maintenance of a viable multiracial society. They believe that civil rights belong to individuals, not groups, and that the only correct civil rights policy, as a practical as well as a legal matter, is a policy of strict government insistence on neutrality in matters of race.

—LINO A. GRAGLIA

Further Reading

Graglia, Lino A. *Disaster by Decree: The Supreme Court Decisions on Race and the Schools.* Ithaca, N.Y.: Cornell University Press, 1976.

Scalia, Antonin. *Scalia Dissents: Writings of the Supreme Court's Wittiest, Most Outspoken Justice.* Edited by Kevin A. Ring. Washington, D.C.: Regnery, 2004.

See also: affirmative action; diversity; education, public; equal protection; incorporation doctrine; quotas; Storing, Herbert J.; Supreme Court; Thurmond, Strom

Civil War

Some observers may find it odd or even amusing that one of the central issues of contention within the conservative movement is a war fought well over a century ago. Yet one's views on this war—and whether one prefers to call it "The Civil War," "The War between the States," or "The War of Northern Aggression"—says much about one's vision of America's central traditions and their worthiness for conservation.

Was this a war to end slavery and preserve the unitary, national government established by the Declaration of Independence and solidified under the Constitution? Or was it a war between those convinced that states remained essentially sovereign controllers of their own destiny under the Constitution and those convinced that the union was indissoluble? Or was it an attempt by the southern states to exercise their constitutional right to secede, to which the northern states responded with force so that they might continue to use the machinery of the federal government to enrich themselves at the South's expense?

The facts of the Civil War make any of these readings seem at least minimally plausible. Certainly there was a great deal of rhetoric on the Union side to the effect that the South had become uncivilized through its practice of slavery. Certainly much of this rhetoric was hypocritical, given hostile northern attitudes and laws regarding black people. Certainly the practice of chattel slavery in the South was brutal and a violation of the natural law in that it denied many blacks the essential ingredients of a decent life—not only basic personal freedom, but family integrity and the right to worship as they pleased, among other things. And certainly there were substantial differences among Americans—and not just between southerners and northerners—regarding the right of secession. Some northern states had threatened to leave the union during the War of 1812, drafting declarations during their Hartford Convention that defended state sovereignty. Southern states, under the leadership of Thomas Jefferson and James Madison, had asserted their right to "annul" federal legislation harmful to their fundamental interests. Representatives of all the states came together in record time to rebuke the Supreme Court and its decision in *Chisholm v. Georgia* (1793), which declared that only one American government could be sovereign, and that that was the federal government. Yet many contended that secession was illegal, disallowed by the Constitution, certainly without the consent of all the other states. Abraham Lincoln argued that the nation was formed by the Declaration of Independence: that Americans were one people ruled by one set of ideas and a common commitment to human freedom. And for decades Supreme Courts, presidents, and Congress's committed to internal improvements and open markets had been building roads, raising common tariffs and attacking state-based barriers to commerce.

The so-called American system of tariffs and internal improvements had accentuated growing differences between southern, western, and northeastern political, economic, and social life. Northeastern businesses profited most from the tariffs, which made goods from their European competitors more expensive, and northeasterners profited more from internal improvements (roads, harbors, and the like) than people in other sections of the country. Moreover, Americans in the various sections were growing more and

more apart in their cultures. Western frontiersmen sought cheap land and increased migration from the northeast—which would increase the cost of eastern labor; they sought to ban all black migration as a danger to free labor. And the south's economy had gone from a varied one resting only partly on a system of slavery its own people often condemned to an increasingly prosperous dependence on cotton and a slave system many began defending as in accordance with nature and God's will.

Thus, the extent of independent state power, states' economic interests, and even the cultural grounding of each section of the United States were, by the mid-nineteenth century, increasingly in conflict. The election of Abraham Lincoln to the presidency may be seen, then, as merely the match that lit the powder keg. Earlier, Lincoln had occasionally spoken somewhat radically on the topic of slavery. But for the most part he had taken a predictable western position against slavery as a moral (and economic) wrong that should not be extended to the territories. Further, he came into office arguing for mutual restraint and promising to do nothing to harm the South or its slave interests. But southerners, having lost a hotly contested election to a man and a party representing a union of western and northeastern interests, were understandably angry and worried. That cool heads did not prevail was the source of great tragedy, but it was hardly surprising.

The point of greatest contention within the conservative movement revolves around the issue of state sovereignty and the connection (or lack thereof) between localism and slavery and the racism intertwined with slavery in the United States. Some on the Right have had a tendency to romanticize the southern cause and to overlook the real moral enormities of chattel slavery. In this view there was a War of Northern Aggression, by which the North sought to destroy the pre-capitalist, conservative, and agrarian southern way of life. While conservatives respect tradition and historical inheritance, idealizing a lost subculture and using this idealized vision as a means of condemning the mainstream of the American tradition verges on utopianism. To other conservatives, it compromises the coherence of our current tradition and denies our society potentially important defenders. Yet these southern partisans defend central principals of conservatism and of the American tradition: local autonomy and respect for tradition.

Others within the conservative movement reject southern traditions and localism altogether on the grounds that they at one time led to the toleration of slavery. Such thinkers prefer to base their vision of America and its traditions on a reading of the Declaration of Independence that sees America as a single, unitary state dedicated to the protection of individual rights. In this view, the North was morally obligated to invade the South in order to stamp out its evil, slave-based society. To condemn chattel slavery as practiced in much of the South prior to the Civil War is undoubtedly to claim the moral high ground. But other conservatives are highly critical of the basis of this condemnation, which rests on a rights-based ideology and seems to subordinate a respect for heterogeneous traditions as essential to the conservative project in favor of a political religion that makes the individual the center of all things and makes some form of liberal politics inevitable.

A third position, which is neither racially intolerant nor intolerant of local diversity, strikes many as more genuinely conservative. This approach combines respect for traditions with an awareness of their failings and a determination to deal with violations of natural law through gradual, nondisruptive means. It also recognizes that centralized power generally does more harm than good no matter how virtuous its claimed end. In terms of the Civil War, then, this conservative position recognizes that the war was a tragedy of great proportions brought on by sin (and most especially the sin of pride) on all sides.

—BRUCE FROHNEN

Further Reading

Genovese, Eugene. *The Southern Tradition*. Cambridge, Mass.: Harvard University Press, 1994.

Kendall, Willmoore, and George W. Carey. *The Basic Symbols of the American Political Tradition*. Washington, D.C.: Catholic University Press, 1995.

See also: Bledsoe, Albert Taylor; Calhoun, John C.; Davis, Jefferson; Democratic Party; Douglas, Stephen A.; Gildersleeve, Basil L.; Lincoln, Abraham; Owsley, Frank; Stephens, Alexander Hamilton; Southern conservatism; states' rights; Webster, Daniel

Claremont Institute

The Claremont Institute for the Study of Statesmanship and Political Philosophy is a conservative think tank in Claremont, California, seeking to "restore the principles of the American Founding to their rightful, preeminent authority in our national life." The institute's guiding text is the Declaration of Independence, especially its claim that "all men are created equal and are endowed by their Creator with certain inalienable rights."

The institute evolved out of an initiative underwritten by the Intercollegiate Studies Institute called Public Research Syndicated (PRS), which was conceived as an alternative news service and also established the Publius Fellows program, now a signature program of the Claremont Institute. Four students of Harry V. Jaffa at Claremont Graduate School founded the institute in 1979 to institutionalize the incipient objectives of PRS.

Today, approximately twenty staff members now coordinate publishing endeavors, conferences, and lecture series. A measure of the institute's vitality is indicated by the fact that it sponsors a dozen or more panels at the annual national meeting of the American Political Science Association.

The institute has benefited over the years from superior leadership. Larry Arnn led the institute to prominence as its longtime president until he was recruited to Hillsdale College in 2000. Ballistic missile expert and veteran institute employee Brian Kennedy is currently president; he is aided by institute board chairman Bruce Sanborn. The institute also publishes the quarterly *Claremont Review of Books,* which is edited by prominent scholar and institute mainstay Charles Kesler and has in a relatively short time become one of the leading book-review publications in the country. Claremont's distinguished fellows, including Jaffa, William A. Rusher, and Sir Martin Gilbert, as well senior fellows such as Thomas G. West of the University of Dallas and Angelo Codevilla of Boston University, regularly conduct research for the institute.

—MATTHEW BOWMAN

See also: Jaffa, Harry V.; Straussianism

Clay, Henry (1777–1852)

Planter and Whig politician from Kentucky, Henry Clay personified the West in American politics throughout his political career, during which he was Speaker of the United States House of Representatives, senator, secretary of state, and four-time presidential candidate. Clay is perhaps best remembered today as the Great Compromiser and proponent of the "American System." His life spanned almost the entirety of the Old Republic. Clay's Whig Party would in some ways serve as a link between the Hamiltonian Federalists and the Lincoln-Seward Republicans. Clay was not a conservative but he did exhibit some conservative tendencies.

Henry Clay was born in 1777 in Hanover County, Virginia, the son of the Reverend John Clay and Elizabeth Hudson Clay. His father died when he was only four, leaving him to be raised by his mother and stepfather, Henry Watkins. From 1792 to 1796 Clay read law under the famous George Wythe, signer of the Declaration of Independence and perhaps the most renowned jurist of his day. In 1797 Clay moved west to the new state of Kentucky and settled in its most vibrant city, Lexington. There he began practicing law and became involved in local politics. He allied himself with the Jeffersonian Republicans and quickly rose through the ranks. In 1799 Clay married Lucretia Hart, the daughter of the wealthy Thomas Hart, who had recently removed his family from Virginia. His wife's wealth and Clay's growing legal practice gave Clay enough social and financial prestige to secure a position among Lexington's elite. He took a seat in the state legislature in 1803 after only six years in the state, and by 1806 he had been elected to represent Kentucky in Washington.

Clay, after supporting (some said forcing) the War of 1812 as Speaker of the House and consequently becoming known as a leading "War Hawk," began developing his "American System" in the years following the war. Though he opposed the renewal of the Bank of the United States charter before the war, he supported it afterwards as the focal point of his system. The American System included a comprehensive plan of internal improvements (the building of roads, canals, and bridges by the federal government) and protective tariffs, which Clay felt to be necessary to spur the development of American industry. Fellow Republicans saw this as a break from strict construction of the Constitution, free trade, and the traditional preference of agriculture over business, all fundamental to the Jeffersonian philosophy. Charges of closet Federalism were reasonably levied at Clay.

The Jeffersonians' fears were confirmed when Clay backed John Quincy Adams for president in the election of 1824. In the so-called "Corrupt Bargain," Adams was elected president by the Clay-led House, and Clay was subsequently appointed secretary of state. Opponents, led by John Randolph and Andrew Jackson, charged foul play. More than anything else, this scandal kept Clay from ever gaining the presidency. Adams and Clay, along with Daniel Webster, formed a "National" wing of the Republican Party in opposition to the "Democratic" wing led by Jackson and Martin Van Buren. The National-Republicans would eventually evolve into the Whig Party in the 1830s, thus forming the second two-party system.

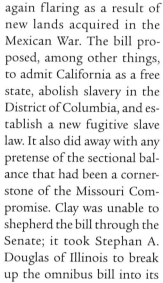

Henry Clay

Clay became known as the "Great Pacificator" and the "Great Compromiser" for his role in the Missouri Compromise of 1820, the Compromise Tariff of 1833, and the Great Compromise of 1850. In each of these compromises Clay was able to gloss over the sectional differences that would eventually explode in civil war. The Missouri Crisis, Jefferson's "fire-bell in the night," was the first true sectional crisis the nation had faced. Clay cooled it by proposing the entrance of Missouri as a slave state, Maine as a free state, and a dividing line within the remaining Louisiana Purchase north of which slavery would be prohibited. This was intended to maintain a balance between slave and free states. A dozen years later, the very protective tariffs called for in Clay's American System precipitated the Nullification Crisis. In order to resist the tariffs that the South felt favored the North and punished the South, South Carolina "nullified" the recently passed tariffs, invoking the power explained anonymously by John C. Calhoun in *The South Carolina Exposition* (1828). Clay proposed a strategic reduction of the tariffs in order to avoid a confrontation between the federal government and that of South Carolina. In 1850 he again proposed a compromise in the form of an "Omnibus Bill" that sought to placate the sectional tempers that were again flaring as a result of new lands acquired in the Mexican War. The bill proposed, among other things, to admit California as a free state, abolish slavery in the District of Columbia, and establish a new fugitive slave law. It also did away with any pretense of the sectional balance that had been a cornerstone of the Missouri Compromise. Clay was unable to shepherd the bill through the Senate; it took Stephan A. Douglas of Illinois to break up the omnibus bill into its component parts and gain its passage. The Great Compromise was Clay's last great moment in politics. He died in 1852.

Clay was a major political actor in the antebellum period and perhaps the consummate American politician. However, he espoused no highly principled political philosophy, certainly none that had lasting power. Even his highly praised speeches contain little substance outside their dealings with the issue of the moment. His sectional "compromises" were superficial, addressing only surface issues and not the fundamental principals that were their root causes. Clay did show a profound dedication to union, which he sought to preserve through his compromises and to strengthen through his American System. His moderate position on slavery gave Clay room to compromise and seek common ground for both sides of the debate. Though a slaveholder, Clay was a leading member in the

American Colonization Society, which hoped to resettle American blacks overseas. He hoped for the eventual end of American slavery but clearly sympathized with the slaveholder's dilemma.

His willingness to compromise does not qualify Clay as a conservative. The very notion of an a priori "system" as developed by Clay deviates from the Burkean notion of an organic society, as do his efforts to industrialize the traditionally agrarian republic.

Clay's influence was cited often by Abraham Lincoln, who had been a Whig. And Clay's American System in many ways prefigures the Republican economic programs instituted after 1861, which are still in many ways dominant. Clay's true significance, then, lies in his pragmatic vision for a united, industrialized, business-dominated America.

—N. ALAN CORNETT

Further Reading

Francis, Samuel. "Henry Clay and the Statecraft of Circumstance." *Continuity* 15 (1991): 45–67.

Hopkins, James F., et al., eds. *Papers of Henry Clay.* 11 vols. Lexington, Ky.: University Press of Kentucky, 1959–92.

Jones, Edwin DeWitt. *The Influence of Henry Clay on Abraham Lincoln.* Lexington, Ky.: University of Kentucky Press, 1952.

Remini, Robert. *Henry Clay: Statesman for the Union.* New York: Norton, 1991.

See also: Randolph, John (of Roanoke); Calhoun, John C.; Lincoln, Abraham

Cleveland, Grover (1837–1908)

Remembered primarily as the only U.S. president to serve two nonconsecutive terms (as the nation's twenty-second and twenty-fourth president), Cleveland left a record as a social and political conservative who fought for honesty and prudent reform in politics as well as free trade.

Elected governor of New York in 1882, Cleveland made his mark in the public arena by aggressively seeking to end the control of the Democratic Party by the corrupt bosses of Tammany Hall. Himself a Democrat, he became upon his election to national office in 1884 the first Democratic president of the United States since the War between the States—winning by the smallest popular margin in American history until the 2000 presidential election. His campaign was hobbled to some extent by news that Cleveland, unmarried at the time, had fathered an illegitimate son. (Acting upon his policy to "above all, tell the truth," he quickly acknowledged his son, and the American public in large part responded favorably to his honesty.) During his first term in office, he married Frances Folsom, who, though not the mother of his son, was a much-admired first lady.

Politically, Cleveland tended to avoid active promotion of proposed legislation, but he acted swiftly to reject legislation with which he disagreed, earning the sobriquet "Old Veto" for wielding the veto-pen more often than any other president to date. His support of free trade cost him reelection, as his proposal to reduce tariffs on foreign goods was contrary to the protectionist tendencies of his Republican opponents, who portrayed Cleveland as a radical and a disloyal American for supporting "the British policy of free foreign trade." In the 1888 election, Cleveland won the popular majority, but his Republican opponent, Benjamin Harrison, garnered more votes in the Electoral College and thus won the election.

Four years later, Cleveland ran again for the presidency on an anti-tariff platform and a call for a fiscally responsible government. He defeated Harrison but was almost immediately forced to face the short, severe economic recession known as the Panic of '93. Amid calls for federal relief, Cleveland was criticized for taking a hands-off policy during this economic downturn. His domestic policy took a different turn when he called out federal troops to break a major railroad strike in the Midwest, which had effectively stopped long-distance shipping of the U.S. mail. His signal achievement in terms of foreign policy lay in his successfully brokering the arbitration of a clear boundary between the South American nations of British Guiana and Venezuela. After leaving office at the end of his second term, he was generally perceived as an honest and virtuous man who despite his personal failings was remembered by many as "Grover the Good."

—JAMES E. PERSON JR.

Further Reading

Brodsky, Alyn. *Grover Cleveland: A Study in Character.* New York: St. Martin's Press, 2000.

Jeffers, H. Paul. *An Honest President: The Life and Presidencies of Grover Cleveland.* New York: William Morrow, 2000.

Welch, Richard E. *The Presidencies of Grover Cleveland.* Lawrence, Kan.: University Press of Kansas, 1988.

See also: free trade

Clinton, William J., impeachment of

The impeachment of and "not guilty" verdict for William Jefferson Clinton, forty-second president of the United States, were the culmination of a series of scandals that began soon after he took office. Many mainstream conservatives believed that the president and his wife, Hillary Rodham Clinton, were so power-hungry that they would bend or break the law to keep the presidency, and so arrogant that they considered themselves above the law. A few conservatives went so far as to accuse the Clintons of treason and to suspect them of murder. Liberals and the Clintons themselves believed that the president and his wife were victims of a "vast right-wing conspiracy."

After promising the American people that he would lead "the most ethical administration" in American history, scandals swirled around the president involving, among other things, land transactions in Arkansas, the sale of access to the White House and other violations of campaign finance laws, and the sale of dual-use technologies such as rockets, computers, and encrypted telephones that potentially could be used against the United States by its enemies. Investigations into these matters by congressional committees and law enforcement officers were stifled by the executive branch, which stonewalled by expanding the doctrine of executive privilege, by suffering simultaneous and profound memory loss, and by taking frequent bathroom breaks during crucial investigative meetings, among other techniques. Without collaborative documentation such as video or tape recordings, investigators could not verify whether the memory losses and weak bladders were real or contrived as a means to avoid testifying.

Ironically, it was not the scandals mentioned above that almost brought down the president but an illicit sexual affair. Throughout Clinton's tenure in Arkansas' government, there were constant rumors that Clinton had had affairs with numerous women. Then, during his campaign for the presidency, an Arkansas woman named Gennifer Flowers came forward claiming to have had an affair with Clinton, an accusation that Clinton denied. Thereafter, stories appeared in the *Los Angeles Times* and the *American Spectator* concerning Clinton's numerous illicit affairs in Arkansas. The *American Spectator* story led a former Arkansas state employee, Paula Jones, to charge Clinton with workplace sexual harassment. The most damaging charge, however, was that Clinton had had an affair with a White House intern, twenty-four-year-old Monica Lewinsky. The president and Lewinsky denied the charge under oath, but DNA evidence was found that proved the president had had sexual relations with Lewinsky.

With hard evidence that the president had committed perjury and obstructed justice, on December 19, 1998, the House of Representatives voted to impeach the president on two counts: for perjury before a grand jury, with 223 Republicans and five Democrats voting for impeachment, and 201 Democrats and five Republicans voting not to impeach; and for obstruction of justice, with 216 Republicans and five Democrats voting to impeach, and 200 Democrats and twelve Republicans voting against impeachment. Two other charges were rejected.

Republicans in the United States Senate were unhappy about the impending impeachment trial, at least in part because public opinion polls showed that the American people opposed it. After efforts to abort it failed, the Senate agreed to a truncated trial with severe limits on evidence, witnesses, and duration. Although the evidence for count one, perjury, was irrefutable—Clinton had lied under oath about the affair with Lewinsky—senators claimed that the crime did not rise to the level of "high crimes and misdemeanors" specified in the Constitution. On February 12, 1999, the Senate voted 45 to 55, with ten Republicans joining the entire Democratic caucus, to acquit the president. On the second charge, obstruction of justice, the vote was 50 to 50, with four Republicans joining the Democrats to vote for acquittal, and Republican Senator Arlen Specter, following the lead of Scottish lairds, voting "not proved."

Although Clinton was not convicted, he signed an "Agreed Order of Discipline" on his last day as president in which he admitted that he had violated the Arkansas code of ethics, and in which he stipulated that he "knowingly gave evasive and misleading an-swers" about the nature of his relationship with Monica Lewinsky. He was also compelled to surrender his license to practice law for five years and was fined $25,000. Earlier, the district judge in the case had fined him more than $90,000 for his perjury. In addition, he settled with Paula Jones for $850,000 and admitted to having had an affair with Gennifer Flowers. Fourteen of his cronies were convicted of other charges, including his deputy attorney general and his successor as governor of Arkansas.

—Robert Waters

Further Reading

Rozell, Mark J., and Clyde Wilcox, eds. *The Clinton Scandal and the Future of American Government.* Washington, D.C.: Georgetown University Press, 2000.

Snyder, K. Alan. *Mission, Impeachable.* Vienna, Va.: Allegiance Press, 2001.

See also: Hyde, Henry; Regnery Publishing; Tyrrell, R. Emmett, Jr.; Wall Street Journal

Cold War

The Cold War refers to the period of high tensions and ideological conflict between the United States and its allies (the West) and the Soviet Union and its allies that existed roughly from the end of World War II in 1945 until at least 1985 and the coming of *glasnost* ("openness") under Mikhail Gorbachev. The phrase "Cold War" was first used and popularized by columnist Walter Lippmann in 1947. The principal condition of the Cold War was the division of Europe into two "blocs," the Western bloc and the communist, or Eastern, bloc. The Cold War is said to have definitively ended during the period from 1989, when the Berlin Wall was torn down and Eastern European nations gained their autonomy from the Soviet Union, to 1991, when the Communist Party collapsed inside the Soviet Union following an abortive coup against Gorbachev.

In the abstract, the division between the democratic West and the communist East seemed foreordained on ideological grounds alone. Many historians and analysts also point to the historic pattern of Russian xenophobia and expansionism as contributing factors to the Cold War. An expanding Soviet empire, even without communist ideology, could have been expected to be a major factor in world tensions. In 1835, for instance, Alexis de Tocqueville wrote in *Democracy in America* that "each [America and Russia] seems called by some secret design of Providence one day to hold in its hands the destinies of half the world."

The proximate origins of the Cold War are to be found in the wartime alliance between the United States, Great Britain, and the Soviet Union against Nazi Germany in World War II. The Atlantic Charter, the agreement that established the alliance of the "Big Three" powers and set out its war aims against Germany, called for unconditional surrender and for self-determination for the Nazi-dominated nations that would be liberated during the war. The ruler of the Soviet Union, Joseph Stalin, made it clear as early as 1941 that one of his key war aims was to expand his territory to the West, at the expense of Poland. At this time the Soviet armies were bearing the brunt of the German war effort, as Britain and the United States were operating on the periphery in Africa. Stalin is said to have been concerned that the United States and Britain would make a separate peace with Hitler, leaving the Soviet Union to fight alone.

President Franklin Roosevelt thought he might be able to forestall Stalin's territorial ambitions by promising to open up a second front in western Europe against Germany in 1942. When military realities precluded the opening of a second front in 1942 (and again in 1943), Roosevelt began to hope

that diplomatic efforts could succeed in keeping the Soviet Union from dominating all of Eastern Europe. Against Winston Churchill's advice, given in 1945, that American and British forces should push as far east as possible before the end of the war, Roosevelt and Supreme Allied Forces Commander Dwight Eisenhower halted the progress of the western armies, thus allowing the Soviet Union to occupy Poland, Czechoslovakia, Hungary, Yugoslavia, eastern Germany and Berlin, Romania, and parts of Iran, Japan, and Austria. At the Yalta conference in January 1945, Roosevelt sought Stalin's agreement that, although the nations of eastern Europe—Poland in particular—would remain under Soviet influence, their governments would be drawn from the various democratic elements within them through democratic elections. Stalin agreed to this, but refused to allow Big Three supervision of the elections, which allowed the Soviet Union a free hand to manipulate the outcome in favor of the communists. This result led the Yalta agreement to be portrayed as a Rooseveltian "sellout" and to become a key step in instigating the Cold War.

Several events in the immediate postwar years determined the course of the Cold War. Soviet support for communist guerrillas in Greece led President Harry Truman to proclaim in 1946 a new policy of opposing communist insurgencies; the policy became known as the "Truman Doctrine," and massive aid to the Greek government succeeded in defeating the communist guerrillas. Truman also bluntly ordered the Soviets out of Iran. In July, 1946, Winston Churchill, turned out of office the previous year, delivered a speech in Fulton, Missouri (President Truman was in the audience) in which he coined the phrase "Iron Curtain" to describe the division of Europe between the Soviet and Western blocs. Also in 1946, George Kennan, then an aide in the American embassy in Moscow, sent his famous cable that articulated the policy of "containment." The policy of containment held that the Soviet Union was an ideological and expansionist power whose extension should be checked by Western counterforce around the world. If the Soviet Union was "contained," Kennan argued, it might eventually evolve into a more traditional and benign Great Power. Kennan's article proved very influential for Western policymakers and was instrumental in inspiring both the Marshall Plan—the program of massive American economic assistance to European nations whose economies had been devastated by the war—and the North Atlantic Treaty Organization (NATO), which was the military alliance Western nations formed to confront the armed might of the Soviet Union and its allies.

Throughout the rest of the 1940s and 1950s, high-intensity ideological warfare and surrogate armed skirmishes in Third World nations characterized the Cold War. Espionage and propaganda took on great importance for both blocs during this period. The United States established a permanent intelligence organization, the Central Intelligence Agency (CIA), and several media directed at the populations of the captive nations behind the Iron Curtain. The most notable of these were the radio networks known as the Voice of America and Radio Free Europe, both supervised by the U.S. Information Agency. Among intellectuals and academics, the Congress for Cultural Freedom was established to promote democratic principles. The CCF founded a journal named *Encounter* that published articles from liberal anticommunist intellectuals. The Hiss case and the Soviet theft of American atomic weapon secrets—culminating in the Soviets' development of the bomb years before our intelligence services expected—raised the issues of espionage and domestic communist activities to a high profile in American politics. Senator Joseph McCarthy of Wisconsin sought to expose Soviet agents in America

through a series of congressional investigations. His tactics were generally regarded as reckless (from whence comes the term "McCarthyism"), and his unpopularity partially discredited anticommunism as a domestic political force.

In 1949, China fell to communist forces led by Mao Tse Tung, setting off recriminations in American politics about "who lost China." Also in 1949, the Soviet Union blockaded Berlin, which was run jointly by the allied powers from World War II, even though it was situated well within the area of Eastern Germany wholly controlled by the Soviets. The blockade was an attempt to get the Western allies to quit Berlin and leave it fully in control of the communists, but a massive airlift of food and other supplies over several months thwarted the Soviet plan. (This was the first of several confrontations over Berlin. The most dramatic came in 1961 when the Soviet Union built the wall dividing the eastern section of the city from the sections administered by the western allies.) When the communist nation of North Korea attacked South Korea in 1950, the United States intervened under the auspices of the United Nations, securing an armistice in 1953 that restored the Korean peninsula to its prewar boundaries.

With the election of Dwight Eisenhower as president in 1952, American foreign policy, under the leadership of Secretary of State John Foster Dulles, entered a phase known popularly as "brinkmanship." Dulles used discrete threats to use the American nuclear arsenal against the Soviet Union to maintain the balance of power in Europe (especially over the Berlin issue) and elsewhere. In 1955, the Soviet Union ended its partial occupation of Austria, but in 1956 the Soviets invaded Hungary to put down an anticommunist rebellion.

With the Cuban revolution of 1959 and the beginning of American involvement in the Vietnam War, the Cold War entered a new phase of superpower skirmishes through proxy states on the periphery of the Third World. In 1961, a poorly executed invasion of Cuba by American-backed Cuban anticommunists ended in disaster. In 1962, the introduction of Soviet medium-range nuclear missiles to Cuba provoked a direct superpower confrontation. The crisis was resolved when the Soviets agreed to remove their missiles in exchange for President John Kennedy's promise that the United States would not try to overthrow the Cuban government of Fidel Castro and that the U.S. would remove its missiles based in Turkey.

The 1970s brought the period known as "détente," after the French word meaning the relaxation of tensions between antagonists. Détente was the product of the diplomacy of President Richard Nixon and Henry Kissinger. Two nuclear arms–control treaties were signed and ratified in 1972. Also in 1972, following secret negotiations by Kissinger, President Nixon went to mainland China, ending America's official enmity with that nation. (Among Nixon's real aims was to exploit the split between the Soviet Union and communist China.) Détente lasted through the Carter administration until the Soviet invasion of Afghanistan in 1979. The collapse of détente was a factor in the election in 1980 of Ronald Reagan, who had long expressed strong anticommunist views. Reagan's presidential campaign platform included a pledge to strengthen U.S. military forces, which had deteriorated during the Ford and Carter administrations.

President Reagan's military buildup was accompanied by tough rhetoric (including a 1983 speech in which he referred to the Soviet Union as "an evil empire," and another arguing that communism would one day be consigned to the dustbin of history), military aid for anticommunist forces in Afghanistan and Central America, and negotiations aimed at an actual reduction in the levels of nuclear weapons on both sides. Following the deployment of American medium-range nuclear missiles in western Europe, the Soviets agreed to Reagan's terms, signing a treaty that eliminated all medium-range missiles in Europe for both sides.

In 1985, the new Soviet leader Mikhail Gorbachev announced the new era of *glasnost* and *perestroika* (restructuring of the economy). Gorbachev intimated his desire for better political and economic relations with the West, and moved eventually to end the Soviet occupation of Afghanistan.

Historians will long argue whether the collapse of communism from 1989 to 1991 should be attributed to the resolute policies of the West under President Reagan's leadership or whether communism was doomed to collapse of its own accord. Conservatives typically maintain that only American strength and resolve could have checked Soviet expansion.

—STEPHEN HAYWARD

Further Reading

Gaddis, John L. *The Origins of the Cold War, 1941–1947.* New York: Columbia University Press, 1972.

Lukacs, John. *A New History of the Cold War.* New York: Doubleday, 1966.

Thomas, Hugh. *Armed Truce: The Beginnings of the Cold War, 1945–46.* New York: Atheneum, 1987.

Wilmot, Chester. *The Struggle for Europe.* New York: Harper, 1952.

See also: anticommunism; arms control; Casey, William J.; Cold War revisionism; containment; Eisenhower, Dwight D.; émigré intellectuals; Foreign Policy Research Institute; Hiss-Chambers trial; isolationism; Kennan, George; LeMay, General Curtis E.; Lippmann, Walter; MacArthur, Douglas; movement conservatism; Nixon, Richard M.; Radio Free Europe; Reagan Doctrine; Reagan, Ronald; Rosenberg case; Thatcher, Margaret

Cold War revisionism

Cold War revisionism refers to the historical scholarship that blames the West, and principally the United States, for starting and sustaining the "Cold War" tensions between the West and the Soviet Union and its allies in the years after World War II. Cold War revisionism was mostly a phenomenon of the "New Left" in the 1960s, but elements of this critique have also been voiced by some on the Right.

The key premise of Cold War revisionism is a benign view of Soviet communism and Soviet war aims during and after World War II. Revisionists hold that the United States and its Western war allies (especially England) were insensitive to legitimate Soviet desires to have friendly nations as a buffer zone between it and Germany, and that the Allies behaved aggressively and threateningly at the various conferences, such as Yalta and Potsdam. In this view, Stalin imposed communist dictatorships on the nations of Eastern Europe only in response to the aggressive hostility of the West. Revisionists further argue that the failure of the United States and Britain to open a second front against Germany in France in 1942 or 1943, as had been pledged to the Soviet Union early in the war, justified Stalin in his distrust of the Western allies.

In addition to a charitable view of the nature and motives of the Soviet Union, revisionism also holds a mendacious view of the nature and motives of the United States and Britain. American opposition to Soviet domination of Eastern Europe is explained as a function of American desire to keep an "open door" for commercial advantage. Britain was hoping to reestablish its imperial might, badly eroded by the war. Revisionists further argue that the use of the atomic bomb against Japan was not necessary militarily, but was done strictly for the political purpose of intimidating the Soviet Union.

The Cold War in general is said to have served the domestic political interest of President Harry Truman and subsequent politicians of both political parties.

Cold War revisionism flourished in the 1960s, as the New Left developed the revisionist theme as a part of its effort to discredit the Vietnam War. Several of the leading books on the subject (see "Further Reading") were published in the 1960s and early 1970s. Cold War revisionism among the isolationist Right, however, began earlier.

Conservative revisionism differs from New Left revisionism in its basic skepticism of U.S. intervention in foreign wars, along with a skepticism about the necessity of warfare in general. Conservative critiques such as Harry Elmer Barnes's *Perpetual War for Perpetual Peace* (1953) see wars as essentially unnecessary and primarily the result of political ambition rather than fundamental causes. America, according to this view, was deceitfully led into both World War I and World War II by the ambitious and self-serving presidents Woodrow Wilson and Franklin Roosevelt. Roosevelt, Barnes charged, collaborated secretly with Britain before 1941, deliberately worsened relations with Japan in the hope that the U.S. would be attacked, and knew that the attack on Pearl Harbor was in prospect. All this to overcome the anti-interventionist sentiment held by the majority of the American people.

With respect to the Cold War, Barnes and other conservative revisionists have written that President Truman's actions were motivated by a need to shore up his and the Democratic party's sagging political prospects at home. Barnes agreed with the New Left that Britain was motivated by imperial considerations and that the atomic bomb was used against Japan to intimidate the Soviet Union. Conservative revisionism differs from New Left revisionism in its view of the Soviet Union. Conservative revisionists hold no illusions about Stalin's ambitions or the nature of the Soviet regime, but they argue that American entanglement in European defense after World War II was not necessary. Conservative revisionists hold that revisionism, and the isolationist policy that revisionism would suggest, is the key to peace.

Despite the efforts of the Cold War revisionists, the "conventional" historical account of the Cold War—that it was started chiefly because of Soviet ideology and aggressiveness in Eastern Europe—remains the factually stronger case.

—STEPHEN HAYWARD

Further Reading

Fleming, D. F. *The Cold War and Its Origins*. New York: Doubleday, 1961.

Gardner, Lloyd. *Architects of Illusion: Men and Ideas in American Foreign Policy*. Chicago: Quadrangle, 1970.

Kolko, Gabriel. *The Politics of War: The World and United States Foreign Policy*. New York: Random House, 1968.

Maddox, Robert. *The New Left and the Politics of the Cold War*. Princeton, N.J.: Princeton University Press, 1973.

Steel, Ronald. *Pax Americana*. New York: Viking, 1967.

See also: Cold War; Crocker, George N.; isolationism

Collegiate Network

A consortium of independent newspapers published at leading America universities, the Collegiate Network provides editorial and financial outreach to conservative and libertarian student journalists. Governed by Collegiate Network, Inc. (CNI) and administered by the Intercollegiate Studies Institute (ISI), the Collegiate Network (CN) offers papers such benefits as operating and incentive grants, internships, training seminars, and an advertising cooperative. Under the ISI umbrella, the CN has reached historic

levels of funding and membership, including nearly 100 publications.

While CN papers vary considerably in editorial perspective and investigative focus, they share a commitment to presenting an alternative to the dominant liberal viewpoint of established campus publications. The *Dartmouth Review, Stanford Review, Cornell Review*, and *Wabash Commentary* are among the CN's longest-running papers. In 1994, *Light and Truth*, a CN-affiliated magazine at Yale, received national media attention after disclosing Yale's misuse of a $20 million grant earmarked for Western Civilization courses.

Although early independent student journals such as the *New Individualist Review* (University of Chicago), *Alternative* (Indiana University), and *Badger Herald* (University of Wisconsin–Madison) flourished on campuses during the sixties and seventies, the origins of the CN can be traced to 1979. That year, University of Chicago students Tod Lindberg and John Podhoretz launched *Counterpoint*. The Institute for Educational Affairs (IEA), a national think tank founded by Irving Kristol and other neoconservative intellectuals, soon extended publishing assistance to *Counterpoint* and to other conservative student papers.

When Leslie Lenkowsky became IEA president in 1986, he invited IEA-supported papers to associate formally as the Collegiate Network. The CN later passed through the IEA's successor organization, the Madison Center for Educational Affairs, before ISI assumed its sponsorship and T. Kenneth Cribb Jr. became president of the newly established parent group, CNI.

In addition to Lindberg and Podhoretz, CN papers have spawned such journalists and policy analysts as *National Review* editor Richard Lowry, authors Dinesh D'Souza, Ann Coulter, and Wendy Shalit, and commentators Tucker Carlson and Laura Ingraham. Other CN editors have transitioned from collegiate to professional journalism through

CN-funded internships with leading national newspapers and journals.

The CN has not been without its critics. Writers affiliated with the liberal Center for Campus Organizing in Cambridge, Massachusetts, have dismissed CN papers as "personal slamsheets and self-promotion tools for writers seeking a job with a New Right think-tank after college." But the hostile reception accorded to conservative papers on many campuses, particularly in the form of property theft, physical threats, and boycotts against advertisers, suggests a different interpretation: that CN member papers threaten entrenched "politically correct" interest groups, as suggested by civil libertarians Alan Charles Kors and Harvey A. Silverglate in *The Shadow University* (1998). Despite such tactics, CN papers continue to thrive by giving university students an alternative to administration-sponsored news.

—MORGAN N. KNULL

Further Reading

Knull, Morgan N. "The New Alternative Press on Campus." *World & I* 16, no. 2 (2001): 58–63.

Ridgley, Stanley K., ed. *Start the Presses: A Handbook for Student Journalists.* Wilmington, Del.: ISI Books, 2000.

See also: foundations, conservative; Intercollegiate Studies Institute; think tanks, conservative

Collier, David S. (1923–83)

Along with Russell Kirk and Henry Regnery, David S. Collier was one of the founders of *Modern Age*, a periodical that was to some extent modeled on T. S. Eliot's quarterly, the *Criterion*. Since its inception in 1957, *Modern Age* has provided a forum for more reflective and scholarly traditionalist conservatives to speak on matters of history, biography, literature, and the state of American culture. Henry Regnery praised his colleague's edito-

rial skill, writing that Collier "never wavered from the purpose of *Modern Age* as Russell Kirk defined it in the first issue, Summer 1957: 'Our purpose is to stimulate discussion of the great moral and social and political and economic and literary questions of the hour, and to search for means by which the legacy of our civilization may be kept safe.'"

Although he hailed from a long-established Maryland family, Collier grew up in the North Chicago suburb of Wilmette. He was a much-decorated soldier during World War II, serving on the staff of General Douglas MacArthur in the Philippines and staying on with American occupation forces in Japan after the war, rising to the rank of captain. After returning to the United States, he received his bachelor's, master's, and doctoral degrees from Northwestern University, studying under William McGovern and Kenneth Colegrove. He was a visiting instructor at the American University of Beirut and the University of Tokyo during the early 1950s. In 1957 he was named executive director of the Foundation for Foreign Affairs, an organization with which he held a long-standing relationship; he was president of the foundation from 1970 until his death.

Also in 1957, Collier joined with fellow Midwesterners Kirk and Regnery to found *Modern Age: A Conservative Review* (later subtitled "A Quarterly Review"), with Collier serving as the magazine's first publisher. As George Nash has written, *Modern Age* "was primarily oriented toward the traditionalist or new conservative segment of the conservative revival. Among the twenty-seven original 'editorial advisors,' only two—Wilhelm Röpke and David McCord Wright—were economists, while none was widely known as a convert from Communism." The board included such figures as Donald Davidson, Eliseo Vivas, Richard M. Weaver, and Anthony Harrigan.

During the first years of its existence, *Modern Age* struggled to attract subscribers and pay its printer invoices; the small staff volunteered its labors, spending much of its time (it seemed) simply raising money to maintain the endeavor. Kirk gave up the editorship of *Modern Age* in 1959, to be succeeded by Eugene Davidson, with Collier serving as coeditor. Collier became editor of the magazine in 1970 and served in that capacity until his death in 1983.

Regnery issued Collier's first book, *Radicals and Conservatives* (cowritten with William McGovern) in 1957. Collier's other books tended to be edited collections of essays by scholars and authorities on international affairs: they include *Berlin and the Future of Eastern Europe* (1963), *The Conditions for Peace in Europe* (1969), and several others. Noted for his knowledge of and prudent approach to foreign affairs, Collier was appointed by President Gerald Ford to serve as a public delegate to the United Nations General Assembly in 1977. Upon the occasion of Collier's death six years later, Henry Regnery wrote, "David Collier was a man of high principles, and through his work as editor of *Modern Age* and in his activities in international relations through the Foundation for Foreign Affairs he made an important contribution to our understanding of the realities of the world in which we live as well as to the intellectual basis of conservatism."

—JAMES E. PERSON JR.

Further Reading

Collier, David S., and Kurt Glaser, eds. *Elements of Change in Eastern Europe: Prospects for Freedom.* Chicago: Regnery, 1968.

———. *Western Integration and the Future of Eastern Europe.* Chicago: Regnery, 1964.

See also: Modern Age

Collier, Peter (1939–)

A leader of the student civil rights movement and antiwar protests of the 1960s at Berkeley, fellow traveler in the New Left and Black Panther movements, and editor of *Ramparts*, Peter Collier began to move away from the Left after the Vietnam War, when he judged that leftists were united more by disdain for America than by concern for the tyranny of communist regimes in Southeast Asia.

In voting for Reagan in 1984, Collier and his fellow radical David Horowitz waved goodbye to the leftist radicalism they had once so defiantly championed. Telling their story in "Lefties for Reagan" in the *Washington Post Magazine*, Collier and Horowitz offered a "conservative assessment" of what they should have known during their twenty-five years of radical rebellion: "We live in an imperfect world that is bettered only with great difficulty and easily made worse—much worse."

Collier continued his alliance with Horowitz throughout the 1980s, this time in publicizing their unyielding disagreement with the Left and in exposing what they thought were its follies and perfidy. In 1986, Collier and Horowitz founded the Center for the Study of Popular Culture and its imprint, Second Thoughts Books. Together they published the periodical *Heterodoxy* and collaborated on biographies of the Fords, Roosevelts, and Kennedys, as well as on political anthologies, commentary, and pamphlets. They even wrote speeches for Bob Dole in 1988.

In 2002 Collier established Encounter Books, the imprint of Encounter for Culture and Education, Inc. (supported principally by the Bradley Foundation), where until his retirement in 2005 he served as publisher and editor in chief of conservative nonfiction works of history, culture, and political analysis. Representative Encounter titles include *Mexifornia: A State of Becoming* (2003), by Victor Davis Hanson, and *Rape of the Masters: How Political Correctness Sabotages Art* (2004), by Roger Kimball.

In addition to the books mentioned above and some fiction, Collier has written *The Fondas: A Hollywood Dynasty* (1991) and *Medal of Honor: Portraits of Valor Beyond the Call of Duty* (2003).

—WILLIAM F. MEEHAN III

Further Reading

Collier, Peter, and David Horowitz. *Deconstructing the Left: From Vietnam to the Clinton Era*. Studio City, Ca.: Second Thoughts Books, 1995.

Collier, Peter, and David Horowitz. *Destructive Generation: Second Thoughts about the '60s*. New York: Summit Books, 1989.

Collier, Peter, and David Horowitz, eds. *Surviving the PC University: The Best of* Heterodoxy. Studio City, Calif.: Second Thoughts Books, 1993.

See also: Horowitz, David

Collins, Seward B. (1899–1952)

Seward Bishop Collins, publisher and editor of the *Bookman* (1927–33) and the *American Review* (1933–37), was raised in New York as the heir to a national chain of tobacco shops. He attended Princeton University, where his literary and theoretical interests were piqued by the works of H. L. Mencken, Bertrand Russell, and Havelock Ellis. He professed liberal views and held editorial positions with the *Brooklyn Daily Eagle* and *Vanity Fair*. In 1927, Collins bought the *Bookman*, a respected highbrow monthly journal devoted to books and literary matters. Initially the publisher only, Collins later assumed editorial responsibility as well.

It was in the summer of 1928 that Collins experienced a philosophical conversion. After reading the works of the humanist writers Irving Babbitt and Paul Elmer More, he renounced the tenets of modernism and proclaimed himself a humanist. Collins's politics naturally became conservative and his political interests began to supercede his literary interests in the pages of the *Bookman*.

The *Bookman* was succeeded by the *American Review* in April 1933. This new monthly became a vehicle by which Collins sought to publish searching critiques of the New Deal and modernity more broadly. The journal was devoted to contemporary American economics, politics, philosophy, and literature, and for a little over four years it served as a major forum for several conservative and traditionalist movements, notably the New Humanists, the Neoscholastics, the Distributists (including G. K. Chesterton and Hilaire Belloc), and the Southern Agrarians (Herbert Agar, Cleanth Brooks, Donald Davidson, Andrew Lytle, Frank Owsley, John Crowe Ransom, Allen Tate, and Robert Penn Warren). Relations with the Agrarians were especially close until Collins began more explicitly to advocate a pro-fascist, strongly centralized government.

The year 1936 was marked both by the divorce of Collins from the Agrarians and the marriage of Collins to his longtime associate editor, Dorothea Thompson Brand. The *American Review* ceased publication a year later. In 1941, Collins and his wife retired to a farm in New Hampshire, where they lived the rest of their lives.

—MARK C. HENRIE

Further Reading

Hoeveler, J. David, Jr. "The American Review." In *The Conservative Press in Twentieth-Century America*, edited by Ronald Lora and William Longton. Westport, Conn.: Greenwood, 1999.

Hoeveler, J. David, Jr. "The Bookman." In *The Conservative Press in Twentieth-Century America*, edited by Ronald Lora and William Longton. Westport, Conn.: Greenwood, 1999.

Schneider, Gregory L. *Conservatism in America since 1930*. New York: New York University Press, 2003.

Stone, Albert E., Jr. "Seward Collins and the *American Review*: Experiment in Pro-Fascism, 1933-1937." *American Quarterly* 12 (1960): 3–19.

See also: American Review; Bookman; *fascism*

Colson, Charles W. (1931–)

Born in Boston, Charles "Chuck" Colson attended Brown University and earned his degree in law from George Washington University. He served in the Marine Corps and worked as a senatorial assistant and as a lawyer before being appointed Special Counsel to President Nixon in 1969. While serving in this position, Colson also became a member of the Committee to Re-elect the President, which led to his involvement in the Daniel Ellsberg case. Several months before the case was tried, Colson converted to Christianity, and in 1974 he pled guilty to obstruction of justice. He served seven months at Maxwell Prison in Alabama.

Colson's experience in prison impressed him with the need for criminal justice reform, while his recent conversion convinced him that the effort to aid prisoners should be the work of the church. This led him to found Prison Fellowship Ministries in 1976. He funded this project with investments from the royalties of his autobiographical book, *Born Again*, published the same year, in which he told the story of his involvement in the Watergate scandal and of his conversion. Directed toward rehabilitating prisoners through evangelization and visitation, Prison Fellowship Ministries includes programs for both prisoners and their families. It has become the largest organization in the world dedicated to prison outreach, with programs around the world and the support of churches of many denominations. In 1993, Colson received the Templeton Prize for Progress in Religion for this work.

In addition to directing this prison ministry, Colson has also been active in addressing modern culture from a Christian perspective. He is the founder of and a commentator for "BreakPoint," a daily radio program which discusses current events from a Christian worldview. He is also the author or editor of a number of books, including *Kingdoms in Conflict* (1987), which addresses the relationship between church and state, and coauthor of *How Now Shall We Live?* (1999), which examines the role of Christians in the secular culture.

Today, Colson is arguably one of the three or four most prominent evangelical conservative figures in the nation, one whose support is assiduously courted by conservative politicians. He has also played a leading and highly visible role in shaping and publicizing the "Evangelicals and Catholics Together" project spearheaded by, among others, Father Richard John Neuhaus.

—ALEXANDRIA CHIASSON

Further Reading
Aitken, Jonathan. *Charles W. Colson: A Life Redeemed*. New York: Doubleday, 2005.

Colson, Charles W., and Nigel Cameron, eds. *Human Dignity in the Biotech Century: A Christian Vision for Public Policy*. Downers Grove, Ill.: InterVarsity Press, 2004.

Colson, Charles W., and Harold Fickett. *The Good Life*. Wheaton, Ill.: Tyndale House, 2005.

Colson, Charles, and Richard John Neuhaus, eds. *Your Word Is Truth: A Project of Evangelicals and Catholics Together*. Grand Rapids, Mich.: W. B. Eerdmans, 2002.

See also: Protestantism, evangelical

Commentary

America's most influential post–World War II neoconservative monthly magazine, *Commentary* was founded in November 1945 by the American Jewish Committee. Despite its neutral title, the magazine was designed to be an explicitly Jewish publication. "The main difference between *Partisan Review* and *Commentary*," Elliot E. Cohen, its first editor, remarked, "is that we admit to being a Jewish magazine and they don't." Cohen believed that, in the aftermath of World War II, Jewish American writers and intellectuals had something important to say to other Jews and to the rest of the nation, and that it was time for them to discard the stance of estrangement that had been fashionable among intellectuals during the 1920s and 1930s. Less parochial than its predecessor, the *Contemporary Jewish Record*, *Commentary* sought to explore the creative possibilities in a symbiosis of American and Jewish identities.

Commentary's staunch anticommunism during the 1940s and 1950s stemmed in part from Cohen's goal of ending the disaffection of the Jewish intellectuals from the American mainstream. To achieve this, Cohen believed, Jews must be in the forefront of America's defenders.

Commentary experienced a crisis in the mid-1950s. Its editorial board fell apart when Nathan Glazer joined Anchor Books, Irving Kristol moved to London to help start *Encounter* magazine, and Robert Warshow died of a heart attack. In addition, Cohen fell into the deep depression that would lead to his suicide in 1959. Norman Podhoretz became the magazine's new editor with the February 1960 issue, and *Commentary* entered a new period in its history. Podhoretz proposed to dilute the Jewish content of the magazine and to move it to the Left.

Indeed, the appeal and intellectual respectability of the New Left was due in part to the support it received from *Commentary*.

The magazine's February 1960 issue contained the first of three installments from Paul Goodman's *Growing Up Absurd*. Future issues featured essays by Staughton Lynd, Norman O. Brown, Robert Heilbroner, and other left-wing gurus of the 1960s. Within six years, *Commentary*'s circulation had skyrocketed from twenty thousand to sixty thousand. By then, however, the magazine had already begun moving to the Right. Initially, this was in response to the New Left's assault on the independence of the university and to the appearance within the civil rights movement of radical "black power" advocates preaching salvation through violence.

Even more important, Podhoretz wrote, was *Commentary*'s dismay over the New Left's "ferocious hatred of 'Amerika' and the coarse and vulgar caricature it was making of the serious radical critique we had been trying to develop of American society and American foreign policy." *Commentary*'s move to the Right was accelerated by specifically Jewish concerns as well, most notably the 1967 Six-Day War in the Middle East and the eruption of anti-Semitism among black and Hispanic "community activists" during New York City's 1968 teacher's strike. "Whatever the case may have been yesterday, and whatever the case may be tomorrow," Podhoretz claimed, "the case today is that the most active enemies of the Jews are located not in the precincts of the ideological Right but in the radical Left." Podhoretz would come to regret his role as one of the godfathers of the New Left.

During the 1970s, *Commentary* gradually moved beyond "Cold War liberalism." There was scarcely a major conservative interest that the magazine did not defend, including religion, capitalism, the military, traditional standards of literature and art, the conventional family, the integrity of the university, opposition to governmental social planning, and antagonism to political radicalism in the Third World.

Commentary

Commentary's prominent position within the American Right did not go unchallenged. Paleoconservatives such as Paul Gottfried and Stephen Tonsor accused it of being a Trojan horse of neoconservatism and of working to displace Old Right conservatives from positions of leadership within the conservative intellectual movement. Paleoconservatives and traditional conservatives pointed in particular to the magazine's seeming lack of concern with the size, cost, and cultural impact of government programs. *Commentary* was also one of the American Left's favorite targets. *Tikkun*, a left-wing Jewish bimonthly, was established in 1986 specifically to fill the vacuum on the Left caused by *Commentary*'s apostasy. Michael Lerner, *Tikkun*'s editor, declared that *Tikkun* would speak for those Jews who, in contrast to *Commentary*, were still moved "by the radical spirit of the Prophets and who insist on keeping their message alive."

Both before and after Podhoretz's formal exit as editor of *Commentary* (he was replaced by Neal Kozodoy in 1995) the magazine has reflected his commitment to a specific reading of American patriotism that emphasizes the need for an aggressive foreign policy aimed at remaking regimes around the world. Podhoretz, who remains editor-at-large, has written of the need for the United States to win what he sees as an already raging "World War IV," pitting America against radical Islam and the states aiding and/or sheltering it.

—EDWARD S. SHAPIRO

Further Reading

Dorrien, Gary. *Imperial Designs: Neoconservatism and the New Pax Americana.* New York: Taylor and Francis, 2004.

Grumet, Elinor. "Elliot Cohen: The Vocation of a Jewish Literary Mentor." In *Studies in the American Jewish Experience*, edited by Jacob R. Marcus and Abraham J. Peck, 9–25. Cincinnati, Ohio: American Jewish Archives, 1981.

Katz, Milton. "*Commentary* and the American Jewish Intellectual Experience." *Journal of American Culture* 3 (1980): 155–66.

Podhoretz, Norman. *Breaking Ranks.* New York: Harper & Row, 1979.

———. "Ideas, Influence and American Politics: The Case of *Commentary*." *Survey: A Journal of East and West Studies* 29 (1985): 20–26.

Shapiro, Edward S. *A Time for Healing: American Jewry since World War II.* Baltimore, Md.: Johns Hopkins University Press, 1992.

Steinfels, Peter. *The Neo-Conservatives: The Men Who Are Changing American Politics.* New York: Simon & Schuster, 1979.

See also: Jewish conservatives; media, conservative; neoconservatism; Podhoretz, Norman

common law

Lawyers tend to define the common law as "judge-made" law—that is, as a set of legal doctrines and rules set forth in precedent and applied by judges. Historians tend to see the common law as specifically the *English* common law, by which they wish to differentiate the custom-based laws of England enforced by its royal courts from various forms of statute- or code-based laws.

Conservative thinkers have a particular affinity for the common law because it is rooted explicitly in custom. From its beginnings in pre-Norman (that is, pre-1066) England, the common law has taken for its rule the established norms of the community in which the dispute originated. For example, if it was established practice in Leeds that a shopkeeper leasing his premises had to abandon any improvements (such as custom shelving) at the end of the lease without receiving compensation, this rule would apply to all relevant disputes in Leeds. But it would not necessarily apply in Kent, where compensation might be required. In either case the courts would follow set procedures in determining the local custom and applying it, over time, to all similar cases.

Custom (or "usage") was therefore given legal effect in a particular area, or in some cases in an entire jurisdiction. Not just any custom was given such effect, however. Common-law judges attempted to enforce only those customs which were found to be rooted in ancient practice, to have been continuously and peaceably applied over the years, and to be reasonable, clear and certain, compulsory (rather than merely voluntary) as a rule of action, and consistent with other customs. Thus, in the common law the time-tested traditions of the people themselves were respected, even as the rule of law was upheld against infringement by any particular actor—private person, public person, or even an arm of the government.

In the American experience, common law has been both more broad-ranging and more localized that many might think. Before independence, each colony had its own customary law, often with very little overlap with the English common law or even with the "common law" of any other colony. Moreover, the English common law itself owed much of its form and content to the combination of church (or canon) law and the Roman (or civil) law once called the *ius commune*—or, as Edmund Burke referred to it, "the common law of Europe." Such factors shaped the law of equity, the principles of fairness, that became part of the common law in America and directly influenced numerous customs.

When the colonies became independent states they faced a decision as to whether and to what extent to adopt the common law. Different states accepted different amounts of English common law, "receiving" it by integrating it into their precedents. That is, states might accept the rulings of English courts handed down in various cases while rejecting those made after a certain date (usu-

ally the date of America's independence). States also might reject some English rules (primogeniture, for example) in their entirety.

State statutes generally determined what rulings would be accepted or rejected in a particular jurisdiction. As time went on, states increasingly looked to statutes to clarify and regularize their common law. Such changes at first left the system of common law intact. Statutes often had been used to "correct" certain common-law rules, but these statutes were almost always interpreted narrowly so as to maintain the primary role of custom or usage. However, over the course of the nineteenth century there was increasing pressure to codify the common law. That is, reformers, particularly of a progressivist bent, sought to regularize states' laws by replacing custom with detailed statutes. Slow at first to gain acceptance, the codification movement essentially won the day during the twentieth century.

There are two primary reasons for the demise of the common law as a ruling system in the United States. The first is the increasing role of the federal government in the lives of the people and in areas formerly governed solely by state law. An increasing reliance on the federal power to regulate commerce in order to establish uniform standards and markets in areas ranging from food safety to taxation resulted in an explosion of federal statutes. And because federal law has been, since the late nineteenth century, purely a creature of statute law, federal expansion has meant statutory expansion. That is why today, for example, sales contracts, even those between two private citizens exclusively operating within the same town, will be adjudicated according to the federal Uniform Commercial Code.

The second important factor in the decline of the common law has been the effort of lawyers to do away with it. Attorneys, as a rule, have attacked custom or usage as embodying outmoded and unfair rules of action. Groups like the American Law Institute brought progressivist lawyers together to "restate" the common laws of all the states in a uniform manner. Moreover, these re-statements, along with various model codes, including the Model Penal Code, often dispensed with rules long established in most jurisdictions in deference to a "better view" defined as such by the lawyers themselves.

In every state, codification has brought ever-greater uniformity to the rules of action used by lawyers, merchants, professionals, and citizens of all types. Most observers have applauded such changes for the increased predictability and efficiency that have accompanied them. Of course, what has been lost is the integrity and often fine-tuned suitability of communal standards and historic traditions, along with the ability of judges, juries, and state legislatures to use prudent judgment in order to determine whether local laws fit local circumstances.

Ironically, the common law survives today in part through misapplication of its principles to constitutional law cases. Most judges today, including many self-identified conservatives, continue to give force to precedents they know to be faulty in constitutional cases when—the Constitution being a written, statutory law—precedent should apply only as a matter of prudence. This crude reliance on *stare decisis* notwithstanding, the common law's greatest legacy remains the form of thought it embodies—one in which we look to long-established practice in determining how we should act under current circumstances, altering our common norms only gradually and according to the tenor of changing conditions.

—BRUCE FROHNEN

Further Reading

Hogue, Arthur R. *Origins of the Common Law.* Indianapolis, Ind.: Liberty Fund, 1986.

Kiralfy, A. K. R. *The English Legal System.* London: Sweet & Maxwell, 1960.

Plucknett, Theodore F. T. *A Concise History of the Common Law.* Boston: Little, Brown, 1956.

Walsh, William F. *Outlines of the History of English and American Law.* Littleton, Colo.: Fred B. Rothman, 1995.

See also: Bill of Rights; Constitution, interpretations of; constitutionalism; custom; Kent, James; law and economics

community

In the years following the French Revolution, conservative thinkers reacted with relatively unanimous skepticism or outright horror at the forces of individualism and progressivism that had erupted with such violence against ancient traditions and institutions during that conflagration. Conservatives like Edmund Burke and Joseph de Maistre recoiled at the new conception of the human person as an atomized and fully free moral agent, possessed of abstract natural rights to be realized unconstrained by social limits. When entrenched as a movement of the people, they argued, this radical expression of individual will would not only destroy the whole structure of moral order on which western civilization was founded, but would also result in the rise of absolutist despotism.

The optimism of the Victorian Age found little that was convincing in this dour conservative outlook. With the popular penetration of the powerful idea of progress, the autonomous individual and his freely expressed will began to seem a self-evident and unmitigated good. The values of the age of progress—the maximum attainment of personal freedom combined with the maximum attainment of efficiency, mobility, uniformity, neutrality, and objectivity in the exercise of political, economic, and social power—were likewise taken largely as articles of faith. When Jeremy Bentham claimed to be able to legislate for all of India from the comfort of his English study, it was hardly puffery or idle boasting. Rather, as Robert Nisbet has noted, it epitomized the profound confidence that the new political theorists had in the objective power of reason to solve all problems of human relations and in the individual as the universal, primary unit of social and political order. Bentham, Mill, and other nineteenth-century apostles of progressive liberalism paid little heed to conservatives such as John Ruskin who were calling attention to the social cost of rationalism and individualism: the scattering of families, increased urbanization, and the disintegration of ancient allegiances—or, in other words, the destruction of communities of belonging that had persisted for centuries. To liberal theorists, this historical process was viewed not as tragic, or even (usually) as regrettable, but rather as signaling the glorious rebirth of man as he became progressively emancipated from the tyranny and irrationality of the past.

The skeptical attitude of European conservatives towards progressivism was never quite as strongly shared by their American counterparts. America, by the very nature of its discovery, settlement, and political birth, was literally a "new world"; a place of nearly limitless opportunity constrained only by the strength of a man's back and the sharpness of his wits. The frontier spirit, buttressed by a Puritan heritage that emphasized individual responsibility and strict moral self-discipline, made the idea of the self-sufficient, rugged individual seem a rather conservative ideal, one which did not necessarily threaten the bonds of family, church, and community. In *Democracy in America*, Alexis de Tocqueville described the New World in biblical terms—a pristine continent provided to Europe's castoffs as if newly risen from the receding waters of the great flood, a nearly empty and seemingly inexhaustible land in terms of both sheer physical space and material wealth. This geographic wonder imprinted itself on the American Puritan soul, Tocqueville explained, creating a new kind of man far less susceptible to the chaotic passions of his cramped and world-weary European cousins. Even so, Tocqueville warned that despite their natural advantages, should Americans ever give themselves over entirely to their private interests, the social bonds and traditional institutions necessary for a democratic republic would fail.

Democracy in America remains the necessary starting point for understanding the dynamics of community in America, and Tocqueville's insights into the push and pull between American individualism and the need for communal ties certainly have been played out across the spectrum of American conservative thought. The dominant direction of this thought, however, has not been kind to strong defenses of community. The American experiences of Revolution against Britain, Civil War and abolition of slavery, suffrage and the political enfranchisement of women, the civil rights struggle, and the sexual revolution all have tended to promote, or be incorporated into, a view of history as the story of man's progressive shedding of oppressive yokes—yokes usually proclaimed as necessary constraints by their defenders. American political thought has always had, and has continued to develop, a muscular theory of the individual rights of man. Conservative thinkers, to gain purchase on the American mind, have been forced to trace their policy and social prescriptions to some basis in individual rights. American conservatism has therefore developed an instrumentalist and mechanical view of community and social bonds: they exist as a means to preserve the maximum freedom and efficiency of individual action. When David Walsh, for example, argues against abortion in *The Growth of the Liberal Soul* (1997), he does so on rights-based grounds: abortion weakens the sanctity of all individuals, but this idea provides the necessary foundation for personal autonomy and freedom, runs the argument, so it must be defended.

The conservative veneration of individual autonomy as the central truth that must be vindicated by the social and political order reached its height with the twentieth-century development of libertarianism, and in particular with that strain of euphoric libertarianism preached in the writings of Ayn Rand. In both her nonfiction essays and especially in her fictional characters, Rand elevated the uncompromising, self-sufficient, immensely capable individualist and capitalist into a conservative hero. For the Christs of Rand's gospel of selfishness, communal restraints and the demands of personal, concrete relationships and small social groups were evil impediments to be overcome on the way to a cross of self-actualization. This vision of conservative virtue as something utterly opposed to communal belonging gained considerable influence on conservative thought during America's postwar struggle against the Soviet ideology of collectivism, and it continues to exert a strong influence on the conservative tradition today.

Not all postwar conservatives, however, were so blinded by their hatred of communism that they abandoned all concepts of true community. Conservative traditionalists like Russell Kirk decried the influence of libertarianism on traditional communities and the networks of social obligations inherent in words like kin, church, village, class, caste, and craft. Kirk's broadsides against libertarian individualists were passionate: he denounced the "decadent fervor" (Marion Montgomery's term) of the libertarians, and declared that any cooperation between libertarians and conservatives was akin to advocating a "union of fire and ice." Two of the most thoughtful defenses of traditional community as a conservative ordering principle were published within a year of Kirk's *Conservative Mind* (1953): Nisbet's *The*

Quest for Community (1952) and Eric Voegelin's *The New Science of Politics* (1953).

Nisbet begins his study on the place of community in American political and social life by examining the failed promises of progress. By the postwar period, America had filled up. A sense of dread and ennui had spread through society, and the dominant tropes of psychospiritual expression were no longer found in terms like optimism, progress, change, and reason, but rather alienation, disintegration, decline, and insecurity. Americans, according to Nisbet, no longer seemed to trust or valorize the selfish Randian hero. The problem, he thought, was not technological tyranny or consumer greed or increasing secularism, but the distribution of political power. Modern man's nervous preoccupation with finding meaning in community is a manifestation of the profound social dislocation caused by the unique power structure of the Western political state. As Western political power had become increasingly centralized, impersonal, and remote, it had atomized the individual and relegated communal interests and relationships to the realm of private personal preference. Nisbet locates the profound unrest in the American soul not so much in the disappearance of communal relationships but in the utter dissociation of those relationships from the exercise of real political and economic power. Traditional communities and the religious, familial, and local ties that bind them have not so much been lost, in Nisbet's view, as they have become irrelevant at the deepest levels of meaning. It is here, in the unmediated exposure of the individual will to the impersonal power of the state (and to a lesser extent, the market), that Nisbet finds the root cause of man's spiritual crisis.

Voegelin's *New Science* tracks a similar course, providing conservative thought with a powerful analytical tool for understanding the spiritual dimensions of the phenomena

Nisbet so clearly describes. For Voegelin, modernity could be summarized as a heretical commitment to Gnosticism, or in other words, a fundamental dissatisfaction with the uncertainties and limits of existence. Impatience for moral meaning and certainty beyond the humble limits of traditional communities leads the Gnostic thinker to imbue human existence in the here and now with the ultimate meaning reserved by traditional Christianity for the next life. By "immanentizing" the Christian eschaton, Voegelin explains, modern man took on the project of remaking existence according to the dictates of political ideology.

Both Nisbet and Voegelin note the paradox that modernity is both marked by nearly continuous warfare and a universally declared desire for peace. Nisbet persuasively argues that with the dissociation of traditional communities from the centers of political power, the modern disciplines of war, mechanization, bureaucracy, and mass communication become invested with a strong sense of moral identity and belonging. Voegelin described how the ardent commitments once reserved for local religious communities had been transferred to mass movements which stood as surrogate moral communities and provided an otherwise missing sense of historical purpose.

During the latter stages of the Cold War, and especially since its end, American conservatism has taken up the mantle of optimism and regained some of its earlier confidence in the rugged individual. Ronald Reagan's seemingly single-handed defeat of the Soviet empire is a powerful symbol in contemporary conservative thought of the moral worth of one individual's iron will. Taking their cue from Reagan, many conservative institutions and publications today seek a new conservative synthesis between the primacy of individual freedom and the need for social belonging. The ideals of this synthesis are put on display in the presidency of George W. Bush, who has managed to conjoin strong religious convictions and a stated commitment to preserving the traditional family and prepolitical communities with an underlying progressivism and a nearly Gnostic commitment to creating unrestrained political and economic freedom abroad.

Whether such a synthesis can successfully be maintained remains to be seen. There is good reason to be skeptical. With one of the most unique, eloquent, and deeply conservative voices of the late twentieth century, Wendell Berry has fashioned from his career a kind of long, poetic lament for the final passing of rural America and of its people, places, rites, and rituals. Community, for Berry, is ultimately about membership: it is a group of people embedded in a place and a network of memory who belong to one another. Within such a community, even individual moral decisions must account for that belonging. As a brilliant essayist and naturalist, Berry has offered in works such as *The Unsettling of America* (1978), *The Gift of Good Land* (1981), and *Sex, Economy, Freedom and Community* (1993) a stinging critique of the false communities of war, international markets, and sexualized consumerism. A central theme throughout is the way in which modern structures break apart that which authentic communities bind together: consumption and production, sex and fertility, freedom and responsibility. Berry demonstrates persuasively that no amount of moralizing will check the corrosive character of abstract freedom, especially economic freedom. As a result, even in a political period of supposed conservative ascendancy, local familial, religious, and rooted communities continue to suffer decline because they are unable to provide a plausibly authoritative account for, not to mention enforce, those norms rooted not in law, markets, or choice, but in tradition, faith, and a deep respect for the particularity of place.

—CALEB STEGALL

Further Reading

Lasch, Christopher. *The True and Only Heaven: Progress and Its Critics.* New York: Norton, 1991.

MacIntyre, Alasdair. *After Virtue: A Study in Moral Theory.* Notre Dame, Ind.: University of Notre Dame Press, 1981.

Percy, Walker. *Signposts in a Strange Land.* Edited by Patrick Samway. New York: Farrar, Straus & Giroux, 1991.

Voegelin, Eric. *Science, Politics and Gnosticism.* 3rd ed. Wilmington, Del.: ISI Books, 2004.

See also: Berry, Wendell; distributism; individualism; Kirk, Russell; localism; mediating structures; Nisbet, Robert A.; Quest for Community, The; Voegelin, Eric

Cone, Carl B. (1916–95)

Carl B. Cone was one of the leading American figures associated with the revival of interest in Edmund Burke during the post–World War II era. A professor of history at the University of Kentucky from 1956 until his death, he was the author of what is still considered to be the best American study of Edmund Burke: *Burke and the Nature of Politics: The Age of the American Revolution* and *Burke and the Nature of Politics: The Age of the French Revolution*, published by the University of Kentucky Press in 1957 and 1964, respectively. Cone was correspondent and friend to leading Burke scholars, such as Russell Kirk, Peter Stanlis, and Ross Hoffman, and a frequent contributor to the *Edmund Burke Newsletter*. Cone was one of the first scholars to draw upon the new mass of original sources found among the Fitzwilliam Papers, a private collection of 2,500 manuscript letters to and from Burke that was released in 1949 and had previously lain dormant for almost a century. Cone's study of Burke was thus the first to present a full, integrated biographical analysis of Burke's thought in the context of his day-to-day political career, masterfully employing the historical method to marshal and interpret a wide range of source material. In Cone's interpretation, Burke elevated party politics above "placemen" and self-interest, rooting it instead in deliberations on the common good of the British empire.

Cone was associated with American conservatism from the scholarly sidelines. His viewed contemporary American politics through the prism of his studies on Burke and the eighteenth century. As he once observed, "Burke studies are a very self-conscious part of our contemporary conservative revival." Of course not every new American Burkean was a conservative, but almost all of the traditionalist "new conservatives" of the 1950s and '60s were Burkeans. Burke's thought, indeed, was central to these new conservatives in that it provided them, according to Cone, with "the unifying, pervasive principle which [they] so desperately sought. Through Burke, modern conservatism became connected with the Middle Ages and antiquity, finding support in immutable law, of divine origin, anterior to positive law, and concerned with the moral duty and the achievement of justice in the social order." The Catholic element in emergent American conservatism was during this early postwar period dominant, and Burke was a focal point for American Catholics seeking to make transatlantic connections between the heritage of Europe and the legacy of the American founding. Cone was among this group of American Catholic scholars. He was president of the American Catholic Historical Association in 1967. He was also the author of *Torchbearer of Freedom* (1952), a study of Richard Price, and *The English Jacobins: Reformers in Late 18th Century England* (1968).

—Jeffrey O. Nelson

Further Reading

Cone, Carl B, ed. *Hounds in the Morning: Sundry Sports of Merry England: Selections from the*

Sporting Magazine, 1792–1836. Lexington, Ky.: University Press of Kentucky, 1981.

———. *The University of Kentucky: A Pictorial History.* Lexington, Ky.: University Press of Kentucky, 1989.

See also: Burke, Edmund; Stanlis, Peter J.

Conquest, Robert (1917–)

Robert Conquest is the preeminent chronicler of the evil inflicted on the world by the Soviet Union. His 1968 classic, *The Great Terror* (updated in 1990), remains the most thorough account of Joseph Stalin's horrific consolidation of power in Soviet Russia through the use of mass murder and intimidation. Another book, *Harvest of Sorrow* (1986), examines the government-sponsored blight and famine imposed on the Ukraine in the 1930s that took the lives of more than 14 million people. In total, Conquest has authored nearly a score of books on history, politics, and international affairs. One of his latest, *Reflections on a Ravaged Century* (2000), approaches the twentieth century as one, as he told C-SPAN's Brian Lamb, that saw "20 million people get killed in peacetime in one country, 50 million in another, [and] 20 million or 30 million . . . killed in wars."

A prolific scholar, Conquest's writings have hardly been confined to the study of Soviet perfidy. Conquest is something of a modern Renaissance man. He served in the British infantry in Bulgaria in World War II and later in the diplomatic corps. He is a fellow of England's Royal Society of Literature and has served as literary editor of the *Spectator* of London. Conquest has produced works of poetry and literary criticism as well as two novels (one authored with Kingsley Amis, the other a science fiction novel). In 1997 Conquest received the American Academy of Arts and Letters Award for light verse. Conquest holds dual American and British

citizenship and is a senior fellow at the Hoover Institution.

—MAX SCHULZ

Further Reading

Conquest, Robert. *The Dragons of Expectation: Reality and Delusion in the Course of History.* New York: W. W. Norton, 2005.

———. Stalin: *Breaker of Nations.* New York: Viking, 1991.

See also: anticommunism

Conscience of a Conservative, The

It could be argued that no other book had a greater impact on the American politics of the second half of the twentieth century than did Barry Goldwater's *The Conscience of a Conservative* (1960). Before its publication, Goldwater was an attractive but controversial senator from a small western state (Arizona), a political comer who might one day become chairman of a Senate committee, a long-shot vice presidential possibility. After its publication, Barry Goldwater became the political heir to Senator Robert A. Taft of Ohio and Senator Joseph R. McCarthy of Wisconsin, the hope of disgruntled Republicans, party-less Independents, and despairing conservative Democrats, and the spokesman for a national political movement.

Goldwater was a skilled politician but not a professional writer. *The Conscience of a Conservative* was ghost-written by L. Brent Bozell. Brother-in-law of William F. Buckley Jr., Bozell had been considered by many to be a better debater and almost as good a writer as Buckley when both were undergraduates at Yale. And having served as Goldwater's speechwriter in the 1950s, Bozell was quite familiar with the senator's political philosophy. Published in April 1960, *The Conscience of a Conservative* sold 85,000 copies in its first month; by June the book appeared on the *New York Times* bestseller list. Eventually, 3.5 million copies sold, making it one of the most popular political works of the 1960s and prompting comparisons to Paine's *Common Sense*.

Why was this slim 125-page political manifesto so popular? Well-written, crisp, clear, and concise, the book insisted that conservatism was not old-fashioned or out of date any more than "the Golden Rule or the Ten Commandments or Aristotle's *Politics* are out of date." The conservative approach, Goldwater (or rather Bozell) wrote, "is nothing more or less than an attempt to apply the wisdom and experience and the revealed truths of the past to the problems of today." Many have tried and failed to offer a more succinct definition of conservatism's role in politics.

Second, *The Conscience of a Conservative* addressed the issues of the day in a breathtakingly direct way. Agricultural subsidies? There should be a "prompt and final termination of the farm subsidy program." Organized labor? Enact state right-to-work laws and limit contributions to political campaigns to individuals, barring both unions and corporations from same. Taxes? The government "has a right to claim an equal percentage of each man's wealth and no more." In the area of foreign policy and national security, Goldwater proposed a seven-point program to achieve "victory" over communism, including military superiority, maintenance of defense alliances like NATO, and the cessation of U.S. aid to communist governments that had used the money "to keep their subjects enslaved." We should, he said, encourage the captive peoples to "overthrow their [communist] captors," foreshadowing the Reagan Doctrine of the 1980s.

Third, it was an original work of politics and philosophy, a persuasive fusion of the three major strains of conservatism in 1960—traditionalism, classical liberalism or libertarianism, and anticommunism. In the most quoted passage of *The Conscience of a Conservative*, Goldwater argued that a decisive turn toward freedom and away from government would come when Americans elected to public office those who proclaimed: "My aim is not to pass laws, but to repeal them. . . . If I should later be attacked for neglecting my constituents' 'interests,' I shall reply that I was informed their main interest is liberty and that in that cause I am doing the very best I can."

This one book introduced conservatism as a major new factor in national politics, helping to lay the foundation for the Reagan Revolution of the 1980s and the Gingrich-led capture of Congress in the 1990s.

—LEE EDWARDS

Further Reading

Edwards, Lee. *Goldwater: The Man Who Made a Revolution*. Washington, D.C.: Regnery, 1995.
Perlstein, Rick. *Before the Storm: Barry Goldwater and the Unmaking of the American Consensus*. New York: Hill & Wang, 2001

See also: Bozell, L. Brent; Goldwater, Barry M.

conservatism

Conservatism is a philosophy that seeks to maintain and enrich societies characterized by respect for inherited institutions, beliefs and practices, in which individuals develop good character by cooperating with one another in primary, local associations such as families, churches and social groups aimed at furthering the common good in a manner pleasing to God.

Often defined simply as a predisposition to conserve existing political and economic structures, conservatism generally is seen as having its roots in opposition to the radical innovations of the French Revolution of 1789. In that revolution, established hierarchies in politics, religion (especially the

Catholic Church, in France heavily influenced by an all-powerful monarchy), and society at large were overthrown in favor of an abstract theory of human equality that proclaimed an age of reason yet ushered in years of oppression and mass executions known as the Reign of Terror. The generally acknowledged founder of modern conservatism, the Irish-born British statesman Edmund Burke, wrote his masterpiece, *Reflections on the Revolution in France* (1790), in opposition to this revolution in its early stages, predicting the terror to come and arguing that the drive to remold society according to any abstract theory, including the revolutionaries' Rights of Man, must lead to tyranny and bloodshed.

Unfortunately, conservatism's modern origin in opposition to revolution has led many to define it in simply negative terms, as a kind of "stand-pattism" or opposition to change. And conservatism *is* "against" many things to which contemporary liberals in particular are attached. Principally, conservatives reject liberals' faith in the ability of political planners to "perfect" human nature through a combination of economic incentives (subsidies and the like) and, more crucially, the reshaping of character through therapy and progressive education. Fundamentally, the liberal's goal is to liberate individuals from inherited institutions, beliefs, and practices. Policies like no-fault divorce and politically correct speech codes and courses of study put into action the liberal desire to remold people into autonomous individuals "liberated" from prejudice and other historical inheritances so that they may build their lives on the basis of radically free, unencumbered choices constrained only by the certainty that all people, choices, and lifestyles are morally equal.

Conservatism is opposed to this radically individualist view of man's nature and goals. Some who are labeled "conservative" stop here. Skeptics of a conservative predis-

position, whether conscious followers of eighteenth-century philosopher David Hume or modern neoconservatives, accept many institutions put in place by liberals (the centralized administrative and welfare state being the prime example) so long as they do not descend into overtly revolutionary policies and activities. These stand-pat conservatives offer no transcendent set of standards by which to judge political and moral developments, resting on skepticism and faith in the inherent strength and goodness of modern American institutions and ideologies, taken in their patriotic mold.

But as a full-fledged philosophical outlook, conservatism does not stop here. It is not constituted by mere pessimism concerning human nature. Nor, despite some conservatives' romanticization of eras bygone, does it aim simply to restore what once may have been. To the contrary, conservatism defends a positive and fully integrated view of the individual and his role in society. True, conservatives are too skeptical of the power of abstract reason to believe that politicians can improve human nature, though they believe that politicians may corrupt it. True, conservatives believe that the individual, shorn of his inherited social ties, will act less morally because he will lose the bonds of affection that keep pride and selfishness in check. But these are mere defensive responses to the overreaching claims of liberalism and its radical outgrowths. The roots of conservative opposition to liberalism lie in a very positive conception of the human person and the possibilities of social life.

Conservatives are attached, not so much to any particular regime or form of government, as to what they believe are the requirements for a good life for all peoples. In the American context, conservatives defend the ordered liberty established by the Constitution and the traditions and practices on which that constitution was built. In particular, the common law understanding of custom as a necessary basis for law and public action and the primary role of local associations in framing the character and lives of the people are central to the conservative vision of America. Because conservatives believe that people live in their families, associations, and communities more than in their government, they seek to maximize the number of important relationships available to individuals as they seek to minimize the role of particular politicians and policies in dominating, destroying, or displacing these associations.

Conservatives' rejection of liberals' claims that they may, if only given the political power, reshape individuals into more caring, healthy members of richer communities rests in part on an appreciation of the importance of private property and free markets. These social institutions serve as important bulwarks of individual and group initiative against state planning. Free markets form an important structural component of a good society, from the conservative perspective, because they allow individuals and the groups to which they belong to work and trade together, free from undue interference from politicians seeking to dictate what people should make or buy, or how they should live. But economic goals are not ends in themselves. In particular, economic efficiency, measured in the short term, may dictate the elimination of jobs or entire sources of production that are of critical importance to a local community and its members. What Joseph Schumpeter called the "creative destruction" of capitalism may often be inimical to a people's existing practices and community. The conservative would choose to conserve that people's way of life rather than the unbridled search for efficiency and profits, even if that search might ultimately issue in more material comforts (at the expense of established traditions).

Ideological defenses of economic freedom are unconservative because they posit one universal spring of human action—the desire for material gain. Such reductionism denies free will and the need for individuals to join with their fellows in common service to the common good. Thus, those in the political coalition often called the conservative movement, be they libertarian or neoconservative, who see in capitalism the source of human goodness and progress toward ever-better societies and individuals are not, in the philosophical sense being defended here, conservative. Such individuals may join with conservatives in fighting a common foe (centralized governmental intervention), but in fact they share more with liberals than with conservatives because they seek freedom (defined merely as the absence of restraints, be they wholesome or harmful) or material progress as man's goals, rather than the leading of rich lives in a multitude of diverse local associations.

Like most movements, the conservative political movement has brought together people of differing viewpoints on the basis of certain important shared goals. The conservative movement has undergone changes in recent decades as the threat posed by communism has waned, which has deprived the movement of an issue that in the past provided significant cohesion and motivation for cooperation. As a result, philosophical cleavages in the movement have become more pronounced and cooperation between segments with differing viewpoints more difficult to sustain. Moreover, conservatism as a distinct body of thought is concerned more with preserving and enriching the Western tradition of political, religious, and social thought and institutions than with "progress" for its own sake, even if that progress is brought about through economic prosperity. Conservatives, following their philosophical godfather, Burke, believe that any society that maintains decent rules of public conduct, allowing families to form and maintain their integrity, encouraging individuals to form groups with their fellows in pursuit of common ends and respecting the central role of religion in the lives of its people, is worthy of deference and loyalty. But it is specifically to the Western tradition—informed and shaped by Judeo-Christian institutions, beliefs, and practices—that they look for the model of a proper society and social order.

Conservatives believe that there is a natural order to the universe, governed by a natural law that gives mankind general rules concerning how to shape their lives in common and as individuals. The natural law is not a detailed code, spelling out how men should act in every possible situation. But it provides general guidelines prohibiting acts such as murder and indicating the central importance of moral decency (best summed up in the Golden Rule) and of institutions, like the family, in which alone decent character can be formed. Traditions flesh out these general principles (for example, some societies rely more on extended families than do others). But should individuals or societies violate natural law principles, such as by devaluing the family and its life- and generations-long ties, they will find themselves suffering (for example, through an increase in juvenile crime and alienation), because natural law tells us what is needed to form decent lives for ourselves and our communities.

Some have argued that this moral vision can be sustained without recourse to religion. But philosophers at least from Cicero onward have acknowledged that natural law is not fully coherent in the absence of a creator and recognition that men are meant not to live as the flies of a summer, but rather for eternity, and that their good must be therefore measured in light of eternity rather than short-term gain or pleasure. Moreover, while some individuals can discover the principles of natural law through reason, to put them into practice in a manner that makes sense for their community requires far more. It requires immersion in a living culture,

habituation to the proper ways of acting, genuine affection for one's fellows that only grows from daily interaction and, perhaps most important, religion. Conservatives are defenders of culture, and culture comes from the cult, or religious practices of a people. A people grows together from its common worship. As individuals develop common liturgical practices, be they a formal liturgy or the simple singing of hymns, they also develop social habits concerning things like cuisine, art, and daily ritual. These common habits bind them together as a people into a common culture. They also tie, forever, the culture of a people with its common religion.

The Judeo-Christian tradition at the root of Western civilization is doubly important because it provides the fullest, most coherent understanding available concerning human nature and the proper goals of man and society. The West inherits from the Israelites, to whom God gave the Ten Commandments through Moses, the understanding that religious norms are superior to those of politics—that we should kneel before God, not Caesar, and that religious, higher law norms must be enunciated and put forward vigorously by religious leaders who are institutionally separated from political leaders. Our civilization owes to Christianity the understanding that the character of each individual is crucial, that each of us is created in the image of God and is capable of salvation as an individual, seeking communion with the creator. Thus conservatives, in keeping with their tradition, value each life as sacred, free, and responsible, with duties, rights, and a central goal of leading a life as much in accordance with the will of God as is humanly possible.

The conservative vision is deeply tied to the tradition of Christian humanism, in which each of us has the right and the duty to serve God in our vocations and daily relations. The institutions, beliefs, and practices to which conservatives are attached are in many ways universal: all of us have the potential to lead good lives of piety and service to the families, associations, and societies into which we are born. But the constitutional freedoms and ordered liberty that have grown from the Western tradition, being intimately tied with Western culture and religion, are not easily transferred to other societies. This means that conservatives, unlike their neoconservative allies, are loath to become greatly involved, particularly at the level of state action, with other cultures. While the saving of souls and the undertaking of other charitable acts are worthy endeavors, to attempt to simply transplant Western political and cultural institutions abroad, in the conservative vision, is prideful and wrongheaded. Thus, while defending families, local associations, private property, and free markets may be conservative, attempting to export a particular version or combination of these natural goods may disrupt or even destroy a society and, by disturbing people's time-tested expectations, the exporter does evil where he should do good. It is central to the conservative temperament that, in politics as in medicine, one should first do no harm.

—BRUCE FROHNEN

Further Reading

Frohnen, Bruce. *Virtue and the Promise of Conservatism: The Legacy of Burke and Tocqueville.* Lawrence, Kan.: University Press of Kansas, 1993.

Kirk, Russell. *The Conservative Mind: From Burke to Eliot.* 7th ed. Washington, D.C.: Regnery, 2001.

Lewis, C. S. *Mere Christianity*. San Francisco: Harper, 2001.

See also: authority; Buke, Edmund; Buckley, William F., Jr.; common law; custom; family; ideology; individualism; Kirk, Russell; liberty; mediating structures; moral imagination; natural law; prejudice; prescription; progress; rule of law; science and scientism; technology; tradition; traditionalism

Conservatism in America

Penned by a distinguished professor of political science at Cornell University, Clinton Rossiter, *Conservatism in America* (1955), subtitled in its 1962 edition "The Thankless Persuasion," reflected the attempt by academic elites in the early 1950s to understand the emerging conservative movement in America. Rossiter was sympathetic with some elements of the conservative critique of the period, but maintained that his goal was "to sober and strengthen the American liberal tradition, not to destroy it."

In *Conservatism in America*, Rossiter argued that, at least in America, conservatism was a matter of subrational "temperament" rather than a set of political principles. In fact, he wrote, "the reasonable man finds conservatism hard to embrace because he is asked to distrust reason." He saw only a slight difference between a "conservative liberal" and a "liberal conservative," and argued that liberalism and conservatism were essentially and properly united within a Whig view of history. Quoting Macaulay favorably, he argued that the conservatives' role was to defend the "progress" made by the previous generation of liberals. In America, liberals would seek to "enlarge" liberties and conservatives to "preserve" them, but the direction of American history toward more liberty—or more liberalism—was clear and inexorable. In Rossiter's view, the conservatives' foremost duty was "to bring stability to the national community."

This role Rossiter was willing to concede to American conservatives; but he would concede little more. Following Louis Hartz, he claimed that "the American tradition" *is* "liberalism." To Rossiter this meant that only a temperamental conservatism in substantial agreement with liberal principles could prosper in America. He recognized that in his time there were some Americans committed to drawing links between genuinely nonliberal European and American conservatism, but he was highly critical of these traditionalists and dismissed Burke as "irrelevant" in America.

On this subject, the patronizing tone of a fundamentally liberal Ivy League professor intrudes into Rossiter's work. For example, he subtitled his chapter on traditionalist "ultra-conservatives" such as Russell Kirk, "With Edmund Burke in Darkest America." In this chapter, he argued that "to accept [the European conservative] tradition unreservedly is to reject the liberal tradition flatly, and thus to move outside the mainstream of American life"—and consequently to become irrelevant or, worse, destabilizing to the regime. Rather than studying European conservative thought, he recommended that the "prudent" Federalists be treated as "a kind of collective Burke" by American conservatives.

The three pieces of advice that Rossiter offered in his conclusion reinforced his fundamental allegiance to the liberal tradition. First, he argued that American conservatism must throw off "pseudo-conservatives," which for Rossiter meant tempering both the John Birch Society and "ultra-conservatives" such as Barry Goldwater and William F. Buckley Jr. Second, he argued that the "natural" conservative class in America was the business class, and so he recommended that American conservatism repudiate the anticapitalist critique that has been a persistent feature of the traditionalist European Right. Finally and most succinctly, Rossiter argued that conservatism in America must "maintain [its] historic links with liberalism."

Rossiter's book contained many perspicacious observations about American political development; it was thoroughly researched and included an extensive bibliography; it sought to make conservatism respectable for liberal academics by defining it as a temperamental attitude toward change. But at a practical level, the useful-

ness of a perspective that finds Adlai Stevenson to be a truer American conservative than Barry Goldwater is questionable. While men of the Right were pleased with the attention generated by *Conservatism in America*, Rossiter's attempt to yoke liberalism and conservatism in a dialectically progressive Whig "center" led some to consider his book a Trojan horse within the American conservative movement.

—Mark C. Henrie

Further Reading

Hartz, Louis. *The Liberal Tradition in America: An Interpretation of American Political Thought since the Revolution*. New York: Harcourt Brace Jovanovich, 1983.

Rossiter, Clinton. *The Political Thought of the American Revolution*. New York: Harcourt Brace, 1963.

———. *The American Presidency*. New York: Harcourt Brace, 1960.

———. *Seedtime of the Republic*. New York: Harcourt Brace, 1953.

See also: Boorstin, Daniel J.; tradition

Conservative Book Club

The Conservative Book Club (CBC) is one of the weapons in Tom Phillips's publishing arsenal, and a major reason why Eagle Publishing, the Phillips subsidiary comprised mainly of CBC, the conservative newspaper *Human Events*, and book publisher Regnery, has been so successful financially.

The Conservative Book Club was founded in 1964 by Neil McCaffrey, an upstate New York activist, editor, and founder of the book publishing imprint Arlington House who had recognized a growing market for works on the Right. Early success came with *Quotations from Chairman Bill* (1970), a collection of William F. Buckley Jr.'s witticisms. McCaffrey later founded the

Nostalgia Book Club and in 1978 acquired the Movie Entertainment Book Club. Newsletter magnate Tom Phillips bought a half-ownership interest in CBC in 1993. After a bruising and contentious power struggle Phillips was able to remove McCaffrey and take control of the operation. Phillips rolled the CBC and Movie Entertainment Book Club into a new company along with two iconic institutions of conservative thought and politics—*Human Events* and Regnery Publishing.

Like CBC, both companies had been foundering when Phillips purchased them; they have all been extremely profitable since. A large part of the credit goes to the synergy Phillips has created between the companies. The Conservative Book Club is a major outlet for Regnery's books, for example, and benefits from paying less for them than for titles from other publishers. Additional middleman costs are eliminated as well. Designating a Regnery title as a CBC main selection can boost the book's sales by many tens of thousands. And Eagle's profit margins on these sales are far higher than if they were sold in stores, despite the fact the list price is higher at a typical bookstore. But CBC doesn't entirely play favorites with Regnery. The Club sells other publishing houses' books as well and has had much success offering non-Regnery works by the likes of Robert Bork and William Bennett.

Today, the CBC has about 80,000 members (more than twice the membership during McCaffrey's reign) who use the club as entrée to the classics of conservative thought, such as works by Russell Kirk and Whittaker Chambers and contemporary conservative writers like Bennett and Thomas Sowell. An added attraction is that many of its selections are not available in bookstores. The club offers titles that appeal to a wide range of interests, from free-market economics to home schooling. One CBC offshoot is the Christian Family Book Club, which, as the name implies, offers religious and inspirational titles unlikely to be found in big chain stores like Borders or Barnes & Noble. CBC goes head-to-head with the behemoth Crossings Book Club for this market, but holds its own. Given its inroads into a market clearly hungering for conservative intellectual ammunition, CBC's prospects in the years ahead look favorable.

—Max Schulz

See also: Regnery Publishing

Conservative Mind, The

In *The Conservative Mind,* a seminal history of conservative ideas, Russell Kirk defined and examined a conservative intellectual tradition that began with Edmund Burke. The book is considered by many to have played a historic role in the postwar revival of conservative ideas in America. Originally titled *The Conservatives' Rout* (because Kirk considered the history of conservatism to be a gloomy record of retreat), the original manuscript was submitted as Kirk's dissertation for the degree of Doctor of Humane Letters from St. Andrews University. *The Conservative Mind* had a dramatic three-fold impact on the tenor and direction of a conservative movement struggling to be born in the 1950s. First, when the dominant ideological currents of the time had nearly extinguished the responsible voices of intellectual conservatism, Kirk's articulation of the tradition of conservative principles reinvigorated a dispirited conservatism adrift and barely conscious of its own existence. The ideas then fashionable in intellectual circles were of a decidedly liberal or socialist orientation. As the historian George Nash has noted, Kirk's book "dramatically catalyzed the emergence of the conservative intellectual movement," which at that time amounted to "at most, scattered voices of protest, profoundly pessimistic about the future of their country."

In this "prolonged essay in definition" Kirk discovered a tradition, battered and often routed by its adversaries but still vibrant, that stemmed from Burke and extended down through the generations, linking writers, poets, and statesman. Among those belonging to this tradition in Britain were Coleridge, Disraeli, Cardinal Newman, James Fitzjames Stephen, W. E. H. Lecky, and T. S. Eliot; in America, its expositors included John Adams, John Randolph, John Calhoun, Orestes Brownson, Henry and Brooks Adams, Irving Babbitt, and Paul Elmer More. From a body of intimately related and mutually supportive ideas common to these men of conservative instincts, Kirk was able to distill the essence of the conservative position.

THE
CONSERVATIVE
MIND

from Burke to Santayana

RUSSELL KIRK

Chicago · HENRY REGNERY COMPANY · *1953*

Second, when the bulk of established intellectuals were prepared to dismiss conservatism as a permanently discredited ideology, Kirk's rediscovery and articulation of a viable intellectual conservative tradition in the English-speaking world restored credibility to a body of ideas once airily dismissed as the mere bleatings of bourgeois Babbitts. By defining and applying its principles to modern challenges, he fortified and strengthened the conservative position. He demonstrated in a compelling fashion that conservatism is an integral part of the Western political tradition.

Lastly, Kirk was writing a history of conservative ideas, the first historian to attempt such a task. But his intent was more than historical: it was didactic and polemical. The rationalism of the *philosophes*, the romantic idealism of the Rousseauists, Benthamism, positivism, Marxism, Social Darwinism, pragmatism, and socialism were among the ideologies he condemned as inimical to the social order of the post-1789 world. From them sprang the belief in the perfectibility of man, enthusiasm for social and economic leveling, the impulse for innovation coinciding with a concomitant contempt of tradition, the denial of the power of Providence in history, and the rejection of what Eliot called "the permanent things," those enduring moral norms that make civilized social existence possible. Against the proponents of radical innovation, Kirk enthusiastically defended tradition, old values, and prescriptive establishments.

The book had an immediate impact. At the suggestion of Whittaker Chambers, *Time* magazine devoted its entire book review section to *The Conservative Mind*. Numerous other journals and newspapers, including the *New York Times,* published reviews praising or at the least expressing respect for the book. As the book's publisher, Henry Regnery, noted, after Kirk's volume appeared "one could call himself a conservative without apology."

Going through no fewer than seven editions during Kirk's lifetime, *The Conservative Mind* changed subtly over the years to reflect new emphases in Kirk's own thought. The original subtitle, "From Burke to Santayana," was replaced by "From Burke to Eliot," reflecting Kirk's growing appreciation for Eliot's work, and especially the poet's desire to reinvigorate concern for and understanding of those goods of human life that are bound up with religion and the institutions and interactions of social and cultural life. The book's concern with natural law and the importance of property rights also became more explicit over time, though each had been present from the first edition. Still in print, *The Conservative Mind* remains of crucial importance for understanding the conservative patrimony and the nature of the society and moral vision it seeks to conserve.

—W. WESLEY MCDONALD

Further Reading

Daly, Anne Carson. "*The Conservative Mind* at Forty." *Intercollegiate Review,* Fall 1993: 46–50.

Guroian, Vigen. "*The Conservative Mind* Forty Years Later." *Intercollegiate Review,* Fall 1994: 23–26.

Kirk, Russell. *The Sword of Imagination: Memoirs of a Half-Century of Literary Conflict.* Grand Rapids, Mich.: Eerdmans, 1995.

McDonald, W. Wesley. *Russell Kirk and the Age of Ideology.* Columbia, Mo.: University of Missouri Press, 2004.

Person, James E., ed. *Russell Kirk: A Critical Biography of a Conservative Mind.* Lanham, Md.: Madison Books, 1999.

See also: community; conservatism; Kirk, Russell; Old Right; Regnery Publishing

Conservative Party of New York

Conceived by conservative Catholic Republicans J. Daniel Mahoney and Kieran O'Doherty in 1962 to complement New York's Liberal Party and counter the state's liberal GOP leadership, which was believed to have cost Richard Nixon the presidency in 1960, the Conservative Party of New York is intent on invigorating conservatism, on giving or withholding endorsements of candidates, and on nominating its own candidates when needed. Thus, during the last four decades the party has challenged the controlling liberal wing of New York's GOP, headed, inter alia, by the likes of Nelson Rockefeller, John Lindsay, and Jacob Javits.

The Conservative Party debuted on the ballot in New York on November 6, 1962, when it boldly ran David Jaquith against Rockefeller, and Kieran O'Doherty, its first chairman, against Senator Javits. The Conservative Party candidates lost, but the New York GOP withheld its approval of the new party for a year, until the powerful Republican state senator Walter Mahoney addressed its first anniversary banquet, thereby conferring an unofficial acknowledgement. In 1964, the party ran scholar Henry Paolucci for Senate against Robert Kennedy, a vigorous effort that brought yet more legitimacy.

The party gained wider publicity and acceptance when in 1965 it ran William F. Buckley Jr. for mayor of Manhattan against Lindsay, a campaign Buckley chronicled in *The Unmaking of a Mayor* (1966). In 1970, Buckley's brother James won a U.S. Senate seat on the Conservative Party ticket, defeating the GOP and Democratic candidates.

A sure indication of the party's political influence occurred in the 1966 elections, when the entire Conservative ticket beat the Liberal ticket, consequently moving it up from Row F to Row C on New York ballots. In two noteworthy state races that year, William Bensely received more votes than Javits, costing the senator a perfunctory bid for membership in the state's Constitutional Convention, while Dean Paul Adams beat a Liberal notable, Franklin Delano Roosevelt Jr.

Still largely ignored, however, the Conservative Party received a legitimizing sign of support in 1968 from Republican presidential candidate Richard Nixon, who, in a letter to State Chairman Mahoney, welcomed the party's endorsement and recognized it as a "responsible political organization."

After three decades of activity, the party in 1994 experienced its most celebrated election victory when it furnished the winning margin for Governor George E. Pataki and Attorney General Dennis C. Vacco.

Since its founding, the party has played a key role in advancing issues germane not only to New York conservatives, such as rent control and the commuter tax, but also to conservatives across the country. Conservative candidates running for national, state, county, city, town, and village offices seek the party's seal of approval. Forming ties not only to conservative Republicans but also to like-minded Democrats, the party has been instrumental in countering the Liberal Party and its Republican partisans and in chastening the liberal impulses of the state government. The party is affiliated nationally with the American Conservative Union and recognizes itself as the New York branch of the American conservative movement.

Besides the 1994 breakthrough, the Conservative Party's other notable victories over four decades include the election of William Carney to the House of Representatives, Serphin R. Maltese to the state senate, and Rosemary R. Gunning and Charles Jerabec to the state assembly.

Ronald Reagan said, "The Conservative [P]arty has established itself as a preeminent force in New York politics and an important part of our political history." William A. Rusher observed that the formation of the Conservative Party indicated "the political sophistication of the intellectual Right."

—William F. Meehan III

Further Reading

Mahoney, J. Daniel. *Actions Speak Louder*. New Rochelle, N.Y.: Arlington House, 1968.

Marlin, George J. *Fighting the Good Fight: A History of the New York Conservative Party*. South Bend, Ind.: St. Augustine's Press, 2002.

See also: Buckley, William F., Jr.

Constitution, interpretations of

One might be forgiven for believing that there can be only one "conservative" interpretation of the Constitution: one that is faithful to the intent and meaning given that document by its framers. And, indeed, conservatives generally are agreed that great respect should be given the wisdom of the drafters, both because that wisdom was very real and because it is unwise for a people to look upon its principal founding document with anything less than genuine respect. Yet recent events concerning Supreme Court decisions and public arguments among conservatives have shown that this view of constitutional interpretation is not sufficiently full and nuanced to take account of differences between conservatives, and even some liberals, in constitutional interpretation.

When Justice Kennedy (no conservative, to be sure) opined in *Planned Parenthood v. Casey* (1992) that the Supreme Court could not overturn even so clearly baseless a constitutional interpretation as that given in *Roe v. Wade* (1973), by which the Court declared abortion a fundamental right, he demonstrated how badly the notion of precedent could be misconstrued by those entrusted with it. Moreover, he showed the limits of contemporary understandings of history and of the nature of our Constitution. The institution with which Kennedy was so concerned—the Supreme Court—has as its central task the correct application of laws, including the Constitution. As such, its duty is to construe properly and thereby defend the integrity of laws, including the Constitution. By perpetuating a clear misreading of the Constitution simply in order to protect its own authority, the Court was misusing its power, to the detriment of its duty, for its own aggrandizement. Moreover, precedent is intended to bind judges to generally accepted understandings of statutes, constitutions, and important legal terms embodied in statute and common law. To perpetuate a bad precedent is to undermine the purpose of a legal institution merely for the sake of defending the status of those currently exercising power over that tool. It destroys predictability, undermines laws arrived at through the democratic process, and elevates judges to the position of unelected super-legislators.

If a constitution is to fulfill its function of setting forth the basic rules by which a people is to govern itself, its terms of art—for example, "due process"—must be interpreted consistently over time. Changes to those meanings, or to the structure itself, must be undertaken through the political process. Should judges change those meanings on their own, the judges, and not the people, become the sovereigns.

Judge Robert Bork's nomination to the Supreme Court was opposed and defeated by Senate liberals, aided by their counterparts in the legal academy and the media, because he had made precisely this argument. Bork had written that judges did not have the authority to redraft the Constitution (or lesser statutes) in accordance with their own beliefs concerning what is just, natural, or required by the nature of the American republic. The only way to achieve predictability, let alone justice, in judicial decision-making, Bork argued, was for judges to strictly adhere to the intent and meaning of the documents' drafters, leaving aside their own opinions concerning what should be done in particular circumstances. Because much if not most of the liberal state had been built on the basis of Supreme Court decisions clearly contradicting the framers' intentions, Bork's views were deemed threatening and characterized as backward-looking and uncaring in terms of the needs of minorities and the poor.

Ironically, it was a set of judicial decisions clearly discounting the needs of just such social groups that established the precedents necessary for liberal judicial activism. Late-nineteenth- and early-twentieth-century courts repeatedly struck down state and local legislation aimed at alleviating labor and racial problems. They did so on the grounds that constitutional "due process," by which the framers had meant the tradi-

tional common law of the land, in fact demanded "substantive due process." By this the judges meant that the freedom of individuals to enter into contracts trumped any and all community concerns. Further, they argued, the Constitution's commerce clause, which the framers had intended to apply very narrowly to interstate trade, in fact demanded a national market of uniform state and local laws—all favoring laissez-faire economics. During the Great Depression, under pressure from President Franklin Roosevelt and in the midst of a substantial change in membership, the Supreme Court reversed itself on the underlying economic philosophy, but not on the activist principles of its jurisprudence. No longer demanding uniform laissez-faire, the Court began imposing nationalist policies aimed at rooting out inequalities and perceived injustices.

The clear subjectivity of the Court's jurisprudence caused concern in conservative quarters, but in Washington at least the perception that good was being done quieted opposition. Bork emphasized the subjectivity of these decisions in showing that the notion of a "living constitution" that would "change with the times" was merely an excuse for allowing judges to act according to their own will rather than the law. Yet Bork's arguments raised concerns among conservatives as well as liberals. A lively exchange in the magazine *First Things* ensued. Hadley Arkes, Russell Hittinger and William Bentley Ball, all broadly conservative scholars, argued that Bork, while correct in much of his criticism of recent decisions, had too easily and completely dismissed natural law as a proper basis for judicial decisions. These critics further argued that judges must look to natural law (some going so far as to defend substantive due process) in order to form proper judicial opinions. Bork insisted that judges had no special access to knowledge concerning natural law and therefore had no right to make decisions on its basis. Edwin Meese

III, attorney general in the Reagan administration, was one lawyer who later sided with Bork, arguing that interpretations of laws and of the Constitution must begin within the "four corners of the document." That is, they should rely on the clear meaning of the words in front of them, rather than on any possible philosophical theories that might lay behind them.

Supreme Court Justice Antonin Scalia has argued for yet another form of originalism. In his view, courts should look to the language of the document they are interpreting as well as to the established traditions of the American people. Important terms in the Constitution should be read as they would have been understood by society at the time of their actual drafting rather than as a contemporary judge may wish to interpret them. This reasoning points to a more subtle—perhaps more accurate—form of natural law originalism, a form that recognizes that judges cannot create or even accurately read natural law in the abstract, but which also emphasizes the importance of the natural law tradition to the framers of the Constitution. Philip Hamburger, among others, has pointed out the extent to which the framers of the Constitution were steeped in the natural law tradition, and the extent to which they sought to bring that tradition to bear in its drafting. But the framers did not see natural law as either a detailed code of conduct or a mere abstraction to which judges and others could give their own, subjective content. Rather, they saw natural law as a general set of precepts demanding, among other things, virtue, civility, and respect for customary institutions, beliefs, and practices. The particular rights and duties needed to form a decent society, in keeping with natural law, were formed over time and were handed down in the form of common law practices and the language used to describe them. Thus, a judge's job entails the proper interpretation of ancient terms (like *due process*, which goes back at least as far as the first Great Charter of liberties, the English Magna Charta of 1215). To interpret important terms of art—from due process to cruel and unusual punishment to free speech—requires a historical understanding of how these terms were understood by those who used them in our Constitution. And this in turn requires a historical understanding of natural law—of what it commands, what it permits, and what it forbids. Most particularly, it requires the ability and willingess to work hard to fully understand the meaning of old words rather than simply to fit their meanings to one's own desires or prejudices.

—Bruce Frohnen

Further Reading

Bork, Robert H. *The Tempting of America: The Political Seduction of the Law.* New York: Free Press, 1990.

Hamburger, Philip. "Natural Rights, Natural Law and American Constitutions." *Yale Law Journal* 102 (1993): 907–60.

Scalia, Antonin. *A Matter of Interpretation.* Princeton, N.J.: Princeton University Press, 1997.

See also: Bork, Robert H.; Federalist Party; judicial activism; Scalia, Antonin; Supreme Court; Thomas, Clarence

constitutionalism

Constitutionalism is the systematic constraint of government power. An older sense of the term constitution, tracing back to Aristotle, is simply descriptive. In that older usage, a constitution refers to the laws, institutions, and practices that organize and direct a government and political system. In this sense, every political system has a constitution. Especially since the American Founding, the idea of a constitution has taken on a more specific and value-laden meaning; it now refers to the establishment of a particular kind of political order. Modern constitutions place limits on and organize government. In modern terms, some nations are constitutional, with limited and accountable governments, and others are not. Constitutionalism is a central mechanism for controlling political power and securing liberty.

Constitutionalism is the political response to Lord Acton's famous observation that power corrupts and absolute power corrupts absolutely. Constitutionalism resists the creation of absolute political power. Absolute power was once widely defended as essential to securing order and advancing the public good. The existence of absolute political power, particularly in the hands of a monarch, was deemed vital to any stable political system, and this proposition was argued at length by writers such as Jean Bodin, Thomas Hobbes, and England's King James I, among many others, in sixteenth- and seventeenth-century Europe. Others, notably including John Locke and the British judge Edward Coke, insisted that the authority of political leaders was limited, that individuals had rights that must be respected, and that government officials should be politically accountable and subject to the rule of law. Although not governed by any single written document, British constitutionalism as it developed in the seventeenth century emphasized the legislature as a check on executive power and individual rights as expressed in the judge-made common law.

The American founders inherited this understanding of constitutionalism and added to it. Two separate aspects of American, and modern, constitutionalism, can be distinguished. Both aspects emphasize the importance of controlling political power and protecting individual liberties from government abuse, but they highlight different paths to that common goal. The first, and in many ways the most distinctively American contribution to constitutionalism, is the notion of the constitution as a fundamental law. In keeping with the early American understandings of natural law and the common law, American constitutionalism recognizes that some rights are fundamental and cannot be appropriately abridged by government. Constitutionalism recognizes that there is a higher law superior to the acts of the government and against which the acts of the government can be judged. The American founding is distinctive, and influential, in creating a single written document grounded in popular consent that is both clearly visible and legally enforceable against government officials. Constitutionalism gives legal status to the principles of just government.

A second aspect of constitutionalism is the fragmentation of political power and the creation of mechanisms of political accountability. Rather than consolidating political power in a single set of hands, constitutionalism widely distributes political power. In sixteenth- and seventeenth-century Britain, the parliamentary power to raise taxes was separated from the monarchical power to spend, forcing the king to win the cooperation of Parliament to support his decisions. In the U.S. Constitution, the power to make laws is divided between the House of Representatives, the Senate, and the president. The Senate must confirm presidential choices of persons to occupy judicial and executive offices. An independent judiciary helps ensure that the executive follows the law produced by the legislature. Elections help hold government officials accountable to the people for their decisions, and the diversity of elected offices helps to represent the diversity of the citizenry. Government responsibilities are divided between the federal and the state governments. The separation of powers, checks and balances, elections, and federalism all serve to distribute political power, to hold political officials responsible for their actions, and to force government to work through compromise, cooperation, and consensus. In this second aspect of constitutionalism, as James Madison observed, ambition is made to counteract ambition by empowering multiple distinct and rival interests.

Both of these aspects of constitutionalism are aimed not at weakening government but at controlling it and channeling its activities toward the public good. Constitutionalism is opposed to arbitrary and absolute political power, whether that power is exercised democratically or not. Constitutionalism asserts that there are limits to what government can justly do and creates institutions to prevent government from overstepping those limits.

—KEITH E. WHITTINGTON

Further Reading

Friedrich, Carl. *Constitutional Government and Democracy*. Boston: Little, Brown & Co., 1941.

Gordon, Scott. *Controlling the State: Constitutionalism from Ancient Athens to Today*. New York: Oxford University Press, 1999.

McIlwain, Charles Howard. *Constitutionalism: Ancient and Modern*. Ithaca, N.Y.: Cornell University Press, 1947.

Wood, Gordon S. *The Creation of the American Republic, 1776–1787*. Chapel Hill, N.C.: University of North Carolina Press, 1969.

See also: Federalist, The; *separation of powers; Supreme Court*

containment

Containment was the doctrinal core of American foreign policy in dealing with the Soviet Union during the Cold War. From 1947, when President Harry Truman proposed the "Truman Doctrine" of aiding any country threatened by communism, until the Soviet Union's collapse in 1991, American presidents sought, with varying degrees of strength and resolution, to prevent the Soviet Union from expanding, whether by conquest, subversion, or election.

Containment was born in a 7000-word telegram sent by George Kennan, who was serving in the U.S. embassy in Moscow (the telegram was published in 1946 as a widely read and influential article in *Foreign Affairs* called "Sources of Soviet Conduct," by "X"). Kennan argued that Joseph Stalin and the other Soviet leaders were insecure because of the illegitimate way that they had come to power and kept it, and because "the Russian-Asiatic world" out of which they had emerged gave them a worldview that rejected the possibility of peaceful coexistence with their neighbors. Overlaid upon their paranoia, Kennan argued, was the Soviet leaders' Marxism-Leninism, which emphasized the implacable hostility of their capitalist opponents, the transcendent justice of communism, and therefore the duty to use any means to communize the globe.

Kennan mitigated his terrifying analysis by arguing that the Soviets approached their expansionist policy with caution, lest pushing too hard lead to a war that would destroy them and their achievements. The result, Kennan wrote, was an offensive foreign policy, but one that "is a fluid stream which moves constantly, wherever it is permitted to move, toward a given goal." To oppose it, Kennan advocated "a policy of firm containment, designed to confront the Russians with unalterable counterforce at every point where they show signs of encroaching upon the interests of a peaceful and stable world." Nothing less would work, because Soviet expansionism "cannot be charmed or talked out of existence." Kennan believed that by frustrating Soviet expansionism, the Soviets' messianic ambitions would recede, leaving nothing but an economically bankrupt and unworkable dictatorship that would ultimately implode.

Kennan's analysis convinced Truman, who issued the Truman Doctrine and organized the North Atlantic Treaty Organization to unite the West against Soviet aggression. When North Korea invaded South Korea in June 1950, Truman ordered U.S. troops into the war. Following the American victory at Inchon, General Douglas MacArthur called on the president to allow him to liberate all of North Korea from the communists. Truman agreed, declaring that Pyongyang would be "the first Iron Curtain capital" to be liberated. When hundreds of thousands of Chinese "volunteers" entered the war and drove U.S. troops back into South Korea, MacArthur publicly demanded that Truman expand the war into China and use nuclear weapons if necessary. Truman, worried that expanding the war could draw in the Soviets, fired MacArthur and returned to containment, ordering U.S. forces to dig in and defend the prewar boundary. Continued stalemate and loss of American lives turned Americans against the war and helped elect Dwight Eisenhower, who promised a more vigorous foreign policy.

Eisenhower and his secretary of state, John Foster Dulles, lambasted containment, calling it an "immoral" and "futile" policy, and Republican Senator Alexander Wiley called containment "mere 'pantywaist' diplomacy." They called for the "rollback" of communism to "liberate" its enslaved victims. Eisenhower reversed course in 1956 when the Soviets invaded Hungary after its leaders declared that they were no longer part of the Soviet empire. The United States protested, but that was all. Henceforth, Eisenhower also adopted the containment strategy, as did every subsequent president.

Vietnam was the second time that American troops were called upon to contain communism. Even more than Korea, Vietnam demonstrated that the American people could not comprehend a policy that sought to restore the status quo rather than to win, an end for which the public proved unwilling to sacrifice American lives.

Following Vietnam's fall, President Jimmy Carter announced that the United States must overcome its "inordinate fear of communism." Carter sought to work with the Soviets rather than to compete against them. The Soviets responded with a massive military build-up, used Cuba as their cat's paw in Central America and Africa, and dramatically expanded support for third-world liberation movements and terrorists. Containment of communism in the third world was effectively dead. Not until the Soviet conquest of Afghanistan in December 1979 did Carter adopt a consistent containment policy, announcing that Afghanistan had caused "a more drastic change in my opinion of what the Soviets' ultimate goals are than anything they've done in the previous time I've been in office."

Ronald Reagan restored the strategy of hawkish containment. He launched a massive arms build-up to meet the surging Soviet threat; assisted anticommunist rebels and governments threatened by communism; refused to compromise in the face of a powerful and vitriolic peace movement that encompassed many European leaders, Democratic Party legislators, and much of the Western intellectual class; and joined the Soviets in rhetorical battle in a way unseen in the West since the death of John Foster Dulles. Reagan called the Soviet Union an "evil empire" and, while visiting West Berlin, demanded of the Soviet dictator, "Mr. Gorbachev, tear down this wall!" Along with this broad-front offensive, Reagan created a form of containment in outer space when he announced that the United States was going to build a space-based antimissile system. Mikhail Gorbachev quickly understood that the Soviet command economy could not keep up. His effort to restructure communism failed and the Soviet empire collapsed, followed in 1991 by the Soviet Union itself.

Just as George Kennan had predicted, containing communism ultimately killed it. Lacking missionary zeal as the Russian Revolution's children died off, unable to provide a decent standard of living for its people, and robbed of its recent and expensive third-world triumphs by a resurgent United States, the Soviet leaders and their people lost their faith in communism's ultimate triumph. With it vanished justification for the Soviet dictatorship.

—ROBERT WATERS

Further Reading

Burnham, James. *Containment or Liberation? An Inquiry into the Aims of United States Foreign Policy.* New York: John Day, 1953.

Gaddis, John Lewis. *Strategies of Containment: A Critical Appraisal of Postwar American National Security Policy.* New York: Oxford University Press, 1982.

Leffler, Melvyn. *A Preponderance of Power: National Security, the Truman Administration, and the Cold War.* Stanford, Calif.: Stanford University Press, 1992.

See also: anticommunism; Cold War; Eisenhower, Dwight D.; Kennan, George; Reagan Doctrine

Coolidge, Calvin (1872–1933)

Calvin Coolidge was the thirtieth president of the United States, serving from 1923 to 1929. A conservative Republican, Coolidge is much reviled by liberal historians who see him, along with his predecessor Warren Harding and his successor Herbert Hoover, as leaders of a reactionary period between the Progressive Era (1900–20) and the New Deal (which commenced in 1933). Coolidge

Calvin Coolidge

especially is portrayed as a shallow, lazy man who was a tool of big business, and his policies are said to have contributed significantly to the onset of the Great Depression. Many historians rank Coolidge among America's worst presidents. Many conservatives would contend that this portrait of Coolidge is highly inaccurate, asserting instead that Coolidge was a thoughtful and principled statesman whose record has been distorted.

Coolidge first came to national prominence in 1919, when, as governor of Massachusetts, he called out the national guard to quell a police strike in Boston. In a telegram to labor leader Samuel Gompers, Coolidge declared that "there is no right to strike against the public safety by anybody, anywhere, any time." The following year, the Republican national convention nominated Coolidge by acclamation to be Warren Harding's running mate. Coolidge became president when Harding died in 1923. He was elected in his own right in 1924.

A key achievement of the Coolidge presidency was a series of income tax cuts, which helped to spur the economic growth of the "roaring '20s" and also provided a model for the "supply-side" tax cut movement of the 1980s under President Ronald Reagan. (One of Reagan's first acts in office in 1981 was to place Coolidge's portrait in the cabinet room.) Federal revenues rose throughout the prosperous 1920s.

Liberal historians, especially Arthur Schlesinger Jr. in his *Crisis of the Old Order* (1956), indict Coolidge chiefly for his supposed attitudes about government and business. The most widely misquoted statement of Coolidge is "The business of America is business." The full context of Coolidge's remark reveals a much different and more comprehensive meaning: "After all, the chief business of the American people is business. . . . Of course, the accumulation of wealth cannot be justified as the chief end of existence. . . . So long as wealth is made the means and not the end, we need not greatly fear it." These and other statements show Coolidge to have been a thoughtful and learned man. Even as an adult, he would translate Cicero and Dante from Latin, and he wrote fondly of the poetry of Homer and Shakespeare.

Some historians, including Schlesinger, argue that Coolidge's policies helped cause the Great Depression. Economic scholarship, especially that of Milton Friedman and Anna Schwartz, has generally refuted this view (see their *Monetary History of the United States*, 1963). It is worth noting that one liberal economist who dissents is John Kenneth Galbraith, who wrote in his account of the Great Depression that it is "grossly unfair" that "a whole generation of historians has assailed Coolidge."

Coolidge also wrote and spoke thoughtfully about the American political tradition. He had high praise for the Declaration of Independence and the nation's founding principles, and he rejected the progressivist ideology. Many of his writings and speeches have an aphoristic quality of substantial merit: "Great men are the ambassadors of Providence sent to reveal to their fellow men their unknown selves. . . . When the reverence of this nation for great men dies, the glory of the nation will die with it." It should be noted that Coolidge wrote all of his own speeches and articles.

The denigration of Coolidge and the other Republican presidents of his era was a necessary part of the effort to aggrandize the New Deal. As the legacy of the New Deal is gradually reexamined by new generations of historians, so too the statesmanship of President Coolidge is likely to be reevaluated in a more favorable light.

—STEPHEN HAYWARD

Further Reading

Coolidge, Calvin. *Have Faith in Massachusetts*. Boston: Houghton Mifflin, 1919.

———. *The Autobiography of Calvin Coolidge*. New York: Cosmopolitan Books, 1929.

Silver, Thomas B. *Coolidge and the Historians*. Durham, N.C.: Carolina Academic Press, 1982.

See also: supply-side economics

Cooper, James Fenimore (1789–1851)

Conservatives have never known quite what to make of James Fenimore Cooper. That he was an important formulator of the conservative identity and typical of the conservative republican ethos that subsisted in America from the reign of the Federalists to the Civil War is apparent. Russell Kirk, in *The Conservative Mind* (1953), is little better than grudgingly appreciative in his account of Cooper's political ideas. In his 1931 introduction to Cooper's *American Democrat*, H. L. Mencken had been more enthusiastic, perhaps because he saw in Cooper a fellow democratic elitist. The most appreciative account of Cooper's ideas, strangely enough, is to be found in the work of the progressive historian Vernon Lewis Parrington. Still, conservatives have seen in Cooper a defender of landowning aristocracy, a partisan of traditional values, an enemy of leveling democracy, and a critic of the dangers of a licentious and libelous press. He has often been read in tandem with Tocqueville, whose *Democracy in America* (1835) is contemporaneous with Cooper's *The American Democrat* (1838).

Cooper was born in 1789 in Burlington, New Jersey. In 1785 his father, William Cooper, came to the shores of Lake Otsego, then a primeval wilderness, with surveyors to take stock of the extensive tracts of land he held. The settlement of his family and the foundation of Cooperstown followed in 1787. Cooper viewed this settlement as a Lockean appropriation, and the themes of wilderness, its original Indian inhabitants, and its conquest by cultivation and culture form the great themes of his works.

Ambivalence and tension mark Cooper's attitudes toward the Indian, the wilderness, the frontiersman, the impact of settlement on the environment, the victory of money, land speculation and development as opposed to manorial agrarianism, and the conflicting values of aristocracy and equality in democratic society. Natty Bumpo, the

James Fenimore Cooper

hero of the Leatherstocking saga in the guise of Hawkeye, Deerslayer, and Pathfinder, is not simply an untutored and noble child of nature in the mode of eighteenth-century Romanticism, for Cooper demonstrates that nature does not necessarily ennoble. The despised Mingoes are no less children of nature than the heroic and tragic Mohicans. The destructive, cruel, and corrupt frontier types, such as Hurry Harry in *The Deerslayer* (1841) and the Bush family in *The Prairie* (1827), are no less children of nature and frontiersmen than Natty Bumpo. Cooper's theory of "gifts" appropriate to a particular culture, gifts that create obligations for ethical action, move his characters beyond the categories of cultural relativism. These gifts are, moreover, progressive in character, the Christian gentleman respectful of but superior to the "naturally" good savage.

Cooper did not glorify the frontier. Indeed, he saw it as the scene of spoliation and ruin. Cultivation and culture made possible the good life. Cooper was much influenced by English landscape gardening, with its emphasis on "nature methodized." Cultivation and culture were the work of the gentleman-squire, whose baronial estates brought order and civility to the wilderness. Cooper was among the first to denounce the devastation of the environment, which he depicts as both stupid and sinful. The ruthless destruction of the sugar maples, the slaughter of the passenger pigeons, and the wasteful overfishing of Lake Otsego are important episodes in *The Pioneers* (1823).

In 1826, Cooper and his family departed for Europe. They were not to return until 1833. During his long stay in Europe, Cooper defended the American experiment from its European critics (*Notions of the Americans: Picked up by a Traveling Bachelor*, 1828). However, he was appalled by the transformation in American life produced by the Jacksonian revolution. Marvin Meyers has argued that Cooper was always Jacksonian in his political sympathies. More accurately, Cooper was anti-Whig because of his gentrified detestation of the moneyed interest, speculation, and commercial development. He styled himself a democrat and a conservative. His aristocratic conception of equality did not extend beyond equality before the law. In *The American Democrat*, Cooper was unflagging in his attack on the social, political, and economic forces working to level American society and the debasement of the public mind by a libelous press. The attack on property that Cooper perceived in radical democracy ran counter to his Lockean conception of appropriation and ownership. The novels *Homeward Bound* (1838) and *Home as Found* (1838) flesh out his political views, providing parodies of his social and political enemies. The "Littlepage Novels" of the 1840s are not simply partisan tracts written in the heat of the rent wars but are rather Cooper's attempt to chronicle the "decay of a sense of values in the American mind."

—STEPHEN J. TONSOR

Further Reading

Meyers, Marvin. *The Jacksonian Persuasion, Politics and Belief.* Palo Alto, Calif.: Stanford University Press, 1957.

Parrington, Vernon Lewis. *Main Currents in American Thought.* New York: Harcourt, Brace & Co., 1927.

Ringe, Donald A. *James Fenimore Cooper.* New York: Twayne Publishers, 1962.

Taylor, Alan. *William Cooper's Town: Power and Persuasion on the Frontier of the Early American Republic.* New York: Alfred A. Knopf, 1995.

See also: equality

Coughlin, Charles E. (1891–1979)

Priest, radio personality, and one of the best-known figures of his time, Charles Edward Coughlin was one of the earliest public figures to use radio as a means to communicate to a mass audience. Coughlin was a fiery anticommunist, one of America's first and most articulate critics of Bolshevism, and an ardent opponent of Franklin D. Roosevelt's New Deal. At the height of his popularity, Coughlin attracted an estimated 40 million listeners to his weekly show and employed approximately 150 secretaries to handle the enormous number of donations and mail that came to his church in a northeast suburb of Detroit.

Charles Coughlin was the only child of Thomas Coughlin, an Indiana native and immigrant Irishman, and Amelia Mahoney. In 1911, he graduated from the University of Toronto and directly entered St. Basil's Seminary, operated by the Basilian Fathers. Never one to suppress his independent and forceful personality, early on Coughlin ran into problems with his superiors. However, he was a faithful and obedient priest who remained a Basilian until 1923, when he left the order and was incardinated under Bishop Michael J. Gallagher in the Diocese of Detroit, Michigan.

Shortly after becoming a secular priest and after two brief church assignments, Coughlin was chosen as pastor of a new church being built in Royal Oak, Michigan, in honor of St. Therese of Lisieux. Having built on his arrival an impressive new church-shrine, Coughlin soon secured a weekly radio show. On October 17, 1926, Coughlin delivered the first broadcast of what would become a long-running, enormously popular, and highly controversial radio program.

Coughlin's impact was felt immediately. Radio was in its infancy and Coughlin became one of its first superstars. At first, he kept strictly to religious topics, but by 1930, after much financial success, the program shifted dramatically from religious to political topics. One of Coughlin's first targets was Russian communism. He warned of the "creeping dangers of communism" and what he called the "Red Menace." By 1930, he had a new contract with CBS radio and an ecumenical audience of more than 40 million people. He became a savage critic of the international banking establishment, seeing in it the source of modern economic exploitation and social injustice. While he criticized the evils of a politically managed monetary system, he extolled the economic wisdom and morality of sound money and a stable currency.

The vitriol he launched at the Russian communists and the international bankers, whom he labeled "the money changers of the modern temples," was underscored by severe criticism of Jewish involvement in and influence on both these groups. Hence, his social analysis often lapsed into a kind of anti-Semitism. This was particularly deplorable in that he spoke during the depths of the Great Depression and his popularity, force of intellect, and oratorical persuasiveness meant that he wielded enormous public influence. Coughlin was able to stir the passions of millions of frightened and desperate hearts by offering sweeping solutions and simplistic indictments of the people and policies he believed had led the country into its perilous economic situation.

Coughlin's first go-around with national politics occurred in 1932, when, dismayed with the Hoover administration's failure to improve the plight of the poor and unemployed, he supported Franklin Roosevelt's candidacy for President. However, he soon became disenchanted with his friend F.D.R., whom he had done so much to help elect, and began to openly criticize the New Deal agenda.

In 1937, Coughlin's bishop and staunch supporter, Michael Gallagher, died; his new superior, (later Cardinal) Edward Mooney, was infuriated by Coughlin. They were frequently at odds, and Coughlin became increasingly inflammatory. Coughlin even went so far as to print the discredited and execrable *Protocols of the Elders of Zion* (1923) in the pages of his weekly newspaper *Social Justice*. In 1940, Coughlin was forced to give up broadcasting after refusing to comply with a new rule of the National Association of Broadcasters that barred all "controversial" speakers unless they agreed to air opposing views. *Social Justice*, however, continued to be published.

After the bombing of Pearl Harbor in 1941, Coughlin attacked Roosevelt and Great Britain in the pages of his paper. Roosevelt initiated a federal investigation of *Social Justice* as a possibly seditious paper and orchestrated a behind-the-scenes deal with Archbishop Mooney to put Coughlin out of business permanently. In return for Mooney's

promise that Coughlin would be silenced, Roosevelt pledged to drop the legal charges pending against him.

On May 1, 1942, Mooney officially silenced Coughlin, ordering him to cease all public pronouncements and publications on non-religious issues. Coughlin lived up to his vow of obedience and silently exited the public arena whose attention he had so powerfully commanded for more than a decade as America's most recognized cleric. He continued to serve as pastor of his magnificent shrine until his 1966 retirement.

—JEFFREY O. NELSON

Further Reading

Brinkley, Alan. *Voices of Protest: Huey Long, Father Coughlin, and the Great Depression.* New York: Knopf, 1982.

See also: anticommunism; New Deal

Cram, Ralph Adams (1863–1942)

Ralph Adams Cram was one of the best-known architects of his time, but one who resisted current trends in art and architecture. His church designs and plans for public buildings sought to combine the spirit of the Gothic and the most apt use of modern materials and modern technology with due regard for the setting. The West Point campus exemplifies Cram's intent: the Chapel might be called Military Gothic and the campus buildings have a Gothic cragginess about them that befits a military academy located on a riverbank high above the Hudson. Cram is also responsible for a number of Gothic churches, and for fine buildings that grace the campuses of Princeton, Bryn Mawr, and Wellesley.

Cram loved the Middle Ages and wrote nearly a dozen books about its art, buildings, cathedrals, and social order. Medieval political theory, Cram argued, held that all authority comes from God, that responsibility for the exercise of that authority focuses on one man, and that the people, knowing misrule when they experience it, may take whatever action is necessary to correct it. His *Heart of Europe* (1915) neatly captures the flavor of the period.

Cram's acid comments on the twentieth century are to be found in two books of social criticism published during the 1930s. *Convictions and Controversies* (1935) contains the celebrated essay "Why We Don't Behave Like Human Beings." Cram believed that we behave as we do because of what we are, only a few of us being truly human. While he qualifies this sentiment, Cram scores heavily against the idea of progressive evolution and the expectation of utopia by way of social engineering. *The End of Democracy* (1937) provides an account of the drift of events from the "high democracy" of the Federalist period to the "peoples' democracies" of the modern world. With the erosion of popular belief in a moral order, wrote Cram, policy tends to be severed from ethics, completely so in Marxist states. Policy, then, is grounded in nothing more stable than "the will of the people," as determined by a show of hands. In practice, this leads to the manipulation of the people by the men in power who control the instrumentalities of information, propaganda, and terror and thus manufacture public opinion at will. In Cram's view, the denizens of people's democracies endure hardships such as they would never suffer under a king because they believe that "we are doing it to ourselves."

—EDMUND OPITZ

Further Reading

Shand-Tucci, Douglass. *Ralph Adams Cram: Life and Architecture.* Amherst, Mass.: University of Massachusetts Press, 1995.

See also: American Review

Crane, Philip (1930–)

A congressman from Illinois, Philip Crane has been one of the House of Representative's most ardently conservative members for over thirty years. Yet he has attracted national attention only once, and then briefly, in 1980, when he ran unsuccessfully for the Republican presidential nomination.

Born in Chicago in 1930, Crane adopted the conservative convictions of his father. After college, the Army, and graduate school, where he earned a Ph.D., the future congressman worked as a history professor and school administrator. In 1969 he won a special election to fill a vacant congressional seat from a suburban Chicago district. A long career in Washington has followed.

From the start, Crane's voting record reflected his conservative ideology almost perfectly. He has consistently supported tax reduction, tax indexing, increased defense spending, and free trade. Crane has routinely opposed increases in domestic-sector spending, he has been a constant critic of the bloated and wastefully inefficient government bureaucracy, and during the fight over government-funding of controversial artists Crane called for the outright abolition of the National Endowment for the Arts.

In 1977, Crane became chairman of the American Conservative Union, a post he held until 1979. That year he launched his bid for the presidency. Crane spent a full year in New Hampshire trying to build support for the first presidential primary. Crane's campaign strategy rested on a single premise: Ronald Reagan, at 69, was too old to win. If this proved true, then Crane—twenty years younger, with impeccable conservative credentials—had reason to think that he might inherit Reagan's national following. At times he came close to billing himself as a younger Governor Reagan.

Initially, at least, the Reagan camp worried that voters might accept Crane's implicit suggestion that Reagan was too old to be president. The possibility also existed that Crane would divide the conservative primary vote and thereby permit a moderate Republican to capture the nomination. Reagan's extraordinary popularity and physical fitness doomed Crane's candidacy. With their hero on the ballot, conservative Republicans had no interest in voting for an imitator. Crane received a scant 1.8 percent of the New Hampshire primary vote, and he soon abandoned his presidential quest to defend his House seat.

During the Reagan years, Crane loyally supported the president's agenda but did not emerge as a leading congressional spokesperson or legislator for the conservative cause. For the most part he avoided the political limelight. In 1984 his brother, Congressman Dennis Crane, representing a downstate Illinois district, became involved in a squalid sex scandal and was turned out of office. Phil Crane suffered no direct political fallout, but the episode hardly brought welcome publicity.

Solidly entrenched in an overwhelmingly Republican district, Crane probably can stay in Congress until he chooses to retire. Undoubtedly he will remain an unswerving conservative until that time.

—George Sirgiovanni

Further Reading

Crane, Philip. *The Sum of Good Government*. Ottawa, Ill.: Green Hill Publishers, 1976.

creationism

Creationism is the belief that the universe, including the earth and all its life-forms, was created by God. The biblical account of origins, in Genesis 1 and 2, was almost universally accepted in the Western world until the nineteenth century. Charles Darwin challenged this account beginning with his *Origin of Species* (1859), which argued that species evolved over long periods of time through the mechanism of natural selection. But creationist controversy is not just a conflict between origins accounts; more broadly, it has become a conflict between theistic and nontheistic cosmologies.

One should not identify creationism with conservatism or Christianity in general. While doubts regarding the Darwinian account of evolution abound on the Right, and span the gamut from scientific "intelligent design" theories to fundamentalist Protestant biblical literalism, the view that God created heaven, earth, and man in seven literal days does not dominate. For example, in 1950 the Catholic Church made clear its position that there is no necessary contradiction between the idea that God used evolution to create the first man and the Catholic faith, provided it is recognized that the spiritual soul is created by God, rather than the human mind being a mere epiphenomenon of matter. Evolution, on this view, is a theory, or rather set of theories, subject to proper scientific analysis.

Creationists in the late nineteenth century were primarily concerned with the philosophical naturalism and materialism Darwinism encouraged. Though reluctant to accept the Bible's scientific material literally, they did stress the divine agency of creation. These early creationists, such as Louis Agassiz and Charles Hodge, mainly critiqued atheistic or naturalistic evolution.

The creationist controversy became more intense, defined, and political in the 1920s. Fundamentalists had stressed a literal interpretation of the Bible, including the Genesis account of human origins. Many had ethical concerns, claiming that Germany suffered moral degeneration prior to World War I because of the teaching of natural selection. Progressives, who were committed to purifying society and protecting children, likewise feared the impact of evolutionary teaching. (Progressive veteran William Jennings Bryan once described his career as patrolling with a double-barreled shotgun: one barrel for an elephant raiding the Treasury, another for a monkey raiding the schoolhouse.) Another progressive reform, compulsory education, dramatically increased enrollment in government high schools and heightened concerns about their curricula.

The creationist controversy erupted at the 1925 Scopes trial in Dayton, Tennessee. Dayton's high school football coach and substitute biology teacher, John Scopes, with encouragement from the ACLU and a local group of business boosters, decided to challenge a Tennessee statute that made it unlawful to deny "the story of Divine Creation of man as taught in the Bible, and to teach that mankind descended from a lower order of animals." His defense attorney was Clarence Darrow, the famous American trial lawyer and agnostic. Siding with Tennessee was Bryan, the three-time Democratic presidential candidate, progressive reformer, and Christian crusader. Scopes was found guilty of breaking the law, but his $100 fine was later overturned on a technicality. When Bryan died a few days after the trial, creationists lost their most famous advocate and seemingly lost the battle.

The creationist crusade, however, continued. Creationist legislative initiatives were rewarded, in 1928, in a spectacularly successful Arkansas referendum measure. Gaining popularity as creationist spokesmen and authors were Harry Rimmer, an itinerant Presbyterian evangelist and self-styled "research scientist," and George M. Price, a Seventh Day Adventist geology professor. By the 1930s, the issue was dormant, as creationists and evolutionists had reached a tacit understanding. Textbooks dropped or muted references to evolution and Darwinism, while states declined to enforce existing creationist laws.

Creationism experienced a revival in the 1960s and 1970s. The most significant figure was Henry Morris, a college professor with a Ph.D. in hydraulic engineering. His *The Genesis Flood* (1961), coauthored with theologian John Whitcomb, sounded authoritative, made "flood geology" popular in Christian circles, and paved the way for "scientific creationism." Morris helped found the Creation Research Society, an organization that required members to hold graduate degrees in the sciences. Later he established the Institute for Creation Research, a San Diego–based research and educational institution whose members have an aggressive program of publication and debate.

Legal battles over creationism were renewed in the early 1980s. Balanced Treatment Acts were passed in Louisiana and Arkansas (and introduced in nineteen other states) that required that scientific creationism be taught in schools where evolution was taught. Rather than forbidding evolutionary teaching, as in the legislation of the 1920s, the measures required equal time for an alternative perspective. In 1987, in *Edwards v. Aguillard*, the U.S. Supreme Court declared the acts unconstitutional, contending that they violated the First Amendment by requiring the teaching of religious doctrine. Sharp dissenting opinions on the Louisiana court and the Supreme Court, however, reflect the divided opinion of Americans on creationism.

Creationists have also appealed to the philosophy of science, particularly to Thomas Kuhn's *The Structure of Scientific Revolutions* (1962). There can be, they argue, two interpretive models to explain scientific phenomena. Though evolution is the established paradigm, other hypotheses may be equally valid and cannot be discounted.

Essentially, though, creationists are driven by religious concerns. First, they wish to defend the authority and accuracy of the Genesis account. Second, naturalistic evolution, when consistently applied, challenges cardinal Christian doctrines about sin and salvation. Third, and perhaps most importantly, they believe that evolution is a dehumanizing doctrine, which in eroding the belief that man is made in the image of God threatens the underpinnings of society.

Creationists have never been in complete agreement about what the Bible teaches, and, over the years, three distinct and competing schools of thought have emerged. Day-age theorists argue that the "days" of Genesis 1 actually refer to long eras or epochs of time. This theory has attracted some ardent fundamentalists, such as William Bell Riley. Others squeeze a great deal of evolutionary science into these indeterminate days of Genesis and are labeled "theistic evolutionists" or "progressive creationists." But all such theorists hold that God guided the process.

Gap theorists argue that there was a gap between Gen 1:1 and Gen 1:2 that could accommodate a large span of time and would explain phenomena such as dinosaurs and cavemen. The fossil record pertains to God's original creation, while Gen 1:2 tells the story of God's re-creation. This system allows great harmonization with science, while still allowing for a literal interpretation of the Bible. The gap theory, outlined in Scofield's biblical reference notes, became an article of faith for most fundamentalists and dispensationalists.

Young-earth theorists interpret the Bible most literally and represent the strictest school of creationism. Following Morris, they argue for a young earth (about six thousand years old), and claim that radical and catastrophic geological changes occurred because of the Noahic flood.

—ROGER SCHULTZ

Further Reading

Bird, Wendell. *The Origin of Species Revisited.* 2 vols. New York: Philosophical Library, 1987-1988.

Eve, Raymond, and Francis Harrold. *The Creation-ist Movement in Modern America.* Boston: Twayne Publishers, 1991.

Gatewood, Willard. *The Controversy of the Twenties: Fundamentalism, Modernism, and Evolution.* Nashville: Vanderbilt, 1969.

Johnson, Philip E., and Denis O. Lemoureux. *Darwinism Defeated?* Vancouver, B.C.: Regent College Publishing, 1999.

Larson, Edward. *Trial and Error: The American Controversy Over Creation and Evolution.* New York: Oxford, 1985.

Numbers, Ronald. *The Creationists: The Evolution of Scientific Creationism.* New York: Alfred Knopf, 1992.

See also: Bryan, William Jennings; Scopes trial

Cribb, T. Kenneth, Jr. (1948–)

T. Kenneth Cribb Jr. has been in the vanguard of the modern conservative intellectual movement for more than three decades. Since 1989, he has served as president of the Intercollegiate Studies Institute, where he has sought to preserve and promote the American ideal of ordered liberty on college and university campuses. Cribb has transformed ISI from an important but relatively small organization in the conservative movement into one of the most influential. Under his leadership, ISI's budget and staff have grown tremendously, while the organization has matured into a prominent cultural and educational presence. Among his enduring accomplishments at ISI have been his role in purchasing a permanent headquarters for the organization and establishing a sizable endowment.

Cribb is also president of the Council for National Policy and president of the Collegiate Network. He is the counselor to the Federalist Society for Law and Public Policy and played a crucial role in establishing its early national credibility and nurturing its growth for over twenty years. Cribb is a former president of the Philadelphia Society, former vice chairman of the Fulbright Foreign Scholarship Board, and former governor of the American Red Cross.

Born and raised in Spartanburg, South Carolina, and educated in Virginia, Cribb earned a B.A. from Washington and Lee University in 1970 and a J.D. from the University of Virginia law school in 1980. In between, he led field operations at ISI and enthusiastically advanced the conservative intellectual movement on campuses across the country. In 1980, Cribb signed on as deputy chief counsel of the Reagan-Bush campaign and later supervised thirty of the president-elect's transition teams.

Cribb joined President Reagan's White House staff in 1981, eventually becoming assistant counselor to the president and right-hand man to presidential counselor Edwin Meese III, Reagan's closest advisor. Cribb soon became known for advancing substantive principles while obtaining practical results. He participated in every major domestic policy initiative and was an early architect and core implementer of Reagan's decision to return federal circuit court appellate judgeships to the constitutional domain of the president instead of letting them remain the bailiwick of senatorial political prerogative.

Cribb served in the Reagan Justice Department from 1985 to 1987 as counselor to Meese. There he spearheaded the effort to promote the fundamental importance of the rule of law and a renewed respect for the Constitution. Cribb returned to the White House in 1987 to serve as Reagan's top domestic policy advisor, becoming Assistant to the President for Domestic Affairs, with four major White House offices reporting to him. In this capacity he helped to reinvigorate the White House policy operation for the home stretch of the second Reagan term. After leaving the White House in 1988, Cribb became a senior fellow at the Heritage Foundation until returning to ISI as president early in 1989.
—JOHN RICHARDSON

Further Reading

Edwards, Lee. *Educating for Liberty: The First Half-Century of the Intercollegiate Studies Institute.* Washington, D.C.: Regnery Publishing, 2003.

See also: Intercollegiate Studies Institute

Crisis

Catholicism in Crisis, a monthly magazine of politics, culture, and the Catholic Church, was founded in 1982 by theologian Michael Novak and philosopher Ralph McInerny to serve as a neoconservative platform from which to criticize the liberal pronouncements of the U.S. Bishops Conference and also as a counterweight to the cultural prominence then wielded by left-leaning Catholic periodicals like *Commonweal* and *America*. The magazine was first published by the Brownson Institute at the University of Notre Dame. In 1984, the magazine moved its headquarters to Washington, D.C., and changed its name to *Crisis*. Its first editors during this time were Novak, Dinesh D'Souza, and Scott Walter. Eleven years later, Deal Hudson, a former Baptist minister and philosophy professor at Fordham University, took the helm of *Crisis* as publisher and editor, and the Brownson Institute passed ownership of the magazine to the Morley Institute (which later became the Morley Publishing Group), a nonprofit organization created to support *Crisis*'s operations.

From the beginning, *Crisis*'s mission has been to "interpret and shape the direction of contemporary culture from a standpoint of Catholic tradition," but the continuity of that mission notwithstanding, the magazine has undergone some striking identity changes through the years. Before Hudson came on board *Crisis* tended to publish primarily high-brow articles and reviews aimed at academics and other highly educated readers; its overall tone was much like that of the current *First Things*. Under Hudson, who was closely connected to the Bush White House, the magazine became more politically focused and less high toned; one of Hudson's major concerns was the formation of a governing coalition in which Catholic conservatives played a fundamental role. In its current format the magazine is glossy, graphics heavy, and journalistic. Despite all the changes, certain columns have remained stalwarts, including those by Frs. James V. Schall and George Rutler. In addition, Terry Teachout and Robert R. Reilly continue to review films and music, respectively.

During his tenure as editor, Hudson was exceptionally successful in putting the once-dowdy magazine on a solid financial footing and increasing the magazine's circulation, which stood at almost 30,000 in mid-2004. However, the resurfacing, in 2004, of a lurid scandal in which Hudson had been involved while at Fordham in 1994 forced him to resign. The current editor is Brian Saint-Paul.
—Xandy Gilman

Further Reading

Feuerherd, Joe. "The Real Deal." *National Catholic Reporter,* August 27, 2004.

Hudson, Deal. *American Conversion: One Man's Discovery of Beauty and Truth in Times of Crisis.* New York: Crossroad, 2003.

See also: McInerny, Ralph; Neibuhr, Reinhold; neoconservatism; Novak, Michael; Roman Catholicism

Criterion

T. S. Eliot founded the quarterly *Criterion* in 1922 with the aim of "bringing together the best new thinking and new writing in its time, from all the countries of Europe that had anything to contribute to the common good." The first issue carried Eliot's famous poem "The Waste Land"; works by major figures like Pound, Auden, Yeats, Forster, Lawrence, Huxley, Chesterton, Dawson, and Allen Tate appeared in subsequent volumes. The *Criterion* also brought translations of Dostoyevsky, Thomas Mann, Paul Valéry, Luigi Pirandello, Cavafy, and other modern European writers to new audiences. Eliot maintained close contacts with and reported on kindred European magazines: *Nouvelle Revue Française, Neue Rundschau, Revista de Occidente,* and *Il Convegno*. During its first few years, the *Criterion* exerted a powerful influence on literature and culture in England and the United States. Later, it became more occupied with politics and theology. In 1939, on the eve of World War II, Eliot halted publication because of "a depression of spirits."

Like Eliot himself, the *Criterion* was concerned with the crisis of modern European culture and, broadly speaking, sought to spread among educated persons a renewed respect for classicism in several senses of the word. For Eliot, classicism meant first a recognition of the ancient bases of civilization: "*all* European civilizations are equally dependent upon Greece and Rome—so far as they are civilizations at all. . . . Neglect of Greek means for Europe *a relapse into unconsciousness.*" Recovering full consciousness would mean not merely retrieving the past but its use to help elaborate a comprehensive discipline of character and a clarification of reason.

Though Eliot had long affirmed that literature must be pursued and judged on its own terms, the *Criterion* took as its scope a wide-ranging scrutiny of every dimension of society, politics, and culture. After the first year of publication, Eliot contended that those who affirm an antinomy between "literature," meaning any literature that can appeal only to a small and fastidious public, and "life," are not only flattering the complacency of the half-educated, but asserting a principle of disorder.

Yet Eliot never imposed a strict editorial line on literary contributions or social commentary, preferring to encourage a "tendency" toward classicism. Throughout the 1930s, he published the work of the then-communist W. H. Auden, Stephen Spender, and Louis MacNeice. He seemed to think Marxism a worthy adversary and even opined that "in times like ours we need ideas, not only our own, but antagonistic ideas against which our ideas may keep themselves sharp."

At the same time, the journal was often accused of nostalgia toward aristocracy and religion and even of a sympathy for fascism. The truth, more probably, is that Eliot, like many intellectuals in the decade before the war, felt that "the immense panorama of futility and anarchy which is contemporary history" could not be corrected by liberal democracy. He therefore groped for solutions elsewhere.

In America, the *Criterion* was an influence before what John Crowe Ransom was to call the New Criticism. Southern writers in particular had felt the attraction of close reading of texts, as opposed to philological, biographical, and political approaches. Sympathy for traditional social arrangements—rather than the rationalized structures of modernity—seemed to flow from the same orientation. The Fugitives, particularly Allen Tate, sought to promote in the United States some of the same values Eliot was championing in Britain. Though Eliot had earlier rejected some of his poetry, Tate persisted in sending him his work, became a regular contributor, and later called the *Criterion* a "model" for the modern literary magazine. Eliot returned the admiration, calling Tate as promising as anyone in his generation in America.

Eliot's quarterly was clearly in Tate's and many others' minds when the *Sewanee Review* was founded. Edmund Wilson, displaying some jealousy about Eliot's influence, warned Tate by letter not to follow Eliot's example of not publishing his own poetry:

"The result was that people bought the *Criterion* because it was Eliot's magazine and then found very little in it except tiresome articles by young men who were hanging around Eliot and whom he didn't have the energy to brush off." Wilson's view was common in the forties, when the Nazi horror had underscored the ultimate failure of the *Criterion* to establish the pan-European classicism it initially sought; it is a view that has been echoed by other critics ever since. But many of the questions addressed by the magazine, and no small number of the articles themselves, retain interest.

Europe and the West generally seem to have given up on the classical revival Eliot somewhat abstractly advocated. The question remains, however, whether a civilization built upon certain concepts and habits derived from those concepts can long endure their disappearance and the rise of alien principles. The chaos of standards in the liberal democracies of the 1930s seems to us today preferable to the many alternatives that have been attempted since. But the basic question of the roots of the liberal order, as examined by Eliot and his contributors over nearly twenty years are, if anything, more pressing and obvious than when they were first posed. And the reflections by Eliot and his contributors on the regional (as opposed to the provincial) and its relationship to the universal (as opposed to the abstract) continue to vex Europe and America today.

F. R. Leavis may have had greater influence on restricted circles in the literature profession through his journal *Scrutiny*, but no intellectual quarterly in English in the years between the World Wars, and probably since, had as general importance and significance as the *Criterion*.

—Robert Royal

Further Reading

Ackroyd, Peter. *T. S. Eliot: A Life*. New York: Simon & Schuster, 1984

Harding, Jason. *The* Criterion: *Cultural Politics and Periodical Networks in Inter-War Britain.* Oxford: Oxford University Press, 2002.

See also: Eliot, T. S.; New Criterion

Crocker, George N. (1906–70)

George N. Crocker is chiefly remembered as the author of *Roosevelt's Road to Russia* (1959), a work of historical revisionism that fingered President Franklin D. Roosevelt as a willing dupe of Josef Stalin, a facilitator of policies designed to model American society upon the Soviet model while sacrificing American interests abroad to the ambitions of the Soviet dictator.

Born into a prominent San Francisco family in 1906, Crocker was educated at Stanford University and Harvard Law School, returning to Stanford to earn his law degree in 1929. During the 1930s, he became an assistant U.S. attorney, afterward entering private practice, and then serving as dean of Golden Gate College's law school for two years. During World War II, he served as an officer in the U.S. Army. After the war, Crocker retired from private practice and, according to publisher Henry Regnery, spent several years preparing to write a diplomatic history of World War II, conducting research "to discover, if possible, why, after overwhelming military victory, none of our professed war aims had been achieved." The result of his labors, *Roosevelt's Road to Russia*, was published by Regnery in September 1959.

In this work, Crocker argued that the reason the U.S. entered the war against the Axis Powers and the reason why an Iron Curtain was allowed to fall from Stettin to Trieste, with all the misery and death that attended this event and its aftermath, was because Roosevelt was enamored of—not deceived by—Stalin and wished to see the world political stage largely modeled along Soviet lines. Published at a time when the late president was still widely revered as a fatherly figure whose policies had ended the Great Depression and achieved total victory in World War II, *Roosevelt's Road to Russia* was destined to receive a rigidly divided critical reception. The book was ignored by many reviewing venues, though R. L. Duffus of the *New York Times Book Review* wrote dryly, "There is plenty to be said against the Russian regime under Stalin and later. But to write of the Nazi butchers and the Japanese overlords as though they were friends with whom we had a minor difficulty is neither history nor scholarship—it is sheer nonsense." Other reviewers were more favorable in their assessments: Walter Trohan called the work "strong meat" that "should be read by everyone who wants to understand the world today," and revisionist historian Harry Elmer Barnes described it as "a powerful, absorbing, timely, and convincing book" and "a masterpiece of picturesque but reliable narration." Crocker's book sold well and was reprinted several times.

From 1962 until his death following a heart attack in 1970, Crocker worked as a columnist for the *San Francisco Examiner*, writing on national and international affairs. In his memoir, Henry Regnery wrote, "George Crocker, unfortunately, did not live to write the second book he had planned, but his one book is a worthy memorial to a man of conviction who searched for the truth and did not shrink from telling what he found."

—JAMES E. PERSON JR.

Further Reading

Regnery, Henry. *Memoirs of a Dissident Publisher.* New York: Harcourt Brace Jovanovich, 1979.

See also: Cold War revisionism

culture wars

The idea that America is in the midst of a "culture war" was popularized persuasively by the sociologist James Davison Hunter in the early 1990s. Americans are divided rather fundamentally on the meaning and purpose of human life, and on moral and religious issues, and they vote these cultural views more reliably than their economic interests. The 2000 election, for example, divided Americans over culture more than anything else but race. The urban and urbane secular relativists tended to vote for Gore, and the small-town religious moralists voted for Bush. Bush carried an overwhelming amount of the territory of the United States, while Gore won the popular vote because he did so well in the major population centers.

At first glance, the cultural divide reflected in the presidential election presents a confusing picture to cultural conservatives. Conservatives characteristically are in favor of conserving "culture" in the sense of the great artistic and literary achievements of our civilization, and so they have disdain for popular vulgarity or philistinism. We think here of the conservatism of Henry Adams and that of the southern aristocratic poet William Alexander Percy. But conservatives also, quite rightly, think of the intellectuals of our time as less sophisticated than they are nihilistic. Most intellectuals now actively engage in the destruction of our cultural inheritance. And so conservatives today are resigned to allying with ordinary people—who have retained considerable respect for God, their families, and their country—against the dominant faction of intellectuals. Today's conservatives usually see that the foundation of any decent society is the virtue—the cultural conservatism—of ordinary people.

A longer and deeper view of our cultural divide shows conservatives to be those Americans who take the side of religion and morality against intellectual liberationism.

At the time of the American founding, there were those, such as Jefferson, who wanted to free Americans from the authority of genuine religion. That elitist liberation movement was opposed then and now by those who believe our moral and political life would be damaged beyond repair if separated from Christian culture. The cultural hopes of the most secular of our founders were at least diminished considerably by the influence of the Puritans, the Calvinists, waves of immigrants, and religious revivals in America. Christianity, as Alexis de Tocqueville noticed, has always been America's genuine counterculture. It is an indispensable antidote to democratic self-obsession and materialism. Aristocracy, too, is strong where democratic liberalism is weak, but Tocqueville was right that all family- or tradition-based aristocracy was destined to fade in America. That is one reason why the Adams family finally dropped off the political and literary map, and why the philosopher-novelist Walker Percy—who was raised by the Stoic aristocrat William Alexander Percy—became a Christian democrat.

To call Christianity our counterculture is not to accuse our dominant or elite culture of public atheism. Tocqueville noted that there is no such atheism in America, and things have not changed all that much since his day. All Americans who want to have public influence speak of God. The real division in American life, as Hunter astutely observed, is between those who view religion in an orthodox and those who view it in a progressive way. Cultural liberals use religion as a vehicle for achieving progressive political goals; God is presented as supporting the latest views on rights and social justice. Cultural conservatives typically really believe in God and that they are bound by his will; his word, the orthodox say, gives us the right way to live. Religion, for them, is a nonnegotiable standard for criticizing contemporary permissiveness and self-righteousness. For the orthodox, the one true human progress is personal—toward sanctity and virtue; those who speak confidently of historical or political progress are usually diverted from the one thing most needful for each one of us.

What is new in our time is the extent to which this progressive-orthodox division creates factions within America's major religious denominations. Such factionalism has animated American political life from its beginning. The claims of reason and revelation have not, in truth, existed in harmony in America. Our rationalists have too often been dogmatically anti-Christian materialists, and our defenders of faith have too often confused being guided by reason with scientific atheism. How could a country that is so shaped both by modern science and Protestant theology possibly be free from cultural conflict and confusion?

American liberals often hold that the idea of Americans being divided politically by their different views of culture is un-American. The American way is to separate religion from political life, reducing the latter to the adjustment of economic interests. The liberal view posits that when religion enters the political arena the result is usually tyranny and war. Cultural or religious issues are those concerning which we oppress and kill one another. Conservatives respond that the idea of a human life or human education indifferent to religious controversy is an unrealistic abstraction. The idea of what cultural conservatives call a "naked public square" is simply inhuman. Most of our public policies—as our political leaders both liberal and conservative are often unafraid to say—are based on some understanding of God and the human soul.

The phrase "culture war," of course, is, for Americans, not literal. There is no real civil war going on, and our country, to its great credit, has avoided wars of religion. Many reasons might be given for this example of American exceptionalism, but one

is that most Americans have found themselves somewhere in between rigid religious orthodoxy and secular humanist liberationism. Moral issues that cannot be compromised in principle have often been compromised in fact. These issues have usually been resolved at the state and local level without being raised to high constitutional principle; that resolution has also typically been influenced by the people's Christian inheritance. (The one moral issue on which compromise proved impossible over the long term—slavery—did provoke a war more bloody than almost all wars of religion.)

In our time, cultural division is more intense because secular elites have become more aggressive in employing the media, public bureaucracies, and especially the courts in advancing their agenda. The permissive views of the allegedly countercultural sixties have become those of our establishment intellectuals, and the size of that class has grown steadily throughout the "information age." The notorious *Roe v. Wade* (1973), for example, made real compromise on the contentious issue of abortion impossible. That decision emboldened "pro-choice" cultural liberals and energized "pro-life" (and pro-family) cultural conservatives. The resulting emergence of a clearly pro-*Roe* Democratic Party and a clearly anti-*Roe* Republican Party sparked a political realignment along cultural lines. Because other cultural issues—such as patriotism—were involved in that realignment, it is hard to tell which party benefited more from this sharpening of American disagreement on human life and the family. Cultural liberals complain that inappropriate moralizing has allowed the Republicans to become the nation's dominant party through populist demagoguery; cultural conservatives complain, with more justice, that their tenuous and surely temporary dominance has done their cause almost no good. Orthodox religious leaders complain with increasing frequency that public policy in America has become hostile to the ways of life they hope to conserve.

Today, many cultural conservatives, despite the result of the 2000 and 2004 presidential elections, seem to be, if not exactly surrendering, at least withdrawing from political combat. They are focused on building small-scale alternative institutions and schooling their children at home. But the challenge of biotechnology will probably return them to action. Our political division into culturally liberal and culturally conservative camps will become clearer. The "new" Democratic Party founded by Bill Clinton is rather consistently libertarian, embracing both personal permissiveness and the free market. The Republican Party, meanwhile, may well become more concerned with using the power of government to protect human culture and community against the "designer" future promised us through genetic therapy and regenerative biology. American cultural conservatives will have to become more self-conscious, although there is no reason to believe they will prevail over cultural liberals in the immediate future. Many sociologists, including Hunter, have observed that Americans are becoming more libertarian, and the Republicans may well suffer as they become more "culturally" and less "economically" conservative. Because the biotechnological issues will soon involve the very future of all that is good about being human, we can expect the culture war to become progressively more warlike.

—PETER AUGUSTINE LAWLER

Further Reading

Hunter, James Davison. *Culture Wars: The Struggle to Define America.* New York: Basic Books, 1992.

Himmelfarb, Gertrude. *One Nation, Two Cultures.* New York: Knopf, 1999.

Lawler, Peter Augustine. *Aliens in America: The Strange Truth about Our Souls.* Wilmington, Del.: ISI Books, 2002.

George, Robert P. *The Clash of Orthodoxies: Law, Religion, and Morality in Crisis.* Wilmington, Del.: ISI Books, 2001.

See also: abortion; Bloom, Allan; Buchanan, Patrick J.; liberalism; New Right

custom

Customs are established standards of behavior that are justified by their past contribution to civility and their embodiment of the normative in historical experience. Although customs may vary by region, organization, or institution, even within a particular nation, they provide a cultural standard for human behavior. They are rooted in common sense (i.e., agreement on universal truth) and thus while they take particular forms in different cultural contexts (because the historical and cultural experience from which they are engendered varies), they have a universal quality. Customs represent a consensus of generations and ages, past and present, that have participated in the search for justice, liberty, truth, and order. They are the product of trial and error and experimentation with different responses to common circumstances. They presume that human beings and human societies are not naturally ordered nor naturally good but rather require the influence and direction of proven human experience that is the product of historical consensus. Without custom, individuals become more anarchic because they must rely exclusively on unaided reason, instinct, and their immediate senses.

Custom plays an important role in the ideas of Edmund Burke, David Hume, and Russell Kirk. In *Enquiries Concerning Human Understanding and Concerning the Principles of Morals* (1751), Hume wrote that custom "is the great guide of human life. It is that principle alone which renders our experience useful to us, and makes us expect, for the future, a similar train of events with those which have appeared in the past. Without the influence of custom, we should be entirely ignorant of every matter of fact beyond what is immediately present to the memory and senses."

While custom is based in reason, its social efficacy has more to do with Burkean prejudice; it provides a ready-made standard for human behavior. The assumption is that "naked reason" alone is incapable of directing individuals to the good. Custom presumes humility, the admission that right action requires reference to the wisdom and prejudice of past generations. Custom is, as Burke said of prejudice, "of ready application in the emergency; it previously engages the mind in a steady course of wisdom and virtue, and does not leave the man hesitating in the moment of decision, skeptical, puzzled, and unresolved." Custom shapes imagination and character in a way that creates a predisposition and habit to the good; custom makes virtue habit, reminding individuals of their civic duties and leading them to their moral responsibilities.

Custom is, then, an important aspect of civility. It provides a cultural ethos that inculcates the disposition toward civility that is necessary for ordered life. Custom also provides the cultural context for law and government. While setting boundaries and parameters to government power, it provides a cultural check against tyranny. Lawmaking, for example, occurs in a context replete with preexisting customs and traditions. Legislators must gauge the force of custom before they craft laws and public policies. The efficacy of law depends, in part, on its compatibility with custom.

Custom can take the form of a legal tradition or law but is differentiated from law in that it does not usually carry the sanction of legal penalty. In fact, customs are important to self-governing in the sense that they provide a nongovernmental source of order. They are one way that private groups and associations shape culture and politics, as Tocqueville notes in *Democracy in America* (1835). Consequently, customs cannot exist and thrive without a significant degree of liberty. Totalitarian governments typically attempt to undermine customs because customs rival state authority. The maintenance of customs depends on the existence of a class of cultural leaders which acts as their stewards. Good leaders live by customary obligations and animate customary ideals in their behavior. By conforming to custom, they provide examples of civil men and women whose character is worthy of emulation. Without a class of natural aristocrats to cultivate and animate customs, customs become stale and ineffective and are reduced to instruments of self-interest and pretension.

Custom is important to conservatism for two primary reasons. First, it provides continuity with the past by bringing historical experience to bear on the present. Second, it is a check on the impulsive tendencies of reformers and radicals who operate from the progressive assumption that the present generation knows better than past generations how to govern society. Conservatives are reluctant to break with ways of life that are the product of time-tested experience. Custom is a primary check against wholesale change.

Liberals and progressives argue that commitment to custom prohibits progress. Rousseau, a romantic naturalist, was one of the most prominent critics of custom because he believed that it inhibits the spontaneous will of human beings, who are naturally good. Scientific naturalists also depreciate the value of custom because they believe that innovations in science and reason demonstrate that established customs are obstacles to progress. Egalitarians and socialists view custom as a tool used by the powerful to maintain their privileged position in society. Custom, they argue, has tended to subordinate women, minorities, animals, and other oppressed groups to inferior social positions. By creating a social hierarchy, custom stands in the way of establishing social equality and social justice.

Followers of the philosopher Eric Voegelin, including some conservatives, tend to view ideological attachment to custom as problematic. Voegelin warned that tradition and custom, while socially useful, should not be elevated to a position of theoretical privilege. Custom is not itself the good. Historical experience, from which custom is derived, is primary and has the existential force to order souls. Custom is secondary, and ideological adherence to it risks the separation of experience from symbolic representations of truth. Customs can become reified once they are separated from experience. Consequently, a custom can come to be viewed as truth itself rather than as a symbolic representation of truth. In its reified form, custom can encourage a fundamentalism and legalism that subvert the good by closing off the search for truth.

Yet custom can change over time as circumstances and human experience alter human perception of the good. Prudence will require changes in custom, but a change that maintains continuity with the past. In other words, conservatives are not blindly wed to custom. Paleoconservatives especially recognize that the universal needs to be repeatedly reconstituted in accord with changing historical circumstances. Conservatives embrace change that preserves continuity because universality, as Irving Babbitt noted, is a "oneness that is always changing."

—MICHAEL P. FEDERICI

Further Reading

Frohnen, Bruce. *Virtue and the Promise of Conservatism: the Legacy of Burke and Tocqueville.* Lawrence, Kan.: University Press of Kansas, 1993.

Kirk, Russell. *The Conservative Mind: From Burke to Eliot.* 7th ed. Washington, D.C.: Regnery, 2001.

———. *Edmund Burke: A Genius Reconsidered.* Rev. and updated ed. Wilmington, Del.: Intercollegiate Studies Institute, 1997.

See also: Burke, Edmund; conservatism; Kirk, Russell; law and order; natural law; paleoconservatism; prejudice; prescription; traditionalism; Voegelin, Eric

D

Dartmouth Review

With its mutinous flair and notoriously un-civil treatment at the hands of administra-tors and faculty, the *Dartmouth Review* is a widely known conservative student newspa-per. Founded by discontented *Daily Dartmouth* editors in 1980, the independent paper has around 10,000 subscribers nationwide, be-sides its free distribution to students on cam-pus. Among the biweekly's former staff are conservative movement notables Dinesh D'Souza, Hugo Restall, James S. Panero, and Laura Ingraham. Dartmouth professor emeritus Jeffrey Hart serves as chairman.

Events at Dartmouth involving the *Dartmouth Review* and its staff have helped to expose the institutional bias against con-servative students in contemporary academe and the double standard to which conserva-tive editors are often held. At Dartmouth, the "Bill Cole Affair" thrust the paper into the media spotlight in 1989.

As the *Dartmouth Review*'s editor in chief, Christopher Baldwin printed some of Pro-fessor Cole's classroom rants unrelated to the subject matter of a music course he was teaching, brought to Baldwin on a tape by a student unaffiliated with the paper. Baldwin and some of his staff were suspended for a "vexatious oral exchange" with the profes-sor, who is black, thus revealing the episode as a sin against political correctness. With the national publicity surrounding the un-fair proceedings and undeserved punish-ment (Baldwin and one colleague were sus-pended for six terms), initiated by columnist William F. Buckley Jr., the students raised nearly $300,000, sued Dartmouth, and won their case in a New Hampshire court, which overturned the college's decision and or-dered the students' reinstatement.

A bellwether of conservative student journalism with a rebellious spirit of politi-cal incorrectness, the *Dartmouth Review* also promotes merchandise featuring the Dartmouth Indian mascot. The following quote from Theodore Roosevelt appears on the paper's masthead: "Far better is it to dare mighty things, to win great triumphs, even though checkered by failure, than to take ranks with those poor spirits who neither enjoy much nor suffer much, because they live in the gray twilight that knows neither victory nor defeat."

—WILLIAM F. MEEHAN III

Further Reading

Hart, Jeffrey. "James O. Friedman: President of Dartmouth." In *Surviving the PC University: The Best of Heterodoxy*, edited by Peter Collier and David Horowitz, 62–63. Studio City, Calif.: Second Thought Books, 1993.

Panero, James, and Stefan Beck, eds. *"The Dartmouth Review" Pleads Innocent: Twenty-Five Years of Being Threatened, Impugned, Van-dalized, Sued, Suspended, and Bitten at the Ivy League's Most Controversial Conservative News-paper.* Wilmington, Del.: ISI Books, 2006.

See also: Collegiate Network; D'Souza, Dinesh; Hart, Jeffrey

Davenport, John (1597–1670)

An English Puritan clergyman, John Davenport advocated theonomy, the binding authority of Old Testament legislation on Christians. Sickened by moral corruption and religious laxity, Davenport, vicar of St. Stephen's, London, and 250 of his parishioners set sail for Boston in 1637. Landing during the Antinominian furor, Davenport vigorously opposed Anne Hutchinson, believing that her views on immediate revelation undermined scripture and social order. Yearning for "yet stricter conformity to the word of God, in settling of all matters, both civil and sacred," he and his supporters established an unincorporated plantation at New Haven in April 1638. He drafted its theocratic constitution, the Fundamental Articles of 1639, which limited political rights to converted male church members, eliminated English common law, including trial by jury, and made the Mosaic code the colony's sole legal foundation. At the Boston Synod of 1662 that recommended the "Half Way Covenant," Davenport led conservative opposition, convinced that baptizing children of unconverted parents would threaten the foundations of his biblical church-state. His considerable prestige in England served to protect New Haven's autonomy during the Commonwealth, but with the Restoration and Davenport's ill-conceived reception of "regicide judges," New Haven was absorbed into the somewhat more liberal, and politically astute, Connecticut. With the collapse of his theocracy, Davenport believed "Christ's interest miserably lost." Deeply disillusioned, he accepted election in 1668 to the pulpit of First Church, Boston, but died shortly thereafter.

Once Davenport adopted Puritan positions on ritual and church governance early in his career, nonconformity became his orthodoxy. Two elements were central to his thinking: the necessity of a Bible-ordered, visible Church of the Elect and a government likewise based on scripture and ruled by the saints. Davenport's belief in a pure church anticipated the views of Jonathan Edwards and New Lights of the Great Awakening. His theonomist ideals foreshadowed the thinking of Rousas John Rushdoony and other advocates of Christian Reconstructionism, a biblical program for cultural reform which, if applied consistently, would supplant the Constitution with the Pentateuch.

—P. Bradley Nutting

Further Reading

Calder, Isabel M. *Letters of John Davenport.* New Haven, Conn.: Yale University Press, 1937.

Dexter, Franklin B. "Life and Writings of John Davenport." In *New Haven Colony Historical Society Papers II.* New Haven, Conn.: Historical Society, 1877.

See also: Christian Reconstruction; Puritanism; Rushdoony, Rousas John

Davidson, Donald G. (1893–1968)

Fugitive poet, Agrarian social philosopher, and member of Vanderbilt University's English faculty for forty-four years, Donald Grady Davidson was a major participant in two famous literary groups associated with that university: the Fugitives and the Agrarians. With Allen Tate, John Crowe Ransom, and Robert Penn Warren, he was a leading member of the Fugitive poets—those Southern writers who edited and contributed poems, essays, and reviews to the *Fugitive* (1922–25), a literary magazine that played a significant role in the inauguration of the Southern literary renaissance. Later in the 1920s, Davidson led the Fugitives in adding social, economic, and political concerns to their literary interests, which resulted in the formation of a second group, the Agrarians. Attracting Andrew Lytle, Stark Young, John

Donald Wade, and other conservative southerners, the Agrarians opposed the New South gospel of industrial progress and defended the South's traditional agrarian way of life in their manifesto *I'll Take My Stand: The South and the Agrarian Tradition* (1930).

The Agrarians described their defense of the Southern way of life by juxtaposing it to the "industrial." *Agrarian* signified a traditional agricultural way of life based on stable, religious, politically conservative communities principally composed of land-owning families. *Industrial* signified a number of features of the modern industrial state that threatened a healthy family- and community-based political and cultural life: political centralization, secularism, materialism, consumerism, cosmopolitanism, urbanization, and standardization. Of the twelve southerners who contributed essays to the Agrarians' manifesto, Davidson was the most faithful and stalwart explicator and defender of agrarianism. And while some of the Agrarians lost interest in the movement in the mid-1930s, Davidson campaigned for the cause until the end of his life, persistently defending traditional conservative principles.

Donald G. Davidson

Before the Agrarians publicly took their stand in defense of the traditional South, Davidson was preparing the ground for the movement as editor and chief reviewer of "The Spyglass" (1924–30), a book page for the Nashville *Tennessean*. His "Spyglass" essays and reviews anticipated many Agrarian themes. In them, he opposed science as an arbiter of moral and social values, and scientism, which destroys myth and religion. He expressed skepticism concerning the ideology of progress and the cult of novelty. He criticized the commercial spirit that regulates everything, even art, in the interest of the cash nexus, and he scorned the taste and values of New York City literati. He also rejected Marxism and every kind of economic and historical determinism. While he noted the deleterious effects of the machine age on the arts, Davidson celebrated folk song, the ballad, handicrafts, and other features of folk heritage. Finally, Davidson cherished sectional differences and praised the artist still in touch with and at home in his community.

Davidson's contribution to American conservative thought is best discussed in terms of regionalism. When he took up the Agrarian cause, Davidson also embraced a regional poetic and social vision that appears in all of his post-Fugitive writings, whether its setting is middle Tennessee (as in his long poem *The Tall Men* [1927] and the two-volume history *The Tennessee* [1946]) or rural New England (some of the verse in *The Long Street* [1961] and his most frequently anthologized essay "Still Rebels, Still Yankees" [1957]). In literary, social, and political matters he always focused on the local scene, recognizing the community before the state, the state before the region, the region before the nation, and the nation before the world. His essay in *I'll Take My Stand*, "A Mirror for Artists" (1930), advocates decentralization of the arts and stresses that the artist owes allegiance to his community as citizen as well as to his art as craftsman.

Davidson made the argument for political decentralization in "That This Nation May Endure: The Need for Political Regionalism," his contribution to *Who Owns*

America? (1936), a sequel to *I'll Take My Stand.* In Davidson's many contributions to the *American Review* (a short-lived conservative journal [1933–37] that published his best known work, "Still Rebels, Still Yankees" and "Lee in the Mountains") he continued to attack national and cosmopolitan approaches to literary and social issues. These *American Review* essays, plus new material, went into *The Attack on Leviathan: Regionalism and Nationalism in the United States* (1938), Davidson's most important work on American social theory. Like much of Davidson's work, this book contains both stinging criticism and an affirmation. Negatively, he attacks Leviathan, the centrally governed industrialized state that (sometimes wittingly, sometimes accidentally) enforces political, cultural, artistic, and social conformity. Positively, Davidson defended the diversity of America: regionalism in education, in literature, in the arts, and in political economy.

Davidson wrote more than one hundred essentially pro-agrarian or traditionalist essays and reviews for a variety of journals of scholarship and opinion. His views on agrarianism, tradition, and the transmission of tradition, his appreciation for the regional past, and his celebration of folk art and community influenced Tate, Lytle, Wade, Frank L. Owsley, and other contemporaries. And as a teacher, poet, and scholar, he influenced later generations of teachers and men of letters, notably Richard Weaver, Randall Stewart, Russell Kirk, M. E. Bradford, Tom Landess, Robert Drake, Peter Stanlis, Madison Jones, and Marion Montgomery.

—MICHAEL JORDAN

Further Reading

Bradford, M. E. "Donald Grady Davidson." In *Fifty Southern Writers after 1900.* Edited by Joseph M. Flora and Robert Bain. New York: Greenwood, 1987.

Davidson, Donald. *Still Rebels, Still Yankees and Other Essays.* Baton Rouge: Louisiana State University Press, 1957; reissued with a foreword by Lewis Simpson, 1972.

Winchell, Mark Royden. *Where No Flag Flies: Donald Davidson and the Southern Resistance.* Columbia, Mo.: University of Missouri Press, 2000.

See also: agrarianism; American Review; I'll Take My Stand; *Southern Agrarians; Southern conservatism*

Davidson, Eugene A. (1902–2002)

Editor, publisher, and historian, Eugene Davidson is distinguished first by his career at Yale University Press, where he was editor from 1931 to 1959 and became director in 1938. Remarkable during this period was his courageous publication of Karl A. Wittfogel's *Oriental Despotism* (1957), a book that scientifically investigated a one-thousand-year phenomenon of political despotism based not on class rule but on a governmental bureaucracy that controlled the great waterworks at the economic core of arid countries.

From 1960 to 1970, Davidson was editor of *Modern Age,* which developed during this period into the most important quality journal willing to publish works by conservative authors. Davidson was also effective as president of the Foundation for Foreign Affairs (1957–70) and as chairman (honorary president from 1986) of the Conference on European Problems, an organization that together with the German *Studiengesellschaft fuer Fragen osteuropaischer Politik* has conducted international conferences meeting alternately in Germany and the United States since 1962. These sessions yielded a number of books on both sides of the Atlantic as well as papers published in scholarly journals, most of them dealing with problems of East-West relations.

As a historian, Davidson became known through a number of works on modern Germany. Prominent among them are *The Making of Adolf Hitler* (1977) and its sequel, *The Unmaking of Adolf Hitler* (1996). Others of his books include *The Death and Life of Germany* (1959), *The Trial of the Germans* (1966), and *The Nuremberg Fallacy* (1973). He also contributed book reviews, articles, and poetry to a number of magazines.

Davidson emphasized his objection to "the patent tendency to accept the downgrading of Western, particularly American culture, as normal. In the name of rainbow coalitions or polycentrism or cultural norming, the intellectual establishment in general has come to advocate a society where one life style is as worthy as another and where social engineering replaces the higher learning."

—GERHART NIEMEYER

Further Reading

Davidson, Eugene A. *Narrow Path of Freedom and Other Essays.* Columbia, Mo.: University of Missouri Press, 2002.

———. *Reflections on a Disruptive Decade.* Columbia, Mo.: University of Missouri Press, 2000.

See also: Modern Age

Davis, Jefferson (1808–89)

Planter, military officer, congressman, senator, secretary of war, and president of the Confederate States of America, Jefferson Davis served as the premier defender of the Southern conservative, or "states' rights," position during the mid-nineteenth century.

Davis spent much of his antebellum political career as a staunch states' rights Democrat who consistently defended slavery and its protection within a union of equal states. Deploring what he called an attack on "communal liberty," Davis believed the letter and spirit of the Constitution created a union in which the states were left to determine their own domestic affairs. His defense of strict construction, however, was not based entirely on his defense of slavery. On several issues, including tariff legislation that granted protection to Northern manufacturers, Davis claimed the Constitution prevented the federal government from being used as an instrument of purely sectional interests.

To Davis, nothing illustrated the problems of antebellum American politics better than the issue of slavery in the territories. Davis insisted that the western territories were the common property of all the states (like Washington, D.C.) and that citizens could not be denied the right to move to the territories with their slaves. He carefully distinguished between the South's cultural and economic minority status on the one hand and the South's unique minority representation in Congress on the other. All regions in the United States, he thought, could be classified as a minority, thus necessitating the need for restraint in any federal legislation dealing with national issues. However, Davis insisted that Congress had deprived the South of its natural expansion by restrictions on slavery in the territories.

Davis's career illustrates the unique pressures placed upon Southern conservatives during the late antebellum period. For example, while he criticized the expansion of federal powers, he also supported federal sponsorship of a transcontinental railroad as well as subsidies for internal improvements used in only one state. The temptations offered by a sizeable federal treasury lured Davis away from earlier Jeffersonian beliefs that the federal government had no authority to fund any internal improvements. Whenever the object of tariff reductions went unmet, he pressed for federal expenditures in Southern states to match those states' contributions to the federal coffers.

Often seen as the legitimate successor to John C. Calhoun, Davis tried to build bridges between Southern Democrats and their potential allies outside the South. Hoping to protect Southern interests while averting secession and civil war, he commonly spoke highly of Northerners, going so far as to call Massachusetts the birthplace of states' rights. The prospect of building a national political majority through the Democratic Party had a special appeal to him as well as to many Southern Democrats. For this reason, Davis always saw secession as a last resort and preferred state nullification. But he subordinated both tactics to that of working through a national party, even to the point of sacrificing some Southern interests in order to maintain a Democratic coalition. His labors for an alliance between Southern and Northern Democrats culminated in the election of his close friend, Franklin Pierce, to the presidency in 1852.

In more than one respect, Davis's dedication to political parties and his national service as secretary of war hindered his efforts to protect his native South. Only with Abraham Lincoln's election in 1860 did Davis come to believe that neither constitutional protections nor national political majorities could restrain what he saw as a crusade against the basis of Southern society. For him the election of 1860 illustrated how a political minority, the Republican Party, could rule the country. A state might nullify perceived unconstitutional laws, but national presidential elections were beyond repair.

He defended the actions of the seceding states by conceiving them as a means of conserving the accomplishments of the American Revolution and the founding. He continually linked the South's actions after 1860 with those of the revolutionary generation and insisted that Southerners were preserv-

ing their prescriptive rights rather than promoting a radical overthrow of American society. His farewell address to the Senate upon Mississippi's secession noted that ". . . we [Mississippians] but tread in the path of our fathers when we proclaim our independence . . . defending and protecting the rights we inherited. . . ."

Chosen provisional president of the Confederate States, then duly elected in 1861, Davis's actions during the Civil War reveal the cataclysmic effect war renders on conservative leaders. Critics have described Davis as unfit for the leadership of a government fighting one of the first modern wars. That he was tactless, brisk, overly intrusive in military operations, and reluctant to dismiss incompetent generals is beyond dispute. However, many of his faults originated in the pressures of war and the animosity of his enemies in the press and the Confederate Congress.

Jefferson Davis

What is more paradoxical is how Davis, though a believer in states' rights, was still willing to consolidate political power in order to further the needs of the Confederacy. Whether supporting the Treasury Department's inflationary financing of the war effort, proposing conscription of Confederate soldiers, or pressing for the suspension of habeas corpus, Davis supervised the rapid construction of a modern warfare state that exerted control over many aspects of Southern society. Only the demands of war could have prompted Davis to part with his conservative principles, and, even then, he justified his actions as a defense of his home and society, not out of an allegiance to abstract political ideals.

Following the defeat of the Confederacy, Davis was captured and imprisoned by Union soldiers. Bound in chains awaiting a trial that never occurred, he became a living martyr for the Southern cause of diffused political power and states' rights.

Davis's political thought can be found in numerous political speeches delivered between 1845 and 1865, but the best expression is his two-volume memoir, *The Rise and Fall of the Confederate Government* (1881), written between 1878 and 1881. In this work, Davis meticulously traced perceived constitutional violations and threats to the South. Characterizing the slavery issue as an expression of larger sectional concerns, he condemned those who, out of jealousy, undermined the legitimate needs of the Southern states and, through civil war, overthrew "... a Constitution with limited powers, the reserved rights of the states, and the supremacy of law equally over both rulers and ruled." For Davis and a long line of Southern conservatives to follow, the American Civil War consolidated political power in the federal government at the expense of the people's sovereignty.

—CAREY ROBERTS

Further Reading

Cooper, William J. *Jefferson Davis, American*. New York: Knopf, 2000.

Davis, Jefferson. *Jefferson Davis: Private Letters, 1823–1889*. Edited by Hudson Strode. Philadelphia: Da Capo Press, 1995.

See also: Civil War; Southern conservatism; states' rights

Dawson, Christopher (1889–1970)

Dawson was one of the major historians of the twentieth century and an important influence on modern conservative thought. T. S. Eliot once called Dawson the most powerful intellectual influence in Britain. During the 1930s, Dawson contributed a number of articles to Eliot's *Criterion* and later served as editor of the influential Catholic journal the *Dublin Review* (Dawson had converted to Catholicism in 1914). Dawson's fame in America grew while he served as the first holder of the Charles Chauncey Stillman Chair in Roman Catholic Studies at Harvard University from 1958 to 1962. His work on the relationship between religion and culture made an impact on later American conservatives such as Russell Kirk, as well as Eliot himself.

Educated at Winchester and Trinity College, Oxford, Dawson never received the doctorate. He published his first book, *The Age of the Gods*, in 1928. Two others quickly followed—*Progress and Religion* in 1929 and *The Making of Europe* three years later—before the chaos of the 1930s and '40s disrupted his plan for a five-volume history of culture. The completed volumes were received to great acclaim and earned praise from historians as well as anthropologists and sociologists, who marveled at Dawson's immense erudition and the wider vision that Dawson brought to his scholarship. His two sets of Gifford lectures, delivered first in 1946–47 and then again in 1948–49, were published, respectively, as *Religion and Culture* (1948) and *Religion and the Rise of Western Culture* (1950). Others of his books include *The Movement of World Revolution* (1959), *Mediaeval Religion* (1934), and *The Spirit of the Oxford Movement* (1933).

The core of Dawson's thought is that religious cult lies at the heart of every culture. Countering the materialist interpretations of human society, culture for Dawson was not limited by its geographic location or material resources. To genetic, geographic, and economic factors Dawson added "a fourth element—thought or the psychological factor—which is peculiar to the human species" and cannot be explained by the other components. This fourth factor organizes the remaining three; each society must contain a core of belief that forms its identity. Dawson applied this insight and his innovative historical methodology, which adopted sociological and anthropological concepts, to both Christian and non-Christian cultures. Indeed, because he thought that the religious impulse was universal and multifaceted, there is a sympathy in his understanding of non-Western cultures that standard anthropology sometimes lacks.

Following World War II, and after years of analyzing the ideologies of communism, fascism, and Nazism, Dawson became convinced that the connection between cultural and religious development he had discerned was more important for the coming democratic age than it had been for previous eras. In 1957, he wrote that because America "lies nearer to the cyclonic path of the forces of world change" than any other nation, its culture is the pattern of what is to come in the "historical new age which is global or universal." America contained within itself all the impulses of the modern age without much of the cultural inheritance that reminded older cultures of their past. The nation reveled in the development of the powers of technology and science to control behavior and society. Paradoxically, America also regarded itself as the culmination of the project of human freedom, where old loyalties were cast aside and where self-invention had become part of the national creed. Dawson instead tried to reconnect the American experience of freedom with its roots in the religious traditions of Christianity.

Dawson's insights into the importance of religion in the history of culture have been vindicated by recent empirical research, which has largely refuted the "secularization" thesis of social theory. The contemporary value of Dawson's work lies in his recognition of the continuing importance and influence of the religious impulse in the postmodern age, and its enduring ability to shape culture, even when diverted into what Dawson saw as pseudo-religions, such as consumerism.

—GERALD J. RUSSELLO

Christopher Dawson

Further Reading

Russello, Gerald J., ed. *Christianity and European Culture: Selections from the Work of Christopher Dawson.* Washington, D.C.: Catholic University of America Press, 1998.

———. "Christopher Dawson's 'America and the Secularization of Modern Culture.'" *Logos* 3 (2000): 3.

Scott, Christina. *A Historian and His World: A Life of Christopher Dawson,* 2nd ed. New Brunswick, N.J.: Transaction, 1992.

See also: American Review; Criterion; *Eliot, T. S.; Kirk, Russell*

Declaration of Independence

The official document by which the thirteen American colonies broke with the English monarchy and seceded from the British Empire, the Declaration of Independence is an object of significant debate within the conservative movement because of the central and unique role some would give it within the American tradition of ordered liberty. Some, particularly neoconservative, commentators have sought to portray the Declaration as a statement of radically new principles, binding the American people together into a single union dedicated above all to protecting the rights of individuals against governmental intrusion. Central to this thesis is a heavy emphasis on the second paragraph of the Declaration, wherein the Continental Congress stated on behalf of the American people: "We hold these truths to be self-evident, that all men are created equal, that they are endowed by their Creator with certain unalienable Rights, that among these are Life, Liberty and the Pursuit of Happiness. That to secure these rights, Governments are instituted among Men, deriving their just powers from the consent of the governed." The Congress went on to state (in a final version that was radically different from the first draft submitted by Thomas Jefferson) that men have the right to alter or abolish governments violating these rights.

From these words some within the conservative movement (perhaps most tenaciously, Harry Jaffa) construct what conservative critics refer to as a civil theology or political religion according to which the great men who secured America's freedom from Great Britain also reformulated the Western tradition of political thought, building on the work of English liberal thinker John Locke so as to secure individual rights as the ultimate end of government. The Founders are deemed to have based these rights in an equality that, while given by the creator of the universe, is superior in importance to duties imposed by that creator, other than the duty to recognize one another's inherent and individual equality. The result, on this reading, is a philosophical statement of limited government and individualism, secured by a belief that these primary goods are demanded by God.

Traditional conservatives generally reject this view of the Declaration as excessively abstract, antihistorical, and lacking in philosophical or political context. Pointing out the pragmatic origins of the Declaration in the colonists' need to make their break with Great Britain official in order to secure French aid, traditional conservatives (including George W. Carey and Russell Kirk, among others) further note the relative lack of importance assigned the document at the time of its promulgation (for example, it was signed by delegates only over the course of several weeks). Moreover, Jefferson himself noted the intentionally uncontroversial nature of the Declaration's preamble; the initial paragraphs on which such great emphasis is placed were intended to merely restate commonly accepted truisms. The Declaration is more properly seen as one in a long line of declarations within the Anglo-American tradition, intended to defend the inherited and chartered rights of Englishmen against attempted usurpations by the monarchy.

Traditional conservatives tend to see the Declaration as part of a tradition going back at least as far as the Magna Carta of 1215. In that document the English barons forced King John to agree that he would abide by a number of rights traditionally accorded to the Catholic Church, the English nobility, and landowners in general. Rights such as habeas corpus (no detention without legal authority), trial by a jury of one's peers, and consent to taxation were secured by this charter; these rights also were declared to have been the traditional law of the land stretching back to time immemorial. This historical view of rights was carried forward in other charters and declarations, including the English Bill of Rights, which resulted from the dethroning of James II in 1688. It was to that document and to the principles of the Glorious Revolution of 1688 that Americans had looked for many decades in detailing the rights they were guaranteed as British subjects.

The bulk of the Declaration is made up of charges leveled against the king. George III is charged with violating a number of important customary and chartered rights of the colonists, including the right to trial by jury, the right of the people not to be taxed without their consent, freedom from excessive interference with local lawmaking, and prohibitions against maintaining a standing army and quartering it in the people's homes. In both style and substance this list of charges closely mirrors that of the English Bill of Rights and, like that earlier document, the Declaration claims that, by violating these long-established rights, the king has become a tyrant to whom the people can no longer look as a legitimate ruler. These charges bind the Declaration, and the United States, to a historical vision of rights and of their necessary place within a long tradition of ordered liberty, rather than to a vision of rights as mere rational deductions supported only by abstract reason.

Moreover, the Declaration's prefatory language regarding equality and rights, so often examined in and of itself, must be read in context. The opening paragraph, and the document as a whole, is a declaration of political independence of one people from another, not an abstract statement of universal rights. It begins by stating that it will detail the causes for the separation of one people from another—not of one set of individuals from another, or of individuals from their government. Through the Declaration, the people of America dissolved the political bands connecting them with the people of Great Britain. As a people they assumed "among the Powers of the Earth, the separate and equal Station to which the Laws of Nature and of Nature's God entitle them."

It was to defend and maintain the rights historically developed and accepted by and for Englishmen that the former colonists declared independence, fought their mother country, and established a new republic. And these rights were not so much those of each individual, atomistic person as of the people. Americans, being as good as Britons in the eyes of God, and having always lived according to traditions spelling out and protecting rights such as that of habeas corpus and representative government, were entitled to maintain those same rights for themselves by forming, if necessary, a separate nation. And it is the character of that nation, as presaged by the Declaration, that is most affected by differing interpretations of the Declaration. Thirteen separate colonies came together to state their grievances and to declare their status as "free and independent states"—the document uses the plural, "states"—from thence forward. Here was the point of tension that would both bless and plague America until a unitary state was finally established over the course of the twentieth century: Americans were one people, existing in several different, sovereign states. The Constitution would seek to bind these states together into a more perfect union in order to address pressing problems in foreign affairs, taxation, and internal trade. But it would do so in keeping with the same principles on which the Declaration was based—principles emphasizing the importance of inherited rights, of the primacy of representative government, and of the continuing sovereignty of each state over its own affairs, save where it had specifically ceded power to the mechanism of federal government, aimed at achieving limited, common ends.

Opponents of the conservative reading of the Declaration argue that it is, in essence, ethnocentric, or rooted only in the history of a particular people, and that it leaves conservatives unable to argue against moral enormities like slavery. But it is central to the conservative understanding that all men have a right to the protections of family and local social life. Thus, chattel slavery, which strips individuals of their fundamental social ties by reducing them to commodities that can be traded away at will, is wrong no matter what form of government a people may have, and no matter what ideological abstraction may be popular at the time. Not wishing to trust the possibility of a good life to any single political document or ideology, conservatives look to the broader tradition of natural law for general principles like ordered liberty and to a people's history for the means by which those principles can best be put into action.

—BRUCE FROHNEN

Further Reading

Kendall, Willmoore, and George W. Carey. *The Basic Symbols of the American Political Tradition.* Washington, D.C.: Catholic University of America Press, 1995.

Schwoerer, Lois G. *The Declaration of Rights: 1688–89.* Baltimore, Md.: Johns Hopkins University Press, 1981.

Shain, Barry Alan. *The Myth of American Individualism.* Princeton, N.J.: Princeton University Press, 1994.

See also: American Revolution; Bradford, M. E.; Civil War; Jaffa, Harry V.; Jefferson, Thomas; Kendall, Willmoore; Lincoln, Abraham; natural law; Natural Right and History; states' rights

Decter, Midge (1927–)

Described as "the first lady of Neoconservatism and one of the most influential social critics of our times" by Heritage Foundation president Edwin Feulner, Decter is known as a deft critic of contemporary feminism and liberal baby-boomer culture, and as a champion of democracy. She is the author of several distinguished essays in *Commentary* and *Esquire,* among other periodicals, as well as a number of books, including *The New Chastity and Other Arguments against Women's Liberation* (1972) and *Liberal Parents, Radical Children* (1975). Commending her "common sense and practical approach" to life, Feulner has written that Decter "ties her insights to the concrete realities of life—motherhood, marriage, striving, and hoping—and argues without illusions and without fear."

Decter was raised in St. Paul, Minnesota, and attended the University of Minnesota and Jewish Theological Seminary of America before traveling to New York to seek a career in writing and editing. In the mid-1950s she worked as an assistant editor at *Midstream* magazine, gaining editorial experience and eventually migrating to the staff of *Commentary,* where she met her future husband, Norman Podhoretz, and became a part of the New York literary scene. In her memoir, *An Old Wife's Tale: My Seven Decades in Love and War* (2001), she recounts how she witnessed the rise of the New Left, the Youth Movement, and contemporary feminism. Like other anticommunist liberals of the era, she began to distance herself from the cultural destructiveness of what she witnessed: the rise of collectivist political sentiment—sometimes tainted with anti-Semitism—thrust forward as the path to freedom; sexual promiscuity touted as a positive good even as it destroyed families; the push for women's equality descending into reflexive contempt for men and denigration of masculinity; and the spectacle of the most well-heeled generation yet to emerge in American history assuming the pose of a cynical, hardbitten proletariat. As Elizabeth Fox-Genovese was to write, "Some might find it tempting to see Decter as emblematic of an entire generation—the one that cut its teeth on the left-wing politics of the 1930s and 1940s, settled into a more or less comfortable anti-Communist liberalism during the 1950s and early 1960s, and was subsequently jolted by the turbulence of the student and women's movements into a new form of conservatism."

During the 1960s, Decter published a number of essays in *Newsweek, Commentary,* the *Atlantic,* and *Harper's* that established her credentials as a telling critic of American Left-liberal culture; these essays are gathered in *The Liberated Woman and Other Americans* (1971). Her next book, *The New Chastity,* focused exclusively upon American feminism and argued the case for traditional gender roles; Stanley Kurtz has described it as "an important critique of feminism at a time when virtually no one but Decter had the thoughtfulness or courage to stand in opposition." Published in 1975, *Liberal Parents, Radical Children* addressed the knotty question of how it came to be that the generation which came of age during World War II—collectively called by a later commentator "the Greatest Generation"—managed to raise children who embraced the counterculture values of the '60s, including contempt for established authority, indulgence in drugs, and a sense of endless entitlement.

By the end of the 1970s Decter, along with Podhoretz, Irving Kristol, Gertrude Himmelfarb, and Jeane Kirkpatrick, was at the forefront of the group of writers and public figures known as neoconservatives: former liberals who had confronted and rejected a liberalism that had evolved into a self-destructive caricature of itself and thus had moved away from many of its former adherents. Today, with the widespread triumph of feminist thought and the politics of entitlement in the academy, the private sector, and government, Decter continues in her role as a social critic, a gadfly who stings the complacent into anger and sometimes even leads them to question their assumptions.

—JAMES E. PERSON JR.

Further Reading

Decter, Midge. *Always Right: Selected Writings of Midge Decter.* Edited by Phillip N. Truluck. Washington, D.C.: Heritage Foundation, 2002.

See also: neoconservatism; Podhoretz, Norman

democracy

The term democracy has been given various meanings over the centuries. Perhaps most influentially, Alexis de Tocqueville, in his *Democracy in America* (1835, 1840), used the term to refer to American society as one characterized by great social, economic, and political equality, an attachment to equal rights, and a relative lack of class-based privileges. But democracy generally has been associated with political rule by the majority of citizens.

Majority rule, as a decision-making principle, has posed serious concerns for conservatives over the decades. These concerns have been central to major conservative works on American institutions and practices, such as John Adams's *A Defence of the Constitutions of Government of the United States of America* (1787) and John C. Calhoun's *A Disquisition on Government* (1851). James Madison in *The Federalist* 10 (1787) deals directly and openly with a perplexity surrounding majority rule that has preoccupied many conservatives, namely, how can republican governments, based on the principle of political equality and majority rule, avoid rule by oppressive majorities—or, as Madison put it, majorities that would rule in a manner "adverse to rights of other citizens, or to the permanent and aggregate interests of the community"?

Conservatives, on the whole, oppose a plebiscitary democracy because its foundations rest on a view of society as merely an undifferentiated collection of individuals. In this form of democracy, often associated with the underlying values and assumptions that guided the French Revolution, majorities rule directly on matters, both great and small, through electoral processes designed to register their "will." Conservatives, by contrast, fearing that such direct rule would result in rash, oppressive, or ill-considered decisions that would only serve the immediate interests of the ruling majorities, are decidedly inclined to favor institutional arrangements that provide for delay and deliberation in decision-making processes. For this reason, most conservatives, quite unlike the proponents of plebiscitary democracy, see merit in representation of the people by qualified and informed individuals who should not necessarily be bound by their constituents' wishes. They also see merit in and defend bicameralism, the separation of powers, and other institutional processes often charged with producing "gridlock." These views stem, in turn, from the tendency of conservatives to view society as a complex hierarchical organism comprising a multitude of institutions, associations, and groups such as church, family, communities, voluntary associations, and the like. For this reason, they are prone to support processes and institutions that are designed to achieve a consensus among the relevant parties when there is conflict or disagreement, rather than submitting matters to an up-or-down vote. Moreover, virtually all conservatives draw a distinction between state and society. Though this distinction at times may be blurred, it recognizes that individuals as well as varied social institutions, groups, and associations have spheres of authority that limit the reach of political majorities.

Conservatives have often wrestled with other problems associated with majority rule. A perennial question has been, who should be allowed to participate in constituting a majority? While universal suffrage is now the norm in the Western world, some conservatives would favor limitations, ranging from literacy tests to property qualifications, on who should be allowed to vote. On this score, still other questions arise: Is a people justified in denying the vote to those whose allegiances are to another country? What crimes, if any, should serve as a basis for disenfranchisement? Should individuals have to demonstrate a basic knowledge of their constitutional institutions and processes in order to vote? Should those unwilling to abide by the decision of a majority, if it should turn out to be unfavorable to their position or interest, be allowed to vote?

The most basic concerns surround the notion of limited majoritarianism. Virtually all conservatives subscribe to the proposition that majorities should not possess unlimited authority; that, simply put, there are things majorities ought not to do. But baffling questions arise in this connection. What kind of limitations should be imposed and how should these limitations be enforced? In the American context, some conservatives see these questions answered with the Bill of Rights combined with judicial enforcement. Others, looking to the historical record, maintain that bills of rights are really parchment barriers and that institutions designed to curb majorities either fail in their mission or assume authoritarian powers destructive of republican self-government. Conservatives of this persuasion maintain that the recognition of limitations depends upon the virtue and good sense of the people, which, in turn, are informed by religion, tradition, and received wisdom.

Finally, most conservatives recognize that a stable and just majoritarian system must make accommodations to the rule of law that require the equal, uniform, and predictable application of the laws. The rule of law constrains majorities from passing ex post facto laws or bills of attainder. Similarly the rule of law enjoins legislators from administering the laws that they pass, lest they show partiality to their family, friends, and political allies. Nor, by the same token, should legislators or administrators serve as judges in settling disputes that arise from the laws and their application. In sum, the requirements of the rule of law impose limitations on the functions and powers of both institutions and majorities.

—George W. Carey

Further Reading

Kendall, Willmoore, and George W Carey. *The Basic Symbols of the American Political Tradition.* Baton Rouge, La.: Louisiana State University Press, 1970.

Carey, George W. *A Student's Guide to American Political Thought.* Wilmington, Del.: ISI Books, 2005.

Kendall, Willmoore. *The Conservative Affirmation.* Chicago: Regnery, 1963.

See also: Adams, John; Calhoun, John C.; equality; Federalist, The; individualism; liberalism; neoconservatism; paleoconservatism; progressivism; Protestantism, mainline; separation of powers; Tocqueville, Alexis de; rule of law

Democratic Party

As the oldest major political party in the United States, the Democratic Party has a complex and varied history. Founded by Thomas Jefferson in 1792 as the Democratic-Republican Party, it immediately established itself as the party of small and constitutionally limited government. Jefferson's most influential opponent was Secretary of State Alexander Hamilton, who advanced an ambitious program that established a protectionist tariff (as opposed to Jefferson's modest revenue tariff) and the First Bank of the United States, and assumed war debt. Early Democrats, particularly James Madison, successfully incorporated the Bill of Rights into the Constitution and reversed many of the Hamiltonian policies of the Washington administration.

The slavery issue divided the Democratic Party into antislavery "barnburners" and more compromising "hunkers." Franklin Pierce brought the Democratic Party together and led it to victory in 1852. Pierce pushed for territorial expansion and tried to ease the growing tensions over slavery. However, disagreements over slavery in the Kansas-Nebraska bill led to open conflict over this issue and split the Democratic Party. The pro-tariff stance of newly elected Republican president Abraham Lincoln added fuel to the fire of Southern passions, bringing secession and the Civil War.

In the years following the Civil War, the Democratic Party had little success. The "Radical Republicans," led by Thaddeus Stevens, imposed a strict version of Reconstruction on the Democratic South rather than the weaker version advanced by President Andrew Johnson. Republicans controlled the executive and legislative branches of government for most of the next sixty-five years. As the Democrats regained political influence, they began to institute segregation and "Jim Crow Laws" in the South. By 1914, the Democrats had successfully segregated the entire South. Segregation continued well into the twentieth century, with the support of prominent Democrats like George Wallace.

Woodrow Wilson led the Democrats back into the White House in 1912 on his promise to keep America out of war. Wilson was responsible for the creation of the Federal Reserve Bank and the Federal Trade Commission, and, of course, finally led America into the Great War. The policies of the Wilson presidency indicated a new direction in the Democratic Party, as the Democrats became increasingly partial to the governmental regulation of economic affairs. With America's entry into World War I came the nationalization of the railroads and the establishment of the War Industries Board.

In 1932, in the midst of the Great Depression, Franklin Delano Roosevelt defeated Herbert Hoover to become the thirty-second president of the United States. Roosevelt seduced the nation with his promise of a "New Deal." This entailed an expansion of the size and scope of governmental authority unlike any other in American history. The Roosevelt administration imposed harsh policies on the already beleaguered economy. FDR confiscated all gold in the U.S.; imposed severe penalties for holding gold; signed legislation to establish the Federal Deposit Insurance Corporation; set interest rate ceilings at 25 percent; banned commercial banks from underwriting stocks; imposed agricultural price supports and wage controls; and established the National Recovery Administration (NRA), which regulated industry and labor markets. A recovery began in the mid-'30s thanks to a reversal in the Federal Reserve's deflationary monetary policy and a Supreme Court ruling that abolished the NRA in May 1935. However, a second crash came when the Fed doubled reserve requirements for banks, a move that withdrew three billion dollars from circulation.

The crash of 1937 was short, but severe. Unemployment rose nearly to 1932 levels. Roosevelt attempted to reinstate his earlier policies but could not. Roosevelt reacted to his failure by moving to "pack the Supreme Court" with his supporters, and to "purge the Congress of opposition." Many Democrats, to their credit, opposed their leader in his efforts to assume these extraordinary powers.

Roosevelt also took an aggressive stance with the Empire of Japan, enacting an embargo against Japan in response to its invasion and occupation of Manchuria. Following a surprise attack by the Japanese on Pearl Harbor, Roosevelt asked the Congress to declare war on Japan. He would spend the reminder of his life as a wartime president.

Roosevelt's presidency made the Democratic Party the dominant political party for a generation. The Democrats controlled Congress for sixty years, with one brief interruption. They would control the executive branch for much of this time as well.

Harry Truman succeeded FDR in April of 1945, and saw the war to its close on August 6 of that year. Truman pushed unsuc-

cessfully for an increase in the minimum wage, the extension and expansion of Social Security coverage, a national housing plan, and a National Health Insurance plan.

In 1960, John Fitzgerald Kennedy led the Democrats to victory against Richard M. Nixon. Kennedy succeeded in passing large tax cuts, thus promoting strong economic growth for that decade. Under Kennedy, the Democrats pursued an aggressive foreign policy that included a tense standoff over Cuba and military support for South Vietnam. When Lyndon B. Johnson succeeded Kennedy, he expanded the war effort in Vietnam—a move that split his party—and instituted vast new domestic spending programs dubbed "The Great Society."

James Earl Carter led the Democratic Party to victory in 1976. This election left the Democrats in the enviable position of controlling both the legislative and executive branches of the federal government. But Carter's moves away from "tax, spend, and regulate" policies made the rift between Northern and Southern Democrats more apparent. Democratic Senator Edward Kennedy opposed Carter for his own party's nomination in 1980. Internal division and embarrassment over the Iranian hostage crisis contributed to a decisive defeat for the Democrats at the hands of Ronald Wilson Reagan. During most of the 1980s, the Democrats attacked President Reagan relentlessly, as he reduced income tax rates, pushed for further deregulation, and stood firmly against Soviet aggression.

In 1985, moderate Democrats formed the Democratic Leadership Council (DLC). This group offered moderate Democrats an alternative to the more leftist Democratic National Committee (DNC). The Democrats then made a strong comeback against President George Bush, when they extracted a reversal on his "no new taxes" pledge and successfully characterized Bush as presiding over "the worst economy in fifty years." Out of this effort came the presidency of William Jefferson Clinton.

After a failed attempt to socialize the health care industry, the Clinton administration focused largely on the defense of Clinton himself. The Whitewater, Cattlegate, and Castle Grande scandals followed Clinton from his home state of Arkansas. Numerous Clinton administration officials were either convicted or confessed to crimes, and many others exercised their Fifth Amendment rights regarding self-incrimination. Clinton was impeached by Congress for committing perjury.

The Democrats lost the 1994 congressional election in a landslide, thus ending a sixty-year period of Democratic control of the Congress. The Democrats then lost close presidential elections in 2000 and 2004 to George W Bush, in neither election able to offer a particularly charismatic or attractive candidate (Al Gore and John Kerry, respectively).

The Democratic Party continues to wield enormous influence in American politics. As the popularity of liberal beliefs has declined, the Democratic Party has moved away from the far-Left policies of FDR and his New Deal. Thus, the Democrats have moved slightly in the direction of their nineteenth-century limited government roots. DLC reformers within the party have succeeded in moderating some of its far-Left tendencies, but there remains a core of mulish DNC support for failed big government enterprises, like Social Security, and extreme social policies, like partial-birth abortion and same-sex marriage.

—DOUG MACKENZIE

Further Reading

Miller, Zell. *A National Party No More: The Conscience of a Conservative Democrat*. Macon, Ga.: Stroud and Hall, 2003.

Witcover, Jules. *Party of the People: A History of the Democrats*. New York: Random House, 2003.

See also: culture wars; Jefferson, Thomas; liberalism; New Deal; Reagan Democrats; Republican Party

DeMuth, Christopher (1947–)

A former Nixon and Reagan administration official, Christopher DeMuth's tenure as president of the American Enterprise Institute has reestablished the Washington, D.C., think tank among the elite of Washington public policy institutions. DeMuth himself is an expert on regulatory affairs, writing and speaking regularly on the topic.

When DeMuth took the helm of AEI in 1986, he inherited an organization that had lost its way. By the early 1980s AEI had atrophied from the nation's premier think tank into a staid establishmentarian organization. It was part of Washington's firmament, but contributed little of importance to the capital's policy debates (indeed, its ineffectiveness was a major factor in convincing Ed Feulner and others to start the Heritage Foundation). DeMuth has returned AEI to prominence as an idea factory that churns out thoughtful and provocative policy analysis. And he has cemented AEI's position as a leading conservative organization. Under his direction the institute has attracted some of the conservative intellectual movement's most prominent figures, including Judge Robert Bork, Dinesh D'Souza, James Glassman, Lynne Cheney, and Charles Murray. The organization also received much attention for helping to staff George W. Bush's administration.

After graduating from Harvard University and taking his J.D. from the University of Chicago Law School, DeMuth served a short stint as a staff assistant in the Nixon White House. Following several legal jobs in the mid-1970s, DeMuth joined Harvard's Kennedy School of Government as Director of the Harvard Faculty Project on Regulation. From there he joined the fledgling Reagan administration in 1981, heading the White House Task Force on Regulatory Relief and serving as the administrator for regulatory affairs at the Office of Management and Budget. From 1984 until leaving for AEI in 1986 he was managing director of Lexecon, Inc.

—MAX SCHULZ

Further Reading

DeMuth, Christopher C., et al. *An Agenda for Federal Regulatory Reform.* Washington, D.C.: AEI Press, 1997.

DeMuth, Christopher C., and William Kristol, eds. *The Neoconservative Imagination: Essays in Honor of Irving Kristol.* Washington, D.C.: AEI Press, 1995.

See also: American Enterprise Institute

Dew, Thomas Roderick (1802–46)

President of the College of William and Mary during a period of intense antislavery debate, Dew was a noted promoter of free trade and defender of property rights and slavery, crafting arguments that sought to portray the "peculiar institution" as a positive good.

Born the son of a Virginia plantation owner, Dew was educated at William and Mary, graduating in 1820. After pursuing further studies in England and the European continent, he returned to Virginia in 1826 to join the faculty of William and Mary as a professor of political law, a position which required that he lecture on matters related to economics, history, and government. These lectures formed the basis of his first book, which brought him to widespread public notice, *Lectures on the Restrictive System* (1829). In this work, Dew built a case for free trade and against the protective tariff in America, deeming the latter a policy that needlessly pitted the more populous, manufacturing North against the largely agricultural South, to the North's economic advantage. According to the author, the tariff not only made for economic inefficiency, it also violated the rights of the constituent states as specified in the Constitution.

In 1832, one year after the bloody Nat Turner slave revolt in Southampton County, Virginia, Dew published *Review of the Debate in the Virginia Legislature, 1831–1832* (1832), which was written in response to the call by some Virginia lawmakers for gradual manumission and the deportation of slaves from American shores. In this, his best-known work, the author argued that slavery was an institution that provided for an orderly society in the South, and that attempts to emancipate slaves or deport them would serve to disrupt the Southern social order and to create interracial discord, thus laying the groundwork for further violent conflicts. Republished in 1852 as *The Pro-Slavery Argument,* Dew's book reached a national audience and served to provide ammunition to Southerners who defended the right to own slaves, as well as to Northern abolitionists who were convinced more than ever of Southern intransigence on the issue. In part because of the arguments put forward in *The Pro-Slavery Argument,* both sides came to foresee the likelihood of an acrimonious and even violent solution to the question of slavery's continued existence in North America.

In the mid-1830s, Dew was appointed president of William and Mary. Because of his stature as a learned and articulate spokesman on issues of national import, he was encouraged to run for national office, a course he refused to take. However, shortly before his death, Dew served in the "kitchen cabinet" of his friend and fellow Virginian, President John Tyler.

—JAMES E. PERSON JR.

Further Reading

Genovese, Eugene D. *Western Civilization through Slaveholding Eyes: The Social and Historical*

Thought of Thomas Roderick Dew. New Orleans, La.: Graduate School of Tulane University, 1986.

Harrison, Lowell. "Thomas Roderick Dew: Philosopher of the Old South." *The Virginia Magazine of History and Biography* 57 (1949): 390–404.

See also: free trade; Southern conservatism

Diamond, Martin (1919–77)

Martin Diamond was an influential political theorist who probed the meaning of American federalism. A colleague and friend of many seminal conservative thinkers, including Willmoore Kendall and Irving Kristol, Diamond obtained his doctorate in 1956 from the University of Chicago. Like Kristol, in his youth he was attracted to the political Left, once working for and supporting Norman Thomas (a biographical fact he shared with Russell Kirk, who voted for Thomas and his failed presidential bid in 1944). Diamond's distinguished teaching career began at the Illinois Institute of Technology (1952–55) while he was still pursuing his Ph.D. He was appointed assistant professor at Claremont University and Claremont Graduate School in 1955, and it was at this institution that he would spend most of his academic career as Wohlford Professor of American Political Institutions (1955–71). Diamond moved to Northern Illinois University in 1972. In 1977 he was appointed to a chair at Georgetown University, but he died in July of that year just moments after testifying before a Senate subcommittee against a proposed amendment that would have eliminated the Electoral College. Diamond was an Earhart Fellow, a Rockefeller Fellow, and a fellow at both the Center for Advanced Study in the Behavioral Sciences and the Woodrow Wilson Center.

Diamond was known to a generation of students as a superb teacher and one of the first students of Leo Strauss at the University of Chicago to turn his attention to the American political tradition, particularly the founding period.

In a seminal essay published in the *American Political Science Review* (1959), "Democracy and *The Federalist*: A Reconsideration of the Framers' Intent," Diamond challenged the progressive understanding of the founders' intentions, viz., that the Constitution was a "reactionary" document designed to protect vested minority interests. Using *The Federalist* as his point of departure, he endeavored to show that the aim of the founders was to provide for deliberative self-government with prudential safeguards against the excesses that had proved fatal to the smaller republics of antiquity. His analysis and conclusions, fleshed out more fully in subsequent articles, have had a lasting impact on contemporary students of the founding period. Diamond, deeply concerned about the growing concentration of powers at the national level, was also a strong proponent of the principle of federalism and administrative decentralization. In groundbreaking essays such as "*The Federalist's* View of Federalism" (1961) and "What the Framers Meant by Federalism" (1962), Diamond demonstrated how our modern conception of federalism differs significantly, in both substance and scope, from that held by the framers.

—GEORGE W. CAREY
AND JEFFREY O. NELSON

Further Reading

Nash, George H. *The Conservative Intellectual Movement in America since 1945*. Rev. ed. Wilmington, Del.: Intercollegiate Studies Institute, 1996.

Schambra, William A., ed. *As Far As Republican Principles Will Admit: Collected Essays of Martin Diamond*. Washington, D.C.: AEI Press, 1992.

Stevens, Richard G., ed. "Martin Diamond's Contribution to American Political Thought: A Symposium.""*Political Science Reviewer* 28 (1999).

See also: Constitution, interpretations of; federalism; Federalist, The

Dickinson, John (1732–1808)

An early spokesman for the conservative tradition in America, John Dickinson practiced law in Philadelphia and entered politics in 1760 when he was elected to the Delaware assembly. He also served in the Pennsylvania assembly (1762–65, 1770–76), where he defended the proprietary government as preserving established liberties and argued that change could jeopardize liberty by destroying lawful order. As a delegate to the Stamp Act Congress (1765), Dickinson drafted the petition asking Parliament to repeal the tax, but he opposed violent resistance. In 1767, responding to the Townshend Duties, Dickinson published "Letters from a Farmer in Pennsylvania. . . ." The "Letters" conceded that conciliation was possible but denied Parliament's right to tax. The king and Parliament were making radical innovations, Dickinson wrote, while Americans were defending ancient traditions and rights.

John Dickinson

The "Letters" brought Dickinson to the forefront of the revolutionary movement. In 1771, acting for the Pennsylvania legislature, he wrote a "Petition to the King" seeking redress of grievances. He was the principal penman for the First and Second Continental Congresses. Among the many petitions he authored was the "Olive Branch Petition" (1775), the colonists' final plea to the king. Even as he resisted English domination, Dickinson urged moderation and, in 1776, absented himself from the final vote for independence. That same day, however, he left Congress to serve as a private soldier. In December 1776, his home near Philadelphia was burned by British soldiers acting on direct orders. His was the only private home to be torched in retaliation for leadership in the "rebellion."

During the war, Dickinson represented Delaware and drew up the first draft of the Articles of Confederation (1776). He was president of the Delaware Executive Council (1781) and president of Pennsylvania (1782–85). In 1787, he attended the Constitutional Convention as a delegate from Delaware. There, as throughout his entire life, he rejected the abstract theorizing of the Enlightenment, instead relying on the lessons of history. "Experience must be our only guide," he said, for "Reason may mislead us."

His earlier attempts to preserve the empire and restore the ancient constitutions having failed, Dickinson sought to preserve traditional American liberties through the creation of a substitute for the old order. He regarded the task of drafting a constitution as an essentially conservative one: recreating in America, as far as could be done with American materials, the ancient uncorrupted constitution of England. He wanted to model the new national legislature as closely as possible upon Parliament. It was Dickinson, too, who first saw that America had a structural substitute for the English baronies: the states were, in a sense, hereditary and permanent. It was prudent, therefore, to draw one branch of the legislature from the people and to have the other represent the states. Such a mixed system, he thought, "was as politic as it was unavoidable."

Dickinson signed the new Constitution and supported it by a series of essays titled "The Letters of Fabius" (1797). In his Fabius letters, Dickinson justified the Constitution in terms of history and prudence. Paraphrasing Sir William Blackstone, he described the Constitution as uniting "force, wisdom, and benevolence." He echoed Edmund Burke when he wrote of its "animated moderation" and described it as "ever new, and always the same." And he offered, at the end of the second essay, a conservative challenge to future generations when he noted that the Constitution is written "in the most clear, strong, positive, unequivocal expressions, of which our language is capable. . . . While the people of these states have sense, they will understand them; and while they have spirit, they will make them to be observed."

—FORREST MCDONALD

Further Reading

Bradford, M. E. "A Better Guide Than Reason: The Politics of John Dickinson." In *A Better Guide Than Reason: Studies in the American Revolution*. La Salle, Ill.: Sherwood Sugden & Co., 1979.

Colbourn, H. Trevor. *The Lamp of Experience: Whig History and the Intellectual Origins of the American Revolution*. Chapel Hill, N.C.: University of North Carolina Press, 1965.

Dickinson, John. *Empire and Nation: Letters from a Farmer in Pennsylvania. . . .* Edited by Forrest McDonald. Indianapolis, Ind.: Liberty Press, 1999.

Flower, Milton. *John Dickinson: Conservative Revolutionary*. Charlottesville, Va.: University of Virginia Press, 1983.

McDonald, Forrest and Ellen Shapiro McDonald. "John Dickinson and the Constitution." In *Requiem: Variations on Eighteenth-Century Themes*. Lawrence, Kan.: University Press of Kansas, 1988.

Stille, Charles J. *The Life and Times of John Dickinson, 1732–1808*. New York: Burt Franklin, 1969.

See also: American Revolution; Burkean conservatism; Constitution, interpretations of; historicism

Dies, Martin (1900–72)

Dies, a Democratic congressman from Texas's Second District, was known for his brand of populism, or "Americanism," which blended conservative and liberal ideas. However, most conservatives identified with Dies's strong opposition to domestic communism. Dies used his power as chairman of the Special House Committee for the Investigation of Un-American Activities, or the "Dies Committee," to hold hearings investigating the presence of fascism and communism in the United States.

Born in East Texas, Dies's exposure to politics began at an early age when his father was elected to Congress in 1908. The younger Dies went on to graduate from the University of Texas and to attend law school at National (Catholic) University in Washington, D.C. He returned to Orange, Texas, and became an attorney. After establishing his practice, Dies was elected to the congressional seat his father had held.

Dies's "Americanism" closely resembled the views of his father and many of his constituents. Americanism included a belief in Christianity, tripartite government with a system of checks and balances, and capitalism. He saw the growth of big business as threatening Americanism and criticized the rise of "an industrial and financial oligarchy" that would ultimately undermine both capitalism and democracy.

Dies was skeptical of the Roosevelt administration's plans for coping with the Great Depression. He believed the New Deal was an attempt to replace capitalism and its emphasis on individual initiative with socialism and collective regimentation. He argued that small businesses and farmers could still prosper if new antitrust legislation was introduced to disband the industrial cartels and if government regulation was limited to areas that "affected the public interest," such as banks and railroads.

A growing fear that communists and fascists had infiltrated the executive branch of the national government and the labor unions led Dies to introduce a number of resolutions asking for the creation of House committees to investigate union activity. One of the resolutions, which called for a special committee to examine the spread of subversive propaganda, was passed by the House in 1938. The Speaker appointed seven members to the committee and named Dies its chair. The House subsequently recreated the committee at the start of the next three sessions of Congress.

As chair, Dies mounted a series of investigations into the activities of government agencies such as the National Labor Relations Board, the Federal Writers Project, and the Board of Economic Warfare. However, Dies used most of the hearings to investigate communist infiltration into the leadership of labor unions, especially those belonging to the Congress of Industrial Organizations. In response to the hearings, the political action committee of the CIO began organizing oil workers in Beaumont against Dies and succeeded in defeating other antiunion members of the committee. Dies opted to retire from Congress in 1945 instead of facing strong primary opposition from a labor-supported challenger.

Dies established important precedents in two areas. First, his committee represented one of the first attempts by conservatives to use the tool of congressional oversight to check the mid-century expansion of executive power. Second, Dies deserves some credit for the Truman administration's purge of communist sympathizers in the executive branch and for the later hearings of the House Un-American Activities Committee. Dies returned to Congress in 1953 but his major accomplishments were behind him. He died in Lufkin, Texas, in 1972.

—ANDREW J. DOWDLE

Further Reading

Barone, Michael. *Our Country*. New York: Free Press, 1990.

Dies, Martin. *Martin Dies' Story*. New York: Bookmailer, 1963.

———. *The Trojan Horse in America*. New York: Dodd, Mead and Company, 1940.

Gellermann, William. *Martin Dies*. New York: John Day, 1944.

See also: anticommunism; Matthews, J. B.; New Deal; populism

Dietze, Gottfried (1922–)

A political philosopher and professor of political science at The Johns Hopkins University, Gottfried Dietze's major contributions as a conservative thinker concern American liberal theory. The author of several important books tracing the classical liberal origins of American democracy, Dietze has been professionally associated with both the Brookings Institution and the Intercollegiate Studies Institute.

Dietze's scholarly career spans several decades and two continents. His academic background includes a J.D. from Heidelberg, a Ph.D. in politics from Princeton, and an S.J.D. from Virginia. His first book, *The Federalist: A Classic in Free Government* (1960), was a systematic examination of the political theory of the *Federalist* papers, exploring the nature of free government and the necessary balance between liberty and authority. His concern with the principles of free government and the challenges presented by democratic "permissiveness" was explored in subsequent works. In *America's Political Dilemma* (1968), Dietze questioned whether the founders' vision of a constitutional, limited democracy was in jeopardy due to the modern trend toward pure democracy. In his 1970 monograph *Youth, University and Democracy*, he presented a case study of contemporary dangers to ordered liberty by the democratic license then sweeping the university community.

A concept of profound importance uniting Dietze's many works is that of the rule of law. According to Dietze, the rule of law, which is central to the constitution of (classical) liberal government, facilitates the "Law State" and its beneficent provision of a sphere of individual liberty. Dietze explores the nature of the Law State and its relationship to democratic rule in *Two Concepts of the Rule of Law* (1973). Noting that the great allure of liberalism—freedom—is also its greatest threat, Dietze argues that propriety is essential to ordered liberty, or "proper liberalism." Propriety and proper liberalism entail the protection of all human rights central to freedom, including both property rights and civil rights. Only in this way can popular sovereignty coexist with free government.

Dietze's mature writings continue to address the complementary relationship between democracy and liberalism. In *Liberalism Proper and Proper Liberalism* (1985), he posits that the rule of law defines both proper liberalism and proper democracy. The realization of liberal democracy in the American context is the subject of *American Democracy: Aspects of Practical Liberalism* (1993). Unlike *Liberalism Proper*, in which Dietze's focus is the history of liberal political thought, *American Democracy* is a study of American political culture in the tradition of Alexis de Tocqueville. Arguing that liberalism has been the source of both Americanism and American democracy, Dietze argues that America is the country where pure liberalism has been most closely approximated. Dietze defines pure liberalism as the drive toward unlimited, enforceable freedom and unlimited opportunity, both material and associational. In America, this liberal quest for freedom of action has developed in conjunction with the extension of popular sovereignty as the protection of free government. Yet unlike Tocqueville, who emphasizes the tension between liberty and equality, Dietze sees the trends toward egalitarian, direct, and unlimited democracy in the United States as exemplifying the wide scope of liberalism. His closing comments, on the inevitability and insatiability of the drive for freedom, are both a testament to and a warning for the American polity.

Dietze belongs to the school of postwar conservatives who would describe themselves as classical liberals devoted to the principles of limited government, rule of law, free enterprise, and the Jeffersonian pursuit of happiness. Dietze is most appropriately compared with thinkers like Friedrich Hayek and Carl J. Friedrich, with whom he shares much in the way of outlook, philosophy, and methods of analysis. As a European commentator on American government, Dietze may also be seen as working in the tradition of Tocqueville and Bryce—attempting to capture the essence of American democracy with the clear and unsentimental vision of an outside observer of American mores.

—NANCY MAVEETY

Further Reading

Dietze, Gottfried. *In Defense of Property*. Chicago: Regnery, 1963.
———. *Magna Carta and Property*. Charlottesville, Va.: University Press of Virginia, 1965.

See also: democracy; Federalist, The; *liberalism, classical; rule of law*

distributism

Distributism is a social disposition held by those who emphasize life as lived out in a local community. Distributists see this emphasis as the best response to the modern tendency of man to be attenuated by participation in larger abstract associations. Distributists hold that there is an organic link between the person, the family, the homestead, the city, and the state; they therefore view concentrated political and economic power with suspicion and seek to influence private and public initiatives in such a way as to encourage a decentralized polity and the widespread distribution of property. Distributism encourages the orderly desire for ownership (in particular, the ownership of the means of production) among individuals, free families, and independent worker cooperatives.

Distributism was shaped initially in Great Britain by Hilaire Belloc, G. K. Chesterton, Cecil Chesterton, Vincent McNabb, and Arthur Penty. The movement arose as a response to the perceived twin evils of communism and unrestricted capitalism. Two complementary traditions of European thought deeply influenced distributist writings: Thomism, restored to prominence under Pope Leo XIII, and the anti-Whig medievalism of late-eighteenth and nineteenth-century British cultural conservatives such as Cobbett, Coleridge, Ruskin, and Newman.

Distributist ideas entered into North America chiefly through the works of the English distributists and the growing influence of Roman Catholic social teaching in political and economic thought. The American Herbert Agar, as London correspondent for the *Louisville Courier-Journal* and a regular columnist for the *American Review*, became a close literary friend to Chesterton and gave public prominence to distributism. While distributist ideas enjoyed broadening circulation in the 1930s and early '40s, the most successful American distributists in the early twentieth century were Catholics such as Peter Maurin and members of the original Catholic Worker movement, Graham Walker and the New England Distributist League, and Virgil Michel, as well as those associated with the National Catholic Rural Life Conference.

The distributists were among the first individuals to identify the destruction of the countryside and the erosion of the agrarian life as a wider social problem to be confronted through a posture of localist self-reliance. In the cities, American distributists were prominent in the fight to prevent unions from embracing communism, while simultaneously working to safeguard workers from the predatory conditions of industrial and urban existence. In the face of the socialist tendencies of the unions and the collusion of government and big business, the urban distributists championed smaller entrepreneurial enterprises and the creation of worker shareholding associations.

The closest allies of the distributists were the Southern Agrarians and their northern associates such as Agar and Ralph Borsodi. Together, the distributists and the agrarians stood for local traditions, self-sufficiency, an economic life centered on the household, stewardship of the land, and localist political activism. They stood against the mechanization of society, laissez-faire capitalism, consumerism, cultural homogenization, the destruction of rural and small town life, and the veiled socialism of the Roosevelt administration. Together the distributists and agrarians attempted to preserve what was described as a Jeffersonian position in American political life. The journal *Free America* became the flagship publication for the alliance. Whereas the distributists anchored their thought in what they saw as a wider natural tendency for man to flourish in a local community, the Southern Agrarians worked out of a specifically regional milieu.

The Southern Agrarians' quintessential regionalism made a lasting and effective union impossible, the two groups achieving little public effect after the appearance of *Who Owns America?* in 1936, although *Free America* remained in circulation until the mid-1940s.

After the Second World War enthusiasm for distributism ebbed as most conservatives formed a common front in the struggle against communism. But a growing concern for the environment, the crumbling of the Soviet Union, and alarm at the destructive tendencies of a resurgent laissez-faire capitalism has renewed interest in distributism since the last decade of the twentieth century.

The thought of distributist thinkers can be set out according to the following canons: (1) subsidiarity, or the understanding that higher associations should not, without grave cause, usurp a smaller organization's ability to accomplish its task; (2) proprietary interest, or commitment to the widespread ownership of property and the means of production; (3) defense of the local, or a suspicion of private or public entities that threaten (1) or (2), and a willingness to support public policy that encourages small, locally controlled economies over the domination of large retail chains and global corporations; (4) craftsmanship, or the confidence that local, community-based economies tend toward greater beauty, quality, and trust between the makers and users of goods; and (5) agrarianism, or the belief that a rural society is the best environment for safeguarding tradition, typically understood as comprising a family-centered life, self-sufficiency, anti-majoritarianism, the dignity of labor and craftsmanship, good health, small communities, and religious vitality.

Distributist thought is also identified with microcapitalism, mutualism, natural capitalism, and the economy of communion. Similarities have also been observed between the social and economic thought of Wilhelm Röpke, who admired Chesterton and Belloc, and distributism. North American institutions promoting distributist positions include the American Chesterton Society, the writers and readers identified with the now-defunct journal *Caelum et Terra*, the Houston Catholic Worker, the Agrarian Foundation, the Röpke Institute, the E. F. Schumacher Society, and the Institute for Local Self Reliance.

—WILLIAM FAHEY

Further Reading

Agar, Herbert. *Land of the Free*. Boston: Houghton Mifflin, 1935.

Berry, Wendell. *The Art of the Commonplace: The Agrarian Essays of Wendell Berry*. Edited by Norman Wirzba. Washington, D.C.: Counterpoint, 2002.

Maurin, Peter. *Easy Essays*. New York: Sheed and Ward, 1936.

See also: Agar, Herbert; agrarianism; Belloc, Hilaire; Borsodi, Ralph; Chesterton, G. K.; community; localism; Röpke, Wilhelm; Southern Agrarians

diversity

As we learn from *The Federalist,* the American political system is predicated on the flourishing of a multitude of diverse groups or factions, each freely assuming responsibility for itself, each entering the political arena and seeking its own perceived interests. Government, even while restraining itself for their sake, is to oversee the competition of these factions in such a way that, in the balancing of many interests, the tyranny of any exclusive and partial interest might be prevented and the common goods of domestic tranquility and prosperity achieved. The continuing agitation of diverse contesting interests is necessary for the vitality of the nation and for the freedom that that contest preserves and expresses. In recent decades, however, the term "diversity" has come to be associated with a conception of government seriously at odds with America's founding principles.

In America, the institution of slavery has long made the question concerning the condition of Blacks a matter of paramount political importance. Immediately after emancipation, it was widely recognized that the former slaves and their descendants needed education into citizenship, into the quality and practice of freedom. But the response to this problem came finally to be framed in terms of an equality understood not merely as a matter of governmental self-restraint that would allow the equal participation of all groups in the political process, but rather as a matter of governmental imposition, as if the political participation of blacks or any other group or faction were something the law might require. However, it is the conservative understanding that entry into the political process and continuing participation within it is a matter of free choice. It is, one might say, the whole substance of political freedom.

To the degree that the civil rights movement was a success, it achieved that success because black citizens stirred themselves to exercise their political will and because in response to that action government removed legal barriers that had been improperly set in their path. On the other hand, to the degree that civil rights were conceived as a work to be undertaken on the behalf of blacks by government, America's founding principles and the freedom they ensure were undermined. For black citizens, like all citizens, exercise their freedom when they express their political will and, typically, ally themselves, each one individually, with whatever factions or parties they might choose. The responsibility of government is to hear the voices of those freely self-constituted groups— or at the least, to feel the pressure they exert. But when it is government itself, and not the

citizens, that in effect defines and establishes a faction and designates who are to be its members, it subverts the rights of all those who are so designated.

In the face of large numbers of blacks who, largely because of the legacy of slavery and segregation, had not been educated into the habit of political engagement, various levels of government in the postwar era established institutions that took political action on their behalf. What was called "affirmative action" was action undertaken by government for blacks as blacks, in contrast to political action taken by blacks as citizens. Government identified blacks as a "minority," which is to say, not as members of a group that had freely constituted itself for the sake of political participation, but rather as a group identified by government and defined by it as unable to act on its own behalf. The cultivation of effective political will in citizens was in this way neglected in favor of a governmental presumption of interests automatically attributed to a group because of a supposed identity rooted not in political choice but in race, that is, in some prepolitical given.

There are many such prepolitical givens, including not only race but also ethnicity, gender, disability, and so on. In the new politics of diversity that has arisen in the last several decades, each minority, identified according to such givens, is presumed to be driven by interests that arise not as a matter of the rational choice of citizens but as a necessary consequence of the group identity assigned a priori. Of course, seen in this way such interests are not matters of free choice but of sheer fact. They are inarguable and not subject to compromise. The contest among them is not political and reasonable, therefore, but prepolitical, a contest of identified powers, mere powers. It follows as well that, precisely because each of these diverse groups is by definition a "minority," it is unable on its own to bring forward its interests against the power of that which opposes the minority, namely the supposed "majority," by definition the greater power. Minorities thus require government to act on their behalf or else to cast them aside as powerless victims.

In fact. nearly every political faction, just because it is a faction, is a minority of a sort. But in the view of the founders, such minority status is no reason to give up political effort. Rather, it is the ordinary condition of each group in its struggles with other groups in the political arena. There, in the assertion of its interests, each group is compelled to argue its case as just and right, as consistent with the common good and so as having a reasonable claim on one and all. That is, in the political arena the common good is the common ground actively shared by every participant regardless of his unshared prepolitical identity. It is the common good that renders political debate possible and that directs argument concerning particular interests toward compromise, general agreement, and an approximation to what justice requires in truth.

However, the politics of "identity" and "diversity" presupposes that there is no common ground and no basis for argument and persuasion, that the minority in its weakness cringes before the supposed majority in a realm where power, not reason, is the rule and measure. Interest loses its properly political character as it loses its connection to the free choice of the citizen and to the common good. Interest remains lodged within a prepolitical identity and so expresses not rational choice but irrational need. This irrational need then becomes the basis for claims to rights. The task of government, seen in this light, is not to direct the political contest toward a common good, but rather to resist the power of the majority and to bestow "compassionate" protection upon the helpless and needy minority.

Government of this sort, unhinged from any conception of the substantive common good—and responsible instead for the satisfaction of boundlessly diverse and inarguable needs asserted by irresponsible and apolitical minorities—must claim vast power for itself. No matter how compassionately it might claim to use that power, it cannot but take dominion over all its charges. The politics of diversity, having its origins in the problems caused by the slavery of some, inclines in the end to the enslavement of all.

It is important to note that the rise of the politics of diversity was not the result of a working through of the principles of the American founding over the long course of practical experience, even if much of that politics emerged by way of the court system and what was supposed to be judicial interpretation of the Constitution. Rather, it was made possible by the importation of something alien—the nihilistic antirationalism of late- or postmodern philosophy. The integration of this antirationalism into American thought and education made possible a fundamental shift in the way political matters generally are conceived. An anthropology of will and power that excludes reason and the common good was disseminated throughout the universities before it came to roost in the courts and legislatures. In turn, the universities have been transformed by the antirationalism to which they opened their doors.

It is difficult to overestimate the seriousness of this transformation. The American university is charged with preserving, cultivating, and transmitting the tradition that gave rise to the United States and to the principles of freedom and human dignity that mark its founding and form its vision of the common good. But the politics of diversity is the direct outcome of a philosophical divergence from that tradition. It is the unambiguous rejection of both the classical pursuit of truth and of abiding fidelity to the revelation that man is formed in the image and likeness of God. It abandons the understanding that men are duty-bound to freedom and that their human dignity requires of them that they rise to the demands of citizenship and its virtues. In the university, under the aegis of diversity and multiculturalism, the work of education for virtue is replaced by the practice of education as a deracinated and relativistic social science. In the classroom it binds students' minds to a narrow ideological correctness, while in the area of "student life"—that is, the management of student behavior on campus—it is forced by the very moral aimlessness and corruption it encourages to engineer and manipulate their behavior through planned "activities," distractions, and entertainments and through ever-expanding and increasingly irksome regulation. In the attempt to impose diversity as a policy, it spawns a flat and dissipated cultural uniformity and implants the psychic and spiritual predisposition to tyrannical rule.

—BARRY BERCIER

Further Reading

Bloom, Allan. *The Closing of the American Mind: How Higher Education Has Failed Democracy and Impoverished the Souls of Today's Students.* New York: Simon & Schuster, 1987.

Hazony, Yoram. *The Dawn: Political Teachings of the Book of Esther.* Jerusalem: Shalem Press, 2000.

Wolfe, Tom. *I Am Charlotte Simmons.* New York: Farrar, Straus, Giroux, 2004.

Wood, Peter. *Diversity: The Invention of a Concept.* San Francisco: Encounter Books, 2003.

See also: affirmitive action; civil rights; education, higher; Federalist, The

Djilas, Milovan (1911–95)

A Yugoslav communist leader jailed after he called for democratic socialism and pluralism, Djilas is most famous for his books *The* *New Class* (1957) and *Conversations with Stalin* (1962).

Djilas was born a peasant in Montenegro, a tiny southern European principality that became part of Yugoslavia following World War I. He grew up in a clannish culture marked by blood feuds, the ultimate goal of which was to kill the enemy and return home, literally, with his head. Growing up in this milieu, which he described in his autobiographical *Land without Justice* (1958), the intellectually gifted Djilas gravitated to the transcendent justice offered by communism. At university, he became a radical student leader, was jailed by the monarchy, and tortured. During World War II he was a leader of the Partisans—communist guerrillas who fought both the Nazi occupiers and anticommunist Chetniks. Djilas was celebrated for his courage and ruthlessness in battle and was regarded as a puritanical communist zealot with outstanding propaganda abilities. The communists' leader, Josip Broz-Tito, subsequently elevated Djilas to the party's leadership. With the collapse of Nazi occupation and the defeat and massacre of the Chetniks, the communists took power. In 1953, Tito appointed Djilas vice president, and he was widely regarded as Tito's heir. But only months later, Djilas renounced communism, claiming in a series of articles that, rather than bringing universal equality, communism produced a "New Class" of exploiters. After being expelled from the party leadership, he resigned from the party and was jailed the following year. Ultimately, Djilas spent almost ten years in Tito's jails, two-and-a-half in solitary confinement.

Djilas's departure from communism began with three visits to the Soviet Union to meet with Stalin, which he described in *Conversations with Stalin.* The first, which he undertook as Stalin's acolyte in wartime Moscow, shocked him. Rather than the simple proletarian of legend, he found Stalin to be a worthy successor to the Borgias: a brilliant and devious actor, cruel with purpose but also simply for the fun of it, immensely confident, frighteningly manic and depressive. Perhaps more important for Djilas's political thought was what he saw in the Soviet Union: a devastated land whose oligarchs lived sumptous lives yet were terrified of and craven before Stalin. At first ascribing these pathologies to Stalin's rule, time and the Yugoslav experience convinced Djilas that such behavior was endemic to communism itself, an argument he put forth devastatingly in *The New Class*. Djilas argued that because the bureaucracy "controls both nationalized and socialized property as well as the entire life of society," it inevitably evolves into "a new class of owners and exploiters" characterized by "unscrupulous ambition, duplicity, toadyism, and jealousy." With remarkable prescience, Djilas predicted, "When the new class leaves the historical scene—and this must happen—there will be less sorrow over its passing then there was for any other class before it. . . . [I]t has condemned itself to failure and shameful ruin." Djilas lived to see his works published in Yugoslavia and to see communism's collapse, which he described as having occurred "in the most beggarly, shameful, and irrevocable way."

—ROBERT WATERS

Further Reading

Djilas, Milovan. *Memoir of a Revolutionary.* Translated by Drenka Willen. New York: Harcourt Brace Jovanovich, 1973.

———. *The Unperfect Society: Beyond the New Class.* Translated by Dorian Cooke. New York: Harcourt, Brace & World, 1969.

See also: Burnham, James; managerial revolution

Dobson, James C. (1936–)

James C. Dobson attended Pasadena College as an undergraduate and earned his doctorate in child development at the University of Southern California. He then worked as assistant clinical professor of pediatrics at the USC School of Medicine and was a staff member of the Children's Hospital of Los Angeles in the division of child development and medical genetics.

With the publication of *Dare to Discipline* (1970), Dobson became well known, especially among evangelical Christians. Espousing a traditional approach to discipline and parental authority that challenged modern permissive childrearing, the book provoked controversy. But despite opposition, Dobson's practical methods resonated with parents, and the book remained a best seller for nearly twenty years.

In 1977, Dobson founded Focus on the Family, a nonprofit Christian organization committed to supporting and defending family life. Beginning with a short weekly radio program produced from a small office in California, the organization has grown to include seventy-four different ministries, ten periodicals, and a daily broadcast, all directed toward helping families to preserve traditional values. Focus on the Family is now located in Colorado Springs, but its programs are internationally syndicated on more than five thousand radio facilities worldwide.

Dobson's dedication to protecting and promoting the family as an institution has also involved him in a number of political endeavors. In 1983 he helped found the Family Research Council, an organization that seeks to further public policy in defense of the family as the basic unit of society. Presidents Ronald Reagan and George W. Bush have sought his counsel on matters related to the family, and he has served on various committees, including the Attorney General's

Advisory Board on Missing and Exploited Children, Health and Human Services' Panel on Teen Pregnancy Prevention, and the Commission on Child and Family Welfare.

Dobson is the author of thirty-five books. Some of these, notably his recent *Bringing Up Boys* (2001), have continued to generate controversy for unapologetically presenting a conservative Christian perspective that challenges modern assumptions on topics ranging from gender differences to homosexuality. Although Dobson currently serves as chairman of the board of Focus on the Family, he devotes most of his time to his writing and speaking activities.

—ALEXANDRIA CHIASSON

Further Reading

Buss, Dale. *Family Man: The Biography of Dr. James Dobson.* Wheaton, Ill.: Tyndale House, 2004.

Dobson, James C. *The New Strong-Willed Child: Birth through Adolescence.* Wheaton, Ill.: Tyndale House, 2004.

———. *Marriage Under Fire: Why We Must Win This War.* Sisters, Ore.: Multnomah Publishers, Inc., 2004.

See also: family; Family Research Council; Protestantism, evangelical

Dos Passos, John (1896–1970)

The illegitimate son of a Southern widow and a distinguished corporate lawyer, John Dos Passos always considered himself an outsider, a "man without a country," a "double foreigner." Perhaps it was the desire to overcome this enduring sense of isolation

John Dos Passos

and loneliness that prompted him to chronicle American history and life. More than any other novelist of his generation, wrote Edmund Wilson in 1930, Dos Passos was "concerned with the larger questions of politics and society."

Regarding capitalism as inhumane, Dos Passos championed the Soviet Union throughout the 1920s and 1930s, a misjudgment he later attributed to the exuberance of youth and the allure of communist propaganda. His denunciation of the execution of Italian anarchists Nicola Sacco and Bartolomeo Vanzetti in 1927 and his exposure of the conditions among striking coal miners in Harlan County, Kentucky, in 1931 irrefutably established Dos Passos's radical credentials. The publication of his *U.S.A.* trilogy between 1930 and 1936 further enhanced his reputation with modernist writers and proletarian intellectuals. Dos Passos's relentless critique of capitalism led many to assume that he was a member of the Communist Party. He was not. Disturbed by the cruel suppression of the Kronstadt Rebellion, Dos Passos had in fact begun to doubt the beneficence of the Soviet regime as early as 1921. A visit to Russia in 1928 and the Stalinist purges of the 1930s only confirmed his mounting suspicions. Outrage at the murder of his friend Jose Robles by communist secret police during the Spanish Civil War, and disgust at subsequent attempts to vilify Robles, ended Dos Passos's romance with communism.

Increasingly mistrustful of bureaucracies, ideologies, and the power they represented, Dos Passos reserved his deepest sympathy for ordinary men and women trying to live decently in a world that no longer valued the individual. "What's the use of losing your 'chains,'" he wrote to Wilson, "if you get a firing squad instead." By the mid-1930s the United States seemed to embody the only real hope for the future. Dos Passos accordingly turned his attention to American history in an effort to discover the essence of American institutions and the genius of the American character.

In a series of probing studies Dos Passos explored the qualities he believed had made America great. Composed of tough, practical men schooled in the "realities of life on a virgin continent," the founding generation envisioned a radiant future for the new country. They were, however, unwilling to sacrifice the freedom, happiness, and dignity of the individual in order to achieve it. Although vexed by "giant bureaucratic machines" wielding "antihuman power," modern Americans still had the best opportunity to solve the problem of "individual liberty vs. bureaucratic organization." For despite concerns about the corruption and greed that infected the capitalist system, despite the failure of the United States to meet the challenge of communism, and despite the evil inherent in human nature, Dos Passos believed to the end of his life that in America "the theme is freedom" and that faith in freedom ultimately means faith in the goodness and nobility of man.

—MARK G. MALVASI

Further Reading

Dos Passos, John. *The Ground We Stand On: Some Examples from the History of a Political Creed.* New York: Harcourt Brace, 1941.

———. *The Theme Is Freedom.* New York: Dodd Mead, 1956.

Ludington, Townsend. *John Dos Passos: A Twentieth-Century Odyssey.* New York: E. P. Dutton, 1980.

Wagner, Linda W. *Dos Passos: Artist as American.* Austin, Tex.: University of Texas Press, 1979.

Douglas, Stephen A. (1813–61)

Known as the "Little Giant," a reference to his physical stature (he was 5'4" tall), Stephen Douglas represented a generation of enormously talented statesmen who ultimately proved unable to avert civil war.

A Jacksonian Democrat, Douglas represented Illinois as a congressman (1843–47) and in the United States Senate (1847–61), where he chaired the Committee on Territories for more than a decade. Demonstrating his genius as a legislator, Douglas secured passage of the Compromise of 1850, which Americans hailed as the "final settlement" regarding the divisive sectional question concerning the extension of slavery into the western territories. Ironically, the truce between North and South collapsed just four years later as a result of Douglas's own legislation: the Kansas-Nebraska Act. Resuscitating the controversial issue, the 1854 statute advocated the principle of "popular sovereignty," shifting the determination of slavery in the West from Congress to the citizens of individual territories. Outrage in the North spawned the Republican Party. The Kansas-Nebraska Act, the resultant violence in Kansas, and the increasingly controversial Douglas himself contributed to the eventual splintering of the Democrats along sectional lines.

Garnering the nomination of the northern wing of the party in 1860, Douglas faced home-state rival Abraham Lincoln and two other candidates for the presidency. Douglas had defeated Lincoln for reelection to the Senate in 1858, traversing Illinois with his opponent in a series of celebrated debates. However, Douglas could not reprise his mastery over Lincoln in the national election: Lincoln won a decisive Electoral College victory. Douglas died only a few months later in 1861 at the age of forty-eight, retaining his Senate seat until his death and remaining a stalwart and vocal supporter of the Union.

In recent decades Douglas's idea of "popular sovereignty" has been seen as providing grounds for contemporary arguments in favor of "states' rights," but this argument has been taken up more by the opponents of conservative localism than by its proponents.

—ASHLEY CRUSETURNER

Further Reading

Holzer, Harold. *The Lincoln-Douglas Debates: The First Complete Unexpurgated Text.* New York: Fordham University Press, 2004.

Johannsen, Robert Walter. *Stephen A. Douglas.* Urbana, Ill.: University of Illinois Press, 1997.

See also: Lincoln, Abraham; states' rights

D'Souza, Dinesh (1961–)

A prolific author who has written on issues ranging from political correctness to economic prosperity, Dinesh D'Souza has consistently attempted to illuminate the impact of Western cultural systems on social and economic structures.

In *Illiberal Education* (1991) D'Souza drew attention to the consequences of affirmative action in America's universities, which had discarded well-established courses based on universal criteria found in the Western scholarly tradition and replaced them with an ideologically informed and intellectually vacuous teaching and research agenda. D'Souza compellingly argued that the so-called multicultural perspective is not a useful tool of intellectual inquiry but rather a political arrangement designed to accommodate the self-cultivated sensitivities of increasingly vocal extremists claiming to represent minority groups on campuses.

In *The End of Racism* (1995), D'Souza employed a broad combination of comparative methods, comparing and contrasting sociocultural systems from a cross-national and historical perspective. His argument: that mainstream America's values of individual responsibility and self-reliance have to be embraced by Americans of African descent if they want to lead prosperous and productive lives. He further contended that reliance on government redistributive programs justified by ever more elaborate narratives relating past sufferings to present failings is a futile strategy.

More recent works by D'Souza include *Ronald Reagan: How an Ordinary Man Became an Extraordinary Leader* (1997) and *The Virtue of Prosperity: Finding Values in an Age of Techno-Affluence* (2000), an analysis of the social and cultural foundations of contemporary American prosperity.

Dinesh D'Souza, a research fellow at the Hoover Institution, graduated Phi Beta Kappa from Dartmouth College in 1983. He was senior domestic policy analyst at the White House from 1987 to 1988. He frequently speaks at top universities and is featured on numerous television programs.

—ANDREW SAVCHENKO

Further Reading

D'Souza, Dinesh. *Letters to a Young Conservative.* New York: Basic Books, 2002.

———. *What's So Great about America.* Washington, D.C.: Regnery, 2002

See also: affirmative action; Dartmouth Review

due process

"Due process" is cherished by conservatives as one of the most significant legal principles to emerge from the English common law tradition. The origins of due process are generally understood to be contained in chapter 39 of the *Magna Carta*, which declares that "No freeman shall be arrested, or detained in prison, or deprived of his freehold, or outlawed, or banished, or in any way molested;

and we will not set forth against him, nor send against him, unless by the lawful judgment of his peers and [or] by the law of this land." Largely through the efforts of the famous English jurist Edward Coke, the phrase "law of the land" was replaced in legal parlance over time with the expression "due process of law." At his urging, the fourth article of the *Petition of Right* (1628) reads "That no man of what estate or condition that he be, should be put out of his land or tenements, nor taken nor imprisoned, nor disinherited, nor put to death without being brought to answer by due process of law." The modern counterparts of this article, found in the Fifth and Fourteenth Amendments of the U.S. Constitution as well as in various state constitutions, read that no person shall be "deprived of life, liberty, or property without due process of law."

As it emerged from the English tradition, the essence of "due process of law" lay in the right of individuals to be notified of the charges against them, as well as their right to a fair hearing. For the most part, during both the colonial years and the period leading up to the adoption of the Constitution, the meaning of due process was cast in terms of notification and fair hearing, and the due process clauses (actually "law of the land" clauses) in the state organic laws were understood to relate to process, not to matters of substance. Save for the infamous *Dred Scott* decision in 1857, the Supreme Court maintained the same view with regard to the Fifth Amendment's due process clause. Even after the passage of the Fourteenth Amendment, the Court was reluctant to look at due process in any other way.

Since the latter part of the nineteenth century, however, the original understanding of the due process clause, including the meaning of "liberty," has changed enormously, so that today even conservatives are divided on its proper use. Towards the end of the nineteenth and into the twentieth century, the courts used the due process clause to review state regulation of businesses, industries, and utilities in the area of economics to see if such regulations were "fair" and "reasonable" or whether they violated the "property" rights or "liberty" of the proprietors. While the Supreme Court no longer practices "substantive" due process in the economic area, there are some libertarians of a conservative bent who argue that property rights deserve priority and that the courts should again turn their attention to the fairness and reasonability of economic regulations promulgated by both the state and national governments. They contend, for instance, that the "rent control" practiced by some municipalities violates the due process clause because it unreasonably deprives individuals of their "property."

The major controversy concerning "due process of law" centers around the Supreme Court's use of the clause in the Fourteenth Amendment to apply most of the provisions of the Bill of Rights to states through the process of "incorporation." This process—started in 1925 and proceeding at a greatly accelerated pace during the period of the Warren Court (1953-68)—in effect defines the word "liberty" as it relates to the due process clause in terms of the liberties and procedures embodied in the Bill of Rights. In fact—and what upsets many conservatives—the Supreme Court has even found rights, liberties, and conditions that are not actually spelled out in the Bill of Rights. Into this category fall the "right of privacy," "freedom of expression," and "wall of separation between church and state." What is more, many, if not most, conservative legal scholars view the entire process of incorporation as illegitimate and contrary to the intention of those who drafted the Fourteenth Amendment. In addition, they point out that if "liberty" was originally thought to include the basic rights in the Bill of Rights, then the founding fathers were guilty of gross redundancy by spelling these rights out in separate amendments.

Most conservatives are critical of the Supreme Court's use of the due process clause for still other reasons. First, the Court has expanded its powers enormously, even to the point of legislating. Some conservative scholars even contend that the expansion of judicial powers, via the Fourteenth Amendment, has created a condition of judicial tyranny. Moreover, conservatives find decisions of the Supreme Court in most significant areas to be repugnant to the intentions of the founders. Such is the case, for instance, with respect to the Court's interpretation of the establishment clause of the First Amendment, which the Court has used to strike down voluntary prayer in the public schools and most state aid programs for religious schools. Conservatives also believe that the Court has severely damaged the system of criminal justice by concocting an elaborate code of defendants' rights that makes it unduly burdensome to convict the guilty.

Second, conservatives view the Court's use of the Fourteenth Amendment as further eroding the power of the states and localities to handle their own affairs. The Court has set down standards with regard to matters such as speech and expression, including pornography, that many communities find far too permissive. Thus, conservatives argue that the Court's use of the due process clause not only contributes to greater centralization and the establishment of a unitary state, but also deprives states and communities of the basic freedom of self-government.

Finally, through the due process clause, conservatives charge that the Court has advanced a liberal agenda by reading into the Constitution rights that simply are not there. For instance, through the "liberty" purportedly protected in the due process clause, the Court in *Roe v. Wade* (1973) declared a "right" of privacy that, in effect, allows for abortion on demand.

—George W. Carey

Further Reading

Carey, George W. *In Defense of the Constitution.* Indianapolis, Ind.: Liberty Fund, 1995.

Holt, J. C. *Magna Carta.* Cambridge: Cambridge University Press, 1976.

See also: Bill of Rights; common law; Constitution, interpretations of; equal protection; Field, Stephen Johnson; incorporation doctrine; judicial activism; natural law; rule of law; Supreme Court

E

Eagle Forum

The Eagle Forum is a national organization committed to the perpetuation of conservative and pro-family values. It was established in 1975 by Phyllis Schlafly as the organizational successor to STOP ERA, a group formed by Schlafly in 1972 to thwart the ratification of the Equal Rights Amendment (ERA). With the aid of volunteers in all fifty states, the Eagle Forum waged a formidable campaign against the ERA, which collapsed in 1982 when the period for its constitutional ratification expired.

The Eagle Forum persisted upon the defeat of the ERA, expanding its agenda to encompass a wide range of political and social concerns. In harmony with conservative Protestantism, the Forum lobbies for a ban on abortion, educational choice, and a powerful United States military. Additionally, the Forum defends the dignity and legal rights of stay-at-home mothers and housewives. Recurring themes in its mission to advance conservative ideas are the devolution of government and the citizenry's moral obligation to become active in politics.

In addition to a national headquarters in Alton, Illinois, the Eagle Forum maintains a Washington, D.C., office and a St. Louis, Missouri, office, which houses the Eagle Forum Education and Legal Defense Fund. Eagle Forum is the parent organization for numerous state Eagle Forums, Eagle Collegians, and Teen Eagles.

—Sara Henary

Further Reading

Critchlow, Donald T. *Phyllis Schlafly and Grassroots Conservatism: A Woman's Crusade.* Princeton, N.J.: Princeton University Press, 2005.

Felsenthal, Carol. *The Sweetheart of the Silent Majority.* Garden City, N.Y.: Doubleday, 1981.

See also: Equal Rights Amendment; family; Schlafly, Phyllis

Earhart Foundation

Earhart Foundation (no "the") was founded in 1929 by Michigan entrepreneur and philanthropist Harry Boyd Earhart. It concentrates its support on the work of graduate students, scholars, and researchers; of 305 grants in 2000, 78 percent were in support of individuals. Daniel J. Boorstin, historian and former Librarian of Congress, wrote that the foundation has "shown a faith in the individual scholar which has itself been an inspiration in this collaborative age." And in a field where the intent of the founder is often ignored or perverted, Earhart Foundation respects scrupulously the free-market, pro-America philosophy of H. B. Earhart.

Born in 1870 in Armstrong County, Pennsylvania, Harry Earhart was the son of a village storekeeper. He was the first cousin, once removed, of the famous woman pilot, Amelia Earhart. Guided by only an eighth grade education and a brief commercial course, Harry Earhart launched a business career that included stints as a cargo broker on the Great

Lakes and as a designer and salesman of logging machinery before he began manufacturing lubricating oil in Detroit.

The growth of the automobile industry led to the distribution of allied petroleum products, and in 1912 Earhart organized the White Star Refining Company. Under his energetic leadership, the company came to operate its own oil refineries and to sell its products throughout the Midwest and in Canada. White Star operates today as a part of Exxon Mobil Corporation. Earhart retired from White Star in 1932 at the age of 62.

Earhart devoted the final two decades of his life to philanthropy and the Earhart and Relm foundations. Earhart Foundation, founded in 1929, was a "family" foundation that initially concentrated its support on charitable and religious causes. But it soon broadened its mission to include research and education for leadership that would "eliminate" social ills rather than simply "relieve the results of social ills."

In 1949, in response to what Harry Earhart regarded as increasing threats to the free enterprise system and "the great American heritage," Earhart Foundation was reorganized, now emphasizing the support of research into economic freedom as the sine qua non of a truly free society. The following year, the Relm Foundation was created with a corporate life of twenty years and a similar mission. With the same trustees and staff, the two foundations differed only in their activities, with Earhart dispensing the H. B. Earhart Fellowships and Relm being responsible for nearly all the programs. In 1977, Relm's trustees terminated the foundation and transferred all its remaining assets to Earhart Foundation to implement H. B. Earhart's philanthropic goals.

Harry Earhart died at his home near Ann Arbor, Michigan, on October 21, 1954; he was eighty-four. Writing about his entrepreneurial spirit and philanthropic philosophy, Earhart Foundation president James A. Kennedy explained that Harry Earhart was an individualist with "a strong sense of responsibility to his fellow man and with a profound affection for his native land." Underlying his many philanthropies was an insistence that "giving should serve to strengthen recipients rather than to make them increasingly and perhaps permanently dependent upon help from others."

With the coming of the chaotic 1970s, Earhart trustees realized that the ideas of liberty were being challenged in the field of culture as well as economics and politics. They decided to expand the foundation's program to include support of research and writing in history, philosophy, and literature—the essential transmitters of traditional values.

In 1985, the foundation adopted a statement of the basic philosophy that guided H. B. Earhart and "which should continue to guide Earhart Foundation, its trustees and its members." It begins, "Harry Boyd Earhart believed profoundly that the free, competitive American enterprise system, based upon the Christian ethic, was the highest form of social organization in history." It is to preserve and foster such beliefs, states the foundation's history, "that he entrusted his resources to Earhart Foundation."

With current assets of about $73 million, Earhart Foundation is small compared to giants like MacArthur, Pew, and Lilly, with their billions of dollars, but in the words of Michigan history professor Stephen Tonsor, few foundations "have been so imaginatively and brilliantly managed" in the pursuit of nonestablishment solutions to social problems.

In the early days, Earhart and Relm "were nearly alone" in their patronage of the conservative movement. They assisted members of all three groups that then constituted that movement—the anticommunist cold warriors, the cultural conservatives, and the free-market economists. However, as Richard Ware, longtime president of the Earhart Foundation, pointed out, both Earhart and Relm worked with "outside" individuals and organizations sharing "some but not all of the conservative philosophy." Scholarship of high quality and a willingness to allow "chips to fall where they may" have been the hallmarks of staff recommendations and trustee decisions. "I believe," said Ware in summary, "we have played a defensible role in the use of venture capital in the competition for ideas." That mission was ably carried forward by Ware's successor as president, David Kennedy, and more recently by foundation president Dr. Ingrid Gregg.

Among those supported by Relm-Earhart over the decades have been six Nobel laureates in economics: F. A. Hayek, Milton Friedman, George J. Stigler, James M. Buchanan, Ronald H. Coase, and Gary Becker. Since the early 1950s, more than 2,500 graduate students have received assistance as H. B. Earhart Fellows. In the field of political philosophy, support was extended to Leo Strauss and Eric Voegelin. In international affairs, the work of Peter Bauer was funded along with such institutions as the Mont Pelerin Society and the Institute of Economic Affairs in London.

In 1964, the Relm Foundation joined the Intercollegiate Studies Institute (then known as the Intercollegiate Society of Individualists) in creating the Richard M. Weaver Fellowships, of which almost four hundred have been awarded, including those awarded to Edwin J. Feulner, president of the Heritage Foundation, Larry Arnn, president of Hillsdale College, and James Gwartney, author of one of the most popular college economics textbooks in the country.

One of those who received an Earhart fellowship in 1960 was Thomas Sowell, probably the most influential black conservative intellectual in America. When Richard Ware retired as Earhart president in 1985, Sowell

wrote him that the foundation's support had made "the difference between my finishing and not finishing my graduate work." In a larger context, added Sowell, Earhart was one of the few institutions "that helped keep alive certain kinds of scholarship that might otherwise have been buried under the prevailing academic orthodoxy and intolerance." In so acting, Sowell said, the foundation "rendered a service not simply to individual scholars but to the nation."

—Lee Edwards

See also: foundations, conservative; Intercollegiate Studies Institute

East, John P. (1931–86)

Conservative writer and politician John P. East was born in Springfield, Illinois, on May 5, 1931, and attended Earlham College (B.A., 1953). He served in the U.S. Marine Corps from 1953 to 1955 as a lieutenant and while stationed at Camp Lejeune, North Carolina, contracted poliomyelitis, which permanently paralyzed him. He attended the University of Illinois School of Law (LL.B., 1959) and later studied political science at the University of Florida (M.A., 1962; Ph.D., 1964). From 1964 to 1980, East was professor of political science at East Carolina University in Greenville, North Carolina.

East was active in conservative causes in North Carolina and the Republican Party and published several articles in conservative journals. In 1980 he ran for the U.S. Senate and won with less than 51 percent of the vote. East was chairman of the Subcommittee on the Separation of Powers of the Senate Judiciary Committee and presided over controversial hearings on antiabortion legislation.

East's term of office was marred by staff problems and by his own increasingly poor physical and mental health. After he collapsed in 1985, hypothyroidism was finally diagnosed and treated, but he was hospitalized for much of the summer. In October 1985, East announced that he would not run for reelection in 1986. Suffering from chronic depression, East committed suicide on the morning of June 28, 1986, while on vacation at his home in Greenville, North Carolina.

—SAMUEL T. FRANCIS

Further Reading

East, John. *Council-Manager Government: The Political Thought of Its Founder, Richard S. Childs.* Chapel Hill, N.C.: University of North Carolina Press, 1965.

———. *The American Conservative Movement: The Philosophical Founders.* Washington, D.C.: Regnery, 1986.

Francis, Samuel T. Obituary for John P. East. *Modern Age* 30, no. 3/4 (1986): 195–97.

Eastman, Max F. (1883–1969)

A writer, lecturer, and political activist, Max Forrester Eastman is best remembered for his anticommunist activities during the 1940s and 1950s, which included supporting Senator Joseph McCarthy of Wisconsin, and for his contributions to the *Reader's Digest* and *National Review.* However, for much of his life Eastman was a radical, not a conservative. He was famous among leftists as the editor of the *Masses* and as a leading protester against American participation in World War I, though later he was shunned by the Left as a premature anti-Stalinist.

Eastman graduated from Williams College in 1905. He studied philosophy at Columbia University under John Dewey (1907–10), completing all requirements for the Ph.D. except the dissertation, which he wrote but declined to file as a protest against academic formalism. Influenced by his sister Crystal, and by the political culture of Greenwich Village where he lived, Eastman became a feminist and socialist and in 1912 received a tele-

gram which read: "You are elected editor of the Masses. No Pay." Eastman transformed the foundering monthly into the liveliest and most attractive left-wing periodical the United States has ever had. Its other editors and contributors included such radical luminaries of art and culture as John Sloan, Art Young, John Reed, Sherwood Anderson, Carl Sandburg, and Randolph Bourne.

Because Eastman and the *Masses* opposed American entry into World War I, the government took away its second-class mailing privilege and indicted Eastman and six other editors and contributors for conspiring to obstruct military recruiting and related offenses. Unlike most defendants in such trials, Eastman and his colleagues escaped prison, two juries in succession failing to agree on a verdict. His eloquence on the stand was crucial to their success, yet by the time he stood trial the charges against him were obsolete, for after the Bolshevik Revolution in Russia Eastman supported the war against Germany. Early in 1918 he founded the *Liberator* to carry on where the *Masses* had left off.

In 1922, tired of hearing about it at second hand, Eastman went to Soviet Russia to see the great "experiment" in action. There he learned Russian, met many leading Bolsheviks, married Eliena Krylenko, and sided with Leon Trotsky in the struggle for power following Lenin's death. After two years Eastman left for Western Europe bearing a copy of what became known as Lenin's Testament, in which the dictator warned against Stalin and named Trotsky as his heir. Eastman published parts of it in *Since Lenin Died* (1925), an attack on the new Soviet leadership that he believed was betraying the revolution.

Eastman returned to the United States in 1927, continuing to serve as Trotsky's English-language translator and literary agent while supporting himself by lecturing, as he had done and would do for many years more, on literature, politics, and humor. His connection with Trotsky separated Eastman from his old following, as most of the American Left sided with Stalin. In the "Red Decade" of the 1930s, things grew worse. Stalin himself lent a hand by personally attacking Eastman as a "gangster of the pen"—a unique event in the history of American letters. Because of his fluent Russian and extensive Soviet connections (his wife was the sister of a prominent Bolshevik) Eastman had reliable information on Stalin's terrible purges and became progressively more disillusioned.

Eastman published his two most important political books in 1940. *Marxism: Is It Science?* announced his renunciation of a doctrine to which he had subscribed since the Bolshevik Revolution. In his own mind, it was as a scientist that he had embraced Marxism. Eastman's conclusion that Marxism was only another false panacea marked the end of his belief in socialism. *Stalin's Russia* was a thorough analysis of Soviet misrule, chronicling it in detail and explaining, for the first time, the meaning of the purges and show trials of the 1930s. Reviewing these books, and Eastman's career as a whole, Edmund Wilson said they were "the best informed discussion of the implication of the Marxist movement and the development of the revolution in Russia that has yet appeared in English."

In 1941 Eastman joined the *Reader's Digest* as a roving editor and moved steadily to the Right. His most important article for the *Digest* was called "To Collaborate Successfully We Must Face the Facts about Russia." Appearing in July 1943, at the peak of America's enthusiasm for its wartime ally, the article caused a sensation and began the process of creating a more realistic national attitude toward the Soviet Union. In 1952 he publicly endorsed Senator McCarthy, and when *National Review* made its appearance three years later Eastman was listed as an "Associate and Contributor." Eastman admired William F. Buckley Jr. and agreed with him on capitalism and individual freedom, as also on the need to fight communism. But as an atheist of long standing and a man of bohemian tastes and habits, he was not comfortable with the magazine's emphasis on religion and traditional morals.

Eastman was most intensely admired as a hero of the antiwar movement in 1917 and 1918, and for editing the *Masses*, but he was most courageous during the years 1924–39, when he was the chief—and at first the only—anti-Stalinist on the American Left. Eastman was not afraid of controversy, a trait that enabled him to break with his friends and associates over Stalin, as later over McCarthy. However, his support of McCarthy, whose methods were widely deplored, ruined his standing among liberals, while his failure to agree with conservatives on sexual morality and religion made his position on the Right somewhat ambiguous.

Eastman hoped he would go down in history as a writer, and to that end he produced twenty-six books, including poetry and fiction. He also translated five major Russian books, edited two anthologies, and made a film documentary of the Bolshevik Revolution. He was a great autobiographer and a masterful essayist.

—WILLIAM L. O'NEILL

Further Reading

Diggins, John P. *Up from Communism: Conservative Odysseys in American Intellectual History.* New York: Harper & Row, 1975.

Eastman, Max. *Enjoyment of Laughter.* New York: Simon & Schuster, 1936.

———. *Love and Revolution.* New York: Random House, 1964.

———. *Seven Kinds of Goodness.* New York: Horizon Press, 1967.

O'Neill, William L. *The Last Romantic: A Life of Max Eastman.* New York: Oxford University Press, 1978.

See also: *anticommunism; Buckley, William F., Jr.; McCarthy, Joseph;* National Review

education, higher

That professors tend to be liberals or even leftists there is no doubt. According to one recent and unusually thorough study by political scientists Stanley Rothman, Seymour Martin Lipset, and Neil Nevitte, self-identified "leftists" outnumber self-identified "rightists" on American faculties by nearly five to one. In the social sciences the ratio was eight to one. In the humanities nine to one. With respect to party preference, professors and administrators preferred Democrats over Republicans by a ratio of five to one. When more prestigious institutions are separately examined, their faculties tend to be even more ideologically lopsided. And though all these tendencies have been present for decades, in recent years they have been exacerbated.

The result of this imbalance is that conservative views take a steady drubbing in most American classrooms, and the effects are not negligible. However skeptical many undergraduates might be about their professors, the continual repetition of leftist pieties tends to establish them as received wisdom. And then there are all the things to which the modern multiculturalist curriculum gives short shrift, like the historical and philosophical foundations of freedom, market economics, and the core religious and cultural traditions of the West. Conservatives understand that civilization needs to be renewed each generation. Unfortunately, the transmission of Western civilization no longer ranks high within the priorities of academe.

The first question likely to occur to any conservative confronted by this situation is "How in the world did it come to pass? There is certainly no lack of sophisticated conservative thought applicable to questions that universities study. Conservative perspectives on the great issues of government policy are in abundant supply. Conservative intellectu-als are prominent in all areas of public controversy and have no difficulty holding their own against opponents. Conservatives are well represented within the electorate, among taxpayers, and among the donors who support America's great private institutions of higher learning. Is something sinister going on?"

Well, yes. But also, no. Unquestionably, the procedures by which faculty are trained, hired, and tenured at most American universities and colleges have, for a long time, discriminated against conservatives in fields where conservatism has any bearing on subject matter. "Disciplines" such as women's studies, ethnic studies, "queer studies," cultural studies, and social work, are, by virtual declaration, places where conservatives need not apply. Their explicit missions have less to do with intellectual discovery than with radical social change. Sociology, cultural anthropology, literature, and teacher education are also thoroughly politicized, the first by its largely Marxist sensibility, the second through its commitment to relativism, and the third and fourth via their postmodern obsessions with race, gender, and class. Although oases of tolerance exist within these fields, no one minimally acquainted with their professional politics can have the least doubt about the enforcement of an orthodoxy hostile to tradition, individualism, and sometimes reason itself. History is only slightly less tainted by leftist dogmatics. Political science and economics are more pluralistic, the former with a strong liberal tilt, the latter with a considerably weaker one.

In the face of these prevailing prejudices, comparatively few conservatives choose to pursue academic careers, and of those who do, many finally become discouraged and drop out. Those conservatives who do dwell in academe are frequently older, having entered in more tolerant times or else turned to the Right during the campus tumults of the sixties. Upon retirement, they are rarely replaced by fellow conservatives. Undoubtedly, were the system of higher education not so inhospitable to conservatives, there would be many more within it. (The term "conservative" is being used here rather broadly, comprehending traditionalists, libertarians, and many others strongly allegiant to free ideals and Western civilization who might not be wholly comfortable with the conservative label. In the skewed intellectual context of the American campus, all are considered conservatives and probably deserve to be.)

Focusing on the very real issue of discrimination risks overlooking an equally important factor in the academic underrepresentation of conservatives: the natural predisposition of intellectuals toward the kinds of totalizing visions that the Left provides. Conservatives are not merely the defenders of society as is; they are, in a deeper sense, the defenders of life as daily lived. It is the "little platoons," the private purposes, the local communities, the vast disaggregate of spontaneous cooperation and enterprise in which conservatives find greatest social value. Their politics center on preserving ample social space for these to flourish.

Intellectuals can, of course, make their own contributions to life as lived. Many produce marketable products and services employing scientific, analytic, and literary skills. But they most command attention and power when painting on a broad canvas, characterizing, interpreting, and judging society as a whole. At one time in Western history this was largely the province of the clergy, the profession within which the great majority of intellectuals were once employed. Because most clergy were, in effect, under political control, their roles were generally discharged in a manner that supported established systems of authority. The gradual secularization of intellectual life starting in the Renaissance, and the breakdown in religious authority that accompanied the Ref-

ormation, began to undermine this pattern. The victory of rationalism and free thought during the Enlightenment reversed it.

Inspired by the palpable reality of the scientific and industrial revolutions, and convinced that society could now be reengineered as readily as could nature, intellectuals increasingly surrendered to a promethean temptation. In practice this meant latching onto theories claiming a scientific understanding of the basic social dynamic (Marxism being the paradigmatic case), or at least subscribing to the view that scientific inquiry held the key to acquiring new knowledge capable of remedying otherwise intractable social defects. These claims proved remarkably persuasive, especially for political leaders seeking updated justifications for exercising power or for ways to extend the sway they already possessed. For intellectuals the payoff was a plenitude of new career opportunities involving studying, teaching, preaching, and advising about these improving power ploys. In some cases it also involved the direct exercise and enjoyment of power.

Most of these opportunities came to center on the university, and it is to the universities that intellectual activists have disproportionately flocked. Even those spending significant periods in government perches have often repaired to academe for intermittent rest and recreation. By contrast, the highly intelligent but less visionary have directed their efforts toward spheres of more immediate practicality, such as business, technology, and the professions. Their contributions to society have been in the form of concrete "products," while their academic counterparts have concentrated on delivering cultural and political "meaning."

To be sure, there is a place in this larger scheme for conservative intellectuals: criticizing their ideological opposites. When academic leftists interpret society to itself, urging the people to surrender ever more power to enlightened authorities, there is a natural opportunity for considered dissent. To be effective, however, this dissent must be familiar with authority-serving doctrines and be able to develop countervailing ones. Only full-time intellectuals can perform these functions. The Left has often preened itself on "telling truth to power," but this is far more precisely the conservative intellectual vocation.

Since the natural tendency of humanistic and social science intellectuals is to proffer sweeping visions, and since these have a way of becoming handmaidens of power, the most effective way for conservatives to protect themselves and their society would be to try to contain the size of the institutions that employ them. But common sense also requires that they exert their influence to make these institutions as open to reasoned dissent as possible.

In theory this should not be necessary. Our universities have long viewed themselves as part of the grand enterprise of science and thus optimally designed for intellectual self-correction. Science advances because its methods allow for the rigorous testing of rival hypotheses, with the consequences that those which fail are discarded. In the natural sciences, where the experimental method works well, there has indeed been steady and remarkable progress. Orthodoxies can be challenged and overthrown, however powerful their supporters. Unfortunately, the same cannot be said of the humanities and social sciences.

A basic problem is their subjects' sheer complexity. Human phenomena cannot be readily reduced to numeric formula or neatly testable propositions. Good analysis requires hard-to-define qualities of judgment, often based on bodies of experience that cannot be formally taught. Moral and aesthetic judgments, outside science's province, also come into play. There are, of course, canons of good practice in these fields; as in true sci-

ence, clarity, logic, and fidelity to evidence are indispensable. But there always remain large residua of ambiguity, often pertaining to questions of the highest importance, where little or nothing can be definitively proved or disproved. And this opens the door to politically correct mischief.

The motive for this mischief is the entanglement of humanistic and social science inquiry with vested interest and personal passion. The resolution of its issues inevitably affects the distribution of power, wealth, and status, and even touches upon matters of morality in consequential ways. Conclusions drawn also bear on the rise or fall of individual academic reputations and careers. With the stakes so high—and lacking the dispositive techniques for reaching consensus that are available to physicists, chemists and their ilk—humanist and social science scholars labor under strong temptations to settle their controversies through organizational imposition.

Unfortunately, university governance takes little cognizance of this. Its premise, rather uniquely for the academy, is laissez faire. Since minimal oversight is more than enough to ensure that physics and chemistry stay on course, the same, it is reasoned, should also suffice for literature and sociology. Let the free market of ideas, alive and well in every field, determine what theories and careers flourish or collapse.

If the history of American higher education during the last third of the twentieth century has demonstrated anything, it is the naïveté of this assumption. Absent the reality checks provided by natural science and allied fields, literature, sociology, and several kindred "disciplines" have fallen under the thumb of suffocating creeds, closely confining what is intellectually acceptable. Accompanying this trend is a related one: the substitution of cleverness for understanding. Fields incapable of genuinely advancing theoretical knowledge can still impress outsiders through the simulacra of theory disguised by pretentious vocabulary and, sometimes, mathematical artifice. Contrived complexity also allows these fields to maintain an organized system of competition among their practitioners. The intelligent and energetic can rise through a hierarchy of status and remuneration by displaying mastery of the regnant jargon and techniques, or by employing unusual imagination in their continued elaboration. Embracing science more in semblance than substance, these fields seek an external respect, and an internal order, that they could not otherwise obtain.

Reformers in these troubled fields should aim at two related goals: (1) the encouragement of as much rational discourse within them as is possible (something from which conservatives will largely benefit); and (2) the inhibition of the formation of intellectual monopolies based purely on organizational clout (something from which radicals will certainly lose). Practices should be considered that, on the one hand, draw academic adversaries into sustained reasoned discourse and, on the other hand, afford limited shelter for diverse views. Needless to say, a balance has to be struck between shelter and competition. Simply protecting viewpoint differences will not suffice. Ideas, conservative or otherwise, must be able to defend themselves in fair fights to earn their academic keep. But they must also be protected from lynching.

Concretely, there are several initiatives worth contemplating. One is the encouragement of university and college governing boards to play an active role in overseeing the intellectual standards of their institutions. Such boards already technically possess these powers, but almost never exercise them, lacking both the confidence and organizational tools to do so. Yet, as the ultimate guardians of institutional mission, they bear the responsibility of ensuring that its integrity is preserved. If there is—as there is currently—clear evidence of internal default they have no choice but to rectify the situation.

The norms of reasoned discourse are not so obscure that trustees cannot grasp them or assess the extent to which they actually prevail in the academic subdivisions they oversee. The degradation that afflicts the humanities in particular often involves obviously fallacious intellectual practices, such as the ad hominem attack, special pleading, and inappropriate appeals to authority (especially of certified "victim groups") of a type once routinely debunked in freshman logic. Indeed, some of it proceeds from the explicit repudiation of concepts like truth, disinterestedness, and other premises of objective inquiry.

Much would be accomplished if trustees made an understanding of, and commitment to, reasoned discourse the litmus test for hiring presidents and chancellors (who would presumably do the same for their subordinates). They might then join with these hires to create academic advisory bodies to evaluate the health and vigor of reasoned discourse within their institutions. Composed of senior scientists and scholars distinguished for the integrity and fruitfulness of their work, such bodies would give boards and presidents an independent perspective on the adequacy of existing intellectual quality controls, supplementing the opinions received on these matters via existing administrative-faculty channels. Generally realists par excellence, conservatives would be helped by the counterattack on reality denial that such bodies could mount.

This remedy, however, carries a strong caveat. In the hands of the politically correct an academic oversight agency would simply add the ultimate weapon to the dogmatists' arsenal. Reform has always had a tendency to be captured by those in most need of it. If concern over debauched standards rouses somnolent boards to new energy, conservatives should stay tuned long enough to ensure that this energy is intelligently directed and sufficiently sustained.

It is unlikely that the politicization of the humanities and social sciences can ever be entirely eliminated. The nature of the subject matter and the inevitable passions of its students prevent it. But if there will always be some politicization, there may also be "constitutional remedies" for its worst consequences. In the larger world, after all, there are forms of governance that allow "a hundred flowers to bloom" and those that repeatedly cut them off at the stem. Given their likely minority status in academe, conservatives should seek to craft academic charters that closely model the former. This will require some doing. Defying the wisdom of constitutionalism generally, and the American constitutional tradition in particular, current academic arrangements typically allow majorities to work their untrammeled will. Chairmen, personnel committees, and curriculum committees are usually elected by a simple majority vote, sometimes of all faculty and sometimes just of tenured ones. In the natural sciences and other comparably rigorous domains, this majoritarianism is benign. But in the humanities and social sciences it sorely tempts fate.

Procedures may therefore be needed that explicitly recognize the value of philosophic pluralism in these fields and provide the institutional means to preserve it. One relatively straightforward remedy would be to change the voting systems by which key academic decisions are made to give intellectual minorities greater weight. John Calhoun would no doubt be pleased and academic conservatives might be as well.

Another reform would allow distinct "schools of thought" within politicized fields to explicitly organize themselves in a state of partial independence from their rivals with respect to hiring, tenuring, and graduate training. Academics of a multitude of factional persuasions would then be at lib-

erty to develop their views with a greater sense of freedom from peer coercion than is now the case. Needless to say, some Madisonian imagination, plus a good deal of trial and error, would be required to get the details right.

To be sure, a system like this would also be subject to dangers. No one wants "affirmative action for ideas." The safeguard lies in the intensified competition that the coexistence of rival schools of thought should produce. Dominant factions could not suppress their rivals but would be compelled to answer them. The prospects for conservative ideas and academics would be vastly improved under such circumstances.

But the single most important thing academic conservatives can do is not mechanical. It is rather to remind themselves and others that they possess a vision of academic life vastly superior to that of their opponents. Neither coercively utopian, nor sterilely scientistic, it combines respect for liberty of mind with a commitment to the great traditions of learning and civilization that permit its reasoned exercise. It places mankind within a grand frame that confers an intellectual nobility unattainable elsewhere. And, amidst the mean and self-indulgent, it calls upon student and teacher alike to make the very best of themselves. Unfurled without hesitation or apology, this vision will prove far more inspiring than its spiritually bereft competition.

—STEPHEN BALCH

Further Reading

Balch, Stephen, and Rita C. Zurcher. *Dissolution of General Education: 1914–1993*. Princeton, N.J.: National Association of Scholars, 1996.

Hanson, Victor Davis, and John Heath. *Who Killed Homer? The Demise of Classical Education and the Recovery of Greek Wisdom*. New York: Free Press, 1998.

D'Souza, Dinesh. *Illiberal Education*. New York: Free Press, 1991.

Ellis, John M. *Literature Lost: Social Agendas and the Corruption of the Humanities.* New Haven, Conn.: Yale University Press, 1997.

Kimball, Roger. *Tenured Radicals: How Politics Has Corrupted Our Higher Education.* Rev. ed. Chicago: Ivan R. Dee, 1998.

Windschuttle, Keith. *The Killing of History: How Literary Critics and Social Theorists Are Murdering Our Past.* New York: Free Press, 1997.

See also: academic freedom; diversity; intellectual; National Association of Scholars

education, public

Concerns about American public education are at least as old as the founding of the republic. Although George Washington, Benjamin Franklin, Benjamin Rush, and Noah Webster thought extensively about public education, Thomas Jefferson emerges as the most comprehensive thinker on the subject. Jefferson and other leaders in the founding generation were influenced by the Aristotelian conception of virtue and education, Greek and Roman ideals of civic virtue, Lockean principles of liberty and virtue, and Judeo-Christian morality. In general, the founders all shared the belief that education must be decidedly *moral*, with attention to the cultivation of personal character; *civic*, with the purpose of encouraging both solicitude and respect for one's country; and appropriately *practical*, so that the ideals of a liberal education might fit appropriately into the challenging context of the new nation.

Jefferson believed a thorough program of education was vital to the well-being of the country. He argued that the general public needed education to conduct its private affairs with competence and intelligence, to lead a life of personal virtue, and to acquire the discretion to elect good leaders and hold them accountable to the general principles upon which the government was founded. Additionally, Jefferson believed, as did others of his generation, that the civic purpose of education should include the inculcation of a certain attachment to one's country, an attitude that must reside in tension with a watchfulness that predisposes a citizen to be quick to protest if his fundamental liberties are threatened by his own government.

Jefferson was no egalitarian, despite the way in which modern educational activists sometimes portray him. Although he advocated universal education he also believed that the future of the country rested on the emergence of leaders of moral and intellectual excellence, a "natural aristocracy," whose gifts would be cultivated by education, and whose legitimacy would be recognized by the citizenry. Citizens moreover, would be equipped by their own education to elect and support those who merited positions of leadership. Jefferson's interest in education for leadership was seconded by James Madison—who (unsuccessfully) introduced a measure at the Constitutional Convention to establish a "national university," the purpose of which would be the formation and refinement of talented individuals. George Washington also lobbied for such an institution in messages to Congress, and later, in his will, he provided financial support for the endeavor.

Jefferson's views proceeded from his understanding of human nature; although he was optimistic in its expectations of virtue and progress, he also recognized "innate obliquities in our moral organization," impediments that made the deliberate acquisition of moral and intellectual habits essential. Jefferson's view of human nature and its importance to a sound philosophy of education should be noted because of the wholesale changes in educational philosophy and practice that John Dewey would later introduce. Dewey's educational system also rests upon his assumptions about human nature. These assumptions, though ambiguous, nonetheless included far less concern for the vicious dimensions of man's make-up.

In the 1830s, Horace Mann, working with the Massachusetts school system and establishing a model for the country at large, was able to further Jefferson's dream of universal education, and in doing so he carried forth several of the ideals of the founding generation, including a belief in the importance of historical knowledge; a respect for the principles of liberty, duty, and virtue; and, a concern for fostering the civic-mindedness of students. Conspicuously absent in his educational thought, however, was Jefferson's emphasis on the recognition and education of leaders, and Mann also added to the curriculum "health" and "physical education." Thus, Mann helped set the tone for much of the professionalization and bureaucratization of education that has become its modern hallmark.

After the founding period, the largest shift in educational thinking, and subsequently in practice, occurred during the Progressive Era, a period during which changes in education were guided largely by John Dewey. Although he was trained as a philosopher and made his mark in psychology, John Dewey is best known as an educational philosopher and pedagogue. It is difficult to overstate his influence on education. Although he saw himself as heir to the democratic tradition—and specifically as heir to Jefferson's role in tying education to democracy—Dewey is responsible for radical changes in American education that still dominate both the philosophy and practices of colleges of education, educational interest groups, and public schools today. Furthermore, most of these changes have been for the worse and are responsible in large part for the decrepit state of contemporary American education.

Dewey's entire educational philosophy must be understood in light of his preoccupation with social change, his pragmatic or instrumentalist philosophy, and his willingness to rearrange every possible dimension of education in the interest of pursuing social reform. Dewey turned virtually every educational tradition upside down. While retaining its vocabulary, he rejected the common understanding of character, substituting "habits of social interaction" for the then prevailing concepts of moral and intellectual virtue. The delicate balance of civic education between affection for and suspicion of one's government was replaced by a demand for social change that alone satisfied Dewey's vision of education for citizenship. While the founding generation generally respected the utility of religion, Dewey staged a militant campaign against both religion and tradition, considering them pernicious impediments to social progress. George Washington had asserted that "Knowledge is . . . the surest basis of public happiness," but in John Dewey one finds a radical depreciation of the value of "facts," historical and otherwise, unless such facts have immediate and demonstrable social utility.

Dewey's stated primary interest was in the unrestricted and creative learning of the child, but this assertion cannot be taken at face value. To be sure, his "creative" educational environment fostered social progress by directing students' inclinations toward predefined social objectives. In *Schools of Tomorrow* (1915), Dewey even notes that not only may students be trained in the classroom to serve as vanguards of social progress upon graduation, but they may also be coached to change their home and community environment while still students. It is in this text also that Dewey frankly acknowledges the influence on him of Jean-Jacques Rousseau's radical educational views, ideas found in the eighteenth-century French philosopher's educational treatise *Emile* (1762), from which Dewey occasionally quotes.

Although Dewey explains that his primary influence was the philosopher William James, one does not find Dewey's intense hostility toward tradition in James's pragmatic philosophy. Dewey's thought now pervades schools of education, though most are not equipped to recognize his influence. Given the overwhelmingly destructive impact of his thought, and given his disdain for outworn notions of "good" and "evil," Dewey may well have crossed a line from mere pragmatism to nihilism. Indeed, in his book *Human Nature and Conduct* (1922), he speaks of the child's creative classroom opportunities as chances to exercise a kind of adolescent "will to power."

In April 1983, the Reagan administration issued "A Nation at Risk," a report making explicit what many already knew anecdotally or intuitively: American public education had badly degenerated compared both to its own past and to other industrialized nations. The report initiated a wave of concern and debate over educational reform, discussions that at the turn of the twenty-first century had grown ever more intense if not better informed.

Many of the problems in education can be attributed to Dewey's influence, yet numerous educational experts still draw upon Dewey's ideas as the cure for the ills his theories have caused. A surprising number of contemporary innovations in public education find their intellectual heritage in Dewey's progressivism. "Outcomes Based Education" (OBE), an idea that appeared in the 1980s, while perhaps conceptually sound, quickly became an opportunity to ensure not so much that students achieved basic competency in math and history, for example, but that they emerged from school with certain politicized attitudes. The phrase "critical thinking skills" has become a conspicuous slogan in reform efforts, but the modern conception of critical thinking has little to do with logic or rhetoric. Instead, such initiatives usually call upon students to "think for themselves" by questioning tradition and authority. Most curiously, programs of critical thinking frequently denigrate the accumulation of mere "information" on the assumption that "facts" have little to do with true intelligence. These programs unfortunately ignore the impossibility of employing one's critical thinking skills in a fact-free vacuum. A similar disdain attends to discussions of "rote memorization" since such uncreative practices also emphasize "information."

The contemporary movement in favor of "standards," "assessment," and "accountability" has produced similarly ideologically charged programs. The national "Goals 2000" initiative under the Clinton administration in 1994, among other problems, quickly became infected with anti-Western and anti-American sentiments. Opponents argued that, aside from its misguided philosophy, Goals 2000 constituted an intrusion into state education responsibilities, thus violating the Tenth Amendment. The program bears Dewey's teeth marks: President Clinton introduced it, not as a program to enhance character or promote civic education, but as "the best change agent we can have." The illustration on the cover of the introductory booklet is also telling. It pictures, not a student busy with his books, nor a supportive family environment, but a schoolhouse encircled by members of the community, none of whom can be recognized as a parent.

Another preoccupation among professional educators is that of the "self-esteem" of the student. While all would agree that a healthy self-image is necessary for well-being, contemporary educators sometimes ignore the fact that self-esteem is best built upon actual achievement. Advocates argue that the teacher should artificially construct a student's self-esteem with praise in the absence of success (or sometimes even effort) with programs such as "I Like Me."

Although many now employ the rhetoric of standards and assessment, educators increasingly shy away from meaningful teacher testing and have fought to minimize the importance of objective tests, especially the SAT. This "test evasion," as one critic of reform has dubbed it, has taken a variety of forms. One is the "re-norming" of the SAT in 1994 so that mediocre scores are now better than they once were. In addition, the SAT and other objective tests are routinely condemned as racially and culturally biased. Many have recommended that they be replaced by as yet unproven psychological measures of "multiple intelligences."

The decision to stage the drama of America's struggle with civil rights in the classroom has had enormous impact on public education, most notably through the activity of busing. *Brown* v.. *Board of Education of Topeka, Kansas* (1954) overturned the "separate but equal" doctrine of *Plessy* v. *Ferguson* (1896) and initiated the integration of public schools. By 1971, mandatory busing had become a frequent judicial remedy to achieve integration. The practice was challenged in *Swann* v. *Charlotte-Mecklenburg Board of Education* (1971) but upheld, which opened the way for busing on a national scale. Whatever its broader merits may have been, busing has been traumatic for public schools and disruptive of primary education objectives. By the 1990s many communities had begun to abandon busing, arguing that either desegregation had been achieved or that busing could do no more to facilitate meaningful integration. The federal courts have generally agreed.

Equally significant but slightly less traumatic has been the Supreme Court's application of the First Amendment establishment clause to public education. The Court has cut a confusing path. By its own admission, the Court has failed to provide parents and the public school system with clear and coherent guidelines, although the general tone of its jurisprudence has been to create a school atmosphere hostile to religion in general and to prayer in particular, an extreme position that reaches well beyond what the founders would have required. The 1990s saw a mild shift in jurisprudence, as several Supreme Court decisions countenanced a greater commingling of educational and religious activity; no significant change in the Court's position, however, seems to be in the offing.

American public education finds itself badly in need of sound philosophy and effective practice; yet reform movements are often thwarted by the political influence of those who have a vested interest in the status quo. The most reactionary forces remain schools and colleges of education and educational interest groups, especially the powerful National Education Association (NEA). Even the Parent Teacher Association (PTA), at least at the national level, has become politicized in such a way that it is often, like the NEA, an opponent of sensible educational improvements and an activist in a whole range of left-leaning political causes, many of which have little to do with education.

The political power of groups such as the NEA is evident in the debate over school vouchers. Some believe that the best solution for the problems besetting American education is to give parents greater discretion through vouchers that could be redeemed at schools of the parents' choosing. So far, however (and despite the popularity of vouchers in cities like Cleveland and Milwaukee, especially among lower income families), such programs have remained rare because of the harsh opposition of educational interest groups able to prevent even reasoned discussion of their possibility, much less their enactment and implementation. In the landmark Supreme Court case *Zelman* v. *Simmons-Harris* (2002), the court decided by a bare majority that a pilot school voucher program in Ohio did not violate the establishment clause of the First Amendment, even though parents might redeem those vouchers at religious schools. Opposition to voucher programs, however, remains intense.

A compromise of sorts has been more successful: the number of "charter schools," which enjoy considerable autonomy from state supervision through special arrangement, even though they are public, is increasing throughout the nation. As of April 2005, forty states and the District of Columbia had charter schools, and in total there were approximately 3400 charter schools operating in the U.S. Some state laws, however, are far friendlier to the creation of genuine charter schools than others. The number of such schools varies from several hundred in some states to only a handful in others.

"No Child Left Behind" (NCLB) was enacted in 2002 and has become the centerpiece of President George W. Bush's education reform. The law constitutes major federal intervention in state education activity, mandating a variety of measures designed to ensure that students are educated as they ought to be. The verdict is still out on whether NCLB will bring about true education reform.

Two leading spokesman for education reform at the turn of the millennium are William J. Bennett, former secretary of education under Ronald Reagan, and E. D. Hirsch Jr. Bennett's work (e.g., *The Education Child*, 1999), while devoting some attention to leading issues in educational reform, is highly practical in nature, providing parents systematic guidance on pedagogical and curricular issues. Hirsch's leading book on reform (*The Schools We Need and Why We Don't Have Them,* 1996), is more theoretical and rightly attributes many of today's educational problems to the progressive movement. Hirsch's work, however, is marred because he tries to save Dewey from his own bad ideas by attributing the problems of pro-

gressivism to Dewey's disciple, William Heard Kilpatrick. Other important voices in U.S. education reform include Chester E. Finn Jr. and the education historian Diane Ravitch.

—HENRY T. EDMONDSON III

Further Reading

Brann, Eva T. H. *Paradoxes of Education in a Republic.* Chicago: University of Chicago Press, 1979.

Edmondson, Henry T., III. *John Dewey and the Decline of American Education: How the Patron Saint of Schools Has Corrupted Teaching and Learning.* Wilmington, Del.: ISI Books, 2006.

Finn, Chester E., Jr. *We Must Take Charge: Our Schools and Our Future.* New York: Free Press, 1991.

Smith, Lorraine, and Thomas L. Pangle. *The Learning of Liberty: The Educational Ideas of the American Founders.* Lawrence, Kan.: University Press of Kansas, 1993.

See also: Bennett, William J.; homeschooling; Jefferson, Thomas

Edwards, Lee (1932–)

A public relations figure in the early conservative movement, Lee Edwards is now a historian of American conservatism and a biographer of its major figures. A prolific writer, Edwards has authored or edited more than a dozen books and written more than 500 articles.

Edwards was born in 1932 in Chicago, Illinois, and educated at Duke University and the Sorbonne. His parents, dedicated anti-communists, introduced him to conservatism early in his life, and his father, Willard, a longtime reporter and columnist for the *Chicago Tribune* based mostly in Washington, D.C., introduced him to the skills of the written word.

Edwards was director of public information for the 1964 Goldwater for President campaign, a founding member of Young Americans for Freedom (YAF), and the first editor of both the *New Guard* and *Conservative Digest*. In 1969, the *New York Times* called him the "voice of the Silent Majority." Edwards has served as a public affairs consultant for key conservative organizations, including YAF, the American Conservative Union, the Committee for a Free China, American Council for World Freedom, and the Heritage Foundation, as well as for the Republican National Committee, Senators Strom Thurmond and Robert Dole, and the Nixon White House.

After receiving his Ph.D. from the Catholic University of America, Edwards launched a second career, writing several significant books, including biographies of Barry Goldwater, Ronald Reagan, and Walter Judd. His *Conservative Revolution: The Movement that Remade America* (1999) chronicles conservatism from Robert Taft through Newt Gingrich, and his histories of the Heritage Foundation, Grove City College, and the Intercollegiate Studies Institute document these organizations' contributions to the conservative movement.

Edwards is currently senior editor of the *World & I* and a senior fellow at the Heritage Foundation.

—ELIZABETH SPALDING

Further Reading

Edwards, Lee. *The Essential Ronald Reagan: A Profile in Courage, Justice, and Wisdom*. Lanham, Md.: Rowman & Littlefield, 2004.

———. *Mediapolitik: How the Mass Media Have Transformed World Politics*. Washington, D.C.: Catholic University of America Press, 2001.

Eisenhower, Dwight D. (1890–1969)

Immensely successful and popular as Supreme Allied Commander during the Second World War, General Dwight Eisenhower vaulted onto the political stage after his homecoming and won a landslide victory in 1952 to become the thirty-fourth president of the United States. Affectionately called "Ike" by millions of Americans, Eisenhower secured an even more lopsided victory in his 1956 bid for reelection. President Eisenhower presided over a period of robust growth and "happy days" at home, and he steered American foreign policy through a series of global crises in an increasingly perilous bipolar postwar world. His statecraft cemented the strategy of "containment" as the fixed American response to the threat of Soviet expansion during the Cold War.

Although he cast himself as a Republican committed to less government and more local control, Eisenhower drew sharp criticism from conservatives before, during, and after his presidency. His low marks emanated from what detractors called his acceptance of "New Dealism," his cozy relationship with big business, and a "deficient understanding of Communism." Eisenhower supported two massive national public works projects, the Interstate Highway System and the St. Lawrence Seaway Act, both of which poured billions of federal dollars into internal improvements designed to promote commerce. For many conservatives, the Eisenhower circle was blindly committed to a market-based economy and society. They were gratuitously materialistic and far too willing to sacrifice tradition on the altar of capitalism. He also appointed arguably the most liberal chief justice in the history of the United States Supreme Court, Earl Warren (an appointment he later called a "damn fool mistake"). In 1957, he boldly and unequivocally asserted federal supremacy over state rights when he dispatched the 101st Airborne to Little Rock, Arkansas, to enforce a federal court order desegregating Central High School. Eisenhower also ran afoul of the anticommunist wing of the Republican Party.

Mindful of conservative anxiety in 1952, candidate Eisenhower chose celebrated anticommunist Richard Nixon as his running mate to offset his closemouthed but palpable revulsion to Joseph McCarthy. Eisenhower loathed the communist-hunting senator from Wisconsin. After McCarthy's dramatic fall from grace, the president wryly observed that "McCarthyism is now McCarthy-wasm." More importantly, Eisenhower selected John Foster Dulles for secretary of state, who famously condemned Harry Truman's policy of containment as soft in the face of Soviet intentions. Dulles proposed an aggressive policy of "liberating captive nations" from the communist bloc. However, even as Dulles set about forging mutual defense pacts in hot spots all over the world and pursuing "brinksmanship" in Soviet-American relations, Eisenhower rejected the combative mentality prevalent among anticommunists on the American Right. On the other hand, the former general was no pacifist. He did not hesitate to employ an atomic threat against North Korea to speed peace talks in 1953, nor was he fooled by the manifestly disingenuous Soviet offer of "peaceful coexistence." The Eisenhower administration engineered an enormous missile buildup and announced the policy of massive nuclear retaliation in response to the expanding Soviet arsenal. Eisenhower introduced the "domino theory" as a scenario for understanding the

Dwight Eisenhower

threat in Southeast Asia (1954); he bemoaned the Soviet crackdown in Hungary (1956); he announced his intention to aid any nation in the Middle East threatened by communism (the so-called Eisenhower Doctrine, 1959); and he instituted an embargo against Cuba—a newly minted Soviet client state just seventy miles off the U.S. coastline (1961). Still, some conservatives complained that little difference existed between the Eisenhower foreign policy and that of his predecessor. The president played tough defense with the Soviets when confronted, his critics asserted, but he stopped well short of actively contesting communist domination in Eastern Europe or working toward regime change in Moscow. In short, for reasons of pragmatism and economy, Eisenhower clearly favored containment over conflict. (Likewise, on the domestic front, Eisenhower preferred to contain the costs of the New Deal as opposed to dismantling it.)

Eisenhower was openly religious, composing and reciting a prayer before his first inaugural, opening cabinet meetings with prayer, and establishing the interdenominational White House Prayer Breakfast. Honest and good-natured, he loved western novels, television, and movies. He played golf, fished, hunted, played bridge, and painted landscapes of mediocre quality. Many sneered at the folksiness of Ike. Compared to the cerebral Adlai Stevenson, whom Eisenhower twice defeated for the oval office, contemporaneous commentators on the Left found the president simple and intellectually limited. Eisenhower's disjointed public speaking style and his purported detachment from the details of office undergirded the assumption that he was dull and uninterested. However, historical reconsiderations of Eisenhower and his presidency over the past four decades have consistently demonstrated his firm hand in events and enhanced his reputation. One scholar, Fred Greenstein, titled his book on the Eisenhower years the *Hidden-Hand Presidency* (1982). Behind the iconic, benevolent, national grandfather image, historians have asserted, beat the heart of a great and competent manager who moved quickly and resolutely behind the scenes.

—ASHLEY CRUSETURNER

Further Reading

D'Este, Carlo. *Eisenhower: A Soldier's Life*. New York: Henry Holt, 2002.

Eisenhower, Dwight D. *Crusade in Europe*. Baltimore: Doubleday, 1948.

See also: Cold War; containment; McCarthy, Joseph; Nixon, Richard M.

Eliot, T. S. (Thomas Stearns) (1888–1965)

It may be that T. S. Eliot is the last great poet of the English language, due to profound social, technological, cultural, and linguistic changes, some of which he himself envisioned and which are already illuminated in his poetry and discussed in his prose. In Eliot's poetry and nonfiction prose, as in the fiction of his countryman and fellow-expatriate Henry James, a high culture that had been developing since the Middle Ages, the Renaissance, and the Reformation reaches a level of complex articulation, verbal ingenuity, and moral sophistication that is probably no longer practicable in an age of mass media and mass taste, an age in which distinctions between high and popular culture have been obliterated. The culture of reading and the word, rooted in the traditions of the Hebrew Bible, Greek and Roman philoso-

phy and rhetoric, and their medieval, Renaissance, Reformation, and Enlightenment sequels, variations, and developments, reached an apogee in the English-speaking world in the Victorian and Edwardian period (ca. 1840–1914) of which Eliot and James are both exemplars. This high bourgeois culture valued education, reading, and literature, pursuits that for some replaced religion.

The catastrophic events of subsequent history, especially the nightmarish period 1914–45, spelled the end of Christian humanist culture. This culture was replaced by radio, television, commercial advertising, and fanatical ideologies (e.g., communism, fascism, and National Socialism) and their flattery of and pandering to democratic and romantic impulses. Increased geographical and social mobility and personal and familial instability also played a role in this culture's demise.

After graduation from Harvard, Eliot studied at the Sorbonne and Oxford before settling permanently in London in 1915. His early poetry, represented by *Prufrock and Other Observations* (1917), is ironic, allusive, and elusive in the high aesthetic mode inherited from the French decadents and symbolists (e.g., Laforgue). *Poems* (1919) continued this ironic current, but *The Waste Land* (1922), which was to become the most influential English poem of the twentieth century, strikes a new set of notes and reaches toward ethics, philosophy, and religion. On one level this poem expresses the disillusionment with the dogma of inevitable, collective, and secular progress that had become so widespread in the nineteenth century but which the horrors of World War I and its attendant furies, such as Bolshevism and fascism, so decisively contradicted and destroyed. Also a satire in the mode of Jeremiah and Juvenal, it harshly mocks liberal, democratic, and romantic ideas, using a stream-of-consciousness technique to illuminate and deplore modern confusion, aimlessness, and hedonism. In full-scale revolt against the optimistic and leftist romanticism of Whitman and Swinburne, Eliot's poem documents modern fragmentation and lostness in "the insufferable inane" of a post-Christian culture, which he depicts, following and drawing on Dante, Baudelaire, and James Thomson, as a hell on earth. His satire on the urban, industrial, and commercial rape of the natural and human landscapes and of human personality and society themselves makes Eliot's poem an ecological protest *avant la lettre*, but one fully consistent with the older Christian humanist critique of scientism and utilitarianism represented variously by Goldsmith, Burke, Blake, Wordsworth, Coleridge,

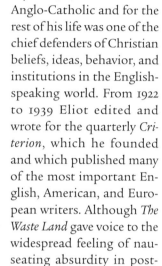

T. S. Eliot

Carlyle, Dickens, Ruskin, Chesterton, Belloc, and other Christians and idealists from the 1790s to the 1920s and into our own time.

Some passages in *The Waste Land* have a ghastly, eloquent pertinence to the tragic chaos of twentieth-century history and life that is both prophetic and classic, as in a passage that his own notes to the poem describe as commenting on "the present decay of eastern Europe":

> What is that sound high in the air
> Murmur of maternal lamentation
> Who are those hooded hordes swarming
> Over endless plains, stumbling in
> cracked earth. (II. 366-69)

Here and elsewhere, Eliot is a world-historical poet who helps to illuminate the history and meaning of a tragic era of human history.

In *The Waste Land*, Eliot employed mythical, anthropological, and religious allusions, themes, and symbols to contrast a chaotic

and nightmarish present to a saner and more humane past, but it is apparent by the end of part 5 of the poem, "What the Thunder Said," that Eliot himself saw a return to religion as the only solution for modern individuals and society. In 1927 he became an Anglo-Catholic and for the rest of his life was one of the chief defenders of Christian beliefs, ideas, behavior, and institutions in the English-speaking world. From 1922 to 1939 Eliot edited and wrote for the quarterly *Criterion*, which he founded and which published many of the most important English, American, and European writers. Although *The Waste Land* gave voice to the widespread feeling of nauseating absurdity in postwar Europe and America, and although Eliot painted a very unflattering picture in this poem and in his prose of a decadent commercial-utilitarian society, he never became an absurdist or a Marxist. Nor did he succumb to the attractions of continental fascism and National Socialism. His literary and social criticism provide, instead, a balanced, highly sophisticated analysis and critique of modern "heresies" or alternatives to the Christian worldview, and in this regard he was not only a moralist and a theologian but also a sociologist, a fit heir to Burke and, more proximately, to G. K. Chesterton. Having mocked Chesterton early on, Eliot changed his mind and finally paid generous tribute to him in two eulogies on the occasion of the elder man's death in 1936.

From the early 1920s until his death in 1965 Eliot dominated English letters in a way analogous to the roles played by Samuel Johnson (1709-84) and Matthew Arnold (1822-88) in their eras. Although a great deal of his literary-critical writing concerned

Shakespeare, other Elizabethan and Jacobean dramatists, and seventeenth-century poets, theologians, and preachers (e.g., John Donne and Lancelot Andrewes), Eliot's Anglo-Catholic position is in direct succession to the views and writings of Johnson, Burke, Coleridge, John Henry Newman, and Chesterton, in their confrontation with what has subsequently come to be called "secularization," "secular humanism," and "modernity." He printed in the *Criterion*—and sometimes made common cause with—the French Thomists (e.g., Maritain), English Distributists, and the American New Humanists and Agrarians and their successors (e.g., Irving Babbitt and Paul Elmer More, Allen Tate, and Russell Kirk). Though he disputed certain features of the thinking of conservative humanists in the tradition of Arnold, especially Babbitt (one of his former teachers at Harvard) and F. R. Leavis of Cambridge (one of his most sympathetic critics), their views and sensibilities had much in common with his own.

In addition to his literary-critical and sociological writing, his editing of the *Criterion*, and his influential service as chief editor of the publishing firm Faber and Faber, Eliot published major works of poetry and drama in his middle and late periods, after the absurdist "The Hollow Men" of 1925. Himself an austere and ascetical man in a promiscuous and hedonistic culture, Eliot published devotional poems ("Ash Wednesday," 1930), didactic and doctrinal poems (choruses from "The Rock," 1934), religious drama ("Murder in the Cathedral," 1935), and, in the period 1939–58, four controversial and still problematic plays. But surely the masterpiece of his late period is the series of philosophical poems called *Four Quartets*: "Burnt Norton" (1935), "East Coker" (1940), "The Dry Salvages" (1941), and "Little Gidding" (1942). Kenneth Muir has called these the most satisfying and substantial poems of the twentieth century, and though

large claims have been made for the lyrics of Yeats, Stevens, and Frost, Eliot's "quartets" are unrivaled in our century in their scope, evocative power, religious and philosophical depth, sanity, and generosity of spirit. Eliot was awarded the Nobel Prize for literature in 1948.

Eliot maintained strong links with American conservatism through his close associations with Babbitt, but more particularly with his fellow converts More, Tate, and Kirk. His negative or slighting comments on and depictions of "free-thinking Jews," the phrase he used in *After Strange Gods: A Primer on Modern Heresy* (1934), have created great controversy and invited widespread disapproval, but Eliot disavowed them and the adjectival phrase deserves emphasis. As Christopher Ricks has recently written, "presumably [even] a rabbi does not believe that any large number of free-thinking Jews is desirable." What Eliot opposed (and hated) was secularization and desacralization, and as the American Jewish sociologist Daniel Bell has said, the essence of modernity is that nothing is sacred. Revolutionary or nihilistic intellectuals and commercial exploiters, whatever their ethnicity, were odious to Eliot, though he maintained, like Chesterton, courteous relations with many of his ideological opponents and even published some of them in the *Criterion*.

—M. D. AESCHLIMAN

Further Reading

Eliot, T. S. *Notes towards the Definition of Culture.* London: Faber and Faber, 1948.

Frye, Northrop. *T. S. Eliot: An Introduction.* Chicago: University of Chicago Press, 1981.

Gardner, Helen. *The Art of T. S. Eliot.* Rev. ed. London: Cresset, 1968.

Grant, Michael, ed. *T. S. Eliot: The Critical Heritage.* London: Routledge, 1982.

Kirk, Russell. *Eliot and His Age.* La Salle, Ill.: Sherwood Sugden, 1984.

Ricks, Christopher. *T. S. Eliot and Prejudice.* Berkeley, Calif.: University of California Press, 1988.

Southam, B. C. *A Student's Guide to the Selected Poems of T. S. Eliot.* 5th ed. London: Faber and Faber, 1990.

See also: Babbitt, Irving; Conservative Mind, The; Criterion; *Dawson, Christopher; fascism; Kirk, Russell; More, Paul Elmer; New Criticism; New Humanism; Pound, Ezra; Tate, Allen*

émigré intellectuals

The impact of the arrival of a group of Central European émigré scholars on American cultural life has long been the subject of social scientific discussion. Such celebrated figures as Theodor Adorno, Max Horkheimer, and Leo Lowenthal—men on the political Left—proved to be highly influential in shaping public policy on the welfare state and civil liberties in the post–World War II years. Until comparatively recently, however, little scholarly attention has been given to a number of conservative scholars who were simultaneously part of this important exodus.

With the growth of the conservative movement highlighted by the "Reagan Revolution," attention has come to focus increasingly on this group of scholars. Although there is considerable overlap in their ideas, they can be classified into three rough categories. There were traditionalists like philosopher Leo Strauss and historian Eric Voegelin, both refugees from Germany. Although a supporter of liberal democracy, Strauss found it lacking in certain fundamental, underlying strengths that could bind it together. Although not a religionist, he found that cement in traditional religious teachings. He taught also in his best-known book, *Natural Right and History* (1950), that Edmund Burke was correct in favoring the "authors of sound antiquity" to the "Parisian philosophers" of the Enlightenment who had distorted the ancient idea of natural right accepted by all into hedonism and relativism. Both Strauss and Voegelin never really considered themselves part of the American conservative movement but the revolt they led against modernity won considerable attention among conservatives.

A variant of traditionalist thought was found in the work of Ernest van den Haag, an émigré sociologist from Mussolini's Italy. Not quite a religionist either, van den Haag nevertheless believed religion could be useful in helping to provide the glue to hold society together and move it to a higher level. His work took on fuller form in the 1960s during the period of racial disorders and the rise of Black militance. Van den Haag refused to accept the tactics of the latter. He was critical of the Kerner Commission appointed by President Johnson to study the causes of the rioting, which proposed a number of liberal formulas for social change. He called, for example, for the arrangement of welfare payments so as not to reduce incentives for work and he sought the abandonment of restrictive labor practices that kept African Americans out of the mainstream.

A second group of émigré scholars were apostles of free-market economics. They included Friedrich von Hayek and Ludwig von Mises, who liked to call themselves "liberals" in the European and conservative sense of the term. The older of the two, Mises, published his "capitalist manifesto" of almost a thousand pages, *Human Action*, in 1949. Conditioned by his generation's experience of the omnipresent state and the threat it posed to individual freedom, he was an uncompromising advocate of laissez-faire economics. By 1935, Mises had become the main rival of the prominent statist John Maynard Keynes.

About the time he accepted a chair at the University of Chicago, Hayek burst upon the American scene with the publication of his highly popular *The Road to Serfdom* (1944). In it, Hayek argued that political freedom was part and parcel of economic freedom. He declared also that Russian communism and German National Socialism were manifestations of collectivist patterns found in all forms of socialism. One might also include in this group of thinkers another émigré, Ayn Rand, whose novels *Atlas Shrugged* and *The Fountainhead* sold millions of copies and were made into films. Rand literally worshipped the free-enterprise system—she wore a silver necklace shaped in the form of a dollar sign. Her heroes, both men and women, were unbridled practitioners of an individualism that reflected an extreme libertarian ideology.

Finally, there were the Cold Warriors, a group that included Gerhart Niemeyer, Stefan Possony, Thomas Molnar, William S. Schlamm, and Robert Strausz-Hupe. Scarred by their experiences with totalitarianism, they helped to shape and lead the fight against the aggressive designs of the Soviet Union in the postwar years. For the most part, they did not seek to go to war. But they cautioned that "peace congresses" and other propaganda devices could lower the guard of the West; they sought, by contrast, confrontation with the Soviets through defense buildups, and they promoted the countering of aggressive Soviet moves in every part of the world in order to force the Soviets' retreat. Otherwise, as Schlamm put it, communism would continue to expand until the United States would be forced to fight a suicidal war. One might include in this group also—although she was not strictly speaking a conservative—the political theorist Hannah Arendt, a native of Hanover in Wilhelmine Germany. Her book *The Origins of Totalitarianism* (1951) came as a revelation to many on the Left. Arendt found totalitarianism to be an entirely novel form of autocracy that sprung from subterranean sources within Western society. The book's importance lay in the fact that she made no distinction between the Soviet and Nazi models, a view that ran counter to prevailing leftist thought in the early days of the Cold War.

A number of these scholar/activists came from Roman Catholic backgrounds; some, however, including Rand, Arendt, Strauss, Mises, and Schlamm, were Jewish.

In the wake of the conservative ascendancy in the last two decades, and through networks of scholars, think tanks, and admirers, these conservative émigré scholars and intellectuals have found a new relevance and contemporary audiences. Leo Strauss, in particular, has been alternately credited and blamed for various domestic and international policies launched by self-identified conservatives.

—MURRAY FRIEDMAN

Further Reading

Ebenstein, Alan. *Friedrich Hayek: A Biography*. New York: St. Martin's Press, 2001.

Hodgson, Godfrey. *The World Turned Right Side Up: A History of the Conservative Ascendancy in America*. New York: Houghton Mifflin, 1996.

Hughes, H. Stuart. *The Sea Change: The Migration of Social Thought, 1930-1945*. New York: Harper and Row, 1975.

McAllister, Ted V. *Revolt Against Modernity: Leo Strauss, Eric Voegelin and the Search for a Postliberal Order*. Lawrence, Kan.: University Press of Kansas, 1996.

Nash, George H. *The Conservative Intellectual Movement in America since 1945*. Wilmington, Del.: Intercollegiate Studies Institute, 1996.

See also: Hayek, Friedrich A. von; Mises, Ludwig von; Molnar, Thomas; Niemeyer, Gerhart; Schlamm, William; Strauss, Leo; Van den Haag, Ernest; Voegelin, Eric

English, Raymond (1917–90)

An English-born political scientist, educator, and scholar of the state of American education, Raymond English was the author of works that focus on the conservative roots of Western cultural order and the ends of education. He entered the world of letters at a time when statist liberalism was in the ascendancy, tradition was dismissed as the dead hand of the past, and imagination was considered the realm of children. Undeterred, English set out to take his stand against this prevailing mindset. In a signal 1952 essay, he famously referred to conservatism as "the forbidden faith," noting that in many quarters within America, adherence to a conservative worldview was viewed as a sign of stupidity at best, viciousness at worst.

Raised and educated in Stretford, Lancashire, English was schooled locally, going on to receive his B.A. and M.A. from Trinity College, Cambridge University during the early years of World War II. During the war he served with the British Army in India, Burma, and Germany. After returning to civilian life, he lectured on political science and history at Harvard University for two years on a Henry fellowship and published a book, *The Pursuit of Purpose: An Essay on Social Morale* (1947). English went on to serve as a professor of political science at Kenyon College from 1948 to 1964, eventually becoming director of the social science program. During this time he contributed scholarly articles in his field to numerous respected quarterlies and served as the editor of an essay symposium, *The Essentials of Freedom* (1960). After leaving Kenyon, he was named director of the social science textbook program of the Educational Research Council of America, in which post he served for fifteen years, fighting to uphold scholarly standards while fending off the efforts of various oversight committees to smuggle into new textbooks political or social ideologies of one form or another.

In 1979 English left the Educational Research Council to join the Ethics and Public Policy Center, where he served as vice president and later as a senior fellow responsible for educational studies and associated mat-

ters. During the final decade of his life, English also wrote book reviews and essays for the *Washington Times,* the *Journal of General Education*, and the *Washington Star*, among other periodicals. A political scientist with a high regard for the natural law, he held that the poetic and the moral imagination are essential for apprehending truth. His long-time colleague Ernest Lefever wrote that English "was a man of singular virtues, virtues that are not always fashionable in the hurly-burly of Washington.... Raymond was an anachronism, but a relevant anachronism."

—James E. Person Jr.

Further Reading

English, Raymond, ed. *Teaching International Politics in High School*. Washington, D.C.: Ethics and Public Policy Center, 1989.

Kirk, Russell. *Redeeming the Time*. Wilmington, Del.: Intercollegiate Studies Institute, 1996.

Lefever, Ernest W, Raymond English, and Robert Schuettinger. *Scholars, Dollars, and Public Policy: New Frontiers in Corporate Giving*. Washington, D.C.: Ethics and Public Policy Center, 1983.

See also: education, higher; education, public

Enlightenment

The Enlightenment was the intellectual movement that dominated Western European and British North American thought during the eighteenth century. Largely secular, the Enlightenment (French *Lumières,* German *Aufklaerung*) developed long after medieval scholasticism had waned in the West. But the medieval theologian's systematic attempt to reconcile all knowledge in revelation and reason found its analogue in the early modern philosopher's systematic effort to comprehend universal order in the laws of nature. Christopher Dawson, Carl

Becker, and Stanley Jaki, among others, have pointed out that both assume the unity and knowability of reality. There is thus an important intellectual link, often overlooked, between the medieval schoolmen on the one hand and the scientists and philosophers of the Enlightenment on the other.

In addition to its medieval roots, the eighteenth-century Enlightenment grew out of a number of seventeenth-century developments, some of them at variance with one another. Francis Bacon's inductive method, Descartes' rationalism, Newton's scientific formulations, Spinoza's pantheism, Locke's empiricism—all suggest the array of differing methods toward and assumptions about man and nature in Enlightenment thought.

Nevertheless, by the eighteenth century the movement's leading lights tended to share a core of beliefs. In general they were: (1) convinced that their age was more advanced than past ages; (2) hopeful of man's ability to use common sense and reason to improve himself and society; (3) skeptical of religious dogmas and a priori metaphysical systems; (4) critical of the social injustices and political backwardness of the ancien régime; and (5) supportive of practical efforts that would lead to greater prosperity, fairer laws, milder government, more efficient administration, better education, more religious tolerance, and greater intellectual freedom. As is well known, some of the Enlightenment's aspirations found expression in the American Revolution (1775–87) and French Revolution (1789–99).

As an intellectual movement, the Enlightenment is so multifaceted that it is desirable to draw distinctions between its dominant tendencies. Such distinctions, while somewhat arbitrary, nevertheless aid our analysis and criticism of Enlightenment thought, especially as it bears on modern thought. Following historian Henry May, it is useful to discern four distinct but interrelated strands of Enlightenment thinking

that surfaced in the early decades of American history.

(1) The "moderate Enlightenment" was dominant in England and lasted from the end of the seventeenth century to the end of the eighteenth century. Inspired initially by Newton and Locke, it championed order, balance and, with some significant exceptions, religious toleration and compromise. (Locke, for example, extended toleration neither to atheists nor Catholics in the body politic.) In America, many of the founding fathers espoused the ideas of the moderate Enlightenment even during the height of the War of Independence. George Washington was one of its leading figures.

(2) The "skeptical Enlightenment" developed around the middle of the eighteenth century. It thrived in France but existed in Britain as well. Its pantheon included Hume, Holbach, Diderot and, above all, Voltaire. The French philosophes typically used wit to attack the decadence of the ancien régime, satirizing a host of aristocratic pretentions and clerical abuses in Europe. The more systematic thinkers among them developed such modern modes of thought as epistemological skepticism (Hume) and radical materialism (Holbach). In America its leading representative was Benjamin Franklin, one of the few Americans who felt truly at home in prerevolutionary Paris.

(3) The "revolutionary Enlightenment" encompasses the decades that saw the American and French revolutions. Adumbrated by Rousseau, it culminated in Thomas Paine, Joseph Priestley, Richard Price, and William Godwin. Thomas Jefferson's relation to the revolutionary Enlightenment is rather more complex: as a younger man he was a partisan of wide-scale revolution, but with age (and with reflection upon the excesses of the French Revolution) his utterances on the subject became considerably more temperate. In general, partisans of the revolutionary Enlightenment championed the

possibility of creating a new world out of the destruction of the old. Freedom from all outward restraint was their goal. This strand of Enlightenment thought inspired not only the French Jacobins but also the American Jacobins who, desirous of liberating all humankind from the shackles of prejudice, custom, and arbitrary authority, wanted to crush any who blocked the advent of the new order.

(4) The "didactic Enlightenment," though centered in Scotland during the middle of the eighteenth century, bore fruit in America in the first years of the nineteenth century. Its adherents opposed radical skepticism and revolution but sought to salvage the idea of an intelligible universe, faith in civilizational progress, and clear moral precepts and judgments. In America, prominent clergymen like Samuel Miller championed the didactic Enlightenment in books and sermons.

British historian A. J. P. Taylor once said that study of the Enlightenment mostly attracts those who are worried about the fate of Christendom. Certainly, for decades traditionalist American conservatives have tended to cast aspersions on the Enlightenment as a whole, believing it responsible for spawning the sterile materialism, secularism, and totalitarianism of the modern era: more than one conservative author has mockingly called the movement the "Endarkenment." And yet the Right does not always apply its criticism with precision. After all, many conservatives laud the eighteenth-century ideas espoused by their country's founding fathers, who were undeniably children of the very movement they criticize.

Consider two conservative responses to Thomas Jefferson, who for many is the quintessential Enlightenment thinker in America. On the one hand Russell Kirk argues that while Jefferson wished to emancipate men from external controls, "he never understood, as Burke knew, how power without and power within always must remain 'in ra-

tio.'" This lack of understanding led to considerable errors in political judgment, especially with regard to the French Revolution. On the other hand commentator George Will has gone so far as to call Jefferson "the Person of the Millennium." Will asserts that the story of humankind is essentially "the history of the human mind, of ideas. Jefferson was, preeminently, the mind of the [American] Revolution that succeeded. It resulted in the birth of the first modern nation, the nation that in the twentieth century saved the world from tyranny. Jefferson expressed the American idea: political and social pluralism; government of limited, delegated and enumerated powers; the fecundity of freedom."

Debate about the Enlightenment's leaders notwithstanding, conservatives have wittingly or unwittingly used Enlightenment categories of thought to argue against the Left. For example, it is not unusual to hear criticism of the "tenured radicals" who increasingly dominate the American academy and try to impose a "politically correct" agenda on scholarship and teaching. John Silber, Thomas Sowell, and others have referred to these intellectual tyrants as the "new barbarians"—an allusion to a term used by the great Italian philosopher of the Enlightenment, Vico, who described the dying phase of a civilization as a descent into intellectual barbarity.

By the 1990s many on the Right seemed less reluctant to acknowledge the Enlightenment's positive contributions to American thought and institutions. Now there is vigorous debate among conservatives concerning the salutary influence of the Enlightenment on modern civil society. The question is not an easy one to settle. After all, if Thomas Paine was a child of Enlightenment, so were Adam Smith and John Adams; if the Declaration of Independence was a ringing affirmation of enlightened ideals, the U.S. Constitution was a manifestation of its moderating genius. Even Edmund Burke showed in such works as *A Vindication of Natural Society* (1756) that he "was a child of the Enlightenment: a child, that is, of the early, English or English-inspired, phase of the Enlightenment," as Conor Cruise O'Brien points out.

On the other hand the philosophes' skepticism, not to mention hostility, toward tradition and authority wherever religion and politics are concerned makes reconciliation between Burkean conservatives and the French-inspired strands of Enlightenment thought unlikely.

It would be a mistake to see Burkean conservatives as standing alone in their repudiation of much in Enlightenment thought. Throughout American history, large bodies of the American people—religious revivalists, Jacksonian democrats, Transcendentalists, populists—have rejected the Enlightenment and by extension the intellectuals who have often been its partisans. As Henry May points out, "This fact has been very hard for American scholars to think about, or even to admit. To think about it seriously means to take account of the deficiencies of the Enlightenment."

—GLEAVES WHITNEY

Further Reading

Becker, Carl. *The Heavenly City of the Eighteenth-Century Philosophers.* New Haven, Conn.: Yale University Press, 1932.

Cassirer, Ernst. *The Philosophy of the Enlightenment.* Translated by Fritz C. A. Koelln and James P. Pettegrove. Princeton, N.J.: Princeton University Press, 1968.

Gay, Peter. *The Enlightenment: An Interpretation.* 2 vols. New York: Norton, 1966.

May, Henry F. *The Enlightenment in America.* Oxford: Oxford University Press, 1978.

McManners, John. "Enlightenment, Secular and Christian." In *Oxford Illustrated History of Christianity,* edited by John McManners. Oxford: Oxford University Press, 1990.

Porter, Roy. *The Enlightenment.* Atlantic Highlands, N.J.: Humanities Press International, 1990.

White, Morton. *The Philosophy of the American Revolution.* Oxford: Oxford University Press, 1978.

See also: American Revolution; Burke, Edmund; Burkean conservatism; French Revolution; Jefferson, Thomas; progress; science and scientism; Scottish Enlightenment; tradition

enterprise zones

Enterprise zones have been a cornerstone of the conservative and Republican anti-poverty agenda since Ronald Reagan made them the subject of public debate in the early 1980s. The program was designed to apply free-market economic doctrine—instead of more government money—to help reverse the economic stagnation of the inner city. A poverty-stricken geographic region would be outlined and firms there would be eligible for a range of tax and regulatory breaks. The added incentives would attract new businesses to the area and stimulate bottom-up entrepreneurship, using the power of the private sector to correct government failures. The primary advocate has been former congressman Jack Kemp, who made enterprise zones a policy priority during his tenure as secretary for Housing and Urban Development in the elder Bush's administration.

Liberals and Democrats have generally opposed enterprise zones, never having appreciated the potential for private-sector growth to address problems of poverty and fearing that the real point was to dismantle federal welfare programs. Federal legislation allowing for enterprise zones was never put into effect during the 1980s, but skepticism on the federal level did not prevent thirty-six states and the District of Columbia from starting their own programs with varying degrees of success.

The idea first came to America in 1979, when veteran zone advocate Stuart Butler (later director of domestic policy at the Heritage Foundation) dispatched from London a Heritage Foundation–commissioned policy paper suggesting that America adopt Sir Geoffrey Howe's idea of free-market zones, which were used widely in Great Britain.

Butler proposed that needy areas abolish nearly all government intervention. His plan would have eliminated zoning, minimum wage laws, and rent controls. All public land, including parks, would be sold to private investors. Economic regulations would be ignored by officials. And, according to the plan, "no company entering a zone would be eligible for any subsidy, grant, or other form of government assistance whatsoever." In this plan, tax breaks played a relatively minor role, applying only to property taxes.

By 1981, when the idea reached the policy stage, Butler's far-reaching plan had been seriously modified. The Reagan administration supported large and diverse tax breaks and minor deregulation, but every other provision was eliminated. A careful look at state-level enterprise zones demonstrates an even odder trend: in practice, enterprise zones rely heavily on pro-business transfer payments, not just tax incentives, to create what amounts to temporary economic boomlets.

Nearly all state-level zones provide even greater preferential treatment for government grants. For example, zones in Vermont, Connecticut, New York, New Jersey, Rhode Island, Pennsylvania, Illinois, Kansas, Arkansas, Louisiana, Alabama, Oregon, and Nevada all offer businesses huge state-funded "job training" grants. California, in addition to direct grants, gives public funds for "infrastructure improvement," program targeting, and "marketing assistance." All state-level programs offer firms loans at below-market interest rates. Some, like Florida, offer fifteen-year interest-free loans, and others like Maryland offer an actual "guarantee" against business failure.

Zones in Massachusetts, Connecticut, Vermont, Indiana, and Pennsylvania finance construction of new buildings and repave roads at taxpayer expense; Texas and New York offer lower utility rates than regular businesses pay. Oregon offers special educational opportunities for employees, Tennessee guarantees student loans, and Kansas offers free childcare. Maine offers only business welfare and no tax cuts.

The promise of regulatory relief in state-run programs has not panned out. "In practice, there has been little, if any, elimination of red tape," concluded Michael Allan Wolf of the University of Richmond in his 1990 study of enterprise zones. Instead, select businesses are given special consideration. They are assigned a bureaucracy specialist to help the company through the complex system of zoning and safety standards. This privilege is not available for all zone-based businesses.

Any federal enterprise zone legislation likely to be passed will have a heavy welfare component. Even while supporting some tax breaks, the plans typically outlaw changes in federal labor law within the zone, make no mention of privatization or easing rent control, and mandate additional provisions of social support services.

Some charge that enterprise zones do not create new businesses, but rather shift corporate money from outside the zone into it. While there is anecdotal evidence to support that view, Kemp and other supporters maintain that the point of the program is otherwise, and with federal legislation expanding tax breaks the original ideal could be fulfilled. And certainly a more comprehensive program along the lines that Butler spelled out would address that problem. The best case for far-reaching enterprise zones remains what it always was: the welfarist program for repairing the inner city seems to have failed completely and there is no reason to not give alternative plans a chance.

—Jeffrey A. Tucker

Further Reading

Butler, Stuart M. *Enterprise Zones: Greenlining the Inner Cities.* New York: Universe, 1981.

Friedman, Miles. "Enterprise Zones Spur Business Growth." *Area Development,* August 1989, 96ff.

Guskind, Robert. "Zeal for the Zones." *National Journal* 21 (1989): 1358-67.

Kemp, Jack. "Tackling Poverty." *Policy Review,* Winter 1990, 2-5.

Wolf, Michael Allan. "Enterprise Zones: A Decade of Diversity." *Economic Development Quarterly* 4 (1990): 3-14.

See also: Kemp, Jack F.; poverty; welfare policy

entitlements

Our Declaration of Independence asserts that as Americans we are entitled to life, liberty, and the pursuit of happiness. To be sure, any entitlement implies a corollary obligation. The Declaration's entitlement allows each of us to use our talents and our property however we choose, while at the same time obligating each of us to forbear from violating the equal entitlements of our fellows. This obligation is negative and not positive in nature. We are obligated to avoid interfering with the equal rights of others, but we are not required to perform positive actions for their benefit. For instance, we would be entitled to use our talents and whatever capital we could raise to open and operate a school. We could properly expect other people to forbear from interfering with our right to do so. At the same time, we would be obligated not to violate other people's equal entitlements. We could not forcibly prevent other people also from opening schools. Nor could we force them to attend our school or to contribute to its financial support.

Nowhere in this formulation does one person's entitlement entail the performance of a positive duty by someone else. A call for "a chicken in every pot" represents a very different form of entitlement. For one person can be guaranteed a chicken only if someone else is obligated to provide it. This form of entitlement entails a corollary positive duty. This duty could take the direct form of being compelled to provide chickens for those whose pots are empty. More realistically, it would take the indirect form of being taxed to finance the purchase of chickens that subsequently are given to those whose pots are empty. The outcome is the same in either case, with one person's entitlement imposing positive duties on others.

To be sure, a chicken in every pot is a quite small entitlement program. But most entitlement programs start small and grow rapidly. Aid to Families with Dependent Children (AFDC) began as a small program to aid widows with children. By the time it was transformed into something else in 1996, AFDC was a large program that mostly aided unmarried, teenaged mothers. In recent years entitlement programs have been the most rapidly expanding portion of the federal budget and now constitute about half of all federal spending. Some arise when one reaches a certain age, as with the various social security programs, including Medicare. Others arise when one fails to reach a certain level of income. These entitlement programs are commonly characterized as forming a *safety net*, and, taken together, they create a form of guaranteed minimum income.

To call entitlement programs a safety net is certainly to cultivate a pleasant image, one that makes it seem almost impolite to question the contribution of such programs in promoting the pursuit of happiness. For some caution or insurance, as represented by a safety net, is surely a good thing in nearly anyone's judgment. Yet that net, to continue with the analogy, is woven through the toil of others. Any formulation in terms of entitlements can be formulated alternatively and equivalently in terms of duties. However, alternative statements often evoke different images and responses. To frame a question in terms of how much income people should be guaranteed is almost inescapably to focus on competing notions of adequacy, with the associated tax burden being determined through competition between the forces of generosity and niggardliness.

Yet a guaranteed income is equivalent to a program of compulsory labor to make good on those guarantees. And to focus on the desirable extent of compulsory labor is surely to bring to the foreground beliefs that such labor should be severely limited. Charles Murray argues cogently in his book *In Pursuit of Happiness and Good Government* (1988) that our entitlement to the pursuit of happiness probably does entail some guarantee of material support at a *subsistence* level. Such a level of entitlement would fall far short of justifying the vast array of what are called entitlement programs under the auspices of the welfare state.

Furthermore, there is often a sharp disjunction between the rationales advanced in support of entitlement programs and the actual consequences of those programs. For one thing, entitlement guarantees have often made matters worse by retarding individual initiative and responsibility. Moreover, political forces have pushed entitlement programs well beyond any subsistence support and given the bulk of support to people who are relatively well off. Payments are made predominantly to those who are influential politically and not to those who are truly needy economically.

—RICHARD E. WAGNER

Further Reading

Epstein, Richard A. *Principles for a Free Society: Reconciling Individual Liberty with the Common Good*. Reading, Mass.: Perseus Books, 1998.

Kidd, Alan. *State, Society and the Poor in Nineteenth-Century England*. London: Macmillan, 1999.

Mead, Lawrence. *Beyond Entitlement: The Social Obligations of Citizenship*. New York: Free Press, 1986.

Murray, Charles. *In Pursuit of Happiness and Good Government*. New York: Simon & Schuster, 1988.

Tullock, Gordon. *Economics of Income Redistribution*. Boston: Kluwer-Nijhoff, 1983.

See also: New Deal; welfare policy

environmentalism

Conservative positions may reasonably be divided into two broad views on environmentalism. The dominant view objects to "environmentalism" for three broad reasons: the Constitution, economic growth, and the social agenda of environmentalist ideology. First, guided by constitutional principles, conservatives seek to limit the power of government, especially at the federal level, and thus often see environmental regulation as an unconstitutional extension of governmental power. Second, it is believed that such extension of power is also ineffective environmentally because it does not harness legitimate self-interest, introducing social and economic rigidities that may cause yet more damage to the environment. Instead, such conservatives hold that the private market is better able to promote environmental quality and pollution abatement without interfering with economic growth and, in fact, it is the free, unfettered growth of the economy which naturally provides such improvement. That environmental regulations now often include some market incentives is an implicit acknowledgement of the importance of the market in achieving desirable environmental results. Third, environmentalism is an ideology and a social movement that is objectionable to some, though by no means all, mainstream conservatives who oppose its agenda for social reform, involving as it does radical changes in the way we live, sometimes including the promotion of abortion and other forms of population control. Other mainstream conservatives agree with, however, or at least do not have any principled objection to, this agenda, so long as it is accomplished through free-market choices and not through government coercion. In this respect, conservatives—or at any rate libertarians—may join with the environmentalists' social agenda.

The economic conservative's vision is one of economic growth based on continuous technological change and individual freedom in the context of a market economy. The social changes arising from this growth are considered the necessary price of economic advancement; nature's existence is justified only insofar as it is instrumental in promoting this material well-being. Environmental quality is merely another economic good best provided in a free-market economy. Since man's destiny and purpose are fulfilled along these lines, public policy should be shaped accordingly.

The second group of conservatives—a minority—both agrees and disagrees with the dominant view on various points. It agrees with them in wanting to limit governmental power and abhors the growth of federal government in many areas. But it also disagrees with them on the complete sufficiency of the market to deal with the problem, and so agrees with many environmentalists that the market is not entirely the solution to the problem and economic growth is often part of the difficulty, resting on the often rapacious exploitation of natural resources and acting as a corrosive force on traditional institutions and social

forms. This second group of conservatives also rejects an unqualified commitment to global capitalism, preferring instead a large measure of local and regional economic independence. It rejects the Faustian imperative to dominate nature that seems to impel economic conservatives and views the impulse to endless economic and social change as objectionable per se, regardless of whether such change is accomplished through the market or through the state. The same modern technology that provides material benefits also threatens social continuity and stability. Preserving humane social forms is given priority by such conservatives over the demands of the economy and business, in contrast to the first group of conservatives, who favor economic growth and business needs at the expense of social stability. The second group of conservatives delights in a permanent, settled way of life that includes respect for creation, historically received institutions, and natural and received limits. This group strives for piety, a discipline of the will through respect, including respect for nature and a recognition of other creatures' right to exist independently of their usefulness to man. Such conservatives see little difference between many mainstream conservatives and Marxists, since both work for the dissolution of traditional society, though in different ways.

Pro-environment conservatives and more conventional, left-leaning environmentalists are not without common ground: they both favor things small and local, restrictions on some types of technology, and a simpler way of life. But these potential areas of political agreement are at the same time limited by moral differences concerning issues and movements such as feminism, homosexuality, abortion, and the divinization of nature. Such conservatives do not see man as a slave to nature forbidden to use her in all but very selective ways, as some extreme environmentalists do, but neither do they view men as gods free, perhaps even called, to do whatever possible to satisfy their material desires. Instead, they see humans as caretakers and guiding partners of nature sensitive to the limits of sustainability.

The obvious tension within the conservative camp that is represented by these opposing views quickly becomes religious in character. At stake is the question of what man's ultimate good is and how it is best achieved, the meaning and nature of the created world and its purpose in relation to man's nature and purpose. In the Cold War period, the two camps were held together by their common opposition to communism and the threat posed by the Soviet Union. With the end of the Cold War, this basis of cooperation has been removed and only a common opposition to intrusive federal control and a broad commitment to a market economy remain. Disagreement concerning man's proper relation to the environment may well be an important factor leading to a deeper cleavage on the political Right.

—RALPH E. ANCIL

Further Reading

Bandow, Doug, ed. *Protecting the Environment: A Free Market Strategy.* Washington, D.C.: Heritage Foundation, 1986.

Bliese, John R. E. *The Greening of Conservative America.* Boulder, Colo.: Westview Press, 2001.

Röpke, Wilhelm. *A Humane Economy.* Chicago: Regnery, 1960.

Smith, Wolfgang. *Cosmos and Transcendence: Breaking through the Barrier of Scientist Belief.* La Salle, Ill.: Sherwood Sugden, 1984.

Truluck, Phillip, ed. *Private Rights and Public Lands.* Washington, D.C.: Heritage Foundation, 1983.

See also: agrarianism; localism; New Urbanism; Property and Environment Research Center; Southern Agrarians; technology; traditionalism

envy

Envy, one of the Seven Deadly or Capital Sins, is the hatred of those who possess health, beauty, money, goods, success, intelligence, education, or some other attribute that the envier does not. It is to be distinguished from jealousy, which seeks to possess what is another's. Envy seeks destruction. The seeming near-universality of envy, and its spiritually and socially corrosive effects, has concerned philosophers and theologians from ancient times, but the systematic treatise of Helmut Schoeck has had a special influence on the American Right, as has the more recent work of Gonzalo Fernandez de la Mora.

Cicero defined envy as "sadness caused at the happiness of others," which "produces sadness and a certain joy in the misery of others." Ovid writes that "the residence of Envy, spattered with black pus, is at the end of a pit, empty of sun, where the air does not reach, sad, flooded by an inert cold, lacking fire and covered with fog."

Clement, a father of the church, wrote that envy is the root of the most profound evils in history. Because of envy, Cain killed his brother Abel, Jacob had to take flight, Joseph was sent into slavery, Moses had to leave his people, Aaron was set aside, Saul and David warred. Envy fueled the persecution of the Apostles, the suffering of Peter, and the deaths of the martyrs.

Cyprian, Bishop of Carthage, called envy "a great evil," a "contagious plague," "a viper's infection," a "moth of the soul and the rottenness of thought"; Lucifer was banished from Heaven because he was "guilty of evil envy against God."

Is America more or less afflicted with this vice than other societies? Tocqueville saw democratic societies as less susceptible because in them "there is an innumerable crowd who are much alike, who, though not exactly rich nor yet quite poor, have enough property to want order and not enough to excite envy." But Ludwig von Mises disagreed. Mises argued that in societies with rigid class distinctions the envious can blame their condition on forces outside their control, so they are rendered relatively harmless. But in a market society like America, "the sway of the principle, to each according to his accomplishments, does not allow of any excuse for personal shortcomings." Thus does envy excite anticapitalist sentiments. Erik von Kuehnelt-Leddihn agreed with Mises, even theorizing that democracy itself promotes envy.

Leftists have always held that one man's wealth causes another man's poverty. In a free market with a growing division of labor, one man's wealth promotes another man's prosperity, but regardless of its bad economics, the leftist thesis has been persuasive because it appeals to envy. The same process is at work in the ideology of victimization. In today's America, it seems as if the key to political success is to declare oneself wronged by a society dominated by rich, white males. The welfare state itself is institutionalized envy. Its failures are obvious, but they have not undermined its political support among leading politicians and academics because the real ambition of redistributionist envy is to destroy.

In an envious social order, de la Mora explains, merit and qualifications are inverted: "The most impudent actor is rewarded and so is the most informalist painter, the grossest language user, the most dissolute preacher. The most secret and private becomes the most respectable, and the monstrous becomes normal."

To combat the political effects of envy, Mises believed that private property must be made absolutely secure. To George Santayana, the ultimate answer was the celebration of inequality: "There is no greater stupidity or meanness than to take uniformity for an ideal, as if it were not a benefit and a joy to a man, being what he is, to know

that many are, have been, and will be better than he. Grant that no one is positively degraded by the great man's greatness and it follows that everyone is exalted by it. Beauty, genius, holiness, even power and extraordinary wealth, radiate their virtue and make the world in which they exist a better and a more joyful place to live in. . . ."

—LLEWELLYN H. ROCKWELL JR.

Further Reading

Kuehnelt-Leddihn, Erik von. *Leftism*. New Rochelle, N.Y.: Arlington House, 1974.

Mises, Ludwig von. *The Anti-Capitalistic Mentality*. Spring Mills, Pa.: Libertarian Press, 1972.

Fernandez de la Mora, Gonzalo. *Egalitarian Envy: The Political Foundations of Social Justice*. New York: Paragon House, 1987.

Santayana, George. *The Life of Reason*. New York: Charles Scribner's Sons, 1932.

Schoeck, Helmut. *Envy: A Theory of Social Behavior*. Indianapolis: Liberty Press, 1987.

Tocqueville, Alexis de. *Democracy in America*. New York: Doubleday, 1969.

See also: equality; Marxism; Mises, Ludwig von; property rights, private

Epstein, Joseph (1937–)

Joseph Epstein is a teacher, editor, and writer whose literary criticism and familiar essays are marked by a nonideological cultural conservatism. A Chicago native who attended the University of Chicago and lectured in the creative writing program at Northwestern University for many years, Epstein writes for the intelligent general reader rather than for academics. He turns to writers and thinkers not for theory or doctrine but for "that body of knowledge known as unsystematic truths." Reading "endless stories, poems, and plays" has left him with "an abiding skepticism about general ideas, systems, and theories." Epstein values authors not for their theories or even ideas but rather for what he calls simply "point of view." He insists that "Everyone has opinions . . . but not everyone has a point of view." The philosopher George Santayana, for example, is important not because of the "isms" he defended—naturalism and materialism—but because his work demonstrates a "talent for facing unpleasant facts" with "an almost happy pessimism" that leaves one not depressed but enlivened.

In contrast to those cultural radicals who suppose that literature, if it is worth anything at all, must embody a protest against everyday life and particularly against bourgeois morality, Epstein finds that the great works clarify, enrich, and illuminate rather than overturn the conclusions of common sense and traditional morality. Although Joseph Epstein has written at book-length on divorce, envy, ambition, and snobbery, and although has also published several collections of short stories, he is likely to remain best known for his expertly crafted essays. These familiar essays, many of which first appeared in the *American Scholar* during his long and celebrated tenure as editor of that journal (1975-97), are collected in such volumes as *The Middle of My Tether* (1983), *Familiar Territory* (1979), *Once More Around the Block* (1987), and *Narcissus Leaves the Pool* (1999). His essays on literary topics appear in *Partial Payments* (1989), *Plausible Prejudices* (1985), and *Life Sentences* (1997).

—JAMES SEATON

Further Reading

Epstein, Joseph. *Snobbery: The American Version.* New York: Mariner, 2003.

Winchell, Mark Royden. *Neoconservative Criticism: Norman Podhoretz, Kenneth S. Lynn, and Joseph Epstein.* Boston: Twayne, 1991.

See also: literary criticism; neoconservatism

equal protection

"No State shall . . . abridge the privileges or immunities of citizens of the United States; nor shall any State deprive any person of life, liberty, or property, without due process of law; nor deny to any person within its jurisdiction the equal protection of the laws." This is the so-called equal protection clause found in section one of the Fourteenth Amendment.

The Civil Rights Act of 1866 outlawed the oppressive "Black Codes" enacted by Confederate states after the Civil War. This act provided that all persons "shall have the same right . . . as is enjoyed by white citizens" with respect to property, contracts, personal security, and participation in legal proceedings. The Fourteenth Amendment was intended to remove all doubt as to the constitutionality of the 1866 act. As Professor Raoul Berger put it, the "original design" of the amendment "was to make the 'privileges or immunities' clause the pivotal provision . . . to shield the 'fundamental rights' enumerated in the Civil Rights Act. . . . The privileges or immunities clause conferred *substantive* rights which were to be secured through the medium of two *adjective* rights: the equal protection clause outlawed statutory, the due process clause judicial, discrimination with respect to those substantive rights."

The language of the equal protection clause, however, is much broader than the 1866 act. It is open to expansive treatment by an activist Supreme Court. Conservatives find that treatment troubling because it has allowed the Court to alter laws and legal structures to fit the Court's own ideological vision of justice and fairness. In recent years, in the words of Dean James Bond, "the Court has given an unwarranted imprimatur to egalitarian doctrines through . . . the equal protection clause, once again depriving the states of their traditional authority to make reasonable legislative classifications in support of legitimate public policies."

Every statute, or other state action, involves a classification, treating some persons or subjects differently from others. The rules employed by the Supreme Court to evaluate classifications under either the equal protection clause or the similar guarantee implicit in the Fifth Amendment are fairly clear. In general, a classification "is presumed to be valid and will be sustained if [it] is rationally related to a legitimate state interest" (*Cleburne v. Cleburne Living Center, Inc.,* 1985). This "rational basis" test, in effect, confers a presumption of constitutionality. But if the classification is based on a "suspect" criterion, such as race (see *Miller v. Johnson,* 1995) or (with some exceptions) alienage (see *Graham v. Richardson,* 1971, and *Ambach v. Norwick,* 1979), it is subject to "strict scrutiny" and "must serve a compelling governmental interest, and must be narrowly tailored to further that interest" (*Adarand Constructors, Inc. v. Pena,* 1995). This "strict scrutiny" test creates a presumption of unconstitutionality. A classification based on religion, incidentally, no longer triggers this test if it is imposed by "generally applicable prohibitions of socially harmful conduct" (*Employment Division v. Smith,* 1988). "Strict scrutiny" will be applied also to classifications that burden a "fundamental right," such as the right to vote (*Kramer v. Union Free School District,* 1969) or the right to travel (*Shapiro v. Thompson,* 1969). An intermediate scrutiny applies to classifications based on sex or illegitimacy. They "must serve important governmental objectives and must be substantially related to achievement of those objectives" (*Craig v. Boren,* 1976; *U.S. v. Virginia,* 1996).

The Court, regrettably, has imported into the equal protection clause a liberal ideological bias in some critical areas. Examples include public school desegregation (*Missouri v. Jenkins,* 1995), legislative apportionment (*Reynolds v. Sims,* 1964), the male-only policy of the Virginia Military Institute, and numerous other matters. In the VMI case, dissenting Justice Scalia said the majority decision shows that a "self-righteous Supreme Court, acting on its Members' personal view of what would make a 'more perfect union' . . . can impose its own favored social and economic dispositions nationwide. . . . The sphere of self-government reserved to the people of the Republic is progressively narrowed" (*U.S. v. Virginia,* 1996).

In *Romer v. Evans* (1996), where the Court struck down a constitutional amendment restricting preferential or protective laws for homosexuals, Justice Scalia, joined by Chief Justice Rehnquist and Justice Thomas in his dissenting opinion, aptly described the recent equal protection jurisprudence of the Court: "When the Court takes sides in the culture wars, it tends to be with the knights rather than the villains—and more specifically with the Templars, reflecting the views and values of the lawyer class from which the Court's members are drawn. How that class feels about homosexuality will be evident to anyone who wishes to interview job applicants at virtually any of the nation's law schools."

Despite its open language, however, the equal protection clause should not be faulted because of the Court's misuse of it. The clause can be, and has been, a useful bulwark against racial quotas and other ideologically driven infringements on personal rights (see *Adarand Constructors, Inc., v. Pena*). Here, as in other areas, the fault lies, not with the Constitution, but with an activist Supreme Court and a submissive Congress.

—CHARLES E. RICE

Further Reading

Berger, Raoul. *Government by Judiciary: The Transformation of the Fourteenth Amendment.* 2nd ed. Indianapolis: Liberty Press, 1999.

Bond, James E. *No Easy Walk to Freedom: Reconstruction and the Ratification of the Fourteenth Amendment.* Westport, Conn,: Greenwood, 1997.

See also: abortion; Brown v. Board of Education; *Equal Rights Amendment; localism; quotas*

Equal Rights Amendment

First proposed to Congress in 1923, the Equal Rights Amendment (ERA) was designed to confer on women the Fourteenth Amendment's promise of "equal protection of the laws" by abolishing the use of sex as a factor in determining the legal rights of individuals. Its author, National Women's Party leader Alice Paul, argued that the right to vote alone could not prevent discrimination against women. The Nineteenth Amendment to the Constitution, ratified in 1920, guaranteed women the suffrage, but Paul and other feminists contended that the Equal Rights Amendment would secure more equal treatment for women in society at large.

For forty-nine years, the ERA remained buried in committee in both houses of Congress, having been defeated in 1946 by a vote of 38 to 35 in its one hearing before the Senate. However, the resurgent feminism of the early 1970s prompted renewed interest in the amendment, and newly formed organizations such as the National Organization for Women (NOW) began demanding its discharge from committee. In 1971, the ERA gained a hearing before the House of Representatives, which offered its approval by a vote of 354 to 24. In like manner, the Senate approved the following language of the Equal Rights Amendment on March 22, 1972, by a margin of 84 to 8:

> Section 1: Equality of rights under the law shall not be denied or abridged by the United States or by any State on account of sex.

Section 2: The Congress shall have the power to enforce, by appropriate legislation, the provisions of this article.

Section 3: This amendment shall take effect two years after the date of ratification.

Upon the Senate's endorsement, Congress sent the ERA to the states for ratification. A resolving clause preceding the amendment placed a seven-year time limit on its ratification by the constitutionally mandated three-fourths (thirty-eight) of the states necessary for an amendment to become law. Prior to the seven-year deadline, thirty-five states ratified. However, five states rescinded their initial ratifications, leaving the ERA eight states short of the thirty-eight necessary for constitutional amendment. ERA advocates attempted to counter this weakening of support. As the ratification deadline drew nigh, they lobbied for a time extension from Congress, which acquiesced and set a final ratification deadline of June 30, 1982.

Despite broad support from Congress, the news media, and Presidents Richard Nixon, Gerald Ford, and Jimmy Carter, popular enthusiasm for the Equal Rights Amendment began to wane upon the inception of the state ratification process. STOP ERA, an organization formed in 1972 by conservative activist Phyllis Schlafly, led the opposition to the amendment, advancing the argument that women would actually lose rights and privileges with the ERA. Opponents of the ERA insisted that women already maintained equal rights, citing the Nineteenth Amendment and the Civil Rights Act of 1964. They further argued that the ERA failed to make allowances for legitimate differences between the sexes, most notably women's capacity for childbirth and other gender-based physical differences. Finally, STOP ERA asserted that the amendment would have a number of undesirable effects, such as making women subject to military conscription, forbidding the law to force husbands to support their wives and children, and advancing the rights of homosexuals. Such claims ignited anxieties about the unintended consequences of the ERA. No state ratified after Indiana did so in 1977, and the ERA expired on June 30, 1982.

—SARA HENARY

Further Reading

Mansbridge, Jane J. *Why We Lost the ERA.* Chicago: University of Chicago Press, 1986.

Schlafly, Phyllis. *The Power of the Positive Woman.* New Rochelle, N.Y.: Arlington House, 1977.

Steiner, Gilbert Y. *Constitutional Inequality: The Political Fortunes of the Equal Rights Amendment.* Washington D.C.: Brookings Institution Press, 1985.

See also: Eagle Forum; family; Moral Majority; Schlafly, Phyllis

equality

The idea of equality is a convenient intellectual fiction unknown in nature and in contradiction to the historical experience of mankind. From the chicken yard to the world of power, privilege, and status characteristic of the Soviet *nomenklatura,* degree and rank are of fundamental importance. Survival, whether in the wolf pack or around the office watercooler, is the consequence of biological and social hierarchy.

The neo-Darwinians have made a rather conclusive case for the importance of aggression, conflict, and achieved status for the success of animal species. Their work is based on the empirical observations of Nobel Prize winners Niko Tinbergen and Konrad Lorenz. The sociobiologists, particularly Edward O. Wilson in *Sociobiology* (1975), have provocatively documented these evolutionary assumptions, which have been extensively popularized by Robert Ardrey in books like *The Territorial Imperative* (1966).

Natural inequality manifests itself in physical differences of intelligence, differences in beauty and physical grace, and the happenstance of being born in the right place at the right time. These are inequalities that no amount of equalization will entirely abridge.

Jean Jacques Rousseau in his *Discourse on the Origin of Inequality among Men,* to which he appended *And Is It Authorized by Natural Law* (1755), produced one of the most influential, suppositious, and fatuous disquisitions on equality; always in error, never in doubt. Rousseau's theme of the original equality of men in the state of nature was taken up by Karl Marx and fashioned into the basis of his Hegelian synthetic historical system. Marx, influenced by the work of the American Lewis Henry Morgan, made notes and intended to write a book on the anthropological underpinnings of his system. Marx died before the work could be brought to completion. After the death of Marx in 1883, Frederick Engels published *The Origin of the Family, Private Property and the State* (1884), in which the Marxist notions of the original equality and promiscuity of mankind are argued. Today, no one other than "cultural materialists" holds these empirically unverifiable ideas. The evidence of anthropology and history points in the opposite direction.

Moreover, early human societies—the Sumerian, Egyptian, Babylonian, Assyrian, Greek, and Celtic and Germanic societies of Northern Europe—were all highly stratified and hierarchical in character. Karl August von Wittfogel in *Oriental Despotism* (1957) argued that the civilizations of the ancient Near East, hierarchical and despotic in character, made possible the great "hydrolic civilizations" based on the efficient supply and control of water and dominated by priests and kings. Social and religious movements toward equality in early human societies are often evidence of political collapse and cultural decadence. This was the case in Mayan civilization and the civilization of the Mississippian mound-builders of Cahokia. Egyptian civilization in the first intermediate period presents conclusive evidence of a relationship between the growth of equality and civilizational collapse.

The most important source of notions of equality aside from political contrivance is religious revelation. The Old Testament asserts that man was created in the image and likeness of God and that all men (Hebrews) through the fatherhood of Abraham are to be respected. But there was no universal equality of participation, and many Jews denied inclusiveness through proselytizing and conversion. Although there are universalizing visions and calls for a widening of participation in the community and worship of the one God, even Jesus, rebuking a pagan woman who sought a miraculous cure for her daughter, said "it is not right to take the children's bread and throw it to the dogs" (Matthew 15:27). To be sure, Jesus is in the course of his teaching more inclusive and increasingly universalistic in proclaiming God's love for all mankind. However, Jesus seems to say that God's grace is unequally apportioned: "To you it is given to know the mysteries of the Kingdom of heaven, but to them it is not given. For to him who has shall be given, and he shall have abundance; but from him who does not have, even that which he has shall be taken away" (Matthew 13:12).

The Christian community came to believe, particularly through Paul and Peter, that God's saving grace is given to all without distinction, as in Paul's famous dictum "There is neither Jew nor Greek, there is neither bond nor free, there is neither male nor female, for you are all one in Christ Jesus" (Galatians 3:25). This was, however, a religious and not a political or social program, and the political inequalities of the ancient world together with its emphasis upon degree and status were left intact.

Moreover, the predestinarian tendencies in Paul's teaching—"Therefore He has mercy on whom He will, and whom He will He hardens" (Romans 8:18)—carried over with emphasis into the teachings of Augustine. Increasingly, men came to see political and social inequality as a consequence of the fallen nature of man, one of the many consequences of original sin.

The New Testament is not a program for social or political revolution, as the Anabaptists came to believe, an idea that Luther rejected in the strongest possible terms. Indeed, Luther believed that God's providential order for society was such that he strengthened the prince and subordinated all, even the church, to him.

The quest for order and degree, for authority and subordination, was, in fact, strengthened rather than weakened by Christianity. The Church, East and West, was from the outset hierarchically organized. This pattern of organization was powerfully strengthened by neo-Platonic currents of thought, with their strong emphasis on "the great chain of being," and reinforced by the writings of Dionysius the Areopagite in his *De coelesti hierarchia*. It is tempting to see the medieval-feudal society of order and degree as strongly influenced by the religious models.

This, however, may not have been the case, and there may be no profound relationship between religious belief and social structure. The reforms of Luther abolished the distinction between clergy and laity with the teaching of the "priesthood of all believers." This act of religious leveling, however, did not carry over into the secular realm. Calvin embraced an absolute predestinarianism and the inequality of God's gift of grace and yet Calvinism was the seedbed of republicanism.

The political and social realities of feudalism contrived a system that exaggerated inequalities and made inherited status the governing political system. In medieval Germany, Eike von Repgow in the Sachsenspiegel, early in the thirteen century, argued that the unfreedom of men in feudalism was due to the unjust use of power rather than the consequences of God's providential order or the result of the Fall. Nonetheless, serfdom persisted in parts of Europe until well into the nineteenth century.

Theoretically, consensus and consent were, in the medieval period, the basis of both doctrine and law. Consultation did not, however, imply equality of participation. The dictum of Thomas Aquinas that "the voice of the people is the voice of God" may have, as Lord Acton said, made Thomas the "first Whig." Nonetheless, like most Whigs Thomas did not believe in equality of participation.

The Renaissance deepened, if anything, the gulf between ruler and ruled, though the hereditary principle was weakened and arbitrary power and money became increasingly dominant. Power ceased to be spiritualized, authority was secularized, and, as Eric Voegelin phrased it, "the eschaton [wa]s immanetized."

It is in the light of these developments that we must read the Army Debates that followed in the wake of the Puritan Revolution in England. The "Levellers" and the "Diggers" gave clear evidence of the tendency of expressions of political equality to drift into demands for equality of condition. Little wonder Cromwell repressed these movements and paved the way for a return to order and degree.

The Enlightenment made the secularization of power absolute and immanentized the eschaton. From the outset the French Revolution drifted into equality of participation and equality of condition. For a number of reasons the American Revolution, which had preceded the French Revolution, retained much of the older English constitution, with its emphasis upon social status and property, even though the frontier acted as a powerful solvent of both.

Alexis de Tocqueville, in his profound study *Democracy in America,* analyzed the danger of the drift of democratic politics and sought in the American example of the decentralization of power, intermediary institutions, and private property a remedy to the extremes of democratic politics that he found in France.

The Marx-Engels *Communist Manifesto* (1848) is the response to Tocqueville's *Democracy in America* (1835). Taken together, these two documents establish the only two possibilities for democratic politics. The danger of totalitarian equality in the *Manifesto* has been mitigated but not destroyed by the failures of socialism.

Socialism brings into sharpened awareness one of the chief problems associated with equality. Far from being complementary, liberty and equality are antithetical. Every increase in equality brings with it a diminution in liberty. We purchase equality at the price of liberty, and absolute equality brings with it the total loss of liberty.

By the third quarter of the nineteenth century developments in philosophy, science, and literary and artistic culture had all become elitist in character. Science, especially physics, had become esoteric. Darwin's elaborate studies of animal and human evolution proclaimed "the survival of the fittest." Friedrich Nietzsche invented the Übermensch, who would displace and trample "slave natures." In literature, the moderns—Ezra Pound, T. S. Eliot, James Joyce—appealed to the cognoscenti rather than to a popular audience. Modernist art and painting were anything but popular, as Stalinist "socialist-realism" well understood. The period after 1900 became the age of the scientific, philosophical, and artistic elite.

At the same time scientific and technological development called forth the expert and the specialist. The worker is now a member of a strictly defined hierarchy and those without specialized skills are members, not of the proletariat, but an untrained and uneducated underclass. The gulf between the competent and the incompetent has broadened immeasurably. Competence, moreover, is rewarded with an increasing share of the social product. The notion that one should share equally in the social product and in political power is less and less conceivable.

The political problem of the twenty-first century is the problem of maintaining the fiction of equal political participation while encouraging the increased growth of creative inequalities in society. Equality before the law, equality of opportunity, and a sense of political participation are essential to the dignity of the citizenry and the stability of the state.
—STEPHEN J. TONSOR

Further Reading

Flew, Antony. *Equality in Liberty and Justice*. New York: Rontledge, 1989.

Jencks, Christopher. *Inequality*. New York: Basic Books, 1972.

Kaus, Mickey. *The End of Equality*. New York: Basic Books, 1992.

See also: *Declaration of Independence; democracy; feminism; French Revolution; Lincoln, Abraham; Marxism; progressivism; socialism; sociobiology; Southern conservatism; Tocqueville, Alexis de*

Ethics and Public Policy Center

The Ethics and Public Policy Center (EPPC) is an independent research organization located in Washington, D.C. Since its founding at Georgetown University in 1976, the center has contributed significantly to the resurgence of conservatism in the United States. Through conferences, the publication of hundreds of books and essays, and the writings and speeches of its research staff, EPPC has tried to articulate the moral and political wisdom of those Western ethical imperatives held in trust by generations of conservatives: respect for the human person, individual freedom, justice, the rule of law, and limited government.

In 1980, EPPC became independent of Georgetown. Under the leadership of its founder, Ernest W. Lefever, it achieved prominent visibility just as the Reagan era commenced. In 1979 the center was hailed as one of the eleven "bastions of neo-conservatism" in the United States in the national media. With its publishing and conference programs already in place, the center helped to reinvigorate the discussion of long-overlooked ideas in this new era of American politics.

Although willing to cooperate with those who held similar first principles, Lefever discerned three distinct elements in the center's mission that distinguished it from other conservative think tanks. First, EPPC sought to bring reasoned debate to those controversial issues of the day that had been monopolized by single-issue groups; that is, it strove to enrich the moral and political debate by drawing on wisdom across the ideological spectrum. Second, the center sought to analyze those issues against the background of long-standing Western concepts and values, and therefore, to clarify the relationship between political necessity and moral principle. Finally, EPPC's belief in the crucial role of religion in American society addressed a moral, cultural, and political factor usually neglected by most secular research organizations.

It is this final element of the center's vision, the role of religion in public life, that has taken on the greatest emphasis in recent years, especially after George S. Weigel Jr., a Roman Catholic writer and thinker, assumed the presidency of the center in 1989. The direction set by Weigel, now a senior fellow at the center, has been maintained by M. Edward Whelan III, a former advisor to the White

House Counsel and Attorney General, who became president of the center in March 2004. Under his leadership, EPPC continues its program of research, writing, publishing and conferences with an eye toward "clarifying and re-enforcing the bond between the Judeo-Christian moral tradition and the public debate over domestic and foreign policy issues."

In recent years the center has tried to exert a formative influence on the national news media through a series of conferences designed especially for print and broadcast journalists seeking to understand the impact of religion on American values, and, in particular, the influence of the religious Right in American politics, both present and future. The center also sponsors research and reflection on bioethics, Islam, and democracy at home and abroad, especially in the Middle East. Recent EPPC conferences have considered end-of-life issues, NASA, "The Role of Religion in Forming Good Fathers," and "Teaching about the World after 9-11." In 2003, EPPC launched, under the editorship of Eric Cohen, the *New Atlantis*, a quarterly journal highlighting ethical issues concerning science and technology, especially biotechnology.

—WILLIAM M. BRAILSFORD

Further Reading

Cohen, Eric. "The New Politics of Technology." *New Atlantis*, no. 1, Spring 2003, 3–8.

Cromartie, Michael, ed. *Religion and Politics in America*. Lanham, Md.: Rowman & Littlefield, 2005.

———, ed.. *Religion, Culture, and International Conflict*. Lanham, Md.: Rowman & Littlefield, 2005.

See also: think tanks, conservative; Weigel, George

Evans, M. Stanton (1934–)

A native Texan, M. Stanton Evans majored in English at Yale University and then studied economics at New York University. He later received an honorary Doctor of Laws degree from Syracuse University.

A journalist specializing in matter-of-fact commentary, Evans became a contributing writer to *National Review* in the fortnightly's early years, after first writing for the *Freeman*. He was also a contributing editor and columnist at *Human Events* before becoming editor of the *Indianapolis News*, where he also ran the opinion page, from 1960 to

M. Stanton Evans

1974. From 1973 to 1985 he was a columnist for the Los Angeles Times Syndicate.

One of the first conservatives to break into broadcast journalism, Evans was a commentator at CBS television from 1971 to 1974, on the CBS radio network show *Spectrum* from 1971 to 1979, and at Voice of America from 1980 to 1982.

For a time Evans served as chairman of the Education and Research Institute and of the American Conservative Union, where he was also named to the board of directors. He has also served as a member of the Young Americans for Freedom National Advisory Board and of the Council for National Policy; as president of The Philadelphia Society; and as a trustee of the Intercollegiate Studies Institute. A humorous speaker (example: "I didn't much care for Joseph McCarthy's *ends,* but I always admired his *methods*") and highly sought-after master of ceremonies, he created "Evans's Law," which reads, "Whenever 'one of our people' reaches a position of power where he can do us some good, he ceases to be 'one of our people.'"

A publisher of *Consumers' Research* magazine and visiting professor of journalism at Troy State University, Evans is probably best known for founding in 1977 the National Journalism Center, where he served as director for twenty-five years. Conceived in response to liberal bias and shallow reporting in newspapers across the country, Evans's twelve-week program emphasized more than the technical skills of journalism and sought intelligent, liberally educated students who were required to approach some assignments from an economic perspective.

Though a disciple of Frank Meyer and his "fusionist" conservatism, Evans holds that using the label "fusion" to describe Meyer's attempted rapprochement between the traditionalist and libertarian wings of conservatism mistakenly implies the joining of disparate positions, positions that are in his opinion naturally and necessarily unified. Central to this understanding, and thus to Evans's conservatism, is the view that the American political system and therefore libertarian government "sprang from Western religious belief and at all the stops along the way has been dependent on religious values and traditional practice for its survival" (*The Theme Is Freedom: Religion, Politics, and the American Tradition*, 1994). This conviction has led Evans to become involved in the battle over school prayer and other issues concerning religious freedom.

—WILLIAM F. MEEHAN III

Further Reading

Evans, M. Stanton. *The Future of Conservatism: From Taft to Reagan and Beyond.* New York: Holt, Rinehart and Winston, 1968.

———. *Revolt on the Campus.* Chicago: Regnery, 1961.

See also: *fusionism; Meyer, Frank S.; Young Americans for Freedom*

F

Falwell, Jerry (1933–)

Pastor of an independent Baptist mega-church and a pioneering televangelist with a national audience of tens of millions, Jerry Falwell became one of the most visible political activists of the Religious Right in the 1970s and '80s, largely by virtue of his leadership of the Moral Majority.

Falwell prepared for the ministry at Baptist Bible College before returning to his hometown of Lynchburg, Virginia, in 1956 to found Thomas Road Baptist Church in the old Donald Duck Bottling Company building. With an aggressive evangelism program, the church grew rapidly; within a year its membership jumped from 35 to 864. By 1983, the Thomas Road Church boasted some 20,000 members and was a $90-million-a-year operation.

At the same time he was building up Thomas Road, Falwell also tried his hand at Christian education. In the 1970s he founded Liberty University (1971), Thomas Road Bible Institute (1972), and Lynchburg Baptist Theological Seminary (1973), funding and promoting the schools through his broadcast ministry. Falwell predicted that Liberty University would enroll 50,000 students by the year 2000 and become "the Notre Dame of fundamentalism." But by 1993 fiscal problems and dwindling enrollments were crippling the institution. Student enrollment continued to fall throughout the '90s, but since 2000, resident enrollment has increased 15 to 20 percent each year. The number of students enrolled in the university's distance learning program has increased significantly since then as well. Still, current resident enrollment, standing at around 7,600 (including graduate students) is a far cry from Falwell's lofty goal.

Falwell was also a pioneer of "televangelism" and the "electronic church." Beginning in 1956, he televised the "Old Time Gospel Hour," which by 1984 was aired on 400 television stations and 500 radio stations, reaching an estimated weekly audience of 25 million. Falwell's replacement of Jim Bakker as head of P.T.L. in 1987 demonstrated his leadership among religious broadcasters, though Falwell was hurt by the P.T.L. scandals.

Falwell was important for his role in politics and the mobilization of the Christian Right. Traditionally, fundamentalists had eschewed political activism, fearing that zeal to save society would supplant the zeal to save souls. Falwell insisted that God had called Christians to do both. Building upon his bicentennial "I Love America" tours in 1976 and his "Clean Up America" campaigns in the late 1970s, in 1979 Falwell helped create the Moral Majority (later called the Liberty Federation), which was "a coalition of God-fearing Americans." Committed to traditional family values, school prayer, strong national defense, and the state of Israel, the Moral Majority also opposed homosexuality, abortion, the nuclear freeze and, most successfully, the E.R.A. The Moral Majority had its greatest influence in 1980, when it contributed to the election of Ronald Reagan and the defeat of several liberal U.S. senators.

For most Americans, Falwell was the symbol of the Religious Right. In 1983, readers of *Good Housekeeping* voted him the second most admired man in America (behind Reagan). Falwell also made enemies. Liberals charged him with fascism and seeking to violate the separation of church and state. Some fundamentalists attacked him for political pragmatism and for inviting "unwashed" conservatives to speak in his church. Fellow Christian Right leaders criticized Falwell's early endorsement of George Herbert Walker Bush for president in 1988. By the late 1980s, Falwell's interest in politics had declined, as had his influence. In 1989, he disbanded the Liberty Federation, claiming it had fulfilled its purpose. Falwell spent the early '90s out of the media limelight, preaching to individual churches rather than at political rallies. In 2000, he was active in the Bush presidential election. After Bush's 2004 reelection, Falwell launched the Faith and Values Coalition, dubbed "The 21st Century Moral Majority," in order to encourage evangelical Americans to "vote Christian." Thus far the organization has claimed little influence on the political scene.

Falwell's most important works are *Listen America* (1980) and *Strength for the Journey* (1987), his autobiography. A leading foe of abortion, Falwell stressed pro-life and family issues, helping draw socially conservative, blue-collar Catholics (who comprised 30 percent of the Moral Majority's membership) into the Reagan coalition and pushing social issues to the forefront of the Republican Party. In 1987, assessing his contribution thus far, Falwell said that, thanks in part to his efforts, "[r]eligious conservatives had become part of the political fabric in America, and ever shall be."

—ROGER SCHULTZ

Further Reading

D'Souza, Dinesh. *Falwell: Before the Millennium*. Washington, D.C.: Regnery, 1984.

Lienesch, Michael. *Redeeming America: Piety and Politics in the New Christian Right*. Chapel Hill, N.C.: University of North Carolina, 1993.

Martz, Larry. *Ministry of Greed: The Inside Story of the Televangelists and Their Holy Wars*. New York: Weidenfeld and Nicolson, 1988.

Strober, Gerald, and Ruth Tomczack. *Jerry Falwell: Aflame for God*. Nashville, Tenn.: Thomas Nelson, 1979.

See also: family; fundamentalism; Moral Majority

family

For most contemporary American conservatives, the family forms the cornerstone for society and morality. Inspired by the teachings of scripture (cf. Genesis 2:24–25; 3:16–20; Exodus 20:12, 14; Mark 10:2–9; Ephesians 5:22–33; 6:1–4) and the traditions of their historic faiths, religiously committed conservatives recognize marriage and the family as divinely ordained. They therefore resist secular and amoral movements in modern culture that threaten the home. Thoughtful defenders of liberty, including some secularists, defend the family as a vital social institution whose sphere of autonomy must be protected against the encroachments of the modern state. Conservative intellectuals typically regard the great anti-utopian novels of the twentieth century—including Zamyatin's *We* (1924), Huxley's *Brave New World* (1932), Orwell's *Nineteen Eighty-Four* (1949), and Burgess's *The Wanting Seed* (1962)—as cautionary tales, warnings against political and technocratic assaults upon the family. Though not numerous, some prominent conservative thinkers, borrowing from the modern discipline of sociobiology, have defended the family as a natural pattern for which evolution has fitted men and women.

Notable disputes broke out in the nineteenth century concerning the limits of parental authority against the power of the state to require compulsory education or to permit "child savers" to remove children from allegedly unfit homes (typically those of poor immigrants). Similar debates took place in the early decades of the twentieth century over female suffrage, divorce, and the right of the state to regulate or ban child labor. Still, until the late 1960s, the sanctity of marriage, motherhood, and the family were largely taken for granted as part of the American consensus. But with the rise of the New Left in the late 1960s and early 1970s, the family came under attack as an "oppressive" institution, one that purportedly served the interests of a capitalist and imperialistic regime. Such attacks helped to remove the stigma from divorce (made much easier under new no-fault statutes) and out-of-wedlock childbearing. Both became much more common, while national marriage and fertility rates fell.

At about the same time, the contemporary women's movement grew vehement in its denunciations of marriage as a form of "prostitution" and of the home as the "prison of domesticity." Betty Friedan, Alice Rossi, Muriel Fox, and others joined together in 1967 to organize the National Organization for Women (NOW), which identified as its primary objectives the passage of the Equal Rights Amendment (ERA) and the legalization of abortion on demand.

Republican activist Phyllis Schlafly provided decisive leadership in the campaign against the Equal Rights Amendment (ERA). In 1975 Schlafly founded the Eagle Forum, a national organization devoted to defeating the ERA. Passed by thirty-five state legislatures between 1972 and 1977, the ERA failed largely because of Schlafly's efforts. Schlafly argued with particular effect that the ERA would require drafting women into the military and sending them into combat. The possibility that the ERA would require public funding for abortion further undercut support.

But the U.S. Supreme Court—responding in part to feminist and Malthusian social critiques—ruled in 1973 in *Roe v. Wade* that a supposed "right of privacy" meant that legal abortion was a constitutionally protected right. Probably as much as any single event, *Roe v. Wade* galvanized conservatives in pro-family political activity. Active in the cause before *Roe v. Wade,* Catholics provided much of the leadership in the fight against abortion.

Conservatives of other religious backgrounds also joined the National Right to Life and other pro-life groups. Reverend Jerry Falwell identified *Roe v. Wade* as the event which spurred him to become a pro-family activist. In 1979, Falwell organized the Moral Majority as a political movement affirming the traditional family and opposing abortion, the ERA, homosexuality, and pornography. The Moral Majority sought to bring together conservative Americans from all religious traditions in political causes supportive of traditional morality and family life. Particularly active in 1980 in registering Christian voters in the South, the Moral Majority was credited by pollster Louis Harris with having provided the margin of victory in that year for Ronald Reagan.

Pro-family activists achieved notable success during the 1980s in their fight against pornography and obscenity. In the 1966 suit popularly known as the "Fanny Hill" case, the Supreme Court stripped local governments of much of their power to control pornography by requiring prosecutors to meet a complicated three-part legal test in obscenity cases. In 1973, however, the Supreme Court ruled that local officials could ban materials violating "contemporary community standards of decency." Groups such as the National Federation for Decency (later renamed the American Family Association), Moral Majority, Morality in Media, and Concerned Women of America marshaled support for the prosecution of pornographers. Psychologist and radio personality James

Dobson served with other conservatives on the Attorney General's Commission on Pornography, which in 1986 issued a landmark report decrying the way that widespread obscenity had helped to "undermine the values underlying the family unit."

Legal sanctions aside, conservative groups discovered the power of the boycott in the 1970s and '80s in fighting obscenity subversive of the family. Donald Wildmon of the American Family Association demonstrated particular effectiveness in challenging the sponsors of obscene television programs and store chains that sold pornographic magazines.

The closing decades of the twentieth century witnessed the emergence of the homosexual movement as a potent enemy of conservative family positions. In 1973 homosexual activists persuaded the American Psychological Association to remove homosexuality from its list of mental disorders, so giving their movement new visibility and legitimacy. In the years that followed, conservative pro-family activists slowed but could not stop this movement. For instance, pro-family activists were able to mobilize public opposition to the Clinton Administration's attempt to bring openly homosexual soldiers into the military in the early 1990s; however, the compromise "Don't Ask, Don't Tell" policy still represented a partial relaxation of the previous ban. When pro-family activists in Colorado succeeded in passing a 1992 ballot initiative forbidding government agencies from granting homosexuals a special protected status, homosexuals orchestrated an effective boycott of the state; the Colorado Supreme Court subsequently struck down the statute. In the 1990s, as part of an effort to block a homosexual marriage in Hawaii, pro-family activists pushed a Federal Defense of Marriage Act through Congress, enshrining monogamous heterosexual union as the federal definition of marriage, with similar measures winning enactment

through referenda or state legislation in more than thirty states. Still, in 1999, the Vermont Supreme Court required the state legislature to permit homosexuals to form "civil unions," conferring all the legal advantages of wedlock. Connecticut joined Vermont in 2005, becoming the second state to allow civil unions between same-sex couples. Massachusetts is the only state currently to allow same-sex marriages, the state supreme court having dictated this in November 2003.

The curriculum battles over condoms and homosexuality reprised many earlier conflicts over permissive sex-education programs. Parent groups also opposed educational programs ostensibly designed to prevent child abuse. Conservative critics faulted these programs for instilling in children an unnecessary distrust of their parents. More broadly, pro-family conservatives advocated greater parental choice in education through vouchers or through greater legal accommodation for parochial education and home schooling.

Perhaps the most symbolically important battle fought by pro-family traditionalists was that waged over the very definition of *family*. Radical redefinitions of the word (applicable to unmarried couples, cohabiting homosexuals, and various other domestic arrangements) were proposed at the White House Conference on Families convened by President Carter in 1976. Traditionalists rallied to prevent such a redefinition of the family; however, only at the session of the conference held in Minneapolis were they able to secure official endorsement of a normative definition.

Because of media hostility to traditional conceptions of the family, Vice President Dan Quayle was subjected to considerable ridicule in 1992 for objecting to television's glamorization of single motherhood. But pro-family activists helped disseminate sufficient evidence of the social costs of family breakdown so that within a few years even many prominent liberals (including President Clinton) publicly acknowledged that Quayle had been justified in his remarks. As a religious reaction against the rise in single-mother families, in the 1990s conservative Protestant men joined in large Promise Keeper rallies, affirming their commitment to fatherhood and marriage. At the intellectual level, many pro-family activists in the late 1990s backed sociologist David Popenoe, author Barbara Dafoe Whitehead, and their colleagues who launched the National Marriage Project to win support for public policies supportive of wedlock.

In some ways the most difficult challenge for conservatives during the latter years of the twentieth century was the attempt by liberal politicians to co-opt the "pro-family" label on behalf of subsidized daycare, parental leave, and other initiatives designed either to institutionalize government as a family surrogate or to force businesses to make special accommodations for employed mothers. Resistance to this co-opting of pro-family rhetoric persisted during these decades, but suffered from the disbanding in the late 1980s of the Moral Majority and the demise of several Washington-based conservative organizations, including United Families of America, the Child and Family Protection Institute, and the family division of the Nation Forum Foundation. Groups that continue today to uphold conservative ideals while advocating public policies conducive to family autonomy (such as additional tax credits for families with young children) include the Heritage Foundation, the Family Research Council, the Library Court Group, and the Howard Center for Family, Religion, and Society.

—Bryce J. Christensen

Further Reading

Carlson, Allan C. *Family Questions: Reflections on the American Social Crisis.* New Brunswick, N.J.: Transaction, 1988.

Christensen, Bryce J. *Utopia against the Family: The Problems and Politics of the American Family.* San Francisco: Ignatius, 1990.

Felsenthal, Carol. *The Sweetheart of the Silent Majority: A Biography of Phyllis Schlafly.* Garden City, N.J.: Doubleday, 1981.

Luker, Kristin. *Abortion and the Politics of Motherhood.* Berkeley, Calif.: University of California Press, 1984.

Popenoe, David. *Life without Father: Compelling New Evidence That Fatherhood and Marriage Are Indispensable for the Good of Children and Society.* Cambridge, Mass.: Harvard University Press, 1999.

See also: abortion; Eagle Forum; Equal Rights Amendment; Family Research Council; feminism; homeschooling; Moral Majority; pornography

Family Research Council

In the Washington, D.C., world of think tanks, the Family Research Council (FRC) distinguishes itself "inside the Beltway" with its specific concern for the impact of public policy and law upon marriage and the family. An institution of historically hybrid purposes, FRC both works to help develop social policy on behalf of a "constituency" of traditional families and moves that constituency to political activity as an interpretive conduit of current policy trends.

Unapologetic in its espousal of the historic Christian faith, FRC is decidedly entrenched in the "theo-con" (that is, theologically oriented) wing of American conservatism. It maintains the Judeo-Christian intellectual tradition as integral to the American experiment—both in its genesis and its perpetuation.

The White House Conference on Families in 1980 inspired the creation of FRC by impressing upon James Dobson (founder of Focus on the Family) the need for an institution to initiate, inform, and direct public discourse concerning the family. The organization was incorporated in 1983, with Dobson, Armand Nicholoi Jr. of Harvard University, and George A. Rekers of the University of South Carolina as its founding board members.

Its first president, former Reagan administration official Gerald P. Regier, led FRC in developing an authoritative body of interdisciplinary thinkers to aid policymakers in crafting "family-friendly" social policy. Regier was succeeded in 1988 by Reagan administration domestic policy advisor Gary L. Bauer. Bauer guided FRC through a period of substantial growth in the 1990s, during which it emerged as the hub of a national family-oriented activist network.

When Bauer resigned to seek the Republican presidential nomination in 2000, Kenneth L. Connor—a successful Florida attorney and one-time gubernatorial candidate—was tapped as FRC's third president. Connor was succeeded by former Louisiana state representative Tony Perkins in 2003. Perkins's legislative career was distinguished by his drafting of the nation's first "covenant marriage" law.

Although its history suggests a close identification with American evangelicalism, FRC is properly understood as ecumenical in its Christianity. Both Protestants and Roman Catholics enjoy positions of significant responsibility within its ranks.

While social policy that is indifferent or of no consequence to the institutions of marriage and the family may be nonexistent, historically FRC's policy attention has been focused on education, the sanctity of life and bioethics (especially abortion, human procreation, and euthanasia), human sexuality, parental rights, religious liberty, and pornography. In the wake of recent judicial decisions, FRC has assumed leadership in efforts to amend state and federal constitutions to protect traditional marriage as a special legal category.

In addition to its participation in matters of law and policy, FRC is also home to a residential academic and internship program—the Witherspoon Fellowship—designed to prepare students for positions of leadership in public life. Named for signer of the Declaration of Independence John Witherspoon, the fellowship provides both domestic and international university students with interdisciplinary instruction in political theory, an integrated role in FRC's policy and advocacy work, and membership in a fraternity of alumni with a shared vision for cultural renewal.

—Douglas Minson

Further Reading

Bauer, Gary. *Our Hopes, Our Dreams: A Vision for America.* Colorado Springs, Colo.: Focus on the Family, 1996.

Sprigg, Peter. *Outrage: How Gay Activists and Liberal Judges Are Trashing Democracy to Redefine Marriage.* Washington, D.C.: Regnery, 2004.

See also: Dobson, James C.; family; think tanks, conservative

farm policy

In many respects, U.S. farm policy remains remarkably similar to that in the New Deal era when agricultural and economic conditions in the United States were much different than they are now. Protectionist U.S. farm programs are inconsistent with a market-oriented economic policy and do nothing to increase the long-run profitability of American agriculture.

U.S. farm programs are incredibly complex and frequently work at cross-purposes. For example, price supports increase the cost of milk, butter, sugar, peanuts, and other farm products for low-income consumers, while food stamps and other subsidized food programs lower food costs. Food stamps and other subsidized food programs strengthen demand and increase farm product prices, but subsidized credit, crop insurance, and research programs lower costs of production and have just the opposite effect.

Farm programs also have other important economic effects. Most of the gains from agricultural programs go to those who own land, production rights, and other specialized agricultural assets at the time the programs are initiated or when benefit levels are increased. An increase in a price support or input subsidy, for example, is quickly incorporated into higher input prices. Thus, it is the owners rather than the users of farm resources who derive the major benefits from farm programs. Farmers who rent land and other farm resources receive little benefit from price supports because the higher prices they receive for farm products are largely offset by higher production costs. Similarly, farmers who purchase land and other farm resources after farm programs are initiated also find that higher prices received for farm products are offset by higher costs of production.

Farm programs ostensibly are intended to increase the incomes of small family farmers. However, farmers whose income, on average, far exceeds median family income in the United States, receive most of the benefits. Although workers possessing specialized skills for the production of some farm products, like milk and tobacco, do benefit from programs that increase the demand for labor, most agricultural workers do not possess highly specialized skills and move readily between farm and nonfarm sectors, thus enjoying little benefit from farm programs.

U.S. agricultural policies are also highly beneficial to the politicians and government employees who develop, administer, and evaluate the effects of farm programs extending to every county in the United States. Politicians use these programs to maintain support among agricultural interest groups and to provide a livelihood for the more than 100,000 federal, state, and county employees of the U.S. Department of Agriculture.

Government farm programs also encourage *favor-seeking* activity at the expense of *profit-seeking* activity. Profit-seeking through the entrepreneurial market process is socially beneficial because it leads to an increased output of goods and services. Favor-seeking, in contrast, refers to attempts by individuals and groups to increase their wealth through income transfers, credit subsidies, and other government programs. The spending of money for lobbying, campaign contributions, and so on to achieve these restrictions on competition is socially wasteful because the result is a reduction in output of goods and services. Consequently, farm program benefits to the farm sector come at the expense of consumers and taxpayers. In addition to an expenditure of some $70 billion per year on U.S. farm programs, including subsidized food programs, food costs to consumers are increased—sometimes substantially—as is the case for sugar, dairy products, and peanuts.

Higher prices bring about both reduced consumption of U.S. farm products and increased use of lower- priced substitutes. The milk program, for example, reduces consumption of fresh milk and increases consumption of substitutes for butter, cream, and cheese. Moreover, U.S. farm programs are inherently protectionist. When domestic prices of farm products are raised above world price levels, import controls must be used to prevent U.S. consumers from purchasing lower-priced sugar, dairy products, peanuts, and other products from abroad.

Despite the huge treasury outlays, government farm programs do nothing to increase the long-run profitability of U.S. agriculture because program benefits, whether in the form of increased product prices or reduced costs of production, are quickly reflected in higher prices of farm inputs. That is, when a farm program is instituted, the competitive market process ensures that resource costs will tend to increase as long as the expected rate of return in agricultural production is higher than that from competing investments of similar risk. Although protectionist farm programs do not increase long-run profitability, abolition of these programs would impose huge windfall losses on current owners of farm land and other specialized agricultural resources. Moreover, the losses would be incurred by *all* these resource owners—not just those who received windfall gains.

Finally, farm programs often are rationalized as necessary to enable farmers to cope with changing economic conditions. However, government policies as they are implemented through the political process often introduce artificial instability into agricultural (and other) markets. Indeed, evidence suggests that decentralized competitive markets in agriculture—as in other sectors of the economy—may be the most effective means of coping with constantly changing economic conditions. Noninflationary monetary and fiscal policies and a more open economy are consistent with conservatism and in the long run might be more beneficial to farmers than stabilization policies designed specifically for agriculture.

Government does have an important role to play in a conservative farm policy—to reduce trade restrictions on agricultural commodities throughout the world and to facilitate the adoption of contractual arrangements in agriculture that enable farmers to cope with weather, market, and political risks.

—E. C. PASOUR JR.

Further Reading

Gardner, B. Delworth. *Plowing Ground in Washington: The Political Economy of U.S. Agriculture.* San Francisco: Pacific Research Institute for Public Policy, 1995.

Luttrell, C. B. *The High Cost of Farm Welfare.* Washington, D.C.: Cato Institute, 1989.

Pasour, E. C. Jr. and Randall R. Rucker. *Agriculture and the State: Market Processes and Bureaucracy.* Rev. ed. San Francisco: Independent Institute for Public Policy, forthcoming.

See also: free trade; New Deal

fascism

A type of totalitarianism, fascism arose out of the chaos that followed World War I (1914–18), when economic hardship, thwarted idealism, and bruised national pride combined to radicalize European politics. The fascist era in Europe is usually dated from 1922, when Mussolini came to power in Italy, to 1945, when Hitler's Nazis were crushed at the end of World War II. But it was an international movement of somewhat longer duration, finding supporters throughout the European continent as well as in Britain, North America, and South America.

The word "fascism" was coined by Mussolini. It derives from the Latin *fasces*, referring to the bundle of rods and projecting ax-head that in antiquity was carried before Roman consuls as a sign of state authority. The rods symbolized social unity; the executioner's ax, firm political leadership. (Use of the fasces as a political symbol is not restricted to fascist parties: in America fasces adorn the wall behind the Speaker's platform in the U.S. House of Representatives and are stamped on the so-called Mercury dime.)

As British philosopher Roger Scruton has pointed out, fascism is characterized more by a common ethos than a consistent political philosophy. Nevertheless, around Italian fascism, German Nazism, and Spanish falangism clustered several distinctive traits. Fascist parties showed implacable hostility toward parliamentary democracy, egalitarianism, and the values of the liberal Enlightenment; and because fascists viewed the world as a Darwinistic jungle in which only the most militant could survive, they tolerated no domestic competition. To secure control of a people, fascists advocated one-party rule by an elite, the use of secret police to eliminate dissent, strict control over the media, and unquestioning obedience to a charismatic leader. To incite enthusiasm for their rule they made appeals to youth and promoted a cult of violence. Nazi calls for organic social harmony (in the name of *das Volk*), militaristic chauvinism, and *Lebensraum* (living space) appealed to the popular imagination as did the use of vivid symbols, torchlight parades, uniforms, and military discipline to express unity in a fragmented age.

Hitler's Brown Shirts and to a lesser extent Mussolini's Black Shirts added two further doctrines to these traits: a barely disguised hostility to Christianity, whose traditional forms they intended eventually to stamp out, and anti-Semitism, which led to the state-sponsored execution of between five and six million Jews.

Despite fascists' harangues against democracy and egalitarian economic arrangements, they were able to win massive popular support in Europe before the 1940s, a fact that has vexed many students of the movement. Moreover, to the embarrassment of the avant-garde, a number of modernists flirted with fascism at one time or another. In Britain, for example, Ezra Pound, George Bernard Shaw, William Butler Yeats, T. S. Eliot, and Wyndham Lewis were drawn to certain fascist ideas. Influential antimodernist Catholics like G. K. Chesterton, Hilaire Belloc, and Roy Campbell were also receptive to fascist notions when the movement was still young. Indeed, for a brief time, fascism enjoyed a radical chic in British high society. But Eliot, Lewis, Chesterton, Belloc, Campbell, and others recoiled from *Il Duce*

and *Der Fuhrer* when they recognized fascism's nihilism and hostility to the West's historical religions.

Scholars have long debated the extent to which fascism was the outgrowth of the Left or Right. Since the 1930s, Marxists, following Trotsky, have tried to make the case that fascism was the inevitable result of the structural crises that wracked latter-day monopoly capitalism. But even Trotsky himself recognized that "Stalinism and fascism, in spite of a deep difference in social foundations, are symmetrical phenomena. In many of their features they show a deadly similarity." Another influential writer, the Hungarian-British writer and philosopher Arthur Koestler, abandoned the Communist Party in the late 1930s and traced the similarities between Stalinism and Nazism in novels such as *Darkness at Noon* (1940) and *Arrival and Departure* (1943)—"perhaps the best analyses of the totalitarian mind ever written," according to Bernard Crick.

Indeed, many scholars see not just Stalinism but Marxist-Leninism as a totalitarian cousin to fascism. It would thus be misleading to place Marxism and fascism at opposite ends of the Left-Right political spectrum. Mussolini, after all, began his political career as a socialist, and his mature fascist doctrines bear the unmistakable stamp of Marx, Sorel, and Lenin. Other fascist leaders learned, in turn, from Mussolini: for Valois in France, Franco in Spain, Mosley in Britain, Degrelle in Belgium, Hitler in Germany, and their followers, "Nationalism plus Socialism equals Fascism," a formula that reveals fascism's affinity with the Left. Even the word "Nazi" has a leftist connotation, derived as it is from the full party title, the National Socialist German Workers' Party (*Nationalsozialistische Deutsche Arbeiterpartei*). Erik von Kuehnelt-Leddihn summarized the relationship between fascism and Marxist-Leninism by referring to them as "socialism national and international."

The historian Stanley Payne wrote that fascism's ties to the traditional Right were frequently tenuous. In Europe, the marriage between fascists and conservatives during the 1920s and 1930s, when it occurred, tended to be one of convenience, not of love. Often such political alliances were forged to jettison indecisive liberal institutions and to combat what was perceived to be the common enemy—Bolshevism. The alliance was bound to be temporary once fascism's full revolutionary agenda was revealed. One radical difference between fascists and traditionalist conservatives turned on religion. For the former, Christianity was anathema since it provided a source of moral criticism prior to and higher than the state; consequently, Nazi leaders wanted eventually to eradicate Christianity and replace it with a pagan pseudoreligion wholly subservient to the state.

There were pockets of fascist sympathy and collaboration in America prior to and during World War II, issuing mainly from anti-Semitic and extremist populist sentiment. Gerald L. K. Smith, Charles Eugene Bedaux, and T. Lothrop Stoddard were among the most prominent. Historians have also identified protofascist tendencies in politicians like Huey Long, who attempted to abolish the power of local government in Louisiana. Mistakenly, Charles A. Lindbergh's antiwar speeches for the America First Committee were branded pro-Nazi, yet his goal was not to promote Hitler's programs but to urge America to stay out of a costly European conflict: in this he was no different from countless American isolationists. The fact is, fascism never took root on American soil and was never an attractive alternative to the Right. Its ethos was too alien to American political traditions and values to win wide support. The American Nazi party, founded in 1958 by George Lincoln Rockwell, probably never numbered more than a hundred members at a time.

Unfortunately, the term "fascist" has been widely used by student radicals since the Vietnam War era to attack college administrators and (mostly Republican) politicians. But such use of the term is not only unfounded but irresponsible since it blunts our understanding of what fascism historically entailed.

—Gleaves Whitney

Further Reading

Ferkiss, Victor C. "Populist Influences on American Fascism." *Western Political Quarterly* 10 (June 1957): 350-73.

Gregor, A. James. *The Ideology of Fascism.* New York: Free Press, 1969.

Hamilton, Alastair. *The Appeal of Fascism: A Study of Intellectuals and Fascism, 1919–1945.* Foreword by Stephen Spender. New York: Macmillan, 1971.

Kedward, H. R. *Fascism in Western Europe, 1900–1945.* Glasgow: Blackie & Son, 1969.

Payne, Stanley. *Fascism: Comparison and Definition.* Madison, Wis.: University of Wisconsin Press, 1980.

Pois, Robert A. *National Socialism and the Religion of Nature.* London: Croom Helm, 1986.

See also: American Review; *ideology; nihilism; Pound, Ezra*

Faulkner, William (1897–1962)

William Faulkner was, by many estimates, the greatest American novelist of the twentieth century. His work exerted a powerful and humane conservative influence on American letters in an era when the literary establishment of the Northeast had strong communist sympathies. Bold and stylistically innovative in his novels, willing to risk subject matter (such as miscegenation and incest) that had been avoided by the "moonlight and magnolias" romanticists of the South, Faulkner writes about "the old verities and truths of the heart," as he called them in his Nobel Prize acceptance speech in 1950: "the universal truths lacking which any story is ephemeral and doomed—love and honor and pity and pride and compassion and sacrifice."

Born in New Albany, Mississippi, on September 25, 1897, he was christened William Falkner after a distinguished great-grandfather. He grew up in Oxford, Mississippi, where he would spend most of his life. Although his talents showed themselves early, he disliked school and never graduated from high school or college. During a brief stint in the Royal Air Force during World War I (without combat experience), he added the *u* to his name, becoming William *Faulkner*. After the war, he returned home to Oxford in his early twenties and worked for a time as a postmaster—a notoriously neglectful one—before being forced to resign. Herman Melville might have been above the "slightest censure" in the New York Custom House, but his rival as America's greatest novelist, William Faulkner, was less impressive as a civil servant.

In 1925, he moved to New Orleans and became part of a literary circle that included Sherwood Anderson. His career as a novelist began with the publication of *Soldier's Pay* in 1926, followed by *Mosquitoes*, usually considered his weakest book, in 1927. But he found his real subject matter in his third novel, *Flags in the Dust*, which was not published in its entirety until 1973. A shorter version, edited down to two-thirds of its original length by his friend Ben Wasson, was published in 1929 as *Sartoris*. At Sherwood Anderson's advice, Faulkner had begun to explore the fictional possibilities of the place and people he knew best, as Anderson had

done in *Winesburg, Ohio* (1919). But Anderson could never have imagined the scope, depth, and majesty of what Faulkner would achieve. "Yoknapatawpha County" would be the setting for all of his novels, with the exception of *Pylon* (1935), *The Wild Palms* (1939), and *The Fable* (1954), for the next thirty-three years.

With its county seat of Jefferson, its plantations, its outlying communities such as Frenchman's Bend, its various yeoman farms, and its access to the big woods of the Mississippi Delta, Yoknapatawpha afforded Faulkner an inexhaustible fictional universe. He brought to bear on it the deep influences of the King James Bible, the rhetoric of the South (both political and religious), and the tradition of storytelling he found everywhere around him. He brilliantly wedded his local background to the new resources that modernism had opened up for the novel. In his first undisputed masterpiece, *The Sound and the Fury*

William Faulkner

(1929), Faulkner recounts the decline of one of Jefferson's noble families, the Compsons, with an artistic force, depth of theme, and lucidity of imagination that established his world stature.

Even while working intermittently as a screenwriter in Hollywood during the Depression, Faulkner turned out a succession of major novels. The problem of time, the difficulty of interpreting the past, and the necessity of constructing the story often preoccupy him. His themes range from the attempt of the poor white Bundrens in *As I Lay Dying* (1930) to get Addie Bundren's body to Jefferson for burial; through the tragic uncertainties of a figure of possibly mixed race, Joe Christmas, in *Light in August* (1932); to the great dynastic ambitions of Thomas Sutpen in *Absalom, Absalom!* (1936) or Lucius

Quintus Carothers McCaslin in *Go Down, Moses* (1942) and the effect such ambitions have on the descendants who must deal with their human consequences. *Go Down, Moses*, in particular, has increasingly emerged as one of Faulkner's greatest works—a Southern counterpoint to *Moby-Dick* (1851). It deals with towering ambition, the American wilderness, settled land, and inheritance, incest, and miscegenation as they play out through the "three races" that Tocqueville described. Also undergoing critical revaluation is Faulkner's treatment of the rise and spread of the Snopes family in *The Hamlet* (1940), *The Town* (1957), and *The Mansion* (1959). The trilogy comprises a major reflection on the ultimate impotence of "Snopesism," a kind of small-souled cunning (dynastic in an almost verminous sense) that seems to have had its historical moment in the culture of the twentieth century. Faulkner's last novel, *The Reivers* (1962), points forward to a future in which a strong sense of piety, courtesy, and honor balances the American infatuation with motion.

When Faulkner was awarded the Nobel Prize for Literature, he spoke memorably about the complexity of "the human heart in conflict with itself." Committed not to utopian speculations but to his "postage stamp of native soil" in rural Mississippi, he embodied the imaginative freedom that the conservative tradition best fosters. He died in 1962.

—GLENN C. ARBERY

Further Reading

Blotner, Joseph. *Faulkner: A Biography*. New York: Random House, 1984.

Brooks, Cleanth. *William Faulkner: Toward Yoknapatawpha and Beyond*. New Haven, Conn.: Yale University Press, 1978.

———. *William Faulkner: The Yoknapatawpha Country*. New Haven, Conn.: Yale University Press, 1963.

See also: Bradford, M. E.; Brooks, Cleanth

federalism

Although a number of contemporary states have been labeled "federal," the United States, Switzerland, Canada, and Australia have generally been considered the "classic" or "genuine" federal states. Among these, the government of the United States represents the archetypical form, a mean between the extremes of consolidation in the central government and autonomy in the constituent states. In between the polar opposites of unity and fragmentation, various divisions and balances of power are theoretically possible. In practice, many attempts at federalism have failed because they could not, in practice, achieve actual balance.

Prior to 1787, the terms "confederation" and "federation" had the same meaning: both referred to a league of states in which each constituent political entity retained its independence or sovereignty. The modern definition of federalism, effectively shaped by the U.S. Constitution, has classified a confederation as something less than a government. The proponents of the Constitution, called the Federalists, contended that although a political union already existed, the arrangement under the existing Articles of Confederation did not constitute a government. Indeed, the Union, as marked by the Declaration of Independence in 1776, predated the Articles of Confederation, which became effective in 1783. As *The Federalist* argued, a government must act directly on individuals rather than on the governments of states, as did the Articles of Confederation. The American debate over ratification of the Constitution highlighted the distinction between a political union and a government. The opponents of the Constitution, who in some ways inappropriately and in other ways appropriately were labeled the Anti-Federalists, charged that the proposed government was a consolidated one. The Federalists countered that the Constitution created a compound government that was partly federal and partly national.

The Constitution's new form of federalism clashed with the Anti-Federalists' conception of (con)federalism, which involved a union of states. They and their heirs, the Jeffersonian Republicans, emphasized "states' rights," which is actually a form of confederalism. By ignoring the federalism of the Constitution, "states' rightists" allow the centralizers of power to claim they are faithful to the Constitution's nationalist principles. In fact, both the "states' rightists" and the centralists distort the Constitution's compound structure, which is a union of the people *in the states* rather than either simply a union of the states or of the people as a mass. In *McCulloch v. Maryland* (1819), the Supreme Court stated that "[n]o political dreamer was ever wild enough to think of breaking down the lines which separate the states, and of compounding the American people into one common mass. Of consequence, when they act, they act in their states. But the measures they adopt do not, on that account, cease to be the measures of the people themselves, or become the measures of the state governments."

The Federalist declared that the chief defect of previous federations as governments had been the attempt of one government to govern other governments, a confederation. "The great and radical vice in the construction of the existing Confederation," Hamilton wrote, "is in the principle of LEGISLATION for STATES or GOVERNMENTS, in their CORPORATE or COLLECTIVE CAPACITIES, and as contradistinguished from the INDIVIDUALS of which they consist." The writers of *The Federalist* acknowledged the usefulness of confederations for limited purposes and duration. But such arrangements did not qualify as governments because "Government implies the power of making laws."

The Constitution clearly did not establish an agreement, compact, contract, or covenant among the states, which is the essence of what is now called a confederation. Instead, the Constitution was the act of "the people" voting state by state to create a limited but direct relationship between the central government and individuals. That relationship meant that the Constitution created a limited government. With few exceptions, the original Constitution left the relationships among individuals within each state to be governed by the states. As discussed by James Madison, however, liberty in the states was vulnerable to the danger of factions, especially majorities in local communities that might act unjustly towards those in the minority. By removing state control over their borders and through other devices, the Constitution limited the coercive power of local majorities by ensuring the free movement of goods and persons across state lines. This new form of federal constitution joined communities and their citizens in a union that nevertheless preserves the basic identity and authority of the constituent communities.

A federal state, as distinct from other forms of federalism, requires separation of powers. Otherwise, the central power will be able to dominate the constituent states. It is not coincidental that there is a concurrence of federalism and separation of powers within the U.S. Constitution. Indeed, federalism as redefined by *Federalist* 39 to be a compound republic, part national and part federal, forges the two doctrines of federalism and separation of powers. Separately considered, each doctrine deals with relationships along a horizontal plane. That is to say, federalism, in the sense of confederalism, involves the linking together of separate sovereigns; their (at least theoretically) equal status means the relationship between and among the states is one of reciprocity, rather than superiority. The doctrine of separation of powers also operates horizontally, involving the division and equality among different departments within the same government. The doctrine of separation of powers and the principle of federalism connect with each other: in the presidency through the Electoral College; in the Senate, where the states have equal representation; and in the Supreme Court, which judges between the states and the federal government on conflicts over the Constitution.

The original structure of federalism was modified but not abolished by the post–Civil War amendments, i.e., the Thirteenth, Fourteenth, and Fifteenth Amendments. Under the original Constitution, the states had almost complete control over their internal police powers. Thus were the southern states able to maintain a system of slavery. While the founders had expected slavery to wither away, that did not happen. Therefore, through these three amendments the federal government limited state power by abolishing slavery; by making all state citizens also citizens of the United States; by guaranteeing due process to all persons; and by extending equal protection of the law, certain privileges and immunities, and the right to vote to all citizens. While these amendments altered the balance of federalism, it was not until the middle of the twentieth century that the federal judiciary used the broad language of the Fourteenth Amendment to federalize many matters not obviously covered by its text or history.

As significant as the role of the federal judiciary has been, it is generally overlooked that the decline of federalism is principally due to the Seventeenth Amendment's provision for direct popular election of U.S. senators. Prior to the Seventeenth Amendment, senators were very solicitous of the wishes of the state legislatures that had elected them. They would not impose burdens on state government that their own states were not willing to bear. With direct popular election, U.S. senators have much less incentive to be responsive to the con-

cerns of state governments, which often are better informed than is the general electorate of the states. Thus, ironically, some members of the Senate chastised the Supreme Court for a series of "federalism" decisions, such as *Alden* v. *Maine* (1999), in which the Court ruled that Congress has no constitutional power to subject the states to lawsuits for money damages. These decisions prevent Congress from stripping the states of their sovereign immunity, which as Hamilton assured the states in *Federalist* 81, is an inherent right of sovereignty. Prior to the Seventeenth Amendment, no senator would have attempted such a direct attack on the residual sovereignty of the states.

Despite some contentions to the contrary, and despite its decisions in cases such as *Alden v. Maine* and *U.S. v. Lopez* (1995), the Supreme Court has not pursued a consistently federalist direction in recent years. Its ruling striking down state sodomy laws in *Lawrence v. Texas* (2003) is perhaps the most striking evidence of the judiciary's continued role in undermining federalism.

—JOHN BAKER

Further Reading

Davis, Rufus. *The Federal Principle*. Berkeley, Calif.: University of California Press, 1978.

Madison, James, John Jay, and Alexander Hamilton. *The Federalist*. New York: Modern Library, 1937.

See also: constitutionalism; Federalist, The; *Federalist Party; incorporation doctrine; progressivism; Rehnquist, William H.; separation of powers; states' rights; Supreme Court*

Federalist, The

The Federalist or Federalist Papers, consists of eighty-five essays of Alexander Hamilton, James Madison, and John Jay written, under the pseudonym "Publius," to secure ratification of the proposed Constitution by the state of New York. These essays originally appeared in various New York state newspapers between October 1787 and May 1788.

For most conservatives, the significance of *The Federalist* far transcends the immediate purpose of its authors because it is the best commentary available concerning the intentions of the founding fathers in drafting the Constitution. The constitutional morality it conveys concerning how the institutions and processes established by the Constitution should operate is generally taken to reflect the consensus of the founding fathers. Thus, for many conservatives, the explicit and implicit teachings embodied in these essays represent the genuine principles of the American political order that American conservatives, as conservatives, are obliged to honor and uphold.

This obligation poses no problems for conservatives since the basic teachings of *The Federalist* derive from assumptions about human motivation that are thoroughly consonant with long-standing conservative political philosophy. Perhaps the most significant of these assumptions or teachings is that, unless sufficiently restrained, men will pursue their passions and immediate interests to the detriment of the common good and eventually of their own well-being. That Publius held to such a view is apparent in his observations at various points in *The Federalist*. "Is it not," he asks rhetorically at one point, "the true interest of all nations to cultivate . . . a spirit of mutual amity and concord?" He answers this question with another: "Has it not, on the contrary, invariably been found, that momentary passions and immediate interests have a more active and imperious control over human conduct than general or remote considerations?" In still another context he asks, "Why has government been instituted at all?" "Because," he replies, "the passions of men will not conform to the dictates of reason and justice, without constraint."

Conservatives are not only at home with the principles embodied in the Constitution but also with the assumptions that undergird its structure and processes. Like Publius, they are fearful of any concentration of power and support the principle of the separation of powers that prevents any one branch from exercising the whole power of another. This fear of concentration is rooted in a commitment to a government by laws, not by men. Moreover, conservatives share with Publius the need to ensure that the process of deliberation within the institutions of government is safeguarded against mindless passions prevailing in the heat of the moment. They see undoubted merit, for instance, in Publius's defense of the Senate as a deliberative body that can serve "to check the misguided career, and to suspend the blow mediated by the people against themselves, until reason, justice and truth, can regain their authority over the public mind." Likewise, they look upon the presidential veto as means to thwart any "sudden breeze of passion" or "transient impulse" that may overtake the people "in order to give them time and opportunity for more cool and sedate reflection."

In a more general vein, conservatives share with Publius a fear of plebiscitary democracy, that is, direct and immediate rule by popular majorities on matters of public policy. They see such a democracy ending in incurable "turbulence and contention," (the same fate Publius predicts for "pure" democracies), and as "incompatible with personal security, or the rights of property." Instead, like Publius, they envision representatives of the people making decisions after due deliberation, not bound to blindly follow the "instructions" of their constituents but free to exercise their own judgment based upon what they consider to be best for all. They also agree with Publius that representatives should "refine and enlarge the public views" through debate and deliberations in the legislative assemblies.

Conservatives are at home with the tacit assumptions that seemed to have guided the framers in drafting the Constitution. Throughout *The Federalist,* for instance, it is taken for granted that the institutions of government have to be fashioned on the basis of man's actual nature and behavior rather than on the basis of how men ought to behave. Publius seems to believe, as do most conservatives, that human nature has been relatively constant over the centuries. Moreover, in keeping with one of conservatism's most fundamental tenets, that which eschews the notion that heaven can be built here on earth, Publius rejects the notion of a "golden age" that "promises . . . an exception from the imperfections, the weaknesses and the evils incident to society in every shape." Nor did he believe it was possible to alter human nature in order to eliminate political friction. "The latent causes of faction are," he contended, "sown in the nature of man," and the most institutions of government can or should try to do is to control their effects. On these and related counts Publius's thinking is thoroughly consonant with conservative principles.

Publius also manifests a degree of prudence that endears him to conservatives. There are features of the proposed Constitution, the three-fifths compromise among them, that he would prefer otherwise, but he knows that he must balance these shortcomings against far greater dangers or evils such as permanent disunion, probable war between the states, or even foreign conquest. He knows, moreover, that no amount of change or tinkering will make the Constitution "perfect"; that a "perfect work" is not to be expected from "imperfect man."

The Federalist also advances a conception of constitutionalism that is the cornerstone of the American conservative belief in limited government. The Constitution and its provisions are, he writes, "paramount" to the government; the authority of those vested with power is limited by the terms of the Constitution, and majorities may exercise their will only in those areas authorized by the Constitution. In short, because it provides insights into the assumptions and values of the founding fathers that find expression in the Constitution, *The Federalist* is and always has been a work central to American political conservatism. Indeed, no other single work in the tradition enjoys such stature.

—BRUCE FROHNEN

Further Reading

Carey, George W. *The Federalist: Design for a Constitutional Republic.* Champaign, Ill.: University of Illinois Press, 1995.

See also: Anti-Federalists; Bill of Rights; Carey, George W.; church and state; Constitution, interpretations of; democracy; Dietze, Gottfried; federalism; Federalist Party; Hamilton, Alexander; judicial activism; separation of powers

Federalist Party

Born out of a division within the administration of George Washington between secretary of the treasury Alexander Hamilton and secretary of state Thomas Jefferson, the Federalist Party composed half of the first two-party system in American politics. Closely associated with the views of Hamilton, the Federalist Party advocated a program of commercial nationalism, elitist control of the political process, and a "broad construction" of the Constitution. The Federalist Party offers a mixed legacy for modern conservatives. Variations of the designation "federalist" permeate the history of post-revolutionary America (see federalism and *The Federalist*). The common appropriation of the term and the multifaceted roots of the Federalist Party make for a complicated heritage. For example, it is ironic but not altogether inconsistent for the Federalist Society, a modern conservative organization founded in 1982 that is dedicated to judicial restraint, to share the name of the party most associated with an activist reading of the Constitution. Likewise, many historians trace the genealogy of the modern Republican Party, the self-described party of small government, back to the Federalist Party, the primordial proponent of a bigger and more powerful central government.

The Federalists officially emerged as an organized party in 1792 with the first contested national election. (The race was for vice president. President Washington faced no opposition and earned unanimous reelection.) The framers of the Constitution had hoped for a government without "factions," but they quickly proved the one-party ideal unworkable. The Federalist Party formed reluctantly as a reaction to the systematic opposition of Jefferson and James Madison (the Republican Party). Although the formal genesis of the Federalist Party must coincide with the establishment of a viable opposition, the starting point of 1792 is misleading. For the Federalists of the mid-1790s were in great measure the same leaders who called for a stronger central government during the 1780s. Fearing the excesses of democracy and the inability of the post-revolutionary governments to maintain order, national-minded leaders called for and dominated the Constitutional Convention of 1787. Foremost among them, of course, were Washington, Madison, and Hamilton. Calling themselves Federalists and branding opponents to the Constitution Anti-Federalists, the nationalists carried the question of ratification in 1788, as a procession of individual state conventions adopted the federal compact. Inaugurating the new government in 1789, Federalists stood for election to Congress and won overwhelmingly as "friends of the Constitution."

The roots of the intra-administration conflict that transformed the Federalist movement into a political party sprang from dissent over economic policy. Convinced that only a healthy and diversified economy could ensure a prosperous American future, Hamilton advocated an energetic national government intent on aiding business. Envisioning an industrial America that would in time eclipse Great Britain, Hamilton offered an aggressive and comprehensive financial plan, which he outlined in four "Reports" to Congress. Almost from the beginning, Jefferson and House of Representatives floor leader Madison attempted to block Hamilton's specific programs and made clear their opposition to his overall vision. The dissension over economic planning revealed the underlying incompatibility between the philosophies of Jefferson and Hamilton, which would define the struggle between the Federalist Party and the Republicans. In addition to advocating a strong national government focused on promoting business, the Federalist Party also fretted over popular misrule and instability. Believing that government by the ablest citizens provided the surest path to peace and prosperity, Hamiltonian Federalists embraced an unabashed elitism. Jefferson feared that a government empowered to keep order and facilitate enterprise would prove equally proficient at seizing liberty. Arguing that Hamilton's vision for strong government came at the expense of hard-won independence, Jefferson and Madison presented themselves as republican defenders of freedom and painted Federalists as monarchists. The economic struggle also framed a fundamental question regarding Constitutional interpretation. Battling Hamilton's proposal to charter a national bank, Madison and Jefferson advanced a "strict constructionist" view of the Constitution, contending that the authority of Congress included only those powers expressly enumerated within the document. Citing the "necessary and proper" clause, Hamilton countered that the Constitution provided for the routine execution of governmental business through implied powers. In response, Jefferson presciently argued that broad construction blazed a path for a massive expansion of federal power in the future. The division also foreshadowed sectional conflict, as Madison and Jefferson were Virginians and Federalists tended to be from New England and the Northeast.

Although George Washington never formally embraced the Federalist Party, he buttressed the Federalist position in myriad ways. The president supported Hamilton over Jefferson on almost every point of contention during his administration, indicating his de facto support for the party of Hamilton. The administrations of Washington and John Adams are rightly termed the Federalist Era, and Washington's retirement in 1796 dealt the party a critical blow. Adams, his well-intentioned successor, possessed far less political capital than Washington; and after a power struggle between Adams and Hamilton, the Federalist Party splintered once again. Even with an antagonistic Hamilton on one flank and the Republicans pressing on the other, Adams only narrowly lost his bid for reelection to Thomas Jefferson. The "Republican Revolution" of 1800 inaugurated a twenty-four year run of Republican presidents and marked the last time the Federalist Party would hold a national elective office.

Jefferson's purchase of the enormous Louisiana territory in 1803 further isolated the Federalist Party as a regional political actor, allowing the Republicans to build a coalition between the Old South and the developing West. Over the next decade party fortunes continued to slip, and a segment of Federalists increasingly discussed secession and embraced a defensive "states' rights" position. During the final days of the War of 1812, Federalist delegates met at the Hartford Convention and pressed the government for redress. With an implied threat to secede if left unsatisfied, New England Federalists proposed several amendments to the Constitution, all intended to limit the power of the Republicans. Following news of peace with England and the extraordinary victory at New Orleans, an exultant nation found the actions of the Hartford Convention inexcusable. In the next presidential race the Federalist Party candidate won only thirty-four out of 217 electoral votes, which marked the last time the party contested a national election.

While completely discredited as a viable national party, the Federalists continued to influence the American political scene long after 1816. Chief Justice John Marshall, one of President John Adams's "midnight" appointees, recast the United States Supreme Court, endowing the institution with greater independence and a more activist role. Known as the last Federalist, Marshall served on the Court until his death in 1835, championing judicial nationalism for more than three decades. Ironically, Hamilton's ambitious economic agenda found able proponents in the second generation of Republican politicians. Henry Clay and others rehabilitated Hamilton's commercial nationalism and placed his program at the center of the National-Republican Party in 1828, inaugurating the second two-party era in American politics. The short-lived National-Republican Party became the Whig Party in 1832. After disintegrating during the early 1850s, the old Whig Party platform provided the economic fundamentals for the modern Republican Party, formed in 1854.

—Ashley Cruseturner

Further Reading

Banning, Lance, ed. *Liberty and Order: The First American Party Struggle.* Indianapolis, Ind.: Liberty Fund, 2004.

Fischer, David Hackett. *The Revolution of Ameri-*

can Conservatism: The Federalist Party in the Era of Jeffersonian Democracy. New York: Harper & Row, 1965.

Livermore, Shaw, Jr. *The Twilight of Federalism: The Disintegration of the Federalist Party, 1815–1830.* Princeton, N.J.: Princeton University Press, 1962.

See also: Adams, John; Anti-Federalists; Bill of Rights; Clay, Henry; federalism; Federalist, The; Hamilton, Alexander; Jefferson, Thomas; Kent, James; Marshall, John; states' rights; Storing, Herbert J.; Washington, George

Federalist Society

The Federalist Society for Law and Public Policy Studies is a group of conservative and libertarian attorneys and law students dedicated to reforming the current legal order. The society claims more than 25,000 members divided into a Student Division, a Lawyer Division, and a recently formed Faculty Division. The Student Division has chapters at approximately 145 law schools.

Led today by longtime director and president Eugene Meyer, the society was founded in 1982. The founding chapters were at Yale University and the University of Chicago, where they benefited from the support of conservative faculty members—Robert Bork at Yale and Antonin Scalia at Chicago. The founders included Lee Liberman Otis and David McIntosh at Chicago and Steven G. Calabresi at Yale.

The founders observed firsthand the virtually unchallenged supremacy of contemporary liberalism in legal education and by extension in the American legal profession. Believing that this bias was contrary to the preservation of the form of government intended by the framers of the Constitution, they decided that it was necessary to form a society dedicated to reforming the current legal order. Looking to the founding for their example they chose to name their society after the Federalists and to name James Madison as their patron and mascot (Madison's silhouette is the society's emblem). Accordingly, the society's goals are shaped by a commitment to the principles of freedom, separation of powers, and judicial restraint.

The society furthers these aims by providing a forum for legal debate as well as a network of like-minded lawyers. Federalist Society debates and panels are common at leading U.S. law schools. In these forums the society tries to attract experts of opposing views, encouraging interaction among members of the legal profession, the judiciary, students, policymakers, and academics.

After law school, many society members remain active through the Lawyer Division's chapters in many major cities. This division sponsors an annual National Lawyers Convention, a Speakers Bureau, and multiple practice groups that facilitate the collaboration of members working on specific issues.

The Faculty Division, added in 1999, reflects both the society's growth and success over the years, as well as its ongoing commitment to education. The Faculty Division was developed to encourage constructive academic discourse about the American legal tradition.

To achieve its goals, the society has created a conservative and libertarian intellectual network that extends to all levels of the legal community. The result has been an increase in both the prestige of the organization and criticism from liberals who resent the conservative influence the society's members exercise. Such criticism was especially intense when many members of the society found appointments in George W. Bush's administration, including Attorney General John Ashcroft, Department of Energy secretary Spencer Abraham, Department of the Interior secretary Gail Norton, and solicitor general Theodore Olson.

The society's commitment to free and open debate on legal questions, however, has earned praise even from liberal critics such as Nadine Strossen of the ACLU, who said of the society, "one thing your organization has definitely done is to contribute to free speech, free debate, and most importantly public understanding of, awareness of, and appreciation of the Constitution."

—Christopher Thacker

See also: judicial activism; Olin Foundation

feminism

Conservatives have consistently railed against feminism and vigorously opposed many feminist programs and pieces of legislation, although often with something less than unanimity. Reagan's "big tent" covered a multitude of viewpoints, including such important and divisive issues as abortion. But notwithstanding the clamor, many conservatives most likely still underestimate or misunderstand the magnitude of feminism's claims and impact on our society and culture. To be blunt, feminism ranks as the most radical and potentially corrosive movement of our time—one that, not unlike a virulent computer virus, is steadily erasing all of our accumulated thoughts and knowledge.

From the start, the movement for women's rights, which since the late nineteenth century has been known as feminism, has ranked as a radical ideology, primarily because successive drives for the "liberation" of women have aimed to dismantle fundamental social, political, and religious institutions. Feminism has consistently sought a social, cultural, and political transformation that would free women from the control of men and establish them as men's equals. These campaigns differ significantly from mere defenses of women's excellence, which have surfaced in most Western societies throughout history, sometimes in association with attacks on men's abuse of their authority—their patriarchalism—but invariably without offering a serious challenge to the social order. The modern campaigns for women's rights emerged in tandem with the rise of modern individualism in mainstream thought and politics, and they have consistently focused on winning for women the same rights as individuals that the men of the English, American, and French Revolutions were claiming for themselves. Increasingly, however, proponents of women's rights focused upon freeing women from any form of domination by men and ensuring women's equality with men.

The emergence of socialism, abolitionism, and various other movements for social, political, and religious reform only accelerated the process. Many early feminists nurtured modest enough goals: securing a married woman's right to hold property in her own name, a woman's right to divorce an abusive or deserting husband, or a mother's right to custody of her children in the case of divorce. Some sought improvements in pay and working conditions, some even sought women's suffrage, and many campaigned for temperance. Others, however, including some of the most accomplished leaders, developed a far more radical vision. Thus, Elizabeth Cady Stanton launched a sweeping attack on Christianity and the Bible that would delight the most radical of contemporary feminist theologians.

During the first half of the twentieth century, as women throughout Western Europe and the United States gained the vote and a variety of other rights and protections, feminism remained largely dormant, although social and economic changes were beginning to erode the institutions, notably families and churches, that had circumscribed women's freedom. But when beginning in the 1960s feminism began to revive, it rode the crest of a dual sexual and economic revolution that secured the realization of even the most extreme feminist demands. As if with a snap of the fingers, feminists secured the legalization of abortion on demand, the widespread distribution of artificial contraception (notably the pill), the social acceptability of premarital sex (at ever younger ages) and single motherhood, and no-fault divorce. Together with affirmative action programs intended to "equalize" the opportunities—and, increasingly, the attainments—of women and men, women's sexual liberation was expected to free women from the domination of men.

Success came rapidly and dramatically. By the early 1990s, women had moved from earning the notorious fifty-nine cents on the male dollar to virtually equal pay (and occasionally a bit more) for equal work. When women did earn less than men, it was invariably because of their commitments to family, especially children. Not content with this record, feminists raged that schools treated girls unfairly, fostering their insecurities and encouraging them to continue to behave like girls. Equality demanded that women's sports receive equal funding with those of men—or that the better-funded men's programs be abolished. Equality demanded that women receive identical access to all branches of the military, from the service academies to armed combat. Equality demanded that men be harshly punished for "acquaintance" rape and all forms of behavior that might be labeled as harassment. Sensitivity training programs proliferated in the public and private sectors and in schools and colleges.

What feminists are reluctant to recognize is that this vast effort at social engineering has worked—at least up to a point. Girls have come to out-perform boys in school and women to outnumber men on college campuses, and women are beginning to equal men in graduate and professional programs. Women who commit themselves single-mindedly to careers are as likely to succeed in them, and as fully, as men. But if feminists are loathe to acknowledge the magnitude of their success, they are even more loathe to acknowledge the havoc they have caused in American society and, increasingly, throughout the world. Their campaign for women's sexual liberation has mushroomed into a full-scale assault on the sanctity of human life, a discrediting of marriage as a covenanted heterosexual institution, a scandalous repudiation of children as the proper objects of adult attention and sacrifice, and a repudiation of the ideals of military heroism and service.

In elevating the liberation of women to the most important measure of social, economic, and political justice, feminism has mightily contributed to the decomposition of the social fabric into a congeries of atomistic individuals without ties or responsibilities to any other. As noted by Pope John Paul II, among others who are often viewed as conservatives, we cannot go back. Feminism would never have attained the success it has, had not women throughout the world suffered centuries of disadvantage, injustice, and sometimes abuse. Nor, as conservatives should note, could feminism have succeeded without the economic transformations, notably globalization, which feed upon footloose employees, drawing both men and women away from the binding ties of marriage and family life. Feminism has fed upon a widespread sense that women deserve greater independence, opportunities, and respect, and it has profited from economic change, but in its unending quest for "freedom from" it has lost sight of "freedom for," and its ultimately nihilistic vision has decisively influenced our culture and society.

—ELIZABETH FOX-GENOVESE

Further Reading

Fox-Genovese, Elizabeth, Stanley Grenz, Mary Steewart Van Leeuwen, and Mardi Keyes.

Women and the Future of the Family. Grand Rapids, Mich.: Baker Books, 2000.

See also: abortion; academic freedom; Decter, Midge; Equal Rights Amendment; family; literary criticism; sociobiology

Feulner, Edwin J., Jr. (1941–)

If the Heritage Foundation stands as a permanent monument to conservative thought in America, Edwin J. Feulner Jr. is the architect of that monument. As president of the Heritage Foundation, Feulner has, in the words of the *Boston Globe,* created "the most perfectly tuned politico-intellectual institution since the Manhattan Project." Coming from a major liberal newspaper, this is high praise indeed.

A graduate of Regis University in Denver, Feulner did postgraduate work at the London School of Economics, the Wharton School of the University of Pennsylvania (M.B.A.), and the University of Edinburgh (Ph.D.). The Chicago-born Feulner originally went to Washington, D.C., as a public affairs fellow at the Center for Strategic and International Studies (CSIS) and later for the Hoover Institution at Stanford University. His first job was as a confidential assistant to then secretary of defense Melvin R. Laird. Two of his colleagues on Laird's staff were David Abshire and William Baroody, who later also headed think tanks, the CSIS and the American Enterprise Institute, respectively.

Feulner later served as administrative assistant to U.S. Rep. Philip M. Crane and as executive director of the Republican Study Committee in the House of Representatives, the subject of Feulner's 1983 book, *Conservatives Stalk the House.* From 1982 to 1991 Feulner served as chairman of the U.S. Advisory Commission on Public Diplomacy.

In 1973, while still running the Study Committee, Feulner helped found the Heritage Foundation. Since assuming command of the tiny conservative think tank in 1977, Feulner has turned the Heritage Foundation into a public policy heavyweight—with a staff of about 180 and annual revenues in excess of $40 million—and a recognized trendsetter among U.S. think tanks. An organization representing all of the various strains of conservative thought—from classical liberal, or libertarian, to traditionalist—Heritage is considered "home base" for Washington's conservative establishment.

Creating a permanent institutional presence in the nation's capital for conservative thinkers and policy experts has earned Feulner wide acclaim as America's leading "public policy entrepreneur." In 1989, he was awarded the Presidential Citizens Medal by President Reagan. The citation read as follows: "By building an organization dedicated to ideas and their consequences, he has helped to shape the policy of our Government. He has been a voice of reason and values in service to his country and the cause of freedom around the world."

Active in numerous conservative organizations, Feulner is past president of the Philadelphia Society, past chairman of the Intercollegiate Studies Institute, and is currently senior vice president of the Mont Pelerin Society.

—HERB BERKOWITZ

Further Reading

Edwards, Lee, *The Power of Ideas: The Heritage Foundation at 25 Years.* Ottawa, Ill.: Jameson Books, 1997.

Feulner, Edwin J., Jr. *The March of Freedom: Modern Classics in Conservative Thought.* Dallas: Spence Publishing Company, 1998.

———, ed. *Leadership for America: The Principles of Conservatism.* Dallas: Spence Publishing Company, 2000.

See also: Heritage Foundation; think tanks, conservative

Field, Stephen Johnson (1816–99)

A late-nineteenth-century jurist, Stephen Johnson Field was a principal architect of the substantive due process doctrine. Field's father was a Congregational minister of modest means who moved the family to Stockbridge, Massachusetts, in 1819 after accepting a call from a congregation earlier served by Jonathan Edwards. Stephen, the sixth of eight children, was preceded in fame and fortune by two brothers: David Dudley Jr., an attorney, and Cyrus, an inventor and transatlantic cable pioneer. His nephew, David Brewer, served a term on the Supreme Court overlapping with his own.

Field spent nearly three years abroad before enrolling at Williams College in 1833, where he came under the influence of the moral philosopher Mark Hopkins. Afterwards he read law under his brother David and became his junior partner in 1841. Gifted with a logical mind and great ambition, he grew restless in his brother's shadow. David became a leader of the codification movement (replacing the traditional common law with a statutory code) in New York and was the principal author of the Field Code, which was adopted by the New York state legislature in 1848. Stephen Field moved to California where he won a reputation for shrewdness, feuding with judges and other lawyers and mixing common and civil (code) law.

After trying sixty cases before the California Supreme Court, he won a seat on the bench in 1857 as a Democrat. Regarded as a radical at the time of his appointment, Field showed his independence early.

Field was nominated (and confirmed) for a seat on the U.S. Supreme Court in 1863 on the strength of his loyalty to the Union and his family ties. The highly moralistic attitudes of his youth had by now acquired an individualistic cast. The development of Field's jurisprudence is best understood by studying the role he played in three series of cases.

In a number of postwar civil liberties cases, Field repeatedly and often successfully sought to restrain Reconstruction policies and practices. He joined the Court's unanimous decision in *Ex parte Milligan* (1866) that the power to suspend habeas corpus does not authorize the president to substitute military commissions while civil courts are operative. Field wrote the Court's opinion in two test oath cases, *Cummings* v. *Missouri* and *Ex parte Garland* (1867), which involved the dismissal of teachers and attorneys who had supported the South. Characterizing the oaths as bills of attainder and ex post facto laws, he anticipated the doctrine of substantive due process by setting forth a theory of inalienable rights that held that the plaintiffs had property rights in their professions.

Another series of cases involved legal tender legislation. During the war greenbacks were issued as an emergency measure, but Chief Justice Salmon Chase, who had acquiesced in the practice while serving as Lincoln's secretary of treasury, now sought a return to specie payments. In *Hepburn* v. *Griswold* (1870) the Court voted 4-3 to strike down a provision of the Legal Tender Act that applied it retroactively to debts contracted before its passage. A year later an expanded Court reversed the decision 5-4 in the *Legal Tender Cases* (1871). Field condemned the practice in a lengthy dissenting opinion that adopted a natural rights position. The controversy culminated in *Juilliard* v. *Greenman* (1884) with the Court's acceptance of a peacetime issue of paper money. Field's lone dissenting opinion is a classic statement of the theory of limited government, warning of evil to follow if hard money principles were abandoned.

Finally, a series of cases involving state regulation of business provided Field the opportunity to establish a laissez-faire judicial philosophy through a doctrine of substantive due process. The Court had traditionally treated the due process of the Fifth

Amendment as a procedural rather than a substantive limitation of government power. This began to change with the *Dred Scott* decision of 1857, when the Court first connected due process with the concept of vested rights. While early hints of substantive due process may be detected in the test oath and legal tender cases, the doctrine was given impetus by two dissenting opinions in the *Slaughterhouse Cases* (1873). The Court upheld a Louisiana law that chartered a New Orleans slaughterhouse monopoly and confined butchering to a single district for reasons of public health. In one of the dissents, Field held that the Fourteenth Amendment enacted "the sacred and inalienable rights of man," although he also acknowledged the importance of state police powers. Citing Adam Smith, he found that among these rights is the individual's right to pursue a lawful profession. Justice Bradley took an even bolder step when he insisted on the priority of national over state citizenship and claimed that the federal government must protect a wide range of citizenship rights that the state may not invade, including what he called "substantive due process." Together, Field and Bradley agreed that the Fourteenth Amendment gave ample scope for federal intervention in defense of economic liberty.

The doctrine was not readily accepted at first. Only after repeated dissents by Field in cases involving Granger laws and railroad rates did it begin to take root. It reached the apex of its development when linked with freedom of contract in *Allgeyer* v. *Louisiana* (1897). Although it subsequently fell into disrepute, the Warren Court revived it in all but name, using it to support a host of claims to personal autonomy and social liberty.

Field's ambitions led him in later years to make unsuccessful bids for the Democratic presidential nomination in 1880 and for appointment as chief justice in 1888. But his tenure was marred by a sensational confrontation involving a one-time judicial colleague and unsuccessful litigant who attacked Field aboard a train and was shot and killed by a bodyguard protecting Field. The affair revived old controversies and placed the Court in an unfavorable light.

Field served more than thirty-four years before he retired in December 1897. His legacy consists primarily of 1,042 opinions, personal reminiscences of the early days in California, and a penchant for judicial activism that has survived him.

—STEVEN ALAN SAMSON

Further Reading

McCloskey, Robert Green. *American Conservatism in the Age of Enterprise: A Study of William Graham Sumner, Stephen J. Field, and Andrew Carnegie*. Cambridge, Mass.: Harvard University Press, 1951.

Swisher, Carl Brent. *Stephen J. Field: Craftsman of the Law*. Washington, D.C.: Brookings Institution, 1930.

White, G. Edward. *The American Judicial Tradition: Profiles of Leading American Judges*. New York: Oxford University Press, 1976.

See also: due process; Reconstruction

First Things

In its premier issue (March 1990), the editors of the monthly journal *First Things* announced that the magazine would be devoted to fostering an intellectually rigorous conversation about "religion and public life." The most fundamental assumption of that conversation would be that public life must point beyond itself to the "first principles" that ground it. Those first principles are grounded, in turn, in culture, which the editors described as nothing less than "the cognitive, moral, aesthetic, and emotive air that we breathe." Lastly, the magazine would be guided by the conviction that "at the heart of culture is religion." *First Things* would thus be a magazine devoted to a discussion of the necessarily religious foundations of public life.

In making this statement, the editors built on an argument first proposed by the magazine's founder and editor in chief, Richard John Neuhaus. In a series of articles and books published in the 1980s—most prominently, *The Naked Public Square* (1984)—Neuhaus developed a distinctive conservative outlook. Despite the considerable political gains made by the New Right under Ronald Reagan's leadership, a persistent "ideology of secularism" threatened to exclude religion from public life in the United States. Believing Christians and Jews were increasingly encouraged—and, in the case of Supreme Court rulings openly hostile to religion, even forced—to bracket these beliefs in public discussion. The result was, he argued, the "naked public square" of his title.

The magazine has consistently sought to correct this debasement of public discourse. In articles and book reviews that strive to be both scholarly and literary, *First Things* provides its readers with highly intelligent cultural commentary on a range of topics, including religion, politics, philosophy, science, education, and the arts. Moreover, Neuhaus's monthly column, "The Public Square," which typically runs to several thousand words, provides the journal's readers with what he calls a "continuing survey of religion and public life."

In addition to these regular features, *First Things* periodically publishes documents and symposia on specific topics—some of which have been the occasion for the magazine's most influential and controversial moments. For example, the journal contributed to the ecumenical movement among conservative Christians in May 1994 by publishing the statement "Evangelicals and Catholics Together," which Neuhaus helped to draft. Then, as part of a November 1996 symposium ("The End of Democracy: The Judicial Usurpation of Politics"), the editors raised the possibility that judicial activism had gone to such extremes in the United States that the time may arrive when "conscientious citizens can no longer give moral assent to the existing regime."

The resulting controversy dominated discussion among conservative intellectuals for many months and inspired some liberal journalists to proclaim that a divide had opened up between moderate "neocons" and the more radical "theocons" who contributed to the *First Things* symposium (these included Judge Robert Bork, Russell Hittinger, Hadley Arkes, Charles Colson, and Robert George). Such a split never materialized, and the magazine's circulation increased in the wake of the dispute. Other symposia provoking widespread discussion have addressed, for instance, doctor-assisted suicide and the cultural influence of the homosexual movement.

—DAMON LINKER

Further Reading

Muncy, Mitchell S., ed. *The End of Democracy? The Celebrated* First Things *Debate, with Arguments Pro and Con.* Dallas: Spence Publishing Company, 1997

Neuhaus, Richard John. *The Best of the Public Square: Selections from Richard John Neuhaus' Celebrated Column in* First Things. New York: Institute on Religion and Public Life, 1997.

———. *The Best of "The Public Square": Book Two.* Grand Rapids, Mich.: Eerdmans, 2001.

See also: Neuhaus, Richard John

Fish, Hamilton, III (1888–1991)

The scion of a prominent Republican political family, Hamilton Fish served in Congress from 1920 until 1945, representing New York's twenty-sixth congressional district, located in the heart of the Hudson Valley. During the 1930s, he gained national prominence as a fierce enemy of communism and a bitter opponent of President Franklin Roosevelt's domestic and foreign policies.

In 1930, Fish chaired the first House committee to investigate communism, or more specifically, communist propaganda. Politically ambitious, eyeing a Senate seat or perhaps a vice presidential nomination in 1932, he thought that the considerable publicity generated by nationwide hearings might thrust him into the spotlight. Another more complex reason was rooted in ideology. The Bolshevik seizure of power, the subsequent attack on property, and the dictatorship of the proletariat presented a frightening image of an ideology run amok. Like many who had expressed concerns about the nature of American capitalism, Fish had visited the Soviet Union in the early 1920s to learn whether the Bolsheviks had in fact discovered the way to a better world. Thoroughly disgusted with what he saw there, he returned to the United States convinced that the Soviet experiment had failed miserably.

Despite his committee's failure to prove that the Soviet Union was involved in domestic subversion, Fish created a precedent for having subsequent investigations into communism conducted by the House of Representatives. He also pioneered many of the methods used by later Red-hunters.

When Franklin Roosevelt became president, Fish accused him of harboring dictatorial ambitions and branded the New Deal the brainchild of communist sympathizers and socialists. Though not indifferent to the enormous suffering experienced by many during the Depression, he refused to support most New Deal programs on the grounds that they tended to enlarge executive, and weaken congressional, power.

Beginning in 1935, Fish became the leading isolationist in the House of Representatives, attempting to use his position as the ranking Republican member of both the House Foreign Affairs and Rules committees to obstruct every measure aimed at enlarging Roosevelt's discretionary control over foreign policy. Between 1935 and 1940, Fish supported a variety of arms embargoes, neutrality, and war referendum legislation. Once war broke out in Europe, he formed the National Committee to Keep America Out of War and became a prominent spokesman for America First. In 1941, he sought to block American military assistance to Great Britain by leading the opposition in the House to the Lend-Lease bill. Careless in his associations, he collaborated with a number of far-right antiwar activists.

Fish would later pay a price when he was targeted for prosecution under the Alien and Sedition Act for allegedly working as a Nazi agent. (This charge was never proved.)

The war years found Fish under increasing attack from political opponents who claimed his prewar opposition to the administration's defense policies had undermined American military preparedness. Sensitive to this charge, he pledged total support to the war effort, although he remained a vituperative critic of the administration. In addition to the legions of enemies he made among Democrats, a number of powerful GOP officials grew uncomfortable with him. In 1944, Governor Thomas Dewey, believing Fish an embarrassment to the party, orchestrated the gerrymandering of Fish's district, and as a result Fish suffered a narrow defeat in his bid for reelection that year. His political career ended, Fish devoted the rest of his life to championing the cause of nuclear disarmament, denouncing the twin evils of internationalism and Communism, and writing a series of polemical books chiefly targeting Franklin Roosevelt. On January 19, 1991, soon after completing work on his memoirs, the 102-year-old Fish died at his home in Cold Spring, New York.

—ANTHONY C. TRONCONE

Further Reading

Fish, Hamilton. *FDR: The Other Side of the Coin: How We Were Tricked into World War II.* New York: Vantage, 1976.

———. *Memoir of an American Patriot.* Washington, D.C.: Regnery, 1991.

See also: anticommunism; isolationism

Fitzhugh, George (1806–81)

Lawyer, sociologist, and political writer, George Fitzhugh was a leading figure in what has been called the "Reactionary Enlightenment" of the antebellum American South. In two books and numerous articles defending the Southern cause, Fitzhugh's thought (an odd mixture of Romantic conservatism and radical political economy) resembled the work of fellow Confederates Albert Bledsoe and George Frederick Holmes, but his defense of Southern claims was unique. He did not restrict himself to Constitutional arguments, nor did he consider slavery simply a necessary evil. Rather, he championed the South's peculiar institution as a positive social good and called for its expansion. He argued this without relying on racist beliefs about Negro inferiority; on the contrary, he explicitly doubted whether one man in twenty, black or white, was really fit to govern himself.

Fitzhugh's formal schooling was meager, and he was not a systematic thinker: his books are rambling and eccentric. In *Sociology of the South, or the Failure of Free Society* (1854) and *Cannibals All! or Slaves Without Masters* (1857), Fitzhugh argued for the moral and practical superiority of "slave society" over "free society." Citing with approval the account of capitalist injustice produced by the utopian socialists Robert Owen and Charles Fourier and their American follower, Horace Greeley, Fitzhugh held that all capital accumulation was the result of exploited labor. The scale of Northern economic success therefore itself proved free society the greater exploiter of human beings. Fitzhugh further argued that capitalist advance would inevitably drive the wage level below that necessary for human subsistence. At that point, the true humanity of the Southern slave system would be clear to all, since, according to Fitzhugh, slavery essentially extended the sphere of paternal care and protection while "slaves without masters," those industrial workers trapped in Northern "wage slavery," were abandoned to inhuman conditions.

For Fitzhugh, the only solution to nineteenth-century social problems was the extension of slavery. In a typically striking passage, he suggested that Northern philanthropists would better help mankind by purchasing slaves rather than freeing them. Against Lockean objections that men could not rationally consent to slavery, Fitzhugh posed "the strength of weakness," and maintained that a system of civilized manners was adequate to protect slaves from the arbitrary willfulness of masters. The natural affection of the household or domestic sphere extended to slavery, he argued, made it benign while the absence of a natural familial tie in the Northern system of free labor made it intolerable. Fitzhugh did admit that "slavery without domestic affection would be a curse."

Laced through these arguments are remarkable digressions recalling the theses of the continental European Reaction, such as Fitzhugh's rejection of free trade as a Manchesterian heresy, his belief in a divine source of political authority, and his admiration of the Middle Ages. His writing emphasized the importance of familialism, and he frequently suggested that opposition to slavery was simply the first step in a more general social revolution against the family and Christianity—a laissez-faire system of "unmitigated selfishness" that neglected man's social nature and resulted in social atomization.

One interpreter has suggested that Fitzhugh can best be understood as the inheritor of the Tory tradition of Sir Robert Filmer, whose *Patriarcha* (1680) contains arguments against which John Locke composed his *Two Treatises of Civil Government* (1690). It is certainly true that Fitzhugh hoped that "the revolution of 1861" would "roll back the Reformation in its political phases." But Louis Hartz has suggested that such a voice in an America "born liberal," without a feudal past, could amount only to a "fraud." To Hartz, the South's development from 1776 into the 1860s was the story of "imperfect Lockes" becoming "grossly imperfect Maistres." The fundamentally un-American quality of Fitzhugh's thought, Hartz argued, was manifest in his relegation to complete intellectual marginality after 1865. In the early 1990s, however, ex-Marxist historian Eugene Genovese responded to the collapse of communism by aggressively championing the insights of Fitzhugh. Genovese saw in Fitzhugh the best foundation in the American tradition on which to construct a needed antiliberal critique of the alienation and anomie within bourgeois society.

—MARK C. HENRIE

Further Reading

Genovese, Eugene. *The Southern Tradition.* Cambridge, Mass.: Harvard University Press, 1996.

Hartz, Louis. "The Feudal Dream of the South," Part 4 of *The Liberal Tradition in America.* New York: Harcourt, Brace, Jovanovich, 1955, 1983.

Wish, Harvey. *George Fitzhugh: Propagandist of the Old South.* Mangolia, Mass.: Peter Smith, 1990.

See also: Genovese, Eugene D.; Southern conservatism

Fleming, Thomas (1945–)

For twenty-five years, Thomas Fleming, editor of *Chronicles*, has been the intellectual leader of American paleoconservatism. Fleming earned a doctorate in classics from the University of North Carolina at Chapel Hill, and he spices his essays on culture and politics with the pepper of Aristotelian and Stoical insight. Not exactly Spenglerian in his view, Fleming nevertheless understands that analogy is not illegitimate in historical analysis and sees that the effects of empire—Diadochic, Roman, Soviet, or American—manifest themselves with a certain grim inevitability. When the imperial center gets used to policing the marches, it regularly starts policing the metropolis, and constitutional protections of the republic fall by the wayside. The whole point of imperium is that the rulers get to exercise their libido dominandi.

Like the classics-oriented poet William Carlos Williams, Fleming advocates the local. A Ninth and Tenth Amendment man, he sees in encroachments of federal over state sovereignty both a cause and a symptom of American civilization's moral decline. The uprooted, amoral professionals and the welfare class alike come to regard the state as a god who "solves" all problems; the state rains down the manna of redistribution to underscore its appearance as a divinity. The procedure is as mendacious as it is entropic.

Chronicles, published by the Rockford Institute, consistently reflects Fleming's determination to spur individuals, communities, and states into a defense of their self-determination against the Gnostic prescriptions of the new therapeutic totalitarianism. This means a defense of voluntary religion against mandatory profanation and of communal against imperial judgments. Fleming opposed both the Gulf War against Iraq and the Balkan Campaign against Serbia as examples of power-mongering by a new multinational clique hostile to all traditional forms of civilization, especially to Christianity.

Fleming is the author or coauthor of three books, including *The Morality of Every-*

day Life: Rediscovering an Ancient Alternative to the Liberal Tradition (2004). His *Politics of Human Nature* (1988) is a Thomistic treatise on the distortions of modern life. For many of his readers, Fleming is the preeminent spokesman for unalloyed conservatism.

—THOMAS BERTONNEAU

Further Reading

Gottfried, Paul, and Thomas Fleming. *The Conservative Movement*. Boston: Twayne, 1988.

See also: Chronicles; *Gottfried, Paul E.;* neoconservatism; *paleoconservatism; sociobiology;* Southern Partisan

Flynn, John T. (1883–1964)

In his books, radio broadcasts, and newspaper and magazine columns, John T. Flynn personified a type of conservatism reflected in pure competitive capitalism, anti-imperialism, and anti-interventionism, and an increasing penchant for conspiracy theories.

Born in Bladenburg, Maryland, in 1882, and educated at the Georgetown University Law School, Flynn had worked for several newspapers before becoming an editor of the *New York Globe*. In the 1920s and 1930s, Flynn contributed a weekly column, "Other People's Money," to the *New Republic* and became well known among intellectuals for his attacks on Wall Street manipulation. By the late 1930s, he was writing a column for the Scripps-Howard press. Flynn backed Roosevelt in 1932 and helped staff Judge Ferdinand Percora's investigation of Wall Street finance. He soon broke with the New Deal, claiming that such agencies as the National Recovery Administration were simply way-stations on the road to fascism. Flynn's suspicion of business monopolies, expressed in such works as *Graft in Business* (1931) and *Security Speculation* (1934), was rooted in the doctrines of Louis D. Brandeis.

Flynn's isolationism grew out of his general economic perspective. As one of a three-man advisory council to the Nye Committee, the journalist proposed severe and rigorous limitations on war profits. In 1939, Flynn suspected that Roosevelt would attempt to bolster the nation's economy by seeking martial adventures abroad, and in 1940 he headed the New York chapter of the America First Committee. In this capacity, he took a more militant posture than the national organization, opposing draft extension and blaming the president for the breakdown of relations with Japan. Flynn's belief in Roosevelt's mendacity led him to investigate Pearl Harbor.

In the last twenty years of his life, Flynn portrayed Congress as the one remaining major restraint on presidential power (*Meet Your Congress,* 1944), offered an impassioned critique of the Roosevelt presidency (*The Roosevelt Myth,* 1948), and warned against a socialist America (*The Road Ahead,* 1949; *The Decline of the American Republic,* 1955). He also claimed that American bungling and a pro-Soviet State Department had created communist domination of China and the Korean War (*While You Slept,* 1951; *The Lattimore Story,* 1953). In his effort to find individual villains, he often neglected the wider economic analyses that he had provided earlier in his career.

—JUSTUS D. DOENECKE

Further Reading

Doenecke, Justus D. *Storm on the Horizon: The Challenge to American Intervention, 1939–1941*. Lanham, Md.: Rowman & Littlefield, 2000.

Moser, John M. *Right Turn: John T. Flynn and the Transformation of American Liberalism*. New York: New York University Press, 2005.

Stenehjem, Michele Flynn. *An American First: John T. Flynn and the America First Committee*. New Rochelle, N.Y.: Arlington House, 1976.

See also: America First Committee; isolationism

Foreign Policy Research Institute

Robert Strausz-Hupé (1903–2002) founded the Foreign Policy Research Institute (FPRI) at the University of Pennsylvania in 1955 to provide support for policymakers and to educate the American public on international politics in the context of the Cold War. He sought to bring scholarship from a range of academic disciplines to help create a new strategy that would integrate a long view of the national interest with the management of current problems.

Born in Austria, Strausz-Hupé came to the United States in the 1920s, where he worked in finance and married Eleanor Cuyler Walker in 1938. Europe's drift toward war profoundly affected Strausz-Hupé, who shifted his focus from business to diplomacy and entered the University of Pennsylvania, earning a Ph.D. in 1946. He also worked with Franklin Roosevelt's advisor, the geographer Isaiah Bowman, as chief of research for Bowman's committee on refugee affairs. Strausz-Hupé introduced the concept of "geopolitics" to Americans. He advised James Forrestal and Dean Acheson during the early years of the Cold War and these experiences lay behind his establishment of FPRI.

FPRI pioneered the sort of interdisciplinary approach that draws on various academic disciplines and area studies to illuminate world politics. It assembled leading scholars, including William Y. Elliot and Hans Kohn, along with policy experts like William R. Kintner and the young Henry Kissinger and James Schlesinger. FPRI became an incubator of talent in the field, with former fellows and researchers moving into important posts. Strausz-Hupé founded the quarterly *Orbis* in 1957 to give FPRI's perspective—historically grounded realism—a regular publishing outlet. FPRI broke with Penn in 1970 to become an independent foundation, later relocating to downtown Philadelphia. Statistical analysis and logical positivism had made Strausz-Hupé's more humane and less quantitative approach unpopular within political science, and Vietnam-era unrest helped make Penn's campus an inhospitable place.

Strausz-Hupé joined the Nixon administration as ambassador to several countries as well as NATO, and he returned to government service in the Reagan administration. At NATO, he developed a close relationship with General Alexander Haig, a Philadelphia native who spent a year as a resident fellow at FPRI before joining the Reagan administration as secretary of state. John Lehman, who served as FPRI's deputy director, became Reagan's Navy secretary. Haig brought Harvey Sicherman from FPRI to serve as his advisor, and Sicherman later worked with Lehman, George Schultz, and James Baker before returning as FPRI's president in 1993. (Daniel Pipes, a Middle East specialist and son of the Harvard historian Richard Pipes, had led FPRI during the last years of the Cold War.)

Sicherman has recast FPRI for a post–Cold War world while remaining true to Strausz-Hupé's vision for the institute. Realizing that history, along with cultural and economic issues, set the context for policy, Sicherman has recruited Walter McDougall and James Kurth, each of whom has served as editor of *Orbis*. After setting its finances and administration on a sure footing, Sicherman has expanded FPRI's education programs and outreach. FPRI now supports work on the history of United States strategy and foreign policy, along with explorations into America's role within the Western tradition. This focus—especially important after 9/11—has kept FPRI in the forefront of America's foreign policy discussions.

—WILLIAM ANTHONY HAY

Further Reading

Gress, David. *From Plato to NATO: The Idea of the West and Its Opponents.* New York: Free Press, 1998.

McDougall, Walter A. *Promised Land, Crusader State: The American Encounter with the World since 1776.* Boston: Houghton Mifflin, 1997.

Strausz-Hupé, Robert. *Geopolitics: The Struggle for Space and Power.* New York: G. P. Putnam's Sons, 1942.

———. *In My Time.* New York: W. W. Norton, 1965.

———. *The Protracted Conflict.* New York: Harper, 1959.

See also: Cold War

Foundation for Economic Education (FEE)

Founded by Leonard Read in 1946, who conceived the idea of an organization set up to preach the gospel of liberty and beholden to no other institution, no faction, and no interest group—and which would have no endowment, instead depending for financial support on the interest generated by the quality of the work it produced—the Foundation for Economic Education was to consist chiefly of five or six scholars of independent mind who would read, research, write, and speak on liberty. Each of these scholars would share in the minor institutional chores; as to how they were to spend the rest of their time, well, in Read's words, "If I had to tell you how to use your time, you wouldn't have been hired in the first place!" Read assembled about a dozen men—business executives, college presidents, professors of economics—for a board of trustees, described his dream to anyone who would listen, raised $40,000, and bought an old and vacated estate in Irvington-on-Hudson, New York.

Read's dream of publishing a literature of liberty in the modern idiom began with a book on wage theory by one of his trustees, economist Fred Fairchild of Yale. Another trustee, Henry Hazlitt, had a book on the bestseller lists, *Economics in One Lesson* (1946).

FEE promoted it and later republished it. Ludwig von Mises was on the FEE payroll as an advisor, and FEE subsidized the republication of his *Human Action* (1949). In 1950, FEE issued a new translation of *The Law* by Frederic Bastiat, which had greatly impressed Read. In 1953, FEE also published a revised edition of Henry Grady Weaver's *The Mainspring of Human Progress.* The three books by Hazlitt, Bastiat, and Weaver have together sold considerably more than two million copies.

Read grew up with the Protestant ethic of self-reliance, individual responsibility, hard work, and biblical values bred into his very bones. He also venerated the Declaration of Independence, especially its central theme that man, as a created being, possesses rights endowed by the creator prior to government, which is instituted to secure for man the rights to life, liberty, and property and to provide equal justice under the law. Read stressed the moral and spiritual antecedents of such a political philosophy, with its natural economic corollary—free-market capitalism as taught by scholars from Adam Smith, through Menger and Bohm-Bawerk, to Mises, Hazlitt, and Friedrich Hayek.

Read was a charismatic and enthusiastic figure. He tended to shun debate, argumentation, and confrontation, preferring instead to win adherents through the recitation of striking illustrations, parables, and stories. A lifelong student, Read sought to improve his understanding of the philosophy of personal liberty (what Read called "the freedom philosophy") in an orderly and just society, and he strove continuously to expound his ideas with ever greater clarity and persuasiveness, using both the written and the spoken word.

By 1965, the various writings of the foundation had been published in twelve substantial volumes titled *Essays on Liberty.* A monthly journal, the *Freeman,* was launched in January 1956. FEE published some forty books under its own imprint and listed more than 100 other titles in its book catalog.

Between 1960 and 1980, the FEE Seminar Team conducted approximately 200 weekend seminars in all parts of the nation and, during the 1980s, in Canada and Mexico as well. In the summer months, week-long schools—targeted to high school, under-graduate, or graduate students—are held on the Irvington campus.

Subsidiary activities at FEE have included the Bettina Greaves' Debate Program—a packet of materials dealing with a particular topic and made available to debate coaches; a clerical fellowship called The Remnant, launched in 1957 by Rev. Edmund A. Opitz of the FEE staff, which for twenty-five years sponsored a series of luncheons and seminars with leading conservative scholars in order to supply ideas to clergymen evaluating those governmental and business structures most compatible with their religious convictions; and the Nockian Society, begun in 1963 and operating anonymously from an office at FEE, which commemorated the editor of the old *Freeman* (1920–24), Albert Jay Nock. The society has also served as a clearinghouse for Nock material and helps to keep his books in print.

Today, under President Richard Ebeling, FEE continues many of the programs it started years ago: lectures at its headquarters in Irvington, New York, focus both on the history of classical liberalism and on current legislative initiatives. FEE offers teaching resources and lesson plans in economics for high school teachers and college professors. The *Freeman* publishes monthly, and the foundation sells and distributes books from such scholars as Ludwig von Mises, Frederic Bastiat, and FEE's founder, Leonard Read.

—EDMUND OPITZ

Further Reading

Hazlitt, Henry. "The Early History of FEE." *Freeman* 34, no. 3 (March 1984).

Read, Leonard. *The Free Market and Its Enemy.* Irvington-on-Hudson, N.Y.: Foundation for Economic Education, 1965.

———. *The Love of Liberty.* Irvington-on-Hudson, N.Y.: Foundation for Economic Education, 1975.

See also: Freeman; Harper, Floyd A. "Baldy"; Hazlitt, Henry; Mises, Ludwig von; Read, Leonard E.

foundations, conservative

Philanthropic organizations devoted to propagating conservative principles such as limited government, a free enterprise system, individual choice, and traditional values helped to fund the people and ideas that laid the groundwork for the Reagan Revolution and the 1994 Republican takeover of the House of Representatives. Conservative foundations did this by supporting conservative think tanks, conservative media, and conservative scholars. To the Left, such as professors Jean Stefancic and Richard Delgado, authors of a critical yet admiring book, *No Mercy: How Conservative Think Tanks and Foundations Changed America's Social Agenda* (1996), conservative foundations funded "the vast right-wing conspiracy" that sought to bring down President Bill Clinton and that continues to dominate American politics.

Conservative foundations have invested their money in conservative think tanks and other organizations as a means to create a conservative infrastructure. This is in sharp contrast to liberal foundations such as Ford and Rockefeller, which have focused their energies and resources on large-scale national and international projects. This difference in emphasis stems (a) from the in-hospitality of academia to conservative scholars and their ideas, which has forced conservatives to create alternative intellectual centers, and (b) from the disparate funding available to the Left and Right. Thus, while the Ford Foundation has roughly $14 billion in assets, the three largest conservative foundations combined have less than $1 billion. Thanks perhaps to their success in creating viable foundations with strong endowments, conservative foundations also began to fund social projects by the late 1990s, mostly at the grass-roots level and with faith-based components.

Former treasury secretary William Simon may have played the most significant role in creating the conservative counter-establishment of which foundations are such an important part. Simon was a wealthy businessman who was selected as president of the John M. Olin Foundation after he left the treasury department in 1977. In 1978, he published a bestseller, *A Time for Truth*, in which he called for the creation of a new set of institutions that would create a conservative counter-establishment. That year he cofounded the Institute for Educational Affairs, which in 1990 merged with the Madison Center (founded by Bill Bennett, Allan Bloom, and others in 1988) to form the Madison Center for Educational Affairs (which has since folded), the purpose of which was to create a network of conservative foundations and thinkers and to help fund and assist "alternative" conservative student newspapers on college campuses. The Intercollegiate Studies Institute bought the Collegiate Network in 1995. Simon's institute also established the Federalist Society, a national organization of conservative-leaning law students.

Although both the Left and the Right use the umbrella term "conservative foundations," the idea really conflates groups with often contradictory aims. The largest conservative foundations, such as the Sarah Scaife, Lynde and Harry Bradley, and John M. Olin Foundations, support a wide range of conservative think tanks and organizations that work in fields ranging from welfare reform to foreign policy and with ide-

ologies that range from traditional conservative to libertarian (although they sometimes restrict their funding of libertarian groups to traditional conservative issues such as welfare reform and deregulation). Others focus their energies in a more ideological manner or on a limited range of issues: the Reason, David H. Koch, and Claude R. Lambe foundations generally restrict their funding to libertarian groups and individuals that support mainstream conservative positions but also support positions that are anathema to many traditional conservatives, including restricting the armed forces to homeland security, cutting most restrictions on immigration, decriminalizing narcotics, and legalizing human cloning research. The Henry Salvatori Foundation tends to restrict its funding to educational groups or issues.

History has not been kind to philanthropic foundations created by conservative businessmen such as J. D. Rockefeller, Henry Ford, and Andrew Carnegie. Their foundations were ultimately taken over by people who disdained the sort of values that made the money that created the foundations. The most egregious example, of course, is the Carnegie Foundation for International Peace, which was once led by Alger Hiss, a liberal New Dealer and communist spy. The Ford Foundation moved so far to the Left that Henry Ford II, son of its founder, resigned from its board of directors in protest. To avoid such a painful eventuality, John M. Olin frequently told his staff that he would like the foundation to be shut down after his death and the loss of those whom he selected to lead it. Following Olin's death and the death in 2000 of his handpicked president, William Simon, the board of directors voted to liquidate the foundation's assets to conservative groups and disband by the end of 2005. Conservatives hope that the work done by foundations such as Olin in helping to train conservative leaders will mean that in the future, there will be no danger of conservative foundations being taken over by those who would turn them to the Left.

—ROBERT WATERS

See also: Simon, William; Olin Foundation; Scaife Foundations; Bradley, Lynde and Harry, Foundation; Reason Foundation; Koch Foundation

Francis, Samuel (1947–2005)

Samuel Francis, who died at age 57 in 2005, was an influential scholar of the thought of James Burnham, the former Trotskyite whose ideas laid the groundwork for neoconservative foreign policy. Francis subscribed to Burnham's "Machiavellian" analysis of political power as a clash among interest groups. But Francis went beyond the objective study of intergroup rivalry, taking as his own the cause of European Americans, particularly the descendants of America's founding peoples, the Anglo-Protestant "core" that once was identified with "Americanism."

A strong anticommunist and populist, Francis was one of the leading voices in the "New Right" movement of the late 1970s and early 1980s—an important contingent in the victory coalition of Ronald Reagan. His collection of essays, *Beautiful Losers: Essays on the Failure of American Conservatism* (1993), is of enduring value in understanding the shifting balance of power within what was once called "movement" conservatism—specifically, the decline of both libertarian and traditionalist strains of thought, and the growing institutional power of neoconservatism. Indeed, Francis was one of the first casualties in the increasingly bitter quarrels within the splintering American Right, losing his column in the *Washington Times* for his resistance to the legacy of the civil rights movement. Francis complained, with some justice, that he was simply holding fast to the editorial stances once taken in such mainstream publications as *National Review* in defense of

states' rights and the interests of America's (shrinking) majority culture against the demands of minority groups. Francis became an eloquent critic of globalist economics, affirmative action, and mass immigration. He supported the presidential candidacies of Patrick Buchanan and Ross Perot, seeing in them the rise of "Middle American radicals," a species of disaffected, natural conservative that found itself unrepresented by elite political movements.

For asserting that European Americans, as much as Asian, African, and Hispanic Americans, had a right to view themselves as a cohesive group with identifiable interests, Francis found himself marginalized and labeled as a "white nationalist." While he accepted that alarming designation, in fact Francis was a thinker obsessed not by race but by culture; without accepting its religious faith, Francis revered the Anglo-Protestant *ethnos* which had shaped America and strove to assert its continued leadership. This left Francis outside, and increasingly opposed to, a conservative movement that drew its politics from an expansive reading of the Declaration of Independence and sought to ground its polemics not in the defense of Western, Christian culture, but in the Enlightenment ideology of America's most prominent founders. Francis was a frequent contributor to *Chronicles,* the *American Conservative,* and Peter Brimelow's immigration reform Web site VDare.com.

—JOHN ZMIRAK

Further Reading

Francis, Samuel T. *America Extinguished: Mass Immigration and the Disintegration of American Culture.* Monterey, Va.: Americans for Immigration Control, 2002.

———. *Thinkers of Our Time: James Burnham.* 2nd ed. London: Claridge Press, 1999.

See also: *Burnham, James;* Chronicles; *paleoconservatism; managerial revolution; New Right*

Free Congress Foundation

In the 1960s and 1970s, union-controlled political action committees (PACs), such as the National Committee for an Effective Congress, held great sway in elections and policy. In response, in 1974 Paul Weyrich founded the Committee for the Survival of a Free Congress, meaning a Congress free to represent the public instead of special interests. Its roots are seen in its successor organization, founded by Weyrich in 1978, The Free Congress Research and Education Foundation, Inc., more often simply called the Free Congress Foundation (FCF).

A culturally conservative nonprofit research and education organization, Free Congress has for more than twenty years been training activists and disseminating information via print, broadcast, and other media. It has worked on a wide array of issues, military and civilian, foreign and domestic, economic and social, often in areas the Right has neglected or not widely recognized at the time. Today, Free Congress focuses on three main concerns.

The first of these is culture. Beginning in the late 1970s Free Congress was an important part of the effort to awaken the conservative movement to the relative importance of culture, as opposed to economics or the Soviet threat. In the 1990s, it began to focus on the cultural dangers posed by political correctness, which it regarded as Marxism translated from economic into cultural terms. More recently, the foundation has hosted discussions on duplicating the homeschooling movement's successful "separation" approach in other fields of cultural conflict.

The second concern is privacy. Many conservatives are inclined to give law enforcement a free hand when it asks for expanded authority for eavesdropping, wiretapping, database collection and gathering, and many also tend to approve of the idea of national identity cards. Free Congress, on the other hand, regards much of this as at odds with Americans' constitutionally protected liberties. The foundation has formed a unique left-center-right coalition of organizations to resist and reverse this trend toward increasing governmental and technological intrusion into citizens' lives.

The third concern is the federal judiciary. Free Congress has worked toward the goal of a federal bench composed of judges who practice judicial restraint. With a comprehensive database of federal judges, a research team investigating the background and writings of judicial nominees, and a large coalition of assembled organizations whose grassroots members can help block or advance a judicial nominee, Free Congress believes that it serves as a crucial point organization whose success in the "judges war" will advance liberty for all and enable conservatives to accomplish their goals through the legislative process.

—WILLIAM LIND

Further Reading

Lind, William S., and William H. Marshner, eds. *Cultural Conservatism: Theory and Practice.* Washington, D.C.: Free Congress Foundation, 1991.

See also: judicial activism; political action committees; Weyrich, Paul M.

free trade

The term "free trade" refers to the exchange of money, goods and services across political barriers without restrictions, or in other words, the extension of the concept of the "market" across national boundaries.

The term "market" refers to a process by which production of goods and services follows paths where production best serves the most pressing needs of consumers. In the free world, the market requires an economy based on private ownership of the means of production to best employ the division of labor in society. A "free market"— that is, a market economy neither centrally planned nor hampered by centralized regulations—seeks to guide the command of the means of production into the hands of those private entrepreneurs who are able to use these means most effectively to satisfy the most pressing needs of consumers. The consumers are made sovereign, as it were, since their decisions to purchase or not to purchase determine the profits and losses of entrepreneurs. A dynamic system of "market prices" therefore emerges in such a system. In a market free from barriers and restrictions to entrepreneurial and consumer decisions, the market price best represents the informational relationship between what the consumers want and the means to satisfy the most pressing of those needs.

Restrictions and barriers placed on consumer and entrepreneurial decisions distort the informational content of the market price. The result is a decline in the efficiency of the market to provide for the needs and wants of consumers. Socially, the effect is a decline in the accumulation of capital goods and a decrease in wealth and well-being generally. To advocates of a free market, consumer decisions work best to increase the wealth and well-being of everyone whom the market serves.

Free trade between nations seeks to eliminate barriers and restrictions to the decisions of consumers and entrepreneurs across national boundaries. The effect is a widening of the division of labor, where production is steered onto paths across political barriers to better serve the most pressing needs of the sovereign consumers of all nations. In sum, free trade seeks globally to enfranchise the consumer. In the West, the recent trend toward globalized markets reflects the desire to extend to as many nations

and peoples as possible the wealth of the free world.

The economic policy of free trade contrasts with protectionist policies that use trade restrictions to stimulate or protect domestic production. Historically, the ruling dynasties of Renaissance Europe understood the simple truth that economic activity is not only a source of domestic well-being, but also a source of real political power among ruling regimes in competition for international primacy. In Europe from the sixteenth through the eighteenth centuries, kings and emperors, intent on establishing their primacy in international politics, increasingly exercised government control over trade and industry. Mercantilism was not so much an economic theory as it was a political conception of a regime's capacity to threaten and make war. According to this conception, a regime increased its strength by achieving a preponderance of exports over imports across its borders. Rulers and parliaments believed the wealth of nations depended mainly upon the possession of gold and silver, accumulated chiefly by a favorable balance of exports over imports with colonies and other nations. They considered colonial exploitation a legitimate and indispensable means to provide the fatherland with precious metals and raw materials upon which domestic industry depends to create exports.

Ruling regimes exercised mercantilist policies of strict control over foreign trade to achieve domestic wealth at the expense of other nations over whom they intended to establish a primacy in international politics. Their very success at stimulating domestic industry and obtaining colonies soon gave rise to opposing pressures. Mother countries used their colonies like supply depots and often forbade their trade with other nations. Politically, the American Revolution may be seen as a reaction against the mercantilism of the British Crown and Parliament. Intellectually, François Quesnay and the Physiocrats in France began a reaction against mercantilist policies, and the classical economists Adam Smith, David Ricardo and J. S. Mill argued for a century in Britain that all nations would share in the wealth in real goods brought by free trade. In *The Wealth of Nations* (1776), Smith argued that the individual interests of the mass of market participants work like an *invisible hand* to increase the wealth and well-being of all.

Economic arguments for protection take three main forms. The oldest is the infant industry argument. Advocates of protection maintain that foreign competition, matured by years of activity, holds advantages that must be reduced or eliminated by import tariffs or trade quotas. Other arguments advocate the protection of domestic industry from dumping. Foreign suppliers may wish to provide domestic markets with plentiful imports at prices significantly lower than domestic prices. The intent is to drive domestic suppliers out of a market that foreign suppliers may then dominate without competition. Still other arguments take the form of national defense. These protectionists point to domestic dependence on foreign sources for essential raw materials and finished goods that might become unavailable in times of national crisis.

Advocates of economic globalization contend that the move toward international modernization and free trade will extend to all nations the wealth and well-being of the free world. Many disagree, arguing that the benefits will not outweigh the costs. Concerning the issue of equality, some argue that globalization tends to increase inequality both within and between nations. Indeed, a move toward meritocratic organization of a national economy favors the educated and the able with wealth and advancement. The Chinese equality of incomes achieved in the 1970s will not survive her advance toward modernization, for meritocratic forces are no less elite than those of dynasty or the strong arm. Politically, capital flow across national borders perpetuates power relationships as the ownership of many national assets falls into foreign hands.

Religious and cultural critics advance a different series of arguments that work against the case for free trade. Hilaire Belloc and G. K. Chesterton complained of the spiritual poverty that industrialized England was inflicting on the British character. In the American South, the Southern Agrarians complained that northern industrialization was creating a spiritual emptiness in the post-Reconstruction South and that the modern industrial city begets a wholly different sort of Southern citizen incongruous with those who populated rural farming communities. Agrarians like Allen Tate and John Crow Ransom mourned the loss of the self-reliance and independence that broadly distributed communities of landholding citizens championed, and in which agriculture was the leading vocation.

In international relations theory, Samuel Huntington of Harvard University has revived the argument for *international primacy*. Like the European mercantilists, he recalls the simple truth that economic activity is a source of real political power. According to Huntington, in the present era it matters more than ever which state holds primacy in the international system. One needs only to consider what alternative distributions of power would have meant to the twentieth century. Moreover, in a world where direct military action between competing states and civilizations has become less probable, economic power has now become the determining factor that will form or maintain the primacies and subordinations of the new century. Western primacy has lent prestige to the liberal ideals of liberty, equality, democracy, and private property throughout the world. An alternative distribution of economic primacy might mean for the coming century a dispensation of prestige less favorable to those ideals that Westerners cherish. Benjamin Barber of Rutgers University also has argued that the present trend is producing a global consumer culture that is unlikely to be democratic.

—WILLIAM FUNDERBURK

Further Reading

Barber, Benjamin R. *Jihad vs. McWorld.* New York: Times Books, 1995.

Hayek, F. A. von. *Individualism and Economic Order.* Chicago: University of Chicago Press, 1948.

Huntington, Samuel P. *The Clash of Civilizations and the Remaking of World Order.* New York: Simon & Schuster, 1996.

Mises, Ludwig von. "The Sovereignty of the Consumer." In *Planning for Freedom and Sixteen Other Essays and Addresses.* South Holland, Ill.: Libertarian Press, 1980.

See also: Austrian school of economics; conservatism; Friedman, Milton; Haberler, Gottfried; Hamilton, Alexander; Hayek, Friedrich A. von; Hutt, William H.; liberalism, classical; libertarianism; Mises, Ludwig von; protectionism; Rothbard, Murray; supply-side economics

Freeman

Historian George Nash wrote that the magazine the *Freeman* (also known as *Ideas on Liberty*), along with the Intercollegiate Studies Institute, the Foundation for Economic Education (FEE), and the Mont Pelerin Society, deserved major "credit for giving 'classical liberalism' some influential coherence as a movement." Though the *Freeman*'s circulation was never terribly large, the influence of this monthly journal of ideas cannot be overstated.

Founded in 1950, the *Freeman*'s name was a nod to an earlier publication run by Albert J. Nock in the 1920s and Frank Chodorov in the 1930s. Drawing on the idea that "economic freedom, as embodied in the free market, is the basic institution of a liberal society," this new publication dedicated itself to promoting notions of individual freedom and traditional liberalism. Chodorov also edited the new incarnation of the *Freeman* after FEE took over the magazine in the mid-1950s and merged it with its house journal, *Ideas on Liberty.*

The magazine was originally edited by legendary journalists John Chamberlain and Henry Hazlitt, and it boasted an all-star cast of regular contributors: F. A. Hayek, Ludwig von Mises, Wilhelm Röpke, James Burnham, William F. Buckley Jr., and Leonard Read wrote frequently. Just about every other major classical liberal thinker could be found in the pages of the *Freeman.* Indeed, its roll call of contributors over the years reads like a *Who's Who* in the American conservative movement.

In contrast to *Human Events* and *National Review*, both of which focused on politics and the current topics of the day, the *Freeman*, from a slightly more distanced position, helped flesh out the evolving conservative position on a host of topics by concentrating on basic tenets and first principles, which were conveyed in layman's terms. Among its greatest accomplishments was giving Mises and Hayek a forum, thereby helping to introduce the Austrian school of economics to American readers.

The magazine followed Henry Hazlitt's lead in how it approached the subjects it covered. The publication's longtime managing editor, Paul Poirot, wrote in 1996 that the

Freeman "consistently and continuously has stood against the fallacies and clichés of politics, not by bitter denunciation, but by reasoned and attractive explanations of the better way of limited government, private ownership, voluntary exchange, moral behavior, and self-improvement." The spirit of Hazlitt's *Economics in One Lesson* (1946) would infuse every issue of *The Freeman*.

Ironically, as the ideas the magazine has championed have been more widely adopted, in recent years the magazine has lost much of its standing. The *Freeman*, like the *American Mercury* or *Saturday Evening Post*, is known to many only for once having been an influential journal. In a move to generate interest in the publication (and to avoid connotations with the notorious freemen movements in the western United States), the Foundation for Economic Education changed the magazine's name to *Ideas on Liberty* in 2000. The change was unpopular with some, however, who saw it as a concession to these movements, and by 2004 the foundation had restored the journal's original title, retaining *Ideas on Liberty* as a subtitle.

—MAX SCHULZ

Further Reading

Nash, George H. *The Conservative Intellectual Movement in America since 1945*. Wilmington, Del.: Intercollegiate Studies Institute, 1996.

See also: Austrian school of economics; Chamberlain, John; Chodorov, Frank; Foundation for Economic Education; Hazlitt, Henry; liberalism, classical

French Revolution

The French Revolution was a political upheaval of global significance that, during the last decade of the eighteenth century, ended the ancien régime in France, ushered in the modern era, and, for some historians, suggested the paradigm of modern revolution.

It is hard to overstate the impact of the French Revolution on the modern world in general and on Western civilization in particular. Between the meeting of the Estates General in May 1789 and the rise of Napoleon Bonaparte in November 1799, French revolutionaries attempted to turn France and Europe upside down. In their own country, they succeeded in abolishing feudal privileges, establishing a republic, executing their king, and launching total war. Abroad they brought church-state relations to a crisis and unleashed hitherto untapped sources of nationalism throughout the Continent.

Because of the destructive consequences of the upheaval, many American conservatives tend to look askance at the French Revolution, regarding it as an essentially liberal or radical event. But the Revolution encompassed such a variety of ideas, institutions, personalities, and events that it is difficult to characterize the upheaval in summary fashion. Indeed, when one praises or blames "the French Revolution," it is well to specify which particular ideas, individuals, or events of the Revolution one has in mind.

For convenience, the French Revolution and the crucial events leading up to it may be divided into four major phases.

(1) The proximate cause of the Revolution lay in the conflict that arose between the most elite elements in French society (the monarchy and the aristocracy) over taxes. When France's defeat in the Seven Years' War (1756–63) left the nation deeply in debt, King Louis XV tried to raise revenues. He was stymied, however, by nobles in a number of provincial *parlements* (courts) that declared the taxes illegal. During the ensuing struggle, these aristocratic *parlements* set themselves up as the voice of the nation, defending French liberties against the illegal and absolutist claims of the monarchy. The nobles' struggle at this point was conservative in the sense that their aim was to restore ancient

liberties that had been usurped by the crown. The nobles also took their lead from Montesquieu's influential *Spirit of the Laws* (1748), which argued that one of the political functions of their order was to assert freedom against any unwarranted usurpations on the part of the monarchy.

In 1787, the conflict deepened when an Assembly of Notables refused to approve Louis XVI's request for new taxes. The Assembly claimed that the only institution that had the right to approve taxes was the Estates General, which had not met since 1614. Royal absolutism was now effectively crippled in the very country of its origin, and Louis reluctantly agreed to convoke the Estates General for the first time in 175 years. The First Estate (the clergy), the Second Estate (the nobility), and the Third Estate (everyone else) were called to meet at Versailles in May 1789. The reformation of the governance of France was clearly afoot.

(2) The Revolution per se began when the Third Estate refused to sit as a separate order within the Estates General. Like the nobles, the middle-class professionals and businessmen who made up the Third Estate had copious grievances over the way they were taxed. But they also wanted more local control of government, unified weights and measures, a freer press, and equality of rights among the king's subjects. They had watched the American experiment with economic and political freedom and, influenced by Enlightenment ideas, were eager to reform France. The decisive breakdown of the medieval Estates General occurred on June 17, 1789, when the Third Estate, impatient with foot-dragging on the part of clergy and nobles, declared itself the National Assembly of all France. Ten days later, Louis reluctantly accepted the National Assembly's claims for itself. Had the Revolution stopped then, the government of France would nevertheless have been transformed, since government by privileged orders had been abolished.

But new events pressed the Revolution further. The storming of the Bastille prison and periodic food riots reflected the unrest of the populace in Paris. In response to these crises, many churchmen and nobles in the National Assembly renounced their feudal rights, dues, and tithes during the dramatic evening of August 4, 1789. Thereafter, all French citizens were equal before the law. Then, on August 27, the Assembly issued the *Declaration of the Rights of Man and Citizen*, proclaiming that all men were "born and remain free and equal in rights."

Over the next two years, the National Assembly set about restructuring France within the framework of a constitutional monarchy, a largely unregulated economy, and equality before the law. Moreover, up to 1792 the legislators, wary of the turbulent masses, eschewed social equality and extensive democracy. But Parisians and peasants occasionally rioted and tried to radicalize the course of the Revolution, with halting success. It was during this period that Edmund Burke composed his famous *Reflections on the Revolution in France* (1790), condemning the violence of the unruly crowds and the reorganization of an ancient country with ancient traditions along rationalistic lines.

(3) By mid-1792, the Revolution was in danger of being undermined from a number of quarters. Many priests resented the anti-clerical Civil Constitution of the Clergy they had been forced to sign, since it transformed the Roman Catholic Church in France into a branch of the secular state; numerous émigrés who had settled along the borders of France had tried to foment counter-revolution; workers resented the fact that their associations were outlawed; and war against Austria and her allies led to inflation and persistent food shortages. In the public's view, the royal family's putative support for the constitutional monarchy was given the lie by their unsuccessful attempt to flee the country. Thereafter, King Louis

XVI and Queen Marie Antoinette remained under house arrest in Paris until their execution in 1793.

It was in this topsy-turvy milieu that the more radical groups in the legislature grew confident in their bid for power. Eventually the group known as the Jacobins, by allying themselves to the Parisian lower middle-class (the *sans-culottes*), emerged as the rulers of France. Under the leadership of Robespierre, Danton, and Carnot, the Jacobins set up a dictatorship to deal with a host of domestic and foreign threats, and the Revolution entered its most radical phase. On August 23, 1793, Carnot issued a *levée en masse* that conscripted males into Europe's first citizen army. This was followed on September 17 by a maximum on prices that placated the *sans-culottes*. At the same time, the notorious Reign of Terror was unleashed to execute opponents of the Revolution, usually by means of the guillotine. Between the fall of 1793 and the summer of 1794, at least 20,000 to 25,000 political prisoners were murdered in quasi-judicial executions. Ironically, the majority of victims were neither aristocrats nor clergymen, but "disloyal" radicals, liberals, and peasants. Robespierre justified state-sponsored terrorism by declaring that in revolutionary times virtue requires terror. "Terror," he said, "is nothing but prompt, severe, inflexible justice; it is therefore an emanation of virtue."

The Reign of Terror was unloosed to crush any who dared to halt the advent of the new age. Inspired by the writings of Jean-Jacques Rousseau, Robespierre and fellow Jacobins sought to establish nothing less than a utopia, a "Republic of Virtue" that the world had never known. By means of extraordinary revolutionary legislation, the Jacobins tried to de-christianize France (the Cathedral of Notre Dame was declared to be a Temple of Reason), to found a new religious cult by legislative fiat (the Cult of the Supreme Being resembled Rousseau's call for a civic religion), to issue a new calendar dating from the first day of the French Republic, to suppress plays that were insufficiently republican, to rename streets to bolster egalitarian images, to copy the dress of the Roman Republic, and to stamp out prostitution, which was supposedly endemic in decadent aristocratic societies.

In advocating and enforcing such extreme measures, Robespierre and his fellow Jacobins were among the first apostles of secular ideologies that, in the name of humanity, would bring so much suffering to Europe and the world during the next two centuries. Never before had Western civilization seen a nation take such measures to compel conformity at home and organize for total war abroad.

(4) The most radical phase of the Revolution subsided when Robespierre himself was arrested and executed in July 1794. The Thermidorian Reaction that followed dismantled the machinery of Jacobin terror but at the same time unleashed "the white terror," in which many former revolutionaries were executed. Thermidorians also repealed the ceiling on prices, reaffirmed property rights, set up a new constitutional republic, and tolerated Catholic services once again in France.

Order was not yet secured, however. Numerous food riots in Paris gave rise to a revolutionary movement led by Gracchus Babeuf. Babeuf was arrested, tried, and guillotined, and his movement came to naught—for the time being. To secure order, the Directory that ruled France between 1795 and 1799 grew increasingly dependent on the army. It was this dependence that gave Napoleon his window of opportunity in the fall of 1799 to establish a dictatorship over France, for all practical purposes ending the Revolution. As historian Herbert Butterfield points out, the Revolution that began with the liberal "principles of 1789" ended by creating government mechanisms "more dreadful than any of the absolute monarchs had had at their command for the repression of the individual, inaugurating a type of polity more formidable as an organ of power than ancient feudalisms and ill-jointed dynastic systems could ever have hoped to achieve." Such is one of the ironies of the French Revolution.

What was America's response to events in France? Many observers in Europe believed that the American revolutionaries had wittingly or unwittingly inspired the French upheaval. Edmund Burke's ideological opponent, Richard Price, claimed that one of Benjamin Franklin's great honors was to have contributed to bringing about the Revolution in France. Nevertheless, reactions among prominent Americans to the French Revolution varied considerably. Jefferson, who was in Paris in 1789 as minister to France, was a partisan of the Revolution from the start. He welcomed the reforms of the National Assembly and prophesied on July 12, 1789, "Should this revolution succeed, it is the beginning of the reformation of the governments of Europe." Subsequent events did not seem to halt his enthusiasm. With each radical turn of events, Jefferson endorsed the Revolution. It was only many years later, when corresponding with Adams, that Jefferson admitted that he was disturbed by the excesses of the French Revolution and Napoleon.

The initial response of John Adams, on the other hand, was to "rejoice with trembling." He was skeptical from the outset, and as the Revolution grew more radical, Adams became more doubtful of its goals and merits. Writing in April 1790, Adams recognized that the French Enlightenment had contributed much more to the Revolution than had Anglo-American traditions, and confessed: "I know not what to make of a republic of thirty million atheists. . . . Too many Frenchmen, after the example of too many Americans, pant for equality of persons and property. The impracticality of this, God Almighty has decreed, and the advocates for liberty who attempt it, will surely suffer for it."

As early as 1791, Adams's eldest son, John Quincy Adams, published (under the name of "Publicola") a series of articles in which he exposed the fallacies and vagaries of the French political reformers. The young Adams had attended school in Paris, and his essays attracted considerable attention in Europe and the United States.

The legacy of the French Revolution still evokes considerable comment among conservative scholars, especially since Marxist interpretations of the upheaval, dominant from the 1930s to the 1960s, are being challenged and are everywhere in retreat. Reductionist explanations that see the Revolution solely in terms of class conflict no longer obtain. More recent interpretations of the French Revolution avoid economic determinism and are effecting, to quote historian Stephen Tonsor, "one of the most important revisionist historical efforts of our time." Scholars today are rediscovering the Revolution's political and cultural facets that fascinated the writers of earlier generations, such as Edmund Burke, Thomas Carlyle, Alexis de Tocqueville, Hippolyte Taine, and Augustin Cochin.

Furthermore, conservatives tend to see the Revolution as a source of much that has gone awry in post-1789 political theory and practice. In coming to terms with the Revolution's totalitarian impulses, however, it is important to recognize, as Tonsor insists, that the ideological substratum of the Terror was laid long before the outbreak of revolution in 1789. "For nearly a century the heirs of Hobbes, Louis XIV, and, more recently, Rousseau, had been preparing a revolution that would usher in a centralized and autocratic state, govern in the name of the people, deny any transcendent purpose to man's existence, and create a political world based upon a thoroughgoing equality. In short, the . . . intellectual groundwork for the French Revolution had been laid for a long time." Thus, any effort to understand this world-historical event must be seen in the larger perspective of modernity.

—GLEAVES WHITNEY

Further Reading

Brinton, Crane. *A Decade of Revolution, 1789-1799.* New York: Harper & Row, 1963.

Furet, François. *Interpreting the French Revolution.* Translated by Elborg Forster. Cambridge: Cambridge University Press, 1981.

———, and Mona Ozouf, eds. *A Critical Dictionary of the French Revolution.* Translated by Arthur Goldhammer. Cambridge, Mass.: Belknap Press, 1989.

Schama, Simon. *Citizens: A Chronicle of the French Revolution.* New York: Vintage, 1989.

Tonsor, Stephen, ed. *Reflections on the French Revolution: A Hillsdale Symposium.* Washington, D.C.: Regnery, 1990.

See also: Adams, John; Burke, Edmund; conservatism; Enlightenment; individualism; Jefferson, Thomas; Morris, Gouverneur; natural law; tradition

Friedman, Milton (1912–)

Milton Friedman is the father of the modern Chicago school of economics. From 1946, when he joined the University of Chicago faculty, until he retired in 1977, Friedman was the intellectual leader of those Chicago economists who challenged postwar theories that called for large and active government. The Chicago school of economics arguably forms the core of the classical liberal, or free market, strand of American conservatism. It is distinguished by the application of price theory to economic policy issues, the integration of theory with institutional and factual detail, and the use of monetary theory to explain business cycles.

Friedman began his career at a turning point in American history. The Great Depression was a fresh memory that had shaken confidence in the ability of free market capitalism to provide stability and prosperity. American and European intellectuals increasingly looked to socialism in search of a more productive and humane economic system. Economists embraced Keynesian macroeconomic theory, which subordinated monetary policy to fiscal policy. The U.S. government initiated a broad array of tax-cum-subsidy and regulatory programs during the Depression and World War II.

In this postwar and post-Depression setting, Friedman's views were not conservative in any literal sense, but rather radically liberal, because he placed a high value on individual liberty and believed the primary role of the state should be to protect liberty. Friedman joined other liberals, led by Friedrich von Hayek in 1947, in forming the Mont Pelerin Society. His views, then and now, are radical in two senses. Increasingly, a powerful and intrusive state apparatus has come to be taken for granted in the United States. As the title of one of his popular books (*Tyranny of the Status Quo*, 1984) indicates, Friedman offers a radical challenge to this status quo. His approach to public policy is also radical in the sense that Friedman uses economic analysis to uncover the roots of problems.

Friedman became the intellectual leader of the classical liberal strand of American conservatism in no small part because of his ability to engage both scholarly and lay audiences. The range of his writings is remarkably broad in an age of intellectual specialization. He is a preeminent scholar, having won two of the most coveted awards for scholarship in economics: the John Bates Clark Medal (1951), given biennially by the American Economic Association to an economist under forty years of age for contributions to economic knowledge, and the Nobel Prize (1976). He was also elected president of the

American Economic Association in 1967. Especially notable in scientific economics are his *Theory of the Consumption Function* (1957) and *A Monetary History of the United States* (with Anna J. Schwartz, 1963). Both of these works are marked by Friedman's characteristically thorough use of data to develop and test theories.

Friedman has written on a broad array of public policy issues, including rent control, exchange rates, education finance, monetary policy, and public assistance to the poor. He reached many lay readers through a regular column in *Newsweek* (1966–84), through the widely acclaimed book and television series *Free to Choose* (with Rose D. Friedman, 1980), and through frequent newspaper editorials.

Few of Friedman's writings are far removed from public policy issues. Always provocative and fiercely independent, Friedman has attracted passionate disciples and equally passionate critics. The publication of his Columbia University Ph.D. dissertation (*Income from Independent Professional Practice*, with Simon Kuznets, 1945) was held up for several years because of objections at the National Bureau of Economic Research, where he did the study, to conclusions about monopoly practices of the American Medical Association. His proposals for monetary and fiscal policy rules, first made in 1947, were intensely unpopular among economists and government officials confident in their ability to "fine tune" the U.S. economy. Friedman argued that the best of intentions were insufficient to overcome the deficiencies of knowledge and foresight necessary for fine-tuning. His and Anna Schwartz's argument in *A Monetary History* that inept monetary policy turned an ordi-

Milton Friedman

nary recession beginning in 1929 into the Great Depression was likewise provocative and controversial. They called into question two widely held beliefs: the Keynesian ideas that the Depression was caused by inherent recessionary instability in the private sector and that monetary policy is less powerful than fiscal policy.

Friedman brought together several strands of his public policy lectures and writings in his 1962 book, *Capitalism and Freedom*. This book became a classic apologia for competitive capitalism. He developed the theme that economic freedom, the freedom to make and spend one's income as one sees fit so long as one does not restrict others' freedom, is fundamentally important both as an end in itself and as a necessary condition for political freedom. With this precept and some simple but powerful economic theories, Friedman explored the role for government in a society dedicated to the preservation of freedom.

The economic analysis in *Capitalism and Freedom* consists of an unblinking application of economic principles concerning what are commonly called "market failures." There are two general classes of market failures. Externalities, or neighborhood effects, are instances where property rights are incomplete. Benefits or costs of activities fall on people who are not party to the activities. Since markets cannot flourish without clear and secure property rights, Friedman assigns to government the responsibility for establishing and protecting rights to property and for enforcing contracts. Government action is appropriate if it brings costs to bear on the people who take actions. Markets also fail to operate properly when there is a tendency toward concentration of economic power. So Friedman assigns to government the responsibility for preventing monopolies.

The course of American politics and public policy after *Capitalism and Freedom* produced more defeats than victories for Americans who favored the limited role for government that Friedman outlined. Milton and Rose Friedman continued the quest to persuade the American public of the virtues of competitive capitalism in two other popular and influential books and companion television series. In *Free to Choose* (1980), the Friedmans added explanations of why welfare state policies resist reform initiatives toward greater reliance on markets. In *Tyranny of the Status Quo* (1984) they developed this theme more fully, drawing on the record of the first two years of the Reagan presidency. They recommended Constitutional changes to break the "iron triangle" of groups receiving subsidies from welfare state programs, politicians who confer benefits on these groups at the expense of the broader population of consumers and taxpayers, and bureaucrats who administer the programs.

Milton Friedman's ability to identify the roots of public policy problems gives his writings an enduring immediacy. It also has allowed him to anticipate issues before they gather broad public attention. He wrote a classic critique of fixed but adjustable exchange rates ("The Case for Flexible Exchange Rates," 1953) at the very beginning of the Bretton Woods era, long before that system came apart from pressures of the type enumerated in Friedman's critique. He first advocated educational vouchers to improve primary and secondary education in 1955. A movement for this reform took shape beginning in the 1990s. Friedman's arguments in favor of a constant growth rate monetary policy rule had much to do with a reorientation of thinking about policy goals and strategy among economists and central bankers.

Friedman's public policy writings have been widely translated, providing a rationale for free markets and limited government to people around the world.

—J. Daniel Hammond

Further Reading

Butler, Eamonn. *Milton Friedman: A Guide to His Economic Thought.* New York: Universe, 1985.

Friedman, Milton. *The Essence of Friedman.* Edited by Kurt R. Leube. Stanford, Calif.: Hoover Institution Press, 1987.

———, and Rose D. Friedman. *Two Lucky People: Memoirs.* Chicago: University of Chicago Press, 1998.

Hirsch, Abraham, and Neil de Marchi. *Milton Friedman: Economics in Theory and Practice.* Ann Arbor, Mich.: University of Michigan Press, 1990.

Thornborrow, Nancy M. "Milton Friedman." In *Nobel Laureates in Economic Sciences: A Biographical Dictionary*, edited by Bernard S. Katz, 53–65. New York: Garland, 1989.

See also: capitalism; free trade; Keynesian economics; liberalism, classical; libertarianism; monetarist economics; Mont Pelerin Society; Road to Serfdom, The; supply-side economics

Frost, Robert (1874–1963)

In eleven books of poetry and miscellaneous other writings published between 1913 and 1962, Robert Frost established himself as the unofficial poet laureate of the United States. Four of his books won the Pulitzer Prize, and he received many other awards from literary organizations, colleges, and universities, as well as from Congress. During the last decade of his life, Frost became a well-known public figure through poetry readings, interviews, television appearances, and as a goodwill ambassador to Latin America, England, Israel, and the Soviet Union. Nevertheless, few Americans recognize that in his views on religion, politics, science, education, and the arts, and in his conception of human nature and the role of history in shaping society, Frost was an original and profound conservative thinker.

Distrustful of abstract labels, Frost never referred to himself as a conservative. He knew that such terms as *radical*, *liberal*, *conservative*, *reformer*, and *revolutionary* were often the basis of ideological systems, and ideology had no place in his philosophy. Fearing that misconceptions regarding these categories would be attributed to him, Frost once said that two lines from some early verses summed up his whole viewpoint: "I never dared be radical when young / For fear it would make me conservative when old."

A philosophical dualist, Frost regarded spirit and matter as the two basic elements of reality. Human nature itself was composed of spirit and matter, or body and soul. As for religion, science, art, politics, and history, each was a different form of revelation. They were metaphors aimed at illuminating the True, the Good, and the Beautiful for the mind of man. Though he belonged to no church or sect, Frost admitted to being "an Old Testament Christian." He accepted the Law of Moses in the Decalogue and believed justice between God and man, and justice between men, was paramount. He was highly critical, therefore, of those who sentimentalized Christ's teachings through doctrines like universal salvation that neglected justice not only in religion but in every aspect of man's life in society.

Frost greatly respected science and its contributions toward man's knowledge of the laws and operations of the universe. Scientists were to Frost among the "heroes" of modern civilization; their "revelations" proved the ability of man to penetrate and harness matter through the mind. But as a religious man and humanist, Frost also believed there were mysteries about both matter and spirit that were beyond the reach of science. And while the methods of the physical sciences applied to matter, they could not be applied with equal validity to human nature and society because man is more than a biological animal. There is a qualitative difference between matter and human nature, most evident in the religious, moral, intellectual, aesthetic, and social values recognized or created by man. Therefore, Frost believed, science could not shape the world toward utopian ends any more than could politics.

It was the function of poetry and the arts, Frost felt, to strive for the final synthesis and unity between spirit and matter. In fact, he defined poetry as the only way mankind has of "saying one thing and meaning another, saying one thing in terms of another." The revelations of art, as well as those of religion, transcend those of science by providing human values and meaning in the universe and in human affairs. Art's revelations are not merely of knowledge, but include insight and love; they involve not only recognition but also response, beginning in ecstatic aesthetic pleasure and ending in calm moral wisdom. Whereas science is like a prism of light cast on a particular point of nature to reveal its laws and operations, the arts are like the sun that shines on all alike, unleashing man's aesthetic and moral imagination upon the whole of creation.

In his social and political philosophy, Frost provided a powerful defense of the American republic through his criticism of attacks upon it by Marxists, international pacifists, and New Deal liberals. Against Marxist collectivism and the welfare state, Frost defended individual liberty as an end in itself. He rejected the rationalist politics of the Left and put his faith in the historical continuity of Western civilization, in the tested moral traditions of the Judeo-Christian religion, in classical liberal education, in the philosophical thought of such thinkers as Aristotle, Kant, Burke, and William James, and especially in the political philosophy of the founding fathers of the American republic. In his reverence for the American constitutional system, Frost was a strict constructionist.

Frost's strong opposition to Marxists and New Deal liberals appears in *A Further Range* (1936). His political conservatism, subtly muted in earlier poems, is starkly evident in his harsh treatment of the kind of sensibility and social consciousness behind New Deal programs that aimed at solving the problems of the Great Depression. *A Further Range* provoked scorn on the American political Left. Granville Hicks, Malcolm Cowley, Edmund Wilson, Richard P. Blackmur, and other Marxist and liberal critics heaped scorn on him for refusing to write poetry that supported revolutionary social and economic change. Frost's response, "It is not the business of the poet to cry reform," flew in the face of what many of his peers believed.

Frost not only refused to write propaganda, he satirized the very premises of New Deal programs. He showed contempt for Roosevelt's "brain trust," calling it "the guild of social planners." He attacked New Deal egalitarianism as a violation of justice between men in favor of mass mercy for the poor. He feared that egalitarianism would result in "a homogenized society," that compulsory benevolence would weaken and possibly destroy individual freedom. Frost clearly opposed everything and everybody that made persons rely more than was necessary upon somebody or something other than their own resources, integrity, and courage.

Frost's conservative religious, moral, and political convictions are most evident in

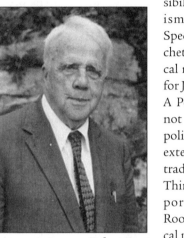

Robert Frost

his poems "The Death of the Hired Man," "A Masque of Reason," and "A Masque of Mercy," which explore the complex issues in what he called "the justice-mercy contradiction." In "The Black Cottage," Frost celebrated the ancient and recurring truths embedded in custom and tradition. He satirized the self-righteous spirit and social sensibility of modern collectivism in "A Considerable Speck." He described the archetypal American ideological revolutionary in "A Case for Jefferson." In "Build Soil: A Political Pastoral," Frost not only attacked the farm policies of the New Deal, but extended poetry's pastoral tradition into politics. "To a Thinker" is at once an ironic portrait of Franklin D. Roosevelt and a philosophical probing of the genius for willful self-deception of all politicians ambitious to play God. "A Lone Striker" is a criticism of industrial regimentation and an assertion of individual freedom and integrity. "New Hampshire" and "The Lesson for Today" are reflective poems on his general philosophy. "New Hampshire" celebrates individual self-sufficiency and pride in provincial and rural life and manners. "The Lesson for Today," in imitation of Horace, shows how the nature of man remains basically the same throughout history, so that "One age is like another for the soul," contrary to the ideology of progress.

In all of these poems, the subjects and themes are means to Frost's artistic ends. His poems on politics are not merely "vehicles of grievances" against the centralized state. Politics was for him simply a metaphor through which he dealt with far greater issues of culture and philosophy, such as the nature of man, the moral order of society, individual freedom and self-fulfillment, and the justice and mercy that transcend politics in the great "griefs" that afflict humanity.

—PETER J. STANLIS

Further Reading

Frost, Robert Lee. *Selected Poems.* New York: Henry Holt & Company, 1938.

———. *Selected Poems.* Edited by Hyde Cox and Edward Connery Lathem. New York: Holt, Rinehart & Winston, 1949.

Lentricchia, Frank. *Robert Frost: Modern Poetics and the Landscape of Self.* Durham, N.C.: Duke University Press, 1975.

Lynen, John F. *The Pastoral Art of Robert Frost.* New Haven, Conn.: Yale University Press, 1967.

Stanlis, Peter J. *Robert Frost: The Individual and Society.* Rockford, Ill.: Rockford College Press, 1973.

See also: New Deal; Stanlis, Peter J.

Fukuyama, Francis (1952–)

The publication of a sixteen-page essay titled "The End of History?" (*National Interest*, Summer 1989) transformed Johns Hopkins University political theorist Francis Fukuyama into one of America's foremost international relations thinkers. Developments in the Soviet Bloc soon made Fukuyama's work profoundly timely: it seemed to predict—certainly to explain—the momentous events of the coming months. His thesis, elaborated in *The End of History and the Last Man* (1992), was simple: the collapse of communism as a viable political system marked the complete victory of the Western ideal of liberal democracy, an ideal that fulfilled the History of man himself. In this interpretation, Fukuyama inserted the demise of communism into the conception of History formulated in Alexandre Kojève's interpretation of G. W. F. Hegel, who believed Napoleon's victory at the battle of Jena heralded the eventual triumph of democratic ideals of liberty and equality as the only rationally justifiable political system. This triumph would be the End of History, the end of struggles over how to order man's political life. Subsequent events, in Fukuyama's reading of Hegel, including fascism and communism, have merely been irrational detours and temporary obstacles to the inevitable fulfillment of History in liberal democracies across the globe, regimes recognizing the essential equality of all men.

The most frequent criticism leveled against Fukuyama—though not one often heard among conservatives—has been prudential: his triumphalism might lead to a complacency that neglects the hard work done to establish liberal democracy and the hard work that remains to bring its fruits to all men. He is insufficiently concerned with the great deeds of passionate believers in the equal rights of man, be they the American founders, the French revolutionaries, or the students in Tiananmen Square. Since the triumph of liberal democracy is inevitable, it needs no strident partisans.

Other lines of criticism attack not Fukuyama's means but his end, asking, in essence, "Does the global triumph of liberal democracy (i.e. Hegel's universal homogenous state) satisfy man as man?" The three most powerful critiques to take this approach center respectively on man's need for religion, culture, and *megalothymia* (the desire to be superior, rather than equal, to others), all of which are eroded by global liberal democracy. The first two of these criticisms are present in Samuel Huntington's 1993 "Clash of Civilizations" article (*Foreign Affairs*, Summer 1993), widely seen as a response to Fukuyama. Huntington argued for the enduring power of civilizations that embody different religions and cultures (the later encapsulating the unique history, language, traditions, and ethnicity of a people). The implication of his thought is that man is not satisfied to live in Fukuyama's universal homogeneous state; man desires to "live within a horizon" of a religion or national culture. The second and third critiques first emerged in a review accompanying Fukuyama's original article, in which Allan Bloom warned Fukuyama of the danger that "fascism has a future." Fascism here means, first, the jingoistic return to "national myths" (religious or otherwise) as a reaction to the homogenizing globalism that strips men of their unique cultures. Second, it means the radical affirmation of man's desire to excel others, to distinguish himself, especially through his triumph over the fear of death in his willingness to struggle. This last criticism of liberal democracy (namely, that it is the regime of the "last man") is present in Fukuyama's work as his own self-criticism of the End-of-History thesis and of Hegel; it is really Nietzsche's criticism, as Fukuyama admits.

Nevertheless, while Fukuyama recognizes the decisive power of the third critique (indeed, it is the one force he envisions bringing down the liberal democratic project, even and precisely from within), in his original work he indicates that passionate argument on its behalf is unnecessary: "While one can throw nature out with a pitchfork, it will come running back." That is, *megalothymia* is of the essence of man; every regime (even one devoted to equality), if it is to survive and excel (for it needs soldiers and statesmen, artists and philosophers), must eventually allow for *megalothymotic* types. However, in later works like *Our Post-Human Future* (2002), Fukuyama concludes that nature itself is under the most extreme threat: biotechnology, through neuropharmacology and genetic engineering, now enables the alteration of human nature, as seen already in the widespread availability of mood-altering drugs like Ritalin and Prozac. The former, in Harvey Mansfield's formulation, tempers the high spirits of boys, while the latter raises the low spirits of women. Both move toward creating new human beings content in the

universal homogenous state. Fukuyama now rightly awakens us to the danger of this project and urges us to resist.

—JOSHUA VANDIVER

Further Reading

Fukuyama, Francis. *The Great Disruption: Human Nature and the Reconstitution of the Social Order.* New York: Free Press, 1999.

———. *State-Building: Governance and World Order in the 21st Century.* Ithaca, N.Y.: Cornell University Press, 2004.

———. *Trust: The Social Virtues and the Creation of Prosperity.* New York: Free Press, 1995.

See also: progress; sociobiology

Fund for American Studies

The Fund for American Studies is an educational forum intended to inculcate college students with the values of "freedom, democracy, and a free-market economy." Based in Washington, D.C., the multimillion-dollar organization sponsors students to attend various programs, which in the past have featured such speakers as Gen. Colin L. Powell and Czech Prime Minister Václav Klaus. The Fund also places students in government and nongovernment internships and gives awards to other conservative groups.

Charles Edison, former secretary of the navy and governor of New Jersey, conceived the idea of the organization in the late 1960s in response to what he believed was widespread opposition to the system of American government. The organization commenced in 1970 after his death. Founding members William F. Buckley Jr., Dr. Walter H. Judd, David R. Jones, and Marvin Liebman named it the "Charles Edison Memorial Youth Fund." The name was changed to the Fund for American Studies in 1987 in accordance with Edison's wishes.

More than 5,000 students have attended the fund's programs, including the Engalitcheff Institute on Comparative Economic Systems; the Bryce Harlow Institute on Business and Government Affairs; the Institute on Political Journalism; and the International Institute for Political and Economic Studies. The fund publishes the *Teaching Freedom* series, which features lectures from its programs, as well as a newsletter. Not slowed after the death of its guiding spirit, David Jones, the organization now conducts its programs under the leadership of President Roger Ream and Chairman Randal Teague.

—MATTHEW BOWMAN

fundamentalism

Fundamentalism is both a national movement in American Protestantism with origins traceable to the Bible conference movement and interdenominational revival meetings of the late nineteenth century and a set of core beliefs central to conservative Protestant Christians.

Fundamentalism as a movement likely took its name from the publication between 1910 and 1915 of twelve booklets titled *The Fundamentals*, which defended the cardinal doctrines of the faith against the modernist onslaught of the World War I era. Most fundamentalists, then and now, believe not only in the absolute authority of the Bible and in the importance of evangelism, but in a complicated eschatological (end times) scheme known as dispensational premillennialism. A tension between these aspects of fundamentalist thought is provided by the degree to which fundamentalists adhere to *separatism*, the belief that a Christian must resist not only worldly personal conduct but the ecclesiastical taint of ecumenism, apostasy, and denominationalism.

Because of this tendency toward separatism, movement fundamentalists and "evangelicals," though in close kinship, are each reluctant to claim the other. "Fundamentalism," according to A. James Reichley, "is an extreme form of evangelicalism, all fundamentalists are evangelicals, but not all evangelicals are fundamentalists." Samuel Hill sees fundamentalists as more "truth-oriented" and evangelicals as more "conversion-oriented," suggesting that for the fundamentalist religion is something you *believe*, while for the evangelical religion is something you *get*.

Much of the confusion in definition has come about in the last fifty years or so with the rise of the "New Evangelicals." Before that time, or at least since the end of World War I, the contrast was stark. There were *fundamentalists*, those who held to the verbal plenary inspiration of the scriptures, and *modernists*, those who began to question all or part of the "old-time religion." Fundamentalists had varying styles, from the learned J. Gresham Machen of Westminster Seminary to revivalists like Billy Sunday, but all battled modernists. These fights included struggles for control in denominations and in seminaries, as well as in society at large. The precise character of the battle between modernists and fundamentalists differed by region. In the South, save the Scopes trial of 1925, fundamentalism reigned without furor through the vast reach of the Southern Baptist Convention. That is, most southern Christians were nominally fundamentalist but did not need to organize themselves into a militant movement. In the North the battle was clearer, as some fundamentalists separated from mainline denominations and others stayed to fight.

Then came Billy Graham. Graham cut a middle course. With Graham and others like him, evangelicals arose in the late 1940s, calling for adherence to doctrine but with more cooperation, more tolerance, and more of a social conscience than was typical of fundamentalism. Joel Carpenter suggests that the fundamentalist-evangelical tension magnified by Graham and others was caused by the paradox created by two phenomena present in early fundamentalism, a spirit of innovation that came from early revivalism, and the spirit of militancy that resulted from the modernist-fundamentalist controversy.

Because of these latent distinctions, assigning membership to fundamentalism in the early years of the twenty-first century can prove difficult. It is a task made even more complicated by the struggle among those who embrace the term, and by popular authors who use the term indiscriminately. For example, the late Bob Jones Jr., son of the founder of Bob Jones University, called himself a fundamentalist but consigned Rev. Jerry Falwell's more inclusive strain to the category "pseudo-fundamentalist." Falwell prefers the fundamentalist label as well, but somewhat less self-consciously, naming his ministry's now defunct journal the *Fundamentalist*, but joking that the best definition of a fundamentalist is "a Christian who is mad about something."

Some popular writers err on the other extreme, tending to fold all conservative Christians who support inerrancy of scripture into the fundamentalist camp, including Billy Graham, Jerry Falwell, Pat Robertson, the Southern Baptist Convention, the Presbyterian Church in America, the Lutheran Church Missouri Synod, Pentecostals, Operation Rescue, Jimmy Swaggart, Jim and Tammy Bakker, Donald Wildmon's American Family Association, and psychologist James Dobson. (One source even lists Amway distributors as fundamentalists.) The unifying factor here is not religion, but politics, for members of most all of these groups have lent support to the goals of Falwell's Moral Majority, Robertson's Christian Coalition, and their successors.

There is a reason for interchanging the religious and the political where fundamentalism is concerned. The Moral Majority's activism is credited with drawing enough born-again Christians (particularly Southern Baptists) away from Southern Baptist Jimmy Carter in 1980 to elect Ronald Reagan. Christian Right politics began in the wake of Supreme Court decisions outlawing school prayer and legalizing abortion, strengthening the long-held fundamentalist belief that government was becoming hostile to the faith. Time has done nothing to reverse fundamentalists' political inclinations. On election day 2000, a *CNN-Time* survey revealed that 80 percent of those identifying themselves as part of the religious Right (14 percent of voters) supported the Bush-Cheney ticket, while only 18 percent of such voters supported Al Gore. Republican politics and fundamentalism have bonded. Few recent treatments of fundamentalism fail to mention politics; some mention little else.

The three-volume scholarly *magnum opus* of Martin Marty is a comprehensive attempt to grapple with fundamentalism. He and his colleague Scott Appleby analyze the subject both broadly (as "fundamentalisms," which includes Islamic and Jewish fundamentalism) and narrowly (examining the various directions in which American Protestant fundamentalist activists have taken their movement). As Marty and others have written, fundamentalism in its broadest connotations is everywhere. Fundamentalist churches are the fastest growing in Protestantism, outpacing mainline denominations and building some of the largest congregations in the country, often with fellowship halls that resemble shopping malls. Denominationally, fundamentalists have moved to take over (or perhaps merely solidify their hold) the Southern Baptist Convention and others. Educationally, fundamentalists have worked all fronts, establishing numerous church-administered private academies and demanding equal treatment and equal access in the public schools as well as the option to home school. Pat Robertson's televangelist empire once included the Family Channel. He also founded the American Center for Law and Justice (a conservative ACLU), and achieved working control of several state Republican parties through the Christian Coalition.

No matter how fundamentalism is defined, the defenders of the old-time religion—those who bear the mantle of the authors of *The Fundamentals*—are certain to have a continued impact on religion and society, even in what has been called the "post-Christian" era.

—ORAN P. SMITH

Further Reading

Carpenter, Joel. *Revive Us Again: The Reawakening of American Fundamentalism*. New York: Oxford University Press, 1997.

Marty, Martin E., and R. Scott Appleby, eds. *Fundamentalisms Observed*. Chicago: University of Chicago Press, 1991.

———, eds. *Fundamentalisms and Society: Reclaiming the Sciences, the Family and Education*. Chicago: University of Chicago Press, 1993.

———, eds. *Fundamentalisms and the State: Remaking Polities, Economies and Militance*. Chicago: University of Chicago Press, 1993.

Reichley, A. James. *Religion in American Public Life*. Washington, D.C.: Brookings Institution, 1985.

Smith, Oran P. *The Rise of Baptist Republicanism*, New York: New York University Press, 1997.

See also: Bryan, William Jennings; creationism; Falwell, Jerry; Hodge, Charles; Machen, J. Gresham; Moral Majority; Protestantism, evangelical; Robertson, Marion Gordon "Pat"; Scopes trial

fusionism

Traditionalist and libertarian ideas largely dominated the American Right's agenda in the era immediately after World War II. Fusionism is the term applied to the attempt during the 1950s and 1960s to reconcile the philosophical gap that existed between these strands of "conservative thought." Traditionalists emphasized the importance of religious and moral beliefs in the quest for virtue. Libertarians stressed the importance of reason and freedom. There was unified opposition on the Right against the expanding welfare state. However, traditionalists often were (and are) willing to use state power to attain their goals—which was (and is) anathema to libertarians. Frank Meyer, a leading figure of the American Right in the early post–World War II era, led the attempt to reconcile these divergent strands of conservative thought.

The early postwar Right reflected several important influences. First, critiques of statist policies by libertarian economists provided intellectual support for the decentralized market economy. The Right was highly critical of the collectivism of the Roosevelt New Deal, and especially benefited from contributions of the Austrian School of Economics. Ludwig von Mises in *Socialism* (1936) proved that central direction dooms an economy to failure. F. A. Hayek in *The Road to Serfdom* (1944) showed that central planning was inconsistent with individual liberty. Henry Hazlitt, Wilhelm Röpke, and Chicago Nobel laureate economist Milton Friedman also made notable contributions.

Anticommunism, including opposition to Soviet imperialism, was a second critical factor shaping the Right. Communism appeared to pose a unique threat to most on the Right, as the Iron Curtain of collectivism descended on Eastern Europe and the specter of domination by the Soviet Union haunted the West. The publication of Whittaker Chambers's book *Witness* (1952) was a defining moment in the anticommunist movement in the United States, revealing that communist views and practices were implacably hostile to the very foundations of a free society. *Witness* provided a graphic account of Chambers's transformation from a communist agent into a dedicated enemy of collectivism. In 1955, when William F. Buckley Jr. founded *National Review*, a periodical that became especially influential among traditionalist conservatives, Buckley considered the Soviet threat so important that he was willing to accept the idea that Big Government would be necessary in the struggle against collectivism.

The historical foundations of society, the "permanent things" that traditionalist conservatives emphasize, were a third important influence on the postwar conservative movement. Richard Weaver's *Ideas Have Consequences* (1948) and Russell Kirk's *The Conservative Mind* (1953) were especially influential. Weaver was a critic of moral relativism and mass culture, and Kirk echoed Weaver in holding that change does not imply progress. Kirk contributed a set of first principles that reflected the conservatism of Edmund Burke. This set of integrated beliefs, traceable to biblical antiquity, addressed the religious and moral concerns of traditionalists. For Kirk, the classical and Christian virtues were not incompatible with a decentralized market economy; indeed, he affirmed that private property was a moral and social good.

Libertarians and traditionalists found a significant amount of common ground in the postwar Right. However, traditionalists were clearly more concerned with ethical than economic issues and emphasized the moral implications of collectivism for traditional institutions and practices. Libertarians, on the other hand, stressed the importance of economic freedom and individual liberty and emphasized statism's inevitable infringement upon the individual's right to choose, whatever the area of choice.

An ideological rift between traditionalists and libertarians threatened the conservative movement in the 1950s. F. A. Hayek's *The Constitution of Liberty* (1960), which made a formidable case for limited government, a free market, and the impersonal rule of law, reflected this tension. Hayek emphasized that knowledge is subjective and highly specific to time and place. Thus, decentralized market signals play a uniquely important role in the discovery, coordination, and transmission of information throughout society. However, Hayek criticized conscious planning on utilitarian grounds rather than appealing to universal and immutable truths. Moreover, in a postscript titled "Why I Am Not a Conservative," Hayek concluded the book with a forceful rejection of conservatism. He criticized traditionalist conservatives for being willing to use state power to achieve their goals.

The ideological differences between traditionalists and libertarians appeared irreconcilable as they debated the relative merits of freedom and tradition in the early 1960s. Libertarians charged that traditionalists were not mainly interested in limiting statism but were seeking to use state power to promote the conservative agenda. On the other hand, traditionalists maintained that libertarians paid too little attention to the foundations necessary for society to survive—foundations rooted in religious belief, including order, morality, truth, and virtue.

Would it be possible to develop a conservative tent under which libertarian and traditionalist philosophies could be united in a single political theory? Frank Meyer, a Christian libertarian, led the movement to find such a common ground. Meyer argued that the differences were not fundamental because they shared a common tradition and were united against a common enemy, collectivism. Indeed, the alleged inconsistency between freedom and reason (emphasized by libertarians) and tradition and virtue (stressed by traditionalists) was false. The history of the West has been a history of reason operating within tradition, and conservatism should embrace both. Moreover,

Meyer believed that James Madison and the other founding fathers already had largely reconciled the two overriding principles, freedom and authority, in debates over the U.S. Constitution.

Furthermore, Meyer argued, "social engineering" is anathema to all on the Right, whether they place paramount importance on freedom or virtue. In either case, emphasis is placed on the importance of the individual. Meyer, a former communist, found the welfare state incompatible with both freedom and virtue. He thought that most Americans shared his views concerning freedom, virtue, and anticommunism.

Meyer explained his fusionist views in numerous articles and, most notably, in his book *In Defense of Freedom: A Conservative Credo* (1962). Meyer shared with traditionalists the view that the achievement of virtue is ultimately the most important of problems; he shared with libertarians a concern for freedom. Meyer considered a free economy necessary for the preservation of freedom and freedom a prerequisite for a virtuous society. Moreover, unlike many traditionalists, he maintained that achievement of virtue is not a *political* problem because virtue cannot be secured through political means. Instead, the appropriate role of the state is to establish and maintain the conditions of freedom.

Meyer stressed that freedom implies *not* virtue but choice—the option to choose between virtue and vice. Unless people are free to be vicious they cannot be virtuous because no coerced action can be virtuous. Thus, any attempt to legislate virtue destroys the very freedom that the individual must have to seek the good.

Wilhelm Röpke, a German economist, also played an important role in the development of fusionist thought. Indeed, his book *A Humane Economy* (1960), was a model of fusionism. It combined a defense of economic freedom acceptable to many libertarians with a traditionalist defense of Christian humanism. Röpke, a critic of "modern mass society," emphasized the importance of family, church, communities, and tradition as the indispensable supports of a free society. In this view, individuals can "breathe the air of freedom" only to the extent that they are willing to bear the required burden of moral responsibility.

The fusionist movement only temporarily reduced tensions within the American Right. The yoking of cultural traditionalism, economic freedom, and an activist foreign policy never convinced many libertarians, such as Murray Rothbard. In the 1960s, fusionism lost much of its momentum, as stresses on the Right resulting from the Vietnam War mounted and an organized libertarian movement developed. Many of these libertarians were just as disdainful of traditionalist conservatives as they were of liberals.

The problems in uniting groups of the Right under a common tent are even more pronounced at the beginning of the twenty-first century. The Right now includes not only traditionalists and libertarians, but also neoconservatives, paleoconservatives, "nativists," antiabortionists, and the religious Right, among other groups. It is unlikely that any future philosophical alliance will be as successful as the earlier fusionist movement in reconciling the differences between these groups. First, differences between libertarians and other "conservatives" became more pronounced with the passage of time and therefore more difficult to reconcile. Second, some tension and conflict is inevitable between individuals who place primacy on tradition and virtue and those for whom the freedom to exercise reason is of paramount value. Many people in the latter group no longer identify themselves as conservatives.

—E. C. PASOUR JR.

Further Reading

Gottfried, Paul. *The Conservative Movement.* Rev. ed. New York: Twayne, 1993.

Nash, George H. *The Conservative Intellectual Movement in America since 1945.* New York: Basic Books, 1976.

Smant, Kevin J. *Principles and Heresies: Frank S. Meyer and the Shaping of the American Conservative Movement.* Wilmington, Del.: ISI Books, 2002.

See also: Bozell, L. Brent; Evans, M. Stanton; libertarianism; Meyer, Frank S.; movement conservatism; Philadelphia Society; traditionalism; Young Americans for Freedom

G

Garrett, Garet (1878–1954)

A prolific financial journalist, novelist, historian, and economist, Garet Garrett was prominent in the libertarian, pre–Cold War "Old Right." Born Edward Peter Garrett, he was a financial writer for the *New York Sun*, *New York Times*, *Wall Street Journal*, and *Evening Post*. From 1912 to 1914 he edited the *Annalist*, the *Times*'s weekly business and financial review. After 1919, Garrett freelanced and appeared frequently in the *Saturday Evening Post*, becoming its chief editorial writer in 1940.

A convinced believer in individualism and laissez-faire capitalism and an admirer of American prosperity, Garrett nevertheless warned in *Ouroboros* (1926) that machinery's high productivity was causing overproduction and sharpening international rivalry for export markets. His *A Bubble that Broke the World* (1932) blamed the 1929 Crash and the Great Depression on overextension of credit. Opposed to both the New Deal and interventionism, Garrett left the *Saturday Evening Post* when it abandoned isolationism.

The People's Pottage (1953), Garrett's most famous book, perceptively depicted the New Deal as perpetrating "revolution within the form," i.e., retaining established institutions and language but radically altering their meaning so as to gain power and make Americans economically dependent on the state. Garrett condemned inflationary public finance and lamented the death of limited government and America's transformation from a republic into an empire hemor-

rhaging wealth and blood overseas. Posthumously published, *The American Story* (1955) interpreted American history from a libertarian perspective, focusing on the twentieth century, especially the New Deal era.

—JOHN ATTARIAN

Further Reading

Ryant, Carl. *Profit's Prophet: Garet Garrett (1878–1954)*. Selinsgrove, Pa.: Susquehanna University Press, 1989.

See also: Old Right

Genovese, Eugene D. (1930–)

Eugene Genovese is one of the foremost American historians. A former Marxist, he is often branded a conservative—"a label applied to me frequently these days by people who understand nothing," he wrote in 1994. Though he may eschew being labeled a conservative, Genovese admits to having always admired much in conservative thought and being a longtime friend and frequent ally of conservatives.

A specialist in the American South, Genovese is the author or editor of more than a score of books and countless articles. Among his most important books are *The Political Economy of Slavery* (1965); *Roll, Jordan, Roll* (1974); *The Slaveholders' Dilemma* (1992); *The Southern Tradition* (1994); and *A Consuming Fire* (1998). In these books he has argued for an interpretation of the Old South as a fundamentally conservative, Christian society. He has also consistently maintained the controversial position that Southern theologians got the best of their Northern counterparts in the debate over whether slavery could scripturally be classed a sin.

Roll, Jordan, Roll, arguably his most important book, posits an economic instead of a racial interpretation of the master-slave relationship. Genovese also dealt seriously with religion in this book—viewing it as more than simply an opiate of the slaves or a justification for rebellion. In *The Slaveholders' Dilemma*, he argues that antebellum Southerners did not think their society antimodern or antiprogressive. Rather they considered themselves progressives seeking a different path to modernity and material progress, one that avoided the perils of radicalism and class conflict that had plagued the West since the French Revolution. Southerners believed slavery to be the only secure foundation for a free Christian society. Yet they also recognized that the societies achieving the greatest material progress were those that were eradicating human bondage and at the same time those most susceptible to radicalism. In *The Southern Tradition*, Genovese describes the principal tradition of the South as being "quintessentially conservative," particularly in its Christianity and anti-industrialism. This conservative Southern tradition offers a critique of modernity that he insists "contains much of intrinsic value that will have to be incorporated in the world view of any political movement, inside or outside the principal political parties, that expects to arrest our plunge into moral decadence and national decline."

Genovese was a founder and the first president of the Historical Society, a professional society for historians launched in 1998. He believed a new, nonideological professional organization was needed because the American Historical Association and the Organization of American Historians, of which he is a former president, had become too politicized. Genovese's goal is to reorient the historical profession toward producing accessible studies free from ideological proscription. In this, as in much else, he has proven himself a steady ally of conservatives.

—SEAN R. BUSICK

Further Reading

Genovese, Eugene D. *The Southern Front: History and Politics in the Cultural War.* Columbia, Mo.: University of Missouri Press, 1995.

———. *The World the Slaveholders Made: Two Essays in Interpretation.* 2nd ed. Middletown, Conn.: Wesleyan University Press, 1988.

See also: Fitzhugh, George; Southern conservatism

George, Henry (1839–97)

While George would scarcely have categorized himself as a "man of the Right," many persons on the Right (including Albert Jay Nock, Frank Chodorov, and William F. Buckley Jr.) have acknowledged being profoundly influenced by the thought of this self-taught political economist and social philosopher. His following, indeed, cuts across the political spectrum. He is best known for the theory, most powerfully and exhaustively developed in his first full-scale book, *Progress and Poverty* (1879), that most of the annual market value of land exclusive of improvements ("economic rent") should be applied to general public purposes, with corresponding abolition of taxation on the fruits of private effort.

George's ideological system rests upon the Lockean premise that private property is ultimately justified by the right of the individual to his labor as an extension of himself. Since land (in economics a synonym for nature) is not created by human effort, but by God as a fund of opportunity for the use of all, the moral argument for private ownership cannot apply to it. However, private ownership may be permitted on grounds of efficiency, provided that economic rent is paid to the community. Economic rent constitutes an exact measure of the disadvantage sustained by those who are denied the chance to use a site or natural resource on equal terms because of its preemption by the owner; therefore, it should be appropriated by the community as an indemnity to them, subsidizing protective and other social services that would otherwise have to be paid for by levies on the direct and/or indirect produce of their labor, i.e., wages and capital. George characterized this as "the taking by the community for the use of the community of that value which is the creation of the community," for he contended that rent (when not artificially inflated by land withholding, speculative or otherwise) is, apart from natural factors such as terrain, fertility, access to navigable waters, etc., essentially a social product—the result of population, public services, and the aggregate improvements and activities of all individuals in a given area, not the result of anything the owner, as such, may do to a particular site.

Henry George

Thoughtless or self-serving critics lump George with the socialists because he advocated the socialization of economic rent, ignoring the fact that every penny thus socially appropriated would be offset by the removal of a corresponding penny of taxation on productive effort and saving. Manifestly, to socialize only one source, even if completely or nearly so, is no more socialistic than to socialize the same sum of value spread among many sources. In fact, if the single source is the product of nature and society whereas the many sources are the product of private effort, it would seem that any system should

be considered *less* socialistic to the extent that it left the latter in private hands. Not without reason did Nock call George "the very best friend the capitalist ever had."

Since he advocated the use of the tax mechanism to collect economic rent, George's proposal is popularly known as the "single tax," but it is really not so much a tax as a public fee. Although he thought, doubtless correctly in his day, that this source would be more than adequate to support all legitimate government functions, his position would not necessarily preclude other benefit fees ("user charges") if economic rent should prove insufficient. A small percentage of the rent would be left to the landowner as an agency commission and an incentive to retain title.

George's rhetoric reflects a strain of utopian psychological environmentalism, but his program, although radical in the sense of attacking the root cause of economic maladjustment as he saw it, is conservative in accepting self-interest as the normative economic motive, and in avoiding drastic methods that might rend the social fabric. As Joseph A. Schumpeter remarks in his *History of Economic Analysis* (1954), George "was careful to frame his 'remedy' in such a manner as to cause minimum injury to the efficacy of the private enterprise economy"—in fact, its object was to enhance that efficacy. Modest local applications of his approach in Australia and elsewhere have tended to stimulate production, improve land use, and encourage better and more affordable housing. George rigorously advocated free trade but did not favor unrestricted immigration. He was a decentralist, an unrelenting foe of Marxism, a staunch believer in natural law, and a devout though undogmatic Christian. His system represents a balance between individualism and communitarianism, holding that for the individual to secure what rightfully belongs to him, the community must secure what rightfully belongs to it. It has contemporary implications that go beyond its original purview—e.g., public appropriation of the rent of the electromagnetic spectrum and of airport landing slots, and ecological conservation through taxation to internalize pollution costs.

George learned to set type as a youth in Philadelphia. Moving west to seek his fortune, he earned a precarious living as a journeyman printer in San Francisco, then became a newspaper reporter, editor, and eventually the publisher of his own daily. A political appointment afforded him the leisure to write *Progress and Poverty*, long the world's bestselling book on economics. Settling in New York City, he spent the remainder of his life lecturing (frequently abroad) and writing. His literary style has seldom been matched in force and clarity. In 1886, George ran for mayor of New York City on a reform ticket. According to most authorities, he actually got the most votes, but since the official count was rigged by the Tammany machine he came in second, ahead of the Republican candidate, Theodore Roosevelt. He was persuaded to run again in 1897, but died of a stroke five days before the balloting. His funeral was marked by an outpouring of public grief unprecedented in the city's history. Even those who opposed his ideas applauded his motives and acknowledged the nobility of his character.

During George's lifetime, his teaching won considerable adherence but was subsequently eclipsed by Marxism and Keynesianism. Now that their bankruptcy has been amply demonstrated, the relevance and fundamental soundness of George's teaching may have greater chance for recognition. Leland Yeager has shown that it is compatible with and complementary to Austrian economics.

—ROBERT V. ANDELSON

Further Reading

Andelson, Robert V., ed. *Critics of Henry George: A Centenary Appraisal of Their Strictures on Progress and Poverty*. Rutherford, N.J.: Fairleigh Dickinson University Press, 1979.

Barker, Charles Albro. *Henry George*. New York: Oxford University Press, 1955.

Nock, Albert Jay. *Henry George: An Essay*. New York: William Morrow & Company, 1939.

Yeager, Leland B. "Henry George and Austrian Economics." *History of Political Economy* 16 (1984): 157-74.

See also: Chodorov, Frank; Memoirs of a Superfluous Man; *Nock, Albert Jay; property rights, private*

Gilder, George (1939–)

During several decades in the public eye, George Gilder has established himself as one of the more interesting and enigmatic conservative social commentators. The varied nature of his interests and fields of study defy any simple characterization. Gilder is a supply-side futurist who has explored topics ranging from the causes of poverty to the inherent morality of capitalism to the unlimited promise of high technology. He might be described as a little bit Charles Murray, a little bit Ronald Reagan, and a little bit Arthur C. Clarke. But even that description would fail to capture the dynamic breadth of vision of one of this era's true original thinkers.

A Harvard-educated New Yorker who served as a speechwriter to Nelson Rockefeller, George Romney, and Richard Nixon, Gilder started making waves in the 1970s with the books *Sexual Suicide* (1973) and *Visible Man* (1978). But it was the 1981 publication of *Wealth and Poverty* that established Gilder as a serious and innovative intellectual. His relentlessly optimistic writings on economic matters helped inform many of the successful policies championed by Ronald Reagan. One recent study of Reagan's speeches concluded that Gilder was the president's most frequently quoted living author.

Gilder has emerged as something of a technology guru in recent years. His acclaimed 1989 book *Microcosm* explored the quantum roots of the new electronic technologies. He is a frequent contributor to *Forbes ASAP* and a Senior Fellow at Seattle's Discovery Institute. From his home in the Berkshire Mountains of western Massachusetts, he directs a small publishing empire producing newsletters dedicated to technology and energy issues. In 2000 he purchased the flailing *American Spectator*, intending to refocus its content more on issues of economics and technology, but this effort failed, and in 2003 he sold the magazine.

—MAX SCHULZ

Further Reading

Gilder, George. *Men and Marriage*. Gretna, La.: Pelican Publishing Company, 1986.

See also: American Spectator; *sociobiology; technology*

Gildersleeve, Basil L. (1831–1924)

An educator and classical scholar, Basil Gildersleeve was born in Charleston, South Carolina, where he was homeschooled by his father, a minister and journalist. By the age of five young Basil had read the Bible in English and the Gospel of John in Greek. Gildersleeve graduated from Princeton in

1849. The following year Gildersleeve began his studies in Germany, then the world center of classical learning. He studied at the Universities of Berlin, Bonn, and Gottingen, receiving the Ph.D. in 1853.

In 1856, Gildersleeve began his career as a college teacher at the University of Virginia. He continued his teaching duties while serving in the Confederate army. In 1875, Gildersleeve accepted an appointment at Johns Hopkins University. There he reached the pinnacle of an American academic career in classics. He founded the *American Journal of Philology*, the first professional journal for classicists in the United States. His scholarly publications, especially on Greek grammar, made him the first American classicist to achieve an international reputation. He received honorary degrees from European and American universities and was a member of the American Academy of Arts and Letters.

Basil L. Gildersleeve

When he died at age 92, Gildersleeve was described by fellow classicist Paul Shorey as the model of an "American scholar and gentleman." Classicists continue to treat Gildersleeve's memory with a reverence verging on hagiography. The edition of his letters by Ward Briggs is a monument of misplaced diligence. The letters reveal a fairly typical backbiting, petty academic, more concerned with gossip and traducing his colleagues than with the pursuit of truth and noble ideas. However, his intellectual defense of the Confederate cause, of classical education, and of the true calling of the teacher earns him an honorable place in the history of American conservatism. Until the end of his life, Gildersleeve proudly called himself "a man of the Old South, identified with the

Southern people by birth, by feeling and by fortune." Like Robert E. Lee, Gildersleeve saw the Civil War as a struggle over states' rights, not over slavery. The South fought for the cause of civil liberty, the right of each state to be sovereign. The South could be compared to the Athens of Pericles, defending the independence of the sovereign states against an aggressive North bent upon consolidation and domination.

In his commemoration of the political and moral values of the Old South, Gildersleeve took his stand along with such later intellectual figures as Richard Weaver and Allen Tate. Gildersleeve linked the northern mentality with ignorant assaults upon classical education. To those "Cape Cod Catos," who would replace the classics by a "scientific education," Gildersleeve answered, "So long as the ancient languages are the means of access to the ancient mind, they must ever be of priceless value to humanity; and, we would add, of prime necessity to all who wish to rise above the lower flats of life." Gildersleeve lived his beliefs, drawing upon the Greeks for his conviction that teaching, not research and publication, is the highest calling of a scholar: "the noiseless scholarship that leavens generation after generation of pupils is of more value to the world of letters than folios of pretentious erudition."

—J. RUFUS FEARS

Further Reading

Briggs, Ward. "Basil L. Gildersleeve." In *Classical Scholarship: A Biographical Encyclopedia*, edited by Ward Briggs and William Calder. New York: Garland, 1990.

Briggs, Ward, ed. *The Letters of Basil Lanneau Gildersleeve*. Baltimore, Md.: Johns Hopkins University Press, 1987.

Gildersleeve, Basil L. *The Creed of the Old South*. Baltimore, Md.: Johns Hopkins University Press, 1915.

See also: Southern conservatism

Gingrich, Newt (1943–)

Former politician and historian Newt Gingrich received his Ph.D. in history from Tulane University in 1971. He first ran for Congress while teaching at West Georgia College, winning his third bid for Congress in 1978. Gingrich founded the "Conservative Opportunity Society" in 1983 and played a prominent role at the Republican convention in 1984. In 1986, Gingrich took the reigns of GOPAC—the Republican Party's congressionally based political action committee. He went on to use this organization to bring his party to power in the House of Representatives. Important in this process was Gingrich's leading role in the House investigation of Speaker James Wright. Wright's resignation in 1989 was an important victory for Gingrich and his colleagues.

In 1994, Gingrich successfully led his party in Congress to victory by focusing on a national campaign of congressional reform. House Republicans gained fifty-four seats that year, giving them a majority in the House for the first time since 1952. Following this victory, Gingrich was elected Speaker of the House. In his "Contract with America," Gingrich promised house votes on ten items in the first one hundred days of his first session as Speaker. Prominent among these items was a measure to require that laws applying to the rest of the country equally be applied to the Congress. Most of these reforms passed the House, but their lasting impact on American politics is debatable.

Gingrich's congressional opponents later leveled accusations of illegal use of GOPAC funds against him. These charges proved false, but in January 1997 Gingrich paid a fine for violating House rules.

In 1998, in the midst of a sex scandal and after Republicans had almost lost control of the House, Gingrich retired from Congress. Since then, he has kept active by writing articles in the popular press and appearing frequently as a television pundit. Newt Gingrich combined the skills of a politician with the vision of a historian to bring about a minor revolution in American politics.

—DOUG MACKENZIE

Further Reading

Gingrich, Newt. *To Renew America.* New York: HarperCollins, 1995.

Steely, Mel. *The Gentleman from Georgia: The Biography of Newt Gingrich.* Macon, Ga.: Mercer University Press, 2000.

See also: movement conservatism

Glazer, Nathan (1923–)

An eminent sociologist, Nathan Glazer teaches at Harvard University. Formerly professor of sociology at the University of California, Berkeley (1963–69), staff member of *Commentary* magazine (1944–53), editor at Doubleday Anchor Books (1954–57); editorial advisor to Random House (1958–62), and urban sociologist with the Housing and Home Finance Agency in Washington, D.C. (1962–63), Glazer has been perhaps most closely associated with the *Public Interest*, at which journal he served as an editor from 1973 until its demise in 2005. He was born in 1923 in New York City. He took his bachelor's degree from City College of New York and graduate degrees from the University of Pennsylvania (in 1944) and Columbia University (in 1962). The recipient of a number of honorary doctorates, Glazer has served on presidential task forces on urban affairs and education. He has also served on the Committee on the Status of Black Americans of the National Academy of Sciences.

His profound insight into urban and ethnic affairs, expressed in *The Lonely Crowd* (written with David Riesman and Reuel Denney, 1950), *Faces in the Crowd* (1952), *The*

Social Basis of American Communism (1961), *Beyond the Melting Pot* (written with Daniel P. Moynihan, 1963), and *Studies in Housing and Minority Groups* (edited with Davis McEntire, 1960), has defined the agenda for his generation. He also is the author of major works on American Jews and Judaism, particularly, "Social Characteristics of American Jews, 1654-1954," *American Jewish Yearbook 1955*, and *American Judaism* (1957, revised 1989). His other books include *Remembering the Answers: Essays on the American Student Revolt* (1970), *Ethnicity: Theory and Experience* (edited with Daniel P. Moynihan, 1975), *The Limits of Social Policy* (1988), and *We Are All Multiculturalists Now* (1997). Many of his books are regarded as definitive, and *American Judaism* is widely held to be the best introduction to its subject. While he regards himself as nonpartisan, he is identified with neoconservative social scientists because his trenchant discussions of "affirmative action" and the student revolt elicited a wide response on the Right.

—JACOB NEUSNER

Further Reading

Glazer, Nathan. *Affirmative Discrimination: Ethnic Inequality and Public Policy.* New York: Basic Books, 1975.

———, ed. *Clamor at the Gates: The New American Immigration.* San Francisco: ICS Press, 1985.

See also: Jewish conservatives; neoconservatism; Public Interest

Gnosticism

An extreme religious sensibility from the early Christian era that has influenced twentieth-century thinkers in their understanding of the modern world, Gnosticism has its origins in the second century AD. Gnosticism has been adopted by conservative thinkers to diagnose and to criticize certain characteristics of modernity. Philosophers such as Eric Voegelin, Hans Jonas, and Thomas J. J. Altizer have compared the secularism and revolutionary messianism of modern intellectual and political movements with the fundamental features of ancient Gnosticism.

Ancient Gnosticism blossomed during the second through the fifth centuries AD in the Mediterranean world and became the heretical foil against which Christian dogma defined itself. A series of diverse sects formed around charismatic leaders such as Simon Magus, Valentinus, Basilides, Marcion, and Mani. Although the ancient Gnostics rejected dogma in favor of individual speculation and revelation, they did share some fundamental metaphysical and theological beliefs. The Gnostics believed the created world was evil as a result of a divine catastrophe: a transcendent god either became entrapped in pre-existing matter or gave birth to an evil god, the Demiurge, who proceeded to fashion an evil realm of materiality. The Gnostic believer's attitude toward his body and the material universe, therefore, is one of hostility and resentment.

Yet salvation from this evil material condition was possible. A divine spark remained in the human soul that sought to return to a transcendent good god. The remembrance of this divine spark required *gnosis*: a special type of knowledge of the divine mysteries of the world. This knowledge is reserved only for an elite. Since the elite Gnostic possesses absolute knowledge of the mysteries of the world, he does not have to make compromises with the status quo in the pursuit of his dream of ultimate liberation from his body and the material universe. In this sense, ancient Gnosticism is both world-rejecting and subversive in its outlook toward reality.

Prior to the mid-nineteenth century, ancient Gnosticism was known exclusively through the antiheretical writings of the Church fathers Hippolytus, Irenaeus, Tertullian, and others. Ironically, ancient Gnostic texts first came to light in 1842 in the form of extensive quotations and explanations included in Hippolytus's *Refutation of All Heresies*, which was a concerted attack on Gnosticism. The first discovery of ancient Gnostic texts was the Coptic *Pistis Sophia* in 1851. Soon other Gnostic texts such as the *Hymn of the Pearl*, *Apocryphal Acts of the Apostles*, and *Odes of Solomon* were discovered and entered into the cultural mainstream at the beginning of the twentieth century. The initial discovery of the original Gnostic texts occurred when the twin canons of the Western tradition—Christianity's faith and Enlightenment's reason—were coming under severe attack and became increasingly regarded as sterile and exhausted.

Confronted with what they believed was a dying tradition, cultural and intellectual elites began to look for alternative roots in their history to make sense of the modern world. The rediscovery of the Gnostic texts provided a narrative source by which to understand modernity and ultimately became the predominant paradigm of the twentieth century. Gnosticism has influenced C. G. Jung's analytical psychology, Gershom Scholem's revolutionary messianism, Harold Bloom's literary criticism, Han Jonas's and Thomas J. J. Altizer's existentialism, and Eric Voegelin's "new science of politics." All these thinkers identify Gnosticism with a particular mindset of displacement, alienation, and recognition of one's unique place in the universe.

Jung believed he had discovered in the ancient Gnostics and their conception of redemption through self-knowledge the earliest forerunners of modern psychologists. The Gnostic drama unfolds in the dualistic opposition between the conscious and unconscious poles of the human psyche. According to Jung, the differentiated ego emerges out of the primordial unconscious, just as the Gnostic Demiurge emerges out of the transcendent god. The conscious self forgets its original home, becomes alienated from itself, and believes itself to be autonomous and powerful until the unconscious reveals itself again through *gnosis*. Jung's three-stage process of ego formation and individuation culminates with the reintegration of the self, like the ancient Gnostic reincorporation of the human divine spark with a transcendent god.

Like Jung, Gershom Scholem also employs a three-stage process in his historical unfolding of religious consciousness. The first stage is the immediate presence of gods in nature, the second stage is the introduction of religion that isolates man from nature, and the third and final stage is the bridge between God and man in the secret path of spiritual mysticism. For Scholem, the Gnostic paradigm has influenced Jewish mysticism in providing a consoling framework to understand the Jewish condition of exile. Just like the cosmic exile of the human spirit, the Jewish people have been exiled from their land of Israel. Scholem traces the course of these Gnostic impulses from late antiquity's *merkabah* mysticism to medieval Kab-balahism to the seventeenth- and eighteenth-century messianic Jewish movements to modern-day Hasidism.

Harold Bloom incorporates Gnosticism into his literary theory of the *agon*. For Bloom, the reading of poetry is a form of *gnosis*. The reader achieves "a realization of events in the history of your spark or *pneuma*, and your knowing is the most important movement in that history. However, this realization is more than a transcendental experience: it is an attempt to usurp the foremost place of one's temporal predecessor in the literary world." By attempting to supplant his temporal predecessor, the reader will challenge his predecessor's authority, ultimately reaching back to the most authoritative text in the West, the Bible.

For Hans Jonas's and Thomas J. J. Altizer's existential philosophies, Gnosticism

is merely a diagnostic tool to understand the modern world. In comparing ancient Gnosticism with the Gnostic character of modernity, they focus on two points: (1) the central experience of exile, homelessness, and alienation from the world; and (2) the experience of the "death" of God in the modern world that is comparable to the ancient Gnostic's alien god. But whereas the alien and transcendent God of the ancient Gnostics held out the promise of redemption through *gnosis*, modernity lacks this metaphysical dimension, and that lack establishes its specifically nihilist and immanent character.

Eric Voegelin also utilizes the concept of Gnosticism to diagnose the modern world. For Voegelin, the essence of modernity is "the growth of Gnosticism." All intellectual and political movements that aim to correct the world's flaws are Gnostic. The self-deifying modern Gnostic redeemers exploit the passions of the people and resort to violence in their transformation of the wretched world into a utopian dream. Voegelin included progressivism, scientism, positivism, communism, fascism, and psychoanalysis as Gnostic in his exhaustive critique of the modern age. For Voegelin, Gnosticism was primarily a mindset characterized by the beliefs that (1) man was not responsible for the evil he finds in himself, (2) he has a right to blame someone or something else, and (3) his salvation depends upon his own efforts to correct the flaws in reality. Dissatisfied with present reality, the modern Gnostic can confidently hope that with increased knowledge he will be able to transform the world into his own image.

Several other philosophers have used Gnosticism in their understanding of the modern world: Gerald Hanratty emphasizes the Gnostic characteristics of Promethean rebellion, self-deification, and salvation through knowledge in the millenarian movements from the late Middle Ages to postmodernity; Carl Raschke claims that the

German Romantics, American religious cultists, and pop psychologists are latter-day Gnostics; and Micha Brumlik traces Gnostic elements of thought in writers from Schopenhauer to Heidegger in their support of political tyranny by self-deified world redeemers. Theologians like Elaine Pagels and Michael Williams point out that Gnosticism reveals the diverse elements in the origins of Christianity, and they claim that the Gnostic emphasis on direct religious experience could have enriched the Christian tradition. Finally, there are those who have employed the Gnostic narrative in their aesthetic theories, a group that includes Norbert Bolz, Kirsten Grimstad, Cyril O'Regan, Michael Pauen, and William Worringer. Gnostic motifs appear in contemporary fiction in the works of Walker Percy, Flannery O'Connor, William Gaddis, and Thomas Pynchon.

Although thinkers are divided over whether Gnosticism is positive, there are some problems studying Gnosticism as a modern phenomenon. According to Stephen McKnight, Carl Raschke, and Gerald Hanratty, some features of modern Gnosticism are seemingly incompatible with the fundamental features of ancient Gnosticism, such as the modern Gnostic desire to transform the world, which would have been repudiated by ancient Gnostics, who sought to escape the world. Moreover, the pro-cosmic, monistic, and evolutionary underpinnings of modern intellectual and political movements are difficult to reconcile with the anti-cosmic, dualist, and devolutionary characteristics of ancient Gnosticism. However, thinkers like Cyril O'Regan contend that the Gnostic narrative not only permits room for differences between modern and ancient forms of Gnosticism but can assist thinkers to understand and to diagnose the modern world.

—LEE TREPANIER

Further Reading

Hanratty, Gerald. *Studies in Gnosticism and the Philosophy of Religion*. Dublin: Four Courts Press, 1997.

Raschke, Carl. *An Interruption of Eternity: Modern Gnosticism and the Origins of the New Religious Consciousness*. Chicago: Nelson-Hall, 1980.

Segal, Robert, June Singer, and Murray Stein, eds. *The Allure of Gnosticism: The Gnostic Experience in Jungian Psychology and Contemporary Culture*. Chicago: Open Court, 1995.

Voegelin, Eric. *The New Science of Politics*. Chicago: University of Chicago Press, 1952.

See also: community; New Science of Politics, The; *Voegelin, Eric*

God and Man at Yale

In the fall of 1951, Yale University, proud member of America's higher education elite, prepared to celebrate the 250th anniversary of its founding. Members of the Yale community looked forward to a joyous, yet placid, celebration. Little did they know that Yale was about to be rocked by a book that would begin the process of launching the American conservative movement.

William F. Buckley Jr. entered Yale in the freshman class of 1946. He had been brought up to be a free-market, individualist conservative. But things were different at Yale. There, Buckley battled what he saw as the pernicious liberal orientation of its students, faculty, and administration. Buckley did his best. He became a well-known student advocate of the conservative viewpoint and won a reputation as a skilled and witty debater. In addition, by 1949 Buckley won election as chairman of the *Yale Daily News*; his editorial blasts against liberals inside and outside Yale outraged and amused the university community. Buckley appreciated and enjoyed his opportunities. Yet he was troubled that liberalism seemed so dominant at Yale, which had a reputation for being conservative.

Yale also affected Buckley in another way. There he came under the influence of Willmoore Kendall, a brilliant and eccentric political scientist who promoted a theory he called "absolute majoritarianism." Kendall argued that a society's survival depended upon the existence of a "public orthodoxy," which it must enforce and to which its members must adhere. If ideas were simply left to compete with each other, goodness and truth need not automatically emerge victorious. Instead, Nazism or communism might triumph, as the twentieth century demonstrated. Hence, society must protect itself against such dangers, even if that meant repressing the freedom of speech of (for example) communists. This theory proved to be a powerful influence upon Buckley, especially since he believed liberalism to be, in its own way, dangerous to America's survival in a communist-infested world.

So, irritated by liberalism's seeming domination, and under the influence of his mentor Kendall, soon after graduation Buckley began to write *God and Man at Yale*. Through quotations from Yale textbooks and classroom anecdotes, he argued that Yale was abandoning God and man and instead was inculcating its students with the equivalent of atheism and socialism. This was directly opposite to what Yale's orthodoxy should be. The truth of Christianity and free enterprise, Buckley argued, had been established by history and tradition. Furthermore, God and economic liberty were clearly what the alumni of Yale desired as Yale's "public orthodoxy." And did not the alumni have a right to decide Yale's destiny?

Buckley was challenging one of academia's most sacred beliefs: academic freedom. But he wrote that academic freedom was only a "superstition." Yale already had an orthodoxy—liberalism. Buckley was not urging the imposition of new standards, but rather the narrowing of those already existing. The alumni, as the purchasers and consumers of Yale's product, and as the supporters of Yale through their contributions, deserved the same sovereignty as did the consumer in the marketplace. Thus, Buckley urged Yale to hire only those academicians who would teach this "orthodoxy." Socialists and atheists could remain, provided that they taught what the alumni stipulated. If they would not, then Yale had the right to fire them. As Kendall might have said, the majority of alumni should rule Yale, not the liberal establishment in the faculty and administration.

The book was published by Henry Regnery of Chicago, one of only three recognizably conservative publishers in business in 1951. Regnery was barely solvent and only able to publish with the financial aid of Buckley's father, William F. Buckley Sr. The book caused a sensation. It not only challenged academic freedom; it also championed individual liberty and the traditional value of religion and excoriated liberalism—ideas with great appeal to a growing conservative constituency in America. Hence, the book sold out its initial printing and within a few weeks reached sixteenth place on the *New York Times* bestseller list. While winning praise from most conservatives, *God and Man at Yale* received bitter denunciations from Yale's administration, its faculty, and assorted liberals. Some dismissed the book as a manifestation of Buckley's "militant Catholicism." Others raised the specter of fascism. Yale trustee Frank Ashburn likened it to the "glow and appeal of a fiery cross on a hillside at night."

Yet its real importance lay in the book's impact upon Buckley himself. It made William F. Buckley Jr. a leader in the conservative movement in America, sought out and respected by all on the Right. Within four years, he had founded *National Review,* assuming the role of becoming conservatism's great popularizer. The reception of *God and Man at Yale* demonstrated to him that he could succeed in that task.

—KEVIN SMANT

Further Reading

Bramwell, Austin W. "The Revolt against the Establishment: *God and Man at Yale* at 50." *Intercollegiate Review* 37, no. 1 (2001): 40–44.

Macdonald, Dwight. "God and Buckley at Yale." *Reporter* 6 (1952): 35–38.

Nash, George. *The Conservative Intellectual Movement in America since 1945.* 2nd ed. Wilmington, Del.: ISI Books, 1996.

See also: academic freedom; Buckley, William F., Jr.; Kendall, Willmoore; Regnery Publishing

God That Failed, The

A symposium of confessional essays by ex-communists and fellow travelers, *The God That Failed* (1949) helped to make anticommunism intellectually respectable. Richard Crossman, a socialist and member of Parliament, conceived the idea for the book in reaction to Arthur Koestler's taunt that he was like all "comfortable, insular, Anglo-Saxon anti-communists. You hate our Cassandra cries and resent us as allies—but, when all is said, we ex-communists are the only people on your side who know what it's all about."

In addition to Koestler, the Hungarian-born author of *Darkness at Noon* (1940), Crossman recruited two other "initiates," or ex-Communist Party members: Ignazio Silone, a former leader of the Italian Party and author of *Bread and Wine* (1936), a clas-

sic novel of politics; and Richard Wright, the black American author of *Native Son* (1939). To complement the testimonies of these men, he solicited essays from three "worshipers from afar": French novelist André Gide, American journalist Louis Fischer, and English poet Stephen Spender.

Like the collection's title, now a familiar metaphor, Crossman's section headings were designed to place primary emphasis on communism's religious character. And with good reason, for one contributor after another likened his commitment to the devotion others reserved for traditional creeds. Koestler set the tone by reporting that he embraced the new religion because he "lived in a disintegrating society thirsting for faith." Others, too, called attention to the spiritual crisis that deepened at the time of the Depression, Hitler's rise to power, and the Spanish Civil War.

In common with other, less savage, gods, communism demanded total obedience, even when that meant sacrificing the intellect. In the beginning, therefore, the converts viewed Soviet realities through rose-tinted glasses and "reinterpreted" evidence of communist tyranny. The ends, they persuaded themselves, justified the means.

In time, however, they came to believe that the means dictated the ends and began to reclaim their heritage as critical intellectuals. Silone awoke from his dogmatic slumber after being asked to denounce, sight unseen, a document from Trotsky's pen. When Gide traveled to the Soviet Union in 1936, he was appalled by the hospitality extended to him; unlike other political pilgrims, he could not square his privileged status with communism's egalitarian rhetoric. The scales fell from Fischer's eyes in 1939, when he received word of the Nazi-Soviet Non-Aggression Pact.

Despite their loss of faith, however, the contributors to *The God That Failed* did not enter the conservative ranks; instead, they retreated to liberalism or democratic socialism. But precisely for this reason, they served as independent witnesses to a communist threat that, during the 1940s and 1950s, preoccupied many spokesmen on the American Right, some of whom—Will Herberg, James Burnham, and Whittaker Chambers, for example—were themselves ex-communists. However much men such as these dissented from the anticommunist Left on a range of other issues, they could enlist *The God That Failed* in their effort to make anticommunism central to a new American conservatism, one that was confrontational at home and interventionist abroad.

—LEE CONGDON

Further Reading

Crossman, Richard, ed. *The God That Failed.* New York: Harper, 1949.

Deutscher, Isaac. "The Ex-Communist's Conscience." In *Russia in Transition and Other Essays.* New York: Coward-McCann, 1957, 203–16.

Niebuhr, Reinhold. "To Moscow—and Back." *Nation* 170 (1950): 88–90.

Podhoretz, Norman. "Why 'The God That Failed' Failed. . . ." *Encounter* 60 (1983): 28–34.

See also: anticommunism; Koestler, Arthur

Godkin, E. L. (Edwin Lawrence) (1831–1902)

E. L. Godkin, one of the great editors of the nineteenth century, struggled with the difficulty of communicating serious ideas in an age of mass democracy. Born and raised in County Wicklow, Ireland, he obtained his college education at Queen's College, Belfast (1851), and then enrolled to study law at the Middle Temple (he later received an M.A. from Harvard in 1871). Godkin was of English stock. His father was a dissenting Presbyterian minister who actively managed and contributed to several newspapers, in which he advocated Home Rule for Ireland. In this controversial cause his father was influential with English liberals, including Gladstone.

After graduating from Queen's College, Godkin left for London, where he soon abandoned his legal studies to work for the famous London publisher John Cassell. He was a writer and editor for Cassell's famous *Illustrated Family Paper*, and his first book, *The History of Hungary and the Magyars* (1853), was published by Cassell's house. After serving for two years as a correspondent for the *London Daily News* in the Crimea, Godkin was offered the editorship of a Belfast newspaper, but turned it down to immigrate to the United States in 1856. After a brief tenure of study with a New York lawyer he was admitted to the bar, but again he quickly strayed from a legal to a journalistic career. He was early on befriended by the great landscape architect, Frederick Law Olmstead, and was even inspired by Olmstead's letters in the *New York Times* about the South to make his own horseback travels through that region. He published many of his observations in the *London Daily News* during the years leading up to the outbreak of Civil War.

In this way Godkin gained literary renown and was offered proposals to lead several big city daily newspapers. However, Godkin was intent upon founding a weekly organ that could provide more reflective opinion and commentary on matters of public interest. And it was in this endeavor that he made his most lasting and significant contribution when, in 1865, with the help of his friend Charles Eliot Norton and a Philadelphia entrepreneur, Godkin founded the *Nation*. From its outset, the *Nation* was a broad and diverse magazine of culture and public affairs that included in its pages the leading thinkers of the day. Like many quality organs of thought and opinion, including other outlets for Godkin's writing such as the *North American Review,* the *Nation's* influence on American life was far greater than its circulation might have suggested. The great contemporary English observer of nineteenth-century America, James Bryce, called it "the best weekly not only in America but in the world." In 1881, Godkin brought the *Nation* under the operating umbrella of the *New York Evening Post,* which he had joined as an editor at the invitation of its new owner, Henry Villard, and of which in 1883 he became editor in chief, a position he retained until his retirement in 1900. Thereafter he wrote daily for the *Post* while also producing the weekly *Nation.* He was sustained throughout by his friendships with the elites of New York and the Brahmins of Boston, for in addition to Norton and Olmstead he was acquainted with James Russell Lowell, Brooks and Henry Adams, and the James brothers, Henry and William.

E. L. Godkin

In the "gilded" and then "yellow" age of journalism, Godkin was an exception: a fiercely independent and nonpartisan journalist. In thought and temperament, Godkin was a liberal of the nineteenth-century variety, a Whig in the tradition of Macaulay and an enthusiastic follower of John Stuart Mill. (Godkin's classical liberalism and the contemporary liberalism of today's *Nation* suggest interesting lines of continuity, as well as discontinuity, between these two kinds of liberalism.) He sympathized with the Union cause in the Civil War and was disposed toward the Republican Party, but he was also a reformer and directed his reformist criticism toward the carpetbaggers in the South, the administration of President Grant, and the rise of Rutherford B. Hayes. He was the leader, in 1884, of the Mugwump revolt of reform Republicans against the Senate candidacy of James G. Blaine. And he was a relentless critic of corruption at all levels of government, notably denouncing and exposing the Tammany Hall leaders even while being persecuted unsuccessfully by the Tammany machine for libel.

Godkin was a free-marketeer, a Manchesterian, and so fought aggressive tariffs and socialism as corruptions of American democracy. He was also a strong advocate of the gold standard. Godkin sought to conserve what he cherished as the original ideals of democracy in America. In books such as *The Triumph of Reform* (1895), *Reflections and Comments, 1865-1895* (1895), *Problems of Modern Democracy* (1896), and *Unforeseen Tendencies of Democracy* (1898), Godkin articulated his notion that democracy was the system of government most natural to man. He championed the notion of an "educated" and disinterested democratic statesmanship. He feared, however, that the "unforeseen tendency" in modern democracy was its degradation into mediocrity. To check this trend, Godkin was an advocate for civil service reform, the referendum, and the initiative—more democracy, that is, to save democracy. Against any criticism of his democratic ideal, real or imagined, Godkin was an implacable opponent. Still, pessimistic about the trajectory of American democracy, Godkin returned to England in 1901, in which year he died and was buried in Northampton.

—JEFFREY O. NELSON

Further Reading

Armstrong, William M. *E. L. Godkin: A Biography.* Albany, N.Y.: State University of New York Press, 1978.

———. *E. L. Godkin and American Foreign Policy, 1865–1900.* New York: Bookman, 1957.

Christman, Henry M., ed. *One Hundred Years of the* Nation. New York: Macmillan, 1965.

Grimes, Alan P. *The Political Liberalism of the New York* Nation, *1865–1932.* Chapel Hill, N.C.: University of North Carolina Press, 1953.

Kirk, Russell. *The Conservative Mind: From Burke to Santayana.* Chicago: Regnery, 1953.

Ogden, Rollo, ed. *Life and Letters of Edwin Lawrence Godkin.* New York: Macmillan, 1907.

See also: gold standard; liberalism, classical; Villard, Henry

gold standard

The term "gold standard" implies that a nation's currency is backed by the precious metal gold. This would mean that anyone holding paper currency could exchange that currency for the amount of gold that the central authority in the nation stated that the currency was worth. Thus, the value of the currency is fixed and is worth a constant amount of gold.

When someone refers to the gold standard they are typically referring to an international monetary system in which participating nations have defined their currencies' values in terms of quantities of gold. Since all currencies can be converted, on demand, into gold, a nation can only issue as much currency as is backed by the stock of gold it possesses. Historically, this was believed to be a useful method for disciplining central banks and preventing governments from over-issuing currency to pay their debts. Most of the world was on an international gold standard from the 1870s until World War I.

It is easy to see how a gold standard facilitates international trade. Since all currencies can be converted into gold, gold becomes the common currency for all nations. With all international transactions being made in gold, inflows and outflows of gold were considered useful in maintaining world economic order. Nations that imported more goods than they exported (ran trade deficits) would experience an outflow of gold. As the gold supply declined the money supply would also have to be reduced. This decline in the money supply would cause falling prices in trade deficit nations, making their exports cheaper on international markets. These lower prices should then stimulate exports and thus restore trade balance.

The opposite effects should occur in nations that exported more goods than they imported (trade-surplus nations). As their gold stocks increased so would their money supply. This would then cause higher prices on international markets and reduce the volume of exports until trade balance was restored.

Though the gold standard was viewed as useful for maintaining trade balances among nations and for preventing governments from practicing inflationary policies, a number of problems were also associated with the gold standard. As international trade expanded, the demand for the international currency expanded as well. Since the supply of gold only increases slowly over time (with a few rare exceptions) the expanded demand could not be met.

A second problem with the gold standard involved the adjustment process in trade-deficit nations. As gold outflows put downward pressure on prices this also led to lower national incomes and higher levels of unemployment. Though the process described above seems logical and simple, in the real world producers are reluctant to accept lower prices for their products and workers are reluctant to accept lower wages for their labor. The resulting reduction in national output and higher unemployment can then make calls to abolish the gold standard politically popular.

At the end of World War I it was apparent to all involved that there was going to be too much demand for international currency to rely only on a gold standard. From this time forward the international monetary system operated as if it were on a gold standard by having nations fix the value of their currency relative to the currencies of other nations. While gold still played an important role in international trade, it was not the sole determinant of the size of a nation's money supply. This system was altered somewhat in 1944 but a system of fixed exchange rates continued to exist until 1971, when the system converted to an exchange system that allowed currency values to float relative to each other.

In many countries price inflation has been and continues to be a nagging economic problem. Because of the belief that this is often caused by excessive increases in the money supply, some critics have called for a return to the gold standard as a solution to what is viewed as mismanagement by the monetary authorities in the guilty countries. While some of these arguments are thought provoking and reasonable for achieving the goals to which they are directed, it is unlikely that we will ever see a return to a pure gold standard.

—HARRY VERYSER

Further Reading

Eichengreen, Barry. *Globalizing Capital: A History of the International Monetary System.* Princeton, N.J.: Princeton University Press, 1996.

Wilson, Ted. *Battles for the Standard: Bimetallism and the Spread of the Gold Standard in the Nineteenth Century.* Burlington, Vt.: Ashgate, 2000.

See also: Haberler, Gottfried; Mises, Ludwig von; populism

Goldwater, Barry M. (1909–98)

By running for president in 1964 as an unapologetic conservative, Goldwater altered the course of modern American politics. In doing so, he prepared the way for the conservative revolution that elected Ronald Reagan in 1980 and established conservatism as the dominant political philosophy in America in the last part of the twentieth century. During his thirty years as a United States Senator from Arizona, Goldwater also played a major role in key policy areas like national defense, U.S. intelligence, and labor-management relations.

Born in Phoenix, Arizona, in 1909, Goldwater was the eldest child of a prominent family that owned the largest department store in the city. He was raised an Episcopalian by his mother, but his great-grandfather, Hirsch Goldwasser, was born in Poland of Jewish parents. Something of a hellraiser in his youth, Goldwater was sent to Staunton Military Academy in Virginia to learn discipline. In his senior year, the onetime rebel won the outstanding cadet award and was offered an appointment to West Point. Instead he returned home to attend Arizona State University and be near his father, who was seriously ill.

Goldwater left college and took over the management of the family business when his father died. In 1930, he joined the Army Reserve and received a commercial pilot's license, beginning a flying career that extended into the 1980s. He became a world-class ham radio operator, once organizing a network of volunteer operators who provided radiotelephone communication between U.S. soldiers in Vietnam and their families in the U.S. He also spent much time with the Navajo and Hopi Indians of Arizona, whose causes he championed in the Senate.

During World War II, he served in the Air Transport Command and flew shuttle runs over the Himalaya Mountains in India, delivering arms, ammunition, and equipment to Nationalist China, with whose leaders and people he developed a special friendship. Restless after the war, Goldwater no longer found satisfaction in minding the family store and entered local politics.

In 1949, he was elected to the nonpartisan Phoenix City Council. Three years later, running for the Senate as a Republican, he challenged and defeated Ernest W. McFarland, the Democratic majority leader of the U.S. Senate, aided by the victory of Dwight D. Eisenhower at the head of the ticket.

A strong supporter of Arizona's right-to-work law, Goldwater became nationally known during his first term for investigating corrupt union bosses like Jimmy Hoffa and challenging the left-wing politics of union leaders like Walter Reuther.

Goldwater crossed the ideological rubicon in 1960 when President Eisenhower proposed a domestic program that Goldwater called a "dime store New Deal" and when Richard Nixon made a deal with New York governor Nelson Rockefeller to obtain the Republican presidential nomination. Goldwater and other conservatives from the west and south vowed they would challenge the Eastern liberal establishment and take over the Republican Party.

Four short years later, they succeeded by nominating Goldwater as the GOP's standard bearer against President Lyndon B. Johnson. Although the outcome of the 1964 campaign was never in question, Goldwater raised the critical issues that have determined American politics ever since, including the proper size of the federal government, law and order, social security and welfare, privatization, the need for a strong national defense, and a commitment to victory in any war.

Although Goldwater won only six states and 39 percent of the popular vote, he established the political fact that a conservative could win the presidential nomination. He raised public awareness of conservatism as a viable political philosophy and galvanized thousands of young people who set to work to put a conservative in the White House. They achieved their goal with the election of President Reagan in 1980.

Goldwater had not sought reelection to the Senate in 1964, but he ran and won in 1968, beginning a second career in the Senate that lasted until 1986. During those years, he rose to a position of unusual power, chairing the Intelligence Committee and then the Armed Services Committee under Reagan. He authored important legislation, especially the first reorganization of the Department of Defense in four decades.

Goldwater was an American original, a man of the west whose loyalties were to duty, honor, and country, a man of salty speech and humor who loved, as he put it, "to shoot from the lip." He affected presidential politics more than any other losing candidate in the twentieth century. He laid a firm political and ideological foundation for the Reagan revolution and led a generation of conservatives to understand that theirs was a winning as well as a just cause.

—LEE EDWARDS

Barry M. Goldwater

Further Reading

Edwards, Lee. *Goldwater: The Man Who Made a Revolution.* Washington, D.C.: Regnery, 1995.

Goldwater, Barry. *The Conscience of a Conservative.* Shepherdsville, Ky.: Victory Publishing, 1960.

McDowell, Edwin. *Barry Goldwater: Portrait of an Arizonan.* Chicago: Regnery, 1964.

Perlstein, Rick. *Before the Storm: Barry Goldwater and the Unmaking of the American Consensus.* New York: Hill and Wang, 2001.

White, F. Clifton. *Suite 3505: The Story of the Draft Goldwater Movement.* With William J. Gill. New Rochelle, N.Y.: Arlington House, 1967.

See also: China Lobby; Conscience of a Conservative, The; *Manion, Clarence; media, conservative; movement conservatism; Republican Party; Rockefeller Republicans; Young Americans for Freedom*

Goodrich, Pierre F. (1894–1973)

An industrialist and philanthropist, Pierre F. Goodrich was the founder of Liberty Fund, Inc., an educational foundation "established to encourage the study of the ideal of a society of free and responsible individuals." Born in 1894 in Winchester, Indiana, Goodrich attended Wabash College and Harvard Law School before establishing an Indianapolis law practice. Goodrich's father James had been governor of Indiana and a successful businessman. In the late 1930s, Pierre assumed control of family investments, ultimately becoming chairman of the Indiana Telephone Company, Peoples Loan and Trust, Ayrshire Collieries Corporation, and other industrial concerns.

Although less politically active than his father, Pierre Goodrich was a patron of cultural and educational causes. He served as a trustee of the Great Books Foundation, Indianapolis Symphony Orchestra, China Institute of America, Intercollegiate Society of Individualists, Foundation for Economic Education, and Institute for Humane Studies. He inherited his father's seat on the Wabash College Board of Trustees in 1940 and served continuously until 1969.

In 1959, Goodrich dedicated a remarkable seminar room in Wabash College's library. A timeline reflecting the development of liberty is carved into high limestone walls that ring the room, and bookshelves underneath hold classic literary and philosophical works selected by Goodrich. "The education here available discards all of the formalized concepts of education, such as courses and departments in this and that," he later explained. "It simply makes available an opportunity to read and think, check, explore, observe, and discuss. It is only the individual who accomplishes his education."

After World War II, Goodrich established two grant-making foundations, the Winchester Foundation and Thirty Five Twenty, to more directly support educational and libertarian endeavors. In 1960 he incorporated Liberty Fund, Inc., which became his primary philanthropic vehicle. Guided by a 129-page "Basic Memorandum" authored by Goodrich, Liberty Fund served as a grant-making foundation in the 1960s and 1970s until the Internal Revenue Service formally classified it as an operating foundation in 1979.

Although not an academic philosopher, Goodrich expounded on the topics of education and politics he had addressed in Liberty Fund's "Basic Memorandum" in a later "Education Memorandum" (1951) and in a 1958 presentation in which he cautioned fellow Mont Pelerin Society members that "there is no middle road between freedom and statism." Nobel economic laureate Milton Friedman remembers Goodrich: "He had thought deeply about philosophical issues and was a convinced libertarian who believed in minimal government."

Introspective and eccentric, Goodrich was a tireless apostle for liberty and reasoned inquiry. He once took a month-long retreat to read Ludwig von Mises's *Human Action* (1949). Combining business acumen with intellectual curiosity, Goodrich reached out to all manner of people—from leading statesmen to his telephone company employees—to discuss liberty. He died in Indianapolis in 1973, but not before instructing his assistants to send books to hospital nurses whom he had engaged in Socratic conversation.

—MORGAN N. KNULL

Further Reading

Liberty Fund. *The Goodrich Seminar Room at Wabash College: An Explication.* Indianapolis, Ind.: Liberty Fund, 2000.

———. *Why Liberty? A Collection of Liberty Fund Essays.* Indianapolis, Ind.: Liberty Fund, 2000.

Starbuck, Dane. *The Goodriches: An American Family.* Indianapolis, Ind.: Liberty Fund, 2001.

See also: Liberty Fund

Gottfried, Paul E. (1941–)

A professor specializing in intellectual history, Paul Gottfried is a student of historical thinking, conservatism, liberalism, and the managerial state. His own conservatism is respectful of the older American political traditions but has important sources in European, especially German, philosophy and political thought. Gottfried defends the historical consciousness and historically rooted cultural identities against abstract rationalism and political universalism. He sees national state sovereignty as most effective in curbing domestic and international conflict. He regards the modern managerial state and mass democracy as destructive of liberty. His thought combines philosophical elements with sociologically and naturalistically oriented theorizing.

In *Conservative Millenarians* (1979), Gottfried examines romantic conservatism in Bavaria in the early decades of the nineteenth century. He shows how a chiliastic faith in the historical consciousness was chastened by a growing sense of mankind's fallen state and by rediscovery of Christian orthodoxy. *The Search for Historical Meaning* (1986) examines the influence of Hegel and German historical thought in the United States and argues that these had a salutary though limited impact on American conservatism after World War II. Gottfried regards the fading of the historical sense among American conservatives since the 1970s as a sign of intellectual decline. He points to the anticonservative implications of the rationalistic ethic propounded by Leo Strauss and developed further by Strauss's American followers. *The Conservative Movement* (1993), whose first edition (1988) was coauthored with Thomas Fleming, surveys the evolution and varieties of American conservatism since World War II. The book offers qualified approval of the "Old Right," represented by thinkers like Russell Kirk, James Burnham, and M. E. Bradford, but criticizes "neoconservatives" for promoting big government and global democracy and for exhibiting patterns of thought and behavior reminiscent of the revolutionary Left. In *Carl Schmitt: Politics and Theory* (1990) Gottfried presents the German thinker as a perceptive though morally flawed commentator on the crisis of the Western state. Gottfried explicates and endorses Schmitt's view that the decline of national state sovereignty is accompanied by domestic disorder and a "tyranny of values." Gottfried finds confirmation for Schmitt's thesis in the United States, where an expanding bureaucratic state champions human rights and global democracy internationally but has difficulty maintaining order at home. *After Liberalism: Mass Democracy in the Managerial State* (1999) contends that a managerial state has destroyed nineteenth-century liberalism in the Western world. A new elite that includes neoconservative ideologues has taken control of society. Nominal adherence to democratic procedures cannot conceal that a "New Class" is imposing its interests and values through a growing administrative state.

Gottfried has also criticized large-scale immigration. He has increased the awareness on the American Right that deep divisions exist within it and that some putative conservatives have much in common with the Left. As a critic of the managerial state Gottfried has made common cause with self-described leftists, some of them associated with the journal *Telos,* who are also critics of the New Class.

—CLAES G. RYN

Further Reading

Gottfried, Paul. *Multiculturalism and the Politics of Guilt: Toward a Secular Theocracy.* Columbia, Mo.: University of Missouri Press, 2002.

See also: historicism; Old Right; paleoconservatism

Grant, George P. (1918–88)

A preeminent Canadian philosopher, and certainly Canada's most important and original conservative thinker, George Parkin Grant was born to a prominent family in 1918. Educated as an undergraduate at Queens University, where his grandfather had been the first principle, Grant took his D.Phil. at Oxford, which he attended on a Rhodes Scholarship (for which program another grandfather had served as the founding secretary). Still in England when the war broke out, Grant, a pacifist, organized an ambulance corps and ministered to those wounded in bombing raids. It was during this period that, while opening a country gate, Grant had a spiritual, almost mystical experience that convinced him of God's presence and loving superintendence of the cosmos. Although is philosophical framework would later shift from Hegelianism toward Platonism, from that point forward he would engage the world as a committed Christian.

After the war, Grant returned to Canada, where he taught philosophy and religion at McMaster University from 1947 to 1980 and at Dalhousie University from 1980 until his death.

Grant's "Red Tory" turn of mind has substantial affinities with traditionalist conservatism in America. *Philosophy in the Mass Age* (1960) put him on the map; *Lament for a Nation* (1961) made him famous. In *Lament,* Grant presents an elegy for the Canadian nation, which, with the failure of the Conservative Diefenbaker government, he describes as has having finally ceded its political and cultural independence. Henceforth, it will essentially be a satellite state of the American technological empire and will thus fail to provide a nonliberal, anti-individualistic counterweight to the restless dynamism of the United States. Despite Grant's couching of this argument in the terms of "destiny" and "fate," the book galvanized a generation of Canadian intellectuals to resist (unsuccessfully, of course) the continental dominance of American liberalism.

English-Speaking Justice (1974), in which Grant targets John Rawls's *Theory of Justice* (1971), presents Grant's most sustained argument against American-style liberalism. Here he argues that Rawls's theory, which provides an account of justice premised on a hypothetical contract between equals, reveals that liberalism's defenseless exposure to Nietzschean radicalization, for it fails to provide an adequately grounded definition of "person." Who is to determine what counts as a person and by what criteria? May not Rawlsian liberalism logically deny personhood to the unborn, the handicapped, and the aged, leading to our progressive dehumanization? In this way Grant argues for the superiority of ancient accounts of justice based on the conception of a human nature oriented toward its "good."

English-Speaking Justice was book-ended by two other slim but powerful volumes:

Technology and Empire (1969) and *Technology and Justice* (1986). In these books Grant makes explicit his view that with the rise of Western science, "knowing" and "making" achieved total co-penetration in a way never before known or contemplated. The break with ancient and medieval civilization is therefore profound—almost literally unthinkable. We are encompassed by technology, argues Grant, and find it impossible as a civilization to think in any but its terms. Capitalist democracy both enshrines technological thinking and is its logical extension into politics and economics. Thus, for Grant, no discussion of cultural decadence—which he believed was most clearly revealed in movements to legalize euthanasia and abortion—was complete without understanding the fateful dynamic of technological civilization, a dynamic characterized by an unrelenting will to power over both human and nonhuman nature. It is this understanding of the fundamental way in which technology orders modern politics, economics, and culture that sets Grant's philosophical and critical thought apart from most conservative reflection in America and has attracted such heterodox thinkers as Peter Augustine Lawler and David L. Schindler.

—JEREMY BEER

Further Reading

Christian, William. *George Grant: A Biography.* Toronto: University of Toronto Press, 1993.

Grant, George. *The George Grant Reader.* Edited by William Christian and Sheila Grant. Toronto: University of Toronto Press, 1998.

———. *Selected Letters.* Edited by William Christian. Toronto: University of Toronto Press, 1996.

O'Donovan, Joan E. *George Grant and the Twilight of Justice.* Toronto: University of Toronto Press, 1984.

Taylor, Charles. *Radical Tories: The Conservative Tradition in Canada.* Toronto: Anansi, 1982.

See also: liberalism; modernity and postmodernity; Schindler, David L.; technology; traditionalism

Great Books programs

A Great Books program is a curriculum consisting only, or at least primarily, of the classic works of the Western intellectual tradition. Advocates of such programs contend that reading and understanding these masterpieces, sometimes called the Western canon, is the sine qua non of a formal education and that, when properly taught, the Great Books best prepare students from a range of educational, social, and cultural backgrounds to think independently and rigorously.

The Great Books as a conscious educational project rose to prominence in the American college curriculum with the efforts of John Erskine at Columbia University in the 1920s. Soon the Great Books had taken hold at the University of Chicago, where the program took wing in the 1940s and 1950s thanks to the dedicated efforts of the two men most closely identified with the idea: Robert M. Hutchins and Mortimer J. Adler.

Adler had been a student in Erskine's two-year program at Columbia, which required reading the classics of Western thought—mainly history, economics, philosophy, politics, and literature—and he later began to teach the seminar himself, as did Mark Van Doren and Clifton Fadiman. Hutchins, Chicago's president, hired Adler in 1930 to develop a Great Books program based on the Columbia model. With the help of Stringfellow Barr and Scott Buchanan, Adler expanded the list of books to include mathematics and the natural sciences, thereby creating an undergraduate course of study in the liberal arts based on great books. Barr and Buchanan in 1937 took the four-year curriculum to St. John's College in Annapolis, where today it remains intact and widely celebrated.

The St. John's program, likened to the trivium and quadrivium, is a single course of study that views the liberal arts as a coherent and interconnected whole, allowing interdisciplinary learning in the essential subjects of literature, history, languages, music, philosophy, natural sciences, and mathematics. Instead of majoring in one discipline, students in small seminars read primary works chronologically from antiquity (starting with Homer's *The Iliad* and *The Odyssey*) to the late nineteenth and mid-twentieth centuries (e.g., William James's *The Principles of Psychology* and Flannery O'Connor's short stories).

Besides the St. John's programs in Annapolis and Sante Fe, Great Books programs as a single course of study leading to the bachelor degree continue on only seven campuses. The approximately 193 other programs utilizing the Great Books are structured as two- or three-course sequences in the literature of Western civilization under a general education core requirement; as Honors curricula; or as major, minor, or certificate programs that draw on existing courses across the disciplines in which a "Great Book" or two is read. Some of these programs follow the St. John's view of the liberal arts as an integrated whole, while others use a discipline-based approach that adheres to conventional departmental divisions in higher education. Moreover, with the rise of postmodernism and multiculturalism, some Great Books programs either have been dismantled (as at Stanford University) or else forced to adopt Western, and non-Western, works not yet considered great because they have not stood the test of time.

—WILLIAM F. MEEHAN III

Further Reading

Adler, Mortimer J., Clifton Fadiman, and Philip W. Goetz, eds. *Great Books of the Western World.* 2nd ed., 61 vols. Chicago: Encyclopaedia Britannica, 1990.

Casement, William. "Whither the Great Books." *Academic Questions* 15 (Fall 2002): 36–51.

See also: education, higher; London, Herbert I.; Regnery, Henry; Senior, John

Grove City College

Grove City College, a once obscure private academy in the hills of western Pennsylvania, has become one of the best small colleges in America, noted for providing a superior education within a Christian environment at a reasonable cost—about $15,000 in 2005-6 for tuition, room, board, books, and a notebook computer and printer for every student. Many other colleges started out with the same objectives but have compromised on quality, atmosphere, or price, and sometimes on all three. Founded in 1876, Grove City has remained faithful to its original mission, in large measure because of its leadership.

For most of the school's first eighty years, Isaac Ketler, followed by his son Weir, served as college president, while Joseph N. Pew and then his son J. Howard Pew chaired the board of trustees. The continuing collaboration of the Ketlers and Pews over eight decades is unprecedented in American higher education and was based on a common commitment to political and economic freedom within a Christian context. President Weir Ketler asserted that it was the college's aim to send out into the world young men and women who would not be afraid "to make a stand for the right in the moral and civic issues of life."

It was in the post–World War II years that Grove City College diverged sharply from public and other private institutions regarding income and operations. State-supported schools received as much as three-fourths of their funding from nonstudent sources—most of it from the government. Private schools depended on endowments or gifts for about 50 percent of their income. But Grove City persisted in operating on what it received each year in student tuition and fees, determined to remain financially independent of government.

The college's defining moment—earning Grove City national attention and conservative approbation—came in 1976 when President Charles S. MacKenzie declined to sign a letter of compliance with Title IX of the Education Amendments Act of 1972. Title IX forbade discrimination against women, but that was not why Grove City refused to comply. The college had been coeducational from its founding and had never discriminated against women. But compliance with Title IX would have inevitably led to compliance with all future amendments and interpretations of the title. At issue was not a seemingly benign government regulation, but the fundamental question: Who runs a private educational institution like Grove City College—the federal government or the institution's trustees and officers?

There ensued an eight-year legal battle that cost the college over $500,000 in legal fees and expenses. In 1984, the Supreme Court ruled that the federal scholarship grants given to Grove City students were direct aid and sufficient to trigger the provisions of Title IX. The college quickly acted to preserve its independence by creating a private student grant plan. Twelve years later, it withdrew from all federal student loan programs and started its own campus loan program. Today, along with Hillsdale College, it is known among conservatives as an institution at which principled conservatism thrives.

—LEE EDWARDS

Further Reading

Edwards, Lee. *Freedom's College: The History of Grove City College*. Washington, D.C.: Regnery, 2000.

See also: education, higher; Hillsdale College

Gulf War (1990–91)

The Gulf War of 1990–91 was the first major military crisis that the United States faced in the post–Cold War era. In turning back Iraqi aggression, the U.S. affirmed its claim to be the dominant power in the oil-rich Persian Gulf. But the American victory was an incomplete one, failing to eliminate Saddam Hussein, the chief threat to regional stability. Furthermore, few of the expected benefits of this seemingly great victory actually materialized. Indeed, the chief "lessons" drawn from the war would prove to be problematic, and the war itself sparked increased tensions between "isolationist" conservatives (most prominently Pat Buchanan) and internationalists of conservative and neoconservative leanings.

On August 2, 1990, Iraqi mechanized forces invaded and quickly overran Kuwait. As a result, Saddam Hussein gained direct control of that nation's substantial oil reserves. More ominously still, Saddam's conquest of Kuwait also put him in a position to threaten or intimidate Saudi Arabia, with its even larger reserves.

The administration of George H. W. Bush viewed Iraqi aggression not only as a threat to vital U.S. economic and security interests in the region, but as a direct challenge to the prospects for a peaceful post–Cold War international order. Declaring that the Iraqi aggression "will not stand," Bush secured Saudi agreement to the immediate deployment of U.S. forces to defend Saudi Arabia (Operation Desert Shield). In an extraordinary display of diplomatic skill, the Bush administration also isolated Iraq through a series of United Nations–imposed sanctions and assembled a diverse coalition of nations to contribute military forces. With few exceptions, the entire "international community" condemned Saddam.

By October 1990, overruling those who favored continued reliance on economic pressure to free Kuwait, Bush decided to use force. More U.S. and allied troops poured into staging areas in Saudi Arabia. On January 16, 1991, with the U.S. troop contingent alone now numbering more than 500,000, Operation Desert Storm commenced. A massive air campaign targeted the Iraqi forces occupying Kuwait, "strategic" targets in Baghdad, and sites throughout Iraq suspected of being used to produce weapons of mass destruction. Only in late February, with the Iraqi army verging on collapse, did coalition ground forces attack. One hundred hours after the ground offensive began, the liberation of Kuwait was complete and Bush suspended hostilities. Coalition casualties were amazingly light; fewer than 150 U.S. troops were killed in action, creating popular expectations that the United States henceforth should be able employ its military power without putting its own forces at risk.

Expectations that Saddam himself would be unable to survive such a devastating defeat proved to be misplaced. Ruthlessly suppressing internal opposition (which the U.S. government had encouraged), he survived until 2003, when George W. Bush followed in his father's footsteps by launching his own war on Iraq.

—ANDREW J. BACEVICH

Further Reading

Gordon, Michael R., and Bernard E. Trainor. *The Generals' War.* Boston: Little, Brown, 1995.

See also: Iraq War

H

Haberler, Gottfried (1901–95)

Haberler was one of the first economists to make a rigorous case for the superior productivity and universal benefits of "free" or politically unrestricted international trade in terms of the modern subjective theory of value. He also developed an approach to analyzing cyclical booms and busts that was based on a synthesis of pre-Keynesian business cycle theories and heavily emphasized the causal role of political manipulations of the money supply. As a world-renowned and influential expert in these areas, Haberler almost always firmly and actively opposed the protectionist and inflationist programs and policies advocated by many of his fellow economists and adopted by the governments of less developed countries and of Western mixed economies in the postwar period.

Gottfried Haberler

Haberler was born in Austria and emigrated to the United States in 1936 to join the faculty of Harvard University as a professor of economics. From 1971, when he retired from Harvard, until his death, Haberler was a resident scholar at the American Enterprise Institute in Washington, D.C.

While in Austria in the 1920s and 1930s, Haberler was a member of the famous Mises-Kreis, the distinguished circle of economists, sociologists, and philosophers who regularly participated in the private seminar organized by Austrian economist Ludwig von Mises. The formative influence of Mises and the Austrian school has always been strongly evident in Haberler's theoretical work and in his policy advocacy, although this influence has at times been obscured by Haberler's vigorous rejection of some aspects of the Austrian theory of the business cycle and by his opposition, in later writings, to the international gold standard. Thus, in terms of economic worldview, Haberler is often, though not very accurately, characterized as a "monetarist" or even a "right-wing Keynesian," and the Austrian connection is altogether ignored.

Haberler made his most important contributions to economic theory in the areas of international trade and business cycles. He was the first to present, in 1933, a modern reformulation of the classical argument that free trade and international division of labor maximize social productivity and the standard of living for all participating nations. Haberler's reformulation was based on the Austrian theory of value and price, which rejects the classical labor theory of value and establishes the crucial link between the subjective values of consumers and the objective monetary cost and revenue calculations of producers, while emphasizing the dynamic interdependence of all economic phenomena.

In a famous study, sponsored and originally published in 1937 by the League of Nations, Haberler undertook a comprehensive survey of the extant literature on business-cycle theory and formulated his own "synthetic" explanation of the causes and nature of cyclical phenomena, which involved a broadly Austrian emphasis on the causal role of changes in the supplies of money and credit combined with price and, especially, wage-rate rigidities imposed by political interventions into the market process.

In the early 1950s, Haberler repudiated his earlier support for an international gold standard featuring national currencies linked to one another by flexible exchange rates, a campaign in which Milton Friedman and other monetarist economists were especially prominent. In addressing the problem of stagflation, which was to become pandemic in Western mixed economies under the latter monetary regime beginning in the early 1970s, Haberler broke with the monetarists and identified the relentless pressure by labor unions for wage rates in excess of market-clearing levels as the initiating cause of inflationary recession. He argued that the politically intolerable level of unemployment inevitably created by the excessive wage settlements gained by legally privileged unions induced the monetary authorities to increase the volume of money and bank credit. The resulting price inflation was intended to alleviate the employment situation by surreptitiously reducing real wage rates back toward market-clearing levels.

In sharp contrast to Keynesian economists, however, who advocated wage and price "guidelines" or controls as the remedy for "cost-push" inflation, Haberler fully accepted the proposition that a persistent rise in general prices cannot occur without an increase in the money supply, and he stood staunchly against any alleged remedy involving political intervention into the distortion of the market's pricing and resource-allocation process. Instead, Haberler prescribed a policy of strict restraint in the growth of the money supply combined with free market–oriented microeconomic policies aimed at radically reducing or eliminating the monopoly power of labor unions and business organizations. These latter policies included further liberalization of international trade, deregulation of domestic industries, abolition of the minimum wage, the abrogation of "prevailing wage" laws mandating that government buy only from firms paying union wages, the termination of welfare and unemployment subsidies to striking workers, and the abolition of special legal privileges and immunities enjoyed by labor unions.

—JOSEPH T. SALERNO

Further Reading

Baldwin, Robert E. "Gottfried Haberler's Contributions to International Trade Theory and Policy." *Quarterly Journal of Economics* 97 (1982): 141–48.

Haberler, Gottfried. *Prosperity and Depression: A Theoretical Analysis of Cyclical Movements.* 5th ed. New York: Atheneum, 1963.

———. *Economic Growth and Stability: An Analysis of Economic Change and Policies.* Los Angeles: Nash, 1974.

———. *The Problem of Stagflation: Reflection on the Microfoundation of Macroeconomic Theory and Policy.* Washington, D.C.: American Enterprise Institute, 1985.

Willett, Thomas D. "Gottfried Haberler on Inflation, Unemployment, and International Monetary Economics: An Appreciation." *Quarterly Journal of Economics* 97 (1982): 161–69.

See also: Austrian school of economics; free trade

Hallowell, John H. (1913–91)

John Hamilton Hallowell was one of the most distinguished conservative political theorists of the mid-twentieth century. A graduate of Harvard University, he also attended Duke University (M.A.) and Princeton University (Ph.D.), completing his dissertation (1939) at the latter institution under the direction of another great conservative political theorist, Gerhart Niemeyer. He later was awarded a Litt.D by the College of the Holy Cross. Hallowell taught politics at Princeton and the University of California at Los Angeles. He was later a visiting professor at Stanford University, the University of Illinois, and the University of North Carolina, and a Charles R. Walgreen lecturer at the University of Chicago. He spent the majority of his teaching career, however, at Duke, where he taught from 1942 until 1981. Additionally, he was director of the Lilly Endowment Research Program in Christianity and Politics from 1957 to 1968.

Hallowell's influence made itself felt in the careers of many young scholars and teachers, including prominent conservatives such as Russell Kirk, who wrote his master's thesis on John Randolph of Roanoke while studying with Hallowell at Duke, and Francis Canavan, who wrote a dissertation on Edmund Burke under Hallowell's direction and who credited Hallowell for awakening him and others of his generation to the conservative and Christian character of Burke's thought. Indeed, it was the connection between religion and political theory that was the principal focus of Hallowell's scholarly work. He once observed that political science cannot "be approached with 'scientific' detachment divorced from all ethical considerations."

Through Niemeyer, Hallowell was influenced by the work of both Eric Voegelin and Michael Polanyi and drew Christian political conclusions from his reading of their work. In books such as *The Decline of Liberalism as an Ideology* (1943), *Main Currents in Modern Political Thought* (1950), and *The Moral Foundation of Democracy* (1953), he established himself as a trenchant critic of liberalism and the French Enlightenment understanding of man and society. Hallowell believed that liberalism, positivism, and totalitarianism were manifestations of the same fundamental theoretical error of the separation of politics from the transcendent. He believed, that is, that liberalism at its core is totalist and tyrannical (echoing a formulation later made famous by James Burnham, Hallowell asserted that "modern liberalism is an invitation to suicide"). He instead embraced an organic understanding of society that led him to stress the existence of a common good above and beyond particular interests. This inclined him to an adherence to the moral natural law tradition; as he once put it, "knowledge of what man should do in order to fulfill his human nature is embodied in what has traditionally been called the 'law of nature' or 'moral law.'" To this end, Hallowell rightly described himself as a "classical realist."

—Jeffrey O. Nelson

Further Reading

Canavan, Francis, ed. *The Ethical Dimension of Political Life: Essays in Honor of John H. Hallowell.* Durham, N.C.: Duke University Press, 1983.

Nash, George H. *The Conservative Intellectual Movement in America since 1945.* 2nd ed. Wilmington, Del.: Intercollegiate Studies Institute, 1996.

See also: Canavan, Francis, S.J..; Kirk, Russell; Niemeyer, Gerhart; Voegelin, Eric

Hamilton, Alexander (1757–1804)

Alexander Hamilton emigrated to New York in 1773 and entered King's College (now Columbia), where he penned pamphlets defending the revolutionary cause. When war broke out he enlisted in the Continental Army and served much of the time as an aide-de-camp to General George Washington. After a term in the Continental Congress (1782–83) he began to practice law. Convinced that the government under the Articles of Confederation was impotent, he attended the Annapolis Convention (1786) and was instrumental in parlaying that meeting into a call for the Constitutional Convention of 1787. His major work in support of the proposed Constitution was his collaboration with John Jay and James Madison to produce *The Federalist* (1788), arguably the most important body of American political writing.

In 1789 Hamilton became the first secretary of the treasury, in which capacity he was committed to free-market capitalism, primarily on moral grounds. He thought that the greatest benefit of a system of government-encouraged private enterprise was the enlargement of the scope of human freedom. "To cherish and stimulate the activity of the human mind" was a distinct good, and "every new scene, which is opened to the busy nature of man to rouse and exert itself, is the addition of a new energy to the general stock of effort."

Instructed by the House of Representatives to devise a plan for coping with the Revolutionary War debts, he produced in 1790 his "Report on Public Credit." In it and subsequent reports he advocated the creation of a stable but flexible monetary system. Hamilton's 1791 "Report on Manufactures" was never fully implemented, for men crying "give the people liberty," but meaning "give us power," banded together to stop him. Still, until he resigned as secretary in 1795, he functioned essentially as the "prime minister" for the Washington administration, and the institutions he created endured and functioned as he had hoped they would. He died in 1804 as a result of a duel with Aaron Burr.

Hamilton trusted neither elites nor the masses. "Give all power to the many," he said, and "they will oppress the few. Give all power to the few, they will oppress the many. Both therefore ought to have power, that each may defend itself against the other." Furthermore, he did not trust individual virtue; he believed that all men were ruled by their passions rather than by reason, and public men were especially motivated by ambition and avarice. His work was thus based upon a "pessimistic" view of mankind. And yet he also believed that if public institutions were properly organized the passions could be channeled, on the average, for the collective good.

Alexander Hamilton

Hamilton saw provincialism and inertia as keeping eighteenth-century America from becoming a great nation. The system as he described it discouraged industry because status derived not from the marketplace, where deeds and goods could be impartially valued, but from birthrights and local hierarchies. He sought, through the office of minister of finance, to reshape that social order. To make society fluid and open to merit, what needed to be done was to monetize the whole. He regarded money as a neutral, impersonal arbiter that would tie individual interests to the interests of the whole. Infused into an agrarian system, money would be the fermenting yeast that gave rise to change and prosperity. And he thought that the most efficacious way of combining freedom and energy in a people was to rely less upon ordering what was to be done than by establishing the way and procedures by which things were done. His view of society was also reflected in his opposition to slavery, and he was an active participant in New York's antislavery movement.

Hamilton rejected laissez-faire theories. "Experience teaches," he wrote, "that men are often so much governed by what they are accustomed to see and practice, that the simplest and most obvious improvements, in the most ordinary occupations, are adopted with hesitation, reluctance, and by slow gradations." Hamilton proposed, therefore, to use government to encourage economic change. Yet, he was emphatic in his reliance upon voluntarism and capitalism.

—FORREST MCDONALD

Further Reading

Brookhiser, Richard. *Alexander Hamilton: American*. New York: Free Press, 1999.

Chernow, Ron. *Alexander Hamilton*. New York: Penguin, 2004.

Hamilton, Alexander. *The Papers of Alexander Hamilton*. Edited by Harold C. Syrett et al. 26 vols. New York: Columbia University Press, 1961–79.

McDonald, Forrest. *Alexander Hamilton: A Biography*. New York: Norton, 1979.

Miller, John C. *Alexander Hamilton: Portrait in Paradox*. New York: Harper, 1959.

See also: Adams, John; Bill of Rights; federalism; The Federalist; *Federalist Party; Washington, George*

Harper, Floyd Arthur "Baldy" (1905–73)

A teacher, economist, educator, and prolific writer interested in the moral, political, and social aspects of liberty, Floyd "Baldy"

Harper was a notable inspiration and guide to conservatives and libertarians throughout the world and a founding member of the Mont Pelerin Society (Switzerland, 1947). Harper also fulfilled his lifelong dream of creating a center for basic research and advanced study in the humane scholarly disciplines with his almost single-handed establishment of the Institute for Humane Studies in Menlo Park, California, in 1961.

After graduation from Michigan State University in 1926, Harper received a Ph.D. in agricultural economics from Cornell University in 1932, where he taught economics and statistics for nineteen years. During his years at Cornell, he became increasingly concerned about statist intervention in the economy and private affairs. From 1946 until 1958, he served as the chief economist for the Foundation for Economic Education. It was here that he wrote two of his most notable works: *Liberty: A Path to Its Recovery* (1949), and *In Search of Peace* (1951). In the former, he stressed the primacy of property rights, and concluded that without property rights, no rights are possible at all. In the latter, he pointed out the danger of false ideas, which can be successfully attacked only with superior ideas, facts, and logic, not by adopting the philosophy or tactics of one's opponent. While not a pacifist or isolationist, Harper considered winning the Korean War as less important than successfully combating the adoption of communist and interventionist ideology at home.

Harper, like Friedrich A. Hayek (whose *The Road to Serfdom* (1944) influenced him greatly), did not consider himself a conservative, but rather a European classical liberal or libertarian. Instead of trying to slow down the authoritarian trends in our society, Harper believed that total liberty was to be sought after as the ultimate goal. To this end, he built the Institute for Humane Studies upon much of Hayek's strategy for achieving social change. Harper saw the importance of developing libertarian ideas and scholarship by focusing the institute's long-range goals on the identification of talented young people and scholars interested in the ideals of the voluntary society, and then nurturing and developing their capabilities.

—CARL WATNER

Further Reading

Harper, Floyd A. *The Writings of Floyd A. Harper.* 2 vols. Menlo Park, Calif.: Institute for Humane Studies, 1978.

See also: Foundation for Economic Education; Institute for Humane Studies; liberalism, classical; libertarianism; Mont Pelerin Society

Harrigan, Anthony (1925–)

As author or editor of nearly two dozen books and as a contributor to more than seventy journals on both sides of the Atlantic, Anthony Harrigan has demonstrated an unusual combination of the traditionalist and anticommunist impulses of the postwar American conservative movement. As a foundation executive, he has also entered into economic debates, warning that unrestricted free trade can weaken American industry and, thereby, American security. Generally, in his writings Harrigan seeks to find how nations in an advanced industrial and global society can be structured politically and economically so as to preserve the settled ways of life of the common man in his local community.

In the 1950s and 1960s, Harrigan was a leading figure behind the "ultraconservative" *Charleston* (South Carolina) *News and Courier.* During the civil rights movement he, like many Southern conservatives, staked out a strongly segregationist position, and his states' rights beliefs led him to view favorably such experiments in regional autonomy as Quebec's independence movement and the division of Cyprus. In this period he also took an acute interest in national security issues, writing about unconventional warfare in *A Guide to the War in Vietnam* (1966) and about nuclear strategy in *Defense against Total Attack* (1965). In *Red Star over Africa* (1964) and elsewhere he warned about communist advances in the developing world.

In the 1980s, as president of the United States Business and Industrial Council and the United States Industrial Council Educational Foundation, Harrigan argued for economic policies appropriate to his commitment to middle-American values. In *American Economic Pre-eminence* (1989), written with William R. Hawkins, he championed a neomercantilist approach to trade policy, a combination of incentives and protective measures centered on the principle that economic policy should serve the national interest in increasing relative national power and wealth. This direct opposition to the classically liberal trade policies favored by neoconservatives marked one front in the dispute between "paleos" and "neos" in the waning days of the Reagan administration.

Harrigan's thought reflects the influence of the works of W. R. Inge and Bernard Iddings Bell, as well as the Southern Agrarians. In evocative and sometimes moving essays reflecting his own experiences, he has appealed to the local traditions and particularities of small-town American life against the values of an urban Eastern elite. He has attacked the "crass materialism" and "shallow cosmopolitanism" of these elites, the latter described as "a disease of the intellectual faculties" that poses a danger to "solid national communities." This defense of the local traditions of concrete communities against the disintegrating rationalism of "cosmopolitans" has proven a recurring theme in his writings.

Throughout his work Harrigan has written as a self-conscious, reflective defender of the inarticulate yet profound conservatism of the common man in America. This entails a fundamentally populist orientation, and in the populism of this very traditionalist paleoconservative we can see the roots of the New Right that emerged in the 1980s.

—MARK C. HENRIE

Further Reading

Harrigan, Anthony, ed. *Putting America First: A Conservative Trade Alternative.* Washington, D.C.: USIC Educational Foundation, 1987.

See also: New Right; paleoconservatism; populism

Hart, Jeffrey (1930–)

An eclectic thinker and personality, *National Review* senior editor, and long-time professor of English at Dartmouth College, Jeffrey Hart has contributed to our understanding of eighteenth-century literary and political figures such as Samuel Johnson, Viscount Bolingbroke, and Edmund Burke. He has also studied the modern American novelist F. Scott Fitzgerald in an attempt to reconcile conservative principles with optimistic American experience. During graduate study in English literature at Columbia University in the late 1950s, Hart was influenced by Lionel Trilling, and an appreciation for modernism in art has remained a distinguishing feature of his work.

In the early 1960s, Hart concentrated on his studies of eighteenth-century England. In *Viscount Bolingbroke* (1965), he argued that, in the thought of the Tory humanists, the traditional values of Western culture, heretofore taken for granted, "become in some part critical, modes of attack upon other values that are beginning to prevail." In other words, "the traditional conception of society, giving way before the commercial and then the industrial revolutions, became a component of the politics of protest." This idea of what might be called a "critical" tra-

ditionalism, a conservatism of protest and opposition, has remained with Hart, though it necessarily underwent reformulation after the conservative ascendancy of the 1980s.

In the later 1960s and early 1970s, Hart became increasingly active in conservative political and journalistic circles. During this period he served as a speechwriter for both Ronald Reagan (1968) and Richard Nixon (1968, 1972); he launched a syndicated column through King Features (1969); he wrote *The American Dissent* (1966), which chronicled the developing thought of the *National Review* circle; and he became a senior editor of *National Review* (1968). In 1968 he was also received into the Roman Catholic Church. In the 1980s, Hart's interests shifted to contemporary social and cultural criticism and to historical narratives of recent American history. His books, *When the Going Was Good! American Life in the 1950s* (1982) and *From This Moment On: America in 1940* (1987) recalled the innocence of a period when "traditional American values" were not under attack, a time when even conservatives could look forward to a bright future for America. His most recent work is *The Making of the American Conservative Mind* (2005), an eclectic and highly personal account of the history of *National Review* that takes to task the magazine and the Bush administration for, as he sees it, entangling conservatism with utopian foreign policy notions and the authoritarian and unrealistic goals of evangelical Christianity.

Hart's thought is difficult to characterize. His deep skepticism about the exercise of state power and his affection for free markets give a libertarian slant to some of his commentary. Yet a clear element of cultural conservatism emerges in his defense of traditional order in the academy, and he calls himself a traditionalist. These seemingly conflicting emphases could be explained within the terms of Frank Meyer's "fusionist" paradigm. But Hart's thought is more protean than this. In the early 1980s he criticized "young fogies," who seemed to believe that the main content of conservatism was "the refusal of experience." To the contrary, Hart maintained that the great modern sin is "the great refusal"—the unlived life—and that an American conservatism must embrace an optimistic sense of "possibility."

Furthermore, claiming that "the average American is a modernist in his bones," Hart argued that American conservatism must work out a "modern" relationship to "tradition." But, he continued, to be modern is to be conscious of a break with tradition. To be modern is to be conscious of one's own novelty. How can one be a "traditionalist" while breaking with tradition? Hart gave no clear answer, though he seemed to believe that elements of a tradition could be appropriated by American conservatives eclectically and creatively.

This ambivalence between traditionalism and modernism has remained a perplexing problem for Hart. In an important essay, "Johnson, Boswell, and Modernity," published in his *Acts of Recovery* (1989), Hart observed that Boswell and Johnson each experienced a heady feeling of nearly limitless possibility when they arrived in London; each could sense an immense freedom for self-creation open to them in the metropolis. This is the modern experience. But while Boswell abandoned himself to a parade of impersonations, of improvised "selves," Johnson intransigently defended a single and fixed—but self-created—role for himself in "the great system of society." If we seek a model for how a critical traditionalist can come to terms with the modern condition, Hart points us ultimately to Dr. Johnson.

—MARK C. HENRIE

Further Reading

Hart, Jeffrey. "The Intelligent Woman's Guide to a Modern American Conservatism." In *The New Right Papers,* edited by Robert W. Whitaker, 36–47. New York: St. Martin's Press, 1982.

———. *Political Writers of Eighteenth-Century England.* New York: Knopf, 1964.

———. *Smiling through the Cultural Catastrophe: Toward the Revival of Higher Education.* New Haven, Conn.: Yale University Press, 2001.

———. *Viscount Bolingbroke: Tory Humanist.* London: Routledge & Kegan Paul, 1965.

See also: National Review

Hawthorne, Nathaniel (1804–64)

Nathaniel Hawthorne, the first great American novelist, made ambiguity one of the hallmarks of his fiction. But as difficult and complex as his narratives may be to interpret, there is a consistent sensibility behind them, one that probed the competing ideologies of the nineteenth century and found them wanting. Though he was not a systematic thinker, Hawthorne strove to find a "third way" that would avoid the errors of Puritan conservatism and Transcendentalist liberalism. The achievement of his work is not that he provided a clear blueprint for that third way, but that he was able, in the language of metaphor, to sketch out some of its outlines.

Born in 1804 in Salem, Massachusetts, Hawthorne's family had long been prominent in New England life; as he notes in *The Scarlet Letter* (1850), one of his ancestors had presided over the Salem witch trials—a fact that haunted him over the years. He was educated at Bowdoin College, where he met and befriended Franklin Pierce, who would later be elected president of the United States.

Hawthorne was not an especially political person but his politics were controversial in his time and remain so today. He was a lifelong Democrat and relied on his connections with fellow party members to help him find government posts that might help support his family. One success involved his being named inspector at the Customs House in Salem. Later, he would write Pierce's campaign biography.

Both he and Pierce opposed the more radical forms of the abolitionist movement. As Brenda Wineapple, his latest biographer, attests, Hawthorne "didn't for a minute condone slavery," but rather "favored a gradual approach," since he felt that the constitutional framework holding the states together was the only bulwark against the anarchy of rampant sectionalism. Hawthorne's gradualism was of a piece with his essentially conservative sensibility, averse as it was to abstract systems and radical politics.

Nathaniel Hawthorne

While he may not have been a political thinker per se, Hawthorne was interested in ideas. Early in his life he developed a fascination with the intellectual currents swirling about the Transcendentalists—whose members included Ralph Waldo Emerson, Margaret Fuller, and Henry David Thoreau. So serious was his interest in the Transcendentalists that Hawthorne chose to join the experimental utopian community they founded, Brook Farm. He left after a mere six months, disillusioned not only with this community but with Transcendentalism in general, a feeling that was reflected in his deft satire on Brook Farm, *The Blithedale Romance* (1852). He came to the conclusion that Transcendentalism's emphasis on the autonomy of the individual, instructed only by Nature (and not the past), ignored the reality of evil and the abiding importance of history and tradition.

It was in his masterpiece, *The Scarlet Letter* (1850), that he would explore the twin dangers of pharisaical religious moralism—represented by the dour Puritans in the story—and the new Transcendentalist philosophy—embodied, for a time at least, by the novel's protagonist, Hester Prynne. By the novel's end, Hester's quietly sacrificial embrace of suffering, tragic though it may be, is set in opposition to the dominant ideologies of the time. Later, in *The Marble Faun* (1860), he would further explore themes of suffering and penance in an Italian setting. (Hawthorne's daughter, Rose, would later convert to Catholicism and become a Dominican nun.)

Many of Hawthorne's short stories are also considered classics of American literature, including "The Minister's Black Veil," "Roger Malvin's Burial," "Young Goodman Brown," "Rappaccini's Daughter," and "Ethan Brand."

—GREGORY WOLFE

Further Reading

Lewis, R. W. B. *The American Adam: Innocence, Tragedy, and Tradition in the Nineteenth Century.* Chicago: University of Chicago Press, 1955.

Miller, Edwin Haviland. *Salem Is My Dwelling Place: A Life of Nathaniel Hawthorne.* Iowa City, Iowa: University of Iowa Press, 1991.

Montgomery, Marion. *Why Hawthorne Was Melancholy.* La Salle, Ill.: Sherwood Sugden, 1984.

Wineapple, Brenda. *Hawthorne: A Life.* New York: Alfred A. Knopf, 2003.

See also: historicism; tradition

Hayek, Friedrich A. von (1899–1992)

The 1974 Nobel laureate in economics, Friedrich A. von Hayek was among the most influential intellectuals of the twentieth century. A multidisciplinary scholar in economics, social theory, and political philosophy, Hayek was dedicated to the idea of a free society. Although Hayek exerted perhaps his greatest influence on the conservative movement in England and the United States, he considered himself a classical liberal. Many view his work as the dominant influence over the Reagan revolution in the United States and the Thatcher administration in Great Britain, as well as the general movement toward a renewed appreciation of the free-market economy and globalization that has marked the last several decades. Hayek was awarded the Companion of Honour in Britain in 1984 and the Medal of Freedom by the United States in 1991.

Hayek's career across multiple disciplines was dedicated to the study of what he called "spontaneous orders." A spontaneous order is an institution, economic outcome, or social norm that serves a social purpose even though it was not intentionally planned to do so by any one set of individuals. In the words of Scottish philosopher Adam Ferguson, the spontaneous order of society and economy is "the product of human action but not of human design." A devotee of the philosophers of the Scottish Enlightenment—such as David Hume and Adam Smith—Hayek spent a career criticizing the idea of "rational constructivism" by government. In his understanding, societies have the capacity to spontaneously build up laws and institutions that contain and reflect the experience and understanding of past generations. Proponents of expansive government and socialist central planning commit what Hayek labeled "the fatal conceit" by attempting to destroy these traditional orders in order to build up "rational" orders in their place. In his understanding, the most important knowledge available to us for the purposes of operating a society are not given to one mind but are distributed among millions of actors and develop by trial and error over time. Rationalist central planners of economies or societies are doomed to fail because no group of minds can contain, process, or even confront the personal and dispersed information and experience of an entire society—let alone the received institutions and mores of past generations.

This general outlook has striking similarity to the traditionalist strain in conservatism, epitomized by Edmund Burke. Burke's conservatism was based on a suspicion of the "leveling instinct" that dominated Enlightenment thought in the eighteenth century. This tendency among would-be social planners threatened to wipe out traditional institutions, such as the British common law constitution, which Burke believed contained the experience and intuitions of past generations. However, Hayek refused to be labeled a conservative. Because interventions by government are almost invariably rationalist replacements of the spontaneous order developed naturally by tradition and complex social interaction, Hayek favored a strictly limited government in *both* economic and moral spheres. His policy outlook was unquestionably classical liberal—the only form of government that he believed allowed a society to contain and use the collective experience, local knowledge, and traditional inheritance of its people.

Hayek was born in 1899 in Austria to a family of intellectuals. His earliest education was in biology—a field that had an inherent saturation in the evolutionary understanding that would eventually suffuse Hayek's work. Later, at the University of Vienna, Hayek specialized in economics, studying under Friedrich Weiser. Hayek took positions in the Austrian government during the 1920s and later acted as director of the Institute for Business Cycle Research in Vienna. During this period, Hayek was deeply influenced by the work done by the Austrian economist, Ludwig von Mises. Mises' work on the impossibility of socialist central planning turned Hayek away from the Fabian socialist leanings of his youth.

Hayek distinguished himself early in his career by elucidating and building the Austrian theory of the business cycle with Mises (1931 and 1933). This theory held that business cycles were caused not by inherent structural problems in laissez-faire economies, but rather by credit expansion by central banks. Through this work and his work on capital theory, Hayek became prominent and was eventually appointed to the faculty of the prestigious London School of Economics. In the 1930s, Hayek's business-cycle theory became the main rival to the developing interventionist theories of the Cambridge economist, John Maynard Keynes, who taught that business cycles were the results of inherent flaws in capitalist economies.

Friedrich A. von Hayek

Hayek also became involved in the famous socialist calculation debates, again building off the work of his mentor, Mises. Hayek contended that socialism was doomed to fail because central planners could not process essential economic information, which was dispersed among all participants in an economy and was changing constantly. Prices—which are absent in socialism—are the only mechanism capable of absorbing, codifying, and communicating the information of time and place essential for healthy economies. Hayek's work on dispersed information led him to write several landmark pieces during the 1940s dealing with the way that local, tacit knowledge of time and place was processed in the spontaneous order of the free market. This insight—that the primary question of economics was how it processed knowledge—was to become the foundation of his later work in political philosophy and social theory.

The general intellectual climate of opinion, including scientific opinion, was not receptive to Hayek's criticisms of either Keynesianism or socialism when they were first developed in the 1930s and '40s. Ironically, during the very period when his influence in the economics profession was declining, his influence within a segment of the general public rose to unexpected heights. In 1944 he published *The Road to Serfdom*, a work widely read in the United States and even abridged and distributed by *Reader's Digest*. In this book, Hayek argued that expansive governments naturally tended toward authoritarianism and even dictatorship. Hayek's major argument was that socialism—which was finding increasing favor among the educated classes—had the same essential features as fascism—which the West had just spent a long and bloody war fighting. In addition to his scholarship, Hayek worked tirelessly to organize the intellectual leaders of classical liberalism to reinvigorate the worldwide movement in support of a society of free and responsible individuals. In 1946, he founded the Mont Pelerin Society. The MPS exerted a tremendous influence on the course of economic policy in the second half of the twentieth century as its active members included such Nobel Prize winners in economics as Milton Friedman, George Stigler, Ronald Coase, Gary Becker, and James Buchanan.

In 1950, Hayek immigrated to the United States and took a position at the University of Chicago on its Committee for Social

Thought. In 1962 he returned to Europe, taking a post at the University of Freiburg in Germany, and then in 1968 at the University of Salzburg in Austria. At Chicago, Freiburg, and Salzburg, Hayek pursued academic research in areas other than technical economics. In 1952, for example, Hayek published both *The Sensory Order*, a study of psychology and the philosophy of mind that has had influence in the field of evolutionary psychology, and his classic work in the philosophy of science, *The Counter-Revolution of Science*. He also published his political treatise, *The Constitution of Liberty*, in 1960, and his major legal study, *Law, Legislation and Liberty*, between 1973 and 1979. In 1988, Hayek published a summary of his life's work, *The Fatal Conceit*, which outlines his understanding of tradition, the evolution of human society, and the ultimate errors of "socialists of all parties."

Hayek died on March 23, 1992, at the age of 92.

—PETER BOETTKE AND RYAN OPREA

Further Reading

Boettke, P., ed. *The Legacy of F. A. Hayek: Politics, Philosophy and Economics.* 3 vols. Northampton, Mass.: Edward Elgar Publishers, 1999.

Caldwell, Bruce. *Hayek's Challenge: An Intellectual Biography of F. A. Hayek.* Chicago: University of Chicago Press, 2004.

Hayek, F. A. *Individualism and Economic Order.* Chicago: University of Chicago Press, 1948.

———. *Monetary Theory and the Trade Cycle.* 1933. New York: Augustus M. Kelley, 1966.

———. *Prices and Production.* 1931. New York: Augustus M. Kelley, 1967.

See also: Austrian school of economics; bureaucracy; émigré intellectuals; fusionism; liberalism, classical; libertarianism; Mises, Ludwig von; Mont Pelerin Society; Road to Serfdom, The

Hayes, Carlton J. H. (1882–1964)

Born in Afton, New York, and raised a Baptist, Carlton Joseph Huntley Hayes converted to Catholicism in 1904 while an undergraduate at Columbia University, and his marriage in 1920 to Evelyn Carroll, a Catholic graduate student at Columbia Teachers College, allowed him to deepen his interest in a religion which became the focal point of his life and work. A historian, Hayes successfully integrated in his work Columbia's New History approach (criticized by many contemporary American Catholic historians for having alleged revolutionary tendencies) with such key tenets of the Christian faith as original sin. This fusion underpinned Hayes's interpretation of European history, which cited nationalism and mankind's perpetual pursuit of progress as major factors behind Europe's descent into mass conflict and the disintegration of the geographical and political entity of Christendom since the sixteenth century.

Hayes's rejection of idealism gained him no little notoriety during his time as ambassador to Spain between 1942 and 1945, when he was vigorously accused of appeasing General Franco by American leftists who had forgotten the importance of Spanish neutrality in the wider battle against fascism. These allegations lingered during the remainder of his career. Hayes criticized this American isolation from, and ignorance of, the wider world in his 1945 presidential address to the American Historical Association (of which he was the first Catholic president), titled "The American Frontier—Frontier of What?" in which he questioned the widespread acceptance of Frederick Jackson Turner's frontier thesis. Rather than being the unique result of the "frontier experience," Hayes argued that the United States' democratic tradition derived from the wider Western tradition and that the Americas should therefore be viewed as Europe's western frontier.

Hayes's final book, *Nationalism: A Religion* (1960), extended his earlier analysis of nationalism to include Asia and Africa. Though a political liberal, Hayes was also a cultural conservative. Indeed, his interpretations influenced some conservatives in the post–World War II years, including especially Ross J. S. Hoffman and John Lukacs. Russell Kirk's understanding of American conservatism and "the roots of American order" can also be read as an extension of the Hayes thesis.
—John Joseph Shanley Jr.

Further Reading

Allitt, Patrick. *Catholic Converts: British and American Intellectuals Turn to Rome*. Ithaca, N.Y.: Cornell University Press, 1997: 240–75.

Hayes, Carlton J. H. *A Generation of Materialism: 1871 –1900*. New York: Harper & Brothers, 1941.

Hughes, Arthur Joseph. "Carlton J. H. Hayes: Teacher and Historian." Ph.D. Dissertation, Columbia University, 1970.

See also: Hoffman, Ross J. S.; Kirk, Russell; Lukacs, John

Hazlitt, Henry (1894–1993)

Henry Hazlitt was one of the most important economic journalists of the twentieth century. From prestigious perches at the *New York Times*, the *Nation*, *Newsweek*, and other periodicals, he penned thousands of articles refuting New Deal economic fallacies and published a wildly successful primer titled *Economics in One Lesson* (1946). The timeless lesson of that book simply states, "[T]he art of economics consists in looking not merely at the immediate but at the longer effects of any act or policy; it consists in tracing the consequences of that policy not merely for one group but for all groups." From this basis, Hazlitt battled against welfare, inflation, foreign aid, economic controls, and Keynesian economics.

Born to humble beginnings in Philadelphia, Hazlitt achieved his prominence through perseverance and natural wit. No Ph.D. or even a bachelor's degree bolstered Hazlitt's résumé; his lucid, incisive writing and clear ideas stood on their own. Prominent economists of the Austrian school, including Ludwig von Mises and F. A. Hayek, as well as H. L. Mencken, counted themselves among Hazlitt's admirers, even if the political Left did not always pay similar deference.

Hazlitt attended New York City College for a year and a half, leaving in order to work. His short time in college, however, only increased his desire for education, and he embarked upon an ambitious plan of study, reading widely and writing every day, which he continued until the end of his life. His interest in economics was aroused by his study of the stock market after working at the *Wall Street Journal*. Two of Hazlitt's major influences were the economic writings of Philip H. Wicksteed and Benjamin M. Anderson. The latter's work, referring often to the thought of von Mises, introduced Hazlitt to the Austrian school of economic theory, which Hazlitt was to publicize in America through his reviews of von Mises' and Hayek's books in the *New York Times*.

In 1950, Hazlitt helped to found and edit the *Freeman*, a journal dedicated to individual liberty and classical liberalism. Five years later the publication was taken over by the Foundation for Economic Education, an organization for which Hazlitt served as vice president on the original board of trustees.

Hazlitt's writing and influence covered a broad spectrum beyond economics, from his critique of the deterministic principles of Freudian psychoanalysis in *The Way to Will Power* (1922), to his books and articles on literary criticism and culture (such as *The Anatomy of Criticism, 1933*), to ventures into philosophy (as in *The Foundations of Morality,* 1964). Yet his primary contribution to history remains his influence in describing in accessible terms the need for a sound dollar, full production, and free-market economics.

—RICH HALVORSON

Further Reading

Hazlitt, Henry. *The Failure of the "New Economics": An Analysis of the Keynesian Fallacies.* Princeton, N.J.: Van Nostrand, 1959.

———. *Man vs. the Welfare State.* New Rochelle, N.Y.: Arlington House, 1969.

See also: Austrian school of economics; Foundation for Economic Education; Freeman; Mises, Ludwig von

Helms, Jesse (1921–)

The most belligerently conservative politician of the post-1960s era, Jesse Helms, former U.S. senator from North Carolina, for a time attained a stature among those on the Right second only to Ronald Reagan's. For those on the other end of the political spectrum, Helms surpassed even Reagan as the foremost villain figure of his time.

Born in 1921 in the small town of Monroe, North Carolina, Helms grew up in a Baptist home dominated by his father, who served as a police and fire official for nearly fifty years. Young Helms attended Wake Forest College and worked as a sports publicist and newspaperman. After military service during World War II, he became the manager of a small radio station in Raleigh, an assignment that gave him his first adult exposure to public affairs.

Since there was no Republican Party of consequence in North Carolina at the time, Helms initially belonged to the Democratic Party. In 1950 he supported the more conservative candidate, Willis Smith, in an exceptionally bitter primary election for a U.S. Senate vacancy. Smith won and brought Helms to Washington as an aide. After Smith died in 1953, Helms became executive director of the North Carolina Bankers Association. He maintained his interest in politics, however, and wrote political editorials for a monthly house organ, *Tarheel Banker*. From 1957 to 1961, Helms also served on the Raleigh City Council.

From 1960 until his election to the Senate in 1972, Helms worked as an executive and TV-radio commentator for the Capitol Broadcasting Company in Raleigh. During these years of upheaval, Helms attracted considerable notice by vigorously expounding an uncompromisingly conservative line. He opposed the 1964 Civil Rights Act and lashed out against Great Society government programs. He derided student protesters, Black Power militants, counterculture activists, and others whom he regarded as enemies of traditional America. Helms supported the Vietnam War as a necessary struggle to prevent communist expansion and eventual world domination.

In 1972, Helms ran for the U.S. Senate as a Republican. He won, aided greatly by President Richard Nixon's massive landslide win in North Carolina. The new senator quickly established himself as a major congressional voice of conservatism. He supported school prayer and a constitutional amendment requiring a balanced budget, and he opposed abortion and school busing to promote racial integration. His pugnaciously anticommunist, anti–Big Government rhetoric endeared him to the New Right forces that emerged in the mid- to late-1970s.

In 1976, Helms supported Reagan's bid for the Republican presidential nomination. Having lost all his early primary skirmishes with President Gerald Ford, Reagan desperately needed a win in North Carolina. Thanks largely to Helms's organization, Reagan narrowly won the state, and his reinvigorated campaign nearly captured the nomination. Had Reagan lost North Carolina, his entire effort against Ford might have collapsed, making it vastly more difficult for him to have mounted a credible race in 1980.

Helms and his national fundraising organization, the Congressional Club, played an important role in the GOP sweep of 1980. With money raised from aggressive direct-mail solicitations to right-wing contributors, the Congressional Club assisted key conservative candidates around the country. On election day Reagan won big at the presidential level, while the GOP scored sizable gains in the House and took control of the Senate for the first time since 1954.

Helms loyally backed President Reagan's tax cuts, defense buildup, and Strategic Defense Initiative, and like Reagan he vigorously championed the Nicaraguan contras in their struggle with the Sandinistan communists. But the senator did not become a mere foot soldier in the Reagan revolution. Helms opposed numerous diplomatic nominations on ideological grounds, and when Senate bills he opposed but could not defeat came to the floor, he frequently engaged in one-man parliamentary maneuvers and other stalling tactics. In 1983, Helms led the opposition to making Martin Luther King's birthday a national holiday. Claiming that the honor was undeserved, Helms demanded the release of King's FBI file, which had been sealed for fifty years by court order because information on King's personal life had been obtained by illegal wiretaps.

For his 1984 reelection bid, Helms squared off against Governor James Hunt, a Democrat with a moderate image. Hunt led in most of the early polls, but Helms charged back with doughty debate performances and saturation television advertisements in the closing weeks of the campaign. He skillfully linked Hunt to Walter Mondale, the lackluster, liberal Democratic presidential nominee. As he had in 1972, Helms profited from a landslide at the top of the ticket: Reagan won the state with 62 percent of the vote, while Helms got 52 percent and another Senate term.

Helms was at the center of a number of high-profile battles in cultural politics during the 1980s and '90s. He was not afraid, for example, to turn his rhetorical fire on gay-rights activists, and the National Endowment for the Arts felt his wrath when Helms learned that the agency had awarded taxpayer-funded grants to artists whose works celebrated the gay lifestyle, derided Christianity, and expressed other politically charged messages in provocative and obscene ways. One especially notorious display, titled "Piss Christ," consisted of a picture of a crucifix lying in a glass container filled with the artist's urine. When Helms sought to eliminate NEA funding for such projects, his opponents cried censorship, and the senator's efforts were only partially successful. Helms's fourth-term bid in 1990 was the year's most ferocious political donnybrook. Running against Harvey Gantt, the African American former mayor of Charlotte, Helms successfully portrayed Gantt as the benefactor of unfair affirmative action programs and himself as an opponent of preferential treatment for either race. Enough voters agreed, and Helms prevailed again. On election night, Helms delighted his followers by publicly ridiculing the media figures unable to hide their disappointment at the outcome.

Helms greeted Bill Clinton's administration by attacking his choice for secretary of state and some of the president's most liberal appointments. But by this time many of Helms's GOP colleagues seemed to have wearied of his relentless assaults on the cultural Left, and despite his seniority Helms's power had noticeably diminished. Nor did the new Bush administration lead to a resurgence of Helms's influence.

Though his actual legislative victories were few, historians will forever cite Helms as an exemplar of congressional conservatism during the years of Reaganite ascendancy. Helms retired from the Senate in 2003.

—James McClellan

Further Reading

Furgurson, Ernest. *Hard Right: The Rise of Jesse Helms*. New York: Norton, 1986.

Helms, Jesse. *Empire for Liberty: A Sovereign America and Her Moral Mission*. Edited by Marc Thiessen. Washington, D.C.: Regnery, 2001.

Snider, William. *Helms and Hunt: The North Carolina Senate Race, 1984*. Chapel Hill, N.C.: University of North Carolina Press, 1985.

See also: culture wars; Republican Party

Helprin, Mark (1947–)

Mark Helprin is a rare figure in contemporary American letters: a writer of fiction who has been hailed as a master of "magical realism" and an unapologetically conservative commentator on foreign policy issues willing to castigate Republicans as often as Democrats. Before his political views were well known, his early books won critical accolades and awards, including the National Jewish Book Award and nominations for both the PEN/Faulkner Award and the National Book Award, but he is now largely shunned by the literary establishment.

Without doubt, Helprin's primary achievement remains his works of fiction. With the publication of *Ellis Island and Other Stories* (1981) and *Winter's Tale* (1983), his gift for penning sweeping narratives and lush, descriptive language was widely recognized. In *Winter's Tale*, an Irish burglar enters a mansion in New York City only to encounter and fall in love with the dying heiress who lives there. The novel spans the entire twentieth century and creates a loving portrait of the city that is both fantastical and grounded in closely observed realism. Helprin's penchant for the themes of love, beauty, and the virtues of loyalty, honor, and courage combine in an almost mystical American romanticism that is sui generis. His novel *A Soldier of the Great War* (1991) is reminiscent of Boris Pasternak's *Doctor Zhivago* in its huge landscape of modern war, erotic love, and political strife.

Helprin's own life story has elements as colorful as any in his stories. As a young man he lived in New York City, the Hudson River valley, and the British West Indies. He served for a time in the British merchant marine. Later, he became an Israeli citizen and served in the Israeli infantry (running "counter-infiltration" missions into Lebanon) and the Israeli Air Force. Helprin has degrees from Harvard University and Harvard Graduate School of Arts and Sciences and also studied at Oxford University. An avid mountain climber, he once nearly died after falling into a crevasse on Mount Rainier.

His credentials as a conservative thinker on geopolitical issues have gained him positions with think tanks such as the Hudson Institute and the Claremont Institute. He has written for *National Review*, the *New Criterion*, and the *Atlantic Monthly*.

Since 1985 Helprin has been an occasional columnist and contributing editor for the *Wall Street Journal*, where he has specialized in foreign policy analysis. A consistent advocate of American military strength, he has supported widespread action against terrorism and militant Islam, and he has issued warnings about the growing threat of China. Though he has supported the Republican Party over the years, he has been deeply critical of the administration of George W. Bush for a lack of historical and strategic insight in its conduct of the War on Terror.

In 1996, Helprin briefly joined Bob Dole's presidential campaign, writing both his Senate retirement speech and a draft of his nomination acceptance speech. These have been described as "unusually lyrical," which is perhaps why his tenure as a speechwriter was limited in duration.

—GREGORY WOLFE

Further Reading

Helprin, Mark. *The Pacific and Other Stories.* New York: Penguin, 2004.

———. *Memoir from Antproof Case.* New York: Harcourt Brace Jovanovich, 1995.

———. *Refiner's Fire: The Life and Adventures of Marshall Pearl, a Foundling.* New York: Knopf, 1977.

See also: Terror, War on

Henry, Patrick (1736–99)

Commonly considered the greatest orator of the American Revolution, Henry offered fiery denunciations of consolidation that provided a rallying point for critics of centralized government following the war. Henry journeyed from proto-nationalist to Anti-Federalist and then back to Federalist during his long career, and his political odyssey reflects the persistent tension between liberty and order so prevalent during his time and beyond.

A self-educated native of Virginia, the "forest-born Demosthenes" emerged as a gifted lawyer during his mid-twenties. Speaking in opposition to the Stamp Act in 1765, Henry gained international recognition with his defiant "if this be treason, make the most of it." A decade later, addressing the Virginia legislature in support of independence, he uttered his most celebrated call to arms: "Give me liberty or give me death."

During the Revolution Henry served as wartime governor of Virginia. As a delegate to the First Continental Congress in 1774, Henry exuberantly declared himself "not a Virginian but an American." He renounced nationalism thirteen years later when he refused election to the Constitutional Convention (called ostensibly to modify the Articles of Confederation), proclaiming that he "smelt a rat." Henry then directed the campaign in Virginia to block ratification of the federal compact. Pronouncing the federal union to be merely a scheme devised by northern states to "despoil" the southern states of their wealth, he also warned that the Constitution provided little protection against tyranny. As Virginia's leading Anti-Federalist, he faulted the document for an unrealistic reliance on "good men" and predicted that some ambitious and able president would inevitably make a "bold push for the American throne." Although he lost the argument (Virginia ratified the Constitution in 1788), Henry remained a hero and a political force in his home state for another decade. Ironically, in his final years Henry returned to his nationalist roots, embracing the Federalist Party and remaining active as a Federalist until his death in 1799.

—Ashley Cruseturner

Further Reading

Mayer, Henry. *A Son of Thunder: Patrick Henry and the American Republic.* Charlottesville, Va.: University Press of Virginia, 1991.

See also: American Revolution; Anti-Federalists; federalism; Southern conservatism

Herberg, Will (1901–77)

Sociologist, theologian, and longtime religious commentator for *National Review*, Will Herberg grew up in New York City the son of multilingual Jewish immigrants and spent his early adult years as an ardent member of and labor organizer for the American Communist Party. Though Herberg broke from the Soviets in the late 1930s, partly in reaction to Stalin's purges, he abandoned Marxism only by stages. Well into the 1940s, he treated Marx's revolutionary view of history as a useful tool for social reform movements. By the late 1940s, however, Herberg had taken irreversible steps toward accepting biblically based revealed religion and the American constitutional order. These commitments are evident in *Judaism and Modern Man: An Interpretation of Jewish Religion* (1951), a work that defends the Hebraic religious core of both Judaism and Christianity and finds therein a "vital drive for social action." Though this book indicates Herberg's continuing attraction to social democracy, it also reaches beyond that stage in his intellectual development with its emphasis on theocentric existence. Heavily influenced by the Christian existentialists Berdyaev, Kierkegaard, and Barth, Herberg dwells in his writing on original sin and the experience of personal conversion, concepts that are unusual in a book that appears to be expounding normative Judaism. Herberg also maintains that Jews and Christians have both been redeemed by different, valid covenants, and he seems equally comfortable addressing the religious concerns of both.

Will Herberg

Herberg's most widely read work, *Protestant, Catholic, Jew* (1955), highlights the integrating functions of mainline religions in teaching civic virtue and fitting their adherents into a common American society. Despite his own patriotism, Herberg warns of "an advancing American secularism, which is not felt to be at all inconsistent with the most sincere attachment to religion." He expressed doubts about an American religion that taught "the essential rightness of everything American" and opened itself to a "strong and pervasive idolatrous element."

By the late 1950s, Herberg was also moving toward a conservative political view, shaped by his reading of Edmund Burke and the interpretations of Burke offered by Reinhold Niebuhr and Peter Stanlis. Both the Burkean preoccupation with historical experience as the test of political institutions and Burke's critique of abstract rights falsely ascribed to mankind in general won Herberg's strong approval. All the same, his political opinions were too much his own to make him a movement conservative in any decade. Sympathetic to labor unions but severely critical of the civil rights movement, particularly Martin Luther King Jr., passionately hostile to communism but enthusiastically supportive of Richard Nixon's opening to communist China, Herberg never again accepted a party line after breaking with the Communist Party. He was also a spirited lecturer and left behind notes and tapes of memorable speeches given to his students at Drew University and elsewhere. His professorship in religion and culture at Drew in the 1960s and '70s was the last phase of an exciting and varied career that went from labor union agitation and journalism into theology and academic honors.

—PAUL GOTTFRIED

Further Reading

Herberg, Will, ed. *Four Existentialist Theologians: A Reader from the Works of Jacques Maritain, Nicolas Berdyaev, Martin Buber, and Paul Tillich.* Garden City, N.Y.: Doubleday, 1958.

———. *From Marxism to Judaism: The Collected Essays of Will Herberg.* Edited by David G. Dalin. New York: M. Wiener, 1989.

See also: Burke, Edmund; Niebuhr, Reinhold

Heritage Foundation

The Heritage Foundation is a Washington, D.C., research institute dedicated to formulating and promoting conservative public policies that promote the principles of free enterprise, limited government, traditional values, and strong foreign defense and national security. Because of the organization's deep and longstanding ties with conservative politicians in Washington, the work of Heritage fellows wields tremendous influence, which both enemies and friends of the foundation have noticed. The *New Republic* referred to Heritage in 1985 as "the most important think tank in the nation's capital." The Soviet newspaper *Pravda* stated in 1984 "that in a matter of ten years the Heritage Foundation has covered a mind-boggling distance which others could not cover in even 100 years." But perhaps the best testimony to Heritage's effectiveness came from one who received tremendous support from the institution, Ronald Reagan. In 1983, Reagan stated: "success in politics is about issues, ideas, and the vision we have for our country and the world. This is, in fact, the very sum and substance of the Heritage Foundation."

The Heritage Foundation began operations in February 1973. It grew out of two earlier efforts by Joseph Coors to establish a policy institution in Washington: the Analysis and Research Association (ARA, founded in 1969 with an $80,000 budget) and the Robert M. Schuchman Memorial Foundation (endowed with an operating budget of $250,000 in 1971–72 by Coors). The two principal founders were Senate staffer Paul Weyrich, who "razzle-dazzled" Coors executives into backing the "untested and unproven small research firm" (ARA) and House staffer Ed Feulner (who would become president of Heritage in 1977, a position he still holds). Both Weyrich and Feulner were frustrated by the fact there were no conservative policy organizations in Washington capable of or interested in actually effecting political change. The American Enterprise Institute (AEI) was the only think tank dedicated to conservative views,

and it deliberately refused to promote policy change with its research. Both ARA and Schuchman therefore provided research directly to conservative politicians, but both proved ineffective, and Schuchman eventually separated from what would become the Heritage Foundation.

Under the leadership of Californian and former Reagan aide Frank Walton, Heritage grew even with the Republican Party (and conservatives) facing the difficulties of post-Watergate fundraising. Its budget went from $413,000 in 1974 to over $1 million by 1976. While much of its funding came from Coors, Richard Scaife, and Milwaukee industrialist Allen Brady, direct-mail fundraising proved instrumental to the success of Heritage's operations; today, with some 200,000 names on its list, the foundation receives much of its support from conservatives across the country, not simply from corporate patrons and foundations.

Throughout the 1970s Heritage focused much of its work on government regulations and taxation, publishing studies designed to challenge the status quo. In 1977 Feulner became president of Heritage, expanding the foundation's operations and soliciting corporate and individual gifts. Under Feulner's leadership, Heritage increased its profile drastically in the late '70s, offering policy alternatives on a range of domestic issues, including the development of entitlement zones in urban areas, supply-side economics, deregulation, and the reduction of government bureaucracy. In foreign policy, Heritage papers urged an end to détente, including a rejection of SALT-II and a more confrontational stance with the Soviets.

Heritage's influence skyrocketed with the election of Ronald Reagan as president in 1980. Heritage took a big gamble, according to historian Lee Edwards, when it produced a massive collection of studies titled *Mandate for Leadership: Policy Management in a Conservative Administration*. Some 3,500 pages long and contained in twenty research volumes, *Mandate for Leadership* was brought together under a team led by Charles Heatherly and included some 2,000 recommendations to move the government in a conservative direction. Ed Meese gratefully accepted the volumes for the Reagan campaign, and dozens of those who worked on *Mandate for Leadership* received staff positions in the Reagan administration. Throughout the 1980s Heritage became the preeminent conservative think tank, vastly outdistancing its rival, AEI, in terms of influence and budget. And it has maintained that preeminence even as dozens of other conservative think tanks have arisen. Heritage played a key role in shaping the policies promoted by Republican legislators after they took back Congress in 1994 and it has been a major influence on the course of George W. Bush's presidency.

Heritage has not limited its activities to the realm of practical politics. For many years it sponsored the publication of *Policy Review*, a major policy journal edited by Adam Meyerson (published since 2001 by the Hoover Institution). Thanks to a gift from the Bradley Foundation, it sponsors the Bradley Fellows Program, which allows scholars one year in Washington to research and produce scholarship and to make connections with likeminded intellectuals and politicians. Prominent Bradley fellows have included Hadley Arkes, Marvin Olasky, and Robert P. George. Heritage also sponsors the popular website townhall.com, a prominent source of conservative news and information.

Heritage is one of the best known and most prestigious organizations associated with the conservative movement. An organization dedicated to conservative principles and ideas, the foundation is a powerful force in shaping the nation's politics and, ultimately, culture.

—GREGORY L. SCHNEIDER

Further Reading

Edwards, Lee. *The Power of Ideas: The Heritage Foundation at Twenty-Five Years.* Ottawa, Ill.: Jameson Books, 1997.

Smith, James Allen. *The Idea Brokers: Think Tanks and the Rise of the New Policy Elite.* New York: Free Press, 1991.

Himmelstein, Jerome L. *To the Right: The Transformation of American Conservatism.* Berkeley, Calif.: University of California Press, 1990.

See also: *enterprise zones; Feulner, Edwin J., Jr.; think tanks, conservative; Weyrich, Paul Michael*

Heyne, Paul (1931–2000)

Called by some "the most effective economic educator in America," Paul Heyne was a long-time lecturer in economics at the University of Washington who specialized in economic history and ethical criticisms of economic systems. His bestselling textbook, *The Economic Way of Thinking* (1973), was considered by many conservatives to be the most effective introduction to economic theory available. A staunch defender of free markets, Heyne also pointed out that markets, while giving individuals more opportunities to choose, do nothing to ensure that their choices will be wise or moral. Markets, he argued, are merely a means to an end, not an end in and of themselves.

Born in St. Louis in 1931, Heyne spent several years as a divinity student at St. Louis's Concordia Seminary. Although he was ordained a minister in 1956, he never became a pastor. Instead, he pursued a master's degree in economics from Washington University in St. Louis, which he received in 1957. From there, he went to the University of Chicago, where he would receive his Ph.D. in ethics and society in 1963.

Heyne's textbook went through nine editions from 1973 to 2000. In a time when many economists eschewed the teaching of undergraduates, Heyne listed "the teaching of introductory economics" as a main field of interest. He frequently participated in seminars on the teaching of economics, not only to doctoral students at the University of Washington, but also to high school economics teachers throughout Eastern Europe.

—JOSHUA HALL

Further Reading

Heyne, Paul. *A Student's Guide to Economics.* Wilmington, Del.: ISI Books, 2000.

See also: capitalism

Hillsdale College

Hillsdale College is often called "conservative." But what does it "conserve"? A friend of the college, Russell Kirk, called what it conserved "the permanent things." Perhaps the best way to understand this old and famous American college is to look at the qualities reflected in its history.

Founded in 1844, Hillsdale was the first private college to be chartered by the Michigan legislature. Its founders were Free Will Baptists, and religious faith has always been one of its chief bases. But the charter of the college was nondenominational in character, and when the college established a seminary in the late nineteenth century, future ministers of all denominations were accepted. By the early 1960s, Hillsdale dropped its Baptist affiliation altogether.

Another quality that characterizes Hillsdale is its deep devotion to the principle of equal opportunity. From the beginning, it admitted blacks and women on an equal basis with white males. This policy of nondiscrimination continues to the present day, despite attempts by the federal government to force the college to adopt racial quotas in the 1970s. The college fought a long legal battle over this issue, and as a result was forced to tell its students that they could no longer accept the federal taxpayer-funded grants and loans that students at almost every other U.S. college and university enjoy. Consequently, Hillsdale bears the burden of true independence by raising money from private sources to fund its students' scholarships and loans.

In order to fund its operations, the college has successfully capitalized on its conservative character. George Roche III, president of the college from 1971 to 1999, used the college's refusal of government aid as an occasion to publicize the school as a bastion of academic freedom and excellence. Roche brought Hillsdale to national attention by instituting a lecture series that invites prestigious conservative speakers to the college. These lectures are published in *Imprimis*, a monthly journal begun in 1972 and freely circulated to one thousand readers. *Imprimis* has served to make Hillsdale widely known and respected throughout the nation, and many donations to the school come from its readers, who number over one million.

During Roche's presidency, the college endowment increased nearly fifty fold from $4 million to $185 million. At the same time, the college became more selective academically, increased its enrollment, and established a reputation as *the* conservative institution of higher education. Roche resigned in 1999 under the cloud of a personal scandal. Larry Arnn was appointed as his succesor in 2000. Arnn has enlivened the intellectual life at Hillsdale and has continued to position the college as the preeminent school concerned with transmitting the heritage of the West and the American experience within it. Even more than Roche, Arnn is dogged in his commitment to liberal education. He has also proved to be an effective fundraiser.

The college has assembled over the years a stellar faculty, and its Center for Constructive Alternatives brings big-name speakers to campus, such as Margaret Thatcher and Sir Martin Gilbert. Soon, life-size sculptures of great statesmen, including Washington and Churchill, will line the college's walkways and serve as a visual reminder of the school's mission to produce liberally educated leaders.

—ARLAN GILBERT
AND DOUGLAS JEFFREY

Further Reading

Gilbert, Arlan K. *The Permanent Things: Hillsdale College, 1900–1994.* Hillsdale, Mich.: Hillsdale College Press, 1998.

Miller, John J. "Horror at Hillsdale." *National Review.* 6 December 1999.

See also: education, higher; Grove City College

Himmelfarb, Gertrude (1922–)

A historian of Victorian England and wife of Irving Kristol, Gertrude Himmelfarb once summarized a critical review of herself by saying, "She is a brilliant historian so long as she is Gertrude Himmelfarb, but she fails dismally when she becomes Mrs. Irving Kristol." But Himmelfarb, while accepting the description "conservative" or "neoconservative," argues that she is not an ideologue at all but "simply an historian."

Himmelfarb has written on such classic conservative thinkers as Edmund Burke and Lord Acton, as well as Charles Darwin and John Stuart Mill. Of particular note are her two books on Victorian approaches to understanding and dealing with poverty, and her studies of that era's personalities and the family. These works make us see the Victorian era as a rich trove of fascinating and instructive figures, not some silly folk who covered piano "legs." Her later work has examined, among other topics, the writing of history, academic fads, and the culture wars dividing American society.

Himmelfarb received her bachelor's degree from Brooklyn College, where she met and married Irving Kristol. A self-described Trotskyite in her youth, she quickly shed that enthusiasm and went on to earn her doctorate in history at the University of Chicago. Among her numerous distinctions are the 1991 Jefferson Lecturership in the humanities, the Templeton Award, and a chair as distinguished professor of history at CUNY.

Himmelfarb's principal contribution to American conservatism has been her studies of the family and the moral and intellectual fabric of civilized society. In *One Nation, Two Cultures* (1999) she applies these reflections from Victorian England to contemporary America. Victorian virtues such as temperance, thrift, work, family, and piety—in a word, respectability—must have their American counterparts in her culture wars. Compassion for the poor involves their assuming responsibility for their improvement. She laments that capitalism's "'creative destruction' has taken its toll on the moral life of society" in America. It is unfortunate that the American founders did not adequately protect their own "Victorianism."

Himmelfarb's most important single book for political purposes is *The De-Moralization of Society* (1995). The book begins with an attack on the contemporary use of the insipid term "values" as a substitute for the robust and more honest language of virtue and vice. A de-moralized society lacks the spirit to recognize and then defend its higher purposes. Himmelfarb discloses the relationship between "morals and manners" and a healthy society, between the private sphere and the public. She argues that the Victorian era brought forth a feminism that is opposed to the sensibility of current feminism; thus, the greatest success for Victorian feminism is the heroine of her book, Margaret Thatcher. Himmelfarb asserts, "Today, confronted with an increasingly de-moralized society, we may be ready for a new reformation, which will restore not so much Victorian values as a more abiding sense of moral and civic virtues."

—KEN MASUGI

Further Reading

Himmelfarb, Gertrude. *The Idea of Poverty: England in the Early Industrial Age.* New York: Knopf, 1983.

———. *Victorian Minds: A Study of Intellectuals in Crisis and Ideologies in Transition.* New York: Knopf, 1968.

See also: culture wars; family; feminism; neoconservatism

Hiss-Chambers trial

Dubbed "The Trial of the Century" at the time, the Hiss-Chambers trial began formally on a sweltering August day in 1948. That was when Whittaker Chambers, an editor at *Time* magazine with a shadowy past as a communist agent, reluctantly testified to a House investigating committee. He quietly explained that a number of former government officials, including the highly regarded Alger Hiss, were secret Communist Party members. When pressed further by House investigators, Chambers admitted that during the 1930s he, Hiss, and others had engaged in espionage for the Soviet Union against the United States.

In brief, events unfolded in the following way: The House Committee on Un-American Activities (HUAC) summoned Hiss. Hiss denied the allegations. Hiss and Chambers were brought together and confronted each other. Chambers recognized Hiss. Hiss emphatically denied knowing Chambers. Hiss challenged Chambers to repeat his charges in public, and Chambers obliged on a radio broadcast. Hiss then sued Chambers for slander in civil court. In the criminal court, a grand jury convened.

Chambers produced additional evidence and Hiss was indicted. But a mistrial was declared after the jury deadlocked. After a second trial, Hiss was convicted in January 1950 of perjury for lying about his relationship with Chambers and his covert actions (the statute of limitations for espionage had lapsed). Hiss was sentenced to five years in a federal penitentiary. A judge then threw out Hiss's slander suit against Chambers.

This thumbnail sketch utterly fails to convey the drama of the Hiss-Chambers case, however. There were congressional hearings and grand jury indictments. A young U.S. representative from California, Richard M. Nixon, cut his political teeth on the case, earning as his reward a national reputation (and the Left's undying enmity). And there were distinguished prosecutors and defense attorneys. Tom Murphy, a New York City prosecutor, had compiled a 99 percent conviction record in the U.S. Attorney's Office. For the defense, the renowned trial lawyer Lloyd Stryker, the Johnnie Cochran or Alan Dershowitz of his day, earned Alger Hiss a mistrial in the first prosecution, but took a pass on a second Hiss defense. That subsequent jury, of course, convicted Hiss of perjury.

Then there were the witnesses—many, many witnesses. Fifteen character witnesses vouched for Hiss, either in person or in writing. These included Supreme Court Justice Felix Frankfurter, Illinois Governor Adlai Stevenson, and 1924 Democratic presidential nominee, John W. Davis. Familial witnesses for Chambers included the singular figure of his wife Esther, who, after sustained badgering by Stryker, exclaimed to the jury, "My husband is a decent citizen, a great man!"

And, finally, there was the evidence: the prothonotary warbler, a rare bird that Hiss had told Chambers he had recently seen in a conversation during the 1930s. By making reference to this bird, Hiss unwittingly confirmed his conversation with Chambers and helped congressional investigators seeking to verify a relationship between the two men. There were the purloined secret State Department memos and documents Hiss passed to Chambers. There were the additional copies Hiss had keyed overnight on his Woodstock typewriter. Most famously, there were the "Pumpkin Papers," actually rolls of incriminating microfilm Chambers had photographed from secret documents Hiss had removed from the State Department. Chambers spirited away these canisters when he made his break with communism, and later stowed them away for safekeeping in a hollowed-out pumpkin on his farm at the height of the investigation's furor.

The prosecution pieced these materials together into a picture of Hiss's clandestine activities that convinced the second jury of his intentional spying for the Soviet Union. Of course, the evidence failed to convince some of Hiss's diehard supporters and mattered little to many on the American Left who argued (as some still argue) that such activities were noble because undertaken for the "right" cause.

After completing his sentence, Hiss began a career as a greeting card salesman (as a convicted felon, he was disbarred from practicing law). He also published his first memoirs, *In the Court of Public Opinion* (1957), essentially a pedestrian lawyer's brief, and continued defiantly declaring his innocence until his death in 1996.

In 1952, Chambers wrote his memoirs, the modern biographical classic titled *Witness*, detailing his life in the Communist Party and the challenges America faced with communism in mid-century. Chambers succinctly summarized those challenges by posing the question: "Faith in God or Faith in Man?" By presenting the stakes in such stark terms and by in effect putting secular liberalism on trial, the soft-spoken Chambers had brought to the fore one of the defining questions of American political discourse in the latter half of the twentieth century. After the trial, an exhausted Chambers retired to his farm in Westminster, Maryland, writing sporadically and publishing commentary in William F. Buckley's fledgling *National Review*. He died in 1961.

Hiss and Chambers were two men scarcely cut from the same political or personal cloth. Hiss was tall, handsome, well pedigreed and highly credentialed. He had graduated from Harvard with a law degree and clerked for Supreme Court Justice Oliver Wendell Holmes. He had worked in the agriculture and state departments, ultimately advising President Franklin Roosevelt at Yalta. Later, in 1945, Hiss served as the secretary-general of the United Nations Conference on International Organizations (UNICO), where he presided over the negotiations that led to the ratification and signing of the UN Charter. Hiss was working as president of the Carnegie Endowment for International Peace when the case broke. Many believed he was a strong contender for secretary of state in a future Democratic administration. And, as numerous files released after the fall of the Soviet regime conclusively show, he was an undercover operative supplying intelligence information for the Soviet Union.

In contrast, Chambers was short, squat, and rumpled. He had dropped out of Columbia University and later out of society in general. A gifted writer, he had penned stirring essays for the communist *New Masses* magazine and *Daily Worker* newspaper in the early 1930s before going underground for "special work" for the Community Party. Emerging in 1939, disillusioned with Stalin's purges and what he saw as the diabolical true meaning of communism, Chambers informed the government of his activities, alerting administration officials to the spy network operating from within, and waited for action. None followed. He subsequently landed a job with *Time* magazine writing thoughtful, sometimes moving, and often provocative book reviews. He later stepped up for a controversial stint at *Time*'s foreign news desk, where he employed his editorial perch weekly to sound the alarm about the not-so-friendly intentions of the Soviet Union. Because *Time* did not assign bylines to its writers and editors in those days, Chambers remained a relatively unknown figure to the American public until the House Un-American Activities Committee subpoenaed the former communist agent to testify in the summer of 1948.

The spy case to which Hiss and Chambers lent their names (and actions) was acrimonious, divisive, and monumental. It defined the post–World War II political battle lines between the emerging anticommunist conservative movement of the Right and the nascent anti-anticommunist reactionaries of the Left, (with beleaguered establishment liberals laboring in between for a middle ground). Its revelations about communism's undemocratic intentions and desire for global domination provided Republican Party candidates, officeholders, and activists with a key component to their sustaining ideology and worldview for roughly forty years. Interestingly, however, Chambers was a severe critic of Senator Joe McCarthy and his use of a Senate committee to attempt to ferret out communist agents. According to Chambers, "For the Right to tie itself in any way to Senator McCarthy is suicide." Indeed, Chambers dubbed McCarthy "a raven of disaster."

—PATRICK SWAN

Further Reading

Swan, Patrick, ed. *Alger Hiss, Whittaker Chambers, and the Schism in the American Soul.* Wilmington, Del.: ISI Books, 2003.

Tanenhaus, Sam. *Whittaker Chambers: A Biography.* New York: Random House, 1997.

Toledano, Ralph de, and Victor Lasky. *Seeds of Treason: The True Story of the Hiss-Chambers Tragedy.* New York: Funk & Wagnalls, 1950.

See also: anticommunism; Chambers, Whittaker; Cold War; Witness

historic preservation

One might imagine that historic preservation is, by definition, a conservative cause. "Remove not the ancient landmark, which thy fathers have set," the Book of Proverbs commands (22:28). The reality, however, is that the preservation movement in the United States is now guided by professionals who subscribe to a historical and cultural relativism largely antithetical to traditional preservation and to a liberal interpretation of American political and social history.

In the United States, historic preservation's nineteenth-century origins lie in the desire to maintain buildings and sites of extraordinary significance. In the decades after the city of Philadelphia purchased Independence Hall and the Liberty Bell in 1816, the former statehouse was restored as a civic shrine. Other major preservation initiatives included the successful mid-century campaign by the Mount Vernon Ladies' Association to purchase and maintain George Washington's Potomac River estate; the passage of legislation, in 1889, allowing the pre-Columbian Casa Grande ruins in Arizona eventually to become a national monument and first national park site; and the creation of the first national military parks at the Civil War battlefields of Chickamauga, Shiloh, and Gettysburg during the 1890s.

The architectural merit of buildings like Independence Hall and Mount Vernon could only strengthen the case for their preservation. Considerations of aesthetic as well as didactic value similarly inspired John D. Rockefeller Jr.'s ambitious project for the restoration of Williamsburg, which got underway in 1926, marking a broadening of preservation's scope from individual buildings to architectural ensembles. In 1931, the city of Charleston, South Carolina, landmarked its magnificent Battery district and enacted the nation's first historic preservation ordinance.

The designation of places like the Battery, Old Town in Alexandria, Virginia (1946), and the Georgetown section of Washington, D.C. (1950) resulted from the architectural standard they set. But it also reflected a new and unprecedented motive for preservation: a loss of confidence in American civilization's capacity to build as well as it had in times past. Though advocates of the steady broadening of preservation's purview see it as an indication of the nation's increasing cultural maturity, one could just as easily regard it as a symptom of cultural decadence. Indeed, preservation's emergence as a major cultural movement is closely associated with one of the great harbingers of the collapse of American architecture: the demolition, in 1963, of Charles Follen McKim's classical masterwork, Pennsylvania Station in Manhattan, and its replacement with a dismal modernist urban-renewal complex. This catastrophe led to the establishment of New York City's Landmarks Preservation Commission, and it also contributed to the passage, in 1966, of the National Historic Preservation Act (NHPA).

Unlike earlier preservation-related legislation in this country, which mainly pertained to the conservation of significant historic, archeological, and natural resources on federal land, the NHPA created a national preservationist infrastructure. It led to the establishment of state historic preservation offices in every state and territory. These offices maintain inventories of historic properties and work with "certified local governments" at the county and municipal level that qualify for federal grants under the act. As a rule, "CLG's," which numbered nearly

2,500 by 1999, have enacted historic preservation ordinances and incorporated preservation guidelines into their zoning codes. Because land use is regulated at the local level in the United States, it is these ordinances that are of immediate consequence for the owners of individually landmarked properties or "contributing" buildings in historic districts. They establish the conditions under which a historic building may be demolished along with design review boards that consider significant exterior alterations.

The NHPA's passage is a matter of almost macabre irony in that the federal government's proverbial right arm used it in an attempt to limit the damage it was inflicting, through urban renewal, with its left. In the very year the act was passed, urban renewal and the plague of ill-considered architectural mega-projects and cross-town expressways it unleashed on the nation's traditional urban fabric got a huge boost courtesy of the Model Cities Act. More than ever, in other words, historic preservation was now a remedial movement that treated symptoms rather than the disease. Needless to say, the movement has been synonymous with public hostility to modernist architecture, a routine ingredient of the urban-renewal recipe. In the decades since the NHPA was passed, legions of urban districts or neighborhoods, varying widely in degrees of architectural distinction, have secured designation in order to protect themselves from the scourge of architecture and urban planning at odds with the sense of cultural continuity most Americans want their built environment to impart.

But that protection has proved inadequate where new construction in designated districts is concerned. This is the result of the advent of an academically trained bureaucracy, itself a result of the vastly increased scope of preservation activities at the national, state, and local levels. This new bureaucracy largely transformed the movement. It introduced a new concept of preservation grounded in the naturalization of Western ideas of history and culture. Professional preservationists thus tend to subscribe, like art and architecture historians in general, to a historical relativism that conflates the deterministic, anthropological, German-romantic concept of culture as a vast organism spanning the range of human activities, which flourish and degenerate in tandem, with non-teleological notions of cultural evolution derived from Darwin.

This relativism does not regard history as normative. It regards it as a mere process. It has therefore deprived the term "historic" of meaning, and largely deprived the preservation movement of its idealistic character in doing so. Indeed, an essentially documentary orientation underlies the *Charter of Venice* (1964), which gave birth to the foremost international preservation organization, the International Council on Monuments and Sites (ICOMOS), which is headquartered in Paris. The charter also exercised a decisive influence on the U.S. Department of the Interior's *Standards for Rehabilitation*, first issued in 1976, which set forth the very exacting criteria the rehabilitation of income-generating "historic" properties must satisfy in order to qualify for federal investment-tax credits.

The *Standards* decree that "each [historic] property shall be recognized as a physical record of its time, place, and use." The traditional idea of transcendent significance is hardly in evidence. One of the *Standards'* crucial stipulations, moreover, is that the "historic integrity" of a given architectural specimen be maintained in *perpetuum*. Any appendage must be readily recognizable as historically distinct in order to avoid unscientific confusion with the original—unless, of course, that appendage is itself "historic." This utterly paradoxical guideline has provided carte blanche for unfortunate modernist additions to old buildings. It underlines the severe limitations of preservation

grounded in "science" rather than a humanistic appreciation of design. Indeed, preservation's documentary ethos has resulted in the exaltation of "authenticity."

Authenticity's merely sentimental value, however, is overlooked. And though many professional preservationists quite subjectively regard modernist architecture as "authentic" and traditionally oriented contemporary design as "fake," there is little indication that the public subscribes to this view. Academic preservation would thus appear to give aesthetic values, values of deeper emotional resonance, far less weight than they carried with preservation's original exponents. One might argue, therefore, that preservation has been the victim of its own success.

In obscuring the distinction between the historic and the historical, the documentary ethos has replaced the normative, culturally integrative concept of "historic" with the relativist and culturally atomistic concept of "heritage," and has served to expand preservation's frontiers very considerably in the bargain. This ethos has led to curiosities such as the listing of the last surviving original MacDonald's on the National Trust for Historic Preservation's annual roster of America's "eleven most endangered historic places." It has led also to confusion between what the public should learn by visiting "historic" sites and what it should learn from printed or audiovisual media. In numerous cases the designation of such sites reflects a preoccupation with addressing social or racial grievances by focusing attention on the "dark side" of American history, as if historians and documentary filmmakers were not equal to the task. The National Park Service, the federal government's principal preservation agent, has thus designated a World War II detention camp for Japanese Americans and the battlefield where a regiment led by George Armstrong Custer massacred 103 South Cheyenne Indians as national historic sites.

Its philosophical vicissitudes notwithstanding, preservation has unquestionably rendered sterling service to the nation. The National Trust, for example, has benefited hundreds of Main Streets across the land by showing how traditional commercial districts can compete successfully against new suburban shopping malls. In this case, it should be noted, preservationists have retained a vital sense of esthetic amenity.

During the 1990s, the preservation movement launched a crusade against "suburban sprawl," which its leaders compare to the struggle against urban renewal. In the present case, however, they are taking on a far more formidable adversary. Whatever the prospects for success in this new crusade may be, the sheer scale of the "sprawl" phenomenon may force at least some of the movement's adherents to conclude that it is not what we save that is of greatest significance for the quality of the nation's built environment, but what we build.

—Catesby Leigh

Further Reading

Fitch, James Marston. *Historic Preservation: Curatorial Management of the Built World.* 2nd ed. Charlottesville, Va.: University Press of Virginia, 1990.

Tyler, Norman. *Historic Preservation: An Introduction to Its History, Principles, and Practice.* New York: W. W. Norton, 2000.

See also: New Urbanism

historicism

Historicism refers most generally to the view that human action, thought, and imagination are inescapably conditioned by the past and the historical situations in which they arise. Modern conservatism is indistinguishable from a strong sense of the dependence of civilized life on historical evolution.

Though mankind has always sensed the power of circumstance and felt a connection between those who live now and previous generations, it was not until the eighteenth century that a more self-consciously historical view of human existence began to emerge. Personal and social characteristics came to be seen as closely bound up with the past and the study of history as indispensable to understanding self and society.

In contrast to conservatism, which assumes a bond between the best of what history has produced and a higher, even providential purpose, "postmodern" thought stresses the historicity of human existence to the exclusion of its element of continuity. Postmodernism asserts the essential arbitrariness of historically evolved authority and order and the impossibility of shared and enduring meaning. Also in contrast to conservatism, thinkers espousing an ahistorical and rationalistic view of moral norms and philosophical insight treat historicism as a source of moral relativism or nihilism.

To ancient Greek philosophers, history seemed a phenomenal flux without meaning. Plato sought reality in a sphere of wholly transcendent forms. Aristotle took more interest in historical evidence as a stimulus to reflection, but Greek thought assumed that there could be real knowledge only of what is ahistorical, timeless, and universal. Since the Greeks, Western thought has had a strong tendency to conceive of what gives moral and other structure to life as separate from historical particularity. Though the ancient world evinced interest in history—vide such men as Herodotus, Thucydides, Polybius, Cicero, and Tacitus—the writing of history did not go much beyond chronicling of events.

Christianity invested history with special meaning, seeing it as governed by divine purpose. Yet a theologian like Augustine, who explicated the spiritual significance of history, resembled Plato in portraying man's historical existence as permeated by sin and imperfection and in placing man's destiny beyond history. Thomas Aquinas attributed greater importance to man's worldly existence, which he regarded as governed by natural, if God-given, law. In his belief that longevity bestowed authority on human laws and institutions Aquinas showed some limited awareness of the value of history and experience. Nevertheless, for him the source of social and political order was not history but an unchanging law of nature. Many of the historicist implications of the Christian notion of the Incarnation, which assumes union of the transcendent Word and individual, historical humanity, have continued to elude Christian reflection.

In the eighteenth century, German thinkers like Immanuel Kant, Friedrich Schiller, and Johann Gottlieb Fichte contributed to the view that human consciousness and the world of particulars are intertwined and mutually dependent. The resulting conception of human experience was wholly different from that of empiricism. The idea emerged that universality may become immanent in history. Georg Wilhelm Friedrich Hegel saw history as the progressive self-realization of Spirit. History was not a record of inert external facts but a gradual revelation of meaning in human consciousness, the present showing itself to be a conspectus and extension of the past. Meaning was immanent in history by virtue of the dialectical coexistence of universality and particularity and became ever clearer as mankind struggled for self-understanding. Although Hegel rejected ahistorical Enlightenment reason, his own notion of Spirit strongly emphasized rationality.

In England the statesman-writer Edmund Burke argued that human society links many generations in an organic whole. In reaction to the French Revolution, Burke pointed to man's dependence on the past and to the "latent wisdom" of inherited ways.

Although recognizing the need for change, he rejected as superficial and dangerous the idea that man might substitute for the accumulated and partly hidden wisdom of the ages the abstract rationality of particular individuals or groups. Burke saw the traditions of the civilized society as embodying moral-spiritual order and as indications of divine Providence, but he did not have Hegel's propensity for viewing his own epoch and society as the incipient culmination of history. He was different from Hegel also in that he did not blur the distinction between good and evil.

In America a groping historical sense, akin in some ways to Burke's, was discernible, for example, in the emphasis that statesmen and thinkers such as John Dickinson, John Adams, and James Madison placed on heeding historical experience and precedent, a concern that was typically connected with admiration for the English tradition of common law. The efficacy of the past in the present and the value of historically and regionally rooted identities were felt by men like John Randolph of Roanoke, Joseph Story, John C. Calhoun, and Nathaniel Hawthorne.

Historicism sometimes evolved in directions destructive of its more humane potentialities. It was prone from the start to romantic-pantheistic evasion of the problem of evil. The fondness for historical schematization and extravagant speculation regarding the meaning of history was evident in Hegel and sometimes acquired a momentum of its own, giving rise to various "philosophies of history." Reactions against the excesses of Hegelianism made possible the advance, even in Germany itself, of French and English positivism as represented by Auguste Comte, the Mills, and Herbert Spencer. These influences transformed the historicist impulse into a concern about gathering empirical historical materials. Theorists of that type sought to divorce the study of history from so-called "value-questions." Writers of naturalistic and scientistic bent claimed to discover causal, impersonal laws of history. Karl Marx turned Hegel "upside down," espousing historical materialism. Sometimes the defense of historically evolved cultural identities was taken to extremes of nationalism.

In the twentieth century the philosophically most mature and original exponent of historicism was the Italian thinker Benedetto Croce. He revived and extended an earlier humanistic historicism and made historicism an integral part of ethics, aesthetics, and logic. Croce revised and supplemented Hegelianism and German idealism in important ways, but a lingering monism left the distinction between good and evil vague.

In mid-twentieth-century America a surge of conservative thought gave new currency to a historical outlook. The most widely read conservative writer, Russell Kirk, was deeply influenced by Burke. Kirk defended Burkean "prejudice" and historical prescription against abstract rationalism. He tried to revive and create respect for older American and Western traditions. Kirk followed Irving Babbitt in seeing the imagination as crucial in bringing the great examples of history alive in the present. Although American conservatism argued in defense of tradition as a guide to life's enduring purpose, it was, on the whole, not disposed to exploring issues of historicism in philosophical depth, which made it sometimes prone to formulaic traditionalism and subject to criticism for not explaining its enduring standard of judgment.

Eric Voegelin showed the influence of historicism in stressing the experiential basis of religious symbols, but he also regarded Hegel's emphasis on the historical immanence of Spirit as an "egophanic" attempt at human self-divinization. Leo Strauss accused historicism, including Burkean con-

servatism, of disparaging natural right and reason and of spawning historical relativism. Both Strauss and Voegelin had strong, though different, Platonic ahistoricist leanings and were prone to reductionistic views of historicism.

The historian John Lukacs has explicitly affirmed historical consciousness as a new stage in human self-understanding and applied it to the study of modern history. Lukacs rejects every form of determinism and stresses that historical knowledge is personal and "participant." Paul Gottfried seeks to combine Hegelian and more naturalistic elements in a defense of historically evolved cultural and national identities. He criticizes the fondness for moral and political abstractions often found among so-called neoconservatives.

Claes G. Ryn argues that historicism need preclude neither intellectual humility nor acceptance of universality or transcendence. In fact, the latter two may be philosophically credible today only as reconstituted by historicist thinking. One may fully recognize the historicity of human existence and still affirm trans-individual meaning. What Ryn calls "value-centered historicism" stresses the possibility of a synthesis of particularity and universality. Goodness, truth, and beauty appear in the historical world of human experience only to the extent that the uniqueness and creativity of individuals embody those universal values. To exist for man, transcendence must become immanent in the concrete. History being a mixture of evil and good, men must discriminate and choose, and this requires a standard of judgment, but, according to value-centered historicism, static rational "principles" are abstract and highly dubious conceptions of universality. Only as known in the concrete experience of goodness, truth, or beauty is universality a living and truly authoritative source of judgment.

—CLAES G. RYN

Further Reading

Croce, Benedetto. *History as the Story of Liberty*. Indianapolis: Liberty Fund, 2001.

Gottfried, Paul. *The Search for Historical Meaning*. DeKalb, Ill.: Northern Illinois University Press, 1986.

Lukacs, John. *Historical Consciousness*. Piscataway, N.J.: Transaction, 1994.

Ryn, Claes G. *Will, Imagination and Reason*. Washington, D.C: Regnery, 1986.

See also: Burke, Edmund; Gottfried, Paul; Kirk, Russell; *literary criticism;* Lukacs, John; Natural Right and History; *Ryn, Claes G.;* Strauss, Leo

Hodge, Charles (1797–1878)

Teaching for many years at Princeton Theological Seminary, the bastion of "Old School" Presbyterianism, Charles Hodge trained 3,000 ministers, who came to constitute a powerful and conservative force in the Presbyterian Church. Most importantly, Hodge helped formulate a doctrinally rigorous "Princeton theology," which in the twentieth century was a foundation for conservative Christianity, particularly fundamentalism.

Hodge spent his entire life at Princeton. He studied at the seminary under his mentor, Archibald Alexander. He became an instructor at the seminary in 1820, professor of biblical literature in 1822, professor of theology in 1840, and taught there until his death. His legacy continued with his students, most notably B. B. Warfield, and two sons, Caspar Wistar and Archibald Alexander Hodge, who followed him as professors at the seminary.

Hodge was a staunch defender of traditional Calvinism and orthodox Christianity.

Charles Hodge

Wary of liberal theological trends he observed while studying in Europe (1826–28), Hodge pledged himself to fighting "rationalism," "mysticism," and "ritualism"—which he considered the main challenges to evangelical Christianity in his day. Both friends and foes of Princeton delighted in Hodge's claim that "a new idea never originated in this seminary." Indeed, until his own *Systematic Theology* appeared in 1872, he assigned students the work of Francis Turretin, a seventeenth-century Swiss theologian.

Most important was Hodge's defense of scriptural authority, which had been eroded in the nineteenth century by higher critical theories. Hodge had an unwavering commitment to the verbal inspiration and infallibility of the scriptures. Later codified as "inerrancy," this Princeton doctrine was the cornerstone of fundamentalism. The whole Princeton theology, buttressed by Scottish "common sense" realism, conveyed a powerful sense of stability and certainty. Hodge's *Systematic Theology* begins with a section on "theology as science."

Hodge also stressed personal piety and practical religion. Converted during a revival at Princeton in 1815, he remained a deeply religious man throughout his life. Though critical of the excesses of revivalists during the Second Awakening, Hodge always impressed upon his students, especially during his Sunday afternoon addresses, the need for heartfelt religious devotion.

Hodge was also a lively polemicist. From 1825 to 1872 he edited the *Biblical Repertory* (later the *Biblical Repertory and Theological Review*, and the *Biblical Repertory and Princeton Review*), a publication committed to "sound Presbyterianism, the cause of Christ, and the honor of our common Redeemer." In addition to theological topics, Hodge addressed contemporary issues, such as abolitionism and Darwinism, which he sharply criticized.

Hodge was the dominant nineteenth-century presence at Princeton, the premier conservative theological seminary in the United States. His stalwart defense of orthodox Christianity profoundly influenced Reformed churches during his lifetime. Most important, in the Princeton theology he laid the ideological foundation for conservative Christianity in the twentieth century.

—ROGER SCHULTZ

Further Reading

Hoffecker, Andrew. *Piety and the Princeton Theologians*. Grand Rapids, Mich.: Baker,1981.

Noll, Mark. *The Princeton Theology, 1812–1921*. Grand Rapids, Mich.: Baker, 1983.

See also: fundamentalism; Intelligent Design theory; Protestantism, evangelical

Hoffman, Ross J. S. (1902–79)

Ross J. (John) S. (Swartz) Hoffman was a leading conservative historian, Catholic convert, and a principal revivalist of interest in the thought of Edmund Burke among conservatives in the post–World War II era. Hoffman was born in Harrisburg, Pennsylvania, into a family of German descent. After graduating from Lafayette College (1923) he took his M.A. (1926) and Ph.D. from the University of Pennsylvania (1932). He then began an influential teaching career as a history professor at New York University (1926–38), but spent the majority of his professional career as a professor of history at Fordham University (1938–67), where he remained as professor emeritus until his death.

As an undergraduate, Hoffman rejected Christianity, adhering instead to socialism. His earliest published work was his dissertation, a study of trade between Great Britain and Germany from 1875 and 1914. As part of this doctoral study, he "roamed over Germany, studying 'conditions,' and watching the mark depreciate. . . ." He left Germany for Paris in 1923 on the day Hitler tried his Munich *Putsch*. Throughout this time he was increasingly influenced by his study of history and travel throughout Europe, as well as by a thorough reading of Scripture; as a result, he converted to Catholicism in 1931.

As Hoffman saw it, the post–World War I world was characterized by "doubt, despair, bewilderment and anarchy." In such a climate, there was for the church a particular obligation to profess the truth of "the Faith" to the present age. Hoffman accepted his own charge, and as much as any American Catholic of his time shaped the thinking of his coreligionists (if not always his secular adversaries). Hoffman's approach was historical. He confidently sought to demonstrate how in the wake of the Great War the Catholic Church was in a unique position to offer a compelling alternative to what he believed was the total failure of nineteenth-century liberalism. Catholicism alone was "totally exonerated from all responsibility and involvement" in the breakdown of European civilization, "for the faith had been sent in exile and the frontiers closed around it."

Hoffman was to America what G. K. Chesterton, Hilaire Belloc, and Christopher Dawson were to England: an assured, reasoned, even lyrical voice for restoration. What he hoped to restore was a modern form of medieval Christendom, which he viewed as a "fresh world" full of "vigor" and "health" and "hard thinking." He regarded the orthodox Catholic as "almost the last rationalist left in the world today." In economics and politics Hoffman rejected both individualist capitalism and collectivist socialism, instead gravitating toward the "distributism" developed by Belloc and Chesterton, which centered questions of political economy around the family, seeking to secure its independence and dignity from both a growing central state and an avaricious capitalist class through a wide distribution of property and ownership. During the interwar period Hoffman produced a number of books—including *Restoration* (1934), *Tradition and Progress* (1938), and *The Organic State* (1939)—and was a frequent contributor to the *American Review* (a "perversely brilliant," in John Patrick Diggins's formulation, journal of pre–World War II cultural conservatism).

Throughout the fertile interwar period Hoffman condemned "pagan" Nazism and "atheistic" communism as but two sides of the same ideological coin. He spared fascism from this criticism because he did not believe it was inherently anti-Christian and might possibly contribute to economic, political, and cultural recovery. He later recanted this early misjudgment of Italian fascism, whose nature he did not detect until Italy formally joined the Germans and the

Ross J. S. Hoffman

Axis powers. With the outbreak of war and America's entry into another European conflagration, Hoffman turned his attention to working out the relationship of America to Europe and the broader civilization of the West. In this effort, Hoffman located in the figure of Edmund Burke an eighteenth-century model for thinking historically about the Atlantic political world—and, more importantly, for connecting that world to ours. Burke, in particular, unlocked for Hoffman a usable past that linked morality and politics, Catholicism and Protestantism, revolution and conservatism, Europe and America.

Hoffman is credited by no less a figure than Bernard Bailyn for ushering in the now influential and ubiquitous subdiscipline of Atlantic history with his 1942 work *The Great*

Republic, his 1944 book *Durable Peace*, and a 1945 essay titled "Europe and the Atlantic Community." For Hoffman and other thinkers, such as Carlton J. H. Hayes and Walter Lippmann, the states comprising the North and South American continents emerged from, and were an extension of, "Western European Christendom." Earlier than the other Atlanticists who followed, Hoffman characterized the Atlantic community as "the inner sea of Christendom." Postwar American strategy, according to Hoffman, ought therefore to be aimed at "fortifying the Atlantic citadel."

Burke was for Hoffman the pivotal figure in this enterprise. To extend Burke's politics into the postwar world, Hoffman organized a new Burke Society at Fordham University in 1945. He was aided by a fellow Burke admirer, the Jesuit political theorist Moorhouse F. X. Millar, who himself had been instrumental in the 1930s in making connections between Burke and the American tradition of ordered liberty. Soon after this, Hoffman was recommended to the publisher Alfred Knopf by his friend Carlton Hayes to compile a new anthology of Burke's writings. The book coedited with his colleague Paul Levack, appeared in 1948 and was titled *Burke's Politics: Selected Writings and Speeches of Edmund Burke on Reform, Revolution, and War*. This groundbreaking compilation became a touchstone for the American Burke revival that blossomed in the ensuing decades. Hoffman also authored a major work on Burke's official relation to the American colonies during the revolutionary period, *Edmund Burke, New York Agent* (1955), and closed his career with a landmark biography of Burke's great political patron, Lord Rockingham, called simply *The Marquis* (1973).

Hoffman had an enduring influence on the American conservative movement, even though for health reasons he was not able to personally contribute to its flourishing in the 1960s and 1970s. He secured teaching jobs for the Austrian "liberal monarchist" Erik von Kuehnelt-Leddihn and the émigré Hungarian historian John Lukacs. And he maintained personal relationships and a lengthy correspondence with Russell Kirk, Peter Stanlis, Francis Canavan, Lukacs, as well as his many students, including Fordham historian and one-time associate editor of the influential *New Individualist Review*, John P. McCarthy. It is generally understood that the protagonist in Evelyn Waugh's novel *Scott-King's Modern Europe* (1947) is roughly based on Hoffman, with whom Waugh traveled in Spain, and with whom he shared an uneasiness about the modern world.

—JEFFREY O. NELSON

Further Reading

Allitt, Patrick. *Catholic Intellectuals and Conservative Politics in America: 1950–1985.* Ithaca, N.Y.: Cornell University Press, 1993.

Halsey, William H. *The Survival of American Innocence: Catholicism in an Era of Disillusionment.* Notre Dame, Ind.: University of Notre Dame Press, 1980.

Hoffman, Ross J. S. *The Book of Catholic Authors*, Third Series, edited by Walter Romig. Grosse Pointe, Mich.: W. Romig and Co., 1945.

McCarthy, John P. "Ross J. S. Hoffman: Conservative Spokesman in a Utopian Period." *Intercollegiate Review* 28, no. 2 (spring 1993): 42–49.

See also: American Review; *Burkean conservatism; distributism; Hayes, Carlton J. H.*

Holmes, George Frederick (1820–97)

A professor of history, literature, and economics at the University of Virginia from shortly before the American Civil War until his death in 1897, George Frederick Holmes was a prolific writer of books and periodical articles advocating free trade, states' rights, and slavery.

Born to English parents in the colony of British Guiana, Holmes was sent to England at age two to be raised by relatives. He was schooled near Durham and attended the University of Durham, where he won a prize scholarship. Because of an obscure misunderstanding with his guardians, Holmes was removed from university at age seventeen and sent to live in Quebec. From there he migrated to Pennsylvania, Virginia, Georgia, and finally South Carolina, where he was admitted to the state bar. He married a woman from a prominent Virginia family in 1844. Faced with the responsibilities of marriage, but finding the practice of law uncongenial, he followed his growing interest in writing and began publishing short stories and reviews for the *Southern Literary Messenger* and other magazines. Many of his articles argued for states' rights in terms of constitutional protections, an end to high tariffs that hobbled the Southern economy, and what he deemed the beneficent nature of slavery. Holmes maintained a voluminous correspondence with the leading writers and public figures of the day—notably Auguste Comte and John C. Calhoun—whose orbit he crossed as a result of his writings.

In 1845 Holmes became professor of ancient languages at the University of Richmond, leaving this for another post at the College of William and Mary two years later. Recognized as a scholar of broad and thorough knowledge, he was named first president of the University of Mississippi in 1848, though this position was short-lived due to an untimely period of ill health. Holmes resigned his position at Mississippi after a short time and spent nine years farming in southwestern Virginia, during which time he wrote continuously to support his wife and children. As he confided in a letter to Auguste Comte, "I have first to work for bread for my family, then to work for books, and finally to work for leisure and independence."

In 1857 he was summoned to the University of Virginia, where he served for the next forty years as a professor of history, literature, historical science, political economy, and the "science of society" (a form of sociology). By the end of his life, he was renowned as the author of numerous periodical articles, several grammar textbooks and spelling books for young readers, and *A School History of the United States of America* (1870, revised in 1885).

—JAMES E. PERSON JR.

Further Reading

Barringer, Paul Brandon. *The University of Virginia: Its History, Influence, Equipment and Characteristics, with Biographical Sketches and Portraits of Founders, Benefactors, Officers and Alumni.* Vol. 1. New York: Lewis Publishing Co., 1904.

Gillespie, Neal C. "The Spiritual Odyssey of George Frederick Holmes: A Study of Religious Conservatism in the Old South." *Journal of Southern History* 32 (1966): 291–307.

———. *The Collapse of Orthodoxy: The Intellectual Ordeal of George Frederick Holmes.* Charlottesville, Va.: University Press of Virginia, 1972.

See also: Southern conservatism; states' rights

homeschooling

One of the most powerful and unexpected American social movements during the last quarter of the twentieth century was homeschooling, by which thousands of parents broke with generations of law and custom and chose to provide the primary and secondary education of their children in their own homes. Despite an ideologically diverse pedigree, by the beginning of the twenty-first century home educators had become an influential component of the American conservative grassroots.

One root of modern homeschooling reaches into late Victorian England. The Christian educator Charlotte Mason, in *Home Education* (1896), urged parents, especially mothers, to understand "that the education of their [young] children . . . is an undertaking hardly to be entrusted to any hands but their own." She especially praised the learning to be gained by an "out-of-door life for the children," a "quiet growing time" focused on spontaneous contact with the natural world.

Other roots were American. The agrarian Ralph Borsodi, in his *Flight from the City* (1933), labeled the home education of his own sons a successful "experiment in domestic production." It saved time and resulted in happier, better adjusted children. The experience also taught the Borsodis that true education "was really reciprocal; in the very effort to educate the boys, we educated ourselves." Raymond Moore, a developmental psychologist and devout Seventh-Day Adventist, made the case for home-centered schooling immediately after World War II. "The family is the best learning nest until near adolescence," he wrote. Where the regimentation and peer pressures found in public schools suppressed children's creativity and joy, home schools would open their minds to the abundance of "God's world."

While Mason and Moore saw homeschooling as an opportunity for Christian expression, the iconoclastic educator John Holt joined Borsodi in building a secular case for bringing children home. He emphasized the incompetence of American public education, the violation of the civil liberties of children by an oppressive bureaucracy, and a growing sense of duty among parents: "Having chosen to have children, they feel very strongly that it is *their* responsibility to help these children grow into good, smart, capable, loving, trustworthy, and responsible human beings." By the mid-1970s, homeschooling under Holt's influence bore the aura of that era's "counterculture." It seemed part of the rebellion against the ponderous postwar liberal order defined by an informal alliance of big government, big business, and big labor.

The same decade also saw the emergence of a more visible Christian homeschooling community. The U.S. Supreme Court's decisions banning prayer in public schools and legalizing abortion, heavy-handed efforts by the Carter administration to regulate religious schools, and the deep intrusion by federal courts into school administration (symbolized by forced busing) stimulated many Christian parents to bring their children home. During the 1980s, the number of homeschooling families climbed sharply. For Protestants, this represented a startling loss of faith in public schools, which had long taught a kind of watered-down Protestant morality. As the evangelical author Susan Schaeffer Macaulay wrote in her popular book *For the Children's Sake* (1984), "the right to parental or family liberty over education is a fundamental right that, because of the pervasiveness of modern government, is being threatened." She also reintroduced the ideas of Charlotte Mason to a new generation of young women, urging them to see "that children are persons who should be treated as individuals as they are introduced to the variety and richness of the world in which we live." Roman Catholics inclined toward homeschooling took heart from the statements of Pope John Paul II affirming "the primary right of parents to educate their children" (*Charter of Rights of the Family*, 1983). Father John Hardon, S.J., saw homeschooling as "the necessary concomitant of a culture in which the church is being opposed on every level of her existence" and so "absolutely necessary for the survival of the Catholic Church in our country."

The homeschooling movement began to take institutional form as well. Two Christian lawyers, Michael Farris and Michael Smith, created the Home School Legal Defense Association in 1983. Several American states used compulsory school attendance laws in the late 1980s to suppress home schools; some parents were imprisoned for a time. But home school associations proved to be effective lobbyists and by the mid-1990s home education was legal (if facing varying degrees of regulation) in all fifty states. When the National Education Association (NEA) pressed in 1994 to use a new federal education bill to discourage home schools, an unprecedented torrent of phone calls to congressional offices crushed the NEA effort (the key House of Representatives vote stopping this effort was a stunning 424 to 1). Homeschoolers had come of political age.

By the turn of the millennium, the U.S. government counted 1.2 million American children in homeschools, up from 25,000 in 1975; other estimates reached as high as two million, or about 4 percent of all U.S. schoolchildren. While highly diverse in composition, clear majorities of homeschool families were both Christian and conservative. Claiming family autonomy, these households frequently banded together for mutual assistance. Hundreds of small, mostly family-run businesses emerged to supply homeschooling households with curricula, books, and other items to assist parent-guided learning.

More broadly, homeschooling has represented a historic effort to rebuild homes. A critical family function ceded to the state nearly 150 years before was coming home. The movement returned to families a common work and purpose. Evidence existed, moreover, that these families grew stronger as a result. Homeschooling households had, on average, nearly twice as many children as the American average, and they were less likely to be affected by divorce. Homeschooled children also found disproportionate success in national spelling, geography, and history competitions, and they were being actively recruited by leading colleges and universities.

At another level, homeschooling has represented a remarkable populist effort at reinventing education in America. A good share of this project meant reclaiming and updating forms of schooling from the past, ranging from the Classical Trivium curriculum of Grammar, Logic, and Rhetoric to a rehabilitation of the *McGuffey Readers* long after their expulsion from the public schools.
—ALLAN CARLSON

Further Reading

Stevens, Mitchell L. *Kingdom of Children: Culture and Controversy in the Homeschooling Movement.* Princeton, N.J.: Princeton University Press, 2001.

See also: Ball, William Bentley; Borsodi, Ralph; education, public; family; traditionalism

Hook, Sidney (1902–89)

One of America's leading anticommunist intellectuals, Hook supported American entry into the Korean War, the isolation of Red China, the efforts of the United States government to maintain a qualitative edge in nuclear weapons, the Johnson administration's attempt to preserve a pro-western regime in South Vietnam, and the campaign of the Reagan administration to overthrow the communist regime in Nicaragua.

Hook's parents were poor Jewish immigrants who had settled in Williamsburg, a working-class neighborhood in Brooklyn. Their son graduated from Brooklyn's Boys High School in 1919 and from the City College of New York in 1923. It was common at this time for young Jews with an intellectual bent to repudiate Judaism and to adopt a surrogate religion. In Hook's case this was Marxism. He became a radical at an early age, protesting American involvement in World War I while still in high school.

Hook received a Ph.D. in philosophy from Columbia University in 1927. While at Columbia, he fell under the sway of John Dewey, the founder of the philosophy of instrumentalism, an offshoot of pragmatism. Dewey's influence was seen in Hook's naturalism, his disdain for metaphysical abstractions, and his faith in intelligence and social planning.

Hook was a Marxist as well as an instrumentalist during the 1930s. He signed the famous 1932 statement "Culture and Crisis" calling for the election of William Z. Foster, the American Communist Party candidate for president. But Hook also recognized that the orthodox Marxism of his day was unacceptable. Its totalitarian monism and determinism conflicted with the openness, freedom, and individualism of Dewey's instrumentalism. In the early 1930s, Hook's most fruitful philosophic period, he sought to purge Marxism of Leninism and Stalinism, and to disentangle Marxism from Hegelianism and from the concepts of the dictatorship of the proletariat, historical materialism, the withering away of the state, and the new socialist "collective man."

The guarantee of individual rights and democratic processes found within the American liberal tradition was more important to Hook than Marxism. For a while he thought liberalism could be fused with Marxism, and he suggested in 1940 that Marxists should look for inspiration to John Dewey. In believing that Marxism could be synthesized with instrumentalism and democracy, Hook's understanding of Marxism was idiosyncratic and, as he would later write, an "intellectual conceit."

After 1945, Hook played no role in formulating a socialist alternative to capitalism and individualism. The great postwar debate, he continually emphasized, was not between collectivism and private enterprise but between democracy and its enemies, or, as he put it in 1959, "between the absolutist and the experimental temper of mind." Hook, however, differed from Walter Lippmann and others who based the defense of democracy on the doctrine of natural rights. For Hook, democracy was not metaphysically but empirically true because it provided more freedom, prosperity, and security than any other political system. His confidence in democracy stemmed not from any belief in the goodness of mankind. He was too familiar with totalitarianism to assume that. Rather, he believed in the possibility of educating the citizenry.

Those both within and outside of conservative circles viewed Hook as one of the gurus of the neoconservative revival during the 1970s and 1980s. In 1985, President Reagan presented Hook with the Presidential Medal of Freedom for being one of the first "to warn the intellectual world of its moral obligations and personal stake in the struggle between freedom and totalitarianism."

Hook died in 1989, that annus mirabilis of recent history that saw the dissolution of the Soviet empire and protests within China against communist rule. Certainly he had not anticipated such developments. He doubted that communist governments could ever be overthrown because of the totalitarian nature of communist rule and the character of Marxist ideology. Communist ideology precluded the peaceful transfer of power to the enemies of the working class, Hook believed. As a philosopher and intellectual historian, Hook in the end took the commitment of communist rulers to Marxist ideology too seriously.

—Edward S. Shapiro

Further Reading

Eastman, Max. *The Last Stand of Dialectic Materialism: A Study of Sidney Hook's Marxism.* New York: Polemic Publishers, 1934.

Hook, Sidney. *Out of Step: An Unquiet Life in the 20th Century.* New York: Harper & Row, 1987.

Reck, Andrew J. *The New American Philosophers: An Exploration of Thought since World War II.* Baton Rouge, La.: Louisiana State University Press, 1973.

Shapiro, Edward S. "The Jewishness of the New York Intellectuals: Sidney Hook, a Case Study." In *American Pluralism and the Jewish Community*, edited by Seymour Martin Lipset, 153–71. New Brunswick, N.J.: Transaction, 1990.

See also: anticommunism; Jewish conservatives; neoconservatism; speech, freedom of

Hoover, Herbert (1874–1964)

Engineer, humanitarian, and statesman, Herbert Hoover is a problematic figure in the history of American conservatism. A hero of libertarians in the 1950s, he is today castigated by libertarians as the true father of the New Deal interventionist state. Acclaimed in his day on the Right as "the greatest Republican of his generation," he has been stigmatized in conservative circles since the 1970s as a cheerless apostle of balanced budgets and high taxes. An examination of his life and political philosophy may help to explain the historical haze that envelops him.

Born in a little farming community in Iowa, Hoover was orphaned before he was ten. By the time he was twenty-one he had worked his way through Stanford University and had entered his chosen profession of mining engineering. By 1914, at the age of 40, he was an extraordinarily successful engineer and financier with a fortune exceeding a million dollars and business interests on every continent except Antarctica.

With the outbreak of World War I, Hoover rose to international prominence as founder-director of the Commission for Relief in Belgium, a humanitarian agency that ultimately brought food to 9,000,000 French and Belgian civilians a day—an unprecedented undertaking in world history. After serving as head of President Woodrow Wilson's wartime Food Administration, Hoover returned to Europe following the armistice as Director-General of the American Relief Administration. Thanks in considerable measure to the Herculean efforts of Hoover and his staff, perhaps one-third of the population of postwar Europe was saved from privation and death. Between 1921 and 1923, he orchestrated American assistance to multitudes of Russians suffering from famine; at its height the project fed at least 10 million people a day. Similar, if smaller, ventures further enhanced his stature in later years.

Returning to America late in 1919, the humanitarian hero soon entered politics. A Bull Moose supporter of Theodore Roosevelt in 1912, and more recently one

Herbert Hoover

of President Wilson's ablest advisers, Hoover at first labeled himself an "independent Progressive." But before long he formally identified himself with the Republican Party and unsuccessfully sought its presidential nomination in 1920.

From 1921 to 1928 Hoover served as secretary of commerce in the cabinets of Presidents Warren Harding and Calvin Coolidge. In short order he became one of the three or four most important men in American public life. In 1922 he articulated his political philosophy in a book called *American Individualism*. According to him the revolutionary upheavals of World War I and its aftermath had produced a world in ferment. In this cauldron, collectivist ideologies alien to America were competing for the minds of men and women. To Hoover the need for a

definition of the American alternative was urgent. He called it "American Individualism."

By this term he did not mean unfettered, old-fashioned laissez-faire. As a self-made man himself, Hoover admired individual initiative. Progress, he said, depended on "creative minds," which must be free to "rise from the mass." But "the values of individualism," he argued, must be "tempered" by "that firm and fixed ideal of American individualism—*an equality of opportunity*." Equality of opportunity, "the demand for a fair chance as the basis of American life"—this, in Hoover's words, was "our most precious social ideal."

In the context of 1921–33 Hoover was a governmental activist. As secretary of commerce he took the initiative in national waterway development, radio regulation, the elimination of industrial waste, and many other projects of postwar reconstruction. He was one of the foremost exponents of governmental public works expenditures as a form of countercyclical economic policy. Nominated for president in 1928 over the opposition of many Republican conservatives, he conceived his term of office as a reform presidency. And when the Great Depression began in 1929, the federal government under his leadership responded with unprecedented intervention in a peacetime economy. This, he said later (and approvingly), "is hardly laissez-faire."

But if Hoover was no free-market purist, neither was he a proto–New Dealer. Time and again he insisted that the form and extent of governmental involvement in the economy must be carefully defined and kept consistent with the broad American tradition of voluntary cooperation, local self-government, and individual initiative. For all his reforming impulses, he had a conserving purpose: the preservation, in an urban, industrial society, of the American tradition of equal opportunity. He sought to use governmental power to facilitate the growth of nongovernmental mediating institutions, and he resisted proposals he deemed socialist or fascist.

Defeated for reelection by Franklin Roosevelt, Hoover soon became a trenchant critic of the New Deal. The election of 1932, he had warned beforehand, was an ideological contest that would determine the nation's course for "over a century to come." Now he saw his dire prophecy fulfilled. "The impending battle in this country," he declared in 1933, would be between "a properly regulated individualism" and "sheer socialism." Discarding the term "American Individualism," Hoover increasingly identified his own philosophy as that of "historical liberalism" and excoriated the collectivist, "false liberalism" of the New Deal. "The New Deal," he said, "having corrupted the label of liberalism for collectivism, coercion, concentration of political power, it seems 'historic liberalism' must be conservatism in contrast." In *The Challenge to Liberty* (1934) and other writings, he tirelessly expounded his message. Thus, in the last third of his life, Hoover, the erstwhile progressive Republican, became a counterrevolutionary: a defender of what he called "true liberalism."

During his lengthy ex-presidency Hoover enthusiastically supported many conservative organizations and causes, including *Human Events* and the Young Americans for Freedom. He was the "principal founder" (in John Chamberlain's words) of the *Freeman* in 1950 and an ally of William F. Buckley Jr. in the founding of *National Review* in 1955. Congressional anticommunists and right-wing newspaper columnists were among those who revered him as "the Chief."

As chairman of the two so-called Hoover Commissions (1947–49 and 1953–55) he attempted to streamline and even roll back the sprawling, post–New Deal federal bureaucracy. He assisted his protégé Robert Taft's campaign for the 1952 presidential nomination. And he nurtured his Hoover Institution in California as an unequaled center of research and documentation on international communism.

There are elements of Hoover's record in office that do not appeal to contemporary conservatives: his energetic expansion of the federal government's role in economic life in the 1920s, for instance, and his assent to the Smoot-Hawley tariff (1930). Yet it is also evident that he was not a modern liberal. As a tireless exponent of voluntarism, he emphatically rejected the statist philosophies of communism, socialism, fascism, and the New Deal, and never abandoned his aversion to the overweening regulatory state. Moreover, unlike many latter-day liberals, he did not believe that government exists for the primary purpose of redistributing wealth. Equality of opportunity, not equality of result, was his governing principle. "The human particles," he wrote, "should move freely in the social solution."

Finally, more than any other man who has held the American presidency, Hoover was profoundly acquainted with the social systems of the Old World. He had seen, as he put it, "the squalor of Asia, the frozen class barriers of Europe." He had seen the terrible consequences of imperialism, war, and revolution as few Americans ever had. And he had seen America in contrast.

This perception of contrast between Old World and New was the experiential core of Hoover's social philosophy, and it had a profoundly conservative effect upon him. It gave him a lifelong understanding of America as a uniquely free, humane, classless society that had come closer to implementing its ideals than any other nation on earth.

In 1964, by then an admired pillar of the American Right, Hoover died at the age of ninety, following an astounding fifty years in public life. In sheer scope and duration it was a record without parallel in American history.

—GEORGE H. NASH

Further Reading

Best, Gary Dean. *Herbert Hoover: The Postpresidential Years, 1933–1964.* 2 vols. Stanford, Calif.: Hoover Institution Press, 1983.

Nash, George H. *Herbert Hoover and Stanford University.* Stanford, Calif.: Hoover Institution Press, 1988.

———. *The Life of Herbert Hoover: The Engineer, 1874–1914.* New York: Norton, 1983.

———. *The Life of Herbert Hoover: The Humanitarian, 1914–1917.* New York: Norton, 1988.

———. *The Life of Herbert Hoover: Master of Emergencies, 1917–1918.* New York: Norton, 1996.

See also: Hoover Institution on War, Revolution and Peace; individualism; isolationism; Republican Party; Rothbard, Murray

Hoover Institution on War, Revolution and Peace

The Hoover Institution on War, Revolution and Peace is an internationally acclaimed research center, library, and archive situated on the campus of Stanford University in Palo Alto, California. Founded in 1919 by Herbert Hoover, thirty-first president of the United States and a Stanford alumnus, the institution has evolved into an extraordinary repository of documents on twentieth-century history as well as a home for some of the nation's most distinguished conservative scholars.

Early in World War I, while directing a gigantic humanitarian relief enterprise in Europe, Hoover happened to read the autobiography of Andrew D. White, the first president of Cornell University. In it White described how he had assembled a vast collection of documents on the history of the French Revolution, including books, pamphlets, and other "fugitive publications." Reading this passage, Hoover realized (he later remarked) that he was "in a unique position to collect fugitive literature" about another revolution: the global cataclysm that he himself was witnessing. He thereupon resolved to undertake an audacious project similar to White's: the systematic collection of contemporary documents on the Great War before they were lost to history.

It was not until the war ended that Hoover could devote his energies to his dream. In 1919 he again found himself in Europe, as a member of the American mission to the Versailles peace conference. Seizing his opportunity, he provided $50,000 of his own money to Stanford University for the purpose of sending a representative to Europe to collect historical material on the war for the university library. Soon Hoover-financed representatives were scouring the continent for historical treasure and sending it back in torrents to his alma mater.

Once begun, his ambitious collecting program never ceased. Although originally focused on World War I and its aftermath, the venture gradually broadened to encompass virtually every twentieth-century social upheaval and every facet of international relations. By the mid-1920s, this library held the greatest assemblage of documents on the Russian Revolution in the noncommunist world. As the scope, value, and volume of acquisitions expanded, the repository underwent several renamings, assuming its present designation in 1957.

Throughout these decades Hoover contributed indefatigably to the development of his prestigious library-archive. The philanthropic founder, however, did not want it to become what he called "a dead storage for documents." Particularly during the early years of the Cold War, he sought to enlist his institution's incomparable resources on communism in an effort to awaken the American people and influence public policy. He hoped by a program of research and publications to demonstrate the evils of Marxism and to "reaffirm the validity of the American system." In this the most famous son of Stanford found himself at ideological odds with his alma mater. Repeatedly during the late 1940s and 1950s he was embroiled in disputes with an increasingly liberal Stanford faculty and administration over his institution's status, programs, and personnel. A bitter struggle for control of the entity developed. For more than a decade, to his chagrin and consternation, the institution he founded was largely staffed and administered by university appointees whose political views were antithetical to his own.

In 1958–59, after a climactic battle, Hoover wrested the institution from his antagonists and took steps to ensure its independence within the frame of the university. As part of this reorientation he selected a conservative economist, W. Glenn Campbell, to become the new director. During Campbell's tenure (1960–89), the Hoover Institution grew rapidly into one of the nation's most influential conservative "think tanks." In 1960, its scholarly staff comprised a few curators; today, its resident fellows and visiting scholars number approximately 100. In 1960, the institution's endowment was $2 million; today it is around $250 million. While Campbell continued the institution's traditional commitment to foreign policy studies, he also increasingly emphasized domestic policy analysis from a free-market perspective. As the conservative political movement coalesced in the 1960s and 1970s, a number of Hoover Institution scholars provided intellectual guidance, notably to Governor Ronald Reagan of California.

Under the directorship of John Raisian since 1990, the Hoover Institution describes itself as "one of the world's leading research centers for the study of public policy." Its library contains more than 1.6 million volumes; its archives include more than 50 million documents. Among its notable holdings are many relating to modern American conservatism, including the papers of James Burnham, Friedrich A. Hayek, Henry Regnery, Eric Voegelin, and the Mont Pelerin Society. The Hoover Institution Press regularly publishes scholarly monographs, documentary collections, and other works. The institution also produces a weekly public television program, *Uncommon Knowledge*.

It is the "think tank" feature of the Hoover Institution, however, that is most visible to the nation's political elites. During the 1980s a significant number of its scholars served the Reagan administration in various capacities. Although by no means monolithically conservative, the institution remains celebrated on the American Right as the home of such individuals as Martin Anderson, Robert Conquest, Milton Friedman, and Thomas Sowell. As a generator and purveyor of conservatively oriented scholarship and policy analysis the institution continues to excel.

Before he died in 1964, Hoover remarked that the founding of the Hoover Institution was probably the most important thing that he had done in his life. Certainly, the establishment of the California institution bearing his name was arguably his greatest gift to American conservatism.

—GEORGE H. NASH

Further Reading

Duignan, Peter C. *The Hoover Institution on War, Revolution and Peace: Seventy-five Years of Its History.* Stanford, Calif.: Hoover Institution Press, 1989.

Nash, George H. *Herbert Hoover and Stanford University.* Stanford, Calif.: Hoover Institution Press, 1988.

See also: Hoover, Herbert; think tanks, conservative

Horowitz, David (1939–)

Perhaps best known for his journey from the political Left to the political Right, David Horowitz is a dynamic and powerful advocate for neoconservative views. A prolific author and well-known commentator, Horowitz is an expert on the methods and rhetoric that liberals use in presenting their views and is adept at turning those same methods against them.

Horowitz was born in New York City to communist parents. While never a communist himself—his parents left the party in the fifties—Horowitz became a leader of the New Left in the sixties while he was attending graduate school at the University of California at Berkeley. He went on to edit *Ramparts*, the movement's largest magazine, and in the 1970s he worked closely with the Black Panther Party in Oakland, California. The murder of a close friend in the winter of 1974–75, however, set him on the path to reconsidering his political views, a journey recounted in his memoir *Radical Son* (1997).

In 1988, Horowitz cofounded The Center for the Study of Popular Culture, a Los Angeles–based think tank. The center's Web magazine, *FrontPage*, receives about 1.3 million repeat visitors per month. From 1992 to 2001, the center also published *Heterodoxy*, a monthly tabloid that focused on political correctness and higher education issues.

Horowitz is highly visible today as a political strategist and commentator, frequently appearing on television and radio and as a speaker at American universities. His primer on political tactics, *The Art of Political War* (2000) is required reading for any conservative activist. He is also a powerful spokesman on race. Several of his other works, including *Hating Whitey and Other Progressive Causes* (1999) and *Uncivil Wars: The Controversy over Reparations for Slavery* (2002), discuss that issue in depth.

—B. KLEIN

Further Reading

Horowitz, David. *The Politics of Bad Faith: The Radical Assault on America's Future.* New York: Free Press, 1998.

———. *Unholy Alliance: Radical Islam and the American Left.* Washington, D.C.: Regnery, 2004.

See also: Collier, Peter

Howard, John A. (1921–)

Born in Evanston, Illinois, John Howard was the descendant of a distinguished family of early American industrialists. (Abraham Lincoln had been an attorney on retainer for one of his ancestors whose reaper design patent Cyrus McCormick had contested in court.) Educated at Princeton and Northwestern, where he earned a doctorate in 1960, Howard had already become at the age of twenty-nine the youthful president of Palos Verdes College. Between 1960 and 1977 he served as president of Rockford College and would oversee and raise funds to finance that institution's move from its decayed nineteenth-century site onto a new campus. As president of Rockford, Howard brought to campus faculty and speakers holding views that were coming to be deemed in an increasingly intolerant academic society as politically incorrect. He also made his traditionalist educational positions known as a public speaker and as a contributing author to *Who Should Run the Universities?* (1969).

Howard received two Silver Stars and two Purple Hearts as a tank commander in the Pacific during World War II, and he has served as president of the American Association of Independent Colleges and Universities, the Philadelphia Society, and the Ingersoll Foundation and taken leadership positions in multiple civic and educational organizations. In 1976 Howard founded (and until 1997 played a leading role in) the Rockford Institute, which grew into a major midwestern center for the advocacy of cultural and educational conservatism. Together with Polish émigré author Leopold Tyrmand, Howard created *Chronicles* magazine as a vehicle of conservative dissent in a culture they perceived as threatened by the anti-bourgeois Left. In 1997 Howard took his mission as a conservative social critic into a new organization, which he cofounded with Allan Carlson, the Howard Center on Family, Religion and Society. Both as head of the Rockford Institute and as a senior fellow at the Howard Center, he has participated in the awarding of the Ingersoll Prize to outstanding scholars and men of letters. These monetary awards, presented in festive surroundings, have gone to such figures as Robert Nisbet, James Burnham, Eugene Ionescu, Walker Percy, Russell Kirk, Murray Rothbard, Forrest McDonald, John Lukacs, Eugene Genovese, V. P. Naipaul, Jorge Luis Borges, Josef Pieper, Edward Shils, and E. O. Wilson. Care has been taken to award the prize to thinkers and writers who express views that seem out of sync with the dominant highbrow and mass cultures.

An inspiring speaker on educational themes and a tireless champion of republican virtue, Howard exemplifies the qualities of mind and spirit associated with American patricians of an earlier age. He and his wife Janice are conspicuous, generous participants in civic life in northern Illinois, devoted members of the United Methodist church in Rockford, and enthusiastic elders of a sprawling family that includes four children and nine grandchildren.

—PAUL GOTTFRIED

See also: Carlson, Allan; Chronicles; *Howard Center on Family, Religion and Society; Rockford Institute*

Hudson Institute

The Hudson Institute was founded in 1961 by Herman Kahn, one of the preeminent mathematicians and nuclear strategists of the late 1950s. Famous for his book *On Thermonuclear War* (1960), Kahn and his associates from the RAND Corporation wanted to establish a think tank dedicated to developing solutions for future problems. Funded by Defense Department grants throughout the 1960s, Hudson fellows produced volumes on defense policy, nuclear strategy, and Vietnam policy. True to its mission, Hudson also published a book, *Toward the Year 2000*, which summarized its projected scenarios for future historical patterns of development. An eternal optimist and inveterate eccentric (Kahn was famous for riding in his convertible during snow storms wearing a coat and wool cap), Kahn's Hudson flourished in the 1960s, obtaining much of its funding from Great Society grants.

The 1970s brought hard times to the Hudson Institute. With new competition from a variety of think tanks, and often late in the production of research (as many as two or three years), Hudson's governmental grants began to dry up. Kahn's death at age sixty-one in 1983 and various financial difficulties necessitated a move from Croton-on-Hudson, New York. With backing from Indianapolis business leaders and the Lilly Endowment, Hudson established its headquarters in Indianapolis, where, under the direction of Herbert London, it would broaden its research beyond defense policy, establishing itself as a prominent authority on matters of education policy, welfare reform, and urban issues. One of Hudson's major successes was its advocacy of the privatization of welfare in Milwaukee with the Welfare-to-Work program. With the leadership of Governor Tommy Thompson, Milwaukee saw its welfare roles drop after the implementation of this program, which eventually spurred the welfare reform embraced by Congress in 1996.

In 2004, the Hudson Institute moved to Washington, D.C., and once again turned its attention to national security and foreign affairs. In its new incarnation Hudson has focused on nuclear proliferation and the advocacy of democracy in the Middle East through its policy center on Islam, democracy, and the Middle East. The institute continues to support a wide variety of research and policy studies, and its list of senior fellows and adjunct scholars includes former policymakers and notable scholars such as Robert Bork, Robert Kaplan, Donald Kagan, and John Fonte. In 2002, the Hudson Institute reported revenues of $6.5 million, much of its activity funded by grants from corporations and private foundations.

—Gregory L. Schneider

Further Reading

DeParle, Jason. *American Dream: Three Women, Ten Kids and a Nation's Drive to End Welfare.* New York: Viking, 2004.

Smith, James Allen. *The Idea Brokers: Think Tanks and the Rise of the New Policy Elite.* New York: Free Press, 1991.

See also: London, Herbert I.

Human Events

America's oldest conservative weekly publication, *Human Events* was founded in 1944 by a group that included libertarians Frank Chodorov and Felix Morley, as well as conservatives Frank Hanighen and William Henry Chamberlin. The paper endured many of the same ordeals faced by the nascent conservative movement during its early years. Nonetheless, *Human Events* survived and became one of the Right's most powerful publications.

Like the conservative movement itself, at the time of its founding *Human Events* represented only a tiny minority voice. At its outset its circulation was a mere 127 copies. Offering its handful of readers bold, punchy articles each week, the paper had little fear of taking unpopular editorial positions. Morley in particular opposed America's intervention in World War II on the grounds that the war provided the government a pretext for future expansion at home and heavy-handedness abroad. Morley was just one of many opinionated writers on the staff, and the publication provided a forum for many, often contradictory, voices.

Over the next few years, though, this chorus of voices became too dissonant to bear. Foreshadowing later strife on the right, the staff grew increasingly divided along conservative and libertarian lines. The Cold War was the major fault line along which these two camps split. Many of the libertarians at *Human Events*, including Morley, tended not to see the Soviet Union as an immediate threat to America's security interests and opposed arming for a showdown with Russia. The opposing conservative faction, which included Chamberlin and Hanighen, tended to view communist Russia as an imminent threat that justified an armed buildup by America's military. Eventually these two camps parted ways, leaving the publication to languish in the shadows of new upstarts like *National Review*.

By the 1960s, however, *Human Events* caught its second wind. The publication rallied to the support of Barry Goldwater in 1964 and climbed to new pinnacles of readership under the watch of Thomas Winter, who joined the paper in 1961 and became an editor in 1964. *Human Events* continued to increase in prominence during the Nixon years, a time before op-ed pages and mass syndication of columnists had become standard fare for general interest newspapers. *Human Events* provided one-stop shopping for a broad spectrum of conservative and right-of-center opinion, and it was widely circulated throughout the 1970s.

During Ronald Reagan's presidency, the paper's publication hit 50,000—including the twenty-four copies delivered each week to the White House. President Reagan once called *Human Events* his "favorite newspaper." Yet the editors were no toadies. In Reagan's first term, the paper ran headlines such as "White House Continues to Fumble Tax Issue" and "Haig Must Go." During a 1982 meeting, Mr. Reagan reportedly told editors Winter and Allan H. Ryskind, "I'm still reading you guys, but I'm enjoying it less."

The end of Reagan's presidency and the rise of other outlets of conservative opinion, including talk radio and new magazines like the *Weekly Standard,* combined to diminish the enormous stature that *Human Events* enjoyed during the 1970s and 1980s. Still the paper remains a staple among conservative activists and beltway insiders. It also continues to provide a broad spectrum of conservatism opinion, much as it did during its early years, thanks to the guiding hand of its publisher, Thomas Phillips. In 1996 the paper reaffirmed its commitment to this ideal when it hired Terry Jeffery as an editor. Mr. Jeffery joined the publication after serving as Pat Buchanan's 1996 presidential campaign manager and immediately took up many of Buchanan's Old Right populist crusades, even as these positions were losing favor within the Republican Party—prompting Buchanan to leave the GOP a few years later. As in the paper's early days, the paper was unafraid to sacrifice its popularity for the inclusion of unfashionable conservative voices.

For this reason it can be argued that the paper has been *the* voice of America's conservative movement since the movement's very beginnings. The paper never has been beholden to one voice or one faction on the Right. Instead it has largely managed to welcome the libertarian and the conservative wings of the movement with open arms. While its influence has waxed and waned over the years, these cycles have tended to coin-

cide with the gains and losses of the political Right. And while its ability to deal with new competition from other venues remains in question, *Human Events'* contribution to the emergence of the conservative political movement already has been indisputably large.

—Scott Rubush

See also: media, conservative; Morley, Felix

Human Life Review

The quarterly *Human Life Review* was founded in 1975 by James Patrick McFadden, longtime journalist and one-time associate publisher of *National Review*. McFadden founded the journal and the organization that serves as its publisher, the Human Life Foundation, partly as a response to the *Roe v. Wade* decision that had appeared in 1973. The quarterly was founded as, and remains, a journal dedicated to reflection on, and support of, pro-life issues, particularly abortion, but also euthanasia, suicide, genetic engineering, cloning, and other forms of biotechnological experimentation. Its pages have also included general commentaries on family and society and meditations on health care developments and their moral consequences.

Despite the intense moral and political debates that surround its subject matter, and despite its own stalwart commitment to the pro-life cause, the *Human Life Review* tends to approach the life issues from a relatively academic point of view, an approach reinforced by the very plainness of its appearance, which recalls academic journals; as a result, William F. Buckley Jr. has called it the "focus of civilized discussion on the abortion issue." Its contributors have included luminaries such as Clare Booth Luce, Cardinal John O'Connor, Nat Hentoff, Wesley J. Smith, and Malcolm Muggeridge, as well as many contemporary journalists and scholars.

McFadden edited the journal until his death in 1998, when his daughter Maria McFadden Maffucci took the helm as editor. Recent articles have included Kass commission member Gilbert Meilaender on "stem cells and Reagan" and George McKenna on "bishops vs. politicians."

—XANDY GILMAN

See also: abortion; Sobran, Joseph

Hutchinson, Thomas (1711–80)

The great-great-grandson of the poet Anne Hutchinson (1591–1643), young Thomas began his career in his father's counting-house at the age of nineteen, having already received both his B.A. and M.A. from Harvard. Through an ennobling marriage and zealous work Hutchinson became, by the 1740s, one of Boston's wealthiest merchants.

A reliable patrician and a forbidding public worker, he emerged into Massachusetts politics as a consummate "networker" and one of a handful of American conservatives seemingly impregnable to either radical rhetoric or loyalist intransigence; thus did he remain until early stages of the American Revolution, when his fortune declined along with the Tory leadership that he represented.

From 1739 to 1749, he served in the House of Representatives, once holding the position of Speaker. Appointed by the House to the Council, he served there until 1766, also holding the post of lieutenant governor in 1758. Although he held no law degree, he was highly regarded throughout the colony for his proficiency as interior court and probate judge, and, from 1760 to 1769, chief justice of Massachusetts. In 1769 he became act-

Thomas Hutchinson

ing governor, a post he held until 1771, when he became royal governor, a post he held until 1774.

One of the most notable colonial Tories, Hutchinson's career gives witness to a fine example of conservative political life before the Revolution. In 1749, he initiated the recall of inflated bills of credit issued periodically by the government since 1690; he then established "hard money" as the medium of exchange for the colony. Using English funds sent as reimbursement for the colony's loyalty in King George's War (1744–45), Hutchinson paid off creditors at a rate of eleven to one, an unpopular action that briefly cost him his seat on the assembly, but strengthened the economy of Massachusetts. At the Albany Convention (1754) he drafted, with Benjamin Franklin, the final version of the Plan of Union, an outline of colonial confederation and a prototype for the Continental Congress.

Often Hutchinson's deep sense of fidelity and service brought him unpopularity. He backed the maligned Sugar Act as well as the Stamp Act, both of which he privately opposed as adverse to colonial and British trade but publicly supported in his capacity as a representative of the Crown. Hutchinson earnestly believed that colonial liberties would best be secured through the patient and reasoned petitioning of loyal ministers such as himself. He would not brook the radical tactics of the Sons of Liberty. He challenged the imaginary community created by the Boston Whigs, engaging in the newspaper wars that anticipated the Revolution. Winning points on principled grounds, but failing to adopt the successful sensationalism of the new American press, Hutchinson lost the conflict on the terrain that seemed to matter the most: literary symbolism.

Unlike many of his revolutionary contemporaries, Hutchinson firmly believed in the need for traditional order, social stability, and hierarchy. Like Edmund Burke, he sought to ground his political vision in historical experience, as he understood it. Hutchinson's most exemplary evocation of historical continuity appears in his letters and pamphlets: especially the *Essay on Taxation* (1764) and the *Dialogue between an American and European* (1768), both of which, for example, frame their arguments partially around an examination of Roman colonial policy. In the *Essay*, Hutchinson voiced opposition to the imminent Stamp Act and attempted to defend a limited extension of colonial liberties. All the while, he balanced deferential rhetoric with a firm argument that the greatest benefits were reaped by all parties when the men of colonies and the mother country shared the same privileges; thus, he politely denounced the concept of "virtual representation," which would later be evident in the Stamp Act. Likewise, in the *Dialogue*, he strove first to define British authority—again, through Roman example—as absolute, but slumbering, and second to counter rigorist interpretations of Locke regarding the constitutional status of the colonies. Sadly for his cause, the discourse was only circulated in private among a dwindling and increasingly marginalized elite.

Commending a consistent and vigorous policy of averting sedition, Hutchinson penned, between 1767 and 1770, a bevy of letters urging that Parliament take stern measures to ensure the loyalty of colonial officials and to curb mounting lawlessness. At one point he even tendered his resignation in an attempt to rouse his torpid superiors in London. The contents of the letters were obtained by Benjamin Franklin and passed on to Samuel Adams, who published them in 1773. The unpopularity they generated, compounded by the unrest that grew in the wake of the Boston Tea Party (December 16,

1773), prompted Hutchinson's replacement with General Thomas Gage. Sailing to England, Hutchinson found himself banished and channeled his energies into writing. Among other works, he completed an acclaimed three-volume *History of the Colony of Massachusetts* (1764–1828), but shattered by the deaths of his wife, sister, and one of his sons, he died a lonely exile.

—WILLIAM FAHEY

Further Reading

Bailyn, Bernard. *The Ordeal of Thomas Hutchinson.* Cambridge, Mass.: Harvard University Press, 1974.

Calhoon, Robert McCluer. "Thomas Hutchinson and the Preservation of Royal Authority." *The Loyalists in Revolutionary America, 1760–1781.* New York: Harcourt Brace Jovanovich, 1973.

Freiburg, Malcolm. *Prelude to Purgatory: Thomas Hutchinson in Provincial Massachusetts Politics, 1760–1770.* New York: Garland, 1990.

Penak, William. *America's Burke: The Mind of Thomas Hutchinson.* Lanham, Md.: University. Press of America, 1982.

Walmsely, Andrew Stephen. *Thomas Hutchinson and the Origins of the American Revolution.* New York: New York University Press, 1999.

See also: Tories, American (Loyalists)

Hutt, William H. (1899–1988)

Born of a working-class family in the East End of London and educated at the London School of Economics, William Harold Hutt began his academic career in 1928 at the University of Capetown in South Africa. After a career of remarkable scholarly productivity, including six books and more than thirty professional journal articles, Hutt retired from Capetown in 1965 and emigrated to the United States, where he was to hold the position of distinguished visiting professor at a number of colleges and universities, including the University of Virginia, Texas A&M, and the University of Dallas. As an American academic, Hutt's scholarly output did not flag. Nonetheless, because he labored most of his career in the academic backwater of South Africa, Hutt's contributions have not yet received in the United States the recognition that they merit, even among free-market economists and others on the American Right.

In economic theory, Hutt drew his basic orientation from the great British economists Phillip H. Wicksteed and Edwin Cannan, the latter Hutt's teacher at the London School of Economics. As Hutt himself has noted, his postwar writings were also heavily influenced by the Austrian approach to economics, especially as expounded in Ludwig von Mises' magnum opus, *Human Action* (1949).

While building on the contributions of the best of his predecessors and contemporaries, Hutt achieved what only a handful of economists have succeeded in: constructing a broad and unified vision of the overall economic process that is original without being idiosyncratic or cranky. The theme that characterizes and unifies all of Hutt's works is the explication, defense, and application of the proposition that rivalrous competition between profit-seeking entrepreneurs operating in a free-market economy, where all prices, including wage rates, are competitively and noncoercively determined, ensures the full utilization of scarce resources in a manner that is continually and strictly in accord with anticipated consumer preferences.

In the 1930s, Hutt coined the term "consumer sovereignty" to denote the concept according to which, in the market economy, the production decisions of entrepreneurs are rigidly governed by the freely expressed spending decisions of consumers. Hutt applied the term "price coordination" to the outcome of the market process by which the prices of scarce resources, including labor, are ultimately determined by the competitive bidding of entrepreneurs on the basis of their forecasts of the future prices of consumer goods. When the prices of productive inputs are thus coordinated with prices of entrepreneurially planned outputs, the result is "full employment" of available resources and the allocation of each resource among the most value-productive of its prospective uses. With respect to the labor market, this means that everyone willing to work at prevailing wage rates can more or less readily find a job that maximizes the monetary value of his or her labor services.

In a later work, Hutt further demonstrated that, contrary to prevailing belief, collective bargaining, or "the strike-threat system" as he labeled it, cannot succeed in increasing the aggregate income share of labor at the expense of the share of capital. Rather, as Hutt showed, the wage gains of unionized laborers come at the expense of nonunion workers and consumers in general.

Hutt was a lifelong and insightful critic of Keynes and of Keynesian economics in all of its variations. To Hutt the fundamental and fatal flaw of Keynesianism was that it completely ignored the coordinating function of the market's pricing process. Hutt exhaustively identified and categorized the diverse kinds of resource idleness which could arise in a market economy. There, Hutt argued that persistent mass unemployment, such as that which existed during the 1930s, was not a result of a failure of "aggregate demand" in the private sector, as Keynes had claimed in the *General Theory* in 1935, but of government and union disruption of the market's price coordination mechanism. Entrepreneurial incentives to employ labor and produce goods were seriously diminished by price rigidities introduced into the economy as a result of legislation mandating minimum wages, compulsory collective bargaining, unemployment insurance, and cartelization and price-fixing in manufacturing and agriculture, which was passed, for example, in the United States during the New Deal era. By effectively preventing the swift competitive adjustment of resource prices to product prices which had declined as a result of monetary deflation and the public's scramble for liquidity, these legislated price rigidities were responsible for the unrelenting nature of the Great Depression.

Hutt explained the apparent success at times of the Keynesian policy of stimulating a depressed economy by increasing "aggregate demand" through deficit spending financed by money creation as attributable solely to the fact that such a policy temporarily inflates product prices relative to incorrect and downwardly inflexible resource prices and brings about a crude type of price coordination. However, anticipating the modern rational expectations position, Hutt argued that once labor unions and other legally privileged groups of resource owners come to anticipate the regular recurrence of such inflationary episodes and to adjust their selling prices accordingly, even the temporary coordinating effect of Keynesian fine-tuning is lost and all that results is inflationary recession or stagflation.

The capstone of Hutt's economic thought is his restatement of Say's Law, a central doctrine of prewar macroeconomic theorizing, whose meaning and importance had been almost completely obscured by the Keynesian revolution. In Hutt's reformulation, Say's Law refers to the truth that, when all inputs and outputs are coordinately priced, the supply of any particular thing constitutes a demand for a noncompeting thing. This implies that it is never an insufficiency of demand but a "withholding" of supply, due to pricing assets or services above market-clearing levels, that depresses economic activity.

—Joseph T. Salerno

Further Reading

Hutt, William H. *Individual Freedom: Selected Works of William H. Hutt.* Edited by Svetozar Pejovich and David Klingaman. Westport, Conn.: Greenwood Press, 1975.

———. *The Keynesian Episode: A Reassessment.* Indianapolis, Ind.: Liberty Press, 1979.

———. *A Rehabilitation of Say's Law.* Athens, Ohio: Ohio University Press, 1974.

———. *The Strike-Threat System: The Economic Consequences of Collective Bargaining.* New Rochelle, N.Y.: Arlington House, 1973.

Mone, Larry, ed. "W. H. Hutt: An Economist for this Century." Special issue, *Manhattan Report on Economic Policy* 3, no. 5 (1983).

Reynolds, Morgan O., ed. *W. H. Hutt: An Economist for the Long Run.* Chicago: Regnery, 1986.

See also: Austrian school of economics

Hyde, Henry (1924–)

A Republican congressman from Illinois, Hyde became the most important pro-life legislator of his day and also led the House of Representatives' impeachment of President Bill Clinton. Hyde was born in 1924 in Chicago to a family of Irish Catholics. He grew up a Democrat and served in the Navy (1944–46). By the 1950s, he was voting for GOP presidential candidate Dwight Eisenhower. He sought elective office himself as a Republican candidate for Congress in 1962, but this first foray into public life resulted in a narrow defeat. Hyde bounced back in 1966 by winning election to the Illinois statehouse. He served there for eight years, and his tenure included a short stint as majority leader (1971–72). He at last won a seat in the House of Representatives in 1974.

A trial lawyer by profession, Hyde gained rapid recognition for his rhetorical skills. His high-pitched voice possessed an unexpected gravity, and many considered him the best debater in Congress. During his first term in office, he offered an amendment to block the federal funding of abortions, which would affect as many as 300,000 abortion procedures annually, mainly for Medicaid recipients. This ban became law in 1978 and was upheld by the Supreme Court three years later. The number of abortions underwritten by federal tax dollars plummeted to just a few thousand per year. Pro-abortion Democrats in Congress and the Clinton administration repeatedly tried to overturn the Hyde Amendment, as it came to be called, but the only major modification occurred in 1993, when an exception was made for rape and incest victims (a life-of-the-mother exception had been in place from the start). This longstanding legislative achievement—combined with his ability to articulate the moral principles behind it—made Hyde a hero to the pro-life movement.

In the 1980s, he emerged as an important Republican voice on foreign policy, especially in support of President Ronald Reagan's Cold War agenda. He played a crucial role in turning back the nuclear-freeze movement. He was also a tireless supporter of the Reagan administration's anticommunist efforts in Central America and a strong defender of the president during the Iran-Contra controversy. Hyde was a widely respected figure among both Republicans and Democrats in the late 1990s when he found himself thrust into the spotlight once more. As the Clinton White House nearly imploded during the Monica Lewinsky scandal in 1998, Hyde became the natural choice to lead the GOP's prosecution against the president on charges of perjury and obstruction of justice. He presided over heated hearings in the House, which resulted in Clinton's impeachment. Then, in early 1999, he helped argue the case against Clinton before the Senate, which ultimately refused to remove the president from office. Despite this, the entire conservative movement has viewed him as one of its most distinguished statesmen and reliable allies. When Republicans who oppose term limits make their case in front of conservative audiences, there is one question they love to pose: "What about Henry Hyde?" In the spring of 2005, Hyde imposed a term limit on himself, saying that he would retire from Congress rather than seek reelection.

—JOHN J. MILLER

Further Reading

Dorning, Mike. "It's All in the Timing, Henry Hyde." *Chicago Tribune,* June 9, 2002, 10.

See also: abortion; Clinton, William J., impeachment of

I

Ideas Have Consequences

First published in 1948 by Richard M. Weaver, then professor of English at the University of Chicago, *Ideas Have Consequences* documents the unfolding of the social, political, religious, and cultural consequences attendant upon rejecting the Christianized philosophy of "logical realism"—which made the West great—in favor of "nominalism."

Weaver's analysis proceeds from the view of the traditional, Christian philosophy holding that there are enduring truths knowable to the human mind that exist independently of man's will and to which man owes allegiance. The best in Western culture derives from the medieval synthesis of Greek thought, mainly Plato and Aristotle, understood and assimilated within the context of a robust Christian faith. Man lives to pursue the ultimate Good, which is absolute and eternal and which transcends the material world. There is a hierarchy of goods leading to this ultimate Good and hitherto the aim of a Christian society was to organize itself in order to help individuals of all stations to participate in and move closer to this Good, to God himself. Social roles involved acting out parts that had spiritual significance. It was possible to know good from evil and it was the duty of public policy to encourage the one and discourage the other, though because of original sin there was no expectation that heaven would be created on earth.

In Weaver's account, the locus of corruption lay ultimately in the nature of nominalism, which, by denying the reality of universals, denies everything transcending human experience. With the advent of nominalism there is nothing higher for man to reach up to, no final truth to guide him. Therefore the material world as experienced and understood by man's subjective feelings and notions is all there is. Man can realize himself more fully by studying and seeking to manipulate what is taken to be a self-sufficient Nature. The victory of nominalism meant that knowledge came to be seen not as a source of truth but of power. Science and technology then became the means to a better life, in which context the concept of "good" was increasingly understood in material terms only. Gradually, argued Weaver, consumption came to be the chief purpose of life and man a mere appetite, while reason, instead of limiting and directing passion, became its servant.

Given the triumph of the nominalist idea, wrote Weaver, it was natural for democracy and the concept of equality to rise in importance. Previously, social hierarchy and a sense of fraternity dominated Western notions of how life should be lived. But with the triumph of nominalism, the concept of social station and the performance of objective duties gave way to the view of absolute equality with a concomitant emphasis on individual rights. Man's focus turned entropically inward toward the self.

Nominalism eroded the value of work as well. Without higher ideals, work was no longer a noble activity whereby the abstract ideal was embodied in the concrete and the particular. Work was no longer worship, or an expression of honor, but the painful grind of a merely utilitarian activity. Even art focused increasingly on the material rather than on the spiritual.

Propagated by the mass media, all of these forces conspired to create the "spoiled-child" effect. Man was taught that he deserves everything; that nothing should stand in the way of satisfying his pleasure. The ability to endure the pain of discipline, which leads to maturity, was lost. Society fragmented into ravenous egos seeking solace for their loss of meaning in material gratification.

Weaver offers three solutions to the dilemma. First is a restoration of private property correctly understood. Not the abstract property of modern finance capitalism but personal, widely distributed ownership of property the responsibility for which teaches important lessons of virtue and thus contributes to character development. Second is a restoration of respect for words as real things, a respect for language that was lost with the rise of Occamism. Third is the restoration of the virtue of piety, including piety toward nature, other people, and the past. If we cannot find an imaginative way out of the troubles caused by nominalism, Weaver warned, we will suffer its consequences.

Weaver's book challenges the dominant secular view of the post–World War II period. It questions the most cherished articles of materialism: that man is inherently good, that what is most recent is best, that progress in science, technology, and democracy will yield an increasingly superior mode of living. It still stands as one of the true classics of conservative cultural criticism.

—Ralph E. Ancil

Further Reading

Scotchie, Joseph, ed. *The Vision of Richard Weaver.* New Brunswick, N. J.: Transaction Publishers, 1996.

Smith, Ted J., III, ed. *Steps toward Restoration: The Consequences of Richard Weaver's Ideas.* Wilmington, Del.: Intercollegiate Studies Institute, 1998.

Weaver, Richard M. *The Southern Essays of Richard M. Weaver.* Edited by George M. Curtis III and James J. Thompson Jr. Indianapolis: Liberty Press, 1987.

———. *Visions of Order: The Cultural Crisis of Our Time.* 2nd ed. Bryn Mawr, Pa.: Intercollegiate Studies Institute, 1995.

See also: fusionism; localism; Weaver, Richard M., Jr.

ideology

The term "ideology" is often used simply as a substitute for the word "philosophy" or even "worldview." Thus, it is often said that conservatism is in need of "an ideology" or a more coherent set of principles on which to base its policy prescriptions. But most intellectual conservatives have a very different view of ideology.

The term "ideology" was first coined by Destutt de Tracy in his *Elemens d'ideologie* (1800–1815). Tracy was referring to a science of ideas. Yet, when Napoleon publicly ridiculed "ideologists," he gave the term a pejorative character it retains to this day. Karl Marx linked the term to the notion of class consciousness in dismissing the ideas of the ruling, bourgeois class as nothing but deceptions of the oppressed proletariat. The twentieth-century rise of communism, fascism, and National Socialism to the level of totalitarian regimes motivated conservative thinkers in particular to consider the distinction between ideology and nonideological political philosophy.

Gerhart Niemeyer, following Eric Voegelin, referred to ideology as "the fallacious immanentization of divine salvation." By this he meant that an ideology is a recipe for bringing heaven down to earth. Modern thinkers, from Rousseau to Hegel to Marx, have rejected Augustine's understanding that the end of history will be the end of the world, at which time man will face his creator to answer for his actions, and at which time alone he may look for the beatific vision. Instead, ideologists seek to bring history to an end here and now. They construct theoretical systems they believe point to the one true and good human society and then seek great men, movements, or events to bring them to reality, thus ending history in a perfect life lived on earth.

A common criticism of thinkers of the Enlightenment—from Descartes to Rousseau at least—is that they sought to make men into gods. Dispensing with spiritual matters, these thinkers reduced the world to data that can be manipulated by the human mind, thus giving man the impression that he can manipulate reality itself. This mistake regarding the nature of reality led to the belief that man also could save himself from the tragedies of life, be they sickness, war, or the drudgery of work. This is the means by which the utopian vision was born. Utopia is the goal of ideology because ideology is the drive to create a new society, based on the system of the ideologist, that will "save" us, bring us into a heaven that is full of abundance but lacking the tragedies of a real life. Yet one should note that few of the actual human beings involved actually would play the role of gods. Marx's unalienated man may be free to shift aimlessly from occupation to occupation, but it is Marx, in combination with the god-like men who bring about the revolution, who has made his life possible. Contemporary ideologies, despite their egalitarian rhetoric, also rely on the god-like ideologist to "liberate" each of us from the ties that bind us to our old institutions, our old ways, and even our old beliefs. And, because anyone who fails to fully and enthusiastically work for the great vision is undermining utopia—denying paradise to everyone around him—that person must be dealt with harshly so that everyone will work all the harder to make paradise a reality. It is no wonder then, in the conservative view, that ideological politics, promising heaven on earth, has produced murderous, hellish police states wherever it has gained power.

Conservatives worry that our society has become overrun with ideology. For example, modern education theory, based in the thought of John Dewey, is at root an ideology. It puts teachers, counselors, and other "facilitators" in the role of gods. These "nonjudgmental" leaders will use various techniques to free us from the prejudices that make us too judgmental and cause us to accept the oppressions of inegalitarian social structures (e.g., the traditional family). By freeing us from these attachments and beliefs, educational ideology would cause us to "choose" the life of unencumbered choice in which one lifestyle is as moral as another and in which we all can agree that the state should protect us from oppression and from the consequences of our own actions.

Real philosophy, in the conservative view, maintains its connection with the broad stream of Western philosophical enquiry. That tradition began with Plato's admission that we are ignorant but should struggle on in the task of measuring what can be measured. Following Aristotle, moreover, it seeks tools appropriate for measuring whatever aspect of reality we currently are examining rather than pretending that we can make reality "fit" the tools we happen to have at hand. Perhaps most crucially, in the conservative view, the Western philosophical tradition recognizes that there is a purpose to nature, to man, and to man's own creations that lies beyond this world. And this means that our inquiries, as well as our daily conduct, must be carried out with the realization that we will not achieve paradise here on earth, but that we will answer to a power higher than ourselves for the actions we take and the spirit in which we take them.

All this makes philosophy, properly understood, an activity far divorced from the dreamy systems and murderous policies of ideology.

—GERHART NIEMEYER
AND BRUCE FROHNEN

Further Reading

Frohnen, Bruce. *The New Communitarians and the Crisis of Modern Liberalism.* Lawrence, Kan.: University Press of Kansas, 1996.

Niemeyer, Gerhart. "Enlightenment to Ideology." In *Within and Above Ourselves.* Wilmington, Del.: Intercollegiate Studies Institute, 1996.

See also: Marxism; Niemeyer, Gerhart; progressivism; Voegelin, Eric

I'll Take My Stand

A 1930 symposium that called attention to the destructive influence of American industrialism on Southern institutions and traditions, *I'll Take My Stand: The South and the Agrarian Tradition* was originally published under the authorship of "Twelve Southerners," four of whom—Donald Davidson, John Crowe Ransom, Allen Tate, and Robert Penn Warren—had been leading figures in the Fugitive poetry group that flourished briefly in the 1920s at Vanderbilt University. The other contributors were poet John Gould Fletcher, writer and economist Henry Blue Kline, psychologist Lyle Lanier, novelist Andrew Nelson Lytle, historians Herman Clarence Nixon and Frank Lawrence Owsley, biographer John Donald Wade, and playwright, poet, and literary critic, Stark Young.

In the diverse collection of tracts that make up *I'll Take My Stand*, only Ransom's introductory "Statement of Principles" espouses views formally endorsed by the entire group. Nevertheless, underlying the symposium's broad spectrum of ideas on

philosophy, art, religion, economics, and history is the premise that modern notions of progress are at war with traditional civilization, and that the South, as the region least affected by this war, was uniquely poised to maintain the defensive. The Southern Agrarians, as the symposium's participants became known, took issue with "New South" advocates who sought to assimilate the region into the "industrial" or "American" way of life. They argued that the gospel of progress through science and technology elevates the pursuit of materialistic comforts above spiritual and artistic values while placing a dangerous amount of confidence in man's ability to build his own utopia.

The authors did not totally reject mechanical innovation and scientific endeavor, but they did protest against making them the ends, rather than the means, of living. Modern society, in the Agrarians' view, had succumbed to a perpetual state of pioneering and invention with little regard for the quality of life so-called progress actually fosters. Timesaving devices and the division of labor increase productivity but often restrict workers to dull routines. Responsible for only a fraction of the completed process, they take little pride in workmanship. The compensation that industrial society offers for this monotonous employment is more "free time," but not "leisure" as traditionally understood.

To justify an industrial arrangement that increases productivity at the expense of human dignity, the surplus goods and services that it creates must be consumed. Modern advertisers need to entice society away from serious reflection by appealing to its appetites. The Agrarians contended that the subsequent lowering of public taste and artistic sensibility cannot be countered with the progressive shibboleths of education and institutionalized patronage because such measures are themselves aimed at mass consumption, and, hence, toward the lowest common denominator. The consequence of succumbing to the industrial ideal, as Davidson wrote, is a life divided between "mechanical and deadening" labor on the one hand, and mere amusement that is "undertaken as a nervous relief."

By contrast, an Agrarian society offers greater harmony between physical existence and the needs of the inner life. The yeoman farmer, an ideal figure for most of the symposium's members, is not motivated to save time and toil for its own sake. His labors, varying with the seasons and carried out on a more personal scale, are not strictly divorced from leisure. Even if, as is conceded to be the case in the South, his manner of living has not inspired the highest culture, the Agrarians argue that it has at least fostered a life of contemplation. Industrialism, on the other hand, not only discourages inner reflection, but its incessant quest for material and social improvements is a form of national hubris that takes no account of the inscrutable forces governing the universe. Its millenarian optimism is doomed to disappointment. Insofar as the agrarian way of life seeks to accommodate rather than subdue the natural order, it is better reconciled to suffering and tragedy. And because it engenders respect for the inexplicable ways of nature, it is more religious.

Published in the first year of the Great Depression, *I'll Take My Stand* was not simply a lament for a passing age. It was a manifesto imploring fellow southerners to resist the siren calls of a social and economic system that promises material well-being but impoverishes the soul, a system that collectivizes humanity into cities and factories yet diminishes the sense of community that existed in a people historically tied to the land. Ironically, upon publication *I'll Take My Stand* was criticized for lacking a viable program of economic reform. The entire thrust of the Agrarian complaint, however, opposes a way of life that places economics before human concerns. The symposium's critics also charged the writers with misconstruing Southern history, in which agrarianism was never so much a widely held ideal as an unfortunate set of circumstances that retarded southern progress. Here again, sympathetic readers point out that the degree to which southerners shared the agrarian ideal was immaterial to whether or not industrialism offers a better quality of life. The symposium's central point was that the South, trailing in the race to industrialize and urbanize, was in a better position to evaluate how much further it should continue.

Of course, Southern history subsequent to the original publication of *I'll Take My Stand* has proceeded along progressive lines and against the admonitions of the Southern Agrarians. At the same time, the symposium has found a growing audience in the nation at large, particularly among cultural and religious conservatives, who find in its essays a formidable objection to the secularizing and homogenizing tendencies of modern society.

—C. H. HOEBEKE

Further Reading

Agar, Herbert, and Allen Tate, eds. *Who Owns America? A New Declaration of Independence.* 2nd ed. Wilmington, Del.: ISI Books, 1999.

Conklin, Paul K. *The Southern Agrarians.* Knoxville, Tenn.: University of Tennessee Press, 1988.

Havard, William C. and Walter Sullivan, eds. *A Band of Prophets: The Vanderbilt Agrarians after Fifty Years.* Baton Rouge, La.: Louisiana State University Press, 1982.

Young, Thomas Daniel. *Waking Their Neighbors Up: The Nashville Agrarians Rediscovered.* Athens, Ga.: University of Georgia Press, 1982.

See also: agrarianism; Davidson, Donald G.; Lytle, Andrew Nelson; Owsley, Frank; Ransom, John Crowe; Southern Agrarians; Southern conservatism; Tate, Allen; Wade, John Donald

Image: A Journal of the Arts and Religion

A literary and arts quarterly featuring original fiction, poetry, creative nonfiction, visual art, essays, interviews, and book reviews, *Image* was founded in 1989 by Gregory Wolfe. The journal's editorial mission grew out of Wolfe's conviction that in the modern era both secular intellectuals *and* religious believers had given up on the idea that great art could still be informed by faith. Both in the pages of *Image* and elsewhere, Wolfe has argued that the postwar conservative movement is overly politicized. Conservatives, he holds, have often failed to see that political reform can only be effective if it is grounded in a revitalized culture, and that culture is ultimately nurtured by religious and artistic vision.

By providing a unique forum for the best writing and artwork informed by religious faith, *Image* sees its mission as that of bridging the rift that both sides in the so-called "culture wars" have opened. In so doing, it champions the belief that the best contemporary art can renew the ancient traditions, challenging believers and nonbelievers alike to find fresh ways for the imagination to embody religious truth and religious experience. Contributors to the journal have included some of the leading literary figures of the era, including John Updike, Annie Dillard, Richard Wilbur, Denise Levertov, Ron Hansen, Richard Rodriguez, Kathleen Norris, and Elie Wiesel. *Image* also cosponsors a summer workshop, as well as an annual conference devoted to the discussion of a particular aspect of aesthetic and religious concerns.

—A. G. HARMON

Further Reading

Wolfe, Gregory. *Intruding upon the Timeless: Meditations on Art, Faith, and Mystery.* Baltimore, Md.: Square Halo Books, 2003.

———, ed. *The New Religious Humanists: A Reader.* New York: Free Press, 1997.

See also: Intercollegiate Studies Institute

immigration

The migration of people to the United States is one of the great social forces in American history—an act that at once made the country's birth possible through the travels of the colonial settlers and later shaped the nation through the arrival of people from cultures spanning the globe. Oscar Handlin hardly overstated the matter in his Pulitzer Prize–winning book *The Uprooted* (1951): "Once I thought to write a history of the immigrants in America. Then I discovered that the immigrants *were* American history." In a sense, immigration is America's creation myth. Yet immigration has posed special problems for conservatives because it highlights tensions between tradition and freedom.

The debate generally turns on whether the nation can successfully transform immigrants through a process of assimilation or whether the sheer number of immigrants disfigures American culture. The truth undoubtedly lies somewhere in between these two poles: the pressure on immigrants to assimilate is a powerful one that often works to great effect, but none can deny that today's America is different from the one that would exist if its racial and ethnic makeup had not changed since the founding. It is a bit beside the point to argue whether America is better or worse than another one that we might imagine, though some conservatives, notably Chilton Williamson Jr. in *The Immigration Mystique* (1996), have criticized the facts of history. Immigration is plainly a national tradition, even as it threatens to disrupt other traditions of equal vintage.

There is a strong anti-immigrant tradition on the Right, which tends to manifest itself when immigration is peaking. The languages, customs, and faiths of immigrants can seem positively alien. Many Americans—and especially conservatives—have suspected that immigration therefore threatens social cohesion. This sentiment existed during the great wave of Irish immigration in the middle of the nineteenth century, it came back at the turn of the twentieth as millions of eastern and southern Europeans streamed through Ellis Island, and it lives again at the dawn of the twenty-first century as millions more arrive from Asia, Latin America, and the Caribbean. The arguments against immigrants were and remain manifold: anti-Catholicism, theories of racial superiority, fears of Bolshevism, economic concerns about wage depression, and general worries about cultural erosion.

There is also a strong tradition among conservatives in support of immigration, often on the grounds that immigration is fundamentally about human freedom—the belief that states should not prevent individuals from choosing where they would like to live, especially when they choose the United States over ancestral homelands because they value political, religious, and economic liberty. America's notion of itself as a "city on a hill"—a phrase coined by John Winthrop in the seventeenth century but embraced by conservatives during the Cold War—suggests a beckoning power that attracts newcomers with appeals to freedom and a set of ideas described in founding documents like the Declaration of Independence. President Reagan marveled at his country's ability to turn foreigners into Americans: "An immigrant can live in France," he wrote in his autobiography, "but not become a Frenchman; he can live in Germany but not become a German; he can live in Japan but not become a Japanese; but anyone from any part of the world can come to America and become an American."

Conservatives who debate immigration often tend to focus on this very question: Are the immigrants in fact becoming American? How well, in short, are they assimilating, or "Americanizing." The United States does have a strong track record at helping immigrants adapt. National unity has withstood more than 60 million immigrant arrivals since 1820, the year the government started counting them. These masses did not tear the country's cultural fabric. A case may even be made that they helped bind it together—an estimated 25 percent of the federal troops during the Civil War were foreign born. At the start of the twenty-first century, immigrants made up slightly less than 10 percent of the country's population, a figure smaller than it was at any point between the 1860s and the 1920s, but also on the upswing due to a 1965 law boosting admission numbers. Because immigration levels have fluctuated over time, alternating between floods and trickles, some conservatives have suggested that the United States requires periods of "digestion" following massive inflows, so that the latest generation of newcomers can invest themselves fully in American life without undue amounts of foreign influence.

The rise of multiculturalism has created a new set of problems for conservatives. In the past, there was often consensus even among people who disagreed about levels of immigration that immigrants themselves must assimilate into American life. Multiculturalism challenges this notion and likens traditional understandings of assimilation to a gentrified form of ethnic cleansing. Its hostility to English-language instruction in public schools has resulted in a bilingual-education regime that inhibits children from learning the language they must know to thrive in the United States.

A number of influential conservatives, such as Michael Barone, Linda Chavez, and

Francis Fukuyama, have tried to balance support for immigration against opposition to multiculturalism. Other voices of conservative restriction, such as the Center for Immigration Studies, believe the problem of multiculturalism will dissipate only when the current period of mass immigration comes to a conclusion.

—JOHN J. MILLER

Further Reading

Barone, Michael. *The New Americans*. Washington, D.C.: Regnery, 2001.

Brimelow, Peter. *Alien Nation*. New York: Random House, 1995.

Chavez, Linda. *Out of the Barrio*. New York: Basic Books, 1991.

Sowell, Thomas. *Ethnic America*. New York: Basic Books, 1981.

Thernstrom, Stephan, ed. *The Harvard Encyclopedia of American Ethnic Groups*. Cambridge, Mass.: Belknap Press, 1980.

See also: Buchanan, Patrick J.; Gottfried, Paul E.; paleoconservatism

incorporation doctrine

Perhaps no judicial doctrine has done more to undermine the legal, political, and social structures conservatives value than has the doctrine that is the subject of this essay. Why are public high school football players forbidden to join in prayer before a game? Why is it practically impossible for a public figure to recover damages when he is libeled? Why are the states effectively forbidden to prohibit any abortion at any stage of pregnancy? In every case the answer is the same: the incorporation doctrine. This doctrine has nothing to do with corporations. It is a judicial invention by which the Supreme Court has misconstrued the Fourteenth Amendment to bind state and local governments, uniformly, by practically every requirement of the first eight amendments of the Bill of Rights as those requirements are interpreted by the Court itself. The Court has also interpreted the Bill of Rights to include additional rights the Court has discovered (or invented) and applied against the states. An example is the right of reproductive privacy found by the Court in *Griswold v. Connecticut* (1965) to exist in the "penumbras, formed by emanations from" the Bill of Rights. This ruling was the precursor of *Roe v. Wade* (1973).

The incorporation doctrine has radically altered our form of government. It is the reason why the Fourteenth Amendment can be called "the second United States Constitution." How did this happen? What can be done about it?

The First Congress and the states intended the Bill of Rights to protect the specified rights only against invasion by the federal government. For protection of those rights against the state governments, the people looked to their state constitutions and the state courts. Thus, in *Barron v. Baltimore* (1833), the Supreme Court held that the Bill of Rights had no application to the states.

The Fourteenth Amendment was designed to provide constitutional protection for the fundamental rights that were included in the Civil Rights Act of 1866, i.e., "to make and enforce contracts, to sue, be parties, and give evidence, to inherit, purchase, lease, sell, hold, and convey real and personal property, and to full and equal benefit of all laws and proceedings for the security of person and property." In the words of Professor Raoul Berger, "the 'fundamental' rights which the framers were anxious to secure were those described by Blackstone—personal security, freedom to move about and to own property; the incidental rights necessary for their protection were 'enumerated' in the Civil Rights Act of 1866; that enumeration, according to the framers, marked the bounds of the grant; and at length those rights were embodied in the 'privileges or immunities' of the Fourteenth Amendment."

The Fourteenth Amendment forbids the states to "deprive any person of life, liberty, or property without due process of law." This was a guarantee of proper judicial and other procedures. From the 1920s and especially after 1940, however, the Supreme Court has used the due process clause of the Fourteenth Amendment to impose substantive, rather than procedural, restrictions, so as to bind the states uniformly by the Court's interpretation of practically every provision of the first eight amendments. Every form of state action, on any and all subjects, is now subject to direct review by the federal courts. Thus, for example, "[t]he Fourteenth Amendment has rendered the legislatures of the states as incompetent as Congress to enact" laws in violation of the establishment clause of the First Amendment ("Congress shall make no law respecting an establishment of religion"; *Abington School District v. Schempp*, 1963).

The establishment clause, incidentally, is especially unsuited for application against the states. The other provisions of the Bill of Rights, e.g., freedom of speech, protect specific liberties. The purpose of the establishment clause was to ensure that the subject of establishing a church would remain within the jurisdiction of the state governments. That clause was merely a demarcation of federal and state jurisdiction rather than a protection of personal "liberty." So even if the incorporation doctrine were legitimate, it should not include the establishment clause. Neither James Madison nor the framers of the Fourteenth Amendment would have walked out of the stadium when the high school players gathered on the fifty-yard line for prayer.

In his classic analysis of its legislative history, Professor Charles Fairman concluded that the framers and ratifiers of the Fourteenth Amendment did not intend to make the Bill of Rights applicable against the states. He contrasted the "mountain of evidence" in support of that conclusion with "the few stones and pebbles that made up the theory that the Fourteenth Amendment incorporated Amendments I to VIII." If the amendment were intended to impose the Bill of Rights, in whole or in part, on the states it would have required a change in the laws of many states with respect to the necessity of indictments, the size of criminal juries, the right to jury trial in civil cases, and other matters. There is no evidence that the states considered it to have any of those effects.

"[W]hen the Court invented the theory that the Bill of Rights limited states as well as the federal government," wrote Judge Robert Bork, "the opportunities for judicial government exploded. The First Amendment speech clause has been made a guarantor of moral chaos, while its religion clauses have been reshaped to banish religious symbolism from public life. The Court invented a right of privacy and used it to create a wholly specious right to abortion. The list of such incursions into the legitimate sphere of democratic control goes on and on."

There can be no restoration of federalism and limited government, conservatives believe, unless the incorporation doctrine is replaced by an enforcement of the basic and limited rights protected by the Fourteenth Amendment.

—Charles E. Rice

Further Reading

Berger, Raoul. *Government by Judiciary: The Transformation of the Fourteenth Amendment.* Indianapolis, Ind.: Liberty Fund, 1999.

Bork, Robert H. "Our Judicial Oligarchy," *First Things* (November 1996): 21–24.

See also: Berger, Raoul; Bill of Rights; due process; states' rights

Independent Institute

The Independent Institute (TII) was founded in 1986 by David J. Theroux as a scholarly research and educational organization. Influenced by classical liberal scholars F. A. Harper and F. A. Hayek, Theroux had previously organized the research, publication, and conference programs for the Cato Institute (1977–79) and the Pacific Research Institute (1979–86).

In the early 1980s, Theroux had become increasingly disenchanted with the public policy research produced by many of the well-funded conservative and liberal policy organizations because of its narrow focus on the Washington, D.C., beltway. In addition, Theroux was impatient with the lack of interest among think tanks in applying modern techniques of marketing and communications to impact the real centers of public debate, which reside outside the beltway. As a result, The Independent Institute had to pursue its research, book publication, conference, and media program without the seed funding normally available to other think tanks. In a 1990 feature article, *Success* magazine termed TII "The Empire of Liberty," acclaiming its uniquely entrepreneurial approach to policy research and education in producing an effective audience of over ten million people.

With over 130 research fellows, TII annually produces many books and other publications. TII research areas include economic, environmental, health, social, legal, and international policy. In addition, TII publishes the quarterly journal, the *Independent Review: A Journal of Political Economy* (*TIR*). Edited by economist and historian Robert Higgs, the *Independent Review* features articles and reviews by many of the world's finest scholars and policy experts. Probing the most difficult and pressing of social and economic questions, *TIR* features in-depth examinations of current policy issues viewed in comprehensive historical, ethical, and economic perspectives. Articles and reviews are devoted to individual liberty and the critical examination of government policy.

Overseeing TII's research program is Alexander Tabarrok. In addition, TII conducts numerous conference programs for scholars, business leaders, the media, and others on such topics as higher education, international finance, war and peace, and the private provision of public services. Its monthly Independent Policy Forum seminar series has featured renowned historians Joyce Appleby and Robert Conquest, economists Roger Noll and Nobel laureate Gary Becker, legal scholars Robert Cooter and Randy Barnett, psychiatrist Thomas Szasz, criminologists Gary Kleck and James Q. Wilson, astrophysicist E. Fred Singer, bestselling authors P. J. O'Rourke and George Gilder, human rights activists Harry Wu and Elena Bonner, business leaders David Packard and Walter Wriston, and many others. In addition, TII regularly hosts national events to honor such individuals as Nobel laureate James Buchanan, economist Lord Peter Bauer, historian Robert Conquest, management innovator Tom Peters, and global financial pioneer Sir John M. Templeton, awarding each the Alexis de Tocqueville Memorial Award.

In 1994, the institute was influential in defeating the Clinton health plan. In the late '90s and early years of the twenty-first century it was active in criticizing the use of antitrust laws in high-technology markets and in opposing the use of price controls on drugs and other health-care products and services.

TII sponsors various scholarship and fellowship programs for students including the biannual Olive W. Garvey Fellowships. The Garvey Fellows program awards scholarship stipends to the top three winners of an international essay competition on the subject of free markets. In addition, in 1999

TII launched the Independent Scholarship Fund (ISF), a private scholarship program for K-12 school children from disadvantaged families to attend the private school of their choice.

—EDS.

Further Reading

Beito, David T., Peter Gordon, and Alexander Tabarrok, eds. *The Voluntary City: Choice, Community, and Civil Society.* Oakland, Calif.: The Independent Institute, 2002.

Roe, Richard. "Empire of Liberty." *Success* (March 1990): 48–52.

See also: liberalism, classical; libertarianism

individualism

"Individualism" is a problematic term in American conservative thought. The cause goes back to the fundamental tension in American conservatism between its libertarian and traditionalist strains. Exponents of the former strain, which often seems to echo and amplify the liberalism of nineteenth-century Europe, are likely to regard individualism in favorable terms, as an affirmation of the human person, and as a counter to the oppressive statism, collectivism, and conformism of socialist and nationalist thought. Exponents of the latter strain, however, see individualism as one of the chief pathologies of modernity, another element in the abstract, rationalistic, nakedly self-interested, egalitarian, leveling, atomistic, antitraditional, and antinomian tendencies that have disordered the present age. At its best, however, American conservatism has sought to navigate between these extremes and has found a variety of ways to reconcile liberty and order and to view them as complementary rather than contradictory.

Hence, "individualism" is not invariably a negative term in American conservative dis-

course. One often sees the term used favorably in what might be called the Hoover-Taft-Goldwater line of antistatist political discourse, often with the adjective "rugged" attached to it. But even traditionalist conservatives are likely to speak well of individualism from time to time, and not only when they are attacking totalitarianism or the welfare state. This should not be surprising, for conservatism places a high value upon the individual, even if it also at the same time tends to question the concept of individual autonomy. Consider the fact that the Intercollegiate Studies Institute, one of the main bastions of traditionalist conservative thought in America, began life as the Intercollegiate Society of *Individualists*. Or that Richard M. Weaver, a hero of traditionalist conservatives, extolled what he labeled "social-bond individualism" as an alternative to both collectivism and atomism. Yet the very awkwardness of Weaver's paradoxical term bespeaks both the necessity of reconciling the two divergent strains and the difficulty entailed in actually doing so.

Some longer historical perspective on the subject, however, should help us to clarify the matter. For, although "individualism" is a relatively new term in Western intellectual and religious history, it has a long and distinguished pedigree, informed by rich antecedents and fertile anticipations. Belief in the dignity and worth of the individual person has always been a distinguishing mark, and a principal mainstay, of what we call Western civilization, the defense of which has become an increasingly central element in what now goes by the name of conservatism.

Elements of that belief can be detected as far back as classical antiquity, particularly in the Greek discovery of *philosophy* as a distinctive form of free rational inquiry, and in the Greco-Roman stress upon the need for virtuous individual citizens to sustain a healthy republican political order. Other elements appeared later, particularly in the intensely self-directed moral discipline of Epicureanism and Stoicism. Even more importantly, the traditions and institutions arising out of biblical monotheism, whether Jewish or Christian, placed heavy emphasis upon the infinite value, personal agency, and moral accountability of the individual person. That emphasis reached a pinnacle of sorts in Western Christianity, which incorporated the divergent legacies of Athens and Jerusalem into a single universalized faith.

None of these expressions of belief in the individual were quite the same as modern individualism, however, for the freedom the premodern individual enjoyed, particularly since the advent of Christianity, was always *constrained*. It was constrained by belief in the existence of an objective moral order not to be violated with impunity by antinomian rebels and enthusiasts. And it was constrained by belief in the inherent frailty of human nature, which indicated that virtue cannot be produced in social isolation. Although almost all influential Western thinkers before the dawn of modernity had conceded the importance of the individual, none used the term "individualism" to express that belief.

Instead, "individualism" first arose in the discourse of opposition to the French Revolution. The nineteenth-century French writer Joseph de Maistre used the word to describe what he found horrifying about the revolution: its overturning of established social hierarchies and dissolution of traditional social bonds in favor of an atomizing doctrine of individual natural rights that freed each individual to be his or her own moral arbiter. For Maistre, individualism was not an affirmation of dignity, but a nightmare of moral anarchy, a nightmare that he rendered in startlingly vivid terms.

The French writer Alexis de Tocqueville, in his classic study *Democracy in America* (1835), had a more subtle and enduring analysis. He believed individualism to be America's self-conscious social philosophy, a view of the social world fostered by the rise of democracy that "disposes each member of the community to sever himself from the mass of his fellow-creatures: and to draw apart with his family and friends: so that . . . he willingly leaves society at large to itself." For Tocqueville, individualism was something new under the sun, a conscious and calculated withdrawal from the responsibilities of citizenship and public life. For Tocqueville—who was, unlike Maistre, a qualified friend of democracy—there was no greater threat to the new order than this tendency toward privatism.

Even Tocqueville's more moderate view seems strikingly at odds with the self-conception of most Americans, who after all had little experience of feudal, aristocratic, monarchical, and other premodern political institutions, and who are likely to see individualism, in one form or another, as a wholly positive thing, the key ingredient in what it means to be American. Such a view is, of course, a bit too simple. It presumes that American history is nothing more than the story of an unfolding liberal tradition, a tale that can be encapsulated in the classic expression of individual natural rights embodied in the Declaration of Independence. Such a view ignores the profound influence of religious, republican, radical communitarian, socialist, and other nonliberal elements in our national saga, including the most illiberal institution of all, slavery. What national commitment to individualistic values we now possess has certainly evolved over time, and there have always been countercurrents challenging the mainstream.

Nor, for that matter, is it always easy to know what is meant by the term "individualism." It is used, albeit legitimately, in a bewildering variety of ways. It may refer to the self-interested disposition of mind that Tocqueville described or to the passionate egotism Maistre deplored or to the self-reliant frontiersman or self-made small businessman praised in American popular lore. Individualism may be taken to refer to an understanding of the proper relationship between the individual and society or state, wherein the liberty and dignity of the former is to be protected against the aggrandizing or social-conformist pressures of the latter. More radically, it may point toward a philosophy of the state or society in which all political and social groups are viewed as mere aggregations of otherwise self-sufficient individuals, whose social bonds are entirely governed by consensual contract. Even more radically, it may point toward the increasingly popular view that, to the maximum degree possible, the individual should be regarded as an entirely morally autonomous creature—accountable to no person and no putative higher law, armed with inviolable rights, protected by a zone of inviolable privacy, and left free to grow and develop as the promptings of the self dictate. All these meanings of individualism have in common a presumption of the inherent worth of the individual person, but they may diverge in dramatic ways.

And yet, disclaimers aside, there can be little doubt that the dominant American tradition in our own day has become one of endorsing the highest possible degree of individual liberty and self-development in political, religious, social, and economic affairs. The pejorative connotation that individualism had at the time of its origins never took deep hold in Anglo-American discourse. If anything, the language of individual rights, and the tendency to regard individual men and women as self-contained, contract-making, utility-maximizing, and values-creating actors, who accept only those duties and obligations they elect to accept, has grown steadily more powerful and pervasive in the early part of the twenty-first century. The recourse to individual rights, whether expressed as legal rights, voting rights, expressive rights, reproductive rights, sexual rights, membership rights, or consumer rights, has become the near-invincible trump card in most debates regarding public policy, and it is only in the rarest instances (such as the provision of preferential treatment for members of groups that have been subjected to past legal or social discrimination) that this trump has been effectively challenged. The fundamental commitment to what Elizabeth Cady Stanton called the "solitary self" has never been stronger.

Conservatives are hard put to mount an effective challenge to this hegemony of rights talk. For one thing, they have to rely on rights talk themselves, as a way of defending their own right to be heard. The loudest and most convincing complaints about political correctness, speech codes, and ideological orthodoxy in the academy now come from conservatives, who might otherwise be silenced entirely. Then, too, there is the fact that so many American conservatives are libertarians, particularly in economic matters and increasingly so in matters of personal morality and social policy as well. Such libertarian commitments often take precedence over questions of social cohesion or the public good, including matters such as land use and environmental or economic policy, or the soundness of the social fabric, matters that used to be at the heart of conservative thought.

More fundamental, though, is the question of how much strength remains in the primary institutions of family, marriage, church, and local community upon which traditionalist conservatism was built and by which the American penchant for individualism has been restrained in the past. Such fragile institutions, and the habits of reverence, accountability, and rootedness they engender, will have little binding power in a utility-maximizing world, where radical individualism is allowed to run riot. As a consequence, much of the gloomy mood of conservative social theory in the past fifty years has taken its cue from Robert Nisbet's classic 1953 work, *The Quest for Community*, seeing the decay of such primary institutions and other "intermediate associations" as profound and irreversible.

Yet Nisbet himself offered grounds to think this view might be too gloomy. As he made clear, there is an enduring point of common ground between the libertarian and traditional critiques of modern America—and that is the aversion both share to the overwhelming dominance of the modern centralized nation-state. As Tocqueville well understood, individualism is itself the product of a particular form of socialization. Radical centralization and radical individualism go hand in hand, precisely because centralization gradually eliminates the functional need for individuals to understand and comport themselves as social creatures, accountable to one another and nourished by and embedded in their proximate social contexts. If, on the other hand, the trend toward centralization could be reversed and social policy be consciously reoriented toward the preservation and strengthening of intermediate associations, it seems reasonable to suppose that the current excesses of individualism might also begin to recede and the tension between individual liberty and social order might be made less intense, and more fruitful, than it is at present. Whether that is possible remains to be seen, of course. But it is not unthinkable.

—Wilfred M. McClay

Further Reading

McClay, Wilfred M. *The Masterless: Self and Society in Modern America.* Chapel Hill, N.C.: University of North Carolina Press, 1994.

See also: Catholic social teaching; Chodorov, Frank; community; Hoover, Herbert; liberalism; libertarianism; mediating structures; Quest for Community, The; Road to Serfdom, The; Spencer, Herbert; Tocqueville, Alexis de

Institute for Contemporary Studies

The Institute for Contemporary Studies is an Oakland-based public policy research institute dedicated to promoting self-government and entrepreneurialism through publications, seminars, and public policy reform. ICS publishes books dedicated to its mission of advancing self-government and improving individual lives. Founded in 1972 by Edwin Meese and Caspar Weinberger as a think tank dedicated to promoting Ronald Reagan's presidential candidacy, the institute is currently headed by Robert B. Hawkins Jr., former chairman of the U.S. Advisory Commission on Intergovernmental Relations (1982–93). Donald Rumsfeld served as CEO of ICS in the late 1980s and broadened the organization's focus to promote economic development in the Third World through the International Center for Economic Growth, a division that promoted market reforms in post-socialist countries. Since the end of the Cold War, ICS has focused its resources on book publishing and on exploring new public policy avenues in education, environmental issues, urban development, and crime. A recent initiative in Oakland aims at developing faith-based programs in the inner city to promote the development of leadership and the development of community organizations aimed at ending governmental dependence. ICS receives most of its operating expenses from private foundation grants, most prominently the Lynde and Harry Bradley Foundation, although it has also undertaken research commissioned by governmental agencies and nongovernmental organizations.

—Gregory L. Schneider

Further Reading

Kelley, John L. *Bringing the Market Back In: The Political Revitalization of Market Liberalism.* New York: New York University Press, 1997.

Smith, James Allen. *The Idea Brokers: Think Tanks and the Rise of the New Policy Elite*. New York: Free Press, 1991.

Institute for Humane Studies

The Institute for Humane Studies (IHS) was founded in 1961 by economist Floyd A. "Baldy" Harper and historian George Resch to cultivate classical liberal and libertarian scholarship.

Ideological differences caused initial funding to fall through. Until 1965 IHS was forced to rely upon the personal support of Harper. In 1965, however, IHS opened its first office, and businessman Charles Koch became a major supporter, in effect saving IHS from what otherwise would have certainly been its financial demise.

Initial support from Koch focused on private vs. public education, later to become IHS's Center for Independent Education. By 1969, Resch rejoined Harper full time, and along with Charles Dickinson, former vice president of Stanford University, and Kenneth Templeton, former vice president at the Lilly Endowment, formed IHS's key staff.

Under Harper's influence, IHS's program of scholarly research, book publication, and conferences was the central force generating a new libertarian intellectual movement at the cutting edge of academic debate. Of particular focus were the Austrian school of economics, revisionist history in economics and war, philosophy of law, and human differentiation.

With Harper's death in 1973, IHS chairman Koch installed his assistant, George Pearson, to oversee operations. Although IHS's program in revisionist history was discontinued, the program on Austrian theory continued, with the operation of a highly successful series of college conferences plus the creation of the influential book series, *Studies in Economic Theory*, which was cosponsored by the Cato Institute. In 1973, IHS also expanded its program into law and economics with the Law and Liberty Project, directed by Davis Keeler, publishing a scholarly newsletter and conducting conferences for legal scholars.

IHS operates fifteen scholarship programs for students and conducts numerous conferences for students, journalists, and junior business people. However, IHS is no longer involved in sponsoring studies by leading libertarian scholars, including the Law and Liberty Project, which was cancelled in 1981. Instead it views itself as a talent-nurturing operation seeking to develop a network of contacts in academia, business, the media, and other fields. As a result, IHS discontinued its book program in 1983, as well as its conference program for scholars by the late 1970s.

Today, the Institute for Humane Studies continues its very successful program in classical liberal ideas to educate college students through its seminar program, various student fellowship programs (Hayek Fund for Scholars and Felix Morley Journalism Competition), and internships (Young Communicators Fellowships) designed to facilitate careers in academia, public policy, law, journalism, filmmaking, and fiction writing.
—David J. Theroux

Further Reading

Moore, W. John. "Wichita Pipeline." *National Journal* (1992): 1168–74.

See also: Harper, Floyd A. "Baldy"; Koch, Charles G., Charitable Foundation; libertarianism

intellectual

As a noun descriptive of persons, "intellectual" implies a person given to abstract thought, presumably of an advanced or radical character, as distinguished from a person attached to tradition, convention, and custom.

In the seventeenth century, the term "intellectual" was chiefly employed to describe a person who holds that all knowledge is derived from pure reason. The more common term for this concept was "intellectualist." Both had derogatory connotations. Francis Bacon criticizes the intellectualist, in *The Advancement of Learning* (1605), for being a mere abstract metaphysician. Bishop Parker remarks how "These pure and seraphic intellectualists forsooth despise all sensible knowledge as too grosse and materiall for their nice and curious faculties." Without actually using the term "intellectual," David Hume demolished eighteenth-century a priori thinkers (after the model of Locke) who took Reason as sole guide to the nature of man. Coleridge—also without using the term—attacked intellectuals as devotees of Understanding, "the mere reflective faculty," as distinguished from Reason, the organ of the supersensuous.

As a noun descriptive of persons, "intellectual" appeared scarcely at all in nineteenth-century dictionaries. So far as the term was employed in Britain and America, it meant the "sophisters and calculators" whom Burke had denounced, the abstract philosophes; it was a category despised equally, though for different reasons, by Romantics and Utilitarians. It was closely linked with an unimaginative secularism: John Henry Newman attacked Sir Robert Peel for embracing it. By implication, an intellectual neglected the imagination, the power of wonder and awe, and the whole realm of being beyond mere rational perception.

Despite the term's derogatory history, a group of persons in the early twentieth century began to describe themselves as intellectuals. They were influenced by the concepts and the terminology of Marx, who said that the intellectual must always gnaw at the foundations of society. This use of the term "intellectual" posits a body of schooled and highly rational persons bitterly opposed to

established social institutions: outcasts, in a sense; alienated men; rootless, radical folk. During the Dreyfus controversy in France, factions of the Right used *"les intellectuals"* with contempt to describe cafe revolutionaries—men who had broken with tradition; foes of patriotism, order, and the judgment of the centuries.

Until fairly recent decades, London and New York did not know the domination of the intellectual. Not until the 1920s, in Britain and America, was there much talk of the treason of the intellectuals, because the word intellectual was seldom used for lack of a distinct class to which it might be applied. Not even Emerson wrote about the "American intellectual." He disliked the concept of "a sort of Third Estate with the world and the soul," a body of persons claiming to speak "exclusively for the intellect, and for the intellect only."

Nevertheless, beginning with the 1920s, there developed in the United States a category or class of intellectuals, chiefly in Manhattan, virtually identified with political and social movements of the Left, ranging from mild secularism to outright advocacy of communism. Lionel Trilling and William J. Newman stated that they employed the words "intellectual" and "liberal" almost synonymously. Correspondingly, educated conservatives have declined to be labeled "intellectuals," preferring such designations as "bookman," "scholar," or "writer."

Not all liberals or radicals, however, embrace the designation "intellectual." In the 1950s, someone wrote to Bertrand Russell inquiring after his definition of that term. "I have never called myself an intellectual," Russell replied, "and nobody has ever dared to call me one in my presence." Russell also stated, "I think an intellectual may be defined as a person who pretends to have more intellect than he has, and I hope that this definition does not fit me."

It has often been said that few conservative intellectuals can be discovered. John Stuart Mill went so far as to call conservatives "the stupid party." But because the thinking conservative rejects the intellectual's premises, necessarily he declines the appellation.

—RUSSELL KIRK

Further Reading

Huszar, George B. de, ed. *The Intellectuals: A Controversial Portrait*. Glencoe, Ill.: Free Press, 1960.

Molnar, Thomas. *The Decline of the Intellectual*. Cleveland: World Publishing Co., 1961.

See also: ideology; liberalism

intelligent design theory

Many American conservatives have adopted "intelligent design theory" as an alternative to Darwinian biology in explaining the order of the living world. The argument for "intelligent design" is at least as old as Book 10 of Plato's *Laws*. In that dialogue, the Athenian Stranger warns that atheists who explain the order of the world solely as a product of nature and chance deny the existence of the gods and the divinely ordained morality necessary to sustain the laws of any healthy community. He recommends that citizens should be taught that the complex order in the universe shows a rational design that could only come from providential gods who reward the virtuous and punish the vicious. In 1874, Charles Hodge—an influential Presbyterian theologian at Princeton University—reformulated this Platonic argument in attacking Charles Darwin's theory of evolution as an atheistic and materialistic denial of God's role as intelligent designer of the universe.

In 1991, Phillip Johnson's book *Darwin on Trial* revived Hodge's argument by warning that Darwinian science was promoting a morally corrupting materialism that ignored the evidence of intelligent design as manifesting the hand of a providential Creator. In addition to Johnson's writings, Michael Behe's *Darwin's Black Box* (1996) and William Dembski's *Intelligent Design* (1999) have contributed to the intelligent design movement. Although some conservatives have adopted the "creationist" view—based on a literal reading of the Bible—that the world was created in six days, many conservatives have welcomed intelligent design theory as more plausible, because it affirms the creative power of a divinely intelligent designer as manifested in the natural world without requiring a literal reading of the Genesis account of Creation.

The Center for the Renewal of Science and Culture at the Discovery Institute—a conservative think tank in Seattle, Washington, whose president is Bruce Chapman—has aggressively promoted Johnson, Behe, Dembski, and others as part of its intellectual strategy for defeating scientific materialism and advancing religious conservatism in the culture wars. The writers sponsored by the Discovery Institute make three kinds of arguments against Darwinian science. The intellectual argument is that intelligent design theory is better supported by the scientific evidence and logic than is Darwinian biology. The moral argument is that while Darwinism is morally corrupting, the idea of intelligent design sustains belief in a divinely ordained moral law. The political argument is that since Darwinism is both intellectually and morally inferior to intelligent design theory, biology classes in the public high schools should teach intelligent design as an alternative to Darwinian biology. The ultimate political aim of the Discovery Institute is to win a case before the United States Supreme Court that would uphold the constitutionality of teaching intelligent design as part of the biology curriculum in public schools.

There are, however, some conservative critics of intelligent design theory who argue that Darwinism is both intellectually and morally defensible. Moreover, they insist that a Darwinian account of human nature actually supports a conservative view of ethics and politics as rooted in a natural moral sense.

—LARRY ARNHART

Further Reading

Arnhart, Larry. "Conservatives, Darwin, and Design." *First Things* 107 (2000): 23-31.

Dembski, William A., ed. *Uncommon Dissent: Intellectuals Who Find Darwinism Unconvincing.* Wilmington, Del.: ISI Books, 2004.

Hodge, Charles. *What Is Darwinism?* New York: Scribner, Armstrong, & Company, 1874.

West, John G., Jr. "The Regeneration of Science & Culture: The Cultural Implications of Scientific Materialism versus Intelligent Design." *Touchstone,* July/August 1999, 33-38.

See also: creationism; sociobiology; Touchstone: A Journal of Mere Christianity

Intercollegiate Review

The *Intercollegiate Review*, the only scholarly journal in America which includes in its core audience undergraduate students (along with graduate students and faculty), was launched in 1965 by the Intercollegiate Society of Individualists, later the Intercollegiate Studies Institute, the publisher of this encyclopedia. Begun at what must have seemed the nadir of postwar "movement conservatism," in the immediate wake of the defeat of Barry Goldwater, the magazine concerned itself not with practical politics but the life of the mind and the philosophical issues disputed among thinkers broadly grouped on "the right." As the magazine promised, the *IR* presented "a thoughtful and thought-provoking interdisciplinary perspective on contemporary issues by digging to the roots: first principles, philosophy and religion, cultural and historical forces." It also served as a lifeline to conservative students isolated at increasingly leftist institutions. Distributed free to all members of ISI, the journal has risen steadily in circulation from 22,000 in the mid-1960s to over 50,000 today.

Even as *National Review*'s Frank Meyer attempted to unite the American right around his "fusionism," a Cold War–infused classical liberalism defended on grounds of the traditional Christian respect for individual dignity and freedom, distinguished authors attached to other positions fenced in the pages of the *Intercollegiate Review*, advocating various versions of traditionalism, libertarianism, and Austrian economics, and debunking the polemics emerging from the nascent New Left that had begun to dominate American campus life. As Lee Edwards notes in his official history of ISI, *Educating for Liberty* (2003), "Aware that an undergraduate generation spans only four years, the *IR* undertook to reintroduce the major themes and figures of the conservative intellectual movement to succeeding generations of conservatives."

The biannual journal's first editor, Robert Ritchie, was a veteran both of the U.S. armed services and of the *New Guard*, the magazine of the almost equally militant Young Americans for Freedom. In his choice of editorial board, however, Ritchie showed a distinctly academic and intellectual bent, choosing such worthies as political philosopher Will Herberg, poet and critic Donald Davidson, political scientist Gerhart Niemeyer, and political philosopher Leo Strauss, among others. The first issues of the magazine set the tone that it would carry forward to the present—intellectual but accessible, committed to broadly right-wing perspectives but nondogmatic, ever infused with a concern for literary culture. Early essays dealt with Hannah Arendt, Arthur Miller and John Dos Passos, alongside discussions of "The Politics of Race" by Paul Cole Beach, "The Civil Rights Movement and the Coming Constitutional Crisis" by Willmoore Kendall, and "Existentialism and the American Intellectual" by Thomas Molnar. Those writers who have appeared in the journal's pages constitute a virtual "who's who" of the conservative intellectual movement; a short, far from exhaustive, list includes Burke scholar Peter Stanlis, historian Stephen Tonsor, philosopher Eliseo Vivas, political journalist and organizer M. Stanton Evans, political theorist Frederick Wilhelmsen, historian of ideas Eric Voegelin, novelist and political historian Erik von Kuehnelt-Leddihn, man of letters (and principal founder of postwar American conservatism) Russell Kirk, sociologist Robert Nisbet, Austrian-school economist Ludwig von Mises, Southern historian Clyde Wilson, even the rightful heir to the Austro-Hungarian monarchy (and an architect, for better or worse, of European unity) Otto von Habsburg.

The tone and content of *IR* has been carefully maintained under successive editors, up through the current editor Mark Henrie, adding to its pages such stars as historian Robert Conquest, economist Paul Craig Roberts, literary critic Marion Montgomery, political scientists Claes Ryn, Harvey Mansfield, George Carey, and Paul Gottfried, historian of science Stanley Jaki, future congressman Jack Kemp, and future senator Phil Gramm. Other important contributors have included novelist Robert Penn Warren and his sometime partner in literary criticism Cleanth Brooks. The journal has also published (posthumously) essays by rhetoric scholar and seminal conservative thinker Richard M. Weaver.

Some of the most important divisions within the conservative intellectual world were first explored within the pages of the *Intercollegiate Review*. Its famous spring 1986 issue featured a symposium, "The State of Conservatism," edited by Gregory Wolfe with contributions by Wilson, Niemeyer, George Panichas, Kirk, Carey, Gottfried and M. E. Bradford. These writers explored the growing influence of neoconservatism, which had by that point veered from an empirically based analysis of the perverse effects of liberal social policy into an alternative account of what in America was worth conserving, different in vital details from what both traditionalists and libertarians had long defended and committed to an activist, neo-Wilsonian foreign policy. The fall 1992 issue explored another important cleavage on the right: the meaning of the American founding, in essays by Bradford, a Southern traditionalist, and Harry Jaffa, advocate of the maximalist reading of the Declaration of Independence first advanced by Abraham Lincoln. The question they disputed as to whether American liberty finds its source in Anglo-Saxon traditions and institutions, which must therefore be preserved as its native soil, or in universal, self-evident truths adaptable to any cultural environ still motivates disputes over the nature of the American founding and identity.

—JOHN ZMIRAK

Further Reading

Nash, George H. *The Conservative Intellectual Movement in America since 1945.* Wilmington, Del.: Intercollegiate Studies Institute, 1996.

See also: Intercollegiate Studies Institute; media, conservative; Milione, E. Victor

Intercollegiate Studies Institute

The Intercollegiate Studies Institute was founded in 1953 by libertarian journalist Frank Chodorov in order to counter the widespread and growing popularity among America's educated elites of socialist and other collectivist ideologies. Chodorov's libertarianism had been inspired in part by the writings of his friend Albert Jay Nock, a sharp critic of the New Deal, foreign interventionism, and other "statist" political programs that enjoyed near-universal acceptance among intellectuals and policymakers after the massive success of the Allied war effort. If the state could manage the conquest of Hitler, went the dominant line, surely it could establish permanent prosperity. Nock and Chodorov, among others, disagreed. Already sixty-three years old and an editor at the conservative paper *Human Events*, Chodorov conceived in 1950 the idea of a chain of campus clubs, a lecture bureau, and a journal aimed at rediscovering and disseminating the classical Western principles of "ordered liberty" among future American leaders.

In an article titled "A Fifty-Year Project to Combat Socialism on the Campus," Chodorov announced the goals of the organization that he would later found as the Intercollegiate Society of Individualists. Chodorov's goal was not simply negative, nor was his inspiration the radical individualism of then-popular novelist (and guru) Ayn Rand, who preached the "virtue of selfishness." Instead, Chodorov, who had returned to his Jewish faith after years as an atheist, saw the religiously informed liberalism of Adam Smith as the best formula for general affluence and freedom.

Chodorov's timing was fortunate. Richard M. Weaver had in 1948 published his stunningly contrarian *Ideas Have Consequences*, tracing the decline of liberty in the West to the rise of skepticism and materialism; this analysis shocked consensus thinkers, who followed the Whig view that religion was the enemy, and science the friend, of freedom. And within a year, Russell Kirk would publish his landmark study, *The Conservative Mind*, which through copious documentation and cogent argument dispelled the popular notion that there was no conservative tradition in America; Kirk himself would in 1957 found *Modern Age*, a scholarly journal intended to carry on this tradition among intellectuals.

Chodorov saw ISI's primary mission as identifying freedom-minded faculty and undergraduates at American colleges, helping them meet each other, and keeping them supplied with fresh arguments and insights regarding the roots of liberty in the Western tradition. Starting with a small donation from Sun Oil Company founder J. Howard Pew, Chodorov launched ISI with the young William F. Buckley Jr. as its first president. Buckley was already famous as the spokesman for conservatives on campus thanks to his 1951 book *God and Man at Yale*. Buckley's involvement with ISI was largely symbolic; he was already busy planning his biweekly *National Review*, which he intended to serve as a journalistic organ for the new movement. But as he would later write in a letter to ISI's E. Victor Milione, "It is quite unlikely that I should have pursued a career as a writer but for the encouragement [Chodorov] gave me just after I graduated from Yale." During the subsequent decades ISI would perform a similar service in the career paths of countless young conservatives, listing among alumni of its summer schools, honors programs, lectures, scholarships and other initatives such luminaries as Paul Gottfried, William Kristol, Edwin Feulner, Angelo Codevilla, John F. Lehman, Larry Arnn, Paul Craig Roberts, and Claes Ryn, among many other important academics, journalists, and activists.

According to its mission statement, ISI was founded to "further in successive generations of American college youth a better understanding of the economic, political, and spiritual values that sustain a free and virtuous society." It began to do so in 1952 with a mailing list of "about six hundred undergraduates—out of a total college population of approximately 2.5 million," as Lee Edwards notes in his history of ISI, *Educating for Liberty* (2003). The group began modestly, providing free subscriptions to students of existing publications such as *Human Events* and the literature of the free-market Foundation for Economic Education. However, Chodorov knew that he wanted to provide something deeper than policy analysis and polemics on economics. He founded a newsletter for ISI titled the *Individualist*—which Russell Kirk criticized as being too, well . . . individualist. Kirk wrote Chodorov urging him to include more voices from the traditionalist Right, more articles about the cultural underpinnings that make a free society possible. Chodorov consequently began to reach out to prominent conservative academics such as Thomas Molnar, Richard Weaver, and Kirk himself, building a faculty network that would number, as of this writing, more than 20,000. With the help of Chodorov's energetic assistant Milione, ISI also started a lecture bureau that offered college students the chance to hear in person the dissenting voices the group was trying to gain a hearing on campus. In its early years, ISI was also instrumental in fostering conservative journalism, aiding in the startup of numerous campus conservative papers—a role it would take up again in the 1990s through its Collegiate Network.

Milione succeeded Chodorov as president, and thanks to his indefatigable work (aided greatly by founding trustee and prominent Philadelphia-area banker Charles H. Hoeflich and longtime ISI chairman Henry Regnery) in fundraising, networking, and organizing, in just a few years ISI would emerge as one of the leading intellectual conserva-

tive organizations in America. (Full disclosure: it is also the publisher of this book.) Throughout the political ups and downs of the conservative movement, ISI has remained nonpartisan, preferring to approach current events from the longer perspective of centuries of Western and American history. In 1964, Milione announced the Richard Weaver Fellowships, designed to help academics sympathetic to ISI's ideals—and those of the untimely departed Weaver—complete their graduate educations. In the next year, Milione launched the *Intercollegiate Review*, a journal distributed free to all ISI members—which by now numbered in the tens of thousands—intended to make the great ideas accessible to undergraduates. The organization itself was renamed the Intercollegiate Studies Institute in 1966 to reflect the strong presence of traditionalist conservatives among the partisans of liberty who made up ISI's membership.

In 1969, a veteran of ISI—its former Western Director, Peter DeLuca—founded a liberal arts institution, Thomas Aquinas College in California, in order to put into practice the educational ideals the group had long been preaching. This school became the inspiration for many other traditionalist colleges that would spring up around the country at about the same time. Another ISI alumnus, former *Intercollegiate Review* editor Gregory Wolfe, is founder and editor of a widely respected journal of the arts called *Image*—one of many initiatives across the country, from academia to practical politics, whose roots lie in the work done by ISI in cultivating young intellectuals.

At the initiative of one of ISI's most important leaders over the decades, executive vice president John Lulves, in 1976 ISI took on the publication of *Modern Age*, whose financial condition had not kept up with its editorial excellence. The quarterly is aimed more at graduate students and faculty—complementing the mission of the *Intercollegiate Review*—and publishes long, analytical pieces on broad issues of culture and philosophy.

With the "arrival" of the conservative movement in 1981 after the inauguration of Ronald Reagan, ISI saw many of its alumni enter positions of influence and power, including Richard V. Allen, Donald Devine, and T. Kenneth Cribb Jr. Other important activists in the (mis-titled) "Reagan Revolution" with ISI roots included Robert Reilly, Rep. Robert Bauman, and Morton Blackwell. But the organization's gaze remained steadily on the deeper cultural issues underlying ephemera of policy and power, leaving its mission unaltered and spirits undimmed by the centrist retrenchment of the first Bush administration. According to Lee Edwards, ISI also managed to avoid the worst effects of the growing division on the Right between traditionalists and libertarians on the one hand, and increasingly influential neoconservatives on the other. Because it had always opened itself to multiple voices—in the beginning, monarchists such as Erik von Kuenhelt-Leddihn alongside rationalist liberals like Ludwig von Mises, and later, traditionalists like Frederick Wilhelmsen and M. E. Bradford beside American Whigs like Harry Jaffa—the organization could never be pigeon-holed or rendered marginal.

In 1989, Cribb, a former Reagan administration justice department official, became president of ISI, employing his extensive connections to increase fundraising and extend ISI's reach without compromising its core missions. He added to ISI's programs the new publication *CAMPUS*, a national magazine written by and for conservative college students. To help incoming students navigate the shoals of academia, in the late '90s ISI began to publish a college guide titled *Choosing the Right College* as part of its new, ambitious publishing program conceived and led by Jeffrey O. Nelson. A couple of years earlier, beginning with a series of high-quality reprints of conservative classics, ISI's book imprint, ISI Books, began to produce a wide range of titles by political scientists, philosophers, literary critics, theologians, and economists. Prominent in its catalogue are the Library of Modern Thinkers series, which features examinations of important twentieth-century thinkers on the right such as Eric Voegelin, Bertrand de Jouvenel, Robert Nisbet, and Wilhelm Röpke; its series of student guides to the major disciplines, which has featured authors John Lukacs, Wilfred McClay, Paul Heyne, and Ralph McInerny; and its Crosscurrents series of translations of classic and contemporary works by non-English-speaking intellectuals on the right. ISI Books publishes approximately twenty new books per year and now has more than 100 titles in print.

By 2005, ISI could boast volunteer representatives at over 900 colleges, more than 50,000 ISI student and faculty members on nearly every campus in the country, and over 300 educational programs held on campus each year. At the conclusion of Chodorov's "50-Year Plan," America no longer faced the threat of an aggressive communist empire; yet the organization he had founded faced new, unimagined challenges, including the challenge posed by a "wired" world whose core philosophies had been "deconstructed" and whose most basic social institutions—such as marriage and motherhood—were under attack by new species of social radicals, some of them purportedly conservative. Through new media and old, ISI carries on its original mission of forming America's elites in the wisdom of their ancestors.

—JOHN ZMIRAK

Further Reading

Nash, George H. *The Conservative Intellectual Movement in America since 1945*. 2nd ed. Wilmington, Del.: Intercollegiate Studies Institute, 1996.

Panichas, George, ed. *Modern Age: The First Twenty-Five Years*. Indianapolis, Ind.: Liberty Press, 1988.

Iraq War

The roots of this ongoing conflict, a war which has raged at various levels of intensity from 1990 to the present, lie in the early twentieth century, when then colonial power Great Britain created from the ruins of the Ottoman Empire the artificial nation of "Iraq." At the urging of Winston Churchill, then secretary for war and air minister, Britain cobbled together three disparate provinces—Mesopotamia, Mosul, and Basra. Two incompatible cultures (Arab and Kurdish) and two hostile strains of Islam (Sunni and Shi'ite) were thus placed side-by-side in one country to be ruled as a British "mandate" by a Jordanian-born monarch, King Faisal. Like other recently created composite states, such as Czechoslovakia and Yugoslavia, Iraq faced an uncertain future, having been created to suit the purposes not of its resident populations, but those of distant empire-builders. In this case, British policymakers wished to secure access to the region's oil—hedging their bets by slicing off another oil-rich region, which they erected as the Emirate of Kuwait.

Iraq achieved nominal independence in 1930, and its Anglophile monarchy survived until 1958, when secular Arab nationalists overthrew its relatively liberal oligarchy and established one of the Cold War world's many postcolonial dictatorships. In 1963, the Ba'athist Party seized control, setting the stage for Machiavellian upstart soldier Saddam Hussein to claw his way to power during the next ten years. He would maintain control by ruthless bloodletting and purges modeled on Stalin's Great Terror.

Unlike Islamic monarchies such as Saudi Arabia, the Ba'athist regime granted tolerance to Christians and some other minorities (Jews had been expelled in 1950) and access to education for women. And the United States maintained moderately good relations with Hussein, who triangulated between the West and the Soviet bloc in order to maximize foreign aid from both. In 1980, with the support of other Sunni regimes in the region and the Reagan administration, all of whom had been fearing a general Shi'ite uprising after the 1979 overthrow of the Shah, Hussein declared war on Iran.

This inconclusive war, which ended in 1988, was devastating to both countries, leaving between 500,000 and one million people dead and both regimes economically drained. In 1990, Hussein sought to make up the financial aid promised (but still undelivered) by neighboring Sunni regimes by raising the price of his country's only significant export, oil. Iraq's tiny, autocratically ruled, pro-American neighbor Kuwait refused to cooperate by diminishing production. Hussein therefore invaded Kuwait in August 1990, displaying his typical bloody-mindedness toward the local population. Almost the entire Arab world, with the exception of the Palestine Liberation Organization, condemned Hussein's attack—a fact which helped George H. W. Bush organize a multilateral coalition, with U.N. support, to invade and liberate Kuwait in February 1991, restoring its emir to power. While significant voices (e.g., Patrick Buchanan, Russell Kirk, Pope John Paul II) opposed the U.S.-led invasion, it was widely supported across the political spectrum and generally considered a success. Yet some supporters of the war were bitterly disappointed that President Bush had not "finished the job" and invaded Iraq in order to depose Hussein.

The U.S. withdrawal from Iraq in 1991 was conditioned on a strict regime of sanctions and no-fly zones, which rendered the

Kurdish regions of Iraq virtually autonomous and successfully crippled Hussein's efforts to obtain advanced weaponry, but also exacted a fearsome toll on the country's civilian population, crippling an economy already hobbled by Hussein's wasteful expenses on militarism and palaces. When Clinton administration secretary of state Madeleine Albright was confronted with international estimates that these sanctions had caused the deaths of one half million Iraqi children, she answered, "I think this is a very hard choice, but the price—we think the price is worth it."

This situation would continue to fester, as Iraq sought to evade and undermine sanctions and hawkish American politicians of both parties looked for a pretext under which to unseat Hussein, who had been transformed from a distasteful ally into an inveterate enemy of American interests. In a crass attempt to cast himself as a new "Saladin" fighting against "Zionists and Crusaders," Hussein had begun to pay bounties to the survivors of suicide bombers who targeted civilians in restaurants and buses inside Israel. In response, American neoconservatives Douglas Feith and David Wurmser, working for the Israeli government in 1996, produced a strategic proposal called "Securing the Realm," which envisioned invading Iraq and toppling Hussein as a stepping stone toward regional dominance.

After this plan, adapted for American purposes, began to be kicked around in conservative circles in the wake of the September 11, 2001 attacks, leading libertarians and "realist" conservatives who questioned this line of argument found themselves tarred as defeatist "unpatriotic conservatives" by Canadian émigré (and former Bush speechwriter) David Frum. Neoconservative columnist (and Soviet émigré) Max Boot rankled many with his complaint that U.S. forces had conquered Afghanistan too cheaply, without inuring Americans to the loss of life necessary to trans-forming the Middle East into a democratic, pro-Western region. Thus, the build-up to war deepened divisions between traditional conservatives and libertarians on the one hand, and Jacksonian nationalists and neoconservatives on the other—as Francis Fukuyama would later observe.

In the immediate aftermath of September 11, Bush administration officials worked hard to find a direct connection between Hussein's regime and al-Qaeda—in part because, as Defense Secretary Donald Rumsfeld famously said, there were "no good targets in Afghanistan," the state which actually harbored Osama bin Laden and his minions. The drumbeat for war echoed loudly in a nation traumatized by the slaughter of civilians and the destruction of national landmarks; it was fed by assertions (later discredited) by neoconservative analysts such as Laurie Mylroie that Hussein had also been implicated in the first (1993) attack on the World Trade Center, the Oklahoma City bombings of 1994, and the 9/11 atrocities. Bush administration officials such as Condoleeza Rice and Vice President Dick Cheney and the president himself blanketed receptive media with warnings about the advanced state of Iraq's programs for "weapons of mass destruction"—a term which lumped together battlefield weapons such as mustard gas shells with weaponized anthrax and nuclear bombs. "We don't want the smoking gun to be a mushroom cloud," Rice warned Americans in January 2003.

Pointing to Iraq's resistance (until the eleventh hour) to extensive U.N. inspections, the Bush administration prepared for war. A dramatic, if factually flawed, presentation by one-time war skeptic Secretary of State Colin Powell did not persuade the international body. A French veto on the United Nations Security Council did not slow war preparations, though it did provoke a brief eruption of hostility toward America's oldest ally on the part of nationalist commentators. America ate its first "freedom fries" in March 2003.

In lieu of a broad coalition with U.N. support such as marked the U.S. invasion in 1991, the Bush administration won large-scale military support from Great Britain and token contingents from several friendly governments in Europe and the developing world. The "Coalition of the Willing" invaded Iraq in March 2003. Iraqi resistance collapsed quickly, echoing neoconservative predictions that the invasion would prove a "cakewalk." U.S. troops captured Baghdad on April 9, 2003. Saddam Hussein himself would be captured in December and imprisoned for future trial. However, a series of disastrous postwar moves—including the decision to disband the Iraqi army and the failure to commit enough troops to secure the entire country against Sunni insurgents—prevented the pacification of the country.

The once-dominant Sunni minority, led by officers and veterans of its former army, reacted to the prospect of rule by Iraq's Shi'ite majority and permanent autonomy for its Kurdish region by creating an effective insurgency throughout large sections of the country, an insurgency that continues unabated as of publication. The country's first democratic election was boycotted by Sunnis, who mostly opposed the draft constitution written by the winning factions. Fighting between rival Shi'ite factions, the prospect of Kurdish secession, the increasing influence of neighboring Iran among Shi'ite parties, and the total unreliability of the newly recruited Iraqi security forces continued to bedevil occupying forces. Furthermore, the policy favored by the United States—a firmly united Iraq, with minor concessions to federalism—was supported mainly by America's enemies, the Sunni minority, while America's allies among the Shi'ites and Kurds actually opposed U.S. policy, seeking a loose confederation.

Popular support for the Anglo-Ameri-

can occupation—and recruitment for the U.S. military—declined steadily as casualties mounted. The justifications offered for the war mostly proved unfounded, as U.S. intelligence discovered no significant weapons programs or links to al-Qaeda or other anti-American terrorists. This did not prevent popular nationalistic commentators from reiterating exploded claims to the contrary—leading some to compare their fixation to that of the French Right in the late nineteenth century, which had continued to assert for decades, against all evidence, the guilt of Col. Alfred Dreyfus. Whether the nationalist Right in America will suffer a comparable loss of moral credibility is an open question.

The remaining rationale for occupying Iraq—effecting a "democratic transformation" of the region by creating the second Arab democracy (after Lebanon)—now stands as the only justification for the war. Conservative critics of the administration point to the likelihood that establishing democratic governments in nations with strong Islamist movements is more likely to increase terrorist activities than to suppress them.

—JOHN ZMIRAK

Further Reading

Bacevich, Andrew J. *The New American Militarism: How Americans Are Seduced by War.* New York: Oxford University Press, 2005.

Cerf, Christopher, and Sifry, Micah, eds. *The Iraq War Reader: History, Documents, Opinion.* New York: Touchstone, 2003.

Keegan, John: *The Iraq War.* New York: Knopf, 2004.

Scheur, Michael: *Imperial Hubris: Why the West Is Losing the War on Terror.* Washington, D.C.: Brassey's, 2004.

See also: American Conservative; *Bush, George W.; Cato Institute; Gulf War; neoconservatism; paleoconservatism; Terror, War on;* Weekly Standard

isolationism

Traditionally, as noted by historian Manfred Jonas, isolationists have opposed political and military commitments to, or alliances with, foreign powers, particularly those in Europe. Although they have recognized the necessity for foreign trade and are not (usually) pacifists, they have sought to guard American sovereignty and freedom of action.

Only with the formation of the League of Nations did isolationism as a distinct position come to the fore, for membership in the League entailed binding political and military commitments. Among the foes of League membership were such conservatives as senators Henry Cabot Lodge (R-Mass.), Miles Poindexter (R-Conn.), Frank P. Brandegee (R-Conn.), and James A. Reed (D-Mo.); publishers Frank A. Munsey and George Harvey; and industrialist Henry Clay Frick. However, these figures were part of a much wider coalition; conservatism and isolationism are by no means synonymous.

Yet from the 1930s to the early 1950s, conservatives were strong in isolationist ranks. A conservative was more likely to be an isolationist if he was also a Republican, a midwesterner, and an inhabitant of a small town or rural area, and also if he stemmed from German-American or Irish-American stock. Conservative isolationists usually opposed American entry into the World Court, favored the neutrality acts of the 1930s, and predominated in the America First Committee. By the late 1930s, the more militant isolationists among conservatives included such senators as Bennett Champ Clark (D-Mo.) and Arthur H. Vandenberg (R-Mich.); such representatives as Hamilton Fish (R-N.Y.); publisher Robert R. McCormick; and aviator Charles A. Lindbergh. More moderate isolationists, who in 1939 favored "cash and carry" and in 1940–41 sought to aid Britain without risking war, included in their ranks Senator Robert A. Taft (R-Ohio),

former president Herbert Hoover, editor Felix Morley, retired diplomat William R. Castle, merchandising executive Robert E. Wood, and ex-governor Alfred M. Landon (R-Kan.).

Conservative opponents of American intervention adhered to one basic premise: participation in war would weaken the United States' traditional political structure and economy, perhaps beyond repair. Indeed America's very survival as a free republic might be in jeopardy. Such conservatives saw war as imperiling the capitalist system, as full-scale mobilization was bound to bring in its wake inflation, price and wage controls, compulsory unionization, and—in practicality—a wartime socialism that would remain after the conflict ended.

To many isolationists, Europe was always at war and would always be so. World War II was, to use the language of Lindbergh, simply one "more of those age-old quarrels within our own family of nations." The fact was, isolationists claimed, that the Allies had no positive war aims. They only sought the defeat and partition of Germany, a Carthaginian peace bound to create more dictators and more wars of revenge.

Aside from blaming Nazism first on Versailles, then on Allied appeasement, the great bulk of conservative isolationists, like their liberal counterparts, held no brief for Germany and frequently coupled isolationist sentiments with condemnations of Germany's actions. Yet, with Soviet Russia lurking in the background, many on the Old Right saw an anti-Hitler crusade as futile. Stalin's dictatorship, so such figures as Lindbergh and journalist Freda Utley argued, was even harsher than Hitler's, and the apparently ecumenical appeal of communism in the long run made it a far greater threat. One should not choose between evils; one should simply stay out of the fracas.

Turning to the Pacific, conservative isolationists did not yet espouse "Asialationism." They often attacked the shipping of American war supplies to Japan, claiming that Franklin D. Roosevelt had hypocritically refused to invoke the neutrality acts when profits were at stake. At the same time, they feared a direct confrontation. For the United States to commit itself to the Dutch East Indies and Singapore would be a back door to war, and involvements in Europe would come automatically into play with any Japanese attack on such possessions. Several arguments were presented: Japan's actions in China involved purely "Asiatic" matters and hence did not affect the Western hemisphere; the United States had no vital interest in Asia worth fighting for; belligerent attitudes risked offending the United States' best customer; China, no democracy, was permeated with communist influence, dictatorial Koumintang rule, and general "backwardness"; Japan held no military threat but was difficult to invade.

In their efforts to offer alternatives to administration policy, conservative anti-interventionists stressed economics and self-sufficiency. Challenging those interventionists who stressed access to natural resources, they claimed that synthetic Brazilian rubber could replace that made in Malaya, and they saw Bolivian tin as a good substitute for that of the East Indies. Besides, they argued, even if Japan conquered East Asia, it would still need the American market.

As far as defense was concerned, conservative isolationists usually opposed a mass army, finding it of necessity too bulky and ill-trained to be of help in any conflict. Indeed, unless one envisioned a new Allied Expeditionary Force to fight in France, such a unit could only be superfluous. Conservative isolationists debated the wisdom of a large navy, with some finding more destroyers unnecessary. Far more consensus was developed over air strategy, and several called for a separate air department. In arguments maintained through the Cold War, conservative isolationists claimed that air power was less costly than ground and naval forces, would eliminate any need for conscription, and could be used with a minimum of coordination with troublesome allies.

Once the Cold War began, some conservative isolationists, such as senators Vandenberg, Charles Tobey (R-N.Y.), and Henry Cabot Lodge Jr. (R-Mass.) and journalist William Henry Chamberlin, started supporting Truman's foreign policy. Furthermore, not all of those conservatives who remained isolationists shared the same degree of militancy. Historian Ted Galen Carpenter has divided Cold War isolationists into three distinct categories. First were the "doctrinaire isolationists," who insisted that the basic principle of nonentanglement was as relevant as ever. Indeed, so they asserted, isolationism could have preserved the United States from involvement in both world wars. In this category would be included elitist theorist Lawrence Dennis; congressmen Frederick C. Smith (R-Ohio), Clare Hoffman (R-Mich.), and Howard Buffett (R-Neb.); senators Hugh Butler (R-Neb.), William E. Jenner (R-Ind.), and George ("Molly") Malone (R-Neb.); journalist John T. Flynn; investor Sterling Morton; and publisher McCormick.

Second were the "pragmatic isolationists," people who found modern circumstances limiting the relevance and applicability of nonintervention. This group sought to modify, rather than to reject totally, plans for the United Nations and such programs as the Truman Doctrine, the Marshall Plan, and the North Atlantic Treaty Organization (NATO). In its ranks were senators Taft, Arthur Watkins (R-Utah), and Kenneth A. Wherry (R-Neb.); congressmen Lawrence Smith (R-Wis.) and Daniel Reed (R-N.Y.); and steel manufacturer Ernest Weir.

Third, Carpenter notes the "marginal isolationists," individuals who accepted the need for economic and even occasional political commitments, but who balked when it came to arms aid and military alliances. Hoover was foremost in this category, though others included senators John W. Bricker (R-Ohio) and Forrest Donnell (R-N.Y.), Congressman John Taber (R-N.Y.), and attorneys Clarence Manion and Frank Holman.

Military and economic commitments, claimed the more militant foes of interventionism, risked bankruptcy at home, supported socialist and statist regimes overseas, neglected the "communist menace" at home, and risked dangerous confrontation with the Soviet Union. In 1947, such figures fought aid to Greece and Turkey; in 1948, they opposed the initial Marshall Plan appropriations; and in 1949, they criticized the creation of the NATO alliance. In December 1950, just after the communist Chinese had entered the Korean War, financier Joseph P. Kennedy, Senator Taft, and ex-president Hoover began a "Great Debate" by calling either for withdrawal from the Korean peninsula or for limiting American commitments there to air and sea power. Yet many conservative isolationists, Taft included, compromised their traditional anti-interventionism by endorsing General Douglas MacArthur's wide-ranging schemes for victory in Asia and demanding United States support for Chiang Kai-shek's regime on Taiwan. Far more often than not, they backed Senator Joseph R. McCarthy's accusations of subversion in the highest levels in Washington. In 1952, the more isolationist candidate for the Republican presidential nomination, Senator Taft, lost to General Dwight D. Eisenhower, and in 1954 the isolationist Bricker Amendment was defeated by Congress.

Beginning in the mid-1950s, the conservative isolationist view of foreign policy suffered many setbacks, including the deaths of Taft in 1954 and McCormick in 1955; the birth in 1955 of the far more strident *National Review* as the major voice of the Right; and the co-optation of many conservative legislators by the Eisenhower administration and the inevitable departure of many others from Congress. Historian Wayne S. Cole points to "the challenges to peace and security from the Axis states and then from communist Russia, the development of nuclear weapons and effective delivery systems, the growth of cities and their accompanying industrial and financial capacities, the further erosion of rural and small-town America, talented leadership by the foreign policy establishment, and the power of the presidency under Truman" as reasons for isolationism's decline. By 1964, many conservatives backed the interventionist Barry Goldwater for president, and by the time Ronald Reagan was elected president in 1980 globalism was supported more by conservatives than by their opponents. However, by the year 2000, certain powerful Republican congressional leaders—Congressman John Kasich (Ohio), Congressman Tom DeLay (Tex.), and Senator Trent Lott (Miss.) among them—criticized American participation in international peacekeeping forces in Kosovo, claiming that the nation's security was not threatened. Such figures have often opposed funding for the United Nations and participation in the International Monetary Fund, arguing that the United States could only weaken itself by such involvement.

Pat Buchanan and many of the writers associated with his magazine, the *American Conservative,* also emerged in the early years of the twenty-first century as new voices for nonintervention on the Right. They continued to maintain that interventionism could only mean the further erosion of the America that the traditional Right treasured. Fiscal responsibility, limited government, rural mores, a village culture, individual economic opportunity, an autonomous foreign policy—all seemed still to be linked, and all appeared beyond recall.

—Justus D. Doenecke

Further Reading

Buchanan, Patrick J. *A Republic, Not an Empire: Reclaiming America's Destiny.* Washington, D.C.: Regnery, 1999.

Carpenter, Ted Galen. "The Dissenters: American Isolationists and Foreign Policy, 1945-1954." Ph.D. diss., University of Texas, 1980.

Doenecke, Justus D. *Anti-Interventionism: A Bibliographical Introduction to Isolationism and Pacifism from World War I to the Early Cold War Era.* New York: Garland, 1987.

———. *Not to the Swift: The Old Isolationists in the Cold War Era.* Lewisburg, Pa.: Bucknell University Press, 1979.

Guinsberg, Thomas N. *The Pursuit of Isolationism in the United States Senate from Versailles to Pearl Harbor.* New York: Garland, 1982.

Jonas, Manfred. *Isolationism in America, 1935–1941.* Ithaca, N.Y.: Cornell University Press, 1966.

Kauffman, Bill. *America First! Its History, Culture, and Politics.* Amherst, N.Y.: Prometheus Books, 1995.

See also: America First Committee; Cold War revisionism; Fish, Hamilton, III; Flynn, John T.; Lindbergh, Charles A.; localism

Ives, C. P. (Charles Pomeroy) (1903–82)

C. P. Ives II (1903–82), nephew of the American composer whose name he shared, was chief editorial writer for the *Baltimore Sun* from 1939 to 1973 and an important contributor to the revival of interest in Edmund Burke studies after the Second World War. He was also a perceptive commentator on the significance of contemporary debates over the nature of law, legal reasoning, and our constitutional order. Ives was the long-time book-review editor of the influential journal *Studies in Burke and His Times*, founded and edited by his friend Peter J. Stanlis. He was also a contributor to the conservative quarterly *Modern Age*, founded by another friend of his, Russell Kirk. He was a graduate of Brown University and Yale, where he wrote an M.A. thesis critical of the school of jurisprudence known as "legal realism."

Like his intellectual mentor Edmund Burke, Ives believed that constitutional law assumed the existence of or was based on the moral natural law. In his columns and writings, Ives provided insightful criticism of the jurists and legal scholars who, particularly during the period from about 1920 through the 1950s, styled themselves "legal realists." This self-generated title, Ives pointed out, was inaccurate from a philosophical standpoint. For centuries, philosophers had recognized that "realism" rests in the recognition that categories and categorical concepts (e.g., "justice") are substantively real—that is, have an existence and an integrity before and beyond human attempts at definition and description. But the "legal realists" based their theories on an outright denial of the reality of generalities, other than as totems of superstition. Thus, the legal realists rejected any philosophical basis for legal reasoning beyond a strict nominalism positing the power of lawyers and judges to create law with each argument and legal decision. Ives exposed this movement's hostility toward abstract thought and generalizations of any kind while also highlighting its practitioners' adherence to a particular theory of human nature and the foundations of social order.

Ives pointed out that legal realism had contributed greatly to the breakdown of legal authority and certainty in America. In teaching students, judges, and policymakers that there is no such thing as justice, responsibility, or any legal rule capable of consistent application, the legal realists have freed these actors to manipulate the legal system and attack its consequences whenever these have not been in their own

445

interest. Ives's work constitutes a telling dissection of one of the most powerful and destructive legal doctrines of this or any other century. Numerous contemporary legal scholars, including proponents of critical legal studies and various forms of "noninterpretive" jurisprudence, owe their core assumptions to legal realism.

—JEFFREY O. NELSON
AND BRUCE FROHNEN

See also: Burkean conservatism; Stanlis, Peter J.

J

Jacobs, Jane (1916–)

Urbanologist, activist, and author, Jane Jacobs's most influential book, *The Death and Life of Great American Cities* (1961), attacked urban planners and large-scale government-financed renewal programs that gutted mixed-used traditional neighborhoods in American cities.

Armed with only a high school degree from Scranton, Pennsylvania, Jacobs moved to New York City in 1935, where she closely observed urban life as she supported herself by writing. From 1943 to 1952, she worked for the Office of War Information and the State Department. Jacobs then became an associate editor at *Architectural Forum*. Her essay "Downtown Is for People" appeared in *Fortune* magazine and won her a grant from the Rockefeller Foundation to write her most famous book, which attacked planners, officials, and public agencies for neglecting human beings—in Jacobs's view the vital component of urban life—in favor of an ideology of order, efficiency, and environmental determinism.

As a Greenwich Village resident, Jacobs further developed her criticism of contemporary planning practices while defending her own neighborhood against Robert Moses, the highway, and the urban renewal machine. By the late 1960s, however, Jacobs found New York City too bureaucratic and she moved to Toronto, where she continued her urban activism. More recently, New Urbanists have cited Jacobs as an important influence, although their ideas diverge from hers on many important points. In 1997, Jacobs's influence on urban planning was commemorated with a five-day symposium in Toronto.

—Anne Krulikowski

Further Reading

Jacobs, Jane. *Cities and the Wealth of Nations: Principles of Economic Life*. New York: Random House, 1984.

———. *Dark Age Ahead*. New York: Random House, 2004.

———. *The Economy of Cities*. New York: Random House, 1969.

See also: New Urbanism

Jaffa, Harry V. (1918–)

Harry Jaffa was a student of the political philosopher Leo Strauss. The principal theme of Strauss's work is "the crisis of the West," a crisis precipitated by modernity's rejection of natural right. Jaffa has extended Strauss's analysis to America, devoting the bulk of his productive scholarly career to uncovering and articulating the natural right principles of the American founding, particularly as those principles are expressed in the Declaration of Independence. For Jaffa, the "crisis of the West" and the "crisis of America" are identical. Even his first book, *Thomism and Aristotelianism* (1952), an analysis of Aquinas's interpretation of natural right in Aristotle, seems to have been merely prelude to his study of the American founding.

Jaffa's best known book is *Crisis of the House Divided: An Interpretation of the Lincoln-Douglas Debates* (1959). In this seminal study, Jaffa argued that Abraham Lincoln had in some sense refounded the American regime by rejecting the radically modern Lockean principles of the founders and grounding the new political regime in Aristotelian natural right. Jaffa argued that Lincoln had thus provided a crucial moral dimension that was missing from the Declaration. In *Crisis*, Jaffa's reading of Locke followed Strauss's view that Locke was a thoroughgoing modern who was barely distinguishable from Hobbes. Strauss, of course, discovered the radically modern Locke buried deep in his esoteric message. In the years after *Crisis*, Jaffa came to believe that the founders could not have read Locke the way Strauss did—indeed there is no evidence that *anyone* ever read Locke with the care and penetration that Strauss did. Thus, if we are to understand the founders as they understood themselves, it is necessary to read them in the light of the exoteric Locke, not the esoteric Locke revealed by Strauss. And it was through their understanding of the exoteric Locke that the founders understood the law of nature in an Aristotelian sense.

In his recent book, *A New Birth of Freedom: Abraham Lincoln and the Coming of the Civil War* (2000), Jaffa sees a greater theoretical unity in the American founding than he did in *Crisis*. Those "classical" elements that Jaffa once attributed exclusively to Lincoln's "refounding" are now seen as elements intrinsic to the founding itself, a founding that Lincoln "perpetuated" and extended but without changing its essential character. According to Jaffa, what guided the founders

Harry V. Jaffa

and introduced an Aristotelian element into the regime was prudence: the Declaration embodies an "Aristotelian emphasis on the dictates of prudence." The Declaration, Jaffa argues, "is both teleological and prudential. It is teleological because it is oriented . . . toward the end of human happiness, which according to Aristotle is the ultimate end of human action, whether individual or political. It is prudential because it measures the goodness of human actions, whether individual or political, by their consequences. The consequences, in turn, are judged by whether they advance or retard happiness."

Jaffa, more than any other student of Strauss, understands political philosophy's primary concern with what Strauss called the "theological-political" problem. Jaffa argues that the egalitarian natural right of the founding is the only form of natural right that is compatible with Christianity. The principle that "all men are created equal" thus provided the founders with the only possible access to nature or natural right available in the modern world. "The doctrine of natural law and natural rights enshrined in the Declaration," Jaffa writes, "is a doctrine of natural *and* divine right." The founders thus were able to resolve—at least on a political level—the theological-political problem that arises from the competing claims made by reason and revelation. The American founding did this by recognizing equally the claims of both. This resolution was made possible, in large part, because the "Lockeanized" ministers of the founding era understood the separation of church and state as no less a dictate of New Testament theology than reason and natural right.

Jaffa's scholarship has been controversial because of his conviction—following Aristotle—that truth is more important than friends. Jaffa has been a severe critic of fellow conservatives—and fellow "Straussians"—and many of his tracts are highly polemical, even though always dialectical. He argues that contemporary conservatism has fallen into the same kind of nihilism that animates liberalism. Both liberalism and conservatism reject natural right as the ground of politics and constitutional government. According to Jaffa, the crisis of America has forced us to choose between nihilism and natural right. Jaffa is strident in his critique of nihilism and its supporters, both those who are aware of their nihilism and those who are not.

—Edward J. Erler

Further Reading

Jaffa, Harry V. *American Conservatism and the American Founding.* Durham, N.C.: Carolina Academic Press, 1984.

_____. *Equality and Liberty: Theory and Practice in American Politics.* New York: Oxford University Press, 1965.

Silver, Thomas B., and Peter W. Schramm, eds. *Natural Right and Political Right: Essays in Honor of Harry V. Jaffa.* Durham, N.C.: Carolina Academic Press, 1984.

See also: Bradford, M. E.; Claremont Institute; Declaration of Independence; Jefferson, Thomas; Lincoln, Abraham; Strauss, Leo; Straussianism

Jaki, Stanley L. (1924–)

A theologian and moralist as well as one of the world's most distinguished historians and philosophers of science, Stanley Jaki is the author of more than forty highly esteemed (but also controversial) books and dozens of essays, reviews, book introductions, and encyclopedia articles.

Born in Hungary in 1924, Jaki was educated at an ancient and famous Benedictine abbey and became a monk and priest. He continued his studies in Rome, taking a doctorate in theology in 1950. Resident in the United States since 1950, Jaki taught college theology and French before severe health problems required him to retire from teaching. Jaki turned this apparent defeat in his career to good advantage when he decided to pursue a doctorate in physics, which he completed under the Austrian émigré and Nobel laureate Victor F. Hess at Fordham University in 1957. This was the beginning of a second career that has led to many books and articles and the highest intellectual honors available, including the Lecomte du Nouy Prize from Rockefeller University in 1970, the Templeton Prize in 1987, two series of Gifford Lectureships at the University of Edinburgh, two series of lectureships in Oxford, and many other lectureships and honors in the United States, Britain, France, Germany, Italy, and Hungary.

Jaki's first major scientific book was the groundbreaking *The Relevance of Physics*, published by the University of Chicago Press in 1966. In this and his vast body of subsequent writing Jaki became influential and controversial for arguing and documenting a new narrative of the history of Western science that conceived of it in ways deeply unsettling to the consensus view that had been inspired and developed initially by Bacon, Descartes, and their admiring successors, the eighteenth-century French "Encyclopedists" and British utilitarians. Briefly put, Jaki's argument is that three biases have afflicted the development of science and especially the explanation of its successes: empiricism, idealism, and anticlericalism. Unearthing and promoting the groundbreaking studies of the French Catholic physicist and science historian Pierre Duhem (1861–1916), on whom he wrote an important biography, Jaki argued for the importance of medieval religion and science as preparing the way for the breakthroughs in physics and astronomy of Copernicus, Kepler, Galileo, and Newton. Neither ancient nor Baconian empiricism nor ancient or modern idealism could find the "middle road" of metaphysical realism that fostered the breakthrough of science in the seventeenth century, supremely in Newton.

In addition to his critique of empiricisms and idealisms ancient and modern, Jaki has argued that the history of science has repeatedly been used unfairly and inaccurately as an anti-Christian ideological tool, especially by a long line of French anticlerical propagandists, from the "Encyclopedists" to George Sarton and Alexander Koyre. No short summary can do justice to the insight, detail, and philosophical power and importance of Jaki's body of work on these issues and the relations between science, philosophy, ethics, religion, and culture. Though foreshadowed by Duhem's immense work and Whitehead's short *Science and the Modern World* (1925), Jaki's oeuvre has an astonishingly learned and original power and relevance that have as yet been inadequately recognized.

—M. D. AESCHLIMAN

Further Reading

Jaki, Stanley L. *A Mind's Matter: An Intellectual Autobiography*. Grand Rapids, Mich.: W. B. Eerdmans, 2002.

———. *Means to Message: A Treatise on Truth*. Grand Rapids, Mich.: W. B. Eerdmans, 1999.

———. *The Road of Science and the Ways to God*. Chicago: University of Chicago Press, 1978.

See also: Enlightenment; science and scientism

Jeffers, Robinson (1887–1962)

A poet of extraordinary if occasionally misdirected power, Robinson Jeffers achieved critical and popular acclaim in the 1920s with verse that found in wild nature the Absolutes

man was elsewhere denied. A political individualist and noninterventionist, Jeffers's reputation declined during the Great Depression and World War II as the balmy statism of the New Deal gained favor among intellectuals. Since his death in 1962, however, Jeffers's popularity has rebounded among students and scholars alike.

Jeffers was born on January 10, 1887, in Pittsburgh. He was the eldest son of an Old Testament theologian at Western Theological Seminary. As a child, Jeffers was educated in Europe and learned several languages, including Greek and Latin. In 1905, he graduated from Occidental College and later attended medical school at the University of Southern California. Jeffers married Una Call Kuster in 1913 and moved to Carmel a year later. There, he completed his first mature work, *Tamar and Other Poems*, which was published in 1924.

All of Jeffers's adult verse is characterized by the poet's prophetic voice and by themes of pantheism and Manicheanism-in-reverse, in which man ascends from a puny interior soul to the greater exterior world of matter and beauty. Though a believer in scientific as well as poetic efficacy, Jeffers viewed man as pessimistically—and sometimes cruelly—unwilling to set aside his ephemeral preoccupations. For those who could, however, a kind of dark goodness awaited.

Jeffers's metaphysical conservatism—his sensitive attention to human limitation—was wedded to a cultural conservatism that abhorred the rise of commercialization and its most successful product, mass man. In poems like "Shine, Perishing Republic," Jeffers advises flight from the American empire in words that acknowledge men as individually worthy but collectively monstrous.

Out of step with his time, the poet came under fire in the 1930s from New Criticism and Marxist writers who attacked what they perceived as his mock primitivism and callous stoicism. Jeffers was also criticized for exhibiting what one critic has called violent pacifism when he published a number of poems opposing American involvement in the Second World War. The collection, *The Double-Axe and Other Poems* (1948), though one of his weakest, remains a fascinating case study in liberal self-censorship: Bennett Cerf and Saxe Commins, the poet's editors at Random House, forced Jeffers to drop ten antiwar (and sometimes anti-Roosevelt) poems from the manuscript and added in their place a disclaimer distancing themselves from Jeffers.

Although poet Robert Hass has correctly noted that Jeffers was never a meticulous user of language, Jeffers's poetry appears to have considerable staying power, with readers still turning to his verse for its beauty.

—David A. Hoefer

Further Reading

Coffin, Arthur B. *Robinson Jeffers: Poet of Inhumanism*. Madison, Wis.: University of Wisconsin Press, 1971.

Hunt, Tim, ed. *The Collected Poems of Robinson Jeffers, 1920–1960*. 3 vols. Stanford, Calif.: Stanford University Press, 1988–91.

Nolte, William H. *Rock and Hawk: Robinson Jeffers and the Romantic Agony*. Athens, Ga.: University of Georgia Press, 1978.

See also: anarchism

Jefferson, Thomas (1743–1826)

Thomas Jefferson was not a conservative. In fact, he spent most of his life attacking the principles that conservatives hold dear. A child of the Enlightenment, he dismissed revealed religion as a tool of priests and kings to manipulate the people. He warred against the political wisdom of the ancients. He particularly hated Plato, and he opined that Aristotle's political writings could be of no use to Americans. Metaphysics and ontology incensed him. He stood proudly with the modern materialists: Bacon, Locke, and Newton. The claims of custom and tradition he rejected, including those his own enlightened age helped to inaugurate. It was a mistake, he said, to regard the Constitution with "sanctimonious reverence." The founders were no wiser than the present age; they just had more experience. Embracing the principle that "the earth belongs to the living," he thought each generation should be free to remake its constitution and laws as well as to renegotiate its debts. He despised the so-called conservatives of his day, the Tories and the Federalists, attributing their political opinions to timid and sickly natures. When abroad, he supported rebellion at home, and when home, he endorsed the French Revolution, even in its most radical phase. He took a generally sunny view of human nature and rejected the doctrine of original sin. Evils there might be, but they were largely the result of a vicious environment. In a properly constructed republic, he was confident that men could govern themselves.

This said, three strands of Jefferson's political thought recommend themselves to conservatives today. To start with the most fundamental (and most controversial), Straussians, and especially Harry Jaffa, emphasize the opening two paragraphs of the Declaration of Independence. Jefferson's assertion that all men are created equal and are endowed with certain inalienable rights, they claim, serves as a bulwark against nihilism. Nature and Nature's God are the source of rights that give dignity to all human beings. Equality in this sense, Jaffa insists, is a conservative principle. Both equality and the rights that flow from it are bounded by a higher moral law accessible through reason and the moral sense. Prudently applied, equality and natural rights are reasonable principles that conservatives should embrace and not cede to their liberal opponents.

(Other conservatives, most notably Russell Kirk, disagree, as do legal positivists such as Robert Bork.)

Second, Jefferson was a friend of limited government. Even after his election in 1800, Jefferson insisted that the only way America could be governed was if the federal government exercised only a few delegated powers and did not try to extend its reach. To do so would invite tyranny and corruption. He defended the separation of powers and a robust version of federalism. He regarded the Union as a compact between each state and the sister states, and in fateful language he asserted the "natural right" of each state to declare "null and void" federal laws that overstepped the legitimate scope of federal powers. In this, he paved the way for John C. Calhoun and generations of Southern conservatives. He took a generally narrow view of federal powers, opposing the establishment of a national bank, federal aid to manufactures, and internal improvements. In 1820, he opposed the Missouri Compromise. In his battles with John Marshall, Jefferson embraced the principle of coordinate construction, according to which each branch of government determines the constitutionality of its acts. In disputes over the meaning of the Constitution, he thought the people should decide through the amendment process. Otherwise, he feared, the Constitution would become a "ball of wax" in the hands of federal judges. As president, he dismantled the Federalist patronage system, reducing both the size of the federal government and the national debt. He also pared down the size of the army and the navy.

Third, Jefferson believed that republicanism was more than just a set of institutional arrangements and that it depended at bottom on the character of the people. To this end, he sought to promote those virtues that would enable the people to govern themselves. He famously insisted that farming was morally superior to urban life, a rallying point for Southern Agrarians. He defended private property because it encouraged industry and liberality, but, most importantly, because it satisfied his understanding of justice, understood as the equal right of all to the fruits of their labor. To keep alive the spirit of the people, he championed public education and local self-government. For Jefferson, republicanism required more than representative institutions; the people must have the opportunity to govern themselves on those matters most interesting to them, such as the protection of their property and the education of their young. Finally, Jefferson recognized that private life held its own considerable charms, and he retired from politics to enjoy his family, friends, and books. In this, he manifested an admirably conservative disposition.

—JEAN YARBROUGH

Thomas Jefferson

Further Reading

Boorstin, Daniel. *The Lost World of Thomas Jefferson.* Chicago: University of Chicago Press, 1981.

Jefferson, Thomas. *Political Writings.* Edited by Joyce Appleby and Terence Ball. New York: Cambridge University Press, 1999.

See also: Adams, John; agrarianism; church and state; Declaration of Independence; education, public; Enlightenment; Jaffa, Harry V.; libertarianism

Jewish conservatives

The term "Jewish conservatives" appears at first glance to be an oxymoron. American Jews have voted overwhelmingly for candidates of the Left, and Jewish intellectuals have been prominent in left-wing movements, ranging from moderate liberalism to communism. Although acculturation and economic and social mobility have moderated their leftist enthusiasms, Jews have continued to identify with the Left. In 1988, for example, the Jewish political scientist Leonard Fein reminded his fellow Jews that a commitment to economic and social justice was "our preeminent motive, the path through which our past is vindicated, our present warranted, and our future affirmed."

Jewish voting patterns are one of the most unusual aspects of American politics. Based on their social and economic position, their traditional social and moral outlook, and their role as entrepreneurs and businessmen, Jews should have been part of the conservative camp. Russell Kirk's *The Conservative Mind* (1953) noted that, except for anti-Semitism, Jews would have been staunch conservatives. "The traditions of race and religion, the Jewish devotion to family, old usage, and spiritual continuity," Kirk wrote, "all incline the Jew toward conservatism." The anomaly of left-of-center American Jewish politics is a product of Jewish history, both in Europe and in the United States.

The majority of American Jews descend from central and eastern European immigrants who settled in the United States between 1850 and 1920. In the nineteenth and early twentieth centuries the European socialist and liberal parties, in contrast to their right-wing opponents, supported Jewish emancipation and the lifting of economic and social restrictions on Jews. Even traditionalist elements of European Jewry looked to the Left to protect their interests. Jewish immigrants carried this left-wing bias with them to America and passed it on to future generations.

This affinity of Jews toward the Left was cemented during the 1930s when, as part of the urban working class, they enthusiastically supported Franklin D. Roosevelt's New Deal. They believed that the New Deal had succeeded in alleviating the social and economic conditions in which anti-Semitism flourished and, in the election of 1936, Jews supported Roosevelt by a ratio of nearly 9 to 1.

Another element shaping Jewish political attitudes was a deep distrust of authority. This was a product of the anti-Semitism that had permeated government, the military, and the church in Europe. American Jews manifested this distrust of authority in a fervent commitment to civil rights, membership in and financial support of such organizations as the American Civil Liberties Union, political support of civilian police review boards, and a reluctance to carve out careers in the military, law enforcement, and politics. The fear of authority was particularly marked when it involved church-state relationships. Mindful of their experiences in Europe and Islamic states, Jews believed that even the most innocuous involvement of religion in government was potentially dangerous.

Because of their knee-jerk suspicion of authority, Jews tended to give the benefit of doubt to the powerless in any conflict with government or with powerful economic interests. One public opinion survey in the 1980s on American Jewish attitudes regarding censorship, pornography, and the use of drugs reported that only 11 percent of Jews favored stricter law enforcement, while 60 percent wanted less. Jews, particularly affluent Jews, became even more sympathetic to liberalism during the 1980s and '90s as issues of culture, lifestyles, and individual rights came to the fore.

Since the 1950s, Republicans, sociologists, and political scientists have proclaimed that a transformation of Jewish voting patterns to comport with their social and economic status was imminent—only to be proven wrong. Since the 1960s, however, a minority of Jews and Jewish intellectuals has moved to the right-of-center or been politically deserted as political bedfellows moved further left. The same phenomenon occurred in England, Canada, Australia, and other Western nations. Symptomatic of this turn toward conservatism in America was the metamorphosis during the 1960s and 1970s of *Commentary* into America's leading conservative monthly, as well as the founding in 1965 of the largely Jewish-edited quarterly magazine *Public Interest*. It was a misconception, Jews were now being told, that their fate was inextricably linked with that of the political Left. The most important factors encouraging this minority of Jews to rethink their politics were the support of black leaders for affirmative action and even racial quotas in employment and college admissions; the leftist campaign to delegitimize Israel; and the acceleration of moral and family breakdown since the 1960s.

Jews were particularly troubled by what the sociologist Nathan Glazer termed "affirmative discrimination," as well as by public opinion surveys claiming that blacks were more anti-Semitic than other Americans. "Quotas," Norman Podhoretz said, "are the most serious threat to Jews since World War II." Jews employed in public schools and government bureaucracies found themselves under increasing pressure from blacks seeking a bigger piece of the pie. In the 1980s, Jesse Jackson, a darling of the American Left, exhibited an almost reflexive dislike of Jews and Israel and refused to repudiate Louis Farrakhan and other black anti-Semites. While Jews continued to champion the principle of merit, black leaders insisted on affirmative action to redress past grievances. In practice, affirmative action meant discrimination in behalf of blacks and other aggrieved minorities. It evoked memories among Jews of the quotas that had once limited their economic, social, and educational opportunities in Europe and the United States. Because of their overrepresentation in academia, Jewish intellectuals were especially concerned with the impact that affirmative action would have on academic standards and hiring practices. Not surprisingly, Jews such as Sidney Hook were important in opposing the assault on the merit principle in academia and in founding the traditionalist Campus Coalition for Democracy.

After the Six-Day War of 1967, the lowest common denominator among American Jews was support for the state of Israel, and Israelism had become the most important component in the "folk religion" of American Jews. Even Jews such as Abbie Hoffman who were otherwise estranged from things Jewish called themselves Zionists after the 1967 war. Since 1967, the most egregious attacks on Israel have been from leftists. They have described the Jewish state as militaristic, racist, capitalistic, pro-American, and an outpost of Western colonialism. American Jews often have been deeply offended by this defaming of Israel, and particularly by the United Nations's 1975 resolution branding Zionism as "racism." American conservatives, on the other hand, became increasingly friendly with Israel because of its opposition to the spread of Soviet influence in the Middle West and its close ties with the United States. For right-wing Christians, the establishment of Israel was an important element in Christian eschatology. Much to the chagrin of Jewish liberals, Menachem Begin, while prime minister of Israel, honored the fundamentalist Jerry Falwell, founder of the Moral Majority, for his support of Israel. "Whatever the case may have been yesterday, and whatever the case may be tomorrow," Podhoretz said, "the case today is that the most active enemies of the Jews are located not in the precincts of the ideological right but in the radical left."

The third element in the move of some Jews to the right was the seemingly pervasive moral breakdown in American society dating from the 1960s. Under Podhoretz's editorship, *Commentary* strongly defended conventional middle-class morality and the traditional family. Religious Jews were especially distressed by the increase in illegitimacy, divorce, pornography, sexual deviancy, and crime. Conservative Republican candidates frequently received more votes in Orthodox areas of Brooklyn than in Jewish neighborhoods in more affluent suburbs. Jacob Neusner, Irving Kristol, and other conservative Jewish intellectuals have even challenged the conventional wisdom that Jewish interests are best protected by a high wall of separation between church and state. They have argued that American Jews were now threatened more by paganism and the unraveling of the moral and social order than by Christianity. This rethinking of church-state relationships has been reflected in the involvement of Jews in *First Things*, a monthly publication encouraging the opening of the "public square" to religious ideas and religiously committed persons.

Don Feder, a columnist for the *Boston Herald*, expressed the concerns of religious Jews in his 1993 book *A Jewish Conservative Looks at Pagan America*. America, he lamented, had ceased being a Christian nation or even a Judeo-Christian nation. Its reigning ethos was now paganism. "The gods of late twentieth century America," he said, "include the doctrines of radical autonomy, of absolute rights divorced from responsibilities, of gender sameness, of self-expression which acknowledges no higher purpose, of moral relativism and sexual indulgence." His own conservatism, Feder continued, was "God-centered, premised on a passion to nurture the best in human nature, which flows from our acceptance of divine injunctions. It is

based on the ethical worldview of the patriarchs and prophets, grounded in the heritage of a people who first taught humanity to think in moral terms."

While Jewish paleoconservatives such as Paul Gottfried were rare, Jews were prominent in the anticommunist, free-market, and neoconservative varieties of conservatism. The ranks of Jewish anticommunists included Alexander Dallin, Will Herberg, Isaac Don Levine, Jay Lovestone, and Bertram Wolfe. Frequently, Jewish anticommunists had been members of the Communist Party, or at least Party sympathizers, and knew its dangers firsthand. Leading Jewish free-market economists included Frank Chodorov, the founder of the Intercollegiate Society of Individualists, Nobel laureates Gary Becker and Milton Friedman, Alan Greenspan, Israel Kirzner, Murray Rothbard, and Murray Weidenbaum. The traditional Jewish suspicion of established authority was perhaps one factor in shaping their skeptical attitude toward government involvement in the private sector.

More Jewish intellectuals were to be found in the ranks of neoconservatism than in any other variant of conservatism. Many of neoconservatism's leading lights were Jews, including Midge Decter, Nathan Glazer, Seymour Martin Lipset, Norman Podhoretz, and Aaron Wildavsky. Irving Kristol was frequently described as the "godfather" of neoconservatism. The Jewish neoconservatives, in contrast to the paleoconservatives, generally came from the social sciences and were not adamantly opposed to government involvement in the economy. While accepting the broad outlines of the welfare state, they rejected many of the Great Society programs of the 1960s.

Irving Kristol predicted in 1972 that Jews could provide conservatism with "an intellectual vigor and cultural buoyancy it has so sadly lacked until now." It is no coincidence that conservatism attained an intellectual respectability at precisely the same time that a significant number of Jewish intellectuals turned to the Right. The insights of the Jewish neoconservatives provided conservatism with the intellectual ballast it had lacked in the past.

—EDWARD S. SHAPIRO

Further Reading

Hook, Sidney. *Out of Step: An Unquiet Life in the Twentieth Century.* New York: Harper & Row, 1987.

Kristol, Irving. *Neoconservatism: The Autobiography of an Idea.* New York: Free Press, 1995.

Podhoretz, Norman. *Ex-Friends: Falling Out with Allen Ginsberg, Lionel and Diana Trilling, Lillian Hellman, Hannah Arendt, and Norman Mailer.* New York: Free Press, 1999.

See also: Commentary; *First Things; neoconservatism; paleoconservatism;* Public Interest

John Birch Society

An extremist anticommunist organization, the John Birch Society was kicked out of the ranks of reputable conservative groups in the mid-1960s, enabling conservatism to continue making inroads in mainstream culture as a legitimate political philosophy.

The group was started in 1958 by businessman Robert Welch and named in honor of an American intelligence officer killed in 1945 by the communists in China. Welch and his followers would say that John Birch was "the first casualty of World War III." The society aimed to prevent subversive communism from making headway in the United States but, unfortunately, Welch was given to making sweeping generalizations about communist influence in the United States, and his reckless charges often boomeranged and harmed the cause of anticommunism. Historian George Nash, in *The Conservative Intellectual Movement in America since 1945,*

called his group "the prime symbol of right-wing extremism."

Welch first got his group in trouble with others on the Right when he charged that President Eisenhower and Secretary of State John Foster Dulles had actively abetted the communist conspiracy in the United States. The society also suggested "the true cause of our imminent danger [is] a semi-secret international cabal whose members sit in the highest places of influence and power worldwide. The American branch of this power elite is most visibly manifested in the Council on Foreign Relations (CFR), which for many years was headed by David Rockefeller, with its members holding key positions in government, the military, business, labor, education, finance, and the media. The CFR's international cousin is the Trilateral Commission." The mainstream press used Welch's conspiratorial statements in an attempt to discredit conservatism as a whole.

William F. Buckley Jr.'s *National Review,* conscious of the harm Welch was bringing to legitimate anticommunism, sought to read him out of the mainstream conservative movement. *National Review* was careful to condemn Welch but not his organization, on the theory that most members were likely unaware of Welch's irresponsible charges. But by 1965, according to Nash, "the distinction between Welch and his followers no longer seemed tenable, and the editors of *National Review,* in a special feature section, condemned the entire society." In a withering attack on the society and its "psychosis of conspiracy," *National Review* listed its various wild claims (such as the society's contention that the country was dominated by communists) and demonstrated why the John Birch Society should play no role in formulating a workable conservative and anticommunist agenda in the United States.

The successful repudiation of Welch and his organization by the standard bearers of American conservatism has gone down as one of the defining episodes in the march of the conservative movement to national acceptance. Though its influence was all but destroyed by its expulsion from the conservative movement, the organization has soldiered on throughout the years. Among its priorities are getting the United States out of the United Nations, and, according to its promotional materials, providing "both the core and the cutting edge of principled opposition to the 'new world order.'" During Ronald Reagan's administration, the society further marginalized itself by denouncing Reagan as soft on communism. Welch died in 1985, just a few short years before Reagan's policies helped defeat Soviet communism.

—MAX SCHULZ

Further Reading

Nash, George H. *The Conservative Intellectual Movement in America since 1945.* 2nd ed. Wilmington, Del.: Intercollegiate Studies Institute, 1998.

Smant, Kevin J. *Principles and Heresies: Frank S. Meyer and the Shaping of the American Conservative Movement.* Wilmington, Del.: ISI Books, 2002.

See also: National Review; *Oliver, Revilo P.; Tansill, Charles*

John Paul II, Pope (1920–2005)

On October 16, 1978, Cardinal Karol Wojtyla, archbishop of Krakow in Poland, became the 264th pontiff to lead the Roman Catholic Church—a stunning selection for an institution that, beset by internal strife and tottering from the aftermath of the sexual revolution, had not selected a non-Italian pope in 400 years. Born in Poland in 1920, John Paul II (the name Wojtyla chose to commemorate his three immediate predecessors) was the first Slavic pope in the Church's history. Few knew exactly what to expect from the fifty-

eight-year-old pope, though the head of the KGB, Yuri Andropov, wisely anticipated conflict and warned his superiors that the election of John Paul II spelled trouble for the Soviet empire.

Three decades later, the image and person of John Paul II had become inseparable from the image and teachings of the modern Catholic Church. To millions of young people, he was until his death in 2005 the only pope they had ever known and the embodiment of what every pope should be, a latter-day apostle who spoke directly to the moral conscience of his auditors. Serving longer than all but two of his predecessors, John Paul II traveled and wrote more than any pope in history. As a "witness to hope," he survived an assassin's bullet and stared down communist regimes. Through his example, intellect, and personality, John Paul II provided a model for living the Catholic faith in the modern age, personifying the "new evangelism" called for by the Second Vatican Council (1962–65). The voice of John Paul II was heard at each crisis of the age. Confidently and intelligently, he guided men and women of faith through the fundamental moral challenges of our time, from the evil of totalitarianism to the meaning of sexual love. Laboring forth from a millennium that ended with a calamitous and bloody century, John Paul renewed an ancient faith through an eternal truth: the transcendent dignity of the human person.

The drama of John Paul II's life unfolded amid the dynamic events of history. As a young man, he excelled as a student, skier, soccer player, and amateur actor before the Nazi invasion of Poland drove him from university life. During the occupation, he risked his life to organize an underground theater group that opposed Nazism. He was ordained a priest in 1946 at the age of 26 and assigned to a small Polish parish before becoming a professor at the Catholic University of Lublin in 1954, the only extant Catholic university in the post-Nazi communist eastern bloc. Behind the Iron Curtain, individuals were but helpless cogs in the state's brutal machine. John Paul II saw what the communists refused to see: man bears in his soul the *imago Dei*. The "fundamental error of socialism," he would later write, "is anthropological." Through the providence of communist ineptitude, his capacious talents were overlooked and he was ordained a bishop at age thirty-eight and archbishop at age forty-three.

Refusing to serve the Polish people from afar, the energetic bishop developed close relationships with ordinary men and women, devoting hours of time to hiking, kayaking, and vacationing with lay people. In particular, Wojtyla developed a close bond with married couples and young people seeking to understand the gift of love. "As a young priest I learned to love human love," he recalled. Wojtyla's carefully developed humanism—a philosophy often referred to as "personalism"—also enabled him to make crucial contributions to the Second Vatican Council, where he drafted the Pastoral Constitution on the Church in the Modern World and the Declaration of Religious Freedom. At the council, the intellectually formidable Polish archbishop set forth his conviction that the dignity of each human person is revealed in his or her lifelong quest to know and live the truth.

The priestly character of Wojtyla's pastoral experience was highlighted to the world in his inaugural papal homily, when he made the bold challenge that would define his pontificate: "Be not afraid." Less than a year later, he undertook the first of his legendary and exhausting travels by returning to

Pope John Paul II

his homeland to deliver a message of courage and nonviolence.

John Paul II's support for Poland's Solidarity movement was instrumental to the free world's bloodless victory over communism. After the Soviets imposed martial law on Poland in 1981, President Reagan called John Paul II for advice, believing that the Soviet Union would collapse if it lost Poland. With the Reagan administration applying political pressure on the Soviets, John Paul II added the necessary moral pressure, emerging as the primary spiritual force behind the Revolution of 1989. "Step by reluctant step, the Soviets and the communist government of Poland bowed to the pressure imposed by the Pope and the President," explained one archbishop to an American diplomat. In a 1992 syndicated column that appeared in major newspapers throughout the world, Mikhail Gorbachev concurred that John Paul II was essential to the end of communism in Eastern Europe.

The fall of communism did not delude John Paul II into thinking that the battle was over. He understood that the human person always bears the responsibility of seeking the truth and he set the Catholic Church on a path of evangelical renewal and the creation of a "culture of life" to oppose the "culture of death" that pervaded the free countries of the West as much as it did those elsewhere. In opposing the tragedies of euthanasia and abortion, John Paul II repeatedly returned to the fundamental issue: the nature of the human person and the meaning of life. Between 1979 and 1984, the Pope devoted 130 addresses to the "theology of the body," contesting the myopic vision of sexuality promoted by sexual liberationists with a penetrating perception of the body as loudspeaker of the soul. John Paul II taught that to be truly human was to be self-giving, an insight he called "the Law of the Gift."

In the later years of his pontificate, the aging pope focused on themes of human suffering. He asked for forgiveness for the mistreatment of Jews at the hands of Christians, and other Christians at the hands of Catholics. He reached out to members of other faiths, seeking to make the new millennium a "springtime of the human spirit." Speaking before the United Nations in 1995, John Paul II explained the source of his hope: faith in Jesus Christ. His words, so emblematic of his personal mission, could well epitomize how he will be remembered in history: "I come before you as a witness: a witness to human dignity, a witness to hope, a witness to the conviction that the destiny of all ... lies in the hands of a merciful Providence." Despite his declining physical capacity, the "man of the century" (in one biographer's words) continued to witness to the Third Millennium. In his stirring 2001 apostolic letter "Novo Millennio Ineunte," John Paul II once again challenged the faithful to "go out into the deep" and transform all noble and honest activities by bringing them to Christ.

—MICHAEL TOTH

Further Reading

Buttiglione, Rocco. *Karol Wojtyla: The Thought of the Man Who Became Pope John Paul II.* Grand Rapids, Mich.: Wm. B. Eerdmans, 1997.

John Paul II. *Crossing the Threshold of Hope.* New York: Alfred A. Knopf, 1994.

Weigel, George. *Witness to Hope.* New York, N.Y.: Harper Collins, 1999.

Wojtyla, Karol. *Love and Responsibility.* Rev. ed. San Francisco: Ignatius, 1993.

See also: Catholic social teaching; liberation theology; personalism; Roman Catholicism

Judd, Walter H. (1898–1994)

A staunch internationalist and fervent anticommunist, Walter Henry Judd led the way during the post–World War II era for congressional adoption of the Truman Doctrine, the Marshall Plan, and NATO, all of which laid foundations for the policy of containment and helped bring about the collapse of communism in Eastern Europe and the breakup of the Soviet empire. He also played a key role in Congress's approval of the United Nations, the World Health Organization, the Voice of America, P.L. 480 (Food for Peace), and the removal of all racial discrimination clauses from U.S. immigration and naturalization laws.

Born in Rising City, Nebraska, in 1898, Judd worked his way through college and medical school and spent ten years in war-torn China in the 1920s and 1930s as a medical missionary for the Congregationalist Church. No other American in the twentieth century was more identified with China than Judd, who advised presidents from Harry Truman to Ronald Reagan and secretaries of state from George Marshall to Henry Kissinger on U.S.-Sino relations, always in defense of the Republic of China and in opposition to the People's Republic of China.

In the two years following his return from China in 1938, Judd made 1,400 speeches urging the United States to stop trading with Japan and giving it the means to conduct war against China. Gifted with rare insight into the Asian mind and character, he warned that if America did not stop giving Japan "the sinews of war" it would soon face Japan on the battlefield.

Following Pearl Harbor, Judd was drafted to run for Congress in 1942 and represented the Fifth District of Minnesota for ten consecutive terms as a Republican. By reason of his integrity, knowledge, and eloquence, he was voted the most admired

House member by his Republican colleagues and one of the ten most influential members of Congress by Democrats and Republicans. He was seriously considered for the vice presidential candidacy by Dwight D. Eisenhower in 1952 and by Richard Nixon in 1960. Commenting on his narrow loss to John F. Kennedy in 1960, Nixon remarked that if he had picked Judd rather than Henry Cabot Lodge, "we might have won." Many political analysts agree.

An inveterate organizer, Judd founded or cofounded Aid Refugee Chinese Intellectuals; World Neighbors' American Bureau for Medical Aid to China; the Committee of One Million (Against the Admission of Communist China to the United Nations); the Committee for a Free China; Republican Workshops; and Former Members of Congress. He was a contributing editor to *Reader's Digest*, a member of the judicial council of the American Medical Association, and the host of "Washington Report," a daily radio commentary that became the largest public-affairs public service program in U.S. broadcasting history, reaching up to 1,100 radio stations in the late 1960s.

Judd was moderate and even liberal on many domestic issues, such as the minimum wage and social security, but on foreign issues he was an unyielding internationalist. After World War II, he helped lead the Republican Party out of its isolationism and helped persuade the United States to accept its role as leader of the free world during the Cold War. Throughout his public life of nearly seventy years, Judd adhered faithfully to Thomas Jefferson's words: "I have sworn upon the altar of God unending hostility against every form of tyranny over the mind of man."
—LEE EDWARDS

Further Reading

Edwards, Lee. *Missionary for Freedom: The Life and Times of Walter Judd*. New York: Paragon House, 1990.

Rozek, Edward J., ed. *Walter H. Judd: Chronicles of a Statesman*. Denver, Colo.: Grier & Company, 1980.

See also: *China Lobby; containment*

judicial activism

Judicial activism refers to a judge's deciding a case on the basis of his own (usually moral) preferences rather than the governing law. In America, the federal judiciary is the most frequent recipient of the "judicial activist" label for improperly interpreting either the U.S. Constitution or a particular law to achieve the judge's desired result. Although this method has been used to achieve conservative results, since President Franklin Roosevelt's administration judicial activism of this sort has tended to impose the agenda of modern political liberalism. Frequently, judicial activism has been criticized as most undemocratic when used as a strategy to strike down state laws as "unconstitutional" even where there is no constitutional provision justifying the invalidation of such laws.

George Carey described the limits of federal judicial conduct, action beyond which constitutes judicial activism, in his *In Defense of the Constitution* (1989). He argued that Alexander Hamilton's *Federalist* 78 defined the proper judicial role. Hamilton contrasted "will"—what the legislature exercises—with "judgment"—the judges' proper role. Judges are to be "bound by strict rules and precedents" and may only strike down as unconstitutional laws that contain an "irreconcilable variance" to the "manifest tenor" of the Constitution. Yet the authority of the judicial branch to define what law is also has its limits. Carey claimed that when a court does engage in judicial activism beyond these limitations it has lost its claim to judicial supremacy and the other branches of the government can and must regulate the court.

Judicial activism entered the popular spotlight in 1986 when Judge Robert Bork was rejected as a nominee for the U.S. Supreme Court. Bork came under fire for criticizing activist decisions of the Court. His nomination was defeated by the Senate after a heated media campaign engineered by the political Left. Bork later defended his views in *The Tempting of America* (1990), which made him something of a conservative icon.

Bork condemns judicial activism from the standpoint of "originalism," which holds that a judge should apply the Constitution as it was plainly intended by its drafters (this applies to whatever law governs the judge's inquiry: whether it be the Constitution, a legislative statute, or precedent, which binds lower court judges). Judicial activism occurs when a judge derives, defines, or applies a governing principle in a nonneutral manner. A judge himself only has the power plainly given to him by the Constitution's text and may not void a law based on his conception of fairness, the natural law, or any other nontextual source. Judicial activism amounts to legislation from the bench and undermines the will of the majority, which is especially odious because judges are ill-suited to legislate and are unaccountable to the governed (federal judges hold lifetime appointments).

Some conservatives criticize Bork's view as overly positivistic. In *Beyond the Constitution* (1990), Hadley Arkes agrees that it is improper for a judge to "free" himself from the Constitution's text in order to impose his own views and then cover up that imposition with a specious explanation of how it is justified by the Constitution. But Arkes also argues that the Constitution itself assumes the "natural rights" outlook of America's founders. Judges may properly draw judgments from "general principles of our political institutions," and these principles can be known by the "logic of morals" and distinguished from ever-changing cul-

tural norms applied by liberals and conservatives alike. Arkes criticizes Bork's view as straying from the founders' view in the same fashion as does modern liberalism: by relying on a purely positivistic theory of law that denies the ability of a judge to know moral truth and apply it properly.

Several Supreme Court decisions stand out as examples of judicial activism. Such decisions often portray the justices' conclusions as authentic interpretations of the constitutional right of "substantive due process." Under that guise and seemingly without constitutional support, the Court issued *Dred Scott v. Sandford* (1857, invalidating state laws that granted "free" status to slaves whose owners transported them there from a slave state, so as to protect the slaveowner's due process right to property), *Lochner v. New York* (1905, striking down a state law restriction on the maximum hours that bakers could work, as violating the employer and employee due process right to liberty of contract), and *Roe v. Wade* (1973, nullifying state laws against abortion, as contrary to the due process right of women to privacy and the liberty to commit abortion).

Judicial activism permeates not only the federal and state judiciaries but also academia and the legal culture—including law school faculties and journals. There, conservative jurisprudence is ridiculed as archaic and irrelevant while activist theories abound in their complexity, variety, and derivation—from Marxism and positivism to radical feminism and innumerable other sources. Defenders of judicial activism point to the unfairness of judicial outcomes if judges are not permitted to strike down unjust laws even absent a constitutional basis for doing so. Organizations in the legal culture that oppose activism and generally support originalism include the Federalist Society.

In 1997, the Republican-led U.S. House and Senate conducted hearings into the problem of "judicial activism" and considered solutions, such as amending the Constitution to impose term limits on the tenure of federal judges. No substantive reforms resulted.

—MATTHEW BOWMAN

Further Reading

Arkes, Hadley. *The Return of George Sutherland:* *Restoring a Jurisprudence of Natural Rights.* Princeton, N.J.: Princeton University Press, 1994.

Bork, Robert H. *Coercing Virtue: The Worldwide Rule of Judges.* Washington, D.C.: AEI Press, 2003.

See also: abortion; Arkes, Hadley; Bork, Robert H.; Brown v. Board of Education; *Constitution, Interpretations of;* Supreme Court

K

Kemp, Jack F. (1935–)

A prominent politician noted for his advocacy of tax cuts, the gold standard, and aggressive efforts to eliminate poverty, Jack French Kemp was born on July 13, 1935, in Los Angeles, California. He attended Occidental College, graduating in 1957, and played professional football for the next thirteen years, principally with the Buffalo Bills. In 1970, Kemp was elected to Congress from the 31st District of New York as a Republican, serving until 1989.

Kemp is notable for his advocacy of tax rate reductions as a means of stimulating the economy. Kemp's tax reduction efforts led to the development of supply-side economics. In the late 1970s, he teamed with Senator William Roth (R-DE) to press for across-the-board cuts in federal income tax rates. The Kemp-Roth bill would have cut the top federal income tax rate from 70 percent to 50 percent and the bottom rate from 14 percent to 10 percent. This proposal was endorsed by Ronald Reagan, who pressed for its enactment after becoming president in 1981. A version of the Kemp-Roth bill became law in August 1981.

In the 1980s, Kemp worked with Senator Robert Kasten (R-WI) on a tax reform proposal that would lead to further tax rate reductions while broadening the tax base. In 1984, President Reagan endorsed a similar proposal, which was enacted in 1986. This led to a further reduction in the top federal income tax rate, from 50 percent to 38 percent.

In 1987, Kemp decided to leave Congress to run for the Republican presidential nomination. After losing the nomination to George Bush, he joined Bush's cabinet as secretary of housing and urban development. From this position, Kemp vigorously advocated new policies to alleviate poverty. Among his innovations were programs to sell public housing to tenants.

Robert Dole chose Kemp as his vice presidential running mate for his unsuccessful run for the presidency in 1996.

Jack Kemp's major significance to conservatism is that, in terms of policy, he helped to push it in new directions. Before him, many conservatives and Republicans were generally opposed to tax cuts, favoring instead a balanced budget. Before him, few conservatives proposed concrete measures to alleviate the cycle of dependency endemic among the poor. Kemp showed that tax cuts could both invigorate the economy and be a vehicle for the achievement of political power, and that policies aimed at helping the poor could reflect conservative values.

—Bruce Bartlett

Further Reading

Kemp, Jack F. *An American Renaissance.* New York: Harper & Row, 1979.

See also: enterprise zones; Laffer curve; supply-side economics

Kendall, Willmoore (1909–67)

A principal figure in the post–World War II conservative movement, Willmoore Kendall was a political scientist noted for his views on the meaning and nature of the American political tradition.

Kendall grew up in Oklahoma the son of a blind Methodist minister. His father carefully supervised his primary and secondary education so that Kendall advanced rapidly through the grades. At the age of thirteen, he entered Northwestern University, the youngest college student of that era, eventually receiving his B.A. from the University of Oklahoma in 1927. At the age of nineteen, he received an M.A. in romance languages from Northwestern University. Subsequently, he accepted a fellowship from the University of Illinois' department of romance languages, but he left this program in 1932 when he was awarded a

Willmoore Kendall

Rhodes scholarship. He studied at Oxford (Pembroke College) from 1932 to 1935, a period during which he embraced communism. After working briefly in the Madrid office of United Press, he returned to the United States in 1936 and began studies at the University of Illinois toward a doctorate in political science. He received his Ph.D. in 1940, and his dissertation, *John Locke and the Doctrine of Majority Rule*, was published by the University of Illinois Press in 1941.

Prior to World War II, Kendall taught at Louisiana State University (1937–40) and Hobart College (1940–41). In 1942 he resigned his position as assistant professor at the University of Richmond to work in the offices of Inter-American Affairs in Washington, D.C. During and after the war he con-

tinued to devote his attention to Latin America, finally being appointed chief, Inter-American Division, Office of Reports and Estimates, for the Central Intelligence Agency. In 1948, he resigned this position to accept an appointment as associate professor of political science at Yale University.

His tenure at Yale (1948–61) was marked by considerable controversy and turmoil, much of which was spurred by the conservative convictions he had acquired sometime in the 1940s. He took frequent leaves of absence, never teaching two consecutive years during his stay. During this period, he met William F. Buckley Jr. and, in 1955, became one of the founding editors of *National Review*, for which he wrote a regular column for approximately five years. In 1961, he reached an agreement with Yale whereby he would be paid five times his salary (which had been frozen since 1948) to resign his professorship. Subsequently, in a visiting capacity, he taught one semester at Georgetown and a year at Los Angeles State College before assuming the chairmanship of the politics department at the University of Dallas in 1963. At the time of his death in June 1967, he was developing a graduate program that would combine the study of politics and literature.

Kendall first made his mark in political science with his work on John Locke and majority rule. In the early stages of his postwar career, he gained a reputation as the foremost advocate of unlimited majority rule. Over the years, though he never abandoned the majority rule principle, he refined his views considerably in light of the American political system. He held that the founding fathers had placed a premium on achieving consensus rather than simply counting heads. He argued persuasively that the framers intended Congress to articulate the popular will through consensual processes, but that, over the decades, liberals had staked out a claim for the president as the most authentic representative of the people's values and aspirations. Thus, he saw a tension within the American system, a tension he described in terms of "two majorities": the congressional, which collects the sense of structured communities in terms of the hierarchical values and interests of those communities, and the presidential (necessarily cast in terms of lofty principle), which speaks for the people as an undifferentiated mass. According to his analysis, Congress was, as an institution, inherently more conservative than the presidency.

Kendall used a battlefield metaphor to depict the contours of the struggle between liberals and conservatives in the United States. In this metaphor the conservative forces were strung out in small, isolated outposts over a wide front that the liberals could easily overrun one at a time because they possessed a general staff to concentrate and coordinate their forces for attack. Only when these conservative outposts united in the recognition of their common enemy would conservatism prevail.

This battle, as Kendall saw it, was of critical importance, involving no less than the destiny of the United States. Liberals, as he perceived the central issue, sought an "open" society of equals. A fair portion of his writings is devoted to refuting the liberals' interpretation of "equality" as it is found in the Declaration of Independence and to countering their claim that our commitment as a nation is to making the unequal equal. He insisted that to place the Declaration of Independence in its proper perspective and to comprehend its meaning, one must take into account those fundamental documents that both preceded and followed it. He thought

it significant, for example, that equality was not among the ends of government set forth in the preamble to the Constitution.

Kendall was also unrelenting in his attacks on the "open society," an idea that he believed embodied liberalism's commitment to relativism ("all opinions are equal") and virtually unlimited freedom of expression. No society, he maintained, could long survive without subscribing to fundamental values that it held to be true and beyond debate. But the professed "truth" of the open society—namely, that there are no truths—must sooner or later bring into question these fundamental values. In elevating the open society and freedom of expression to the summum bonum, liberals, according to Kendall, come to regard societies that are not totally "open" as "closed." But such a dichotomy, he held, is dangerously misleading. No society, he insisted, could ever be completely open; in the real world, the choices come down to an infinite number of possibilities as to how open, or how closed, a society is to be.

Kendall focused on the American political tradition almost exclusively during the last years of his life because he believed that there was a distinctive American conservatism whose flavor and essence could not be adequately comprehended by reference to Burke or continental philosophers. Thus, he is of particular interest for students interested in exploring the roots of a specifically American conservatism.

—George W. Carey

Further Reading

Kendall, Willmoore. *The Conservative Affirmation.* Chicago: Regnery, 1963.

———. *Willmoore Kendall Contra Mundum.* Edited by Nellie D. Kendall. New Rochelle, N.Y.: Arlington House, 1971.

———, and George W. Carey. *The Basic Symbols of the American Political Tradition.* Baton Rouge, La.: Louisiana State University Press, 1970.

Murley, John A., and John E. Alvis, eds. *Willmoore Kendall: Maverick of American Conservatives*. Lanham, Md.: Lexington Books, 2002.

See also: Buckley, William F., Jr.; Carey, George W.; Declaration of Independence; democracy; equality; God and Man at Yale; tradition

Kennan, George (1904–2005)

Occupying his own place on the ideological spectrum, George Kennan was the principal architect of the premier Cold War doctrine known as "containment," but in later years he was an icon of dovish liberals and anti-anticommunists like John Lukacs for his isolationism and his advocacy of arms treaties and even unilateral disarmament by the United States. Although his political links were chiefly with the Democratic Party, he wrote about the moral and material decadence of the West in terms that are congruous with the most severe traditionalist conservative critics of the West.

Kennan, who at the time of his death was professor emeritus of historical studies at the Institute for Advanced Study at Princeton, entered the foreign service in 1927 and served the State Department in several European capitals during the 1930s. Fluent in Russian, Kennan went in 1933 with Ambassador William Bullitt to reopen the American Embassy in Moscow. It was while serving as a diplomat in the U.S. Embassy in Moscow in 1946 that Kennan sent his famous "long telegram" about Soviet behavior that was later adapted into the famous "Mr. X" article on "The Sources of Soviet Conduct" in *Foreign Affairs* in 1947.

Kennan argued that the Soviet Union was motivated by a combination of ideology and traditional Russian xenophobia and imperialism. Kennan thought that if Soviet expansionism were "contained" by the West, the Communist Party within the Soviet Union might unravel, and the Soviet Union would transform itself into a more traditional great power.

A key phrase of Kennan's article—"that the Soviet pressure against the free institutions of the Western world is something that can be contained by the adroit and vigilant application of counter-force at a series of constantly shifting geographical points, corresponding to the shifts and maneuvers of Soviet policy"—became the intellectual cornerstone of the "Truman Doctrine," which committed the United States to aid foreign governments battling against communist insurgencies, and of Cold War strategy generally.

In later years Kennan came to repudiate the common understanding of his "Mr. X" article, saying that by "containment" he had not meant to suggest *military* containment, but rather *political* containment. Kennan, and many of the liberal critics of his article at the time, thought the Truman Doctrine too broad, that it represented an unrealistic overcommitment by the West. Counterforce could not be successfully applied to all geographic regions of the globe, Kennan thought. Kennan did, however, support American intervention in the Korean War in 1950. He came to oppose the Vietnam War. More than a few conservatives criticized Kennan and containment for not going far enough, for not proposing a "rollback" of communism in Eastern Europe and the defeat of the Soviet Union itself. These critics saw containment as a recipe for slow defeat.

Throughout the 1960s and 1970s, Kennan began to describe himself as a qualified isolationist, he endorsed "moderate socialism" as the best course for Western Europe, and he supported various disarmament proposals. In the early 1980s, during the height of the controversy over the introduction of medium-range nuclear missiles in Western Europe, Kennan joined with several prominent liberals in calling for a "no first use" (of nuclear weapons) declaration by the United States, which was used by the Left in its campaign against the missiles.

But Kennan also spoke out against the "decadence" of the West, "its self-indulgent permissiveness, its pornography, its rampant materialism." "Isn't it grotesque," Kennan said, "to spend so much of our energy on opposing such a Russia in order to save a West which is honeycombed with bewilderment and a profound sense of internal decay?" Kennan thought the West needed to devote much more attention to its own spiritual regeneration.

The author of more than a dozen books, including two volumes of *Memoirs* (1967, 1972), Kennan was a distinguished diplomatic historian. He wrote extensively on the diplomatic prelude to World War I, as well as on contemporary questions.

—STEPHEN HAYWARD

Further Reading

Herz, Martin F., ed. *Decline of the West? George Kennan and His Critics.* Washington, D.C.: Ethics and Public Policy Center, 1978.

Kennan, George F. *American Diplomacy, 1900–1950.* Chicago: University of Chicago Press, 1951.

———. *Interviews with George F. Kennan.* Edited by T. Christopher Jespersen. Jackson, Miss.: University Press of Mississippi, 2002.

See also: Cold War; containment

Kenner, Hugh (1923–2003)

A prolific polymath, Hugh Kenner was not only one of the leading literary critics of the second half of the twentieth century, but a witty, original thinker in his own right, with abiding interests in politics, art, mathematics, and technology. Like his close friend Marshall McLuhan, Kenner was a Canadian and a Catholic convert; both men were fascinated by the paradox of how innovation in art and science might renew the tradition of Western civilization. Kenner's first book was, in fact, about G. K. Chesterton's use of paradox, but none of his later books would be as public about the theological convictions he shared with Chesterton. Kenner went on to become the premier authority on literary High Modernism, penning nearly two dozen books on such writers as T. S. Eliot, Ezra Pound, James Joyce, Wyndham Lewis, and Samuel Beckett. *The Pound Era* (1971) is generally considered his magisterial work.

A number of critics have criticized Kenner as a "covert fascist" because he wrote with sympathy about some of the Modernists who were initially drawn to fascism, including Pound, Lewis, and W. B. Yeats. But as one obituarist wrote, this charge is "simply absurd." What absorbed Kenner was the way in which these poets and novelists employed modern literary forms, including fragmentation, allusion, and mythic structures, to renew the roots of Western culture. (These arguments would be echoed by the preeminent conservative thinker Russell Kirk in a more accessible fashion, as for example in his book *Eliot and His Age*.) Kenner did befriend William F. Buckley Jr. in the late 1950s and was for a time the literary editor of *National Review*, but his interests were too wide and his attitude to writers across the political spectrum too generous to pigeonhole him as an ideologue of the Right.

—GREGORY WOLFE

Further Reading

Goodwin, Willard. *Hugh Kenner: A Bibliography.* Albany, N.Y. : Whitston, 2001.

Kenner, Hugh. *Historical Fictions.* San Francisco: North Point Press, 1990.

———. *Invisible Poet: T. S. Eliot:.* New York: McDowell, Obolensky, 1959.

See also: Pound, Ezra

Kent, James (1763–1847)

James Kent was born in Dutchess County, New York, the son of local gentry, on July 31, 1763. He matriculated at Yale University, where he engaged in literary pursuits. Following graduation in 1781 he studied law with Egbert Benson, then attorney general of New York, and established himself in Poughkeepsie, where he practiced law from 1785 to 1793. Having made the acquaintance of Alexander Hamilton in 1787, Kent became a lifelong Federalist. He was elected to the state legislature from Dutchess County in 1790 and reelected the next two years. He showed himself from the beginning of his political career to be a conservative favorable to property and stability.

James Kent

In 1793, Kent was appointed professor of law at Columbia University, where he taught until 1798. In his lectures at Columbia, in the years prior to *Marbury v. Madison* (1803), he made the case for a broad power of judicial review in order to protect individual rights from infringement by majoritarian legislatures. In 1796, John Jay, then governor of New York and a patron of Kent's, appointed him a Master in Chancery, and the following year made him Recorder of New York, the chief judicial post in the city. In 1798, Kent was made a judge on the New York Supreme Court, and he would be made chief justice in 1806, a position he held until 1814.

As a Federalist on the New York court, Kent was often outnumbered by Jeffersonians. Kent was able to lead this fractious court by dint of his own massive learning in the law, mastering in particular English legal history and the continental sources of law. As chief justice, Kent was able to incorporate into New York law large parts of the English common law. The applicability of the English common law was then very much in dispute. Jeffersonians in particular were opposed to its continuing vitality in the new United States, perceiving it to contain a number of oppressive doctrines, such as strict rules on debt and prohibitions on organized labor. Kent also made generous use in his opinions of classical Roman law and of such continental writers as Hugo Grotius and Emmerich de Vattel.

Kent authored a number of opinions favorable to the commercial interests of New York. In a famous case, *Livingston v. van Ingen* (1812), Kent upheld the grant to Robert Livingston and Robert Fulton of a monopoly of steamship operations in New York waters. In his opinions Kent also proved to be a defender of religious orthodoxy. In the absence of a statute, Kent upheld a conviction of blasphemy in *People against Ruggles* (1811). The people of New York, Kent reasoned, "profess the general doctrines of Christianity." "Whatever strikes at the root of Christianity," Kent observed, "tends manifestly to the dissolution of civil government." Thus blasphemy, which was a crime at common law, should also be enforced as a criminal offense under New York law.

In 1814, Kent was appointed chancellor of the State of New York. He retired from the judiciary in 1823, returning to the practice of law and to a professorship at Columbia University. In retirement, Kent authored a four-volume treatise on American law, the *Commentaries on American Law* (1826), which stressed the strong historical connectedness between American law and English and European antecedents. Kent was particularly influenced by Matthew Hale's understanding that law must not be "the product of the vision of some one man or society of men in any one age; but of the wisdom, counsel, experience, and observation of many ages of wise and observing men." The *Commentaries* proved to be an extraordinarily popular restatement of American law, going through five editions during Kent's lifetime. Oliver Wendell Holmes edited the twelfth edition (1873). Kent died on December 12, 1847, surrounded by his wife and children.

—CHARLES J. REID JR.

Further Reading

Horton, John Theodore. *James Kent: A Study in Conservatism.* New York: D. Appleton-Century Company, 1939.

See also: Federalist Party

Keynesian economics

Keynesian economics is a term that describes some of the ideas of economist John Maynard Keynes (1883–1946), a British economist who is generally considered the most influential economist of the twentieth century. The principal feature of Keynesian economics is its advocacy of government deficit spending to stimulate economic growth.

Keynes first rose to prominence in the 1920s as a critic of the Versailles Treaty, which ended World War I and required large war reparations from Germany. His first major book, *The Economic Consequences of the Peace* (1919), argued strongly against the reparations policy as damaging to European economic integration and thus contrary to the interests of the Allies as well as the Germans. In addition, Keynes strongly opposed the British government's economic policies, especially the decision to peg the value of the pound at its prewar exchange rate. He be-

lieved that this would require a severe deflation in England that would seriously damage the economy.

In 1936, Keynes published his most important work, *The General Theory of Employment, Interest and Money*, which argued in favor of budget deficits and increases in the money supply to restore economic growth. The prevailing view among both economists and politicians of the time was that government budgets should be balanced and that the money supply should be tied to the gold standard. Keynes believed that workers would never allow wage rates to fall enough to eliminate unemployment. He thus favored inflationary policies that would cause the real level of wages to fall even though nominal rates remained unchanged.

Although initially attacked, the Keynesian view soon exerted significant influence on both economists and policymakers. This is because Keynesian economics offered a rationale for government intervention in the economy that had been constrained by the laissez-faire doctrines of classical economics, the gold standard, and the balanced budget rule. As Joseph Schumpeter wrote in his *History of Economic Analysis* (1954): "Whatever its merit as a piece of analysis may be, there cannot be any doubt that [*The General Theory*] owed its victorious career primarily to the fact that its argument implemented some of the strongest political preferences of a large number of modern economists."

As a response to the deflationary conditions of the 1930s, the Keynesian program had merit. The problem was Keynes's insistence that he had put forward a general theory applicable to all times, rather than just the conditions of a deflationary depression. After the return to prosperity during World War II appeared to vindicate Keynesian policies, they became the foundation of both economic theory and economic policy in all Western nations. The United States, for example, codified Keynesian economics in the Employment Act of 1946, which obliged the government to utilize Keynesian policies to sustain full employment.

By the 1960s, Keynesian economics dominated economic policymaking in the U.S. The Kennedy tax cut of 1964 was explicitly based on Keynesian economics and by 1971 even President Richard Nixon confessed to being a Keynesian. However, the development of rapid inflation and slow growth in the 1970s, combined with rising budget deficits, severely eroded the credibility of Keynesian policies. Critics of Keynesian economics, such as Professor Milton Friedman of the University of Chicago, had always viewed it as dangerously inflationary. The stagflation of the 1970s appeared to confirm this view. In addition, a growing number of economists, such as Professor Martin Feldstein of Harvard, were becoming concerned about the growth of budget deficits and began to view them as a drag on the economy.

By the 1980s, most economists had already turned away from Keynesian economics, although many of its doctrines continue to be embedded in economics textbooks.

—BRUCE BARTLETT

Further Reading

Bartlett, Bruce. "Keynes as a Conservative." *Modern Age* 28 (1984): 128–33.

Buchanan, James M. and Richard E. Wagner. *Democracy in Deficit: The Political Legacy of Lord Keynes*. New York: Academic Press, 1977.

Harrod, Roy. *The Life of John Maynard Keynes*. New York: Macmillan, 1951.

Hazlitt, Henry. *The Failure of the "New Economics": An Analysis of the Keynesian Fallacies*. Princeton, N.J.: Van Nostrand, 1959.

Lekachman, Robert. *The Age of Keynes*. New York: Random House, 1966.

See also: Austrian school of economics; Buchanan, James M.; Friedman, Milton; Hutt, William H.; monetarist economics; supply-side economics

Kilpatrick, James J. (1920–)

James J. Kilpatrick played a vital role in transforming conservatism into a viable mass political movement during his many years as a broadcaster and syndicated political columnist.

Born in Oklahoma in 1920, Kilpatrick went to work as a reporter for the Richmond, Virginia, *News-Leader* in 1941. In 1949, he became that paper's editorial page editor and established its reputation as a reliable voice for staunch conservatism. A self-described Whig and latter-day proponent of states' rights, Kilpatrick's rise to national prominence began in earnest in 1964 when he began writing his syndicated column, "A Conservative View." He found a receptive audience among Barry Goldwater supporters and Richard Nixon's "Silent Majority," and went on to become the nation's most widely syndicated political columnist. While his political writings dealt with all things Washington, Kilpatrick became known primarily for his articles about the judiciary and the Supreme Court. He has also been an outspoken supporter of First Amendment rights, both as a columnist and as a founding trustee of the Thomas Jefferson Center for the Protection of Free Expression.

Even though Kilpatrick has managed to reach millions of readers through his eleven books, frequent articles in *National Review* and *Nation's Business*, and the 500-plus newspapers that ran "A Conservative View," he managed to reach an even larger audience during his nine years as a pundit on CBS's *60 Minutes*. During his tenure there during the 1970s, he faced off against a left-wing counterpart on the show's weekly "Point Counterpoint" feature. He also has appeared on numerous other political talk shows, including *Inside Washington* and *Meet the Press*.

By the time of Ronald Reagan's election to the presidency, Kilpatrick slowly began to turn his attention—and his writings—to matters beyond the Beltway. In 1981 he began writing a column called "The Writer's Art," which he uses to discuss proper usage of the English language. In 1992 he gave up "A Conservative View" for good, and has since moved on to a slower, semi-retired life.

—Scott Rubush

Further Reading

Kilpatrick, James Jackson. *The Sovereign States: Notes of a Citizen of Virginia.* Chicago: Regnery, 1957.

See also: states' rights

Kimball, Roger (1953–)

Roger Kimball is an accomplished essayist and cultural commentator. From 1989 to 2005, he was managing editor of the *New Criterion,* a magazine he now coedits. A widely published author, his books include *Tenured Radicals: How Politics Has Corrupted Our Higher Education* (1990), *The Long March: How the Cultural Revolution of the 1960s Changed America* (2000), and *Experiments against Reality: The Fate of Culture in the Postmodern Age* (2000).

After graduating from Bennington College in 1975 with majors in philosophy and ancient Greek, Kimball studied and taught at Yale. He began contributing to the *New Criterion* in October 1983 with a review of Jacques Barzun's *A Stroll with William James* (1983). In November 1989 he followed Erich Eichman as managing editor of the magazine, while continuing to contribute cultural commentary, art criticism, book reviews, and articles on history and philosophy to its pages. Along with great technical improvements in the mechanics of editing and production, Kimball has brought to the *New Criterion* a detailed chronicling of the culture wars of the later twentieth and early twenty-first centuries, especially in academe. He has also added a seasoning of academic philoso-

phy, as when introducing his readers to the Australian philosopher David Stove. In 2005 Kimball was tapped to be the new publisher of Encounter Books.

—John Derbyshire

Further Reading

Kimball, Roger. *Art's Prospect: The Challenge of Tradition in an Age of Celebrity.* Chicago: Ivan R. Dee, 2003.
———. *Lives of the Mind: The Use and Abuse of Intelligence from Hegel to Wodehouse.* Chicago: Ivan R. Dee, 2002.

See also: New Criterion

Kirk, Russell (1918–94)

One of the principal founders of the post-World War II conservative intellectual revival, Russell Kirk is the author of numerous books on political theory, intellectual history, education, cultural criticism, and supernatural tales. His examination and vigorous defense of tradition, order, and "the permanent things" helped shape the substance and direction of the conservative movement in America.

Born near a railway station in Plymouth, Michigan, a small suburb of Detroit, this son of a railroad engineer spent his childhood mostly among his mother's people in the tiny village of Mecosta situated in the "stump country" of upstate Michigan. He resided there in his ancestral home, "Piety Hill," with his wife Annette and their four daughters until his death on April 29, 1994.

Kirk took his bachelor of arts degree in history at Michigan State College (now University) in 1940. The following year, he received his M.A. in history from Duke University. While at Duke, he studied the politics of John Randolph of Roanoke. His book on this Virginia planter-statesman, *Randolph of Roanoke: A Study in Conservative Thought*

(1951) would endure as one of his most important contributions to contemporary conservative literature. While researching Randolph's politics, Kirk discovered the far more powerful conservative thinker, Edmund Burke, whose principles would strongly influence his subsequent thought.

He left Duke in 1941 to work briefly at the Rouge plant of the Ford Motor Company before entering the U.S. Army. During World War II he attained the rank of staff sergeant in the Chemical Warfare Service in the Great Salt Lake Desert. After his discharge, he became an instructor in the history of civilization at Michigan State. He took a leave of absence from teaching in 1946 to research at St. Andrews University, Scotland, the history of the principal conservative thinkers of England and America. The resulting manuscript, titled "The Conservatives' Rout," earned him in 1952 the degree of Doctor of Letters. Henry Regnery published this lengthy study, retitled *The Conservative Mind*, in 1953.

The critical success of *The Conservative Mind* catapulted this thirty-five-year-old college professor into national prominence. In the next five years he published six more major works and became widely recognized as a formidable rising young literary and social critic. *Newsweek* magazine took note of his achievements and hailed him as "one of the foremost intellectual spokesmen for the conservative position." *Time* magazine, echoing this opinion, praised him as "a gifted and sorely needed spokesman" for American conservatism. He continued to publish books, articles, and columns at a remarkable rate during the subsequent de-

Russell Kirk

cades of his active writing. By the end of his life, he had written twenty-six nonfiction works; three novels; three books of collected short stories; approximately 2,000 articles, essays, and reviews; 2,687 short articles for his nationally syndicated newspaper column, "To the Point" (1962–75); and a monthly *National Review* column, "From the Academy" (1955–81), assessing the decay of American education. The Russell Kirk Center for Cultural Renewal was founded after his death to provide students and scholars interested in Kirk's thought and works a place to study and do research. Situated at Piety Hill, the center hosts seminars and publishes the *University Bookman*, a quarterly journal of book reviews founded by Kirk.

Dismayed by the decay of academic standards at Michigan State College, Kirk resigned from its faculty in 1953 to become an independent man of letters. When not in his private library in Mecosta researching and writing, he lectured at colleges, seminars, and conferences around the country. He especially enjoyed addressing college audiences, believing strongly that the key to the lasting triumph of conservative ideas lay in shaping the cultural and moral beliefs of the rising generation.

The concept of the "moral imagination" formed the basis of Kirk's attack on ideologies of both the Left and Right. This term, coined by Burke and used later by Paul Elmer More and Irving Babbitt as a philosophical concept to be applied as a response to modern ideological challenges, refers to man's intuitive power to perceive ethical truths and abiding law in the midst of the seeming chaos of experience. Imagination, not calculating reason, Kirk held, elevates man above the beasts. The primary conflict of our time exists not between competing programs for the material betterment of mankind, but between opposing types of imagination. The idyllic imagination of Rousseau and the rationalistic utilitarian imagination of Jeremy Bentham inspired the virulent ideologies that continue to threaten the moral and political foundations of Western social and moral order. Kirk especially condemned the utilitarians for failing to acknowledge the existence of an ethical standard beyond mere self-interest. In his understanding of the moral foundations of traditional conservatism, Kirk freely admitted his indebtedness to Edmund Burke and other thinkers presented in *The Conservative Mind* whose contributions he believed formed a conservative political tradition.

While he cautioned against the excessive growth of centralized governmental authority, Kirk stressed that government and society ought properly to serve man's civilized objectives. For Kirk, true conservatism entailed recognition of man's spiritual and social nature. Strongly critical of the atomistic individualism embraced by many libertarians, Kirk argued for a community of spirit in which generations are bound together by a shared acknowledgment of those enduring universal moral norms that form the basis of genuine civilized existence. "The permanent things," reflected in religious dogma, traditions, humane letters, social habit and custom, and prescriptive institutions, nurture the roots of genuine community—the final end of politics.

In his account of human nature, Kirk conceived of man as a flawed creature, his character mingled with good and evil, original sin accounting for man's proclivity toward selfishness and arbitrariness. "Men's appetites are voracious and sanguinary," he held, and must be "restrained by this collective and immemorial wisdom we call prejudice, tradition, customary morality."

Traditions play an indispensable role in developing man's moral nature. "Traditions are the wisdom of the race; they are the only sure instruments of moral instruction . . . ," wrote Kirk, "and they teach us the solemn veneration of the eternal contract which cannot be imparted by pure reason." A reliance on tradition, the funded wisdom of humanity, enables us to escape what T. S. Eliot called "the provincialism of time." Kirk adopted as axiomatic Burke's principle that the "individual is foolish; but the species is wise." "The permanent things," he wrote, "are derived from the experience of the species, the ancient usages of humanity, and from the perceptions of genius, of those rare men who have seen profoundly into the human condition—and whose wisdom soon is accepted by the mass of men, down the generations."

When we speak of traditions, explained Kirk, "we mean prescriptive social habits, prejudices, customs and political usages which most people accept with little question, as an intellectual legacy from their ancestors." They are accepted by the greater bulk of people as good because of their long standing. The fact that the previous generation has maintained these traditions to be transmitted to the rising generation gives them a certain authority, a presumption in their favor.

Kirk's defense of the role of tradition does not imply, as some of his critics have contended, a romantic longing for a lost golden age or a rigid resistance to all change. Rather, Kirk stressed that the work of genuine reform must take place within the context of sound tradition. "Traditions do take on new meanings with the growing experience of a people," he wrote, "And simply to appeal to the wisdom of the species, to tradition, will not of itself provide solutions for all problems. The endeavor of the intelligent believer in tradition is so to blend ancient usage with necessary amendment that society never is wholly old and never wholly new." Therefore, in a healthy society, he held, "tradition must be balanced by some strong element of curiosity and individual dissent." The task of the statesman finally is to preserve and reform at the same time.

Kirk primarily blamed modern industrialization and urbanization for the decay of tradition. The impulse for change, in Kirk's estimation, came largely from cities, where people are uprooted and detached from community and the fellowship of those with whom they share bonds of kinship and common experience. Conservatism, accordingly, prospers best in smaller, more stable communities where men are slow to break with the old ways that tie them to past generations and their religious foundations. "Tradition thrives where men follow naturally in the ways of their fathers, and live in the same houses," Kirk observed, "and experience in their lives that continuity of existence which assures them that the great things in human nature do not alter much from one generation to another." Hence, the guardians of tradition have been "recruited principally, although not wholly from our farms and small towns."

Although his work helped to launch a political and intellectual movement, because of his singular lack of interest in hobnobbing with either power brokers or literary moguls Kirk was virtually snubbed by the intellectual and media establishment. His influence instead can be best measured by the scores of disciples who came to Piety Hill to study and live and went forth to careers in education, communications, publishing, the church, and government.

Kirk's enduring reputation as a major thinker of the twentieth century is assured as a consequence of his rediscovery and persuasive expression of a living conservative intellectual tradition. He was responsible for drawing conservatism away from utilitarian and individualistic premises, toward which it had veered in the 1950s, to a position rooted in community-conserving norms and culture. More broadly, he contended with considerable effect against the challenges of ideologies of both the Left and Right to the enduring moral and social order of Western civilization.

—W. WESLEY MCDONALD

Further Reading

Kirk, Russell A. *Enemies of the Permanent Things: Observations of Abnormity in Literature and Politics.* New Rochelle, N.Y.: Arlington House, 1969.

———. *The Politics of Prudence.* Bryn Mawr, Pa.: Intercollegiate Studies Institute, 1993.

———. *The Roots of American Order.* 4th ed. Wilmington, Del.: ISI Books, 2003.

———. *The Sword of Imagination: Memoirs of a Half-Century of Literary Conflict.* Grand Rapids, Mich.: Eerdmans, 1995.

McDonald, W. Wesley. *Russell Kirk and the Age of Ideology.* Columbia, Mo.: University of Missouri Press, 2004.

Person, James E., ed. *Russell Kirk: A Critical Biography of a Conservative Mind.* Lanham, Md.: Madison Books, 1999.

See also: Burkean conservatism; Conservative Mind, The; *historicism;* Modern Age; *movement conservatism;* Old Right; *prejudice;* Roman Catholicism; *tradition; traditionalism;* University Bookman

Kirkpatrick, Jeane J. (1926–)

Jeane Kirkpatrick rose to prominence as an unabashed proponent of U.S. national interests and democracy while serving as U.S. permanent representative to the United Nations (1981–85). A noted political scientist and neoconservative commentator, Kirkpatrick is currently Leavey Professor of Government at Georgetown University and a senior fellow at the American Enterprise Institute.

Kirkpatrick has authored six books, several monographs, and numerous articles on

American foreign policy, party politics, and political theory. She espouses a public philosophy based on "realism," holding that philosophical or political inquiry must have a solid empirical foundation. Following Aristotle, she looks to what "is" as well as to what "ought to be." Kirkpatrick warns against "rationalism," which rests on belief in human perfectibility and the practicability of abstract principles, and which focuses on utopian goals rather than empirical problem-solving. Since rationalists presume special understanding of the needs and interests of others, they often use power to impose their views upon the polity. Thus, Kirkpatrick suggests, rationalism conduces to tyranny.

A self-described "welfare-state conservative," Kirkpatrick is qualifiedly optimistic about the capability of a democratic government to contribute to building a good society. Under conditions of urbanization, industrialization, and globalization some problems resist solution except by government. Applied prudently, state power can promote both liberty *and* equality, which Kirkpatrick—unlike many conservatives—views as compatible when pursued in moderation. She urges respect for tradition but rejects outmoded or pernicious customs (especially sexual and racial discrimination) that she views as incompatible with democratic values. Kirkpatrick calls for an assertive foreign policy based on realistic assessments of threats to U.S. national interests, forthright defense of those interests, promotion of democratic values, and avoidance of utopian double standards that concede too much to the enemy.

A longtime Democrat, Kirkpatrick supported the presidential candidacies of Senators Hubert H. Humphrey and Henry M. (Scoop) Jackson. In 1972, she and other neoconservative Democrats founded the Coalition for a Democratic Majority (CDM) to resist the party's McGovernite tilt. In 1980 she joined Ronald Reagan's campaign team and in January 1981 became the first woman in his cabinet, serving until 1985. In that year she formally changed party affiliation, explaining that the Democratic Party did not represent her views and had not for more than a decade.

—TIMOTHY GOODMAN

Further Reading

Kirkpatrick, Jeane J. *The Withering Away of the Totalitarian State . . . and Other Surprises*. Washington, D.C.: American Enterprise Institute, 1990.

———. *The Reagan Phenomenon*. Washington, D.C.: American Enterprise Institute, 1983.

———. *Dictatorships and Double Standards: Rationalism and Reason in Politics*. New York: Simon & Schuster, 1982.

See also: neoconservatism; Reagan Doctrine

Knight, Frank H. (1885–1972)

A leading economist of the "Chicago school," Frank Knight was born on a farm in Illinois. After going to college in Tennessee, he received his Ph.D. from Cornell University in 1916. He then taught at the University of Iowa before moving to Chicago in 1927. His main economic research concentrated on the theory of entrepreneurial profit, with his most important results contained in *Risk, Uncertainty and Profit* (1921). His approach to profit, analogous to that of Joseph Schumpeter, pointed out that the profits of capitalists are not similar to the returns to labor and the rent of capital. Rather, profits are inherently uncertain, and so the task of the capitalist cannot be reduced to that of a passive investor. Knight's theory emphasizes the importance of capitalist innovators in a market economy. Naturally, he saw socialistic schemes that relied on "rational planning" as inherently wrongheaded.

Knight played an important role in several controversies regarding capital theory. He was a strong opponent of Austrian capital theory, particularly that associated with Eugen von Bohm-Bawerk, and he was able to largely discredit this theory by his attacks in the 1930s.

Knight also made an important critique of Arthur Pigou's theory of externalities. In developing the theory of external effects, Pigou emphasized the role of taxes in bringing external effects under control. Knight showed that Pigou's solutions were incorrect, and that a more fundamental approach would define the fundamental property rights involved. If the property rights could be properly defined and enforced, then market contracting would internalize the externalities and the free-market solution would be efficient. This line of reasoning was carried further by Ronald Coase in his fundamental work on how efficient contracting could eliminate externalities (which won him the Nobel Prize in 1991), and by Harold Demsetz in his work on the development of new property-rights rules to internalize externalities. Knight's fundamental point is that government control of external effects like pollution is unnecessary in many cases. If government will enforce private property rights, private markets will internalize these costs more effectively than will government. This remains the basic position of economists, in opposition to the government-based schemes proposed by environmentalists.

While Knight was foremost an economist, he was also a philosopher of the Socratic type. He loved argument and disputation, and most enjoyed showing that something widely believed to be true really was not. Perhaps he should be called a skeptical inquirer. Students and colleagues remember him as raising philosophical issues in what might otherwise seem down-to-earth economics, particularly in the introductory economics graduate courses at Chicago. His style of inquiry was that of the common-sense farmer or stubborn Yankee who was not to be taken in by highfalutin nonsense. Thus, his philosophical conservatism was that of the critic of impractical or dangerous public-policy experiments.

His basic philosophical position was to favor freedom. This view followed directly from his view that the essential quality of human life was uncertainty—fundamental uncertainty. People responded with activity, making choices, in the face of ignorance. Knight suggested that much activity, including economic activity, could be seen as games that people engaged in as a form of play. While Knight emphasized human autonomy, he was not a libertarian, as he also pointed out the social and evolutionary nature of human beings. To Knight, our nature contains basic contradictions.

In addition to his research accomplishments, Frank Knight was a great teacher. He inspired generations of young economists at the University of Chicago, such as George Stigler. Stigler emphasizes Knight's passion for the pursuit of the truth, and his concentration on the great issues of the economy and society. These have remained characteristic elements of the "Chicago school" approach to this day.

—Kenneth Koford

Further Reading

"In Memoriam, Frank Knight." *Journal of Political Economy* 82 (1973).

"Frank Knight in Retrospect." *Journal of Political Economy* 83 (1974).

Knight, Frank H. *The Ethics of Competition.* New York: Harper, 1936.

———. *Freedom and Reform: Essays in Economic and Social Philosophy.* New York: Harper, 1947.

———. *On the History and Method of Economics.* Chicago: University of Chicago Press, 1956.

See also: Becker, Gary S.; property rights, private; Stigler, George J.

Koch, Charles G., Charitable Foundation

A foundation established by one of the owners of Koch Industries (not to be confused with the separate, but related, David H. Koch Foundation or Fred C. and Mary R. Koch Foundation), the Charles G. Koch Foundation has a long record of financial commitments to active and diversified philanthropic programs. Led by president Richard Fink and vice president Kevin Gentry, the foundation espouses a philosophy committed to advancing prosperity, opportunities, peace, and freedom through economic growth and improving standards of living.

The foundation expressly rejects any particular partisan approach because it does not wish to preclude the possibility of learning from the rich array of alternative views available in the marketplace of ideas. But although the foundation does not consider itself in any particular ideological camp, its philanthropic philosophy reflects many of the key components of the modern American conservative movement. Furthermore, its charitable acts have laid the foundation for the education of many young people who have gone on to make significant contributions to conservatism and to the creation of a more humane society.

The foundation, or in some cases Koch himself, provided the original startup funds for many of America's most influential conservative organizations. (Koch is the CEO and chairman of the board of Koch Industries, one of the nation's largest privately held companies.) Included among these are the Cato Institute, Institute for Justice, the Mercatus Center, and the Bill of Rights Institute. In addition, the Koch Foundation has supported the Institute for Humane Studies (IHS) for over three decades. Thanks to the foundation's support, Humane Studies Fellowships and the Charles Koch Summer Fellow Program have together assisted more than 1,000 students pursuing careers in academia and public policy.

—Craig T. Cobane

See also: Cato Institute; Institute for Humane Studies

Koestler, Arthur (1905–83)

Arthur Koestler was a polymath writer best known for *Darkness at Noon* (1940), a novel that with devastating force describes the Stalinist show trials through the eyes of Rubashov, an Old Bolshevik falsely accused of treason who finds himself trapped by a True Believer's faith in the logic of the communist dialectic. Rubashov is forced to make confession as "the last service the Party will ask of you," and is executed in the Lubyanka Prison with a bullet to the back of his head.

Koestler was born in Budapest of middle-class Jewish parents. He attended university in Vienna, majoring in physics and engineering. Bored with school, he became a Zionist and moved to Palestine, beginning a peripatetic and sometimes quixotic intellectual life. Bored with the insular Zionist community after a couple of years, he moved first to Paris and then to Berlin, where he worked for a leading liberal German newspaper. He quickly was promoted to science editor, then editor of foreign affairs. Bored with elections, and horrified as he watched Europe descend into depression and the Nazis ascend to power, Koestler began to read Marx, Engels, and Lenin, joined the Communist Party, and became a spy. "To say that one has 'seen the light' is a poor description of the mental rapture which only the convert knows," he later wrote: "It was a satisfactory and blissful state.... [Y]ou were no longer disturbed by facts.... Both morally and logically, the Party was infallible: morally, because its aims were right, that is, in accord with the Dialectic of History, and these aims justified all means; logically, because the Party was the vanguard of the proletariat, and the proletariat the embodiment of the active principle in History." From twenty years' perspective, he added: "Faith is a wondrous thing; it is not only capable of moving mountains, but also of making you believe that a herring is a racehorse."

Koestler covered the Spanish Civil War for the communists, writing brilliant fact-based propaganda. After several narrow escapes, he was captured by Franco's forces and jailed for months, every day expecting to be executed, every night listening as his fellow prisoners were taken, crying for their mothers, and shot. There he began his journey out of communism. He described his transformation thusly: "The lesson taught by this type of experience, when put into words, always appears under the dowdy guise of perennial commonplaces: that man is a reality, mankind an abstraction ... [,] that ethics is not a function of social utility, and charity not a petty-bourgeois sentiment but the gravitational force which keeps civilization in its orbit. Nothing can sound more flatfooted than such verbalizations of a knowledge which is not of a verbal nature; yet every single one of these trivial statements was incompatible with the Communist faith which I held."

During World War II, Koestler published *Darkness at Noon* and *Arrival and Departure* (1943), novels that dramatically analyzed the appeals of communism and Nazism, the latter also the first book to describe the early stages of Hitler's Final Solution, when Jews were gassed in the back of vans. Following the war, Koestler contributed the lead essay to *The God That Failed* (1949), in which he de-

Arthur Koestler

scribed communism's quasi-religious power and appeal. In 1955, he announced that he had said all he had to say about totalitarianism: "Now the errors are atoned, the bitter passion has burnt itself out, Cassandra has gone hoarse—let others carry on." He wrote on the history of science, parapsychology, and Lamarckian biology, and took up crusades to abolish capital punishment, allow pets to reenter England without months of quarantine, remove the stigma from suicide, and whatever else caught his interest. Ill with Parkinson's and leukemia, Koestler committed suicide along with his wife in 1983.

Koestler's epitaph might have been taken from an incident in the 1960s, at a time when his native Hungary had begun to liberalize from the hardcore Stalinism that followed its Soviet-crushed bid for freedom in 1956. Koestler asked a Hungarian cultural attaché what would happen were he to return for a visit. He was told, "We would welcome you with pride, but we could not guarantee your safety. You are on a very short list of those whom the Soviet Union cannot come to terms with. *Darkness at Noon* is as dangerous today as it was a generation ago. . . . It is a very tiny list, but you are on it."

—ROBERT WATERS

Further Reading

Hamilton, Iain. *Koestler: A Biography.* New York: Macmillan, 1982.

Koestler, Arthur. *Arrow in the Blue.* New York: Macmillan, 1952.

See also: anticommunism; fascism; God That Failed, The

Kors, Alan C. (1943–)

A distinguished senior scholar of European history, Alan Charles Kors is also active as a leading advocate for academic freedom. After graduating summa cum laude from Princeton University in 1964, Kors received an M.A. (1965) and a Ph.D. (1968) in European history from Harvard University, where he was awarded the Danforth, Woodrow Wilson, and Harvard Prize fellowships. He joined the department of history at the University of Pennsylvania in 1968 as an assistant professor. He was appointed associate professor in 1974 and full professor in 1988.

A leading authority on early modern European intellectual and Enlightenment history, Kors has published and spoken widely on such topics as the origins of the modern mind in seventeenth-century Western thought, the intellectual origins of the American Republic, theology and skepticism in early modern France, British philosophy and politics in the seventeenth and eighteenth centuries, and toleration and atheism.

Kors is the author of numerous scholarly books and articles including *Atheism in France, 1650–1729* (1990) and *D'Holbach's Coterie: An Enlightenment in Paris* (1976). Kors serves as editor in chief of *The Encyclopedia of the Enlightenment* for Oxford University Press.

In 1998 Kors and Harvey Silverglate coauthored *The Shadow University: The Betrayal of Liberty on America's Campuses*, which focused national attention on problems of academic freedom at American universities. Their efforts led to the establishment of the Foundation for Individual Rights in Education (FIRE), of which Kors has been president and codirector since 1999. He has published frequently on matters of academic freedom in the *Wall Street Journal, Reason, Academic Questions,* and other leading journals of opinion.

The emphasis Kors places on the intellectual foundations of a free and ordered society underscores his promotion of the ideas of limited government, individual responsibility, and the rule of law. In recognition of his many efforts, Kors was appointed to the National Council on the Humanities in 1992, where he served until 1998. In 1995 Kors was given the Engalitcheff Award for Defense of Academic Freedom. It seems certain that he will be known to history as one of the nation's most principled, articulate, and persistent defenders of individual freedom in academia at a time when that freedom was gravely threatened.

—INGRID GREGG

Further Reading

Kors, Alan Charles, and Paul J. Korshin, eds. *Anticipations of the Enlightenment in England, France, and Germany.* Philadelphia: University of Pennsylvania Press, 1987

Kors, Alan Charles, and Edward Peters, eds. *Witchcraft in Europe, 400–1700: A Documentary History.* 2nd ed. Philadelphia: University of Pennsylvania Press, 2001.

See also: academic freedom; education, higher; liberalism, classical

Kramer, Hilton (1928–)

Art critic and cultural commentator, Hilton Kramer was cofounder of the *New Criterion* and has remained editor of that magazine from its first issue.

Kramer's career as a full-time intellectual began in 1953 when *Partisan Review,* then at the peak of its influence, published his first piece of art criticism. He continued to write art criticism for *Partisan Review,* and also for *Art Digest,* through the 1950s and early 1960s, developing a distinctive voice that was open to modernism when it strove to add to the great tradition of artistic endeavor but was critical of artists who altogether repudiated that tradition or held it up to ridicule. Through his work as a critic, Kramer came to know the key figures in the literary, artistic, and intellectual life of the time. (He was the original for the minor character Magnasco in Saul Bellow's novel *Humboldt's Gift* [1975].) From 1965 to 1982 Kramer was art critic at the *New York Times* and observed with many misgivings that newspaper's efforts to broaden its appeal during the 1970s. Striking up a friendship with Samuel Lipman, then music critic at *Commentary*, Kramer suggested they start their own review, and the *New Criterion* was born in 1982, with Lipman as publisher and Kramer as editor. Kramer has continued his work as an art critic (for the *New York Observer*, since 1987), and from 1993 to 1997 wrote a column titled "Timeswatch" for the *New York Post*, pointing out errors and absurdities in that newspaper's much grander rival. Kramer also has written, cowritten, and edited more than ten books, the most important of which are probably his *Age of the Avant-Garde: An Art Chronicle of 1956–1972* (1973), *Revenge of the Philistines: Art and Culture, 1972–1984* (1985), and *Twilight of the Intellectuals: Culture and Politics in the Era of the Cold War* (1999).

—JOHN DERBYSHIRE

Further Reading

Kramer, Hilton, and Roger Kimball, eds. *The Betrayal of Liberalism: How the Disciples of Freedom and Equality Helped Foster the Illiberal Politics of Coercion and Control.* Chicago: Ivan R. Dee, 1999.

Kimball, Roger, and Hilton Kramer, eds. *Lengthened Shadows: America and Its Institutions in the Twenty-First Century.* San Francisco: Encounter Books, 2004.

See also: New Criterion

Kristol, Irving (1920–)

Irving Kristol was the major intellectual inspiration, and remains one of the most influential voices, of the phenomenon labeled "neoconservatism." In contrast to many others who were described by this term, Kristol accepted it for himself, and as much as any individual in the 1970s and 1980s he helped give substance to it.

Kristol embodied the classic model of the neoconservative. He was born in Brooklyn and grew up in a poor Jewish family from Eastern Europe. At the City College of New York he identified with the Trotskyist wing of the radical students and professors, in opposition to the Stalinist Communist Party loyalists. Here began his deep roots with the "New York Intellectuals," many of whom, like him, would gravitate toward conservatism in later years.

Kristol fought in Europe during the Second World War and married the historian Gertrude Himmelfarb. Kristol's growing alienation from the Left was clearly visible in the early 1950s when he refused to join the vociferous attacks on Joseph McCarthy. From 1947 to 1952, as managing editor of *Commentary*, Kristol strove to alert readers to the dangers of communism. In 1953, in London, he started *Encounter* magazine with Stephen Spender under the sponsorship of the Congress for Cultural Freedom, a liberal anticommunist organization sponsored by the Central Intelligence Agency. His place in neoconservatism was fully evident by 1965 when, with Daniel Bell, he began publication of the *Public Interest*. This journal utilized empirical studies in the social sciences to deflate the ambitious political programs and reformist social agenda of the Great Society initiatives. It addressed such subjects as urban renewal, housing, taxation, and education. The *Public Interest* deliberately avoided questions of foreign policy because of the controversy surrounding the Vietnam War at the time, but in 1985 Kristol cofounded the journal *National Interest* to address foreign affairs. In 1972 and afterward he was a contributing editor to the *Wall Street Journal*.

Although Kristol's political views had for some time been shifting away from liberalism, it was in 1972 that he first acquired the title "neoconservative." For many years a loyalist of the Democratic Party, Kristol broke ranks when it chose George McGovern as its presidential nominee. Unwilling to endorse McGovern's foreign policy, Kristol voted Republican, creating a stir in liberal circles. Kristol was not alone, of course, in his movement away from the New Left, but rather was accompanied by fellow intellectuals such as Norman Podhoretz and Nathan Glazer.

Irving Kristol

Kristol became a professor at New York University in 1969, where he taught social thought until 1988. Since then, he has been a senior fellow at the American Enterprise Institute. He remained senior editorial associate of the *Public Interest* until its final issue in the spring of 2005 and continues to serve as a member of the Council on Foreign Relations, with which he has been associated since 1972.

Kristol advanced his conservative ideas mostly through essays, many of which were collected into books. Of these, the most important were *On the Democratic Idea in America* (1972), *Two Cheers for Capitalism* (1978), and *Reflections of a Neoconservative* (1983). Like many neoconservatives, Kristol advocated a strong American foreign policy to meet the threat of the Soviet Union. He made national interest the first priority of American policy, subordinating it to human rights concerns. Although Kristol showed a commitment to a free-enterprise economy and accepted as a fact the death of socialism, he registered a clear ambivalence about capitalism and the society it had produced. He distinguished between the bourgeois moral ethic, based on the traditional values of work, saving, and delayed gratification, and the capitalistic ethic, which was materialistic and hedonist.

Kristol insisted that capitalism had once established its legitimacy on the bourgeois ethic, but it had eroded to the point that American society had become vulgar and self-indulgent. In his lament at this condition, Kristol sometimes echoed Victorian standards of moral judgment. He considered contemporary bourgeois society prosaic and unheroic. And he believed that institutional religion was American society's only hope for a recovery from its spiritual malaise. Perhaps this contributed to his decision, late in life, to become a practicing Jew.

—J. David Hoeveler Jr.

Further Reading

DeMuth, Christopher, and William Kristol, eds. *The Neoconservative Imagination: Essays in Honor of Irving Kristol.* Washington, D.C.: AEI Press, 1995.

Hoeveler, J. David, Jr. *Watch on the Right: Conservative Intellectuals in the Reagan Era.* Madison, Wis.: University of Wisconsin Press, 1991.

Norman, Geoffrey. "The Godfather of New Conservatism (and His Family)." *Esquire* 91 (1979): 7–42.

Steinfels, Peter. *The Neoconservatives: The Men Who Are Changing America's Politics.* New York: Simon & Schuster, 1979.

See also: Commentary; Jewish conservatives; movement conservatism; neoconservatism; nihilism; Public Interest

Kristol, William (1952–)

Born in New York City and educated at Harvard University, Bill Kristol was out of step with his predominantly liberal and leftist classmates, three-quarters of whom supported George McGovern in the presidential election of 1972. But he enjoyed political debate and seemed impervious to insult. He denounced the "mindless conformism" of the campus Left, supported the war against communism in Vietnam, and would have no truck with fellow students as they stormed campus offices and shouted down visiting speakers.

In taking issue with liberal baby boomers, Kristol was his parents' son. His historian mother, Gertrude Himmelfarb, was a critic of the sexually promiscuous cultural elite that had rejected traditional values in the England of Queen Victoria. His father, Irving Kristol, was a leading figure in an intellectual circle of former liberals and leftists ("neoconservatives") who denounced the counterculture that engulfed America after the 1960s. For Irving Kristol, there was no "after the Cold War." Like his parents, Bill Kristol abhorred nonjudgmentalism and relativism. At various times, he said that abortion was morally wrong, that the nation's high rate of illegitimacy was a tragedy, and that the new biotechnology—human cloning, etc.—threatened humanity.

At Harvard, Kristol's graduate professor Harvey Mansfield was a leading follower of the twentieth-century philosopher Leo Strauss. Like Mansfield and Strauss, Kristol emphasized that the virtue of a citizenry was even more important than equality, prosperity, or personal freedom. Unlike other social conservatives, the Straussians did not derive their emphasis on virtue from religion but from reason, and as a young man Kristol thought that faith was for others, not himself. Later he returned to the synagogue of his family heritage, but during both his secular and Jewish phases he rejected relativism, condemned immorality, and extolled the importance of virtue.

After teaching political philosophy for a few years, Kristol joined the Reagan administration as an assistant to William Bennett, the secretary of education. Later, he became Vice President Dan Quayle's chief of staff and, in 1995, he was the founding editor of the *Weekly Standard*. In each job he has emphasized the importance of moral virtue, but he also has established positions at odds with some other conservatives. Thus, for example, Kristol never intended to abolish the Department of Education, but rather to deploy it against progressive education. And on foreign policy he has emphasized not narrow national interests but universal principles of human rights. He has viewed the military and commercial might of the United States as an appropriate vehicle for propagating those principles, and so has been an enthusiastic advocate of the Iraq War and, with David Brooks, public policies founded on the ideal of "national greatness." A frequent television commentator on Fox News, he is the unquestioned intellectual leader of the hawkish wing of the Washington neoconservative establishment.

—RAYMOND WOLTERS

Further Reading

Easton, Nina J. *Gang of Five: Leaders at the Center of the Conservative Crusade*. New York: Simon & Schuster, 2000.

Kagan, Robert, and William Kristol, eds. *Present Dangers: Crisis and Opportunity in American Foreign and Defense Policy*. San Francisco: Encounter Books, 2000.

Kaplan, Lawrence F., and William Kristol. *The War over Iraq: Saddam's Tyranny and America's Mission*. San Francisco: Encounter Books, 2003.

Kristol, William, and Eric Cohen, eds. *The Future Is Now: America Confronts the New Genetics*. Lanham, Md.: Rowman & Littlefield, 2002.

See also: *Iraq War;* Weekly Standard; *neoconservatism*

Kuehnelt-Leddihn, Erik von (1909–99)

Catholic political thinker, novelist, and artist, Erik von Kuehnelt-Leddihn was best known for his radical critique of leftism and his unorthodox defense of an "ideological" Right. Born in Austria, he took his doctorate at the University of Budapest and subsequently served, for brief periods, on the faculties at Georgetown, Fordham, and Chestnut Hill. After 1947, he earned his living as a lecturer and contributor to conservative journals

Erik von Kuehnelt-Leddihn

around the world. In the United States, he was most closely associated with *National Review.*

Kuehnelt-Leddihn regularly took time out from his busy schedule to travel. Over the course of his life he visited virtually every country in the world. This wanderlust and his determination to master foreign languages date to his earliest years, when he first marveled at the Austro-Hungarian monarchy's mosaic of peoples, cultures, and languages. That wonder also created in him a hatred of the totalitarian drive for identity, sameness, and uniformity. Men and women were in their element, he believed, only when they could savor life's variety, the fruit of human liberty. "All varieties of curiosity for the new—the eagerness to travel, to eat other food, to hear different music, to get in touch with varied cultures and civilizations—derive," he wrote in *Leftism Revisited* (1990), "from the tendency to diversify."

Because of his passion for diversity and for the liberty that is its sine qua non,

Kuehnelt-Leddihn described himself as a liberal in the tradition of Alexis de Tocqueville and Jacob Burckhardt, or an anarchist in the tradition of Pierre Joseph Proudhon and Henry Adams. Those noble traditions, he argued, were of the Right, for they stood in stark contrast to the Left, which had *its* roots in democracy. In modern form, he pointed out, democracy owed its birth to the French Revolution, a primal act of rebellion not only against monarchical order, but against God. Once loosed upon the world, democracy soon transformed itself, with a logic both consistent and murderous, into socialism—international and national. Contrary to received opinion, that is, Kuehnelt-Leddihn regarded these revolutionary movements as rivals rather than enemies, brothers under the skin; like their progenitor, democracy, they were both identitarian ideologies of the Left. That is why the Hitler-Stalin Pact should have occasioned no surprise.

For Kuehnelt-Leddihn, then, democracy was not the antidote to totalitarianism. The Wilsonian idea of global democracy filled him with horror and disgust. At the same time, he did not think it enough to speak in Burkean accents of political common sense and respect for historical tradition. Rather, he believed that false ideologies could only be put to rout by a true one. If the democratic—leftist—ideology was to be driven from the field, right-thinking people would have to articulate a "Free World ideology," by which Kuehnelt-Leddihn meant "a coherent set of ideas about God, Man and the world without inner contradictions and well-rooted in eternal principles." In pursuance of that end, he compiled twenty-six propositions, "The Portland Declaration" (1982), as a basis for public discussion. To that

483

"rightist" creed he devoted his distinctive talents to the end.

—LEE CONGDON

Further Reading

Kuehnelt-Leddihn, Erik von. *Black Banners*. Caldwell, Idaho: Caxton Printers, 1954.

———. *Liberty or Equality: The Challenge of Our Time*. Front Royal, Va.: Christendom Press, 1993.

See also: anarchism; democracy; equality; liberalism, classical; liberty

Kuyper, Abraham (1837–1920)

In his ambitious commitment to a comprehensive reform of politics and culture, the Dutch statesman, theologian, journalist, and academician Abraham Kuyper embodied perhaps the starkest orthodox Protestant alternative to Christian social pietism. Kuyper's legacy is not limited to The Netherlands. His impact upon contemporary American evangelicalism and the "religious Right" arguably exceeds his enduring influence in his homeland.

After receiving his doctor of theology degree from the University of Leiden in 1863, Kuyper entered into pastoral ministry. He came to reject the theological liberalism in which he had been schooled and experienced a conversion to an orthodox Calvinism that inspired his pursuit of a seamless integration of religious faith and citizenship.

Kuyper anticipated contemporary notions of "culture war" with his conviction that the intellectual modernism that inspired the French Revolution entailed an understanding of human nature and society antithetical to Christianity. Kuyper believed that only Calvinism provided a sufficient alternative to the challenge of modernism, not simply as a body of doctrinal religious propositions, but as a "world—and life—view."

This sense of the "antithesis" between Christianity and modernism led Kuyper to found a Reformed Calvinist political party—the Anti-Revolutionary Party (ARP). He directed the ARP in thirteen parliamentary campaigns, serving as party leader, member of parliament, and ultimately as prime minister of The Netherlands.

In a public life as wide-ranging as the scope of his worldview, Kuyper added to his work as party organizer and leader with the founding (1872) and editing of a national daily newspaper (*De Standaard*), for which he wrote nearly 5000 front-page editorials. Kuyper also edited another weekly paper (*De Heraut*), and in 1880 he helped to found the Free University of Amsterdam.

Abraham Kuyper

Notwithstanding his insistent critique of modernity, Kuyper enthusiastically embraced a political liberalism in the English Whig tradition, ascribing to it (and to the American experiment) a distinctly Calvinistic Christian pedigree.

To the Reformation belief in a free and unassailable human conscience, Kuyper added an insistence upon human equality and the unique sovereignty of God as the foundations of religious and civil liberty. Kuyper developed a notion of limited government known as "sphere sovereignty," a system that narrowly frames the jurisdiction of the state as an entity that exists not over other social spheres (family, church, scientific enterprise, etc.) but alongside them. For Kuyper, the state enjoys a purely artificial and mechanical status: it exists only to forestall the effects of human sinfulness and maintain the integrity of other, natural and primordial, spheres. Thus, Kuyper's sphere sovereignty both constrains government and provides for robust social pluralism.

In his political efforts to advance the Christian worldview, Kuyper found himself aligned with Roman Catholics against liberal Protestants. His interdenominational social and political cooperation anticipated the "ecumenism of the trenches" that has united conservative American Protestants and Roman Catholics since the Supreme Court's *Roe v. Wade* decision. Kuyper's own ARP never received more than 20 percent of the popular vote, but together with the Roman Catholic party Kuyper wielded enormous political influence and became prime minister from 1901 to 1905.

Through the thought of such figures as J. Gresham Machen, Cornelius Van Til, Francis Schaeffer, Nicholas Wolterstorff, and Chuck Colson, Kuyper continues to bring an appreciation of the Reformed "creation mandate" to American evangelicalism, animating cultural engagement along much the same conceptual divide that inspired his larger-than-life career.

—Douglas Minson

Further Reading

Bolt, John. *A Free Church, a Holy Nation: Abraham Kuyper's American Public Theology.* Grand Rapids, Mich.: W. B. Eerdmans, 2000.

Kuyper, Abraham. *Abraham Kuyper: A Centennial Reader.* Edited by James D. Bratt. Grand Rapids, Mich.: W. B. Eerdmans; 1998.

Lugo, Luis E., ed. *Religion, Pluralism, and Public Life: Abraham Kuyper's Legacy for the Twenty-First Century.* Grand Rapids, Mich.: W. B. Eerdmans, 2000.

See also: modernity and postmodernity; Protestantism, evangelical; Van Til, Cornelius

L

Laffer curve

According to the standard story, economist Arthur Laffer, at the time professor of business economics at the University of Southern California, first sketched his famous curve on a cocktail napkin in the late 1970s. He was trying to make a fairly simple point about tax rates, tax revenues, and economic behavior.

A tax rate of zero will of course earn no revenue. But a marginal rate of 100 percent will also earn, if not quite zero, close enough to make any such revenue negligible. If every additional dollar is completely confiscated, people will flee into alternatives: stop working, shelter their income, engage in fraud, revert to barter—anything but pay the 100 percent rate.

Somewhere between these extremes, therefore, must be a point at which further rate increases paradoxically begin to yield lower government revenue. Laffer referred to this as the "prohibitive range." Since the curve contained no other numbers apart from zero and 100, the determination of where this range lay was a matter of educated speculation.

Although the curve itself was not given explicit formulation until the late 1970s, the idea had precedents in American tax policy. Thus, during the 1920s Treasury Secretary Andrew Mellon was convinced that the wartime tax rates still in force were punitive and economically destructive, and that rate reductions would actually increase net revenue. That is exactly what happened.

The idea of the Laffer curve, popularized by such figures as Jack Kemp and Jude Wanniski, featured prominently in the intellectual apparatus behind the income tax cuts of Ronald Reagan's presidency. Contrary to popular belief, its proponents did not claim that the behavioral changes lower rates would encourage would in every case completely offset the revenue losses that static analysis attributed to a reduction in tax rates. (Reagan's budget expected them to make up for only 17 percent of the lost revenue.) What they did claim is that just as high marginal rates affected behavior (by discouraging investment and business expansion, encouraging the use of tax shelters, and so on), considerable reductions would affect behavior in the other direction. As a result, the increased economic output that would result from the rate cuts would offset some of the revenue loss associated with the lower rates.

Some on the political Right expressed concern that the Laffer curve implicitly presumed that revenue maximization was a desirable outcome and that tax rates ought to be set with this goal in mind; small-government conservatives naturally wondered whether the Laffer curve really represented a triumph for conservative values. But this is not what Laffer meant: his purpose was to show that at some point even liberal Democrats, given the logic of his curve, would have to concede that by their own standards rates were too high.

Laffer's main point, which he considered tautological, has never been refuted, and indeed the 1980s saw modest reductions in top rates even in many European countries.

—THOMAS E. WOODS JR.

Further Reading

Henderson, David. "Limitations of the Laffer Curve as a Justification for Tax Cuts." *Cato Journal* 1, no. 1 (Spring 1981): 45–52.

Wanniski, Jude. *The Way the World Works: How Economies Fail—and Succeed.* New York: Basic Books, 1978.

See also: supply-side economics

Lane, Rose Wilder (1886–1968)

Individualist and libertarian polemicist, journalist and novelist, Rose Wilder Lane was born in De Smet, Dakota Territory (now South Dakota), the daughter of Laura Ingalls Wilder, author of the *Little House* series. Starting her working life in Kansas City as a telegraph operator, Lane moved to California in 1908 and in the early teens started reporting for the *San Francisco Bulletin.* She became one of the most famous journalists of her day, a bestselling novelist, and a well-known and vocal opponent of Roosevelt, the New Deal, and Social Security.

Rose Wilder Lane

In later years, Lane described herself as having been a Christian socialist, supporter of Eugene Debs, and pacifist from 1914 to 1920. In 1917 she became a "convinced, though not practicing, communist," changing her mind after visiting Soviet Russia. In the 1930s and 1940s Lane became more ardently individualistic. Because of her opposition to the income tax and her determination not to pay it, she largely stopped publishing books or magazine articles after 1941. In 1943 she be-

came book-review editor of the National Economic Council's *Review of Books*, a free-market organ. Her two best-known political tracts are *Give Me Liberty* (1936), published in the midst of the Depression, and *The Discovery of Freedom* (1943), published during World War II. In 1965, at the age of 78, she traveled to Vietnam to cover the war for *Woman's Day.*

With Isabel Paterson, Lane was an early financial supporter of Ayn Rand, but once *The Fountainhead* (1943) was published and Rand claimed to have had no help from anyone, she and Lane broke. Lane kept up a voluminous correspondence, and her letters to DuPont executive Jasper Crane, many of which touch on political topics, were published in 1973 under the title *The Lady and the Tycoon.* Her personal influence over men such as Crane and many others in the libertarian movement was considerable. Her wider significance is less as a theorist than as a popularizer; even her novels (such as *Free Land*, published in 1938 and still in print) can be read as arguments for individualism, a belief she grounded in her own family's experience of pioneering and self-reliance. In *The Discovery of Freedom* Lane held that liberty is *"inalienable,"* and she considered illogical the notion that there was any controlling authority outside of the individual. Yet she believed that America had a vital role to play worldwide in promoting freedom, and despite her opposition to the centralization that comes with war, she supported both World War II and the Vietnam War as necessary blows to tyranny.

—KATHERINE DALTON

Further Reading

Anderson, William T. *Laura's Rose: The Story of Rose Wilder Lane.* [Pamphlet] Mansfield, Mo.:

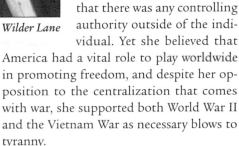

Laura Ingalls Wilder and Rose Wilder Lane Home Association, 1976.

Wilder, Laura Ingalls and Rose Wilder Lane. *Little House Sampler*. Edited by William T. Anderson. Lincoln, Neb.: University of Nebraska Press, 1988.

See also: Paterson, Isabel; Rand, Ayn

Lapin, Daniel (1947–)

A bestselling author as well as a popular radio host and motivational speaker, Rabbi Daniel Lapin is the founder and head of several conservative organizations in the United States aimed at cultural renewal and optimum business practices, notably Cascadia Business Institute and Toward Tradition. He has contributed articles to numerous conservative periodicals and spoken before many groups and businesses, including the Heritage Foundation, the Mont Pelerin Economic Society, and the 1996 Republican National Convention, in which talks he consistently delivers a message of adherence to traditional norms amid the rapid changes of modern life. According to one of his most frequently quoted sayings, "The more that things change, the more you must depend upon those things that never change."

Rabbi Lapin was born in South Africa and educated in London and Jerusalem. Upon completing his formal education, he taught theology and physics in South Africa. The study of these disciplines affirmed his belief that there is no real conflict between the truths of science and the spiritual truths of the natural law. Immigrating to America, he served as a congregational rabbi for over two decades, discovering during that time that the truths of Judaism's ancient texts contain much practical wisdom for the present day. Together with cultural critic Michael Medved, he established the Pacific Jewish Center, a dynamic Orthodox synagogue in Venice, California, in which the congregation is motivated weekly to apprehend the living truths of traditional Judaism and apply them to everyday life.

Settling in Seattle, Washington, Rabbi Lapin founded Toward Tradition in 1991. With numerous chapters scattered about the United States, Toward Tradition is a national cultural and economic movement to provide spiritual and intellectual affirmation and resources to Jews and Christians who seek to embrace the free market and conserve traditional norms as they apply to the family. In 1996 he formed Cascadia Business Institute, which provides seminars encouraging corporate managers to embrace traditional Jewish wisdom to effect excellence in business. In his first book, *America's Real War* (1999), he presented the thesis that either the United States must recover its Judeo-Christian heritage or perish, writing, "Almost every social pathology and nearly every sign of civic disarray can be traced to one thing: the extirpation of religion from American public life during the past three and a half decades."

—JAMES E. PERSON JR.

Further Reading

Lapin, Daniel E. *Buried Treasure: Hidden Wisdom from the Hebrew Language*. Sisters, Ore.: Multnomah Publishers, 2001.

See also: Medved, Michael

Lasch, Christopher (1932–94)

Christopher ("Kit") Lasch was an iconoclastic historian of American political, social, and intellectual life, a prominent critic of liberalism and progressivism with liberal and progressivist roots, and a leading theorist of cultural conservatism during the last half of the twentieth century who defies easy classification into any school of thought. While

Lasch's cultural conservatism was more explicit and fully developed in his later works such as *The True and Only Heaven* (1991) and *The Revolt of the Elites* (1995), a central theme of this conservatism runs like a red thread throughout nearly everything that he wrote: rejection of the liberal doctrine of progress. Other themes relevant to the study of conservatism include an emphasis on human fallibility and the limits of human freedom; a preference for local over centralized authority; a defense of petty-bourgeois virtues, the traditional family, and small proprietary institutions; and the rejection of ethics of personal liberation and the therapeutic state. However, Lasch's sympathy toward radical traditions (including populism and socialism), his intellectual debts to Marx and the Frankfurt School (including Max Horkheimer and Herbert Marcuse), his consistent attacks upon economic inequality and corporate capitalism, his critiques of widely acknowledged classical and modern conservative thinkers (e.g., Edmund Burke and Robert Nisbet), and his rejection of Cold War *Realpolitik* indicate the complexity of his thought and the difficulty of defining him as simply "conservative."

Lasch's critique of the liberal doctrine of progress began with his first book, *The American Liberals and the Russian Revolution* (1962), in which he adopted the approach of Richard Hofstadter in *The American Political Tradition* (see Lasch's 1973 foreword to Hofstadter's book) by focusing on the shared convictions or assumptions of American liberals apparently deeply divided over the Russian Revolution. Lasch argued that, despite significant differences between "war liberals" and "anti-imperialists," all liberals at the

Christopher Lasch

time shared an optimistic belief in the inevitable progress of democracy, including a belief in progress through revolution. For Lasch, the refusal to question this optimism and its assumptions concerning progress defined the primary failure of liberalism well into the twentieth century.

During the late 1960s and 1970s, Lasch continued to analyze the political and intellectual bankruptcy of liberal individualism and focused increasingly on the vulnerability of individuals, families, and local institutions to the growth of a paternalistic welfare state and corporate capitalism. In *Haven in a Heartless World* (1977), Lasch developed a theory of the decline of the bourgeois family that emphasized that the family had gradually succumbed to the pressures of the marketplace and state control through the agencies of bureaucracy, management, and professionalization. In *The Culture of Narcissism* (1978), which was widely read beyond the academy, Lasch proceeded to analyze the dependent culture of narcissism that had emerged under the bureaucratic paternalism of the state and business corporations, arguing that with the rise of a therapeutic ethic of leisure and self-fulfillment American progressivism had finally lost all trace of its origins in the nineteenth-century liberalism of self-disciplined economic man.

Although Lasch drew upon scholars readily identifiable as cultural conservatives (e.g., Philip Rieff, Lionel Trilling) in *The Culture of Narcissism* and its successor *The Minimal Self* (1984), he was able to use them to support a critique of welfare capitalism that seemed to owe more to radical than to conservative traditions. But with the publication of his magnum opus *The True and Only*

Heaven, Lasch achieved a synthesis of radical and conservative motifs that secured his own distinctive theory of liberal demise and therapeutic triumph, while tracing a line of historical resistance to progressivism with important implications for the present.

Lasch achieved this unusual synthesis by attempting to recover a longstanding tradition of opposition to progressive ideology grounded in the moral sensibilities of the petty bourgeoisie and located historically in radical traditions such as populism, syndicalism, and guild socialism, which opposed the excesses of capitalism. These sensibilities included a respect for limits, natural and otherwise; virtuous habits associated with property ownership; a commitment to a calling as opposed to a career; the virtue of loyalty; a preference for hope rather than optimism; and the ability to resist the vices of envy, resentment, and servility. "The central conservative insight," Lasch wrote in 1990, "is that human freedom is constrained by the natural conditions of human life, by the weight of history, by the fallibility of human judgment, and by the perversity of the human will." Lasch saw this conservative wisdom exemplified in the conscience of the lower middle class, both past and present, just as he saw the follies of progressivism embodied in their social superiors, past and present. In order to clarify and to strengthen the historical continuities of a *moral* conservatism, Lasch turned to a range of historical examples for inspiration—Sorel's vision of syndicalism, G. D. H. Cole's guild socialism, Niebuhr's spiritual discipline against resentment, and Martin Luther King's practice of nonviolent resistance, to mention a few. Through such an approach to history, Lasch hoped to remind radicals and conservatives alike of their common roots in a morality of limits and to give the current heirs of progressivism compelling arguments for reforming the errors of their ways.

—ALAN WOOLFOLK

Further Reading

Lasch, Christopher. "Conservatism against Itself." *First Things* 2 (April 1990): 17–23.

———. *The New Radicalism in America, 1889–1963: The Intellectual as a Social Type*. New York: Knopf, 1965.

———. *Women and the Common Life: Love, Marriage, and Feminism*. New York: W. W. Norton, 1997.

See also: family; populism; progress; progressivism; Rieff, Philip; therapeutic state

law and economics

The scholarly movement known as law and economics has experienced three separate phases, each conservative, but in very different senses.

Although there were precursors, the first significant application of economic analysis to legal issues commenced with the work of Aaron Director at the University of Chicago Law School in the late 1940s. Director, Rose Friedman's brother, who attended the initial convocation of the Mont Pelerin Society, began a critique of U.S. antitrust law in a famous course taught with Edward Levi. Director expanded the critique in founding the *Journal of Law and Economics* (*JLE*) in 1958. The early issues of the *JLE* were devoted to articles criticizing all forms of government intervention in the market and providing a normative philosophical defense of capitalism. The most famous article in this series proved to be Ronald Coase's "The Problem of Social Cost." In this article, Coase demonstrated that the most expansive economic justification for state regulation—to control externalities—was fundamentally incoherent. Coase invoked examples from contexts involving the common law of tort and nuisance that, as described below, importantly influenced the direction of the field. Coase succeeded Director as editor of the *JLE*, but shifted its contents from philosophy and pure political economy to empirical studies of the harmful effects of governmental programs, in particular state regulation of industry. These articles ultimately formed the substantive basis for the deregulation movement in the United States and around the world.

Coase's attention to the common law led several other scholars to examine common law topics and over the succeeding years law and economics as a discipline shifted its principal attention from antitrust and government regulation to a broader examination of legal topics. Work during the 1970s and 1980s followed in particular Guido Calabresi's *The Costs of Accidents* (1970) and Richard A. Posner's *Economic Analysis of Law* (1972). Calabresi showed how accident law implicated a wide range of social policies and, in particular, how the law could be employed to achieve various desired forms of wealth redistribution. Posner, in contrast, claimed that the entirety of the common law served to achieve the end of economic efficiency. Posner's work proved far the more arresting since in the many subsequent editions of the book and in hundreds of individual articles, many with his colleague William Landes, Posner claimed that scientific inquiry proved that the doctrines of the common law *were* efficient and, thus, that Calabresi's normative arguments about wealth redistribution were beside the point.

Posner, who also did important work in antitrust and economic regulation, deflected the Director-Coase conservatism of law and economics. Law and economics in the Posner era remained conservative in a way: Posner's defense of common law rules directly criticized Calabresi's endorsement of wealth redistribution and thus resembled the Director-Coase criticism of governmental intervention. But Posner built the case from a seeming scientific standpoint, frequently arguing that, even if one were hostile to or agnostic with respect to economic efficiency,

common law rules *were* efficient, implying that arguing against efficiency was like arguing against natural selection. Posner was never able to present convincing reasons why the common law possessed this efficient character, a failing that has affected the ultimate influence of this work. Posner's work departed from the Director-Coase emphasis, in addition, because, while generally supportive of market as opposed to politically driven outcomes, Posner employed mathematical economic models to establish what the efficient outcome was, a technique that differed from socialist economic planning only in the ultimate desideratum.

The third and current era of law and economics is not so clearly demarcated, but appears dominated by a portion of the Posner tradition. Although the critique of antitrust law and state economic regulation remains an important feature of the discipline, much of modern law and economics work consists of the application of mathematical economic models to issues arising in different legal contexts. Here the conservatism of the field stems from its conservative ambitions and its continued focus on efficiency as the preeminent substantive value. Efficiency is a value in much of this work, however, chiefly because it is susceptible to mathematical modeling and, in this respect, law and economics mirrors much of the normatively antiseptic character of modern economics proper. The Director-Coase attack on state intervention has now only a modest following. Indeed, in some respects, the field has turned around. Mathematical economic modeling can be put to use by the state; indeed, an ambitious regulatory state possesses the greatest demand for the results of models.

—GEORGE L. PRIEST

Further Reading

Bennett, John. *The Economic Theory of Central Planning*. Oxford: Blackwell, 1989.

Hartwell, R. M. *A History of the Mont Pelerin Society*. Indianapolis, Ind.: Liberty Fund, 1995.

Landes, William M., and Richard A. Posner. *The Economic Structure of Tort Law*. Cambridge, Mass.: Harvard University Press, 1987.

See also: Olin Foundation

law and order

Russell Kirk often noted that order is the first human need. Without a basic level of peace and stability—without a general knowledge among the people of what is expected of them and what they can expect of others—freedom, prosperity, and even the minimal standards of decency necessary for living life in common with others would be impossible. Traditionally, then, conservatives have been less willing than their liberal counterparts to look the other way when faced with crime, social disruption, and the breakdown of common norms of behavior. At times, and particularly during the turbulent times of the 1960s and 1970s, conservatives have looked to the law as a necessary statement of shared norms and to its strict enforcement to show society's determination to defend itself in the face of those seeking to undermine or overthrow its fundamental structures. Conservatives (though not their libertarian allies) often look to laws against immoral conduct (prostitution, pornography, and drug use, for example) to send a signal of societal disapproval and discouragement of conduct destructive of common standards of virtue. At all times conservatives oppose extreme, absolutist readings of individual rights—such as those to speech and assembly—that would undermine the peace and order that make individual rights possible and meaningful.

But laws do not and cannot stand on their own; they require for their enforcement and effectiveness a set of respected, commonly held norms. We can see this relationship between law and norms in James Q. Wilson's theory of the broken window. On that theory, proved true time and time again, when one window is left broken in a particular neighborhood other windows nearby soon will also be broken because the local inhabitants have signaled that they do not care about their surroundings. The statute banning vandalism may be in effect in both a well-kept and an ill-kept neighborhood. The crucial difference is not economic—poor neighborhoods often have been very well kept and looked after. The critical difference resides in local standards of behavior, which are enforced (or not) by ordinary citizens in their daily interactions with one another.

Recognition of the link between behavioral norms and the law leads to a tension within the conservative movement regarding law and order; a tension that sometimes crosses typical dividing lines within the movement. Where some conservatives emphasize the need for more and stricter laws to punish evildoers and serve as a warning to potential miscreants, some conservatives worry that the constant emphasis on law may lead the authorities, particularly those in Washington, to usurp the role of local associations and citizens in setting the standards of behavior necessary for good conduct and ordered liberty.

Moreover, a number of conservatives—and not just their libertarian allies—have become increasingly concerned at the means being used by the authorities in enforcing the law and even some of the ends they seek. One should not forget, after all, that the state, which is bound by the law, also may be empowered by the law to the point where it can endanger ordered liberty. And it is ordered liberty that the conservative seeks above all else in the political sphere.

Thus the use of the "RICO" statute, designed to fight organized crime, to prosecute pro-life demonstrators may be seen as evidence that the government has been given too much power in its pursuit of criminal conspiracies. The use of infrared cameras, cameras on streetlights, and other surveillance equipment also raises the specter of an intrusive government, as do laws banning smoking and administrative regulations that seem designed to force each citizen to become a clerk whose duty it is to maintain massive files on his own activities for the convenience of a watchful government.

Taken together, these extensions of state power blur the line between fundamental law and mere unilateral acts of the state and risk calling the legitimacy of our entire system of laws into question. Thus, conservatives, more willing than most to look to custom and tradition as upholders of societal norms, often seek fewer, clearer laws so that the unofficial social sanctions of local associations may again take over their primary role of guiding people in their daily lives. Fewer, clearer, and more clearly necessary laws would encourage the respect for law and authority conservatives see as crucial to social order. They also would leave room for the informal relations that make up the bulk of a life well lived.

—BRUCE FROHNEN

Further Reading

Kelling, George L. *Fixing Broken Windows: Restoring Order and Reducing Crime in Our Communities.* New York: Martin Kessler Books, 1996.

Mac Donald, Heather. *Are Cops Racist?* Chicago: Ivan R. Dee, 2003.

Wilson, James Q., and George L. Kelling. "Broken Windows: The Police and Neighborhood Safety." *Atlantic Monthly,* March 1982.

See also: authority; liberty; Wilson, James Q.

Lee, Robert E. (1807–70)

West Point graduate, engineer, accomplished military officer, superintendent of West Point Military Academy, commander in chief of the Confederate Army, and college president, Robert E. Lee remains the premier symbol of antebellum Southern conservatism. Son of the distinguished Revolutionary War veteran and Federalist politician, Henry "Light Horse Harry" Lee, Robert Lee was reared in Virginia and educated at West Point. His marriage to Mary Ann Randolph Custis, the great-granddaughter of Martha Washington, placed Lee at the top of Virginia's most prominent families. After valorous service in the Mexican War, Lee faced a promising career in the United States Army.

Robert E. Lee

Lee was not only a nationalist; he also deplored Southern slavery, which he considered morally indefensible. However, he envisioned a federal union that accepted cultural accommodations and diversity. Like most Southerners in 1861, Lee was not a secessionist but came to believe disunion was a necessity after Lincoln called for troops to force South Carolina back into the Union. Rather than relying on a compact theory of the Constitution and states' rights, Lee justified Virginia's actions in 1861 based on the prescriptive right to rebel against a government insensitive to the interests of its people. His desire to preserve constitutional government as handed down by the founders and his loyalty to his homeland, Virginia, ultimately overrode any favorable sentiment he held for the Union.

Lee gained command of the Army of Northern Virginia and successfully routed George McClellan's invasion in 1862. After winning the Battle of Second Manassas, Lee pushed north hoping to rally Confederate sympathies in the border states. But after the Battle of Antietam, Maryland, he returned to Virginia where, assisted by his able subordinate, Thomas "Stonewall" Jackson, he defeated Union forces at Fredericksburg and Chancellorsville. In the summer of 1863, Lee again pushed north, this time into Pennsylvania, where he suffered his worst defeat at the Battle of Gettysburg. Though Lee inflicted massive losses on Ulysses Grant's forces during 1864 and 1865, he was unable to stop the capture of Petersburg and Richmond. On April 9, 1865, Lee surrendered to Grant at Appomattox Courthouse rather than divide his army and continue the war with guerilla tactics. His decision to surrender also rested on the expectation of honorable treatment. Years later, he reportedly admitted that he would have continued to fight had he known what Reconstruction would bring to the South.

Following the war, Lee held the position of president of Washington College, later named Washington and Lee. Unlike other Confederate leaders and military officials, Lee refused lucrative offers by businesses and criticized the rise of an industrialized "new" South. For generations of Southerners, Lee symbolized the best of their tradition. Virtuous, devout, courageous, and restrained, Lee chose to follow the concrete over the abstract and defended his home against a government he called too "democratic."

—CAREY ROBERTS

Further Reading

Freeman, Douglas Southall. *R. E. Lee: A Biography.* 4 vols. New York: Scribner's, 1937–40.

Thomas, Emory M. *Robert E. Lee: A Biography.* New York: W. W. Norton, 1995.

See also: Civil War; localism; states' rights

LeMay, General Curtis E. (1906–90)

Born in 1906 in Columbus, Ohio, Curtis LeMay brought his engineering degree to the United States Army Air Force, skipping West Point and earning a commission through reserve officer training (1928). He rose through the ranks as an enthusiastic proponent of air power and his tactics eventually inspired the slogan "Bombs away with Curtis LeMay."

As a young general officer, "Iron Pants" LeMay commanded the Eighth Air Force in Europe, arranging thousand-plane missions to obliterate heavy industry in Hitler's Germany. In 1944, LeMay went to the Pacific and got control of a new weapon, the Boeing B-29 heavy bomber. LeMay ordered the B-29 fleet stripped of defensive armament, filled its bomb-bays with incendiaries, and began the relentless drill of reducing metropolitan Japan to ashes in massive low-level raids. LeMay planned and oversaw the Berlin Air Lift of 1948. He became head of the postwar independent Air Force shortly thereafter. He organized the Strategic Air Command and lobbied for the hydrogen bomb, with which he then armed his more than two thousand B-47s and B-52s. If Richard Rhodes may be believed, LeMay hoped to provoke the Soviet Union into a war, once sending a stream of B-36 "Peacemakers" over Vladivostok. LeMay calculated that it was the threat of unilateral, not of mutual, assured destruction that would deter communist aggression. Sterling Hayden's cigar-chewing General Jack D. Ripper in Stanley Kubrick's *Dr. Strangelove* savagely parodies LeMay. The portrayal no doubt sums up the way in which LeMay appeared to the Left. A consummate Cold Warrior, LeMay teamed with Governor George Wallace as a vice presidential hopeful in 1968. The embodiment of uniformed pugnacity and the aerial equivalent of the tank-general Patton, LeMay died in

1990, after more than twenty years of peaceful retirement.

—THOMAS BERTONNEAU

Further Reading

LeMay, Curtis E., with MacKinlay Kantor. *Mission with LeMay: My Story.* Garden City, N.Y.: Doubleday, 1965.

LeMay, Curtis E., and Bill Lenne. *Superfortress: The Story of the B-29 and American Air Power.* New York: McGraw-Hill, 1988.

Levine, Isaac Don (1892–1981)

A prolific journalist, Isaac Don Levine devoted himself to fighting communism and exposing Soviet crimes. Born in Mozyr, Russia, Levine came to America in 1911. After writing for the *Kansas City Star*, he was foreign news editor for the *New York Tribune*, foreign correspondent for the *Chicago Daily News*, and a prominent columnist for the Hearst newspapers. Meanwhile Levine produced critical books about the Soviets, e.g., *The Man Lenin* (1924) and *Stalin* (1931). Informed by Whittaker Chambers in 1939 of Soviet espionage in the State Department, he went with Chambers to tell Assistant Secretary of State Adolf A. Berle, who could not interest President Roosevelt in the matter. Levine testified to save Chambers as a witness in the Hiss case.

In 1946, Levine and Ralph de Toledano founded *Plain Talk*, a well-informed anticommunist monthly that revealed communist subversion in America, the existence of the Soviet Gulag slave labor camps, and worldwide Soviet espionage. Levine edited *Plain Talk* until 1950, when it was merged with the *Freeman*. He also helped found the American Committee for the Liberation of the Peoples of Russia, which sought the Soviet Union's overthrow.

Despite his crusading anticommunism, Levine rejected the conservative label, describing himself to the *New York Times* in 1968 as "an inveterate libertarian who has never joined any conservative camp and who looks upon statism regardless of its color and upon every form of concentrated power as the blights of our age."

—JOHN ATTARIAN

Further Reading

Levine, Isaac Don. *Eyewitness to History.* New York: Hawthorn, 1973.

See also: anticommunism; Toledano, Ralph de

Lewis, C. S. (Clive Staples) (1898–1963)

Culturally conservative and militantly orthodox in his religious belief, C. S. Lewis is nevertheless difficult to categorize in terms common to political discourse. Precisely to avoid such categorization (he viewed it as polemically inconvenient) he refused an offer of knighthood from Churchill's postwar government. In that light he is best seen as conservatively disposed rather than as a conservative per se.

C. S. Lewis

Touchstones of his conservative thought are his trust in the validity of reason, defense of natural law, general reliance upon tradition ("mere Christianity"), objective view of creation (both natural and supernatural) and the legitimacy of its claims upon us (our moral and aesthetic responses are trainable and ought to be ordinate), distrust of emotion as a guide to truth, refusal to equate progress with innovation or to see it as at all inevitable, and a rejection of egalitarianism as both dangerous and immoral. Wounded in the trenches of World War I, his patriotism compelled him to proclaim the duty of men (pronouncedly not women) possibly to die for their country, but he steadfastly refused "to live for it." He distrusted collectivism (especially mass movements) of any kind, loathed government intrusion into everyday life, and reviled statist presumptuousness (despising, for example, "The Humanitarian Theory of Punishment" on the grounds that whereas the state might very well punish wrongdoers it had no business "curing" them).

Yet he allowed that a genuinely Christian society would somehow be a socialist one. His unvarying orthodoxy notwithstanding, he believed that laws against homosexuality and pornography were not only futile but wrong. His allegiance to scriptural inerrancy did not lead to anything resembling biblical literalism or religious fundamentalism (Bob Jones, Jr., after meeting him, said that although Lewis did drink and smoke he believed that "that man is a Christian"); and he counseled that two lovers would be better off living together outside of marriage rather than violating their sacramental vow of marital fidelity. Somewhat like his great creation, the lion Aslan, Lewis was not tame.

Thus, his thought must be read within the considerable context that he provided, not as lessons or, worse, tricks, but as an organic worldview arising from inherited culture and faith in the Risen Lord. In over forty books, two hundred essays and sermons, and eighty poems, he was one of the greatest Christian apologists ever to have written in English; a formidable religious thinker, psychologist, and devotional writer; a philosopher and poet; a fiction writer who arguably produced benchmarks in religious allegory, the first-person novel, children's fantasy, and science fiction; and one of the foremost literary historians and critics of the twentieth

century. Withal, he is what he famously called himself, an Old Western Man, and he would consistently remind us that "anything not eternal is eternally out of date."

In short, his imaginative effusions are as radical as nature itself; his reason as conservative as the multiplication tables; and his spirit as liberal and as liberated as the open arms of the Cross he worshipped.

—JAMES COMO

Further Reading

Lewis, C. S. *The Abolition of Man*. New York: Macmillan, 1947.
———. *Mere Christianity*. New York: Macmillan, 1952.
Sayer, George. *Jack: C .S. Lewis and His Times*. San Francisco: Harper & Row, 1988.
Vanauken, Sheldon. *A Severe Mercy*. San Francisco: Harper & Row, 1977.

See also: *natural law; Protestantism, evangelical; science and scientism; therapeutic state;* Touchstone: A Journal of Mere Christianity

liberalism

As the meaning of "liberalism" shifts, that of conservatism does too. Leo Strauss writes of ancient liberalism, meaning the liberty claimed by the philosopher against the city. In that view, the ancient conservatives were those such as the playwright Aristophanes who wrote to protect morality against intellectual irresponsibility. Liberalism, from the beginning, has been an elitist claim for intellectual liberation from the common bonds of religion, morality, and tradition.

Modern liberalism originated as modern individualism. According to John Locke, the truth about human nature can be discovered through imagining the human being in a state of nature, where he is a free and equal individual. The individual has natural rights but no natural duties; he has no authoritative guidance from God, nature, tradition, or family. So the foundation of all human obedience is consent; the individual agrees to be ruled in order to have his rights protected better than he could protect them on his own.

The individual is the basis of liberal or limited government. The purpose of such government is the protection of rights, no more and no less. The individual consents to that government not as a member of a race, class, gender, or religion; the government views him as being free from all such oppressive attachments. Government protects the economic, religious, and intellectual liberty of this individual.

Indeed, modern liberalism aims especially to free government from religious influence; it aims to free the individual from the tyranny of politicized Christianity. In America, liberalism meant leaving the individual free to be religious—not to be an individual, but a creature—in his private life. Religious liberty protects the free exercise of religion and therefore the free existence of churches. In Europe and especially France, liberalism for a long while meant purging religion completely from society; it meant going to war against the church. So in Europe far more than in America, conservatives opposed themselves to atheistic liberalism.

In America, conservatives aim to show that American liberalism is so incomplete that it might not be viewed as liberalism at all. Americans characteristically have not viewed their liberal government as atheistic or even secular. When the term liberal becomes identified with hostility to religion in America—as it has recently—it becomes a political liability. American liberalism has always, ironically, been a mixture of conservatism and liberalism. And American conservatism—free as it is from longings for any ancien régime—has always had some liberal ingredients.

Liberalism in America has also been op-posed to democracy. A liberal government is one that protects individual liberty from the tyranny of the majority. *The Federalist* (1788) argues that democracy has been bad government so far, but it can become good if it is designed in such a way as to protect liberty. So in another way American liberalism is really a mixture of liberalism and democracy often called "liberal democracy." In the nineteenth century, liberalism tended to become laissez-faire liberalism; the main purpose of government came to be seen as the protection of the economic liberty of individuals—especially wealthy, entrepreneurial individuals—from an envious majority roused up by populist demagogues. Laissez-faire liberals employed the Supreme Court to strike down laws regulating the economy as majority tyranny. The partisans of laissez-faire deserved the liberal label; they had little of the concern for the perpetuation of tradition and culture that characterizes genuine conservatism.

Franklin Roosevelt successfully renamed laissez-faire liberals—those who opposed the New Deal regulations of the economy on behalf of the unfortunate—conservatives. Nineteenth-century liberalism then became, in large measure, twentieth-century conservatism. Roosevelt drew upon the old meaning of liberality as the virtue of generosity. New Deal liberals still liberally and confidently deploy the resource of government to solve a virtually endless series of social problems. But the Aristotelian virtue of liberality concerns the person's generous use of his own wealth. Spending government's money freely surely is no sign of one's own virtue, and the best conservative criticism of New Deal liberalism is that it undermines in many ways the personal practice of virtue.

From roughly 1936 to 1968, the Democratic Party stood for economic liberalism and the Republican Party stood for economic conservatism—in other words, against the indefinite growth of the welfare state. By

1972, the Democrats had also become the party of social or cultural liberalism, meaning the party of individual permissiveness. Once again, liberalism was identified with elitist liberation. Liberal Democrats became plagued with the contradiction of being sternly moralistic statists when it came to the economy, but as partisans of "Do your own thing" licentiousness when it came to morality and even patriotism. The Republican Party tended to become the party of social or cultural conservatism—it stood against abortion and for family, religion, and patriotism, while remaining devoted to economic liberty. Ronald Reagan's genius was to hold economically conservative or libertarian Republicans in the same party with morally and religiously motivated cultural conservatives. But the Republicans no less than the Democrats depended on blurring the rather fundamental differences separating their two main factions.

The reformed Democratic Party of Bill Clinton redefined liberalism to move it closer to libertarianism. President Clinton supported the globalized free market, ended welfare as Americans knew it, and was famous for his pro-choice or permissive positions on a wide array of social issues. New Deal liberals nostalgic for principled devotion to compassionate liberal programs for the unfortunate have been marginalized in their own party. The main exception here is environmentalism, where most liberals new and old remain in favor of greatly expanded government regulation. Conservatism meanwhile has become more cultural and less economic, and libertarian Republicans are becoming alienated from their party.

Whether social or cultural liberalism will dominate America's political future is unclear. Americans say they dislike liberalism insofar as it is associated with angry feminism, anti-Americanism, and disdain for the way of life of ordinary Americans. But they in a more abstract way are more than ever on the side of liberal tolerance or nonjudgmentalism, and it is likely most of them do not want abortion or biotechnology regulated much by government. American thought is surely more confused than usual right now, but on balance social liberalism seems to be becoming progressively less unpopular. Conservatism detached from libertarianism may be in for a difficult time, unless challenges to our nation continue to inspire patriotism.

We might say that today liberalism is returning to its roots: once again, it is becoming clearly identified as the dogma of liberated individualism. Conservatives are more clearly becoming those who say that human beings, in fact, are not such individuals; they are persons, beings with social, moral, and religious responsibilities given them by nature and God.

—Peter Augustine Lawler

Further Reading

Galston, William A. *Liberal Pluralism*. New York: Cambridge University Press, 2002.

Kramer, Hilton and Roger Kimball, eds. *The Betrayal of Liberalism*. Chicago: Ivan R. Dee, 1999.

Lawler, Peter Augustine. *Aliens in America: The Strange Truth about Our Souls*. Wilmington, Del.: ISI Books, 2002.

Licht, Robert A. *The Framers and Fundamental Rights*. Washington, D.C.: AEI Press, 1992.

Seaton, James. *Cultural Conservatism, Political Liberalism*. Ann Arbor: University of Michigan Press, 1996.

See also: culture wars; democracy; Democratic Party; individualism; liberalism, classical; libertarianism; New Deal

liberalism, classical

"Classical liberalism" is the term used to designate the ideology advocating private property, an unhampered market economy, the rule of law, constitutional guarantees of freedom of religion and of the press, and international peace based on free trade. Up until around 1900, this ideology was generally known simply as liberalism. The qualifying "classical" is now usually necessary, in English-speaking countries at least (but not, for instance, in France) because liberalism has come to be associated with wide-ranging interferences with private property and the market on behalf of egalitarian goals. This version of liberalism—if such it can still be called—is sometimes designated as "social," or (erroneously) "modern" or the "new" liberalism. Here we shall use liberalism to signify the classical variety.

Although its fundamental claims are universalist, liberalism must be understood first of all as a doctrine and movement that grew out of a distinctive culture and particular historical circumstances. That culture—as Lord Acton recognized most clearly—was the West, the Europe that was or had been in communion with the Bishop of Rome. Its womb, in other words, was the particular human society that underwent "the European miracle" (in E. L. Jones's phrase). The historical circumstances were the confrontation of the free institutions and values inherited from the Middle Ages with the pretensions of the absolutist state of the sixteenth and seventeenth centuries.

From the struggle of the Dutch against the absolutism of the Spanish Hapsburgs a polity issued that manifested basically liberal traits: the rule of law, including especially a firm adherence to property rights; de facto religious toleration; considerable freedom of expression; and a central government of severely limited powers. The astonishing success of the Dutch experiment exerted a "demonstration effect" on European social thought and, gradually, political practice. This was even truer of the later example of England. Throughout the history of liberalism, theory and social reality interacted,

with theory stimulated and refined through the observation of practice, and attempts to reform practice undertaken with reference to more accurate theory.

In the English constitutional struggles of the seventeenth century a number of individuals and groups displayed significant liberal traits. One stands out, however, as the first recognizably liberal party in European history: the Levelers. Led by John Lilburne and Richard Overton, this movement of middle-class radicals demanded freedom of trade and an end to state monopolies, separation of church and state, popular representation, and strict limits even to parliamentary authority. Their emphasis on property, beginning with the individual's ownership of himself, and their hostility to state power show that the amalgamation of the Levelers to the pre-socialist Diggers was mere enemy propaganda. Although failures in their time, the Levelers furnished the prototype of a middle-class radical liberalism that has been a feature of the politics of English-speaking peoples ever since. Later in the century, John Locke framed the doctrine of the natural rights to life, liberty, and estate—which he collectively termed "property"—in the form that would be passed down, through the Real Whigs of the eighteenth century, to the generation of the American Revolution.

America became the model liberal nation, and, after England, the exemplar of liberalism to the world. Through much of the nineteenth century it was in many respects a society in which the state could hardly be said to exist, as European observers noted with awe. Radical liberal ideas were manifested and applied by groups such as the Jeffersonians, Jacksonians, abolitionists, and late-nineteenth-century anti-imperialists.

Until well into the twentieth century, however, the most significant liberal theory continued to be produced in Europe. The eighteenth century was particularly rich in this regard. A landmark was the work of the thinkers of the Scottish Enlightenment, particularly David Hume, Adam Smith, Adam Ferguson, and Dugald Stewart. They developed an analysis that explained "the origin of complex social structures without the need to posit the existence of a directing intelligence" (in Ronald Hamowy's summary). The Scottish theory of spontaneous order was a crucial contribution to the model of a basically self-generating and self-regulating civil society that required state action only to defend against violent intrusion into the individual's rights-protected sphere. As Dugald Steward put it in his *Biographical Memoir of Adam Smith* (1811), "Little else is requisite to carry a state to the highest degree of opulence from the lowest barbarism, but peace, easy taxes, and the tolerable administration of justice; all the rest being brought about by the natural course of things." The Physiocratic formula, *Laissez-faire, laissez-passer, le monde va de lui-même* ("the world goes by itself"), suggests both the liberal program and the social philosophy upon which it rests. The theory of spontaneous order was elaborated by later liberal thinkers, notably Herbert Spencer and Carl Menger in the nineteenth century and F. A. Hayek and Michael Polanyi in the twentieth.

One argument between liberals and Burkean and other conservatives who in important respects stand close to liberalism is related to this central liberal conception. While liberals typically expect the market in the widest sense—the network of voluntary exchanges—to generate a system of institutions and mores conducive to its continuance, conservatives insist that the indispensable underpinning must be provided by the state beyond the simple protection of life, liberty, and property, including especially state support of religion.

With the onset of industrialization, a major area of conflict opened up between liberalism and conservatism. Conservative elites and their spokesmen, particularly in Britain, often exploited the circumstances of early industrialism to tarnish the liberal escutcheon of their middle-class and nonconformist opponents. In historical perspective, it is clear that what is known as the Industrial Revolution was Europe's (and America's) way of dealing with an otherwise intractable population explosion. Some conservatives went on to forge a critique of the market order based on its alleged materialism, soullessness, and anarchy.

To the extent that liberals associated conservatism with militarism and imperialism, another source of conflict arose. While a strand of Whiggish liberalism was not averse to wars (beyond self-defense) for *liberal* ends, and while wars of national unification provided a major exception to the rule, by and large liberalism was associated with the cause of peace. The ideal type of antiwar and anti-imperialist liberalism was provided by the Manchester School and its leaders Richard Cobden and John Bright. Cobden, particularly, developed a sophisticated analysis of the motives and machinations of states leading to war. The panacea proposed by the Manchesterites was international free trade. Developing these ideas, Frédéric Bastiat proposed an especially pure form of the liberal doctrine that enjoyed a certain appeal on the Continent and, later, in the United States.

Liberalism's adherents were not always consistent. This was the case when they turned to the state to promote their own values. In France, for instance, liberals used state-funded schools and institutes to promote secularism under the Directory, and they supported anticlerical legislation during the Third Republic, while in Bismarck's Germany they spearheaded the *Kulturkampf* against the Catholic Church. These efforts, however, can be seen as betrayals of liberal principles and in fact were eschewed by those acknowledged to be the most consistent and doctrinaire in their liberalism.

The basis for a possible reconciliation of liberalism and antistatist conservatism emerged after the experience of the French Revolution and Napoleon. Its best exponent was Benjamin Constant, who may be viewed as the representative figure of mature liberalism. Faced with the new dangers of unlimited state power based on manipulation of the democratic masses, Constant looked for social buffers and ideological allies wherever they might be found. Religious faith, localism, the voluntary traditions of a people were valued as sources of strength against the state. In the next generation, Alexis de Tocqueville elaborated this Constantian approach, becoming the great analyst and opponent of the rising omnipresent, bureaucratic state.

In English-speaking countries the hostility of antistatist conservatives has been exacerbated by an extreme emphasis on the role of Bentham and the Philosophical Radicals in the history of liberalism. J. S. Mill's *On Liberty* (1859) actually deviated from the central line of liberal thought by counterposing the individual and his liberty not simply to the state but to "society" as well. Whereas the liberalism of the early Wilhelm von Humboldt and of Constant, for example, saw voluntary intermediate bodies as the natural outgrowth of individual action and as welcome barriers to state aggrandizement, Mill aimed at stripping the individual of any connection to spontaneously generated social tradition and freely accepted authority—as, for instance, in his statement in *On Liberty* that the Jesuit is a "slave" of his order.

It is the socialist state that classical liberalism has opposed most vigorously. The Austro-American Ludwig von Mises, for example, demonstrated the impossibility of rational central planning. Prolific for more than fifty years, Mises restated liberal social philosophy after its eclipse of several decades; he became the acknowledged spokesman for liberal ideology in the twentieth century. Among the many students on whom Mises

exercised a remarkable influence was Murray N. Rothbard, who wedded Austrian economic theory to the doctrine of natural rights to produce a form of individualist anarchism, or "anarcho-capitalism." By extending the realm of civil society to the point of extinguishing the state, Rothbard's view appears as the limiting case of authentic liberalism.

Classical liberalism is often contrasted with a *new social liberalism*, which is supposed to have developed out of the classical variety around 1900. But social liberalism deviates fundamentally from its namesake at its theoretical root in that it denies the self-regulatory capacity of society: the state is called on to redress social imbalance in increasingly ramified ways. The plea that it intends to preserve the end of individual freedom, modifying only the means, is to classical liberals hardly to the point: as much could be claimed for most varieties of socialism. In fact, social liberalism can scarcely be distinguished, theoretically and practically, from revisionist socialism. Furthermore, it can be argued that this school of thought did not develop out of classical liberalism around the turn of the century—when, for instance, the alleged fraudulence of freedom of contract in the labor market is supposed to have been discovered. Social liberalism existed full-blown at least from the time of Sismondi, and elements of it (welfarism) can be found even in great classical liberal writers such as Condorcet and Thomas Paine.

With the end of the classical socialist project, classical liberals and antistatist conservatives may agree that it is contemporary social liberalism that now stands as the great adversary of civil society. The political preoccupation of classical liberals is, of necessity, to counteract the current now leading the world towards what Macaulay called "the all-devouring state"—the nightmare that haunted Burke no less than Constant, Tocqueville, and Herbert Spencer. As older quarrels grow increasingly obsolete, liberals and antistatist conservatives may well discover that they have more in common than their forebears ever understood.

—RALPH RAICO

Further Reading

Acton, John. "The History of Freedom in Antiquity" and "The History of Freedom in Christianity." In *Selected Writings of Lord Acton*, vol. I, *Essays in the History of Liberty*, edited by J. Rufus Fears. Indianapolis, Ind.: Liberty Press, 1985.

Bramsted, E. K., and K. J. Melhuish. *Western Liberalism: A History in Documents from Locke to Croce*. London: Longman, 1978.

Hamowy, Ronald. *The Scottish Enlightenment and the Theory of Spontaneous Order*. Carbondale, Ill.: Southern Illinois University Press, 1987.

Pocock, J. G. A. "The Political Economy of Burke's Analysis of the French Revolution." In *Virtue, Commerce, and History: Essays on Political Thought and History, Chiefly in the Eighteenth Century*. Cambridge: Cambridge University Press, 1985.

Raico, Ralph. *Classical Liberalism in the Twentieth Century*. Fairfax, Va.: Institute for Humane Studies, 1989.

Stewart, Dugald. *Biographical Memoir of Adam Smith*. 1811. Reprint, New York: Augustus M. Kelley, 1966.

See also: capitalism; Freeman; *free trade;* Hayek, *Friedrich August von; liberalism; libertarianism; Mont Pelerin Society; property rights, private*

liberation theology

Liberation theology defined a doctrine and a movement that sought a religious justification, particularly within the framework of Catholicism, for the Marxist revolutionary politics that swept Latin America in the 1970 and '80s. It taught that Christ's message pertained not only to salvation of the soul, but also to political salvation here on earth through the establishment of Christian socialism. The movement pitted the poor against the rich, as if their interests were in intractable conflict, and sought to morally justify violent peasant revolts on behalf of the poor. Christ was rendered not only as the Son of God but also as a political radical who came to liberate the poor from oppression.

The intellectual power of the liberation theology movement derived from its attempt to justify a traditionally atheistic Marxist movement within a framework that would appeal to religiously minded Latin Americans. In this respect, it breathed new life into an economic doctrine that had not yet developed a serious following among ministers of the Gospel. The political power of the movement was built on the objective conditions of the poor in the developing world, which seemed to offer evidence that the Marxist theory concerning capitalism and socialism was correct.

The first and leading intellectual defense of liberation theology came from the pen of Peruvian priest Fr. Gustavo Gutiérrez. His book *A Theology of Liberation* (1971) was a seminal treatise that galvanized theology and seminary students in the United States and Europe, a number of whom traveled to Latin America to support Marxist rebels in non-Marxist countries and the Marxist Sandinista government in Nicaragua. Other writers in this tradition included Brazilian theologian Leonardo Boff and Jesuit scholar Jon Sobrino, whose works were also read by religious students of that generation.

The theology was not complicated. It combined Marxian economic doctrine with a misrendering and politicization of Christ's moral injunctions to help the poor. In this respect, it was easily refuted through simple economic logic. The "structures of oppression" that so outraged the liberation theologians were not capitalism but traditional mercantilist policies in which a government-connected elite used the state to inhibit free competition for land and capital and sought trade policies that would benefit large landholders at the expense of craftsmen and small farmers. The "liberation" that these faith-based Marxist ideologues sought could only be found in the overthrow of mercantilist economics and the invigoration of a business economy that would spread economic opportunity and prosperity.

Uprooting the theological error was more complicated. Formal political and theological criticism came from the Catholic Church under Pope John Paul II. Having lived under the totalitarian socialism of both Nazism and communism, he saw the grave dangers that seemingly naïve misunderstandings of economics, combined with religious zeal, could pose for societies. He used his personal influence among Latin American bishops to weigh against the teaching of the liberation theologians, and he directly confronted leaders of Marxist political and ecclesiastical movements for their distortions of traditional Christian teaching. At issue, he said, was not only the danger that liberation theology would lend moral support to would-be totalitarians; he also rejected the attempt to thoroughly politicize Christ's message on behalf of the poor.

The leading opponent of liberation theology in the United States was Michael Novak, who had once identified with "progressive" movements in the 1960s before their links to statist economic policies became too much to bear. As a former spokesman for the theological Left, however, Novak's voice had a special resonance when denouncing the economic and theological agenda of liberation theology.

The rise and decline of the Sandinista regime (1985–90) in Nicaragua roughly chronicles the popularity of liberation theology in the public mind. Daniel Ortega came to power in what appeared to be a popular revolution but was voted out of power in 1990 because of the severe economic hardships that Sandinista socialism had imposed on the country. His defeat at the polls refuted the notion that the Sandinistas enjoyed popular support. Long after the collapse of the Soviet Union, Ortega ran for office again (1996) and was humiliated.

The threat of communist revolution began to dissipate throughout the 1990s as more and more governments instituted privatization and other structural economic reforms, along with democratic elections. By the beginning of the twenty-first century, it had become clear that the liberation movements in Latin American to take seriously are those that seek a wider distribution of private property and a relaxing of the economic regulations that have hurt the poor. From a theological point of view, the reinvigoration of Catholic orthodoxy under John Paul II exposed the heterodox movements as marginal aberrations from the main current of Catholic social teaching. The Church reasserted its traditional teaching that socialism—being a complete worldview that submerges the individual and the family to the collective state—is heresy.

Liberation theology is not completely dead, however. It survives in different forms in many seminaries in the U.S. and Europe. It takes the form of social democratic movements that teach social activism as the fulfillment of the Gospel, and also of religiously inspired environmental movements that seek to liberate nature from the influence of man. In each case, the distorted teaching of liberation is rooted in a conflict view of society: capitalists against workers, the poor against the rich, environment versus industry, even while it ignores or downplays the eternal spiritual conflict between personal sin and virtue.

—Rev. Robert A. Sirico

Further Reading

Novak, Michael. *Will It Liberate? Questions about Liberation Theology.* New York: Paulist Press, 1986.

See also: *Catholic social teaching; John Paul II, Pope; Marxism; Novak, Michael*

Libertarian Party

The Libertarian Party (LP) is the third largest political party in the United States (if one goes by number of political offices held). The LP was founded by advertising manager David Nolan and a group of disillusioned Republican Party and libertarian student activists after the imposition of wage and price controls during the Nixon presidency. The student contingent had broken away from the *National Review*–dominated Young Americans for Freedom because of YAF's opposition to draft resistance and YAF's support for the war in Vietnam. Strictly devoted to both civil liberties and property rights, the new libertarian activists had been attracted to politics by the antigovernment rhetoric of the 1964 Goldwater campaign and believed government should be strictly confined to the defense of the individual and his property against attack. The bulk of early LP membership was composed of people influenced by the writings of Ayn Rand, Leonard Read (founder of the Foundation for Economic Education), Milton Friedman, Murray Rothbard, Ludwig von Mises, F. A. Hayek, and others.

In June 1972, the first national LP convention was held in Denver. It attracted 89 people and nominated John Hospers (professor of philosophy at the University of Southern California) for president and Oregon radio producer Tonie Nathan for vice president. In the fall, the LP also ran numerous races around the U.S., including the highly innovative and media-grabbing campaigns of Fran Youngstein for mayor and Walter Block for Congress in New York City. After the November general election, Virginia electoral college member Roger MacBride bolted from the Republican Party and voted for the LP executive ticket, providing the only Electoral College vote ever cast for a woman candidate (Nathan) for national office.

In 1973, the LP's Kay Haroff Campaign for Senate in Ohio produced a record 6 percent of the vote, and other races around the country established the LP as a significant third party. And in 1975, under the national LP chairmanship of Edward H. Crane (later to become president and cofounder of the Cato Institute), the LP's presidential ticket of MacBride and attorney David Bergland achieved ballot status in thirty-two states and received 170,000 votes.

In 1978, the LP ran attorney Edward Clark for governor of California, receiving 5 percent of the vote, and Alaska's Dick Randolph became the first elected LP state legislator. Subsequently, in 1979 the LP nominated Clark as its presidential candidate. Appearing on the ballot in all fifty states, and despite the independent presidential candidacy of John Anderson, the LP ticket received almost one million votes, having run extensive national television ads and offering many Americans their first exposure to libertarian ideas. In addition, Randolph was reelected and joined by Kenneth Fanning in the Alaska state legislature.

In 1982, Louisiana LP congressional candidate James Agnew attracted 23 percent of the vote, Alaska gubernatorial candidate Randolph received 15 percent, and Arizona gubernatorial candidate Sam Steiger 5 percent. However, accusations that the Crane-run Clark/Koch and Randolph campaigns hedged on key planks within the LP platform helped to produce a major schism within the LP. The division pitted former Cato employees Williamson Evers and Rothbard, adhering to the platform, against Crane and the so-called "Crane Machine," seeking to modify the LP into a party promoting "low-tax liberalism." As a result, at the 1983 national convention, the Crane candidate for presidential nomination, Cato foreign policy expert

Earl Ravenal, was narrowly defeated by Bergland. In addition, all members of the Crane slate for national LP office were defeated. Crane then quit the LP, which resulted in the party's loss of a major benefactor.

Despite the schism, reduced funding, and greatly increased hurdles to ballot access in many states, the 1984 LP presidential ticket achieved ballot status in thirty-nine states and finished third nationally with 228,700 votes. The campaign also produced the Bergland book, *Libertarianism in One Lesson* (1984), which eventually sold more than 75,000 copies. In addition, Andre Marrou became the third LP member elected to the Alaska legislature and eleven other LP members were elected to office around the country.

In 1987, Congressman Ron Paul resigned from the Republican Party, joining the LP, and the Seattle national LP convention nominated him for president. Paul's tightly controlled campaign, along with charges of financial improprieties and ideological differences, produced yet another LP schism. Several prominent academics, including Llewellyn Rockwell, quit the LP, launching an attack on those critical of the Paul campaign and on the failure of some within the LP to support traditional American family values in conjunction with a pure devotion to liberty.

In 1996, bestselling author and long-time libertarian Harry Browne became the LP's presidential candidate. Browne pursued a highly visible campaign that brought the LP greater respectability, an influx of new members and supporters, and a total of 463,000 votes. Browne was the LP's standard-bearer again in 2000. This time around, the LP was also competing with third-party candidates Patrick Buchanan (Reform Party) and Ralph Nader (Green Party), and in one of the tightest national elections in U.S. history, all third-party candidates struggled at the ballot box, with Browne winning 382,000

votes. Other LP candidates did better, with more than 3.2 million people voting Libertarian around the country and a total of 1,420 LP candidates seeking office. In Massachusetts, Carla Howell received 306,457 votes (12 percent) in the race for U.S. Senator against Edward Kennedy, just 1 percent behind the Republican candidate, Jack Robinson, and in Nevada, James Dan received 45 percent of the vote against an incumbent Democrat.

As of 2004, the LP had 600 people in elected office across the U.S., more than twice all other third parties combined. Today, the LP has 22,000 dues-paying members, publishes the monthly *LP News*, and is headquartered in Washington, D.C.

—DAVID J. THEROUX

Further Reading

Collier, Peter. "The Next American Revolution." *New West*, August 27, 1979, 26–32.

Paul, Mark, "Seducing the Left: The Third Party that Wants You." *Mother Jones*, May 1980, 47–62.

Rothbard, Murray N. *For a New Liberty: The Libertarian Manifesto.* New York: Macmillan, 1973.

See also: Cato Institute; libertarianism; Young Americans for Freedom

libertarianism

Libertarianism is a political philosophy that advocates individual liberty and limited, constitutional government. Advocates of libertarian views generally regard themselves as belonging to the tradition of John Locke, Adam Smith, the American founders, and the classical liberals. The term "libertarian" originated in postwar America as the term "liberal" came to mean an advocate of expansive government. A consciously libertarian political movement also developed in the years after World War II.

Libertarianism may be more specifically defined as the view that each person has the right to live his life in any way he chooses so long as he respects the equal rights of others. Libertarians defend each person's right to life, liberty, and property—rights they believe that people have naturally, before governments are created. In the libertarian view, all human relationships should be voluntary; the only actions that should be forbidden by law are those that involve the initiation of force against those who have not themselves used force—actions such as murder, rape, kidnapping, theft, and fraud. Libertarians believe this code should be applied consistently—and specifically, that it should be applied to actions by governments as well as by individuals. Governments should exist to protect rights, to protect individuals from others who might use force against them. When governments themselves use force against people who have not violated the rights of others, libertarians believe that governments are themselves rights violators. Thus, libertarians condemn such government actions as censorship, the draft, price controls, confiscation of property, and regulation of personal and economic choices.

The key concepts of libertarianism have developed over many centuries. The first inklings of them can be found in ancient China, Greece, and Israel; they began to be developed into something resembling modern libertarian philosophy in the work of such seventeenth- and eighteenth-century thinkers as John Locke, David Hume, the French physiocrats, Adam Smith, Thomas Jefferson, and Thomas Paine. The key concepts of libertarian philosophy include the following:

Individualism: Libertarians see the individual as the basic unit of social analysis. Even the choices and actions of groups can be traced back to the choices and actions of individuals. Libertarian thought emphasizes the dignity of each individual, which entails both rights and responsibility. Libertarians see the progressive extension of rights to more people—to women, and to people of different religions and different races—as one of the great triumphs of the Western world.

Individual rights: Because individuals are moral agents, they have a right to be secure in their life, liberty, and property. These rights are not granted by government or by "society"; they are inherent in the nature of human beings. The burden of explanation should lie with those who would take rights away.

Spontaneous order: A great degree of order in society is necessary for individuals to survive and flourish. It is often assumed that order must be imposed by a central authority. The great insight of libertarian social analysis is that order in society arises spontaneously, out of the actions of thousands or millions of individuals who coordinate their actions with those of others in order to achieve their purposes. Over human history, we have gradually opted for more freedom and yet managed to develop a complex society with intricate organization. The most important institutions in human society—language, law, money, and markets—all developed spontaneously, without central direction. Civil society—the complex network of associations and connections among people—is another example of spontaneous order; the associations within civil society are formed for a purpose, but civil society itself is not an organization and does not have a purpose of its own.

The rule of law: Libertarianism is not libertinism or hedonism. Rather, libertarianism proposes a society of liberty under law, in which individuals are free to pursue their own projects so long as they respect the equal rights of others. The rule of law means that individuals are governed by generally applicable and spontaneously developed legal rules, not by arbitrary commands, and that those rules should protect the freedom of individuals to pursue happiness in their own ways rather than aiming at any particular result or outcome.

Limited government: To protect rights, individuals form governments. But government is a dangerous institution. Libertarians have a great antipathy to concentrated power, captured in Lord Acton's famous dictum, "Power tends to corrupt and absolute power corrupts absolutely." Thus they seek to divide and limit power, and especially to limit government, generally through a constitution enumerating and limiting the powers that the people delegate to government.

Free markets: To survive and to flourish, individuals need to engage in economic activity. The right to property entails the right to exchange property by mutual agreement. Free markets are the economic system of free individuals, and they are necessary to create wealth. Libertarians believe that people will be both freer and more prosperous if government intervention in people's choices is minimized.

The virtue of production: Much of the impetus for libertarianism in the seventeenth century was a reaction against monarchs and aristocrats who lived off the productive labor of other people. Libertarians defended the right of people to keep the fruits of their labor. Libertarians developed a pre-Marxist class analysis that divided society into two basic classes: those who produced wealth and those who took it by force from others. Thomas Paine, for instance, wrote, "There are two distinct classes of men in the nation, those who pay taxes, and those who receive and live upon the taxes." Modern libertarians defend the right of productive people to keep what they earn, against a New Class of politicians and bureaucrats who would seize their earnings to transfer them to nonproducers.

Natural harmony of interests: Libertarians believe that there is a natural harmony of interests among peaceful, productive people in a just society. People's individual plans—which may involve getting a job, starting a business, buying a house, and so on—may conflict with the plans of others, so the market makes many of us change our plans. But we all prosper from the operation of the free market, and there are no necessary conflicts between farmers and merchants, manufacturers and importers. Only when government begins to hand out rewards on the basis of political pressure do we find ourselves involved in group conflict, pushed to organize and contend with other groups for a piece of political power.

Peace: Libertarians have always battled the age-old scourge of war. They have understood that war brings death and destruction on a grand scale, disrupts family and economic life, and puts more power in the hands of the ruling class—which might explain why rulers do not always share the popular sentiment for peace. Free men and women, of course, have often had to defend their own societies against foreign threats; but throughout history war has usually been the common enemy of peaceful, productive people on all sides of a given conflict.

The libertarian tradition draws on the Greek and Hebrew ideas of a higher law, the struggle for religious toleration, the development of representative government and limits on power throughout the West, the economics of the Spanish Scholastics in the sixteenth century, and the response to absolutism, especially in England and the Netherlands. The first clearly libertarian ideas—self-ownership, natural rights, private property, religious toleration, and representative government—were advanced by the Levellers in the English Revolution. Libertarians see John Locke's theories of natural rights and government by consent and Adam Smith's explanation of the spontaneous order of the marketplace as the great building blocks of libertarianism, and of classical liberalism, and indeed of modern Western civilization.

The libertarian pantheon also includes such figures as Thomas Paine, Thomas Jefferson, James Madison, Wilhelm von Humboldt, John Stuart Mill, Frederic Bastiat, Benjamin Constant, and Herbert Spencer. In the twentieth century the most important names are Ludwig von Mises, F. A. Hayek, Ayn Rand, Milton Friedman, Murray Rothbard, and Robert Nozick.

Long experience with government excesses has persuaded libertarians that strict limits on government are needed to protect individual freedom. Many libertarians believe that individuals have natural rights, the legal protection of which is the best check on power. Others believe that although rights are ultimately a social construction, not a natural reality, the constitution of a free society should limit government in a manner consistent with individual rights. Others take a more historical approach, arguing that our constitutional rights reflect a long process of individuals and groups contending with governments to achieve particular liberties, which eventually produced a free society, one in which civil society is left largely free of coercive intervention by the state. Others, especially libertarian economists, would make the case for liberty strictly in consequentialist terms: private property, free markets, and limited government will lead to the highest standard of living for a society. All would agree that individuals should be free to live their lives as they choose, so long as they respect the rights of others to do likewise.

Libertarians disagree about their place in the political spectrum and in particular about the relationship between libertarianism and conservatism. It is often said that libertarians are conservative on economic issues and liberal on issues of personal freedom, which suggests that libertarianism is equidistant from modern liberalism and modern conservatism. Yet there has clearly been a closer relationship between libertar-

ians and conservatives than between libertarians and liberals. The long struggle against communism united libertarians and conservatives. And to the extent that American conservatives defend private property, capitalism, and the Constitution, they are pursuing an agenda congenial to libertarians. Still, libertarians have often disagreed with conservatives over such issues as personal freedom (in areas like the prohibition or regulation of drugs, gambling, and consensual sexual activity), the separation of church and state, and foreign interventionism (though in the post–Cold War era liberals have seemed more enamored than conservatives of foreign military entanglements, at least until very recently).

The modern libertarian movement may be traced to World War II and its aftermath, notably the publication of *The Fountainhead* by Ayn Rand in 1943 and *The Road to Serfdom* by F. A. Hayek in 1944. Rand's *Atlas Shrugged* in 1957 and Milton Friedman's *Capitalism and Freedom* in 1962 were perhaps even more influential. There were libertarians involved in the 1964 Goldwater campaign, as well as in the antiwar movement, and by the late 1960s there were enough libertarians to begin forming their own organizations, including the Libertarian Party in 1972. Other libertarians remained within the Republican Party and played a role in the Reagan administration. Libertarians have also been active in campaigns for lower taxes, school choice, Second Amendment rights, and term limits.

—DAVID BOAZ

Further Reading

Boaz, David. *Libertarianism: A Primer*. New York: Free Press, 1997.

———, ed., *The Libertarian Reader*. New York: Free Press, 1997.

Hayek, F. A. *The Constitution of Liberty*. Chicago: University of Chicago Press, 1960.

Kelley, John L. *Bringing the Market Back In: The*

Political Revitalization of Market Liberalism. New York: New York University Press, 1997. Rothbard, Murray. *For a New Liberty: The Libertarian Manifesto.* New York: Collier, 1978.

See also: anarchism; capitalism; Cato Institute; community; constitutionalism; free trade; Friedman, Milton; fusionism; Hayek, Friedrich A. von; individualism; Institute for Humane Studies; liberalism; liberalism, classical; Libertarian Party; Mises, Ludwig von; property rights, private; Rand, Ayn; Reason; Rothbard, Murray; speech, freedom of

liberty

Few words command such quick and unbridled favor as "liberty." Nor have many terms been so closely identified with America and Americans. When Patrick Henry demanded "Give me Liberty or Give me Death!" he clearly spoke for a vast number of Americans of his day (many of them self-described "sons of liberty") who risked their lives, fortunes, and sacred honor to vindicate inalienable rights, with liberty at their center. Yet in his *Reflections on the Revolution in France* (1790), Edmund Burke, the founder of modern conservatism, asked, "Is it because liberty in the abstract may be classed amongst the blessings of mankind, that I am seriously to felicitate a madman who has escaped from the protecting restraint and wholesome darkness of his cell on his restoration to the enjoyment of light and liberty?"

Suspicion of those who proclaim liberty to be always and everywhere a blessing is not at all equivalent to hostility toward liberty. Indeed, conservatives, as proponents of limited government and self-rule by local political and social associations, are committed to vigorously defending a rational, ordered liberty. But conservatives rarely engage in revolutionary rhetoric like Patrick Henry's. Nor do they share libertarians' enthusiasm for absolute liberty in all its forms. In particu-

lar, conservatives insist on the necessity of taking into account liberty's potential for abuse when interpreted, in a simplistic fashion, as the mere absence of constraint. The prominent liberal philosopher Isaiah Berlin famously distinguished between two forms of liberty—"negative" and "positive." "Negative" liberty is freedom from coercion and constraint, whereas "positive" liberty is the freedom to fulfill one's essential purposes. Berlin made clear his preference for "negative" liberty as promoting self-control, contrasting it with a potentially totalitarian "positive" liberty. For Berlin, liberty must be seen as merely one among many goods (such as equality and fairness) to be pursued.

But it is important to note the rather unsatisfactory understanding of liberty presented by Berlin. Negative liberty, abstractly understood, is simply power. It is a person's ability to act, without check, as he chooses. And individuals may and often do choose to act in ways that may be harmful and even evil. Taken in this asocial sense, negative liberty clearly is not an unmitigated good. Neither is "positive" liberty, in which an individual person may have his essential purposes defined for him by the government. But then reality, as the conservative knows, rarely fits nicely into rationalistic philosophers' neat categories.

Early in American history the Puritan leader John Winthrop, in his "Little Speech on Liberty," also distinguished between two forms of liberty. "Natural" liberty men share with beasts. It is the liberty to do as one pleases, be it good or evil. This "natural" liberty (so named in reference to man's natural, inherent sinfulness) is inconsistent with authority of any kind, including the rightful authority of free, ordered government. The other liberty, which Winthrop termed "civil," refers to the freedom of men guided by moral norms. It is the liberty to do "that only which is good, just, and honest." Civil liberty consists in the freedom of men joined together in political communities to pursue the common good. This civil liberty is not defined by the will of the ruler, empowered to determine the good of each individual he rules. Rather, it is the liberty of social creatures, reared in family, church, and local association, to recognize their duties to their fellows, as well as their right to pursue good ends.

Winthrop's "natural" liberty, like Berlin's "negative" liberty, rests on rejection of any authority outside the self; its possessor seeks to follow his own inclinations only. Only in "civil" society does the individual become part of a constitutive group, part of a community seeking the common good and therefore making liberty beneficial to all. Thus, conservatives follow Burke in accepting the goodness of liberty only when and to the extent that it is not, in fact, unbounded, but instead subject to the moral dictates of natural law and the customary and legal restraints of society. This is in keeping with the conservative view of man's inherently social nature, the necessity of social interaction for the formation of good character, and the imperative that men have good character, or virtue, if they are to be free. As Burke remarked in the *Letter to a Member of the French National Assembly* (1791), "It is ordained in the eternal constitution of things, that men of intemperate minds cannot be free. Their passions forge their fetters."

Conservatives support liberty that is properly—that is socially, politically, and morally—ordered and understood. In other words, ordered liberty is the ability to pursue the good in common with one's fellows. And the good is not defined by those in power merely, but by the permanent standards of natural law made concrete in the norms of social life. Thus, liberty is inextricably communal. In fact, historically, liberty has been the possession of groups as much as it has individuals. When the American colonies won from the English crown the liberty to govern themselves, they were follow-

ing in the wake of those medieval cities which had won "liberties" from kings through charters granting them rights of self-government in important areas of public life. Charters' liberties could be lost through misuse. In similar fashion, an individual person's right to free speech will not protect him from punishment if he uses it to commit slander.

In sum, the most thoughtful conservatives recognize that a sustainable liberty is ordered by the proper ends of natural law and the customs and common good of the community.

—Bruce Frohnen

Further Reading

Berlin, Isaiah. "Two Concepts of Liberty." In *Four Essays on Liberty*. Oxford: Oxford University Press, 1969.

Frohnen, Bruce, ed. *The American Republic: Primary Sources*. Indianapolis, Ind.: Liberty Fund, 2002.

Hamburger, Philip. "Natural Rights, Natural Law, and American Constitutions." *Yale Law Journal* 102 (1993).

Reid, John Phillip. *The Concept of Liberty in the Age of the American Revolution*. Chicago: University of Chicago Press, 1987.

See also: conservatism; law and order; liberalism, classical; libertarianism

Liberty Fund

Located in Indianapolis, Liberty Fund is a private educational foundation established by industrialist-philanthropist Pierre F. Goodrich in 1960 to encourage and facilitate the study of the ideal of a society comprising free and responsible individuals. It has been led faithfully by Goodrich's successor T. Alan Russell since 1984.

Liberty Fund has a strong tradition of providing scholars and serious readers access to books and conference programming focused on the concept of liberty. A cuneiform inscription serves as the foundation's symbol; this is said to be the earliest known written appearance of the word "freedom" or "liberty" and serves as a design motif for the endpapers of the books published by the organization.

Perhaps the most lasting of Liberty Fund's contributions to the American conservative movement thus far has been its extensive conference programming. The small group conferences—of which almost 200 are held every year—take place in locations across the country (and also outside the country), providing a forum for those interested in in-depth discussions related to the ideas of a free society. From these conferences has developed a rich and extensive network of conservative-leaning intellectuals, many of whom have made significant contributions to the conservative movement.

Supporting this ongoing initiative is a program to republish out-of-print classical liberal texts; many of these books were found in the libraries of our nation's founding fathers. Liberty Fund's ever-increasing number of books range across many disciplines, subscribe to the highest standards of production, and are priced to ensure their availability to all serious readers. Examples of recent releases include the letters of David Ricardo, *Theory and History,* by Ludwig von Mises, and Hugo Grotius's *Truth of the Christian Religion.*
—CRAIG T. COBANE

See also: Goodrich, Pierre F.

Lieber, Francis (1800–72)

Educator and pioneer in the fields of political science, penology, and military law, Francis Lieber was born into a middle-class business family that suffered financial reversals during the French Revolution. His intense patriotism was evident even in childhood during the French occupation of Berlin in 1807. In 1820 he surreptitiously earned a doctorate at the University of Jena, then slipped out of the country a year later to fight in the Greek war for independence, an experience that left him disillusioned and destitute. Before his return to Germany he spent a year with the historian Barthold Niebuhr, who was Prussia's ambassador to Italy, and acquired a lifelong interest in the traditions of what he called Anglican liberty.

Because of his youthful political activities, Lieber faced an uncertain future in Germany. In 1826 he emigrated to England and in 1827 to America, where he operated a gymnasium and swimming school in Boston and also became a newspaper correspondent. Lieber founded and began to edit the *Encyclopedia Americana* (1828–33), which brought him into contact with many American political and literary figures. A student of the Lancastrian system in England, he became active in educational circles and wrote an education plan for Girard College in 1834.

Lieber commenced his distinguished teaching career a year later when he was unanimously elected professor of history and political economy at South Carolina College. It was during this period (1835–56) that he wrote his major scholarly works. But from the start he was homesick for the North. Following a long campaign, he secured a teaching position at Columbia College (1857–65), where he held the first political science chair. Conflicts with a new president eventually led to his transfer to Columbia Law School (1865–72).

During the Civil War, Lieber was commissioned by the Lincoln administration to draft the first code of military conduct (known as the Lieber Code) for use in land warfare. It was later incorporated into the Hague and Geneva Conventions.

Lieber's scholarly activities covered a wide range of fields, including linguistics, higher education, economics, sociology, geography, constitutional law, international law, and penology (a word he coined). He translated and wrote a preface to Beaumont and Tocqueville's *On the Penitentiary System* (1833). He campaigned for an international copyright and urged Congress to create an office of statistics.

Following the Civil War, Lieber was given charge of organizing the Confederate archives and served as umpire on the United States and Mexican Claims Commission. He devoted much of his attention to the subjects of nationalism and internationalism and sought to organize scholarly conferences on international law.

In addition to the *Encyclopedia Americana*, Lieber's published work includes an 1823 account of his experiences in Greece; numerous poems in German and English; a popular travelogue, *Letters to a Gentleman in Germany* (1834), which includes an account of his experiences at the Battle of Waterloo; the *Manual of Political Ethics* (two volumes: 1838, 1839); *Legal and Political Hermeneutics* (1839); *Essays on Property and Labour* (1841); and his chief political science treatise, *On Civil Liberty and Self-Government* (1853). A collection of his shorter writings, *Miscellaneous Writings* (two volumes: 1881) and selections from his letters edited by Thomas Sergeant Perry, *The Life and Letters of Francis Lieber* (1882), were published posthumously.

Along with the Lieber Code, Francis Lieber is best known for his theory of institutional liberty, which contrasted the organic development of English government with the highly centralized French tradition. A supporter of free trade, Lieber helped introduce the work of Frederic Bastiat to the American public.

—STEVEN ALAN SAMSON

Further Reading

Brown, Bernard Edward. *American Conservatives: The Political Thought of Francis Lieber and John W. Burgess.* New York: Columbia University Press, 1951.

Freidel, Frank. *Francis Lieber: Nineteenth-Century Liberal.* Baton Rouge, La.: Louisiana State University Press, 1947.

Hartigan, Richard Shelly. *Lieber's Code and the Law of War.* Chicago: Precedent, 1983.

See also: Civil War; free trade; French Revolution

Liebman, Marvin (1923–97)

Born and raised in Queens and Brooklyn, New York, Marvin Liebman grew up in a milieu of Jewish radicalism and in 1937 joined the Young Communist League. Liebman attended New York University until 1942, when he was drafted into the Army Air Corps. He served until 1944, when he was discharged because of his homosexuality. Active in efforts to establish a Jewish state in Palestine, Liebman worked for various communist front groups and raised funds in Hollywood for the United Jewish Appeal. He remained a member of the Communist Party until 1952, when he became an apprentice of fundraiser Harold Oram. He became a strident anticommunist in the 1950s and established dozens of "letterhead organizations," most prominently the Committee of One Million (to Keep Red China Out of the United Nations). He participated in the founding and early guidance of Young Americans for Freedom (YAF). In 1982 he received a job at the National Endowment for the Arts and worked there until his death.

On July 9, 1990, he publicly revealed his homosexuality in an open letter to William F. Buckley Jr. that was published in *National Review.* In 1992 he published *Coming Out Conservative: An Autobiography,* which documented his long and largely secret homosexual lifestyle.

Liebman was an important fundraiser and organizer of various anticommunist and conservative committees. A person who recognized talent, Liebman was crucial to the formation of YAF, and in his organization of the Committee of One Million he for many years helped sustain recognition of Taiwan as the legitimate government of China.

—GREGORY L. SCHNEIDER

Further Reading

Schneider, Gregory L. *Cadres for Conservatism: Young Americans for Freedom and the Rise of the Contemporary Right*. New York: New York University Press, 1999.

See also: Young Americans for Freedom

Liggio, Leonard P. (1933–)

Leonard P. Liggio is a historian and legal scholar who has been active in forming and sustaining a number of organizations promoting the principles of a free and ordered society. In 1952, Liggio assisted Frank Chodorov in the development of the Intercollegiate Studies Institute and founded its first chapter at Georgetown University. In 1960, Liggio participated in the organization of the Institute for Humane Studies. Since that time, Liggio has worked to advance the ideas of limited government, individual responsibility, the price system, and the rule of law around the world through teaching, publishing, and serving in a variety of market-oriented independent research institutes, including the Cato Institute, the Acton Institute for the Study of Religion and Liberty, the Salvatori Center of the Heritage Foundation, the Institute of Economic Studies–Europe, the Philadelphia Society, the Mont Pelerin Society, and the Atlas Economic Research Foundation.

Liggio, educated at All Hallows Institute in the Bronx, New York, and at Georgetown, Columbia, and Fordham universities, has published widely on jurisprudence, the history of legal institutions, political philosophy, economics, and religion. In the 1950s, he became involved with the stateless libertarians led by Murray Rothbard, a group that combined Austrian economics, capitalism, and isolationism. Liggio also cofounded *Left and Right: A Journal of Libertarian Thought* with Rothbard and George Resch. The journal was published only from 1965 to 1968, but Liggio remained a close friend of Rothbard, working with him on such projects as the first volume of *Conceived in Liberty* (1975).

Currently, Liggio serves on the editorial board of the *American Journal of Jurisprudence*. He has been active in the American Catholic Historical Association, and for many years held an appointment as research professor in the Department of History and School of Law at George Mason University.

Liggio has been the recipient of numerous honors, including an honorary doctorate in social science conferred by the Universidad Francisco Marroquin of Guatemala in 1990. A tireless traveler and mentor, Liggio encourages young scholars to investigate the principles of liberty from a variety of academic and policy perspectives. He has paid special attention to the promotion of liberty in developing countries and in postcommunist states.

—INGRID GREGG

Further Reading

Liggio, Leonard P. "Isolationism, Old and New, Part I." *Right and Left: A Journal of Libertarian Thought* (Winter 1966).

Liggio, Leonard P., and James J. Martin, eds. *Watershed of Empire: Essays on New Deal Foreign Policy*. Colorado Springs, Colo.: R. Myles, 1976.

See also: Atlas Economic Research Foundation; Rothbard, Murray; Students for America

Limbaugh, Rush (1951–)

Radio talk-show host and popular author, Rush Limbaugh is known to many as *the* voice of conservatism in America. Limbaugh discusses and debates current events with listeners and injects a considerable amount of humor into the three hours that his show runs daily. This combination of current events, thoughtful debate, and often irreverent humor has proven extremely successful as a media form.

Limbaugh hails from Cape Girardeau, Missouri. He began working in radio at the age of sixteen in a local station. He attended Southeast Missouri State University, but left college for a job as a disk jockey at a Pittsburgh radio station. After this, he moved to Kansas City. There Limbaugh switched from radio to sports when he landed a job directing sales and special events for the Kansas City Royals.

In 1983, Limbaugh returned to radio once again, this time as a political commentator for KMBZ in Kansas City. Over the next few years, he got his own daytime talk show in Sacramento. His career took off in August 1988, when he moved to a new program in New York. More than a break for Limbaugh, this move arguably signaled the start of a revolution in mass media. For with this new show came national syndication on fifty-eight stations, a number that grew steadily to reach more than 600 stations and twenty million listeners. Thus, the success of Limbaugh's show expanded the market for talk radio itself. Indeed, by building up an audience of tens of millions, Limbaugh elevated talk radio to a status in the media equal to that of television or newsprint.

Limbaugh also had a late-night television show for several years (January 1993 to September 1996). At its peak, this show was televised on 206 stations throughout 98 percent of the country. In October 1992, Limbaugh began publishing a monthly newsletter. The circulation of this newsletter, still published, eventually exceeded 400,000.

In September, 1992 Limbaugh published his first book, *The Way Things Ought To Be,* followed by another the following year titled *See, I Told You So.* These two books sold nearly nine million copies and further established Limbaugh's reputation as the leading political controversialist on the Right.

Limbaugh has won numerous awards. The National Association of Broadcasters has bestowed the Marconi Award for Syndicated Radio Personality of the Year upon him twice. Also, in 1993 he was inducted into Broadcasting's Hall of Fame.

The twenty-first century has brought some trials for Limbaugh. In 2001, Limbaugh gradually lost his hearing and in October of that year Limbaugh announced that he was completely deaf. However, in early 2002 Limbaugh regained his hearing through the use of a surgically implanted device. More seriously, Limbaugh faced an investigation in 2003 for drug usage, with his addictive use of painkillers and the sources from which he obtained them coming under scrutiny. Limbaugh was not charged with a crime, and both he and his radio program continue to be exceptionally popular.

—DOUG MACKENZIE

Further Reading

Bowman, James. "The Leader of the Opposition: Political Commentator Rush Limbaugh." *National Review,* September 6, 1993.

See also: media, conservative; movement conservatism

Lincoln, Abraham (1809–65)

More than any other American political leader, the statesmanship of Abraham Lincoln, sixteenth president of the United States, implicates perennial problems and historically contingent issues that define the meaning of conservatism in the American political tradition. Lincoln's signal achievement was to maintain the founders' regime of federal republicanism against forces of democratic popular sovereignty that culminated in the movement of revolutionary secession. As Russell Kirk wrote, in the contest between the claims of order and the claims of freedom posed by the Civil War, "Lincoln prevented the victory of disorder."

In the Springfield Lyceum address of 1838, Lincoln analyzed the problem of preserving constitutional liberty and equal rights against the potentially destructive power of popular sovereignty. As a Whig lawyer-politician in frontier Illinois, he represented middle-class, evangelical Protestant, and pro-capitalist interests concerned with projects of economic and moral improvement. In partisan contests against anticapitalist Democrat agrarians in the Illinois legislature and the U.S. Congress, Lincoln supported the Whig program of government-funded transportation projects, protective tariffs for domestic manufacturing, and a national banking system. Whig political economy was intended to strengthen national unity and economic prosperity against European monarchies abroad and the influence of proslavery partisanship in domestic politics.

In the slavery controversy that led to the Civil War Lincoln recommended a conservative antislavery position. Where Congress had authority to legislate, in the District of Columbia, he favored a plan of gradual, compensated emancipation to be approved by popular referendum. Opposed to abolitionism, Lincoln as a Whig and later as a member of the Republican Party occupied the centrist free soil position in the spectrum of antislavery politics that formed in the 1850s to resist the nationalizing, expansionist demands of the slave states.

In 1854 Lincoln achieved both acclaim and notoriety for his political and moral opposition to the Kansas-Nebraska Act, Democrat Senator Stephen A. Douglas's measure opening unorganized national territory to slavery penetration by repealing the antislavery restrictions of the Missouri Compromise. Appealing to the principles of the Declaration of Independence, Lincoln stated: "no man is good enough to govern another man, *without that other's consent....* Let us turn slavery from its claims of 'moral right,' back upon its existing legal rights, and its arguments of 'necessity.'" Not only moral principle but also free-labor economic interests justified resistance to proslavery aggrandizement. "The whole nation is interested that the best use shall be made of these territories," Lincoln said. "We want them for the homes of free white people."

Seeking election to the Senate in 1858, Lincoln assumed a more radical position based on the conviction that proslavery demands threatened republican government and free society in the nation as a whole. Criticizing the proslavery *Dred Scott* decision (1856), he predicted in the so-called House Divided speech that the sectional conflict would be resolved by the country becoming either all slave or all free. Lincoln relentlessly condemned the popular sovereignty principle of his political rival Douglas as a form of moral neutrality that effectively promoted the cause of slavery expansion. In 1860 Lincoln won the Republican presidential nomination as a moderate alternative to the more extreme antislavery senator William H. Seward of New York. Which of the four parties competing for the presidency—Republicans, northern Democrats, southern Democrats, and Constitutional Unionists—best represented the constitutional principles of the founding and was the true conservative party was the question to be decided.

The Republican platform recognized slavery as a local institution under federal constitutional protection in the states where it existed. It opposed the extension of slavery in national territories and declared the principles of liberty, equality, and consent in the Declaration of Independence to be essential to the preservation of republican institutions in the United States. Before his nomination Lincoln gave hundreds of speeches condemning slavery as a violation of the nation's founding principles, while scrupulously disavowing abolitionist ends and asserting vaguely that slavery be placed in course of ultimate extinction consistent with the founders' intent. Southern Democrats' claim to conservative constitutional fidelity rested on the argument that no practical or moral distinction existed between immediate abolition of slavery in states where it existed and opposition to territorial slavery. In general, southerners held slavery to be the foundation principle both of American constitutional republicanism and of a progressive, racially hierarchical social order.

Abraham Lincoln

After Lincoln was elected president, fear for the safety of their domestic institutions led South Carolina and six other southern states to secede from the Union. Secession was based on claims of a reserved and unalienable right of sovereign state-nations to withdraw at will from a legally nonbinding constitutional compact. The focus of national politics now shifted from the problem of slavery and republican government to the question of the existence of sovereign state immunity to overthrow the government of the Union created by the unanimous consent of all the American states. The issue posed was whether the American people constituted a nation, the conditions under which it was lawful and just for them to maintain their territorial and political integrity, and whether the government of the Union possessed legitimate authority to suppress a movement aimed at destroying the federal republic.

In this political crisis Lincoln acted on conservative grounds to maintain the existence of the Union under the Constitution ordained by the people of the United States. In his first inaugural he rejected the idea of a legal and constitutionally privileged right of secession as anarchical in nature and contrary to fundamental law. Affirming the central principle of the American political tradition disputed by the secessionists, Lincoln declared: "A majority, held in restraint by constitutional checks, and limitations, and always changing easily, with deliberate changes of popular opinions and sentiments, is the only true sovereign of a free people."

Lincoln acknowledged the liberal principle of a right of revolution to which an aggrieved minority could with moral justification appeal should the majority deprive it of a clearly written constitutional right. He denied that deprivation of "vital rights" of minorities had occurred. Observing that southerners still had the protection of the Constitution and laws on slavery they had written, Lincoln asked for "a patient confidence in the ultimate justice of the people." The federal government, he declared, would not assail them. When the Confederate states decided to exercise the right of secession by using military force to occupy Fort Sumter in South Carolina, Lincoln used military force to defend the Union against what he proclaimed to be lawless and unjustified rebellion.

Whether Lincoln or the secessionists acted on a correct constitutional understanding of the nature of the Union, and where responsibility lay for starting the Civil War, remain controversial questions. Sympathetic to claims of local liberty against the dictates of twentieth-century centralized sovereignty, a body of conservative opinion regards Lincoln as a revolutionary nationalist and racial egalitarian whose willful rejection of compromise and denial of the right of secession plunged the country into war. In this view the Confederate states seceded not to preserve the system of Negro slavery, as appearance might suggest, but to defend their sovereignty as independent state-nations in the voluntary and noncoercive Union established by the founding fathers. Lincoln is charged with derailing the American political tradition from its constitutional unconcern with equality, canonizing the equality principle of the Declaration of Independence at the center of American political experience through revolutionary means. Allowed to pursue the path of local libertarianism, conservatives of this persuasion suggest, the Confederate states would have separated from their northern brothers on equitable terms and resolved the slavery question in a humane and racially progressive way, without the catastrophic loss of life and property exacted by Lincoln's decision for war.

Although provocative, the libertarian conservative critique exaggerates in an unhistorical way the role of Lincoln and the Republican Party as the sources of contemporary statist liberalism and egalitarian excess that modern conservatism opposes. If the Union was the nonbinding compact of sovereign states that secessionists said it was—in essence a pure interstate anarchy system—it is difficult to understand why the northern states did not have as much right to defend the interests of free labor in liberal republican society as the southern states

did the interests of slave labor in patriarchal republican society. If, on the other hand, the nature of the Union was ambiguous, the constitutional arguments of North and South canceling each other inconclusively, then superior prudence and a deep understanding of the American political tradition might be considered the decisive factor in resolving the crisis of American nationality. On this score Lincoln's historical reputation as a conservative statesman is not undeserved.

In political circumstances that portended the "mortal feud" and "conflagration through a whole nation" that had concerned the founding fathers, Lincoln acted with conscious and deliberate intent as a constitutionalist, rather than as a revolutionist. As an antislavery reformer and representative of bourgeois capitalist society, Lincoln recognized political and constitutional limits on the federal government—including the power of the chief executive in time of war—that casts doubt on the view of him as an egalitarian nationalist. In the face of extreme antislavery pressure, Lincoln endeavored to prevent the war from degenerating into "a violent and remorseless revolutionary struggle." With single-minded determination he insisted on the priority of maintaining the Constitution and Union as the aim of the war. His actions as president-elect in the secession crisis and as wartime chief executive were politically controversial precisely because the Constitution was not in any comprehensive way suspended. Like its Confederate counterpart in Richmond, the Lincoln administration found it necessary to restrict individual civil liberties in areas of disloyal activity and overt military operations. The temporary suspension of civil rights was undertaken because of the friction and abrasion of war, however, rather than because of a systematic design to subvert the constitutional order and establish executive dictatorship.

Lincoln's actions on the slavery question

reflected the prudence of a moderate reformer concerned with constitutional limitations and existing legal obligations. The very reason for the Republican Party's existence, and the cause of Lincoln's presidency, was to maintain free political and social institutions against the threat of proslavery political domination. With the outbreak of war it was obvious that changes in the institution of slavery might occur. Yet Lincoln scrupulously subordinated action on the slavery question to the strategic objective of maintaining the Union and the Constitution. He issued the Emancipation Proclamation as a measure warranted by the Constitution, upon military necessity, which was "sincerely believed to be an act of justice."

In the view of Richard Weaver, the statesmanship of Abraham Lincoln was distinguished by recognition that a politically effective American conservatism must be based on principles grounded in a fixed concept of the nature of man. Conservatism was evident in Lincoln's challenge to Douglas's relativistic popular sovereignty, his appeal to the moral idea of freedom and the political idea of Union as ideal objectives rising above political expediency, and his respect for established principles of American government. In transcending the passions of war in his second inaugural, Weaver observed, Lincoln offered his fellow countrymen of both the North and South a final demonstration of conservative statesmanship.

—HERMAN BELZ

Further Reading

Jaffa, Harry V. *A New Birth of Freedom: Abraham Lincoln and the Coming of the Civil War.* Lanham, Md.: Rowman & Littlefield, 2000.

Kendall, Willmoore, and George W. Carey. *The Basic Symbols of the American Political Tradition.* Baton Rouge, La.: Louisiana State University Press, 1970.

Kirk, Russell. *The Roots of American Order.* 4th ed. Wilmington, Del.: ISI Books, 2003.

Weaver, Richard M. *The Ethics of Rhetoric.* Chicago: Regnery, 1953.

See also: Civil War; Clay, Henry; Douglas, Stephen A.; Jaffa, Harry V.; Reconstruction; Republican Party

Lindbergh, Charles A. (1902–74)

Because of his solo trans-Atlantic flight in 1927, Charles Lindbergh became the hero of a jaded generation. His visibility as a conservative isolationist, however, only came with the advent of World War II.

The son of a schoolteacher and a populist-minded congressman from Minnesota, Lindbergh grew up in Little Falls, Minnesota. In his early twenties, he was a barnstorming aviator. After his famous flight, he served as technical adviser for Transcontinental and Pan-American airlines and undertook various scientific projects.

In the 1930s, Lindbergh feared that any conflict in Europe would result in the spread of communism, an anxiety that led him to endorse the Munich agreement. In the late 1930s, he made several trips to Germany, doing so at the request of the American military attaché in Berlin, Colonel Truman Smith. He genuinely disliked Nazi fanaticism but admired the "virility" of Germany and Italy. When in September 1939 World War II broke out, Lindbergh publicly opposed aid to the Allies and joined the national committee of America First.

There was no major anti-interventionist figure so controversial as Lindbergh, in part because of his previous fame and in part because of his comments during the debate over intervention. One of the more extreme isolationists, he said he wanted neither Germany nor Britain to win. He refused to return a Nazi decoration bestowed on him in 1936, and three years later he called for building "our White ramparts." In May 1941, he demanded "new leadership," though Roosevelt had recently been elected for a third term. On August 29, he warned that Great Britain could turn against the United States, and on September 11 at Des Moines he linked "the Jews" with the British and the Roosevelt administration as elements leading the nation to war. His enemies were quick to label him as pro-Nazi, anti-British, and anti-Semitic, accusations he firmly denied.

When the United States entered the war, Lindbergh was rejected by the Roosevelt administration for military service, but he flew more than fifty combat missions in the Pacific as a combat test pilot. During the most intense years of the Cold War, he maintained a studied silence, limiting his comments to the causes of ecology and space exploration.

—Justus D. Doenecke

Further Reading

Berg, A. Scott. *Lindbergh*. New York: Putnam, 1998.

Cole, Wayne S. *Charles A. Lindbergh and the Battle against American Intervention in World War II*. New York: Harcourt Brace Jovanovich, 1974.

Lindbergh, Anne Morrow. *War Within and Without: Diaries and Letters, 1939–1944*. New York: Harcourt Brace Jovanovich, 1980.

Lindbergh, Charles A. *Autobiography of Values*. Edited by William Jovanovich and Judith A. Schiff. New York: Harcourt Brace Jovanovich, 1978.

See also: isolationism; Old Right

Lippmann, Walter (1889–1974)

Newspaper editor, syndicated columnist, and political philosopher, Walter Lippmann was born and raised in New York City the son of a wealthy Manhattan businessman. He was educated at Harvard, where he studied under philosopher George Santayana. Graduating in 1910, he joined the staff of *Everybody's* as an assistant to Lincoln Steffens, the famous muckraker, and wrote freelance articles for a number of progressive and socialist publications. In 1912 he served briefly as secretary to the socialist mayor of Schenectady and published his first book, *A Preface to Politics*, in 1913 at the age of twenty-three. A year later, he helped found the weekly public-affairs magazine, *New Republic*.

When war erupted in 1914, Lippmann sided with the Allies. President Wilson considered him a critical asset in persuading the American public to abandon its neutrality. In 1917, he joined the "Inquiry," a secret organization of scholars and diplomats who helped the administration draft an initial postwar settlement. Disenchanted with the Versailles

Walter Lippmann

Treaty's indefensible peace, however, he returned to the *New Republic* and also wrote for *Vanity Fair*. In 1924 he took over the editorial page of the *New York World*.

When the *World* went bankrupt seven years later in 1931, the *New York Tribune* hired Lippmann to write his own column, "Today and Tomorrow." The first column dedicated solely to political opinion, "T & T" was an overnight success, syndicated in hundreds of daily newspapers with an estimated readership of more than ten million. In thirty-six years it totaled several thousand articles. In addition, Lippmann continued to write for both popular magazines and scholarly journals, and he published twenty-four books. His influence on public opinion was such that many Americans professed to being undecided on the issues until they knew what Lippmann thought. He received the Pulitzer Prize for Journalism in 1958 and 1962.

Lippmann's views did not lend themselves to easy categorization as liberal or conservative. In foreign affairs, to which he dedicated a third of his columns, he eschewed both isolationism and interventionism. He was an early proponent of defeating Germany in both world wars to make the Atlantic safe for American trade and travel—not to make the world safe for democracy. In the Cold War, a term Lippmann is credited with inventing, he supported resistance to Soviet-backed insurgencies in areas strategic to American interests, but denounced any open-ended policy of "containment," claiming it overreached American military and economic capabilities while committing American prestige to suppressing third world aspirations driven more by nationalism than communism. Celebrated by the Left for opposing America's land wars in Asia, Lippmann had actually argued against those wars in the terms of traditional conservative statesmanship. He believed international security hinged on a balance of power in which there were mutually respected spheres of influence.

On domestic matters, Lippmann considered himself a liberal, although he was by no means ideologically committed. Even in his youthful flirtation with socialism he preferred practical compromises to dogmatic solutions. In the tradition of Tocqueville, moreover, his writings expressed a deep suspicion of mass democracy, its leveling influences on culture and morals, and its tendency to end in totalitarian dictatorship. Lippmann also argued for the need to halt the erosion of Western values. No civilization, he insisted, could be truly progressive without conserving its philosophical and moral inheritance.

—C. H. HOEBEKE

Further Reading

Dam, Hari. *Intellectual Odyssey of Walter Lippmann*. New York: Gordon Press, 1973.

Lippmann, Walter. *Essays in the Public Philosophy*. Boston: Little, Brown, 1955.

Rossiter, Clinton, and James Lare, eds. *The Essential Lippmann*. New York: Random House, 1963.

Steel, Ronald. *Walter Lippmann and the American Century*. Boston: Little, Brown, 1980.

Syed, Anwar. *Walter Lippmann's Philosophy of International Politics*. Philadelphia: University of Pennsylvania Press, 1963.

See also: Babbitt, Irving; Cold War

literary criticism

The history of contemporary American literary criticism begins with the New Criticism, whose adherents shared a conservative political outlook but advocated a shift in the study of literature from philological research to textual explication that disregarded the author's intentions and refused to anchor the poem's overt message in history.

The New Critics' insistence on the centrality of metaphor in poetry was an important correction to the crudeness of those interpreters who treated poetry as an ornamental way of saying what could have been said in expository prose. Nevertheless, by toning down the importance of history and subjectivity, the New Critics facilitated the demise of content-oriented criticism and the reappearance of the concepts of history and personality within a new semantic framework. Hence, personality returned as a sex-oriented construct of depth psychology to the exclusion of what used to be called the conscious human person, and history returned not as a collection of facts but as a social and political process or an ongoing power struggle whose primacy the authors of literary works routinely sought to hide. Thus, the meaning of the poem came not to be sought in what it said or suggested but in what it concealed.

Structuralism followed in the footsteps of the New Criticism as a kind of subsidiary. It shared with the New Criticism a lack of interest in subjectivity and history and instead investigated the phonemic and compositional structures of poems, stories, and novels. Structuralism had French and Russian roots. By the late 1960s, it was on its way out in the American academy, to be replaced by the trends that have dominated the critical scene ever since: deconstruction, the New Historicism, postcolonial studies, and feminism. Their claims on literature (now called "text") are much more radical than those of structuralism.

The term "deconstruction" was introduced by French critic Jacques Derrida, who sought to interpret literary texts as duels between language and writer. "Deconstructionist" literary critics are supposed to serve as explicators of the relationship between the writer's unconscious and what may be termed the "language unconscious." This highly abstract relationship is exemplified in Derrida's analysis of Jean-Jacques Rousseau's writings. In *Of Grammatology* (1976), Derrida alleged that there existed a relation between Rousseau's addiction to masturbation and his addiction to writing (Rousseau spoke of both as "supplements"). Like the Freudian critics, the deconstructionists tend to see sexual underpinnings in texts that are ostensibly not related to sexual themes.

In the 1970s, the New Historicism appeared, a sophisticated critical trend profoundly influenced by German thought. The New Historicists perceive literary works as bearers of ideology that, they allege, is virtually never consciously perceived by the writer but which the critic must expose. They treat literature as a form of social activity that contributes to the preservation or weakening of regnant ideologies. They make scant allowances for aesthetic, let alone moral, values. They are not interested in language as such or in the personality of the author; indeed, they perceive the author as a product of various ideological forces. Nor are the New Historicists interested in the sequence of political events as they occurred in time. The historicity of which they speak has to do with the general laws of history (the unproven assumption that such exist lies at the core of the historicist creed). The lackluster quality of historicist studies, or "the poverty of historicism," can be best observed by perusing *Representations*, the leading literary quarterly of the American New Historicists.

Feminism can be considered a subcategory of historicism. It, too, sees literary texts as dominated by an ideology that writers are unable to control, let alone overcome. The feminist critics are poised to expose the alleged cultural habit of centering thought and discourse within the male persona. They see history as a process of domination of women by men. The intellectual territory to which feminist criticism has laid claim includes such seemingly nonideological arenas as theology and mathematics.

A number of Marxist orientations (with the Gramscian orientation predominating) constitutes an important background to these trends. Such critics as Fredric Jameson, Frank Lentricchia, and Terry Eagleton are probably best described as simply Marxist. However, Jameson and others have also been called structuralists and historicists. Literary quarterlies such as *Diacritics* publish deconstructionist, historicist, and Marxist criticism, or combinations thereof.

The publication of Edward Said's *Orientalism* in 1978 ushered in the hybrid methodology of postcolonial studies that combines elements of the New Historicism, deconstruction, and, occasionally, feminism, with an orientation toward aspects of literature said to be related to imperialistic greed.

Postcolonial critics see literature as a partner in the colonial enterprise of the empires to which writers belong. While postcolonial critics maintain that they are as anti-essentialist as their other postmodern colleagues, the presence of moral indignation in their writings indicates their affinity with the critical nature of Western political thought.

All of these critical trends have involved a redefinition of concepts such as subject and object, as well as a radical change in the understanding of what constitutes evidence and truth. They also have involved a change in the definition of literature. The assumption that knowledge is cumulative has been rejected in favor of the laws of history or the internal laws of a particular period of time. It is assumed that "texts" have a rich political and sexual unconscious, and that the role of the critic is to lay it bare. It is also assumed that evidence is concealed rather than exposed by literary works, and that literary study should not be concerned with what literary works say or suggest but rather with what they hide. Invariably, in study after study, these hidden themes have to do with social inequities, power struggle, ideological manipulation, and sexuality.

Thus has literary criticism abandoned its role as a custodian of cultural heritage and companion to the reader's journey through literary masterpieces, assuming instead the role of a public prosecutor, political analyst, or midwife of social change. The relation of these trends to the state of American schools or the level of literacy in America has not been systematically studied. In spite of the appearance of several remarkable books combating what Frederic Crews has called "dialectical immaterialism," there is no sustained dialogue between the literary scholars representing the trends in criticism described above and their conservative critics. Conservative journals such as *Modern Age* and the *Intercollegiate Review* and the neoconservative *Academic Questions* have rela-

tively small circulations and can hardly count on financial and other support from the nation's major academic institutions.

On the other hand, the tendency of postmodern literary criticism to move into territories once considered the domain of historians, political scientists, psychologists, and sociologists indicates a possible exhaustion of the discipline whose academic prominence arose in the twentieth century and which may not survive that century's end for long. In that case, literary criticism will retreat back to book-review sections of journals and magazines. The efforts of literary scholars to encroach upon other areas of enquiry may stem from a realization that the era of salaried literary critics at universities is almost over.

—EWA M. THOMPSON

Further Reading

Crews, Frederic. *Sceptical Engagements*. Oxford: Oxford University Press, 1986.

Culler, Jonathan. *Structuralist Poetics: Structuralism, Linguistics and the Study of Literature*. Ithaca, N.Y.: Cornell University Press, 1975.

Donoghue, Denis. *Ferocious Alphabets*. Boston: Little Brown, 1981.

Jameson, Fredrick. *The Political Unconscious: Narrative as a Socially Symbolic Act*. Ithaca, N.Y.: Cornell University Press, 1981.

Thompson, Ewa M. "Dialectical Methodologies in the American Academy." *Modern Age* 28 (1984): 9–22.

Warhol, Robyn R., et. al., eds. *Feminisms: An Anthology of Literary Theory and Criticism*. New Brunswick, N.J.: Rutgers University Press, 1997.

See also: Babbitt, Irving; Brooks, Cleanth; feminism; Marxism; More, Paul Elmer; New Criticism; New Humanism

localism

Localism is the jealous defense of spontaneous, organic communities resting on custom or on "ancient" and distinctive identities. These bodies include vocational guilds, villages, municipal corporations, religious fraternities, communal hierarchies, and family or kin. Such localism builds on attachments to a particular place or geographic location. Its disposition is to favor that which is directly known or experienced and to limit sympathies and ideas to such attachments.

Conservatives have defended localism as a guarantor of liberty and the nexus for the good life. In contrast to liberals and socialists, the conservative holds that natural communities protect individuals from the overweening power of the centralizing state. They also nourish the personality in necessary ways. Accordingly, in the conservative view, these "intermediate institutions," these "states within states," should be able to administer their own affairs and to make binding claims on individuals, so limiting the latter's freedom to act. This means that institutions such as families, which grow out of human nature, should enjoy autonomy; the public law should not cross the threshold of the home. Nor should it intrude on the church.

Localism as embodied in the civic association, town, family, and religious fraternity exist logically and historically prior to the state. Conservatives commonly view Europe's classic medieval era (circa 1300) not as a time of chaos and disorder, but rather as an era when liberty, true pluralism, and fraternity flourished. As Richard Weaver explained in *Ideas Have Consequences* (1948), "Where men feel that society means station, the highest and the lowest see their endeavors contributing to a common end, and they are in harmony rather than in competition. . . . Such was true of feudal Europe." Where liberals see "old prejudices and unreasoned

habits," the conservative finds "jealously guarded liberties" and an "immense range of legal autonomy" rooted in variety and privilege. Where the centralist favors uniform customs and laws, the localist delights in particularity and the differences to be found in moving from village to village.

Conservatives have also tended to admire the local economics of premodern Europe. These markets were neighborhood or municipal in orientation and had little inclination to render the whole of society in their image. Indeed, the chartered municipalities raised every possible obstacle to national or international markets, in order to preserve local stability rooted in ideals of fairness and economic justice.

While Aristotle may properly be cited as the great architect of a localist philosophy, the modern conservative understanding comes from Edmund Burke. He admired the local institutions found in the American colonies. As the French Revolution burned its way across Europe, Burke authored a classic description of the origins of localism: "We begin our public affections in our families. . . . We pass on to our neighborhoods, and our habitual provincial connection. These are inns and resting places. Such divisions of our country as have been formed by habit, and not by the sudden jerk of authority, were so many little images of the great country in which the heart found something which it could fill." It was through this natural chain of loyalties, resting on spontaneous, organic units tied to place, that the good society emerged.

America's great sectional conflict during the middle decades of the nineteenth century embodied for some conservatives this contest between localism and centralization, summed up in the debate over "states' rights." As Robert E. Lee wrote to Lord Acton: "Maintenance of the rights and authority reserved to the states and to the people [is] the safeguard to the continuance of free government. . . . Whereas the consolidation of the states into one vast republic . . . will be the certain precursor of . . . ruin." From this perspective, the Fourteenth Amendment to the U.S. Constitution has served as the great desiccator of localism in America, sucking away the spirit found in local customs, statutes, and privileges in favor of the "equal protection of the law." As Alexis de Tocqueville once explained, "the only condition necessary in order to succeed in centralizing the supreme power in a democratic society is to love equality."

In the early twentieth century, American conservatives were frequently found in the ranks of those opposed to engagement in foreign wars, from the Philippine Insurrection to the 1939 war in Europe. Pejoratively labeled "isolationists," their real concern was the preservation of local life, for looming behind war was the centralizing state. As the agrarian Donald Davidson explained in 1941, war could only feed the Roosevelt administration's "highly industrialized, centralized, and socialistic order." No matter what results might be achieved in Europe, American intervention "would probably be ruinous" to hopes for the preservation and reconstruction of localism.

In the second half of the twentieth century, some conservatives lost enthusiasm for aspects of localism. While still sympathetic to appeals on behalf of "family," they found value in certain forms of central power. Some embraced the "national security state," resting on a large standing military force and a vast intelligence network, as a necessary pillar for the American global struggle against communism and other rival ideologies. Others delighted in the triumph of global capitalism over countless local and regional markets as the surest creator of wealth and opportunity. Still others found the U.S. Department of Education and other federal agencies to be useful platforms for moral reconstruction from the center.

At the same time, there were also conservatives who held fast to a vision of localism rooted in the good community, one that placed "high value on neighborly love, marital fidelity, local loyalty, the integrity and continuity of family life, respect for the old, and instruction of the young," one that "draws its life, so far as possible, from local sources" as Wendell Berry argued. These conservatives looked for ways to restore function-rich homes (e.g., through such seemingly insignificant measures as home-schooling and family gardens), to promote small-scale agriculture and family-held businesses, and to protect religious communities and other spontaneous associations from state interference.

—ALLAN CARLSON

Further Reading

Berry, Wendell. *What Are People For?* San Francisco: North Point Press, 1990.

Carlson, Allan. *The New Agrarian Mind: The Movement toward Decentralist Thought in Twentieth-Century America.* New Brunswick, N.J.: Transaction, 1999.

See also: anarchism; Berry, Wendell; centralization; community; distributism; mediating structures; Southern conservatism; states' rights; traditionalism

Lodge, Henry Cabot (1850–1924)

Scholar and statesman of the Gilded Age and Progressive Era, Henry Cabot Lodge served both as a United States congressman (1887–93) and as a United States senator (1893–1924). The scion of a colonial Boston family, few Americans made a career in politics with the academic credentials of Henry Cabot Lodge. In 1876, having earned his baccalaureate and law degrees from Harvard University, he was one of three students to receive from Harvard the first Ph.D.s in history ever awarded in the United States. He studied under Henry Adams, who shared Lodge's passion for foreign affairs, and assisted Adams in editing the prominent monthly, *North American Review*. From 1876 to 1879 he lectured in American history at Harvard. Throughout his career, he published numerous essays and books on politics and history, most notably biographies of Washington, Hamilton, Webster, and his Federalist great-grandfather, George Cabot.

Never intent on being solely a scholar, Lodge became increasingly active in the Republican Party. He served two years in the Massachusetts House of Representatives (1880–81) and, after failing on two previous attempts, was elected to the U.S. House of Representatives in 1887. In 1893, the Massachusetts legislature elected

Henry Cabot Lodge

him to the Senate, where he served until his death in 1924. Lodge's career in Congress was marked in domestic issues by an attempt to reach a balance between the plutocratic and socialist elements of the era. As the descendant of pre-industrial aristocracy, Lodge disapproved of the methods and manners of the newly rich, but he believed in the overall efficacy of free enterprise. He viewed federal legislation such as the Sherman Anti-Trust Act (1890) and Theodore Roosevelt's "trust busting" campaign as conservative measures to prevent economic revolution. A passionate conservative on constitutional questions, he spoke out against the direct legislation movement in the Progressive Era, as well as attempts to popularize the state and federal judiciaries. He also voted against the direct election of senators, ratified as the Seventeenth Amendment in 1913.

Lodge's primary interest as a senator, however, was in international affairs. In the age of American isolationism, he was an early advocate of an aggressive foreign policy, backed by naval power, to protect the nation's expanding interests overseas. At the same time, he believed that there were limits to both American interests and power. As chairman of the Senate Committee on Foreign Relations during and immediately after World War I, Lodge, who had supported American involvement, orchestrated the defeat of the Versailles Treaty when it went before the Senate for ratification. While not opposed to collective security arrangements that were expedient and temporary, the senator argued that President Wilson's guarantee of maintaining the territorial integrity of every member of the League of Nations usurped the congressional prerogative to declare war and ran counter to America's traditional avoidance of entangling alliances. Lodge's speech to the Senate urging his colleagues not to accept the "Fourteen Points" of Wilson's peace plan without amendments has become required reading in American diplomatic history.

—C. H. HOEBEKE

Further Reading

Garraty, John A. *Henry Cabot Lodge: A Biography*. New York: Knopf, 1953.

Widenor, William C. *Henry Cabot Lodge and the Search for an American Foreign Policy*. Berkeley, Calif.: University of California Press, 1980.

See also: isolationism; populism; progressivism

London, Herbert I. (1939–)

A prominent neoconservative social critic, institution executive, and educator, Herbert

London received his Ph.D. in 1966 from New York University, where he subsequently became a professor of social studies. In 1972, London created NYU's Gallatin Division, a school organized to encourage study of the great books. He was the Gallatin Division's dean until 1992, when he became John M. Olin University Professor of Humanities. A pioneering opponent of "political correctness" in higher education, London cofounded (with Stephen Balch) the National Association of Scholars in 1986 and served on its original board of directors. He was the first editor of its journal, *Academic Questions*.

In addition, London was a Republican candidate for mayor of New York City in 1989 and the Conservative Party candidate for governor of New York in 1990. In 1994, he was the Republican candidate for comptroller of New York, losing narrowly.

London has written or edited sixteen books, including *Myths that Rule America* (1981), *The Overheated Decade* (1976), and *A Strategy for Victory without War* (1989). Reflecting his commitment to balanced, nonideo-logical education, *Why Are They Lying to Our Children?* (1984) rebutted the environmental doomsaying then prominent in public school textbooks; *Armageddon in the Classroom* (1987) surveyed critically the fearmongering "nuclear education" in public schools during the eighties.

Serving on the Hudson Institute's board of trustees since 1974, London has long also been a senior fellow at Hudson, and he founded the institute's Center for Education and Employment Policy. He became president of the Hudson Institute in 1997.

—Robert Waters

Further Reading

London, Herbert I. *The Broken Apple: New York City in the 1980s.* New Brunswick, N.J.: Transaction, 1989.

———. *Decade of Denial: A Snapshot of America in the 1990s.* Lanham, Md.: Lexington, 2001.

See also: education, higher; Hudson Institute; National Association of Scholars

Lowell, James Russell (1819–91)

In a lifetime bracketed by the beginning and end of the nineteenth century, Lowell personified rather than shaped his age. Scion of the Boston Lowells (as close to a natural aristocracy as the United States has ever produced), James Russell went dutifully to

James Russell Lowell

Harvard, graduating in law in 1840, but committed in his heart to the pursuit of poetry. He vindicated his choice by returning to his alma mater in 1856 as Professor of Romance Languages and Belles-lettres in succession to Longfellow. Lowell had in the meantime made the acquaintance of Emerson and Thoreau; he had been active both as a poet and a journalist, contributing a copious amount of prose to the abolitionist cause and a plenitude of lyric to his muse. He edited many journals, most notably the *Pioneer* in 1843.

As a versifier, Lowell's early reputation depended on his satirical dialect poems, known collectively as *The Bigelow Papers* (1848). The technique seems in retrospect ham-handed, the peculiarities overdone; yet in skewering American hypocrisy, the *Papers* do sometimes exhibit a timeless quality: "I du believe the people want / A tax on teas and coffees, / Thet nothin' ain't extravygunt, – /

Providin' I'm in office," a campaign-stumper says in a candid aside. Another stanza from the same monologue suggests the sine qua non of contemporary liberalism: "I du believe in any plan / O' levyin' the texes, / Ez long ez, like a lumberman, / I git jest wut I axes." That this poem, in particular, takes the form of a mock credo further suggests that Lowell knew what an ideology was, whether he had the word for it or not.

Like Karl Marx and Percy Shelley (and like the Romantics generally), Lowell was attracted to the Prometheus myth. Lowell's "Prometheus" (1843) is the most ambitious, and arguably the best, of his early poems; his Titan gives voice to the Emersonian Oversoul, proclaims the perfectibility of the human, and thus remains true to the Unitarian-Transcendentalist vision. "There is a higher purity than thou," says the stealerof-fire to Jove, who stands in for Jehovah; later in the ode Prometheus extols "the supremeness of Beauty." After the Civil War, Lowell made an effort to be the trans-Atlantic Browning, dedicating poems short and long to historical subjects. "The Cathedral" (1869) is impressively Gothic and forecasts the themes of Henry Adams's *Mont-SaintMichel and Chartres* (1904). Ruskin liked these lines. More intimate and revealing is Lowell's elegy for Louis Agassiz.

Lowell also wrote criticism (see *Some Conversations on Old Poets*, 1844) and in the decades after Appomattox helped to establish a sense among the Brahmin classes of a distinct American literature. The opinions that modern people have about Washington Irving and James Fenimore Cooper, for example, are largely Lowell's. The case of Lowell points to the central limitation in American poetry (perhaps in American culture). Where it looks to the past, that past tends to be Yankee, Unitarian, and Transcendentalist; thus, what an artist of the tradition tends to "conserve" is Puritanism with its perfectionist program and a notion of Christianity at

once purged of the Trinity and melded with a pantheism that appears to be otherwise entirely irreligious. Where it wants to be "progressive" (at one point, in the late 1840s, Lowell thought of himself as a "radical"), this poetry oddly finds itself in much the same place, advocating the Promethean project of consummating man as the Man-God. Thus, Lowell could see that many of his countrymen had submitted to an ideology (tax my neighbor's corn to subsidize my crop—it's the moral thing to do) but he could not see that he too worked within strict ideological limitations. (The politician being mocked in the quatrain about taxes is a Southern Democrat, as though they were the only ones who sinned.)

The reason for modern conservatives to investigate Lowell is that the postmodern gatekeepers hate him and would consign him to the trash-heap with all the rest of American "phallogocentrism." Lowell, in contrast to Whitman, understood form.

—Thomas Bertonneau

Further Reading

Heymann, C. David. *American Aristocracy: The Lives and Times of James Russell, Amy, and Robert Lowell.* New York: Dodd, Mead, 1980.

See also: Cooper, James Fenimore

Lowell, Robert (1917–77)

Differing from the Transcendentalist school of American poets even while, in many respects, he continued it, Robert Lowell was a seer-lyricist in the Emerson-Whitman mode, but as inimical as they were not to moral vagueness. A native Bostonian related to the Lowells (he was a distant cousin of Miss Amy), he went to school first at Harvard but left after two years in favor of Kenyon College in Ohio, where he studied with John Crowe Ransom. While honing his art he did what most poets have done: he lectured on aspects of literature at a series of colleges and universities. In addition to Ransom, who championed even as he mentored him, Lowell rubbed bardic shoulders with Randall Jarrell and W. H. Auden, both of whom also praised his work in the boost-phase of his literary trajectory. Like Auden, Lowell objected conscientiously to military service during World War II and politely declined combat. It is also worth noting that bipolar disorder made Lowell's life an often stormy one.

While Transcendentalism always remained closely tied to a certain sucrose Unitarianism, Lowell's poetry displayed a decidedly Roman Catholic or Thomistic orientation. Lowell's diction thus reveals nothing of Wallace Stevens's penchant for quasi-philosophical abstraction in the posture of Kant and Emerson; he preferred the concrete (something that he boasted in common with William Carlos Williams, a poet otherwise entirely unlike Lowell), and he bluntly, insistently addressed modernity's evasion of ethics. In "Mrs. Edwards and the Spider" he says, "It's well / If God who holds you to the pit of Hell, / Much as one holds a spider, will destroy, / Baffle and dissipate your soul." Death pointed back to sin and it was sin, not neurosis, that most threatened a person considered *qua spiritus* and *sub specie aeternitatis*. For Lowell, mankind thus required Christian humiliation, not Gnostic exaltation. Lowell shares some traits with Frost and some, of course, with Ransom and Jarrell, both of whom he surpassed as a poet.

Lowell won a Pulitzer for his collection *Lord Weary's Castle* (1946) and elbowed the critics into reacknowledging his existence with *For the Union Dead* (1964), which appeared at about the time that those afflicted with the French diseases of structuralism and semiotics were dismissing him as an atavistic scribbler of Civil War nostalgia in verse. The title poem of *For the Union Dead* raises an audacious question mark over the price of the Yankee triumph. America became an empire, bombed civilians, as at Hiroshima, and now, in commercial Boston, "a savage servility slides by on grease." Contemporary critical discussion has mostly dropped Lowell, unfortunately. This is a temporary condition; it is Lowell who will trump au courant assessments and it is his contemporary assessors who will populate oblivion.

—THOMAS BERTONNEAU

Further Reading

Lowell, Robert. *Interviews and Memoirs.* Edited by Jeffrey Meyers. Ann Arbor, Mich.: University of Michigan Press, 1988.
———. *Selected Poems.* New York: Farrar, Straus & Giroux, 1977.

See also: Frost, Robert; Ransom, John Crowe

Luce, Clare Boothe (1903–87)

Magazine editor, playwright, author, journalist, congresswoman, ambassador, political appointee, wife, and mother, Clare Boothe Luce was arguably the most influential woman of the postwar American conservative movement; she was certainly one of the more prominent women in modern American political history. Throughout most of her life, she forged her way with grit and brilliance, achieving remarkable success.

Clare was born into a middle-class New York City family. Her mother was a beautiful former actress, her father a musician who took his family along on touring musicals. Clare was largely self-educated and read voraciously. At nine, when her father deserted the family, Clare's ambitious mother planned a career in theater for her. Luce secured several parts, but eventually her mother gave up on this career plan.

When Clare was twelve years old, she began regular schooling, and at fourteen she transferred to the Castle School in

Tarrytown, New York, where she excelled socially and academically, graduating first in her class at sixteen.

After travel abroad in 1923, Clare's mother arranged her marriage to George Tuttle Brokaw. Brokaw was a wealthy bachelor who was twenty-three years older than Luce and heir to a garment business fortune. But after the birth of their daughter, Ann, the marriage went downhill. Brokaw, a frequent and heavy drinker, was often violently abusive of Clare, who suffered four miscarriages before finally divorcing him. Now twenty-six years old, she took a position writing captions for *Vogue* and soon moved on to become an assistant editor at *Vanity Fair*, where she began writing humorous essays spoofing "high society." A collection of her best *Vanity Fair* essays titled *Stuffed Shirts* was published in 1931. Clare shifted to more serious topics as the economic decline brought on by the stock-market crash and the Great Depression overwhelmed America, and she was made *Vanity Fair*'s managing editor in 1931. This was an incredibly swift ascent for a young professional woman to have made in just two years.

In 1932, Clare covered the Democratic Party convention and, not yet having a definite political philosophy of her own, joined *Vanity Fair*'s staff in supporting Franklin D. Roosevelt. Clare actually worked briefly for Roosevelt when his administration appointed her to a wing of the National Recovery Administration (NRA), the Motion Picture Authority. But she quickly came to believe that Roosevelt's NRA constituted excessive governmental interference in the economy. She also disliked Roosevelt's arrogant sexist condescension toward women.

Clare Boothe Luce

Returning to edit *Vanity Fair*, Clare shifted the magazine's emphasis toward more political topics. She wrote stinging attacks and published caricatures, in drawing and text, of Roosevelt and his wife.

In 1933, Clare resigned from *Vanity Fair* to devote herself to journalism and agreed to write a weekly column from Europe for the Hearst newspaper chain. Her writing reflected her now strongly developed convictions that when the United States had legitimate international interests it should intervene to influence events. As a result, the isolationist Hearst organization printed few of her columns, eventually firing her.

Upon returning to New York, Clare began to write plays. Her first Broadway play, *Abide with Me,* opened in 1935, the same year she met and married Henry Robinson Luce, the founder, publisher, and owner of *Time* and *Fortune*. Her next play, *The Women*, opened in 1936 and was a tremendous success, earning millions of dollars for Clare Boothe Luce with more than 650 Broadway performances, two different movie productions, and a television play. Her other two most successful plays were *Kiss the Boys Good-bye* (1938), an allegory about fascism, and *Margin for Error* (1939), a dramatic attack on the Nazi philosophy that credentialed her as a serious commentator on international politics.

Luce then decided to go to Europe to better understand the coming war and spent most of l940 as a roving correspondent viewing the German advance. Her *Europe in the Spring* (1940), a bestseller, laid out the mortal miscalculation of Europe in the face of Hitler's aggression.

After traveling to and reporting from Asia for *Life* magazine, Luce returned home in 1942 and decided to run for Congress as a Republican from her home district in Connecticut in that year's election. She beat overwhelming odds to win in a Catholic working-class district and gained a reputation in Washington as an independent thinker who was exceptionally knowledgeable about international affairs. Her speech at the 1944 Republican national convention consisted of a sharp critique of President Roosevelt, who she said had "lied the American people into war" by knowing in advance of the Japanese attack on Pearl Harbor but permitting it to happen in order to generate American support for the war.

Her attacks on Roosevelt were so effective that the national Democrats targeted her for defeat in her Connecticut district, but again Luce beat the odds to win, becoming an even more prominent national leader in the process. Luce refused Republican Party entreaties to run in 1946 for a third term or for the U.S. Senate. Later that year she was formally received into the Roman Catholic Church. In 1947, Luce explained why she had left politics and converted to Catholicism in a series of articles for *McCall's* magazine.

After returning home from Congress Luce wrote the screenplay that became *Come to the Stable*, a film nominated for an Academy Award. She also wrote a number of other plays that were less well received before joining Eisenhower's presidential campaign in 1952, giving scores of speeches for him all over the nation. Eisenhower asked Luce to join his administration by serving as his U.S. ambassador to Italy.

In 1953, Luce and her husband sailed for Italy where she was the first woman to serve as a U.S. ambassador. While in Italy Luce was named in one poll there as the best-known woman in Europe. She resigned her post in 1956, extremely discouraged over America's failure to support the Hungarian rebellion and ill from arsenic-poisoned paint that she discovered, too late, had been falling on her

for several years from the ceiling of the ambassador's residence while she slept.

During the rest of her active life Luce wrote articles for *Life, McCall's, Sports Illustrated, National Review*, and other magazines, but she stayed out of the limelight. After her husband died in 1967, she lived in Hawaii for ten years, frequently flying to Washington, D.C. She served for eight years on President Nixon's Foreign Intelligence Advisory Board and received the Presidential Medal of Freedom from President Ronald Reagan in 1983, two months before her eightieth birthday. She died in 1987, less than three months after a brain tumor had been discovered.

—MICHELLE EASTON

Further Reading

Lyons, Joseph. *Clare Boothe Luce*. New York: Chelsea House Publishers, 1989.

Martin, Ralph G. *Henry and Clare, An Intimate Biography*. New York: G. P. Putnam's Sons, 1991.

Shadegg, Stephen. *Clare Boothe Luce*. New York: Simon & Schuster, 1970.

Sheed, Wilfrid. *Clare Boothe Luce*. New York: Dutton, 1982.

See also: New Deal; Sheen, Fulton J.

Lukacs, John (1924–)

A maverick historian and historical philosopher, John Lukacs has pressed the claim that the greatest distinction of the modern age lies not in the emergence of science, but in the advent of historical consciousness. Since the seventeenth century, Lukacs argues, we have come to understand ourselves and our world at least as much through history as through science. We are, as he puts it, historians by nature, but scientists only by choice. Since historical consciousness evolved along with self-consciousness, for Lukacs history constitutes the partial, unsystematic, and imperfect knowledge that some human beings have of other human beings. Lukacs is less concerned with the knowledge of history than he is with the historicity of knowledge.

Born in Hungary, Lukacs chose exile in 1946, when his countrymen were awakening to the realities of Russian domination. In such books as *The Great Powers and Eastern Europe* (1953), *A New History of the Cold War* (1966), and *1945: Year Zero* (1978), he returned again and again to the postwar division of Europe between Russia and the United States. That division was a major turning point because it marked the passing of the Modern, Bourgeois, European Age and the full emergence of the American Century, an epochal transformation that Lukacs laments.

A cultural European, Lukacs resents the fact that, as he believes, Americans think themselves "preferable to the old peoples of Europe"—preferable because they are allegedly exempt from the sinful condition that limits Europeans and because they represent the future. Indifferent to history, they worship at the shrines of science and progress. Yet Lukacs also sees signs of hope. In 1876, Americans seemed little interested in history. The Centennial Exhibition in Philadelphia was an encomium to technology, "progress," and the future. A century later, in 1976, Americans were fascinated with the old-fashioned vessels that sailed into New York Harbor. Even among Americans, it seems, there is a growing appetite for history.

Lukacs reserves special ire for many contemporary American conservatives, especially anticommunists and, more recently, neoconservatives. American "conservatives," he maintains, are in reality progressives enamored of technology and unlimited economic growth, ideologues committed to global democracy, the Wilsonian idea that has caused at least as much mischief (if only because its influence has been more widespread) as the discredited Leninist idea of communism. Worse, these conservatives made anticommunism the litmus test of orthodoxy. As a result, they failed, especially during the Cold War, to comprehend the nationalist origins of Russian behavior and exaggerated the communist threat within their own borders.

This critique owes much to Lukacs's experience in Nazi-occupied Europe. "It was," he argues, "the respectability of Hitler's anticommunism—not the respectability of his anti-Semitism—that brought him to power in Germany." Similarly, too many non-German conservatives became obsessed "with the alleged powers of the communist enemy within their own country rather than with the foreign powers, the enemy without." Genuine conservatives, those who viewed the world through historical rather than ideological lenses, did not make that mistake. Churchill and de Gaulle recognized that the German danger was paramount and that without the Russian armies the war for Europe would be lost. They knew that the Russians would emerge from the conflict in control of the East, but concluded that half of Europe was better than none.

Lukacs is not, then, an American conservative. Indeed, he describes himself as a European reactionary who prefers the liberal era of the last century to any conceivable future. It was in the years before 1914 that the bourgeoisie cultivated such patrician virtues as family fellowship, personal dignity, privacy, and the interior life. Lukacs put his admiration for these virtues, and for good breeding in general, on full display in *Budapest 1900* (1988) and *Philadelphia: Patricians and Philistines, 1900–1950* (1981), affectionate portraits of his native and adopted cities.

—LEE CONGDON

Further Reading

Allitt, Patrick. *Catholic Intellectuals and Conservative Politics in America, 1950–1985.*

Congdon, Lee. "History as Personal Knowledge: John Lukacs and His Work." *Continuity* 3 (1981): 63–75.

Lukacs, John. *Historical Consciousness, or The Remembered Past.* New York: Harper & Row, 1968.

———. *Remembered Past: John Lukacs on History, Historians, and Historical Knowledge: A Reader.* Edited by Mark G. Malvasi and Jeffrey O. Nelson. Wilmington, Del.: ISI Books, 2005.

See also: anticommunism; historicism; neoconservatism; progress; traditionalism

Lyons, Eugene (1898–1985)

Described by *National Review* as one of the most formidable American Cold Warriors of the mid-twentieth century, Eugene Lyons was a journalist and editor who wrote blistering polemics against both Josef Stalin's Soviet Union and communism's apologists in America. His book *Assignment in Utopia* (1937), a memoir of his disillusionment as a reporter working in Russia during the era of Stalin's purges and manmade famines, opened many Western eyes to the evils of "scientific socialism" and played a signal role in leading Whittaker Chambers to his own break with communism.

Born in Russia to Jewish parents, Lyons and his family immigrated to America when he was a young boy. Drawn to leftism, he worked at several newspapers and covered a short-lived workers' uprising in Italy before becoming editor of the first popular American periodical about Russia, *Soviet Russia Pictorial,* in 1922. A year later, he left that position to begin a stint as an editor for the Soviet news agency *Tass.* While working for *Tass,* he published his first book, a worshipful dual-biography of the Italian anarchists Sacco and Vanzetti. In 1928 he went to work as a United Press reporter in Russia, serving at that post for several years. During that time, he experienced a conversion of the heart similar to that described by fellow journalist Malcolm Muggeridge in *Winter in Moscow* (1934): the sure conviction that he and other Western reporters and visitors to Stalin's "workers' paradise" were being deceived by a state-contrived façade that masked what amounted to a vast police state.

The result of Lyons's turnabout was the book *Assignment in Utopia,* which earned the author numerous influential enemies within America's intelligentsia. Assessing Lyons's rejection of the Left, Upton Sinclair (for one) ventured that while Stalin's methods were certainly distasteful, Soviet communism could not simply be dismissed as an evil system, as a certain leeway needed to be granted to a government attempting to bring about great things. On the other hand, *Assignment in Utopia* revealed the true nature of Stalinism to a Western audience otherwise subjected to a steady stream of fawning articles published by British and American reporters gulled—often willingly—by the Soviet government's deceptions. Edmund Wilson noted that Lyons returned to the United States after his assignment in "Utopia" "convinced that the immediate task—for those who have the urge to participate consciously in the historical processes of their lifetime—is to defend the basic concepts of freedom, humaneness, intellectual integrity, respect for life."

From 1939 until 1944, Lyons served as editor of the conservative *American Mercury,* a magazine to which he continued to contribute well into the 1950s. He also wrote extensively for *Reader's Digest* and *National Review*—he was a founding associate editor of the latter—focusing primarily on the dangers posed by communism to the Free World. His other widely reviewed book, *The Red Decade: The Stalinist Penetration of America* (1941), was a forerunner of Chambers's *Witness* in exposing the activities of communists and their fellow travelers in the United States during the 1930s. Of that book James Burnham wrote, "What Lyons is in truth writing about, this ludicrous and horrible suicide of a whole intellectual generation, is not the vagary of individuals, but a phase in the death of a culture." Appraising *The Red Decade*, former leftist Max Eastman lauded Lyons's honesty and skill, claiming, "He has a gift of slashing satire, and has no fear of calling foolish acts and famous people by their exact names."

—JAMES E. PERSON JR.

Further Reading

Lyons, Eugene. *Workers' Paradise Lost: Fifty Years of Soviet Communism: A Balance Sheet.* New York: Funk & Wagnalls, 1967.

See also: anticommunism

Lytle, Andrew Nelson (1902–95)

Born and raised in middle Tennessee in the early years of the twentieth century, Andrew Nelson Lytle came to prominence with his essay "The Hind Tit," a contribution to *I'll Take My Stand* (1930), a collection by a group of writers who would come to be known as the "Southern Agrarians." This group of writers, which included such leading literary figures as Robert Penn Warren, Allen Tate, and John Crowe Ransom, grew out of a community of poets that formed at Vanderbilt University and called itself the "Fugitives." Though they were derided by critics as neo-Luddites, the Fugitive/Agrarian writers, with their defense of the small family farm and the centrality of local community as bulwarks against the atomizing effects of modern industrialization and urbanization, have recently been given more credit for their political and cultural acumen.

Though Lytle would write essays on political matters throughout his life, his great-

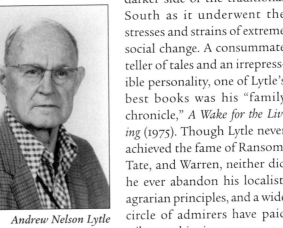

Andrew Nelson Lytle

est achievements were literary. A distinguished teacher at such institutions as the University of Florida and the University of Iowa Writers' Workshop, Lytle's students included Flannery O'Connor, Madison Jones, and James Dickey. For many years he was the editor of the *Sewanee Review*, the venerable literary quarterly based at the University of the South. Ironically, though he was a staunch defender of the agrarian, cultural, and religious traditions of the South, his novels, including *The Long Night* (1936) and *The Velvet Horn* (1957), often explored the darker side of the traditional South as it underwent the stresses and strains of extreme social change. A consummate teller of tales and an irrepressible personality, one of Lytle's best books was his "family chronicle," *A Wake for the Living* (1975). Though Lytle never achieved the fame of Ransom, Tate, and Warren, neither did he ever abandon his localist, agrarian principles, and a wide circle of admirers have paid tribute to him in numerous essays. Many of his books have recently been brought back into print.

—GREGORY WOLFE

Further Reading

Bradford, M. E., ed. *The Form Discovered; Essays on the Achievement of Andrew Lytle.* Jackson, Miss.: University Press of Mississippi, 1973.

Lytle, Andrew. *From Eden to Bablyon: The Social and Political Essays of Andrew Lytle.* Edited by M. E. Bradford. Washington, D.C.: Regnery, 1990.

———. *Southerners and Europeans: Essays in a Time of Disorder.* Baton Rouge, La.: Louisiana State University Press, 1988.

See also: Bradford, M. E.; I'll Take My Stand; Sewanee Review; Southern Agrarians

M

MacArthur, Douglas (1880–1964)

Indomitable soldier and anticommunist, Douglas MacArthur first realized the significance of his vocation of military service in the Philippines (1903), where he was influenced by men like his own father, men who believed that America's destiny was to plant democracy and Christianity in the Pacific. During the Second World War MacArthur attained mythic stature, consciously constructed from his preening imperial self-image and audacious campaigns against the Japanese. After the war, he earned his enemy's admiration through the implementation of a conservative, decentralizing, and humane constitution (1947). He remained focused on eastern affairs throughout the Cold War, seeing there the final theater of conflict between communism and the West.

MacArthur's brand of patriotism often compelled him to act rashly and to judge the political order with myopic simplicity. When army veterans and their families petitioned for economic relief in Washington, D.C. (1932), MacArthur—against President Hoover's orders—roughly suppressed the protesters, branding them as radicals and anarchists. The early vacillations of the Truman government in the Korean conflict, like those of the Taft administration in the Philippine War, convinced MacArthur that politicians would ever handicap America's mission in the Far East. Furthermore, he contended that America's wavering stemmed from a deep moral sickness.

During the Korean War MacArthur's actions and public commentary helped to awaken American awareness to the global threat of communism. He swiftly regained the south of Korea and drove communist forces to the Chinese border until a massive counterattack brought the campaign to a halt. His plans to retaliate against China and his propaganda war against the Truman administration resulted in MacArthur's dismissal (April 10, 1951). This act outraged the nation and MacArthur returned to a popular triumph, making a bid for the Republican nomination.

The reaction to MacArthur's dismissal and the sentiments that he articulated in his famous Farewell Address signaled to some conservatives that the moment had come to galvanize popular opinion through a combination of military-based patriotism and anticommunist hatred. To his credit, MacArthur realized that the struggle against communism was one fundamentally of ideas, not materials and territory. For the remainder of his life he urged the American leadership to abandon the policy of containment and work towards a total moral victory, a vision that only came to fruition under the Reagan administration.

—WILLIAM EDMUND FAHEY

Further Reading

Fredricks, E. J. *MacArthur: His Mission and Meaning.* Philadelphia: Whitmore Publishing, 1968.

MacArthur, Douglas. *Reminiscences.* New York: McGraw-Hill, 1964.

———. *A Soldier Speaks: Public Papers and Speeches of General of the Army, Douglas MacArthur.* New York: Praeger, 1965.

See also: anticommunism

Machen, J. Gresham (1881–1937)

J. Gresham Machen became the intellectual leader of the conservative forces in the Presbyterian Church during the fundamentalist-modernist controversies of the 1920s and 1930s. As the Presbyterian Church began to fall victim to the same creeping modernism that had already infected American Protestantism at large, Machen, who was known as the "scholarly fundamentalist" but disdained the label (he preferred to be known as a Calvinist), widened his horizons to do battle not only for the soul of his own denomination, but for the entire spectrum of traditional Christianity.

J. Gresham Machen

Born the scion of a prominent Baltimore family, Machen studied under Basil Gildersleeve and Daniel Coit Gilman at the Johns Hopkins University, graduating Phi Beta Kappa in 1901. He spent a short time at the University of Chicago before starting his studies at Princeton Theological Seminary, from which he graduated in 1905. After studying at Marburg and Göttingen universities in Germany, Machen returned to Princeton as an assistant professor of New Testament. There he began a twenty-four-year career as one of the preeminent New Testament scholars in the United States. He is most noted for his contribution to Pauline scholarship in *The Origin of Paul's Religion* (1921), and his *The Virgin Birth of Christ* (1930) and *New Testament Greek for Beginners* (1923) remain widely used today.

Machen's *Christianity and Liberalism* (1923) stunned the religious world with its forceful critique of religious liberalism, calling such belief a religion wholly divorced from Christianity. For nearly a decade Princeton Seminary's reputation for orthodoxy gave Machen institutional support for his battle against modernism. In 1929, however, after a battle between the faculty and the board, the seminary succumbed to a reorganization plan with a new board that included signers of the 1924 "Auburn Affirmation," which denied some of the cardinal doctrines of historic Christianity. Machen's booklet, *The Attack upon Princeton Seminary: A Plea for Fair Play* (1927), 20,000 copies of which were printed and distributed at the author's expense, analyzed the crisis and its possible ramifications. His argument proved prescient. In 1929, Machen, along with a majority of the faculty and many members of Princeton's student body, withdrew to Philadelphia and began Westminster Theological Seminary.

Machen soon emerged at the forefront of another controversy. Along with several other prominent conservatives protesting the commissioning of missionaries who denied fundamental beliefs central to the Westminster Confession of Faith (at that time the primary confessional statement of the Presbyterian Church), Machen headed an Independent Board for Foreign Missions. This new mission board, begun after several overtures to the General Assembly of the church were defeated, pitted Machen squarely against the ecclesiastical hierarchy of his denomination. He was accused of subverting the constitution of the church and was summarily defrocked after a lengthy and bitter trial.

In that same year, Machen, many of his fellow faculty at Westminster Seminary, and others began a new denomination, the Presbyterian Church of America, later renamed the Orthodox Presbyterian Church (OPC). The new group sought to be "a truly Presbyterian church at last." Machen lost much-needed support among conservative Presbyterians after his insistence on an Independent Board and a new denomination. The OPC, without a strong popular base, struggled for existence but remains to this day a bastion of Presbyterian orthodoxy. In January 1937, while speaking in North Dakota in support of a small OPC congregation, Machen died of pneumonia.

At his death, such diverse critics as H. L. Mencken, Walter Lippmann, and Pearl Buck praised him in the secular and religious media. A colleague from his days at Princeton Seminary, Caspar Wistar Hodge, wrote that in Machen's death conservative Christianity had lost "the greatest theologian in the English-speaking world."

—William M. Brailsford

Further Reading

Dennison, Charles G., and Richard C. Gamble, eds. *Pressing toward the Mark: Essays Commemorating Fifty Years of the Orthodox Presbyterian Church*. Philadelphia: Great Commission Publications, 1986.

Hart, D. G. *Defending the Faith: J. Gresham Machen and the Crisis of Conservative Protestantism in Modern America*. Baltimore: Johns Hopkins University Press, 1994.

Longfield, Bradley L. *The Presbyterian Controversy: Fundamentalists, Modernists, and Moderates*. New York: Oxford University Press, 1991.

Machen, J. Gresham. *Selected Shorter Writings*. Edited by D. G. Hart. Phillipsburg, N.J.: P&R Publishing, 2004.

Stonehouse, Ned B. *J. Gresham Machen: A Biographical Memoir*. Grand Rapids, Mich.: William M. Eerdmans, 1954.

See also: fundamentalism; Gildersleeve, Basil L.; Kupyer, Abraham; Protestantism, evangelical; Protestantism, mainline

Macon, Nathaniel (1758–1837)

North Carolina planter, Revolutionary soldier, opponent of the Constitution, state representative and senator, U.S. representative and senator, chairman of the House and Senate Foreign Relations committees, president pro-tempore of the Senate, and presiding officer of the 1835 North Carolina constitutional convention, Nathaniel Macon stood for old-fashioned republicanism. A simple and frugal man in his own life with a decided "distaste for pomp and idolatry" (he lived in a modest plantation home, Buck Spring, twelve miles northeast of Warrenton, North Carolina, and labored in his own tobacco fields with his slaves), Macon was the living embodiment of the classical republican ideal: the virtuous agrarian and paterfamilias who was devoted to family and country. To Thomas Jefferson, he was "the last of the Romans."

Much respected by his neighbors for his honesty and courtesy toward all classes, Macon built on that loyalty to become a long-serving political figure who represented his constituents faithfully. In an era of great economic and political change caused by the extraordinary growth of the United States between the Revolution and the Age of Jackson, Macon never deviated from true Jeffersonian republicanism or the principles of 1776, 1787, and 1798. His cause, above all, was that of constitutionalism defined as the act or process of restraining government by means of a written charter approved by the people as the sovereign authority that defines and limits what powers can and cannot be exercised. Only by maintaining inviolate the sacred charter of American government and its wise distribution of powers, he believed, could liberty be preserved. For Macon, this meant interpreting the Constitution strictly and maintaining the rights of states as bulwarks against the abuse of power by the federal government.

True to his principles, Macon opposed taxes, conscription, the protective tariff, a national bank, federal internal improvements, all unnecessary expenditures, and executive power. Agreeing with John Taylor, another republican purist, Macon believed that the republic was increasingly imperiled by a Supreme Court that expanded the authority of the federal government through implied powers based on a loose construction of the constitution. During the heated presidential contest of 1824, he supported William H. Crawford of Georgia as the candidate who best symbolized old-fashioned republicanism. After John Quincy Adams's term, Macon lukewarmly identified with the emerging Democratic Party of Andrew Jackson as the best hope for maintaining republican principles. Although an ardent advocate of states' rights, he nevertheless opposed nullification, believing that the revolutionary right of secession was "the best and almost only guard against improper legislation." Equally distasteful and threatening, however, was President Jackson's threatened use of force in 1833 against South Carolina.

Like many others of his time, Macon also opposed the politics of "King Numbers," or the right of majority rule, which he interpreted to mean majority tyranny. As he lamented in 1826, "The die is cast, and the people will have a magnificent government. The form may remain, but power will be increased. When I say the people will have a magnificent government, I mean only that it seems that a majority of them approve the measures which must lead to it."

—W. Kirk Wood

Further Reading

Dodd, William E. *The Life of Nathaniel Macon*. Raleigh, N.C.: Edwards & Broughton, 1903.

Risjord, Norman K. *The Old Republicans: Southern Conservatism in the Age of Jefferson*. New York: Columbia University Press, 1965.

See also: Southern conservatism

Magnet, Myron (1944–)

If the ability to affect politics and policy is the handiest measure of a think-tank warrior, then the Manhattan Institute's Myron Magnet is certainly one of the most influential public-policy scholars in the country. George W. Bush has stated that, after the Bible, Magnet's 1993 book, *The Dream and the Nightmare: The Sixties' Legacy to the Underclass*, is the most important book he has ever read. Only Marvin Olasky's *The Tragedy of American Compassion* (1992) rivals Magnet's in shaping the president's philosophy of "compassionate conservatism."

Bush is not the only major public figure to have cited Magnet. Former New York Mayor Rudolph Giuliani depended heavily on *City Journal*, the Manhattan Institute's urban-policy magazine edited by Magnet, for innovative ideas on how to run the city. A central theme to Magnet's thought has been government's obligation to care for society's disadvantaged while simultaneously recognizing the abject failure of the last several decades of social policy in dealing with urban problems. Magnet notes the paradox that while the United States has gown more prosperous since the 1960s, the situation in America's cities has gotten worse. The reason, Magnet argues, is that the pernicious values of the 1960s have served to imprison America's underclass in a cycle of hopelessness and social destructiveness.

Magnet may focus squarely on distinctively twenty-first century problems, but his appearance is positively nineteenth. Bald, bespectacled, with monstrous mutton-chop sideburns, Magnet looks like a character out of a Charles Dickens novel. Fittingly, among his several books is *Dickens and the New Social Order* (1985, 2003), adapted from the thesis he wrote to earn his doctorate in English literature at Columbia University. After teaching for a brief period at Columbia, Magnet joined the staff of *Fortune* magazine in 1980. He joined the Manhattan Institute in 1994.

—MAX SCHULZ

Further Reading

Magnet, Myron, ed. *The Millennial City: A New Urban Paradigm for Twenty-First-Century America*. Chicago: Ivan R. Dee, 2000.

———. *What Makes Charity Work? A Century of Public and Private Philanthropy*. Chicago: Ivan R. Dee, 2000.

See also: Bush, George W.; City Journal; Manhattan Institute; welfare policy

managerial revolution

"Managerial revolution," a phrase coined by James Burnham in a book of that title published in 1941, has now entered the language. As commonly used by economists today, the managerial revolution refers exclusively to the process by which professional managers or salaried employees have displaced shareholders as the dominant decision-making element in the corporation and in the corporate economy. This process is also known as the "separation of ownership and control," a phrase used by Adolf A. Berle Jr. and Gardiner C. Means in their 1932 book, *The Modern Corporation and Private Property*, which influenced Burnham's theory.

Yet the theory of the managerial revolution as Burnham formulated it has much

wider application than the sense in which the phrase is commonly used. The essence of the theory is that not only are corporate managers displacing owners (the capitalist or bourgeois elite) but that governmental bureaucrats, functionally analogous to corporate managers, are displacing elected officeholders as the dominant force in the state. Burnham explicitly extended the term "manager" to include not merely corporate but also governmental bureaucrats and not only the formal, board-of-director corporate managers (the group Berle and Means discussed) but also those who actually direct the technical processes of production. Because managers in the economy and government depend on their mastery of technical skills in production and administration, and because modern technological society depends on such skills, the formal rights of property and ownership in the economy and the formal legal and political institutions of the state are becoming obsolete, and those who are masters of technical and managerial skills are acquiring power. Since corporate managers do not own corporate assets, they have no inclination to resist governmental encroachment on property rights, a point also made by Berle and Means as well as by Joseph Schumpeter. Moreover, large-scale business firms, which tend to be managerial corporations, tend to drive out or absorb smaller ones that remain under private (individual, family, or partnership) ownership and control. Labor unions also generate a managerial class that identifies its interests as separate from and opposed to those of the workers they supposedly represent. Thus, all economic and, as a result, political power tends to come under managerial control. The "revolution" consists not only in this transfer of economic and political power, however, but also in the managerial reconstruction of society—in government, law, economy, and social and cultural relations—to reflect the interests of the new ruling class.

Burnham's theory was intended as a corrective of Marxist predictions of a "class-less" society, which was supposed to emerge after the displacement of capitalism. While Burnham generally accepted the Marxist interpretation of history as the struggle for power among successive economic classes (feudal and capitalist) and agreed that capitalism was dying, he rejected the Marxist prophecy that the proletariat would succeed the capitalist class. Instead, the managers would become a new, distinctive class with their own interests, ideology, and institutions and would be just as repressive and exploitative (indeed, even more so) than previous elites. Burnham pointed to Stalin's Soviet Union, Hitler's Germany, and (in much less developed form) Roosevelt's New Deal as examples of rising managerial regimes.

For Marxists and the Left in general, Burnham's theory was a direct threat. In their view, repression and exploitation proceeded from the existence of private property and private ownership; once these were abolished or controlled, repression and exploitation would cease or be diminished. But Burnham was arguing that repression and exploitation could flourish even in the absence of private property, and Stalin's and Hitler's regimes seemed to prove him right. Hence, the harshest polemics against Burnham and his theory have always come from the Left, which nevertheless has granted Burnham a grudging respect.

Burnham predicted that managerial society would be totalitarian, with a ruling class that sought to regiment all aspects of social and economic life under its own power. State and economy would be "fused," if not by formal nationalization then at least through governmental regulation and planning. Production for individual profit would give way to production for "collective" goals such as full employment or efficiency in war. Politically, the parliamentary assemblies and constitutionalism that had characterized liberal bourgeois government would be superseded by "Caesarist" leaders ruling through direct, plebiscitary appeals to the masses and surrounded by the managerial-bureaucratic elite, which would exercise power through administrative decree rather than law. Internationally, the nation-state and national sovereignty would be replaced by supranational organizations that would contend for global power and would also be under the control of managerial elites. Culturally, bourgeois individualism, the cultural core of capitalist society in the arts, religion, ethics, and political thought as well as in the economy, would be replaced by managerial collectivism and a culture based on it.

In his second book, *The Machiavellians: Defenders of Freedom* (1943), Burnham offered a revised, non-Marxist framework for his theory and abandoned the economic determinism that had informed the earlier work. In the preface to a 1960 reprint of *The Managerial Revolution*, Burnham acknowledged that his original formulation of the theory had been "too rigid and doctrinaire" and that some predictions had been falsified by history. Yet he continued to believe that the core of his analysis was correct, though he also now would "allow for a greater range of variation within the general form of managerial society" than the simple totalitarian model he had originally predicted as the exclusive managerial form.

The Managerial Revolution generated immense controversy, sold widely, and became a classic of political and economic sociology. C. Wright Mills and H. H. Gerth wrote a fierce critique of the book, though Mills's own later theory of the "power elite" revealed its influence, as did the work of Daniel Bell, who was also highly critical. Irving Kristol, David Riesman, Karl Wittfogel, Milovan Djilas, George Orwell, and Jacques Ellul, among others, also were profoundly influenced by the book. In the third edition of *The New Industrial State* (1978), John Kenneth

Galbraith acknowledged the importance of Burnham's book, and Galbraith's idea of the "technostructure" was essentially the same as Burnham's "managerial class." The book's central assumption, Berle and Means's "separation of ownership and control," has been debated among economists for decades, but in 1978, shortly before a stroke permanently impaired his memory, Burnham had the satisfaction of reviewing Alfred D. Chandler Jr.'s *The Visible Hand: The Managerial Revolution in American Business* (1977), which massively documented the Berle-Means-Burnham thesis, though Chandler did not explore the cultural and political dimensions of the managerial revolution.

In the 1960 preface, Burnham also acknowledged that parts of the theory had been previously developed by Max Weber, Vilfredo Pareto, Berle and Means, the Polish anarchist Waclav Makhaivsky, and the Italian Trotskyist Bruno Ricci in an obscure book, *The Bureaucratization of the World* (1939). Indeed, Ricci later accused Burnham of "plagiarizing" his ideas, a charge made by others as well. In 1985, however, Adam Westoby showed that Burnham had actually published early versions of his managerial revolution thesis in a Trotskyist journal under a pseudonym in 1937, and Ricci acknowledges this work in his own text. Thus, not only did Burnham not plagiarize Ricci, but Ricci in fact was influenced by Burnham, though he probably did not know Burnham's pseudonym.

"There can be few things more disputed than an idea whose time has come," writes Westoby of Burnham's theory, which has proved to be one of the most resilient and suggestive interpretations of twentieth-century history ever written. It has clear analogues with Hilaire Belloc's *The Servile State* (1912) and similar analyses by the Southern Agrarians (*Who Owns America?* [1936]), Robert Nisbet (*The Present Age* [1988]), and Joseph Schumpeter (*Capitalism, Socialism, Democracy*

[1942]). It is a somber and pessimistic theory that warns of the tyranny and cultural deracination that economic and political bureaucratization and collectivism cause, and, despite its flaws and oversimplifications, remains one of the seminal ideas of contemporary intellectual history.

—SAMUEL T. FRANCIS

Further Reading

Francis, Samuel T. *Power and History: The Political Thought of James Burnham*. Lanham, Md.: University Press of America, 1983.

Mills, C. Wright and H. H. Gerth. "A Marx for the Managers." In *Power, Politics, and People: The Collected Essays of C. Wright Mills*. Edited by Irving Louis Horowitz. New York: Oxford University Press, 1963.

See also: Burnham, James; Djilas, Milovan; Gottfried, Paul E.; Marxism; paleoconservatism; totalitarianism

Manhattan Institute

The Manhattan Institute has quickly become a leading public-policy think tank in New York and has expanded its sphere of influence to gain national acclaim. The institute has propagated conservative values and free-market economics in the public dialogue over welfare reform, school choice, tax reform, and many other issues.

British economist Antony Fisher founded the institute in 1978 as a think tank for policy analysis grounded in free-market principles. The institute now serves as home to many leading conservatives. The original chairman, William Casey, went on to become the director of the CIA in the Reagan administration. Under Casey's successor, William M. H. Hammett, the institute's influence mushroomed. In 1982, the institute commissioned Charles Murray's seminal work *Losing Ground* (1984), which spurred dialogue on welfare reform. Since then, fellows at the institute's Center for Legal Policy, such as Walter Olson and Peter Huber, have been prominent voices on liability and tort reform. Former U.S. Department of Education assistant secretary Chester E. Finn Jr., former congressman Rev. Floyd H. Flake, and senior fellow Jay Greene at the institute's Center for Civic Innovation have been major figures in the nationwide education reform debate. John DiIulio went on from the institute to become for a time the head of the president's Office of Faith-Based and Community Initiatives. The institute's quarterly magazine *City Journal*, edited by Myron Magnet and Brian C. Anderson, was a favorite read of New York's former Republican mayor Rudolph Giuliani and has been credited with playing a substantial role in gestating new ideas regarding urban policy.

—RICH HALVORSON

See also: City Journal; *Magnet, Myron; think tanks, conservative*

Manion, Clarence (1896–1979)

Trained as a lawyer, Clarence Manion spent twenty-seven years as a professor of constitutional law and, for much of that time, as dean of the law school at the University of Notre Dame. Following his retirement from Notre Dame in 1952, Manion began the "Manion Forum," which was dedicated to promoting a conservative brand of individualism in America. Funded with numerous small, private donations, the Manion Forum served as an extensive media outlet for Manion's views. It published pamphlets, copies of the Declaration of Independence and the Constitution, and books, including the first printing of Barry Goldwater's *Conscience of a Conservative* (1960).

Most importantly, the Manion Forum produced and broadcast radio addresses to the nation on a weekly basis, beginning in 1954 and ending in 1979 with Manion's death. Manion stated his objectives for the program in his first broadcast on October 3, 1954: "This upcoming series of broadcasts is unique in the history of American radio. At the insistence of patriots in all parts of the country, I am here now, next week and hereafter, to tell you the simple truth as I see it, limited only by the principles of decency, morality, and good taste." On the program, Manion often interviewed prominent Americans, most of them conservatives. He was especially influential in launching Barry Goldwater onto the national scene. Goldwater once said of Manion, "I just don't know where the cause of conservatism would be without him."

—BRADLEY J. BIRZER

Further Reading

Bauman, Michael. *The Best of the Manion Forum: A Conservative and Free Market Sourcebook.* San Francisco, Calif.: Mellen Research University Press, 1990.

Manion, Clarence. *The Conservative American: His Fight for National Independence and Constitutional Government.* New York: Devin Adair, 1964.

See also: Conscience of a Conservative, The; *Goldwater, Barry M.*

Mansfield, Harvey C. (1932–)

One of the most distinguished political theorists writing today and arguably the most prominent conservative academic teaching in a major American university, Mansfield is a prodigious scholar as well as a noted commentator and writer on contemporary political life. Mansfield received his B.A. (1953) and Ph.D. (1961) in government from Harvard University. Except for a brief period of teaching at the University of California at Berkeley in the early 1960s, Mansfield has spent his entire professional career at Harvard, where he is currently William R. Kenan Jr. Professor of Government.

At Harvard, Mansfield studied with such influential political scientists as Carl J. Friedrich and Samuel Beer but increasingly came under the influence of the political philosopher Leo Strauss. Mansfield followed Beer in pursuing the sympathetic, scholarly study of Anglo-American constitutionalism. From Strauss he learned an appreciation of the philosophical dimensions of politics, ancient and modern. As a result, Mansfield is one of the most politically minded "Straussians" and one of the most philosophically grounded students of modern politics.

Mansfield's first book was *Statesmanship and Party Government: A Study of Burke and Bolingbroke* (1965). In that work, Mansfield examines Edmund Burke's philosophical defense of "party" as a necessary ingredient of free government in the modern world. Mansfield remains one of the most penetrating scholars of Burke's statesmanship and political thought, and he has edited and introduced a selection of Burke's correspondence. In particular, Mansfield admires Burke's manly defense of liberty, his eloquent articulation of prudence as *the* political virtue, and his profound critique of revolutionary and ideological politics.

Mansfield is perhaps best known as a scholar of Machiavelli and Machiavellianism. He is the author of *Machiavelli's New Modes and Orders: A Study of the Discourses on Livy* (1979) and of a remarkable collection of essays titled *Machiavelli's Virtue* (1996). He has also translated and introduced *The Prince* (1985) and (with Nathan Tarcov) *The Dis-*

Harvey C. Mansfield

courses on Livy (1996). Following Strauss, Mansfield emphasizes Machiavelli's role as the self-conscious "founder" of a distinctively modern political and philosophical sensibility. Mansfield believes that Machiavelli's work provides a salutary correction to the apolitical moralism and humanitarianism dominating contemporary liberalism. But he also faults him for allowing anti-theological ire to lead him to deny the very existence of the soul or of universal political principles above one's country.

For a more truthful account of politics, and for a defense of moderation in the soul, Mansfield's work points backwards to Aristotle and forward to Alexis de Tocqueville. Aristotelian-Tocquevillean reflections on contemporary politics can be found in two collections of essays, *The Spirit of Liberalism* (1978) and *America's Constitutional Soul* (1991). In those books as well as in *Taming the Prince* (1989), his work on the philosophical origins of executive power, Mansfield shows that the strength of the American political order lies in its carefully designed "constitutional soul." The founders did not share the ambition of Machiavellian modernity to dispense with (classical) virtue altogether. Instead, they established institutions, such as the presidency, that depend upon and elicit virtue without guaranteeing its presence. America's constitutional soul "stresses the voluntary rather than the habitual or cultivated side of virtue." At its highest, the American political order is thus an invitation to statesmanship.

Mansfield is an articulate critic of "big government" but he is no libertarian. Libertarians mistakenly think there can be self-government without any public realm whatsoever. Mansfield opposes "big government" on Tocquevillean grounds: it undermines self-government and individual responsibility while leaving citizens exposed to the tyranny of bureaucrats and "experts." The theoretical grounds of Mansfield's opposition to "soft despotism" is best expressed in the seventy-page introductory essay that he and his wife Delba Winthrop wrote for their translation of Tocqueville's *Democracy in America* (2000).

In addition to being an outstanding scholar and teacher (his students have included William Kristol, Jeremy Rabkin, Charles Kesler, and Mark Blitz), Mansfield is also a witty and incisive controversialist. He is an eloquent critic of affirmative action and the scourge of political correctness in all its forms. He has led an increasingly successful one-man crusade against grade inflation at Harvard. And he is a fierce critic of the insularity of "women's studies" and of the "liberationist" legacies of the 1960s. His book *Manliness* was set to appear in early 2006.

—DANIEL MAHONEY

Further Reading

Blitz, Mark, and William Kristol, eds. *Educating the Prince: Essays in Honor of Harvey Mansfield.* Lanham, Md.: Rowman & Littlefield, 2000.

See also: Burke, Edmund; constitutionalism; modernity and postmodernity; Strauss, Leo; Straussianism; Tocqueville, Alexis de

Marshall, John (1755–1835)

The fourth man to serve as chief justice of the United States Supreme Court (following John Jay, John Rutledge, and Oliver Ellsworth), John Marshall established the Supreme Court as an independent and strong third branch of the U.S. federal government. His influential decisions are regarded by some conservatives as important bulwarks of the American republic, and by other conservatives as critical steps towards the overconcentration of power in the federal government.

Born near the post-frontier region of Germantown, Virginia, Marshall spent much of his youth watching over his fourteen younger siblings. Though his mother was related to the aristocratic Randolphs, the Marshalls lived in a simple style. Marshall received little formal education; his parents taught him when time permitted, as did a minister who lived with the family. But as a pre-teen, Marshall already displayed signs of brilliance, having by that time memorized much of Alexander Pope's *Essay on Man* (1733) as well as having translated several famous Latin works into English.

During the American Revolution, Marshall served for a year in the Virginia militia and in the Continental Army with George Washington from 1776 to 1779. His service profoundly affected him, as, he wrote, it "confirmed [me] in the habit of considering America as my country, and congress as my government." Prior to the war's end, Marshall spent several months listening to lectures by famed legal scholar George Wythe at the College of William and Mary.

Formally becoming a lawyer in 1780, Marshall spent the next two decades establishing both a law practice and a strong presence and career in Virginia politics. He helped lead the effort to ratify the U.S. Constitution in Virginia and became one of that state's leading Federalists. At the time of the ratification debates, Marshall had espoused a strict constructionist view of the Constitution, a point his opponents would use against him when he was chief justice of the Supreme Court. Marshall declined several positions offered by the Washington administration but finally accepted his first federal post as one of President John Adams's delegates to meet with representatives of the volatile

French Republic in 1797. In what was later known as the XYZ Affair, the three American delegates refused to pay bribes to the French government. His patriotic and morally outraged statement of refusal propelled John Marshall into the national spotlight.

The citizens of Richmond elected Marshall as a Federalist to the U.S. Congress in 1799. Some historians have rated Marshall ineffective as a legislator, but President Adams appointed him as Secretary of State in mid-1800, and Marshall essentially served as the sole executive officer in the very last days of the Adams administration.

On January 27, 1801, the Senate confirmed Marshall as the Supreme Court's chief justice, and he took his post on February 4, 1801, remaining in that position until his death on July 6, 1835. Perhaps more than any other figure in the early history of the American Republic, Marshall shaped not only the role of the Supreme Court but also the public's attitudes toward and understanding of the U.S. Constitution. While many of the cases over which Marshall presided are important for a constitutional understanding of America, five in particular stand out. The first, *Marbury v. Madison* (1803), established the power of the Supreme Court to engage in judicial review, which doctrine served as a defense of the judiciary against the other two branches of government. The second, *Fletcher v. Peck* (1810), ruled that state authority did not supersede the sanctity of a private contract mutually agreed to by consenting parties. *Dartmouth College v. Woodward* (1819) argued along the same lines, holding that, in general, no state could interfere with a charter of incorpora-

John Marshall

tion. That same year, Marshall decided in *McCulloch v. Maryland* that a state could in no way tax a federal entity because of the "great principle that the constitution and the laws thereof are supreme; that they control the constitution and laws of the respective states and cannot be controlled by them." The fifth major decision came in 1824 with *Gibbons v Ogden*. In this case, Marshall denied the power of any state to infringe on interstate commerce or travel.

Marshall's character proved as important as his intellect to his success as an effective chief justice. During his thirty-four-year tenure, Marshall presided over 1,100 cases, ruling with the majority 1,092 times. He also wrote the majority opinion in 519 cases. His mastery came from his ability to form a consensus among his fellow members of the bench.

—Bradley J. Birzer

Further Reading

Dangerfield, George. *The Awakening of American Nationalism*. New York: Harper & Row, 1994.

Elkins, Stanley, and Eric McKitrick. *The Age of Federalism: The Early American Republic, 1788–1800*. Oxford: Oxford University Press, 1993.

Smith, Jean Edward. *John Marshall: Definer of a Nation*. New York: Henry Holt, 1998.

See also: Federalist Party; Supreme Court

Marxism

In 1894, Engels published posthumously the third and last volume of Marx's *Capital*, the work for which Marx was widely known. A number of economists then began to write critical analyses of Marx's system. The best known of these is that by Eugen von Bohm-Bawerk (*Karl Marx and the Close of his System*, 1896).

The two basic concepts of Marx's *Capital* are "value" and "surplus value." Marx begins with an analysis of "commodity" and "commodity production." "Exchange value presents itself in the first instance as the quantitative relation, the proportion, in which values in use of one kind are exchanged for values in use of another kind. . . . As use values commodities are of different qualities, but as exchange values they are merely different quantities," which, however, "must be capable of being expressed in terms of something common to them all." This common "something" is the property "of commodities being products of labor . . . all are reduced to one and the same sort of labor, human labor in the abstract." Hence, Marx's concept of value insists that labor, "and labor alone," is that which determines value, from which Marx concludes that this value determines the prices of production. "The price is merely the money-name of the quantity of social labor realized in a commodity." What about surplus value? "The owner of money must buy the commodities at their value, then sell them at their value, the process must draw out more money than he put in. Such are the conditions of the problem." What enables him to do this is that he can find in the market a commodity "whose use-value possesses the peculiar property of being a source of value," namely, "labor power," which is being sold by its owner, the laborer.

Labor power as a commodity has the value of whatever it costs to maintain the worker and his family in existence. This "more"—which Marx called "surplus value"—was attributed by Marx to the capitalists' keeping workers longer at work than the time required for producing the amount equivalent to their own value, thus "robbing" the workers of value produced though not owned by them. Bohm-Bawerk, however, pointed out that quite a few other factors besides labor determine a commodity's value. He called Marx's limitation of exchange values to commodities a "fallacious reduction, since 'commodity' is a concept narrower than 'goods.'" Moreover, Marx entirely leaves out "the gifts of nature." Marx maintained that surplus value varied with differences in the "organic composition" of capital (i.e., the proportion of labor to machinery and land.). Bohm-Bawerk argued that in the real world "capitals of equal amount, without regard to possible differences of organic composition, yield equal profits." Moreover, wrote Bohm-Bawerk, when Marx "is confronted by the task of explaining why the permanent prices of commodities do not gravitate toward the incorporated quantity of labor but towards the 'prices of production' which deviate from it," he "simply drops the assumption that commodities exchange according to their values." It is interesting that, more than half a century after Bohm-Bawerk, it was Stalin who observed that in Soviet Russia in 1950 commodity production still prevailed.

The economists and the public seemed to believe that Bohm-Bawerk's critique had finished Marx, but the Russian Revolution of 1917 and the great strength of Marxist political parties in Western Europe proved the contrary. A purely economic critique of Marx fails to see the appeal of Marx's ideological construction of history, as well as his theory of revolution. The primary source for these aspects of Marx's work is still the *Communist Manifesto* (1848). Marx's only coherent statement about historical materialism amounts to no more than one and a half pages in Marx's *Preface to the Critique of Political Economy* (1859); also relevant are *The Holy Family* (1844), and *The German Ideology* (1846).

Marx reduced man's essence to labor and society to modes of economic production. He thus removed from history, as he saw it, any element of freedom and unpredictability. Feeling secure in the knowledge of bare material conditions, he proceeded to divide the historical past into clearly distinguished stages, each identified with a particular mode of production. He then concluded that these were the "laws of history":

> At a certain stage of their development, the material forces of production in society come into conflict with the existing relations of production. Then begins an epoch for social revolution. No social order ever disappears before all the productive forces for which there is room in it have been developed. Therefore, mankind always sets itself only such tasks as it can solve. The task itself arises only when the material conditions necessary for its solution already exist.

At this point Marx mentions the following stages of the past: "Asiatic, the ancient, the feudal, and the modern bourgeois modes of production" (at other times the list was slightly different). The revolution of the proletariat against the bourgeoisie will then usher in the fifth stage, which Marx asserts to be also the last one. That future and final destiny of mankind Marx claims to know with "scientific" precision. On this basis, Marxists speak of the future socialist existence of mankind not as a wishful utopia, but as a fact.

In reality, of course, Marxist historical materialism is not scientifically precise, for it depends at crucial points on willful reductions of reality to mere materiality. Marx was fully aware of his own reductionism and its potential unacceptability. In his *Economic and Philosophical Manuscripts* (1844), he confronts a too-critical reader: "[You ask] who created the first man and nature as a whole? I can only reply: your question is a product of abstraction; give up your abstraction and at the same time abandon your question. Do not think, do not ask any questions. For socialist man, the *whole of what is called world history* is nothing but the creation of man by human labor. Socialism is positive human *self-consciousness* attained through the negation of religion." Eric Voegelin calls this Marx's "prohibition of question," at which point the nonphilosophical and ideological character of Marx's thinking reveals itself as what it is: totalitarian compulsion of the mind. Voegelin's critique of Marx goes to the root of the issue:

> When Marx says that his rational dialectics stand Hegelian dialectics on its feet, he does not correctly describe what he is doing. Before the actual inversion begins, he has done something much more fatal: he has abolished Hegel's problem of reality. And since only the answer to this problem (the dialectic of the Idea) is specifically Hegelian, while the problem itself is a general philosophical one, he has by this act abolished the philosophical approach to the problem of reality on principle. The Marxian position is not anti-Hegelian, it is anti-philosophical.

All history, says Marx, is a chain of "class struggles" between the respective owners of the means of production and a burgeoning class possessing a new kind of property and wielding a new mode of production. When capitalism has been rendered ripe for collapse by its own successes, it will be overthrown by the proletariat, an underdog class that does not own any means of production. For this reason the proletariat, says Marx, is the only "really revolutionary class"; its self-liberation will put an end to all class rule, and thereby to the class struggle. Once it is on top,

> the proletariat will use its political supremacy to wrest, by degrees, all capital from the Bourgeoisie, to centralize all instruments of production in the hands of the *State*, . . . and to increase the total productive forces as rapidly as possible. In the beginning, this cannot be effected except by means of despotic inroads on the rights of property and on the condition of bourgeois production; by means, therefore, which appear economically insufficient and untenable, but which, in the course of the movement, outstrip themselves, necessitate further inroads upon the old social order, and are unavoidable as a means of entirely revolutionizing the mode of production.

What is envisaged here is something Marx calls the "period of transition," lasting an indefinite amount of time, during which power will be wielded by "the dictatorship of the proletariat." At this point, the state has been pushed to its utmost conceivable degree of power. Eventually, however, the state will "wither away," and society will be ordered by nothing but the administration of things and processes of production.

Marx's concept of political structure and political power is flawed because his eyes are riveted wholly on the property of the means of production. This property, rather than political rule, is the essence of power, in his mind. Thus Marx severely criticizes government and its power in a society where the means of production are privately owned; but he has no words of criticism for power that is wielded by the non-owning class, the proletariat (or wielded in the name of this class). We do not know whether Marx would have changed his mind had he seen the totalitarian regime that was realized in history on the basis of his ideas. One may, however, reject the thinking of a mind that calls on the proletariat to wield power without any limit of law, but then also expects this dictatorial regime eventually to "wither away." In Marx's mind, the proletariat has an almost divine quality that purifies power from all potential of evil provided that it is wielded only by it, the non-owning class. What is more, the society resulting from this rule of the proletariat is also supposed to be free from all evil of private actions. Marx expects it to be a wholly "good" society, in which all conflicts and contradictions of human existence will have disappeared. This fact, then, gives to Marxism its character of a message of "salvation," the pattern obviously derived from the Christian religion, but the reality declared to be human rather than divine, and pertaining to history rather than to eternity. As Voegelin stated, "At the root of the Marxian idea we find the spiritual disease, the gnostic revolt. . . . The soul of Marx is demonically closed against transcendental reality."

—GERHART NIEMEYER

Further Reading

Berlin, Isaiah. *Karl Marx: His Life and Environment.* 4th ed. New York: Oxford University Press, 1996.

Kolakowski, Leszek. *Main Currents of Marxism: Its Rise, Growth, and Dissolution.* Translated by P. S. Falla. 3 vols. Oxford: Clarendon Press, 1978.

Sowell, Thomas. *Marxism: Philosophy and Economics.* New York: Morrow, 1985.

See also: Burnham, James; capitalism; Catholic social teaching; Eastman, Max F.; fascism; Hook, Sidney; liberation theology; managerial revolution; Reagan Doctrine; socialism

Mason, George (1725–92)

George Mason was a Virginia planter, legislator, political writer, and natural rights philosopher who played important roles in the independence movement from Great Britain (as an ardent advocate of colonial rights from 1765 to 1776) and in constructing constitutional governments both for the state of Virginia (as a delegate to its convention of 1776 and as principal author of the Virginia Constitution and Declaration of Rights of that same year) and the new nation itself (as a delegate to the Federal Convention of 1787). Mason is chiefly remembered, albeit negatively and perhaps unfairly, as an opponent of the Constitution, which he refused to sign in Philadelphia. His "Objections to this Constitution of Government," written in September 1787, became a leading document for Anti-Federalist opposition during the great ratification struggles of 1787–88.

In opposing the Constitution of 1787, Mason was not so much a rejectionist as he was a perfectionist. Without a bill of rights, he believed, as did many others, that the new government was not only incomplete but also inconsistent with the principles of 1776.

Although Mason recognized the need for a new government to replace the Articles of Confederation (his efforts at reconciling border disputes between Virginia and Maryland were no doubt instructive in this regard, as was his long familiarity with the problem of western lands), he believed the constitution approved by the Philadelphia delegates erred too far on the side of conferring power to the central government without provid-

George Mason

ing adequate safeguards for individual and state rights. In his view, consistently maintained over the period 1776–87, government was supposed to serve the people, who represented the only legitimate source of political power. "All men," he wrote in 1776, "are by nature born equally free and independent" and "all government . . . is or ought to be calculated for the general good and safety of the community. . . . [L]et us never lose sight of this fundamental maxim—that all power was originally lodged in and is consequently derived from the people." Moreover, "whenever any power or authority extends further, or is of longer duration than is in its nature necessary for those purposes, it may be called government, but it is in fact oppression."

If Mason is not as well known as some of his fellow Virginians, he nevertheless contributed significantly to the creation of the American republic and its unique form of government. Disdaining politics, which he abhorred, his steady devotion to principle even at the cost of reputation helped to make possible the government that is so much admired around the world today.

—W. Kirk Wood

Further Reading

Rutland, Robert Allen. *The Birth of the Bill of Rights.* Chapel Hill, N.C.: University of North Carolina Press, 1955.

Mason, George. *The Papers of George Mason, 1725–1792.* 3 vols. Edited by Robert Allen Rutland. Chapel Hill, N.C.: University of North Carolina Press, 1970.

Miller, Helen Hill. *George Mason, Constitutionalist.* Cambridge, Mass.: Harvard University Press, 1938.

Rowland, Kate Mason. *The Life of George Mason,*
   1725–1792. 2 vols. New York: G. P. Putnam's
   Sons, 1892.

See also: Anti-Federalists; Bill of Rights

Matthews, J. B. (Joseph Brown) (1894–1966)

Joseph Brown (J. B.) Matthews was a forerunner of Whittaker Chambers in moving from
fervent involvement with socialist and hard-
Left organizations to embrace with equal fervor the cause of anticommunism during the
1930s. He became a close adviser to Martin
Dies in investigating the possible infiltration
of American institutions by foreign subversives from 1938 through 1945. But to the
embarrassment of President Franklin
Roosevelt and other early supporters, the Dies
Committee, originally given administration
support on the assumption that it would expose Nazis and fascists, instead found communist infiltration a much more pervasive
danger and pursued it accordingly. Claiming
that differences between liberals, pacifists,
socialists, and communists were fundamentally a matter of semantics, Matthews, testifying before Dies's House Un-American Activities Committee in 1938, identified some
ninety-four such groups he deemed commu-
nist-front organizations and with which he
had been associated during the previous seven
years. For this he was attacked by the political Left as a henchman of anti-Semites, as a
colleague of fascists, and as a traitor to the
progressive cause who had turned his coat in
exchange for prestige and wealth. Other commentators were more sympathetic to
Matthews's shift in loyalty; alluding to the
popular thumbnail definition of communism as "socialism in a hurry," George
Sokolsky wrote, "Matthews was apparently
in a hurry—but the world was not. He had
that to learn, and I think he has learned it."

"I had an inheritance of conservative
traditions," Matthews wrote in 1938, in his
autobiography, *Odyssey of a Fellow Traveler.*
"Now, after almost twenty-five years of political nomadism, I am back at the beginning.
But political and economic conservatism is
no longer merely an inheritance. It is a personal faith." Raised in Kentucky, educated
at Drew University, Union Theological Seminary, and the University of Vienna, and
trained to be a Methodist missionary, he
adopted the liberal social gospel doctrines
of the early twentieth century. He spent the
period between 1915 and 1938 teaching at the
college level and becoming involved in numerous left-wing social-justice organizations, joining the Socialist Party in 1929.
Matthews published numerous articles and
several poorly received books during those
years on the iniquities of capitalism; but in
the mid-1930s he began moving toward the
belief that "private competitive enterprise,
with all of its faults, appears to be the best
available servant of consumers' interests." By
1938 Matthews had completed his change of
philosophical direction, becoming Research
Director of the House Un-American Activities Committee. His *Odyssey of a Fellow Trav-*
eler exposed the communist connections of
many individuals who presented themselves
as liberals, including Arthur Kallet of Consumers Research and David L. Saposs, chief
economist of the National Labor Relations
Bureau—incurring the wrath of communists
and their sympathizers. Over the next three
decades, he served as a fervent spokesman
for HUAC as well as for Senator Joseph
McCarthy's investigations into communist
penetration of the American government.
During those years, Matthews's articles appeared frequently in the *American Mercury,*
and some of his essays were appropriated for
publication in Nazi-supported and anti-
Semitic periodicals—thus giving ammunition to his Left-liberal enemies. In 1953 he
resigned from his position as executive di-

rector of McCarthy's Subcommittee on Investigations in response to pressure by the Eisenhower administration after he claimed that Protestant clergymen constituted the greatest concentration of communist supporters in America. At the end of his career, Matthews served as a consultant to the Hearst newspaper chain. His name appeared on the masthead of *National Review* from its debut in 1955 until his death in 1966.

—JAMES E. PERSON JR.

Further Reading

Matthews, J. B. *Communism and the NAACP.* Atlanta: Georgia Commission on Education, 1958.

See also: anticommunism; Dies, Martin; Mises, Ludwig von

Mayflower Compact

Arguably the first constitutional document firmly within the American tradition, the Mayflower Compact is principally an oath taken in 1620 by forty-one of the men aboard the ship *Mayflower* before landing and founding Plymouth Colony in what is now Massachusetts. By signing this document, these men bound themselves into a people or body politic, vowing to serve with one another in pursuit of the glory of God, the advancement of the Christian faith, and the honor of their king and country. For their better ordering as a people, the signers vowed to work for such "just and equal" laws as were thought necessary for the good of the colony. That is, each would work for laws they thought were just and would seek to apply them equally to all members of the community.

The Mayflower Compact provides no frame of government. It does not set forth what shall constitute a good law. But conservatives in particular see its signing as a seminal event in American constitutional history. The compact is a self-conscious adaptation of a church covenant, by which dissenting Protestants in Great Britain formed their congregations, to the civil requirements of founding a colony. Conservatives emphasize the document's importance because it shows the deeply religious and communal habits of thought and action at the root of Americans' conduct from the earliest times in the new world. It begins with the phrase "In the name of God, Amen." In this way the compact's signers call on God as a witness and indicate that they have engaged in serious deliberations, for which they are willing to answer to Him. The compact then states the purposes of its signing—the common ends for which the signers have agreed to work. These common ends—God's glory, the propagation of Christianity, and the service of king and country—are both religious and communal in nature. Moreover, the heart and purpose of the compact is the oath by which the signers bind themselves into a civil body politic; by which they agree to work with one another for their common good in the formation of a civil government and the consideration, promulgation, and enforcement of laws.

The form in which the Mayflower Compact is written—it begins by identifying the signers, and then provides a statement of purpose, an oath creating the body politic, and an indication of what kind of body politic is being created—is followed by numerous later political documents within the American tradition, including the Constitution. The gradual de-emphasis, over many decades, of the role of God as witness could be seen as one marker of the decline of faith's explicit role within the American political tradition (or perhaps as the inevitable corruption of a once virtuous people). But one also should note that the compact is in a sense more fundamental even than our Constitution, which leaves out any opening reference to God. The compact forms a people, whereas the Constitution merely forms a government—a set of rules for the business of law- and policymaking that assumes the preexistence of a people worthy of that frame of government.

—BRUCE FROHNEN

Further Reading

Kendall, Willmoore, and George W. Carey. *The Basic Symbols of the American Political Tradition.* Washington, D.C.: Catholic University Press, 1995.

Lutz, Donald S. *The Origins of American Constitutionalism.* Baton Rouge, La.: Louisiana State University Press, 1988.

Miller, Perry. *The New England Mind: The Seventeenth Century.* Cambridge, Mass.: Belknap Press, 1983.

See also: church and state; constitutionalism; tradition

McCarthy, Eugene J. (1916–2005)

Eugene Joseph McCarthy was the embodiment of conservative liberalism at the level of public affairs in the last third of the twentieth century. He was an anticommunist liberal and a reformer in the mold of Burke. Russell Kirk admired him and voted for him in 1976, referring to him rightly as a "poet-politician." McCarthy was born in Watkins, Minnesota, the son of a farmer. He received his A.B. from St. John's University in Minnesota (1935) and his A.M. from the University of Minnesota (1939). He taught high school in Minnesota and North Dakota (1935-40, 1945), and economic education at St. John's University, Collegeville (1940-42). In 1944, he served as civilian technical assistant in the Military Intelligence Division of the War Department. After the Second World War, McCarthy taught sociology and economics at the Benedictine-operated College of St. Thomas in St. Paul from 1946 to 1948. A lifelong Catholic, McCarthy also spent a short period of time in a Benedictine monastery, but, deciding against that vocation, later married and purchased eighty acres in the anticipation of being a farmer and teacher.

As it turned out, he would not be content with that life, either, and in 1949 he was elected to the U.S. House of Representatives, where he served until 1958. In that year, he was elected to the U.S. Senate, where he stayed until 1970, and during which time he famously ran as Democratic candidate for president in 1968—a race in which he became a national focal point for his strong and principled anti–Vietnam War stance and his near-defeat of incumbent Lyndon B. Johnson in the New Hampshire primary (an accomplishment that forced Johnson out of the race). As a congressman and senator, McCarthy was deeply concerned about maintaining constitutionally proper legislative procedures, and he conservatively interpreted the Senate's role in foreign policy. Such a position, which made him a centrist in the mid-1950s, would later leave him increasingly outside the liberal mainstream, with the rise of the New Left and its concern for substantial social change—not constitutional administrative procedure—and the increasing corporate dominance of both major parties.

McCarthy failed, of course, in his 1968 presidential bid, and, indeed, his positions put him at odds with his own party, which he was all but forced to leave (think of a Democratic leader of his time or ours opining that America is becoming a country in which "everyone belongs to a corporation and everyone else belongs to the federal government"). However, his legacy was established and his trajectory toward a more overtly conservative liberalism fixed. McCarthy ran for the presidency in 1976 as an Independent (a campaign that emerged from his "Committee for a Constitutional Presidency"), and in 1980 he endorsed the candidacy of Ronald Reagan. Beyond these later political activities, he wrote several volumes of poetry, lectured widely, and wrote on various subjects of political and cultural importance, including the constitutional crisis presented by the presidency's growth in power, the problem of liberal immigration policies, foreign entanglements and foreign policy, the perils of American bureaucratization (he had a particular loathing for intrusive government agencies such as the IRS), and the corrupting influence of the mainstream media.

On numerous occasions McCarthy stated that his intellectual heroes were Burke and Tocqueville, and that their ideas formed the foundation of his own brand of American conservative and constitutional liberalism. He would also point out that he was heavily influenced by Dorothy Day and the Benedictine monk Virgil Michel (his teacher at St. John's). These influences, combined with his own experiences growing up on and later owning a farm, fashioned him at his core—like Robert Frost and his friend and occasional debate partner, Russell Kirk—as a "Northern Agrarian." McCarthy, influenced as many Catholics of his generation were by the writings of Chesterton, was also something of an American distributist. Like the English distributists and the Southern Agrarians, McCarthy was dedicated to life lived on a humane scale, and while he may justly be accused of being a big spender, he was no proponent of big government. He was, rather, a decentralizer.

Day's and Chesterton's writings also made McCarthy an advocate of "distributive justice." He was, therefore, a relentless critic of corporate capitalism and all forms of communism. If in his early years he was comfortable with the New Deal legacy of Roosevelt

Eugene J. McCarthy

and an advocate of government spending to achieve social renewal, the Vietnam War marked a profound awakening of conscience, bringing into focus much that imperiled the republic's prospects. His anticommunism had led him to be an early advocate for interventionism and an implacable foe of the isolationists of his time (though he had no affection for some other famous anticommunists, including Joseph McCarthy and John Kennedy). McCarthy regarded Soviet communism as Burke did French Jacobinism: as a global threat to the Christian commonwealth of Europe and its offspring in North America. But Vietnam was another matter. As he put it in 1967, "America's contribution to world civilization must be more than a continuous performance demonstration that we can police the planet." He thus became one of the first major American politicians to criticize Cold War orthodoxy at home and abroad—and, as he admitted at the time, he was "committing political suicide" in doing so.

The "left conservative" Norman Mailer contended that McCarthy was "the most serious conservative to run for president since Robert Taft." (Champions of Barry Goldwater might have something to say about that.) McCarthy, if a liberal, was always a republican, a champion of American federalism and its system of checks and balances. It was this political arrangement, embedded in an agrarian and Christian culture, which he sought to conserve. In his late years, which he called "hard years" and during which he penned ruminations he hoped might serve as "antidotes to authoritarians," his truest nature emerged resplendent: that of a deeply sensitive poet of nature and of man's glory and folly. Ever the foe of ideology, armed or unarmed, he would write in "Ares," a poem infused with the high imagination of a Burke or a Lowell: "ideologies can make a war/ last long and go far/ ideologies have not boundaries/ cannot be shown on maps/ before and after/ or even on a globe/ as meridian, parallel/ or papal line of demarcation."

—JEFFREY O. NELSON

Further Reading

Kauffman, Bill. *Look Homeward, America: In Search of Reactionary Radicals and Front-Porch Anarchists.* Wilmington, Del.: ISI Books, 2006.

Kirk, Russell. *The Sword of Imagination.* Grand Rapids, Mich.: Eerdmans, 1995.

McCarthy, Eugene. *No-Fault Politics: Modern Presidents, the Press, and Reformers.* Edited by Keith C. Burris. New York: Times Books, 1998.

Rising, George. *Clean for Gene: Eugene McCarthy's 1968 Presidential Campaign.* Westport, Conn.: Praeger, 1997.

Sandbrook, Dominic. *Eugene McCarthy: The Rise and Fall of Postwar American Liberalism.* New York: Knopf, 2004.

See also: agrarianism; distributism; Kirk, Russell; Roman Catholicism; separation of powers; Vietnam War

McCarthy, Joseph R. (1908–57)

Joseph McCarthy, Republican senator from Wisconsin from 1947 until his death in 1957, is best known for his crusade against suspected communists and their sympathizers in the government of the United States, whom he held responsible for Soviet gains following World War II. The conduct of his investigations, which critics characterized as irresponsible demagoguery, led to his censure by the Senate in 1954 for actions "contrary to senatorial traditions."

McCarthy's early life was marked by dire poverty, enormous ability, and driving ambition. He was born on a farm in Grand Chute, Wisconsin, on November 15, 1908, and completed the eighth grade in a one-room school. He started a chicken farm but went to work in a grocery when the chickens died. He then completed a four-year high school course in one year and attended Marquette University, where he earned a law degree and served as class president, boxing coach, and member of the debating team. As a student, he supported himself with jobs as a janitor, salesman, short-order cook, and construction worker. McCarthy was admitted to the bar in 1935 and became partner in a law firm in 1937. Defeated in his bid for district attorney as a Democrat in 1936, he was elected circuit judge as an independent in 1939, which made him the youngest elected judge in state history.

In 1942 McCarthy joined the Marines and served with distinction as an intelligence officer in the Pacific, even flying combat missions that were not part of his job. In 1946 he returned to defeat Robert La Follette Jr. and in so doing became the youngest member of the United States Senate. In 1949 he took up the cause of German soldiers imprisoned at Dachau. These prisoners, who had confessed to shooting American prisoners, had been stripped of their prisoner-of-war status, but they claimed that their confessions had been coerced after they were subjected to severe abuse. Indeed, one had committed suicide rather than sign his confession; unsigned, it was used as evidence against the others. McCarthy's stand for due process in this case was controversial at the time, and this experience may well have encouraged him in his general suspicion of conspiracy and his sense of victimhood.

On February 9, 1950, McCarthy gave the speech in Wheeling that is often cited as the beginning of "McCarthyism." In this speech, the poor boy from the chicken farm lashed out at the American children of privilege who, he alleged, had sold China and Eastern

Europe into slavery, and who, like Secretary of State Dean Acheson, still remained loyal to Alger Hiss, recently convicted of perjury:

> The reason why we find ourselves in a position of impotency is not because our only powerful potential enemy has sent men to invade our shores, but rather because of the traitorous actions of those who have been treated so well by this Nation. It has not been the less fortunate or members of minority groups who have been selling this Nation out, but rather those who have had all the benefits that the wealthiest nation on earth has had to offer—the finest homes, the finest college education, and the finest jobs in Government we can give.
>
> This is glaringly true in the State Department. There the bright young men who are born with silver spoons in their mouths are the ones who have been the worst.

According to the local newspaper, McCarthy claimed to have in his hand a list of 205 communists and their sympathizers still in the Department of State, though he would soon reduce that number to fifty-seven and never mounted a successful public case against any. Nevertheless, it is now fairly clear that a good many senior men who had entered government service during the Depression still believed that some form of communism was mankind's best hope, and that the less palatable aspects of Stalin's rule would not last for long.

On the floor of the Senate, where his speech was protected from civil suit, McCarthy went so far as to say that former secretary of state George Marshall had been a traitor and President Harry Truman his dupe. "How can we account for our present situation unless we believe that men high in this Government are concerting to deliver us

to disaster?" McCarthy asked. "This must be the product of a great conspiracy, a conspiracy on a scale so immense as to dwarf any previous such venture in the history of man. A conspiracy of infamy so black that, when it is finally exposed, its principals shall be forever deserving of the maledictions of all honest men."

Such attacks were useful to his party at the time, but in 1952 the Republicans nominated General Eisenhower, a protégé of General Marshall, for president. After Eisenhower's election McCarthy found himself increasingly marginalized. Over the next few years the Eisenhower administration would negotiate an end to the Korean conflict, in effect conceding half the country to the communists, refuse to come to the aid of France in Vietnam, and fail to support popular uprisings against communist rule in Eastern Europe. In McCarthy's eyes, at least, by 1956 the advance of communism could no longer be attributed solely to the treason of the Democrats.

In January 1953, with the Republicans in control of Congress, McCarthy was appointed chair of the Senate Committee on Government Operations, but he chose instead to head its Permanent Subcommittee on Investigations. Resurrecting an investigation that had been dropped by the House Committee on Un-American Activities, McCarthy targeted first the mainline Protestant churches. "The largest single group supporting the Communist apparatus in the United States today is composed of Protestant clergymen," wrote J. B. Matthews, the former HUAC staff member whom McCarthy had made his executive director on the same day his article, "Reds in our Churches," was published. An Irish Catholic himself, McCarthy did not anticipate the strong reaction his fellow Republicans would have to this attack on the religion of most Americans.

McCarthy's next target was the United

States Army, and he chose the new medium of television to reach out to the American public directly. Unfortunately, the main item under dispute turned out to be trivial, involving the routine promotion of a dentist despite his Communist Party affiliation, and the Army charged that McCarthy's chief counsel Roy Cohn was demanding special treatment for a close friend, a consultant to the subcommittee who had been drafted. Furthermore, McCarthy was an amateur with respect to television; his enemies were not. In March 1954, CBS aired an attack by veteran journalist Ed Murrow consisting largely of footage from the hearings (Murrow and producer Fred Friendly paid for the advertising with their own funds). Public opinion turned sharply against McCarthyism, and the full Senate censured him in December 1954.

After his censure, Senator McCarthy declined into acute alcoholism, dying of hepatitis on May 2, 1957. He was survived by his wife Jean and their daughter Tierney, whom they had adopted that January. It is likely that heavy drinking had affected his judgment for years, influencing his decisions to attack the churches and the Army and contributing to the coarse manner and bullying style that made him so vulnerable to ridicule. Documents made public since the end of the Cold War have vindicated McCarthy's initial concern about the willingness of many in the United States government to advance the Soviet agenda. His later career is all the more tragic because for decades it brought that concern into widespread disrepute.

—FRANK PALMER PURCELL

Further Reading

Buckley, William F., Jr. and L. Brent Bozell. *McCarthy and His Enemies: The Record and Its Meaning.* Chicago: Regnery, 1954

Cook, Fred J. *The Nightmare Decade: The Life and Times of Senator Joe McCarthy.* New York: Random House, 1971

McCarthy, Joseph. *America's Retreat from Victory: The Story of George Catlett Marshall.* Boston: Western Islands, 1952.

Rosteck, Thomas. *See It Now Confronts McCarthyism: Television Documentary and the Politics of Representation.* Tuscaloosa, Ala.: University of Alabama Press, 1994.

Rovere, Richard H. *Senator Joe McCarthy.* New York: Harcourt Brace, 1959.

See also: anticommunism; Bozell, L. Brent; Buckley, William F., Jr.; Cold War; Eastman, Max F.; Eisenhower, Dwight D.; Matthews, J. B.; McCarthyism; Sokolsky, George; Viereck, Peter

McCarthyism

McCarthyism designates a movement organized around Senator Joseph McCarthy and his attempt to expose communists and communist sympathizers in the U.S. foreign policy apparatus. Both the career of McCarthy as a crusading anticommunist and the appearance of his advocates came after he delivered a provocative address to Republican women in Wheeling, West Virginia, on February 7, 1950. In this speech the Wisconsin senator referred to a list in his possession of communists and communist fellow-travelers who were or had been formerly connected to the making of American foreign policy. This speech elicited strong reactions, coming as it did only two weeks after the sentencing on perjury charges of Alger Hiss, a state department official the discovery of whose misdeeds had set the stage for McCarthy's accusations. While almost all of the American Left and even some eastern Republicans were hostile to McCarthy's anticommunist rhetoric, much of the Republican old guard, as exemplified by Robert Taft, went along with his campaign against communists and Soviet sympathizers. For them, McCarthy was restoring America morally and politically by discrediting the procommunist Left that had attached itself to New Deal Democrats during World War II. McCarthy was also rightly or wrongly perceived as a useful Republican vote-getter, having pockets of support that Republicans might be able to reach among ethnic Democrats. The fact that some state department officials and some of those who did research on the atomic bomb were shown to be communists provided evidence of the charge that subversives had been allowed to infiltrate government security operations.

There were also other, more fervent intellectual backers of the controversial senator, and some of them persistently defended him even after he had made what Whittaker Chambers described as "irreparable blunders" in taking on the U.S. military, and even long after he had died, partly as a result of his debilitating alcoholism, in 1957. Within the emerging *National Review* circle, which included William F. Buckley Jr., Buckley's brother-in-law L. Brent Bozell, Buckley's former professor at Yale Wilmoore Kendall, Ralph de Toledano, John Chamberlain, Willi Schlamm, Suzanne La Follette, and Eugene Lyons, McCarthy's devotees were closing ranks. These writers helped him to prepare speeches and to substantiate his charges; they authored and signed endorsements of his work; and in the Buckley-Bozell vindication of his campaign titled *McCarthy and His Enemies* (1954) they brought out a meticulously documented defense of the charges McCarthy had made in his well-publicized Wheeling speech. Not all traditionalists expressed such unqualified support: T. S. Elliot, Russell Kirk, and Chambers were openly contemptuous of McCarthy's slashing style of debate and were inclined to compare it to that of the anti-fascist and procommunist Left. But his defenders were struck more by the duplicity of the Left than by the senator's defects, and they had no use for the moderates whom they thought were happy to cover up communist espionage, particularly during the period of Soviet-American alliance in World War II. McCarthyites were also outraged by the comparisons "progressive" intellectuals made between anticommunism and Nazism and between McCarthy and Hitler. Such reckless comparisons spurred left-of-center anticommunists in the fifties, such as Will Herberg and Irving Kristol, into taking the field for anticommunism, if not directly for McCarthy.

Although not all self-declared McCarthyites were disillusioned communists who had moved to the right, many of them, like Schlamm, Frank Meyer, and James Burnham, answered to this description. The movement also showed a Catholic connection, from McCarthy's own religious self-identification, to the clerical professor at Georgetown who had lectured him over lunch on the inescapable conflict between the Church and international communism, to his Irish Catholic backers (typified by the Kennedy family), to those Catholic conservative intellectuals, some of them converts, who were rushing to his defense. Among McCarthy's advisors, however, were also numerous Jews, while the majority of his ideological supporters were southern and midwestern Protestants. The McCarthy movement represented a populist Right that liberal historians have never quite been able to fit into their customary demonologies. It was neither anti-Semitic nor racist nor anti-Catholic, and given its highly cerebral defenders, it cannot be accused of being anti-intellectual, unless intellectual is associated exclusively with the politics of the Left. McCarthyism gave impetus to the postwar reconfiguration of the American Right. It expressed the anticommunist fervor at the heart of this new Right, which centered on such publications as *National Review* and *Human Events*. And because of this focus postwar conservatism would become heavily oriented toward foreign affairs and abandon the isolationist politics of its prewar antecedents. This may have been a partly unintended effect of McCarthyism, since among its political supporters were such known critics of activist internationalism as Senator John Bricker of Ohio.

—PAUL GOTTFRIED

Further Reading

Herman, Arthur. *Joseph McCarthy: Reexamining the Life and Legacy of America's Most Hated Senator.* New York: Free Press, 2000.

See also: anticommunism; Cold War; Eisenhower, Dwight D.; McCarthy, Joseph R.; populism

McClellan, James (1937– 2005)

Between 1961 and 1974, James McClellan taught government and constitutional law while a member of the faculty at the University of Alabama, Emory University, and Hampden-Sydney College. He held a Ph.D. in political science from the University of Virginia, where he was a Thomas Jefferson Fellow, and a J.D. from the University of Virginia School of Law.

McClellan served on the staffs of Senators Jesse Helms, Orrin Hatch, and the late John East, where his profound grasp of the principles and history surrounding our national founding informed his policy contributions in areas including the Voting Rights Act, public school prayer, busing, arms reduction under the Taiwan Relations Act, the Panama Canal treaties, abortion, and the reform of the federal judiciary and the federal criminal code.

In 1983, McClellan established the Center for Judicial Studies, which focused on the original intent of the Constitution's framers and their conception of the federal judiciary. The Center for Judicial Studies began publishing *Benchmark* in 1985, a groundbreaking constitutional journal which produced several seminal studies, including a critique of Lawrence Tribe, the restriction of jurisdiction under Article III, Section 2, and surveys of the careers of Judge Robert Bork and Professor Raoul Berger.

McClellan's first book, written with Russell Kirk, was *The Political Principles of Robert A. Taft* (1967). Their chapter titled "The Struggle for Responsible Party" emphasized the pedagogic role of political parties in instructing the people in the traditional virtues of freedom in a social context marked by industry, self-reliance, strong character, and religious values; that is, it emphasized that prosperity depends on a stable social matrix. To this teaching McClellan held fast, as may be seen in his critique of the so-called big-tent theory of moderate Republicanism that sought to marginalize Taft's social traditionalism.

In *Liberty, Order and Justice: An Introduction to the Constitutional Principles of American Government* (1989), McClellan provided the only college-level political science textbook then available that emphasized the intent of the framers and refuted the pervasive misinterpretation of the founders as followers of the Enlightenment intoxicated by an egalitarian or Lockean vision of politics.

With George W. Carey, McClellan coedited *The Federalist: A Student's Edition* (1990). He also contributed to the recovery of the founders' Constitution by bringing out, in partnership with M. E. Bradford, the first three volumes of a new edition of Jonathan Elliot's *The Debates in the Several State Conventions on the Adoption of the Federal Constitution* (1989), which includes Madison's *Notes* and the records of the ratifying conventions. From 1990 to 1992, McClellan served as the director of the Jesse Helms Center, the repository of the records of Senator Jesse Helms. For several years the director of publications at Liberty Fund, at the time of his death he was James Bryce Visiting Fellow in United States Studies at the University of London.

—DOUGLAS E. BRADFORD

Further Reading

McClellan, James. *Joseph Story and the American Constitution: A Study in Political and Legal Thought.* Norman, Okla.: University of Oklahoma Press, 1971.

See also: Bradford, M. E.; Carey, George W.; Political Science Reviewer; Taft, Robert A.

McCormick, Colonel Robert R. (1880–1955)

As publisher of the *Chicago Tribune*, Colonel Robert McCormick built his newspaper into the most widely circulated standard-sized paper of his day, a period that lasted from 1910 until his death in 1955. During the 1930s, at the very time that the press empire of William Randolph Hearst was in decline, McCormick was emerging as the largest practitioner of personal journalism of a decidedly conservative cast.

Educated at Ludgrove, a British preparatory school, Gront, and Yale, and beginning his career as a Bull Mooser and Chicago alderman, McCormick soon turned his editorial page into a forum for his personal crusades. A man of impassioned invective, he called President Hoover "the greatest state socialist in the world" and compared Henry Wallace, Franklin D. Roosevelt's secretary of agriculture, to Lenin, Mussolini, and Hitler. He once claimed that Rhodes scholars were conspiring to return the American colonies to Mother England. He accused the United Nations of seeking to enforce polygamy in the United States. And he said that the United Nations Convention on Genocide, which sought to outlaw the mass extermination of entire nationalities, would render sections of the Bible illegal.

There is, however, far more to McCormick's views than mere eccentricity. The archetype of a militant nationalist, the colonel—a World War I veteran—long supported universal military training, a large navy, and a bellicose foreign policy. Never harboring pacifist leanings, McCormick long supported extraterritorial rights in China, conscription, and a strong navy, only abandoning his militarism when he believed that Roosevelt was leading the nation into a destructive war. He defended United States intervention in any Latin American nation that, in his eyes, was incapable of self-rule.

His militarism aside, the key to McCormick's thought lay in his fear of state power. More consistent than many conservatives, the man who in his forties opposed prohibition denied in his seventies that Harry S. Truman had the right to involve the United States in the Korean War.

—JUSTUS D. DOENECKE

Further Reading

Edwards, Jerome E. *The Foreign Policy of Col. McCormick's Tribune, 1929–1941.* Reno, Nev.: University of Nevada Press, 1971.

Gies, Joseph. *The Colonel of Chicago.* New York: Dutton, 1979.

Smith, Richard Norton. *The Colonel: The Life and Legend of Robert R. McCormick, 1880–1955.* Boston: Houghton Mifflin, 1997.

Waldrop, Frank J. *McCormick of Chicago: An Unconventional Portrait of a Controversial Figure.* Englewood Cliffs, N.J.: Prentice-Hall, 1966.

Wendt, Lloyd. *Chicago Tribune: The Rise of a Great American Newspaper.* Chicago: Rand McNally, 1979.

See also: Chicago Tribune; isolationism; Old Right

McDonald, Forrest (1927–)

Few contemporary historians have been either as prolific or as controversial as Forrest McDonald, whose career has been one long exercise in demythologizing. Unlike most of his colleagues, McDonald is an unabashed conservative whose name has appeared prominently in periodicals such as *Continuity* and *National Review*.

Born in Orange, Texas, McDonald received his bachelor's, master's and doctoral degrees at the University of Texas. He has held academic positions at Brown University (1958-67), Wayne State University (1967-76), and the University of Alabama (1976–present), where he is currently distinguished senior fellow of the Center for the Study of Southern History and Culture. McDonald has addressed many topics, including American business history, the early national period of American history, and the ethnic roots of the American South.

Much of his work offers a strong pro-business perspective. In his history of the electric utilities industry in Wisconsin, *Let There Be Light* (1957), McDonald defended holding companies for making cheap power available at low cost. His life of Samuel Insull (1962) challenged the stereotype that the Chicago utilities magnate was among the most crooked of the latter-day robber barons. In reality, McDonald claimed, Insull was the father of government regulation of public utilities, a progenitor of rural electrification, a promoter of welfare capitalism and trade unions, and a pioneer in public relations. In a series of books on the Constitution (*We the People* [1958], *E Pluribus Unum* [1965], *Novus Ordo Seclorum* [1985]), McDonald conceded that economic forces played a vital role in ratification but—contrary to the claims of Charles A. Beard—denied the existence of any correlation with class.

College students have come across McDonald's general interpretation in a series of textbooks, including *The Torch is Passed* (1968), *The Last Best Hope* (with Leslie Decker

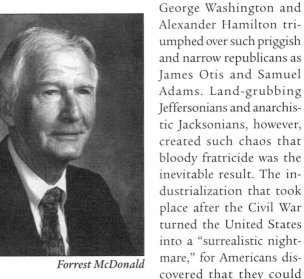

Forrest McDonald

and Thomas P. Govan, 1972), *The American People* (with David Burner and Eugene Genovese, 1980), and *A Constitutional History of the United States* (1982). Here he offers his general schema of American history, which—in capsulized form—reads as follows: The British empire was an efficient, orderly, and manageable organization destroyed, at least in part, by men of base, sordid, and corrupt motives. Fortunately, amid the chaos of the American Revolution, such nationalists as George Washington and Alexander Hamilton triumphed over such priggish and narrow republicans as James Otis and Samuel Adams. Land-grubbing Jeffersonians and anarchistic Jacksonians, however, created such chaos that bloody fratricide was the inevitable result. The industrialization that took place after the Civil War turned the United States into a "surrealistic nightmare," for Americans discovered that they could neither live with the corporation nor without it. Finally, such farsighted businessmen as J. P. Morgan and public administrators as Lyman Gage restored order, but with the Panic of 1907, progressivism took a destructive turn, culminating in the dangerous moralism of Woodrow Wilson. McDonald admires the foreign policy of Franklin Roosevelt and thought the Soviet threat in the 1940s quite genuine, but he is critical of post–World War II America for taking on itself "the role of liberal and Lord Protector of the Third World."

In commenting on legislation in the 1960s and 1970s, McDonald criticized Congress, regulatory agencies, and the courts for creating lower meat standards, increasing pollution, levying prohibitive taxes, making race a factor in education and employment, and declaring abortion a constitutional right. Because of such activity, he charged, federalism was eroded, checks and balances were destroyed, and "the Constitution ceased to be a fundamental law governing government." Were such trends not reversed, "the United States would have forfeited the legitimate reason for its own existence."

—JUSTUS D. DOENECKE

Further Reading

McDonald, Forrest, ed. *Empire and Nation.* Indianapolis: Liberty Fund, 1999.

———. *Recovering the Past: A Historian's Memoir.* Lawrence, Kan.: University Press of Kansas, 2004.

See also: Hamilton, Alexander; paleoconservatism; states' rights; Washington, George

McInerny, Ralph (1929–)

Thomistic philosopher, educator, author, and Catholic public intellectual, the quick-witted and gregarious Ralph McInerny has been exceeded by no one in making the thought of Thomas Aquinas and such contemporary Neo-Thomists as Jacques Maritain and Yves Simon well known and attractive today. The author of more than 150 articles, some twenty books on philosophy and theology, and more than fifty novels (some of which have been filmed for television, including those in the popular Father Dowling mystery series), McInerny has inspired countless people by his popular lectures as well as by his long years of teaching at the University of Notre Dame, where he is the Michael P. Grace Distinguished Professor. He received his Ph.D. in philosophy from the Université Laval in 1954 and joined the Notre Dame faculty in 1955. Since 1979 McInerny has been the director of the Jacques Maritain Center and he has overseen

the publication of Maritain's collected works. Entrepreneurial in spirit, he was influential in establishing the Fellowship of Catholic Scholars, the *Catholic Dossier* magazine, and many other publishing ventures, including *Crisis* magazine, to which he has contributed a regular column since 1982.

Philosophically, McInerny is a Thomist and stands in the scholarly tradition of the Laval professor Charles DeKoninck. He has emphasized the Aristotelian dimensions of the synthesis achieved by Thomas Aquinas, with stress on the importance of Aristotelian logic and physics for the understanding of Thomistic metaphysics. Convinced of the philosophical distinctiveness of Aquinas in drawing attention to the analogical nature of the term "being," McInerny has explored crucial works on this topic by Aquinas, such as Aquinas's commentary on the *De Trinitate* of Boethius. Among McInerny's earliest books were *The Logic of Analogy* (1961) and *Studies in Analogy* (1968). Later works such as *St. Thomas Aquinas* (1977) and *Ethica Thomistica* (1982), not to mention his delightful *First Glance at Thomas Aquinas: Handbook for Peeping Thomists* (1990), have been extremely reliable guides for those seeking an introduction to the thought of Aquinas.

More recently McInerny has also penned a number of insightful studies on Aquinas that are of a highly technical nature. Like his *Being and Predication* (1986), his *Boethius and Aquinas* (1990) advances further arguments for the type of approach to Aquinas that he has been proposing since his early studies on analogy. His *Aquinas on Human Action* (1992) both contributes to the contemporary debates on action theory and develops in a more technical vein the approach to Thomistic ethics that McInerny had laid out in more popularly accessible form in *Ethica Thomistica*. His *Aquinas against the Averroists* (1993) explores the quarrel between Thomas Aquinas and thirteenth-century figures like Siger of Brabant over the proper interpretation of the Aristotelian doctrine of the agent intellect. This issue is crucial for the explanation of how human beings are able to know what they know, and McInerny's discussion bears not just on the historical controversy but on lively issues in the philosophy of mind today.

—JOSEPH W. KOTERSKI, S.J.

Further Reading

McInerny, Ralph. *Art and Prudence*. Notre Dame, Ind.: University of Notre Dame Press, 1988.
———. *Thomas Aquinas*. New York: Penguin, 1998.
———. *What Went Wrong with Vatican II: The Catholic Crisis Explained*. Manchester, N.H.: Sophia Institute Press, 1998.

See also: Crisis; *natural law; natural law theory, new*

media, conservative

Conservative media have been at the forefront of conservative politics since William F. Buckley Jr. founded *National Review* magazine in 1955. The postwar conservative movement has seen three waves of conservative media come to the fore: print, which includes magazines, scholarly journals, book publishers, and newspapers; talk radio, a field virtually created by Rush Limbaugh; and the internet, which includes online magazines with original content and "bloggers," individuals who create their own Web sites.

During the early 1950s, conservative journalism was moribund. While liberals and the Left had the *New Republic* and the *Nation*, small but tremendously influential weekly journals of news and opinion with national readerships, the few surviving conservative journals of opinion were either rather obscure or else did more harm than good. *Human Events* was a tiny broadsheet read mostly in Washington, D.C., the *American Mercury* had turned anti-Semitic, and the *Freeman* had suffered editorial convulsions

that had reduced it to irrelevancy. It was in this atmosphere that the thirty-year-old Buckley launched *National Review*.

Buckley had become famous through his authorship of *God and Man at Yale* (1951), a witty and irreverent polemic that the recent Yale graduate wrote to show how far America's elite college campuses had moved away from America's traditional values and the purposes for which those colleges had been founded. His notoriety, along with his father's wealth and connections, allowed Buckley to raise the money and put together the stable of conservative editors and writers needed to launch *National Review*. The magazine was a mix of serious thought, political commentary on current events, and humor, often sarcastic. In its pages, *National Review* created a new version of American conservatism, an umbrella that *National Review*'s Frank Meyer called fusionism. The magazine brought together three major segments of conservative thinkers: anticommunists, traditionalists, and free marketeers. It also excluded as beyond the pale the anti-Semitism, racism, and conspiratorial view of politics and history that came to be identified with the John Birch Society. *National Review* played a significant role in creating the conservative movement, especially the rise to prominence of Republican senator Barry Goldwater and President Ronald Reagan.

Predating *National Review* was *Human Events*, a broadsheet founded in 1944 by Frank Hanighen, William Henry Chamberlin, and Felix Morley with a subscription base of 127. *Human Events* focused on Washington politics and current events to a greater extent than *National Review*, providing both with important niche markets. When Barry Goldwater ran for president in 1964, *Human Events*'s circulation rose to more than 100,000. During the administration of Richard Nixon, *Human Events* was considered the most influential conservative publication within the Washington political community.

Russell Kirk founded conservatism's most important scholarly journal, *Modern Age*, in 1957, serving as editor until 1959. At the time, *Modern Age* was America's only conservative scholarly journal, a tradition-based quarterly focusing on academic rather than topical subjects. Today *Modern Age* is published by the Intercollegiate Studies Institute, which also publishes the *Intercollegiate Review* and the *Political Science Reviewer*.

Providing financial assistance for the launching of *Modern Age*, *Human Events*, and *National Review* was Henry Regnery, who founded Regnery Publishing in 1947, the only conservative book publisher of the time. Among the important conservative books that Regnery published were Buckley's *God and Man at Yale*, Whittaker Chambers's *Witness* (1952), and Russell Kirk's *The Conservative Mind* (1953). In the 1990s, a very different Regnery published some of the most important exposés of President Bill Clinton and his administration, including Gary Aldrich's *Unlimited Access* (1996), Anne Coulter's *High Crimes and Misdemeanors* (1998), and Barbara Olson's *The Final Days* (2001) and *Hell to Pay* (1999). Regnery became part of Eagle Publishing, which also includes *Human Events* and the Conservative Book Club. Other major conservative book publishers include Liberty Fund, Encounter, Spence, the Intercollegiate Studies Institute, Crown, and Sentinel, the latter two imprints of large mainstream publishing conglomerates.

National Review is of course no longer the only important conservative opinion magazine. Others include the *American Spectator*, which began life in 1967 as the *Alternative*, a college newspaper published from Indiana University's campus by R. Emmett Tyrrell Jr., and Rupert Murdoch's *Weekly Standard*. The radicalism of the 1960s saw disillusioned liberals and their media outlets join the conservative camp. The most important of these was *Commentary*, formerly a New Left magazine and edited by Norman Podhoretz, which

became the flagship of the neoconservative movement.

Newspapers have been an area of conservative weakness within the print media. The cult of objectivity has kept the overwhelming majority of newspapers from following avowedly liberal or conservative lines, although the nature of reportage and the conscious and unconscious biases of those who enter the journalism profession have led conservatives to believe that most of the working press is liberal—a conclusion amply documented since 1987 by the Media Research Center and its president, L. Brent Bozell III. The most important conservative newspapers are the *Washington Times* and the editorial page of the *Wall Street Journal*. The *Washington Times* was founded in 1982 by the Rev. Sun Myung Moon, leader of the Unification Church. Because of its "Moonie" financing and conservative slant on the news, including a four-page opinion section, the newspaper was disdained by most of the political establishment. By its twentieth anniversary in 2002, the *Washington Times* had overcome the "Moonie" stigma, thanks largely to the editorial leadership of important journalists like Smith Hempstone, Arnaud de Borchgrave, and Wesley Pruden, and thanks also to its unmatched sources within the national security bureaucracies. The *Wall Street Journal*'s editorial page has also been a key conservative player, perhaps most importantly as the leading media proponent of supply-side economics. In 2002, the conservative *New York Sun* was launched as an intelligent alternative to the *New York Times*.

The second wave of conservative media was launched on August 1, 1988, when Rush Limbaugh's radio call-in program went into national syndication in New York City and on fifty small- and middle-market radio stations. Within five years, Limbaugh's blend of conservatism and political satire had spread to 650 stations and was heard by 25 million people each week. Limbaugh's rise was a textbook case of the moment meeting the man. National talk shows had long been late-night radio staples, but they primarily focused on general interest topics or self help. The motto of the radio business was "local, local, local," the assumption being that people listened to the radio for local topics, traffic, and temperature. Since there was little money to be made late at night, talk stations were happy to accept nationally syndicated programming. This programming was almost always apolitical because of the "Fairness Doctrine," a regulation that required political commentary and coverage to be ideologically balanced. Rather than risk running afoul of regulators, station managers simply stayed away from politics. When the Reagan administration repealed the Fairness Doctrine in 1987, the ground was clear for a program like Limbaugh's. The last factor in the equation was the decline of AM radio. While FM had been stereo-capable for years, thus providing music with better sound, AM did not acquire stereo capability until the mid-1980s. By then, popular music and its listeners had switched to FM, leaving AM as the home of muzack, fundamentalist preachers, and the occasional news or talk station. There was a niche to be filled, and Limbaugh filled it brilliantly.

After Limbaugh, hundreds of conservative talkers went on the air, nationally and locally, but none came close to matching Limbaugh's audience or influence. Limbaugh eventually became so powerful that President Bill Clinton telephoned a liberal call-in show to complain that Limbaugh was destroying his healthcare plan because Limbaugh had greater access to the airwaves than he had. The first lady, Hillary Clinton, interviewed liberal talk-show hosts at the White House in hopes of finding a "liberal Limbaugh." She was unsuccessful, and by the turn of the millennium, few liberals had been able to acquire a national audience. In 1994, when the Republicans recaptured the House of Representatives for the first time in forty years, the freshman class voted Limbaugh an honorary member.

The Internet revolution of the late 1990s provided another media venue for conservatives. While most magazines and newspapers would use the Internet to reprint a few articles from their current print issue as a means to tease print sales, *National Review* created *National Review Online (NRO)*, which publishes new material five days per week. *NRO* is perhaps the most widely read conservative Web site. Matt Drudge's "Drudge Report" also has garnered success as an outlet for opinion, analysis, and rumor.

The early 2000s saw the advent of Internet "bloggers," a name derived from "Web log," the term of art for online diaries. Once known as "vanity Web sites," blogs are running commentaries that provide links to other Internet sites. Thanks to the power, ease of use, and relative cheapness of the Web log technology, blogging has grown at a prodigious pace. Within the technology industry, blogs have become the primary news medium. Blogs allow the blogger to post news or opinion and receive almost instantaneous discussion, correction, and rival points of view. The most prominent bloggers tend to be libertarians such as law professor Glenn Reynolds, whose thoughts are recorded on "InstaPundit," former *New Republic* editor Andrew Sullivan, and *Reason* editor Virginia Postrel. *National Review Online* has created a successful blog in which all of its writers participate called "The Corner."

The medium in which conservatives have had the hardest time making inroads is television. Conservative efforts to buy CBS during the late 1970s failed, and conservative television networks such as National Empowerment Television, the Conservative Television Network, GOP-TV, and America's Voice all fared poorly. Conservatives have had more success with television programs. William F. Buckley Jr. was in the forefront with *Firing Line*, which began its thirty-year run in 1966. The vast expansion of the cable television dial in the 1980s and 1990s also brought more conservatives into television. Fox News counterpoises a conservative slant to the other networks' evening news, and Fox has made libertarian and conservative commentators Bill O'Reilly and Sean Hannity into stars.

—ROBERT WATERS

Further Reading

Goldberg, Bernard. *Arrogance: Rescuing America from the Media Elite.* New York: Medium Cool Communications, 2003.

Judis, John B. *William F. Buckley Jr.: Patron Saint of the Conservatives.* New York: Simon & Schuster, 1988.

Kurtz, Howard. *Hot Air: All Talk, All the Time.* New York: Times Books, 1996.

Limbaugh, Rush H. *The Way Things Ought to Be.* New York: Pocket Books, 1992.

Regnery, Henry. *Memoirs of a Dissident Publisher.* New York: Harcourt Brace Jovanovich, 1979.

See also: Buckley, William F., Jr.; Commentary; *Conservative Book Club;* Human Events; *Limbaugh, Rush;* Modern Age; National Review; *Regnery Publishing;* Wall Street Journal; Washington Times; Weekly Standard

mediating structures

The phrase "mediating structures" was in recent decades popularized by Peter Berger and Richard John Neuhaus, but the concept has been fundamental to conservative thought since Edmund Burke. The term refers to the social groups and associations that lie between the individual and the state—the family, parish, guild, village, voluntary associations, and all other such local and parochial communities. At times, such groups are also referred to as "intermediate" or "secondary" groups, as in the writings of Alexis de Tocqueville. Whatever the precise language employed, the defense of mediating structures has been essential to modern conservatism, and, while certain liberals (such as J. S. Mill) and radicals (especially P. J. Proudhon and P. Kropotkin) have mounted at least tepid defenses of mediating structures, conservatism has been both more consistent and more vigorous than either liberalism or radicalism in efforts to preserve the corporate rights of social groups.

Burke first stated the conservative case for mediating structures in his *Reflections on the Revolution in France* (1790). Burke observed that the French revolutionaries subscribed to a version of modern natural law that refused to recognize the salutary influence of any traditional social institution. The Jacobins believed that rights reside within individuals and that there are no legitimate interests beyond the particular interests of individuals and the national interest. Accordingly, the revolutionaries abolished the guilds, attacked the monasteries, institutionalized divorce, bound the clergy to the Revolution by oaths, and eliminated primogeniture and other laws protecting family property. As Burke discussed in the *Reflections*, the revolutionaries also redrew districts according to population size and geometric symmetry in order that "the people would no longer be Gascons, Picards, Bretons, Normans but Frenchmen." Burke says, however, that instead of being Frenchmen with one country and one heart, the people "will have no country. No man ever was attached by a sense of pride, partiality or real affection to a description of square measurement. We begin our public affections in our families . . . [,] we pass on to our neighborhoods, and our habitual connections. . . . The love of the whole is not extinguished by this subordinate partiality." Indeed, Burke asserted that "to love the little platoon we belong to in society is the first principle (the germ as it were) of public affections."

To disband the little platoons is to foster individual "weakness, disconnection and confusion," according to Burke. Mediating structures provide the individual guidance through custom, tradition, and habitual practices—"the coat of prejudice." In a word, Burke believed that mediating structures militate against what Tocqueville in the next century called "individualism."

Tocqueville was preoccupied with the dangers of the loss of mediating structures, especially civil associations. In *Democracy in America* (1835), he describes "individualism" and the centralization of state power as rising in tandem, both rooted in the passion for equality. According to Tocqueville, the individual and the state are not opposed to one another. Rather, they are reinforcing poles, each opposed to the social groups and associations lying between them. The state secures individual rights and, without mediating structures to buffer the individual, the individual looks to the state to secure his needs—including the need for community. Tocqueville maintained that individualism fosters "democratic despotism" and that the centralized state vanquishes mediating structures, isolating individuals. Conversely, and more optimistically, Tocqueville argued that mediating structures simultaneously combat the chief evils of democratic egalitarianism—individualism and the overweening, tutelary state.

Much of modern thought has been hostile to mediating structures. For example, Hobbes, Rousseau, and Bentham each envisioned an ideal condition in which the state guards the rights and fulfills the needs of unencumbered, desocialized individuals. Nonetheless, recently in America the rhetoric of "community" has become commonplace, even fashionable. At times this rhetoric has certainly been abused, as in the widely noticed *Habits of the Heart* (1985), a book by Robert Bellah and several others that used the language of community to justify an egalitarian state dedicated to the redistribution of property. But such rhetoric is clearly not always disingenuous, and the recent concern with "community," "civil society," and "mediating structures" bespeaks a genuine and profound presence of conservatism in America today. Indeed, the strength of concern for mediating structures in any modern society is an excellent barometer for measuring the vigor of that society's conservative philosophy.

—BRAD LOWELL STONE

Further Reading

Nisbet, Robert. *Conservatism: Dream and Reality*. New Brunswick, N.J.: Transaction, 2001.
———. *The Quest for Community*. New York: Oxford University Press, 1953.

See also: Berger, Peter L.; Burkean conservatism; centralization; community; localism; Neuhaus, Richard John; Tocqueville, Alexis de; traditionalism

Medved, Michael (1948–)

Media critic, author, radio talk show host, and "cultural crusader" born in Philadelphia and raised in San Diego, Michael Medved began studying at Yale University at age sixteen and graduated with honors in U.S. history in 1969. After receiving a Yale Fellowship, he continued his studies at the law school. While in New Haven, his classmates included both Bill and Hillary Clinton as well as George W. Bush. His service as co-chair of the Vietnam Moratorium antiwar demonstration on campus led to his obtaining a job as head speechwriter for the local Joe Duffey senatorial campaign, and despite Duffey's loss, this position initiated a series of writing and political consulting jobs. Medved never returned to his studies.

After moving to Berkeley in 1971, Medved left the Democratic Party after serving as a campaign consultant to California congressman Ron Dellums (later described by Medved as a "Stalinist Democrat"). During this time he also supervised a minority recruitment campaign for Bay Area police departments. Compounding his disillusionment with the Left was his experience with a company that hired Medved to create an ad department in order to land set-aside contracts. Still, it wasn't until 1980 that Medved officially registered as a Republican.

In 1976, Medved cowrote, with David Wallechinsky, *What Really Happened to the Class of '65?* The book used narratives from former classmates from their West Los Angeles Palisades High School to examine the American counterculture. As a result, Medved gained notoriety and published several other works ranging from movie critiques (*The Fifty Worst Films of All Time* [1978], *The Golden Turkey Awards* [1975], *The Hollywood Hall of Shame* [1983], and *The Son of Golden Turkey Awards* [1986]) to more scholarly works on the history of White House chiefs of staff (*The Shadow Presidents*, 1979) and the medical industry (*Hospital: The Hidden Lives of a Medical Center Staff*, 1982).

These successes led to both popular and critical acclaim. Medved became the first on-air film critic for CNN in 1980 and three years later, along with Jeffrey Lyons, he hosted for over a decade, *Sneak Previews*, a nationally syndicated movie review show on PBS originally featuring Gene Siskel and Roger Ebert. Medved published *Hollywood vs. America* in 1992. In an interview with *Investor's Business Daily*, Medved commented that "[w]hat's wrong is not the body of the films but the soul, and the fact that films so infrequently reflect or even respect the values of the American people."

By 1993, Medved had become chief film critic for the *New York Post*. After sitting in several times for talk show host Rush Limbaugh, Medved was offered his own radio show at KVI-Seattle in 1996. Three years later, *The Michael Medved Show* was among the top ten syndicated shows in America.

In 2001 Medved, a Jewish theist who attends an Orthodox synagogue, coauthored a book with his rabbi, Daniel Lapin. *Buried Treasure* is a collection of essays highlighting the wisdom contained within the Hebrew language.

—Nicholas Slepko

Further Reading

Medved, Michael, and Diane Medved. *Saving Childhood: Protecting Our Children from the National Assault on Innocence.* New York: HarperCollins, 1998.

See also: Lapin, Rabbi Daniel

Meese, Edwin, III (1931–)

Edwin Meese III served as the seventy-fifth attorney general of the United States and was President Ronald Reagan's closest advisor and confidant. During Reagan's presidency, Meese gained prominence as the single most effective change agent in the Reagan administration—other than Reagan himself. Meese is widely credited with spearheading the contemporary movement to restore the Constitution's original meaning to preeminence. He also played a pivotal role in discovering, and reporting to Reagan, the Contra diversion from the Iran initiative, a discovery he immediately made public, an act that likely saved the Reagan presidency from a serious impeachment attempt by its opponents in Congress.

A California native, Meese was born and raised in Oakland. He was educated at Yale University, where he earned a B.A. in 1953, and at the University of California at Berkeley, where he took a law degree in 1958 after serving two years active duty as an artillery officer in the army. Meese became a prosecutor after law school and was serving as deputy district attorney of Alameda County,

California, when he joined then-governor Reagan's staff in 1967 as legal affairs secretary. In this role, he was instrumental in crafting and implementing Reagan's response to widespread student disruption on campus.

In 1969, Meese became chief of staff to Governor Reagan, serving in that capacity until 1974 and functioning as Reagan's principal policy advisor. Meese's professionalism, evenhandedness, and focus on practical accomplishments earned him bipartisan respect and statewide recognition. Outgoing Governor Reagan credited Meese for much of his success as governor.

When Reagan became president, Meese was named counsellor to the president and a member of both the Cabinet and the National Security Council. As such, he became the senior member of the White House staff. In the White House, Meese functioned as President Reagan's chief policy advisor on all matters, foreign and domestic. He was instrumental in every major policy initiative of the Reagan administration, from tax reform to the Strategic Defense Initiative. Meese also played a central role in the selection of federal judicial candidates.

In early 1985, Meese became attorney general of the United States at the Justice Department. As the nation's chief law enforcement officer, he also managed the Federal Bureau of Investigation, the Drug Enforcement Administration, and the Immigration and Naturalization Service. In this new position Meese pursued a characteristically aggressive agenda that included advancing the Constitution as the supreme law, championing crime victims' rights, coordinating the federal fight against drug trafficking and abuse, creating groundbreaking international law enforcement cooperation against terrorism, and establishing a new federal task force to prosecute child pornography. Meese left office in late 1988, having effectively revolutionized the legal and law enforcement landscape for decades to come.

After the Reagan presidency, Meese joined the Heritage Foundation and began a second career focused on institutionalizing these accomplishments. He also became a visiting fellow at the Hoover Institution and remains a leading authority on constitutional law, law enforcement, terrorism, and the Reagan administration.

—JOHN RICHARDSON

Further Reading

Edwards, Lee, *To Preserve and Protect: The Life of Edwin Meese III*. Washington, D.C.: Heritage Foundation, 2005.

Kmiec, Douglas W., *The Attorney General's Lawyer: Inside the Meese Justice Department*. New York: Praeger, 1992.

Meese, Edwin III, *With Reagan: The Inside Story*. Washington, D.C.: Regnery, 1992.

See also: Constitution, interpretations of; Cribb, T. Kenneth, Jr.; Heritage Foundation; Institute for Contemporary Studies; pornography; Reagan, Ronald; rule of law

Memoirs of a Superfluous Man

Memoirs of a Superfluous Man (1943) is an autobiography of the ideas and mind of Albert Jay Nock, and only incidentally of his life or achievements.

Nock's contribution to conservative philosophy consists mainly in his analysis and rejection of all forms of statism. From the 1890s to the 1940s, Nock witnessed the growth of the state, as power became centralized and government absorbed through taxation more and more of the national wealth. Nock said he was thankful that he never had contact with any institution under state control and had not been indoctrinated with state-inspired views.

Nock looked back fondly to an America whose people had the virtues of independence, self-reliance, dignity, and diligence, virtues which flourished in liberty. For Nock, communism, the New Deal, fascism, and Nazism were merely so many trade-names for collectivist statism. Nock credits Jefferson with the insight that in proportion as the state is given power to do things *for* citizens, the state will do things *to* citizens.

In the *Memoirs,* Nock reports that he had been of a skeptical frame of mind since childhood. He learned Latin and Greek early and became educated in the ancient classics. His motto was always to "see things as they are," the mark of a truly educated man who sees the reality beneath superficial appearances.

Nock refers to himself as being a "superfluous man" in several ways: superfluous in that he had no desire to change others in a society that itched to change people; in that he had been educated rather than merely trained; and in that he maintained an interest in culture and ideas amidst a vulgar society centered on an "economism" that championed material wealth.

Nock was disdainful of leftist movements for social reform and their careless superficial use of abstract terms such as "capitalism." He regarded most of what they said as sheer nonsense. These "reformers," in his view, failed to recognize that the evil lie in capitalists and others obtaining state-granted advantages rather than in the ownership of capital as such. Particularly noxious "reforms" to Nock included the income tax and the popular election of U.S. senators.

The social philosopher and economist that Nock especially admired was Henry George, author of *Progress and Poverty* (1879) and other works that analyzed the economic as well as moral damage of government intervention, especially the taxation

of production and trade. George proposed a "single tax" only on land rent, which, since the land was there by nature and since its value derived from community activity, would not hamper production and investment. To Nock, Henry George was the "real thing" and the Georgist fiscal program the best path to economic freedom.

—FRED FOLDVARY

Further Reading

Crunden, Robert M. *The Mind and Art of Albert Jay Nock.* Chicago: Regnery, 1964.

Wreszin, Michael. *The Superfluous Anarchist.* Providence, R.I.: Brown University Press, 1972.

See also: Nock, Albert Jay

Mencken, H. L. (Henry Louis) (1880–1956)

A prolific and widely read journalist and critic who flourished from the 1910s to the 1940s, and often referred to as the "American Voltaire," H. L. Mencken was a son and lifelong resident of Baltimore. His identification with that city contributed to the shift-

H. L. Mencken

ing of the literary center of gravity of the United States southward from the Northeast. Mencken made his first mark in 1908 with a book, *The Philosophy of Friedrich Nietzsche,* which was significantly responsible for introducing Nietzsche to America. However, Mencken's métier was journalism, and within a decade he was the leading light in the American highbrow press. His work appeared mainly in the *Smart Set* and the *American Mercury,* the magazine he founded in 1923 with the help of Alfred A. Knopf. From 1919 to 1927, Mencken compiled collections of his work in six volumes of *Prejudices.*

Mencken's journalistic writings came in the form of the aphoristic line or paragraph and the essay. His writing was characteristically brazen and jocular. For example, from his mock memorial to William Jennings Bryan, who died shortly after defending creationism at the Scopes Monkey Trial of 1925: "[Bryan] staggered from the court ready to die, . . . witless and in poor taste. . . . He came into life a hero, a Galahad, in bright and shining armor. He was passing out a poor mountebank." Mencken's style gained him throngs of aficionados in the "ballyhoo" 1920s. Collegians, men- and women-about-town, and litterateurs of all sorts carried the *American Mercury* under arm and aped the editor's skepticism, irreverence, and know-it-all tone.

As for the content of Mencken's body of work, it remains difficult to evaluate, aside from the certainty that Mencken's worldview was complex and impressive. Mencken loathed democracy, which he thought stifled the most interesting spirits in the population. Yet he cultivated indifference toward the rich and high society, was highly skeptical of religion, and was slow to give honor to recognized intellectuals. The one piece of writing that may be seen as a confession of faith is his excoriation of the New South, "The Sahara of the Bozart" (1920), in which Mencken made plain that he longed for a society such as the departed Old South, where a premium was placed on cultural appreciation, philosophy, manners, and the art of conversation. Mencken also had formidable opinions on American literature. His reviews on contemporaries such as Willa Cather and Sinclair Lewis and his essays on literary history, such as "The National Letters" (1920), set forth compelling and highly original views.

During the Depression, the nation lost its taste for Mencken, who in turn tried his hand at political journalism, only to be ex-

asperated by the popularity of Franklin D. Roosevelt. In the 1940s, Mencken published several volumes of autobiography as well as supplements to his monumental study, *The American Language,* which had first appeared in 1919. Mencken's very considerable influence has extended to Richard Hofstadter in history and to Tom Wolfe, R. Emmett Tyrrell, and the early *National Review* in journalism.

—BRIAN DOMITRIVIC

Further Reading

Teachout, Terry. *The Skeptic: A Life of H. L. Mencken.* New York: HarperCollins, 2002.

See also: American Mercury; American Spectator; *Babbitt, Irving*

Meyer, Frank S. (1909–72)

Frank S. Meyer, one of America's most influential postwar conservative philosophers and popularizers, was born in 1909 in Newark, New Jersey. For a short time he attended Princeton University, but eventually he left in order to study in England. While there, influenced by his readings about the First World War and then by the shock of the Great Depression, Meyer joined the Communist Party in 1931.

He rose quickly within the party. While a graduate student at the London School of Economics, he won election as president of the Student Union as an avowed communist. When he returned to the United States in 1934, he became the party's director of education for the Illinois-Indiana region, with responsibility for recruiting new members and for developing new methods of education and propaganda.

But despite these responsibilities and his acceptance within the party, as the years passed Meyer began to have doubts. As he would write later in his book *The Moulding of*

Communists (1961), the Communist Party sought to mold its members into an ideal image. This meant a constant struggle to eliminate all "subjectivism" and "bourgeois" influences and to follow the party's dictates without hesitation. But Meyer had never completely abandoned his belief in the value of the individual; the party's zeal for discipline and control began to seem far too confining and dictatorial. Meyer's doubts were strengthened during the time he served in the army during World War II, which allowed Meyer to escape the party's immediate control and to see new people and encounter new ideas. By 1945 Meyer made a final break with the Communist Party.

He now began a slow yet steady journey to the right. Meyer was deeply influenced by the conservative literature that began to appear in the postwar years—especially Friedrich von Hayek's *The Road to Serfdom* (1944) and Richard Weaver's *Ideas Have Consequences* (1948). These works confirmed Meyer's belief in the sanctity of the individual—a belief that would remain deeply ingrained in him. Meyer soon became a fervent anticommunist, partly in aversion to his own communist past, partly because of the developing Cold War between America and the Soviet Union after 1945. His dissatisfaction with Harry Truman's prosecution of the conflict led him to become a Republican by 1952 and to begin contributing to the *Freeman* and the *American Mercury*. By the mid-1950s he was well known in conservative intellectual circles.

In 1956 Meyer joined William F. Buckley Jr.'s *National Review* and quickly settled down as the editor of its book review section and the writer of a regular column called "Prin-

Frank S. Meyer

ciples and Heresies." He would remain at *National Review* until his death in 1972, but while the magazine was important to him Meyer's immediate goal became to affect and influence American conservatism as a whole. In so doing, he became something of a legend.

This status was in large part due to Meyer's persona. He usually cloistered himself in his home nestled among the hills around Woodstock, New York. There he carried on an owl-like existence—sleeping by day and working at night. His rejection of his Marxist past led him to adopt a strict individualism. He educated his children at home and fought against even the smallest manifestations of state control—even zip codes. He conducted most of his business over the telephone, seeking out reviewers and debating their viewpoints with them late into the night. He would also make late-night phone calls to his fellow members of the American Conservative Union, or the Conservative Party of New York, or Young Americans for Freedom. He also frequently had visitors. Conservatives of all stripes made the trek to Meyer's lair, staying up all night and debating conservative philosophy or discussing classical literature—with Meyer rumbling out his views from behind an ever-present cloud of cigarette smoke.

Meyer's influence upon contemporary American conservative philosophy was considerable. By 1960 the conservative philosophical house was in a state of disorder. A split existed in the movement between libertarians, led by figures such as Friedrich von Hayek and Ayn Rand, and traditionalists, led by Russell Kirk. Libertarians championed freedom as the highest good and focused on the primacy of a minimalist government and the worth of the individual person. Traditionalists, however, emphasized the need for order. They argued that the state, while not being omnipotent, should still seek to instill virtue and order in society in the midst of a "revolutionary age."

Meyer felt both groups had mistaken emphases, and in a series of essays (and a book titled *In Defense of Freedom* [1962]) during the early 1960s he sought to put forth the basis for a rapprochement. Traditionalist conservatives, he argued, emphasized the need for authority too much. In so doing, they subordinated the individual to the state's conception of a higher good and made themselves powerless to argue against collectivist liberals, who championed state power with the same type of argument. At the same time libertarians, although commendably advocating a limited state, allowed their exaltation of freedom to lead them to skepticism and secularism. They were ignoring the "organic moral order," said Meyer; while they rightly opposed the "authoritarianism" of man, they failed to recognize the "authority of God and truth."

Meyer wished to link these two principles of freedom and organic moral order. He argued that this could be done and indeed already had been done by America's founding fathers. Our country's founding documents preached that virtue was none of the state's business. Rather, in the political realm liberty was the ultimate goal. But it was not an end in itself; our founders taught that America's citizens must use liberty to choose virtue. Yet the government must not impose this virtue by force. For virtue and morality to mean anything, they must be freely chosen; men must have the right to be vicious.

What conservatives must then do, Meyer continued, was to apply these philosophical principles to contemporary life. Hence, Meyer assailed all and sundry bureaucrats, social engineers, and of course communists for ignoring the worth of the individual person and seeking to impose upon him their versions of morality. Meyer attempted to apply these principles to politics and foreign policy. Not all on the Right subscribed to his version of conservatism. Some traditionalists and libertarians shunned his *fusionism* (as L. Brent Bozell termed it) as too contrived and unworkable. Others felt that his application of principles in politics was too rigid. Fellow *National Review* senior editor James Burnham, for example, argued for a more pragmatic approach that would, in the long run, gain the Right entry to power circles and advance conservative ideas. Yet even today the outlines of Meyer's philosophy remain discernible as the (constantly endangered) common ground of a disparate conservative movement.

—KEVIN SMANT

Further Reading

Gottfried, Paul. *The Search for Historical Meaning: Hegel and the Postwar American Right.* DeKalb, Ill.: Northern Illinois University Press, 1986.

Meyer, Frank S. *The Conservative Mainstream.* New Rochelle, N.Y.: Arlington House, 1968.

Nash, George. *The Conservative Intellectual Movement in America since 1945.* 2nd ed. Wilmington, Del.: Intercollegiate Studies Institute, 1996.

Smant, Kevin J. *Principles and Heresies: Frank S. Meyer and the Shaping of the American Conservative Movement.* Wilmington, Del.: ISI Books, 2002.

See also: Bozell, L. Brent; Evans, M. Stanton; fusionism; National Review; Zoll, Donald Atwell

Milione, E. Victor (1924–)

E. Victor Milione was the guiding force of the Intercollegiate Studies Institute for thirty-five years, from 1953 through 1988. As executive vice president and then president,

Milione initiated ISI's most important programs, including the Weaver Fellowships, the *Intercollegiate Review* and other publications, the campus clubs and lectures, the seminars, the summer schools, and the regional offices. He oversaw the steady increase of the institute's annual budget from a miniscule $12,000 in its first year of operation to just under $1 million in his final year.

Under his leadership, ISI forged enduring relationships with students, professors, trustees, and donors that enabled the institute to survive the apathetic fifties and the revolutionary sixties and attain significant influence in the receptive Reagan years. Through all the ups and downs, it was Vic Milione who ensured that ISI stuck to its mission of educating for liberty, of helping students and professors to acquire the knowledge and understanding of the values and institutions necessary for a free society to endure.

Born in Penfield, Pennsylvania, a suburb of Philadelphia, Milione attended public and private schools and served in the air force during World War II. He graduated from St. Joseph's University in 1950 with a B.S. in political science. He worked for Americans for the Competitive Enterprise System before meeting in 1953 the libertarian author-journalist Frank Chodorov, who persuaded him to become the first campus organizer of a new youth organization—the Intercollegiate Society of Individualists (the name was changed to the Intercollegiate Studies Institute in 1966).

Although not a trained political philosopher, Milione more than held his own in correspondence and conversation with the prominent intellectuals associated with ISI. He became known for providing apt quotations from thinkers and writers such as Richard Weaver, Jose Ortega y Gasset, Jacob Burckhardt, Jacques Barzun, and John Henry Newman.

On ISI's tenth anniversary, newly in-stalled President Milione stated that liberty could only be maintained if the people "accept individually the responsibilities" that liberty imposes. ISI's primary emphasis was on youth, he explained, because as Alexis de Tocqueville wrote, "Every fresh generation is a new people." Whenever he was asked for the answer to the problems of the academy—whether the radicalism of the sixties or the political correctness and postmodern nihilism of the nineties—Milione always had the same answer: "stand firm upon the truths, standards, and institutions of our culture that are time-tested and of proven worth."

—LEE EDWARDS

Further Reading

Edwards, Lee. *Educating for Liberty: The First Half-Century of the Intercollegiate Studies Institute.* Washington, D.C.: Regnery, 2003.

See also: Intercollegiate Studies Institute; Philadelphia Society

Mises, Ludwig von (1881–1973)

One of the most notable economists and social philosophers of the twentieth century, Ludwig von Mises developed an integrated, deductive science of economics based on the fundamental axiom that individual human beings act purposively to achieve desired goals. Even though his economic analysis itself was "value-free"—in the sense of being irrelevant to values held by economists—Mises concluded that the only viable economic policy for the human race was a policy of unrestricted laissez-faire, of free markets and the unhampered exercise of the right of private property, with government strictly limited to the defense of person and property within its territorial area. Mises was able to demonstrate (a) that the expansion of free markets, the division of labor, and private capital investment is the only possible path to the prosperity and flourishing of the human race; (b) that socialism would be disastrous for a modern economy because the absence of private ownership of land and capital goods prevents any sort of rational pricing, or estimate of costs, and (c) that government intervention, in addition to hampering and crippling the market, would prove counterproductive and cumulative, leading inevitably to socialism unless the entire tissue of interventions was repealed.

Holding these views, Mises became famous for his "intransigence" in insisting on a noninflationary gold standard and on laissez-faire and was effectively barred from any paid university post in Austria and later in the United States. As the chief economic adviser to the Austrian government in the 1920s, Mises was single-handedly able to slow down Austrian inflation; and he developed his own "private seminar" that attracted the outstanding young economists, social scientists, and philosophers throughout Europe. As the founder of the "neo-Austrian School" of economics, Mises' business cycle theory, which blamed inflation and depressions on inflationary bank credit encouraged by central banks, was adopted by most younger economists in England in the early 1930s as the best explanation of the Great Depression. Having fled the Nazis to the United States, Mises did some of his most important work there. In over two decades of teaching, he inspired the emergence of an Austrian school of economics in the United States.

Mises was born in 1881 in the city of Lemberg (now Lvov) in Galacia, where his father, a Viennese construction engineer for the Austrian railroads, was then stationed. Both Mises' father and mother came from prominent Viennese families; his mother's uncle, Dr. Joachim Laudau, served as deputy from the Liberal Party in the Austrian Parliament.

Entering the University of Vienna at the turn of the century as a leftist intervention-ist, the young Mises discovered *Principles of Economics* (1871) by Carl Menger, the founding work of the Austrian school of economics, and was quickly converted to the Austrian emphasis on individual action rather than unrealistic mechanistic equations as the unit of economic analysis, as well as to the importance of a free-market economy. During this period, in his first great work, *The Theory of Money and Credit* (1912) Mises performed what had been deemed an impossible task: to integrate the theory of money into the general theory of marginal utility and price (what would later be called integrating "macroeconomics" into "microeconomics"). Since Bohm-Bawerk and his other Austrian colleagues did not accept Mises' integration and remained without a monetary theory, he was obliged to strike out on his own and found a "neo-Austrian" school.

In his monetary theory, Mises revived the long-forgotten British Currency School principle, prominent until the 1850s, that society does not at all benefit from any increase in the money supply, that increased money and bank credit only cause inflation and business cycles, and that therefore government policy should maintain the equivalent of a 100 percent gold standard. Mises added to this insight the elements of his business cycle theory: that credit expansion by the banks, in addition to causing inflation, makes depressions inevitable by causing "malinvestment," i.e., by inducing businessmen to over-invest in "higher orders" of capital goods (machine tools, construction, etc.) and to under-invest in consumer goods. The problem is that inflationary bank credit, when loaned to business, masquerades as pseudo-savings, and makes businessmen believe that there are more savings available to invest in capital goods production than consumers are genuinely willing to save. Hence, an inflationary boom *requires* a recession, which becomes a painful but necessary process by which the market liquidates unsound investments and reestablishes the investment and production structure that best satisfies consumer preferences and demands.

Mises and his follower Friedrich A. Hayek developed this cycle theory during the 1920s, on the basis of which Mises was able to warn an unheeding world that the widely trumpeted "New Era" of permanent prosperity of the 1920s was a sham and that its inevitable result would be bank panic and depression. When Hayek was invited to teach at the London School of Economics in 1931 by an influential former student at Mises' private seminar, Lionel Robbins, Hayek was able to convert most of the younger English economists to this perspective. On a collision course with John Maynard Keynes and his disciples at Cambridge, Hayek demolished Keynes's *Treatise on Money* (1930) but lost the battle and most of his followers to the tidal wave of the Keynesian Revolution that swept the economic world after the publication of Keynes's *General Theory* in 1936. From 1936 on Mises was totally in opposition to the worldwide fashion in macroeconomic policy.

Ludwig von Mises

Socialism-communism had triumphed in Russia and in much of Europe during and after World War I, and Mises was moved to publish "Economic Calculation in the Socialist Commonwealth" (1920), in which he demonstrated the impossibility of a socialist planning board's planning a modern economic system; furthermore, no attempt at artificial "markets" would work, since a genuine pricing and costing system requires an exchange of property titles, and therefore private property in the means of production. Mises developed the article into his book *Socialism* (1922). This book converted many prominent economists and social philosophers out of socialism, including Hayek, the German Wilhelm Röpke, and the Englishman Lionel Robbins. In the United States, the publication of the English translation of *Socialism* in 1936 attracted the admiration of the prominent economic journalist Henry Hazlitt, who reviewed it in the *New York Times* and converted one of America's most prominent and learned communists of the period, J. B. Matthews, to a Misesian position and to opposition to all forms of socialism.

If socialism was an economic catastrophe, government interventionism could not work and would tend to lead inevitably to socialism. Mises elaborated these insights in his *Critique of Interventionism* (1929) and set forth his political philosophy of laissez-faire liberalism in his *Liberalism* (1927).

In addition to setting himself against the political trends of the twentieth century, Mises combated with equal fervor and eloquence what he considered the disastrous dominant philosophical and methodological trends in economics and other disciplines: positivism, relativism, historicism, "polylogism" (the idea that each race and gender has its own "logic" and therefore cannot communicate with other groups), and all forms of irrationalism and denial of objective truth. Mises also developed what he considered to be the proper methodology of economic theory—logical deduction from evident axioms, which he labeled "praxeology"—and he leveled trenchant critiques of the growing tendency in economics and other disciplines to replace praxeology and historical understanding by unrealistic mathematical models and statistical manipulations.

Mises' most monumental achievement was *Human Action* (1949), the first comprehensive treatise on economic theory written since the end of World War I. Here Mises took up the challenge of his own methodology and research program and elaborated an integrated and massive structure of economic theory on his own deductive, "praxeological" principle. Published in an era when economists and governments generally were totally dedicated to statism and Keynesian inflation, *Human Action* was unread by the economics profession. Finally, in 1957 Mises published his last major work, *Theory and History*, which, in addition to refutations of Marxism and historicism, set forth the basic differences and functions of theory and of history in economics as well as all the various disciplines of human action.

In the United States as in his native Austria, Mises could not find a paid post in academia. New York University, where he taught from 1945 until his retirement at the age of 87 in 1969, would only designate him as a visiting professor; his salary had to be paid by the conservative-libertarian William Volker Fund until 1962, and after that by a consortium of free-market foundations and businessmen.

Mises was also sustained by and worked together with free-market and libertarian admirers. From its origin in 1946 until his death, Mises was a part-time staff member of the Foundation for Economic Education at Irvington-on-Hudson, New York; and he was in the 1950s an economic adviser to the National Association of Manufacturers (NAM), working with their laissez-faire wing, which finally lost out to the tide of "enlightened" statism.

Mises was a libertarian who championed reason and individual liberty in personal as well as economic matters. As a rationalist and an opponent of statism in all its forms, Mises would never call himself a "conservative," but rather a liberal in the nineteenth-century sense. Indeed, Mises was politically a laissez-faire radical who denounced tariffs, immigration restrictions, and governmental attempts to enforce morality. On the other hand, Mises was a staunch cultural and sociological conservative who attacked egalitarianism and strongly denounced feminism as a facet of socialism. In contrast to many conservative critics of capitalism, Mises held that personal morality and the nuclear family were both essential to, and fostered by, a system of free-market capitalism.

—MURRAY N. ROTHBARD

Further Reading

Kirzner, Israel. *Ludwig von Mises: The Man and His Economics.* Wilmington, Del.: ISI Books, 2001.

Mises, Margit von. *My Years with Ludwig von Mises.* Cedar Falls, Iowa: Center for Futures Education, 1984.

Moss, Lawrence, ed. *The Economics of Ludwig von Mises: Toward a Critical Reappraisal.* Kansas City: Sheed & Ward, 1976.

Rothbard, Murray N. *Ludwig von Mises: Scholar, Creator, Hero.* Auburn, Ala.: Ludwig von Mises Institute, 1988.

Sennholz, Mary, ed. *On Freedom and Free Enterprise: Essays in Honor of Ludwig von Mises.* Princeton, N.J.: Van Nostrand, 1956.

See also: Austrian school of economics; capitalism; émigré intellectuals; envy; Foundation for Economic Education; Freeman; *Haberler, Gottfried; Hayek, Friedrich A. von; Hazlitt, Henry; liberalism, classical; libertarianism; Mises, Ludwig von, Institute; Rothbard, Murray; socialism*

Mises, Ludwig von, Institute

The Ludwig von Mises Institute in Auburn, Alabama, founded in 1982, has developed into the world's leading research and educational center of the Austrian school of economics and libertarian political theory. Its publications include the *Quarterly Journal of*

Austrian Economics, the *Journal of Libertarian Studies*, *Austrian Economics Newsletter*, the *Free Market*, the *Mises Review*, and many books, articles, and monographs on history and economics.

In 1981, Ludwig von Mises' widow, Margit, gave her approval to found the Mises Institute, which was formally established on August 24, 1982, with founder Llewellyn H. Rockwell Jr. serving as president until the present day. With the support of Margit von Mises, who served as board chairman until her death in 1993, and leading thinkers such as F. A. Hayek, Lawrence Fertig, Henry Hazlitt, and Murray N. Rothbard, who headed its academic programs until his death in 1995, the Mises Institute has more than 250 associated faculty members working with it on one or more academic projects.

The institute's primary research, publication, and educational goal is to promote and advance the ideas of economist Ludwig von Mises (1881–1973) and his many followers and like-minded colleagues and allies in the academic world. These ideas are widely disseminated through the Institute's Web site and its publication programs.

Mises' Austrian school of economics offers a vision of the discipline that is tied closely to the idea of purposeful human action. Instead of regarding economics as a highly mathematized version of the physical sciences (as most economists do), Austrian-school economists see economics as a deductive enterprise focusing on real-world actors. Consequently, they place a stronger emphasis on free-market entrepreneurship than do mainstream economists (who often pay no attention at all to entrepreneurship), have a higher regard for the organizing and coordinating potential of free-market exchange, and regard government intervention as economically and socially destructive.

The institute emphasizes these themes in its many educational programs for students, such as Mises University, the History of Liberty conference, and the Rothbard Graduate Seminar. The purpose of these programs is to counter the pervasive bias that students encounter in economics, history, sociology, and other disciplines in which politicians and government bureaucrats are usually championed at the expense of entrepreneurs.

The institute also sponsors a professional academic gathering—the Austrian Scholars Conference—at its campus in Auburn. Each year more than 200 economists, historians, philosophers, and legal theorists gather to present the results of their latest research projects and to offer comments on each other's work. The institute also offers residency programs for Ph.D. students, postdoctoral students, and professors on sabbatical, as well as an internship program for undergraduates. Since 1982 the Mises Institute has assisted more than 7,000 students at more than 900 colleges and universities with aid ranging from one-year book scholarships to full multiyear Ph.D. fellowships.

The institute's teaching conferences and seminars on subjects ranging from monetary policy to the costs of war have generated hundreds of scholarly papers and thousands of published popular articles on economic and historical issues. Two important books to have appeared in recent years are *The Costs of War* (1997) and *Reassessing the Presidency* (2001). The Mises Institute also publishes books by Ludwig von Mises and other works by Austrian economists, maintains the complete Mises bibliography, and manages the archive and literary rights of Murray N. Rothbard. The institute has produced three documentary films, published or subsidized the publication of 125 books and monographs, from *Man, Economy and State* (1962) by Murray Rothbard to *Theory and History* (1957) and *Human Action* (1949) by Ludwig von Mises, and distributes the most comprehensive scholarly book catalog in Austrian economics.

The success of the Mises Institute has inspired the creation of Mises Institutes in Brussels, Bucharest, and Mexico City, which have no financial connection to the organization in Auburn but are sister organizations in spirit. Major centers of Misesian economics and social philosophy also thrive in Paris, Moscow, Prague, Madrid, Rome, Milan, Beijing, and Tokyo.

—THOMAS J. DiLORENZO

See also: Austrian school of economics; Mises, Ludwig von; Rothbard, Murray

Missile Defense, National

In its currently accepted configuration, National Missile Defense (NMD) is designed to protect U.S. territory from attacks by small numbers of intercontinental ballistic missiles (ICBM) by destroying their warheads (which are likely to be nuclear) at the terminal phase of their flight, i.e., when they are about to enter the upper level of the atmosphere. The system, currently in various stages of development and construction, includes land-based interceptors (exoatmospheric kill vehicles carried by small rockets), radar and command facilities, as well as space-based tracking and detection devices.

Despite the limitations inherent in the current design, NMD serves to assert continuing U.S. technological superiority over potential rivals and to maintain a foreign policy designed to protect U.S. national interests anywhere in the world, if necessary by military force unhindered by potential threats from the rogue states possessing ICBM and nuclear capabilities.

First attempts to deploy defensive systems capable of destroying incoming ICBMs were made in the early 1960s. At that time, the main threat was presented by the Soviet Union's rapidly expanding ICBM arsenal. By the end of the decade, when the inability of available antiballistic missile (ABM) technology to cope with the increased scale of the Soviet threat became apparent, deterrence policy became based on the doctrine of mutually assured destruction (MAD), whereby the equal vulnerability of the U.S. and the Soviet Union to massive ICBM attacks was regarded as the guarantee of mutual safety. Indeed, the ABM treaty of 1972 enshrined MAD as the only U.S. deterrence policy. In the 1980s the preeminence of MAD was challenged by Ronald Reagan's Strategic Defense Initiative (SDI), which envisioned an ABM defense with space-based components. The SDI was shelved when the collapse of the Soviet Union eliminated the threat of a massive ICBM attack against the U.S.

In the 1990s the threat of ICBM attack, although on a limited scale, resurfaced, as many nations, disregarding nonproliferation treaties, made steps towards the acquisition of nuclear and ICBM technology. Among those states, North Korea is believed to have made significant strides in research of weapons of mass destruction and ICBM technology. Iran is also on the list. As ruling elites in those countries are unlikely to be deterred by the prospect of overwhelming U.S. retaliation, their nuclear and ICBM capabilities are potentially damaging to America's ability to protect its interests in strategically important regions. Other potential threats include unauthorized or accidental ICBM launches from Russian or Chinese sites or a takeover of one of these sites by a terrorist group and subsequent blackmail. The decision to counter these threats by deploying a limited-scale missile defense was taken in 1996 by the Clinton administration under strong pressure from the Republican-controlled Congress. In 2001 President George W. Bush formally withdrew from the ABM treaty, thereby clearing the way for the future development and deployment of a missile defense system.

Some critics of the NMD in its current, land-based shape insist that the existing capacity of tracking and targeting equipment makes it prone to frequent mistakes in distinguishing between true targets (nuclear warheads) and balloon decoys deployed by the same missile. Another line of criticism is that a potential aggressor may load the atmosphere entry vehicle with multiple bomblets containing chemical or biological weapons which would be released at the entry stage and present more individual targets than the missile defenses could cope with. However, even if these criticisms were based on correct assumptions about the present capabilities of the NMD, they would not invalidate the idea itself. Provided that the currently proposed and tested NMD system is designed as a means of protection against unauthorized launches (by definition, single-missile events) and threats from rogue states with very few ICBMs in arsenal, and even if its capabilities of distinguishing between real warheads and decoys are not perfect, they are still sufficient to counter small numbers of potential targets. Besides, decoys occupy the payload that otherwise could be allocated to real nuclear warheads, so even a relatively unsophisticated NMD indirectly reduces overall attack capabilities, which in the rogue nations are already limited.

In response to the assessment that the planned NMD was not enough to eliminate all potential future threats, the Bush administration established the Missile Defense Agency in 2002. The objective of this new agency is to establish a defense system under a single program that is capable of intercepting missiles in all phases of their flight. One of the goals of this system is the development of space-based defenses.

Space-based defenses, by deploying anti-missile kill vehicles in space, would solve the problem of targeting at the entry stage, when the target (the warhead) is small, cold (and therefore hard to detect), moving fast, and potentially accompanied by decoys. Instead, space-based defenses would target the missile at its boost phase, when it is large (still having all its stages in addition to the warhead), hot, moving relatively slowly, and without the option of deploying decoys. Proposed alternatives to space-based defenses—namely, planes and/or naval vessels carrying anti-missile vehicles and kept in the vicinity of potential launching sites—are not quite practical due to obvious deployment limitations. While the development of space-based defenses still awaits funding, in the near future NMD is likely to include a combination of land-based defenses and space-based sensors.

—Andrew Savchenko

Further Reading

Cordesman, Anthony H. *Strategic Threats and National Missile Defenses: Defending the U.S. Homeland.* Westport, Conn.: Praeger, 2002.

Lindsay, James M., and Michael E. O'Hanlon. *Defending America: The Case for Limited National Missile Defense.* Washington, D.C.: Brookings Institution Press, 2001.

See also: Claremont Institute; Teller, Edward

Modern Age

Arguably the premier scholarly journal on the right since its founding in 1957 by conservative man of letters Russell Kirk, publisher Henry Regnery, and political scientist David S. Collier, *Modern Age* is intended, as Kirk wrote in its first editorial, "to stimulate discussion of the great moral and social and political and economic and literary questions of the hour, and to search for means by which the legacy of our civilization may be kept safe." Published quarterly, the journal prints extensive, intellectually demanding essays by prominent thinkers. Kirk edited the journal for two years, then passed control to Eugene Davidson. While the magazine has always been both nonpartisan and nonsectarian, its editorial line has consistently remained conservative, and its pages have been especially open to people of faith. The journal has reflected on a broad range of issues, ranging from revolution, tradition, and totalitarian rule to the relationship between Western tradition and American liberty, the significance of literary movements such as the Fugitives and modernism, and the correct interpretation of the American founding.

Over the years, contributors to the journal have included novelist John Dos Passos, conservative theoretician Frank Meyer, economist Ludwig von Mises, sociologist Robert Nisbet, political scientist Henry Jaffa, literary critic M. E. Bradford, novelist Andrew Lytle, political philosopher Francis Graham Wilson, Vatican II *peritus* John Courtney Murray, S.J., economist and social thinker Wilhelm Röpke, theologian Will Herberg, journalist William Henry Chamberlin, political philosophers Eric Voegelin and Eliseo Vivas, and the literary critic Marion Montgomery.

The journal was published independently—on a frayed shoestring, insiders recall—for many years. *Modern Age*'s second editor (1960–69), Eugene Davidson, was a historian with a specialty in modern Germany. Under Davidson, *Modern Age* explored issues of individual liberty and resistance to Soviet expansion, working to diffuse the unearned prestige that Marxist theory had attained in academic circles. *Modern Age* offered serious, sustained theoretical explorations of the flaws inherent in socialisms of every variety and in doing so helped sustain a growing movement of resistance within the academy to the dominance of leftist thought. Memorable essays in this vein include the great libertarian Murray Rothbard's "Freedom, Inequality, Primitivism, and the Division of Labor," Herberg's "Christian Faith and Totalitarian Rule," and critic J. M. Lalley's "The Anatomy of Perdition."

The journal's third editor, David Collier, took over in 1969, as American intellectual life was torn over U.S. involvement in the Vietnam War. A political scientist, Collier published essays exploring the roots of the suddenly popular protest movements, such as "Marxism, Anarchism, and the New Left" by German historian Karl A. Wittfogel, and "Marxist Revisionism: A Commentary," by Molnar.

By the mid-1970s, the journal was facing financial trouble; with circulation hovering around 6,500, its future was in doubt. At the initiative of John Lulves, then executive vice president of the Intercollegiate Studies Institute (the publisher of this book), ISI approached Collier about a merger with *Modern Age*—to which it could offer fundraising and organizational expertise and a large base of student and faculty supporters. The merger took place in 1976, and the magazine's circulation soon rose to exceed 10,000. According to Lee Edwards, *Modern Age*'s "issues from 1976 to 1983 were marked by a concentration on 'conservative theory' at a time when the conservative movement was on the cusp of coming to political power. . . . There were, for example, a long string of articles about the relationship between libertarians, traditionalists, and the then-novel neoconservatives, by such authors as Robert Nisbet, Murray Rothbard, George Carey, Russell Kirk, and Paul Gottfried." The journal also devoted significant space to the important debate begun by M. E. Bradford and Harry Jaffa over the meaning of the "equality" favored by the American founders—a debate that marked the beginning of the acrimonious, enduring split between traditionalist and neoconservatives.

When Collier died in 1984, there was some internal debate over which direction *Modern Age* ought to take—deeper into political theory, or more broadly into general culture. In the end, the magazine's literary editor, George Panichas, was asked to lead the journal in the latter direction. In the decades since, *Modern Age* has become, in the words of one contributor, "the journal of moralist literary criticism." One of the most important issues of the journal under Panichas's tenure came in 1988, the winter issue of which featured a symposium of twelve leading thinkers on the right discussing the import of Allan Bloom's *Closing of the American Mind*. While campus leftists had denounced Bloom as a reactionary, in *Modern Age* authors Stephen Tonsor, Marion Montgomery, Peter Augustine Lawler, and others argued that in fact Bloom was a rationalist partisan of the radical Enlightenment. This episode illustrates well how, ever since its founding, *Modern Age* has sought to keep in creative tension both the Greek and the Judeo-Christian elements of the Western tradition.

—John Zmirak

Further Reading

Edwards, Lee. *Educating for Liberty: The First Half-Century of the Intercollegiate Studies Institute.* Washington, D.C.: Regnery, 2003.

Nash, George H. *The Conservative Intellectual Movement in America since 1945.* 2nd ed. Wilmington, Del.: Intercollegiate Studies Institute, 1996.

Panichas, George, ed. *Modern Age: The First 25 Years.* Indianapolis, Ind.: Liberty Press, 1988.

See also: Collier, David S.; Davidson, Eugene A.; Kirk, Russell; media, conservative; Regnery, Henry

modernity and postmodernity

The modern must be contrasted with the ancient or the traditional, and so conservatives are characteristically skeptical if not contemptuous of every modern claim. Thinkers usually regarded as conservative, from Leo Strauss to Jacques Maritain, trace the beginning of modern thought to Niccolo Machiavelli. The Machiavellian innovation was to devote human beings to the conquest of nature, to turn human efforts toward the acquisition in freedom in this world of what God had promised in the next. Machiavelli redefined human virtue as whatever works in transforming the world in the name of human security. He reduced religion to a useful tool in achieving political goals. Machiavelli even deprived philosophy of its high and independent status of contemplating the truth about nature and God by holding that the truth is that we only *know* what we *make*. Every human claim for wisdom must be tested practically; we can only know the world by changing it.

Thus, moral and political life in modern times no longer aims to cultivate human souls but to protect human bodies. The attempt to use political means to elevate the soul turned out to be ineffective and needlessly cruel. We cannot make human beings good through an appeal to moral and religious motives, but we can make them act as if they were good by using fear to predictably control their bodies. So the modern premise is that human beings are free individuals with no duties given to them by God or nature; their only duty is to obey those contracts, ultimately based in fear, which they have made with other individuals.

Characteristically, modern government uses strong political institutions—such as the separation of powers and checks and balances—to limit and direct human action. The main goal is to protect human beings from the tyranny of unlimited government without expecting too much of either rulers or ruled. Modern government, in fact, is to be limited but strong; free human beings consent to be ruled in order for their bodies to be more secure and comfortable. But they would not consent to be needlessly afraid of government or to have their souls cruelly tortured. So the American Constitution, for example, creates a strong presidency that is limited both by Congress and by the necessity of securing reelection.

This moderate and modern form of government must be praised for its effectiveness, for its protection of human security and liberty, and for providing a context for unprecedented human prosperity. But conservatives would add that no decent modern government has been wholly modern. *Decent* modern governments have relied heavily on their premodern inheritances, including respect for tradition, religion, and various kinds of uncalculating virtue. Strong institutions are not enough for a free society to work; good government always depends also on the existence of free and responsible citizens, and these do not just happen. Modern society, conservatives add, erodes its premodern capital. It sows the seeds of its own destruction.

Conservatives have plenty of evidence that modern thought and action are not in the long run compatible with moderation. Modern, limited government gave way to revolutionary efforts to use unprecedented forms of cruelty to perfect human existence on this earth. Marxist thought might be viewed as a more consistent form of Machiavellianism. All means necessary might be used to bring heaven to earth, and terrible cruelty in the short term might be used to obliterate cruelty altogether over the long term. Without something like revolutionary success, the modern fear became, the modern world might be judged a failure. The moderns' success in reducing the recognized presence of God in the world and in allowing people to acquire more wealth and

power, argue conservatives, has made them more anxious and restless and on balance less happy.

That the deepest modern impulse is necessarily revolutionary might first have been noticed by Jean-Jacques Rousseau: The bourgeois individual that moderate modernity brought into being is miserable and contemptible; he has no idea what virtue and happiness are. But Rousseau still embraced the modern premise that there is no going back to the simple and noble world of the citizen and the saint. He concluded that modern efforts must be radicalized to eradicate human individuality altogether. *The modern paradox is that a world that began with the celebration of the free and unencumbered individual seemed to culminate in the worst form of anti-individualistic or misanthropic tyranny. Modern thought created the bourgeois individual, and then it became radically antibourgeois.*

The best student of Machiavelli of our time, Harvey Mansfield, has remarked that if Machiavelli were alive today he would admit he was wrong. The Florentine's view was that Christianity was the cruelest form of domination over the human soul imaginable, but today he would know that it was nothing compared to the ideological tyranny of the twentieth century. That fact surely would have caused him to reevaluate premodern Christian virtue, says Mansfield, which offered the most steadfast foundation for dissident resistance to communism. What Machiavelli regarded as unnecessary classical and Christian constraints on human freedom are in fact largely based on the realistic premodern distinctions that separated beast, man, and God.

The modern project has been to turn human beings into gods, but the foundation of that effort has been the proposition that the human being is merely a body, just another animal. It is characteristically modern to be so devoted to freedom that the limitations and directions nature and God have given human beings seem like tyranny. It is equally modern to believe that anyone who thinks that human beings have souls—are more than bodies—has fallen victim to tyrannical delusion. As Blaise Pascal predicted near the beginning of modernity, the result of that confusion has been more to brutalize than to divinize human beings.

Another view of the modern paradox is the Hegelian/Marxian claim that the aim of the modern world is to bring history to an end. Modern thought understands the human being as free from natural determination to create himself or make history. So the end of history would have to be the end of human liberty. The end of our free or godlike striving is to make ourselves merely animals again. Rebellion against this conclusion is the beginning of *postmodern* thought. Most postmodern thought follows Friedrich Nietzsche in an effort to liberate human will or greatness from the reductionistic tendency of modern scientific reason. Postmodernity so understood is the celebration of free human creation for no particular purpose. History cannot end because history can have no real point; anything rational or predictable is inhuman.

But this alleged postmodernism is, in truth, an intensification of the modern tendency to liberate human will from natural and divine constraints. The modern project is in effect criticized by the postmoderns for not being modern enough, for having a residual faith in the goodness of human efforts and in the possibility of human progress. The postmodern view is that the modern project is even crueler than Christianity because it ruthlessly and futilely aims to impose scientific order or direction on chaotic human reality. Thus, most postmodern thinkers, on rather Machiavellian premises, reject modern science and replace it with the human imagination. Only the imagination can give human beings the

experiences of security and comfort they crave. We can use the imagination to control our experiences, even if we cannot really eradicate human contingency and mortality.

Postmodernism as it has evolved would have repulsed Nietzsche, who connected great or authentically human willing with the reality of the human experience of the "abyss," of the nothingness that surrounds our brief and accidental existence. The greatest of postmodern thinkers—Martin Heidegger—renounced resolute Nietzschean willing after his ineffective performance as a Nazi. But the murky later thought of Heidegger seems too much like fatalism to be very inspirational.

There is also a less noticed conservative postmodernism—postmodernism rightly understood. This authentic postmodernism is based on a criticism of modernity for its lack of realism, for its inability to tell the truth about the greatness and misery of being human. The basic human experiences are of limitation and of responsibility; to live well, human beings must accept the distinctively human duties that come with living in light of the truth. The bad news is that human beings are not free to impose their own will on nature; they cannot make and remake the world to suit their convenience. The good news is that they are fitted by nature to know the truth they did not make and to be open to God. They were born to know and love, not just to suffer and die. This sort of postmodern thought is associated with Aleksandr Solzhenitsyn and American literary Thomists such as Marion Montgomery, Walker Percy, and Flannery O'Connor.

Conservative postmodernism does not entail the wholesale rejection of all that the modern project accomplished. The achievements of modern science and technology, for better and worse, will remain with us, and the postmodern task is to subordinate them to properly human purposes. The genuine successes of the best modern forms of constitutional government deserve to be perpetuated, but the liberty they protect has to be understood as the liberty of human beings, not beasts or gods. Human liberty must be freed from any confusion with either liberationism or libertarianism. Postmodernism is in many ways a revolution in thought, but it is not intended to produce revolutions in practice. Perhaps *the* shortcoming of late modern political thought is the completely unsubstantiated belief that political revolutions could ever be relied upon to cure what ails human beings.

—PETER AUGUSTINE LAWLER

Further Reading

Guardini, Romano. *The End of the Modern World.* Wilmington, Del.: ISI Books, 1998.

Lawler, Peter Augustine. *Postmodernism Rightly Understood: The Return to Realism in American Thought.* Lanham, Md.: Rowman & Littlefield, 1999.

Lilla, Mark. *The Reckless Mind: Intellectuals in Politics.* New York: New York Review Books, 2001.

McMahon, Darrin M. *Enemies of the Enlightenment: The French Counter-Enlightenment and the Making of Modernity.* New York: Oxford University Press, 2001.

Mahoney, Daniel J. *Aleksandr Solzhenitsyn: The Ascent from Ideology.* Lanham, Md.: Rowman & Littlefield, 2001.

Strauss, Leo. *Natural Right and History.* Chicago: University of Chicago Press, 1953.

See also: agrarianism; Brownson, Orestes A.; Enlightenment; Gnosticism; individualism; New Science of Politics, The; O'Connor, Flannery; science and scientism; Strauss, Leo; technology; tradition; traditionalism

Molnar, Thomas (1921–)

A political philosopher by training, Thomas Molnar was born June 26, 1921, in Budapest and studied in France just before the Second World War, by the end of which he found himself interned in Dachau for anti-German activities. His first book, *Bernanos: His Political Thought and Prophecy* (1960), was a pioneering study of the work of the famous French Catholic novelist, who had moved from membership in the Action Française to writing on behalf of the French resistance. Taking his cue from Bernanos, Molnar would, like the novelist, go on to become a fiercely independent and contrarian writer, as well as a critic of modern political and economic systems that attempted to deny or transform man's nature and his place in the cosmos. As Molnar would write of Teilhard de Chardin in perhaps his most wide-ranging book, *Utopia: The Perennial Heresy* (1967): "[Teilhard's] public forgets . . . that man cannot step out of the human condition and that no 'universal mind' is now being manufactured simply because science has permitted the building of nuclear bombs, spaceships and electronic computers." Throughout his career, Molnar would remain the enemy of such transformative philosophical endeavors—whether they came in the form of Soviet communism or Western technological hubris. In this respect, his critique of classical and modern "Gnosticism" mirrored the work of the philosophical historian Eric Voegelin.

Revolted by the communist conquest (and 1956 suppression) of his homeland, Molnar early found himself interested in twentieth-century counterrevolutionary movements such as the Action Française and the Spanish Falangists. He examined such movements in his penetrating study *The Counter-Revolution* (1969), pointing to the quality they shared with their counterparts on the Left: a loathing of the rise of the commercial class and its mores. Regardless of the important constituencies such movements might find in the middle class—Engels was a factory owner's heir, Maurras got his funding from French manufacturers—Molnar concluded that the animating sentiment of each such movement was hostility to the "bourgeois spirit."

Molnar's study of these secular counterrevolutionary movements revealed their limitations and their participation in the modern spirit that aims to "manage" human nature by means of state or party in accord with an ideological plan. Molnar rediscovered his childhood Catholic faith in the early 1960s, and it would ever after serve as the lodestar guiding his political, cultural, and philosophical writings. Among his most important books are *Twin Powers: Politics and the Sacred* (1988) and *The Church: Pilgrim of Centuries* (1990), which examine the struggle between church and state in medieval and early-modern history—and this battle's continuing implications for politics and ecclesiastical governance. Molnar identifies two destructive tendencies rooted in the medieval and early-modern periods whose implications only became obvious in the twentieth century: first, Erastianism, the subjection of spiritual authority to the power of the state or the preferences of civil society; and second, Puritanism, a claim by the state to spiritual power and redemptive purpose.

Molnar was one of the earliest writers and academics to associate himself with the Intercollegiate Society of Individualists (later Intercollegiate Studies Institute), joining its lecture program and frequently publishing in the *Intercollegiate Review* and *Modern Age*. His writing also appeared in dozens of other publications and in several European languages on topics ranging from classical history and French literature to foreign policy and modern philosophy. Molnar has traveled to every inhabited continent and has moved increasingly in recent years toward a global, world-historical (rather than particularly Western) view of events; he retains, however, a firmly Catholic faith that renders him skeptical of secular undertakings, including

the conservative movement. A personal friend of luminaries Russell Kirk and Wilhelm Röpke, Molnar has been more pessimistic than either of those thinkers about the prospects of saving the essentials of Western civilization from the advancing effects of the "ideology of technology," which promises with more apparent plausibility than did previous systems (such as Marx's) to make man into a different animal, if not in fact a god. Molnar is the author of more than thirty books.

—JOHN ZMIRAK

Further Reading

Molnar, Thomas. *The Decline of the Intellectual.* Cleveland: World, 1961.
———. *The Emerging Atlantic Culture.* New Brunswick, N.J.: Transaction, 1994.
———. *The Pagan Temptation.* Grand Rapids, Mich.: Eerdmans, 1988.

See also: Gnosticism; modernity and postmodernity; technology

monetarist economics

Monetarist economics is a label for both an economic theory and a type of economic policy. As economic policy cannot be divorced from political considerations, the school of monetarist economics has come to be associated with a particular political philosophy, namely one of governmental nonintervention.

The importance of monetary economics to conservatism lies in the common vision of political society underlying both views. That the market should be the primary allocative agent is generally agreed upon. However, the social and cultural norms supporting market society can break down rapidly during periods of sharp economic distress, as in Germany between the two world wars. Why does the capitalist system suffer from cycles of prosperity and depression? If these events were due to some exogenous force, such as earthquakes, the social fabric would not necessarily be disturbed. It is the belief that these oscillations need not be, yet appear regularly, that is the source of the problem. Radicals see such a boom-bust cycle as inherent in capitalism, hence their call for radical change. Conservatives, on the other hand, believe the market to be fundamentally stable—hence instability arises from the misguided attempts of governments to intervene.

Historically, the most common mode of government intervention has been tampering with money. Monetarist economics is the modern embodiment of the philosophical view that rules rather than discretion should guide governments' economic policy. Among such rules, perhaps the most important is that which makes the value of money (inflation) predictable and controlled. The primary analytical tool used by monetarist economics is the "quantity theory of money." For example, David Hume argued that, regardless of its goodness or badness, the quantity of money a country can retain is beyond the control of the authorities, being subject to the self-regulation of international markets. Hence, concern for the balance of trade (which changed the available quantity of money) was needless.

The practical use of the quantity theory is based on the assumption that the level of real goods and services being produced is unaffected by changes in the money supply. As such, faith in the underlying stability of the free market to attain the best possible level of employment (which may or may not be "full employment") is an implicit article in the arguments of all those who have subscribed to the quantity theory of money.

The modern debate on the quantity theory centers largely on the work of Milton Friedman and his followers, and it is the set of doctrines associated with them that has come to be called "monetarist economics." Friedman begins by emphasizing that the quantity theory of money is basically a theory of the demand for money. Friedman's theory derives much of its bite from the succeeding claim that the demand for money is a stable relationship and that it is one of the few stable relationships available in economics. Furthermore, since the demand function is stable, the value of money or price-level must as a consequence be set primarily by the supply of money.

To appreciate the importance of Friedman's claims, one has to realize that John Maynard Keynes had raised doubts about the stability of free markets in 1936 and that one part of his attack was a denial of the stability of the demand for money. By arguing that the demand for money was stable and that the Keynesian replacement, the marginal propensity to consume, was not, Friedman reasserted the fundamental stability of the market system.

This idea has certain policy implications, which Friedman developed in his critique of Keynesian ideas. Thus, support for government intervention in order to push the economy toward full employment typically takes place in Keynesian policy by increasing direct government spending—on public works, for example. Such fiscal policy involves direct government action either in the shape of taxation or expenditure. As such, it is less desirable than monetary policy which typically involves indirect actions such as selling government bonds. While interventionists wish to use fiscal policy to stabilize the economy, monetarists emphasize the dangers of such direct attempts to "smooth out" the economy. The monetarist critique of this policy is built on the notion that the delays between knowing of the need for intervention and the actual act of intervention are so unavoidably long and unpredictable that such policies could well exacerbate the business cycle rather than dampen it. For example, there is a lag between the time a region becomes economically depressed and when it is officially pronounced to be so, a further lag between the time the depressed conditions are recognized and congressional action is taken, and yet another lag between the vote of Congress and the actual implementation of a given proposal. Because of such reasoning, it is widely agreed that the fine-tuning of an economy is impossible. The monetarists have therefore strongly supported "rules rather than discretion" as guides for economic policy. And the particular rule most associated with monetarism is that of a stable rate of growth of the money supply. A publicly announced and faithfully implemented rule of this sort will anchor the market's inflationary expectations and permit smooth functioning.

While monetarist economics generated great interest in the 1960s and 1970s, in recent years much less attention has been given to specific monetarist ideas. In a sense, monetarist ideas were not so much new or unconventional as they were selective. Monetarists emphasized certain economic relationships as primary, and supported their assertions with much empirical research. But the experience of the 1980s did not support monetarist predictions. Increasingly, volatile financial markets and new financial instruments made it increasingly problematic to define what it was that should be tested or how a policy should be implemented.

Thus, the value of the quantity theory and hence of monetarism has come to be questioned sharply in recent years. The rule of monetarism stated that the money supply ought to be steadily increased at some preannounced rate. But this implies that money is at the control of the authorities. Now the same market that the monetarists wish to defend is the very market in which intelligent agents are free to substitute money-substitutes for approved forms of money. After all, money is what money does.

The financial markets have provided substitutes for money in such profusion in recent years that control of the money supply has become almost meaningless. Credit cards enable one to make direct purchases so long as one remains within one's credit limits. But then every consumer has the power to buy—to create money—to the limit of their credit ratings. Money has now become endogenous in many market transactions. Control over the market has to be exercised by responsible individuals, not by a well-behaved monetary authority. In this sense, then, the limitations of monetarist economics emphasize the utility of social conservatism.

Despite these considerable setbacks, it remains true that the permanent legacy of monetarist economics lies in its role in turning professional consensus away from a belief in government intervention to a faith in the stability of markets.

—Salim Rashid

Further Reading

Blinder, Alan S. *Central Banking in Theory and Practice.* Cambridge, Mass.: MIT Press, 1998.

Friedman, Milton. *Money and Economic Development.* New York: Praeger, 1973.

Kaldor, Nicholas. *The Scourge of Monetarism.* New York: Oxford University Press, 1982.

Mayer, Thomas, ed. *The Structure of Monetarism.* New York: Norton, 1978.

See also: *Austrian school of economics; Friedman, Milton; Haberler, Gottfried; supply-side economics*

Mont Pelerin Society

The Mont Pelerin Society was founded in 1947 through the cooperative efforts of economists Friedrich Hayek and Wilhelm Röpke and the Swiss writer and activist Albert Hunold. These men sought to promote personal and economic freedom in the Western liberal tradition. Since then, the society's periodic meetings, annual and semi-annual, regional and international, have brought together academics, businessmen, politicians, journalists, and other thinkers for the purpose of exploring classical liberal ideas and policies.

As R. M. Hartwell records in his authoritative *The History of the Mont Pelerin Society* (1995), the group had its origins in the 1938 efforts of French philosopher Louis Rougier to found the *"Centre International d'Etudes pour la Rénovation du Libéralisme."* This group came to nothing thanks to the onset of World War II, which would amount to a three-sided test of strength among fascism, communism, and Anglo-American war socialism. The one worldview left quite unrepresented in the postwar settlement was classical liberalism. Hayek and Röpke, who took a lively part in the public debates about the reconstruction of Europe—see Hayek's *The Road to Serfdom* (1944) and Röpke's *The Solution to the German Question* (1946)—tried to remedy this lack by founding a liberal journal. When they were unable to raise enough money, they used their funds instead to revive Rougier's idea of a colloquium, even including twelve of Rougier's original twenty-six participants, among many other luminaries. Attendees at the Mont Pelerin Society's organizational meeting (which took place April 1–10, 1947) included Bertrand de Jouvenel, Ludwig von Mises, Michael Polanyi, George Stigler, Henry Hazlitt, Frank Knight, Milton Friedman, Karl Popper, and Walter Eucken, as well as Hayek and Röpke. Originally, Hayek had wished to call the group the Acton–de Toqueville Society, in order to show its roots in the Western tradition, but various members objected to naming the group after two Catholic aristocrats. To avoid further contention, the group was titled after the Swiss city that hosted its first meeting.

Within a year, neoliberal policies would be enacted in the nascent West Germany, as its economics minister Ludwig Erhard (later a member of the society) heeded Röpke's recommendations and removed wage and price controls while establishing a sound currency, the Deutschmark. The enormous success of West Germany fueled the postwar recovery of Europe and gave new credibility to liberal ideas. Other political figures of note soon joined the society, including Luigi Einaudi, president of Italy; M. J. Rueff, former prime minister of Monaco; Sir Theodore Gregory, economics advisor to the Greek government; and Frederick Benham, who advised the government of Malaya. Important intellectuals to join the society would later include Raymond Aron, Walter Lippmann, and James Buchanan. By the 1980s, the society would include among its members three Nobel Prize–winning economists. The Mont Pelerin Society continues to thrive today as an ongoing seminar—an open-ended conversation across the decades and among thinkers attached to individual freedom.

—John Zmirak

See also: Hayek, Friedrich August von; Röpke, Wilhelm

Montgomery, Marion H. (1925–)

Teacher, poet, fiction writer, critic of literature and culture, Marion Montgomery is a native and resident of the state of Georgia. He received his B.A. and M.A. at the University of Georgia and did postgraduate work in creative writing at the University of Iowa. For thirty-three years (until his retirement in 1987), he taught literature and creative writing at the University of Georgia. While teaching he followed the muse, writing hundreds of poems (three collections of his verse have been published), three novels, and one novella. He has also written well over a dozen books of literary and cultural criticism. Politically, he calls himself an independent conservative. He is a second-generation Agrarian and, in theology and philosophy, a neo-Thomist. This combination of Southern Agrarianism and Thomism is a distinctive feature of his traditional conservatism: he is faithful to the traditional heritage of the South, and a sacramental piety toward creation and veneration for the Creator and Redeemer are major themes in much of his writing.

Although Montgomery has received honors, awards, and some regional recognition for his fiction and poetry (written for the most part in the 1950s and 1960s), it is his later work as a critic that has attracted a following among conservatives. Like the works of Eric Voegelin, whose philosophy of order and history has influenced him, Montgomery's criticism is broad-ranging, dense, and sometimes challenging. He writes alternately as citizen, poet, and philosopher. As citizen, he is concerned with the relationship of language to the individual living in community; he insistently places the writer's flights of individual imagination in the context of a corporate reality. He speaks, too, in the voices of vatic poet and philosopher—now using metaphor for illustration, now using definition for clarification. Refusing to accept arbitrary divisions between academic disciplines, or between the world of the mind and the world at large, he endeavors to address his concerns with an associated sensibility, with head and heart in concert. The dissociation of sensibility (of head and heart, of reason and faith) is one of the modern spiritual diseases Montgomery often diagnoses in his work. Thus his criticism is more than literary scholarship. It may be described as a blend of prophecy, preaching, poetry, and philosophy.

To date, Montgomery's greatest critical achievement is his trilogy *The Prophetic Poet and the Spirit of the Age* (1981–84), an examination of Western (especially post-Renaissance) culture, literature, and philosophy. Though the scope of this work is enormous, each volume has a focal point in the thought and fiction of one of three American writers: Flannery O'Connor (vol. 1), Edgar Allan Poe (vol. 2), and Nathaniel Hawthorne (vol. 3). This trilogy is a study of the roots of modernity, of modern gnosticism and alienation; it examines modernity in light of the intellectual heritage of the West and calls readers back to known but forgotten truths.

—MICHAEL JORDAN

Further Reading

Montgomery, Marion. *Liberal Arts and Community: The Feeding of the Larger Body*. Baton Rouge, La.: Louisiana State University Press, 1990.

———. *Making: The Proper Habit of Our Being: Essays Speculative, Reflective, Argumentative*. South Bend, Ind.: St. Augustine's Press, 2000.

Niemeyer, Gerhart. "Why Marion Montgomery Has to 'Ramble.'" *Center Journal* 4 (1985): 71–95.

See also: Hawthorne, Nathaniel; modernity and postmodernity; O'Connor, Flannery; Southern Agrarians

moral imagination

"Moral imagination" is a term of humane letters and politics implying that men and women are moral beings and that the power of the imagination enables them to perceive, beyond mere appearances, a hierarchy of worth and certain enduring truths.

The term appears first to have been employed by Edmund Burke, in his *Reflections on the Revolution in France* (1790). Burke speaks of "that generous loyalty to rank and sex," a "mixed system of opinion and sentiment" that "had its origin in the ancient chivalry." He continues,

> But now all is to be changed. All the pleasing illusions, which made power gentle, and obedience liberal, which harmonized the different shades of life,

and which, by a bland assimilation, incorporated into politics the sentiments which beautify and soften private society, are to be dissolved by this new conquering empire of light and reason. All the decent drapery of life is to be rudely torn off. All the superadded ideas, furnished from the wardrobe of a moral imagination, which the heart owns, and the understanding ratifies, as necessary to cover the defects of our naked shivering nature, and to raise it to dignity in our own estimation, are to be exploded as a ridiculous, absurd, and antiquated fashion.

In recent years, some popular writers have referred to man as "a naked ape." That is precisely what man would become, Burke implies, were it not for the gift of the moral imagination. The "barbarous philosophy" of the Jacobins of the French Revolution, Burke declares, "is the offspring of cold hearts and muddy understandings . . . as void of solid wisdom, as it is destitute of all taste and elegance. . . . In the groves of *their* academy, at the end of every vista, you see nothing but the gallows."

In Burke's rhetoric, the civilized being is distinguished from the savage by his possession of this moral imagination. Drawn from centuries of human experience and reflection, these concepts of the moral imagination are expressed afresh from age to age.

Irving Babbitt, in his *Democracy and Leadership* (1924), contrasts with Burke's "moral imagination" the "idyllic imagination" of Jean-Jacques Rousseau (whom Burke had called "the insane Socrates of the National Assembly"). Rousseau's sort of imagination, Babbitt contended, fancies that man is by nature innocent and great-souled, if uncorrupted by church, state, and private property: a fatal delusion.

T. S. Eliot, influenced by Babbitt and to a lesser degree by Burke, writes in his *After*

Strange Gods (1934) of the "diabolic imagination" of degradation, cruelty, and perversion—at the opposite pole from the moral imagination. In the Book of Genesis is found the earliest reproof of the corrupt imagination: "The imagination of man's heart is evil from his youth."

Such Christian writers as G. K. Chesterton have employed this term "moral imagination" from time to time. An elaboration of the theme by a Catholic writer, with some deductions therefrom that Burke, Babbitt, and Eliot might not have found agreeable, is Philip S. Keane's *Christian Ethics and Imagination* (1984).

—RUSSELL KIRK

Further Reading

Kirk, Russell. *Redeeming the Time*. Wilmington, Del.: Intercollegiate Studies Institute, 1996.

See also: Babbitt, Irving; Burke, Edmund; Eliot, T. S.; Kirk, Russell; Ryn, Claes G.

Moral Majority

The Moral Majority was the political arm of the Reverend Jerry Falwell's ministries throughout the better part of the 1980s, making a substantial contribution to electoral politics though at the price of exceeding notoriety. Falwell is rivaled only by Pat Robertson and Jesse Jackson as men of the cloth who have made a considerable impression on recent American political culture. The quintessential televangelist, Falwell founded the Moral Majority in 1978, taking its name somewhat from Richard Nixon's "Silent Majority" following of a decade before. Despairing of a culture he perceived to be sliding in the last generation or so, Falwell helped mobilize followers to participate in the political process in order to combat legalized abortion, the expulsion of prayer from schools, same-sex marriage, the Equal

Rights Amendment, and other evils.

Falwell initially built up the Moral Majority by using the mailing lists from his *Old Time Gospel Hour* television program based in central Virginia. By the mid-1980s, the organization had more than 300,000 dues-paying members, including tens of thousands of ministers useful for mobilizing voters from their pulpits. Thanks in large part to the Moral Majority's efforts, the 1980 presidential and congressional elections saw the rise of a potent new political force—evangelical and fundamentalist Christians, many located in the South—that had previously lain untapped. Many of them had not voted before 1980 and some had actively disavowed politics. But as a group newly mobilized around particular issues of concern, the Christian Right represented a formidable constituency.

Falwell and Robertson were two of the Christian Right's most prominent leaders. Their overt mixture of politics and religion drew much criticism from moderate Republicans and from Democrats who accused Christian conservatives of pursuing a theocracy. The Moral Majority was a particular target of feminists and homosexual rights groups (a favorite slogan was, "The Moral Majority Is Neither"), and Norman Lear founded People for the American Way largely to counter Falwell's organization. Even today Falwell remains a loathed bogeyman of the Left, despite the fact that his influence has waned considerably. Falwell has been conscious of that image. In 1984 he told the *Washington Post*, "Before we were painted as political cartoons—missiles growing out of church spires, painted as anti-Semitic, in some cases, racist. But we earned some of it. We were on the outside looking in a few years ago and by necessity had to knock the door down. We had to be more strident. Today we are sitting down at the table talking."

Despite its success, Falwell realized the group's growing notoriety was beginning to serve as a handicap. In 1987 he shut down the organization, announcing that he was getting out of full-time politics and going "back to preaching, back to winning souls." Pat Robertson's Christian Coalition would step in to fill much of the void left by Falwell's exit. But in the national elections held since the Moral Majority closed its doors, the Christian conservative voting bloc has arguably not been quite so effective.

—MAX SCHULZ

Further Reading

D'Souza, Dinesh. *Falwell: Before the Millennium.* Washington, D.C.: Regnery, 1984.

Lienesch, Michael. *Redeeming America: Piety and Politics in the New Christian Right.* Chapel Hill, N.C.: University of North Carolina, 1993.

Strober, Gerald, and Ruth Tomczack. *Jerry Falwell: Aflame for God.* Nashville, Tenn.: Thomas Nelson, 1979.

See also: Falwell, Jerry; family; fundamentalism; populism; Thomas, Cal

More, Paul Elmer (1864–1937)

Paul Elmer More edited the *Nation*, wrote the largest body of literary criticism composed by an American, and was cofounder of the New Humanism, an important and controversial conservative intellectual movement of the 1920s. His ideas influenced writers such as T. S. Eliot and Russell Kirk.

More was born December 12, 1864 in St. Louis, Missouri, the child of Enoch Anson More and Katherine Hays More (nee Elmer). He was graduated *cum laude* from Washington University of St. Louis in 1887 and earned his M.A. there in 1891. He studied classical and oriental languages at Harvard, where he met his best friend and the greatest influence on his intellectual development, Irving Babbitt. After receiving his M.A. from Harvard in 1895 he taught Sanskrit, Greek, and Latin at Bryn Mawr for two years. He then retired to little Shelburne, New Hampshire, for two years (1897–99) to meditate, read, and write for literary journals such as the *Atlantic Monthly* and the *New World*.

In 1900, he married Henrietta Beck of St. Louis and moved to East Orange, New Jersey. For the first decade of the twentieth century he worked as literary editor for the *Independent, New York Evening Post*, and *Nation*. In 1909 he was appointed editor of the *Nation*, which he maintained as America's premier literary journal. In 1914, More resigned and moved to Princeton, New Jersey, where he lectured on Greek and patristic philosophy at Princeton University. In 1926 he moved to the classics department, which was more in sympathy with his historical researches. He died in Princeton on March 9, 1937.

In 1904 he published his first volume of literary criticism, *Shelburne Essays*, the eleventh volume or "series" of which appeared in 1921. From 1921 to 1931 the four volumes of *The Greek Tradition* and a complementary volume on *The Catholic Faith* (1931) were published. *Platonism*, which More republished twice as introduction and complement to the series, had been published in 1917. Three volumes of *New Shelburne Essays* appeared from 1928 to 1936.

The volumes are a remarkable record of a highly cultured mind developing as it confronts great literature. More's style was dignified, even highfalutin. His views began as a conventional romantic agnosticism. But by *Shelburne Essays* volume 9, titled *Aristocracy and Justice* (1915), he had developed a hardheaded but ethical Burkean critique of American progressivism. His favorite targets included Theodore Roosevelt and the academic culture of the "German Ph.D." When More began working on the Platonic tradition, he was a deist who saw dualism as the heart of both Platonism and Christianity. By the late 1920s he had become a communing

Episcopalian, although his committed dualism kept him from accepting the doctrine of the Trinity. His intellectual journey is recounted in *The Sceptical Approach to Religion* (1934), volume 2 of *New Shelburne Essays,*.

During the 1920s More collaborated with his old friend, Irving Babbitt of Harvard, to popularize their views as the New Humanism. The movement was widely noticed, attracting negative responses from George Santayana, H. L. Mencken, and Sinclair Lewis and sympathetic criticism from T. S. Eliot. More combined high literary standards with an ethical and religious commitment that still influences the Burkean tradition in America today.

—E. Christian Kopff

Further Reading

Foerster, Norman, ed. *Humanism and America*. New York: Farrar & Rinehart, 1930.

Davies, Robert M. *The Humanism of Paul Elmer More*. New York: Bookman Associates, 1958.

Duggan, Francis X. *Paul Elmer More*. New York: Twayne Publishers, 1966.

Shafer, Robert. *Paul Elmer More and American Criticism*. New Haven, Conn.: Yale University Press, 1935.

Young, Malcolm. *Paul Elmer More: A Bibliography*. Princeton, N.J.: Princeton University Press, 1941.

See also: American Review; Babbitt, Irving; Bookman; Conservative Mind, The; New Humanism

Morley, Felix (1894–1982)

Felix Morley was a founding editor of the conservative weekly *Human Events* and an American political journalist respected for his acumen and fairness by his peers across the political spectrum. In numerous articles and books he advocated resistance to expanding government power, mistrust of uninformed democracy, the rollback of New Deal and Fair Deal legislation, and an American foreign policy characterized by nonintervention in the military struggles of other nations—a position strongly shaped by his staunch Quaker faith.

Morley was born and raised in Haverford, Pennsylvania, to parents active in the Society of Friends. One of his brothers, Christopher, became a well-known novelist. Felix Morley matriculated at the Quaker Haverford College, served as an ambulance driver for the British Army during World War I, and then went up to New College, Oxford University, on a Rhodes Scholarship, receiving his A.B. in 1921. From the mid-1910s until 1940 he wrote several politically focused books and worked as a writer and editor for several newspapers, including the *Baltimore Sun* and the *Washington Post*. In 1936 Morley won the Pulitzer Prize in editorial writing while working at the *Post*. But because the *Post*'s support for American military intervention in World War II ran counter to his Quaker pacifism, he resigned his editorial position in 1940 and assumed the post of president of Haverford College, which he held for five years. An opponent of the rapidly expanding welfare state and the entanglement of the United States in military alliances with other nations, Morley joined with fellow cultural critic Frank C. Hanighan and former America-Firster Henry Regnery to found *Human Events: A Weekly Analysis for the American Citizen* in 1944, contributing actively as a writer, editor, and president. But over time, a rift developed between Morley and Hanighan; the latter wanted *Human Events* to become an organ advocating foursquare active resistance to the Warsaw Pact threat, while Morley wanted it to focus on resistance to government expansion at home while advocating the exercise of a prudent rein on the American military. Recognizing that the editorial direction of *Human Events* was moving away from his own beliefs,

Morley resigned from the magazine in 1950, spending the rest of his life serving in various civic and academic positions and as a trustee of the Herbert Clark Hoover Memorial Foundation.

Former president Herbert Hoover provided a foreword to an edition of one of Morley's best-known books, *Power in the People* (1949), which examines the conflict between the American claims for liberty and self-government as against the rule of the unrestricted majority, in which prudence is cast aside for popular demands for bread and circuses and leaders who promise the same. Reviewer Edith Hamilton described *Power in the People* as "a remarkable book, nobly written and profoundly thought out." Morley's *Freedom and Federalism* (1959), one of his other major books, explores much the same theme. A few years before he died, Morley published his autobiography, a well-received work titled *For the Record* (1979), which is both a fascinating story of life as a newspaperman and editor during the mid-twentieth century and, in John Chamberlain's words, "an eloquent testimony to the need for Reaganism in economics and in the political allocation of power between Washington, the fifty state capitals, and the 200-million-odd citizens who have never relinquished any of the rights that come within the scope of the first ten amendments to the Constitution."

—JAMES E. PERSON JR.

Further Reading

Morley, Felix. *The Foreign Policy of the United States.* New York: Knopf, 1951.

Regnery, Henry. *Memoirs of a Dissident Publisher.* New York: Harcourt Brace Jovanovich, 1979.

See also: Human Events; isolationism

Morris, Gouverneur (1752–1816)

Gouverneur Morris displayed an unsentimental view of human nature, remarking that "[h]e who wishes to enjoy natural rights must establish himself where natural rights are admitted. He must live alone." And yet, his perception that government should "depend upon the established institutions and the political maturity of the people" was moderate and prudential. At base, his philosophy rested on the premise that the sanctity of property was the "main object of Society."

Morris graduated from King's College in 1768 and was admitted to the bar in 1771. He represented Westchester County in the Provincial Congress of New York (1775-77) and helped draft the New York Constitution. He served in the Continental Congress (1777-78), where he sponsored military reforms and supervised diplomatic missions. And he aided Robert Morris (no kin) as assistant superintendent of finance from 1781 to 1785. As a delegate from Pennsylvania to the Constitutional Convention, Morris urged the creation of a strong central government. During the Convention his bold style caused some discomfort, but his frankness also broke some deadlocks. His reputation as a literary craftsman won him immortality: he wrote the final draft of the Constitution.

Morris went to Europe on private business in 1789 and remained there until 1798; his diary is a major source for the study of the French Revolution. He served in the United States Senate as a High Federalist from 1800 to 1803, and his last national political involvement came with the publication of an antiwar, secessionist pamphlet, "Address to the People of the State of New York" (1812).

—FORREST MCDONALD

Further Reading

Brookhiser, Richard. *Gentleman Revolutionary: Gouverneur Morris, the Rake Who Wrote the Constitution*. New York: Free Press, 2003.

McDonald, Forrest. "The Political Thought of Gouverneur Morris." *Continuity: A Journal of History* 22 (1998): 39-54.

Mintz, Max M. *Gouverneur Morris and the American Revolution*. Norman, Okla.: University of Oklahoma Press, 1970.

Sparks, Jared. *The Life of Gouverneur Morris with Selections from his Correspondence and Miscellaneous Papers*. 3 vols. Boston: Gray & Bowen, 1832.

See also: Federalist Party

movement conservatism

In 1950, critic Lionel Trilling asserted that "liberalism is not only the dominant but even the sole intellectual tradition" in America. While Trilling conceded that a conservative "impulse" existed here and there, conservatism, he insisted, usually expressed itself only in "irritable mental gestures which seem to resemble ideas." Fifty-plus years later, conservatives and their ideas occupied the White House, controlled the U.S. House of Representatives and the Senate, constituted a majority of the nation's governors, and generally dominated the political landscape of America. What had happened to produce such a sea change in American politics?

The shift depended largely on two epic events that shaped the last half of the twentieth century—the waging of the Cold War and the growth of the modern welfare state. Conservatives declared that communism was evil and had to be defeated, not simply contained. And they argued that the welfare state had grown dangerously large and had to be reduced in size and influence, not just managed more efficiently.

Because conservatives played a decisive role in ending the Cold War peacefully and alerting America to the perils of a leviathan state, they reaped enormous political rewards, from Ronald Reagan's sweeping presidential victories in 1980 and 1984 to the Republicans' historic capture of Congress in 1994 and George W. Bush's upset win in 2000.

The conservative movement's rise was helped by the decline of American liberalism, which lost its way between the New Deal and the Great Society, between the Korean War and Kosovo, between Harry Truman and Bill Clinton. Liberals went into free fall, their descent marked by a shift from a concern for the common man and Middle America to a preoccupation with minorities and special interests.

The tectonic shift from liberalism to conservatism was not inevitable. Indeed the conservative movement frequently seemed to be on the edge of extinction—after the untimely death of Senator Robert A. Taft of Ohio in 1953, after the crushing presidential defeat of Senator Barry Goldwater of Arizona in 1964, the razor-thin loss of Ronald Reagan to Gerald Ford for the 1976 Republican presidential nomination, and the demonization of House Speaker Newt Gingrich and the Republican Congress in the mid-1990s. But the movement not only survived these crises but gained strength and momentum each time, in large measure because of its principled leaders.

First came the men of ideas, intellectuals and philosophers like Friedrich A. Hayek, the Austrian-born classical liberal; Russell Kirk, the midwestern traditionalist; and Irving Kristol, the New York Trotskyite-turned-neoconservative. Next came the men of interpretation, the journalists and popularizers like the polymath William F. Buckley Jr., founder of *National Review*; the columnist and television commentator George Will; and the radio talk-show host Rush Limbaugh. Last came the men of action, the politicians and policymakers, led by the Four Misters: "Mr. Republican," Robert A. Taft; "Mr. Conservative," Barry Goldwater; "Mr. President," Ronald Reagan; and "Mr. Speaker," Newt Gingrich.

Equally important was the political maturation of American conservatism as the movement learned how to combine into a winning electoral force traditionalists, libertarians, and neoconservatives; the South, Midwest, and West; and blue-collar Catholics and Protestant evangelicals.

Conservatism triumphed—as in 1980 and 1994—when the movement contained all the essential elements of political success: a clearly defined, consistent philosophy; a broad-based, cohesive national constituency; experienced, charismatic, principled leadership; a sound financial base; and proficiency in the mass media. It failed to advance—as in the 1998 congressional elections—when one or more of these elements was missing.

Whatever their specific label—Old Right, New Right, neoconservative, paleoconservative, compassionate conservative—conservatives have shared certain basic beliefs: in the great majority of cases the private sector can be depended upon to make better economic decisions than the public sector; government serves the governed best when it is limited; good men and women produce a good society rather than the opposite; and peace is most surely protected through military strength.

Conservative ideas that were labeled extreme fifty years ago are now accepted as mainstream. They determine much of the debate in Congress and the executive branch, in the statehouses, in national and regional think tanks, in newspaper op-ed and magazine articles, in television and radio programs. They are discussed respectfully in a growing number of colleges and universities. Still, the political future of movement conservatism depends on its success not only in maintaining a governing majority in Washington, D.C., but in maintaining this majority's foundation on shared conservative principles.

—LEE EDWARDS

Further Reading

Edwards, Lee. *The Conservative Revolution: The Movement that Remade America.* New York: Free Press, 1999.

See also: anticommunism; Cold War; conservatism; fusionism; neoconservatism; paleoconservatism; Republican Party

Murray, Charles (1943–)

A fellow at the American Enterprise Institute, Charles Murray is one of the most accomplished and visible of the new breed of conservative social scientists that emerged in the 1970s and 1980s. After receiving his doctorate in political science at the Massachusetts Institute of Technology, Murray never took a permanent academic position but instead took up residence at various think tanks.

Murray has written eight books, two of which aptly reflect the areas in which he has been most influential—and controversial: government social policy and the sociology of intelligence. Murray became famous with his first book, *Losing Ground: American Social Policy 1950–1980* (1984), which popularized the concept of a self-perpetuating urban "underclass" and inspired welfare reform efforts. It played an important role in galvanizing conservatives—especially neoconservatives—and even moderate liberals in their opposition to the existing welfare system, an opposition that eventually bore fruit in the welfare reform bill of 1996.

The Bell Curve: Intelligence and Class Structure in American Life, published in 1994 and coauthored with Richard Herrnstein, brought to the American public—in remarkably accurate and accessible form—truths about the social importance of intelligence which, although increasingly undeniable in academic psychology and sociology, remained largely unknown outside these disciplines. For their efforts Murray and Herrnstein suffered an enormous, highly publicized backlash and numerous personal attacks, but the core of the book's thesis—that intelligence is highly heritable and is generally a more important variable than socioeconomic status in predicting any number of socially important outcomes—remains a faithful portrayal of the academic consensus.

Murray identifies himself politically as a libertarian (see his *What it Means to Be a Libertarian: A Personal Interpretation*, 1997). Consequently, his nonempirical work has sometimes met with mixed reaction among conservatives, some of whom look skeptically on his prescriptions for societal ills, especially those that tend toward (noncoercive) eugenics.

—JEREMY BEER

Further Reading

Murray, Charles. *Human Accomplishment: The Pursuit of Excellence in the Arts and Sciences, 800 BC to 1950.* New York : HarperCollins, 2003.

See also: entitlements; social Darwinism; welfare policy

Murray, John Courtney, S. J. (1904–67)

John Courtney Murray was a Jesuit theologian, author, editor, and educator whose great lifework, a creative reinterpretation of Roman Catholic church-state theory, was deeply influenced by profound reflection on the nature of the American experiment. Murray's scholarship and proposals, highly controversial in Roman Catholic circles in the mid-1950s, were subsequently vindicated by the Second Vatican Council in its "Declaration on Religious Freedom."

Born in New York City, Murray joined the Society of Jesus in 1920 and was educated at Weston College, Boston College, Woodstock College, and the Pontifical

Gregorian University in Rome, from which he received the doctorate in 1937. Murray then served as professor of theology at Woodstock College for the next thirty years, until his untimely death of a heart attack in 1967. During that period Murray was also the editor of the prestigious quarterly, *Theological Studies*, and worked as religion editor of the Jesuit weekly, *America*, in the mid-1940s.

A man of wide and deep learning, Murray was the embodiment of the classic Christian humanist, but with a distinctively American flavor. At ease in a library pouring over ancient and medieval theological texts, Murray was also at home with his good friends Henry and Clare Boothe Luce, with the staffers of the Center for the Study of Democratic Institutions (where he sometimes lectured), and with the members of the many governmental agencies and commissions who sought his counsel on issues ranging from nuclear weapons to selective conscientious objection. A man who did not suffer fools gladly, Murray was nonetheless, according to all accounts, a charming companion and steadfast friend in whom—as his eulogist, Walter Burghardt, S.J., put it—"an aristocracy of mind was wedded to a democracy of love."

Murray did not leave an extensive corpus of published works; his métier was the essay, a form in which he wrote with singular elegance. But commentators at the time, and since, have judged Murray's 1960 book, *We Hold These Truths: Catholic Reflections on the American Proposition*, to be the single most influential Catholic reflection on American public life ever published. *We Hold These Truths* is emphatically not "for Catholics only." Its central premise—that the American democratic experiment could not be sustained without a "public philosophy" capable of disciplining the natively pluralistic public discourse of the republic—was (and is) shared across a considerable spectrum of public life. So, too, was Murray's concern

that no such "public philosophy" existed and that, in its absence, the public square would be filled with all manner of reckless agitations. More controversial at the time, although perhaps less so now, was Murray's brilliant attack on the anti-Catholicism of the "new secularists," like Paul Blanshard. Murray's proposal—that the American "public philosophy" reflect the categories and style of reasoning of Thomistic epistemology and natural law theory—was generally disregarded in the intellectual climate of the 1960s and 1970s. And yet, a generation later, the Murray proposal has been revived by a number of Protestant as well as Catholic scholars, generally neoconservative in their political orientation.

Murray also had a tremendous if indirect influence on international life through his work in creating a Catholic defense of religious liberty as the first of human rights. Absent Murray's historical and theoretical work in the 1940s and 1950s on the Catholic theory of church-and-state (which sought to disentangle the Church from its principled preference for the altar-and-throne arrangements of the European ancien régime), it is unlikely that the Second Vatican Council would have given such prominence to the religious liberty issue. The Council's "Declaration on Religious Freedom" subsequently became the key text in Pope John Paul II's defense of human rights throughout the world and in the Polish pope's endorsement of democracy as the political system most likely to secure those rights under modern conditions. The impact of that papal teaching can, of course, be discerned throughout central and eastern Europe, in Latin America, and in east Asia. In that sense, then, John Courtney Murray can be considered one of the prophets of the revolution of 1989 that brought down Soviet communism.

Given the correlation of intellectual forces in the Church and the country at the time of his death, Murray might well have been surprised had someone suggested that he would be an entry, a generation later, in an encyclopedia of American conservatism. Like all great intellects and spirits, Murray defies easy ideological classification. Yet Murray's argument that the American Revolution, unlike the French, was a "revolution of conservation" which owed intellectual and moral debts to Christian medieval philosophy, would be found entirely congenial by American Christian neoconservatives (who "rediscovered" Murray when he was being largely ignored by more radical theologians) in the 1980s. So, too, would Murray's vigorous anticommunism and his mature American patriotism. The Murray revival that began in the mid-1980s and has continued until the present day seems likely to keep the question of Murray's intellectual and political legacy alive for the foreseeable future.

—George Weigel

Further Reading

Neuhaus, Richard John. *The Naked Public Square: Religion and Democracy in America.* Grand Rapids, Mich.: Wm. B. Eerdmans, 1984.

Pelotte, Donald E. *John Courtney Murray: Theologian in Conflict.* New York: Paulist Press, 1976.

Weigel, George. "The John Courtney Murray Project." In *Tranquillitas Ordinis: The Present Failure and Future Promise of American Catholic Thought on War and Peace.* New York: Oxford University Press, 1987.

See also: Catholic social teaching; Roman Catholicism; Schindler, David L.

N

Nash, George H. (1945–)

George Nash is an independent historian and the author of *The Conservative Intellectual Movement in America since 1945* (1976, 1996), which examined the varieties of intellectual conservatism in modern America and summarized the careers of such figures as Friedrich Hayek, Whittaker Chambers, Russell Kirk, William F. Buckley Jr., Henry Regnery, Richard Weaver, Frank Meyer, Willmoore Kendall, and Irving Kristol. Nash's work definitively shaped the future of the historiography of conservatism by identifying as conservatives most if not all of those who had voiced opposition to communism, urged a return to traditional ways of life, criticized the bureaucratic state, or in one way or another questioned notions of liberalism and progress. In other words, the book cast a wide net. For example, Nash emphasized Arthur Schlesinger Jr.'s anticommunism, even though Schlesinger identified himself explicitly as an opponent of conservatism in his histories. Religious skeptics Leo Strauss and Max Eastman were included on account of their disbelief in progress and their antitotalitarianism; they stood alongside traditionalists such as Russell Kirk and (for the times) liberal Catholic priests such as John Courtney Murray.

The dynamic of the book is a dramatic crescendo. The book begins with the early stories of Hayek, Buckley, and Regnery struggling to find an audience. With the popular anticommunism of the 1950s and the grassroots conservatism of the 1960s, conservative intellectuals found a following and began to emerge. By the 1970s, as Jeffrey Hart wrote in a review of Nash's work, "the modern American conservative movement [had become] a major political and intellectual force in the United States."

On publication, Nash's book elicited much reflection from conservatives. *National Review* took heart from the growing momentum chronicled in the book, while Henry Regnery cautioned that the book should not mislead conservatives into thinking that they had achieved very much in terms of political and social reform. With the accession of Ronald Reagan in the 1980s, *The Conservative Intellectual Movement* became recognized as a classic and was reissued in 1996. A meticulous historian respected across the political divide, Nash has also published numerous articles and a three-volume biography of Herbert Hoover.

—BRIAN DOMITROVIC

Further Reading

Nash, George H. *Herbert Hoover and Stanford University.* Stanford, Calif.: Hoover Institution Press, 1988.

See also: movement conservatism

National Association of Scholars

The National Association of Scholars (NAS) was founded in 1987 by Steven Balch and Herbert London. Originally known as the Campus Coalition for Democracy, it was through the efforts of a small group of New York area scholars that NAS took form, providing a forum for academics critical of contemporary academia. Unlike some other organizations seeking to reform the academy, NAS membership is limited to college professors, graduate students, and college administrators. Its prime purpose is to foster renewed respect for the proposition that rational discourse and scholarship are the basis of academic life. NAS is especially concerned about the prevalence of extremist ideological currents in the academy and the damage it does to constructive scholarly exchange.

Though sometimes viewed as a conservative organization, NAS sees itself as a liberal body, i.e., as an organization committed to the free play of ideas. Consequently, it is open to all those who are interested in the restoration and preservation of the academy as the center for rational discourse and reasoned debate. While NAS does not expect members to hold to a narrow political creed, it unabashedly maintains a commitment to freedom and sees the academy as an important ally in the perpetuation of a free society. That such a commitment might exclude some academics is more a commentary on the current state of campus life than of the philosophy of NAS.

A major concern of NAS is the politicization of scholarship, especially as it affects the curriculum. In recent decades, many colleges and universities throughout the country have been engaged in curriculum reform, the efforts of which have frequently resulted in a diminution of respect for the heritage of Western civilization. Under the innocuous banner of multiculturalism, curriculum reform has sought the elevation of non-Western cultures to the denigration of Western traditions and achievements. It is in areas like this that NAS asserts itself.

NAS wants to recall higher education to its classic function of grounding students in the heritage of their civilization. In particular, members want to stimulate an informed understanding of the Western commitment to freedom and democracy. For this to be done, many fashionable curriculum reforms need to be reassessed. Not to be misunderstood, NAS believes that it is entirely proper that new programs and courses of study be contemplated and often implemented. It only insists that additions be made so as to expand the corpus of knowledge, and not to service some politically partisan objective. In short, scholarship that does not conform to established standards of evidence or else departs in any way from the rigor of academic excellence has no legitimate role to play in the academy.

Though a young organization, NAS already has many state affiliates and is active in college towns throughout the country. Its annual conferences have drawn considerable attention, providing a forum for constructive alternatives to prevailing orthodoxies. Locally, members meet periodically at each other's homes, combining conviviality with spirited discussion; formal lectures, symposia, and debates are also featured. NAS operates a fellows program as well as a faculty and executive search office. Its quarterly journal, *Academic Questions*, is generally regarded as one of the most authoritative voices in higher education today.

—WILLIAM A. DONOHUE

See also: academic freedom; education, higher; London, Herbert I.

National Conservative Political Action Committee

The National Conservative Political Action Committee was perhaps the best known and most effective of the independent expenditure groups that sprang up in the wake of Watergate-era political reforms. Also known as NCPAC (pronounced "Nick-Pack"), the group helped shape the political landscape after the Nixon scandal. NCPAC's hard-hitting political campaigns tested the boundaries of the sweeping electoral reform laws passed in the mid-1970s and even ended the political careers of several liberal titans.

NCPAC was founded in 1975 by young conservative political activists Terry Dolan, Charlie Black, and Roger Stone. Within a short period of time, however, the organization became synonymous with Dolan, an unapologetic conservative firebrand and brilliant political strategist. NCPAC was among the first groups to capitalize on revised federal election laws that set no limit on the expenditures independent political groups could make. Indeed, NCPAC was a party to a major Supreme Court ruling affirming this point.

In the 1980 elections, NCPAC targeted six Democratic United States senators for defeat, spending $1.2 million on advertising that exposed their liberal voting records to increasingly conservative constituencies. Four of the six senators went down to defeat. The group's efforts helped deliver control of the U.S. Senate to the Republicans for the first time in decades and ensured congressional cooperation for Reagan during his first year in office. The 1980 elections might have been the high-water mark for NCPAC: its influence was never as decisive in later elections. Indeed, the organization even ran into some trouble for skirting election laws. In the 1982 election cycle NCPAC was fined $15,000 for coordinating with New York Senator Daniel Patrick Moynihan's challenger.

Despite this setback, the group achieved a major success in 1985 when the Supreme Court ruled that political action committees could not be limited to spending $1,000 in presidential campaigns, a ruling with huge significance for the future of presidential politics. Throughout the first half of the

1980s NCPAC made news with its fierce issue- and political-advocacy campaigns. Dolan and NCPAC were also involved in drumming up support for Nicaraguan freedom fighters, as well as in defeating members of Congress who opposed U.S. support for the Contras.

Unlike many others who ran independent expenditure groups, Dolan was always up front about his sources of funding. Among his patrons was Unification Church head Sun Yung Moon. Dolan's NCPAC was a proving ground for a number of prominent conservative activists and consultants, including Craig Shirley and Greg Mueller. Financially, NCPAC was not doing well by 1986 and reportedly owed creditors and vendors as much as $4 million, including $1 million to direct-mail king Richard Viguerie. NCPAC's death knell began to sound in late 1986 when Dolan, a closeted homosexual, died of AIDS. Brent Bozell III served as the organization's chairman after Dolan's death, but within a year he left as a result of a public spat with the board of directors. Dolan's sister Maiselle Dolan succeeded Bozell for a short while, but the group eventually suffocated and folded under the weight of its substantial debts.

—MAX SCHULZ

See also: political action committees

National Federation of Independent Business

The National Federation of Independent Business (NFIB), founded in 1943 by Wilson Harder in his home, has become the leading advocate for small-business owners in the United States at both the federal and state level. The organization has approximately 600,000 small-business members. The NFIB also maintains the NFIB Education Foundation (an educational and public-policy research foundation), the NFIB Legal Foundation (a public-interest litigation foundation) and the Save America's Free Enterprise (SAFE) Trust (a political action committee). Jack Faris has been president and chief executive officer since March 1992.

The NFIB, widely regarded as one of the most influential lobbies in Washington, works to reduce the tax and regulatory burden on small enterprises. It supports tax cuts, fundamental tax reform, repeal of the estate and gift tax, and regulatory reform. It opposes increases in the minimum wage, unfair competition by government enterprises against small business, and tax advantages presently afforded to the commercial enterprises of not-for-profit organizations that are unrelated to their tax-exempt purposes.

The NFIB became particularly influential in the late 1970s under the leadership of then federal legislation director James Douglas (Mike) McKevitt. Its influence grew during the Reagan years, as it helped the Reagan administration to achieve major tax reductions (1981), tax reform (1986), and a significant reduction in the regulatory burden on small businesses. During the Clinton years, the NFIB was a major factor in the defeat of the administration's health care plan.

—DAVID BURTON

National Review

Launched in November 1955, the conservative journal National Review first appeared at a time conservatives found bleak. The Eisenhower administration, under the sway of "modern" (liberal-leaning) Republicans, was consolidating rather than dismantling the New Deal, and after a stab at "political warfare" to "roll back" Soviet rule in Eastern Europe, was reverting to the "containment" strategy initiated by the Democrats while simultaneously seeking "peaceful coexistence" with the Soviets. To make things

worse, conservatives wielded no influence among opinion makers. Free-market enthusiasts, Southern agrarians, hard-line anti-communists, old-fashioned isolationists, and Burkean traditionalists—these groups seemed to have scarcely more in common with each other than they did with liberals. Nor did they have adequate means of publicizing their views: some daily newspapers (but not the most prestigious ones); a handful of journals, such as the biweekly and then monthly Freeman (which, however, in 1954 narrowed its purpose to preaching libertarian economics) and the newspaper-like weekly Human Events; some small publishing houses; a modest number of radio newsmen and commentators; and a thin scattering of academics. They lacked entirely what they needed most: a weekly journal that brought the conservative viewpoint to bear on the deeper trends in American life and culture.

Then came National Review, the brainchild of a twenty-eight-year-old Yale graduate named William F. Buckley Jr., who had served as editor in chief of his college newspaper, worked briefly in the covert action branch of the CIA, and become famous for his book God and Man at Yale (1951), which protested his alma mater's bias toward collectivism and atheism. His aim, Buckley said, was to invigorate the conservative viewpoint and reach the people who shaped the country's thinking. National Review, he announced in NR's maiden issue, would stand "athwart history yelling Stop." Like the Nation and the New Republic, the liberal journals that to some extent served as its models, National Review came out weekly. The magazine reported and commented on news of the moment; ran editorials, columns, book reviews, cultural criticism, and articles on theoretical questions; and published political cartoons, verse, and a crossword puzzle. (After financial pressure caused it to become a biweekly in 1958, National Review sent subscribers a second publication, the *National Review Bulletin*, the week the magazine did not appear. An eight-page newsletter, usually edited by *NR* senior editor and foreign-affairs columnist James Burnham, the *Bulletin* came out until 1978.) *National Review* resembled its liberal counterparts in tone as well as in content, being, by turns, solemn, accusatory, illuminating, indignant, and ironic. But its tone could also differ markedly from theirs, assuming an irreverent playfulness they scrupulously eschewed. When, for example, Pope John XXIII issued his 1961 encyclical *Mater et Magistra* (Mother and Teacher), which questioned the compatibility of Christianity and free markets, *NR*, playing on a much repeated pro-Castro slogan of the day, "Cuba si, Yanqui no," responded with an editorial called "Mater si, Magistra" no.

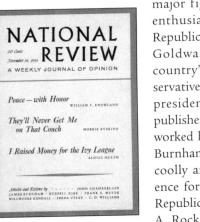

Joining the breadth of interests and the reportorial and analytical strengths of *Human Events* and the pre-1954 *Freeman* (many of whose writers it inherited), *National Review* supplied conservatives with the kind of journal required by their competition with liberals. Not only did *NR* give conservative ideas a sorely needed visibility, it also made evident the Right's intellectual diversity, for in a latitudinarian spirit it published conservative writing of all stripes, barring only inveterate spokesmen for the lunatic fringe. Thus, *NR's* readers could move from the hard-line foreign policy pronouncements of Burnham, who rejected all compromise when the issue was Soviet communism but defended federal insurance programs such as Medicare; to Frank S. Meyer and William F. Rickenbacker, who combined an anticommunism no less fierce than Burnham's with an equally fervent loathing of all government programs; to the traditionalist Russell Kirk, who, as *National Review's* education critic, left economic issues to others but in any case seemed to have little interest in them; to such champions of the free market as Tom Bethel and Alan Reynolds, who clearly preferred libertarianism to traditionalism; to Buckley, whose column always ran the gamut of issues.

Testifying further to the range of opinion at *National Review*, not all the magazine's major figures reacted with enthusiasm when Arizona Republican senator Barry M. Goldwater (then the country's best-known conservative politician) ran for president in 1964. If *NR's* publisher, William A. Rusher, worked hard for Goldwater, Burnham viewed the senator coolly and voiced a preference for New York's liberal Republican governor, Nelson A. Rockefeller. *National Review*, then, provided conservatives with a public arena for intramural debate. Many of them availed themselves of the opportunity, attacking one another's views in an *NR* feature called "The Open Question." But paradoxically, in encouraging such clashes, the magazine also fostered a feeling of shared ground among conservatives, since it brought all the adversaries together within a common framework. Meanwhile, *National Review's* own animating convictions were clear and steady: preservation of freedom and the historic constitutional order, deference to traditional moral and cultural norms, rejection of the New Deal legacy of highly centralized federal power (especially as embodied in the multiplication of regulatory agencies and in what came to be called the "nanny state"), adherence to free-market economic principles, support for a strong defense, and active opposition to Soviet global designs.

Though its positions often sounded like those trumpeted by Republicans, *National Review*'s relations with the GOP were often strained. The journal that had lambasted the "modern" Republicans of the Eisenhower administration showed no great liking for the Nixon administration either. Indeed, opposed to Nixon's efforts at détente with the Soviet Union and Mao's China and to a number of Nixon's domestic initiatives, several *NR* editors met with other prominent conservatives in July 1971 to announce their "suspension of support" for the administration. Nor did *National Review* long defend Nixon during the Watergate affair or endorse the policies of his successor, Gerald R. Ford. Not until Ronald Reagan (a prime beneficiary of the conservative movement *NR* had done so much to shape) entered the White House twenty-six years after *NR*'s debut did the magazine have a Republican president it backed with enthusiasm. *National Review* conceived of itself not as a tabernacle for enshrining conservative ideas, but as an instrument for their diffusion. As a way of spreading the conservative word, gaining new readers, and raising money to meet ever-rising publication costs, the magazine helped organize gatherings around the country called "Evenings with *National Review*," at which several editors would address an audience on current issues, and later perhaps hold a question-and-answer session with local media. In addition, individual editors went on speaking tours of their own, which, though not intended as a means of advertising *National Review*, inevitably did so.

NR made special efforts to reach students, in its view the key to the future. *NR* editors often spoke at colleges and universities, and the magazine regularly called upon older readers to cover the cost of a subscription for a student. Such efforts bore fruit. By the 1970s, a conservative renaissance was visible on campus, and in the 1980s conservative student journals began to crop up, the features of which identified them as the offspring of *National Review*.

National Review's hard work brought success off campus, too. Beginning with a circulation of about 18,000, the magazine reached the hundred thousand mark in 1968, and in the early yeas of the millennium, with Rich Lowry (having succeeded John O'Sullivan) at the editorial helm, could boast a circulation of 155,000. All the while, *NR* was evolving in various ways: picking up advertising; dropping its originally austere, pictureless covers, which had only announced an issue's main writers and articles, for covers illustrated with photographs or drawings; adding regular film and art critics; giving more space to reporting and less to columns; and going online with a popular Web site that brings viewers further news and daily commentary.

The end of the Cold War and the implosion of the Soviet empire closed the file on one of *NR*'s most hoary preoccupations. But the emergence of new international problems and the perennial trend toward a more intrusive federal government, along with a slew of more recent domestic issue—abortion, racial preferences, uncontrolled immigration, and the controversies associated with "political correctness," to mention only a few—ensured that *NR* editors had no time to doze at their desks.

Though the number of conservative journals currently published dwarfs the miniscule group of the 1950s, *National Review* is still the most widely read. And, realizing its founder's hopes, *NR* has become one of those rare journals that has not just reported and commented on American political life but has helped substantially to change it.

—DANIEL KELLY

Further Reading

Judis, John B. *William F. Buckley, Jr.: Patron Saint of the Conservatives*. New York: Simon & Schuster, 1988.

Kelly, Daniel. *James Burnham and the Struggle for the World: A Life.* Wilmington, Del.: ISI Books, 2002.

Nash, George H. *The Conservative Intellectual Movement in America since 1945.* 2nd ed. Wilmington, Del.: Intercollegiate Studies Institute, 1996.

Smant, Kevin J. *Principles and Heresies: Frank S. Meyer and the Shaping of the American Conservative Movement.* Wilmington, Del.: ISI Books, 2002.

See also: Buckley, William F., Jr.; Burnham, James; Chambers, Whittaker; John Birch Society; media, conservative; Meyer, Frank S.; New Right; Rusher, William A.; Schlamm, William

National Rifle Association

The National Rifle Association (NRA) promotes the shooting sports and works to protect the right to keep and bear arms. True to its founding purpose, the association continues to emphasize its role as a training and educational organization. However, today the NRA is primarily known for its political efforts against gun-control laws that would threaten the Second Amendment–rights of gun owners. With Wayne LaPierre as its executive vice president and Charlton Heston as its president from 1998 to 2003, a position currently occupied by Sandra S. Froman, the NRA's membership has grown to 4 million, and it is among the most powerful single-issue lobbies in American politics.

The NRA was founded in 1871 by Union army veterans Col. William C. Church and Gen. George Wingate. Disappointed by the marksmanship of their troops during the war, they decided that it was necessary to find a vehicle to "promote and encourage rifle shooting on a scientific basis." The new organization was granted a charter by the state of New York and Gen. Ambrose Burnside became the NRA's first president.

A year later, with financial help from New York's state government, the association purchased property on Long Island for a rifle range. As early as the late nineteenth century, however, there was political opposition to the promotion of marksmanship in New York, and the NRA was forced to move its first range to New Jersey in 1892.

The NRA's political activity began in the pages of its magazine, the *American Rifleman.* The *Rifleman* informed members of new firearms legislation being considered in Congress and in the states. In 1934, the association decided to take a more aggressive approach in defending the Second Amendment–rights of members and so formed a legislative affairs division. This new division provided members with information about particular legislation in a timely manner, though it stopped short of any direct lobbying. It was not until 1975 that the Institute for Legislative Action, the lobbying arm of the NRA, was created.

Despite the high profile of the NRA's political efforts, the association continues to devote most of its resources to training, education, and marksmanship. While continuing to expand the outreach to youth it began in 1903, the NRA has also taken a leading role in training and educating the hunting community. In 1949 the NRA established the first hunter-education program, and in 1973 the association launched a new magazine dedicated solely to hunting.

Today, the NRA also participates in law enforcement training, with more than 10,000 NRA-certified police and security firearms instructors across the country. And the association remains the leader in civilian training with more than 50,000 instructors training about 750,000 gun owners every year.

—CHRISTOPHER THACKER

Further Reading
Heston, Charlton. *The Courage to Be Free.* Kansas City, Kan.: Saudade Press, 2000.

LaPierre, Wayne R. *Guns, Crime, and Freedom.* Washington, D.C.: Regnery, 1994.

natural law

In Book V of the *Ethics*, Aristotle distinguishes between natural and legal justice. Some measures of justice, he observes, are rooted in nature rather than in human stipulation. Natural terms of justice are universal, for they do not depend on the customs and laws of a particular polity. Historically, the rubric "natural law" is often used to designate very generally the idea that there are some universal norms of moral conduct that are not mere creatures of human custom or positive law. In this respect, natural law is not limited to propositions concerning justice or law, but is equated with the position that there are objective ("natural") grounds for moral judgments.

Natural law can also denote the idea of a natural legal order. From late antiquity to the nineteenth century, many philosophers and theologians held that God promulgates at least some moral precepts via the secondary causality of nature. Hence, in the writings of St. Paul, St. Augustine, and St. Thomas Aquinas we find the notion of an instilled law (*lex indita*) written on the human heart or conscience. It was from the synthesis of classical notions of natural justice and biblical belief in a divine creator and lawgiver that we inherited the phrase "natural law." Natural law was held to be one of the ways that God governs rational creatures. Aquinas contended that the ten precepts of the Decalogue represented natural law conveyed in the mode of a divine positive law.

In the modern period, the idea of natural law is often reduced to the notion of human rights. By dint of their humanity, individuals have certain rights the state must respect. Such diverse theorists as Locke and Kant, and such diverse institutions as the Catholic Church and the United Nations, have been sources or advocates of the doctrine of natural rights. In the nineteenth and twentieth centuries, discourse and debate about natural rights is often dissevered from the idea of a natural "law," particularly its theistic formulation.

In American legal culture, natural law is regularly identified either with the position that there are unenumerated rights that can be cognized and vindicated by the judiciary or with the method of jurisprudence by which a judge takes note of moral principles that are beyond the written text of the Constitution. According to the jargon of constitutional lawyers, this method of jurisprudence is called "noninterpretivism." The judge must from time to time do more than interpret the written text; that is, he must search out the moral meaning and implications of a legal text or case. However, it must be noted that not all "natural lawyers" believe that judges are authorized to appeal to natural law, and by the same token not all "noninterpretivists" believe in anything resembling the traditional notion of a natural law.

These are but a few of the meanings assigned to the phrase "natural law." They have received quite different and sometimes contradictory formulations. Considered historically, natural-law theory has involved more than one problem or theme, but there are family resemblances among theories of natural law. For example, most natural lawyers hold some version of the thesis that norms of justice do not come into existence exclusively by dint of human art or statute. Most natural lawyers also hold that natural standards of justice constitute a necessary condition for a positive law being a genuine law. Indeed, philosophers as different as Cicero, Augustine, and Kant have held that human laws have moral as well as more narrow legal requirements. Hence, Augustine asserts, "an unjust law is no law at all." By this, Augustine did not mean to say that justice is the sole criterion for law; rather, he meant that the absence of justice vitiates a positive law.

On the other hand, those who argue that a positive law need only meet technical or procedural criteria internal to a system of (positive) laws are generally called "positivists." In answer to the question of what makes a command a "law," or what makes a legal system able to identify an ordinance as a "law," positivists such as Hans Kelsen and J. L. Austin insist that there is no necessary connection between the moral and legal properties of an enactment. To say that an ordinance or rule is a law is simply to say that it is the command of a sovereign, backed by sanctions, and habitually obeyed. The claim by positivists that the substantive moral merit or demerit of an enactment is incidental to its status as law is sometimes dubbed the "separationist thesis." There are crude as well as relatively sophisticated versions of the thesis. The late H. L. A. Hart, who gave a very influential and nuanced account of the separation of law and morality, took care to point out that positivism does not necessarily entail the belief that morality is unimportant to law, much less that an unjust law should always be obeyed. Rather, he argued that the moral property of a command is not what endows the command with the status of law. An unjust law can be a genuine law. If it is unjust, then lawmakers ought to change it.

At least in the English-speaking world, modern conservatives have been ambivalent, skeptical, and sometimes hostile to natural law. While most conservatives have held the philosophical or religious conviction that there are timeless moral truths, many have been cautious about the political and legal implications of natural law discourse. In the Anglophone political culture, the common law was thought to contain and, as Sir Matthew Hale said, to "radiate" the natural law, making explicit appeal to natural law unnec-

essary. Although American colonists frequently used the rhetoric of natural rights, their justification for American independence relied chiefly on arguments concerning the history and rights of Englishmen.

Among conservatives, nothing discredited theories of natural rights more than the French Revolution, in which appeals to the "rights of man" were used to overthrow the social, political, and ecclesiastical orders. Both Jeremy Bentham's positivism and Edmund Burke's defense of custom and tradition represented reactions to the revolutionary effects of natural-rights theories on the Continent. The waning of natural-law jurisprudence in the English tradition was due in large part to the revulsion caused by the French experiment. Moreover, the nineteenth-century abolitionist movement in the United States frequently appealed to a "higher law" to justify the expansion of federal authority over state governments. Although Jefferson Davis himself defended the Southern cause in the language of natural rights, the Civil War and Reconstruction convinced many conservatives, particularly southerners, that "higher law" doctrines were mere ideologies crafted for the purpose of undermining custom and positive law. Not only southerners expressed disapproval of "higher law" doctrines. The New England Catholic convert Orestes Brownson wrote an important treatise, "The Higher Law," which took abolitionists to task for undermining the authority of the Constitution in the name of natural law.

In the contemporary debate, conservative suspicion of natural law has been aroused by the activist judiciary, which has used various kinds of natural-law reasoning to justify federal supervision and abrogation of the moral police powers of the states. The Robert Bork and Clarence Thomas nomination hearings indicated the extent to which natural law, as a tool of jurisprudence, has become a mainstay of Left-liberal theorists.

Both nominees were criticized for being "originalists" in jurisprudence and for failing to respect the alleged moral grounds of modern privacy rights.

Of course, there is no necessary reason why natural law requires judicial supremacy—Aquinas, for example, argued that judges ought not to be given principal authority to make the natural law effective in the political community. Yet the continuous and seemingly arbitrary use of "natural law" by the judiciary, usually for the purpose of reaching egalitarian social results and in order to vindicate individual rights against traditional morals legislation, has deeply soured conservatives on the subject.

Generally speaking, within the conservative movement today, only some libertarians enthusiastically embrace the notion of judicially cognizable natural rights. The libertarian interest in natural rights can be explained, in part, by the Supreme Court's use of a substantive due process doctrine earlier in the century in vindicating property and contract rights. Substantive due process is the doctrine that the due process clause of section 1 of the Fourteenth Amendment ("nor shall any State deprive a person of life, liberty or property without due process of law . . .") mandates more than procedural justice and reaches the substantive goods being deprived or regulated by the state. Thus, according to this doctrine, judges are authorized to consider not merely whether life, liberty, or property are being fairly deprived, but also whether the state has any compelling reason to limit these substantive values. For some theorists, life, liberty, and property are natural rights, and therefore there is a prima facie ground for putting the burden of justification on the state whenever these rights are touched by statutes.

While conservatives have been, at best, ambivalent about natural-law doctrines in the areas of law and politics, the opposite is true in the area of philosophy. The three most important philosophical schools of postwar conservatism in the United States—Straussian, Voegelinian, and neo-Thomist—have all insisted, in different ways, on the importance of natural law. Hence, once the issue is shifted from practical matters of politics and jurisprudence to the more speculative arena of moral and political theory, conservatives have tended to be more prepared to defend natural law—at least the ancient and medieval conceptions of natural law. Leo Strauss and his disciples have been very effective in pointing out the differences between modern conceptions of natural rights and premodern conceptions of natural law.

In sum, modern conservatives gravitate toward custom and positive law in matters of law and politics, while gravitating toward nature in the more abstract discussions of the foundations of moral and political order. Since the French Revolution, conservatism has not been of one mind on this subject. Much of what counts as "conservative" opinion on natural law is shaped by reactions to the use of the concept by Left-liberals.

—Russell Hittinger

Further Reading

Barnett, Randy E., ed. *The Rights Retained by the People: The History and Meaning of the Ninth Amendment.* Fairfax, Va.: George Mason University Press, 1989.

Haines, Charles Groves. *The Revival of Natural Law Concepts.* Cambridge, Mass.: Harvard University Press, 1930.

Hittinger, Russell. "Natural Law in the Positive Laws: A Legislative or Adjudicative Issue?" *Review of Politics* 55 (1993): 5–34.

Kirk, Russell. "Burke and Natural Rights." *Review of Politics* 13 (1951): 441–56.

Strauss, Leo. *Natural Right and History.* Chicago: University of Chicago Press, 1953.

Tuck, Richard. *Natural Rights Theories.* Cambridge: Cambridge University Press, 1979.

Voegelin, Eric. *The Nature of the Law and Related Writings*. Edited by Robert A. Pascal, James L. Babin and John W. Corrington. Baton Rouge, La.: Louisiana State University Press, 1991.

See also: Burkean conservatism; conservatism; Constitution, interpretations of; natural law theory, new; Natural Right and History; Roman Catholicism

natural law theory, new

The so-called new natural law theory or "new classical natural law theory" or (sometimes) the "Grisez-Finnis theory" is a late-twentieth-century intellectual development, though it has antecedents in the thought of mid-twentieth-century philosophers such as Elizabeth Anscombe. New natural law theory is closely associated with the thought and writings of the American Catholic theologian German Grisez and the Oxford legal philosopher John M. Finnis, as well as figures such as Robert P. George, Joseph M. Boyle Jr., and William E. May.

New natural law theory disputes the claim of "neoscholastic" natural law theorists (such as the seventeenth-century scholar Francisco Suarez, S.J.) that practical principles, including moral principles, can be deduced from purely theoretical truths about human nature. New natural law theory also rejects, however, the "emotivist" position of figures such as David Hume, which holds that if moral norms cannot be deduced from facts, they must instead be projections of human feelings rather than objects of human reason.

Instead, new natural law theory holds that practical principles (including moral norms) are rational principles whose directiveness is independent of human feelings. New natural law theory maintains that the most basic practical principles stipulate actions that people have reasons to perform precisely because they are opportunities for people to realize for themselves (and often others) benefits whose rational value cannot be reduced to purely instrumental purposes. Under the new natural law account of practical reasoning, a variety of factors figure in the genesis of acts performed by people for noninstrumental reasons. These include acts of the will, which new natural law theorists typically understand in Aquinas's sense of man's rational appetite.

New natural law theory brought in its wake a renewed philosophical interest in theories of natural law. This was especially true following the publication of John Finnis's *Natural Law and Natural Rights* (1980). On one level, this book revitalized reflection on natural law within the Roman Catholic Church, where it had been somewhat neglected following the Second Vatican Council. New natural law critiques of the moral theories of "proportionalism" and "consequentialism" advocated by dissenting Catholic theologians prepared the way for the formal papal condemnation of such theories in John Paul II's encyclical *Veritatis Splendor* (1993).

New natural law theory also began to attract attention within decidedly secular circles, especially among analytical philosophers, in the 1980s. This owed much to the reawakening of interest in practical reason in the English-speaking world and the willingness of figures such as H. L. A. Hart, Joseph Raz, and Philippa Foot to take practical reason seriously in areas such as jurisprudence and political philosophy. It may be that new natural law theory's attention to practical reason allowed its followers to figure among the more formidable critics of liberal-secular political philosophy and jurisprudence, especially on such controversial matters as contraception, abortion, euthanasia, and homosexual unions, as articulated by liberal-secular scholars such as John Rawls, Ronald Dworkin, and Robert Nozick.

At the beginning, new natural law theorists found that much of their attention was devoted to matters of sexual morality, precisely because it was in this area that liberal-secular scholars (be they of the Kantian, Humean, or libertarian variety) were devoting the most time and effort. In the early 1990s, new natural law theory also became increasingly applied to matters such as constitutional questions, economic theory, and the foundation of human rights.

Among the strongest critics of new natural law theory, one finds not only secular thinkers but also neo-Aristotelians and Catholic scholars such as Ralph McInerny and Russell Hittinger. The latter are sometimes referred to as "old natural law" or "neoscholastic" theorists. Though they do not question the commitment of Grisez, Finnis, et al. to orthodox Catholic teaching on faith and morals, old natural law theorists maintain that new natural law theory appears to rely on a type of Kantian deontologism. In this connection, neoscholastic scholars argue that new natural law theory holds that practical reason operates on its own first principles without any dependence on antecedent knowledge drawn from disciplines such as theology, metaphysics, or human anthropology. Hence, the "basic goods" proposed by natural law theory are regarded by some neoscholastic scholars as "Platonic-like." Another neoscholastic charge concerns the plausibility of the incommensurability of the basic goods proposed by Grisez and Finnis. While Grisez, Finnis, May, and Boyle have responded in detail to these claims, essays written by Robert P. George in the late 1980s and early 1990s constitute especially important components of the defense of new natural law theory in the face of these critiques.

In more recent years, the debates between new and old natural law theorists have subsided. This owes less to the resolution of the differences between the two camps than it does to the increasing attention given by natural law scholars of both schools to combating the ongoing advance of secularist philosophies within the public square, the academy, the law, and the moral ecology of Western societies.

—SAMUEL GREGG

Further Reading

Finnis, John. *Aquinas: Moral, Legal, and Political Theory.* Oxford: Oxford University Press, 1998.

_____. *Fundamentals of Ethics.* Oxford: Clarendon Press, 1983.

George, Robert P. *In Defence of Natural Law.* Oxford: Clarendon Press, 1999.

Grisez, Germain, Joseph Boyle, and John Finnis. "Practical Principles, Moral Truth, and Ultimate Ends." *American Journal of Jurisprudence* 32 (1987): 99–151.

See also: natural law

Natural Right and History

Published in 1950 as an expansion of the six Charles R. Walgreen Lectures that Leo Strauss had delivered at the University of Chicago in 1949, *Natural Right and History* is a classic work in the twentieth-century's literature of critical evaluation of and reasoned attack on the modern turn toward positivism and relativism. The focus of the book is what Strauss considers the basic controversy in political philosophy: Is there any natural right? Strauss evaluates the major thinkers on both sides of the question—the development of theories of natural right, or natural law, in classical philosophy and the modern world's modification or outright rejection of these theories beginning with Hobbes—with a closely reasoned presentation of the arguments and their underlying assumptions and implications. By the force of his reasoning and detailed analysis Strauss makes a strong case for the restoration of natural right.

Strauss begins by quoting the famous unalienable rights passage from the Declaration of Independence, pointing out that in the mid-twentieth century the belief in "natural right" and "humanity" had been almost universally abandoned in Western thought in favor of "the historical sense" or "relativism," or conventionalism, a universal tolerance that, inconsistently, rejects all "intolerant" or "absolutist" or natural right positions. This widespread rejection of natural right, partly brought about by modern science, which Strauss argues has destroyed the teleological view of the universe, has what he considers "disastrous consequences," since with no higher standard we are incapable of choosing what is truly good or just. When all options are equally good or permissible the result is nihilism and alienation.

Strauss's own antihistoricist position is that the same philosophical themes and problems are the concern of "all human thought," and "if the fundamental problems persist in all historical changes, human thought is capable of transcending its historical limitation or of grasping something trans-historical." Strauss sees natural right and philosophy as essentially interdependent, with historicism or relativism destructive of both as well as of rightly ordered existence in the world. For this reason he analyzes in detail—and rejects—the position of Max Weber (whom he considers "the greatest social scientist" of the twentieth century) that there are conflicts between ultimate values that human reason cannot resolve. This position, Strauss contends, leads to nihilism.

Having outlined the crisis in modern thought brought about by the rejection of natural right, Strauss goes back to the beginning, devoting the next two chapters to a detailed discussion of classical natural right as it was discovered by the early philosophers,

who developed and analyzed the distinction between nature and convention. Strauss distinguishes and discusses three types of natural-right teaching: the Socratic-Platonic (including the Stoics), the Aristotelian, and the Thomistic, all of which uphold some form of objective standard of morality.

The fifth chapter considers in detail the theories of Hobbes and Locke, who broke away from the traditional natural-right belief to develop the doctrine of political hedonism, and the sixth and last chapter, "The Crisis of Modern Natural Right," evaluates Rousseau's and Burke's different attempts to correct the "radical error" of the modern rejection of natural right. The first chapter has already made clear that these and other attempts have been largely unsuccessful in reversing modernity's adoption of relativism.

—MICHAEL HENRY

Further Reading

Deutsch, Kenneth L., and Walter Nicgorski, eds. *Leo Strauss: Political Philosopher and Jewish Thinker.* Lanham, Md.: Rowman & Littlefield, 1993.

Devigne, Robert. *Recasting Conservatism: Oakeshott, Strauss, and the Response to Postmodernism.* New Haven, Conn.: Yale University Press, 1994.

McAllister, Ted V. *Revolt against Modernity: Leo Strauss, Eric Voegelin, and the Search for a Postliberal Order.* Lawrence, Kan.: University Press of Kansas, 1996.

See also: historicism; modernity and postmodernity; Strauss, Leo; Straussianism

neoconservatism

Neoconservatism is a right-wing branch of American liberalism that emerged in the late 1960s and early 1970s, largely as a reaction to liberal utopianism and the irrationality of the new Left. Most neoconservative writing has been concerned with social issues, such as the inefficiencies and unintended consequences of the welfare state, the problem of equal opportunity, and the amelioration of racial tensions. In foreign affairs, neoconservatives have consistently advocated strongly internationalist policies to contain communism and promote democracy abroad. Neoconservatives allied themselves with the traditional Right in the early 1980s, thereby increasing their own influence within the Reagan administration but also causing some resentment among those who saw them as latecomers to the conservative movement.

Neoconservatism is rooted in post–World War II liberalism. After the death of Franklin Roosevelt, liberals split over the question of how best to preserve and extend the reforms of the New Deal. Some liberals, disturbed by the rise of Cold War tensions with the USSR and fearing a takeover by the Right at home, were willing to form a coalition with communists to work for more domestic reforms and an accommodation with Moscow. Led by former vice president Henry A. Wallace and organized as the Progressive Party, they were opposed by liberals who saw communism as the true danger to liberalism. The latter group remained loyal Democrats and supported President Truman's policies. Truman's victory in the 1948 presidential election established their dominance among liberals and the leading role of their organization, the Americans for Democratic Action. Many of the individuals in this group who later became prominent neoconservatives, such as Jeane Kirkpatrick, Daniel Bell, and Daniel Patrick Moynihan, were professors or New York intellectuals active in literary, artistic, and cultural criticism. Several, including Bell and Irving Kristol, had been Marxists when they were students in the 1930s, but had since broken with the radical Left.

The postwar generation of liberal intellectuals tended to be reformist and mildly socialist. Their writings portrayed American society as complex and its problems—mainly relating to political, economic, and racial inequality—as complicated as well. Consequently, they rejected what they viewed as the simplistic or utopian approaches to social problems advocated by the Left and Right, dismissing them as based on ideology rather than realistic analysis. This view received its fullest expression in Bell's book, *The End of Ideology* (1960). Moreover, unlike traditional conservatives, these liberals were more concerned with shaping the future than with preserving traditional institutions. Instead, they emphasized a social-engineering approach to issues, using social science methods to identify problems and to develop government programs to solve them. In the 1960s, for example, they supported Kennedy and Johnson administration proposals to extend social welfare programs and to establish antipoverty and urban programs. Not surprisingly, many of the leading liberal intellectuals of the 1950s and 1960s, such as Daniel Bell and Nathan Glazer, were sociologists.

Neoconservatism began to emerge in the later 1960s when some liberal intellectuals began to consider the lessons of the decade's failed reforms. Continued urban deterioration, increasing welfare enrollments and costs, and the rise of black militancy made it clear that many of the reforms had not met their goals. In addition, the social disorder and urban riots of the mid- and late-1960s led some liberals, particularly Moynihan and Kristol, to a new appreciation of the role of institutions and traditional authority in society. In seeking to explain reform's failure, these liberals raised questions about the theories behind the programs and the federal government's ability to administer programs effectively. Moynihan, for example, believed that the failure of urban anti-poverty programs had been caused by the government's reliance on unproven theories that, in practice, turned out to be wrong. Glazer saw that some policies actually worsened problems, as when affirmative action programs failed to help the most disadvantaged while increasing racial and ethnic tensions. In sum, these liberals became much more skeptical about the ability of social scientists and the government to shape society. This skepticism became especially identified with the *Public Interest,* a magazine founded by Bell and Kristol in 1965 to examine social issues.

Many liberals were further disturbed in the late 1960s by the rising influence of the new Left. Postwar liberals had frequently seen themselves as radicals, but the new Left seized that label for itself while embracing a utopian ideology and attacking the concepts of liberal democracy. To some liberals, this was similar to the threat posed to reformist liberalism by communists twenty years earlier. For some the threat was also personal. Professors such as Glazer witnessed the student rebellions firsthand and saw in them a threat to their academic freedom and their integrity as researchers and teachers. Some Jewish intellectuals saw the New Left's attacks on Israel as thinly veiled anti-Semitism. This was particularly true for Norman Podhoretz, the editor of *Commentary.* In June 1970, Podhoretz began using *Commentary* as a platform for a broad counterattack against the new Left. By late 1970, he and other defenders of New Deal- and late-1940s-style liberalism were being called "new conservatives," a label which evolved into "neoconservative" by the middle of the decade.

Neoconservative ideology had four major characteristics. First, neoconservatives remained wedded to the social-science approach. Neoconservative analyses were marked by rigorous research and careful writing and sought to identify the true causes of problems. Their conclusions reflected skepticism of new, large federal programs, and thus ran counter to accepted liberal wisdom. Neoconservative policy suggestions, reflecting the lessons of the 1960s, also had limited ambitions—they reflected the belief that social problems could be eased, but not erased—and frequently concentrated on criticizing liberal promises to "cure" a problem.

Neoconservatism's second major element was the acceptance of economic and social inequality. They saw "a society of equals as unwieldy and unworkable," in the words of Amitai Etzioni, and instead favored establishing true equality of opportunity and letting individuals succeed or fail on their own.

Third, neoconservatives continued to support the welfare state. They did not seek to reverse what they viewed as the achievements of liberalism, such as social-security programs or medical assistance to the poor and elderly, but resisted costly new programs that they believed had only dubious chances for success. Instead, they wanted to improve the efficiency and responsiveness of existing programs by taking administrative authority from federal agencies and placing it in local hands whenever possible and by maximizing the choices of individuals.

Finally, in foreign policy neoconservatism was marked by its strong defense of Western democracy. These views were largely unchanged from the liberal outlook of the late 1940s, which was heavily influenced by the writings of Protestant theologian Reinhold Niebuhr and historian Arthur M. Schlesinger Jr. Niebuhr took a pessimistic view of man's tendencies and rejected communism largely because it placed no moral restraints on the state's actions, a condition that he believed led to despotism. Niebuhr further argued that liberal democracy—however flawed—was man's best hope for progress. This defense of democracy was reinforced by Schlesinger's book *The Vital Center* (1949), which urged the containment of communism, strong support for democratic governments, and financial and technical aid to underdeveloped states in order to undercut the appeal of communism. This consensus dominated liberal foreign-policy thinking from 1948 until the late 1960s. After 1967, as a result of the escalation of the Vietnam War, many liberals began to reconsider their foreign-policy views. The consensus broke up and most liberals began to support new foreign-policy ideas, which usually sought to reduce American commitments overseas in favor of an international regime stabilized by economic interdependence and stronger legal mechanisms. Those liberals who still favored a strongly anticommunist, activist foreign policy were in the minority.

Led by Kristol, neoconservatives argued that the United States had to maintain its role as global policeman or chaos and dangerous instability would result, benefiting only the Soviet Union. The neoconservatives were further concerned by what they viewed as the liberal elites' loss of willingness to defend themselves after the Vietnam disaster. Political scientist Robert W. Tucker, for example, believed that the West's weak response to the 1973 Arab oil embargo was an indication of such a loss of nerve. The oil embargo also led to increased neoconservative hostility to Third World claims against the West, which neoconservatives perceived as going unanswered by Washington and the liberal elites. Moynihan identified both socialist ideology and the belief that the Third World had been exploited by Western imperialism as the roots of the demand for increased economic transfers from wealthy to underdeveloped countries. Moynihan and other neoconservatives were further concerned with Third World and communist bloc attacks on Israel, which they viewed as an assault on Western democracy as well as a manifestation of anti-Semitism. As ambassador to the United Nations from 1975 to 1976, Moynihan vigorously refuted charges that continued Western imperialism, racism,

and exploitation were to blame for the ills of the underdeveloped states.

Because they saw themselves as the guardians of true liberalism, the neoconservatives struggled to maintain a role for themselves in the Democratic Party during the 1970s. As a result of party reforms following Hubert Humphrey's defeat in the 1968 presidential election, the Democrats became dominated by younger, more liberal activists, at the expense of traditional postwar-style liberals. Washington Senator Henry "Scoop" Jackson, the favorite of the neoconservatives, was defeated in his attempts to gain the presidential nomination in 1972 and 1976. A neoconservative attempt to reclaim traditional liberal influence over the party after Senator George McGovern's defeat in the 1972 presidential election—the founding of the Coalition for a Democratic Majority—failed as well, largely because of poor organization. As a result, the party remained in the hands of its left wing and the neoconservatives became increasingly isolated. In 1980, angry with President Carter's refusal to shift to a more hard-line foreign policy after the Iranian revolution and Soviet invasion of Afghanistan, most neoconservatives supported Ronald Reagan's candidacy, although they remained registered Democrats. Several received high-level appointments in the Reagan administration, including Kirkpatrick as ambassador to the United Nations, Elliott Abrams as an assistant secretary of state, and Richard Perle as an assistant secretary of defense.

Neoconservatism's impact on domestic politics was made clear after the movement's break with the Democrats. Because they reflected popular disenchantment with failed government programs, as well as widespread anger with President Carter's economic and foreign policy failures, the neoconservatives were in a position to help mobilize support for alternative policies and candidates. Their access to influential journals, newspapers, and "think tanks" was valuable for developing and spreading new ideas. As a consequence of their rejection by the Democrats, the neoconservatives brought these resources to the Republicans, Ronald Reagan, and the traditional Right.

Neoconservatism's effect on traditional conservatives has been more ambiguous. On the one hand, these conservatives (some of whom frequently distinguish themselves as paleoconservatives) have clearly benefited from the alliance. The coalition has eased the isolation of the intellectual Right and brought valuable assistance in the struggle to limit the size and powers of government and to bolster traditional social institutions, such as the family. On the other hand, many paleoconservatives believe that the conservative movement has been taken away from them. Paul Gottfried and Thomas Fleming suggest, for example, that the paleoconservatives may be swallowed by the neoconservatives as conservative activists adopt the social science–based arguments of the neoconservatives in place of their traditional reliance on a more philosophically based point of view. Many paleoconservatives have come to resent the influence of neoconservative publications and the neoconservatives' ability to obtain foundation money to support their programs. Furthermore, the popular media's labeling of prominent neoconservatives, such as William Bennett, as conservatives has raised fears among paleoconservatives that the neoconservatives have come to be seen as representing all American conservatives. Finally, as Ernest van den Haag has pointed out, there is a lingering resentment among paleoconservatives of the prominence of what they view as a group of ex-Marxist latecomers.

The collapse of communism in the late 1980s and early 1990s commenced a process by which the split among neoconservatives and the traditional Right has continued to intensify. After the communist threat disappeared, some conservatives advocated an "America First" policy that, in 1990, led them to oppose American intervention in the Persian Gulf and worry that American policy was serving Israeli interests at the expense of the United States. These worries were voiced again, possibly even more strongly, during the Iraq War a decade later. Such conservatives are often highly skeptical of efforts to spread American democracy abroad, especially by force. Most neoconservatives, on the other hand, not only supported the Gulf and Iraq wars but also, as exemplified by Joshua Muravchik, have advocated a neo-Wilsonian policy wherein the United States has a moral obligation to assist by whatever means necessary the globalization of democracy.

—John Ehrman

Further Reading

Buchanan, Patrick J. *Where the Right Went Wrong: How Neoconservatives Subverted the Reagan Revolution and Hijacked the Bush Presidency.* New York: Thomas Dunne Books, 2004.

Glazer, Nathan. *Affirmative Discrimination.* New York: Basic Books, 1975; reprint, Cambridge, Mass.: Harvard University Press, 1987.

Gottfried, Paul and Thomas Fleming. *The Conservative Movement.* Boston: Twayne Publishers, 1988.

Hoeveler, J. David. *Watch on the Right.* Madison, Wis.: University of Wisconsin Press, 1991.

Kristol, Irving. *Reflections of a Neoconservative.* New York: Basic Books, 1983.

———. *Neoconservatism: The Autobiography of an Idea.* New York: Free Press, 1995.

Moynihan, Daniel Patrick. *Maximum Feasible Misunderstanding.* New York: Free Press, 1969.

Podhoretz, Norman. *Breaking Ranks.* New York: Harper & Row, 1980.

See also: conservatism; Jewish conservatives; Kristol, Irving; liberalism; movement conservatism; Novak, Michael; paleoconservatism; Public Interest; Schindler, David L.

Neuhaus, Richard John (1936–)

Theologian, author, editor, and activist, Richard John Neuhaus has been a central figure in debates about religion and American public life for more than a generation. Neuhaus's 1984 study, *The Naked Public Square*, recast the argument about the proper relationship of church and state, warned against the advance of a judicially imposed secularism in America, and assessed the new activism of evangelicals and fundamentalists in national politics. In *The Catholic Moment* (1987), Neuhaus proposed that this ought to be the time in which "the Roman Catholic Church in the United States assumes its rightful [leading] role in the culture-forming task of constructing a religiously informed public philosophy for the American experiment in ordered liberty." Neuhaus has also made important con-

Richard John Neuhaus

tributions to the dialogue between Jews and Christians in America.

A native of Pembroke, Ontario, Neuhaus was educated at Concordia Theological Seminary in St. Louis and ordained to the Lutheran ministry in 1960. From 1961 through 1978, he served as senior pastor of St. John the Evangelist Lutheran Church in the Bedford-Stuyvesant section of Brooklyn, a predominantly black and Hispanic low-income congregation. During that period he was politically active in the civil rights movement, the antiwar movement, and Democratic Party affairs. With James Forrest, he led a 1975 appeal for human rights to the government of Vietnam that split the American Left. An appointee to federal advisory bodies in both the Carter and Reagan administrations, Neuhaus combined his pastoral work at St. John's with a senior editorship

at *Worldview*, the monthly journal of the Council on Religion and International Affairs. He was also a leader, with Peter L. Berger, in the 1975 "Hartford Appeal for Theological Affirmation," an ecumenical challenge to the modernist orthodoxies then regnant in American Protestant, Catholic, and Orthodox theological circles. The Hartford Appeal and commentaries on it were later published in a volume Neuhaus coedited with Berger, *Against the World for the World* (1976). In the early 1980s Neuhaus was one of the founders of the Institute on Religion and Democracy, a Washington-based agency instrumental in alerting the country to the radical politics of the National and World Councils of Churches.

In 1984, Neuhaus became director of the Rockford Institute Center on Religion and Society in New York, which rapidly became an influential voice in the debate about religion and American public life through its newsletter (*The Religion & Society Report*), its quarterly journal (*This World*), and a series of scholarly conferences which were the source of the Encounter Series of books published by Eerdmans. In 1989, Neuhaus and his colleagues were summarily dismissed from their responsibilities and locked out of their offices by representatives of the Rockford Institute. Neuhaus then founded the Institute on Religion and Public Life in New York, which, in addition to its conferences and seminars, publishes *First Things: A Monthly Journal of Religion and Public Life*, which has quickly established itself as the premier publication in its field.

In 1990, Neuhaus was received into full communion with the Roman Catholic Church; in 1991 he was ordained to the priesthood by Cardinal John O'Connor.

Often identified (by both friends and adversaries) with fellow neoconservatives Michael Novak and George Weigel, Neuhaus has had a major formative impact on American public theology through his many books, articles, and essays, and as the personal and intellectual center of an increasingly influential network of evangelical Protestant, ecumenical Protestant, Roman Catholic, and Jewish scholars.

—GEORGE WEIGEL

Further Reading

Neuhaus, Richard John. *Appointment in Rome: The Church in America Awakening.* New York: Crossroad, 1999.

———, ed. *The Chosen People in an Almost Chosen Nation: Jews and Judaism in America.* Grand Rapids, Mich.: W. B. Eerdmans, 2002.

See also: Berger, Peter L.; First Things; *Novak, Michael;* Roman Catholicism; *Schindler, David L.; Weigel, George*

Neusner, Jacob (1932–)

An astonishingly prolific writer (at last count, the Library of Congress listed 550 titles under his name), Jacob Neusner is Research Professor of Religion and Theology at Bard College. Since the 1950s, when he earned degrees at Harvard, the Jewish Theological Seminary, and Columbia University, he has earned more than fifty honorary degrees, prizes, scholarships, and other academic awards from various institutions of higher learning for his numerous articles and several hundred books, which often focus on explicating biblical truths and relating them to life in the modern age. Much of his ever-growing literary canon comprises treatments of Mishnah, Midrash, and Talmud, as well as explorations—both fictional and historical—into the realm of Jewish-Christian dialogue and the possibilities of these two great

faiths finding common ground while recognizing a healthy respect for the traditions of each. In addition to writing myriad books, Neusner lectures widely and contributes essays to many periodicals, including *Commentary* and *Chronicles: A Magazine of American Culture.*

The energetic Neusner, called "this Niagara of Judaic teaching" by one interviewer, seeks to present and explicate Jewish wisdom literature as a fount of transferable, universal truths in a world he sees increasingly given over to specialization and ethnic Balkanization, especially within the American academy. As he told Roy Bongartz in an interview, "If all I study is private to Jews, or private to women or to blacks, then I'm not addressing the world at large. I've tried to find what is human and general in what is particular—in my case, Jewish. We're all human beings. The lessons I learn in my life can illumine your life too. Your experience can illumine my life. In universities our goal is to speak to everybody all the time, not to engage in special pleading." He also views the purpose of education to be not occupational training, but the inculcation of wisdom and virtue.

Neusner's many textbooks and works of translation, interpretation, and history include such titles as *Judaism and Christianity in the Age of Constantine: History, Messiah, Israel and the Initial Confrontation* (1987), *The Rabbi Talks with Jesus: An Intermillennial, Interfaith Exchange* (1993), and *Judaism in Modern Times: An Introduction and Reader* (1995), among many others.

—JAMES E. PERSON JR.

Further Reading

Neusner, Jacob. *The Emergence of Judaism.* Louisville, Ky.: Westminster John Knox Press, 2004.

———. *The Way of Torah: An Introduction to Judaism.* 7th ed. Belmont, Calif.: Wadsworth/Thomson, 2004.

New Criterion

A monthly review of arts and culture based in New York City, the *New Criterion* was founded in 1982 by Samuel Lipman, music critic of *Commentary*, and Hilton Kramer, formerly chief art critic at the *New York Times*. Their intention was to provide an alternative voice in the world of high-cultural criticism, in opposition to the dominance of leftist viewpoints and nihilist fads that increasingly had vexed them, and many others, since the 1960s. Modeling their new enterprise consciously on T. S. Eliot's defunct quarterly the *Criterion* (1922–39), they appealed in their first editorial to "anyone capable of recalling a time when criticism was more strictly concerned to distinguish achievement from failure, to identify and uphold a standard of quality, and to speak plainly and vigorously about the problems that beset the life of the arts and the life of the mind in our society." Hilton Kramer's name appeared as editor on the masthead of that first issue, Samuel Lipman as publisher, a state of affairs that remained constant until Lipman's death in 1994.

TNC enjoys the unusual distinction of having been denounced by the critical establishment (Carlin Romano in the *Philadelphia Inquirer*, Leon Wieseltier in the *New Republic*) even before its first issue appeared. It has continued to play the role of critical gadfly ever since, offering thoughtful, highly literate critiques of intellectual and artistic trends by a deep bench of writers of a mainly conservative inclination: which is to say, writers who do not believe that any useful, interesting, or inspiring work can be done by authors and artists who disdain, or are ignorant of, or seek to hold up to scorn, the accumulated wisdom of civilized humanity. This bench has included critics, novelists, working artists, historians, philosophers and political scientists, essayists and journalists. Since the April 1984 issue *TNC* has also published poets,

mainly those associated with the "new formalist" school and its successors.

An especially satisfying feature of *TNC* has been its unchanging appearance. Other than the introduction of poetry, only one new department has been instituted: the "Notes and Comments" section, offering editorial remarks about current events, which began in September 1989. There have been no "makeovers." The covers of the ten annual issues (TNC does not publish in July or August) remain color-coded—September is cyan, October yellow, November mauve, and so on. Surveying the first 200 issues, the author of this entry was able to discern only a single change of format: the list of contributors was broken into two columns from the September 1990 issue on. These constancies have been maintained in spite of many technical improvements in the mechanics of editing and production (and the addition of an excellent Web site), by *TNC*'s two managing editors: Erich Eichman, who served until October 1989, and his successor, Roger Kimball (now, with Kramer, coeditor of the journal). The magazine's offices, currently on Manhattan's Seventh Avenue, are a haven for civilized discourse, erudition, and wit, a bunker in the cultural wars of this age.

—John Derbyshire

Further Reading

Kramer, Hilton. *The New Criterion Reader: The First Five Years.* New York: Free Press, 1988.

———, and Roger Kimball, eds. *Against the Grain: The New Criterion on Art and Intellect at the End of the Twentieth Century.* Chicago: Ivan R. Dee, 1995.

See also: Kimball, Roger; Kramer, Hilton

New Criticism

The New Criticism is an approach to the interpretation and teaching of literature that was formulated in the United States in the 1930s and 1940s and dominated literary study in American colleges and universities in the middle of the twentieth century. The New Critics emphasized the formal structure of literary works, isolating the work from the author's personality and social influences.

The American New Critics were inspired by the critical essays of the Anglo-American poet-critic T. S. Eliot and the Cambridge don I. A. Richards. In the essays of *The Sacred Wood* (1920), especially "Tradition and the Individual Talent," Eliot stressed, in contrast to Romanticism, the aesthetic integrity of the poem and its independence from the personality of the poet. Richards likewise insisted on the self-contained structure of a poem, as opposed to its reference to the external world, and he emphasized, like Eliot, close reading of the text. Beginning in the 1930s, American academics such as Cleanth Brooks, John Crowe Ransom, Allen Tate, Robert Penn Warren, and William K. Wimsatt Jr. developed theories of literature in which the poem is treated essentially as a unified structure of conflicting meanings in tension. Hence ambiguity, irony, and paradox are the most prized qualities of great literature, which provides an imaginative knowledge of the conflicts and complexities of human experience transcending straightforward scientific rationality and empirical knowledge of material fact.

New Criticism was associated with the Agrarian branch of American conservatism from the beginning. Ransom, Tate, and Warren, for example, contributed to *I'll Take My Stand* (1930), a collection of essays produced by writers connected with the literary magazine, the *Fugitive*, in defense of the rural culture of the antebellum South against the commercial and industrial societies of the Northeast and Midwest. Moreover, Cleanth Brooks directed the doctoral dissertation of Richard Weaver at Louisiana State University in the early 1940s. Dedicated to John

Crowe Ransom, with whom Weaver had studied earlier at Vanderbilt, this dissertation would be published posthumously as *The Southern Tradition at Bay* (1968). Two of the most prominent New Critics thus enjoyed an important academic influence upon a man who would exercise an enormous influence on the postwar conservative movement in America.

The relationship between the New Criticism and conservatism is not, however, merely the result of fortuitous personal contacts. Because it stresses the formal properties of literature, the new critical approach is inherently antimaterialist. If a work of literature is to maintain an identity independent of the author who conceives it, or the reader who experiences it, or the society in which it is produced, or—in the case of drama—specific performances, then it must exist in an ideal realm transcending material causes and circumstances. The tendency of modern leftist thought, of which Marxism is the most extreme version, is to submerge the individual human being along with the creations of his mind and spirit in the relentless stream of history determined by material necessity. By defending the integrity of a work of literature as a structure of meaning apart from the unconscious psychological drives of writer or reader or the economic forces of any particular society, the New Criticism joins conservatism in affirming the creative power of human reason and imagination to resist the imperatives of our physical condition.

Some commentators have equated the New Critics' insistence on objectivity and rejection of the sentimentality of Romanticism with a quasi-scientific stance, attaching the label "positivism" to their approach to literature. To be sure, I. A. Richards was influenced by the logical positivism, or logical empiricism, of the Vienna Circle, which confines valid knowledge to empirically verifiable facts and logical propositions. Although many of the New Critics admired Richards's innovative critical methods, they were generally traditionalists on social and moral issues and regarded the imaginative representation of human experience in literature as an alternative but equally significant form of knowledge to that generated by empirical science and mathematical logic. In other words, a tragedy by Shakespeare, an ode by Keats, or a novel by Faulkner embodies a vision of reality—the reality of the human spirit—that is quite as important and objective as the knowledge of the physical universe provided by Newton, Einstein, or Watson and Crick. In their affirmation that literature furnishes knowledge of that element of mankind that cannot be explained in terms of chemistry and biology, the New Critics carried on the work of Edmund Burke, who opposed the moral imagination to the reductive rationalism of the French Revolution. Finally, if a movement may be defined by its enemies, then the New Criticism will seem conservative because the postmodern theorists who now dominate academic literary study routinely denounce the New Critics' commitment to disinterested knowledge and traditional literary values.

—R. V. YOUNG

Further Reading

Brooks, Cleanth. *The Well Wrought Urn: Studies in the Structure of Poetry*. New York: Reynal & Hitchcock, 1947.

Cowan, Louise. *The Fugitive Group: A Literary History*. Baton Rouge, La.: Louisiana State University Press, 1959.

Ransom, John Crowe. *The World's Body*. New York: Charles Scribner's Sons, 1938.

Winchell, Mark Royden. *Cleanth Brooks and the Rise of Modern Criticism*. Charlottesville, Va.: University Press of Virginia, 1996.

Tate, Allen. *Essays of Four Decades*. 3rd ed. Wilmington, Del.: ISI Books, 1999.

See also: Brooks, Cleanth; Eliot, T. S.; literary criticism; Ransom, John Crowe; Tate, Allen

New Deal

In 1932, Democratic presidential candidate Franklin Delano Roosevelt offered a "New Deal" to the American people that centered on the use of the federal government to combat the Great Depression. Because the three-year-old Depression had reached such devastating proportions (a quarter of the nation's people were unemployed) Roosevelt concluded that a new "economic bill of rights" was necessary, one that guaranteed the welfare of every American. These new rights, Roosevelt insisted, required a transformation of the very principles of American government. In addition to the guarantee of the rights to life, liberty and property, the New Deal promised that each individual may look to the central government for job security, retirement insurance, and extensive regulation of private enterprise in order to achieve economic prosperity.

Upon taking office, Roosevelt and the New Dealers, as they were called, took measures to stabilize the banking system and created a number of programs, such as the Civilian Conservation Corps and the Works Progress Administration, which put individuals to work directly. Other long-term reforms included the creation of the Federal Deposit Insurance Corporation, the National Labor Relations Board, and the Securities and Exchange Commission. The pillar of the New Deal, Social Security, was created in 1935. In Roosevelt's first two terms as president, real federal government spending almost doubled.

In addition to these immediate initiatives, the New Deal may be understood as the birth of the welfare or administrative state in America. FDR's transformation of the federal government went beyond combating the Depression. The New Deal reversed the longstanding American opposition to centralized administration. The traditional Jeffersonian view required that the central government should be empowered to undertake only those things necessary for the common good of the Union as a whole, such as national defense. Americans traditionally believed that state and local governments were better suited to handle economic regulation, which concerned primarily private and parochial interests. The New Deal, on the other hand, made the federal government the arbiter of such interests by reversing the principle of decentralized administration. This meant that the central government would now involve itself in the economic and social lives of individual Americans.

As FDR said, the "day of enlightened administration has come," which required the expansion of the executive power. This emphasis on administration set the New Dealers apart from the normally partisan process of legislation. Because of this, Roosevelt antagonized many of his fellow partisans, so much so that he attempted a "purge" of the party by running against conservative Democrats in the 1938 primaries. Though he failed in this attempt, FDR's purge signified the extent to which the ideology of the New Deal opposed the decentralized nature of the American governmental system. Conservative Democrats, like many Republicans, were hesitant about allowing the federal government to overshadow state and local governments.

This transformation of the idea of government in America is now largely complete. The New Deal legacy is still influential today, as many issues that divide the parties revolve around the same ideas that became commonplace during the 1930s. Indeed, the Great Society programs of the 1960s and the more recent reforms of health care can be understood as continuations of the New Deal, if not radicalizations of it. Though the anti-poverty programs of the 1960s are considered by many Americans to have failed, most of them continue to be funded. And although many Americans are concerned that changes may go too far, the frequent success of Democrats in attacking Republicans for relatively minor Medicare or Social Security reforms is a testament to the now conventional belief in the role of the federal government in economic and social regulation.

During the resurgence of conservatism in the 1980s, many thought President Reagan and the Republicans would eventually remove or at least reform the major institutions of the New Deal. However, real federal government spending during and after the Reagan era continued to increase. In fact, Reagan considered himself to be the heir to Roosevelt's legacy; he said that he did not leave the Democratic Party, but that the party had left him. While often decrying the welfare state, many conservatives like Reagan accept the main elements of the New Deal.

Moreover, this contradiction has represented a principal roadblock to the success of the conservative movement in America. The New Deal established a series of welfare benefits that have come to be known as *entitlements*. Widespread acceptance of the notion of entitlements is one measure of the transformation of the idea of republicanism that occurred during the New Deal. Roosevelt's concept of "enlightened administration" facilitated the belief that each individual is entitled to positive assistance from the central government. Indeed, by the end of FDR's presidency, the principal aim of the national government had come to be understood as the continual expansion of the national economy and the more equitable distribution of wealth within that economy. To the extent that conservatism today is wedded to the idea of positive central government policies to expand economic output, it is wedded to the principles of the New Deal.

On the other hand, certain recent developments have indicated at least some movement away from the New Deal view of government. In the 1990s, major reforms of the welfare system were passed. And in his campaigns for the presidency in 2000 and 2004, Republican nominee George W. Bush proposed partial privatization of Social Security. In the past, such a proposal would have been considered too politically dangerous for any serious presidential candidate. Regardless of whether such a reform occurs in the near future, Bush's ability to win both the 2000 and 2004 elections while making such a suggestion may signal an important shift away from the ideals of the New Deal.

—SCOT ZENTNER

Further Reading

Eden, Robert, ed. *The New Deal and Its Legacy: Critique and Reappraisal.* New York: Greenwood Press, 1989.

Karl, Barry. *The Uneasy State: The United States from 1915–1945.* Chicago: University of Chicago Press, 1983.

Milkis, Sidney M. *The President and the Parties: The Transformation of the American Party System since the New Deal.* New York: Oxford University Press, 1993.

See also: American Liberty League; Democratic Party; Frost, Robert; Hoover, Herbert; liberalism; neoconservatism; Old Right; paleoconservatism; progressivism; welfare state

New Humanism

The New Humanism was a movement of literary and social criticism that had its first expressions in the very late nineteenth century and reached the height of its influence in 1930. Its major leaders were Irving Babbitt, Paul Elmer More, Stuart Pratt Sherman, and Norman Foerster. The New Humanists opposed the cultural forces of romanticism and naturalism, which they saw as reinforcing influences in the twentieth century, and they sought to effect a humanistic countermovement. The Humanists were traditionalists in matters of culture and the arts and Burkean in their political orientations.

The movement was first defined by the early writings of Babbitt, a Harvard professor in the department of romance languages and literature. His first book, *Literature and the American College* (1908), collected some of these early writings, but his intellectual position found its richest illustrations in his two major books, *Rousseau and Romanticism* (1919) and *Democracy and Leadership* (1924). Babbitt was more dogmatic than his colleague More, who provided learned and subtle literary criticism for the Humanist repertoire. More was editor of the *Nation* magazine and later a professor of classical literature at Princeton. His major essays were anthologized in several volumes titled *Shelburne Essays*, published between 1904 and 1928.

The two younger individuals in the movement were both students of Babbitt at Harvard. Sherman was more eager and willing than Babbitt and More to take Humanist principles into the literary arena of his day. His major nemesis was H. L. Mencken, and the two debated each other, in lively and sometimes vitriolic prose, on the subject of contemporary literature. Sherman's essays, gathered in such collections as *On Contemporary Literature* (1917), *The Genius of America* (1923), and *Points of View* (1924), invigorated the New Humanism and gave it a wider notoriety.

Foerster's main interest was American higher education, on which all of the major Humanists expressed views. His most trenchant criticism of the American colleges appears in *The American State University* (1937). He described the colleges as victims of the materialistic and democratic forces in American life. He charged that they had forsaken their responsibility to promote high intellectual training and had succumbed to pressures to serve a large democratic constitu-ency with an indefinite array of vocational subjects. Foerster organized the effort that became the intellectual manifesto of the New Humanists, an anthology of fifteen essays titled *Humanism and America*, published in 1930. That same year, C. Hartley Grattan ed-ited a rival anti-Humanist anthology, *The Critique of Humanism*. Malcolm Cowley, Edmund Wilson, Kenneth Burke, R. P. Blackmur, Lewis Mumford, Yvor Winters, and Allen Tate were among the thirteen con-tributors.

By this time the Humanist movement had been reinforced by other younger con-tributors—Robert Shafer, Gorham Munson, and G. R. Elliott among them. They gave varied applications to Babbitt's dualistic phi-losophy but without the erudition and depth of Babbitt's own writings. T. S. Eliot, a former student of Babbitt, was also an affiliate of the Humanists.

In their often strident, negative assess-ment of American culture, the New Human-ists called for a recovery of standards in the arts and the return to what Babbitt called "first principles." In literature they invoked neoclassical ideals of universalism and looked to the arts to recover the sense of a representative human nature as the goal of creative expression. They believed that ro-mantic influences had reduced much of art to solipsistic individualism, depriving it of its communicative qualities. On the other hand, in the works of novelist Theodore Dreiser especially, they decried the natural-istic reduction of human beings to the sum-mary influences of environmental forces.

The Humanists themselves, however, revealed some interesting internal divisions. Babbitt and More were thoroughgoing crit-ics of democracy and its cultural effects. Both defended the economic interests of the prop-erty-owning classes and warned against movements of social reconstruction. Sherman, on the other hand, represented the liberal wing of the Humanists. He energeti-cally championed a literature of democracy and hailed Ralph Waldo Emerson, Walt Whitman, and Mark Twain as the bearers of a healthy democratic idealism in American letters.

On the subject of religion Babbitt and More had important disagreements. Babbitt always insisted that Humanism must stand on empirical grounds and could not appeal to supernatural faith for support. To a de-gree, his point was strategic. He believed that Humanism could not hold its own in a sci-entific-minded age if it were tied too closely to religious faith. More, however, moved in-creasingly in that direction. His book *The Sceptical Approach to Religion* (1934) was the culmination of his gradual move to Chris-tianity.

The New Humanists lost influence with the onset of the Depression in the 1930s, even though their adherents published important works well into the ensuing decade. As clas-sical conservatives they enhanced the case for tradition in an age of economic change and artistic experimentation. Babbitt and More were especially influential among later con-servative intellectuals.

—J. David Hoeveler Jr.

Further Reading

Dakin, Arthur Hazard. *Paul Elmer More.* Princeton, N.J.: Princeton University Press, 1960.

Hoeveler, J. David, Jr. *The New Humanism: A Cri-tique of Modern America, 1900–1940.* Charlottesville, Va.: University Press of Vir-ginia, 1977.

Nevin, Thomas R. *Irving Babbitt: An Intellectual Study.* Chapel Hill, N.C.: University of North Carolina Press, 1984.

See also: Babbitt, Irving; Bookman; Eliot, T. S.; More, Paul Elmer

Newman, John Henry (1801–90)

John Henry Newman came to prominence as a leader of the Oxford Movement, whose raison d'être was to defend the Church of England against the growing danger posed by religious liberalism. The movement began at Oxford University following John Keble's 1833 "national apostasy" sermon against the Whig disestablishment of the Anglican Church in Ireland. Like Keble, Newman saw Christian orthodoxy threatened by "latitudinarianism, indifferentism, and schism, a spirit which tends to overthrow doctrine, as if the fruit of bigotry and discipline."

Newman was no party man. Yet his political debt to Burke can be seen in his warnings against "dangerous innovations." In matters of intellectual debate, "[a]bstract argument is always dangerous." "I prefer to go by facts," wrote Newman

John Henry Newman

in *A Grammar of Assent* (1870). Here, Newman defends religious knowing by comparing what he called the "illative sense" with common sense in precisely the same way as Burke described "prejudice." He abandoned his sympathy for Toryism following the rise of religious pluralism, a practical recognition that the theory that protected Anglican privileges "came to pieces and went the way of all flesh." His study of doctrinal development contributed to his 1845 conversion to Catholicism. Newman discovered that a really living system like the Catholic Church changes in response to changing conditions. As circumstances change "old principles reappear under new forms." This dynamic conservatism made the Catholic Church, in his opinion, the only effective guardian of traditional values.

His opposition to what Christopher Dawson called "progressive secularism" was also directed against rationalist advances in public life. The Tamworth Reading Room, established in 1841 by the radical utilitarian Lord Brougham and the Conservative Party leader Sir Robert Peel, was an instance of liberal benevolence that, by design, excluded religion. The purpose of the institution was to promote "useful knowledge" for the moral improvement and social advancement of the emergent political classes. But how does one advance morally without religion? Newman opposed "a state of society such as ours, in which authority, prescription, tradition, habit, moral instinct, and the divine influences go for nothing."

From the time of the Reform Bill of 1832, Newman opposed popular sovereignty. His 1837 article on the papal condemnation of Abbé de Lamennais revealed an early belief in the sinfulness of agitating for political rights. As late as 1885, Newman writes in frustration at the British prime minister's renewed campaign to broaden the franchise: "What a dreadful thing this democracy is! How I wish Gladstone had retired into private life. . . ." This opposition to democracy was largely a pragmatic belief that ignorance should not direct public affairs.

His work with the Catholic University in Ireland was motivated by "the wish . . . to strengthen the defences . . . of the Christian religion." Newman's *Idea of a University* (1858) is a classic defense of the liberal arts. A true university will encourage the study of both science and religion since they are compatible. "I want the intellectual layman to be religious, and the devout ecclesiastic to be intellectual." Newman's educational model came from Oxford and from the vibrant intellectual life of medieval Europe, when religious authority had been decentralized.

Just as he opposed clericalism in Catholic higher education, he championed the independent spirit of the English people, who believe "a government is their natural foe; they cannot do without it altogether, but they will have of it as little as they can. They will forbid the centralization of power. . . . [A] free people will maim and cripple their government lest it should tyrannize." Newman wrote this in 1854 in a series of letters entitled "Who's to Blame?" about the disasters suffered by the English in the Crimean War. His most explicit political statement was in essence a Burkean defense of the British constitution that favored a strong nation but a weak state.

Peter Viereck and Robert Nisbet have acknowledged Newman's rightful place in the conservative pantheon, while the young Garry Wills wrote favorable pieces in the early numbers of *National Review*. But perhaps the only notable man of the Right in America to have written at length about Newman is Russell Kirk, most especially in *The Conservative Mind* (1953). This neglect is unfortunate since Newman left to posterity his university lectures to help prepare a lasting defense of Christian civilization against the bigotry and ignorance of modern liberal ideology. Alasdair MacIntyre sees Newman as "a far more important theorist of tradition" than Burke precisely because the former knew that healthy traditions contain within themselves a vibrancy prepared to meet rising dangers by adopting powerful new methods and arguments while casting off old strategies inadequate to the task.

The reasons for the failure of American conservatives to better appreciate Newman can easily be surmised. A public intellectual who had no party affiliation is hard to categorize, unlike a Coleridge or a Disraeli. A churchman who is known for equating the Protestantism of his day with the heresies of the early Church, despite employing powerful conservative arguments to bolster his case, will not likely attract interest from right-wing evangelicals. Newman's Christian apologetics present an obstacle to nonreligious conservatives who have secular mentors of their own to admire and emulate. Newman's classical liberalism is often misconstrued as twentieth-century liberalism by progressive Catholics who seek to advance their agendas in his name. Ironically, the elder Garry Wills is guilty of this, and conservative observers who don't know Newman have little reason to object to the co-optation.

—John M. Vella

Further Reading

Newman, John Henry. *Apologia pro Vita Sua*. Edited by Martin J. Svaglic. Oxford: Clarendon Press, 1967.

MacDougall, Hugh A. *The Acton-Newman Relations: The Dilemma of Christian Liberalism*. New York: Fordham University Press, 1962.

Norman, Edward. "Newman's Social and Political Thinking." In *Newman After a Hundred Years*, edited by Ian Ker and Alan G. Hill. New York: Oxford University Press, 1990.

See also: Conservative Mind, The; *Roman Catholicism; tradition*

New Right

The "New Right" is a name that has been given to three discrete occurrences. In the 1950s the term was used to identify the band of conservatives who broke from the old right of the years before World War II and gathered around William F. Buckley, Jr. and his magazine, *National Review*. In the 1980s the term was applied to a pro-Reagan coalition of libertarian economic conservatives (who formed the traditional core of the Republican Party) and social conservatives (many of whom had been lifelong Democrats). Later, the term was also applied more specifically to people who took a stand for traditional values and against moral decay and the decline of the family.

The Old Right of the 1930s had opposed both the New Deal and intervention in foreign wars. The new right of the 1950s, however, supported a policy of anticommunism abroad even as it also favored a comparatively unregulated form of free enterprise at home. By accepting the need for a big government to oppose communism, the New Right drifted away from policies that had been central to the Old Right. The New Right also had a distinctive style, with the *National Review* evincing a brash assertiveness that some older conservatives considered sophomoric. And the New Right set limits by condemning both anti-Semitism and the John Birch Society.

Within the New Right, there was an important division. On one side were the classic libertarian individualists who insisted that people should enjoy the maximum amount of personal freedom with little government intervention. On the other were traditionalists who believed in a transcendent moral order and emphasized the importance of the Judeo-Christian heritage. Yet Buckley and the *National Review* managed to patch over the difference and to persuade libertarians and traditionalists to join together in opposition to communism.

This coalition remained a minority group until the 1970s, when a new New Right emerged. This new new right was made up of social conservatives, many of whom had been Democrats in the past. Some resented high taxes after having only recently achieved middle-class status. Others took exception to the reverse racial preferences that had come to characterize the liberal left. Still others were disaffected from their traditional Democratic moorings because of concern about crime, divorce, pornography, and other changes in the culture.

Ronald Reagan recognized the opportunity to build a Republican majority. In a 1977 speech to the American Conservative Union, he explained that he wanted to maintain the support of the Republican base by continuing to favor lower taxes and less government regulation of business. But he also wanted to use "the so-called social issues—law and order, abortion, busing, [and] quota systems" to appeal to millions of other Americans "who may never have thought of joining our party before." His goal was "to combine the two major segments of contemporary American conservatism into one politically effective whole." This was the new New Right of the 1980s.

Yet electoral victories were of little use against social policies that resulted from changing mores and from new judicial interpretations. Consequently, social conservatives were disappointed even after Reagan triumphed at the polls. For them conservatism had been a three-pronged attack against too many government regulations at home, against communism abroad, and against the counterculture. But Reagan achieved only two of the goals. Business was deregulated and the Soviet Union disintegrated, but abortion, promiscuity, pornography, and trashy music seemed even more prevalent after Reagan's presidency. Consequently, at the turn of the twenty-first century, many social conservatives were engaged in a new "culture war."

—RAYMOND WOLTERS

Further Reading

Hodgson, Godfrey. *The World Turned Right Side Up: A History of the Conservative Ascendancy in America.* Boston: Houghton Mifflin, 1996.

Judis, John. *William F. Buckley Jr.: Patron Saint of the Conservatives.* New York: Simon & Schuster, 1988.

Phillips, Kevin. *The Emerging Republican Majority.*

New Rochelle, N.Y.: Arlington House, 1969.
Rusher, William A. *The Rise of the Right*. New York:
William Morrow, 1984.

See also: Blackwell, Morton; National Review; *Republican Party*

New Science of Politics, The

The New Science of Politics comprises the Walgreen Lectures Eric Voegelin delivered in Chicago in 1951 under the title "Truth and Representation." The book, published in 1952, has ever since exerted enormous influence on the orientation and theoretical development of conservative political thought, not only because it is among the most concise and accessible of Voegelin's works, but also because it sketches a compelling account of the historical forces behind the rise of modern totalitarianism.

The New Science of Politics outlines a new—or rather, "restored"—concept of political science and further achieves a theoretical assessment of modernity. At present, Voegelin says, as a result of positivism "the consciousness of principles" of politics "is lost," and the principles "must be regained by a work of theoretization which starts from the concrete, historical situation of the age." Positivism's destructive effects are traced by Voegelin to (a) the assumption that the mathematizing method of the natural sciences should also be the model for the sciences of man, and (b) the assumption that the method of the natural sciences provides "the criterion of theoretical relevance in general." Hence "metaphysical questions which do not admit of answers by the methods of the sciences of phenomena are not to be asked," and "realms of being which are not accessible to exploration by the model methods" are considered "irrelevant," and, at the extreme, nonexistent. The subordination of theoretical relevance to method "perverts the

meaning of science on principle" since logically "all facts are equal . . . if they are methodically ascertained." Even more destructive, claims Voegelin, has been the "operation on relevant materials under defective theoretical principles." Thus Voegelin treats in detail the problem of a science of man that rigorously excludes all value-judgments and of a "rationalism which relegated religion and metaphysics into the realm of the 'irrational.'"

In his book, Voegelin enumerated several reforms necessary to restore political theory successfully:

> The understanding of ontology as well as the craftsmanship of metaphysical speculation had to be regained, and especially philosophical anthropology as a science had to be re-established. By the standards thus regained it was possible to define with precision the technical points of irrationality in the positivistic position. . . . Positivistic thinking had to be determined as a variant of theologizing (which) diagnosis could be conducted successfully only if a general theory of religious phenomena was sufficiently elaborated to allow the subsumption of the concrete case under a type.

In turn, this project required a return to Greek and medieval philosophy and an understanding of the difference between them. The "final task had to be faced of searching for a theoretically intelligible order of history into which these variegated phenomena could be organized."

Voegelin's analysis of the problem of representation moves beyond "elemental" (i.e., merely descriptive) representation, to "existential" representation centering on the meaning of society's existence, and finally to the problem of representing "truth." While "societies as representatives of truth . . .

actually occur in history," says Voegelin, for Socrates, Plato, and Aristotle "a truth represented by the theorist was opposed to another truth represented by society. It is "the truth to the soul . . . to be defined in terms of certain experiences which have become predominant to the point of forming a character." Man experiences himself "as open toward transcendental reality," hence "the truth of man and the truth of God are inseparably one." Plato and Aristotle developed the standard "of the man who can be the measure of society because God is the measure of his soul."

Modernity is held by Voegelin to consist in a process of "re-divinization" of the temporal sphere of power after Christianity had brought about its "de-divinization." This process began in the Middle Ages, with the "three ages" of Joachim of Fiore (d. 1202), from which this notion moved through the period of Enlightenment to twentieth-century communism and Nazism. The result of this process was a radically de-Christianized "immanent fulfillment" of history that Voegelin calls "a theoretical fallacy." "Secularization," then, consists of the attempt "to bring our knowledge of transcendence into a firmer grip than the Christian faith will afford." Thus, the seventeenth-century English Puritans are theoretically analyzed by Voegelin as Gnostics. Modern "Gnosticism . . . most effectively released human forces for the building of a civilization because on their fervent application to intramundane activity was put the premium of salvation." Thus, Voegelin concludes that "the essence of modernity [is] the growth of Gnosticism." The two chief dangers of this situation are "the destruction of the truth of the soul" and a false picture of reality that amounts to the creation of "a dream world." Ultimately, modern totalitarianism turns out to be "the journey's end of the Gnostic search for a civil theology."

—WILLIAM LUCKEY

Further Reading

Federici, Michael P. *Eric Voegelin: The Restoration of Order*. Wilmington, Del.: ISI Books, 2002.

McAllister, Ted V. *Revolt against Modernity: Leo Strauss, Eric Voegelin, and the Search for a Postliberal Order*. Lawrence, Kan.: University Press of Kansas, 1996.

Voegelin, Eric. *Science, Politics and Gnosticism*. 3rd ed. Wilmington, Del.: ISI Books, 2004.

See also: community; Gnosticism; Puritanism; Voegelin, Eric

New Urbanism

When Andrés Duany and his wife Elizabeth Plater-Zyberk designed the Florida Panhandle town of Seaside, the first of what have come to be called New Urbanist developments, they aspired to capture the charm of the old Southern communities along the Gulf of Mexico. But that was back in the early 1980s. Since then, the reasons New Urbanists cite for recovering the pedestrian scale and sense of architectural amenity and spatial enclosure imparted by streets in older American neighborhoods and downtowns have gone far beyond esthetics. Too far, many conservatives and libertarians would be inclined to think.

In resorting to historic precedents in laying out new neighborhoods and towns and redeveloping core-city districts, Duany, Plater-Zyberk, and their cohorts have restored an artistic dimension to American urbanism, which has been very seriously undermined by modernist and functionalist tendencies—especially the modernist planning mantra of single-use zoning—since the 1930s. This is a major cultural achievement which has won the admiration of many conservatives, but at this writing it would be impossible to venture even a guess as to how extensive its ramifications for America's built environment might be.

Planners' renunciation of big cities' traditional complexity—their fine-grained diversity of uses—for the "sorting out" of buildings and classes of people into self-contained precincts was denounced decades ago by Jane Jacobs, whose *Death and Life of Great American Cities* (1961) has exerted an enormous influence on the New Urbanists. Indeed, this same sorting-out syndrome, calibrated to the scale of the automobile, underlies what Duany and Plater-Zyberk call the "artificial simplicity" of low-density suburban development, or "sprawl," with its spatially segregated residential subdivisions, office parks, and strip malls. These precincts, in turn, are linked not by thoroughfares amenable to the pedestrian, but by what the two New Urbanist pioneers qualify as "traffic sewers." New Urbanists also object to the social stratification fostered by the residential pod and its homogenous abodes.

The New Urbanist antidote to sprawl is the pedestrian-scale, mixed-use neighborhood, where every resident lives within five minutes' walking distance of a public square or green with a civic building and transit stop. This is their fundamental module for urbanism, whether at the scale of village, town, or city. Different residential types—single-family, townhouse, and apartments—are located in close proximity to one another. Easy access to public transportation, which can serve only more compact neighborhoods efficiently, is provided as a boon to those too old, too young, or too poor to drive, or to those averse to doing so. Corner stores, live/work units, shops and offices with rental apartments overhead, granny flats that can house either tenants whose rent payments help home-buyers meet their mortgages or elderly in-laws who would prefer not to live in retirement homes—are all part of the New Urbanist neighborhood blueprint. The problem is that this functionally and socially complex blueprint, derived from American communities antedating the Depression, is banned under conventional postwar zoning codes.

There is much more to sprawl, however, than the planning regime largely created by the Federal Housing Administration since the 1930s and the vast federal mortgage and highway construction subsidies that are geared to it. Sprawl reflects deeply ingrained cultural preferences as well as the centrifugal ramifications of new technologies ranging from the train, subway, and automobile to the Internet. All indications are that low density urbanization will continue for a long time to come. Opinion polls, however, indicate widespread dissatisfaction with suburbia among its denizens. On the other hand, the Congress for the New Urbanism (CNU) claims a total of some 400 projects—both "greenfield" developments and "infill" projects in areas already urbanized—as conforming to the movement's architectural, functional, and social guidelines. There are many more ersatz New Urbanist developments, including gated communities excluded from the official roster, but the fact remains that all this amounts to a drop in the bucket, as Duany has been the first to admit, compared with the "million new tract houses a year."

One major problem, as the CNU notes, is that American builders have become overly specialized under the single-use-zoning regime, with one builder accustomed to erecting enfilades of single-family residences in precincts restricted to this housing type, while another erects rowhouses, another condominiums, and still others shopping malls and office parks in precincts zoned exclusively for those uses. Under these circumstances, functionally and esthetically integrated places like Kentlands, a town Duany and Plater-Zyberk designed in Montgomery County, Maryland, are in short supply and all the more expensive as a result.

Politically, the New Urbanism does not exist in a vacuum. It is broadly allied with the "smart growth" movement, which also includes planners, historic preservationists, environmentalists, and public-transit advocates. This anti-sprawl movement opposes new highway construction and seeks to impose growth boundaries and conserve open space. It emphasizes "infill" development in order to increase population densities and facilitate the use of public transportation. Along with smart-growth advocates, New Urbanists support a top-down social and political agenda involving the creation of regional governments to distribute economic assets and social responsibilities among central cities and surrounding jurisdictions, along with the reorientation of federal transportation subsidies toward public transit and "transit-oriented" real-estate development—and especially toward light rail systems academic researchers regard as exorbitantly expensive, inefficient, and inflexible.

Based on their track record to date, moreover, the notion that regional governments will necessarily advance the New Urbanist or smart-growth agenda is dubious. Indeed, the argument for regional government is based largely on a zero-sum interpretation of the competition between cities and suburbs that is possibly simplistic. What is more, New Urbanists' apparent indifference to the constitutional principle of keeping governmental authority as close to home as possible—despite their assertion that federal policies' net impact on American urbanism and the American landscape has been overwhelmingly negative—has sometimes been interpreted by conservatives and libertarians alike as a token of arrogance.

The environmental and socioeconomic alarums Duany and Plater-Zyberk sound in their denunciation of sprawl in their book, *Suburban Nation*, the most important statement of the New Urbanist design philosophy to date, are unconvincing precisely because the authors fail to take serious account of opposing arguments. They advocate an urbanism based on a Western European model geared to trolleys, subways, and commuter trains without acknowledging the fact that that model is giving way to dramatically increased automobile ownership. Their distaste for "diesel-belching" buses—the most flexible and efficient form of public transit—seems cavalier. And their polemic against the car, which takes after that of Jane Holtz Kay, architectural critic for the *Nation*, at times assumes the tone of a cultural crusade rather than a sensible plea for striking a better balance between the amenities afforded the driver, on the one hand, and pedestrians on the other. This is something the New Urbanism has in fact achieved, on a modest scale.

But in discarding merely quantitative planning and zoning restrictions in favor of three-dimensional design akin to that employed in a wide variety of historic urban settings—in Francis Nicholson's Williamsburg, for instance, as in Baron Haussmann's Paris—the New Urbanists have raised the possibility that good design, and cultural memory, will once again become relevant to America's built environment on the broad scale. They also have restored a vital element of idealism to American design, while giving a major boost to traditional architectural practice. The socioeconomic ramifications of their approach to designing neighborhoods and communities, however, are likely to be far less significant than New Urbanists would care to think. Their ideas will largely manifest themselves for the time being as isolated patches of traditional urban fabric. Such patches will quite possibly proliferate as an inflexible and bureaucratic land-use regime becomes the brunt of increasingly widespread dissatisfaction in municipalities and counties across the land. Only time will tell whether such a phenomenon could culminate in an at least partial restoration of the traditional hierarchy of city, town, village, landscape, and wilderness in the United States.

—CATESBY LEIGH

Further Reading

Duany, Andrés, Elizabeth Plater-Zyberk, and Jeff Speck. *Suburban Nation: The Rise of Sprawl and the Decline of the American Dream.* New York: North Point Press, 2000.

Kunstler, James Howard. *The Geography of Nowhere: The Rise and Decline of America's Man-Made Landscape.* New York: Simon & Schuster, 1993.

See also: environmentalism; historic preservation; Jacobs, Jane

Niebuhr, Reinhold (1892–1971)

An American theologian, Reinhold Niebuhr would protest his inclusion in an encyclopedia of conservatism. And indeed, a man active in liberal causes and organizations throughout his career would seem an unlikely candidate for these pages. Yet a case can be made for his presence. Though Niebuhr disdained the Right, his critique of liberalism echoed characteristic themes of twentieth-century American conservatism; and such important present-day conservatives as Michael Novak and Richard John Neuhaus count him an indispensable influence.

Reinhold Niebuhr

Niebuhr's work partook of the neo-orthodox theological mood arising in continental Europe after the First World War. For Niebuhr, the turn to neoorthodoxy was the fruit of disillusionment with the banal triumphalism of liberalism, progressivism, and the Social Gospel. It drew upon his theological heritage as a Missouri-born German-American brought up in the Evangelical Synod of North America. German (and Lutheran) affinities led him to reject the moralistic progressivism of Woodrow Wilson; and a pastorate in the Detroit area radicalized him on labor-capital issues. His *Moral Man and Immoral Society* (1932), drawing upon Marx and Beard, charged that the comfortable middle-class morality of Deweyan liberals could not address the need for radical social change.

During his many years as a professor of "applied Christianity" on the faculty of Union Theological Seminary, which he joined in 1928, and as editor of the journal *Christianity and Crisis*, which he founded in 1941, that combative position coalesced into a nuanced "Christian realism" that insisted simultaneously upon the imperative of social action and the fallenness of human nature. Although more liberal than conservative in his theology, Niebuhr nevertheless asserted that the tenets of orthodox biblical Christianity—especially the doctrines of original sin and the utter irredeemability of this world, short of the coming Kingdom of God, which transcends and stands in judgment over it—offered the truest understanding of the world and of human nature. Niebuhr was equally insistent that Christians behave like liberals, committing their lives in love to the redemption of an irredeemable world. Yet they needed to realize that this struggle does not offer easy choices between pure good and pure evil, but rather heartbreaking choices between greater and lesser evils, which inevitably enmesh them further in the webs of sin.

This hard paradox was evident in Niebuhr's tough-minded view of the Cold War. In *The Irony of American History* (1952), Niebuhr argued that the choice between the

United States and the Soviet Union was of epochal importance. Yet he also insisted that America not prosecute the Cold War in a spirit of crusading self-righteousness. Americans' belief in their moral superiority had been the chief source of their moral weakness, and American civilization, Niebuhr argued, was only marginally better than that of its enemies; both were mired in materialism, moral complacency, and structural injustice. The only solution was an awareness of sin, and constant repentance for it, before a transcendent God who stands above and apart from all human causes and cultures.

—WILFRED M. MCCLAY

Further Reading

Brown, Charles C. *Niebuhr and His Age: Reinhold Niebuhr's Prophetic Role in the Twentieth Century.* Philadelphia: Trinity Press International, 1992.

Brown, Robert McAfee, ed. *The Essential Reinhold Niebuhr: Selected Essays and Addresses.* New Haven, Conn.: Yale University Press, 1987.

Fox, Richard W. *Reinhold Niebuhr: A Biography.* New York: Pantheon, 1986.

Kegley, D. W. and R. W. Bretall, eds. *Reinhold Niebuhr: His Religious, Social, and Political Thought.* New York: Harper & Row, 1956.

See also: liberalism; neoconservatism; Protestantism, mainline

Niemeyer, Gerhart (1907–97)

One of the foremost conservative political theorists of the twentieth century, the German-born Gerhart Niemeyer studied at Cambridge and Munich before earning a doctor of laws from the University of Kiel with a dissertation on international law. He left Germany for Spain after Hitler's rise to power in 1933, and after the Spanish Civil War broke out in 1936 he immigrated to the United States, where he published his first American book in 1941, *Law without Force*, which was received as a prominent work on international law. Niemeyer taught at a number of schools, including Princeton, Yale, Oglethorpe, Vanderbilt, Hillsdale, the National War College, the University of Munich, and for more than thirty years at the University of Notre Dame.

Much of Niemeyer's work is concerned with communist ideology, on which he was long acknowledged as a leading authority. He published *An Inquiry into Soviet Mentality* in 1956, and in 1958 he and I. M. Bochenski collaborated on *The Handbook on Communism* (published in English in 1962). The House Committee on Un-American Activities commissioned *Facts on Communism, Vol. I: The Communist Ideology* in 1959 and Niemeyer also wrote *Communists in Coalition Governments* (1963) for the American Enterprise Institute. In 1971 he published another study of communism, *Deceitful Peace*, and an analysis of the ideological total critique of society in *Between Nothingness and Paradise.*

In addition to his writings specifically devoted to communist ideology, Niemeyer wrote also on classical and modern political theory, foreign policy, public policy, Christianity, the relation between faith and philosophy, the philosophy of history, literature, teaching and the meaning of true education, Aleksandr Solzhenitsyn, and the thought of Eric Voegelin. One of the central themes of all of Niemeyer's writing and teaching is the striving for intellectual and spiritual fulfillment through critical inquiry into the nature of order, the roots of disorder and alienation, and the way back to order. His work is particularly concerned with preserving a living sense of the Western Christian tradition because in his view what is preserved in that tradition is essential to our understanding of our humanity. To Niemeyer human beings are participants in a whole that we cannot fully understand, but the good life requires that we constantly seek to improve our understanding of order and Being.

On these and related themes he published more than one hundred articles and reviews in a variety of periodicals, including the *Center Journal*, the *Intercollegiate Review*, *Modern Age*, *National Review*, the *Review of Politics*, *Orbis*, and several other journals, as well as a number of essays for books, such as the *festschrift* for Eric Voegelin titled *The Philosophy of Order: Essays on History Consciousness and Politics* (1981) and *Marx and the Western World* (1967), among others. A representative selection of Niemeyer's essays, *Aftersight and Foresight*, was published in 1988 by the Intercollegiate Studies Institute (ISI). *The Good Man in Society* (1989), a collection of essays in Niemeyer's honor also published by ISI, contains a complete bibliography of his writings up to 1986.

—MICHAEL HENRY

Further Reading

Niemeyer, Gerhart. *Within and Above Ourselves: Essays of Political Analsysis.* Wilmington, Del.: Intercollegiate Studies Institute, 1996.

See also: anticommunism; émigré intellectuals; ideology

nihilism

Nihilism is a term around which orbits a body of beliefs, all connoting the rejection of traditional religious faiths, moral principles, and political arrangements. Derived from the Latin *nihil* (nothing), it has been used in English at least since 1817. At base it is the belief in nothing, as opposed to the absence of belief.

In metaphysics, nihilism is an extreme form of skepticism that denies existence. It can be traced to the ancient Greek sophist, Gorgias, who held that nothing exists; but even if something existed, it would be unknowable; and even if it were knowable, it could not be communicated. In ethics, nihilism is associated with the Marquis de Sade and Friedrich Nietzsche and involves the repudiation of all norms derived from divine revelation, classical philosophy, and social custom. Virtuous behavior for Nietzsche's *Übermensch* or superman is not to obey received mores of natural law, but to "will his own desire as a law for himself."

In nineteenth-century politics, nihilism became associated with the radical Russian intelligentsia who, during the 1860s and 1870s, denied all authority over the individual but affirmed terrorism to promote science, materialism, and revolutionary change in behalf of "the People," abstractly conceived. Perhaps the most celebrated nihilist is a fictional character, Bazarov in Turgenev's *Fathers and Sons* (1862). Although repudiated by his creator, Bazarov became a paragon for a whole generation of radicals. The character was probably modeled on the Russian literary critic V. G. Belinsky (1811–48), who was noted for the enthusiasm with which he defended his frequently changing convictions.

In twentieth-century politics, nihilism is associated with fascist and Nazi doctrines, especially since the latter are linked to aspects of Nietzsche's thought.

Many Americans on the Right assume that nihilism is a European export, foreign to their country's values, institutions, and traditions. In a sense this assumption is true. But conservative denunciations of nihilism are not restricted to the left-wing disciples of Nietzsche, Bazarov, and the Marquis de Sade. Nihilism is a protean concept, adaptable to changing historical contexts. Within conservative discourse, the idea is used to assail radical apologies for modern, capitalistic political economies. The nihilistic implications behind Ayn Rand's Objectivism, for example, have long been criticized in such conservative journals as *National Review* and the *Intercollegiate Review*.

Irving Kristol has written one of the most frequently cited conservative critiques of nihilism. One aim of his *Two Cheers for Capitalism* (1978) was to expose the apparent inability of libertarianism to oppose nihilism in principle. Kristol called attention to the fact that modern liberal democracies are rational and secular to a hitherto unprecedented degree. "Modern, liberal, secular society," he noted, "is based on the revolutionary premise that there is no superior, authoritative information available about the good life or the true nature of human happiness [worked out, for instance, by Aristotle and Thomas Aquinas], that this information is implicit only in individual preferences, and that therefore the individual has to be free to develop and express these preferences" in the marketplace. Unfortunately, in the marketplace just about anything goes if it sells—including, ironically, those books and magazines, recordings and television shows that are subversive to the very idea of ordered freedom. Kristol believed that most libertarians—even those of the caliber of Friedrich von Hayek and Milton Friedman—had not sufficiently answered the nihilistic challenge in the unregulated marketplace.

Also, libertarianism's silence in the face of secularization renders it impotent to oppose nihilism. Modern liberal democracies are increasingly neutral in matters of religion. The widespread disestablishment of religion in the West, asserted Kristol, has probably contributed to "a diminution of religious faith and a growing skepticism about the traditional consolations of religion." Ironically, once the religious spirit is weakened—especially where that spirit is characterized by the Puritan or Protestant ethos—such esteemed values as honesty, sobriety, diligence, and thrift begin to wane in the marketplace.

Ultimately, however, the secularization of modern life has given rise to "the blithe and mindless self-destruction of bourgeois society which we are witnessing today." The real enemy of liberal capitalistic societies, wrote Kristol, is not socialism but nihilism: "Only liberal capitalism doesn't see nihilism as an enemy, but rather as just another splendid business opportunity." That is the challenge, according to Kristol, to which most Austrian economists and committed libertarians have "no answer." Since few apologists for libertarianism have responded satisfactorily to the dangers of nihilism in the marketplace, Kristol is willing to give only "two cheers" for capitalism.

While some conservative discourse has been directed at the nihilistic implications of the secularized free market, most has been focused on the decadence of post-1968 American culture. Here the religious Right has been especially vocal. Among Catholics a landmark essay on nihilism is Michael Novak's *The Experience of Nothingness* (1970), which sharply critiques the widespread debasement of meaning and value in American culture. The cinema, television, and music industry have been virtual midwives to nihilistic sentiments. As a result, argues Novak, America "is a civilization of massive dissolution." Among Protestants, books such as Jerry Falwell's *Listen, America!* (1980) and Charles Colson's *The Struggle for Men's Hearts and Minds* (1986) and *Against the Night* (1989) have also assailed the nihilistic currents in contemporary American morals and manners.

Finally, it should be pointed out that the Right has been influenced by a number of culture critics who, while themselves not "movement conservatives," have written penetrating critiques of American culture. Works like Aleksandr Solzhenitsyn's *A World Split Apart* (1978), Allan Bloom's *The Closing of the American Mind* (1987), Jacques Barzun's *The Culture We Deserve* (1989), and John Silber's *Straight Shooting* (1989), among others, have stimulated conservative responses to spiritual malaise, decadent culture, and the mass media. Anymore, the proselytes of nihilism do not have to be imported from Europe; they are home grown. Bloom noted, for example, that filmmaker "Woody Allen helps to make us feel comfortable with nihilism, to Americanize it."

—GLEAVES WHITNEY

Further Reading

Cunningham, Conor. *A Genealogy of Nihilism: Philosophies of Nothing and the Difference of Theology*. New York: Routledge, 2002.

Hibbs, Thomas S. *Shows about Nothing: Nihilism in Popular Culture from* The Exorcist *to* Seinfeld. Dallas: Spence Publishing, 1999.

Rosen, Stanley. *Nihilism: A Philosophical Essay*. 2nd ed. South Bend, Ind.: St. Augustine's Press, 2000.

See also: Bloom, Allan; Jaffa, Harry V.; Kristol, Irving; libertarianism; Novak, Michael; Solzhenitsyn, Aleksandr

Nisbet, Robert A. (1913–96)

The author of multiple works on social theory, the history of sociology, and social commentary, Robert Alexander Nisbet might be best remembered for *The Quest for Community* (1953), *The Sociological Tradition* (1966), and *The Social Bond: Introduction to the Study of Society* (1970), all books long assigned as college texts. Notwithstanding his unmistakable defense of hierarchical societies, Nisbet had his work recommended and read by those on the opposite side of the political divide. His literary skills and obvious learning both account for this success, as does his unmistakably utilitarian approach to social institutions.

Though Nisbet did recognize religious mystery as an integral part of its foundation, he also defended social authority from a secular perspective, viz., as necessary for civilized life and human stability. While a conservative Republican in his politics, despite his early enthusiasm for the New Deal, Nisbet tried to distance himself from both libertarians and the religious Right. He criticized the former for its abstract, atomistic view of society and the latter for its eagerness to enlist the state for its moral work. Between *Prejudices: A Philosophical Dictionary* (1982) and *The Present Age* (1988), Nisbet moved from at least provisional agreement with neoconservatives on policy issues back into closer accord with an older tradition of American conservatism. Throughout his career he underlined the need for a multiplicity of local, social groups as the natural realm of human action and as a bulwark against the centralized, unitary state of the twentieth century.

After a distinguished academic career at the University of California-Riverside in his native California, Nisbet went to Columbia University as Albert Schweitzer Professor of the Humanities. Among other accolades he was a recipient of the Ingersoll Prize (1985) and in 1988 the Jefferson Day lectureship of the National Endowment for the Humanities. Nisbet was also a senior fellow of the American Enterprise Institute, and with his wife Caroline he resided in Washington, where he spent his time studying in "self-imposed isolation from political intrigue." His highest achievement may have been his works on social theory, which continue to be widely read and which document the conservative origins of nineteenth-century sociology. Sociologists, observed Nisbet, once set

Robert Nisbet

out to demonstrate the truth of Aristotle's axiom that man is a social being. Ironically, he also noted, a discipline once identified with Aristotle's view about the value of custom and inherited order has been dragged into a war against social authority.

A major theme of Nisbet's work, one that extends from *The Quest for Community* to *The Present Age* (1988), is the social impact of the "centralized territorial state." Since the Middle Ages but particularly in the modern era, this "leviathan" has altered social relations and weakened the "intermediate institutions" that had once marked and enriched European civilization. Although Nisbet was not blind to the faults of the Middle Ages, he also viewed them as a period in which social and cultural life developed communally, without the steady interference of public administration. Like his mentor Alexis de Tocqueville, Nisbet did not deny that democracies sought universal justice on the basis of equality, nor did he think this an ideal to be entirely spurned. But when this goal was relentlessly pursued in alliance with state power, the result, both Nisbet and Tocqueville warned, would likely be Jacobin totalitarianism. Moreover, as *The Quest for Community* makes clear, the weakening of family and community in the modern West has created a sense of alienation that further serves the interests of the unitary state. The reintegration of uprooted individuals into reconstructed communities now takes place under political or administrative auspices. While the quest for community is both natural and understandable, Nisbet feared that it is also an invitation to the state to extend its control and to smother what remains of autonomous social institutions.

—PAUL GOTTFRIED

Further Reading

Nisbet, Robert A. *Conservatism: Dream and Reality.* 2nd ed. New Brunswick, N.J.: Transaction, 2002.

———. *History of the Idea of Progress.* 2nd ed. New Brunswick, N.J.: Transaction, 1994.
Stone, Brad Lowell. *Robert Nisbet: Communitarian Traditionalist.* Wilmington, Del.: ISI Books, 2000.

See also: community; individualism; progress; Quest for Community, The

Nixon, Richard M. (1913–94)

Thirty-seventh president of the United States (1969–74), after serving in the House (1947–51) and Senate (1951–53), and as vice president for eight years under Dwight Eisenhower (1953–61), Richard Nixon distinguished himself in the House and Senate as an outspoken anticommunist. He was largely responsible for building the case against the former state department official Alger Hiss, a case that culminated in Hiss's perjury conviction in 1950. Nixon's persistence in investigating Hiss's concealment of his longtime communist associations when testifying before the House Un-American Activities Committee brought Nixon to the attention of conservatives. So, too, did his befriending of the conservative intellectual Whittaker Chambers, who played a decisive and controversial role in exposing Hiss.

While Nixon identified himself on most domestic issues with mainstream Republicans, he enjoyed the good will of the Republican Right from his political beginnings in Orange County, California. Seen as a hardline anticommunist and often reviled by the liberal press, he came to embody for friends and enemies alike the politics of the Cold War era. In his two successful presidential bids in 1968 and 1972, he appealed to the "silent majority," those who opposed the counterculture and defended, albeit inarticulately, the values of family and country. Nixon's vice president, Spiro Agnew, meanwhile spoke out against "epicene" social protesters who mocked manly patriotism; and Nixon's campaign advisor Kevin Phillips emphasized the need to court Southern and blue-collar constituencies in creating a new Republican majority.

Despite Nixon's conservative instincts and patriotic oratory, his actions as president did not always please the Right. Under his administration the federal budget and federal deficit soared, the dollar was devalued, and a New Economic Policy, initiated in August 1971, imposed price and wage controls. Nixon's major foreign policy accomplishments, the reopening of communications with communist China and the completion of a nuclear arms limitation treaty with the Soviets, further alienated many conservatives. The complaint was heard that the president had moved too far away from his earlier anticommunism. Nor were Nixon's anticommunist critics at all reconciled when he and Secretary of State Henry Kissinger spoke of dividing spheres of power with the Soviets in a changed world. Despite the willingness of the editors of *National Review* to support Nixon in the 1968 and 1972 presidential races, by the time of his resignation this conservative fortnightly had turned against him.

Nixon's forced resignation on August 9, 1974, served to widen the wedge between him and American conservatives. Although many on the Right had rallied to Nixon when the liberal press, especially the *Washington Post*, had begun to savage him, some conservatives were genuinely shocked to discover that Nixon had concealed facts about the Watergate break-in. There were also grounds for the suspicion that he had tried to direct the FBI away from the case. Others, and not only conservatives, continued to view Nixon's participation in the cover-up as a mere replay of what other presidents had done with impunity.

Despite the harsh judgments of his critics across the political spectrum, in his later years Nixon reclaimed some loyalties on the Right that had slipped away in the 1970s. Pat Buchanan's *Right from the Beginning* (1988) is full of praise and fond memories about his former boss. Nixon remained intellectually vigorous into old age, publishing his voluminous memoirs and well-crafted books on politics and political personalities. He also put forth a compelling theory of political realism, together with an incisive criticism of Cold War liberals' stress on global democracy as the essence of American foreign policy. A constant reader in law, history, and political science, Nixon may have been the most erudite American president since Woodrow Wilson. Despite the obvious differences in their worldviews, Nixon admired Wilson as a political theorist capable of attracting a broad electoral following.

The dedication of the Richard Nixon Library and birthplace at Yorba Linda, California, in 1990 brought together President George Herbert Walker Bush and three former chief executives with tens of thousands of well-wishers. Both the enthusiastic turnout for the ceremonies and the surprisingly positive responses of the media indicate that the tide might have turned for Richard Nixon. His professional resilience and critical intelligence have perhaps finally overshadowed the image of him as a mere opportunist. His ability to weather crises in his career is now understood, even by liberal biographer Stephen Ambrose, as a mark of Nixon's acumen rather than a lack of principle. On the intellectual Right a new assessment of his achievements that stresses his geopolitical realism has been underway since his death.

—Paul Gottfried

Further Reading

Ambrose, Stephen. *Nixon.* New York: Simon and Schuster, 1987.

Nixon, Richard M. *In The Arena: A Memoir of Victory, Defeat, and Renewal.* New York: Simon & Schuster, 1990.

———. *Seize The Moment: America's Challenge in a One-Superpower World.* New York: Simon & Schuster, 1992.

See also: *Buchanan, Patrick J.; Cold War;* National Review; *Republican Party; Vietnam War*

Nock, Albert Jay (1870–1945)

During a lifetime that spanned Woodrow Wilson's policy of foreign intervention, John Dewey's progressive educational theories, and Franklin Roosevelt's New Deal bureaucracy, Albert Jay Nock vigorously challenged the growing belief that the expansion of government power could cure social and economic ills. As a journalist and editor, Nock was a vehement and influential spokesman against collectivism and mass society. Protesting America's involvement in both world wars, he contended that intervention in foreign affairs only subverted the cause of liberty. In domestic matters, he objected especially to progressive taxation, which he argued would institutionalize pauperism, as well as to compulsory government education, which he predicted would lead to a dangerous reverence for the state.

Nock was born in Scranton, Pennsylvania, and raised in Brooklyn. He also spent time as a child in a town near Lake Huron, where he observed around him the virtues of individual and community independence and self-reliance, virtues he grew to appreciate as a necessary foundation for liberty. In 1887, he entered St. Stephen's College (now Bard College), to which he would return as a professor from 1931 to 1933. After graduating, he attended divinity school and was or-dained in the Episcopal Church in 1897. He then served as pastor at several Episcopal churches before leaving the clergy in 1909 to take up a career in journalism and editing.

From 1909 until 1914, Nock worked as editor of *American Magazine.* He left to write for the *Nation,* then under the editorship of Oswald Garrison Villard. In 1920, Nock became coeditor with Francis Neilson of the original *Freeman,* a new magazine of opinion that focused on politics and economics, among other topics. During this time, Nock published a collection of his articles for the magazine as his first book, *The Myth of a Guilty Nation* (1922).

In 1924, the *Freeman* ceased publication, having failed to become financially self-sustaining, so Nock turned to freelance writing. His articles were published in such eminent periodicals as *Atlantic Monthly, Scribner's,* and *Harper's,* and he embarked upon a series of biographies of his favorite thinkers: *Mr. Jefferson* (1926), *Francis Rabelais: The Man and His Works* (1929, with Catherine Rose Wilson), and *Henry George: An Essay* (1939). Aside from these biographies, Nock's writings consisted mainly of social criticism and political commentary. Among the topics which concerned him most were education, addressed in *The Theory of Education in the United States* (1932) and the dangers of centralized government, discussed in *Our Enemy, the State* (1935).

Albert Jay Nock

Nock's last book was to become his best-known work. In *Memoirs of a Superfluous Man* (1943), he traced the development of his political ideas and criticized the current state of liberty in America. Although Nock never became famous among the general public either during or after his lifetime, his contributions to individualist thought greatly influenced a number of those who would found the conservative intellectual movement of the next generation, including such figures as Russell Kirk, William F. Buckley Jr., and Murray N. Rothbard, who praised Nock as "an authentic American radical."

—ALEXANDRIA CHIASSON

Further Reading

Crunden, Robert Morse. *The Mind and Art of Albert Jay Nock*. Chicago: Regnery, 1964.

Nock, Albert Jay. *Free Speech and Plain Language*. New York: William Morrow, 1935.

———. *On Doing the Right Thing and Other Essays*. New York: Harper & Brothers, 1928.

See also: Foundation for Economic Education; Freeman; Memoirs of a Superfluous Man; *Spencer, Herbert; Villard, Oswald Garrison*

Novak, Michael (1933–)

Philosopher, theologian, prolific author, and quondam diplomat, Michael Novak has played a leading role in American neoconservatism for more than a generation. His 1982 book, *The Spirit of Democratic Capitalism*, was an enormously influential philosophical and theological defense of what Novak liked to term the "trinitarian" American system: a democratic polity, a market-oriented economy, and a pluralistic culture. In addition to its prominent place in American debates, *The Spirit of Democratic Capitalism* influenced scholars, churchmen, and activists throughout Latin America and in central and eastern Europe. (During the martial-law period in Poland in the early 1980s, *The Spirit of Democratic Capitalism* circulated in a Polish samizdat edition.)

Born in Johnstown, Pennsylvania, Novak studied for the Catholic priesthood at Stonehill College, in Rome, and at the Catholic University of America in Washington before leaving the seminary and pursuing advanced studies at Harvard. Married to the artist Karen Laub-Novak, Novak is the father of three children. Novak taught at Stanford, SUNY-Old Westbury, and Syracuse before taking up the George Frederick Jewett Chair in Religion and Public Policy at the Washington-based American Enterprise Institute, where he also serves as director of social and political studies.

Novak's voluminous and often translated writings touch on virtually every aspect of the American experiment: religious belief and atheism, ethnicity, sports, presidential politics, labor relations, foreign and defense policy, economics, culture, and human rights. As a founder of the journals *Crisis* (formerly *Catholicism in Crisis*) and *This World*, as a widely syndicated newspaper and magazine columnist, as religion editor of *National Review* from 1979 until 1986, and in his scholarly and managerial roles at the American Enterprise Institute, Novak played a seminal role in shaping neoconservative thought and bringing it to a wider public audience, while concurrently nurturing the careers of younger scholars. In the mid- and late-1980s, following on the success of *The Spirit of Democratic Capitalism*, Novak devoted increasing attention to issues of the Catholic Church and public policy. He played an important role in the debates that led to the National Conference of Catholic Bishops' 1983 pastoral letter, "The Challenge of Peace." Even more prominently, Novak and his colleagues in the Lay Commission on Catholic Social Teaching and the U.S. Economy were crucial actors in the debates before and after the 1986 U.S. bishops' pastoral letter, "Economic Justice for All."

Amidst all of this scholarly activity, Novak has devoted considerable time to public affairs. In 1981–82, he served as head of the U.S. Delegation to the United Nations Human Rights Commission in Geneva, where his eloquent interventions (later gathered into two volumes) announced a new American assertiveness on human rights issues in the world body. In January 1984, he was named by President Reagan to the Board for International Broadcasting, which supervises the work of Radio Free Europe and Radio Liberty; he continued in this role until 1994. Since 2002, he has served on the Board of the National Endowment for Democracy, advocating the expansion of programs promoting free-market democracies in Latin America and the Middle East. Recently, he has been active in defending the 2003 U.S. invasion of Iraq, arguing that Christian just war doctrine can be extended to include preventive war.

Novak's most enduring contribution to American intellectual and public life will most likely be his work to define and defend "democratic capitalism." Far more than a mere defense of the market mechanism in economics, Novak's *Spirit* and his subsequent writings on the subject have explored in depth the moral and practical linkages among culture, economics, and politics. He also brought this distinctive "trinitarian" conception of American society to bear on a host of public policy issues, including race relations, education, and welfare reform, in ways that helped redefine the meaning of "liberal" and "conservative" in contemporary public discourse.

—GEORGE WEIGEL

Further Reading

Novak, Michael. *Business as a Calling: Work and the Examined Life*. New York: Free Press, 1998.

———. *On Two Wings: Humble Faith and Common Sense at the American Founding*. San Francisco: Encounter Books, 2002.

———. *The Rise of the Unmeltable Ethnics*. New York: Macmillan, 1972.

———. *The Universal Hunger for Liberty: A Surprising Look Ahead at the Culture, Economics, and Politics of the Twenty-first Century*. New York: Basic Books, 2004.

———. *Will It Liberate? Questions for Liberation Theology*. New York: Paulist Press, 1986.

See also: Crisis; *liberation theology; neoconservatism; Neuhaus, Richard John; nihilism; Schindler, David L.; Weigel, George*

Novak, Robert (1931–)

Robert Novak worked his way from covering college basketball as a student at the University of Illinois to become one of the most respected and feared names in twentieth-century, and early twenty-first century, political journalism. A staunch conservative, this so-called "Prince of Darkness" spent fifty years building an unequaled reputation for digging deeper than the mainstream press and has distinguished himself from his peers by a reporting style that has always valued honesty over party loyalties. Novak began writing "Inside Report" with longtime partner Rowland Evans for the *Chicago Sun-Times* in 1963. The column became a national hit—the longest-running syndicated column ever. Novak's partnership with Evans also extended to the writing of several books, including *Lyndon B. Johnson: The Exercise of Power* (1977), *Nixon in the White House: The Frustration of Power* (1972), and *The Reagan Revolution* (1981). In addition to writing about domestic affairs, Novak has reported on events around the world, traveling widely and interviewing many world leaders, including Deng Xiaoping in 1978.

An old-school journalist who started out as a paper boy in the days of the printing press, Novak became a household name in the age of the television pundit when he began hosting CNN's *Crossfire* and *Capital Gang* in the 1990s. He recently drew attention in 2003 for disclosing the identity of Valerie Plame as a Central Intelligence Agency operative in what became known as the Plame Affair.

Despite having been raised Jewish and having attended the Catholic Church for nearly two decades, Mr. Novak surprised his readers when he made a sudden decision to convert to Catholicism in the late 1990s. "A college student at one of my lectures told me to do it," he later confided. "She said I was getting too old to procrastinate. I took that as my sign from God."

Still considered one of the best sources of political news inside the Beltway, Novak was asked at a recent visit to Wabash College how long he planned to continue writing. "As long as I'm able," he replied. "It is still as exciting for me as the day I started, and I would not give it up for anything."

—SEAN SALAI

Further Reading:

Novak, Robert D. *The Agony of the G.O.P. 1964.* New York: Macmillan, 1965.

———. *Completing the Revolution: A Vision for Victory in 2000.* New York: Free Press, 2000.

O

Oakeshott, Michael (1901–90)

Michael Oakeshott was among the most notable political philosophers of the twentieth century, and a distinguished exponent of the "conservative disposition." Among his important contributions are his interpretation of the thought of Thomas Hobbes, critique of modern rationalism, magisterial essay on "The Rule of Law," theory of civil association and political authority, philosophy of history, and philosophy of education. Oakeshott read modern history at Cambridge University and then taught there from 1926 until 1948. After a brief period at Oxford he was appointed, in 1951, as the professor of political science in the government department at the London School of Economics, a post he held until retiring in 1968.

Michael Oakeshott

His most important books are *Experience and Its Modes* (1933), *Rationalism in Politics and Other Essays* (1962), and *On Human Conduct* (1975). The most accessible introduction to Oakeshott's thinking is the collection of essays in *Rationalism in Politics*. There one finds the pieces titled "On Being Conservative," "The Political Economy of Freedom," "Political Education," and "The Tower of Babel." These, together with the posthumously published *The Politics of Faith and the Politics of Scepticism* (1996), constitute a clear statement of his conservative disposition.

Oakeshott described himself as a "skeptic." He meant, following St. Augustine and Montaigne, skepticism about human pretensions to succeed in "the pursuit of perfection as the crow flies," to build towers into a putative heavenly kingdom, or to control and manage the contingencies of human existence. Such aspirations he admired in individuals, for he applauded individuals seeking their fortunes as they defined them for themselves, but he deplored such aspirations in governments. He did so because he saw the state as a basically involuntary but necessary arrangement presiding over diverse people and interests. To invest in a single ideal would necessarily impose on some for the sake of others, suppressing the natural diversity which is the ground of human freedom. What is preferable is a "civil association" in which diverse people with diverse interests acknowledge and subscribe to a rule of law to insure the basic order they must have, with a view to affording the greatest freedom to live according to their own self-understandings. Oakeshott thought that this was the principal achievement of modern Europe, first emergent in the fifteenth century, gaining grand theoretical expression in the seventeenth and eighteenth centuries, and persisting against fierce attacks in the nineteenth and twentieth centuries. The achievement may be described as the transformation of relations of command and obedience into relations of authority and acknowledgment, and it was possible because the ideal of the self-regulating individual, competent to pursue individual interests within mutually acknowledged procedural restraints, and not dependent on coercive enforcement, was increasingly instantiated in practice in modern European history.

Nevertheless, as the technical and military power of modern governments began significantly to increase, they brought with them the temptation to invest modern governments with grand purposes for the redesign or reconstruction of social orders. This practical turn of events was encouraged theoretically by the influential growth of "rationalism" in modern Europe under the influence of the thought of Francis Bacon and Descartes and later of Jeremy Bentham and the modern social sciences. Rationalism, as Oakeshott described it, proposes techniques or methods of analytic reasoning, inspired by the natural and mathematical sciences, by means of which we may overcome the contingent character of historical existence. In extreme form, it holds that the hitherto endless activity of preserving and changing in politics can be brought to a satisfactory conclusion, and that this is to be done by a coalition of the intellectually enlightened with governments, a coalition that will direct the use of power in steering people to the right end.

The result is that modern politics is conducted in a charged field polarized between a skeptical attitude towards governmental power and the view that such power is the means to infinite improvement. The contest between the skeptic and the rationalist has proven historically irresolvable, although Oakeshott thought that in recent times rationalism had clearly—and, he thought, regrettably—dominated over political skepticism. But because of the power in practice of the ideas of civil association, of rule of law, of authority grounded in acknowledgment rather than in coercion, and because he thought these to be more consistent with the human spirit, Oakeshott believed that this remarkable modern achievement would maintain itself. Modern politics is thus constituted in the tension between competing traditions of thought. They play off of each other and the character of each is shaped by the presence of the other. Regardless of his personal preferences in the matter, he thought that this was the reality of our situation.

For Oakeshott, the main task of modern governments was, then, to "keep the ship afloat" so that individuals and voluntary associations could seek their fortunes and define for themselves their destinations within a procedural system of laws. This must be done within the context of dispersed power wherein the state, while not especially strong, and with few resources to distribute, was strong enough to resist informal conglomerations of power that would turn the civil association into a managerial enterprise, a modern form of the Tower of Babel. Here then is the "conservative disposition." It is not the same as a philosophical understanding. For Oakeshott, philosophy is seeking in detachment simply to understand, and to describe, what is going on in the world. Rather, conservatism is a considered practical response to the opportunities and perils of modern political life. What Oakeshott offered was a picture of the philosophical and historical context within which to identify more clearly what prompts the conservative disposition. He did not think philosophy could resolve the issues but could only clarify them in ways their practitioners would likely not consider. In expressing his preference for one pole, however, he associated himself with an ancient tradition in the West which denies to politics the highest honor. He called politics a "necessary evil," meaning thereby to say both that we cannot do without politics and that from its necessity does not follow its candidacy to be the source of all meaning.

—TIMOTHY FULLER

Further Reading

Devigne, Robert. *Recasting Conservatism: Oakeshott, Strauss, and the Response to Postmodernism.* New Haven, Conn.: Yale University Press, 1994.

Oakeshott, Michael. *Hobbes on Civil Association.* Berkeley, Calif.: University of California Press, 1975.

———. *Religion, Politics, and the Moral Life.* Edited by Timothy Fuller. New Haven, Conn.: Yale University Press, 1993.

See also: authority

O'Connor, Flannery (1925–64)

Though she lived less than forty years, (Mary) Flannery O'Connor is widely considered one of the giants of American literature. A writer of fiction deeply rooted in the language and culture of what she called the "Christ-haunted South," O'Connor combined modern literary preoccupations and styles, including the use of violence and the grotesque, to become known as one of the greatest short story writers of all time. She was also a devout Catholic with widespread intellectual interests, including theology and philosophy. While her narratives are highly dramatic and can be appreciated simply for their emotional and psychological dimensions, they also contain profound insights into the condition of the modern world.

Born in Savannah, Georgia, the Catholic O'Connor grew up as an outsider in the dominantly Protestant South, but she retained a lifelong admiration for the often stark and powerful religiosity of her region. She studied at Georgia State College for Women (now Georgia College and State University), graduating in three years. However, in many ways she was an autodidact; she read voraciously, not only in the realm of literature but also in the philosophies of St. Thomas Aquinas and modern thinkers such as Eric Voegelin, Henri de Lubac, and Hans Urs von Balthasar.

She went on to study writing at the University of Iowa's Writers' Workshop, where she came into contact with a number of outstanding writers, including Andrew Lytle and Austin Warren. Later she would befriend the literary couple Robert and Sally Fitzgerald, with whom she stayed in Connecticut while trying to establish herself as an author. Robert was a gifted poet and translator; Sally would become O'Connor's posthumous editor and literary executor.

O'Connor's first novel, *Wise Blood* (1955), manifests a fully mature talent and was received with high praise from critics and reviewers. Its protagonist, Hazel Motes, is a desperate loner cut off from family and community and driven by anger and rebellion to profess a Nietzschean philosophy. A dark prophet, Motes attempts to found the "Church of Christ without Christ," but his prideful quest is doomed to fail. When a violent act shocks him into recognizing his own guilt and sinfulness, he turns to equally dark gestures of asceticism.

O'Connor's short stories, which many consider superior to her novels, follow a similar pattern of prideful protagonists encountering violent epiphanies. At such moments, her characters are often offered a glimpse into divine grace, but the stories remain open-ended: we, as readers, are forced to reflect on whether we would be willing to accept such severe mercies from God.

Her most famous story, "A Good Man Is Hard to Find," is about a family that gets lost while on vacation, only to encounter a serial murderer who calls himself "The Misfit." Here O'Connor demonstrates her animus against various modern ideologies that would explain away the reality of evil by substituting theories of social or psychological maladjustment.

After her untimely death from lupus in 1964, a series of posthumous volumes emerged, including a gathering of her essays and addresses, *Mystery and Manners* (1969), and a collection of her letters, *The Habit of Being* (1979). In these books O'Connor's aesthetic and philosophical convictions are revealed in all their astonishing depth and sophistication. For many conservative thinkers, Flannery O'Connor forged an enduring critique of modernity—in the dramatic and metaphorical language of fiction.

Flannery O'Connor

—GREGORY WOLFE

Further Reading

Brinkmeyer, Robert H. *The Art and Vision of Flannery O'Connor*. Baton Rouge, La.: Louisiana State University Press, 1989.

Montgomery, Marion. *Why Flannery O'Connor Stayed Home*. La Salle, Ill.: Sherwood Sugden, 1981.

O'Connor, Flannery. *Collected Works*. New York: Library of America, 1988.

———. *The Presence of Grace and Other Book Reviews*. Athens, Ga.: University of Georgia Press, 1983.

Wood, Ralph C. *Flannery O'Connor and the Christ-Haunted South*. Grand Rapids, Mich.: William B. Eerdmans, 2004.

See also: Lytle, Andrew Nelson; modernity and post-modernity; Montgomery, Marion H.

Olasky, Marvin (1950–)

Marvin Olasky is a journalism professor, evangelical Protestant, and, in the *New York Times*'s words, "the godfather of compassionate conservatism." Raised Jewish, Olasky was an atheist by age fourteen. He embraced Marxism and joined the Communist Party. But by 1973 Olasky had discarded communism, and three years later he converted to Christianity, becoming a Presbyterian.

Meanwhile, Olasky earned a Ph.D. in American studies at the University of Michigan in 1976. After lecturing at San Diego State University, he wrote speeches for Pete DuPont from 1978 to 1983, then became a professor of journalism at the University of Texas at Austin.

Olasky has written books about abortion, journalism, and history, but is most famous for his dissection of the concept of "compassion." His *Tragedy of American Compassion* (1992) pointed out that in nineteenth-century America, religious organizations and individuals attacked poverty by practicing compassion in its true, literal sense, *suffering with* the unfortunate, involving themselves personally with them and offering both material and spiritual help, challenging them to be better. This approach worked well, Olasky argued, and should be retrieved. William Bennett recommended *The Tragedy of American Compassion* to Speaker of the House Newt Gingrich, whose endorsement won Olasky's ideas national attention. Olasky's *Compassionate Conservatism* (2000) articulated a strategy of attacking poverty with local, faith-based efforts, an idea that would soon thereafter become a focus of national debate and would help lead to the creation of the White House's Office of Faith-Based and Community Initiatives. Since 1993, he has been an advisor to George W. Bush, who strongly endorsed "compassionate conservatism" as the governor of Texas and as president.

Olasky has been the editor of *World* magazine, a weekly that covers national and international news from an evangelical Christian perspective, since 1994.

—JOHN ATTARIAN

Further Reading

Olasky, Marvin N. *Abortion Rites: A Social History of Abortion in America*. Wheaton, Ill.: Crossways Books, 1992.

———. *Renewing American Compassion*. New York: Free Press, 1996.

See also: abortion; Bush, George W.; poverty

Old Right

The Old Right was a coalition of libertarians and nationalists who united in the 1930s to oppose the New Deal of President Franklin D. Roosevelt and to try to prevent American intervention in World War II. Although most members were Christians, and the coalition is sometimes called the "Old Christian Right," the moral component was of secondary importance at a time when the vast majority of Americans accepted the validity of traditional Judeo-Christian ethics. The focus of the Old Right was on the iniquity of big government at home and the imprudence of intervention abroad.

Libertarians fervently believed that people should have freedom in their economic pursuits and should succeed by their own initiative. They favored a comparatively unregulated form of free enterprise that emphasized free markets, private property, limited government, and self-reliance. They op-

posed the welfare state and the government regulatory agencies of the New Deal, and they were especially vehement in criticizing socialism and communism.

When war clouds gathered over Europe, most of the Old Right also supported a program of American nationalism. Their motto was "America First." Their most popular spokesman, the aviator Charles A. Lindbergh, called for an impregnable defense but believed that American democracy could best be preserved by staying out of the European war. In the 1930s most members of the Old Right favored France and Britain over Nazi Germany but thought the Western powers had the resources and strength to protect their interests. "This is not our war," said *Chicago Tribune* publisher Robert McCormick, "It is their war. They are competent to fight it." When it developed that Nazi Germany could not be defeated without the assistance of communist Russia, the Old Right balked at intervention. Rather than aid Russia, and thereby allow Stalin to extend his brutalities, the Old Right hoped that the Nazis and Communists would destroy one another.

After Pearl Harbor, the Old Right rallied in support of the United States and its armed forces. Nevertheless, many members were harshly criticized for their earlier "isolationism." Some were banished from government service and President Roosevelt personally made sure that Colonel Lindbergh did not receive a commission in the U.S. armed forces.

The Old Right survived the Second World War but succumbed during the Cold War. Because they were strongly anticommunist, most members were willing to do whatever was needed to contain the Soviet Union. They supported the Truman Doctrine, the Marshall Plan, and the North Atlantic Treaty Organization (NATO); that is, they embraced big government and internationalism, and in the process they drifted away from the policies that had defined the Old Right.

Yet a remnant of libertarians endured. In the early 1950s economists Friedrich Hayek and Ludwig von Mises warned of the dangers inherent in the central direction of economic activity. The *Freeman* was established as a small but respectable fortnightly for individualists, and the Intercollegiate Society of Individualists (ISI) became a clearinghouse for conservative publications and a support group for young libertarians who might otherwise have been isolated in an era when collectivism was in vogue. ISI was also influenced by Russell Kirk, whose book *The Conservative Mind* (1953) argued that many traditions, and especially the tradition of local self-government and individual rights, were the distilled essence of wisdom. Later, when socialism turned out to be a "god that failed," and when the enhanced state power of New Deal liberalism proved problematic, this remnant would become an important component in a new, stronger conservative movement.

—RAYMOND WOLTERS

Further Reading

Berg, A. Scott. *Lindbergh*. New York: G. P. Putnam's Sons, 1998.

Cole, Wayne S. *America First: The Battle Against Intervention, 1940–1941*. Madison, Wis.: University of Wisconsin Press, 1953.

Raimondo, Justin. *Reclaiming the American Right: The Lost Legacy of the Conservative Movement*. Burlingame, Calif.: Center for Libertarian Studies, 1993.

Ribuffo, Leo P. *The Old Christian Right: The Protestant Far Right from the Great Depression to the Cold War*. Philadelphia: Temple University Press, 1983.

See also: America First Committee; anarchism; Chicago Tribune; Flynn, John T.; isolationism; Lindbergh, Charles A.; McCormick, Robert R.; New Right; paleoconservatism

Olin, John M., Foundation

The John M. Olin Foundation, which at press time was scheduled to cease operations by the end of 2005, offered grants to organizations that champion the American systems of constitutional government and private enterprise. John Merrill Olin (1892–1982), a chemical industrialist, inventor, and conservationist, established the foundation in 1953 and began directing it to promote American ideals around 1973. For many years the foundation held less than $50 million in assets and awarded about $3 million annually. In 1994, with a bequest from Olin's wife its assets rose to more than $100 million and this foundation subsequently donated between $10 million and $20 million annually.

John M. Olin chose William E. Simon, former secretary of the treasury, to head the foundation in 1977. Michael Joyce succeeded Simon but left for the Lynde and Harry Bradley Foundation in 1985, at which time Simon again assumed the helm. Simon was aided immeasurably by former University of Pennsylvania professor James Piereson. After Simon died in 2000 the foundation declared its plans to phase itself out of existence—in accord with Olin's original desires—by giving its money away over a few years' time to its favorite grantees. Joyce indicated that Olin had seen Henry Ford II disillusioned by the leftward tendencies of the Ford Foundation in its later years and that Olin hoped that his foundation would avoid a similar fate.

The foundation fostered research into political and economic policy, American institutions, the rule of law and the legal system, and international economic and social policy. Universities lead the foundation's giving chart, where it has promoted conservative programs and the John M. Olin faculty chair for such scholars as Gary Becker (University of Chicago), Eliot Cohen (Johns Hopkins University), Walter E. Williams (George Mason University), Mary Ann

Glendon (Harvard Law School), Herbert London (New York University), and George Priest (Yale Law School). The foundation also financed such intellectuals as Milton Friedman, Jeane Kirkpatrick, and Irving Kristol. The Olin Foundation is credited with bolstering the Federalist Society and advancing "Law and Economics" studies at leading law schools, which at the University of Chicago has featured U.S. Court of Appeals judges Richard A. Posner and Frank H. Easterbrook.

Between 1985 and 2000 the foundation granted $1 million or more to each of twenty-three academic institutions and thirty-two private organizations. Notable private grantees include the American Enterprise Institute, Heritage Foundation, Intercollegiate Studies Institute, Producers Incorporated for Television (which produced William F. Buckley Jr.'s "Firing Line"), and the Institute on Religion and Public Life.

The Left attacked the Olin Foundation, as it has most conservative organizations, for helping to fund politically incorrect research. For example, antigun lobbyists criticized the foundation in 1997 for supposedly undermining objective research when John Lott, the John M. Olin Fellow at the University of Chicago Law School, argued that relaxed laws against concealed weapons might reduce crime. The lobbyists alleged a conflict of interest between the foundation and the Olin Corporation, which owned Winchester Ammunition. The foundation minimized the significance of these ties—common among liberal as well as conservative foundations—and pointed out its lack of control over the selection of John M. Olin professors.

—MATTHEW BOWMAN

Further Reading

Miller, John J. *A Gift of Freedom: How the John M. Olin Foundation Changed America.* San Francisco: Encounter Books, 2005.

See also: foundations, conservative; Simon, William E.

Oliver, Revilo P. (1910–94)

Professor of classics at the University of Illinois in Champaign-Urbana and a founding member of the governing council of the John Birch Society, founded in 1958, Revilo P. Oliver was a noted scholar in the field of classical studies. Oliver enjoyed a less successful career in political activities. Throughout the early 1960s, in addition to being a member of the John Birch Society governing council, Oliver contributed book reviews and articles to *American Opinion*, the society's monthly news and opinion magazine.

Oliver came to national attention in 1964 when he published a two-part article on the assassination of President John F. Kennedy in the February and March issues of *American Opinion*. Oliver contended that Kennedy was a tool of the international communist conspiracy but that he was not working fast enough to suit his masters in the Kremlin. Oliver's argument was prototypical of the conspiratorial view of history with which the John Birch Society became synonymous.

In the articles on the Kennedy assassination, Oliver maintained that no matter what Kennedy did, he could not satisfy Moscow. Consequently, according to Oliver's thesis, Lee Harvey Oswald, a defector to Russia who was trained as a terrorist, was readmitted to the United States (with the silent complicity of the U.S. Department of State, which Oliver insisted was also under communist control) and killed Kennedy, an act which was to have set the stage for the mass murder of "true" patriots. According to Oliver, the plan was spoiled when Dallas police captured Oswald. To prevent Oswald from spilling the whole story, the communists killed him as part of their grand cover-up.

Time and *Newsweek* featured Oliver and his conspiratorial charges. The controversy they generated represented Oliver's high-water mark in terms of publicity in the popular press. In the wake of the controversy,

Oliver testified before the Warren Commission on September 9, 1964. His testimony was speculative in nature and did not give the commission any new information or documentation on the Kennedy assassination.

Oliver's involvement with the John Birch Society ended abruptly after a speech he delivered on July 2, 1966, at the New England Rally for God, Family and Country in Boston, Massachusetts. In the speech, he declared that the United States was "the victim of some vast and evil conspiracy" whose nucleus was "the great Jewish conspiracy of 117-118 AD," a conspiracy Oliver claimed nearly succeeded in bringing down the Roman empire.

Oliver's speech proved disastrous for the John Birch Society, which had been plagued with allegations of anti-Semitism since its inception. Had he not voluntarily resigned on July 30, 1966, permanently ending his involvement with the John Birch Society, Oliver would probably have been forced out.

Oliver's brand of conservatism belongs to what may be described as the "conspiratorial school" of American politics. Most mainstream conservatives agree that Oliver and other proponents of conspiratorial views in the 1960s may have temporarily damaged the credibility of the modern conservative movement and slowed its efforts toward building a popular American conservative consensus.

In his later years, Oliver himself expressed regret that he had allowed political activism to subtract time from his classical studies.

—CHARLES SCOTT HAMEL

Further Reading

Oliver, Revilo P. *America's Decline: The Education of a Conservative*. London: Londinium Press, 1981.

Russell, Dick. *The Man Who Knew Too Much*. New York: Carroll & Graf Publishers, 1992.

See also: John Birch Society

Orton, William Aylott (1889–1952)

A Catholic classical liberal economist, William Aylott Orton was born in England and educated at Cambridge and the University of London. Orton immigrated to America in 1922 and became a professor of economics at Smith College the same year. He held this post until his death and was also a visiting professor at Amherst (1929-30) and Williams (1939-1940).

Orton's richly learned *The Liberal Tradition* (1945) was both a history of the West from a classical liberal perspective and a history of liberalism. Liberalism's fundamental values, he argued, are the dignity of the individual person and the equality of all persons before the law and are essentially Christian. Arguing that liberalism's goal is "expanding liberty within expanding community," Orton called for minimal government involvement in economics, free trade, and liberal internationalism, and he rejected the welfare state.

The Economic Role of the State (1950) examined the "fundamental principles" of its subject. Because we value the development of free individuals, Orton argued, coercion, on which the state holds a monopoly, should be minimal. Policies promoting "free personality in a free society" ought to be promoted. Since "applied intelligence" has made the ideal of independent small business untenable, the alternative is to "moralize bigness." Although endorsing Social Security and legislation and regulation to achieve "fairness," Orton maintained that both ethical imperatives and economic realities demand the maximization of freedom and personal responsibility.

Russell Kirk praised Orton as a "humane economist," "at once liberal and conservative," seeking to "liberalize and humanize the Dismal Science."

—JOHN ATTARIAN

Further Reading

Orton, William Aylott. *America in Search of Culture.* Boston: Little, Brown, 1933.

See also: liberalism, classical

Orwell, George (1903–50)

Eric Arthur Blair, better known as George Orwell, was born in India, where his father served as a member of the Opium Department of the Indian Civil Service. Orwell was raised in England and attended Eton, but he opted to join the imperial police in Burma rather than go on to university.

Orwell's five years in Burma (1922–27) convinced him that he hated imperialism and that he wanted to be a writer. Those years also provided him with material that he would draw upon for the rest of his life. The novel *Burmese Days* (1934) and two of his most famous essays, "A Hanging" and "Shooting an Elephant," derived from his stay in Burma.

George Orwell

Orwell's attempts at a writing career were at first not marked by great literary success, although he produced a book a year from 1933 through 1939, the best of which was *Coming Up for Air,* written on the eve of World War II. It portrayed a sleeping, materialistic England unready for the crisis it was about to face. His fictionalized memoir, *Down and Out in Paris and London* (1933), a study of life among the unemployed and tramps, revealed a talent for brilliantly descriptive prose. His portrait of conditions in the depression-ridden north of England in *The Road to Wigan Pier* (1937) broke new ground for investigative journalism.

In 1937 Orwell went to Spain and fought on the Loyalist side. He suffered a serious throat wound and had to flee the country one step ahead of the communist police. Spain turned Orwell into a convinced if idiosyncratic socialist, but it also made him a bitter enemy of communism. In a series of articles on Spain, and especially in his memoir, *Homage to Catalonia* (1938), he accused the communists and their English left-wing allies of betraying the cause of revolution and becoming mouthpieces of Stalin's perversion of communism in the Soviet Union. Orwell described himself at this time as a "democratic socialist," with emphasis on the adjective. His attacks on communist treachery in Spain made him anathema in certain socialist circles in England and he was never fully trusted by the Left thereafter.

During World War II Orwell was rejected for military service because of poor health. He worked for the BBC for two years (1942–44) before deciding to devote himself to writing full time. His essays "Notes on Nationalism," "Patriots and Revolutionaries," "My Country, Right or Left," and especially his book *The Lion and Unicorn,* examined the power of patriotism as a unifying theme in England's struggle against Nazism. Orwell argued that contrary to what his fellow socialists thought, patriotism was a necessary force to win the war. Orwell's early World War II essays and reviews showed his emerging power as a literary stylist and maturing, original thinker.

His last two books, *Animal Farm* (1945) and *Nineteen Eighty-Four* (1949), won him a worldwide reputation as an adroit critic of totalitarianism, especially Stalin's brand of communism. Orwell's critique of communism made him popular in conservative circles in both England and the United States. Both books were chosen as Book-of-the-Month-Club selections in the United States and remain in print, continuing to sell briskly more than a half century after Orwell's untimely death from tuberculosis in January 1950.

Orwell gave the English language some memorable phrases, including "Big Brother," "All Animals are equal but some are more equal than others," "doublethink," and "newspeak," and he remains as popular today as he was in his lifetime.

—JOHN P. ROSSI

Further Reading

Bowker, George. *Inside George Orwell: A Biography*. New York: Palgrave Macmillan, 2003.

Newsinger, John. *Orwell's Politics*. New York: St. Martin's, 1999.

Orwell, Sonia, and Ian Angus (eds). *The Collected Essays, Journalism and Letters of George Orwell*. 4 vols. London: Secker and Warburg, 1968.

Rodden, John. *The Politics of Literary Reputation: The Making and Claiming of "St. George" Orwell*. New York: Oxford University Press, 1989.

———. *Scenes from an Afterlife: The Legacy of George Orwell*. Wilmington, Del.: ISI Books, 2003.

See also: Burnham, James; totalitarianism

Owsley, Frank (1890–1956)

A major historian of the American South and a Southern Agrarian, Frank Owsley was educated at Alabama Polytechnic Institute and the University of Chicago. Owsley taught history at Birmingham Southern College (1919–20), Vanderbilt University (1920–49), and the University of Alabama (1949–54).

Owsley significantly advanced Southern historiography. His *State Rights in the Confederacy* (1925) maintained that the states rights doctrine crippled the Confederacy's war effort and led to its defeat. *King Cotton Diplomacy* (1931) drew on British and French archives to make a persuasive case that profits, not antislavery sentiment or dependence on American wheat, kept Britain neutral during the Civil War. Most importantly, his *Plain Folk of the Old South* (1949) established that the antebellum South contained a large middle class of small farmers, demolishing the myth of a South of plantation owners, slaves, and poor whites.

"The Irrepressible Conflict," his contribution to the Southern Agrarian manifesto *I'll Take My Stand* (1930), vigorously disputed the mainstream view that slavery caused the Civil War. Rather, the interests of the industrial North and the agrarian South collided irreconcilably on several points, especially protective tariffs and internal improvements. In *I'll Take My Stand*'s sequel, *Who Owns America?* (1936), Owsley's "The Foundations of Democracy" argued that widespread personal ownership and control of productive property is the "keystone of the arch" of true democracy and a guarantor of the rights to life, liberty, the pursuit of happiness, and self-government, and he warned that America had abandoned this Jeffersonian ideal of decentralized property ownership.

—JOHN ATTARIAN

Further Reading

Carlson, Allan. *The New Agrarian Mind: The Movement toward Decentralist Thought in Twentieth-Century America*. New Brunswick, N.J.: Transaction, 2000.

Owsley, Frank Lawrence. *The South: Old and New Frontiers: Selected Essays of Frank Lawrence Owsley*. Athens, Ga.: University of Georgia Press, 1969.

See also: American Review; I'll Take My Stand; Southern Agrarians

P

paleoconservatism

The term "paleoconservative" has been applied to more than one conservative grouping, from the pre–World War II opposition to the New Deal and the formation of an American welfare state to current critics on the right of the neoconservatives. Most often the term pertains to post–World War II conservatives centered on *National Review* and *Modern Age* and concerned with reconciling economic and political liberty with traditional social and religious values. Paleoconservatives did not agree on all philosophical and policy questions, as witnessed by the bitter, prolonged debates between Frank Meyer and Russell Kirk, but they do appear, in retrospect, to have shared a number of sentiments and principles. Among these was skepticism about democracy and equality and a belief in freedom, both personal and corporate, coupled with respect for social authority.

Most paleoconservatives backed an active American role in combating communism and the Soviet Union as its most menacing armed advocate, but had little patience for big government and nonmilitary foreign aid. They advocated victory over communism for two reasons: because they viewed the communists as irreconcilably hostile to both traditional Western order and political liberty, and because they saw the communists as the extension of a violent revolutionary impetus going back to the French Revolution and now threatening the United States and the rest of the Western world. Though not all were Catholic, most paleoconservatives expressed respect for the Catholic Church. They praised it as a moral bulwark against communism and as an institution coextensive with and long dominant over Western civilization.

Paleoconservative becomes a conceptual and political counterpoint to *neoconservative* in *The Conservative Movement* by Thomas Fleming and Paul Gottfried (1988). Here the term no longer refers merely to conservative traditionalists of the 1950s and 1960s, e.g., Southern Agrarians, Catholic anticommunists associated with *National Review*, and Taft Republicans who rallied to the Cold War. Instead, the term is now applied to embattled conservatives who opposed the growing influence of anticommunist New Deal Democrats on the Reagan presidency and on the conservative movement of the 1980s. Some of these paleoconservatives— e.g., Russell Kirk, Thomas Molnar, Stephen Tonsor, George Carey, Forrest McDonald, George Panichas, and Robert Nisbet—were clearly among the traditionalists of the postwar conservative movement; others—e.g., Claes Ryn, Samuel T. Francis, Clyde Wilson, and Thomas Fleming—were too young to have belonged to that generation, though they were shaped by it. In contradistinction to first-generation paleoconservatives, this second generation is less Catholic in its point of reference. It is also more open to the social sciences and sociobiology and less preoccupied with the self-described Left than with the neoconservatives. Unlike the traditionalists of the 1960s, who supported Barry Goldwater, the new paleoconservatives speak about a return to the anti-interventionism of Robert Taft, a political position now defended principally by Patrick J. Buchanan. They have also reached out to libertarians who share their disdain for the "welfare-warfare state."

Since 1989 paleoconservatives have been eager to abandon anticommunism as an issue. The waning of the Cold War and neo-isolationism are certainly factors here; but equally important is the perception among paleoconservatives that anticommunist enthusiasm has benefited their neo-conservative detractors. The centrality of fighting Soviet and communist aggression, it is believed, forced an earlier generation of conservatives to make their peace with the welfare state. Paleoconservatives blame the same anticommunist fixation for the loss of the conservative movement to anticommunist welfare-staters, exemplified by figures such as Norman Podhoretz and Ben Wattenberg.

In the present conservative wars, *National Review,* which played a critical role in the founding of postwar conservatism, has leaned unmistakably toward the neoconservatives. This split has allowed the paleoconservatives to move more daringly toward new policy positions without the baggage of Cold War politics. It has also encouraged paleoconservatives to take their bearings not from postwar conservatism but from the pre–World War II, anti–New Deal Right. What has been called the "conservative crackup" has actually reproduced almost exactly the political alignments of the 1930s, which pitted pristine New Dealers (neoconservatives) against anti–New Deal Republicans (paleoconservatives). It has also brought forth (unsubstantiated) charges of anti-Semitism against the paleoconservatives from their pro-Zionist neoconservative opposition. The paleoconservative consensus against Third World immigration is a further source of dissension. Neoconservatives, who are overwhelmingly pro-immigration, have at times accused their rivals on the Right of xenophobia as well as anti-Semitism. In fact, there are Jews and Christians in both camps, and Middle Eastern politics is by no means the only point of contention between them. More basic to the split are opposing attitudes about domestic equality and the exportability of democracy.

The war in Iraq has served to exacerbate this antagonism, and the two sides have generally taken opposed positions here. On the whole the paleoconservatives have been reactive in this debate. They have questioned the wisdom of a struggle that their adversaries with influence in the current administration helped initiate. A new paleoconservative magazine with a broad readership, the *American Conservative,* has focused predominantly on the Middle East and on the follies of American interventionism. For the older generation of paleoconservatives, what makes the present "struggle for democracy" particularly irritating are its ideological premises. It seems to be a variation on Marxism and a harmful diversion from the task of dismantling the managerial regime at home.

—PAUL GOTTFRIED

Further Reading:

Buchanan, Patrick J. *Where the Right Went Wrong: How Neoconservatives Subverted the Reagan Revolution and Hijacked the Bush Presidency.* New York: Thomas Dunne Books, 2004.

Gottfried, Paul E. *After Liberalism: Mass Democracy in the Managerial State.* Princeton, N.J.: Princeton University Press, 1999.

Ryn, Claes G. *America the Virtuous: The Crisis of Democracy and the Quest for Empire.* New Brunswick, N.J.: Transaction, 2003.

See also: American Conservative; Chronicles; *neoconservatism; traditionalism*

Parkman, Francis (1823–93)

Historian Francis Parkman bequeathed to the United States a confident vision of the American past narrated with grandeur. Like William Prescott and George Bancroft, Parkman viewed America as the fruit of European achievement, not a mere extension of it. The seven books that constitute his magnum opus, *France and England in North America* (1865–92), tell a tale of Homeric proportions in which Protestant liberty, French absolutism, and Indian barbarism lock in a death struggle to determine the cultural order that would rise to greatness from the primeval forests of America. A champion of the cultivated individual and a political understanding of an America made robust through Republican aristocrats, Parkman and his legacy demand continued attention from historian and social critic alike.

Born in 1823 to stern Unitarians, Parkman turned quite early from the rigid urban scene of federalist Boston to two apparently separate sources of renewal: the ancient civilization of Europe and the virginal wilderness of America. His life was largely spent idealizing struggle (both in his personal life and in history) and illustrating the greatness that can arise from sacrifice and suffering. From Parkman's Harvard days through his entire life, personal illness heightened his own awareness of man's limitations. Yet Parkman placed himself under an extreme regime aimed at overcoming his weaknesses. His college days were marked by arduous expeditions to observe first hand the battlefields of the French and Indian War and, most notably, a long hunting trip from St. Louis to Wyoming (1846) during which he lived with the Sioux

Francis Parkman

Indians. A result of such exertions was permanent physical debilitation; but to the extent that he decimated his body, he sharpened his mind. His travels at home and abroad convinced him of the folly and fallen nature of man. His study of history confirmed these observations and led Parkman to reject both social romanticism and historical materialism.

A sharp contrast between civilization and barbarism is found in all his works, from *The Oregon Trail* (1849) through his histories and even his botanical writings. The early deaths of his wife and only son and his near blindness meant agony during his research and writing. But his disabilities did little to abate his productivity. From *The Conspiracy of Pontiac and the Indian War after the Conquest of Canada* (1851) through many pamphlets and journal articles to his crowning achievement, *Montcalm and Wolfe* (1884), Parkman worked with restless energy in the defense of greatness against determinism, democracy, and pusillanimity. Whether religious zealotry, martial cruelty, or social enervation blackened the hearts of the men who illuminated Parkman's forests and plains did not matter. The colonial period offered examples of natural aristocrats dedicated to the advancement of what was most noble in their societies. Though Parkman ultimately championed the Anglo-American order that emerged, French Catholic and Indian cultures provided a foil to the nascent democratic egalitarianism of his own day. In part, Parkman's historical writings should be seen as a conscious assembly of *exempla*, a casebook for the renewal of the heroic in American society.

—William Edmund Fahey

Further Reading

Doughty, Howard. *Francis Parkman*. Cambridge, Mass.: Harvard University Press, 1962.

Jacobs, Wilbur R. *Francis Parkman, Historian as Hero: The Formative Years*. Austin, Tex.: University of Texas Press, 1991.

Morison, Samuel Eliot. *The Parkman Reader*. Boston: Little, Brown, 1955.

Parkman, Francis. *France and England in North America*. Edited by David Levin. 2 vols. New York: Viking, 1983–91.

———. *The Oregon Trail and the Conspiracy of Pontiac*. Edited by William R. Taylor. New York: Viking, 1992.

Tonsor, Stephen. "The Conservative as Historian: Francis Parkman." *Modern Age* 25 (1983): 246–55.

See also: West, American

Parry, Stanley J. (1918–72)

Rev. Stanley J. Parry, a priest of the Congregation of Holy Cross and a professor in the political science department at the University of Notre Dame, considered himself a political "theorist," one who "attempt[s] to interpret man's relation to man in civil society" in the larger perspective "of man's relation to the universe and to God." He regarded the transmission of classical and Christian wisdom as his primary educational mission and was a warm supporter of the conservative movement in American public life, sometimes bringing men like Willmoore Kendall, whom he baptized in 1951, to the campus for the edification of his students and colleagues.

During his tenure as the head of the department of political science, Father Parry published a richly documented study of the nineteenth-century American Catholic publicist, Orestes A. Brownson. Beginning with the secondary literature of the 1940s and 1950s, Father Parry made use of the corpus of Brownson's works with the intention of providing further evidence of his metaphysics and deepening the interpretation of his political thought. Thus, it was only natural that Father Parry would draw from Brownson as well as from his own reasoning and experience in 1958 when he and colleague Gerhart Niemeyer drafted a memorandum regarding the Civil Rights Commission. This document, "Politics and Morality in Civil Rights," predicted disruptions of public order should the government act "as an instrument of salvation" rather than circumscribing itself in deference to "mutually exclusive concepts of justice, each based on sincere conviction even though on faulty thinking."

Father Parry's last major work was his 1961 treatise on tradition in which he made clear that "the goods" we seek in the temporal order are in themselves limited and imperfect. They point to "the good" which transcends this life, to the "ultimate good . . . not yet" ours in which to "rest." But as a teacher, recognizing that analysis of the ultimate good would go beyond political theory to religious experience, Parry "restricted" himself to the "world immanent aspects" of the problem of human order.

In the early 1960s Parry left Notre Dame to work closely with William Baroody at the American Enterprise Institute as one of Baroody's principal advisors.

—MARK C. HENRIE

Further Reading

Parry, Stanley. "Politics and Morality in Civil Rights." *Scholastic*, January 17, 1958, 12–21.

———. "The Restoration of Tradition." *Modern Age* 3, no. 2 (Spring 1961): 125–38.

———. "The Premises of Brownson's Political Theory." *Review of Politics* 16, no. 2 (April 1954): 194–211.

See also: Baroody, William J.; Brownson, Orestes A.; tradition

Party of the Right

A conservative debating society at Yale, the Party of the Right (POR) is one of the parties within the Yale Political Union. Founded in the early 1950s out of a perception that the then-existing Conservative Party was drifting toward Eisenhowerian "respectability," the POR has always drawn to itself the more flamboyant and reflective conservatives at Yale—be they monarchists, libertarians, Old Rightists or New Rightists. Under the chairmanship of Wayne James Holman (Autumn 1955), the party adopted King Charles I of England as its official hero, and his Scaffold Speech—which expresses conservative values with a populist tint—is ceremonially recited by the chairman whenever the party gathers for a "toasting session" at Mory's, Yale's traditional watering hole.

While respectful of political activism (indeed, many POR members are also active in the College Republicans), the POR is basically about the life of the mind. Under Chairman Karl Rex Ziebarth (Autumn 1958), the "debate caucus" took shape as the party's central activity. A topic likely to spark disagreement among conservatives is chosen in advance, and speeches are entertained on the floor. Topics vary from the concretely political to the abstractly philosophical. The party's debating rules reject, on principle, time limits. Dogmas are welcome, but dogmatism is not. Use of written notes is prohibited: the aim is to encourage rhetoric in the Periclean sense, in contrast to the woodenness of high school debating. Debate caucuses are nominally "adjourned to Mory's"; in reality, pizza has replaced Mory's as the standard post-caucus convivium.

Liberals and leftists who welcome debate and desire to participate in the life of the POR have often been admitted as members. The closest thing the party has to an absolute prerequisite for membership is a formal connection with Yale University.

Under Chairman Charles Alan Garland (Spring 1963), the POR adopted the Socratic maxim, "The unexamined life is not worth living," as part of its operating creed. Through debate and through friendship, members encourage one another to examine their beliefs and themselves. In an age in which the Left may be seen as increasingly degenerating into "politically correct" dogmatism, the connection between conservatism and "Garlandism" is becoming ever more clear.

The POR persisted throughout the era of the counterculture; the only impact of that era on the party was that its recruits became, if anything, more conservative rather than less. While the party has had its share of controversies and upheavals over the decades, it continues, in the age of "PC," as a place of fellowship and rational dialogue among idea-oriented conservatives.

—DAVID WAGNER

Paterson, Isabel B. (1886–1961)

Born in Canada, Isabel Bowler Paterson's childhood experiences as a pioneer in the Canadian Northwest indelibly shaped her perspective on freedom, individualism, and responsibility. A voracious reader from an early age, she broke into the newspaper business as an editorial writer in the American Northwest during the early part of the twentieth century. Her first regular column, appearing in the *Vancouver World*, established Paterson's long-lived literary persona as, simply, "I.M.P." Her first book, a novel titled *The Shadow Riders*, was published in 1916. Eight additional books, seven of them novels, appeared over the next thirty years, some to wide critical acclaim. She moved to New York shortly after World War I to write for magazines and newspapers. Paterson, or "Pat," as close friends called her, became a formidable and outspoken literary critic.

From 1926 until 1949, her influential weekly literary column, "Turns with a Bookworm," appeared in the Sunday book review supplement of the *New York Herald-Tribune.* There she lashed out at poets and novelists who she felt violated literary standards and turned her wrath equally on books by representatives of the Left and Right, treating each author as an individual rather than as a spokesperson for a particular political stance. She paid close attention to the tools used by authors in their works and their ability to "make the essential truth acceptable." Her column frequently discussed political issues as well, especially during the 1930s and 1940s. Her biographer, Stephen Cox, notes that "her idea of literature as an individual accomplishment was clearly relevant to her advocacy of economic and political individualism."

Isabel Paterson

Such forays into political thought culminated in Paterson's 1943 book on political economy, *The God of the Machine.* In it, she used the idea of an open electric circuit to depict the ideal working of a free society. The founding fathers, she argued, designed political and legal structures that allow peaceful human energies to flow and interact freely in an unhampered market economy. The energy system is short-circuited whenever government begins to intervene by directing individuals' lives and regulating the economy. "Government by force is a contradiction in terms and an impossibility in physics," Paterson wrote, "Force is what is governed. Government originates in the moral faculty." Hence, she concluded, "A machine economy cannot run on a mechanistic philosophy." "The root of the matter," Paterson believed, "is ethical, philosophical and religious, involving the relation . . . of man's creative faculty to his Creator." Appearing in the same year as Ayn Rand's *The Fountainhead* and Rose Wilder Lane's *The Discovery of Freedom* (each a friend of sorts), Paterson's analysis won accolades from libertarian and conservative thinkers. Albert Jay Nock, for example, praised the work as "the ablest, most acute and closely-reasoned piece of political writing that has been produced in this country" in his lifetime. The book propelled Paterson into heady correspondence with leading conservative intellectuals, including Russell Kirk.

Forcibly retired from her *Herald-Tribune* column in January 1949, Paterson set to work on a ninth novel, *Joyous Gard.* In 1955, William F. Buckley Jr. convinced Paterson to become a contributor to his new journal, *National Review*, for which she wrote a handful of articles, ranging in topic from North-South relations to teaching children to read. Angered by a slight editorial change in a book review she had written, she severed her ties with Buckley and the magazine in 1959. During her last years, Paterson sought the assistance of her sometime friend Ayn Rand in the publication of *Joyous Gard*, but to no avail. After several weeks of serious illness, Paterson passed away on January 10, 1961. She is buried in an unmarked grave, her name and contributions to literary and political thought all but forgotten.

—EDMUND OPITZ

Further Reading

Cox, Stephen D. *The Woman and the Dynamo: Isabel Paterson and the Idea of America.* New Brunswick, N.J.: Transaction, 2004.

See also: Lane, Rose Wilder; Rand, Ayn

Pegler, Westbrook (1894–1969)

An outstanding sportswriter and controversial political essayist, Westbrook Pegler was one of the most recognizable names in the American press from the Jazz Age through the dawn of the Cold War. As a sportswriter, he was known for his colorful expressions and the equally colorful "you-are-there" descriptions of sporting events. It was Pegler who described how a fur-clad football crowd at Yale "rose as one raccoon" during the 1920s, an era he termed "the Era of Wonderful Nonsense." In 1933 he moved beyond sportswriting to cover political issues, to which he brought a Menckenesque invective-charged skepticism toward the prominent and powerful combined with a very un-Menckenesque faith in the common man.

During the 1930s Pegler became one of the most widely read journalists of his day—his writings syndicated in some seventy-five newspapers—largely because of his unfashionably irreverent treatment of Franklin and Eleanor Roosevelt as well as Henry Wallace, the Progressive Party's presidential candidate in 1948. (Wallace's political career was effectively destroyed after Pegler delved into Wallace's past and uncovered a collection of bizarre letters to a spiritualist.) Long associated with Scripps-Howard newspapers and United Press International, he achieved his greatest triumph in 1941, when he received the Pulitzer Prize after writing a series of articles on union racketeer George Scalise.

Having broken into journalism at about the time of the 1919 "Black Sox Scandal," Pegler inherited from other journalists of that era a strong sense of skepticism in men and institutions, typified by the belief that if the highly placed individuals who oversaw sporting events or government policies showed signs of benefiting in terms of wealth or influence, the "fix" was probably in. He early recognized the poisonous philosophy of Adolf Hitler as well as the iniquities of racial segregation in professional sports in America. (It is ironic that Pegler, a scourge of Nazi anti-Semitism, succumbed to publishing anti-Semitic remarks late in his own career.) Unlike many of his press colleagues, he wrote of communism not as the wave of the future but as an evil ideology that needed to be opposed vigorously.

As he passed his prime, Pegler drifted from a conservative suspicion of big-government intrusiveness and the skewering of political frauds into mere abusiveness, eventually being sued for libel and concluding his long career by writing for two little-known Southern publications. Although he is not much remembered today, Pegler put his stamp upon a caustic journalistic prose style that foreshadows the work of several later conservative writers, including Patrick J. Buchanan. At the height of his powers, Pegler prompted Stanley Walker to claim, "Mr. Pegler is valuable because he is the man who is always asking 'Is that so?' . . . He is a tough man who calls them as he sees them." "He has made his mistakes," wrote M. Stanton Evans, "but he has never wavered in his commitment to American institutions, or lost touch with the striking virtues of his native idiom."

—James E. Person Jr.

Further Reading

Farr, Finis. *Fair Enough: The Life of Westbrook Pegler*. New Rochelle, N.Y.: Arlington House, 1975.

Orodenker, Richard. "Westbrook Pegler." In *Twentieth-Century American Sportswriters*. Vol. 171 of Dictionary of Literary Biography. Edited by Richard Orodenker, 264–74. Detroit: Gale, 1996.

Pilat, Oliver. *Pegler: Angry Man of the Press*. Boston: Beacon Press, 1963.

Percy, Walker (1916–90)

Born in Birmingham, Alabama, Walker Percy was one of the preeminent American novelists and essayists of the twentieth century. His first novel, *The Moviegoer* (1961), won a National Book Award and immediately established the author as a distinctive literary voice. *The Last Gentleman* (1966), *Love in the Ruins* (1971), *Lancelot* (1977), *The Second Coming* (1980), and *The Thanatos Syndrome* (1987) confirmed him as a philosophical novelist. His two major volumes of nonfiction, *The Message in the Bottle* (1975) and *Lost in the Cosmos* (1983), demonstrated that literary artistry might still be brought to the writing of philosophy—a philosophy that rejected the dominant liberal literary ethos and social mores at that.

To call Percy a philosophical novelist seems to consign him to the world of ideas clumsily clothed in fictional form. But his major achievement is to have brought grace, humor, and a profound concern for recovering the authentically human to the existential questions of life in late-twentieth-century America. As a southerner, Percy had a strong sense of place, family, and history. But as a man who had occupied himself with science for most of his education and who had graduated from the Columbia College of Physicians and Surgeons, he was also aware of the contemporary power of abstract reason. Much of the richness of his philosophical stories derives from the interplay, and attempt at resolution, of the simultaneous concreteness and abstractness of the human animal.

For Percy, language was the key to the modern predicament. Language is the one human phenomenon, he believed, that cannot be explained by a reductive science. Hence, his attempts in *Message in the Bottle* and *Lost in the Cosmos* (subtitled *The Last Self-Help Book*) to show the self-defeating—indeed, profoundly distorting—nature of the various modern projects to reduce man to the status of "an organism within an environment." Though Percy had converted to Catholicism in 1949 and regarded the historically rooted religion of the Bible as the ultimate antidote to modern abstraction and alienation, he repeatedly emphasized that the mystery of language and of the human person was not only a religious question but also an empirical one.

Walker Percy

That mystery receives its full embodiment in his novels. One of the major problems Percy addresses there is that advances in modern technology and the increased ability to satisfy human "needs" do not make people feel better. Placing himself in the tradition of Kierkegaard, Gabriel Marcel, Heidegger, Sartre, and Camus, Percy explores how it is that modern man must "come to himself," generally through physical or emotional ordeal. The mere abstract truths of medicine, psychology, philosophy, democratic politics, even religion are all well and good so far as they go. The problem is that once they have become accepted as abstract scientific truths "about" us, they become denatured, lose their value as living guides to the sovereign wayfarer, man.

Percy is merciless and hilarious in excoriating the pretensions of his medical colleagues who have claimed for science more knowledge about the human condition than it can possess. The doctors and scientists have also accepted a mechanistic interpretation of "compassion" and have barely noticed as euthanasia, abortion, and other violations of the sacredness of human life become common and seemingly required.

But Percy also attacks the "bad faith" of a spectrum of seemingly good people: southern Stoics, Christian evangelists, advocates of democratic living, and purveyors of self-help who, whatever their intentions, do not much help people to a living appreciation of the mystery of their own being. Percy's conservatism is not so much a political stance (he was, for example, active in the civil rights movement) as a reminder that every generation must act and suffer and come to understand the truths of limited and fallen human existence for itself.

—ROBERT ROYAL

Further Reading

Foote, Shelby, and Walker Percy. *The Correspondence of Shelby Foote and Walker Percy.* Edited by Jay Tolson. New York: W. W. Norton, 1997.

Percy, Walker. *Conversations with Walker Percy.* Edited by Lewis Lawson and Victor Kramer. Jackson, Miss.: University Press of Mississippi, 1985.

Percy, Walker. *Signposts in a Strange Land.* Edited by Patrick Samway. New York: Farrar, Straus and Giroux, 1991.

Tolson, Jay. *Pilgrim in the Ruins: A Life of Walker Percy.* New York: Simon & Schuster, 1992.

See also: modernity and postmodernity

personalism

"Personalism" names a number of independent philosophical schools that take the human person as a central explanatory principle, including American personalists such as Walt Whitman, Josiah Royce and W. E. Hocking as well as French neoscholastic personalists such as Emmanuel Mounier, Jacques Maritain, and Gabriel Marcel.

The term "person" comes from the Latin *persona*, originally meaning "mask, actor, or dramatic role," for *per-sonare* (to "sound through") describes the use of masks as a kind of megaphone to amplify the voices of actors in an open-air theater. The term gained special importance in early Christian theological controversies about the proper description of the members of the Divine Trinity and the unity of divine and human natures in Christ. Boethius devised what has become the classical definition of "person" as "an individual substance of a rational nature" in order to include within a single term divine and angelic as well as human beings. As suggested by this definition, personalists have regularly emphasized both the dignity that attaches to all persons by virtue of rationality and the status of persons as individual beings or substances.

Although there are atheistic personalists, such as J. M. McTaggart, personalists are generally theistic and many hold that the principle of ultimate reality is a spiritual, supernatural being (a personal God) who created human persons as distinct substances in his own image. But there are also personalists among the absolute idealists in the tradition of Hegel who hold that all reality is one absolute spirit or mind and that all finite beings, including human beings, are simply the manifestations of this one absolute being. Likewise, there are panpsychist personalists such as A. N. Whitehead and Charles Hartshorne who work in the tradition of Leibniz, who took the supreme monad (God) to have created all other monads in a preestablished harmony.

The Boston University School of Theology has been an important center of American personalism ever since the nineteenth-century efforts of Borden Parker Browne to elaborate an explicitly theistic version of personalist idealism. One of his students, Ralph Tyler Flewelling, founded the journal *The Personalist.* Another, Edgar Sheffield Brightman, stressed the view that the natural world needs to be understood as an order within the mind of God but that God needs to be understood as existing temporally rather than atemporally in eternity.

Mounier's personalism is closely related to existentialism, but is explicitly Christian and communitarian. He stresses the "vocation" to seek communication with other unique persons. Distinguishing "person" from the "abstract, legal" individual of the political realm, Mounier stressed that a person is a "spiritual being" who must respect a hierarchy of values and live a life of "responsible commitment." In reaction to excessive claims in the name of individualism and equal excesses in the service of collectivism, Maritain's *The Person and the Common Good* (1947) attempts to make the necessary distinctions between the inalienable rights inherent in every human being as person and the duties intrinsic to membership in civil society. Among the most important contemporary proponents of scholastic personalism is W. Norris Clarke, whose *Person and Being* (1993) proposes a creative completion of Thomistic metaphysics by careful use of certain ideas from the traditions of process philosophy and personalism. Because of its obvious influence on Pope John Paul II and its conveyance of the idea of the individual-as-always-already-in-relation-to-others, personalism has also of late become a philosophical school of substantial interest to religious, and especially Catholic, thinkers suspicious of the liberal philosophical tradition.

—Joseph W. Koterski, S. J.

Further Reading

Marcel, Gabriel. *Man against Mass Society.* Translated by G. S. Fraser. Chicago: Regnery, 1962.

Mounier, Emmanuel. *Personalism.* Translated by Philip Mairet. Notre Dame, Ind.: University of Notre Dame Press, 1970.

Wojtyla, Karol. *The Acting Person.* Translated by Andrzej Potocki. Boston: D. Reidel, 1979.

See also: Acton Institute; John Paul II, Pope

Philadelphia Society

The Philadelphia Society was founded in 1964 by Donald J. Lipsett, working together with William F. Buckley Jr., Edwin J. Feulner, Frank S. Meyer, and Milton Friedman. The society has provided a forum for conservative thinkers to discuss the meaning of ordered liberty in a frank and open exchange of ideas. Lipsett saw a need to provide among conservative thinkers and activists the encouragement to continue the battle of ideas generated by the Barry Goldwater phenomenon in American politics.

The society's name derives from the fact that Lipsett was living in Philadelphia at the time of the society's founding and thought that the city, as the cradle of the Constitution, symbolized the broad conservative coalition he wished to nourish. From the beginning, the society provided a congenial place for traditionalist and libertarian conservatives to discuss their differences. Thus, the society is characterized by the sort of fusionism that animated the first successful postwar conservative political coalition. "The Philadelphia Society still today tries to maintain the tension and vitality of the two groups as a hallmark characteristic of its intellectual activity," says the organization's current and longtime secretary, William F. Campbell.

The Mont Pelerin Society and the Intercollegiate Studies Institute (ISI) were important forerunners of the society. From the former, Lipsett drew the society's dedication to the market economy and its belief that the society was not to be a lobbying organization that took specific stands on the pressing political issues of the day or issued manifestos in support of particular policies. From ISI and its president E. Victor Milione, Lipsett took the society's broader commitment to the moral foundations of Western civilization.

The society sees its mission as "deepening the intellectual foundation of a free and ordered society and of broadening the understanding of its basic principles and traditions." It sponsors twice-yearly regional and national meetings similar to scholarly symposia, the panels featuring influential conservative thinkers whose analysis shapes ongoing debates in economics, education, politics, culture, religion, and philosophy. Encouraging the thoughtful and candid discussion of topics, the society's meetings are based on the assumption that understanding and insight, not conformity and coercion, will engender a heightened awareness of various and often conflicting views. As a result, its meetings have not been without their moments of tension and controversy; it was at a 1986 meeting of the society, for instance, that the split between paleo- and neoconservatives—spurred by the latter group's successful campaign to derail the nomination of M. E. Bradford as chairman of the National Endowment for the Humanities—became highly public and seemingly irreparable.

The Philadelphia Society's membership list has included a remarkable proportion of the most influential conservative thinkers of the last forty years, including Nobel Prize-winning economists Milton Friedman, Friedrich von Hayek, and Ronald H. Coase. Prominent conservative thinkers Russell A. Kirk, M. E. Bradford, M. Stanton Evans, Claes Ryn, Ellis Sandoz, and Forrest McDonald have not only been frequent speakers but also have served as president of the society. Other core members in its early years included Erik Ritter von Kuehnelt-Leddihn, Henry Regnery, Gerhart Niemeyer, and Eliseo Vivas. The quality of its membership is doubtless one reason that the society has become, in the words of historian Lee Edwards, "American conservatism's premier organization of intellectuals."

—WILLIAM F. MEEHAN III

Further Reading

Edwards, Lee. *Educating for Liberty: The First Half-Century of the Intercollegiate Studies Institute.* Washington, D.C.: Regnery, 2003.
Kuehnelt-Leddihn, Erik von. "The Philadelphia Society. *National Review,* November 2, 1965, 986.

See also: Intercollegiate Studies Institute; Mont Pelerin Society

Phillips, Howard (1941–)

Howard Phillips is a longtime conservative activist best known for his gadfly runs for president as the candidate of the U.S. Taxpayer Party and its successor, the Constitution Party.

Phillips is a Harvard-educated populist who, after helping found Young Americans for Freedom and toiling in conservative and Republican political circles throughout the 1960s, was rewarded with several positions in the Nixon administration. He was director of the U.S. Office of Economic Opportunity in 1974 when he resigned and repudiated the Republican Party. His principle disagreement with the Nixon White House and with the GOP stemmed from Nixon's desire to cement Lyndon Johnson's Great Society programs, rather than roll them back. Phillips soon after founded the Conservative Caucus, the group with which he would be most associated until his first run for president in 1992.

For a long period the Conservative Caucus was a leading conservative activist group, weighing in forcefully on issues such as the Panama Canal and the Start II treaties. The Conservative Caucus also pushed right-to-life and anti–United Nations literature, as well as a number of initiatives protesting excessive government regulation and taxation. In addition, Phillips and his group helped coordinate private-sector support of anticommunist freedom fighters in places like Angola and Nicaragua. In recent years the group has moved from a conventional Reaganite conservatism to positions more closely associated with Patrick Buchanan. Recent Conservative Caucus campaigns have aimed at a national version of California's Proposition 187 (to end federal subsidies for non-American citizens) as well as opposition to the North American Free Trade Agreement.

In 1992 Phillips started the U.S. Taxpayers Party (USTP) with the idea, according to Phillips's biographical material, of "restoring the Federal Republic to its delegated, enumerated functions and returning American jurisprudence to its original 'common law' Biblical foundations." Phillips was the USTP's candidate in 1992 and again in 1996. When Pat Buchanan lost the race for the Republican nomination for president in 1996, Phillips offered to step down as the USTP candidate and allow Buchanan to run in his place. Buchanan toyed with the idea but ultimately declined, not choosing to run as an independent candidate until 2000. Phillips would run again for president in 2000, this time under the banner of the Constitution Party, the new name of the USTP.

—MAX SCHULZ

Further Reading

Phillips, Howard, et al. *The New Right at Harvard.* Vienna, Va.: Conservative Caucus, 1983.

See also: Buchanan, Patrick J.

Podhoretz, Norman (1930–)

The editor in chief of *Commentary* magazine from 1960 to 1995, Norman Podhoretz is considered one of the preeminent neoconservative social and literary critics in the United States. In such works as *Making It* (1967), *Breaking Ranks: A Political Memoir* (1979), and *Ex-Friends: Falling out with Allen Ginsberg, Lionel and Diana Trilling, Lillian Hellman, Hannah Arendt, and Norman Mailer* (1999), he details his odyssey from heir-apparent of the leftist "New York Intellectuals" to staunch advocate of meritocratic values and a strong national foreign policy and opponent of statism and anti-Semitism. Considered a turncoat by his former colleagues on the Left, Podhoretz seeks in his work to provide a counterblast to the libertine collectivist vision that sprang into bloom within American culture during the tumultuous 1960s and early 1970s.

Born in Brooklyn, New York, and educated in literature at Columbia, Jewish Theological Seminary, and Cambridge under Lionel Trilling and F. R. Leavis, Podhoretz joined the staff of *Commentary* in 1955, making his mark there as a discerning and thoughtful literary critic. The criticism written during his early career melds literary and political concerns, with Norman Mailer once writing, "Podhoretz is probably as good as any critic in America at this kind of writing." In 1960 he was named editor in chief of *Commentary*, at the time a periodical that supported the policies of the Adlai Stevenson wing of the Democratic Party, with its emphasis upon anticommunist policies abroad and the expansion of the role of government in domestic affairs. Around 1964, at the time of the rise of the new Left, Podhoretz began to shift his emphasis from literature to politics and cultural criticism; he also began to distance himself from the liberalism evident in the academy, government, and American letters. The collection of literary essays he published in 1964 reflected this; of *Doings and Undoings: The Fifties and After in American Writing*, Frank Kermode wrote that Podhoretz "speaks from his own limitations, as a person of this time and this place: the Jewish New Yorker, the ex-revisionist liberal, collecting in his book the thoughts of a series of Podhoretzes who, over a few years, have seen New York, Jewry, liberalism and many other things move through the different positions plotted for history by what people have said and written. What gives it all unity and value is the only quality that can ever do so—a humanely intelligent personality."

While *Doings and Undoings* received a warm critical response, his next work, *Making It* was the pivot of his career, wrote Andrew Ferguson, who added that "it would have guaranteed his place in American literature no matter what he wrote or edited before or after." Recounting in unsparing detail Podhoretz's break with the doctrinaire liberalism of his upbringing and training, *Making It* evoked disdain and hostility from the author's longtime liberal associates and sympathizers in the world of magazine journalism, including Saul Maloff, Daniel Stern, and Mordecai Richler. "The memoir's unblinking candor has been noted often," wrote Ferguson, "and even now . . . it has the capacity to unnerve any reader who blunders into it unawares." Podhoretz's second memoir, *Breaking Ranks*, earned Podhoretz further disdain from the Left, with Christopher Hitchens describing the author as "a born-again conformist with some interesting disorders of the ego." In this work, Podhoretz described his political odyssey away from the world of calculated, toney expressions of contempt for the American middle class, the breezy mindset which equated "Amerika" with Nazi Germany, and the expressions of sympathy with various "people's democratic republics" around the world that characterized the heyday of the new Left. The book describes his break with various figures within the New York Jewish literary world, such as Irving Howe, Jason Epstein, and Lillian Hellman. "*Breaking Ranks* cannot fairly be dismissed as a piece of self-indulgence or mere intellectual

Norman Podhoretz

gossip," wrote Joseph Epstein. "The events its author describes are important. I think he describes them without falsehood, even though many of his portraits of contemporaries are etched in acid." Hilton Kramer added, "In dealing with [the] fateful link between culture and politics in the period of the Vietnam War and its aftermath, Mr. Podhoretz has few equals among the writers of his time."

By the time Podhoretz published *Breaking Ranks*, *Commentary* was well established as a leading magazine of American neoconservatism, publishing works by Rael Jean Isaac, Terry Teachout, and Podhoretz's wife, Midge Decter, among many others. In *Commentary*, Jeane Kirkpatrick published an essay that described the American liberal as a peculiar being whose instinctive reaction to any international crisis is to "blame America first"—an expression used against his opponents by President Ronald Reagan in the years that immediately followed. Early in the 1990s, Podhoretz entered into a respectful, widely publicized debate in the pages of *National Review* with William F. Buckley Jr. concerning anti-Semitism within the ranks of conservatism. Retiring from the active editorship of *Commentary* in 1995, Podhoretz has spent recent years explicating further his disagreements with the Left and his deep love of America.

—James E. Person Jr.

Further Reading

Podhoretz, Norman. *My Love Affair with America: The Cautionary Tale of a Cheerful Conservative.* New York: Free Press, 2002.
———. *The Norman Podhoretz Reader: A Selection of His Writings from the 1950s through the 1990s.*

Edited by Thomas L. Jeffers. New York: Free Press, 2004.

Winchell, Mark Royden. *Neoconservative Criticism: Norman Podhoretz, Kenneth S. Lynn, and Joseph Epstein.* Boston: Twayne, 1991.

See also: Commentary; *Jewish conservatives; neoconservatism*

political action committees

A political action committee (PAC) is an organization that receives voluntary contributions and makes donations and expenditures to influence the outcome of elections. In the 1960s, virtually all PACs were organized by labor unions, who gave the vast bulk of their money to candidates on the Left. Soon thereafter conservative activists and business interests began to form and use PACs effectively.

The first major conservative movement PAC was the Conservative Victory Fund of the American Conservative Union, which began in the 1960s. After 1970, conservative PACs multiplied rapidly and became major factors in congressional campaigns for a decade or more. Some organized effective training programs for conservative activists. Their successes include the defeats of liberal incumbents by Sen. Orrin Hatch in 1976, Sen. Roger Jepsen in 1978, and Sen. Steve Symms in 1980.

Among the most prominent PAC organizers in the early '70s were Paul Weyrich, who formed the Committee for the Survival of a Free Congress, and Terry Dolan, who formed the National Conservative PAC (NCPAC). Citizens for the Republic, the continuation as a PAC of the 1976 Reagan presidential campaign, became for many years the largest conservative movement PAC.

Business PACs began in earnest after the famous 1975 SUNPAC advisory opinion in which the new Federal Election Commission determined that businesses could organize PACs.

The founders of major conservative movement PACs created other organizations, including lobbying groups and tax-exempt foundations of various types. Organizational entrepreneurs found it much harder to raise funds for their PACs than for their other groups. Conservative movement PACs began a long and slow decline. Nevertheless, many conservative movement PACs survive and significantly support their candidates in primaries and general elections. Numerous active PACs organized around specific clusters of conservative issues also continue.

In federal elections, the law limits any individual's gifts to a PAC to $5,000 per year and limits a PAC's contributions to a candidate to $5,000 per election. The U.S. Supreme Court's 1976 *Buckley v. Valeo* decision struck down some serious, further restrictions pushed through Congress in the first wave of legislative attacks on citizen participation through PACs. State laws regarding PACs' activities in nonfederal elections vary widely, some more restrictive and some much less restrictive.

There is, however, no limit on how much a federal PAC can spend on an independent expenditure for or against a specific federal candidate. Though limited in what they can *receive* from a single donor, PACs can *spend* unlimited amounts in a given election contest, provided their spending is uncoordinated with any candidate's campaign. A conservative example would be the Conservative Leadership PACs' independent expenditure campaign against Al Gore in the 2000 presidential election.

Another way conservative PACs avoid the federal limits is by "bundling" contributions. A PAC can solicit checks made out to a specific candidate, up to $1,000 per person, from an *unlimited* number of donors, then bundle and deliver those personal checks to the candidate. This technique, made famous by the Left's Emily's List PAC, was successfully copied by such conservative PACs as the Susan B. Anthony List and Mike Farris's Madison Project.

For conservatives, the great variable in campaign contributions has been the behavior of the business PACs, which dramatically vary the percentage of the massive campaign contributions they give to conservative and Republican candidates. The new business PACs shocked conservatives and Republicans by giving a lot of money to liberals and Democrats. After public exposure of this, most of the business-related PACs came into the conservative Republican camp. But in 1981–82, then Congressman Tony Coelho, chairman of the Democratic Congressional Campaign Committee, warned the business PAC community that strongly antibusiness legislation would be passed if they didn't give more money to Democrats. By the 1988 elections, business-related PACs, in aggregate, gave much more to Democrats than to Republicans.

Business PAC growth slowed, and they gave mostly to Democrats until Republicans captured both houses of Congress in 1994. Since then Republicans have received somewhat more from business PACs than have Democrats. In 2001–2, congressional candidates received $969.5 million from all sources. Business PACs gave $163 million in this election period, with 64% of their donations going to support Republican candidates.

The Bipartisan Campaign Reform Act, also known as the McCain-Feingold bill, has increased restrictions on political donations and advertising by all outside groups, including PACs. Signed by President Bush in 2002, this legislation provoked much controversy concerning whether it violated free speech and free association as protected by the First Amendment. Nevertheless, the major provisions of the act were upheld by the Supreme Court in December 2003. The effect that this act has had on PACs is equivocal: while it clearly limits the activity of PACs, it has also hindered other forms of political involvement to a greater degree, so that PACs remain one of the most effective methods for groups to influence politics, and they continue to increase in number.

Until McCain-Feingold, at least, the number of PACs seemed to be increasing. In the 2001–2 election cycle, a total of 4,594 federal PACs of all kinds were active, compared with 4,499 in 1999–2000.

—MORTON BLACKWELL

Further Reading

Sabato, Larry J. *PAC Power: Inside the World of Political Action Committees.* New York: W. W. Norton, 1984.

See also: American Conservative Union; Free Congress Foundation; National Conservative Political Action Committee; Weyrich, Paul M.

Political Science Reviewer

An annual review of books related to the field of political science, broadly understood, and founded in 1973 by James McClellan and George Carey, the *Political Science Reviewer* continues to publish under the auspices of the Intercollegiate Studies Institute. In 2004 Carey relinquished his editorship and Bruce Frohnen became acting editor. The journal publishes article-length (usually more than 10,000-word) reviews of both classic and contemporary works, with special attention to books dealing with constitutional law and political thought. In addition to such reviews, each issue generally contains a symposium on the work of one author or work (e.g., the 1930 Southern Agrarian manifesto *I'll Take My Stand*). Other symposium subjects have included John Stuart Mill, Michael Oakeshott, and Eric Voegelin.

Several important issues have received

their first scholarly hearing in the pages of this journal. For example, Joseph Hamburger's 1995 article on "Individuality and Moral Reform: The Rhetoric of Liberty and the Reality of Restraint in Mill's *On Liberty*" first made clear the argument that Mill's supposed libertarianism actually is part of his attempt to establish a new orthodoxy rooted in a religion of mankind, in which he would indoctrinate all persons. Other articles have looked at social conservatives on the left end of the political spectrum, the thought of Václav Havel, and—a particular concern of the journal—the political thought of the American founding.

—Bruce Frohnen

Further Reading

Edwards, Lee. *Educating for Liberty: The First Half-Century of the Intercollegiate Studies Institute.* Washington, D.C.: Regnery, 2003.

See also: Carey, George W.; Intercollegiate Studies Institute

populism

The political movement called populism began as a reaction to the depression of the 1870s. Farmers were particularly hard hit when prices for agricultural goods plummeted, the cost of operating farms rose, and the value of manufactured goods increased. In response, farmers formed cooperative organizations such as the National Grange and the Farmers' Alliance, which sold supplies at reduced prices, offered loans at below-market rates, and stored crops in silos when prices were depressed.

Over the next twenty years, populism became a political movement whose members established the People's Party. Its primary goal was to end the gold standard. Populists argued that issuing silver and paper money would spur the economy and help alleviate the enormous debts that farmers had incurred during lean economic years. Populists favored direct popular election of senators, an eight-hour workday, nationalization of railroads to help transport goods to market more cheaply, and a graduated income tax as a mechanism for limiting the power of the rich.

The People's Party made a respectable showing in the election of 1892 when its presidential candidate received 1,041,028 popular and twenty-two Electoral College votes. Sensing a chance to gain the White House, Populists endorsed William Jennings Bryan, who had become famous for his fiery "Cross of Gold" Speech that attacked the gold standard. In 1896 Bryan, representing both the Democratic and the People's parties, received 6,467,946 popular votes but lost the election to William McKinley. Bryan was nominated again in 1900 but lost the election by an even larger margin. By 1908 the People's Party had vanished from the political landscape.

Populism does not refer only to the political movement that used its name. Populism has roots in America's past stretching back to the founding, and echoes of populism resound through political discourse today. Populism emphasizes the power of individual citizens.

The framers of the Constitution rejected populist principles. They argued that while individuals often intend to do the public good, they are not equipped to put good policies into practice. Also, it is impossible for the whole population to meet and discuss issues, whereas a smaller representative body can deliberate on proposals and formulate better laws. Most people are not schooled in public affairs and are too busy with their own enterprises to become expert in lawmaking or administration. A republic allows for a division of labor in which representatives concentrate on public affairs. Moreover, the people are sometimes blind to their own shortcomings and may fail to see that the particular interest of their group might not be in the interest of the nation. Because they are accountable to their constituents, representatives are under the watchful eye of the people. They are expected to get things done. In order to form a ruling majority they must negotiate and compromise. Republican government is thus more moderate than popular rule.

The framers were aware that democracies tend to place greater and greater power in the hands of the people. They hoped that the Constitution would curb the inclination of popular rule either to transform itself into majority tyranny or to disintegrate into factional anarchy.

As the framers feared, populist movements have arisen claiming that the people are the only legitimate source of authority. During the 1960s, the new Left battled what it perceived to be the illegitimate "Establishment" (made up of business, government, and military elites) pursuing an imperialist war in Vietnam. The new Left adopted the slogan "Power to the People" and hoped to end the war by instituting that principle.

By the 1980s, a form of right-wing populism arose under the banner of the Moral Majority, which claimed that liberal groups in the bureaucracy, the media, and especially in entertainment had foisted an immoral and libertine culture on America. As its name implies, the Moral Majority claimed that it only had to organize at the grassroots to reverse the moral slide of the nation and wrest power from the liberal oligarchy.

Ross Perot exemplified a populism of the middle. In the presidential election of 1992, Perot ran as the candidate representing those citizens who believed that government had abandoned its responsibility to meet their needs. The government could not solve the debt crisis, the crime problem, or the competitiveness crunch. The people's representatives had sold out to special interests and foreign lobbyists. America's prob-

lems could be resolved only if someone acted exclusively for the common good. Perot claimed that he could "just do it!" His plan for how he would do it was not altogether clear. For the most part he offered mainstream solutions, such as cutting spending, raising taxes on gasoline, and investing in research. While the policy changes he proposed were quite moderate, the way he attempted to implement them was not. Perot scorned the traditional way of running for office and of governing once in power.

If elected, Perot pledged to clean up politics by banishing corruption, ridding the government of special interests, and ending gridlock in Washington. One of the nation's major problems, according to Perot, was that its political institutions subverted the will of the people—for Perot, a pure expression of the common good. The problem was a lack of democracy, and the cure was more democracy.

The heir to the Perot movement—which fell apart when Perot behaved erratically—was Jesse Ventura, a one-time professional wrestler who rode to the governor's mansion in Minnesota by flaunting his flamboyant personality and his disdain for conventional politics. Ventura immediately attacked the institutions of government as undemocratic and sought to institute a unicameral legislature in his state. He did not seek another term.

A new and powerful tool for populism is the Internet. It allows people to disseminate information and express their views freely to a wide audience without intervening institutions such as government bureaucracies or media organizations. Some people have argued that the Internet will eventually replace representative government by allowing people to decide public policy issues directly. Conservatives are led to wonder whether such an innovation would be wise.

—JAMES PONTUSO

Further Reading

Goodwyn, Lawrence. *The Populist Moment: A Short History of the Agrarian Revolt in America.* New York: Oxford University Press, 1978.

McKenna, George, ed. *American Populism.* New York: Putnam, 1974.

Lasch, Christopher. *The True and Only Heaven: Progress and Its Critics.* New York: W. W. Norton, 1991.

See also: Bryan, William Jennings; Buchanan, Patrick J.; Lasch, Christopher; Moral Majority; Phillips, Howard; Wallace, George C.; West, American

pornography

Conservatives in the United States are divided on the appropriate response to the proliferation of pornographic and sexually explicit material reaching American homes via neighborhood video outlets, the U.S. mail, cable and satellite TV, telephones, and the Internet. Libertarian conservatives, on the one hand, contend that pornography, like drugs, will always be available to users in some form, that consumption is a matter of free choice, and that government and the legal system have no part to play in the regulation of pornography distribution or the prosecution of pornography producers. Pornography is in the mind of the consumer, libertarians argue, and the selling of representations of sex is as old as recorded history.

Public opinion polls, however, consistently reveal that a substantial majority of Americans favor a crackdown on all illegal pornography, and on the question of sexual violence and child pornography, the figure jumps to over 90 percent. Official studies of pornography and sexually explicit material have determined that pornography is by no means a victimless crime. Federal commissions in 1970 and in 1986 determined that minors comprise the largest category of consumers of pornography in America, and that

even so-called "soft" porn could well have a serious, harmful, and lasting effect on the mind of a child. Pornography was found to be physically, psychologically and socially damaging. Rape and child molestation are the principal physical harms associated with use of pornography. Psychological damages suffered by porn users range from suicidal thoughts and behavior to the abuse of alcohol and other drugs. Social problems include financial losses, divorce, promotion of racial hatred, promiscuity, prostitution, and sexual harassment.

The production and distribution of pornography causes many serious public health problems—mainly through the spread of AIDS and venereal diseases during anonymous sexual contacts in "adult" bookstores—and illegal pornography has become a multibillion dollar industry that is almost exclusively controlled by organized crime.

While many legal experts are reluctant to define "pornography" and "obscenity," the U.S. Supreme Court in 1973 ruled that material is obscene if all three of the following conditions are met: (1) the average person, applying contemporary community standards, would find that the work, taken as a whole, appeals to the prurient interest [in sex]; and (2) the work depicts or describes, in a patently offensive way, sexual conduct specifically defined by the applicable state [or federal] law; and (3) the work, taken as a whole, lacks serious literary, artistic, political, or scientific value.

The Court also ruled that pornography is legally akin to libel, slander and false advertising and cannot be considered "free speech" protected by the First Amendment.

Thus, the Supreme Court in effect ruled that prevailing community standards determine what pornography is "obscene." What is illegal is determined by what is successfully prosecuted in a community. Pornography is presumptively protected by the First Amendment until a court—normally in a jury trial—determines it to be "obscene." Once a court determines items of pornography to be obscene, these items then serve as a guide for community standards.

The Final Report of the U.S. Attorney General's Commission on Pornography, which was set up by Attorney General Edwin Meese in 1985, found that the enormous differences between states and between geographic areas in obscenity law enforcement are due not to differences in the laws, but to differences in how vigorously and how often these laws are enforced. Prosecutorial successes in Atlanta and Cincinnati, for example, plainly indicate that the laws are available for those areas that choose the course of vigorous enforcement. The Commission found, however, that with few exceptions, obscenity laws that *are* on the books go unenforced. Manpower shortages in most large cities were cited. The commissioners concluded that with respect to the criminal laws relating to obscenity, there was a striking "underenforcement" that resulted from "undercomplaining, underinvestigating, underprosecution," and "undersentencing."

Much of this debate, however, is quickly becoming less and less relevant, as pornographers shift more of their resources and attention to the Internet, where anonymity protects both purveyor and client from not only prosecution, but public attention. While some extreme libertarians have made clear that they welcome this change, the burgeoning Internet porn industry has clearly also led to a disturbing increase in sexual addictions, especially among males, a social problem that has of yet not attracted the attention it deserves.

—LARRY MORAHAN

Further Reading

Shapiro, Ben. *Porn Generation.* Washington, D.C.: Regnery, 2005.

See also: family

Pound, Ezra (1885–1972)

Ezra Pound will forever remain controversial. What most critics agree on is that he was a central figure in the world of literary High Modernism: a distinguished poet (though some prefer his earlier to his later work) and a brilliant and generous networker who gave timely practical and artistic help to T. S. Eliot, James Joyce, and Wyndham Lewis, among many others.

However, Pound's anti-Semitism, his sympathy for fascism, and his political and economic ideas in general have earned him (in many cases, rightly) harsh denunciation. While living in Italy during World War II he made ill-advised radio broadcasts that were treated by the American government as traitorous. After the war he was incarcerated in St. Elizabeth's Hospital in Washington, D.C., for eleven years. Upon his release he returned to Italy, where he spent the rest of his life.

In the academy today, attacks on Pound are de rigeur. A few literary critics with conservative sensibilities, including Denis Donoghue and the late Hugh Kenner, have attempted to defend large aspects of Pound's achievement as a poet, but this has also earned them vilification.

A few other independent voices have questioned the campaign against Pound. A leading literary critic with no ties to conservatism, Marjorie Perloff, has recently stated: "I still believe—and I speak here as a refugee from Hitler whose family fled the morning of the Anschluss—that Pound's "fascism"— most of it completely nonsensical, juvenile, and failing to understand how government works—was not nearly as dangerous as Heidegger's willed, conscious, perfectly 'reasoned' fascism."

The incoherence and extremism of Pound's political ideas have caused his influence on American conservative thought to be minimal.

—GREGORY WOLFE

Further Reading

Kenner, Hugh. *The Pound Era*. Berkeley, Calif.: University of California Press, 1971.

Donoghue, Denis. *Connoisseurs of Chaos: Ideas of Order in Modern American Poetry*. New York: Macmillan, 1965.

See also: fascism; Eliot, T. S.; Kenner, Hugh

poverty

Long occupying a position on the public agenda, as a national political issue poverty came to the fore with Lyndon Johnson's announcement in 1964 of a War on Poverty. Whether paradoxically or predictably, what had been a steady reduction in poverty throughout the postwar period came more or less to a halt soon afterwards.

Much of the controversy over poverty and public policy stems from different beliefs about its sources. Poverty can arise involuntarily, as a matter of chance, a manifestation of the luck of the draw or an accident of birth. "There but for the grace of God go I" is an expression of this truth. It is surely unreasonable to hold people responsible for their poverty when it arises through one of nature's involuntary lotteries. Policy prescriptions in such cases would seem almost naturally to run in terms of programs of income redistribution. Indeed, such programs could be construed as a form of social insurance against poor luck, through which the differential bestowal of God's grace is counteracted.

Alternatively, poverty may result through personal choice. People can choose directly to be poor by, e.g., forgoing a full-time job to have more time for fishing, or in refusing to attend evening classes three nights a week for six months to qualify for a steady job. They can also make such a choice indirectly as a by-product of other choices, e.g., a choice to get pregnant and drop out of school at sixteen.

Consider Henry Fawcett's tale of Robinson and Smith, both of whom worked for the same wages and had the same number of dependents. "Robinson is extremely prudent, and does everything in his power to set aside some provision for his old age. By dint of constant thrift he is able . . . to secure for himself an annuity of 5s. a week. Smith never makes the slightest effort to save, but spends every shilling he can spare at the public-house. When the time comes that he is too old to work he . . . applies to the parish for maintenance." In Fawcett's continuation of the story, Smith is granted 5s. per week. Robinson points out the manifest unfairness of this grant, and asks for a 2s. supplement, which is denied.

To be sure, the distinction between involuntary poverty by chance and voluntary poverty through choice is simpler to make conceptually than it is to perceive empirically. Poverty is generally a mixture of choice and chance, with that mixture varying from case to case. Chance is ubiquitous in all of our lives, starting with the family situations into which we are born. Those born into loving, nurturing homes will get a better start in life than those born into indifferent or malevolent homes.

What would constitute a successful public policy toward poverty? It is often claimed that measures of poverty based on income exaggerate the incidence of poverty because of the widespread availability of a large number of programs that award in-kind benefits, such as food stamps, Medicaid, and public housing. By some measures, the incidence of poverty falls roughly in half once the monetary equivalent of such programs is taken into account. It would seem to follow that the only thing preventing the complete eradication of poverty is sufficient government spending. Yet the persistence of many on on the welfare rolls would hardly seem to indicate that poverty might be completely eliminated.

A more reasonable approach is to define poverty in terms of the ability of people to be self-supporting. And it is here that problems of poverty policy become especially difficult. It might seem reasonable that policy should seek to aid cases where poverty is the result of chance, while refraining from aiding cases where poverty is the result of choice. The trouble with this prescription is that it cannot be implemented without knowledge of souls and minds. Nature does not generate birthmarks or other signals that allow such categorization. Mistakes will infect any assistance program, even in a world governed by the best of intentions. The receipt of aid by those who are poor through choice will encourage more such choices. But to withhold aid to prevent such outcomes will imperil those who are poor through chance.

This tragic dimension is present in Fawcett's tale of Robinson and Smith. When Smith reaches retirement age, it seems cruel to deny him some support. After all, Robinson has an annuity and Smith has none. Some redistribution might seem only fair. Yet Smith's poverty was voluntary, the outcome of earlier choices he had made. Is it heartless to refuse aid because Smith's poverty is voluntary? Smith might claim, poignantly and truthfully, that he would not have allowed this to have happened to him had he realized the consequences. Should a second chance, so to speak, be given in this case? What would be the point of refusing to aid? It might punish Smith, but what has been done cannot be undone. Might not some show of compassion toward Smith be in order?

A problem in giving an affirmative answer to this question lies in the lessons that are thereby communicated throughout the society when the aid to Smith becomes generalized as a policy principle. For the primary lesson then becomes that a failure to provide for the future will not be a burden to be borne by those who so fail, but will partly be shifted onto those who do not. Failure becomes rewarded, success penalized. Giving aid to those who make impoverishing choices will encourage others to do the same, thereby worsening the problem. Yet there is no unmistakable way of separating choice from chance. The odds of successful separation can be improved, however, by replacing public with private forms of assistance. Public assistance must be impersonal and bureaucratic, for requirements of fair treatment must be expressible through objectified rules and procedures. Such an approach is not suitable for making discriminating judgments about who genuinely would use a helping hand profitably and who is simply looking for a handout. Privately organized assistance, where those who supply the assistance not only have greater knowledge of local circumstances and the people with whom they are dealing, but also are free to use the tacit knowledge they have that cannot be reduced to a table in a memo, offers a better though far from utopian option.

—Richard E. Wagner

Further Reading

Fawcett, Henry. *Pauperism: Its Causes and Remedies*. London: Macmillan, 1871.

Himmelfarb, Gertrude. *Poverty and Compassion: The Moral Imagination of the Late Victorians*. New York: Vintage, 1992.

Murray, Charles. *Losing Ground: American Social Policy, 1950–1980*. New York: Basic Books, 1984.

Olasky, Marvin. *The Tragedy of American Compassion*. Washington, D.C.: Regnery Gateway, 1992.

Rector, Robert and William F. Lauber. *America's Failed $5.4 Trillion War on Poverty*. Washington, D.C.: Heritage Foundation, 1995.

See also: Catholic social teaching; enterprise zones; Olasky, Marvin; welfare policy

prejudice

As Edmund Burke employed the term in his *Reflections on the Revolution in France* (1790), prejudice is not to be confused with merely arbitrary opinion. Rather, by prejudice Burke meant the "untaught feelings" and "mass of predispositions" supplied by the collective wisdom of a people. He was deeply critical of the Enlightenment view that the lives of men and societies could be ordered by "abstract speculation." Burke held instead that a person's private stock of wisdom is meager and unreliable. "The individual is foolish, but the species is wise," he declared. Far from being necessarily irrational feelings or fancies of the moment, the prejudices of a people may be derived from that body of accumulated wisdom found in long-established habits, customs, and traditions. Burke considered prejudice to be an indispensable guide to social and moral decision-making. People are advised to cling to their prejudices to avoid the pitfalls of moral confusion, doubt, and error.

Elaborating on Burke's definition, Russell Kirk wrote that prejudice "is prejudgment, the answer with which intuition and ancestral consensus of opinion supply a man when he lacks either time or knowledge to arrive at a decision predicated upon pure reason." Hence, in much, man must rely on this body of ancestral wisdom because, as Burke taught, "We are afraid to put men to live and trade each on his own private stock of reason; because we suspect that this stock in each man is small, and that the individuals would do better to avail themselves of the general bank and capital of nations and of ages."

Prejudice is a necessary part of the predisposition of the civilized person. Insofar as the traditions of a people are civilized, the prejudices that shape and restrain their thought and actions will also be civilized. "Prejudice," Burke explained, "is of ready application in the emergency; it previously engages the mind in a steady course of wisdom and virtue, and does not leave the man hesitating in the moment of decision, skeptical, puzzled, and unresolved. Prejudice renders a man's virtue his habit; and not a series of unconnected acts. Through just prejudice, his duty becomes a part of his nature."

Burke believed that the English had been inoculated against the "armed doctrines" of the French revolutionaries because they cherished their prejudices. Because of their "sullen resistance to innovation," Englishmen abjured the radical doctrines of the French philosophes, convinced "that no discoveries" in morality, or "the great principles of government, nor in the ideas of liberty" have been made or will be made. Such truths "were understood long before we were born" and will continue to be long after the present generation perishes. The civilized prejudices of the English provided a safeguard against unwise, rash, and potentially destructive innovation.

Kirk incorporated this Burkean principle into his political thought. Among the prejudices to which we should cling, Kirk advised, is the "prejudice against organic change, a feeling that it is unwise to break radically with political prescription, an inclination to tolerate what abuses may exist in present institutions out of a practical acquaintance with the violent and unpredictable nature of doctrinaire reform."

—W. WESLEY MCDONALD

Further Reading
Kirk, Russell. *The Conservative Mind.* 7th rev. ed. Washington, D.C.: Regnery, 1995.

See also: Burke, Edmund; Burkean conservatism; custom; Kirk, Russell; traditionalism

prescription

The concept of prescription forms the basis of Edmund Burke's reply in his *Reflections on* the *Revolution in France* (1790) to the French Jacobin call for the radical restructuring of society. The contempt shown for this principle by the National Assembly of France was a leading cause of Burke's hatred for the revolution. Prescription entails a presumption in favor of long-standing institutions and customs that neither precludes reform or improvement nor gives license to those in power to abuse their authority.

Burke was no doubt influenced in the formation of this concept by his legal training. The principle is taken from the law of real property that gives title to property as a consequence of its ancient or unquestioned possession. Burke expanded this definition to include the granting of authority to government. He was presumably convinced further by the emphasis on the role of historical development found in David Hume's *History of England* (1754).

Burke denounced the French Jacobins' "Rights of Man" as a violation of the principle of prescription. He rejected entirely the notion that a body of prepolitical rights can be apprehended through the exercise of abstract reasoning. People have only historical rights, he affirmed, which are determined not by rational speculation but grow out of the conventions and compacts made by many successive generations. Civil society as well is "the offspring of convention." The science of government cannot be "taught *a priori*," because its mastery requires "even more experience than any person can gain in his whole life, however sagacious and observing he may be." Burke warned that "it is with infinite caution that any man ought to venture pulling down an edifice which has answered in any tolerable degree for ages the common purposes of society, or on building it up again without having models and patterns of approved utility before his eyes."

The will of our ancestors creates moral obligations, Burke believed, that bind the present generation. Even if certain parts of the constitution seem outdated and not relevant to current circumstances, they are to be obeyed until legitimately changed. Contrary to the arguments of the social contract theorists, Burke did not believe consent of the majority was necessary to legitimize the authority of government. In life, he reminds us, we are frequently obligated to obey the rules of others to whom we have never given our consent. Children are obligated to obey their parents, even though they never formally consent to their rule.

Burke's teaching was that social reform should take place within the context of historical experience. We may no longer remember the reasons for the existence of certain institutions, customs, or norms, but we risk reviving ancient forgotten evils by altering recklessly that which has been long established and works tolerably well. In practice, "we transmit," Burke observed, "our government and our privileges, in the same manner in which we enjoy and transmit our property and our lives." By conforming to this "part of the law of nature," the political system "is never old, or middle-aged, or young."

The English constitution, Burke pointed out, "is prescriptive" in that "its sole authority" is that it "has existed time out of mind. Your kings, your lords, your juries, grand and little, are all prescriptive." Without assent to the principle of prescription, Burke believed, property and liberty would be insecure. Order in society depends on the bulk of the people giving unthinking, instinctive obedience to prescriptive claims.

Burke's idea of prescriptive rights entails a presumption in favor of settled usages, conventional wisdom, and existing customs and mores. While it may be possible that things have changed and "past experience in that particular is invalid," as Russell Kirk explained, the "presumption ordinarily is to the contrary; and in any case, it may be wiser to continue an old practice, even though it seem the child of error, than to break radically with custom and run the risk of poisoning the body social, out of doctrinaire affection for mathematical precision or bluebook uniformity." To rudely impose alteration upon society, while blindly ignoring existing patterns of social behavior, Burke condemned as a positive evil. The "rage and phrensy," displayed during the French Revolution, he declared, "will pull down more in half an hour, than prudence, deliberation, and foresight can build up in a hundred years." Prescription, prejudice, and presumption, all of which embody a society's traditions, help to sustain and direct man's ethical thought and action. Burke taught that in their absence a powerful check upon man's proclivity for selfish, destructive, and arbitrary behavior would be lacking.

—W. Wesley McDonald

Further Reading

Russell Kirk, *The Conservative Mind.* 7th rev. ed. Washington, D.C.: Regnery, 1986.

See also: Burke, Edmund; Burkean conservatism; tradition; traditionalism

privatization

Privatization refers to the shift of functions and responsibilities from the public sector to the private sector. The term was virtually unknown prior to the 1980s, but by the end of the decade it had become part of the everyday political vocabulary around the world.

Broadly speaking, there are five types of privatization. The most far-reaching is divestiture, in which government completely gives up a function or enterprise either by shutting down its own operation in preference to private operators or by selling or giving the asset or enterprise to private owners. This form of privatization is most common over-

seas, especially in formerly socialist and communist countries.

When government remains responsible for funding a particular function but turns over its delivery to the private sector, it can do so in one of two ways. The first is to purchase the service from one or more private providers; this form of privatization is called contracting out (or sometimes outsourcing). The other way is to empower individuals to purchase the service from the provider of their choice; in this case, government gives eligible individuals a voucher that the providers can redeem for cash from the government.

A fourth form of privatization occurs when government retains responsibility for providing a service, but no longer funds it via taxation; instead, it shifts to user charges, so that only those who benefit from the service pay for it, and pay in proportion to their usage. User charges are most often used for discretionary services (e.g., municipal golf courses) rather than core government functions.

Finally, the fifth type of privatization is the long-term franchise by means of which private capital and private enterprise produce and operate major new infrastructure projects. Waste-disposal plants, toll roads, and airport terminals are among the types of infrastructure that have been privatized in this manner. Franchises typically run for twenty to forty years, after which, in most cases, the project may revert to the state.

The precise origin of the term privatization in its modern sense is not completely clear. Peter F. Drucker used the term "reprivatization" in his 1968 book, *The Age of Discontinuity*, to refer to the eventual denationalization of industrial enterprises in social welfare states. In the early 1970s, Robert W. Poole Jr. of the Reason Foundation and E. S. Savas (then at Columbia University, now at Baruch College, CUNY) both began writing about contracting out and started referring to it informally as privatization. Poole wrote a handbook (*Cut Local Taxes without Reducing Essential Services*) for the National Taxpayers Union in 1976 that explained the concept, which he expanded into book form in *Cutting Back City Hall* (1980). Savas, by then at the U.S. Department of Housing and Urban Development, followed with his book *Privatizing the Public Sector* in 1982.

These ideas migrated from the United States to England in 1977–79, where they helped to inspire the founders of the Adam Smith Institute, Eamonn Butler and Madsen Pirie, who did a great deal to popularize privatization during the early years of the Thatcher government. In addition, Canada's Fraser Institute in 1980 published a book, *Privatisation*, on the denationalization of the British Columbia Resources Investment Corporation.

Privatization has been championed in the United States by the Reason Foundation, which has made it one of that organization's major, ongoing issues. Other think tanks that have done significant work on this issue include the Heritage Foundation and the National Center for Policy Analysis.

The most common forms of privatization in the United States are contracting out and infrastructure franchises. The federal government codified its contracting-out policy in the form of OMB Circular A-76 in 1966. Under these provisions, agencies are supposed to seek bids for any service that is supplied by private enterprise and to contract out if cost savings can be demonstrated. The policy has been emphasized by some administrations, virtually ignored by other administrations, and limited by numerous congressional mandates.

State and local governments began experimenting with contracting out during the 1970s and using it fairly extensively in the 1980s, spurred along by various tax revolts. During the 1990s, both Democratic and Republican governors and mayors turned in-creasingly to this form of privatization. Liberal organizations like the Progressive Policy Institute repackaged the idea as part of a paradigm of "entrepreneurial government." Vice President Gore's National Partnership for Reinventing Government embraced the idea as well, inspired by books such as *Reinventing Government* (1992) by David Osborne and Ted Gaebler.

Infrastructure privatization began in the early 1980s with wastewater and waste-to-energy plants. Private capital was attracted partly because of tax benefits. When those benefits were greatly reduced in the tax reform act of 1986, the waste-treatment market suffered a setback, but new projects began appearing by 1990, as environmental needs collided with scarce government resources. Another area for private infrastructure investment has been private toll roads. By 2000, some sixteen states had enacted private toll road laws, and such projects had been opened or were under construction in California, Missouri, Puerto Rico, South Carolina, Texas, and Virginia.

Although more than one trillion dollars' worth of state-owned enterprises were sold by governments worldwide during the 1980s and 1990s, there have been relatively few divestitures in the United States. The federal government sold Conrail in 1987, the Alaska Power Marketing Administration in 1996, the Elk Hills Naval Petroleum Reserve in 1997, and the U.S. Enrichment Corporation in 1998. In addition, a series of spectrum auctions has netted the federal government several tens of billions of dollars thus far, with further auctions expected.

—ROBERT W. POOLE JR.

Further Reading

Hudson, Wade, ed. *Privatization 2000: The 14th Annual Report on Privatization.* Los Angeles: Reason Public Policy Institute, 2000.

Johnson, Robin A. and Norman Walzer. *Local Government Innovation: Issues and Trends in*

Privatization and Managed Competition. Westport, Conn.: Forum Books/Greenwood Publishing, 2000.

Osborne, David and Peter Plastrik. *Banishing Bureaucracy: The Five Strategies for Reinventing Government.* Reading, Mass.: Addison-Wesley, 1997.

Savas, E. S. *Privatization and Public-Private Partnerships.* New York: Chatham House/Seven Bridges Press, 2000.

See also: Austrian school of economics; Reason Foundation; Thatcher, Margaret

progress

Progress is defined as movement forward, toward some goal deemed to be good. It connotes the steady development or gradual improvement of a civilization. While many Americans take the idea and reality of progress for granted, there are, nevertheless, profound difficulties attending the concept.

In the first place, what is "movement forward"? Whose criteria will be enlisted to determine whether a society is progressing or regressing? Unavoidably the question of progress involves deeper questions concerning the nature of human existence and the existence of human nature. If the ultimate goal of human beings is to find and remain in a state of happiness, by what means can that state be achieved? Answers to this question differ markedly. For traditionalist conservatives, the recovery of the sacred may be reckoned as true forward movement; for libertarians, the recovery of the unregulated marketplace.

This leads to a second difficulty, which involves the spheres of life in which true progress is possible. Since antiquity, most observers of the human condition have recognized that progress is possible in science, technology, and the professions. If or when progress occurs in a society's laws and insti-

tutions is more debatable and depends on the context and consequences of change over time. Whether significant forward movement takes place in literature and the fine arts is dubious. And whether advancement is possible in the realm of human nature and morality is, for most conservatives, altogether doubtful. In fact, since antiquity, technological progress among a people has been seen as perfectly compatible with moral regress.

A third difficulty arises out of decades of historiographic debate. Scholars are not agreed as to when the idea of progress was invented. It was once popular to assert, after J. B. Bury's landmark study, *The Idea of Progress* (1920), that the notion was not invented before the seventeenth-century scientific revolution. That opinion has been vigorously challenged by Ludwig Edelstein, E. R. Dodds, and others who believe that the conception was at least imperfectly known to the ancient Greeks.

The conservative historian and sociologist, Robert Nisbet, argues in his *History of the Idea of Progress* (1980) not only that the notion originated in ancient Greece, but that it "subsequently achieved its fullest expression in [the] Christian philosophy of history." In their writings church fathers such as Tertullian, Eusebius, and St. Augustine combined the Greco-Roman appreciation for cultural advancement with the Jewish conception of sacred history to develop the notion of material and moral progress for all mankind. Salvation history was for them a drama that gradually unfolds in time and reveals direction and purpose. This notion of progress, asserts Nisbet, would exert a powerful influence on Western thinking long after the decline of the Middle Ages, not only in believers such as Bodin, but in non-believers like Condorcet. The latter's *Sketch for a Historical Picture of the Progress of the Human Mind* (1795, trans. 1955), composed ironically when he was anticipating his execution by French revolutionaries, is widely considered to be the first major statement of modern secular progress.

Another enduring influence from the Judeo-Christian heritage issued from the *Apocalypse* of St. John of Patmos and shaped the thought of medieval millenarians like Joachim of Fiore, who developed a progressive, three-stage view of human history that culminated in the thousand-year reign of Christ on earth. Historian Stephen Tonsor points out that secularized versions of millenarianism persist in modern utopian thought of all stripes, especially Marxian.

It would thus be a mistake to overlook the intellectual link between early Christian conceptions of progress and their modern secular counterparts. Both entail historical necessity whereby either supernatural Providence or a natural law of progress effects changes in human affairs and directs the course of human development.

Faith in secular progress gained converts in the milieu of the seventeenth-century scientific revolution, gathered momentum during the eighteenth-century Enlightenment, then peaked in the heyday of the Victorian Age, the early decades of which historians have dubbed the "Age of Progress." During the nineteenth century there was widespread confidence in America and Britain that the methods of science, applied to all areas of life, would usher in an epoch of unending material, social, and moral improvement. The doctrine of progress was variously expressed in the rhetoric of classical liberalism (with its emphasis on the providence of the free market), in the rhetoric of statist liberalism (with its emphasis on political planning and social welfare), and in the rhetoric of socialism (with its emphasis on state control of the means of production).

During the closing decade of the nineteenth century, however, a darker mood shrouded Europe and *la belle époque* was transformed, in some minds, into the *fin de siècle*. This, followed by two world wars, viti-

ated the idea or progress but did not "kill" it, as is sometimes asserted. In the twentieth century the idea continued to be championed in the works of thinkers as diverse as H. G. Wells, Friedrich von Hayek, and Pierre Teilhard de Chardin. But its diminution over the past decades is undeniable and is causally linked, in Nisbet's judgment, to the "general weakening of the Christian foundations of Western culture." Nisbet asserts that

> [t]he idea was, in short, born of religion in the classical world, sustained by religion from the third century on, and now threatens to die from the loss of religious sustenance. For no century in Western history has proved to be as non-religious, irreligious, and anti-religious in its major currents of philosophy, art, literature, and science as was the twentieth. Faith in progress cannot long last when its historical foundations have weakened or dissolved.

Recovery of the idea, which in Nisbet's view is "one of the West's oldest and most fertile ideas," will only occur when intellectual leaders recover the premises necessary for the notion of progress to flourish.

In the course of American history, the Right's view toward the idea and reality of progress has been complex and admits of no easy generalizations. Historically Puritans, Jeffersonians, classical liberals, and social Darwinists have all believed in and championed some form of progress, as have some modern conservative scholars like Nisbet. Reactionaries, Catholic traditionalists, and Burkean conservatives, on the other hand, tend to repudiate the very idea of progress if it implies that man's nature can be improved or that society can be significantly perfected. John Lukacs has warned that while human conditions change, human nature never does. In his autobiography, *Confessions of an*

Original Sinner (1990), Lukacs strikes a "reactionary" posture toward progress with which many conservatives would agree: the reactionary

> knows, and believes in, the existence of sin and in the immutable essence of human nature. He does not always oppose change, and he does not altogether deny progress: what he denies is the immutable idea of immutable progress: the idea that we are capable not only of improving our material conditions but our very nature, including our mental and spiritual nature. We must never deny the potentiality of possible improvements of the human condition. But we must be aware—especially at this time, near the end of the twentieth century—of the need to think about what progress means.

Among cultural critics one of the most provocative theories of the late twentieth century—which some have mistaken for an unqualified apology for progress—has come from Francis Fukuyama. In a much discussed 1989 article in the *National Interest*, Fukuyama gave new life to an old theme, the end of history, which he defined as "the end point of mankind's ideological evolution and the universalization of Western liberal democracy as the final form of human government."

Based on Alexandre Kojeve's and G. W. F. Hegel's idealistic view of history, Fukuyama's end-of-history thesis asserts that the triumph of Western liberalism in the realm of idea and consciousness is now virtually complete. In the twentieth century, the collapse first of fascism in Germany and Italy and of communism in China, the Soviet Union, and Eastern Europe have left the ideological field empty of any significant competition. With the possible exception of the Islamic Revolution, there are no fundamental ideological contradictions (of the

thesis-antithesis sort) in the modern world. So, Fukuyama states,

> What we may be witnessing is not just the end of the Cold War . . . but the end of history as such: that is, the end point of mankind's ideological evolution and the universalization of Western liberal democracy as the final form of human government. . . . [T]he victory of liberalism has occurred primarily in the realm of ideas or consciousness and is as yet incomplete in the real or material world. But there are powerful reasons for believing that it is the ideal that will govern the material world in the long run.

It is easy to exaggerate Fukuyama's views—and detractors have done so. First, despite some critics' assertions to the contrary, the theory is not apocalyptic: Fukuyama sees neither the terrible *Dies Irae* at the end of time nor the emergence of a new heaven and a new earth: at the "end of history" human nature will not have changed. Second, "at the end of history it is not necessary that all societies become successful liberal societies, merely that they end their ideological pretensions of representing different and higher forms of human society." Third, Fukuyama is hardly unambivalent about the ramifications of his thesis; he writes that

> The end of history will be a very sad time. . . . [T]he worldwide ideological struggle that called forth daring, courage, imagination, and idealism, will be replaced by economic calculation, the endless solving of technical problems, environmental concerns, and the satisfaction of sophisticated consumer demands. . . . Perhaps this very prospect of centuries of boredom at the end of history will serve to get history started once again.

It is worth noting that many conservatives question whether the triumph of the idea of bourgeois liberal democracy really constitutes "the end of history" as Fukuyama defines it. They question, further, whether this triumph would necessarily represent progress. For many on the Right, the envisaged stasis is too reminiscent of totalitarianism, of the world of Orwell's Big Brother, of Huxley's Mustapha Mond, to hold great appeal. More to the point, because of human freedom, history and life are too full of the unexpected to condescend to our forecasts. Hegelian schemes may be aesthetically, logically, or pedagogically satisfying—but that does not make them true. As J. B. Bury wrote in his landmark study of the subject, belief in the true progress of humanity is, in the end, "an act of faith."

—GLEAVES WHITNEY

Further Reading

Dawson, Christopher. *Progress and Religion*. Garden City, N.Y.: Image, 1960.

Dodds, E. R. "Progress in Classical Antiquity." In *Dictionary of the History of Ideas*, vol. 3, 623–33. New York: Scribners, 1973.

Ginsberg, Morris. "Progress in the Modern Era." In *Dictionary of the History of Ideas*, vol. 3, 633–50. New York: Scribners, 1973.

Himmelfarb, Gertrude. "History and the Idea of Progress." In *The New History and the Old*. Cambridge, Mass.: Harvard University Press, 1987.

Lasch, Christopher. *The True and Only Heaven: Progress and Its Critics*. New York: W. W. Norton, 1991.

Wagar, W. Warren. *Good Tidings: The Belief in Progress from Darwin to Marcuse*. Bloomington, Ind.: Indiana University Press, 1972.

See also: community; conservatism; custom; Enlightenment; Fukuyama, Francis; I'll Take My Stand; Lasch, Christopher; Nisbet, Robert A.; progressivism; science and scientism; Scottish Enlightenment; technology

progressivism

Progressivism is an ideology based on the idea that historical and social progress are inevitable. The idea of progress assumes movement toward some ideal or end that usually includes the perfectibility of human nature and human society. Progressives conceive of this end in various ways: history may culminate in an era of absolute freedom, social and economic equality, or some form of utopia. Given the predilection to progress, the past is viewed as an inferior state of existence with various afflictions that wither away over time. While some progressives consider progress inevitable, others believe that political, economic, and social reforms are necessary to achieve it. Scientism is a progressive ideology premised on the idea that use of the scientific method will lead to progress not only in technology and scientific understanding, but also in moral and social life.

Important American progressives include Herbert Croly and Woodrow Wilson. Croly pronounced in *The Promise of American Life* (1909) that

> Democracy must stand or fall on a platform of possible human perfectibility. If human nature cannot be improved by institutions, democracy is at best a more than usually safe form of political organization. . . . But if it is to work better as well as merely longer, it must have some leavening effect on human nature; and the sincere democrat is obliged to assume the power of the leaven.

There is a democratic and egalitarian strain to progressivism. Early-twentieth-century American progressives, like populists, advocated participatory and direct democracy. They favored direct primaries, recall elections, ballot initiatives, and referendums.

The direct election of senators was a progressive reform.

American progressives in the early twentieth century argued that corporations and monied interests concentrated power to the detriment of workers, consumers, and the poor. They presumed that authentic progress must be brought about in part by economic and social leveling. Thus, they saw as obstacles to progress tradition, traditional ways of life, and big business, including a class system that privileged a monied aristocracy. Ironically, the instrument for progressive reform was the administrative state, or what is sometimes called the welfare state. To decentralize power in the private sector, thought progressives, power had to be centralized in the government sector. To achieve this required the destruction of federalism and the evisceration of intermediate groups and associations.

The philosophical fathers of progressivism include Francis Bacon, Hegel, Marx, Comte, Rousseau, Condorcet, Bentham, Mill, and Edward Bellamy. These thinkers ushered in the modern historical era, an era in which progressivism was a main current. One of the characteristics of these thinkers' progressivism was its pseudospirituality, or religion of humanity. In this substitute religion, faith in a transcendent moral order is replaced by faith in nature, science, technology, and reason. This faith also involves a sort of humanitarian sentimentalism that attempts to satisfy an inner desire to serve mankind and the world by engaging in reforms meant to uplift the less fortunate. Yet these reforms are not intended to effect inner spiritual reform but rather to change institutions and thus improve society through outer reform. Conservatives argue that progressive humanitarianism is both a diversion and escape from individual moral responsibility.

Progressivism also includes the idea that human perfectibility is possible in history. This doctrine holds that it is unnecessary to wait for the afterlife for human perfection; the fulfillment of human nature can take place in earthly life. Scientific progressives, like Bacon, believe that progress is a predicate of scientific knowledge and technological developments. Social progressives, like Croly, believe that human nature can be transformed through political reform.

Progressivism is intimately tied to modern liberalism and the politics of the welfare state, which holds that the transformation of society can only be achieved by a centralized government that has sufficient power to remake society. In this vein, progressives take up causes that conservatives consider misguided. Examples of progressive reforms would include the Great Society's war on poverty, the abolition of private gun ownership, and the Eighteenth Amendment. Conservatives criticize progressive reforms because they believe these reforms do not account for unintended consequences, are based on a misunderstanding of the human condition, and fail to accept a degree of evil in the world. Consequently, conservatives often conclude that progressive reforms end up doing more harm than good. For example, abortion, which has been a central reform in the progressive cause of liberating women from traditional sex roles, has helped achieve liberation at the cost of infanticide and the depreciation of human life. Thus, in many ways progressivism is an inclination diametrically opposed to that of conservatism.

The progressive imagination is also manifest in the thought of those who advocate a "living" Constitution. For such thinkers, it makes no sense to adhere to a permanent, fixed constitution if the current generation knows better than past generations what are the true, the good, and the beautiful. The Constitution must therefore be adapted to the times. Justice Douglas expressed this idea in his *Gray* v. *Sanders* (1963) opinion. In that case the Court embraced the principle of one-person-one-vote and rejected the framers' political theory. Douglas wrote that "[p]assage of the Fifteenth, Seventeenth, and Nineteenth Amendments shows" that the conception of political equality expressed by Hamilton in *Federalist* 68 in describing the Electoral College "belongs to a bygone day, and should not be considered in determining what the equal protection clause of the Fourteenth Amendment requires in statewide elections."

Finally, progressivism has in it a gnostic element. That is, progressives believe that they possess the knowledge needed to transform society and human nature. They are greatly dissatisfied with the world as it is and are impatient with life and the very structure of reality because these fall short of perfection or the progressive ideal. These gnostic attributes are part of an existential disposition that fails to accept the permanence of evil in earthly life—in theological terms, original sin. By contrast, most conservatives believe that the structure of reality, including human nature, is permanent. Attempts to transform the human condition end up in disaster, as Huxley and Orwell suggest in their dystopias *Brave New World* (1932) and *Nineteen Eighty-Four* (1949).

Today, progressive ideas are especially prevalent in international politics. Liberal internationalists and neoconservatives both tend to embrace Wilsonian democracy. They believe that if democracy and capitalism are spread through the world, peace and stability will be much more likely. Here again lies the underlying assumption of progressivism: evil is the result of a poorly organized world. Reorganization of the world in accordance with progressive ideas will usher in a new age of freedom, equality, and peace.

—Michael P. Federici

Further Reading

Carey, George W. *A Student's Guide to American Political Thought.* Wilmington, Del.: ISI Books, 2004.

Gamble, Richard. *The War for Righteousness: Progressive Christianity, the Great War, and the Rise of the Messianic Nation.* Wilmington, Del.: ISI Books, 2003.

Ryn, Claes. *America the Virtuous: The Crisis of Democracy and the Quest for Empire.* New Brunswick, N.J.: Transaction, 2003.

See also: Benthamism; Gnosticism; Lasch, Christopher; liberalism; judicial activism; progress; science and scientism; welfare state

Property and Environment Research Center

The Property and Environment Research Center (PERC), formerly known as the Political Economy Research Center, is the institutional outgrowth of an intellectual collaboration begun in the early 1970s between John Baden and Richard L. Stroup. Both men believed that if a market economy, characterized by secure and transferable property rights, limited government, and the rule of law could be trusted to provide the great bulk of the goods and services desired by a free society, then the market should also be fruitful in providing for the protection of environmental quality and a large array of environmental amenities. This view eventually became known as free-market environmentalism (FME) and is often contrasted with conventional environmentalist thinking, which emphasizes government management of natural resources and command-and-control regulation of pollution. In order to promote a research agenda based on this insight, Baden and Stroup established, in 1978, the Center for Political Economy and Natural Resources at Montana State University. With the help of other scholars, most notably Terry L. Anderson, Peter J. Hill, and Michael D. Copeland, Baden and Stroup later created PERC as a free-standing research institute that eventually replaced the center. Baden

681

left PERC later to run his own organization, the Foundation for Research on Economics and Environment (FREE).

Today, PERC, with Terry L. Anderson as executive director, is a leader in research and public advocacy on FME issues such as endangered species, water, public lands, and pollution. Other major programs include the annual Political Economy Forum, conference programs for journalists, policy analysts, and academics interested in FME, and residential programs for summer research interns, senior scholars, and journalists. A program of public outreach includes environmental education, newsletters, and policy studies. *Free Market Environmentalism,* by Anderson and Donald R. Leal (1991, revised 2001), serves as an important summary of the FME approach and PERC research accomplishments.

—William C. Dennis

Further Reading

Anderson, Terry L., and Peter J. Hill, eds. *Environmental Federalism.* Lanham, Md.: Rowman & Littlefield, 1997.

Hill, Peter J., and Roger E. Meiners, eds. *Who Owns the Environment?* Lanham, Md.: Rowman & Littlefield, 1998.

See also: environmentalism

property rights, private

The issue of private property rights has arisen, of course, in different conceptual terms throughout human history. One of the most pronounced and evident examples of its discussion can be found in Aristotle's *Politics.*

Aristotle criticizes Plato's proposal for communal ownership of property on the grounds that it leads to reduction of responsibility and a corresponding lack of care for and attentive involvement with whatever is so owned.

In the twentieth century this Aristotelian observation, which comprises only a few lines in the *Politics,* was developed into a major thesis by the University of California, Santa Barbara, environmental biologist Garrett Hardin. His article "The Tragedy of the Commons," published in *Science* (December 13, 1968) argues that if things are commonly owned a moral tragedy will obtain. His case in point is a grazing area being used by private citizens, owners of cattle. This area, which belongs to everybody, will be exploited much sooner, indeed abused, than if it were privately owned. The reason is that no one knows the limits of his or her authority and responsibility and will, therefore, tend to use more than would be prudent in terms of the general interest.

Both Aristotle's and Hardin's thesis point up a practical or utilitarian feature about what private property rights do for human beings in societies. They place a limitation around what people may do and also what may be done to them so as to produce overall benefit. Just as one's own backyard puts a limitation as to what one may do, thus confining one's good or bad activities, there is everywhere a practical use for the idea of private property rights.

Initially this appears to be a mere practical necessity for human social life. If we were all angels and omniscient, there would be no problem because we would know what ought to be done within the commune. But we are human beings who can fail and can make mistakes, and it is vital to confine these mistakes within a sphere attached to the agent. Yet there is more to all of this than practical usefulness. Some defenders of private property rights have stressed the moral importance of the institution. This is evident in the social world.

From the point of view of morality one needs to know one's scope of personal authority and responsibility. One needs to know that some money is one's own to use before one can be charitable or generous to other people. If one does not know that some particular area of human concern is under one's proper authority or under the authority of people who have voluntarily come together, then one cannot know if it will be courageous, foolhardy, or silly to protect it.

In other words, private property rights are a social precondition to the possibility of the moral life. If one wants to be generous to the starving human beings in the Sudan but has nothing of one's own from which to be generous, generosity will not be possible. So there is in effect a necessary connection between practical morality and the institution of private property rights.

John Locke (1632-1704), perhaps the most prominent English philosopher to have defended the theory of private property rights, made a connection between acting freely and responsibly as moral agents and having the right to private property. For Locke one has a right both to one's person and to one's estate.

Karl Marx, of course, emphasized the destructive possibilities entailed by the right to private property. He tried to discredit the idea by observing that if one has a right to private property—if there are things one has acquired either via one's good judgment, one's hard work, others' kindness and generosity, or good luck—it implies that no one may interfere in how one uses what one owns, provided one does not encroach on other people's rights in the process. Yet clearly aside from being free to misuse one's property, having a right to it also makes possible its prudent, productive, and wise use— indeed, as Aristotle suggests, the right to private property encourages just that.

Another argument against property rights, advanced by Pierre Joseph Proudhon (1809-65), the prominent French anarchist, is that all property is theft: Even if we could assign private property originally, by now matters relating to exchange have gotten very confused. No one knows whether what is currently assigned to someone is in reality his or hers since it was probably stolen or acquired via conquest several times over throughout history. By the time it gets down to our generation, it is so corrupted, so unclear that any claim to it is insupportable.

Is there some method whereby a correct assignment of property rights is possible? What might be a just assignment of property rights to various items that can be owned by people? John Locke advanced the theory that when one mixes one's labor with nature, one gains ownership of the part of nature with which the labor was mixed. While initially nature is a gift from God to us all, once we individually mix our labor with some portion of it, it becomes ours alone.

Yet this idea has not carried sufficiently wide conviction partly because the idea of "mixing labor with nature" seems ambiguous. Does discovering an island count? Does exploring it? Does fencing it in? Does identifying (discovering) a scientific truth count as mixing one's labor with nature? What about inventing something? And how about trade—should the act of coming to mutually agreed-to terms count as mixing one's labor with something of value?

A revised idea has been advanced in current libertarian thought, via the theory of entrepreneurship. This idea was advanced by Fordham University philosopher James Sadowsky and New York University economist Israel Kirzner at about the same time. One's judgment, fixing something as of potential value to oneself or others, establishes a moral claim to property. Judgment, after all, is not automatic, nor need it involve actual overt physical labor. It is a freely made choice involving the quintessential human capacity to think, to reason things out, in this case with respect to some aspect of reality and its relationship to one's goals and purposes in life. One makes the choice to identify something as having potential or actual value. One may be right or wrong, but in either case the judgment brings the item under one's jurisdiction on a kind of first-come, first-served basis. George selects some hole in the ground as of potential value, and then George has rightful jurisdiction over it and may explore it for oil or minerals, or perhaps build a museum on it or a private home. George may have been right or wrong to make this selection—indeed, the hole may not come to anything at all. But by his selecting it he has appropriated it. And the appropriation has moral significance because it exhibits an effort of prudence, of taking proper care of himself and those for whom he is responsible. George's attempt to act prudently, to exercise the virtue of prudence, by his judgment and subsequent exploitation of what he has chosen to appropriate, is potentially morally meritorious. George must be free to make such attempts without intrusions by others.

This is the beginning. In complex social contexts such as industrial society, such acquisition occurs via thousands of small and large acts of discovery, investment, saving, buying and selling, with willing participants who embark upon the same general approach to life. Yet no one is coerced into one particular approach. This is evident in all the experimental communities, churches, artistic colonies, scientific organizations, etc., that abound in what has come to be perhaps the most capitalistic, private property-respecting large society in human history.

—TIBOR R. MACHAN

Further Reading

Anderson, Terry L., and Fred S. McChesney, eds. *Property Rights: Cooperation, Conflict, and Law.* Princeton, N.J.: Princeton University Press, 2003.

Ely, James W. *The Guardian of Every Other Right: A Constitutional History of Property Rights.* 2nd ed. New York: Oxford University Press, 1998.

Kirzner, Israel M. *Competition and Entrepreneurship.* Chicago: University of Chicago Press, 1978.

See also: *capitalism; conservatism; libertarianism; managerial revolution; regulation; socialism*

protectionism

In his *Wealth of Nations*, published in 1776, Adam Smith explained that free trade would be superior to the policies of restricted and managed trade followed by the mercantilist nations of his time. After its articulation by David Ricardo in his 1817 book *Principles of Political Economy and Taxation*, this proposition about free trade later became known as the law of comparative advantage. Ricardo illustrated this law for England and Portugal. He assumed that Portugal was the more efficient producer of wine, while England was relatively more efficient in producing cloth. Ricardo showed how England and Portugal could both gain if Portugal specialized in producing wine and England cloth, with England buying wine from Portugal in exchange for cloth.

An alternative illustration of comparative advantage, one often found in international trade textbooks, is a lawyer who can type faster than his secretary. Suppose the lawyer earns $200 per hour and the secretary $20, and that the lawyer types twice as fast as the secretary. The secretary will still be able to trade with the lawyer. If the lawyer does one hour of his own typing, he saves the $40 he would have had to pay the secretary for two hours but he loses the $200 he could have earned in one hour as a lawyer. The law of comparative advantage holds that we all gain by specializing our productive talents and trading with other people who are similarly specialized, regardless of where those other people live.

By contrast, protectionism claims that comparative advantage is a poor guide for policy and supports instead a policy that restricts trade by awarding protected shelters to selected domestic industries. It is easy enough to see why domestic producers who face tough foreign competition might like to be protected from that competition. A protectionist policy enriches people associated with the protected industry by forcing consumers to pay higher prices. Protectionists do not deny this effect of protection, but argue that in some instances there are other sources of national advantage that make protection worthwhile.

Perhaps the most prominent protectionist claim is that a temporary period of protection may be necessary to allow a young industry to reach maturity and achieve its comparative advantage, after which protection will cease and the industry must engage in free international competition. Protection in this case is a form of capital advance that consumers make to the industry, after which they are repaid through lower prices and better products. This argument for protection, however, is contradicted by experience. Protection is rarely short lived. It is typically granted to established industries that have found their competitive position to be slipping, not to nascent industries that have yet to form a significant political constituency.

A newer cousin of the infant industry argument is the strategic-trade claim that government can increase the wealth of a nation by picking industries to protect that will subsequently achieve international dominance. For instance, by favoring industries that pay high wages and produce little pollution, a strategic trading policy could make the nation wealthier and cleaner. Among other things, this claim for protection involves the presumption that government is an extremely smart and capable businessman who can identify future winners more quickly and accurately than anyone else. The evidence is strongly to the contrary: government is a laggard and not a leader in anticipating future commercial conditions. A related protectionist claim is that there is a scientifically designed tariff, labeled an "optimal tariff," that can increase the price received for exports sufficiently to outweigh the inefficiencies that protection would otherwise generate. This possibility requires a precision of commercial knowledge about present and future conditions that is not possessed by even the most astute of commercial enterprises.

Protection has often been supported by claims that it is important for national defense. In this case, the claim is made that it is prudent to retain some domestic productive capacity even though comparative advantage would call for complete importation. Even if this claim is granted, however, there are other options to secure national defense that are generally superior. For instance, a program of stockpiling those items is almost surely to be more economical than one that encourages domestic production through protection. Political considerations, however, often work in the reverse direction because stockpiling shows up as a budgetary cost whereas the cost of protection is hidden.

Political expediency and not commercial astuteness is a far more accurate explanation for trade protection. Bananas could be grown in North Dakota with the use of greenhouses. They would be expensive and would require protection against bananas imported from such places as Central America. North Dakota is clearly better for growing wheat. Now, as a matter of fact there are no politically influential banana growers in North Dakota, but there are influential sugar growers in Louisiana. And as a result the United States maintains a program of sugar quotas that protects domestic sugar growers against foreign competition. This protection aids those associated with the industry at the expense of American consumers generally.

Indeed, restrictions on trade are typically the result of a domestic political calculus, not some notion of the general welfare. Barriers to trade are erected to provide economic advantage to well-organized industrial groups at the expense of relatively unorganized groups, including consumers. Nonetheless, protectionism has gained new adherents among conservatives in recent years as a means of asserting national power and combating the increasing role of international bodies in controlling trade and other economic activities.

—RICHARD E. WAGNER

Further Reading

Bhagwati, Jagdish. *Protectionism.* Cambridge, Mass.: MIT Press, 1988.

Rowley, Charles K., Willem Thorbecke, and Richard E. Wagner. *Trade Protection in the United States.* Hants, U.K.: Edward Elgar, 1995.

See also: farm policy; free trade; Smith, Adam

Protestantism, evangelical

Evangelical Protestantism is a conservative theological movement devoted to the classical Protestant doctrines of salvation through justification by faith alone, the Bible as the infallible Word of God and the final authority for the believer in all matters of faith and practice, the priesthood of all believers, and the fundamental obligation to preach the Christian Gospel to all peoples. This obligation necessitates the affirmation of the doctrines of the incarnation and virgin birth of Christ, his sinless life, his substitutionary atonement and bodily resurrection as the basis of God's forgiveness of sinners, and the spiritual regeneration of all those who trust in the redemptive work of Jesus Christ.

"Evangelical" comes from the Greek word *evangelion*, which means gospel, glad tidings, and good news. All evangelicals believe and proclaim the Gospel, the good news of reconciliation and redemption through the atoning work of Jesus Christ on the cross, as summarized by the Apostle Paul in 1 Corinthians 15:3-4: "For what I received I passed on to you as of first importance: that Christ died for our sins according to the Scriptures, that he was buried, that he was raised on the third day according to the Scriptures." For evangelicals the proclamation of this biblical Gospel is of utmost concern. They hold that classical orthodox Christianity has always seen this message to be the essential core of the faith.

Because the Gospel message focuses on God's unconditional grace rather than on any form of human merit or achievement, evangelicals have steadfastly affirmed four principles of Martin Luther's: *sola gratia, sola fide, sola scriptura, sola Christus* (grace alone, faith alone, Scripture alone, Christ alone).

Protestant evangelicals have a varied ancestry. The distinctives of their doctrinal beliefs are rooted particularly in (1) the Protestant Reformation of the sixteenth century, (2) the evangelical revivals and awakenings associated with George Whitefield, Jonathan Edwards, and John Wesley in the eighteenth century, and (3) the conservative theological movement that grew out of the "fundamentalist-modernist" controversy in the first three decades of the twentieth century.

The teachings of the Reformers, chiefly Luther, Calvin, Zwingli, and the leaders of the Radical Reformation, found expression in four major denominational groupings: Lutheran; Reformed or Calvinist; Anglican; and Anabaptist (the forerunners of modern Mennonites, Quakers, and Baptists). The essential theological convictions of the Reformation were expressed in denominational confessions—most significantly the Lutheran Augsburg Confession of 1530, the Anglican Thirty-Nine Articles of 1563, and the Westminster Confession of Faith of 1643. During the centuries that followed, the central emphases of the Reformation were renewed, modified, and promulgated by groups as diverse as Puritans, Methodists, Pietists, Baptists, revivalists, Pentecostals, and holiness churches. These denominations and traditions played a vital role in setting and shaping the moral standards of American life and culture.

Evangelicalism is indebted for much of its own distinctive development to the revivals that took place in the United States and Europe in the eighteenth and nineteenth centuries. The vigorous defense and recovery of the Gospel that had occurred during the Reformation had later given way to a rationalistic faith that had become lifeless and cold. Religious convictions had become encased in formalized creedal expressions. In America, George Whitefield, John Wesley, Jonathan Edwards, and William Tennet were instrumental in bringing a revitalized Gospel message to the masses of working people. These "awakenings," with their strong emphasis on expository preaching, appeals for instantaneous conversion, and pietistic stress on a warmhearted faith and a holy life stirred widespread religious interest. People flocked to churches, and a vibrant new piety, combined with a renewed emphasis on the transforming power of the conversion experience, swept the country for more than a century (1720–1860).

Twentieth-century evangelicalism has been primarily shaped by theological battles that occurred in the first three decades of the century, most notably by what is called the fundamentalist-modernist controversy. This controversy was fought largely in Presbyterian and Baptist denominations over what many conservative Protestants perceived as a dilution and modification of classical doctrines of the Christian faith. Evangelicals felt that liberal Protestants, or "modernists," were altering core doctrines of the faith in order to accommodate the findings of modern science, especially Darwinian evolution. Evangelicals found modernists to be increasingly untrustworthy in their theological orientation as they reinterpreted the faith in accordance with the new "higher

criticism" of scripture and the naturalism of the new science.

Evangelicals attempted to resist the increasing influence of the modernists. In 1910 they began a major effort to regain control of the denominations. Their most noteworthy response was a series of twelve books published between 1910 and 1915 called *The Fundamentals*. These were designed to set forth the major doctrinal issues from an evangelical point of view and to counteract the rapid spread of modernist liberal theology. The volumes, containing ninety articles, systematically expounded on the authority and inspiration of the Bible, the historicity of Jesus Christ, the person and work of the Holy Spirit, eschatology (the doctrine of the Second Coming of Christ), the need for missions and evangelism, and the errors of higher criticism.

In the face of the threatening theological liberalism, evangelicals suppressed their own intramural differences to defend the essential doctrines of their common orthodox faith. For example, *The Fundamentals* included an article by B. B. Warfield, a Reformed Calvinist scholar from Princeton Theological Seminary, and also one by C. I. Scofield, the editor of the popular *Scofield Reference Bible* (revised ed., 1917) and champion of a theological position, dispensa-tionalism, from which Warfield dissented in many significant respects. *The Fundamentals* were circulated widely without charge among church leaders, pastors, seminary professors and students, evangelists and missionaries. As many as three million copies were distributed. Yet despite their wide distribution, the books had little effect in the larger academic debate with liberalism. The net accomplishment seems to have been only a temporary pause in the decline of conservative evangelical influence in the Protestant denominations. These evangelical defenders of Protestant orthodoxy were soon disparagingly dubbed "fundamentalists" by liberal modernist theologians.

A leading spokesman in the battle for the theological future of the denominations was conservative Presbyterian theologian J. Gresham Machen, a New Testament scholar at Princeton Theological Seminary. Machen described the clash between conservative orthodoxy and liberal theology as a contest between two completely incompatible religions and suggested that, as a matter of honesty, liberals should leave denominations founded on biblical Christianity. Instead, the opposite occurred. As tolerance toward liberal beliefs increased, many conservatives chose to separate from their denominations to start new ones, though many others remained to continue the debate. Machen left Princeton and led a group of conservative Presbyterian leaders to found Westminster Theological Seminary in Philadelphia in 1929.

Many evangelical Protestants became concerned that these ongoing debates might signal the end of conservative Protestant dominance in American culture. That their concern was not unfounded was most evident in the growing popular acceptance of the theory of biological evolution formulated by the nineteenth-century naturalist Charles Darwin. Vigorous campaigns were organized against the teaching of evolution in public schools, and bills were introduced in twenty state legislatures. The most famous event in this controversy was the 1925 Scopes trial in Dayton, Tennessee. Two prominent lawyers, Clarence Darrow and William Jennings Bryan, clashed over whether John Scopes could teach evolution in a public school in defiance of Tennessee law. Bryan, arguing against Scopes, won the case, but nationwide public sentiment, spurred on by a national press that shared his views, was clearly in favor of Darrow, who made a mockery of his opponent's crusade. Conservative Protestantism won the battle but lost the war. Its social dominance plummeted drastically, and its adherents withdrew from involvement in the larger culture. From 1926 through the early 1940s, some conservative Protestants became strident fundamentalists whose posture toward the larger church, and the general culture, was both separatist and sectarian.

Emerging from two decades of quiescence, the years following World War II were the beginning of a dramatic turnaround. Theologians Edward J. Carnell, Carl F. H. Henry, and Harold J. Ockenga were the leaders of what came to be called "neo-evangelicalism," which took issue with an older fundamentalism that had become embittered, uncharitable, anti-intellectual, and excessively separatist. According to these leaders, the theological separatism of fundamentalism had led to a separation from cultural and social responsibilities and also to an unnecessary lack of engagement with important issues of the day. Carl Henry's *The Uneasy Conscience of Modern Fundamentalism* (1947) was a clarion call for evangelicals to confront modernism with a Christian apologetic that was intellectually respectable and socially responsible.

These neo-evangelical leaders were pivotal in the founding of the National Association of Evangelicals in 1942, the Fuller Theological Seminary (of which they were all faculty members) in 1947, and the important evangelical magazine *Christianity Today* (of which Henry was the first editor) in 1956. Also important was the growing worldwide impact of the ministry of Billy Graham. His popular evangelistic crusades helped to forge a broad-based evangelical constituency and to give renewed vitality to a movement that was beginning to reclaim a role in the mainstream of American culture. Graham and his organization were instrumental in convening two significant international meetings: the World Congress on Evangelism in Berlin in 1966 and the International Congress on World Evangelization in Lausanne, Switzerland, in 1974. *The Lausanne Covenant*, signed by more than three thousand evangelicals from all over the world, provides one of the best summaries of more recent evangelical theological convictions.

By the 1970s evangelical churches were growing rapidly, while liberal Protestant churches began experiencing a serious decline. A renewed self-confidence, combined with growing numbers, allowed evangelicals to become an increasingly strong political force. They became more outspoken about issues such as legalized abortion, the decline of traditional family values, the elimination of prayer in public schools, and increased government intrusion into private schools. While evangelicals are by no means monolithic in their political and social views, they have largely maintained an alliance with political conservatism—evidenced in their overwhelming support for Presidents Ronald Reagan and both George Bushes.

Despite its diversity, the community of evangelical Protestantism is still discernible in various transdenominational movements—numerous missionary societies, hundreds of Bible colleges, Christian liberal arts colleges and seminaries, world hunger and relief agencies, parachurch youth organizations and prison ministries, radio and television programs, and dozens of magazines, newsletters, and book publishers (whose sales of evangelical books run into millions every year).

The diversity of modern evangelicalism has been compared by historian Timothy L. Smith to a mosaic or even a kaleidoscope. Many of its parts appear to be disconnected, which makes it hard to pin down as a single, unified phenomenon. But beneath the surface diversity is a strong commitment to a common core of beliefs, and so it is possible to speak of evangelicalism as a single phenomenon, conceptually unified and transdenominational in scope.

—MICHAEL CROMARTIE

Further Reading

Bloesch, D. G. *The Evangelical Renaissance*. Grand Rapids, Mich.: Eerdmans, 1973.

Hunter, J. D. *American Evangelicalism*. New Brunswick, N.J.: Rutgers University Press, 1983.

Marsden, George M., ed. *Evangelicalism and Modern America*. Grand Rapids, Mich.: Eerdmans, 1984.

Noll, Mark A. *The Rise of Evangelicalism: The Age of Edwards, Whitefield, and the Wesleys*. Downers Grove, Ill.: InterVarsity Press, 2003.

Sweet, Leonard I., ed. *The Evangelical Tradition in America*. Macon, Ga.: Mercer University Press, 1984.

See also: Books & Culture; *Colson, Charles W.; Falwell, Jerry; fundamentalism; Kuyper, Abraham; Machen, J. Gresham; Protestantism, mainline; Robertson, Marion Gordon "Pat"; Schaeffer, Francis A.; Scopes trial*

Protestantism, mainline

The term "mainline Protestantism" refers to the Protestant denominations and agencies of historic vintage in the United States, and more specifically to those Protestants who remained the most influential during the 1920s and the fundamentalist controversy. As such, the label "mainline" sets off a certain group of Protestants from evangelicals (or fundamentalists). A variety of issues contributed to the controversies that split Protestants during the 1920s, but on the doctrinal level evangelicals emerged as the party of theological conservatism while mainline Protestants have been known as more liberal about doctrinal matters. In recent discussions about the relation between religion and politics, it has become a common trope for commentators to correlate theology with attitudes toward government, thereby linking evangelicals with the conservatism of the religious Right and mainline Protestants with the liberalism of the Democratic Party. Although this correlation may work well for Protestant history since 1970, it errs if it reads the contemporary positions of the mainline denominations back into the middle decades of the twentieth century. In fact, evangelical and mainline Protestants from 1860-1960 shared a common set of political convictions that were conservative, at least in the sense of supporting limited government, free markets, and personal responsibility. Sometimes religious convictions conflicted with conservative ideals. But until the late twentieth century practically all American Protestants of British stock believed that their faith went hand in hand with liberty and democracy.

The origin of Protestant support for American ideals goes back to the American Revolution, when Protestant clergy, especially Congregationalists, Baptists, and Presbyterians, led the charge against British tyranny. Unlike Europe, where the Enlightenment was strongly anticlerical, in the United States religion and the new philosophy often wound up working together. Both republican political philosophers and British Protestant dissenters interpreted history in Whiggish or progressive terms. The American Revolution's view of freedom also contained a notion about the direction of history that was shared by Protestants and Enlightenment philosophers. In the decade prior to American independence, many Protestant colonists equated the cause of freedom with the defeat of the papacy and the dawn of the millennium. In similar fashion, Enlightenment thinkers such as Tom Paine believed that the rise of science and the application of scientific principles to human and social relations would usher in a new age in history. This outlook equated the Protestantism of the sixteenth-century Reformation with political and intellectual freedom, while Catholicism was linked with superstition, bigotry, tyranny, and ignorance. According to John Adams, second president of the

United States, before the Reformation human nature had been "chained fast" in "cruel, shameful, and deplorable servitude."

The American Protestant identification with the United States' political values was further strengthened at the time of the Republican Party's origins. The crucial link between Anglo-American Protestantism and the emerging Republican political philosophy was the evangelical notion of individual conversion and its effect in producing disciplined and holy persons. Protestant devotion, accordingly, dovetailed with the Republican/Whig emphasis on individual responsibility and self-denial that drove an expanding economy and unified the nation. The earlier Protestant embrace of liberty became much more complicated during the sectional division that led to war, as the antislavery measures favored by Republicans and northern Protestants conflicted with a commitment to limited government. Nevertheless, the notion that Protestantism was on the side of America's freedoms emerged unscathed after the Civil War.

In fact, the Protestant-Republican synthesis was responsible in no small measure for the establishment of a Protestant mainline during the late nineteenth and early twentieth centuries. Just after the Civil War, Protestants from different denominations began to cooperate at various levels for both religious and cultural reasons. One motivation was the belief that Christians, or at least Protestant Christians, should heed Jesus' admonition that his followers be one. Important, too, was the fear of many Protestant leaders that the United States was spinning out of the orbit of Christian civilization thanks to the inroads of materialism, atheism, and Catholicism. Beginning in 1873 with the founding of the American branch of the British-based Evangelical Alliance, the largest Protestant denominations laid the foundation for a demonstration of Protestant unity. The culmination of these efforts was the founding in 1908 of the Federal Council of Churches (FCC), later the National Council of Churches.

Part of the impetus for the FCC was a growing sense of alarm over the deteriorating conditions of urban industrial wage-earners. In fact, one of the council's first actions was a social declaration that advocated a minimum wage and standard work day. Although these policies appeared to be at odds with Protestantism's earlier commitment to free markets, individual responsibility, and limited government, they were also of a piece with the sort of moral reforms that Protestants had historically supported, including blue laws, temperance legislation, and the abolition of slavery. Rather than representing a reversal of the earlier politics of Protestantism, the FCC's social creed demonstrated the inconsistency of mainline Protestant political thought; Protestants were inclined to support limited government as a check upon arbitrary power, but their understanding of political liberty rarely precluded legislating public morality, even if to do so meant increasing the power of the state. This inconsistency helps to explain why during the 1920s both mainline Protestants *and* fundamentalists could vigorously support Prohibition and displays of Protestant piety in public schools. Granting the state greater power was legitimate if such a bequest advanced Christian civilization.

However inconsistent, Protestants proved their loyalty to American liberty again during the middle decades of the twentieth century when they championed liberal democracy in opposition to fascism and communism. Illustrative of the renewed commitment of the mainline churches to American ideals was John Foster Dulles, who within a decade went from the chair of the FCC Commission on a Just and Durable Peace, founded in 1941, to secretary of state during the Eisenhower administration, starting in 1952. Dulles spoke for many Protestants when in 1940 he declared that the greatest threats to democracy and freedom were totalitarianism and secularism. Accordingly, the only strong foundation for Western civilization was a renewed commitment to Christianity's social and moral truths. As a spokesman for the Eisenhower administration and as a prominent Protestant layman, Dulles's opposition to the tyranny of communism would become even more pronounced. For him, as for many American Protestants, the United States had a role to play in the Cold War that was virtually messianic. In the struggle between the United States and the Soviet Union, the faith that had made the American nation great was at war with the ideology of atheism that drove Soviet expansion.

In the decade after Dulles's death in 1959, the close identification between mainline Protestantism and the American political tradition came unyoked quickly. The Supreme Court rulings on prayer and Bible reading in public schools were indicative of a changing perspective, at least in elite circles, that Protestantism, instead of being good for a nation committed to liberal democracy, was actually oppressive. Civil rights legislation, the feminist movement, champions of sexual liberation, and opponents of America's involvement in Vietnam furthered the impression that the United States was not as free or as democratic as it had once appeared. As a result, having once identified with a moderately conservative political order, leaders in the mainline churches embraced radical politics as the genuine expression of Christian political conviction. For instance, in the National Council of Churches' resolution on Czechoslovakia the year after the Soviets crushed an effort for independence, this mainline body observed that the Soviet Union continued its "oppressive" rule, but added that the United States "itself has been guilty of oppression." For the established institutions of mainline Protestantism, America had changed from the hero to the villain: the nation's rhetoric in favor of freedom and democracy actually obscured its oppressive ways.

Mainline Protestantism's recent reputation for espousing liberal, even anti-American, politics still reflects a certain continuity with American Protestantism's historic opposition to tyranny and oppression. Protestants in the United States have generally been supportive of the ideals that inspired the American Revolution, and although mainline Protestant church leaders came to use language against the American nation that a previous generation might have hurled against the King of England, its theme was still that of liberty and self-determination. What it did not reflect was a consistent application of that theme. At the same time, the recent political shift among mainline Protestants shows that American political ideals fuel these churches more than theology, since even when they were liberal theologically these Protestants up through the 1960s continued to support political conservatism. Where liberal theology may have helped to determine liberal politics was in the notion that the church must adapt its message and ways to contemporary culture. This may explain why mainline Protestantism was politically conservative during times that demanded a defense of American ideals and why it shifted when those ideals became more contested in American society. Even here, however, a better theological explanation for mainline Protestantism's political evolution may be the old Protestant teaching that the gospel, if it were the genuine article, would inevitably transform individuals and nations. In which case, we might say that mainline Protestants believed first that conservative, and then liberal, politics best accomplished the goal of transformation.

—DARRYL G. HART

Further Reading

Hart, D. G. "Mainstream Protestantism, 'Conservative' Religion, and Civil Society." *Journal of Policy History* 13 (2001): 19–46.

Hutchison, William R., ed. *Between the Times: The Travail of the Protestant Establishment, 1900–1960.* New York: Cambridge University Press, 1989.

Noll, Mark A., ed. *Religion and American Politics: From the Colonial Period to the 1980s.* New York: Oxford University Press, 1990.

Toulouse, Mark G. *The Transformation of John Foster Dulles: From Prophet of Realism to Priest of Nationalism.* Macon, Ga.: Mercer University Press, 1985.

See also: Bushnell, Horace; fundamentalism; liberalism; Protestantism, evangelical

public choice economics

Public choice theorists use the tools of economics to study the decision-making of collective organizations, particularly governments. The objective of their analysis is to enhance our knowledge of how collective organizations really work and how alternative decision-making rules influence political outcomes.

This subfield of economics and political science was developed between 1960 and 1990. Prior to 1960, almost all social scientists conceived of government as a supra-individual pursuing policies reflecting the public interest. They also generally assumed that politicians and bureaucrats faithfully followed the mandates of their superiors and served the public interest. Public choice theorists challenged this view, arguing that it reflected a naïve conceptualization of reality. They developed and tested various models of political organization based on the self-interest postulate—the view that voters, politicians, bureaucrats, and lobbyists, like their market counterparts, are motivated by personal self-interest.

Leading contributors to the public choice literature include Nobel laureates Kenneth Arrow and James Buchanan, Duncan Black, Anthony Downs, Mancur Olson, William Niskanen, Robert Tollison, Gordon Tullock, and Richard Wagner. Disappointment with the results of government action in several areas (for example, budgetary policy, antipoverty programs, agriculture, and business regulation) during the 1960s and 1970s provided a fertile field for the development of public choice analysis. Researchers began to question why the results of governmental policies were sometimes quite different than the stated objectives. Public choice analysis often helped to explain why this was the case.

Several important discoveries have resulted from public choice analysis. First, it explains why political outcomes tend to reflect central (rather than extremist) positions. When decisions are made by referendum, the outcome will tend to reflect the option preferred by the median voter. To illustrate this point, assume there are three people in a bridge club, and the members want to decide how many games to play each night. Person A wants to play one game nightly; person B wants to play two games nightly; and person C wants to play three games nightly. Assuming our players will vote for the option closest to their most preferred point, it can be easily seen that the option of playing two games nightly can beat either playing one game or three games. Essentially, the median voter is the decisive voter. In his 1957 book, *An Economic Theory of Democracy*, Anthony Downs used the median voter analysis to explain why, in a competitive two-party setting, the platforms of the two parties will generally be quite similar. Since the party offering the median voter's most preferred platform will win the election, both parties will gravitate toward the center—the platform favored by the median voter. As a result, there will be substan-

tial similarity between the platforms of the two parties.

Second, public choice analysis explains why many voters will be uninformed about issues and the positions of candidates on issues. This lack of voter information merely reflects the incentive structure confronting each individual voter. When decisions are made collectively, the direct link between the individual voter's choice and the outcome of the issue is broken. The probability that a single vote will decide an election is virtually zero when the decision-making group is large. Recognizing that the outcome will not depend on his or her vote, the individual voter has little incentive to seek information (which is costly) on issues and candidates in order to cast a more informed vote. Thus, voters are likely to be uninformed (or misinformed) on many issues and candidates. Economists refer to this phenomenon as the "rational ignorance effect," a term initially coined by Downs.

Perhaps most importantly, public choice analysis explains why even democratic representative governments will often adopt inefficient programs. For decades, economists recognized that markets generally failed to allocate resources efficiently when monopoly, externalities, or public goods were present. These "market failures" were often used to justify government intervention. Public choice analysis, however, indicates that "government failure" is also a problem.

The political clout of special-interest groups is one source of government failure. Consider an issue that provides substantial personal benefits to members of a special group, while imposing small personal costs on members of a large majority of citizens. Since their personal stake is large, members of organized interest groups (and their lobbyists) have a strong incentive to inform themselves and their allies and to let legislators know how strongly they feel about the issue of special importance. Many of them will vote for or against candidates strictly on the basis of whether they support their interests. In addition, such interest groups are generally an attractive source of campaign resources, including financial contributions. In contrast, most other voters will care little about a special-interest issue, and, as the result of the rational ignorance effect, have little incentive to acquire information on the issue. For the non-special-interest voter, then, the time and energy necessary to examine the issue will generally exceed any potential personal gain from a preferred resolution. Thus, most non-special-interest voters will simply ignore such issues. Given this incentive structure, there will be a strong incentive for politicians to support the special interests even when their views conflict with economic efficiency. Political support for counterproductive government programs such as business and agricultural subsidies, tariffs, and pork-barrel spending reflect government failure due to the special-interest effect.

When government regulation and spending programs exert impact on the income of individuals, people have an incentive to invest time and energy seeking government favors. Public choice theorists refer to this source of government failure as "rent-seeking." By way of illustration, suppose that government was going to issue a monopoly right to sell shoes in a specific state. Government decisions about such policies do not take place in a vacuum. Individuals on all sides of the issue will expend their own resources attempting to influence the outcome. Indeed, individuals who want the monopoly right might be willing to spend an amount up to what the expected value of the monopoly profits will be. But this rent-seeking expenditure carries with it an opportunity cost. The resources used seeking the government favor will be unavailable for productive activity. As the result of wasteful rent-seeking, the size of the economic pie will be

smaller. (See Gordon Tullock, *The Political Economy of Rent-Seeking*, 1988, for additional details on this topic.)

The failure of government to achieve efficient economic outcomes under representative democracy and majority rule highlights the potential importance of constitutions. In recent years, constitutional economics has emerged as a new subfield of public choice analysis. Constitutional economics, like orthodox economics, is about how individuals make choices. But unlike orthodox economics, which examines how choices are made under a given set of legal, institutional, and social constraints, constitutional economics concerns itself with the choice to be made among the various legal, institutional, and social constraints themselves. The pioneering work of James Buchanan and Gordon Tullock in *The Calculus of Consent* (1962) provides the foundation for this area of study. This book analyzes the effects of different voting systems (for example, supramajority rather than simple-majority) and the impact of bicameral legislative bodies on political outcomes.

Compared to the traditional view of government as a corrective device, public choice provides a more realistic method of conceptualizing government. Public choice provides a coherent theory about how the political process works that both enhances our understanding of public policy and provides a framework for the development of constitutional structures more consistent with economic efficiency. Important research is ongoing. Those interested in keeping abreast of current research in this area will want to consult two key professional journals, *Public Choice* and *Constitutional Political Economy*.

—JAMES GWARTNEY
AND ROBERT LAWSON

Further Reading

Mueller, Dennis C. *Public Choice III*. New York: Cambridge University Press, 2003.

Tullock, Gordon, Arthur Seldon, and Gordon L.
Brady. *Government Failure: A Primer in Public
Choice.* Washington, D.C.: Cato Institute,
2002.

See also: Buchanan, James M.; Tullock, Gordon

Public Interest

The *Public Interest*, a quarterly journal of social and political thought, was launched in
1965 by Irving Kristol and Daniel Bell. It came
into existence alongside both the Great Society and the rise of the counterculture, and
many of its earliest articles were efforts to
critique the excesses and misconceptions of
these two "utopian" movements in American life, while at the same time defending
the dignity and importance of public life.

As the inaugural issue put it:

> Obviously, there never has been a soci-
> ety in which the public interest ruled
> supreme; equally obviously, so long as
> men are not angels, there will never be.
> But it is also true that there has never
> been a society which was not, in some
> way, and to some extent, guided by this
> ideal. . . . We feel that a democratic so-
> ciety, with its particular encouragement
> to individual ambition, private appetite,
> and personal concerns has a greater
> need than any other to keep the idea of
> the public interest before it.

The magazine's founding is generally
considered to mark the beginning of the
neoconservative movement in American
politics—a reaction against the New Left that
arose in the late 1960s and 1970s. By the time
of Ronald Reagan's election in 1980, the *Public Interest* had exerted a significant influence
on the thinking of mainstream conservatives
and on the political ideals and programs of
the Republican Party.

Until it published its last issue in spring
2005, the magazine addressed or considered
many issues during its four-decade run: the
urban crisis; the problem of modern bureaucracy; the unintended consequences of the
welfare state; the virtues and limits of bourgeois life; the intellectual and moral crisis of
the university; the spirit of American capitalism; the rise of both a new underclass and
a new overclass; the theory and practice of
supply-side and free-market economics; and,
in general, the prospects for American democracy and culture.

While any such typology is an oversimplification, there were, over the years, two
kinds of *Public Interest* essays: the social science essay, which tested various public policies via the rigorous examination of evidence
and experience; and the thematic essay, which
sought to define the political and cultural
moment, or to reflect on the present state of
affairs in the clarifying light of the past.

Even until the last issue, the *Public Interest* remained one of the most influential
magazines in American political and intellectual life. Its contributors included both
the first generation of neoconservatives
(James Q. Wilson, Nathan Glazer, Gertrude
Himmelfarb, Daniel Patrick Moynihan) and
a new generation of public intellectuals
(Francis Fukuyama, Wilfred McClay, Daniel
Mahoney, and others). At the time of its demise, the magazine was edited by Adam
Wolfson.

—ERIC COHEN

Further Reading
Kristol, Irving, Nathan Glazer, and Adam
Wolfson. "Looking Back." *Public Interest,*
Spring 2005.

*See also: Jewish conservatives; Kristol, Irving; neocon-
servatism*

Puritanism

The term Puritan was first used by the opponents of those English and American Protestants who desired to reform (though not necessarily separate from) the Church of England in worship, doctrine, and polity. In theology, Puritans followed Calvin rather than Luther, though their particular emphasis on experiential conversion and personal piety often distinguished them from Scottish and other European Calvinists. Scholars link Puritanism to English and American concepts of morality, politics, religion, education, business, and the arts. Puritanism has been associated, favorably or unfavorably, with most modern philosophies and movements in politics and religion. What is uniquely Puritan in England is not always easy to discern. But Puritan (also called Pilgrim) thought has uniquely influenced America since the foundation of her first colonies. The Puritan vision of America as a "city on a hill" has uniquely shaped the American view of life and politics and continues to influence what Sacvan Bercovitch calls "the American self."

The term Puritan has typically been used as a term of derision intended to communicate an overly zealous reformist spirit. Those conservatives who have focused on the Puritans' revolutionary character have tended to scorn Puritanism. In *The New Science of Politics* (1952), for example, Eric Voegelin elaborates on the criticisms of Richard Hooker and labels the Puritans gnostic revolutionaries. But other conservatives see Puritan traits as inherently conservative. In *The Roots of American Order* (1974), for example, Russell Kirk sees Puritanism in America as a bulwark against moral revolution and the modern spirit. Kirk also sees the "Puritan inheritance" as integral to understanding American political thought. Regardless of the intent or consequence of Puritan reforms, Puritan views on society, church, and state have become integral to the British and American worldview, especially the Puritans' pessimism towards human nature and their hope for the victory of the church in history.

Puritan worship services took place in buildings devoid of traditional ornamentation and were neither ceremonial nor liturgical. Exegetical and expository preaching rather than the sacraments formed the center of Puritan worship. Puritan church leaders rejected the traditional church calendar and its holidays as interfering with a simple and spiritual worship style that emphasized personal knowledge of the Bible and the pious duties of the laity. While the Puritans saw their efforts as the restoration of worship in the spirit of the early church, critics have charged that their reforms inevitably led from piety to rationalism. Whether this rationalism led to Unitarianism and transcendentalism in America is a subject of lingering debate.

In church governance, Puritans rejected formal and extensive hierarchy as "Popish." Instead, Puritan churches favored a Congregational or Presbyterian structure that gave congregations varying degrees of autonomy and emphasized the leadership of ruling and teaching elders within the local church. Church members were expected to have a close knowledge of the Bible and to attend worship regularly. The Puritans' emphasis on congregational autonomy and personal religious experience has led many to see them as a source of the democratic spirit in American politics. But such a claim must also take into account the Puritans' emphasis on "calling" and their distrust of democratic civil government and antinomian theology. The Puritans did require education for all, but their requirement for the extensive training of clergy in particular discouraged the egalitarianism more characteristic of Methodists and Baptists. Indeed, the Puritans' emphasis on higher education inspired them to found Harvard, Princeton, and other famous institutions.

English Puritans confronted questions about political liberty and religious tolerance in the Putney and Whitehall debates in 1647 and 1648 during the Puritan Revolution. American Puritans debated similar questions in famous controversies surrounding Anne Hutchinson and Roger Williams. In *Democracy in America* (1835), Alexis de Tocqueville writes about the importance of Puritanism to the American spirit and suggests that Puritanism was as much a political theory as a religious doctrine. He suggests that Puritanism encouraged both a republican and a democratic virtue and has enabled the kind of civic responsibility necessary for limited and federal government.

The Puritan Jonathan Edwards is considered by many to be America's greatest theologian. Together with Puritan George Whitefield, Edwards was also instrumental in inspiring American revivalism and its emphasis on personal virtue. The Mathers—Increase, Cotton, and Richard—embody a rich multigenerational history of American intellectual thought. In England, John Milton is associated with Puritanism in literature, while Oliver Cromwell is famous for his revolution against Charles I. English Puritan John Bunyan is famous for his enormously influential *Pilgrim's Progress* (1678). Finally, the political ideas of Puritans John Winthrop and William Bradford are essential for an understanding of America's colonial experience.

—Glenn Moots

Further Reading

Adair, John. *Founding Fathers: The Puritans in England and America*. Grand Rapids, Mich.: Baker, 1982.

Miller, Perry. *The New England Mind: From Colony to Province*. Cambridge, Mass.: Belknap Press, 1953.

———. *The New England Mind: The Seventeenth Century*. Cambridge, Mass.: Belknap Press, 1939.

Miller, Perry, and Thomas H. Johnson, eds. *The Puritans: A Sourcebook of their Writings*. Mineola, N.Y.: Dover Publications, 2001.

Ryken, Leland. *Worldly Saints: The Puritans as They Really Were*. Grand Rapids, Mich.: Academic Books, 1986.

See also: New Science of Politics, The; *Rushdoony, Rousas John; tradition*

Q

Quayle, James Danforth (1947–)

James Danforth "Dan" Quayle was born in Indianapolis, Indiana, an heir to the Pulliam newspaper fortune. After graduating from law school, Quayle went to work for the chain as associate publisher of the *Huntington* (Indiana) *Herald-Press*, using the position as a stepping stone to the House of Representatives in 1976 at age twenty-nine. After two terms in the House, he was elected to the Senate in 1980 and reelected in 1986. Quayle acquired a reputation as a strong conservative who was willing to work with Democrats for his programs and was well liked by senators from both parties.

In 1988, Quayle was the surprise choice for vice president by the Republican presidential candidate, Vice President George Herbert Walker Bush. Although he added youth and conservatism to the ticket, many questioned whether Quayle was too young and inexperienced to be vice president, a situation made worse by a hyperkinetic performance at the campaign rally where Bush introduced him to the nation. Revelations that Quayle had avoided service in Vietnam by joining the National Guard in 1969, allegedly using family connections, and the release of a photograph of Quayle in uniform and sunglasses added to his woes. His debate with Democratic vice presidential candidate Lloyd Bentsen, in which Quayle defended himself against the charge that he was too young and inexperienced by comparing himself to John Kennedy, who had been younger and even less experienced when he ran for president,

brought the devastating reply from Bentsen, "You're no Jack Kennedy." Quayle "looked like a deer in the headlights," said one conservative supporter.

Despite the setbacks, Quayle worked diligently behind the scenes and quietly began to grow into the job. As chairman of the National Space Council, Quayle led the effort to reform and streamline NASA—a bureaucracy increasingly seen as bloated and irrelevant by many—and he was much praised for his leadership of the council on competitiveness, working with business leaders to cut unnecessary and economically unproductive regulations. All the while, his public speaking improved, the national press corps began to appreciate his affable manner and low-key hard work, and he provided a conservative voice in a Republican administration often unsympathetic to conservatives. Many conservatives began touting the vice president as a legitimate presidential aspirant for 1996.

Quayle's rehabilitation came to nothing when, during the Bush-Quayle ticket's 1992 reelection campaign, in judging an elementary school spelling bee he read a misprinted flash card and tried to help a child by telling him to add an "e" to the end of "potato." The furor that followed was politically devastating. Ironically, one of the comments that cost him most in the eyes of the liberal media—his questioning the decision of television character Murphy Brown to refuse to marry the father of her child and instead raise the baby herself—came within a few years to be accepted as obvious, commonsense wisdom even among some liberals. Candice Bergen, who played Murphy Brown on television, herself later admitted that Quayle had been right. Still, the damage had been done. Following his defeat for reelection, Quayle toyed with the idea of running for president in 1996 and ran unsuccessfully in 2000.

—ROBERT WATERS

Further Reading

Broder, David S., and Bob Woodward. *The Man Who Would Be President: Dan Quayle.* New York: Simon & Schuster, 1992.

Quayle, Dan. *Standing Firm: A Vice-Presidential Memoir.* New York: HarperCollins, 1994.

See also: family

Quest for Community, The

Published by Oxford University Press in 1953, *The Quest for Community: A Study in the Ethics of Order and Freedom* was the magnum opus of America's premiere conservative sociologist, Robert Alexander Nisbet. While Nisbet would later maintain that he "had not particularly written it as a conservative book," *The Quest for Community* made such a significant historical contribution to the postwar conservative renaissance in the United States that Nicholas Lemann was prompted to conclude in 1991 that "the triumph of Nisbetism" was "the stated creed of American politics at the highest level."

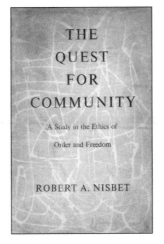

The central thesis of *The Quest for Community* would figure prominently in all of Nisbet's later work and bore strong influences from his "two greatest intellectual heroes," Edmund Burke and Alexis de Tocqueville. In its pages, Nisbet argued that modernity's preoccupation with alienation, isolation, and loneliness results from the gradual erosion of the ties that bind—traditional, intermediate communities of kinship, place, and faith—by the ascendancy of the Western political nation-state. Leviathan had absorbed the functions, usurped the authorities, and severed the ties of traditional associations embodied in the family, village, parish, and guild. "The quest for community will not be denied," Nisbet insisted, "for it springs from some of the powerful needs of human nature—needs for a clear sense of cultural purpose, membership, status, and community." The bitter irony in all this, Nisbet maintained, was that the modern quest for community—itself a result of the state's growing consolidation and ubiquity—is all too often misdirected back towards the state itself. Thus, as traditional social institutions erode, our longing for the sense of belonging they once provided manifests itself in distinctly *political* solutions: namely the increasing consolidation of national government. Yet, Nisbet warned, such a triumph of the political bond over the social bond only leads to a further unraveling of the social fabric and thus to our heightened sense of anxiety.

Arriving on the scene in the same year as Russell Kirk's *The Conservative Mind*, Nisbet's first book immediately met with praise from T. S. Eliot, Kirk, Reinhold Niebuhr, and others, who rated it a thoughtful critique of modern liberal individualism. Nisbet's writings in general, and this book in particular, have also made a significant contribution to modern communitarian discussions by focusing attention on the state not as a guarantor of community but instead as a primary contributor to its dissolution. The thread that ties together virtually all of Nisbet's later work can be found in the first page of his preface to *The Quest for Community*. While acknowledging the myriad dislocations caused by economic, religious, and technological agents, Nisbet informs his readers that he has chosen "to deal with the *political* causes of the manifold alienations that lie behind the contemporary quest for community." To view the state as merely a legal relationship, he warns, is "profoundly delusive." The true "significance of the modern state," he insists, is "inseparable from its successive penetrations of man's economic, religious, kinship, and local allegiances, and its revolutionary dislocations of established centers of function and authority."

—CORY ANDREWS

Further Reading

Nash, George H. *The Conservative Intellectual Movement in America since 1945.* Rev. ed. Wilmington, Del.: Intercollegiate Studies Institute, 1996.

Stone, Brad Lowell. *Robert Nisbet: Communitarian Traditionalist.* Wilmington, Del.: ISI Books, 2000.

See also: community; individualism; mediating structures; Nisbet, Robert A.

quotas

Affirmative action programs seeking to increase the representation of women and minorities have often taken the form of numerical quotas in hiring, promotions, public contracting, and college admissions. Conservatives oppose quotas because they violate the principle of equality before the law.

The history of quotas is tortuous. The 1964 Civil Rights Act ensured that individuals would be treated equally regardless of their race, sex, or other social categories. Titles IV, VI, VII, and X of the amended act expressly forbade the use of racial or other

quotas. Largely because of these provisions, the act was approved by 80 percent of Republicans and 60 percent of Democrats in both houses.

The transition from equal opportunity to numerical preferences began soon after the passage of the Civil Rights Act. In 1965 President Johnson issued an executive order that created the Office of Federal Contract Compliance. In 1969 this office began implementing the "Philadelphia Plan," which required that employers set "numerical goals" for hiring minorities in order to keep their federal contracts. Additionally, the Civil Rights Act created the Equal Employment Opportunity Commission, which quickly transformed the legal standard for discrimination from one where employers were liable for intentional acts to one where they were responsible for statistical inequities. Since 1972 the EEOC has had the power to initiate suits, and it follows what is known as the "80 percent" or "four-fifths" rule. For example, in a community that includes 12 percent African Americans, if an employer hires 9 percent African Americans (or a ratio of less than four-fifths), the burden is on the employer to prove that he or she is not discriminating.

Although several states have recently sought to curtail affirmative action in higher education, racial quotas have been common in college admissions since the early 1970s. When admissions offices employ quotas, they must go deep into the minority applicant pool, creating a mismatch between student talents and institutional demands. The average black SAT score is typically 100 to 280 points lower than the average white SAT score at the same institution. Consequently, the black failure rate is five times higher than the white rate at colleges that are not traditionally African American.

The theory underlying quotas is that without "institutional racism" group representation in colleges and the workplace would mirror the proportions in the population at large. Statistical disparities are taken as evidence of discrimination. Yet, statistical disparities are commonplace without discrimination. For example, women who work full time earn 75 percent of the amount earned by comparable men, but this difference is a function of marital status and childbearing, not gender; never-married women have perfect income parity with never-married men. Similarly, black households earn only 61 percent of that earned by white households, but this difference is a function of the high proportion of single-parent black households, not race; married black couples are approaching income parity with married white couples. Meanwhile, white households earn only 67 percent of that earned by American-born Asian households.

By thin majorities in *Regents* v. *Bakke* (1978), *United Steel Workers* v. *Weber* (1979), and *Fullilove v. Klutznick* (1980) the Supreme Court has upheld the use of quotas in college admissions, hiring and public contracts. However, since 1989 the Court has set limits on quotas by invoking the equal protection clause of the Fourteenth Amendment. The fate of quotas depends upon future Supreme Court appointments.

—BRAD LOWELL STONE

Further Reading

D'Souza, Dinesh. *The End of Racism*. New York: Free Press, 1995.

Sowell, Thomas. *The Quest for Cosmic Justice*. New York: Free Press, 2000.

Thernstrom, Steven and Abigail Thernstrom. *America in Black and White*. New York: Simon & Schuster, 1997.

See also: affirmative action; civil rights; equal protection; Jewish conservatives

R

Radio Free Europe

Radio Free Europe (RFE) and Radio Liberty (RL) were created to act as surrogate "hometown" radio stations for communist-controlled countries in Central and Eastern Europe (RFE) and the Soviet Union (RL), offering an alternative to communist-controlled local stations.

Ostensibly independent so that they would be allowed to say things that the U.S. government–controlled Voice of America could not, the creation of RFE and RL was the idea of George Kennan and Joseph Grew of the State Department and the CIA's Frank Wisner. RFE began operations in 1950, and Radio Liberty (then known as Radio Liberation) followed in 1953. Until 1972, both received covert CIA funding. The stations' purpose was to function as a means of harassing the communist governments of Central and Eastern Europe. Their creators' insight was that the provision of local news, commentary, and cultural analysis by émigré broadcasters would act as a powerful assault against communism. Radio Free Europe's broadcasts went out to each Soviet bloc state in Europe, and Radio Liberty broadcast in more than a dozen languages to the Soviet Union. Their audiences numbered in the millions, and communist governments spent billions of dollars jamming their broadcasts.

In the stations' early years, broadcasters encouraged resistance, generally passive, and the stations' tone and rhetoric were vigorously anticommunist. Disaster struck during the Hungarian revolution of 1956, when RFE broadcasters, acting independently but adhering to the Eisenhower administration's stated policy goal of "rolling back" Soviet power, encouraged violent resistance to the Soviet invasion and implied that NATO forces would intervene against the Soviets. In the ensuing battle, Soviet tanks killed more than 20,000 freedom fighters while the United States did nothing. Tightened broadcast oversight followed at RFE.

Following congressional hearings by Senator J. William Fulbright, who sought to shut down the stations because he had concluded that their anticommunist slant on the news endangered détente, the stations were made independent of the CIA and shifted to a less ideological and more "professional" style of broadcast. The latter policy was overturned by the Reagan administration, which sought a stronger anticommunist focus and also created Radio Marti, which broadcasts to communist Cuba.

In November 1988, without warning, the Soviets stopped jamming RL and RFE. The following year, RFE played an important role in Poland's "nonpartisan" legislative elections by opening the airwaves to anticommunist candidates, who were prevented from using Polish state media, and by repeatedly broadcasting lists that identified which candidates were pro- and which anticommunist. The anticommunists won 96 percent of the vote. RL broadcasters were also with Boris Yeltsin broadcasting throughout the hardline communists' attempted coup in 1991.

With the end of the Cold War, President Bill Clinton made significant cuts in the stations' budgets, but he also added a South Slav service for the nations that emerged from the break-up of Yugoslavia. Radio Free Afghanistan, which had broadcast from 1985 to 1993, was reestablished in 2002.

—ROBERT WATERS

Further Reading

Puddington, Arch. *Broadcasting Freedom: The Cold War Triumph of Radio Free Europe and Radio Liberty*. Lexington, Ky.: University Press of Kentucky, 2000.

See also: anticommunisim; Cold War; Kennan, George

Rand, Ayn (1905–82)

Ayn Rand, née Alissa Zinovyevna Rosenbaum, had her roots in the secular, middle-class Jewry of St. Petersburg, Russia; it was from the civic afflictions of that city under incipient communism that she fled with her family to North America in 1926. Linked in the popular imagination with conservatism, a persistent but difficult-to-uphold affinity that she herself explicitly rejected, Rand early nourished herself on the work of Friedrich Nietzsche, who enjoyed considerable currency in pre-Bolshevik Russia. The Promethean theme in Rand's fiction—the superman-triumph of Howard Roark in *The Fountainhead* (1943) or of John Galt in *Atlas Shrugged* (1957)—reflects her Nietzschean contempt for conventional (i.e., Judeo-Christian) morality and her dream of a new human type, beyond good and evil, who would transcend the limitations imposed on ego-development by social orthodoxy.

That Rand possessed a powerful creative drive admits of no contestation. She began writing, first in Russian and then in English,

in her twenties. A novel, *We the Living* (1936), while derivative, usefully dramatizes the dictatorial grotesque of life under the Leninist regime, yet it hardly constitutes the original masterpiece that Rand's followers sometimes make it out to be. The same could be said of *Anthem* (1937), a sequel of sorts to *We the Living* that cleaves even closer than its precursor to the already long-consolidated dystopian genre worked by Yevgeny Zamyatin, Aldous Huxley, and H. G. Wells. A play, *The Night of January 16,* belongs to this formative period. All of these early works champion the individual against socialism, or, more particularly, against the Bolshevik variety of socialism. The characters in these fictions lack palpability, however, with various cardboard personae incarnating this idea or its opposite and the conflict adhering to an elementary political-allegorical scheme.

A superficial reading of *The Fountainhead* convinced many among its excited initial audience that Rand espoused an ethos congenial to Wendell Wilkie conservatism, as though to take up the cudgel against Franklin Delano Roosevelt and the New Deal meant swearing allegiance to the Protestant dispensation and to the local Booster Society. A casual interpreter might lazily have seen it that way. But in Rand's view, the local Booster Society is just as corrupt, because just as socialistic, as the New Deal; and to compromise with either is to offend against moral and epistemological integrity. Roark thus seeks vindication neither in tradition nor in normality, going so far as to dynamite a public works project over an esthetic issue; he is rather the first fully realized ego-dogmatist in Rand's work, *Atlas*'s Galt being the second. His antagonists are the adherents of altruism; they are the betrayers of ego for the sake of *others,* who, by their betrayal of that without which human life as such is impossible, are in fact nihilists.

The nihilists are hard at work undermining civilization—and attacking the ego—in

Atlas, the novel on which Rand commenced shortly after the appearance of *The Fountainhead.* Of the two, *Atlas* is the grander in conception, while *The Fountainhead* is the greater literary achievement, being more satisfactorily centered on Roark as its point of view character, whereas *Atlas* multiplies its point-of-view protagonists. *Atlas* assuredly has many merits, not least among them a truly Wagnerian conception of mythic action on the vastest scale, as the postwar industrial-civic infrastructure of the Western nations—most especially of the United States—slips away into the rust, breakdown, and riot of a rapaciously redistributive policy that fails even to conceive that wealth might be increased rather than appropriated, hoarded, and wasted. Rand's fondness for the cinematic vision of Fritz Lang, especially for his Wagnerian *Siegfried* (1926), finds fruition in the epic story of engineer-*cum*-superman John Galt. Galt embodies Randian decisiveness; Dagny Taggart and Henry "Hank" Reardon follow his elusive trail, as they also follow him into a rejection of the altruistic *ethos* and the espousal of heroic egoism.

Ayn Rand

In the aftermath of *Atlas Shrugged,* Rand floundered creatively; no further fictions, on any scale, would emerge. In the abeyance of her storytelling impulse, Rand turned to the task of systematizing the implicit philosophy of *The Fountainhead* and of *Atlas.* "Objectivism," as she dubbed it, while again not the unprecedented achievement that either she or her acolytes boast, qualifies nevertheless as a respectable and somewhat unusual contribution to twentieth-century philosophy. Objectivism's roots lie in two soils, one acknowledged and the other not: the first is Aristotle, whose ontological axiom that existence is identical with itself ("A = A"), becomes an all-purpose touchstone for distinguishing truth from ideology; the second, not surprisingly, is Nietzsche, whose glorification of the will against the strictures of what he sees as arbitrary morality supplies Rand with the basic theme of her paean to the ego. It should be noted that Rand never managed an actual book codifying her position, a task she left to Leonard Peikoff, who fulfilled it in *Objectivism* (1991). She found her métier in longish essays, producing them steadily in the 1950s, '60s, and '70s and collecting them in anthologies perpetually reissued, including *For the New Intellectual* (1961), *The Virtue of Selfishness* (1964), *Capitalism: The Unknown Ideal* (1967), and *The Romantic Manifesto* (1971; revised 1975).

Rand made herself felt: her one-time protégé Alan Greenspan has brought something of Rand's outlook to the Federal Reserve; her conception of the businessman appears in the studied mien of a public figure like Donald Trump. In life she violated her oaths, cuckolding her husband Frank O'Connor, a one-time film-actor, with her younger protégé Nathaniel Branden, and expelling heretics from her circle; she was vituperative, without humor, and increasingly Stalinist in her behavior as she aged, resembling an L. Ron Hubbard or a Jim Jones in the jealous demands she exercised over those who formed what in effect was her cult. While regarding her warily, readers can nevertheless find a range of valid insights in her work, particularly her analysis of envy as the taproot of socialist and related ideologies.

—THOMAS F. BERTONNEAU

Further Reading

Branden, Nathaniel. *Judgment Day: My Years with Ayn Rand.* Boston: Houghton Mifflin, 1989.

Rand, Ayn. *Introduction to Objectivist Epistemology.* Edited by Harry Binswanger and Leonard Peikoff. Expanded 2nd ed. New York: New American Library, 1990.

———. *Return of the Primitive: The Anti-Industrial Revolution.* Edited by Peter Schwartz. New York: Meridian, 1999.

———. *The Voice of Reason: Essays in Objectivist Thought.* Edited by Leonard Peikoff. New York: New American Library, 1989.

Sciabarra, Chris Matthew. *Ayn Rand: The Russian Radical.* University Park, Pa.: Pennsylvania State University Press, 1995.

See also: Chambers, Whittaker; community; émigré intellectuals; libertarianism; nihilism; Reason

Randolph, John (of Roanoke) (1773–1833)

Virginian political leader and orator John Randolph of Roanoke entered public life as a radical and ended his career as a conservative. First in the federal House of Representatives and later in the Senate, he opposed the administration of every president of the United States from John Adams through Andrew Jackson.

Descended from two great Virginian families, the Randolphs and the Blands, the young Randolph, restless and talented, entered politics as a passionate opponent of the Federalists. Elected to the House of Representatives in 1799, he became the majority leader in the House during Jefferson's first administration and continued to dominate the House even after he fell out with members of Jefferson's cabinet and with President Jefferson himself. His opposition to the purchase of Florida and to settlement of the Yazoo land claims out of federal funds presently led him to become the leader of the faction in Congress called the "Old Republicans" or "Tertium Quids," beginning in 1806; he and his allies, chiefly members of Congress from Virginia and North Carolina, set themselves against the "War Hawks" and the War of 1812. They held by strict construction of the Constitution, reproaching the "Virginia Dynasty" presidents for straying from that doctrine.

Aristocratic, fearless, a brilliant speaker, a remorseless adversary of corruption, Randolph in practical politics was a champion of the rural interest and of the society of the Southern states. He began his political career as a self-proclaimed *ami des noirs* and opponent of chattel slavery; he was active in the abolition of the slave trade in the District of Columbia and in attempts to settle free blacks in Africa; at the end of his life he bequeathed all his property to his slaves (whom he had inherited, together with his plantation of Roanoke, in southern Virginia), attempting to settle them in the free state of Ohio. As political pressure from the Northern abolitionists upon the South increased, however, he resisted with his sardonic eloquence the increasing political power of the North. The national controversy over statehood for Missouri, nationalist plans for "internal improvements" at federal expense, and his opposition to Henry Clay's "Panama Mission" designs brought Randolph increased popularity as a sectional leader dur-

John Randolph

ing the 1820s. Although Randolph mordantly criticized Vice President John C. Calhoun during Randolph's year (1826) in the Senate, the Virginian's speeches powerfully influenced Calhoun's later political convictions and conduct. In that sense, Randolph was a forerunner of Southern nationalism; but his allegiance lifelong was rather the Old Dominion of Virginia. Occasionally he found political allies in New England and New York.

An ardent Anglican during his mature years, and strongly attached to the Virginia of yesteryear, Randolph looked with foreboding upon the westward expansion of the United States, saying that no government which should extend from Atlantic to Pacific would be fit to govern him. At the Virginia Constitutional Convention of 1829–30, he denounced "King Numbers," the notion of one man, one vote. He was the most conspicuous delegate to that convention, though many Virginians of mark were present; and on the floor he expressed memorably the conservative understanding of politics—which he had acquired, in part, from the study of Edmund Burke. Here he is on one proposal of the innovators at the convention:

> Mr. Randolph said, that he should vote against the amendment, and that on a principle which he had learned before he came into public life; and by which he had been governed during the whole course of his life, that it was always unwise—yes, highly unwise—to disturb a thing that was at rest. This was a great cardinal principle that should govern all wise statesmen—never without the strongest necessity to disturb that which was at rest.

Unmarried, living solitary much of each year at his Roanoke plantation in a cabin, he was loved by some and feared by many.

He made three trips to England, and from May 1830 to the autumn of 1831 was American minister to the Court of St. Petersburg. Possessing what was said to be the finest library in Virginia, he was an omnivorous reader (intimately familiar with the collections of the Library of Congress) and a master of English prose style. His *Letters to a Young Relative*, published at Philadelphia the year after his death, illustrate both his literary talents and the complexity of his character. "They will never love where they ought to love," Edmund Burke had written, "who do not hate where they ought to hate": Randolph both loved and hated earnestly. He fought at least two duels (one with Henry Clay, a combat memorably recorded by Senator Thomas Hart Benton); also he was capable of compassion and generosity.

—RUSSELL KIRK

Further Reading

Kirk, Russell. *John Randolph of Roanoke: A Study in American Politics, with Selected Speeches and Letters*. 3rd ed. Indianapolis, Ind.: Liberty Press, 1978.

Randolph, John. *Collected Letters of John Randolph of Roanoke to Dr. John Brockenbrough, 1812-1833*. Edited by Kenneth Shorey. New Brunswick, N.J.: Transaction, 1988.

Risjord, Norman K. *The Old Republicans: Southern Conservatism in the Age of Jefferson*. New York: Columbia University Press, 1965.

See also: Kirk, Russell; Southern conservatism

Ransom, John Crowe (1888–1974)

A distinguished poet and literary scholar, John Crowe Ransom was also, at least initially, the leading spokesman of the Agrarians, a group of twelve writers from the Middle South who sought to conserve the predominantly agrarian way of life in their region against the destructive inroads of industrialization and scientism. The Agrarians, who flourished at Vanderbilt University during the late 1920s and early to mid-1930s, achieved their high-water mark with the publication of *I'll Take My Stand: The South and the Agrarian Tradition* (1930). Ransom's fellow Agrarians (and contributors to the volume) included Robert Penn Warren, Donald Davidson, Allen Tate, Andrew Lytle, Frank Lawrence Owsley, and John Gould Fletcher, among others. Ransom's own contributions, the manifesto's "Statement of Principles" and the essay "Reconstructed but Unregenerate," took pride of place in the volume. The latter, which calls for Southerners to be prudent in accepting cultural change—to carefully admit only as much industrialization as will not alter the distinctive character of the South—is the most quoted and best known of all the essays in *I'll Take My Stand*.

John Crowe Ransom

During the 1930s, the Tennessee-born Ransom and his fellow Agrarians wrote frequently on Southern traditionalism in the pages of the *American Review* and elsewhere. And while the year 1930 marked the high tide of Southern Agrarianism, it was also the apex of Ransom's stature as a conservative writer, for in that year he also published *God without Thunder: An Unorthodox Defense of Orthodoxy* (1930), which called on Western culture to eschew milk-and-water religion and instead pledge allegiance to the utterly transcendent and unfathomable God of the Bible (especially the God of the Old Testament). Though the book became a minor conservative classic, it was not well received and eventually went out of print; even Ransom's fellow Agrarian John Gould Fletcher, reviewing *God without Thunder* in the *Criterion*, was

moved to write that Ransom had written "an interesting book, though scarcely a convincing one."

As the 1930s passed and Ransom's colleagues left Nashville for other cities to pursue separate careers, the Agrarian cause faded. Although he contributed to a second Agrarian symposium, *Who Owns America? A Second Declaration of Independence* (1936), Ransom found his own interest in the cause fading as well. He left Tennessee to take a position on the English faculty at Kenyon College in Gambier, Ohio, in 1937. Two years later Ransom founded the *Kenyon Review*, which, under his editorship, became renowned as an outstanding literary quarterly. As an editor and literary scholar he helped develop and then gave a name to a textually focused critical school— "The New Criticism"— that dominated the world of literary scholarship for several decades. By the mid 1940s, Ransom's engagement in traditionalist cultural and political analysis had all but ended.

A brilliant Rhodes Scholar as a young man, and trained in classical and Anglo-American literature, Ransom had begun his career writing poetry in the years immediately before World War I. After the war, he began teaching English at Vanderbilt University. There he became part of a small group of men interested in writing and discussing poetry and how the inroads of poetic modernism ought to influence the Southern poet, a group that included Tate, Davidson, Alec B. Stevenson, and Stanley Johnson, among several others. In time the group, which styled itself the "Fugitives," began publishing a magazine. The *Fugitive* (1922–25) contained their own verse and that of like-minded contributors. In its brief efflorescence, the *Fugitive* became the most influential and distinguished poetry magazine in the South, publishing poetry that built on Southern themes while also embracing the poetic styles of modernism, with its complex textures and stylistic freedom. Ransom's own verse was no exception to this; and it was during his years as a Fugitive that Ransom wrote most of his best poetry, including "Necrological," "Bells for John Whiteside's Daughter," "Antique Harvesters," and "Janet Waking." Ransom's poetry, along with the cultural and literary essays he wrote throughout his life, had as an underlying theme the idea of human folly and the foolishness of modern gnosticism, as manifest by moderns' prideful belief in inevitable progress in matters of the spirit and human behavior. In an assessment written late in his subject's life, Tate praised Ransom's achievement, writing, "[No] poet of our age, not even his exact contemporary T. S. Eliot, has surpassed [Ransom] in the awareness of the shadowy back room of the human condition, where 'invisible evil, deprived and bold' makes its bid for domination." Tate added that Ransom "warns us to slow up, to take thought, to come out of our Gnostic dream of perfection back into the actual world, where human reality is in the commitment to the limited human condition, which allows us only the irony of imperfect love."

—JAMES E. PERSON JR.

Further Reading

Ransom, John Crowe. *The New Criticism*. 2nd ed. Westport, Conn.: Greenwood Press, 1979.
———. *Selected Essays of John Crowe Ransom*. Edited by Thomas Daniel Young and John Hindle. Baton Rouge, La.: Louisiana State University Press, 1984.
———. *Selected Poems*. 3rd rev. ed. New York: Knopf, 1969.
Young, Thomas Daniel. *John Crowe Ransom: Critical Essays and a Bibliography*. Baton Rouge, La.:
Louisiana State University Press, 1968.
———. *Gentleman in a Dustcoat: A Biography of John Crowe Ransom*. Baton Rouge, La.: Louisiana State University Press, 1976.

See also: agrarianism; I'll Take My Stand; *literary criticism; Lowell, Robert; New Criticism; Southern Agrarians*

Read, Leonard E. (1898–1983)

Growing up in rural Michigan, Leonard Read, founder of the Foundation for Economic Education, lost his father at the age of ten. Honing his work ethic by doing farm chores and clerking in a nearby country store, Read finished secondary school right as the United States entered World War I. He volunteered and served in the aviation corps in England and with the Army of Occupation after the war's end. Read returned to Michigan when his service ended and started a wholesale produce business, but this business failed.

Read then moved to California with his wife and two sons, selling real estate for a time and eventually finding his niche at the Chamber of Commerce. Indeed, Read, a charismatic speaker, eventually became manager of the western division of the national Chamber. It was at this time that he wrote his first book, *The Romance of Reality* (1937). Two years later, Read became the general manager of the Los Angeles Chamber, the nation's largest. Eschewing the traditional tub-thumping for the city's climate and orange groves and the starlets of Hollywood, Read sought to use the Chamber as a platform from which to make the case for the classical-liberal philosophy of individual rights, private property, limited government, and the free-market economy in an idiom that drew heavily from the Declaration of Independence and the Constitution. Toward this end the Chamber published books, pamphlets, and a journal and held seminars and lectures. Soon the publications of the Los Angeles Chamber began to have a national circulation and Read found himself addressing audiences all over the country.

Still, Read was troubled by the fact that the Chamber was really only the agent of the hundreds of southern California industries that supported it. He became convinced that the classical-liberal philosophy he was expounding needed a base that was strictly independent, supported voluntarily only by those who believed in it. In 1946 his dream took shape with the formation of the Foundation for Economic Education (FEE) in Irvington-on-Hudson, New York. During the next thirty-seven years Read wrote twenty-seven books, numerous pamphlets and articles, delivered hundreds of speeches, and traveled more than two million miles in preaching the doctrines of classical liberalism. Under his leadership, FEE flourished, and the voices of Milton Friedman and George Stigler, Ludwig von Mises, and Henry Hazlitt were unified, strengthened, and given a new outlet in their defense of economic freedom.

—EDMUND OPTIZ

Further Reading

Read, Leonard. *Elements of Libertarian Leadership: Notes on the Theory, Methods and Practice of Freedom.* Irvington-on-Hudson, N.Y.: Foundation for Economic Education, 1962.

———. *Seeds of Progress.* Irvington-on-Hudson, N.Y.: Foundation for Economic Education, 1980.

See also: Foundation for Economic Education

Reagan Democrats

Ronald Reagan (1911–2004) was the most conservative American president elected in the second half of the twentieth century. He entered office vowing to roll back many of the social welfare programs that the Democratic Party had put into place during the New Deal and after. Reagan's electoral victories in 1980 and 1984 astonished political commentators because a large block of his support came from traditional Democrats—union members and working-class ethnics—who had never before abandoned their party in such massive numbers.

The reasons for Reagan's success with Democrats are complex, because opinion polls show that Reagan Democrats often disagreed with the particulars of Reagan's policies even while supporting him at the polls. Perhaps the most obvious reason for Reagan's victory in 1980 was President Jimmy Carter's perceived weakness. During the Carter years energy prices rose, interest rates soared, inflation increased, and unemployment was high. Carter appeared helpless when the Soviet Union invaded Afghanistan. In addition, at the time of 1980 election fifty-three Americans were still being held hostage in Iran, having been seized the previous November.

Carter's haplessness alone, however, cannot account for Reagan's inroads among traditional Democrats. As Stanley B. Greenberg revealed in his 1985 study, "Forging Democratic Ideas," Reagan's platform appealed to many Democrats who were feeling increasingly alienated from their party in the 1980s. Greenberg points to middle-class Americans, particularly blue-collar workers and ethnic Catholics, who formerly constituted a significant portion of Democratic voters but objected to the tax increases and affirmative action advocated by their party. Resenting both the rich, who they believed to be virtually tax exempt, and the poor, who received welfare, many middle-class workers believed that the Democratic Party no longer represented them and so cast their votes for Reagan, whose pro-family and limited government policies appealed to their sense of values.

With the exception of West Virginia and, in 1980, Georgia (Carter's native state), Reagan carried the entire South in both elections. Since then, the South has continued to vote almost exclusively Republican, a change which has significantly affected the House of Representatives, as more than half of the members from southern states are now Republican.

Once in office, Reagan proved to be a masterful politician, even though he often left the day-to-day administration of policy to his subordinates. Not only was he able to halt the growth of the welfare state, but he also convinced a large segment of the voting public that government bureaucracies were wasteful and that social spending was counterproductive. As he put it, "the government is the problem, not the solution." So pervasively complete was Reagan's influence that no presidential candidate since 1980 has described himself as a "liberal."

In foreign affairs Reagan promised to restore American strength and prestige after its humiliating defeat in the Vietnam War. Although most voters prudently feared a direct confrontation with the Soviet Union, they accepted Reagan's view that weakness, not strength, was more likely to lead to conflict. Many Reagan Democrats' families had emigrated from countries dominated by communist tyranny, and they agreed with the president that the Soviet Union was an "evil empire."

Reagan's most enduring political skill was his ability to instill confidence. After years of turmoil—including the assassination of one president and the resignation of another, unprecedented crime rates, the breakdown of moral consensus, defeat in a foreign war, and the stagnation of the once-vibrant U.S. economy—American self-esteem was badly shaken. Reagan restored faith in the American system of government. His simple message proclaimed that the days of confusion, distrust, and malaise were gone:

"America is back." He made people believe that their efforts mattered and that their nation was great. Even when he criticized others, he presented an optimistic tone and a can-do attitude. Reagan's affability and his call for a return to patriotism struck a chord with the American public.

Although traditional Democrats had differed with Reagan over policy, they supported him because they acknowledged that he possessed one of the rarest of human qualities: the capacity to inspire a people and successfully lead a nation.

—JAMES PONTUSO

Further Reading

Brookhiser, Richard. *The Outside Story: How Democrats and Republicans Re-Elected Reagan.* Garden City, N.Y.: Doubleday, 1986.

Busch, Andrew. *Reagan's Victory: The Presidential Election of 1980 and the Rise of the Right.* Lawrence, Kan.: University Press of Kansas, 2005.

See also: Democratic Party; Reagan, Ronald; Republican Party

Reagan Doctrine

The Reagan Doctrine was both a continuation of and a departure from America's Cold War foreign policy. Every president since Harry Truman in the 1940s had attempted to contain communism, arguing that its spread threatened democracy. As part of the broad strategic plan called "containment," America covertly aided anticommunist groups throughout the world. President Ronald Reagan took this principle one step further. He openly declared America's intention to roll back communism by propping up all noncommunist governments and by overthrowing Marxist governments wherever communism had not become firmly established. He supported anticommunist political movements in El Salvador and Guatemala and anticommunist insurgencies in Afghanistan, Angola, Cambodia, Ethiopia, Grenada, Laos, and Nicaragua.

The Reagan Doctrine was implemented in a number of ways, depending on local conditions. It employed political, economic, military, and psychological warfare in support of indigenous anticommunist forces. These wars were called "low intensity" conflicts because they occurred primarily in the Third World and did not involve direct military confrontation between the United States and the Soviet Union. Only in Grenada, where American citizens were in jeopardy and where the Caribbean island's proximity threatened American interests, did Reagan commit United States armed forces to battle.

The Reagan Doctrine was very controversial. Critics insisted that the United States was collaborating with groups that violated human rights and restricted democracy in more brutal ways than did communism. There were, in fact, many instances when American-backed forces acted brutally against their enemies.

United Nations Ambassador Jeane Kirkpatrick responded to charges that the Reagan administration was insensitive to violations of human rights by making a distinction between right-wing dictatorships and Marxist regimes. She argued that right-wing dictatorships—such as Franco's Spain—could, and often did, transform themselves into democracies; however, once firmly established in the communist camp, no Marxist government had ever relinquished power.

Kirkpatrick's thesis seemed to have validity. In assisting "fraternal" allies throughout the world, the Soviet Union sent the Red Army into Afghanistan to crush an anticommunist coalition that threatened to overthrow the Marxist regime in Kabul. Soviet leader Leonid Brezhnev justified direct intervention in Afghanistan by proclaiming

the "Brezhnev Doctrine," which held that the victory of Marxism was inevitable and that the Soviet Union would not allow any communist regime to be overturned by "the imperialist forces" of the West.

The Reagan Doctrine was not merely a set of policies aimed at protecting American interests. Reagan considered opposition to communism a moral crusade. He called the Soviet Union "an evil empire" and was persuaded that it was intent on spreading its inhuman principles throughout the world. Reagan proclaimed that the ideas of Marx were inconsistent with human nature and that they led to the most vicious forms of political repression. Whatever the original goal of Marx might have been, wherever Marxist principles were applied totalitarian government quickly followed.

Reagan's clearly stated opposition to the Soviet Union rallied anticommunist forces across the world, and, in British Prime Minister Margaret Thatcher's words, helped "break the world free of a monstrous creed."

—JAMES PONTUSO

Further Reading

Lagon, Mark P. *The Reagan Doctrine: Sources of American Conduct in the Cold War's Last Chapter.* Westport, Conn.: Praeger, 1994.

Scott, James M. *Deciding to Intervene: The Reagan Doctrine and American Foreign Policy.* Durham, N.C.: Duke University Press, 1996.

See also: Casey, William J.; Cold War; containment; Reagan, Ronald

Reagan, Ronald (1911–2004)

Born in rented rooms above a bank in Tampico, Illinois, Reagan would become the most important American conservative political leader of the twentieth century. His ascendancy to the presidency in January 1981 and his subsequent two terms in office would mark the decisive breakthrough of conservative ideas into the realm of national policy. His program of steep tax cuts, industry deregulation, staunch anticommunism, and a broad defense build-up defined his largely popular but controversial eight years in office. His strong appeal, widely attributed to his personal eloquence and style as well as his vigorous and principled agenda, not only succeeded in uniting the disparate elements of the Republican Party but also helped win him support from many traditional Democratic constituencies.

The second son of an Irish Catholic father and a Scots-English Protestant mother, Reagan spent his formative years in the cities and towns of northern Illinois. From his father Jack, an itinerant shoe salesman, he would inherit his jovial sense of humor, his gifts as a storyteller, and the support for Franklin D. Roosevelt's New Deal liberalism that would define the political outlook of his young adulthood. From his mother Nelle Wilson, a homemaker and amateur actress, he received his Protestant faith, his love of the stage, and the almost boundless optimism that would sustain him throughout his life.

Although marred by poverty, Reagan's was a happy childhood made happier by his family's decision in 1920 to settle permanently in Dixon, Illinois. There he found solace in reading and religion, won a place on the high school football team, dated the pastor's daughter, and worked in the summers as a lifeguard along the Rock River. In 1928 he matriculated at Eureka College, a small liberal arts school owned by the Disciples of Christ (the church into which Reagan was baptized at age twelve). At Eu-

reka, he majored in economics, continued his play on the gridiron, swam, joined the Drama Society, Booster Club, yearbook, and the Tau Kappa Epsilon fraternity. In his senior year he was elected student body president. After graduation in 1932, during the depths of the Depression, he found work as a sports announcer at an Iowa radio station. For more than four years (mostly at WHO in Des Moines) he honed his skills on the airwaves, until a 1937 trip to Los Angeles and a hastily arranged screen test with Warner Brothers changed his life.

Ronald Reagan

During his tenure in Hollywood, Ronald Reagan appeared in fifty-three films, all the while developing the comfort and poise before the camera that later served him so well in his political career. It was his involvement in the Screen Actors Guild, however, that introduced him to the hurly-burly of politics. Elected as the guild's president in 1947, he wrangled with movie moguls and studio executives over pay and benefits, confronted government regulators, and fought what he believed was the attempted takeover of Hollywood by communists. These struggles with Hollywood leftists decisively transformed his earlier benign views of communism into outright antipathy. In 1952, several years after his first marriage to Academy Award–winning actress Jane Wyman had ended in divorce, Reagan married the young actress Nancy Davis.

In 1954, his film career waning, Reagan signed a lucrative contract to host the television show General Electric Theater. A stipulation requiring him to address GE employees across the country sixteen weeks a year not only allowed him to perfect his oratorical and speechwriting skills; it also resulted in a wholesale transformation in his thinking. As he crisscrossed the continent, reconnecting with the world of average Americans, he became more aware of the frustrations that many were feeling under the burdens of postwar taxes and bureaucracy. Having experienced the intrusions of Washington in the affairs of Hollywood as well as the inefficiency of Army bureaucracy while a stateside officer during the war, Reagan began to shed his liberal faith in government as the primary instrument with which to address social ills. Over time, his GE speeches became less company pep rallies and more his own ruminations on the conservative themes of political and economic freedom.

In 1962, realizing that his political views were no longer compatible with the Democratic Party, Reagan officially became a Republican. On October 27, 1964, before a national audience, he delivered his celebrated address (later called "A Time for Choosing") in support of Barry Goldwater's candidacy. The overwhelming success of this frontal attack on President Johnson's Great Society brought him to the attention of important financial backers and transformed him overnight into a serious contender for the California governorship.

His landslide victory over incumbent Democrat Pat Brown in 1966 was followed by two eventful terms as governor. Balancing the budget, reforming welfare, and quelling campus unrest, as America's most visible conservative politician Reagan slowly built a national political base from which to launch a presidential bid. Although unsuccessful in his attempt to secure the Republican nomination in 1976, he claimed the prize four years later and went on to defeat incumbent President Jimmy Carter in 1980.

In his first inaugural address in 1981, Reagan exhorted his fellow Americans to begin an era of national renewal, to help lift the country out of what many believed to be the worst economic crisis since the Great Depression. Signaling that his administration planned a new direction in foreign policy, he warned potential adversaries that if action were required to preserve its national security, America would act.

Reagan had come to the presidency believing that the United States had lost its sense of mission in world affairs. America, he wrote in his 1990 autobiography, had begun to abdicate its historical role as the spiritual leader of the Free World and its foremost defender of democracy. Reagan's remedy, however, did not consist of a return to the conventional Cold War paradigm. In a bold revision of national policy, he argued that the communist world should not merely be contained: it should be aggressively rolled back.

This new strategy, dubbed the Reagan Doctrine, called for the expansion of aid to the Mujahedin in Afghanistan, the support of anticommunist fighters in Nicaragua, Angola, and Mozambique, and the channeling of funds (via the Catholic Church) to the Solidarity Free Trade Union in Poland. In 1983, in a move that symbolically ended America's post-Vietnam reluctance to engage in military action, he ordered the invasion and overthrow of the Marxist regime on the Caribbean island of Grenada. His unflinching support of America's allies in their struggles against Marxist insurgents was part of a grand strategy to strengthen existing democratic institutions or, in the case of authoritarian regimes, to lay the groundwork for democracy's future emergence.

In order to counter the perceived threat from an adventurous Soviet Union (which in 1983 he famously labeled an "evil empire"), Reagan called for and received significant increases in defense spending. Believing that America's military readiness had languished dangerously in the post-Vietnam era, he asked Congress for a wide variety of new weapons systems, including the MX Peacekeeper missile, the B1-b and Stealth bombers, and more Trident nuclear submarines. In the face of strong overseas opposition, he succeeded in persuading Western European leaders to accept the placement of Pershing II intermediate-range missiles on their soil to counter the threat of the comparable class of Soviet SS-20s. His most controversial proposal, however, was his Strategic Defense Initiative (SDI). Announced in 1983, Reagan calculated that this plan to research and eventually construct an antiballistic missile system would not only transform current strategic thinking—particularly its decades-old reliance on stability through deterrence or Mutual Assured Destruction (MAD)—but would also lure the Soviet Union into arms control negotiations.

Aware that his foreign policy would never succeed if the U.S. economy continued to contract, Reagan's first and, in his opinion, most important presidential initiative was the Economic Recovery Act of 1981. Enacted in the weeks following his own recovery from a would-be assassin's bullet, the bill called for deep tax cuts to be phased in over three years; it was also the centerpiece of a comprehensive economic policy that included a reduction in the growth of public expenditures, the deregulation of industry, and tighter control of the money supply.

During 1981–82, however, the recession worsened, raising speculation that Reagan would not seek a second term. Then, in the final months of 1982, the economy began a dramatic and abrupt turnaround: growth rates spiked, unemployment fell, and inflation, the scourge of the previous ten years, plummeted. Largely on the strength of this recovery, Reagan enjoyed a 1984 landslide reelection victory over Minnesotan Walter Mondale.

In the next four years, the economy continued its impressive upward spiral, growing at a pace few had predicted. Critics, however, would call increasing attention to the large federal deficits, which rose dramatically over the course of the decade. Reagan countered that the deficits resulted from Congress's unwillingness to cut wasteful government spending rather than his costly but much-needed defense build-up and tax cuts. Besides, he argued, continued economic expansion would eventually eliminate deficits.

In 1986, dark clouds gathered when it was revealed that the administration had sold arms to the Iranian government in exchange for the release of Americans being held hostage in Lebanon. The scandal, which became known as the Iran-Contra Affair, further intensified when it was learned that some of the money from the sale had been diverted to the anticommunist fighters (or Contras) in Nicaragua. Although technically no laws were broken in either transaction, several administration officials were indicted by a special prosecutor for withholding information from Congress and obstructing the investigation; some were convicted; all were later pardoned or had their charges dismissed.

One notable accomplishment of Reagan's second term was the Tax Reform Act of 1986. This compromise with congressional Democrats simplified the tax code, substantially reducing the number of tax brackets and lowering the highest personal bracket to 28 percent (from a high of 70 percent in 1981). In foreign affairs, Reagan's hard-won personal bond with the communist reformer Mikhail Gorbachev led to an unprecedented thaw in U.S.-Soviet relations. This new relationship, coupled with Reagan's earlier resolve in the Pershing II deployment and his refusal to give up SDI, resulted in the historic Intermediate-Range Nuclear Forces (INF) Treaty of 1987 and laid the groundwork for the future and more far-reaching Strategic Arms Reduction Talks (START). In 1988, the Soviets withdrew from Afghanistan; in 1989 and 1990, Eastern European communism collapsed.

As the cracks in the communist edifice began to widen, a host of authoritarian regimes, under pressure from the Reagan administration, gave way to democracy. In 1986, the administration was instrumental in convincing Filipino strongman and American ally Ferdinand Marcos to hold free elections and then brokered the transfer of power to the rightful winner Corazon Aquino. Reassured by Reagan's anticommunist policies and energized by popular sentiment, Latin America experienced a democratic resurgence; while in 1981, less than one-third of all Latin countries were democratic, by 1988, over 90 percent had joined the ranks of the democracies. In 1990, Nicaragua held free elections and ousted the Marxist Sandinista regime.

While Reagan was remarkably successful in transforming the debate in America over social policy, he placed perhaps his most lasting domestic conservative stamp on the courts. In addition to his appointment of more than four hundred federal judges, most of whom subscribed to the idea of judicial restraint, he elevated William Rehnquist to Chief Justice of the United States and appointed conservative justice Antonin Scalia, as well as justices Sandra Day O'Connor and Anthony Kennedy. His legacy was further enhanced when in January 1989 his vice president of eight years, George Herbert Walker Bush, was sworn in as forty-first president of the United States.

On November 5, 1994, Reagan announced that he was suffering from Alzheimer's disease and would retire from public life: "When the Lord calls me home," he wrote in a letter addressed to the American people, "I will leave with the greatest love for this country of ours and eternal optimism for its future. I now begin the journey that will lead me into the sunset of my life. I know that for America there will always be a bright dawn ahead." He died at his home in Los Angeles on June 5, 2004.

—MARK C. MOLESKY

Further Reading
Cannon, Lou. *President Reagan: The Role of a Lifetime.* New York: Public Affairs, 2000.
Dallek, Matthew. *The Right Moment: Ronald Reagan's First Victory and the Decisive Turning Point in American Politics.* New York: Free Press, 2000.
Edwards, Lee. *The Essential Ronald Reagan: A Profile in Courage, Justice, and Wisdom.* Lanham, Md.: Rowman & Littlefield, 2004.
Kengor, Paul, and Peter Schweizer, eds. *The Reagan Presidency: Assessing the Man and His Legacy.* Lanham, Md.: Rowman & Littlefield, 2005.
Reagan, Ronald. *Reagan, In His Own Hand.* Edited by Kiron K. Skinner, Annelise Anderson, and Martin Anderson. New York: Free Press, 2001.
———. *Reagan: A Life in Letters.* Edited by Kiron K. Skinner, Annelise Anderson, and Martin Anderson. New York: Free Press, 2003.

See also: anticommunism; Cold War; containment; Heritage Foundation; Meese, Edwin, III; movement conservatism; neoconservatism; New Deal; New Right; Reagan Democrats; Reagan Doctrine; Republican Party; supply-side economics; think tanks, conservative; welfare policy

Reason

A monthly magazine on current affairs published by the Reason Foundation, *Reason* is the largest circulation periodical with a libertarian editorial philosophy. *Reason* focuses primarily on domestic economic, political, social, and cultural issues. Recent areas of emphasis have included environmental policy, drug laws, cyberspace, culture, and biotechnology.

Reason was founded as a mimeographed publication by Boston University journalism student Lanny Friedlander in 1968. The name derived from Ayn Rand's emphasis on reason as "man's only tool of survival." The first typeset and offset-printed issue appeared in 1969, by which point the magazine had several hundred paid subscribers, thanks to classified ads in libertarian newsletters and word of mouth. Near the end of 1970 several of the magazine's contributing editors, led by Robert W. Poole, Jr., Tibor Machan, and Manny Klausner, purchased *Reason* from Friedlander and moved it to Santa Barbara, California, under the auspices of a partnership, Reason Enterprises. Thanks to direct-mail marketing, by the end of 1971 circulation reached several thousand.

The partnership built the circulation to 12,000 by 1978, at which point they decided to create the Reason Foundation as a way of creating a financial base for a full-time staff and significant growth. Under the foundation's auspices, and with Poole as editor and publisher, the magazine began using four-color covers and glossy pages, paying its authors, and conducting larger marketing efforts. It also launched an investigative journalism program, with several stories receiving national newspaper and television coverage, and two of them receiving national journalism awards, the Mencken Award and the John Hancock Award for Excellence. Marty Zupan became editor in 1984, with Poole continuing as publisher. Zupan left in 1989 to become a vice president of the Institute for Humane Studies.

In 1989 associate editor Virginia Postrel was promoted to editor. Circulation then stood at 30,000. During the 1990s Postrel helped to make the magazine more visible, with three *Reason* articles making the finals of the National Magazine Awards. Postrel wrote an influential book, *The Future and Its Enemies* (1998), introducing the terms "dynamism" and "stasis" into political discourse. By the time she stepped down as editor in chief in January 2000, circulation had reached 60,000. Associate editor Nick Gillespie then took over, becoming *Reason*'s fifth editor.

Reason contributors over the years have included Milton Friedman, Thomas Szasz, Edith Efron, James K. Glassman, Peter Huber, Walter Williams, Charles Murray, George Gilder, and Thomas Sowell.

—ROBERT W. POOLE JR.

Further Reading

Poole, Robert W., Jr., and Virginia I. Postrel, eds. *Free Minds and Free Markets: Twenty-Five Years of* Reason. San Francisco: Pacific Research Institute for Public Policy, 1993.

See also: libertarianism; Reason Foundation

Reason Foundation

Founded in 1978 by Robert W. Poole, Jr., Manuel S. Klausner, Tibor R. Machan, and R. Clyde Packer, the Reason Foundation was created to promote privatization, the free market, and the rule of law from a stoutly libertarian perspective. The foundation at first concentrated on the publishing of *Reason* magazine, a periodical that brought the foundation's thoroughgoing libertarian philosophy to bear on current affairs. Soon after its founding, however, the organization's mission grew to include research on topics related to privatization and deregulation.

One of the first research projects the foundation embarked upon was a series of books critiquing the extension of the federal government: *Instead of Regulation* (1982) focused on regulation agencies, *Defending a Free Society* (1984) on foreign policy, and *Unnatural Monopolies* (1985) on the regulation of public-utility companies. In addition to these books, the foundation produced a series of papers proposing ways that such federal programs as the U.S. Postal Service and the Federal Aviation Administration's air traffic control system could be operated as private-sector enterprises.

In 1986, the foundation added its "Economics in Argumentation" program, which teaches high school students how to analyze matters of public policy in light of economic issues. In 1990, it began producing Professor William R. Allen's weekly economic commentary, the *Midnight Economist*. More recently, the Reason Public Policy Institute was officially founded in 1997. Focusing on public policy, members of the RPPI engage in public discussion and present their research to state legislative bodies and congressional committees.

Located in Los Angeles, the Reason Foundation has a staff of twenty-five. Research at the foundation currently focuses primarily on school choice, environmentalism, urban policy, and transportation as these issues relate to privatization.

—Alexandria Chiasson

See also: libertarianism; privatization; Reason

Reconstruction

Interpretations of Reconstruction have changed dramatically. The Dunning School, dominant in the early twentieth century, sympathized with white Southerners and saw Reconstruction as a period of organized looting by "carpetbaggers," "scalawags," and freedmen. The Redeemers, who fought back via electoral efforts and irregular violence, were thus the heroes. After World War II, the "revisionist" or "neo-abolitionist" school reversed these judgments and portrayed Reconstruction as a necessary but tragically postponed social revolution.

The theory on which Abraham Lincoln conducted the war obscured some important questions, and his government had to invent a basis for reincorporating the South. When the hoped-for Southern Unionist masses failed to materialize, Lincoln based new "loyal" state governments on 10 percent of the population. This policy continued under President Andrew Johnson.

Southern civil governments created on the Lincoln-Johnson plan held elections in 1866. On the official theory of the war, they had every right to participate in the Union. The Thirteenth Amendment had settled the matter of slavery; but emancipation had actually increased Southern representation in the House—with blacks now counted as whole persons—and Republicans were appalled to see their old enemies arriving to help govern the Union. Furthermore, planters seemed to be establishing quasi-slavery via Black Codes, with draconian restrictions on labor mobility meant to insure a speedy return to agricultural production. These laws struck Republicans as a deliberate affront.

Thus, outraged Republicans determined to reconstruct the South properly through social revolution imposed by military rule and local collaborators. Whatever it did for former slaves, the program would guarantee permanent Republican ascendancy through control of Southern state governments and congressional seats. Wartime northern Congresses had enacted a program of American mercantilism with high tariffs, business subsidies, and a national banking system, and hardly wished to see these measures tampered with by unrepentant Democrats.

The Radical Republicans' new program pitted Congress against Johnson, a product of the plain folk of Tennessee. Almost unseated through impeachment, Johnson was reduced to utter ineffectiveness. Radicals asserted that the Southern states had committed political suicide by seceding. Under this novel theory, Congress enacted the Reconstruction Act of 1866, cutting the South into five military districts. With most white males disenfranchised and male freedmen voting, new state constitutions would be drawn up, new legislatures would ratify the Fourteenth Amendment, and Congress would "readmit" the delinquents into the Union. These governments rested on a coalition of so-called "carpetbaggers" (northern fortune-seekers and idealists), "scalawags" (white Southern collaborators), and freedmen.

Revisionists downplay Republican corruption and stress the Radicals' egalitarian idealism. There were, however, serious limits to Republicans' social radicalism. On the revisionists' own showing, Republicans mostly succeeded in issuing railroad bonds and selling them to one another. The Fourteenth Amendment made the 1866 Civil Rights Act constitutional, thereby protecting nationally the basic rights of former slaves. The clause allowing Congress to reduce the representation of any state violating the amendment reflects the Republicans' keen interest in controlling Southern elections.

Southern resistance and sabotage stopped Reconstruction short. Where the Dunning School glossed over the methods used, revisionists have denounced them as atrocities. In any case, state by state Redeemers took power from their enemies. Their governments were *cheaper*. Northern politicians weighed their options and, to settle the disputed 1876 presidential election, effectively ended Reconstruction.

The pivotal force in the defeat of Reconstruction was probably the Southern "plain folk": independent, property-owning farmers and herdsmen. These yeomen answered to the broad group of armed property-owners central to republican theory, an ideology the yeomen largely embraced. Southern politicians could not ignore the opinions of this class.

"Class conflict" in the Old South had centered on taxes, property rights, and religious differences. Slave patrols had shifted enforcement costs of slavery onto non-slaveholders. In addition, there were sundry "souths": Tidewater, Piedmont, Mountain, Louisiana, and Texas. Not surprisingly, then, support for the Confederate cause had not been unconditional. Jefferson Davis's strategy required colossal efforts to hold territory and precluded guerrilla warfare. Con-federate leaders apparently feared the loss of control that came with the guerrilla option. But Confederate centralization arguably undercut the cause. Conscription (with class-based exemptions), in-kind taxes, and inflation alienated the Southern people. Confederate strategy squandered not just lives and fortunes, but also morale.

Reconstruction further alienated the plain folk. Along with former planters they resisted the social revolution offered by their conquerors, defeating the Radicals' egalitarian measures. They failed, however, to reverse outsiders' political-economic control.

Taxation and the desire for local self-government were decisive for the yeomen. The Radicals were committed to ambitious projects: public education, "infrastructure," and railroad subsidies. To fund these, they levied general taxes on land, which replaced antebellum taxes on slave property. Hard-pressed farmers found themselves faced with an unprecedented tax burden. Whatever the Redeemers' peculations, Southerners preferred a little *local* rent-seeking to the Radicals' full-fledged national mercantilism.

Thus, Reconstruction was fundamentally a phase in the consolidation of the U.S. continental-imperial state apparatus. The federal government, having saved itself from territorial loss, needed to make its victory permanent. Interest groups, politicians, and bureaucrats attached to the new state governments sought personal profit and perpetual public employment. Northern politicians and businessmen got a consolidated national state and high tariffs and subsidies to industry, generally characterized (oddly) as laissez-faire capitalism. Secretary of State William Seward already foresaw a U.S. commercial world empire as the goal of this neomercantilist political economy.

Reconstruction ushered in a revolution: a revolution in the relation of people, states, and localities to the federal government.

—Joseph R. Stromberg

Further Reading

Dunning, W. A. *Reconstruction, Political and Economic, 1865–1877.* New York: Harper, 1962.

Burgess, John William. *Reconstruction and the Constitution, 1866–1876.* New York: C. Scribner's Sons, 1902.

Woodward, C. Vann. *Reunion and Reaction: The Compromise of 1877 and the End of Reconstruction.* Boston: Little, Brown, 1951.

See also: Civil War; Democratic Party; Southern conservatism

Red Scare

In 1919–20, America experienced its first full-blown "Red Scare," a national hysteria over a supposed communist plot to overthrow the United States government.

The Red Scare's immediate origins can be traced to World War I (1914–18) and the Russian Revolution (1917). During the war, the government of Woodrow Wilson actively promoted a climate of suspicion, fear, and intolerance toward the German "Huns." After the armistice, these attitudes quickly refocused on the new menace of "Reds," foreign and domestic, especially in the wake of the Bolsheviks' triumph and their creation of the USSR.

Four major labor disputes in 1919—a general strike in Seattle, a policemen's strike in Boston, and national walkouts by steel and coal workers—came in rapid succession, fueling widespread apprehension that Marxist-Leninist forces controlled the labor unions. When a number of bomb packages, sent through the mail to prominent business and political leaders, were discovered, national alarm turned to panic. Newspapers, civic and patriotic organizations such as the newly formed American Legion, and countless ordinary citizens demanded that swift countermeasures be taken against impending Soviet-sponsored revolution.

The government responded with a frenzied campaign against this supposed conspiracy. The principal targets included communists, socialists, anarchists, foreign-born radicals, and members of the Industrial Workers of the World. Wilson's attorney general, A. Mitchell Palmer, directed a massive roundup of suspected "revolutionaries," many of them immigrants.

During these "Palmer raids," thousands of people were arrested, roughed up, and held for deportation if they were aliens, usually without evidence of wrongdoing.

In December 1919, 249 foreign-born anarchists, including Emma Goldman, were put aboard an Army transport vessel (dubbed the "Soviet Ark") and deported. In New York, the state legislature refused to seat five Socialists duly elected to the assembly. The Justice Department created an antiradical division headed by a young bureaucrat, J. Edgar Hoover. The government-sponsored activities continued into early 1920; on one January night alone, some 4,000 suspected communists were arrested throughout the nation.

Thereafter, tensions began to ease. A sober look at the cases stemming from the Palmer raids plainly revealed that few of the arrestees had committed crimes. Respected leaders, including conservatives like Charles Evans Hughes, voiced disgust with the government's wholesale violation of civil liberties. Palmer himself inadvertently helped restore calm when he predicted massive communist-inspired violence on May Day 1920. When the day passed without incident, the country realized that the threat of revolution had been greatly exaggerated. By the end of 1920, the Red Scare was over. However, the murder trial of the anarchists Sacco and Vanzetti, arrested in Massachusetts during the Red Scare, stirred up an international controversy that historians continue to debate even today.

—George Sirgiovanni

Further Reading

Murray, Robert K. *Red Scare: A Study in National Hysteria, 1919–1920*. Minneapolis, Minn.: University of Minnesota Press, 1955.

Pfannestiel, Todd J. *Rethinking the Red Scare: The Lusk Committee and New York's Crusade against Radicalism, 1919–1923*. New York: Routledge, 2003.

See also: anticommunism

Reed, Ralph (1961–)

A southern Republican Party powerbroker, Ralph Reed served as executive director of Pat Robertson's Christian Coalition and built that institution into one of the more formidable forces in politics in the early 1990s. Soothing and savvy, Reed is extremely articulate and exudes mainstream sensibilities. These proved to be invaluable characteristics as Reed attempted to bring a constituency viewed with much suspicion into the political mainstream. Today Reed serves as a political consultant and as head of Century Strategies, his public relations, marketing, and political consulting firm. The success Reed has had as a consultant, however, would not have been possible without the success he earned with the Christian Coalition.

After a stint in the early 1980s as executive director of the College Republican National Committee, and following a number of jobs on various campaigns (where he learned the trade under legendary political strategists Carter Wrenn and Tom Ellis in North Carolina), Reed hooked up with Robertson after the 1988 elections. Robertson's failed bid for the Republican presidential nomination yielded a substantial mailing list, which he turned over to Reed to use to build an organization. And build an organization he did. Reed's first annual budget was $200,000; by 1997, when he left the Christian Coalition, it was $27 million.

Much of Reed's success with the Christian Coalition was owing to his ability to galvanize voters—particularly southern evangelicals and fundamentalists—around a core of pro-family issues. Under Reed, this range of issues was expanded from traditional areas of concern to Christian conservatives to include such areas as taxes, deregulation, and welfare reform. The Christian Coalition met with so much success in this regard that by the 1996 presidential election cycle, Reed was considered a conservative kingmaker. That assessment wasn't entirely off the mark. As *Time* magazine wrote in 1995, the Christian Coalition held "a virtual veto on the Republican nominee for president, and will exert an extraordinary influence over who will occupy the Oval Office beginning in 1997." The organization's aid helped Bob Dole—its all-but-announced favorite—secure the nomination but could not save Dole from being soundly defeated by Bill Clinton in the general election. Both Robertson and Reed stepped down from the helm of the Christian Coalition in 1997—Robertson to retire and Reed to explore new opportunities. A measure of how well Reed ran the organization is that in his absence the Christian Coalition has foundered badly.

Reed set up his consulting and public relations firm Century Strategies in Atlanta. His candidates had middling success in the 1998 and 2000 elections. Reed also took on a number of high-profile corporate clients, including Microsoft and Enron. Enron paid him $10,000 per month for four years until its bankruptcy. In addition, he served as a senior adviser to George W. Bush's 2000 campaign and as chairman of Bush's campaign in the southeast region in 2004.

—Max Schulz

Further Reading

Reed, Ralph. *Active Faith: How Christians Are Changing the Soul of American Politics*. New York: Free Press, 1996.

Watson, Justin. *The Christian Coalition: Dreams of Restoration, Demands for Recognition*. New York: St. Martin's, 1997.

See also: *Protestantism, evangelical; Robertson, Marion Gordon "Pat"*

Regnery, Henry (1912–96)

Publisher, conservative, musician and music patron, author and civic leader, Henry Regnery was born in Hinsdale, Illinois, a Chicago suburb, in 1912. His father, William H. Regnery, was a successful businessman and manufacturer, a second-generation American descended from German Catholic ancestors. His mother, Francis Susan Thrasher, of older Pennsylvania and Maryland stock, married William H. Regnery in Kansas City on June 30, 1903.

After being educated in the public schools of Hinsdale, in the fall of 1929 Regnery entered Armour Institute of Technology, now the Illinois Institute of Technology, to study mechanical engineering. Increasingly uncomfortable with the implications of technology, he transferred to MIT where he majored in mathematics. In 1934, influenced by a friend, he went to Germany and studied for two years at the University of Bonn. In the fall of 1936 he entered the graduate school at Harvard in economics. In 1937 he completed the requirements for and was granted an M.A. Shortly thereafter he met Eleanor Scattergood, a descendant of T. P. Cope and the daughter of Alfred G. Scattergood, who had supervised the child-feeding program in Germany after World War I for the American Friends Service Committee. Her character and judgment were the most important influence in the life of Henry Regnery.

The Regnery family was not always politically conservative. Henry's father had, as a young man, been influenced by the reform movements of his day, particularly the ideas of Henry George. He had supported Franklin Roosevelt in the elections of 1932 and 1936. Young Henry had worked for the New Deal Resettlement Administration and later the American Friends Service Committee in community development. Both Henry and his father, however, were increasingly alienated by the intrusiveness and authoritarianism of New Deal domestic policies and Franklin Roosevelt's drive to involve the United States in World War II. The elder Regnery was one of the founders and a financial supporter of the America First Committee.

Henry Regnery

Conservatism slowly began defining itself as a consequence of the political, cultural, and economic wreckage that followed in the wake of World War II. In 1945 Henry Regnery became one of the partners in the publication of *Human Events* among the paper's first pamphlets were those authored by Robert M. Hutchins. On September 9, 1947, the Henry Regnery Company (later Regnery Gateway) was created, becoming overnight the most influential small publishing company in the United States. Regnery not only published the Great Books for the University of Chicago program but also translations of German texts of enduring cultural value. Regnery's press became the organ of World War II historical revisionism and published book after book calling attention to the postwar communist threat. With Regnery's publication in 1951 of William F. Buckley's *God and Man at Yale* and Russell Kirk's *The Conservative Mind* in 1953, American conservatism took on an identity and became a movement.

Not only did his Regnery Gateway publishing house provide the decisive impetus in the formation of twentieth-century conservatism, but Henry Regnery, energetic and self-effacing, spent his time and money identifying talent, serving on committees and boards of trustees, and looking for opportunities to create community and stimulate ideas even after his retirement. This quiet service, often not in a political cause, is best exemplified in his generous trusteeship at the Chicago Conservatory of Music and his membership in the Cliff Dwellers, a Chicago club devoted to the arts. His sustained interest in literature, history, and culture often expressed itself in hospitality, turning his home into a conservative salon frequented by the likes of Buckley and Kirk. After a life spent in service to the "great and noble tradition" of Western culture, Regnery died at the age of 84 in 1996.

—Stephen J. Tonsor

Further Reading

Regnery, Henry. *The Cliff Dwellers: The History of a Chicago Cultural Institution.* Chicago: Chicago Historical Bookworks, 1990.

———. *A Few Reasonable Words: Selected Writings.* Edited by George A. Panichas. Wilmington, Del.: Intercollegiate Studies Institute. 1996.

———. *Perfect Sowing: Reflections of a Bookman.* Edited by Jeffrey O. Nelson. Wilmington, Del.: ISI Books, 1999.

See also: Collier, David S.; God and Man at Yale; *media, conservative; Regnery Publishing*

Regnery Publishing

Perhaps the best-known conservative publishing house, Regnery Publishing embarked on its second half century aiming to be a considerably different kind of company from what it was in its first fifty years.

Henry Regnery founded the company in 1947 with the idea of publishing books countervailing the dominant notions of the day. Regnery was bent on publishing thoughtful and substantial works on politics, philosophy, religion, and culture that challenged conventional wisdom while examining the underpinnings of Western-style liberal democracy. In the process, this publishing company helped give voice and shape to the conservative political movement borne of the United States' Cold War struggle and culminating in the Reagan Revolution and the fall of Soviet communism.

To this day, few American publishing houses are so identified with a series of important and influential titles as is Regnery. The mention of Regnery elicits thoughts of seminal conservative books such as Russell Kirk's *The Conservative Mind* (1953) and William F. Buckley's *God and Man at Yale* (1951); the first English translations of significant works of Continental philosophy, such as Gabriel Marcel's *Man against Mass Society* (1962) and Max Picard's *The World of Silence* (1952); and even masterworks of theology, like Romano Guardini's *The Lord* (1954).

In short, Regnery Publishing provided intellectual ammunition for a rising generation of broadly conservative scholars and writers. And it gave articulation and legitimacy to anticommunism at a time when few Americans (and few leaders in government) appreciated that the epic battle between freedom and communism would ultimately define the twentieth century. In doing so, Regnery, along with *Human Events* and Buckley's *National Review*, would provide a home for serious conservative reflection and analysis.

The eponymous Henry Regnery Company was located in Chicago and held close ties to the University of Chicago until the controversial debut of *God and Man at Yale*. In 1951, the publishing house changed its name to Regnery Gateway and continued to operate out of Chicago until the 1980s, at which point Henry's son Alfred took the helm of the company and moved it to Washington, D.C.

In the early 1990s Regnery Gateway was on the verge of collapse. Henry Regnery famously said that turning a profit would be a sure sign they were doing something wrong. Whether or not he was actually serious, the company foundered for decades. And while Regnery continued to churn out thoughtful and often important books—its impressive stable of authors ranged from Burke to Kirk—the company's adherence to its intellectual mission was financially debilitating.

Newsletter magnate and self-styled conservative activist Tom Phillips stepped into the breech. He bought the company and then bundled it with the Conservative Book Club and the similarly rescued *Human Events* to create Eagle Publishing in 1993. While nominally pledging to continue the company's mission of publishing important books, the new-era Regnery smartly cast off its founder's notorious disdain for profits. Indeed, Regnery went in quite the opposite direction, discarding many of its traditional titles while swinging for the fences with bestsellers.

The strategy has worked, but at a cost. Recent years have seen the company shed its old reputation for a new one—as a publisher of right-wing polemics bent on bruising Left-liberal icons. The Phillips-era Regnery scored its first blockbuster with the 1996 publication of *Unlimited Access*, by retired FBI Agent Gary Aldrich. This first-hand account of shady goings-on in the Clinton White House by an agent who had been detailed there scandalized Washington and surprised the nation by topping the *New York Times* bestseller list. But *Unlimited Access*'s prurient eye for pornographic details and its numer-

ous unsubstantiated claims made it an easy target to discredit. A firestorm of controversy and calumny rained down on the company.

Undeterred by heavy criticism, the company pressed forward with a series of anti-Clinton books. Almost all met commercial success from an audience thirsting for dirt on the corrupt president and his administration. A handful were worthwhile and substantial books (such as *Betrayal* [1999] by Bill Gertz, *Year of the Rat* [1998] by Ed Timperlake and Bill Triplett, and *Sellout* [2000] by David Schippers). Others were not. Post-Clinton targets have included Jesse Jackson (*Shakedown* [2002], by Kenneth Timmerman) and the liberal news media (Bernard Goldberg's *Bias* [2001]).

Owing much of its new success to editorial director Harry Crocker and publisher Margi Ross, Regnery does continue to publish quality titles, such as Michael Barone's *The New Americans* (2001), a well received biography of Allen Dulles, and the autobiography of opera soprano Dame Joan Sutherland. But, in more ways than one, it is no longer the press founded and built by Henry Regnery.

—Max Schulz

Further Reading

Regnery, Henry. *Memoirs of a Dissident Publisher.* New York: Harcourt, Brace, Jovanovich, 1979.

See also: Conservative Book Club; Conservative Mind, The; God and Man at Yale; *media, conservative; Regnery, Henry*

regulation

All economic activity is regulated. There is no such thing as an unregulated economy. There are, however, different methods of regulation. When people speak of economic regulation, they usually mean regulation by government. This is regulation accomplished through public ordering. Regulation also occurs through private ordering. Much of economics since Adam Smith's *Wealth of Nations* (1776) has been concerned with the discovery of how private ordering operates successfully to regulate economic activity. With private ordering, there is no center of regulatory authority. That authority is dispersed throughout society. Private ordering is achieved through competition within a legal framework provided by the principles of private property and freedom of contract. Through private ordering, the number of new products that software developers create in a year is regulated by such things as the creativity of those developers and the willingness of consumers to buy their products. It is also regulated by the ability of computer manufacturers to develop new hardware and to control costs, as well as by the attractiveness to consumers of other offerings generated elsewhere throughout the economy. Private ordering through free and open competition generates a dense network of cooperative relationships throughout society. This method of economic regulation leads producers to produce what consumers want, and to do so efficiently.

The same cannot always be said of government regulation through public ordering. With respect to the software illustration, it would be as though new software had to be approved by a government agency, much as new pharmaceuticals must be approved by the Food and Drug Administration. Proponents of government regulation claim that it improves upon the self-regulation that market competition generates. It is easy enough to advance this claim. It is not so easy actually to demonstrate its truth.

There are three principal lines of argument for why government regulation might improve upon market regulation. These arguments claim that a market economy may be plagued by monopoly, ignorance, and external costs. For each of these three plagues, government regulation is advanced as an

antidote. A careful examination of these claims shows generally not only that they are false, but also that regulation is a source of trouble for consumers and not a solution.

The claim that market processes often lead to monopolistic outcomes seems to be an inherited part of American folklore. While instances of monopoly have been found, most of them have been short lived. Longevity seems to require government regulation. Indeed, a rich variety of empirical studies have shown that regulation is more often a source of monopoly than an antidote. For instance, from the time it was created in 1938 until its demise in 1979, the Civil Aeronautics Board never licensed a single new domestic trunk airline, despite the phenomenal growth in passenger air travel that took place over that period. It is doubtful that even the fiercest of private cartels could have prevented entry into the passenger airline business under the conditions of massive growth that prevailed during 1938–79.

The claim that consumers often lack expert-level knowledge is often true but also generally irrelevant. If consumers do not know how to test their eyes and to make glasses, not to mention their inability to diagnose their intestinal pains or episodes of dizziness, it might seem as though they do not possess the basis of expertise on which to choose among suppliers. Government regulation might be promoted as enabling a regulatory agency to act as a wiser agent on behalf of consumers.

There are two problems with this claim in support of government regulation. One is that regulators may lack the interest or ability to promote consumer well-being. The other is that private ordering is a robust generator of consumer protection. The economic regulation that emerges through open competition and private ordering takes many forms. Customers, both satisfied and dissatisfied, tell their friends and neighbors of their experiences. Moreover, a person need not know how a car works to know that his car does not work well. Advertising might convince someone to try a particular product, but it will not induce many repeat purchases if the product performs poorly. Products generally work as they are portrayed simply because this is the best road to commercial success in a market economy.

Market competition regulates the harm that misinformation might otherwise create. Still, it might be thought that government regulation could improve matters still further. For instance, it might seem reasonable to claim that government regulation of electricians would ensure better and safer service. Incompetent electrical work can prove dangerous, and government licensing might keep incompetent electricians from doing damage. There are two problems with this claim. One is that licensing might not operate to remove incompetent practitioners. After all, teachers are licensed by government, and yet one continually encounters incompetent teachers. Furthermore, government regulation typically makes the regulated products or services more expensive. People will respond to these higher prices by seeking less costly options. Among other things, people will do more of their own electrical work to economize on the high price of professional electricians. One study found that the licensing of electricians led to an increase in electrocutions, because a greater volume of electrical work was done by amateurs. Similarly, the regulatory imposition of safety caps on medications did not reduce the volume of accidental poisonings, and may actually have increased it. By making the removal of caps more difficult, the regulation also induced people to fail to replace the caps they had removed, leading to an increase in the volume of uncapped medication.

Government regulation is also justified on the ground that it is necessary to prevent the social costs that accompany economic activities pursued through market processes. Many of these are environmental in nature. For instance, groundwater pollution can occur many miles from the polluting source. Regulation of effluent discharges is often cited as a necessary means of curbing those costs that would otherwise run rampant throughout a market economy. Yet much water pollution results because water is treated as a common property resource that no one owns. While regulation may improve upon the common property situation, it is often feasible to allow private property rights to operate. The replacement of government regulation with self-regulation through market processes is often feasible, and would often be superior in containing social costs.

Numerous studies of the actual consequences of governmental regulation have provided massive evidence against the common claims in support of regulation. But they have not established, nor could they possibly establish, the contrary claim that government regulation can never improve upon the self-regulating forces of a market economy. Still, it should not be forgotten that the option is never government regulation or no regulation, for self-regulation through private ordering is always an option, and an exceedingly effective form of regulation at that.

It is often different with government regulation. The politics of government regulation often generate outcomes that vary systematically from the claims advanced in support of such regulation. To a large extent, this is because political processes tend to reward well-organized interest groups, regardless of how strongly that reward diverges from the arguments advanced in support of regulation. Much government regulation protects inferior competitors by penalizing superior competitors. Consumers thus pay higher prices and receive inferior products. A good deal of regulation protects established competitors from new sources of competition. There is also much regulation that prevents privately organized businesses from entering into competition with publicly favored enterprises, regardless of whether those enterprises are privately or publicly operated.

From these examples follows a generalization that has support from a wide variety of empirical studies: regulation benefits the politically well organized at the expense of the politically poorly organized. In many cases this translates into a statement that regulation benefits producers at the expense of consumers. But sometimes matters are more complex, as when it benefits large producers and consumers at the expense of small. But in any case the politics of regulation is far different than the common justifications would suggest, and a consideration of that politics surely increases one's confidence in the self-regulation that occurs through market processes.

—RICHARD E. WAGNER

Further Reading

Hill, Peter J. and Roger E. Meiners, eds. *Who Owns the Environment?* Lanham, Md.: Rowman & Littlefield, 1998.

Lee, Dwight R., and Richard B. McKenzie. *Regulating Government*. Lexington, Mass.: D. C. Heath, 1987.

McChesney, Fred S. *Money for Nothing: Politicians, Rent Extraction, and Political Extortion*. Cambridge, Mass.: Harvard University Press, 1997.

Meiners, Roger E., and Bruce Yandle, eds. *Regulation and the Reagan Era: Politics, Bureaucracy, and the Public Interest*. New York: Holmes & Meier, 1989.

Stigler, George J. *The Citizen and the State: Essays on Regulation*. Chicago: University of Chicago Press, 1975.

See also: enterprise zones; free trade; law and economics; New Deal; protectionism

Rehnquist, William H. (1924–2005)

Associate justice of the United States Supreme Court from 1972 to 1986, and chief justice from 1986 until his death in 2005, William Rehnquist graduated first in his class from Stanford Law School in 1951, after having earned master's degrees in political science from Stanford (1949) and Harvard (1950). He clerked for Supreme Court Justice Robert H. Jackson, practiced law in Phoenix for sixteen years, then served as Richard Nixon's assistant attorney general for the Office of Legal Counsel. When he was first nominated as an associate justice, Rehnquist won confirmation by a vote of 68 to 26, but when Chief Justice Warren Burger retired, and President Reagan sought to promote Rehnquist to chief justice, there was a somewhat more vigorous confirmation battle, finally won by a vote of 65 to 33.

Those who sought to prevent his becoming chief justice—and possibly leading the Court in a more conservative direction—pulled no punches, even seeking, as they did in 1972, to question the nominee on a memorandum he had written for Justice Jackson, before the landmark case of *Brown* v. *Board of Education* (1954). In that memo, Rehnquist had allegedly argued in favor of upholding the "separate but equal" doctrine of *Plessy* v. *Ferguson* (1896). Justice Jackson eventually participated in the unanimous decision in *Brown* to overrule *Plessy* and to hold that "separate" was "unequal" in the field of public education. Still, Rehnquist's critics repeatedly tried to paint him as unalterably opposed to civil rights. Opposition to Rehnquist's nomination as the sixteenth chief justice seems also to have sprung from his reputation on the bench as one of the more conservative members of the Court, from the fact that he had written fifty-four lone dissents as an associate justice—he presented a dissenting opinion in the *Roe* v.

Wade abortion-rights case of 1973—and because he was the Court's most consistent advocate of "federalism," or of restricting the federal government to a secondary role in American policymaking, as Rehnquist and other conservatives believe the framers intended.

What might be described as Rehnquist's sympathy for "states' rights," as critics of federalism often label the doctrine, led one scholar, H. Jefferson Powell, to label Rehnquist the "Compleat Jeffersonian," an appellation that probably did not much disturb the chief justice. Rehnquist's conservatism was also evident in his hostility to the notion of a "living Constitution," the doctrine employed by many members of the Warren and Burger courts to refashion the meaning of constitutional provisions in line with their particular policy preferences. Rehnquist occasionally conceded that there was an inevitable lawmaking role for the Supreme Court, but, in the main, he remained faithful to a conservative jurisprudence grounded not in a "living Constitution" but rather in the original intention of the Constitution's framers. Another characteristic of his jurisprudence that might be thought to be "conservative" was his concern for the preservation of order in society, which generally led him to support law enforcement officials when challenged by expansive advocates of the rights of individual criminal defendants. Rehnquist's belief in the deterrent effects of criminal law was also manifested in his participation in opinions rejecting claims that the death penalty violates the Eighth Amendment's proscription against "cruel and unusual punishment."

The Rehnquist Court will probably be remembered as the most important Court since the New Deal in the area of federal-state relations. The expansive interpretation of the Constitution, ongoing for more than six decades to permit an increased role for federal regulation, was reversed during

chief justice Rehnquist's tenure. Most important in that regard was probably the decision in *United States* v. *Lopez* (1995), for which the chief justice wrote the majority opinion that found unconstitutional the Clinton administra-tion's Federal Gun-Free School Zones Act. Also significant was Rehnquist's majority opinion in *United States v. Morrison* (2000), which found parts of another Clinton-era measure, the federal Violence Against Women Act, to exceed federal authority. Other important Rehnquist Court decisions, but from which the Chief Justice dissented, include the Court's upholding of constitutional protection for abortion, in *Planned Parenthood* v. *Casey*, in 1992, and the barring of prayers at public school graduation ceremonies and football games, in *Lee v. Weisman* (1992) and *Santa Fe Independent School District v. Doe* (2000). The Rehnquist Court will likely also be known for overturning racial preferences in cases involving voting rights, employment, and government contracting. The trend of the Court, it might be said, was toward implementing a "color-blind Constitution," in which local, state, and federal governments were forbidden from making any distinctions based on race. This, the chief justice believed, was the intention of the Fourteenth Amendment's framers.

Rehnquist himself was a somewhat playful jurist and surprised Court-watchers when, on his own, he festooned his chief justice's robe with a distinctive set of gold sleeve-stripes. Reports indicated that this was an idea Rehnquist got from a costume he saw in a Gilbert and Sullivan operetta. He is the Court's most literary chief justice since John Marshall and has written several well-received books on American politics and law. He was the first sitting justice on the Court ever to publish a book about the manner in which the Court works.

As Chief Justice, Rehnquist was the administrative head of all the federal courts, and was a forceful advocate before Congress and other audiences for the procurement of needed financial resources for the judiciary in light of the dramatic increase in federal court cases brought during the waning decades of the twentieth century and the beginning of the twenty-first. He is one of only two chief justices of the United States to preside over the Senate impeachment trial of a sitting president. During his two sets of confirmation hearings, senators were harsh in their objections to his jurisprudential views, but his even-handed and occasionally witty conduct of the Clinton impeachment proceedings won him favorable reviews from both sides of the Senate aisle.

—STEPHEN B. PRESSER

Further Reading

Friedelbaum, Stanley H. *The Rehnquist Court: In Pursuit of Judicial Conservatism.* Westport, Conn.: Greenwood Press, 1996.

Rehnquist, William H. *Grand Inquests: The Historic Impeachment of Justice Samuel Chase and President Andrew Johnson.* New York: Morrow, 1992.

———. *The Supreme Court.* Revised ed. New York: Knopf, 2001.

Yarbrough, Tinsley E. *The Rehnquist Court and the Constitution.* Oxford: Oxford University Press, 2000.

See also: church and state; equal protection; federalism; speech, freedom of; separation of powers; Supreme Court

relativism

Relativism is the "absolute" denial that permanent things, either of reality or of the mind, exist. Relativism posits that anything will look differently from different points of view in space, time, or position. There can be no knowledge of what something really is that does not appear otherwise from another viewpoint. Each position is decided by its place within the system. All systems are independent of and irreducible to each other.

"There is one thing a professor can be absolutely certain of: almost every student entering the university believes, or says he believes, that truth is relative," observed Allan Bloom. Even if this "belief" in relativism is incoherent in itself, it still will have moral, political, and intellectual consequences that need to be reckoned with. Certainly, relativism is a common popular opinion in need of examination. Many people live by its presumed validity.

Relativism is of importance to conservatism in part because Edmund Burke is sometimes considered to be, in effect, a "cultural relativist." That is, Burke's view that bad or immoral customs or practices could gradually grow milder or become so attenuated that they no longer bore the heinous connotation originally associated with the custom or practice might be seen as a form of relativism. Burke is thus said to presuppose the same lack of a solid basis on which liberalism is founded, except that Burke achieves the same relativist results more slowly.

But Burke was in fact a natural law thinker, not a relativist. His emphasis on gradual change or adaptation veered away from the relativism toward a belief in certain timeless and universal truths. He merely maintained that slow or gradual change from an invalid to a valid position was often to be preferred, and would often be more successful, than that which was violent or rapid. Burke's was a principle of prudence, a strategy of how better to work toward a valid practical principle when starting from something culturally disordered, as defined by the canons of natural right or natural law.

Relativism has roots in the classical world. Herodotus noted in his travels that marital and burial rites varied widely from place to place, as did money, language, and dress. The Egyptians and the Greeks did not do things in the same way. The more one knew of the varying ways that people lived their lives, the more chaotic and unruly they seemed to be. If each culture, city, or nation had its own "ways," with no common standard of judgment about their validity, then all ways appeared to be equally good or equally bad.

The Sophists, moreover, claimed to be able to teach anything to anyone. They could teach whatever the student would pay for. They were skilled in teaching differing doctrines, even in teaching what was wrong, if indeed anything was wrong. They seemed to lack any principle that would distinguish the false and the true. Because of the variation in things, there was no essential difference between what was said to be wrong and what was said to be right.

Aristotle mentioned this same problem in the case of justice. In Book 5 of his *Ethics*, he described both natural justice and conventional justice. He even noticed that natural justice seemed to be somewhat changeable. It was, he thought, easy to see why many people would think that all things were conventional, that nothing seemed to be "natural." For, after all, the same thing was said to be right in Gaul and wrong in Germany. Likewise, Tacitus noticed that the ancient Germans evidently thought that thievery was not wrong, just as the pirates, whom Alexander the Great chased off the Mediterranean, thought that all was rightly theirs on the high seas if they could take it. These famous examples implied that attitudes towards the justice of theft or robbery were merely cultural or customary.

Aquinas, however, agreeing with Aristotle, argued that the relative and the permanent were not necessarily opposed. Thus, although burial rites might not be the same in Egypt, Greece, Rome, or Germany, it was universally true that all peoples took special care with their dead. When suffi-ciently analyzed, the manifest and indeed praiseworthy variety in human things does not necessarily mean that all is relative. If there are a hundred different ways to do the same thing, this is not "relativism," the view that there is no "same thing" to be doing. The permanent is rather embodied within the contingent and temporal.

When Machiavelli sought to refute Plato's "best city in speech," he insisted on looking at what men, especially politicians, really did. Under this principle, men suddenly become "free" to use the methods of the lion and the fox, the beast and the man, the law and arms, whatever was "successful." They proceeded to do some pretty terrible things. But nothing that they "did" would have surprised Plato or Aristotle, who had already described these same things. The "freedom" to do these dire things did not confirm the relativist position that whatever one did was right because it was successfully done. It only proved that princes did different things in Egypt, Athens, and Florence, but in a standard pattern already described by the philosophers. Plato had already described "the Prince" about as well as Machiavelli described him. What was wrong in Athens was wrong in Florence, even if successfully done in either city. Place and time did not change the quality of what was done in any place or time.

In fact, modern relativism has its origins less in moral reflection than in epistemology or science. For example, the theory of "relativity" as an explanation of aspects of cosmic reality is sometimes seen as a universal principle valid in all fields. But the "theory" of relativity is not itself "relative." Scientific theories useful or valid for one sort of object need not work equally well for other sorts of objects under investigation. The theory of relativity is not intended to deny that there is an order in the universe. It is rather a part of a search for what this order is.

More fundamentally, contemporary

doubts about the possibility of universal truth have their roots in early-modern doubts about our knowing capacities. Beginning with Descartes' methodological doubt, the focus of intellectual attention shifted from the order of cosmic and human things to the question of whether we could know anything about external reality at all. Modern thought is rooted in doubt about whether our senses are connected to our minds in such a way that what we encounter in our mind corresponds with what exists in reality. Clearly, if we cannot trust the testimony of our senses, then we are free of external reality and can proceed to create our own world. Once we have created our own version of what the world "ought" to be, we can "project" it outward onto a world empty of natural principles. This is basically the project of modern philosophy.

Conservatism can be confused with relativism if there is no provision within conservatism for transcendent philosophical principles, or for realism. What ought to be "conserved" is always what is valid and justified, not merely what is practiced. Yet, there is a presumption of right order in things that have long been practiced together, and also a presumption that there is danger in adopting new practices that create a break with the past. In one sense, relativism can lead to stagnation as a justification of the status quo. It can also undermine any system as well as legitimize any alternative. A conservative philosophy is not relativist but rather aware of the difference between legitimately variable conventions and the unchanging truths of nature, including human nature.

—James V. Schall, S.J.

Further Reading

Kirk, Robert. *Relativism and Reality: A Contemporary Introduction*. New York: Routledge, 1999.

Krausz, Michael, ed. *Relativism: Interpretation and Conflict*. Notre Dame, Ind.: University of Notre Dame Press, 1989.

Krausz, Michael and Jack Meiland, eds. *Relativism: Cognitive and Moral*. Notre Dame, Ind.: University of Notre Dame Press, 1982.

La Follette, Hugh. "Truth in Ethical Relativism," *Journal of Social Philosophy* 30 (1999): 146-54.

Stewart, Robert, and Lynn Thomas. "Recent Work in Ethical Relativism." *American Philosophical Quarterly* 28 (April 1991): 85-100.

See also: historic preservation; historicism; natural law; Natural Right and History; nihilism; science and scientism

Repplier, Agnes (1855–1950)

The lone woman to have contributed significantly to Philadelphia's late-nineteenth-century literary flowering, the extraordinarily well-read, chain-smoking, and temperamentally conservative Agnes Repplier published more than twenty-five immensely popular biographies, histories, and collections of literary and social criticism between 1880 and 1940.

Agnes Repplier

At sixteen, Repplier began to make the first of her lifelong financial contributions to her family by writing essays for Philadelphia newspapers and *Catholic World* magazine. Later, Repplier was often asked to explain the Roman Catholic Church's viewpoint on contemporary issues. Beginning in 1886, when one of her essays appeared in *Atlantic Monthly*, readers of literary journals regularly enjoyed Repplier's witty and elegant essays on topics ranging from tea to social ills.

The author offered her readers keen observations on human nature, about which she was highly skeptical. In her essay "Are Americans a Timid People?" Repplier criticized the American fear of offending through frank speech, arguing that the country had become "too democratic for liberty." The author had little patience for reformers, believing their solutions to be simplistic and sentimental. In "Women Enthroned," Repplier argued that women were capable of voting, yet she abhorred the zealotry of feminism. With the outbreak of World War I, the well-traveled Repplier advocated American intervention by coauthoring *Germany and Democracy* (1914) and writing several essays included in *Counter-Currents* (1916).

Repplier was one of the first women offered membership in the National Institute of Arts and Letters and was awarded honorary doctoral degrees from Yale, Princeton, and other universities. A popular lecturer for many decades, Repplier wrote for publication until she was eighty-five years old.

—ANNE KRULIKOWSKI

Further Reading

Lukacs, John. *Philadelphia: Patricians and Philistines, 1900–1950.* New York: Farrar, Straus, Giroux, 1980.

Repplier, Agnes. *American and Others.* New York: Houghton Mifflin, 1912.

———. *In Our Convent Days.* New York: Houghton Mifflin, 1905.

Stokes, G. S. *Agnes Repplier: Lady of Letters.* Philadelphia: University of Pennsylvania Press, 1949.

Walker, Nancy and Zita Dresner. *Redressing the Imbalance: American Women's Literary Humor from Colonial Times to the 1980s.* Jackson, Miss.: University of Mississippi Press, 1988.

Republican Party

Today the Republican Party is the conservative party in the United States. But in 1854, the party was founded as the more progressive alternative to the Democratic party and its support of the nation's slaveholding interests. The passage of the Kansas-Nebraska Acts ushered in the momentous era in American politics culminating in the Civil War. The acts allowed the expansion of slavery into the territories north of the southern border of Missouri, effectively overturning the Missouri Compromise. In opposition to the acts, the Republican Party was formed by remnants of the Whig Party and disaffected Democrats. The Republicans opposed slavery in the territories and disdained the institution generally.

With the election of Abraham Lincoln to the presidency in 1860, the Republicans assumed majority party status. This election (along with the periodic disenfranchisement of Southerners and other consequences of the Civil War) established the Republicans as the dominant party in the United States for most of the next seventy years, the most successful period in the party's history. It asserted its strength at the height of this period when in 1896 William McKinley appealed to the conservative elements of the electorate in opposition to the populist agenda of William Jennings Bryan.

By the early 1900s there arose in the nation a push for economic, social, and political reform in opposition to the concentration of business interests. The Republicans vied with the Democrats for leadership in this new Progressive movement. This phase of the party's history is exemplified best by the presidency of Theodore Roosevelt, who from 1901 to 1909 embarked on what was then considered an ambitious program of trust regulation and labor reform.

Only after World War I and the presidency of Woodrow Wilson did the Republican Party really become identified with political conservatism. This was seen in the "Return to Normalcy" presidential campaign of Warren G. Harding in 1920. This appeal to traditional politics and noninvolvement in foreign affairs continued with Presidents Calvin Coolidge and Herbert Hoover.

The Great Depression, which began during Hoover's tenure in office, marked the beginning of the Democratic Party's ascendancy. The Democrats, under the New Deal banner of Franklin Roosevelt, won a decisive victory over Hoover and the Republicans in 1932. In 1936, Roosevelt and the Democrats consolidated their victory with one of the greatest landslide presidential wins in history. This election seemed to establish the legitimacy of both centralized government administration in the United States and the belief that government in general has the obligation to secure the economic welfare of every American.

Though he offered much reform as well, Hoover had appealed to what he called the "rugged individualism" of the American people to combat the Depression's hardships. In doing this, Hoover put forth principled opposition to further increases in central government administration of the economy and society as the party's most basic tenet. Thus did the Republicans become the opponents of centralized government, a position similar to that once held by the Democratic Party in its support of "states' rights." Indeed, the "New Federalisms" of Presidents Richard Nixon and Ronald Reagan in later years attempted to shift many government programs back to the states, with the belief that when government intervention is economically necessary, that intervention ought to take place at the state level.

However, the Democratic Party could still lay claim to the allegiance of American conservatives as late as the 1960s, when many southern senators and congressmen opposed civil rights legislation initiated by their more liberal colleagues. But with passage of the 1964 Civil Rights Act under the leadership of Democratic president Lyndon Johnson, the Republicans emerged as the party clearly associated with conservatism. Indeed, it is only since the 1960s that the Republican Party has become the obvious home for the American Right in partisan politics. At the time of Johnson's push for civil rights reform, the Republicans put forth their first avowed conservative candidate for president: Senator Barry Goldwater of Arizona. Although he was soundly defeated by Johnson in the 1964 election, Goldwater's campaign energized the Right.

In addition, Goldwater demonstrated the effectiveness of a conservative appeal to Southerners with his relatively strong showing in the former states of the old confederacy. This strategy of gaining conservative southern votes in presidential elections was used by Richard Nixon in 1968. Nixon claimed to represent a "silent majority" of Americans who had become disenchanted with the problems of Vietnam, race relations, and drug use. The riots in Chicago outside the Democratic National Convention that year exemplified the social and political chaos against which Nixon battled.

Yet Nixon did not represent a continuation of the conservative movement in Republican politics begun by Goldwater. This task was taken up by Ronald Reagan. Reagan's famous televised endorsement of Goldwater during the 1964 Republican National Convention is often thought of as a prologue to his later use of the party as an instrument of the American Right. His conservative challenge to President Gerald Ford for the presidential nomination in 1976 marked the beginning of this attempt at the national level.

Prior to Reagan's emergence as leader of the party, many elements within American conservatism (such as the "New Right" and fundamentalist and evangelical religious groups) did not view the Republican Party as a useful vehicle for political change. Yet these groups began a general shift toward conservatism and the Republican Party when it became apparent that the Democrats had moved much further to the left since the mid-1960s. With Reagan's embrace of conservative religious groups like Jerry Falwell's "Moral Majority," such organizations acquired significant influence within the Republican party. Indeed, with the help of his extensive church-based organization, evangelist Pat Robertson made a significant run for the Republican presidential nomination in 1988. By the end of the 1980s, the Religious Right had used its organizational strength to become a major player in the party, particularly at the state and local levels.

The Reagan years represented the apex of conservatives' influence in the Republican Party. Perhaps not coincidentally, the party did very well electorally at all levels of government during these years, even managing to capture the U.S. Senate for the first time in more than twenty-five years. Many observers thought that the 1980 election was a prelude to a complete party realignment in 1984, akin to the Democrats' confirmation election in 1936. The right wing of the Republican Party had virtually replaced the old "Rockefeller Republicans" (named for moderate New York governor Nelson Rockefeller) as the party's power center. And Reagan had embarked on an expansive agenda of cutting taxes, increasing defense spending, and implementing conservative social policies generally.

The realignment, however, did not materialize. Though Reagan was reelected in a landslide, congressional Republicans barely made up their recession-hampered losses from the midterm elections of 1982. In 1986, the Democrats regained control of the Senate. President George Bush, Reagan's successor, then moved away from Reagan's more conservative program, signing onto a major tax increase in 1990 and exhibiting indecisiveness on other issues such as racial quotas. Many in the conservative movement considered Bush's move toward the center to be a major cause of the party's loss of the presidency to Arkansas governor Bill Clinton in 1992.

This was especially problematic since Clinton campaigned, in effect, to the right of the Republicans. He favored middle-class tax cuts, the death penalty and, as he put it, the "end of welfare as we know it." The hopes for both the party and the conservative movement as a whole soared during the landslide 1994 Republican congressional victory, led by Congressman Newt Gingrich. Clinton had made himself vulnerable by raising taxes and sponsoring a proposal to nationalize the healthcare system. Yet, within one year Clinton had orchestrated a successful offensive against the Republicans over budget and Medicare reform. In the three succeeding elections, the Republican Party lost seats in the Congress. Even Gingrich, the sitting Speaker of the House of Representatives, would resign after the 1998 elections and Clinton's successful avoidance of conviction in the Senate after he had been impeached in the House.

With the passing of Reagan from the political scene, the collapse of the communist threat at the end of the Cold War, and the emergence of Clinton's leadership style, a debate emerged among Republicans as to whether ardent conservatism is good for the party. This ambivalence toward conservatism within the party may be seen in its nomination of Texas governor George W. Bush in 2000. His message of "compassionate conservatism" was calculated specifically to contrast his views with that of the right wing of the party, and his interventionist foreign policy (and consequently massive budget deficits) and apparent acceptance of big government programs during his first years in office did indeed make many traditional conservatives think long and hard before supporting him in 2004 (in the end, most did). On the other hand, Bush did implement broad tax cuts and spoke openly of the partial privatization of Social Security, the core program of the New Deal. He also denied federal funding for stem-cell research on new embryo lines. A majority of voters arguably signaled their support for Bush's peculiar type of big-government conservatism in re-electing him in 2004 and increasing the Republicans' majorities in the Senate and House.

—SCOT ZENTNER

Further Reading

Brennan, Mary C. *Turning Right in the Sixties: The Conservative Capture of the GOP*. Chapel Hill, N.C.: University of North Carolina Press, 1995.

Mayer, George H. *The Republican Party 1854–1966*. New York: Oxford University Press, 1967.

Oldfield, Duane M. *The Right and the Righteous: The Christian Right Confronts the Republican Party*. Lanham, Md.: Rowman & Littlefield, 1996.

Rae, Nicol C. *The Decline and Fall of the Liberal Republicans from 1952 to the Present*. New York: Oxford University Press, 1989.

See also: Bush, George W.; Coolidge, Calvin; *culture wars*; Democratic Party; Federalist Party; Goldwater, Barry M.; Hoover, Herbert; *liberalism*; Lincoln, Abraham; New Right; Nixon, Richard M.; Reagan, Ronald; Rockefeller Republicans; Roosevelt, Theodore; Rusher, William A.; Taft, Robert A.; Taft, William Howard

Rickenbacker, William F. (1928–95)

Son of World War I air ace Eddie Rickenbacker and an economic libertarian, William F. Rickenbacker described himself as an "earnest partisan of individual liberty."

Ricken-backer graduated from Harvard in 1949 and entered the U.S. Air Force in 1951, piloting transports in the Korean War. He then worked in the Smith, Barney investment firm before becoming an independent investment consultant.

His refusal to complete the long form of the 1960 census as an invasion of privacy, and his subsequent prosecution (he was fined $100), brought Rickenbacker to the attention of William F. Buckley Jr. In 1961, he became a senior editor at *National Review*. Preferring Ronald Reagan for president, he resigned in 1968 over Buckley's support for Richard Nixon's candidacy. But he continued to publish in *National Review*; his column "Land of the Free," which upheld free enterprise and attacked government economic intervention as costly, intrusive, and harmful, appeared frequently during the 1970s. He was an editorial advisor for *Modern Age* and, from 1992 to 1995, an associate editor of that quarterly.

A shrewd economic observer, Rickenbacker correctly predicted rising silver bullion prices in *Wooden Nickels* (1966) and the collapse of the Bretton Woods international monetary system in *The Death of the Dollar* (1968). He also published a financial advisory letter, *The Rickenbacker Report*. In the early 1970s, he chaired the National Tax Limitation Committee, which sought a balanced-budget amendment to the Constitution. He edited *The Twelve-Year Sentence* (1974), a volume of essays criticizing compulsory schooling, and, with Linda Bridges, coauthored a writing manual, *The Art of Persuasion* (1993).

—JOHN ATTARIAN

Further Reading

Rickenbacker, William F. *The Fourth House: Collected Essays*. New York: Walker, 1971.

See also: National Review

Rieff, Philip (1922–)

Philip Rieff was born in Chicago on December 15, 1922. He attended the University of Chicago for both his undergraduate and graduate studies, which were separated by a stint in the U.S. Air Force during the war. In 1951, as a twenty-eight-year-old instructor at his alma mater, he married a beautiful and intelligent seventeen-year-old sophomore named Susan Sontag. (Before divorcing in 1958 they would have one child, David, who like his parents would go on to become a writer of note.) Rieff then went on to Brandeis University and finally, shortly after divorcing Sontag, to the University of Pennsylvania, where he remains the Benjamin Franklin Professor of Sociology and University Professor. He has also taught at Oxford, Princeton, Yale, William and Mary, and elsewhere. A prickly personality, Rieff was nevertheless a renowned teacher who approached his craft with exceptional seriousness.

Though he wrote a good deal on theology (especially Judaism) and politics, the most important aspect of Rieff's ouevre comprises his sensitive and pioneering scholarship on the thought of Sigmund Freud and the cultural ramifications of psychoanalysis and its theoretical successors. His *Freud: The Mind of the Moralist* (1959) is arguably the best one-volume work on Freud's work published to date. The introductions he contributed to his ten-volume edition of Freud's collected works further established him as a Freud scholar of the first rate. Rieff's Freud is a courageous genius, a Socratic figure who dared to test the received wisdom of a spiritually desiccated age and thereby revealed new truths about man. Freud's painstaking therapeutic approach could help men not only truly know themselves, but also live (relatively) well with that knowledge. Even so, Rieff understood that the consequences of Freud's work had been to encourage the creation of a new human type, psychological man, for whom there were no suprapersonal moral or ethical hierarchies. Rieff also saw that Freud had unintentionally paved the way for a new kind of "therapeutic culture"—a term Rieff coined in his critical classic, *The Triumph of the Therapeutic: Uses of Faith after Freud* (1966). In a sense, therapeutic culture is no culture at all but an anti-culture, since in Rieff's terminology a culture inheres in its prohibitions, while therapeutic culture is marked largely by its feverish attempts to remove all individual restraints and taboos. It is plain to see that Rieff is an—if not the—unacknowledged father of the view, now widely held, that contemporary laissez-faire, egalitarian "emotivism" owes much to the cultural influence of various watered-down therapeutic doctrines. It should be noted also that among those writers particularly influenced by Rieff was Christopher Lasch, who reveals his debt to Rieff most clearly in *The Culture of Narcissism* (1978).

Rieff's former student Jonathan Imber gathered Rieff's essays and articles into a rewarding collection titled *The Feeling Intellect* (1990). Rieff, who essentially stopped publishing toward the end of the 1980s and no longer teaches, currently lives in Philadelphia.

—JEREMY BEER

Further Reading

Freud, Sigmund. *Collected Papers of Sigmund Freud.* 10 vols. Edited by Philip Rieff. New York: Collier, 1963

Rieff, Philip. *Fellow Teachers.* New York: Harper and Row, 1973.

See also: Lasch, Christopher; therapeutic state

right-to-work movement

The right-to-work movement is an outgrowth of federal labor legislation passed in the 1930s and 1940s. Prior to the Great Depression, federal labor law was not supportive of labor unions, and union membership exceeded 10 percent of the nonagricultural labor force only briefly during and shortly after World War I. The National Labor Relations Act, better known as the Wagner Act (after its sponsor, Senator Robert Wagner of New York), was passed in July 1935 and provided powerful legal impetus to the spread of labor unions. The National Labor Relations Board was created to administer laws permitting workers to vote in representation elections determining whether they would bargain collectively. The Wagner Act and some earlier legislation outlawed practices followed by employers to discourage unionization and was considered very "pro-labor" by friends and foes alike. It was upheld by the Supreme Court in 1937 in *National Labor Relations Board v. Jones & Laughlin Steel Corporation* and several related cases. As a consequence, union membership soared, rising to about 30 percent of the civilian nonfarm work force by the end of World War II.

The Wagner Act permitted the closed shop; that is, this law allowed unions to negotiate contracts prohibiting the hiring of nonunion workers, making union membership mandatory. However, public acceptance of unions, relatively high in the depressed 1930s, declined sharply in the early and mid-1940s as the public wearied of strikes, some of which occurred during World War II, when most Americans felt that, given its adverse effects on the war effort, striking was wrong.

In response to this, in June 1947 the Republican-controlled 80th Congress passed the Taft-Hartley Act and then overturned the veto of President Harry S. Truman, who termed the legislation a "slave-labor law."

Taft-Hartley outlawed the closed shop, but permitted a variant of it, the union shop, unless otherwise prevented by state law. The union-shop arrangement allowed non-union persons to be hired by firms with union contracts but required the new workers to join the union within thirty days or face dismissal. However, states could prohibit the union shop by legislation, allowing workers the right to work regardless of union affiliation. The national fight to give workers the right to work that led to passage of the Taft-Hartley Act spread to the states, as they now had the power to nullify a key pro-union provision of federal labor law.

In the first two decades after the passage of Taft-Hartley, right-to-work laws were passed in nineteen states concentrated in the American South, agricultural Midwest, and a few western states. Unions were highly successful in thwarting attempts to adopt such laws in the Northeast and the industrial Midwest. In 1960, for example, only 23 percent of the population lived in right-to-work states. The proportion increased somewhat in the 1960s; the nineteen right-to-work states in 1970 had 28.4 percent of the American population.

In the period since then, the right-to-work movement has been moderately successful in improving the legal environment for workers not wishing to belong to unions. At this writing, three additional states (Idaho, Louisiana, and Oklahoma) have become right-to-work states (bringing the number to twenty-two), and the proportion of Americans living in such states has risen to 38.3 percent. More important than the addition of new right-to-work states has been the migration of Americans to those states. Some of the fastest growing states in the nation (e.g., Nevada, Arizona, Texas, Florida, North Carolina) protect the right of workers to decline union membership if they wish.

While unions have used aggressive lobbying and legal strategies to prevent states from adopting right-to-work laws, they have been losing some ground in their battle in recent decades for several reasons. First, union membership has declined sharply; about 10 percent of Americans in the private sector and below 15 percent overall belong to unions. The political clout of unions has thus undergone some decline. Rising educational levels, the decline in the relative importance of manufacturing, the rise of service industries, globalization, the increase in two-worker families, well-publicized instances of union corruption and other factors all have played a role in this decline. Second, people have voted with their feet by moving in large numbers to states with right-to-work laws. Third, the right-to-work movement itself has grown stronger and more organized over time.

Regarding the last point, traditional employer groups such as the National Association of Manufacturers and the U.S. Chamber of Commerce have generally supported right-to-work laws, but the movement was not well organized. On January 28, 1955, the National Right to Work Committee was created, with retired U.S. Representative Fred Hartley (cosponsor with Sen. Robert A. Taft of the Taft-Hartley legislation) as president. With 2.2 million members, the National Right to Work Committee and its sister foundation today are the leading organizations promoting right-to-work legislation. In addition, the committee has strongly supported individuals perceived to be suffering from the abuse of union power. Its president is Mark A. Mix, and it is headquartered in a Washington, D.C., suburb.

In its early days, the committee concentrated on preventing repeal of Section 14(b) of Taft-Hartley, the provision permitting state enactment of right-to-work laws. A particularly bitter and divisive fight occurred in 1965, when Republican Senate minority leader Everett Dirksen led a successful effort in thwarting attempts by the predominantly Democratic Congress to repeal Section 14(b). Throughout the 1970s and 1980s, much of the committee's effort was devoted to successfully fighting attempts to legalize "common situs" picketing, a move that would have dramatically increased pressures for unionization in the construction industry.

In more recent times, the committee has taken the offensive, promoting legislation that has received considerable (but not sufficient) congressional support. Also, it has provided legal support to workers, enabling them to sue unions where workers have lost their jobs or income because they did not wish to join a union. The organization has also joined in the effort to enforce the *Beck* Supreme Court decision prohibiting unions from using dues for political purposes without the written consent of members (*Communications Workers of America* v. Beck, 1988).

—RICHARD VEDDER

Further Reading

Leef, George. *Free Choice for Workers: A History of the Right to Work Movement.* Ottawa, Ill.: Jameson Books, 2005.

See also: Taft-Hartley Act; unionism

Road to Serfdom, The

The best selling book in the history of the University of Chicago Press, *The Road to Serfdom* was written by F. A. Hayek while the London School of Economics was relocated at Cambridge University during the Second World War out of recognition that National Socialism, fascism, and communism each condemned classical liberalism as its most hated doctrine. In this book and thereafter, the conflict and choice between individualism and collectivism became Hayek's central theme.

Based on his reading of Tocqueville, Lord Acton, and Hilaire Belloc, Hayek feared that Europe and the United States had lost sight of the principles of "the whole evolution of Western civilization." In his view, socialism, increasingly prevalent throughout the West, would inevitably rapidly abandon "the salient characteristics of Western civilization as it has grown from the foundations laid by Christianity and the Greeks and Romans. . . . [T]he basic individualism inherited by us from Erasmus and Montaigne, from Cicero and Tacitus, Pericles, and Thucydides, is progressively relinquished." Hayek's individualism therefore was no mere abstraction, but a historically rooted phenomenon. Hayek traced its rise within the Western tradition through Aristotle, the Stoics, Thomas Aquinas, the School of Salamanca, Hooker, Grotius, Milton, John Locke, and Francis Hutcheson.

Professor Fritz Machlup, who like Hayek had been a member of Ludwig von Mises' Vienna Seminar, presented the page proofs of the English edition of the book to Professor Aaron Director (brother of Rose Director Friedman) who shared the page proofs with his University of Chicago colleague Frank Knight. Knight recommended the book to the University of Chicago Press, which published two thousand copies with an introduction by John Chamberlain (September 1944). Following a first-page review in the *New York Times Book Review* by the paper's economics editor, Henry Hazlitt, Chicago ordered additional printings. A condensed version was published in the *Reader's Digest* (April 1945), and 600,000 copies of the condensed book were distributed by the Book-of-the-Month Club.

Milton Friedman wrote an introduction to the first edition published in Germany (1971). (A German-language translation was published in Switzerland in 1948; postwar Allied Occupation censors barred *The Road to Serfdom* from Germany on the grounds that it was subversive of New Deal policies.)

Friedman wrote

Over the years, I have made it a practice to inquire of believers in individualism how they came to depart from the collectivist orthodoxy of our times. For years, the most frequent answer was a reference to the book for which I have the honor of writing this introduction. Professor Hayek's remarkable and vigorous tract was a revelation particularly to the young men and women who had been in the armed forces during the war. Their recent experience had enhanced their appreciation of the value and meaning of individual freedom. In addition, they had observed a collectivist organization in action. For them, Hayek's predictions about the consequences of collectivism were not simply hypothetical possibilities but visible realities that they had themselves experienced in the military.

Hayek would go on to become arguably the twentieth century's most prominent and influential economist, writing more than twenty books, but it was *The Road to Serfdom* that made him a public figure. The book's appearance at a time when much of the Western world seemed in danger of succumbing to socialism helped to awaken public awareness to the importance of individual liberty, and it therefore played a crucial role in the battle against collectivism.

—LEONARD LIGGIO

Further Reading

Caldwell, Bruce. *Hayek's Challenge: An Intellectual Biography of F. A. Hayek*. Chicago: University of Chicago Press, 2004.

Ebenstein, Alan. *Friedrich Hayek: A Biography*. New York: Palgrave, 2001.

Wood, John Cunningham, and Ronald M. Woods. *Friedrich A. Hayek: Critical Assessments*. New York: Routledge, 1991.

See also: émigré intellectuals; fusionism; Hayek, Friedrich August von; libertarianism

robber barons

The term "robber barons" was popularized by journalist Matthew Josephson, who applied it in his book *The Robber Barons* (1934) to the leading businessmen of the late nineteenth century. The argument of Josephson and others was that America's leading businessmen and entrepreneurs of the late nineteenth century extracted or "stole" more in high prices and corrupt business practices than they gave back in production. Many historians and textbook writers have echoed Josephson and have called the post–Civil War period the "Era of the Robber Barons." Such a term, however, is very misleading.

The major problem with the robber-baron label is that America's late-nineteenth-century entrepreneurs were, as a group, very efficient producers in terms of both quality and price. During the last three decades of the century, prices steadily and sharply declined in such key industries as steel, oil, and railroads. As a result, the United States, a second-rate economic power before the Civil War, transformed itself into the world's leading economic nation by 1900. Specifically, in 1870, the United States produced 23 percent of the world's industrial goods, while Britain led with 30 percent and Germany produced 13 percent. By 1900, the U.S. was in first place with 30 percent of the world's industrial output, and Britain and Germany lagged behind with 20 and 17 percent, respectively. England, for example, dominated the world in steel in 1870, but in 1900 the output of Andrew Carnegie alone exceeded that of all Great Britain. In 1900, John D. Rockefeller's Standard Oil Company refined and exported more than half of all the world's oil. As a result of the successful efforts of Carnegie, Rockefeller, and others,

from 1,000 to 3,000 immigrants each day came to America from Europe—many of them eager to join other immigrants in working in American industries.

Another problem with the robber-baron label is that it lumps all businessmen together. It fails to separate the *market entrepreneurs* from the *political entrepreneurs*. Market entrepreneurs tried to achieve success by competing in the open market to produce reasonably high quality goods at low prices. Political entrepreneurs tried to be successful by using government to gain special subsidies or to regulate competitors. These political entrepreneurs were the true robber barons—they corrupted the political process and stifled others from competing.

In the case of the transcontinental railroads, for example, the Union Pacific and Central Pacific received tens of millions of dollars and tens of millions of acres from the government to build a railroad to span a continent. The result was a shabby, unusable line of rails and a stream of bribes and corruption that led to new laws regulating railroads. The best-built transcontinental line—and one that never failed—was James J. Hill's Great Northern Railroad. Hill was a market entrepreneur and received no federal money or land for his railroad. A similar story was repeated in the steamship industry, the building of the first successful airplane, and even in the steel industry. Robber barons were present, but market entrepreneurs prevailed, created jobs, and led the United States to world leadership in the late nineteenth century.

—Burton W. Folsom Jr.

Further Reading

Folsom, Burton W., Jr. *The Myth of the Robber Barons.* Herndon, Va.: Young America's Foundation, 1991.

See also: Carnegie, Andrew

Robertson, Marion Gordon "Pat" (1930–)

Religious broadcaster and conservative political activist, founder of the Christian Broadcasting Network (CBN), Christian Coalition, American Center for Law and Justice, International Family Entertainment Inc., and Regent University, Pat Robertson has perhaps done more than any other single individual to galvanize conservative evangelicals into a powerful political force. He tested the strength of that support in a failed bid for the Republican presidential nomination in 1987. Following his defeat, Robertson returned to head up the Christian Broadcasting Network.

Robertson was born on March 22, 1930, in Lexington, Virginia, to A. Willis Robertson and Gladys Churchill Robertson. His father, a thirty-six-year veteran of the U.S. House and Senate, introduced Robertson to the world of politics at an early age.

Robertson graduated magna cum laude from Washington and Lee University in 1950. He continued his education at Yale University Law School, where he received a law degree in 1955. He then earned a master's degree from New York Theological Seminary in 1959. Robertson served a brief stint in the U.S. Marine Corps Reserve during the Korean War as assistant adjutant of the First Marine Division. Ordained a Southern Baptist minister in Norfolk, Virginia, in 1961, Robertson resigned his position in 1987 before announcing his candidacy for the U.S. presidency.

One of his greatest achievements was the creation of the Christian Broadcasting Network (CBN). Founded in 1960, CBN became the first Christian television network established in the United States. It quickly became the world's largest television ministry, with programs airing across the United States in 9,000 communities and in fifty foreign countries. Its flagship program, the *700 Club*, began airing in 1963. The show, which offers news and features from a conservative Christian perspective, is cohosted by Robertson.

Court decisions legalizing abortion on demand, forbidding prayer in school, and legalizing much pornography and obscene speech convinced Robertson and Jerry Falwell to enter the political arena. And when Jimmy Carter failed to translate his "born again" religious values into conservative public policy, Robertson and other members of the Religious Right endorsed Republican presidential candidate Ronald Reagan in 1980.

The more than one million viewers of the *700 Club* provided a natural constituency for Robertson and his conservative political and religious views. Encouraged by the conservative momentum of two Reagan terms and buoyed by more than three million signatures on petitions, Robertson declared his candidacy for the Republican presidential nomination in 1987. Raising more than $19 million in support, he campaigned aggressively in thirty-four states on such issues as outlawing abortion, reinstating school prayer, and rolling back the tide of communism. During the primary season, he gained 1.9 million votes, or 9 percent of the Republican vote nationwide. He won caucus victories in five states and placed second in eight.

Robertson and others have been criticized by libertarians and some conservatives for mixing religion and politics, a combination the American people have traditionally eyed with suspicion. Robertson, however, responds that Christians should be active in politics and that his candidacy in no way violated the Scriptures' injunction to "render unto Caesar's what is Caesar's." In fact he said, "In America, *we* are Caesar. To render unto Caesar is to be good citizens. If we are to obey the command of Christ, we *must* be involved. If we want to become a persecuted, hunted minority, then we can stay out of politics."

Following his failure to capture the Republican nomination, Robertson turned his political ambitions elsewhere. In 1989, ten years after Jerry Falwell founded the Moral Majority, Robertson established the Christian Coalition, a grassroots, citizen-action organization aimed at promoting pro-family legislation and giving Christians a voice in government. According to its mission statement, the Christian Coalition "seeks to impact public policy on a local, state, and national level by keeping members informed of the critical issues affecting families." The Christian Coalition flourished especially under Ralph Reed's leadership in the early to mid-1990s, when it was a major player in conservative politics.

In recent years Robertson has sold the Family Channel and resigned his position as president of the Christian Coalition and the Christian Broadcasting Network. He remains active in evangelical causes and organizations and continues to appear on the *700 Club* television program.

—K. Teubner

Further Reading

Gottfried, Paul and Thomas Fleming. *The Conservative Movement*. Boston: Twayne, 1988.

Hutcheson, Richard G. *God in the White House*. New York: Macmillan, 1988.

Reinhard, David W. *The Republican Right since 1945*. Lexington, Ky.: University Press of Kentucky, 1983.

See also: fundamentalism; Moral Majority; Reed, Ralph

Rockefeller Republicans

A "Rockefeller" Republican is a liberal Republican. Conservatives often mean the term to be highly critical, while many in the liberal (or "moderate") wing of the Republican Party are happy to be associated with the term's source, the late governor of New York, Nelson A. Rockefeller. Differing views on the term, then, reflect differing views of Rockefeller and his career.

A member of one of America's wealthiest families, Rockefeller (1908–79) represented the most progressive wing of the Republican Party for two decades. As a congressman, and especially during his three terms as governor of New York, he promoted liberal policies on various social issues and supported increased government spending to fund an expanded welfare state and large public works projects. Most prominent during the 1960s, Rockefeller was a key proponent of programs in keeping with, and at times serving as models for, President Lyndon Johnson's Great Society.

Several times a candidate for president, Rockefeller's divorce hurt his standing in the polls, particularly during his run in 1964 against conservative candidate Barry Goldwater. Having lost to Goldwater, Rockefeller delivered a speech at the Republican national convention in which he decried "extremist" elements within the Republican Party and accused his opponents of dirty tricks and connections with the John Birch Society. Roundly booed by the delegates, this speech helped deepen the conservative/liberal split within the Party; a split that helped lead to Goldwater's poor showing in the general election, which he lost to Johnson in a landslide.

Rockefeller would continue to serve as governor of New York, running for president again in 1968. Chosen by Gerald Ford to serve as his vice president after Richard Nixon's resignation, Rockefeller proved too liberal and too aristocratic in temperament and demeanor for rank-and-file Republicans and was bounced off the ticket when Ford ran for president in 1976.

While memories of Rockefeller and his reputation in general have faded, his name still can spark debate concerning the efficacy of his policies. Liberals in general have seen these policies as compassionate and just attempts to help the poor and the middle class. Conservatives have pointed out that poverty and other social ills increased substantially during Rockefeller's tenure, along with government spending, taxes, and the size of the bureaucracy.

The failure of Rockefeller-like policies to eradicate or slow the growth of poverty has been seen by conservatives as proof that liberal programs, whether administered by Democrats or Republicans, are ineffective or counterproductive. The continued weakness of the Republican Party in the northeast, where Rockefeller and his wing of the party were most powerful, also led to serious doubts among conservatives concerning the electoral viability of Rockefeller's policies. It should be noted, however, that national party strategists continue to urge conservative candidates to "move to the center" by supporting social and welfare spending when and where it is perceived to be popular.

—BRUCE FROHNEN

Further Reading

Persico, Joseph E. *The Imperial Rockefeller: A Biography of Nelson A. Rockefeller*. New York: Simon & Schuster, 1982.

Underwood, James E., and William J. Daniels. *Governor Rockefeller in New York: The Apex of Pragmatic Liberalism in the United States*. Westport, Conn.: Greenwood Press, 1982.

See also: Republican Party

Rockford Institute

Located in Rockford, Illinois, the Rockford Institute is a conservative think tank that focuses on the promotion of liberty and the achievements of Western civilization, political and economic decentralization, and defense of the family. The institute was founded by John A. Howard in 1976 and has since become associated with the paleoconservative wing of the conservative movement.

Originally part of Rockford College, the Rockford Institute became independent in 1980. Its first international conference, "For Your Freedom and Ours," took place in Frankfurt, Germany in 1982. A year later the Institute took on even more responsibility with its guidance of the Ingersoll Milling Machine Company's corporate foundation. Through the Ingersoll Foundation, the institute presents two writing awards annually, the T. S. Eliot Award for creative writing (past winners include Walker Percy, Muriel Spark, and Richard Wilbur) and the Richard M. Weaver Award for scholarly letters (which has been given to such scholars as Robert Conquest and E. O. Wilson).

In 1984, the institute founded the Center on Religion and Society to reestablish "religiously grounded values as the basis for private and public decision making." Rockford later added the Center on the Family in America to support the American family with scholarly research. Personal and philosophical differences led to a schism between the institute and the two centers, which combined to become the Howard Center on Family, Religion and Society, in 1997.

Currently, the Rockford Institute endeavors to fulfill its mission predominantly by publishing a monthly journal, *Chronicles: A Magazine of American Culture* (Wendell Berry, Russell Kirk, John Lukacs, and Robert Nisbet have all appeared in this publication); by holding an annual, week-long "summer school" to discuss conservative thought; and by organizing annual meetings of the John Randolph Club, the "authentic voice of the American heartland," whose founding president was Murray Rothbard.

—LAURA BARROSSE-ANTLE

See also: Buchanan, Patrick J.; Carlson, Allan; Chronicles; Fleming, Thomas; Howard, John A.; Neuhaus, Richard John

Roman Catholicism

Conservative thought parallels Roman Catholic teaching in many respects. Not surprisingly, then, numerous Catholics have played a leading role in conservative politics and intellectual life in America, especially since World War II.

In the early years of the American Republic, Catholics Charles Carroll of Carrollton, a signer of the Declaration of Independence, and his cousin Daniel Carroll, a signer of the Constitution, were identified with conservative elements in Maryland politics and became prominent Federalists, the first conservative American political party. The only other Catholic signer of the Constitution, James Fitzsimons of Philadelphia, also was a Federalist and member of the first House of Representatives. In the nineteenth century, Orestes A. Brownson, a Yankee convert to Catholicism, became one of America's greatest political thinkers. He opposed the radical, innovating spirit taking hold in nineteenth century America and was described by Russell Kirk as "the most interesting example of the progress of Catholicism as a conservative spirit in America."

Catholic doctrine and tradition are close in many respects to the basic tenets of conservatism. Pope Leo XIII, in his famous social encyclicals of the late nineteenth century, strongly attacked liberalism for its arch-individualism, which preached "boundless license" and disconnected men from God and the natural moral law. Rejecting the natural law and making human consent the sole basis for governance permitted no certain restraint to political tyranny. Leo—along with leading contemporary Catholic spokesmen in the United States—also rejected egalitarian leveling in politics and economics, socialism and communism, and innovating, impractical, and utopian social theories; he strongly defended private property; and he stressed the need for limited and sufficiently decentralized government. All of these principles coincide closely with, say, the "canons" of conservative thought as articulated by Kirk.

It should be pointed out, however, that the liberalism of the era that Leo XIII wrote against was classical, or laissez-faire, liberalism. This version of liberalism in the twentieth century has actually been identified with certain branches of conservatism, especially in its economic outlook. While the Church has given her support to the market economy, entrepreneurship, private economic initiative, the profit motive, etc., she has also insisted that the market must be limited to ensure that it is just, moral, and humane; that the rights of workers and the poor must be upheld; and that a proper role for the state—in economics and other areas—must be acknowledged. So, in spite of the Church's affinity with conservatism in many matters, she does not fully embrace it or any particular socio-politico-economic perspective.

In active politics, the American Catholic community has been divided in its outlook and support for liberal and conservative candidates. Catholics were an important element in the Democratic party from the rise of the old urban political machines at the time of heavy Catholic immigration from Europe, and later most embraced the "liberal" New Deal. At the same time, Catholics were more like conservatives in their ardent anticommunism. After 1960, American liberalism became increasingly secularized and embraced positions, such as unqualified support for legalized abortion, that increasing numbers of Catholics could not accept. Catholics began to shift their support toward political conservatives and the Republican party. Still, in the confusion that enveloped American Catholicism in the wake of the Second Vatican Council (1962–65) some Catholics turned away from, or at least selectively rejected, the teaching authority of the Church and espoused both doctrinal and political liberalism. Others accepted their

Church's teachings, but did not carry them over into their political thinking and decision-making.

Among the more prominent American Catholic conservatives in the twentieth century have been the following: Francis Graham Wilson, author of *The Case for Conservatism* (1951); Russell Kirk, a major shaper of the conservative intellectual revival, which he helped ignite with his *The Conservative Mind* (1953); Fr. John Courtney Murray, S.J., one of the most influential Catholic spokesmen and thinkers of the 1950s who argued forcefully for the natural law underpinnings of American politics; William F. Buckley Jr., whose *National Review* became a major conservative opinion journal; William J. Bennett, secretary of education in the Reagan administration and a major cultural critic; Patrick J. Buchanan, syndicated columnist and sometime presidential candidate; Justice Antonin Scalia, the current intellectual leader of the U.S. Supreme Court; Fr. Richard John Neuhaus, a Lutheran minister who later became a Catholic priest and established the influential ecumenical journal *First Things*; Congressmen Henry J. Hyde and Christopher Smith; Neil McCaffrey, conservative activist and founder of the Conservative Book Club; Alan Keyes, Catholic radio commentator and presidential candidate; Edwin Feulner, long-time president of the influential conservative think tank, the Heritage Foundation; Paul M. Weyrich, head of the Free Congress Foundation; Robert P. George, McCormick Professor of Jurisprudence at Princeton and noted Catholic scholar; Hungarian *émigré* scholars John Lukacs and Thomas Molnar; E. Victor Milione, long-time president of the Intercollegiate Studies Institute; historian and columnist James Hitchcock; syndicated columnist Joseph Sobran; traditionalist activist-writer L. Brent Bozell; presidential speechwriter and political commentator Peggy Noonan; political theorist Willmoore Kendall; and traditionalist scholar Frederick Wilhelmsen.

Beginning with the pontificate of John Paul II (1978–2005), a revival of Catholic orthodoxy has spawned or focused renewed attention on many Catholic organizations and publications, some of which are avowedly conservative and others of which share many basic conservative principles. These organizations include Catholics United for the Faith, the Fellowship of Catholic Scholars, the Society of Catholic Social Scientists, Women for Faith and Family, the Catholic Central Union (Verein) of America, the Catholic League for Religious and Civil Rights, and the Catholic Family and Human Rights Institute. Publications contributing to the Catholic renaissance have included the *Wanderer*, *National Catholic Register*, *Crisis*, *New Oxford Review*, *Catholic Social Science Review*, *Catholic Dossier*, and *Catholic World Report*. New or transformed institutions of higher education, committed to doctrinal orthodoxy, have appeared: Thomas Aquinas College, Christendom College, Franciscan University of Steubenville, and The Thomas More College of Liberal Arts chief among them. Numerous graduates or student interns of these institutions have worked in or become part of conservative political efforts in Washington. Ave Maria School of Law, recently founded by Catholic billionaire Thomas Monaghan, presents the promise of producing a new generation of natural law–oriented Catholic lawyers. Catholic lay activists in recent decades have also distinguished themselves in the "conservative" pro-life, pro-family, and educational reform movements. As a result, Catholic voters, especially those who regularly attend mass, have begun to make a stronger connection between Catholic moral teaching and political principles, usually to the benefit of more conservative candidates.

—Stephen M. Krason

Further Reading

Allitt, Patrick. *Catholic Intellectuals and Conserva-tive Politics in America, 1950–1985.* Ithaca, N.Y.: Cornell University Press, 1993.

Krason, Stephen M. *Liberalism, Conservatism, and Catholicism.* Rev. ed. St. Louis: Catholic Cen-tral Verein of America, 1994.

———, ed. *Catholic Makers of America.* Front Royal, Va.: Christendom Press, 1993.

O'Brien, David. *Public Catholicism.* New York: MacMillan, 1989.

Varacalli, Joseph A. *Bright Promise, Failed Commu-nity.* Lanham, Md.: Lexington Books, 2000.

———. *The Catholic and Politics in Post–World War II America.* St. Louis: Catholic Central Verein of America, 1995.

See also: Catholic social teaching; conservatism; John Paul II, Pope; liberalism; natural law

Roosevelt, Theodore (1858–1919)

On September 14, 1901, Theodore Roosevelt took the oath of office as the twenty-sixth president of the United States, the youngest man ever to as-sume that office. To that point, Roosevelt, following his graduation from Harvard, had spent all but five years of his adult life in public service. As a young man he served three terms in the New York state legis-lature, following which he owned and operated a cattle ranch in North Dakota; lost a bid for mayor of New York City; and continued a lucrative writing career as a historian and essayist, which included authoring a respected four-volume history of American westward expan-sion and biographies of Senator Thomas Hart Benton, Gouverneur Morris, and Oliver

Theodore Roosevelt

Cromwell. From 1889 he served consecutively as Civil Service Commissioner; New York City Police Commissioner; Assistant Secre-tary of the Navy; Commander of the Rough Riders; governor of New York; and vice presi-dent of the United States. Consistently pro-gressive in public service, Roosevelt has none-theless been appreciated by conservatives for his prudent foreign policy, unabashed na-tionalism, opposition to socialism and an-archism, and his forthright advocacy of in-dividual virtue.

Roosevelt's politics and political thought are bounded by the twin principles of prom-ise and performance. For individual and coun-try alike, promise is bound to an understand-ing of civilization and virtue. The educated, civilized individual has a duty to engage in public service for the advancement of society toward greater development of its civilized life. This requires individual virtue, or character, as Roosevelt would often refer to it, and the premier virtue was courage. It is courage that inspires the individual to throw his hat in the ring to do his duty, and which supports him through the challenges that such public service presents. Likewise, the country is also to fulfill its duty in the ser-vice of civilization or else suf-fer the justifiable and de-served reprobation of those countries made of sterner stuff. The country, like the individual, brings to its task the fruits of its ancestry. The race characteristics, as Roosevelt termed them, of any country, are of great importance to its effort to fulfill its duty and to shoulder its share of worldly bur-dens. The dissolute individual and country will both face the prospect of losing ground absolutely as well as in relation to those that strenuously pursue their duty to civilization.

Roosevelt believed that the United States of his time was abundantly endowed with the attributes of promise: an energetic, free, and virtuous citizenry dedicated to noble Anglo-Saxon ideals and principles. Fulfillment of its promise, however, required prudence in selecting the means through which the country could perform at a level commensurate with its promise. Domestically, the country had to maintain, if not improve, its level of virtue, which required opposition to political tendencies toward either utopianism or plutocracy. Roosevelt consistently pursued policies intended to improve education and virtue while at the same time restricting anarchist and socialist pursuit of utopian ideals, and regulating the plutocratic influences of wealth and big business. He is perhaps best remembered for the latter, as manifest by the prosecution of the Northern Securities case (1904); passage of the Hepburn Act (1906) authorizing bureaucratic regulation of railroad rates; and the Pure Food and Drug Act (1906). Roosevelt followed much the same line in his foreign policy, asserting American rights and interests in the world in the manner he thought appropriate to a new world power. His foreign policy sought a moderate path toward continued progress in the successful exercise of the United States' power for good while avoiding both stale imperialism and breathless revolution. We see these principles on display in the Roosevelt Corollary to the Monroe Doctrine, which entailed keeping European powers out of Santo Domingo; in his brokering of a peace between Russia and Japan; and in his mediation of a dispute between France and Germany over Morocco.

Following his presidency (1901–09), Roosevelt lived a strenuous life of exploration and adventure—traveling far abroad to Africa and South America. His run for the presidency in 1912 as a progressive once again found him attempting to plot a course between the vices of plutocracy and radicalism, though some believe he had moved significantly in a radical direction. The onset of World War I found Roosevelt once more in the vanguard, advocating that the United States fulfill its duty to act in the service of civilization. There he remained until his death in 1919.

—LANCE ROBINSON

Further Reading

Dalton, Kathleen. *Theodore Roosevelt: A Strenuous Life.* New York: Knopf, 2002.

Morris, Edmund. *Theodore Rex.* New York: Random House, 2001.

Roosevelt, Theodore. *Letters and Speeches.* New York: Library of America, 2004.

———. *Theodore Roosevelt: An Autobiography.* New York: Da Capo Press, 1985.

See also: progressivism; Republican Party; Taft, William Howard

Root, Elihu (1845–1937)

Lawyer, statesman, and diplomat of the Progressive Era, Elihu Root served as secretary of war under Presidents William McKinley and Theodore Roosevelt (1899–1904), secretary of state under Theodore Roosevelt (1905–09), and as a United States senator from New York (1909–15).

Born in Clinton, New York, and educated at Hamilton College, Root received his law degree from Columbia and enjoyed a long and successful private practice, interrupted briefly by his appointment as a federal district attorney in the Arthur administration (1883–85). A lifelong Republican, Root's legal talents, personal integrity, and party loyalty attracted the notice of the party's national leadership. Appointed by McKinley to head the War Department, Root was responsible for administering the newly acquired territories ceded to the United States in its victory over Spain. He reorganized the military more effectively under civilian control by creating the General Staff, an invention widely praised and emulated in Europe. Root succeeded John Hay as secretary of state and continued Hay's efforts to strengthen ties with China, keep the peace with Japan, extend trading agreements in Latin America, and uphold the Monroe Doctrine to protect the Western hemisphere from European encroachments. The prudence of Root's foreign policies both as secretary of state and as a member of the Senate's Foreign Relations Committee earned him the Nobel Peace Prize in 1913.

Elihu Root

Although remembered primarily for his work in foreign affairs, in his own time Root was an outspoken critic of "progressive" politics at home. He was not unsympathetic to calls for stronger federal regulation of American business life, but he staunchly opposed attempts to redress political grievances through amendments to the United States Constitution. Many state constitutions of the early twentieth century, purporting to make government more "responsive," had adopted the popular initiative and referendum in legislation, as well as the popular recall of elected officials. To Root, such innovations weakened the representative system, and he worried that this "direct democracy" movement would escalate to the federal level. As a United States senator, he spoke out against the transference of Senate elections from state legislatures directly to the people, formally ratified as the Seventeenth Amendment in 1913. In 1912, Root chaired the divisive Republican national convention and sided with the "Old Guard" supporters of the presidential incumbent, William Howard

Taft. He thus broke with his personal friend and political ally, Theodore Roosevelt, who bolted the convention to form the Progressive Party and run his own presidential campaign on a platform that called for many of the constitutional amendments Root wanted to prevent.

Root declined renomination to the Senate in 1915, refusing to promote himself in public as the new methods of electioneering required.

—C. H. HOEBEKE

Further Reading

Jessup, Philip C. *Elihu Root*. 2 vols. New York: Dodd, Mead & Company, 1938.

Leopold, Richard Williams. *Elihu Root and the Conservative Tradition*. Boston: Little, Brown & Co., 1954.

Root, Elihu. *Addresses on Government and Citizenship*. Edited by Robert Bacon and James Brown Scott. Cambridge, Mass.: Harvard University Press, 1916.

See also: progressivism; Roosevelt, Theodore; Taft, William Howard

Röpke, Wilhelm (1899–1966)

Perhaps the most important conservative economist of the twentieth century, Wilhelm Röpke's thought combined the classical liberalism of Adam Smith's political economy with the European tradition of Christian humanism. To put his importance in easily understood terms, he was able to maintain in one coherent project the best of the logical rigor of Ludwig von Mises, the social understanding of Friedrich von Hayek, the anticommunism of Frank Meyer, and the conservative temper of Russell Kirk.

Born in Schwarmstedt, Germany, Röpke received his doctorate in political science in 1921 from the University of Marburg. Because he was a staunch opponent of Hitler in the very earliest years, he was forced to emigrate, becoming a professor at the University of Istanbul from 1933 to 1937. In 1937 he went to the Graduate Institute of International Studies in Geneva. Even during the 1930s Röpke had no illusions about either the economic success or the moral superiority of Soviet communism. He was a staunch opponent of all varieties of totalitarianism, whether Nazi or Soviet, all his life.

In Europe after the war Röpke was one of the architects of the "social market economy." He was part of a group of humane scholars—the Ordo liberals, which included Alexander Rüstow, Walter Eucken, and Luigi Einaudi—who during World War II laid the intellectual groundwork for the Christian Democratic movement that would reconstruct Europe and resist Soviet expansion. This group also played an important role in reestablishing the market economy in Germany after World War II, which combined respect for private property, free markets, competition, and a limited, federalized government. They helped persuade Ludwig Erhard to accompany the introduction of the Deutschmark with a lifting of Nazi-era wage and price controls. This bold move made possible the German "economic miracle," a term Röpke did not like because he considered Germany's economic recovery to be the natural result of free markets and competition. His wartime book *The Solution of the German Problem* (1945)—which argued for a loose, Swiss-style confederation of German states—helped convince postwar Germans to

Wilhelm Röpke

decentralize power, granting far more independence and power to the individual states than that enjoyed by French departments or British counties.

Röpke also played a significant role in the early years of the Mont Pelerin Society, in which he served as president. His conservative and religious views were in tension with the more secular, libertarian views of some of its members. Although his methodology and economics were Austrian in large part, he did not have the tendency of some libertarians to exalt the private sector at the expense of legitimate governmental functions nor did he denigrate the substantive truths of morality. In fact, he believed that a market economy could not be planted or would not survive without the moral capital and social cushion provided by tradition, religion, and civic-minded citizenship. He deplored the "cult of the colossal" and the uncritical embrace of technological advancement, and he worried about the consequences of population growth and unrestricted immigration.

Although he was a Protestant, Röpke respected Catholic social teaching and its embrace of small business, small farms, and "subsidiarity"—the doctrine that political decisions ought to be made locally wherever possible and only delegated upward to central authorities when absolutely necessary to the common good. Like the Chestertonian distributists, Röpke held that the widespread dissemination of private property (especially land) and economic power was the best safeguard against socialism and totalitarianism. He warned that the amassing of great wealth in the hands of the few was merely a waystation on the road to collectivism. He held up as a model the Swiss constitution (modeled in 1848 on the then-decentralized American system), noting that citizens in that country paid most of their taxes to their local governments. In terms of public policy, Röpke subscribed to the American view of substantive due process and a federalist understanding of legitimate police powers.

Röpke wrote elegantly and persuasively, and most of his numerous books have been translated into English and many other languages. His textbook, *The Economics of the Free Society* (1937), is probably the best introduction to free-market economics available. The first two books of his trilogy, *The Social Crisis of Our Time* (1942) and *The Moral Foundations of Civil Society* (1944), are excellent syntheses of social conservatism and market economics. Probably his most important work for the conservative intellectual movement in the United States has been his late collection of essays *A Humane Economy* (1958).

—WILLIAM CAMPBELL

Further Reading

Röpke, Wilhelm. *Against the Tide*. Translated by Elizabeth Henderson. Chicago: Regnery, 1969.

———. *International Economic Disintegration*. London: William Hodge, 1942.

Zmirak, John. *Wilhelm Röpke: Swiss Localist, Global Economist*. Wilmington, Del.: ISI Books, 2001.

See also: Austrian school of economics; Catholic social teaching; distributism; localism; Mont Pelerin Society

Rosenberg case

The Venona Archives proved Julius (born 1918) and Ethel (born Greenglass, 1915) Rosenberg to be what the Justice Department said they were during their trial in 1951—collaborators with Stalin who had funneled American nuclear know-how to the Soviet Union. While some doubt might linger about the relevance of the Rosenberg-Fuchs information to the Soviet A-bomb project (the Russians by 1948 needed no further assistance), none, sadly, can remain about the treachery of the husband-and-wife team, both of whom died in the electric chair in 1953 after appeals for President Truman to intervene went unheeded.

Julius earned his engineering degree from City College, New York, in 1939, the same year he married Ethel; he specialized in radio. Both Julius and Ethel participated with enthusiasm in left-wing causes and had joined the Communist Party. On the order of NKVD handler Alexander Feklisov they quit the party and cancelled their subscription to the *Daily Worker*. The year was 1942. The Army Signal Corps had hired Julius as a civilian inspector, with a security clearance, and Feklisov saw a chance to develop intelligence on the American military. In 1948, with Martin Sobell, Julius and Ethel passed secret information from the American nuclear weapons program, received by them from Klaus Fuchs, to the Russians. Only in 1950, after the first series of Soviet A-bomb tests, did Ethel's younger brother David Greenglass "name names" to the FBI, who promptly arrested both husband and wife. The trial that followed, under Federal Circuit Judge Irving Kaufman and with young Roy Cohn as prosecutor, articulated Cold War concerns and, like the Alger Hiss trial, gave the American Left one of its eternal themes.

After the Rosenbergs' conviction, Truman reasoned that, should he commute Ethel's sentence, the KGB would thereafter substitute female for male agents, with the argument that even were they convicted they would avoid a capital sentence. The executions came on June 19, 1953. Sobell received a lengthy sentence, from which he at last emerged in 1969.

Two sons of the Rosenbergs, Robert and Michael Meeropol, have continued to maintain their parents' innocence; but Feklisov corroborated the positive evidence in 1997, admitting that he had "handled" them, thus bolstering information already released from the KGB archives. Still, like Sacco and Vanzetti and Alger Hiss, the Rosenbergs remain icons of the radical Left.

—THOMAS BERTONNEAU

Further Reading

Feklisov, Alexander. *The Man Behind the Rosenbergs: By the KGB Spymaster Who Was the Case Officer of Julius Rosenberg, Klaus Fuchs, and Helped Resolve the Cuban Missile Crisis.* New York: Enigma Books, 2004.

See also: Cold War

Rothbard, Murray (1926–95)

A student of Ludwig von Mises who became a prolific scholar, Murray Rothbard published more than twenty books and hundreds of essays on free-market economics, American history, ethics, and political theory. Many of Rothbard's works, e.g., *Toward a Reconstruction of Utility and Welfare Economies* (1956) and *The Mystery of Banking* (1983), can be seen as extended commentaries on the work of Mises regarding the rationality of the market economy and the distorting effects of government planning. His study *America's Great Depression* (1963) exposed the deficit spending and inflationary policies of the Hoover administration. Rothbard set out to show that the pump-priming economics of the New Deal had their origin in Herbert Hoover's brand of progressive Republicanism. New Deal economic policies continued

Murray Rothbard

and aggravated the Depression by pushing Hoover's recovery plans to new inflationary heights.

Though trained as an economist at Columbia University and under the tutelage of Mises at New York University, Rothbard acquitted himself well as an ethicist and historian. In his works on the ethical foundations of the market economy, which were influenced by Kant and Mises, and in his multivolume work on the American founding, *Conceived in Liberty* (1975-79), Rothbard gave evidence of an expansive and polymath mind. Some may object to what seem the relentlessly libertarian premises of his writings, yet there are characteristics linking him to a traditionalist conservative position. Rothbard wrote with obvious sympathy for Western civilization, particularly its bourgeois and Christian components, and he fought "moral nihilists" within the libertarians' ranks for many years as a critic of the adversary culture.

Like his mentor, Rothbard received few academic honors during his intellectually vigorous career. Only after several decades of teaching at the Polytechnic Institute of New York did Rothbard obtain an endowed chair, and like that of Mises at NYU, his own at the University of Nevada at Las Vegas was established by an admiring benefactor. Like Mises, moreover, Rothbard never hesitated to stand outside the academic or political mainstream; his free-market views earned him the enmity of many leftists in his field; his principled isolationism drove a wedge between him and those on the Right who advocated a steadily interventionist foreign policy; and his fierce defense of marriage and the family and stated dislike for feminism caused him to break with the Libertarian party and to be attacked by the Cato Institute, the editors of *Reason* magazine, and counterculture libertarians. Through his many books and articles, newsletter, and *Journal of Libertarian Studies*, Rothbard made his own views both explicit and widely known.

—Paul Gottfried

Further Reading:

Raimondo, Justin. *An Enemy of the State: The Life of Murray N. Rothbard.* Amherst, N.Y.: Prometheus Books, 2000.

Rothbard, Murray N. *For a New Liberty: The Libertarian Manifesto.* Rev. ed. New York: Collier Books, 1978.

———. *Man, Economy, and State: A Treatise on Economic Principles.* Princeton, N.J., Van Nostrand, 1962.

See also: anarchism; Austrian school of economics; liberalism, classical; libertarianism; Mises, Ludwig von, Institute

Royster, Vermont C. (1914–96)

Before there was Robert Bartley, there was Vermont Connecticut Royster. As editor of the *Wall Street Journal* and president of Dow Jones & Company, Royster established the *Journal* as the nation's foremost newspaper of record on issues of business and economics. Royster was largely responsible for the pronounced editorial bias in favor of free markets that defines the paper to this day and that sets it off in contrast to the *New York Times*.

The oddly named Royster (named in honor of a grandfather, himself born into a family where all the children were named after states of the Union) was born and grew up in North Carolina. Upon graduating from the University of North Carolina-Chapel Hill in 1935, Royster moved to New York City. After a short stint with the New York City News Bureau, Royster moved to the *Wall Street Journal*, where he would stay for the rest of his life, excepting a four-year stint in the U.S. Navy during World War II. Upon signing up with Dow Jones, Royster steadily ascended the *Journal*'s masthead, serving as editor from 1958 until 1971. He remained a contributing editor and columnist until his death.

In six decades with the *Journal*, Royster was awarded two Pulitzer Prizes (for editorial writing in 1953 and commentary in 1984) and a host of other journalistic accolades, along with the Presidential Medal of Freedom from Ronald Reagan. Royster wrote several books, including *Journey through the Soviet Union* (1962), *A Pride of Prejudices* (1967), and *My Own, My Country's Time: A Journalist's Journey* (1983), but he will long be remembered for, in the words of his colleague Michael Gartner, helping "make the *Wall Street Journal* great."

—Max Schulz

Further Reading

Royster, Vermont. *The Essential Royster: A Vermont Royster Reader.* Chapel Hill, N.C.: Algonquin Books of Chapel Hill, 1985.

See also: Wall Street Journal

rule of law

An important catch phrase of modern conservative leaders and thinkers, the "rule of law" captures what conservatives see as the need to return to past assumptions about government.

One commonly held view of the meaning of "the rule of law" is that governments ought to be so structured that citizens perceive society as grounded on the impartial application and enforcement of agreed norms of behavior rather than on the whims or prejudices of political leaders. In most contexts that mention the rule of law, the implied if not explicit contrasting phrase is "and not of men." As outlined in Montesquieu's seminal *The Spirit of the Laws* (1748), influential in the thought of the founders of the American Republic, there should exist a certain balance of power between the various branches of government so that no partisan can disturb the overall structure. This arrangement allows citizens to trust in the fair administration of the laws. Constructing and maintaining this balance are themes in James Madison's famous *Federalist* 10 (1787), which urges ratification of the new Constitution because it will serve as a crucial tool for ameliorating the activities of factions (i.e., political parties and special interest groups) in American political life.

This practical political result requires more than customary observance of the usual technical legalisms—that is, that no act should be designated a crime and no punishment meted out, without law. As important as these legalisms might be, the overall structure of government must be so framed as to inspire and protect the confidence of the people. This requires a written constitution as the fundamental formulation of governmental authority. In Thomas Jefferson's words, "In questions of power, then, let no more be heard of confidence in man, but bind him down from mischief by the chains of the Constitution." The judiciary, then, whose power it is to interpret the law and the Constitution itself, is central to understanding the rule of law in American life.

Contemporary debate about what the rule of law requires frequently hinges on competing philosophies of jurisprudence concerning the role that the Supreme Court properly should play in American life and the freedom of the Court to interpret and apply a "living" Constitution to the alleged necessities of contemporary life. Prominent in this debate during the 1980s were conservatives such as Edwin Meese III, U.S. attorney general under Ronald Reagan, and Robert Bork, judge of the Federal District Court of Appeals for the District of Columbia (retired) and failed 1987 nominee for the Supreme Court. In fact, what turned this continuing and normally dry academic debate into a popular concern were the televised hearings held by the Senate Judiciary Committee on Bork's nomination to the Supreme Court and the abuse heaped upon Bork for his originalist jurisprudence. Bork maintained that cases coming before the Court should be decided from the language of the Constitution according to the meaning intended by its originators. Formulated in various ways and tagged with a variety of labels (e.g., strict construction, original intent, judicial restraint, interpretivism), this conservative theory opposes the view that the Supreme Court may properly *make* rather than *interpret* the law of the land.

To illustrate, the Supreme Court justices' opinions in the well-known case of *Griswold v. Connecticut* (1965) indicate that there is a "right of privacy" in the U.S. Constitution that protects a married couple's decision to use contraceptives. The couple's decision as to whether to use contraceptives was said to be beyond the legitimate control of the state, irrespective of the state's typically justifiable power to manage the health and welfare of its residents, and the rational-policy counterclaims that supported Connecticut's prohibition. The constitutional and thus rule-of-law difficulty was that while seven justices agreed that Connecticut's statutory prohibition could not be allowed to stand, they could not agree exactly as to why it should be struck down, nor quite where the constitutional right to privacy was to be found in the Constitution's text. Justice Douglas found this right in "penumbras" of the guarantees in the Bill of Rights, which are "formed by emanations from those guarantees" in the First, Third, Fourth, and Fifth Amendments; Justice Goldberg, in a separate concurring opinion joined by Chief Justice Warren and Justice Brennan, emphasized the Ninth Amendment; while Justices Harlan and White found reason for overturning the prohibition in the liberty afforded persons under due process, not privacy. None of these four separate opinions commanded a majority of the Court, a point emphasized by the two dissenters (Justices Black and Stewart) in their opinions, which vigorously argued that the Court had no constitutional mandate to overturn this "silly" law and could not do so without simultaneously doing grave damage to the language of the Constitution. This was the "slippery slope" to *Roe v. Wade* (1973), where the Court held that the right to privacy covers the woman's individual, not familial, right to an abortion.

Such cases are explosive not only because of their sexual subject matter: other cases (e.g., involving prayers in public schools, crèches on government property, affirmative action programs, criminal defendants' rights) illustrate the same sort of illegitimate rights creation. And because this explosion of judicially created rights is arguably nowhere to be found in the text or history of the Constitution and its amendments, it is utterly opposed by conservatives who take such "activism" as inimical to the democratic balance struck by the founders in the eighteenth century, a balance seen to be essential to the continued legitimacy and vitality of the Republic. Special rights—for example, those enabling a woman to abort a child without so much as informing her husband—undermine the equality before the law that allows for the rule of law and not of men.

—Daniel W. Skubik

Further Reading

Bork, Robert H. *The Tempting of America: The Po-litical Seduction of the Law*. New York: Free Press, 1990.

Hayek, Friedrich A. von. *The Rule of Law*. Menlo Park, Calif.: Institute for Humane Studies, 1975.

Nieman, Donald G. *The Constitution, Law and American Life: Critical Aspects of the Nineteenth-Century Experience*. Athens, Ga.: University of Georgia Press, 1992.

Shapiro, Ian, ed. *The Rule of Law*. New York: New York University Press, 1994.

See also: Constitution, interpretations of; constitutionalism; democracy; Dietze, Gottfried; judicial activism; libertarianism; Oakeshott, Michael

Rushdoony, Rousas John (1916–2001)

The founder of the Chalcedon Foundation, a "think tank of the Christian Right," Rousas John Rushdoony was also the father of Christian Reconstruction, a neo-Puritan theology that encourages Christian activism.

Rushdoony was born to Armenian immigrants. His father was an Armenian Presbyterian minister, and Rushdoony's own theology reflects the intense spirituality of that heritage. After graduating from Berkeley (B.A., M.A.) and the Pacific School of Religion (B.Div.), Rushdoony was ordained in the U.S. Presbyterian Church in 1944 and served as a missionary in India and as a pastor before joining the small and theologically conservative Orthodox Presbyterian Church.

The major influences on Rushdoony were New England Puritanism, Old School Southern Presbyterianism (especially Robert Dabney), Dutch Reformed social theory (especially Abraham Kuyper and Herman Dooyeweerd) and, most importantly, Cornelius Van Til, an apologist at Westminster Seminary.

Rushdoony founded the Chalcedon

Foundation (named for an early church council) in 1965 to encourage "the reconstruction of all things in terms of God's Word." Chalcedon challenged the retreatist pietism of many evangelicals, who, as was charged at the time, refused to engage their culture. The foundation publishes a monthly magazine—the *Chalcedon Report*, a semiannual scholarly publication—the *Journal of Christian Reconstruction*, and various studies through Ross House Books.

Rushdoony was a prolific author, writing books on theology, philosophy, history, political science, economics, psychology, and education. Among his most important works are *By What Standard* (1959), *The Messianic Character of American Education* (1963), *This Independent Republic* (1964), *The Nature of the American System* (1965), *The Foundations of Social Order* (1968), *The Revolt Against Maturity* (1977), *The Politics of Guilt and Pity* (1970), *Law and Society* (1982), and *Roots of Reconstruction* (1991). Rushdoony's magnum opus, and the manifesto of Christian Reconstruction, is *The Institutes of Biblical Law* (1973), a work that explains Old Testament judicial law and its application to modern society.

Christian Reconstruction has three unique emphases: postmillennialism, presuppositionalism, and theonomy. "Postmillennialism" (literally meaning that Jesus will [return] to earth after the millennium) was the old Puritan system of eschatology. It is an optimistic system, teaching that the church will be triumphant on the earth, and hence encourages political and cultural activism. "Presuppositionalism" is a rigorously Calvinist approach to apologetics and theology, which states that one's presuppositions or theological paradigm governs one's worldview. Finally, "theonomy" (literally, "God's law") means that every area of life must be ordered by God's law or word. Theonomy's emphasis on biblical law has prompted accusations that it promotes "theocracy," distinguishing its followers from other conservatives who stress tradition or natural law.

Rushdoony's greatest influence was as a social critic who used a revisionist and Bible-centered philosophy to critique cultural trends, particularly those of humanism and statism. Rushdoony saw humanism as rooted in a primal spiritual rebellion against God. Statism he saw as but another form of humanism. For Rushdoony, God has ordained three lawful but limited spheres of authority: the family, the church, and the state. The modern humanistic order uses the state to intrude into these other spheres.

The patriarch of the Christian Reconstruction movement and theonomy, Rushdoony formed a new generation of Reconstructionist thinkers, including Gary North (Rushdoony's son-in-law), Greg Bahnsen, James Jordan, and David Chilton. Rushdoony's movement has united Christians of different backgrounds, offering them an objective standard of ethics, an optimistic vision of national renewal, and a radically theistic interpretation of all disciplines.

—Roger Schultz

Further Reading

Barron, Bruce. *Heaven on Earth? The Social and Political Agendas of Dominion Theology*. Grand Rapids, Mich.: Zondervan, 1992.

Bahnsen, Greg. *No Other Standard: Theonomy and Its Critics*. Tyler, Tex.: Institute for Christian Economics, 1991.

De Mar, Gary. *The Debate over Christian Reconstruction*. Ft. Worth, Tex.: Dominion Press, 1988.

See also: Christian Reconstruction; Van Til, Cornelius

Rusher, William A. (1923–)

As long-time publisher of *National Review* and as a conservative political activist, William Rusher has wedded ideas to action. Although his parents moved to New York City from Chicago not long after he was born, Rusher never forsook his Midwestern roots or his family's affiliation with the Republican Party. At the time he matriculated at Princeton University and then Harvard Law School, Rusher was an enthusiastic advocate for Wendell Wilkie, Thomas Dewey, and eventually Dwight Eisenhower.

After 1952, however, Rusher's moderate Republicanism began to undergo a transformation. First, he came into contact with the growing body of conservative literature. He read authors such as Friedrich von Hayek, Russell Kirk, and James Burnham, and their arguments impressed him. He was most powerfully affected by Whittaker Chambers's *Witness* (1952). Rusher was also affected by the controversy surrounding Senator Joseph McCarthy. The liberal attack on McCarthy, he felt, was fundamentally dishonest and misguided. Perhaps this is why in 1956 Rusher agreed (at the urging of his friend Robert Morris) to serve as associate counsel to Senator James Eastland's Internal Security Subcommittee. Rusher spent slightly more than a year in Washington, investigating communist activities and making valuable contacts. Most importantly, he was now a convinced conservative.

By the middle of 1957, Rusher began to look for new work. He sought out William F. Buckley Jr.; Rusher hoped to do legal work for the Buckley family's oil business. To his surprise, however, Buckley asked him to become the publisher of *National Review*. And so began Rusher's thirty-one years of association with *National Review*. He had a considerable impact on the journal, greatly improving the business side of the magazine, and presiding over increases in advertising revenues and (eventually) a substantial jump in subscribers. By the end of his tenure, *National Review*'s circulation had risen to more than 100,000.

In addition, Rusher proved to be an important conduit between *National Review* and the conservative faction within the Republican Party. Believing passionately that firm conservative principles must be translated into effective political action, Rusher worked behind the scenes for the Draft Goldwater movement of 1961–64 and for the candidacy of Ronald Reagan in 1968. Although he often felt *National Review* did not go far enough in actively supporting conservative candidates, Rusher kept the magazine apprised of political developments and extended *National Review*'s influence in Republican circles.

Rusher also carved out an identity apart from *National Review*. By 1968 he began writing his own newspaper column, "The Conservative Advocate," which soon appeared in more than 100 newspapers. Beginning in 1970, Rusher began to appear regularly on PBS's "The Advocates," where he debated the conservative position against various liberal opponents. And from 1976 to 1979 he was under contract to ABC's "Good Morning America," where he participated in the show's regular "Face Off" segment. Rusher always sounded his own themes. He emphasized that a conservative political majority was possible, but that mobilizing economic conservatives was not enough: The right must also reach out to "social" conservatives, who were moved by the issues of crime, drugs, and abortion and who lived primarily in the South and West. For a time Rusher despaired of ever seeing the Republican Party forge such a coalition; the GOP's liberal wing always seemed able to block it. Hence, in 1975 and 1976 he urged conservatives to form their own political party in order to finally unite this "new majority." This failed, but Rusher felt a powerful sense of vindication when in 1980 Ronald Reagan finally did bring together this conservative majority in the GOP and achieved victory.

Rusher retired as publisher of *National Review* in 1988. Since then he has continued speaking, writing, and serving as a senior fellow at the Claremont Institute. It is likely that he will be remembered most for his tireless efforts on behalf of *National Review*, and his struggles for the triumph of conservatism within the Republican Party. Certainly few worked harder to see conservative principles translated into action than did William Rusher.

—KEVIN SMANT

Further Reading

Judis, John B. *William F. Buckley Jr.: Patron Saint of the Conservatives.* New York: Simon & Schuster, 1988.

Nash, George. *The Conservative Intellectual Movement in American since 1945.* Wilmington, Del.: Intercollegiate Studies Institute, 1996.

Rusher, William A. *Special Counsel.* New Rochelle, N.Y.: Arlington House, 1968.

———. *The Making of the New Majority Party.* New York: Sheed & Ward, 1975.

———. *The Rise of the Right.* New York: Morrow, 1984.

See also: National Review; *Republican Party*

Russell, Richard B., Jr. (1897–1971)

Born in 1897 in Winder, Georgia, Richard Brevard Russell Jr. was the son of Judge Richard B. Russell and Ina Dillard Russell. Educated at Gordon Institute and at the University of Georgia Law School, Russell was elected to the Georgia House of Representatives in 1920. This was the beginning of a fifty-year career in politics and public service, which included stints as a state legislator (1921–31), governor (1931–33), and United States senator (1933–71). He died in office on January 21, 1971.

By the late 1940s Russell had become one of the most influential senators in Washington. He supported most of Franklin D. Roosevelt's New Deal, but in later years opposed the growing powers of the federal government. He was a strict constructionist of the United States Constitution. Russell was a strong nationalist and believed in maintaining a powerful national defense. Except for defense, he was a fiscal conservative, as illustrated by his opposition to foreign aid.

His reputation as a conservative was also based in large measure on his unfailing support of racial segregation. From the 1940s onward he fought the growing demand for civil rights legislation and was probably the most influential opponent of any civil rights laws in Congress. Russell strongly believed in the superiority of the nation's Anglo-Saxon heritage and principles and thus opposed increasing immigration, especially from Asia, Africa, and Latin America.

Russell never married but was part of a large extended family and believed strongly in traditional family values. His mark on American history during his thirty-eight years in the Senate is symbolized by the Richard B. Russell Senate Office Building in Washington, D.C.

—GILBERT FITE

Further Reading

Fite, Gilbert C. *Richard B. Russell, Jr., Senator from Georgia.* Chapel Hill, N. C.: University of North Carolina Press, 1991.

Goldsmith, John A. *Colleagues: Richard B. Russell and His Apprentice, Lyndon B. Johnson.* Washington, D.C.: Seven Locks Press, 1993.

Rutledge, John (1739–1800)

John Rutledge of South Carolina had a political and judicial career that spanned the Revolutionary era, from its infancy in the 1760s to its completion with the establishment of the federal government in the 1790s. Rutledge held positions of importance in the colonial, state, and national governments and took part in every major political convention of his time, holding important positions in most. Throughout the Revolutionary era, Rutledge believed that the traditional "Rights of Englishmen" should be confirmed for Englishmen on both sides of the Atlantic. Rutledge and other conservative revolutionaries desired only to restore their place within the empire, only at the last instant favoring a total break. Rutledge represented the ideal of the educated elite who studied the political theories of the day and embodied these ideas in the United States Constitution.

Rutledge was born into the Charleston elite. He was educated by private tutors and later studied law in Middle Temple in London. In 1760, he was called to the English bar and shortly thereafter returned to his native South Carolina to begin his law practice. In short order, he was elected to the South Carolina Commons House of Assembly and quickly established himself as a leading politician and attorney.

John Rutledge

Rutledge made his debut in colonial politics in 1765, when at the Stamp Act Congress he was selected to be chairman of the committee to draft a memorial to the House of Lords. In 1774, he was elected to the First Continental Congress, where he advocated colonial autonomy within the British empire. At the Congress he was a strong supporter of the proposed embargo on trade with Britain, but managed to have South Carolina's rice exempted.

Two years later, as the support for economic pressure on the mother country waned, giving way to more open rebellion, Rutledge was elected to the Second Continental Congress. His tenure at the Congress was brief, for he soon returned to South Carolina to take part in creating its first state government. He aided in crafting the first state constitution and was elected South Carolina's president. Rutledge is given much credit for the defense of Charleston in 1776 when local militia defeated a seemingly invincible British invasion force.

Rutledge resigned as president in 1778 after vetoing a liberal, more democratic constitution crafted by the state legislature, but he was elected governor under that same constitution the next year. With the British invasions of 1779 and 1780–81, the legislature granted Rutledge sweeping powers, so much so that he was widely known as "Dictator" John Rutledge. Rutledge coordinated the defense of the state with the Continental commander, Nathanael Greene, and by late summer 1781 British forces had been expelled from all but the city of Charleston. In September 1781 Rutledge called for the election of a new legislature and the reestablishment of civil government. On January 29, 1782, the new legislature was seated and Rutledge gave up his office, as was constitutionally mandated. However, his career in politics was by no means over.

Between May 1782 and September 1783 Rutledge served in Congress, resigning after his election to a state judgeship and to the state House of Representatives. In 1787, he went to the Philadelphia convention as head of the South Carolina delegation. While at Philadelphia, Rutledge served as chairman of the Committee on Detail; he advocated representation based upon wealth, federal assumption of state debts, election of the executive by the Congress, and election of the Congress by the state legislatures. Rutledge apparently played an important behind-the-scenes role in guaranteeing that the federal government could not interfere with the slave trade for twenty years, a provision vital to his constituents.

After ratification, which in South Carolina was due to Rutledge's unbending support, President Washington appointed him senior associate justice of the United States Supreme Court, a position he held until 1791 when he resigned to take the (then more prestigious) position of chief justice of South Carolina. Four years later, Rutledge wrote to Washington asking that he be appointed to succeed John Jay, soon to retire as chief justice of the United States, to which Washington readily agreed. Rutledge sat on the Supreme Court for one term without Senate confirmation, but his strident and outspoken opposition to Jay's Treaty and intermittent bouts with insanity doomed his chances of being confirmed. Upon leaving the Court in defeat, Rutledge retired from public life, living in Charleston until his death in 1800.

—RICHARD S. DUKES JR.

Further Reading

Barry, Richard. *Mr. Rutledge of South Carolina.* New York: Duell, Sloan, & Pearce, 1942.

Bradford, M. E. *Founding Fathers: Brief Lives of the Framers of the United States Constitution.* Lawrence, Kan.: University Press of Kansas, 1994.

See also: American Revolution; Southern conservatism

Ryn, Claes G. (1943–)

Conservative critic of democratic excess in the American system, influential thinker in conservative political theory, and internationally known moral philosopher, Claes Ryn was born in Sweden in 1943 and undertook doctoral studies in political science at Uppsala University before receiving his Ph.D. in political science and philosophy at Louisiana State University in 1974. He has taught at the Catholic University of America since that time, becoming professor of politics in 1982.

Ryn's interests center on ethics and politics; historicism and values; politics and the imagination; the history of political thought; democracy and constitutionalism; liberalism; conservatism; the epistemology of the social sciences and the humanities; and on the figures Jean-Jacques Rousseau, Benedetto Croce, and Irving Babbitt. The influence of Babbitt, particularly his critique of sentimental ethics as found in Rousseau, is prominent in most of Ryn's writings. Moreover, Ryn's major works—*Democracy and the Ethical Life* (1978), *Will, Imagination, and Reason* (1986), and *The New Jacobinism* (1991)—develop particular aspects of Babbitt's intellectual legacy. Ryn has also done important work developing a value-centered historicism that rejects the ahistorical, abstract theories of ethics and politics that discount the concrete, lived reality of actual social and political life. His widely publicized polemics against "new Jacobin" global democrats were strongly praised by Richard Nixon.

Ryn is also chairman and cofounder of the National Humanities Institute. Based in Washington, D.C., the institute supports humanistic research and teaching and publishes a quarterly journal, *Humanitas.*

Though often identified with the Old Right, Ryn has gone his own way on key philosophic and political questions. Unlike most of the postwar Right, he has acknowledged his debt to the historically based philosophies of the modern era, especially the work of Croce. Both dialectical thinking and a historically situated ethic are basic to Ryn's technical studies. His historicism explores the universal elements operative in changing historical circumstances. Ryn has also clarified the concept of moral imagination found in Burke and Babbitt and demonstrated the interaction of will, reason, and imagination in ethical acts and all forms of judgment. He has doggedly resisted the determinism that he locates not only in Hegel but in the beleaguered second-generation Old Right. Unlike the emphasis on sociobiological and social-structural factors present in the political commentaries of Thomas Fleming and Samuel T. Francis, Ryn's work has adamantly upheld the primacy of ethics and culture in shaping societies and individuals. On this point, he has parted company with others of his generation and general political persuasion. But he has also remained a bridge to the European humanist tradition and to an older generation of American cultural conservatives.

—JACOB NEUSNER

Further Reading

Ryn, Claes G. *America the Virtuous: The Crisis of Democracy and the Quest for Empire.* New Brunswick, N.J.: Transaction, 2003.

———. *A Common Human Ground: Universality and Particularity in a Multicultural World.* Columbia, Mo.: University of Missouri Press, 2003.

See also: Babbitt, Irving; historicism

S

Safire, William (1929–)

A Pulitzer prize–winning (1978) commentator on politics from a moderately conservative-libertarian perspective, and an acute analyst of the uses of power in politics, author and journalist William Safire is a widely recognized authority on the uses of the American language. Safire was born in New York City, studied at Syracuse University, and received an honorary degree from the same institution. He began his career as a reporter for the *New York Herald Tribune* syndicate, worked as a radio-TV producer for WNBC, and headed his own public relations firm (1960–68). As special assistant to President Richard M. Nixon (1969–73), Safire wrote presidential speeches and from 1973 to 2005 made his thrice-weekly *New York Times* column into a significant event in political discourse. Safire's commentary on the Washington scene was considered by many the last word on the uses of power in government.

Safire's novel *Freedom* (1987), a fictional account of the issuance of the Emancipation Proclamation in 1863, provides in narrative form a classic account of the decision-making process in the federal system. Others of Safire's thirty or so books include *Before the Fall* (1975), *Safire's Political Dictionary* (1978), *On Language* (1980), *Freedom* (1987), *Language Maven Strikes Again* (1990), and *The First Dissident* (1992), a political reading of the book of Job. This work drew appreciative attention from the world of biblical scholarship.

—Jacob Neusner

Further Reading

Safire, William. *The Right Word in the Right Place at the Right Time: Wit and Wisdom from the Popular "On Language" Column in the "New York Times Magazine."* New York: Simon & Schuster, 2004.

———. *Scandalmonger.* New York: Simon & Schuster, 2000.

Santayana, George (1863–1952)

A member of the Harvard philosophy department, George Santayana was an antiegalitarian and antimodernist political and social theorist whose books and letters had a strong influence on the traditionalist wing of the American conservative movement. Born in Madrid, Santayana moved to Boston at the age of eight to be with his mother, who had separated from his father years earlier. He graduated from Harvard in 1886, studied in Germany for two years, and later completed his doctorate at Harvard, writing his dissertation on Rudolf Lotze. He joined the Harvard faculty and remained there until 1912, when he retired on an inheritance. He moved to England, settled in Rome in 1925, took refuge in a convent of English nuns during World War II, and remained there studying and writing until his death. His major works are *The Sense of Beauty* (1896) and a five-volume work, *The Life of Reason* (1905).

Even while living his academic life in America, Santayana cherished his Spanish birth and never lost his strong identification with Mediterranean civilization. To him, a good society was marked by beauty and imagination, not a plenitude of consumer goods, science, and technical innovation. It was a place where the life of the mind and art could thrive. His critique of modern life rested on this position. He had a high regard for the place of religion in society, even as he regarded religion as something not to be taken as literal truth. Rather, for Santayana religion had a more organic justification, akin to language and nationality. Religion is best regarded as an imaginative and comprehensive method of reorganizing our moral experience, and as such it is impossible to abandon religion and unwise to attempt to do so, as both liberal democracy and communism have done. Santayana esteemed both piety, practical attachment to the ideal or the sources of being, and spirituality, which directs us toward ideal meaning and prevents us from placing economic goods as the highest end. He condemned those modernists who wanted to replace the truth claims of religious belief with artificial claims lacking in moral and spiritual content.

Santayana's Catholicism had a strong influence on his social doctrine, which emphasized the institutions that form social allegiances: tradition, family, church, chivalry, community, and country. Not surprisingly, Santayana championed the role of hierarchy and authority in social life. The rational and beautiful society is always dominated by an aristocracy, he said, because any alternative collapses into sameness and arbitrary rule. A vociferous opponent of democracy, he viewed it as crushing what was the most imaginative and interesting aspect of society, the diversity of its individuals and

George Santayana

groups, in favor of rule by the majority, the "most cruel and unprogressive of masters." He linked democracy to a Protestant form of social dissolution and to liberalism, where legitimate authority is envied and crushed and a false equality is engineered by the technocratic state. Instead he advocated the "natural" society, where members and groups found the position in life that most suited their abilities and temperament. While not an advocate of capitalism as an ideology, he opposed managerial attempts to regulate and direct uses of private property.

During his long writing career, Santayana distinguished himself as a critic as well as philosopher, and even his detractors have recognized the brilliance of his critiques of utilitarianism, pragmatism, atomism, and positivism. Against the trends of his time, Santayana composed prose of extraordinary power, style, and lucidity. His name and work figure prominently in Russell Kirk's *The Conservative Mind* (1953), which was originally subtitled "From Burke to Santayana."

—JEFFREY A. TUCKER

Further Reading

McCormick, John. *George Santayana: A Biography.* New York: Knopf, 1987.

Munitz, Milton. *The Moral Philosophy of Santayana.* New York: Columbia University Press, 1939.

Santayana, George. *Character and Opinion in the United States.* New York: W. W. Norton, 1934.

———. *Dominations and Powers: Reflections on Liberty, Society, and Government.* New York: Charles Scribner's Sons, 1951.

See also: Conservative Mind, The; *envy; traditionalism*

Scaife foundations

Four foundations associated with Richard Mellon Scaife (of the Mellon banking fortune) subsidize conservative groups, charities, and cultural projects. These include the Sarah Scaife Foundation, Allegheny Foundation, Carthage Foundation, and Scaife Family Foundation. Fund investments in 2003 were above $430 million, with grants exceeding $23 million.

The Sarah Scaife Foundation financed population control and the arts until Scaife's mother's death in 1965. Richard Scaife gained control over the foundation's funding policies in 1973 and began supporting organizations associated with the "New Right," including Richard Nixon's presidential campaign and the fledgling Heritage Foundation. Other beneficiaries have included the American Enterprise Institute, Center for Strategic and International Studies, Center for the Study of Popular Culture, Judicial Watch, Free Congress Foundation, Accuracy in Media, and the Intercollegiate Studies Institute.

A far-sighted and principled philanthropist, Scaife's support for key conservative institutions and initiatives has made this private man a favorite target of the Left in recent years. Scaife and the foundations he heads drew particularly intense scrutiny during President Clinton's tenure, when they were accused of funding a "vast right-wing conspiracy." The charges did not put an end to Scaife's activities, but did cause him some trouble. For example, Scaife was to endow a chair at Pepperdine University for Clinton Special Prosecutor Kenneth Starr, but gave up on the idea after being harshly criticized for a supposed conflict of interest arising from his funding of the *American Spectator*'s investigation of "Troopergate" and Clinton-aide Vincent Foster's death.

Scaife continues to fund a significant number of conservative organizations as well as population control supporters, particularly through the Federation for American Immigration Reform and its activist Stephen D. Mumford. Mumford's ally Donald Collins serves on the Scaife Family Foundation's board and advocates population control in Scaife's Greensburg, Pennsylvania, *Tribune-Review*.

—Matthew Bowman

See also: foundations, conservative

Scalia, Antonin (1936–)

Nominated by President Reagan as associate justice to the United States Supreme Court in 1986, Antonin Scalia is widely acknowledged as the most intelligent and witty of the Rehnquist Court's justices and is the intellectual leader of the Court's conservative wing. His jurisprudential views are profoundly influenced by his Roman Catholicism.

Scalia did his undergraduate work at Georgetown University (A.B.), studied at the University of Fribourg in Switzerland, and earned an L.L.B. (magna cum laude) from Harvard Law School. After some time in private practice in Cleveland, Scalia taught at the University of Virginia School of Law, worked in the Nixon administration, and then served under President Ford as the assistant attorney general for the Office of Legal Counsel. In 1977 Scalia left government to teach at the law school of the University of Chicago before being appointed to the United States Court of Appeals for the District of Columbia Circuit in 1982. Four years later he was appointed to the Supreme Court, becoming the first law professor to become an associate justice since Felix Frankfurter.

On the Court, Scalia's role has principally been to champion constitutional interpretation according to the original understanding of the document, to refer repeatedly to "tradition" as a guide to constitutional exegesis, and to advocate the interpretation of statutes according to their "plain meaning" and not according to their legislative history. Unlike several other conservative nominees proposed for the Court in the late twentieth century, Scalia's nomination secured the concurrence of the Senate with relatively little trouble, as his appointment was made during a brief period when there was a Republican majority during Reagan's presidency.

Scalia is best known, perhaps, for his continuing opposition to the idea, currently associated with Justice Sandra Day O'Connor, that there is a constitutional right to secure an abortion without an "undue burden" being placed on the practice; this was the doctrine established by a plurality of the Court in the 1992 decision *Planned Parenthood v. Casey*. Dissenting from that decision, which essentially upheld the first Supreme Court decision to find antiabortion legislation unconstitutional, *Roe v. Wade* (1973), Scalia clearly indicated that abortion was an area where the federal government did not belong and that such domestic regulation should be left to the states. In *Lee v. Weisman*, another 1992 decision, Scalia dissented from the five-person majority's holding that barred even nonsectarian prayer from a public middle school graduation ceremony. Scalia also dissented from *Santa Fe Independent School District v. Doe* (2000), where the Court barred student-led prayer at a public school football game. Scalia indicated that the American tradition of sanctifying important public events by prayer deserved the deference of, and not interference from, the Court.

Scalia may also be the most independent thinker on the Court: while he is a fairly reliable adherent to conservative views, this is not always the case. His independence was demonstrated when he was the sole dissenter in *Morrison v. Olson*, the 1988 case which upheld the creation of the Office of Independent Counsel, a prosecutor relatively unsupervised by other executive branch officials. Scalia argued that creating a prosecutor independent of the executive violated the Constitution's structural provisions regarding the separation of powers between the three branches of government. At the time, Scalia's dissent was not regarded as persuasive, but by the end of Independent Counsel Kenneth Starr's tenure, Scalia's dissent in Morrison had all but become conventional wisdom. Even Starr himself testified before Congress against the renewal of the statute involved, and Congress decided to let it expire.

In *Texas v. Johnson* (1989), Scalia's was the fifth and thus the deciding vote for the Court's opinion that legislation forbidding flag desecration was an unconstitutional infringement of First Amendment rights. While this departed from the views of most traditionalist conservatives at the time, Scalia's dissent was consistent with some of his other First Amendment opinions. In that limited area Scalia seems prepared to depart from the original understanding of the amendment's coverage in the framers' time, believing apparently that the amendment's free speech guarantees were intended to grow as necessary to secure this most basic American right.

—Stephen B. Presser

Further Reading

Brisbin, Richard A. *Justice Antonin Scalia and the Conservative Revival*. Baltimore, Md.: Johns Hopkins University Press, 1997.

Scalia, Antonin. *A Matter of Interpretation: Federal Courts and the Law*. Princeton, N.J.: Princeton University Press, 1997.

———. *Scalia Dissents: Writings of the Supreme Court's Wittiest, Most Outspoken Justice*. Washington, D.C.: Regnery, 2004.

Schultz, David A., and Christopher E. Smith. *The Jurisprudential Vision of Justice Antonin Scalia*. Lanham, Md.: Rowman & Littlefield, 1996.

Smith, Christopher E. *Justice Antonin Scalia and the Supreme Court's Conservative Moment.* New York: Praeger, 1993.

See also: Brown v. Board of Education; *Constitution, interpretations of; equal protection; speech, freedom of; Supreme Court*

Schaeffer, Francis A. (1912–84)

A Protestant missionary and apologist and leading intellectual figure behind the public resurgence of evangelicalism during the late twentieth century, Francis Schaeffer, with his wife Edith, founded and directed L'Abri Fellowship, an international study center and caring community in the Swiss Alps. From this remote sanctuary, the American-born Presbyterian minister offered a critique of secular culture from a Christian perspective. Schaeffer was especially effective in tracing the decline of Western civilization across a variety of disciplines, including art and architecture, philosophy, science, and religion. The consequence of Schaeffer's life and work was to compel many evangelicals toward greater involvement in American politics and culture. As the Roman Catholic theologian Richard John Neuhaus has observed, "For many Evangelicals, Schaeffer, an astonishing autodidact, made accessible a large part of Western thought construed to his distinctive Christian vision."

In 1960, *Time* magazine featured Schaeffer as an eccentric, goateed, knickers-clad "missionary to intellectuals" who readily welcomed existentialists, beatniks, and other spiritual seekers to his alpine chalet. Over the course of nearly three decades thousands of students and seekers stayed at L'Abri to pray, study, and converse with Schaeffer. One student at L'Abri was President Gerald Ford's son Michael, who ultimately led the Schaeffers to a private White House dinner party with the first family.

Schaeffer's influence was greatly extended through his writings and international public lectures. In 1971, he was introduced to Rep. Jack Kemp and his wife, Joanne. This meeting opened the door to a wider circle of Washington officials. The Kemps hosted a discussion group for ten years that studied the writings of Schaeffer. By 1982, *Newsweek* reported Schaeffer to be the "guru of fundamentalism," the "folk-philosopher" intellectual behind a phenomenal reemergence of religious conservatives in American public life. His thought and writings influenced a number of leading evangelical thinkers and activists, including Charles Colson, Kenneth Connor, James C. Dobson, Jerry Falwell, Os Guinness, C. Everett Koop, Tim and Beverly LaHaye, Richard Land, Pat Robertson, Randall Terry, and Cal Thomas.

Schaeffer's twenty-four books have sold more than three million copies in twenty languages. His early works—*The God Who Is There* (1968) and *Escape from Reason* (1968)—traced the decline of Western humanistic culture to its skepticism of universal truths and moral absolutes. Arguing that the triumph of relativism had robbed the world of meaning and purpose, Schaeffer thought the West to be in cultural despair. A window to this despair could be seen in the films of Bergman and Fellini, in the writings of Camus, Sartre, and Heidegger, in the poetry of Dylan Thomas, in the art of Salvador Dalí and Picasso, and in the music of the Beatles, Bob Dylan, and John Cage.

Schaeffer's later writings, such as *How Should We Then Live* (1976), *Whatever Happened to the Human Race* (1979), coauthored by C. Everett Koop, and *A Christian Manifesto* (1981), detailed the social and political consequences of skepticism and relativism. Abortion, infanticide, and euthanasia were the consequence of a dehumanizing secularism. In these works, Schaeffer argued that Reformation Christianity was essential to maintaining political freedom and just order. According to Schaeffer, the republican democratic tradition was cradled in the Reformation. Ideals of human rights, dignity, and freedom were grounded in a Bible-based culture. The perpetuation of these democratic values could only be assured by a return to Christian culture.

—ALAN R. CRIPPEN II

Further Reading

Burson, Scott R., and Jerry L. Walls. *C. S. Lewis & Francis Schaeffer*. Downers Grove, Ill.: InterVarsity Press, 1998.

Dennis, Lane T., ed. *Francis A. Schaeffer: Portraits of the Man and His Work*. Westchester, Ill.: Crossway Books, 1986.

Ruegsegger, Ronald W., ed. *Reflections on Francis Schaeffer*. Grand Rapids, Mich.: Zondervaan, 1986.

Schaeffer, Francis A. *The Complete Works of Francis A. Schaeffer: A Christian Worldview*. 2nd ed. Westchester, Ill.: Crossway Books, 1995.

See also: Protestantism, evangelical

Schall, James V. (1928–)

James V. Schall, S.J., could be called the American Chesterton, though with the qualification that while he is an essayist and an apologist for the Catholic faith, he has also contributed numerous academic works on the interrelation of reason, revelation, and political philosophy. Born in Iowa, he began his studies at the University of Santa Clara in 1945, but these were interrupted in 1946 when he enlisted in the army. In 1948, Schall entered the California Province of the Society of Jesus at Los Gatos, California. He received his B. A. (1954) and M.A. (1955) from Gonzaga University (he would also earn an M.A. in sacred theology from Gonzaga in 1964). He was an instructor at the University of San Francisco from 1955 to 1956, after

which time he attended Georgetown University, where he was awarded his doctorate under the direction of the famous Catholic political theorist Heinrich Rommen (1960). Schall was ordained to the priesthood in 1963 and thereafter spent time studying and teaching in Belgium and Rome. In 1968, he became professor of government at the University of San Francisco, and in 1978 he accepted a similar position at Georgetown. He has been a distinguished presence at that institution ever since.

Schall's Catholic and conservative mind ranges wide and plumbs the depths of the best that has been thought and said in the Western philosophical, religious, political, and literary traditions. Typically his essays include a number of citations from Plato, Aristotle, St. Thomas Aquinas, St. Augustine, and Cicero, usually interspersed with complementary observations from figures such as Samuel Johnson, Hilaire Belloc, Chesterton, and Leo Strauss—as well as his comic heroes Charlie Brown, Snoopy, and other *Peanuts* characters. Schall has an international following consisting of scholars inspired by his book on education, *Another Sort of Learning* (1988), a work that offers alternative "Great Books" reading lists. His classes at Georgetown are conducted according to the Socratic method. He is a popular and revered teacher.

A recurring theme throughout Schall's works is that the principal consequence of revelation for political life is that it works to prevent politics from conceiving itself as either a metaphysic or an eschatology. Schall is critical of modernity for blinding scholars to the possibility that revelation was directed at reason's own legitimate but unanswered questions, and he argues that the reason why modernity reached political and intellectual dead ends is that it sought, and could not find, an alternative to the Eucharist. Modernity has exhausted all the possible substitutes—the state, science, sex—in this search, leaving in its wake the fragmentation of the integrity of the human person and, for many, a loss of an understanding of what it means to be human. Schall has also written extensively on the topic of natural law. He takes the position that the natural law of St. Thomas was not simply the natural right of Strauss's Aristotle, and still less the natural law or "human rights" of modernity as articulated in the writings of Hobbes or Rousseau. In works such as *Jacques Maritain: The Philosopher in Society* (1998) he questions the wisdom of Maritain's attempted synthesis of the natural law and natural right traditions. Beyond his academic writing, Schall is a prolific columnist, contributing regularly to *Crisis* magazine, the Chesterton Society publication *Gilbert!* and the *University Bookman*. He was appointed by Ronald Reagan to the National Council on the Humanities, serving as a member from 1984 to 1990.

—TRACEY ROWLAND

Further Reading

Guerra, Marc D., ed. *Reason, Revelation, and Human Affairs: Selected Writings of James V. Schall.* Lanham, Md.: Lexington, 2001.

Schall, James V., S.J. *Roman Catholic Political Philosophy.* Lanham, Md.: Lexington, 2004.

See also: modernity and postmodernity; natural law; Roman Catholicism

Schindler, David L. (1943–)

Academic dean and Edouard Cardinal Gagnon Professsor of Fundamental Theology at the John Paul II Institute for Studies on Marriage and Family, editor in chief of the Anglo-American edition of *Communio: International Catholic Review,* and one of his generation's most sophisticated and penetrating critics of liberalism, David L. Schindler and his work have served as an alternative locus of orthodox Catholic engagement with American culture—alternative, that is, to the favored approach and themes of the dominant Catholic neoconservatives.

Schindler took his B.A. and M.A. in philosophy at Gonzaga University before obtaining his doctorate from Claremont Graduate School in religion in 1972. He taught at Mount St. Mary's College and Seminary before taking a post in the Program of Liberal Studies at the University of Notre Dame in 1979, where he taught until 1992, when he left for the John Paul II Institute in Washington, D.C. Schindler became editor in chief of the quarterly theological journal *Communio*— a product of the Papal Theological Commission of the early 1970s that was led by Hans Urs von Balthasar, Joseph Ratzinger, Karl Lehmann, and Henri de Lubac—in 1982. *Communio* was first published in 1972 in German. The first American edition was published in 1974, with James Hitchcock as editor and Schindler as assistant editor, and was followed by other international editions over the years. Today, *Communio* is published in seventeen different languages. The Anglo-American edition counts among its editorial board members and contributing editors religious thinkers such as Stratford Caldecott, Louis Dupré, and Aidan Nichols.

In a number of articles and especially in his important book, *Heart of the World, Center of the Church: Communio Ecclesiology, Liberalism, and Liberation* (1996), Schindler has attempted to articulate, in ontological and theological terms, how and in what ways the project of Catholic neoconservatives like Richard John Neuhaus, Michael Novak, and George Weigel—sometimes referred to by him and others as the "John Courtney Murray project"—is insufficient and ultimately untenable. The proponents of this project maintain that, if understood correctly, there is no fundamental incompatibility between liberalism and Catholicism, which view consequently allows them to adopt an optimistic or (in the terminology of theologian Tracey Rowland) "Whig" view of liberal economic and political institutions, particularly as those institutions have developed in the American context.

Schindler is not, as his opponents sometimes fail to comprehend, a restorationist, integralist, or theocrat. Rather, as he is at pains to point out, his critique of the neoconservatives (or, more accurately, neoliberals) rests on certain fundamental philosophical-theological differences. For instance, drawing on de Lubac and Balthasar, Schindler believes that the neoconservatives subscribe (perhaps unwittingly) to a misunderstanding of natural law that implies an extrinsic model of the relationship between nature and grace, as if grace is something "extra" that God adds on to a preexisting and self-sufficient nature. For this reason they tend to see economic relations, for instance, as something "natural" that ought to be restrained, where necessary, by Catholic social teaching, but not transformed and reshaped by it. Likewise, Schindler believes that the Catholic neoconservatives too readily accept the claim that liberal institutions and technology are "neutral," rather than having an interior logic of utilitarianism and indeed atheism. And he has criticized Catholic neoconservatives for interpreting Pope John Paul II's encyclicals, especially *Centesimus Annus,* as endorsing the assumptions undergirding American-style consumer capitalism.

Though Schindler could rightly be characterized as a conservative in that he is a non-utopian, prudent antiliberal, his focus is not on politics but on the transformation of culture through interior transformation. Besides Balthasar, de Lubac, and Wojtyla, an emerging influence on Schindler's cultural criticism in the last decade has been the work of the farmer-writer Wendell Berry, who argues persuasively that the "key to understand-ing contemporary American culture lies in its homelessness: homelessness, that is, understood first not as an affliction of a discrete group of people living in the streets, but precisely as the modern condition of being."

—JEREMY BEER

Further Reading

Bandow, Doug, and David L. Schindler, eds. *Wealth, Poverty, and Human Destiny.* Wilmington, Del.: ISI Books, 2003.

Rowland, Tracey. *Culture and the Thomist Tradition: After Vatican II.* New York: Routledge, 2003.

Schindler, David L., ed. *Catholicism and Secularization in America: Essays on Nature, Grace, and Culture.* Huntington, Ind.: Our Sunday Visitor, 1990.

———. "Homelessness and the Modern Condition: The Family, Evangelization, and the Global Economy." *Logos* 3, no. 4 (2000): 34-56.

See also: Berry, Wendell; Catholic social teaching; natural law; Neuhaus, Richard John; Novak, Michael; Roman Catholicism; Weigel, George

Schlafly, Phyllis (1924–)

An author, speaker, lobbyist, and conservative leader, Phyllis Schlafly's greatest success was the defeat of the Equal Rights Amendment. She also became an expert on nuclear strategy and worked to convince Americans of the dangers of communism and the necessity of maintaining a strong American defense during the Cold War. Schlafly is the heroine of many supporters of the traditional family and the enemy of nearly all liberal feminists.

Schlafly was born in St. Louis, Missouri, to Roman Catholic parents. Her father opposed the New Deal even though he lost his job during the Depression and her mother was forced to become the family's sole provider. Schlafly's father worked on inventing a rotary engine (patented but never sold) and extolled the free-enterprise system. During

World War II, Schlafly attended hometown Washington University while working nights as a test gunner in a munitions plant. She graduated Phi Beta Kappa in three years and then went on to earn a master's degree in political science from Radcliffe in 1945. In 1949, she married attorney J. Fred Schlafly Jr. and made Alton, Illinois, her home. Their six children were born from 1950 to 1965. Schlafly obtained her law degree in 1978.

In 1952, Schlafly ran for Congress and began a lifelong practice of attending Republican National Conventions, often as an elected delegate. A member of Dwight D. Eisenhower's Kitchen Kabinet, Schlafly organized seminars and compiled study guides to inform Americans of the dangers of communism, and she continued to lecture on this theme throughout the Cold War. In 1964, she published the influential bestseller *A Choice Not an Echo,* in which she revealed how powerful, liberal "kingmakers" controlled the outcome of the Republican conventions. The book also endorsed Arizona Senator Barry Goldwater (whom she admired for his strong support of nuclear defense) and proved instrumental in his nomination as the Republican presidential candidate for the 1964 elections.

With Rear Admiral Chester Ward, Schlafly wrote five intensive studies detailing the threat of Soviet nuclear strategy and the weakening of American defense. *The Gravediggers* (1964) and *The Betrayers* (1968) indicted men such as Defense Secretary Robert McNamara for disarming the U.S. while Soviet nuclear strength grew. *Strike from Space* (1966) warned that while Soviets kept the United States entangled in a conventional war in Vietnam, they planned a nuclear attack via space missiles. *Kissinger on the Couch*

Phyllis Schlafly

(1974) and *Ambush at Vladivostock* (1976) criticized SALT I and Kissinger's influence on disarmament pacts signed by President Ford.

In 1967, Schlafly encountered opposition when she campaigned for the presidency of the National Federation of Republican Women and lost the election, an event she discussed in her book *Safe—Not Sorry* (1967). Nonetheless, she maintained a large following among Republican women and formed the Eagle Trust Fund to amass support for conservative projects. She also began publishing *The Phyllis Schlafly Report,* a monthly newsletter of ideas and relevant news. Schlafly ran for Congress again in 1970. She lost the election, too, but soon after began the work for which she is best known: the battle against the Equal Rights Amendment (ERA).

The ERA had passed in Congress and been ratified by thirty of the thirty-eight states needed to make it law when Schlafly founded STOP ERA in 1972. Drawing on personal and political experience, she revealed its threat against those it seemed to protect: women. She argued that section one, which states, "Equality of rights under the law shall not be denied or abridged by the United States or by any State on account of sex," would deny women exemption from the draft and military combat. It would invalidate labor laws designed to protect women and laws that required husbands to support their wives and pay alimony. It would allow homosexuals the same rights as married couples, such as the adoption of children. A woman could demand abortion to maintain her equality with men claiming that, like men, she had a right not to be pregnant. Moreover, section two would give Congress the power to enforce the amendment, threatening individuals' and states' rights and enlarging central government. And she pointed out that the amendment would not mandate equal pay for equal work.

Through an endless battery of tactics and ideas, Schlafly was able to maintain the attention of the press. She fought the ERA by publicizing her arguments through newsletters, debates, public appearances, and her book, *The Power of the Positive Woman* (1977), which consisted of arguments against the ERA and reflections on womanhood. "It is on its women," Schlafly writes, "that a civilization depends—on the inspiration they provide, on the moral fabric they weave, on the parameters of behavior they tolerate, and on the new generation that they breathe life into and educate."

In 1972, Schlafly founded the Eagle Forum to organize traditional conservative support. Her "Eagle Forum Newsletter" instructs her followers on letter-writing campaigns, rallies, and fundraisers. Under Schlafly's leadership, Eagle Forum has grown to include 80,000 members with chapters in more than forty states. In addition to her work as president of the Forum, Schlafly has remained active in political matters, serving many times as a delegate at National Republican Conventions. She also continues to speak on daily and weekly radio programs and to write a nationally syndicated column for the *Phyllis Schlafly Report.*

—KRISTEN SIFERT

Further Reading

Critchlow, Donald T. *Phyllis Schlafly and Grassroots Conservatism: A Woman's Crusade.* Princeton, N.J.: Princeton University Press, 2005.

Felsenthal, Carol. *The Sweetheart of the Silent Majority.* Garden City, N.Y.: Doubleday, 1981.

Schlafly, Phyllis. *Feminist Fantasies.* Dallas: Spence, 2003.

See also: Eagle Forum; Equal Rights Amendment; family

Schlamm, William (1904–78)

A staunch Cold Warrior and a founder of *National Review,* William Schlamm, born in Austria, was a communist in his teens but, disillusioned, forsook communism at age twenty-five. He edited a left-wing journal in Vienna, shifting to Prague when Hitler took power and finally fleeing to America in 1938, where he joined the staff of *Fortune* three years later. In 1943 he became a foreign policy adviser to Henry Luce, the publisher of *Time, Life,* and *Fortune.* Luce promised Schlamm the editorship of a projected new magazine, which never materialized. Schlamm left Luce in 1951 and helped edit the *Freeman* until 1954. He also edited William F. Buckley Jr. and Brent Bozell's *McCarthy and His Enemies* (1954).

Schlamm's greatest contribution to conservatism was persuading Buckley to create *National Review.* After failing to interest Henry Regnery in a magazine, he approached Buckley, who was enthusiastic. Buckley and Schlamm raised funds and recruited a staff. Schlamm became an editor, with columns on foreign affairs and the arts.

Due to friction with his colleagues, Schlamm left *National Review* in 1957. He emigrated to Germany and a new career in journalism. After a few years Schlamm and Buckley reconciled, and in 1965 Schlamm's work began reappearing in *National Review.* In 1971 he founded his own monthly journal, *Die Zeitbühne.*

Schlamm also wrote *This Second War of Independence* (1940), an examination of Hitler's conquest of Western Europe and its implications for America, and *Germany and the East-West Crisis* (1959), which argued for an American alliance with West Germany against communism.

—JOHN ATTARIAN

Further Reading

Hart, Jeffrey. *The Making of the American Conserva-

tive Mind: National Review *and Its Times.* Wilmington, Del.: ISI Books, 2005.

See also: *émigré intellectuals;* National Review

Schumpeter, Joseph A. (1883–1950)

Austrian economist and social thinker Joseph Alois Schumpeter earned his doctorate in economics at the University of Vienna in 1906. His academic career was interrupted by a brief tenure as Austria's finance minister in 1919 and then as bank president until 1925, when he accepted a position at the University of Bonn. In 1932 he came to Harvard and remained professor there until his death. Schumpeter authored ten books, of which three were published posthumously, and more than 1,900 articles and other writings. Among his works, *Capitalism, Socialism and Democracy* (1942) stands out as a work that bridges the disciplines of economics, sociology, and political science. Written for a broad audience within and outside the economics profession, this work continues to inform public opinion on aspects of economic development. While the message of this most famous of Schumpeter's works can be understood as broadly conservative, a more detailed analysis reveals a rather contradictory picture.

Joseph A. Schumpeter

To Schumpeter, the study of capitalism was not merely a matter of technical economic analysis, but a broad historical investigation of the interaction between economy, polity, and society. In his writings capitalism is presented as a unique stage in human history, the only known society whose emergence, development, and survival depend on continuous innovation. This innovation, in his view, was not just the result of a gradual accumulation of technological advancements, but rather the consequence of radical departures from the status quo undertaken by risk-taking, profit-seeking individual entrepreneurs. Entrepreneurial innovation is only possible in a democratic political system and in a culture valuing individual initiative. The centrality of individual entrepreneurship for innovation is based on Schumpeter's analysis of competition, whereby even large monopolies can be swept away by the "gale of creative destruction." His idea that monopolies emerge as a result of successful innovation and ultimately are doomed to destruction when the next major breakthrough makes them obsolete puts in doubt the plausibility of antimonopoly legislation currently in effect in virtually all developed economies (if innovation makes monopolies susceptible to market forces, government interference is redundant at best). While attributing the very vitality of capitalist economic order to continuous entrepreneur-driven innovation, Schumpeter interpreted the growth of research departments in large industrial firms as an indication that the entrepreneurial function was about to be taken over by the salaried employees of large corporations whose culture is virtually indistinguishable from that of government bureaucracy. Schumpeter thought that this process would ultimately spell the end of the free market economy, together with its institutional arrangements: a democratic polity and cultural system based on individual enterprise. He envisioned "The March to Socialism" as a gradual transformation to a centrally controlled economy. Schumpeter did not advocate this development, but thought it likely, judging by the centralizing trends of his time.

Writing in 1942, Schumpeter estimated that capitalism would achieve the apex of its development in approximately fifty years and would be gradually transformed into socialism as innovation ceased to be an individual endeavor and became a corporate activity. While this might indeed have been the case had innovation been confined to large corporations, in real life qualitative, ground-breaking innovations are still made by small firms that grow large as they reap the benefits of their pioneering endeavors.

While Schumpeter's political convictions were decidedly anticommunist (in 1919, he used his influence as Austria's finance minister to assist a group of Hungarian counterrevolutionaries), he was unwilling to challenge the emerging orthodoxy in contemporary economic and social thought that tended to justify increased state interference in the economy as well as abridgment of individual freedom. Schumpeter was one of the few conservative thinkers who did take Marx seriously, so much so that his biographers, including Edouard Maerz and Wolfgang Stolper, have difficulties drawing a line between Marx's historical dialectics and Schumpeter's historicism. His acceptance of Marx's vision of social and economic change contributed to his mistaken prediction that capitalism would eventually be replaced by socialism.

—ANDREW SAVCHENKO

Further Reading

Maerz, Edouard. *Joseph Schumpeter.* New Haven, Conn.: Yale University Press, 1991.

Schumpeter, Joseph. *Economics and Sociology of Capitalism.* Edited by Richard Swedberg. Princeton, N.J.: Princeton University Press, 1991.

———. *Essays.* Edited by Richard V. Clemence. Cambridge, Mass.: Addison-Wesley Press, 1951.

———. *Ten Great Economists, from Marx to Keynes.* New York: Oxford University Press, 1951.

Stolper, Wolfgang F. *Joseph Alois Schumpeter: The Public Life of a Private Man.* Princeton, N.J.: Princeton University Press, 1994.

See also: Austrian school of economics; capitalism; Marxism; socialism

science and scientism

The emergence and growth of modern science to a position of cultural and technological prominence and potency since the seventeenth century has been the glory, curse, and riddle of modern civilization. Its benefits are most easily seen and stated and have come to distinguish the West as the cynosure of "globalist" world development and attention. The gradual increase in collective, cumulative human power over nature has diminished or eliminated a great deal of the human ignorance, weakness, vulnerability, superstition, and other kinds of misery that surely plagued the overwhelming mass of humanity in the West before the eighteenth century and still afflict masses of people in other parts of the world. Examples of beneficial technological applications of scientific knowledge and methods are too obvious and numerous to require mention; for many people today they are synonymous with civilization itself. To take only one case, advances in horticulture in and since the sixteenth century initiated a still-continuing agricultural revolution that has steadily increased the capacity to feed more and more people decently throughout the world. American plant breeders such as Luther Burbank prepared the way for the vastly productive "Green Revolution" that started in the mid-1940s and is perhaps best represented by the work of the American agronomist Norman Borlaug, who received the Nobel Prize in

1970 for his work in improving the world's food quality and supply.

But as early as the late Renaissance, perceptive thinkers began to worry about both theoretical and practical problems brought by the scientific method and its applications. The French Christian humanist Rabelais worried that "Science without conscience is nothing but the death of the soul," which is to say the death of the regulative, moral, human dimension that should govern and direct scientific and technological developments to beneficial human ends. Rabelais suggested that while the printing press was a clear gain (though one might wonder while looking at a modern newsstand), the invention of gunpowder probably wasn't. Mutatis mutandis, while penicillin was a clear gain, the rapidly repeating rifle was not; while the "Green Revolution" was, the "Red" Bolshevik Revolution, which styled itself "scientific socialist," was not; and so forth.

Although its roots can be found in classical Greek debates between Plato, Aristotle, and Greek scientists, the controversy over the meaning, status, significance, and effects of the modern "Scientific Revolution" began in earnest in England and France in the seventeenth century and in fact has subsequently never ceased, except when prohibited, as in effect it was in the communist "scientific-socialist" states. The shorthand phrases for this debate are "the Ancients-Moderns dispute" in the seventeenth and early eighteenth centuries, the controversies over "Enlightenment" and "progress" in the eighteenth and nineteenth centuries, continuing into our own time, and the late-nineteenth and twentieth-century disputes about "the two cultures," the environment, and biotechnology.

These debates have occurred not only between and within nations, cultures, and eras, but sometimes even within families. Thus the polymathic humanist man of letters Aldous Huxley, having written the powerfully traditionalist satirical-philosophical novel *Brave New World* (1932), also wrote critically of uncritical scientific utopianism to his own brother Julian Huxley, first Director-General of UNESCO, the United Nations Educational, Scientific, and Cultural Organization. "I [feel] rather dubious about the whole [modern] idea of progress," Aldous Huxley wrote to his brother on October 27, 1946. "[We] never get anything for nothing. Gains in one field are paid for by losses in another." He went on to cite revealing remarks by a traditional Chinese scholar visiting California, saying what must seem to us particularly poignant in light of the overwhelming defeat of traditional China and its civilization by the simplicities and brutalities of Marxist "scientific socialism" a few years later. Speaking of Confucian China in light of the "advanced" West, the Chinese scholar said, "We understand more than we know; you know more than you understand." Aldous Huxley commented, "Is the increase in knowledge at the expense of 'understanding' a progress? I don't know, and I see no reason to suppose that anyone else does either." In raising this doubt he continued a line of criticism that had been articulated by many of the greatest Western Christian and humanist writers in varying degrees and with varying emphases but the same substance: John Donne, John Milton, Blaise Pascal, Jonathan Swift, Samuel Johnson, and Edmund Burke, to name a few in the period 1600–1800. It is also interesting to note the recourse of culturally conservative modern thinkers to traditional Confucian views: Irving Babbitt, Ezra Pound, and most recently William Theodore deBary have written in this vein. The brilliant but tragic Pound, for instance, wrote in 1938 that "rapacity is the main force in our time in the Occident," and such critics would now say that this amoral rapacity is everywhere. (The depredations of Chinese communism against Lamaist Buddhism in Tibet are a stark example of the more general assault of a rapaciously modernist ideology against a traditional religious-moral culture.)

At the heart of the religiously and culturally conservative critique of the utopian worship and uncritical application of science is the criticism of what the historian and philosopher of science Stanley L. Jaki calls "the cult of the quantitative method known as scientism, physicalism, and reductionism." Critics of scientism, who include many scientists, do not necessarily criticize it primarily on fideistic religious grounds (as Islam and fundamentalist forms of Judaism, Christianity, and other religions do) or on idealist or pantheist grounds (as Romantic thinkers like Goethe and Blake and idealist philosophers such as Hegel—and all their various followers—have done). Instead, they criticize it initially on classical rational grounds. Briefly put, the critique lodged by Western rationalists from Socrates, Plato, and Aristotle down to the present has been that the proper elementary understanding of rationality indicates that science is a valid and purposeful subset of rationality, but that it is clearly contradictory to assert that "only scientific statements have validity": science is a subset but is not equivalent to the set "rationality" or "rational phenomena" or "rational statements." To say that "only factual statements have validity" is a "thematic-performative" self-contradiction, because it is not itself a factual statement. To say that all thought and behavior are determined by the impersonal laws of matter, space, time, mass, and energy that science discerns is self-contradictory because the person who makes this statement assumes that he (and his reader or hearer) is exempt from the force of the generalization just made. He implicitly claims for himself free will, rationality, and an interest in truth, validity, and evidence, although his generalization denies these qualities. As a wise and witty French thinker ironically put it, "C'est librement qu'on est deterministe"—"It is freely that one chooses to be a determinist."

For more than 2,000 years Western thinkers were educated in light of the explanation of the working of rationality and its indispensable minimum understanding of the principle of noncontradiction (PNC) given by Aristotle (who, in this respect as in others, Dante called "the master of all those who know"). Such thinkers were in little danger of succumbing to an obviously contradictory scientistic materialism. Partly through the influence of Descartes—who rejected Scholastic method and Aristotle's definition of knowledge—thinkers began to see the goal of science as the enthronement of man as the "master and possessor of nature." In his philosophical-moral masterpiece *Gulliver's Travels* (1726), the Christian Aristotelian and traditional humanist Jonathan Swift defended Aristotle against the modernist "Enlightened" thinkers throughout Europe who had dismissed him in favor of utopian hopes and projects based on the Baconian slogan that "knowledge is power."

Among early-twentieth-century thinkers it was perhaps the philosopher Alfred North Whitehead who put the main point against scientism most pithily and memorably: "Scientists animated by the purpose of proving themselves purposeless make an interesting subject for study." The organized use of reason is a purposeful endeavor entailing thought, conscience, will, language, conceptual standards of truth and validity, and procedures of logic and argument that are themselves nonphysical ("metaphysical") and undetermined (though not unconditioned or unlimited). That these elementary facts are no longer widely understood in the West is in no conceivable sense intellectual or moral "progress" or the progress of "Enlightenment" and civilization. For so brutal and primitive a mental system as Marxist "scientific socialism" to have attracted so many minds in the West in the last 150 years suggests that the desertion of classical rationality was a catastrophe for the human species.

Jaki has illuminated another aspect of the main point against scientism. As opposed to the false and terrible simplifications of reductionism and scientism, in truth "there remains a mutual conceptual irreducibility between quantities and all other categories, [and] there remains an irreducible difference, indeed an opposition, between the sciences and the humanities." From Rabelais through Pascal, Swift, and Johnson (see *Rasselas* [1759] and his "Life of Milton" in *Lives of the English Poets* [1779]), down to Whitehead, Etienne Gilson, C. S. Lewis, and Jaki, it has also been apparent that, as Jaki puts it, "the scientific method [provides] no guidelines for the proper handling of the awesome tools science provides."

The numerous critics of Machiavelli from the Renaissance onward had noticed that his line of "scientific" thinking about human nature was a profound departure from classical and Christian ethics. Machiavelli viewed the human being as an amoral, competitive, devious animal fundamentally actuated by what St. Augustine called the lusts or drives for power and pleasure ("libido dominandi" and "libido sentiendi"): Hobbes's "homo hominis lupus"—man the wolvish devourer of man. From the 1760s on in France such amoral naturalism was in the ascendant, though usually married to a credulously and falsely optimistic assessment of human nature and history that has subsequently been amply disproved by events. We owe to a series of modern scholars who have studied this period—but especially to Irving Babbitt, Paul Elmer More, Aldous Huxley, Basil Willey, Lester Crocker, and Louis Bredvold—the realization of the pervasive and propulsive force of what Crocker called "The Nihilist Dissolution," seen best in the writings of the Marquis de Sade, himself a student of La Mettrie's *Man a Machine* (1749). This is one version of a fully "scientific" view of the human person, one that became widespread among individuals and ideologies in the twentieth century.

The German physicist Max Born, a refugee from the Nazis who went on to win the Nobel Prize for Physics in 1954, put this issue in its most somber implication: "I am haunted by the idea that this break in civilization, caused by the discovery of the scientific method, may be irreparable." He continued: "The political and military horrors and the complete breakdown in ethics which I have witnessed during my life may be . . . a necessary consequence of the use of science." If so, Born concluded, "there will be an end to man as a free, responsible being." The fear that reductive "science might deanthropomorphize human beings" (John Passmore) has been at the heart of the critique of scientism at least since Rabelais, and probably since Socrates, Plato, and Aristotle tried to vindicate purpose and reason against the ultimate demoralization of mechanistic naturalism. "All our cultural ills and woes," Jaki writes, "the disintegration of Western culture unfolding before our very eyes, are due to a growing loss of the sense of purpose." This is what C. S. Lewis called "the abolition of man." It is an ironic and tragic—but possible—destination of the career of modern science.

—M. D. Aeschliman

Further Reading

Aeschliman, M. D. *The Restitution of Man: C. S. Lewis and the Case against Scientism.* Grand Rapids, Mich.: Eerdmans, 1998.

Crocker, Lester G. *Nature and Culture: Ethical Thought in the French Enlightenment.* Baltimore, Md.: Johns Hopkins University Press, 1963.

Huxley, Aldous. *Ends and Means.* London: Chatto & Windus, 1937.

Jaki, Stanley L. *Means to Message: A Treatise on Truth.* Grand Rapids, Mich.: Eerdmans, 1999.

Lewis, C. S. *The Abolition of Man.* London: Oxford University Press, 1943.

Maritain, Jacques. *Three Reformers: Luther,*

Descartes, Rousseau. New York: Charles Scribner's Sons, 1929.

Whitehead, Alfred North. *The Function of Reason.* Princeton, N.J.: Princeton University Press, 1929.

See also: Enlightenment; Jaki, Stanley; modernity and postmodernity; progress; progressivism; technology

Scopes trial

In 1925, the Tennessee state legislature made it unlawful for any teacher in the public schools "to teach any theory that denies the story of the Divine creation of man as taught in the Bible, and to teach instead that man has descended from a lower order of animals." Answering an invitation of the American Civil Liberties Union, John T. Scopes, a high school teacher in Dayton, Tennessee, arranged to have himself charged with violating this law. At his trial in Dayton in July 1925, his defense was led by Clarence Darrow, the most famous trial lawyer of the time. The prosecution was led by William Jennings Bryan, a former presidential candidate of the Democratic Party who had become a leader of the Protestant fundamentalist movement. The trial became a dramatic battle between those defending Darwinian evolutionary theory as an expression of modern scientific enlightenment and those opposing it as a threat to morality and religion. Although Scopes was convicted, a technical mistake by the judge allowed an appeals court to overturn the conviction, which deprived the ACLU of any chance to appeal the case to the United States Supreme Court.

Historians sometimes depict the trial as a debate between the reactionary conservatism of Bryan and the progressive liberalism of Darrow, yet both Bryan and Darrow were progressive Democrats. Like the contemporary Marxist critics of sociobiology, Bryan believed that Darwinian theories of human nature would hinder social reform by denigrating the importance of cultural environment in shaping human behavior. In fact, the fundamental issue in this case—the proper relationship between science and morality—remains as controversial for American conservatives as for American liberals and radicals.

By the end of the nineteenth century, Darwin's teaching about the evolution of the higher animals (including, for Darwin, human beings) from the lower was introduced into many biology textbooks without provoking much criticism even from religious leaders. But after World War I, the Darwinian "struggle for existence" was associated with German militarism and the Nietzschean "will to power." Protestant fundamentalists insisted that only a literal reading of the Bible as a source of moral guidance could protect Americans from the immoral materialism of Darwinian science. Many, like Bryan, believed it was therefore proper for legislatures to protect public school children from such a dangerous teaching. When Darrow argued that scientific ideas could never be morally harmful, Bryan pointed out that Darrow himself had warned of the dangerous consequences of reading Nietzsche in his famous defense of Nathan Leopold and Richard Loeb, the university students in Chicago who committed a murder to prove that they were "beyond good and evil." In 1953, Richard Weaver, in *The Ethics of Rhetoric*, restated Bryan's arguments as supporting the general conclusion that a legislature's supervision of the moral education of the young is properly concerned not so much with the factual truth of what is taught as with its ethical consequences.

In 1968 the U.S. Supreme Court ruled in *Epperson v. Arkansas* that laws prohibiting the teaching of evolution in public schools were unconstitutional because they represented an establishment of religion contrary to the First Amendment. Opponents of evolution then changed their strategy to passing laws requiring equal time for evolution and "scientific creationism." But in 1987 the Supreme Court decided in *Edwards v. Aguillard* that even these laws were unconstitutional if the legislative intent was clearly to promote the biblical doctrine of divine creation. William Rehnquist and Antonin Scalia, two of the more conservative justices, dissented in this case.

Many conservatives (like Tom Bethell, Irving Kristol, and President Ronald Reagan) have spoken of evolution as both scientifically unsubstantiated and morally dangerous. But others have defended it as a well-supported theory that supports traditional morality. Does it deprive human beings of their moral dignity as created "in the image of God" to explain the human species as "descended from a lower order of animals"? Some conservatives have argued that it does. But other conservatives believe that a Darwinian account of human beings as naturally moral animals supports a conservative view of ethics as rooted in human nature.

—LARRY ARNHART

Further Reading

Johnson, Phillip E. *Darwin on Trial*. Downers Grove, Ill.: InterVarsity Press, 1991.

Larson, Edward J. *Summer for the Gods: The Scopes Trial and America's Continuing Debate Over Science and Religion*. New York: Basic Books, 1997.

Morris, Henry M. *The Biblical Basis for Modern Science*. Grand Rapids, Mich.: Baker Book House, 1984.

See also: Bryan, William Jennings; creationism; fundamentalism; Protestantism, evangelical

Scottish Enlightenment

It is hard to offer a concise definition of the Scottish Enlightenment that does justice to the variety of ideas and themes that come legitimately within its scope, although (together with pretty much everything else in the academic world) the term has been rendered virtually meaningless in recent years by a kaleidoscope of postmodern deconstructions.

What can be stated, generally but fairly, is that Scotland and its universities experienced an extraordinarily vibrant intellectual discourse in the century after 1730, fuelled largely by the following social, economic, and political factors: the political union with England in 1707; the rapid commercial and economic expansion that occurred in the wake of the union; and the development of intellectual, social, and commercial ties with the American colonies. This intellectual discourse had, broadly, three areas of focus: moral philosophy; "philosophical history," or the exploration of progress in the history of civilizations and societies; and political economy. The questions raised reflected the wider tension between continuity and change affecting Scottish society as a whole: What was the source, or place, of "civic virtue" in a rapidly changing and increasingly market-driven society? How could the conflicting human impulses of sociability and self-interest be reconciled rationally to provide an authoritative basis for order in society? What is understood by "progress" in history, what drives it, and did a fast-expanding knowledge of scientific and historical "laws" leave room any longer for the providential working of God in human society?

The changes that affected Scottish society in the eighteenth century exacerbated existing social and political divisions—including those between Highland and Lowland communities, for example, between Whigs and Jacobites, and between high churchmen and radical Protestants. The vast (Lowland) majority of Scottish Enlightenment thinkers were loyal to the Hanoverian settlement and embraced the changes occurring around them as sources of cultural, social, and material enrichment. Such a state of rapid social and intellectual transition has powerful echoes today, as conservatives (in particular) grapple with the implications of technological progress and global commercial activity for virtue, spiritual life, and the cohesiveness of local communities. Whether, however, conservatives should view the writings of the Scottish Enlightenment philosophers as a source of comfort ("We have been through this before, and survived") or as a warning ("The only solutions these thinkers found opened the door to utilitarianism, relativism and historicism") remains a hotly debated point.

In 1727, Francis Hutcheson arrived from Dublin as professor of moral philosophy at the University of Glasgow. Hutcheson, sympathetic to Shaftesbury's critique of the philosophical foundations of classical republicanism, challenged Bernard Mandeville's rejection of a socially cohesive, innate benevolence in human nature and argued that men possess a "moral sense" by which they may perceive virtue and vice as real ideas, independent of an enforced political and legal system of punishment and reward. This theory of the "moral sense" placed universal human passions, appropriately directed by reason, education, and manners, at the heart of civilization and social progress. In so doing, it also downplayed the significance of high politics and law in the promotion of order and liberty in society.

This shift in the identification of the sources of social cohesion and progress—from the exemplary virtues of great men and lawgivers to the "invisible hand" of common human feelings—underpins much of the work of those thinkers, in various disciplines, who followed Hutcheson, although each of these extended the theme in somewhat different directions and jettisoned key aspects of the original position, including the idea of a "moral sense" itself. There is, for example, David Hume's (more skeptical) understanding of the importance of custom and approbation in moral education, Adam Smith's (more Stoical) application of the concept of "sympathy" in the exercise of civic virtue, and Thomas Reid's (more complex) focus on "common sense" rather than "moral sense" in the apprehension of reality and first principles.

Similarly, Adam Ferguson (*Essay on the History of Civil Society*, 1767, and *History of the Progress and Termination of the Roman Republic*, 1783), Adam Smith (*Lectures on Jurisprudence*, 1762–66), and William Robertson (*History of Charles V*, 1769, and *History of America*, 1777), among others, broadened the scope of historical method by developing an understanding of the "progress" and "decline" of civilizations through distinct stages of social arrangement. They imputed the distinctiveness of each stage to the complex interaction of a variety of natural, social forces, ranging from the advancement of manufacture and commerce to the awakening of curiosity in natural phenomena and the consequent expansion of scientific knowledge. Likewise, commerce, morality, and history were tightly combined in the works of political economy. Smith is, of course, the preeminent figure here, and it is instructive that his treatment of the subject in his *Wealth of Nations* (1776) effectively produced a sea change in thinking, from high-political or law-driven economic and commercial policy to an understanding of material prosperity rooted in the underlying coherence of spontaneous human impulses and moral affections.

The broader historical significance of the Scottish Enlightenment has generally been interpreted in two ways. First, many historians have attempted to trace the influence of thinkers such as Hutcheson, Lord Kames, and Dugald Stewart on prominent members of the founding generation in America, most notably Thomas Jefferson. There is much of value to be discovered here, not least a corrective to the simplistic connections often drawn between the American Revolution and Lockean contractual theory. However, the exercise can also give rise to an impression of the Scottish Enlightenment that is too homogeneous. For example, the "common sense" and "self-evident truths" of Jefferson and Paine had precious little in common with the "common sense" school of Thomas Reid or James Beattie. Indeed, the differences among Scottish Enlightenment thinkers ought to attract more attention than they do. Beattie, for example, was highly critical of Hume's philosophy, and Adam Ferguson's interpretation of the dominant aspects of human nature differed in important respects from that of Hutcheson.

The second interpretation focuses on the relationship between the Scottish Enlightenment and the historicism and utilitarianism of the nineteenth century. In this case, there is a temptation to discover an "inevitable" link between the movement's rejection of "metaphysical" certitude and absolutes and its methodological emphasis on historical circumstances and empiricism with the rise of relativism or pragmatism. As a result, the cohesive aspirations and religious assumptions of many of the leading thinkers are given insufficient attention. The aim of figures such as Adam Smith and Thomas Reid was not to reduce truth and reality to the boundaries of our knowledge of the material and sensory world, the path to extreme skepticism, but reasonably to chart the limits of certainty in philosophical and scientific enquiry, thus curbing the arrogance and potential excesses of rationalism and "metaphysics," while always acknowledging the orienting pull of a divine presence beyond our physical apprehension.

In fact, the emphasis on the natural "sociability" of man, the rejection of a priori "metaphysical" argumentation, the measured skepticism of David Hume, the moral and political implications of "common sense" thought, and the discovery of the constancy of human nature in the cumulative evidence of diverse cultures and eras have all come to form vital aspects of the conservative anti-ideological tradition of thought from Edmund Burke onwards.

—Ian Crowe

Further Reading

Broadie, Alexander, ed. *The Cambridge Companion to the Scottish Enlightenment.* New York: Cambridge University Press, 2003.

Stewart, M. A., ed. *Studies in the Philosophy of the Scottish Enlightenment.* New York: Oxford University Press, 1990.

See also: Enlightenment; liberalism, classical; Smith, Adam

Senior, John (1923–99)

A Catholic writer and educator, and a prominent advocate of the Great Books, John Senior received his B.A., M.A., and Ph.D. in the 1940s at Columbia University, studying under Great Books proponent Mark Van Doren. After teaching at Bard College, Hofstra University, Cornell University, and the University of Wyoming, Senior taught English and classics at the University of Kansas from 1967 to 1983. His teaching won him the Amoco Award and citation by *Esquire* magazine as one of America's fifty best teachers.

Greatly concerned with children's education, Senior argued that the Great Books movement failed because "the cultural soil has been depleted; the seminal ideas of Plato, Aristotle, St. Augustine and St. Thomas thrive only in an imaginative ground saturated with fables, fairy tales, stories, rhymes and adventures: the thousand books of Grimm, Anderson, Stevenson, Dickens, Scott, Dumas and the rest." Therefore children should "enjoy a thousand good books before they study a hundred great ones." His list of good books, which he deemed one of his most important contributions, is still used by numerous Christian homeschoolers.

While at Kansas, Senior, together with colleagues Dennis Quinn and Frank Nelick, created the Integrated Humanities Program (IHP), which in effect created a distinct college, Pearson, within the university. Reflecting its belief that students must be introduced to the good and the beautiful before the great and the true, IHP exposed its students to music, dance, poetry, and others of the fine arts. Although the program enjoyed much success, it also attracted much opposition, which eventually killed it. Specifically, Senior's presentation of the beauty of Christian culture, although it was astoundingly popular among students, brought ferocious criticism from the American Civil Liberties Union and other secularist groups and individuals, who charged that Senior was using the program to proselytize students.

In *The Death of Christian Culture* (1978), Senior presented a comprehensive diagnosis of the modern predicament. Beginning with Flaubert and Baudelaire, he argued, literature gradually became dominated by modernism, which, stressing artificiality and sensationalism, led to boredom, which in turn spawned fascination with pornography and perversion. Christianity betrayed itself by forsaking its principles and becoming engrossed in materialism and social panaceas. Education abandoned the liberal arts and the cultivation of the mind in favor of technique and careerism, leaving students uncultured and unable to cope with classical Greek, Latin, and even vernacular works. Liberalism perverted liberty to mean "everyone has the right to do what he wants," and

denied free will and responsibility, thereby liberating the evildoer to perpetrate abominations, while a society ignorant of justice simply does "not know what to do with him."

In *The Restoration of Christian Culture* (1983) Senior argued that Christian culture was centered on the Eucharist. He indicted television, technology, maleducation, and irreverent modern liturgy as factors in cultural decline. Senior recommended forsaking television, passive entertainments, and excessive consumption for a return to reading, active entertainments such as singing, and simpler lifestyles. Our predicament being ultimately spiritual, he advocated a return to traditional liturgy and a life of prayer, writing that "the simplest, most practical restoration of Christian Culture will be the reestablishment of contemplative convents and monasteries." Since Christian culture was inspired by Marian devotion, consecration to Mary, he concluded, is our "only recourse."

—JOHN ATTARIAN

Further Reading

Senior, John. *The Way Down and Out: The Occult in Symbolist Literature*. Ithaca, N.Y.: Cornell University Press, 1959.

See also: Great Books programs; homeschooling

separation of powers

The phrase "separation of powers" exists neither in the Constitution nor in *The Federalist*, which always speaks of "separation of the Departments of power." The Constitution has separate "departments" or branches: an executive department, a legislative department, and a judicial department. However, *The Federalist* emphasizes that what is separated are these *departments*, which, however, *share* the corresponding executive, legislative, and judicial *powers*. Thus, "separation of powers" both misleadingly omits that it is the *institutions* that are separated and misleadingly emphasizes the separation rather than the sharing of powers.

The Constitution *separates* the departments only partly to avoid, as *Federalist 47* states, "the accumulation of all powers legislative, executive, and judiciary in the same hands," which is "the very definition of tyranny." But the powers are *shared* to enable the departments to check and moderate one another. Thus, both the president's veto power and the Supreme Court's power to declare an act of Congress unconstitutional are legislative ("lawmaking") powers given to them in order to forestall both legislative oppression and legislative hostility or indifference to what *Federalist 10* calls "the permanent and aggregate interests of the community." Indeed, the constitutional "separation of powers," as we now imprecisely call it, was established largely to moderate and control Congress, because that was thought to be the greatest danger. "The legislative Department is everywhere extending the sphere of its activity, and drawing all power into its impetuous vortex," according to *Federalist 10.* And, as is pointed out in *Federalist 51,* "In republican government the legislative authority, necessarily, predominates."

Constitutional conservatives think the federal government should operate within the framework of the Constitution of 1789 as amended. They believe constitutionally "limited government" so understood is more likely than its opposite to conserve life, liberty, and property. Thus, constitutional conservatives seek to preserve and defend the "separation of powers."

Recently, constitutional conservatives like Robert Bork and Justices Rehnquist, Scalia, and Thomas have struggled to return the judicial department to its status as a mere coequal of the other two branches, in contrast to the "imperial judiciary" they believe it has become. What might be done about this "judicial usurpation of democ-

racy" divided thinkers on the right in the 1990s, splitting neoconservative thinkers such as Gertrude Himmelfarb, Walter Berns, and Peter Berger from others (puckishly labeled "theocons") such as Robert Bork, Hadley Arkes, and Fr. Richard John Neuhaus, editor of *First Things.*

Both groups agree in opposing the Supreme Court's claim to define the Constitution in whatever way a majority of justices see fit. They tend to agree that the Court is constitutionally limited to applying the will of the people as contained in the Constitution as understood at the founding and as amended in the manner prescribed by the constitutional text itself. They agree that the judiciary has usurped democracy by exercising powers that constitutionally belong to elected and removable representatives.

Their surface disagreement concerns the prudential judgment about whether this judicial supremacy has become so egregious and irremediable as to call into question the legitimacy of the American system as such. They may also implicitly disagree over the policies in the name of which the Court has most recently usurped democracy. Those policies have to do mainly with abortion and related matters and with the proper relationship of the public square and religion. Religious and social conservatives disapprove strongly of the substance of these policies; the neoconservatives either do not disapprove of them so strongly or do not think of them as so foundational or important.

Sometimes the separation of powers frustrates conservative policy preferences. An outstanding example was provided in the aftermath of the 1994 election. That election was a victory for conservatives, especially in the House, whose "Contract with America" called for, among other things, congressional term limits, constitutional amendments requiring a balanced federal budget and a line-item veto, and elimination of the marriage penalty. However, while conservatives managed to get substantial parts of the "Contract" adopted, they were unable to implement these central parts of their agenda.

These defeats were made possible by the separation of powers, which enables the Senate to "interfere" with what *Federalist* 63 terms the people's "irregular passion . . . until reason, justice and truth can regain their authority over the public mind." Naturally, conservatives had thought that their 1994 agenda stemmed from "regular passion." And had the voters continued to elect conservatives (especially to the Senate, as they did in 1994), their more "regular" passion would have been more fully implemented. Since they did not, the passion succumbed to the mitigating effects of the separation of powers. To quote *Federalist* 71, "The republican principle demands that the deliberate sense of the community should govern . . . but it does not require an unqualified complaisance to every sudden breese of passion, or to every transient impulse which the people may receive. . . ."

Notwithstanding that the separation of powers sometimes defeats temporary conservative political agendas, constitutional conservatives tend to see it as fundamentally serving conservative ends in the long run. The reason is that it is a permanent institutional obstacle to unrestrained government action, and constitutional conservatism's fundamental orientation to government action is that it should be restrained. The operational meaning of "restrained" is "until institutional restraints can be overcome." Such restraint serves both justice and individual liberty and security, which are in danger of being crushed by both society and government. For constitutional conservatism, such restraint is what "limited government" is.

—GARY GLENN

Further Reading

Franck, Matthew J. *Against the Imperial Judiciary: The Supreme Court vs. The Sovereignty of the People.* Lawrence, Kans.: University Press of Kansas, 1996.

Muncy, Mitchell, ed. *End of Democracy? The Judicial Usurpation of Politics.* Dallas, Tex.: Spence, 1997.

See also: constitutionalism; federalism; Federalist, The; *Supreme Court*

Sewanee Review

The *Sewanee Review*, one of America's most distinguished literary quarterlies, was founded at the University of the South in Sewanee, Tennessee, in 1892. The university, founded in 1868, is both a liberal arts college and a seminary for the Episcopal Church. While the *Review*'s founder, William Peterfield Trent, was a highly regarded scholar of English literature, the reputation of the quarterly is largely founded on its history over the last sixty years. In the 1940s two of the South's most respected writers, Andrew Lytle and Allen Tate, became associated with the *Review* and transformed it into a publication with world-class contributors—and readers.

Lytle and Tate were both closely associated with the "Southern Agrarian" writers, a group that also included Robert Penn Warren and Donald Davidson, among others. They were both creative writers—Lytle in fiction and Tate in poetry—but also gifted essayists. Like their fellow Agrarians, they believed that the religious and cultural traditions of the South, while tainted by slavery and other evils, retained virtues that could act as counterweights to the worst excesses of modern industrialism and individualism. They had wide-ranging contacts with other conservative-leaning movements, such as the New Humanism of Irving Babbitt and Paul

Elmer More, and the exponents of the New Criticism, such as Cleanth Brooks. All these thinkers shared a belief that the roots of Western civilization were under attack in the modern world and required a passionate, literate defense.

These writers quickly put their aesthetic and social convictions into the *Sewanee Review*, publishing not only literary works but also philosophical and cultural essays by the likes of Jacques Maritain and T. S. Eliot. The *Sewanee Review*'s roster of contributors has, since the editorships of Tate and Lytle, consisted of a parade of major literary talents, including Donald Davidson, Robert Lowell, Katherine Anne Porter, Caroline Gordon, Wallace Stevens, Dylan Thomas, Walter Sullivan, and Wendell Berry.

Tate actually served as the quarterly's editor for only a brief period (1944–47). Taking the reins from Monroe Spears (1952–61), Lytle edited the journal from 1961 to 1973, when George Core became editor. Under the editorship of Core, the *Sewanee Review* has continued to be a first-class publication devoted to literary excellence rather than passing fads and theories.

—GREGORY WOLFE

Further Reading

Bradford, Robert. "A *Review* of One Hundred Years." *Sewanee* (summer 1992).

Core, George, ed. *The Critics Who Made Us: Essays from* Sewanee Review. Columbia, Mo.: University of Missouri Press, 1993.

Lytle, Andrew, and Allen Tate. *The Lytle-Tate Letters: The Correspondence of Andrew Lytle and Allen Tate.* Edited by Thomas Daniel Young and Elizabeth Sarcone. Jackson, Miss.: University Press of Mississippi, 1987.

See also: Lytle, Andrew Nelson; Southern Agrarians; Tate, Allen

Sheen, Fulton J. (1895–1979)

Roman Catholic archbishop, prolific author, melodious orator, Fulton J. Sheen gained celebrity in mid-twentieth-century America through his Emmy-winning television program "Life Is Worth Living." He trumpeted Catholicism as harmonious with American values and entertained thirty million viewers with a popularized Christian-intellectual perspective on important issues of life and culture. Sheen vigorously attacked communism and was a personal friend of FBI Director J. Edgar Hoover (Sheen did, however, refrain from directly supporting Senator Joseph McCarthy).

Fulton J. Sheen

Sheen was born in El Paso, Illinois, and ordained a priest in 1919. A distinguished scholar, he earned two degrees from the Catholic University of America in Washington, D.C., in 1920; a Ph.D. from the University of Louvain, Belgium, in 1923; and the *agrege en Philosophie* from Louvain in 1925 (the first American to do so). His dissertation, *God and Intelligence in Modern Philosophy*, won the Cardinal Mercer Prize for International Philosophy and the admiration of G. K. Chesterton, among others. Sheen taught philosophy and theology at CUA from 1926 to 1950. During this time he began to write, lecture, and preach widely, anchoring "The Catholic Hour" radio broadcast heard by four million listeners beginning in 1930. Sheen wrote sixty-six books. His *Communism and the Conscience of the West* (1948) railed against the Soviet "religion" and called

Catholics to express equal zeal in their opposition to the Soviet system. Sheen studied and critiqued Sigmund Freud in *Peace of Soul* (1949), which became a bestseller.

Francis Cardinal Spellman of New York arranged for Sheen to be named head of the American branch of the Church's world missionary fund, the Society for the Propagation of the Faith, in 1950. Sheen was ordained auxiliary bishop of the New York archdiocese in 1951 and soon thereafter launched his television career, succeeding against the likes of Milton Berle and Groucho Marx. He led thousands to convert to the Catholic faith, including industrialist Henry Ford II, writer Clare Boothe Luce, and former communists Louis Budenz and Bella V. Dodd. Actor Ramon Estevez changed his name to Martin Sheen in his honor.

Fulton Sheen's admitted weakness was vanity, and he later lamented his expensive limelight lifestyle. Yet Sheen's motivation was spiritual: from his royalties he donated an estimated $10 million to the missionary fund; daily he spent an hour in quiet prayer.

Sheen's celebrity began to wane when in the early 1950s he accused Spellman of misusing missionary funds. Pope Pius XII sided with Sheen, but Spellman pulled the plug on Sheen's television series in 1957 and had Sheen appointed Bishop of Rochester, New York, in 1966, which effectively truncated his magisterial ascent. Sheen, having participated in the Church's Second Vatican Council (1962–65), controversially implemented its reforms in Rochester. Protest fermented over his proposed grant of Church property to a federal HUD project, and he was criticized for opposing the Vietnam War. An unsuccessful administrator, Sheen retired in 1969. Yet in his last ten years Sheen wrote, traveled, and spoke at a tremendous pace while battling heart disease. Two months after meeting newly elected Pope John Paul II (who personally lauded Sheen as "a loyal son of the Church"),

Sheen died on December 9, 1979, in his chapel.

—MATTHEW BOWMAN

Further Reading

Reeves, Thomas C. *America's Bishop: The Life and Times of Fulton J. Sheen.* San Francisco: Encounter Books, 2001.

Sheen, Fulton J. *A Fulton Sheen Reader.* St. Paul, Minn.: Carillon Books, 1979.

———. *Liberty, Equality, and Fraternity.* New York: Macmillan, 1938.

See also: Roman Catholicism

Simon, William E. (1927–2000)

A conservative financier, businessman, and philanthropist, William Simon served as secretary of the treasury from 1974 to 1977, during the Nixon and Ford administrations. His greatest contribution to American conservatism was his support, both financial and intellectual, of conservative-minded philanthropy and scholarship.

Simon left a lucrative Wall Street career in 1973 to become President Nixon's deputy secretary of the treasury. Later that year, he became "energy czar" during the Arab oil embargo. "I'm the guy that caused the lines at the gas stations," he once quipped. In April 1974, Simon was named treasury secretary, a post he held until the end of the Ford administration. In 1975, he created a political firestorm when he tried to persuade President Ford not to bail out New York City from its deep financial crisis.

An accomplished amateur athlete, Simon was an active member of the United States Olympic Committee for more than thirty years. After leaving government, he served as USOC treasurer from 1977 to 1981 and as USOC president during the subsequent four years. He was credited with rescuing the committee from near-bankruptcy, for providing crucial support for President Carter's decision to boycott the 1980 Moscow Olympics, and for playing a key role in organizing the hugely successful 1984 Olympic Games in Los Angeles. During the 1980s, Simon cofounded Wesray Corporation with Raymond G. Chambers. Simon and Chambers were recognized as pioneers of the "leveraged buyout"—that is, as adept at buying undervalued companies, bringing them to health, and selling them for large profits.

Simon wrote two bestselling books, *A Time for Truth* (1978) and *A Time for Action* (1980), both of which defended free enterprise and limited government against policies that stifled economic growth and threatened individual liberties. Simon closed *A Time for Truth* by urging business leaders to pay closer attention to the uses of their philanthropic contributions: "Most private funds," he wrote, "flow ceaselessly to the very institutions which are philosophically committed to the destruction of capitalism." Simon challenged business leaders and donors to "rush by the millions to the aid of liberty . . . [and] to funnel desperately needed funds to scholars, social scientists, writers and journalists who understand the relationship between political and economic liberty."

In this endeavor, Simon led by example. As a philanthropist, he made some $80 million in charitable contributions in a career of giving that began during his days as a bond trader on Wall Street. Perhaps his most important service to the conservative movement was his role as president of the John M. Olin Foundation from 1977 until his death. Under Simon's leadership, the foundation made farsighted grants to support innovative conservative scholarship and other intellectual work that energized a broad critique of the welfare state. While at Olin, Simon also helped groom Michael Joyce, who went on to become a prominent leader in conservative philanthropy as head

of the Bradley Foundation. In 1978, Simon cofounded (with Irving Kristol) the Institute for Educational Affairs, which provided funding to conservative-minded scholars. Simon also spearheaded the group that created the Philanthropy Roundtable. He served on the boards of the Heritage Foundation and the Hoover Institution, and he was also a trustee of the John Templeton Foundation.

—LEE BOCKHORN

Further Reading

Simon, William E. *A Time for Reflection: An Autobiography.* Washington, D.C.: Regnery, 2004.

See also: foundations, conservative; Olin Foundation

Smith, Adam (1723–90)

Adam Smith was, and saw himself as, both a scientist and a philosopher. As a scientist, he was an acute interpreter of natural phenomena; as a philosopher, he sought to uncover an intelligent pattern through the systematization of his material. His beliefs regarding moral philosophy and political economy are to be found not only in his famous *Theory of Moral Sentiments* (1759) and *Wealth of Nations* (1776), but in posthumously published material on jurisprudence, belles-lettres, and the history of science. Taken together, these works indicate how an advanced commercial society may reconcile natural liberty with ordered justice through the application of historically rooted principles that combine a belief in an unchanging human nature with an acceptance of dynamic social change. Consequently, Smith offers some pointers on how conservatives might resolve tensions deep within their own tradition—how to conserve essential values while accepting needed change, and how to defend principles while avoiding ideology.

Smith was born in Kirkcaldy, on the east coast of Scotland, in 1723 and studied at the

University of Glasgow (1737–40) and at Balliol College, Oxford (1740–46). On returning to Scotland from Oxford, he lectured on rhetoric in Edinburgh "under the patronage of Lord Kames," until his appointment, in 1751, as professor of logic at Glasgow. The following year, he was elected professor of moral philosophy there, a position he held for eleven years, during which time he achieved fame with the publication of his *Theory of Moral Sentiments*. In 1764, Smith took up a position as tutor to the duke of Buccleuch and in the same year traveled to France, where he met Voltaire and leading Physiocrats such as Quesnay and Turgot. It was at this time that he began the work that was eventually published in 1776 under the title *An Inquiry into the Nature and Causes of the Wealth of Nations*. From 1777 until the year of his death, in 1790, Adam Smith held the position of commissioner of customs, in Edinburgh, but he never published a third, projected work on the history of jurisprudence.

Smith's analytical system, which shows the strong influence of the thinkers of the Scottish Enlightenment, and of the new school of "philosophical" history in particular, is a powerful response to the problem of the lacuna between empirical fact and binding principles of law that also shaped the work of scholars such as David Hume, Francis Hutcheson, and Thomas Reid. In his claim that the human faculty of imagination brings coherence to diverse empirical facts and sensations, and in his methodological combination of inductive and deductive techniques, he steers clear of the skepticism of Hume and the egoism of Mandeville, on the one hand, and of the more sharply metaphysical doctrines of natural law and a passive belief in Providence on the other.

The key to understanding the workings of this imaginative faculty lies in the basic human impulses that, Smith observed, shape both our moral and our material existence.

The strongest of these impulses is sympathy—a complex, instinctive referral to "the other." In Smith's thought, the *sympathetic* instinct may be found at the root of both the development of moral awareness and the material well-being deriving from an appreciation that one's own needs (or self-interest) require cooperation and integration with the needs of "the other." These two branches are covered, respectively, in the *Theory of Moral Sentiments* and *Wealth of Nations*, and it is important to remember that they have a common, philosophical-scientific root. We should also keep in mind that Smith had not completed this systematic and integrative analysis at the time of his death.

The *Theory of Moral Sentiments* places Smith firmly among the thinkers, such as Hutcheson and Hume, who emphasize the role of aesthetics and the natural human passions in the shaping of principles of moral philosophy. In the way he links sympathy, imagination, and ambition, however, he moves beyond his contemporaries in two main respects. First, in developing the "sympathetic" link between the impartial spectator and the individual conscience, he injects an objective quality of imagination into the impulse of sympathy (in which sense Smith might be seen as a "philosopher of the normal," a term used by Dr. William Campbell to describe the political economy of Wilhelm Röpke). Secondly, his treatment of the motive of "self-love" reveals a subtle combination of utility and benevolence that passes between Hutcheson's reliance on a separate moral sense and Bentham's utilitarianism. Both of these concepts, conscience and self-interest, reveal the powerful influence of Stoicism on Smith's thought, and are vital in appreciating how Smith linked the natural and the moral—motive and judgment—within his system.

In the *Wealth of Nations*, Smith examines the stages of the development of systems of political economy but concentrates on advanced commercial societies to show how public benefit can emerge from the private pursuit of self-interest and how government can foster social harmony through the promotion of natural liberty among its subjects. It is the introduction of the division of labor that creates the conditions for opulence and a commercial society that reflects an advanced and natural (though not inevitable) form of mutual cooperation. The wealth of nations, then, is to be measured in terms of productive capacity and not in bullion—a point that leads Smith to an extended demolition of mercantilism and its interventionist policies (with reference to the exploitation and economic health of colonies and the impoverishing effect of wider restrictive factors such as monopolies and inappropriate forms of taxation). Smith then delineates the proper role of the public power—again, emphasizing areas that will promote the free exchange of goods and the mobility of labor in particular.

We are, however, not presented with a simplistic parallel between material and moral progress. On the contrary, in the final sections of the book, perhaps as a prelude to his unfinished third work, Smith issues warnings about the moral impact of opulence and the division of labor (seeing, for example, a legitimate role for government in ensuring the provision of basic education at a parish level) and emphasizes the need for governors to guard against purely sectional pressure from the mercantile and manufacturing interests.

For conservatives, one of the most attractive aspects of the *Wealth of Nations* lies in the link between "natural liberty" and eco-

Adam Smith

nomic practice, with its consequent skepticism about the beneficial effects of government planning; but the implications of Smith's thought require an awareness of the nature and significance of the links between political economy and his moral philosophy.

These links have often been simplified or overlooked by conservatives in their preoccupation with the struggle against socialism and the planned economy, while their enemies, in their assaults upon capitalism, have tended to ignore the distinctions that Smith attempted to maintain between the principles of motivation and those of judgment. In particular, Smith's famous image of an "invisible hand" conjuring common benefits from self-interested actions should not be interpreted either as a mechanical truth of human existence or as the working out of an unfathomable Providence.

Regarding Smith's broader analytical method, the naturalness of his system and the underlying, empirical contingency of its principles are also attractive to conservatives, as is Smith's integrative method, which produces a blend of attention to circumstance and diversity while recognizing the cohesion and unity of human nature under its Creator. More problematic, however, has been the historicist ingredient within that system. Furthermore, Smith's dynamic faith in progress seems to leave little room for the aristocratic practices and communal patterns of the past, and his idea of true patriotism, mirroring his critique of mercantilism, subordinates the historic claims of political sovereignty to the broader benefits of free trade.

—IAN CROWE

Further Reading

Muller, Jerry Z. *Adam Smith in His Time and Ours: Designing the Decent Society.* Princeton, N.J. : Princeton University Press, 1995.

Smith, Adam. *The Essential Adam Smith.* Edited by Robert L. Heilbroner. New York: W. W. Norton, 1987.

See also: capitalism; free trade; liberalism, classical; libertarianism; Scottish Enlightenment; West, E. G.

Sobran, Joseph (1946–)

Originally from Ypsilanti, Michigan, Joseph Sobran was undertaking graduate studies in English when William F. Buckley Jr. hired him to write full time for *National Review* (*NR*), where he was a senior editor from 1975 to 1993. Throughout his career, Sobran has distinguished himself as a critic of the media, the "culture of death," and the Left (which he calls "the Hive"), analyzing each with an incisive mind and a sharp wit.

Through the 1980s and the Persian Gulf War, Sobran criticized various Israeli policies and America's alliance with Israel. He contended that American taxpayers should not subsidize a state that was committed to socialism and discrimination against ethnic and religious minorities; moreover, he argued, the alliance needlessly alienated the Muslim world. In response to Sobran's criticisms, Norman Podhoretz, the editor of *Commentary*, accused him of anti-Semitism. The ensuing controversy exacerbated preexisting tensions between neoconservatives and paleoconservatives—tensions that liberals were only too eager to foment—during the 1992 presidential campaign of Patrick J. Buchanan, who was also a critic of the American-Israeli alliance. Bill Buckley, still Sobran's boss at *NR*, disagreed with his argument against the alliance; he found Sobran's statements at worst borderline anti-Semitic and at best impolitic and potentially offensive. Sobran denied all accusations of anti-Semitism, and stood his ground. His association with *NR* ended in 1993 when Buckley fired him. Buckley's reflections on the implications of this controversy for conservatism were published in book form as *In Search of Anti-Semitism* (1992). Sobran published a rejoinder to Buckley in a pamphlet called "How I Got Fired by Bill Buckley" (1993).

Academic and artistic interpretations of Shakespeare have been Sobran's favorite topic of cultural commentary. His long-standing interest in Shakespeare culminated in the book *Alias Shakespeare* (1997), in which Sobran argued, against contemporary academic orthodoxy, that the Bard was actually the Earl of Oxford, not a man from Stratford-upon-Avon.

Sobran has contributed to the *Human Life Review* (*HLR*) since its inception in 1975, building a reputation as an articulate defender of the unborn. Early on he recognized that legalized abortion struck at the heart of the unwritten moral constitution of America. Several of Sobran's essays for *HLR*, which were concerned with the protection of a culture of life, were published in a collection titled *Single Issues* (1983). The *Roe v. Wade* decision also highlighted for Sobran the dangers of the judicial usurpation of politics and the expansion of the power of the federal government. Since the end of the Cold War and the removal of the Soviet threat to America, the paleoconservatism and libertarianism latent in Sobran's earlier work have become even more salient. These positions are put forth in Sobran's newsletter, *Sobran's Own.* He also writes a nationally syndicated newspaper column and the "Washington Watch" column for the *Wanderer*, the conservative Catholic weekly.

—BRACY BERSNAK

Further Reading

Sobran, Joseph. *Hustler: The Clinton Legacy.* Edited

by Tom McPherren. Vienna, Va.: Griffin Communications, 2000.

See also: Buckley, William F., Jr.; Human Life Review; National Review; paleoconservatism

social Darwinism

Ever since the publication of Charles Darwin's *The Origin of Species* (1859) and *The Descent of Man* (1871), Darwinian biology has influenced American conservative thought through an intellectual movement commonly called "social Darwinism." Darwin's ideas about "the struggle for existence" and "survival of the fittest" in social evolution seemed to show the natural roots of the free competition of individuals favored by libertarian conservatives, which suggested that laissez-faire economics was dictated by natural law. Herbert Spencer, an English philosopher, was the most important interpreter of social Darwinism as a radical libertarianism that shaped the thought of American conservatives such as William Graham Sumner and Albert Jay Nock. Recently, some conservatives have adopted Edward O. Wilson's sociobiology as a new form of social Darwinism. Other conservatives, however, scorn Darwinian social theory as dangerous because of its association with a deterministic materialism that denies human freedom and dignity. Moreover, some religious conservatives reject Darwinism even as a biological theory because it denies God's activity as Creator. The fundamental issue is whether modern natural science is compatible with the conservative understanding of human nature.

Few people today are willing to identify themselves as social Darwinists because the term has become associated with eugenics and Nazism. Darwin himself praised the work of his cousin Francis Galton in founding the eugenics movement, and he spoke of racial differences in ways that could be interpreted as racist. Adolf Hitler, in *Mein Kampf* (1925), argued that in the Darwinian struggle for existence nature favored the stronger race over the weaker. Consequently, many conservatives avoid any association with social Darwinism for fear of appearing racist.

In defense of social Darwinism, it can be argued that Darwin and Spencer did not glorify brutal selfishness as the primary motive of human nature or deny the importance of social cooperation. In *The Descent of Man*, Darwin emphasized the "social instincts" that human beings share with other social animals; he insisted that the "moral sense" of human beings set them apart from all other animals. Spencer interpreted "survival of the fittest" in its ethical sense as the principle that "each individual ought to receive the good and the evil which arises from its own nature"; and he spoke of the uniquely human capacity for altruistic sympathy as the ground for the human sense of justice. Both Darwin and Spencer saw the family as a natural basis for social cooperation; and social Darwinist John Fiske, in *The Meaning of Infancy* (1909), argued that maternal care for children during their long period of dependency was the natural root of human morality. Edward Westermarck's *The History of Human Marriage* (1889) used Darwin's theory to defend the view that marriage and the family expressed natural human instincts. It is not surprising, therefore, that contemporary conservatives who are at least somewhat sympathetic to social Darwinism—people like George Gilder, Thomas Fleming, Charles Murray, and Francis Fukuyama—defend traditional family life as the primary experience through which human beings fulfill their social nature.

It is true, however, that Darwinism can be interpreted as promoting a crudely materialist view of human nature that would subvert the moral dignity of human beings. Darwin, in one of his private notebooks, wrote: "Why is thought, being a secretion of brain, more wonderful than gravity a property of matter? It is our arrogance, it is our admiration of ourselves." Remarks like that can be quoted by conservative critics like Gertrude Himmelfarb as evidence of a dogmatic materialism that leaves no room for human freedom and rationality.

In considering how to apply natural science to human morality and politics, which is the aim of social Darwinism, conservatives must ponder the ambiguity of our human place in nature: we are both a part of and apart from the order of nature. Our thinking and choosing are not completely determined by nature, but our capacities for thinking and choosing are part of our nature. We are free when we do what we want to do, but what we want to do is to satisfy the desires that constitute our nature.

—LARRY ARNHART

Further Reading

Darwin, Charles. *The Descent of Man*. Princeton, N.J.: Princeton University Press, 1981.

Fleming, Thomas. *The Politics of Human Nature*. New Brunswick, N.J.: Transaction, 1988.

Hawkin, Mike. *Social Darwinism in European and American Thought*. New York: Cambridge University Press, 1997.

Himmelfarb, Gertrude. *Darwin and the Darwinian Revolution*. New York: W. W. Norton, 1959.

Hofstadter, Richard. *Social Darwinism in American Thought*. Boston: Beacon Press, 1955.

Spencer, Herbert. *The Principles of Ethics*. 2 vols. Indianapolis, Ind.: Liberty Press, 1978.

See also: Murray, Charles; Nock, Albert Jay; sociobiology; Spencer, Herbert; Sumner, William Graham

socialism

"Socialism" is the term applied to an economic system where property is held in common and not individually, and where relationships among people are governed by the politically organized compulsion that this common property status entails. Socialism is thus opposed to the market economy, where relationships among people are organized on the basis of individual liberty and private property. The original socialist vision called for the abolition of private property and the replacement of market exchange with collective planning. No one any longer believes this form of social organization is workable. Rather than abandon socialism entirely, socialists have come now to think in terms of market socialism, a system that envisions islands of market exchanges scattered throughout a sea of collective planning.

The term "capitalism" was developed in the second half of the nineteenth century by Marxists and used as a term of criticism against the liberal system of free enterprise. The Marxist use was meant to convey the idea that the market economy was a system run by capitalists for the benefit of capitalists. This idea, when combined with the presumption that capitalists were few in number, with most people being laborers, was thought to prepare the ground for socialism to take root.

Much of the criticism of socialism has concerned its ability to promote the creation of wealth. Much discourse envisions some tradeoff between economic and ethical values. This tradeoff might hold that capitalism is economically more productive than socialism, but that socialism is ethically superior. Much of the literature on socialism has sought to show how socialism could be made more workable economically. With the ethical superiority of socialism being taken for granted, any reduction in the economic advantage of capitalism would expand the sphere over which socialism could be practiced. As a pragmatic matter, then, some socialists might favor a gradual or creeping socialization, with the rate of movement determined by the steepness of the tradeoff between economic and ethical value.

Common ownership does not mean that decisions concerning the use of resources are made collectively by the collectivity. Rather there will be individuals in positions of authority who will make choices in the name of the collectivity. Once this simple point is acknowledged, it becomes necessary to inquire into the operation of collective ownership. For there is good reason to believe that collective ownership will almost inescapably result in oligarchical and tyrannical rule, even if that rule is democratically organized.

Socialism arose as a rebellion against the impersonal relationships that were thought to characterize a market economy. Marx used the term "alienation" to express the idea that production in a market economy was for the market and not for direct use. The product of a worker's labor was alienated from that worker through market transactions. Socialism was envisioned as a form of social organization that would avoid this alienation.

Socialism treats the national economy as an extended family and approaches economic organization from the perspective of household management. The sentiment "from each according to his abilities, to each according to his needs," does surely characterize well-working family relationships. The members of a family generally do contribute to the family economy according to their abilities, both in dealing with the outside world and in handling household tasks. Allocations of family resources are generally made on the basis of needs and not according to the market value of the work performed by individual family members. Socialism takes the ethical and organizational principles of a family and seeks to apply them to a national economy. Organizationally, this requires the replacement of market allocation processes by a planning process, in which the planning agency represents the household manager. But how can this be accomplished in any actual economy?

Private ownership is often portrayed in terms of fences and the like, with the focus on the separation of one person's possessions from another's. Common ownership, by contrast, is typically portrayed as featuring togetherness. Yet the reality is starkly different. Private ownership draws people together to pursue activities of mutual gain. In a well-ordered society private property and the pursuit of personal interest lead to the advancement of all. But throw in common property and the reverse results—common interest is sacrificed for personal.

The well-known "tragedy of the commons" illustrates socialism in operation. Consider the case of commonly owned oyster beds. The problem with common ownership is that small and large oysters are hauled up together, and effective management requires the small oysters to be returned to be caught at a later time. Socialism in this case requires self-denial even to have any chance at working. It requires the oyster fisherman to return small oysters for others to catch, despite the pain in his hands and his back from hauling in his nets.

Capitalism, on the other hand, requires no such self-denial. With private ownership, the oyster fisherman returns the small oysters to be harvested later after they have grown, because they are worth more to his consumers, and, therefore, to him. Capitalism is a workable ethic that promotes the common good. Socialism is an unworkable ethic that destroys the common good. The resonance of socialism in some quarters is testimony to the worship of the abstract notion that preaches the love of mankind while refusing to aid the neighbor who comes into proximity. Capitalism devalues the abstract, at least as a principle to be striven for, and deals with concrete settings. It harnesses people where they are into a coherent pattern of mutual assistance, not for the love of assistance, but because of the recognition that mutuality is the only prospect for peaceful and prosperous survival this side of Eden. Socialism, by denying fundamental truths of human nature, would spread destruction in the name of straining to achieve the impossible.

Within a well-working household, decisions concerning resource allocation are based on intimacy and love. Family members possess detailed, concrete knowledge of each other's abilities and needs, and they are bound together by love. But no matter how desirable an extension of the family model to a nation might sound, it is an utterly impossible extension to make. Socialism cannot resolve the problem of economic calculation, so it cannot achieve the social cooperation that is its pronounced objective. It is in no one's capacity to organize the economic activities of a complex society. Household management may be possible, but national economic management is not. The organization of economic activity can only occur through a bottom-up process, as it were. In a market economy, such organization arises through the interplay among persons when each pursues his interests, and when the relationships among people are governed by the legal principles of private property and freedom of contract. It is within such a framework that prices arise for goods and services, and these prices serve as valuable guides for enabling people to make economic decisions that form a coordinated pattern. The abolition of market exchange would destroy market prices and ipso facto the coordinating function that those prices perform.

The treatment of a socialist economy as an extended household is simply impossible because the requirements for the acquisition and use of precise, detailed knowledge are well beyond human capacity. Economic life in any but the simplest of societies is just too complex to be directed or planned by any social manager. This was true for the Soviet Union even in the days when it declared itself to be practicing central planning. For those plans were compiled from the bottom-up as a validation of what had been done, along with instructions to do 2 percent more the next year. This is not central planning, but rather a prediction of what is likely to happen, with the sum of those predictions being called a plan. As Paul Craig Roberts put the matter, "the Soviet economy can be viewed as a polycentric system with signals that are irrational from the standpoint of economic efficiency."

Alas, the recognition that economic calculation is impossible without markets has led not to the abandonment of socialism, but to the development of market socialism. This version of socialism envisions a sharp distinction between capital goods and consumer goods. There would be social ownership of capital goods, the produced means of production, but consumer goods would be owned individually and allocated through markets. The presumption in this case is that market prices for consumer goods can be used to derive valuations for capital goods, thus overcoming the knowledge problem that plagued socialism without markets.

Yet this version of socialism, too, is an exercise in fiction. Ludwig von Mises noted that the market socialists "want people to play market as children play war, railroad, or school. They do not comprehend how such childish play differs from the real thing it tries to imitate. . . . A socialist system with a market and market prices is as self-contradictory as is the notion of a triangular square."

In fact, the idea that it would be possible to derive capital-good valuations from consumer-good valuations is a fiction derived from a reification of abstract economic models. In a market economy there is a systematic relationship between the prices of consumer goods and capital goods, as all markets are linked together. But to abolish markets for capital goods through the collectivization of ownership does nothing to overcome the problems of economic calculation.

socialism

Indeed, the very distinction between consumer goods and capital goods is an analytical distinction developed by economists as an aid to thinking. But it is not a distinction that is capable of concrete implementation. For instance, is a car a capital good or a consumer good? Some might say it is a capital good when used in a business and a consumer good when used by individuals. But what if those individuals are in business for themselves? Thus, while the rigid separation between capital and consumer goods may be useful for analytic purposes, but is not useful as a concrete guide to economic planning. In a modern economy almost everything is a capital good, in that it yields services over time. Market socialism is as much a fiction as is socialism without markets.

Socialism is often portrayed with a humane face, as represented by the term *democratic socialism*. But however it is portrayed, socialism entails the substitution of group decision-making for individual choice. And group decision-making on a large scale tends to be oligarchic and responsive to special interests, even when it is democratically organized.

Socialism cannot prevent people from competing for what is scarce. All socialism can do is create offices of authority with the right to influence the outcome of such competition. Whereas winners under market allocations will be those who bid more money directly, under socialism the winners will be those who do so indirectly—and perhaps directly as well, depending on the extent of bribery. Whether the socialist system is authoritarian or democratic may well matter in several important respects, but in either case oligarchic governance for the benefit of special interest groups will have replaced the true democracy of the capitalist marketplace.

—Richard E. Wagner

Further Reading
Arnold, N. Scott. *The Philosophy and Economics of*

Market Socialism. New York: Oxford University Press, 1994.
Boettke, Peter J. *Calculation and Coordination: Essays on Socialism and Transitional Political Economy*. London: Routledge, 2001.
De Jasay, Anthony. *Market Socialism: A Scrutiny*. London: Institute of Economic Affairs, 1990.
Hayek, Friedrich A., ed. *Collectivist Economic Planning*. London: Routledge, 1933.
Mises, Ludwig von. *Socialism: An Economic and Sociological Analysis*. London: Jonathan Cape, 1936.

See also: Austrian school of economics; capitalism; Catholic social teaching; equality; Hayek, Friedrich A. von; ideology; liberation theology; Marxism; Mises, Ludwig von; property rights, private

sociobiology

In his book *Sociobiology*, published in 1975, Harvard biologist Edward O. Wilson defined sociobiology as "the systematic study of the biological basis of all social behavior." The leftist critics of Wilson's sociobiology attacked him as a biological determinist who was trying to promote racism, sexism, and capitalist ideology by grounding them in an unchanging human nature. Wilson insisted that sociobiology was ideologically neutral, supporting some liberal prejudices and some conservative prejudices in an unpredictable manner. The reaction of conservatives seemed to confirm this, because while some conservatives feared Wilson's Darwinian materialism as a threat to the moral dignity of human beings, others welcomed his Darwinian naturalism as showing the natural limits to social experimentation.

"The central theoretical problem of sociobiology," Wilson wrote, is "how can altruism, which by definition reduces personal fitness, possibly evolve by natural selection?" In answering this question, the most important contribution was the idea of "inclusive fitness" as developed in 1964 by William D. Hamilton: natural selection favors organisms that act not only for their individual fitness but also for the fitness of their offspring and other kin. Yet although this explains the social cooperation of organisms living in closely related groups, it does not explain the cooperation of organisms that are distantly related or even members of different species. To explain the latter, Robert Trivers in 1971 proposed the idea of "reciprocal altruism," in which altruism arises from a situation of "tit for tat": natural selection can favor an organism being altruistic so long as the altruistic organism receives some sufficiently large benefit in return. Cooperation within a group of individuals can arise whenever it benefits all members of the group, so long as the cheaters who refuse to contribute their fair share can be identified and punished. Even in very large groups, having a reputation for being cooperative can confer great benefits, which thus fosters cooperative behavior. Applying these ideas to human beings, it would seem that the social life of human beings as manifested in kinship, friendship, and citizenship expresses the biological nature of homo sapiens.

Since conservatives commonly lament the moral and cultural relativism that became intellectually fashionable in the twentieth century, it is understandable that some have welcomed the development of sociobiology as a scientific challenge to such relativism. Thomas Fleming, the editor of *Chronicles*, has defended sociobiology as providing scientific support for "natural politics"—a modern version of natural law in which political philosophy could once again be rooted in human nature. When Wilson received the Ingersoll Foundation's 1989 Richard M. Weaver Award for Scholarly Letters, his acceptance speech confirmed Fleming's argument. What bothers the leftist critics of sociobiology, Wilson explained, is "the threat perceived to the core precept of their belief

system—namely, that there is no human nature, that human behavior and human social institutions are entirely the product of economic forces and culture; in other words, that human beings can be shaped by imposing an ideal social order." By contrast, said Wilson, sociobiology suggests "that ideal institutions must conform to some reasonable extent with the biological realities of human nature."

For Fleming and others, including George Gilder, James Q. Wilson, and Francis Fukuyama, one of those "biological realities of human nature" is the difference between men and women. Men are naturally inclined to be more aggressive and competitive; women are naturally inclined to be more nurturant and prudent. Although men seek to dominate women, male violence expresses the sexual insecurity that makes them dependent on women. "The crucial process of civilization," Gilder argues, "is the subordination of male sexual impulses and biology to the long-term horizons of female sexuality." In the family, male nature is domesticated in the service of social order. This defense of sexual differences and family life as rooted in biological nature has become the core of the conservative attack on radical feminism. Even some feminists, however, acknowledge the sociobiological evidence for sexual differences: the true liberation of women requires not the transformation of women into men, or the creation of androgynous beings abstracted from their bodies, but the freedom for men and women to express their natures as two sides of human nature.

Another element of conservative political thought that seems to be supported by sociobiology is the argument for private property and economic exchange. Adam Smith presented his "system of natural liberty" as rooted in "a certain propensity in human nature . . . to truck, barter, and exchange one thing for another." The sociobiologist would see this as an expression of "reciprocal altruism." The failure of Marxist socialism demonstrates the foolishness of denying this biological propensity. Richard Pipes has argued that since acquiring property is a natural instinct for human beings, societies such as Marxist Russia that try to abolish or restrict private property must deny freedom and promote tyranny, because they must repress human nature. Even some leftist philosophers—such as Peter Singer—have conceded that a Darwinian science of human nature refutes the traditional leftist belief that human nature is so malleable that it could be radically transformed through utopian experiments in social reform.

Some conservatives have warned against such biological reasoning about human nature, because it seems to deprive human beings of their moral freedom by reducing human conduct to the level of animal behavior. It should be noted, however, that Darwin recognized the uniqueness of human beings as the only animals who engage in moral reasoning. Furthermore, the existence of biological inclinations does not deny freedom unless we adopt an absurd view of freedom as absolute indeterminacy. As Jonathan Edwards argued, the only uncaused or self-determined being is God; and therefore the only freedom that makes any sense for human beings is the freedom to do whatever one has the desire and ability to do within the range of desires and abilities that defines human nature. The "blank slate" argument—the denial that humans have any inborn tendencies and the claim that what we call instincts are products of environmental conditioning—fosters not human freedom but environmental determinism.

It is true, however, that sociobiological theory is sometimes stated in a reductionistic, even Hobbesian, manner, as if survival and reproduction were the sole motivations for human action, and as if cultural habits and rational reflection were not as impor-

tant as biological nature in shaping human life. Conservatives should be attracted to the work of theorists like Mary Midgley and Robert McShea, who have begun to work out a nonreductionistic account of human nature that draws upon sociobiological theory. The good is the desirable, they would argue, and the desirable varies according to the natural desires of each species. As members of the human species, human beings inherit a species-specific pattern of desires, a genetic structure of feelings that motivate human action. Since the genetic feeling pattern of the human species evolved among our hunting-gathering ancestors, that pattern of motivations remains the same despite obvious historical-cultural differences. Men and women still form families. Mothers still care for their children. Young males still compete for status and sexual identity. Societies are still organized into dominance hierarchies. Competing groups still go to war. And human beings still use language and other symbols to figure out what it all means.

Despite the apparent novelty of such sociobiological reasoning, conservatives such as James Q. Wilson and Francis Fukuyama recognize the tradition of biological theorizing about social life as Aristotelian. As a biologist, Aristotle spoke of human beings as political animals who could be studied in comparison with other political animals such as bees, ants, wasps, and some birds. He also saw important similarities between human beings and apes. So although Aristotle was not an evolutionist, his biological view of human nature anticipated the view adopted by Darwin, by social Darwinists like Herbert Spencer, and by contemporary sociobiologists.

Aristotle's claim that social and political arrangements can be judged as better or worse depending on how well they conform to the natural needs of human beings has been one element of conservative political theory. But within conservative thought Aristotelian naturalism seems to conflict with a Burkean culturalism that asserts the historical diversity of human beings as shaped by cultural traditions. One way to resolve this disagreement would be to revive Aristotle's notion of prudence as the practical activity of judging how best to serve human nature within the constraints of particular historical circumstances. Just as Edward Wilson says that the central problem of the social sciences is understanding the mechanism of biocultural evolution as the interaction of biology and culture, the Aristotelian-Burkean conservative would say that the central problem of conservative political theory is understanding the exercise of prudent statesmanship as guided by the universals of human nature and the contingencies of human history.

—LARRY ARNHART

Further Reading

Arnhart, Larry. *Darwinian Conservatism.* Exeter, U.K.: Imprint Academic, 2005.

Fukuyama, Francis. *The Great Disruption: Human Nature and the Reconstruction of Social Order.* New York: Free Press, 1999.

Gilder, George. *Men and Marriage.* Gretna, La.: Pelican, 1986.

Pipes, Richard. *Property and Freedom.* New York: Knopf, 1999.

Segerstrale, Ullica. *Defenders of the Truth: The Battle for Science in the Sociobiology Debate and Beyond.* Oxford: Oxford University Press, 2000.

Singer, Peter. *A Darwinian Left.* New Haven, Conn.: Yale University Press, 2000.

See also: Fleming, Thomas; Fukuyama, Francis; Gilder, George; social Darwinism; Wilson, James Q.

Sokolsky, George (1893–1962)

Journalist, industrial consultant, and spokesman for capitalism, George Sokolsky was born in Utica, New York, and educated at the Columbia University School of Journalism. He emigrated to Russia in 1917 and wrote for Petrograd's English-language *Russian Daily News.* Disabused of youthful radicalism by the Russian Revolution, Sokolsky moved to China and worked on various English-language newspapers there.

After returning to America in 1931, Sokolsky wrote for the *New York Times* and *New York Herald-Tribune,* serving as a columnist for the latter until 1940. Now a staunch advocate of capitalism, he wrote that "The right to win and use private wealth and to keep and use the benefits that derive from it is part of democracy." Sokolsky described himself as conservative, a capitalist in economics, "a rigid constitutionalist in my political thinking," and fearful of government power concentrated in one man. Sponsored by the National Association of Manufacturers, Sokolsky made weekly radio broadcasts from 1937 to 1941. He was also a consultant for the public relations firm Hill & Knowlton and the American Iron and Steel Institute. His book *The American Way of Life* (1939) upheld American corporate capitalism against the criticisms of consumer advocates. *Time* magazine called him "a one-man intellectual front for conservative capital" and a "star-spangled spieler for capitalism."

Sokolsky wrote a column, "These Days," for the *New York Sun* from 1940 to 1950, then wrote for the Hearst newspapers until 1962, with his column appearing in more than 300 papers. A fervent anticommunist, he was an advisor to Senator Joseph McCarthy and staunchly defended him in print.

—JOHN ATTARIAN

Further Reading

Cohen, Warren I. *The Chinese Connection: Roger S. Greene, Thomas W. Lamont, George E. Sokolsky and American–East Asian Relations.* New York: Columbia University Press, 1978.

See also: capitalism; McCarthy, Joseph R.

Solzhenitsyn, Aleksandr (1918–)

Aleksandr Solzhenitsyn has spent his whole life listening to "the sad music of Russia," his homeland, and writing of it. Therefore, it is unwise to try to place him on the spectrum of American political opinion. Indeed, viewing this fundamentally moral writer through the prism of politics has been the bane of his reception in the West. Even so, the overlap between his outlook and American conservatism is substantial. His view of life is thoroughly traditionalist, and he is famously anticommunist, though he himself considers anticommunism "a poor construction," since "Communism is anti-humanity" and thus "that which is against Communism is for humanity."

The tumultuous twentieth century forged many dramatic life stories, of which Solzhenitsyn's was one of the most improbable. As a boy he was reared on the Christian religion by his relatives, but the Marxism-Leninism learned from his teachers prevailed. He graduated from Rostov University, then married Natalya Reshetovskaya. As World War II broke out, he joined the Red Army, rising to artillery captain. For criticizing Stalin in a letter to a friend, he was arrested in 1945 and spent the next eight years in those prison camps which he was to name "gulag," a word that now appears in dictionaries as a common noun. Imprisonment was the defining event of his life; aided by the example of religious believers, he moved away from Marxism and back to Christianity. Next, he spent three years of what was to have been perpetual internal exile in Kazakhstan, where he taught high school mathematics and physics. He also, as he had intended from

Aleksandr Solzhenitsyn

boyhood, began to write, though now, given his radically altered viewpoint, he wrote "for the drawer" (or, literally, for jars to be buried in the backyard). Other dramatic episodes include narrowly surviving abdominal cancer and attempted assassination by the secret police (KGB).

The unknown schoolteacher burst onto the world scene in 1962 with his novella *One Day in the Life of Ivan Denisovich*, which Nikita Khrushchev himself approved for publication. For this first literary glimpse into the Soviet concentration camps, Solzhenitsyn was widely hailed as a truth-telling freedom-fighter, but Soviet officialdom soon reversed itself and refused further publication. Other works based on what he had experienced and learned through imprisonment, notably his novels *The First Circle* (1968) and *Cancer Ward* (1968), were published only outside his homeland. In 1970 he received the Nobel Prize for Literature. In 1972, with all hope gone of being published in his homeland, he made explicit the Christian beliefs that had been implicit in all his writings.

In 1973, when Solzhenitsyn learned that the KGB had gotten hold of a copy of *The Gulag Archipelago*, his history of the Soviet prison camps, he gave the signal, and Western presses, in possession of a smuggled-out copy, rolled. Therefore, on February 12, 1974, he was sent into exile, a fate that he had said was, for a Russian writer, worse than death. He passed two years in Zurich, Switzerland, then eighteen in Cavendish, Vermont.

As more of his worldview, especially its religious foundations, became known, Western intellectuals turned against Solzhenitsyn. His 1974 *Letter to the Soviet Leaders* gave momentum to this reaction, and his 1978 commencement address at Harvard University solidified it. Journalist Jeri Laber spoke for many when he lamented that Solzhenitsyn "is not the 'liberal' we would like him to be."

Solzhenitsyn would eventually spend most of his life writing on the great subject he had chosen in his youth, the events that culminated in the Bolshevik Revolution. This series of novels, his magnum opus (totaling some 5,000 pages and titled *The Red Wheel*), is now finished, though only *August 1914* (1971) and *November 1916* (1999) have appeared in English. Other published works include his autobiographical *The Oak and the Calf* (1975) and *Invisible Allies* (1995), plus many essays and speeches. Not yet available in English are the third and fourth volumes of *The Red Wheel*, memoirs of his exile in the West, a book about post-Soviet Russia, and a scholarly work on Russian-Jewish relations during the last 200 years.

Solzhenitsyn's first marriage, battered by prison-imposed separation and divergence of outlooks, ended in an acrimonious divorce in 1973. His second marriage was to one of his young "invisible allies," Natalia Svetlova, who became her husband's trusted confidante and coworker. They have three loyal sons: Yermolai, Ignat, and Stephan.

According to Solzhenitsyn, the "anthropocentricity" of the Enlightenment is the root cause of the horrors of the twentieth century, the utopian dreams of "rationalistic humanism" becoming the totalitarian schemes of ideology. In particular, states governed by communist ideology slaughtered innocent citizens on a massive scale. The central issue for him is one of belief: "the principal trait of the *entire* twentieth century," he has written, is that "men have forgotten God." To this atheism he counterposes a moral vision rooted in Christian teaching. He declares that "the line dividing good and evil cuts through the heart of every human being," and thus he attends primarily to "the timeless essence of humanity" and to those "fixed universal concepts called good and justice." Even of *The Gulag Archipelago* he announces, "[L]et the reader who expects this book to be a political exposé slam its covers shut right now." Although his Soviet context requires that he apply his moral vision to ideological politics, he complains about those who "always insist on regarding me in political terms, . . . completely missing the point that this is not my framework."

Solzhenitsyn was one of the few who anticipated the demise of the Soviet experiment, and throughout his exile he predicted that he would someday return home in the flesh. His three conditions for his return—that his citizenship be restored, that the charge of treason against him be dropped, and that all his works be published in his homeland—indicate that these two prophecies were one and the same. On Christmas Day 1991, the red flag over the Kremlin came down for the last time. After completing his magnum opus, Solzhenitsyn returned to Russia in 1994. Surprising everyone, he came not directly to Moscow but through the Pacific back door, embarking on a fifty-five-day train trip so that he could talk with people along the way and prepare to represent their views to the authorities.

Today many consider Solzhenitsyn a hero for delegitimizing the Soviet Union among his countrymen and discrediting it abroad. Certainly, he thought his writing would have world-historical import: "Oh, yes *Gulag* [*Archipelago*] was destined to affect the course of history, I was sure of that." But the negative consensus established in the 1970s has resulted in a degree of academic neglect of his writings. Recent studies of the collapse of the Soviet Union regularly, though sometimes only in passing, mention *One Day in the Life of Ivan Denisovich* and *The Gulag Archipelago* as contributing factors. David Remnick, editor of the *New Yorker* and a self-described liberal, captures the schizophrenic attitude toward

Solzhenitsyn. On the one hand, Remnick acknowledges that "when Solzhenitsyn's name comes up now it is more often than not as a freak, a monarchist, an anti-Semite, a crank, a has-been, not as a hero." On the other hand, Solzhenitsyn's "helping to bring down the last empire on earth" leads Remnick to conclude, "In terms of the effect he has had on history, Solzhenitsyn is the dominant writer of this century. Who else compares? Orwell? Koestler?"

Solzhenitsyn and his wife now live outside Moscow. In old age he continues to write.

—EDWARD E. ERICSON JR.

Further Reading

Ericson, Edward E., Jr. *Solzhenitsyn and the Modern World.* Washington, D.C.: Regnery Gateway, 1993.

Mahoney, Daniel J. *Aleksandr Solzhenitsyn: The Ascent from Ideology.* Lanham, Md.: Rowman & Littlefield, 2001.

Pearce, Joseph. *Solzhenitsyn: A Soul in Exile.* Grand Rapids, Mich.: Baker Books, 2001.

Solzhenitsyn, Aleksandr. *Warning to the West.* New York: Farrar, Straus, Giroux, 1976.

Thomas, D. M. *Alexander Solzhenitsyn: A Century in His Life.* New York: St. Martin's, 1998.

See also: anticommunism; modernity and postmodernity; nihilism

Southern Agrarians

The Southern Agrarians comprise primarily the twelve southern writers who authored the book *I'll Take My Stand* (1930), a kind of manifesto against modernism. The authors were John Crowe Ransom, Andrew Lytle, Henry B. Kline, Stark Young, Lyle H. Lanier, Frank L. Owsley, Allen Tate, Donald Davidson, John Gould Fletcher, Herman C. Nixon, Robert Penn Warren, and John Donald Wade. Many of the contributors had earlier formed a lit-

erary group and magazine called the *Fugitive*. The image of the agrarian as their ideal developed later, as they became increasingly aware that the South had certain features worth preserving and that central to the good things of life they wanted to defend was social stability and closeness to the soil. Not unmindful of the flaws of Southern ways, they wanted to defend a set of characteristics that were in preponderance in the South and that perhaps could have flourished more fully, even eventually choking out more of the blemishes, had certain events not occurred. These events were not just the Civil War and the "Reconstruction" that followed. They included the rising preoccupation with material well-being based on industrialism and applied modern science.

The Southern Agrarians stressed that human nature is as frail as it is constant. The forces of rapid change and heightened consumption oppress a soul that requires stability, closeness to inscrutable creation, and a sense of the holy and mysterious in life. They complained that modern ways of living, aided and abetted by science, never let man rest, since such ways were at peace with neither society nor creation. In industrial modernity, the human soul is brutalized and exploited to an extent equaled only by the suffering of creation in general. Industrialism, in fact, wages continuous warfare on creation, ceaselessly endeavoring to exploit and manipulate her in the name of material progress. This total commitment to a Cartesian matter-in-motion elbows out the satisfaction of higher needs. Opposed to this abyss of infinite change, the Agrarians sought a way of life that could be lived with grace and piety and with enough leisure to allow tradition, custom, and manners to flourish.

While agreeing broadly on a certain vision of life, the Agrarians had no detailed agenda for social change, nor was it their goal to have one. On the specific paths of action to be taken, individual Agrarians differed somewhat in emphasis and degree. John Crowe Ransom felt political action should be taken in concert with other geographic regions of the country that also showed signs of discontent with modern life. He thought that the South could compromise and accept some industrialism, albeit with very bad grace. Donald Davidson, speaking of the effect of modern industry on the arts, believed that since the effect of industrialization was to dehumanize, it was diametrically opposed to the arts. Its "Satanic" nature required uncompromising rejection. Art must be defended by the civic-minded artist seeking to correct the errors of public policy and current trends. Allen Tate revealed a Burkean dislike for abstract reason and metaphysical "principle" in favor of inchoate images of the good life mingled with concrete facts welded together by a deep desire to be loyal to a rather unsatisfactory Southern history. For Tate, modernity had led to an insupportable separation of the religious mind from the secular or practical mind in which the latter devours the former.

Today, even if the name "Southern Agrarians" is not often explicitly mentioned, their influence is evident. A second generation of Agrarians arose and found a most eloquent spokesman in University of Chicago professor Richard M. Weaver, who refined and extended their arguments. (Other latter-day Agrarians with particular importance for cultural conservatives include M. E. Bradford and Wendell Berry.) Weaver's work influenced conservative thought considerably after World War II. The Agrarians' critique of industrialism, science, and the exploitation of nature not only survived in Weaver but antedated the popular rise of environmentalism and may have influenced it. A Southern Agrarian like the late Andrew Lytle can be quoted by a staunch environmentalist such as Jeremy Rifkin. The Agrarian philosophy, however, was not socialist, globalist, feminist, or neopagan. It was thoroughly steeped in and defensive of the best of the culture, tradition, and history of the Christianized West. It took seriously the linguistic connection between "culture" and "agriculture," holding that a humane civilization requires rootedness and permanence in the land and that it must be sustained, nurtured, and protected from thoughtless change. Such a relation, the Agrarians argued, is necessary to satisfy man's spiritual needs and to protect the higher values of life.

—RALPH E. ANCIL

Further Reading

Agar, Herbert, and Allen Tate, eds. *Who Owns America? A New Declaration of Independence.* 2nd ed. Wilmington, Del.: ISI Books, 1999.

Berry, Wendell. *The Unsettling of America: Culture and Agriculture.* San Francisco: Sierra Club Books, 1977.

———. *The Art of the Commonplace: The Agrarian Essays of Wendell Berry.* Edited by Norman Wirzba. Counterpoint: Washington, D.C., 2002.

Bradford, M. E. *Remembering Who We Are: Observations of a Southern Conservative.* Athens, Ga.: University of Georgia Press, 1985.

Lytle, Andrew Nelson. *From Eden to Babylon: The Social and Political Essays of Andrew Nelson Lytle.* Washington, D.C.: Regnery Gateway, 1990.

Malvasi, Mark G. *The Unregenerate South: The Agrarian Thought of John Crowe Ransom, Allen Tate, and Donald Davidson.* Baton Rouge, La.: Louisiana State University Press, 1997.

Weaver, Richard M. *The Southern Essays of Richard M. Weaver.* Edited by George M. Curtis III and James J. Thompson Jr. Indianapolis, Ind.: Liberty Press, 1987.

See also: agrarianism; American Review; *Berry, Wendell; distributism;* I'll Take My Stand; *Lytle, Andrew Nelson; Owsley, Frank; Ransom, John Crowe;* Sewanee Review; *Tate, Allen; traditionalism; Wade, John Donald; Weaver, Richard M., Jr.*

Southern conservatism

Southern conservatism, as opposed to the generic American variety, is a doctrine rooted in memory, experience, and prescription rather than in goals or abstract principles. It is part of a nonnegotiable Southern identity with what it *is* prior to what it *means*. Not the consequence of dialectics or reasoning, it emerges from a historical continuum engendered by a recognizable people who have, over a long period of time, a specific set of experiences. This conservatism antedates the American Revolution, and, after much attenuation, can be found in the region to this day, legalistic, rhetorical, retrospective, defined by its past and unthinkable in any other setting than the one which shaped its unfolding. The political theory of Southern conservatism, from the seventeenth century, has been localist and legalistic: willing to acknowledge that government is natural among men—self-government, though not if organized by extrinsic or a priori ideas—and providing for the preservation of a culture and way of life grown out of its beginnings, not (in the language of *I'll Take My Stand*, 1930) "poured in from the top." Always Southern conservatism has acknowledged a precious Anglo-American continuity, a heritage preserved, first of all, through veneration of the British constitution and of institutions derived from our colonial English past and our struggle to resist presumption and high-handedness from the mother country without surrendering our patrimony as overseas Englishmen.

This conservatism is both historic and principled in not insisting on rights anterior to or separable from the context in which they originally emerged—what the Declaration of Independence says, if we read all of it and not just one sentence. No "city on a hill" to which we, as mortal men, will someday arrive is presumed by it—no New England millennium. We can read much of the story of the beginnings of Southern conservatism in Richard Beale Davis's *Intellectual Life in the Colonial South, 1585–1763* (1978), or in the cautious voices of the Revolution in the South: the Carolinians, such as Edward and John Rutledge, Rawlins Lowndes, William Henry Drayton, Charles Cotesworth Pinckney, James Iredell, and Samuel Johnston, often more characteristic Southern thinkers than the Virginia radicals; also, from Virginia itself, such revolutionaries by inheritance as Carter Braxton, Edmund Randolph, Patrick Henry, Benjamin Harrison, William Grayson, and Edmund Pendleton; and from Maryland such Old Whigs as Luther Martin and Samuel Chase. This is to mention only a few of the Southerners who, through and beyond the Revolution, expressed a great respect for the British constitution; and to ignore other nontheoretical framers and the less familiar followers of Jefferson, Madison, Richard Henry Lee, and George Wythe, who were indeed the sometime champions of "natural rights." But the great point to be derived from this evidence is that colonial Southern political piety is a predicate for the rigorous constitutionalism of Southerners as citizens of the new Union that took shape between 1787 and 1790.

In that portion of the region's political history that includes its early experience as part of the Republic and the years of sectional conflict leading up to secession and the War between the States, powerful conservatives worked and spoke for the South and refined its doctrine. Indeed, such Southern thought that was *not conservative* during this period is generally regarded as eccentric or exceptional. Therefore, a catalogue of these conservatives is unnecessary. But no summary of this period of regional establishment would be complete without mention of the imaginative literature generated in this time and place. John Pendleton Kennedy's *Swallow Barn* (1832) and the revolutionary war romances of William Gilmore

Simms, since these fictions are as representative of their time as are Jefferson's *Notes on the State of Virginia* (1784) and John Drayton's *Memoirs of the American Revolution as Relating to the State of South Carolina* (1821) of the previous era, deserve mention. Both have obvious claims on the attention of those interested in the essence of Southern politics—as do the satiric stories of the frontier humorists George Washington Harris, Johnson Jones Hooper, William Tappan Thompson, Joseph Glover Baldwin, and Augustus Baldwin Longstreet.

Direct political teaching not to be ignored is to be found in *Arator* (1813) and other controversial writings by John Taylor of Caroline, in John C. Calhoun's *Disquisition on Government* (1851), in his *Fort Hill Address* (1831), *Discourse on the Constitution and Government of the United States* (1851) and many occasional writings, in the speeches and letters of the *Tertium Quids* (John Randolph of Roanoke, Thomas Sumter, Nathaniel Macon), in the two inaugural addresses of Jefferson Davis as president of the Confederate States of America, and in the farewell speeches of the Southern senators who left Washington during the Great Secession Winter of 1860-61. Moreover, it is impossible to consider this subject and still ignore the political theory of Southern savants like Thomas Roderick Dew, Henry Hughes, T. R. Cobb, George Fitzhugh, E. N. Elliot, George Tucker, and George Frederick Holmes; or the social teaching of their impressive contemporaries among Southern theologians—James Henry Thornwell, Benjamin Palmer, Robert Dabney, and Thornton Stringfellow. The study of Southern conservatism after its manifestation in the state ratification conventions that approved the Constitution and before the state conventions that adopted ordinances of secession could be a work of several volumes. Southern conservatism in this era is constitutional, antitheoretical, antirationalistic, localist, and religious. Fur-

thermore, even before the debate concerning slavery, it knows itself as Southern—as is even more the case once it has attempted to realize itself politically in creating a nation of its own. The failure of this effort in 1865 completed the basic list of ingredients informing the characteristic Southern worldview in its maturity by adding to that list what is sometimes called the tragic sense of life, what a people learn by losing a terrible war.

There are several inclusive examinations of the Lost Cause written by Southern historians after the fact of defeat, by soldiers, clergymen, journalists, and legal theorists. The great summary of all this literature is Richard Weaver's *The Southern Tradition at Bay: A History of Postbellum Thought* (1968) and later *The Southern Essays of Richard Weaver* (1987). We can recognize a development of the inherited political doctrine in the legal teaching of Albert Taylor Bledsoe, in the polemical analysis of Edward Pollard and Alexander Stephens, and in the personal narratives of Raphael Semmes, Robert Lewis Dabney, and Richard Taylor, which is to make no appropriate mention of the wartime and postbellum memoirs of Southern women or of the voluminous fiction of the "era of good feeling" described by Paul H. Buck in *The Road to Reunion, 1865–1890* (1937). These were of course the best days of the United Confederate Veterans, the United Daughters of the Confederacy, and Sons of Confederate Veterans. Official piety was ubiquitous and flourished under every imaginable circumstance. But after the South's successful resistance to Reconstruction, there was a persistently elegiac quality in subsequent expressions of loyalty to the inherited political tradition and the culture it had sustained.

The continuity of Southern conservatism after 1918 is a matter of intellectual refinement along with a simultaneous practical attenuation. The South remained the backbone of American conservatism, but with less effect and less distinction. Traditional Southern conservatives came to a better historical understanding of their own position and developed a more adequate critique of other, often hostile forces operating in the dialectic of American history. American political leaders continued to presuppose the region's conservatism, and yet were nervous about it, even though racial questions were no longer taken to be peculiarly problems of the Southern Right. From this period the student of Southern conservatism should read William Alexander Percy's *Lanterns on the Levee* (1941); J. Evetts Haley's *Rough Times, Tough Fiber* (1976); *I'll Take My Stand,* by Twelve Southerners (1930) and *Why the South Will Survive,* by Fifteen Southerners (1981); Donald Davidson's *Attack on Leviathan* (1938) and *Still Rebels, Still Yankees* (1957); M. E. Bradford's edition of *From Eden to Babylon: The Social and Political Essays of Andrew Nelson Lytle* (1990), and Andrew Lytle's *A Wake for the Living* (1975); Francis Butler Simkin's *The Everlasting South* (1963), and Charles P. Roland's *The Improbable Era: The South since World War II* (1975). This selection passes over a wide range of imaginative evidence produced by the writers of the Southern Renaissance—evidence which renders in action, tone, and character the traditional vision of the South; and it leaves aside many uncollected essays and works of scholarships—such as Russell Kirk's *John Randolph of Roanoke: A Study in American Politics* (1964), Clyde Wilson's *Carolina Cavalier: The Life and Mind of James Johnston Pettigrew* (1990), and Eugene Genovese's *The Slaveholder's Dilemma: Freedom and Progress in Southern Conservative Thought, 1820–1860* (1992)—the kind of scholarly achievements that illuminate and reinforce the entire tradition in focusing on its characteristic figures or central problems. Paradoxically, as traditional Southern conservatism loses some of its force in the public life of the region and among a people who have honored its premises for more than 200 years, our understanding of the tradition, its origins, and its justifications grows apace.

In summary, Southern conservatism is still decentralist, opposed to concentrated authority inclined to regulate men's lives in a fashion that is arbitrary, indifferent, self-important, and (when challenged) arrogant. Even today this doctrine continues to be antiegalitarian, as the biblical parable of the talents is antiegalitarian: opposed not only to demands for equality of condition but also to vapid generalizations concerning equality of opportunity, a circumstance which cannot be achieved even by a total submission to government: the negative equality of universal slavery. The industrial, cosmopolitan lifestyle, along with those political, scientific and managerial methods of manipulating reality so well suited to a contemporary assault on the providential order of things are also rejected, in part for reasons announced most clearly in the introduction to *I'll Take My Stand.* There the Agrarians speak of religion as "our submission to the general intention of a nature that is fairly inscrutable; it is a sense of our role as creatures within it. But nature industrialized, transformed into cities and artificial habitations . . . is no longer nature but a highly simplified picture of nature. We receive the illusion of having power over nature, and lose the sense of nature as something mysterious and contingent." Modern rationalism rejected the mythopoeic vision that makes religion possible. Filtered through these distortions, God "is merely an amiable expression." At the bottom of agrarianism is a commitment to what Richard Weaver called "the older religiousness." In essence, it is an ontology as well as a preference for the agricultural life and an attitude that rejects most versions of the progressive, Faustian myth. Ignoring the Agrarians, many politicians and journalists predicted that the South would lose its character after the conclusion of the Second Reconstruction. They were guilty of wishful thinking.

Traditional Southern conservatism, even when blurred or mixed with other attitudes, maintains a precarious balance. On the one hand, everyone needs to be as independent as it is possible to be. Yet some will always have five talents, some three, and some only one. Therefore, responsible members of the tribe, brothers and sisters, uncles and aunts, parents and grandparents always have to organize the units of the human family to some formula for stewardship: a patriarchal/matriarchal arrangement with most of the operative pressure not on the state but on voluntary associations, ties of blood and friendship that are prepolitical. Certainly, this conservatism is not going to hold that liberty or human rights can exist apart from the context in which they are created and readily subsist: it is not going to accept that such values can be posited as anterior to their historical development in particular circumstances.

—M. E. BRADFORD

Further Reading

Bradford, M. E. *A Better Guide than Reason: Studies in the American Revolution*. La Salle, Ill.: Sherwood Sugden, 1979.

———. *The Reactionary Imperative: Essays Literary and Political*. Peru, Ill.: Sherwood Sugden, 1990.

Genovese, Eugene. *The Southern Tradition: The Achievement and Limitations of an American Conservatism*. Cambridge, Mass.: Harvard University Press, 1994.

Owsley, Frank L. *Plain Folk of the Old South*. Baton Rouge, La.: Louisiana State University Press, 1949.

Reed, John Shelton. *The Enduring South: Subcultural Persistence in Mass Society*. Lexington, Mass.: Lexington Books, 1972.

Wade, John Donald. *Selected Essays and Other Writings*. Edited by Donald Davidson. Athens, Ga.: University of Georgia Press, 1966.

See also: Bradford, M. E.; Calhoun, John C.; Davis, Jefferson; I'll Take My Stand; Jefferson, Thomas; localism; Randolph, John (of Roanoke); Southern Agrarians; Southern Partisan; Taylor, John (of Caroline); Weaver, Richard M., Jr.

Southern Partisan

The *Southern Partisan* is a South Carolina–based magazine dedicated to defining and defending traditional Southern values, both in a historical and a modern context. Published quarterly, each issue is an eclectic mix of politics, history, literature, religion, and culture—all from a Southern perspective. With subscribers throughout the United States and in most European countries, the magazine is a major intellectual outlet for Southern conservatism.

The *Southern Partisan Quarterly Review* was founded in 1979 by Thomas Fleming, a professor of classics, and Clyde Wilson, editor of the John C. Calhoun papers. Together, they published two issues. The magazine was then purchased in 1981 by the Foundation for American Education and publication was resumed under the shorter title, the *Southern Partisan*. The magazine was independently restructured in 1984 as the Southern Partisan Corporation.

Regular features over the years have included a "Partisan Conversation," or interview, with a notable person; "Obiter Dicta," a collection of stinging editorial comments; "Civil War Trivia," by Webb Garrison; "Anguished English," by Richard Lederer; "Southern Sampler," by Bill Freehoff; and its most famous staple, the "Scalawag Award," which is given each issue to a Southerner who the editors believe has conspicuously betrayed the heritage or the values of the South. Bill Clinton, Tom Wicker, Bill Moyers, and David Gergen have been among its notable recipients.

Much of the writing in the magazine

draws inspiration from the "Fugitives" or Southern Agrarians who produced the famous defense of the South, *I'll Take My Stand*, in 1930. The late M. E. Bradford wrote for the *Southern Partisan* and served as a senior editor; among the magazine's other noteworthy contributors have been Andrew Lytle, Russell Kirk, Pat Buchanan, Tom Landess, Samuel T. Francis, and J. O. Tate.

—S. P. SMITH

Further Reading

Smith, Oran P. *So Good A Cause: A Decade of "The Southern Partisan."* Columbia, S.C.: Foundation for American Education, 1993.

See also: Bradford, M. E.; Fleming, Thomas; Southern conservatism

Southern Review

The original series of the *Southern Review* was founded at Louisiana State University in 1935. This magazine, as shaped by its principal editors Cleanth Brooks and Robert Penn Warren, virtually defined the literary quarterly as a highbrow periodical publishing fiction, poetry, and criticism for the intelligent general reader. So influential was the *Southern Review* that, in 1940, a writer for *Time* magazine observed that the center of literary criticism in the Western world had moved "from the left bank of the Seine to the left bank of the Mississippi." In addition to discovering new writers such as Eudora Welty and Peter Taylor, the *Southern Review* was a frequent outlet for such distinguished international figures as Katherine Anne Porter, the Fugitive poets of Nashville, Ford Madox Ford, Aldous Huxley, Kenneth Burke, Sidney Hook, Delmore Schwartz, F. O. Matthiessen, Mary McCarthy, James T. Farrell, John Dewey, and Philip Rahv.

Although the *Southern Review* espoused no official political ideology, Brooks and Warren were both part of the socially conservative Agrarian movement. Because of its insistence on distinguishing literature from propaganda, the *Southern Review* was sharply critical of the tendentious criticism of such democratic nativists as Archibald MacLeish, Van Wyck Brooks, Alfred Kazin, and Howard Mumford Jones. The original series of the magazine was suspended in 1942 (ostensibly as a wartime austerity measure). A new series of the *Southern Review* has been published continuously by LSU since 1965, but though it has remained a thoughtful journal, it has not had the essentially conservative character of its predecessor.

—MARK WINCHELL

Further Reading

Blotner, Joseph. *Robert Penn Warren: A Biography.* New York: Random House, 1997.

Cutrer, Thomas W. *Parnassus on the Mississippi: The Southern Review and the Baton Rouge Literary Community, 1935–1942.* Baton Rouge, La.: Louisiana State University Press, 1984..

Winchell, Mark Royden. *Cleanth Brooks and the Rise of Modern Criticism.* Charlottesville, Va.: University Press of Virginia, 1996.

See also: Brooks, Cleanth; New Criticism

Sowell, Thomas (1930–)

Thomas Sowell has had a prominent academic career in three fields of inquiry: the history of classical economic thought; the economics, sociology, and politics of race and ethnic groups; and issues of how people in an economy deal with limited knowledge. He is also a syndicated columnist whose column appears in approximately 150 newspapers nationwide.

Sowell was born in Gastonia, North Carolina. His undergraduate studies were at Harvard. He received an M.A. from Columbia, and then went on to the University of

Chicago, where he became a disciple of Milton Friedman. After teaching at Rutgers, Cornell, Brandeis, and UCLA, and leading a project at the Urban Institute, in 1980 Sowell moved to the Hoover Institution at Stanford University.

Sowell's research on racial differences in performance and his opposition to affirmative action brought him into the public policy arena. He showed that different ethnic groups such as the Irish and Italians, or blacks from the U.S. South and the Caribbean, had very different success patterns. Thus, it was not possible to infer racial discrimination from the different incomes of different groups. Also, while such ethnic groups as the Irish Catholics eventually entered the mainstream, it took nearly a century, and some cultural differences in economic success still remain. Sowell documents the disabilities that American blacks have faced and shows how this background has led to the high levels of crime and social disorder blacks currently exhibit. Nevertheless, just as other ethnic groups have gradually overcome these problems, Sowell shows that blacks have gradually been coming "up from slavery" since the 1860s.

Thomas Sowell

Sowell has widely criticized affirmative action policies; his arguments are stated most fully in *Preferential Policies* (1990), which shows how in many countries around the world affirmative action or reverse discrimination has led to violent interethnic disputes. Often the result has been to make a minority group worse off than before such policies were implemented. A striking aspect of Sowell's evidence is how common preferential policies have been historically and how often they appear to cause strong political grievances. Sowell is opposed to affirmative action because "discrimination has been pervasive, but not pervasively effective." People and ethnic groups can be quite successful despite discrimination, as is shown by the history of the Jews and the Japanese.

Sowell's original scholarly work was on the theories of the classical economists, particularly early theories of recession. The dominant view, argued by David Ricardo, was that permanent recessions or general gluts could not occur, so there really *was* no problem of recession. The opposing view claimed that imbalances in growth could lead to financial and banking panics, which would in turn lead to a major contraction in output. Sowell pointed out that the latter view had many merits that classical economic theory lacked. It was not until the twentieth century and Keynes that macroeconomic theory was developed.

Sowell's book *Marxism: Philosophy and Economics* (1985) emphasized that Marx was the last major classical economist. Marx explicitly followed Ricardo on many major points and in his main purpose of analyzing the development of the capitalist economy. Sowell's careful reading shows Marx's (and Engels's) views to have been more sensible and innovative than they are typically portrayed as being. Marx's most important innovation is the idea that contradictions within an economic system lead to new and more productive institutions—including entrepreneurial capitalism. This insight influenced Schumpeter and other "Austrians" to see innovation and "creative destruction" as the essence of capitalism, contrary to the static models of neoclassical economics. And it has clearly influenced Sowell's views on the histories of ethnic groups. Sowell also points out Marx's great defects, the most egregious being his inaccurate theory of revolution—which would serve as the natural rationale for those murderous dictatorships which at one point ruled a third of the world.

A third fundamental strand to Sowell's thought is his analysis of *Knowledge and Decisions* (1980), as one of his books is titled. This work owes much to Hayek. The fundamental insight here is that civilization, and a market economy, are immense devices for economizing on knowledge. A clear system of property rights allows individuals to act effectively to better their own lives while remaining ignorant of how others are managing theirs. Social institutions should be judged by their ability to allow effective economizing on imperfect information. Sowell criticizes trends in law and politics that pursue the mythical goal of fairness.

Sowell has been a major contributor to the political and economic debate on race and affirmative action. His views are based on a deep and essentially Burkean understanding of the heterogeneity of human cultures and the limitations of human knowledge.

—KENNETH KOFORD

Further Reading

Sowell, Thomas. *Conquests and Cultures: An International History.* New York: Basic Books, 1998.

———. *Essays on Classical Economics.* Princeton, N.J.: Princeton University Press, 2005.

———. *A Personal Odyssey.* New York: Free Press, 2000.

———. *Race and Culture: A World View.* New York: Basic Books, 1994.

See also: affirmative action; Hayek, Friedrich A. von; Marxism

speech, freedom of

Next to freedom of conscience, freedom of speech is generally regarded as the most important freedom that a people can possess. Determinations of the precise meaning of the term, however, have varied—and not simply along predictable ideological lines. On the right, for example, traditional conservatives favor a limited interpretation, one that speaks to issues of political discourse. Libertarians, on the other hand, prefer a more expansive reading and think in terms of freedom of expression. Those on the left have their own internal quarrels, though it can safely be said that contemporary liberal thought on the subject is virtually identical to the libertarian position; radicals regard freedom of speech as a "bourgeois liberty."

The legislative history of the First Amendment reveals very little as to what the framers meant by freedom of speech. But from what we do know, nothing approaching the contemporary libertarian position was countenanced. According to Leonard W. Levy, the nation's leading authority on the subject, "If the Revolution produced any radical libertarians on the meaning of freedom of speech and press, they were not present at the Constitutional Convention or the First Congress which drafted the Bill of Rights." Indeed, the fact that the First Congress passed the Alien and Sedition Acts literally seven years after the passage of the Bill of Rights indicates their rejection of an absolutist interpretation of freedom of speech. It would be more accurate to conclude, with Levy, that the First Amendment, as originally conceived, "was more an expression of federalism than of libertarianism."

Traditional conservatives argue that the founders were right to see freedom of speech as a means toward the end of good government. To Jesuit scholar Francis Canavan, there is a limiting principle embedded in this interpretation: reasoned discourse is valued precisely because it serves the needs of a democratic political order, ergo speech that does not contribute to that end or is positively subversive of it, is not worthy of protection (exceptions to this rule would involve instances where the suppression of speech might be an even greater hindrance to the maintenance of good government). Canavan's contribution is perhaps the most cogent explication of the traditional conservative interpretation of freedom of speech.

The Supreme Court did not rule on a free-speech case before the twentieth century, largely due to the fact that the First Amendment was not held to be applicable to the states until after the First World War. Significantly, it was in the Court's first free-speech case, *Gitlow v. New York* (1925), that Justice Oliver Wendall Holmes, in a dissenting opinion, laid bare what was to become the basis of the "freedom of expression" school of thought. For Holmes there was no principle embodied in the First Amendment, no connecting link between freedom of speech and republican government. Truth, in this view, emerges solely from the free marketplace of ideas.

The term "freedom of expression" entered the lexicon of constitutional experts sometime after Holmes's ideas proved triumphant. But it was left to Supreme Court Justice William Brennan to posit that free speech was an end in itself, having, as he said, a "transcendent value" quite apart from any republican considerations. It is no exaggeration to say that the belief that all speech is of equal value is the defining mark of liberal thought on the subject today. It is the basis of the absolutist position and is the intellectual lifeblood of contemporary civil libertarian thought, especially as represented by the American Civil Liberties Union.

Conservatives such as Walter Berns have challenged the liberal view by reminding us of the fact that the Constitution, and its founding principles as represented in the Declaration of Independence, do not support a belief in the equality of all ideas. Slavery, for example, is an idea that may prove victorious in the free marketplace of ideas, but it is not the kind of idea that is compatible with the principles of republican government. The goal of the Constitution is liberty, not despotism, and efforts to subvert that end by perverting the meaning of the Constitution have no legitimate role to play in a free society.

The absolutists see every conceivable expression, whether verbal or nonverbal, as deserving of First Amendment protection. Conservatives, especially those of the traditional school, have been supportive of the need to draw the line and have generally approved of the high court's exceptions to First Amendment protections. Those exceptions cover such areas as libel, obscenity, incitement to riot, "fighting words," copyright infringement, false advertising, solicitation of a crime, creation of a "clear and present danger," etc.

To be sure, there are issues, such as flag burning, on which conservatives like Justice Antonin Scalia (a libertarian) and Chief Justice William Rehnquist (a traditionalist) take diametrically opposing positions. Scalia believes that flag burning is a form of speech, and is therefore entitled to all the protections afforded by the First Amendment. Rehnquist sees flag burning as "the equivalent to an inarticulate grunt or roar," lacking in constitutional insulation. It is clear that much depends on just how elastic an interpretation one gives to the meaning of freedom of speech.

How do we know when, or where, to draw the line? Sidney Hook shed important light on the "slippery slope" dilemma when he wrote that "our *awareness* that we have stepped on a slope is a brake on our precipitous descent." That is why conservative opposition to granting full First Amendment protections to Nazis need not result in tyranny: distinctions can be made between terrorist organizations bent on the subversion of democracy, and unpopular minorities seeking liberty. And as Hook also counseled, our unwillingness to act against those who would undermine democracy may itself result in despotism.

In short, the conservative position on freedom of speech (a) is not a commitment to protecting every conceivable "expression," (b) is supportive of the need to balance speech rights with other competing social interests, the consequence of which may mean a limited and specific abridgment of certain speech rights, and (c) is a commitment made in behalf of the successful functioning of republican government.

—WILLIAM A. DONOHUE

Further Reading

Berns, Walter. *The First Amendment and the Future of American Democracy*. New York: Basic Books, 1976.

Canavan, Francis. *Freedom of Expression: Purpose as Limit*. Durham, N.C.: Carolina Academic Press, 1984.

Donohue, William A. *The Politics of the American Civil Liberties Union*. New Brunswick, N.J.: Transaction, 1985.

Hook, Sidney. *Paradoxes of Freedom*. Buffalo, N.Y.: Prometheus Books, 1987.

Levy, Leonard. *Freedom of Speech and Press in Early American History: Legacy of Suppression*. New York: Harper & Row, 1963.

See also: Berns, Walter; Bill of Rights; libertarianism; Rehnquist, William H.; Scalia, Antonin; Supreme Court

Spence Publishing Company

Waco, Texas, native Thomas W. Spence founded this Dallas-based publisher in 1996. Spence entered the industry at a difficult time for newcomers. But its founder was convinced that it could fill a niche other conservative book publishers had begun to neglect—quality nonfiction that could engage in an intelligent but accessible way the cultural pathologies that had resulted from sixties-style liberalism and its historical forbear, the Enlightenment.

Spence's first book was *The End of Democracy?* (1997), a collection of essays on judicial imperialism that were first published in the neoconservative monthly *First Things* and sparked intense debate among conservatives as to whether recent decisions of the Supreme Court (notably *Planned Parenthood v. Casey*, 1992) had cast doubt on the legitimacy of the American political regime. Nevertheless, the press has for the most part eschewed Spenglerian doom, indicating that the founder of the young publishing company and his editor-collaborator, Fort Worth–native Mitchell Muncy, have a cautiously optimistic view of the culture that they wish to leaven.

Subsequent titles, of which there have been a few dozen, have suggested that Spence will not be painted into an ideological corner. With the publication of a number of books on American culture, including Kenneth Craycraft's *The American Myth of Religious Freedom* (1999), a book that suggested that religious orthodoxy was incompatible with American-style pluralism, Spence has shown itself to be intellectually adventuresome, publishing thoughtful traditionalist titles as well as books by the neoconservative bomb-throwing gadfly David Horowitz (*Hating Whitey* [1999], *The Art of Political War* [2000], *Left Illusions* [2003]). The publication of such critically acclaimed titles as *All Shook Up* (2001), by Carson Holloway, *Domestic Tranquility* (1998), by F. Carolyn Graglia, and *Love and Economics* (2001), by Jennifer Roback Morse, indicate that Spence sees its primary role as informing the deeper debates that form the backdrop of modern political life:

debates concerning the role of the family, the state of the arts, and the primacy of religion.

—Brian McGuire

See also: media, conservative

Spencer, Herbert (1820–1903)

As one of the most influential English philosophers of the nineteenth century, Herbert Spencer promoted the ideas of individualism and evolution. He was raised in a family that taught him the principles of classical liberalism and modern science, and he advanced these principles as a journalist active in radical liberal politics. Then, in the second half of his life, he spent most of his time writing a massive series of books—under the general title *Synthetic Philosophy*—that would apply his understanding of individualism and evolution to all fields of knowledge.

Spencer used the terms "evolution" and "survival of the fittest" long before they were adopted by Charles Darwin. Spencer defined evolution as a change from the homogeneous to the heterogeneous. This evolutionary pattern is clear in the organic development of a seed or egg into a mature plant or animal. He thought this same pattern of growth from a simple, homogeneous structure to a complex, heterogeneous structure through a process of successive differentiations could be found throughout nature. The history of the universe, the history of the Earth, the history of life, and the history of human society were all governed by this law of evolution. Although he spoke of social evolution as progressive, Spencer did not see this progress as inevitable or as a single series of stages. Rather, he thought that societies would be diverse in their adaptations to their particular conditions of life.

Spencer's individualism was based on the principle of equal freedom, which held that each person should be free to do as he wishes, so long as he does not infringe on the equal freedom of anyone else. The proper aim of government, then, is to secure the equal freedom of individuals from the coercion of others. Although he saw that societies had evolved for thousands of years under the pressure of warfare into "militant" societies based on compulsory cooperation, Spencer hoped that modern commercial societies were evolving into "industrial" societies based on voluntary cooperation. Through much of the nineteenth century, political liberalism was devoted to promoting individual freedom in a social order of voluntary cooperation. But by the end of the century, Spencer saw that those who called themselves "liberals" were expanding the coercive powers of the state and thus moving toward socialism. He foresaw that the Tories might become the new defenders of individual liberty against the collectivism of the new Liberals.

Spencer's ideas of individualism and evolution have influenced the American conservative movement. Albert Jay Nock revived Spencer's arguments for individualism and directed them against the collectivist welfare-statism of Franklin Roosevelt. Conservatives such as Frank Chordorov, Russell Kirk, and William F. Buckley were in turn influenced by Nock (though Kirk, at least, rejected Spencer). Chodorov founded the Intercollegiate Society of Individualists (now the Intercollegiate Studies Institute) in 1953 to preserve the individualist tradition that he traced to Spencer and Nock, among others.

In addition, Spencer's thinking about the evolution of social order through voluntary cooperation rather than central planning helped to spur a tradition of thinking about spontaneous order that was continued by the likes of Friedrich Hayek. Like Spencer, Hayek defended the free society as an order that was grown rather than constructed.

—Larry Arnhart

Further Reading

Nock, Albert Jay. *Our Enemy, The State*. Caxton, Idaho: Caxton Printers, 1950.

Spencer, Herbert. *The Evolution of Society*. Edited by Robert L. Carneiro. Chicago: University of Chicago Press, 1967.

———. *The Man versus the State*. Indianapolis, Ind.: Liberty Classics, 1981.

———. *On Social Evolution*. Edited by J. D. Y. Peel. Chicago: University of Chicago Press, 1972.

Weinstein, David. *Equal Freedom and Utility: Herbert Spencer's Liberal Utilitarianism*. New York: Cambridge University Press, 1998.

See also: individualism; liberalism, classical; libertarianism; social Darwinism

Spiritual Mobilization

Spiritual Mobilization (S.M., 1935–61) was a Los Angeles–based "spiritual libertarian" and free market-oriented national organization formed by Rev. James W. Fifield Jr. (1899–1977)—a politically conservative but theologically liberal Congregationalist minister—to counteract not only the political collectivism spawned by the New Deal but also a variety of leftist trends in organized religion (for example, the anticapitalist "Social Gospel" advocacy of the National Council of Churches).

Throughout its twenty-five-year history, S.M. aimed—through its journal *Faith and Freedom*, newspaper columns, radio and TV broadcasts, lectures, regional conferences, and religious retreats—to mobilize a fellowship of American Christian clergy, educators, students, and business leaders to take a stand against statist, collectivist trends in church, state, economics, and culture. During the post–World War II era, S.M. played a leading role in networking with other free-market groups (such as the William Volker Fund and Leonard E. Read's Foundation for Economic Education) to forge a coalition of American libertarian individualists, antistatist conservatives, and religious champions of the philosophy of freedom.

During its heyday in the critical decade of the 1950s, S.M. underwent a dramatic mutation when S.M.'s new president James C. Ingebretsen (1906–99), an influential Los Angeles libertarian lawyer, attempted to steer S.M. in new directions. First, he emphasized libertarian political economy approaches, going beyond Fifield's anticommunist focus. More importantly, he steered the organization toward the emerging transformational human-potential paradigm formulated by Aldous Huxley's intellectual mentor, historian-philosopher Gerald Heard (1889–1971). Though a generation in advance of their time, Ingebretsen's ideas marked a historic watershed that distinguished two different approaches to the libertarian theory of social change. Spiritual Mobilization dissolved soon therafter in 1961.

—JOHN V. CODY

Further Reading

Fifield, James W., Jr., and Bill Youngs. *The Tall Preacher: Autobiography of Dr. James W. Fifield, Jr.* Los Angeles: Pepperdine University Press, 1977.

See also: libertarianism

Stanlis, Peter J. (1920–)

Peter James Stanlis is the dean of postwar Edmund Burke studies in America. He is known particularly for his 1958 book *Edmund Burke and the Natural Law*, in which he situated Burke as a great eighteenth-century advocate of the moral natural law tradition. He is also a widely published scholar on the political and social philosophy of the poet Robert Frost.

Born into an immigrant family from Lithuania in Newark, New Jersey, Stanlis attended Middlebury College, where he came under the direction of the Dean of the Bread Loaf School of English, a graduate school associated with Middlebury where Frost spent his summers. Stanlis conducted interviews with Frost in six consecutive summers and was advised by the poet to attend the University of Michigan. It was there, under the direction of the distinguished conservative English literature professor Louis Bredvold, that Stanlis was introduced to the writings of Edmund Burke.

During his time in graduate school at Michigan, Stanlis found his way back to the Catholic Church of his youth. That reconversion played a powerful role in his thinking. It was concurrent with a return to scholasticism on the part of his intellectual coreligionists, as manifest in the flourishing neo-Thomist movement. Stanlis subscribed early on to a central journal of that movement, the *Natural Law Forum*, which was published out of Notre Dame and eventually became the *Journal of American Jurisprudence*. As a result of his reading of Roman jurisprudence and the English common law, he became convinced that Burke's mind was informed by the moral natural law tradition. When he turned to the secondary literature about Burke, however, he discovered that with few exceptions, Burke was considered an enemy of moral natural law. All the Victorian commentators on Burke were of one mind: Burke, like David Hume, rejected the concept of natural law as it pertained to the moral life. Stanlis thought they were wrong.

The University of Michigan Press published his thesis under the title *Edmund Burke and the Natural Law*. Its appearance was greeted by 53 reviews. Russell Kirk wrote the original foreword, making direct connections between Stanlis's interpretation of Burke and the rise of the "new conservatism" in post–World War II America. Stanlis's book became an influential conservative text, making the case for the central place of mo-

rality in politics. In eighteenth-century study circles, nobody who wrote on Burke thereafter could ignore it. The book continues to exert tremendous influence; in 2003, Transaction Publishers released the fourth edition, with a new introduction by V. Bradley Lewis.

In the 1940s and 1950s, Stanlis found himself on the ground floor of what many now call the "Burke Revival." Following largely from the availability of newly discovered Burke papers in 1949, a veritable Burke industry flourished. For his part, Stanlis has contributed more than twenty scholarly books and monographs to the field. The climate was also ripe for a renewed interest in Burke in another important way. Nazism and Communism were, to reflective conservative and liberal thinkers, shattering the moral basis of Western civilization. Stanlis was among those who found in the natural law tradition powerful elements that might be marshalled in opposition to such forces. And he was among those who believed that Burke, and the scholars inspired by him, spoke to questions that politicians and jurists were not addressing. The discovery of the Burke papers, combined with the climate of the time, created a unique moment for a deeper interest in Burke to take root and flourish in America. This was the principal basis upon which the conservative intellectual attachment to Burke was made.

Stanlis founded the *Burke Newsletter* in the summer of 1959. Its earliest numbers were included as a supplemental appendix in Russell Kirk's conservative journal *Modern Age*. It struck out on its own when Kirk left his position as editor of *Modern Age* a year later. In 1967, the journal found an institutional home at Alfred University in New York. It also changed its name and modified its format, for as editor Stanlis noted, "*The Burke Newsletter* had gradually evolved into a journal on Edmund Burke and his age. . . . This development was in keeping with the strong current interest in Burke and his period." Thus, *Studies in Burke and His Time* became the chief vehicle for Burke studies in America. In 2005 it was revived and published by the Educational Reviewer, Inc. It is now edited by Joseph Pappin III.

As Stanlis first editorialized in 1969, *Studies in Burke and His Time* aimed to publish "various commentaries across the full spectrum of political opinion," and welcomed "judgments differing from our own interpretations of positions taken by Burke on various subjects." Many scholars writing from various viewpoints did indeed appear in its pages, including Isaac Kramnick, Jeffrey Hart (who debated Harvey Mansfield on Burke's commitment to Christianity in one number), Russell Kirk, Ross Hoffman, Carl Cone, Lucy Sutherland, T. O. McLoughlin, George H. Gutteridge, Charles Ritcheson, Donald Greene, Jackson Turner Main, Frank O'Gorman, Gaetano Vincitorio, Burleigh Wilkins, Garry Wills, and Esmond Wright. It was this now uncommon ecumenism that made the *Burke Newsletter* and *Studies in Burke and His Time* such a vital—and enduring—intellectual production. The mere fact that these publications are still so often mined for important scholarship is a testament to Stanlis the scholar-editor's refusal to slavishly advance any particular school of Burke interpretation, even his own.

—JEFFREY O. NELSON

Further Reading

Nash, George H., *The Conservative Intellectual Movement in America since 1945*. Wilmington, Del.: Intercollegiate Studies Institute, 1996.

Nelson, Jeffrey O. "Odyssey of a Burke Revivalist: An Intellectual Biography of Peter J. Stanlis." In *An Imaginative Whig: Reassessing the Life and Thought of Edmund Burke*, edited by Ian Crowe, 228–39. Columbia, Mo.: University of Missouri Press, 2005, .

Stanlis, Peter J., "Acceptable in Heaven's Sight: Frost at Bread Loaf, 1939–1942." In *Frost: Centennial Essays*, vol. 3, edited by Jac Tharpe, 179–311. Jackson, Miss.: University Press of Mississippi, 1978.

See also: Burke, Edmund; Burkean conservatism; Frost, Robert

states' rights

Original states' rights were those governing prerogatives which the states retained even while delegating certain powers to the United States government. States' rights were antecedent to the national governments organized under the Articles of Confederation and the United States Constitution. The origins of states' rights can be traced back to colonial America, during which time townships, counties, and colonial assemblies had increasingly asserted their respective desires for local self-government and independence from British control. When the British passed the Stamp Act in 1763, the colonists considered that act to be an affront to their long-established practice of local self-government. The battle cry "No taxation without representation" rallied the colonies for collective action, which led to the American Revolution and culminated in independence. Under British colonial rule the colonies were administratively linked together through the British Crown, but they had substantial independence when dealing with each other on this side of the Atlantic. When the Crown's authority that linked the states together was dismantled by the American Revolution, the colonies qua states gained their independence not only from the Crown and Parliament, but in large measure from each other. The Declaration of Independence acknowledges the new political arrangement in several ways. First, it is subtitled "The Unanimous Declaration of the Thirteen United States of America"; and second, it stipulates that "These United Colonies are, and of Right ought to be Free and Independent States; that they are Absolved from all Allegiance to the British Crown, and that all political connection between them and the State of Great Britain, is and ought to be totally dissolved; and that as Free and Independent States, they have full Power to levy War, Conclude Peace, contract Alliances, establish Commerce, and do all other Acts and Things which Independent States may of right do." The several states of South Carolina, Virginia, New York, etc., were thereby the equals of the "State of Great Britain."

The Declaration, the Articles of Confederation, the U.S. Constitution, and the various state constitutions collectively support the view that the union was established as a political compact between the states, in contradistinction to a social contract between individuals. The intent of the compact was to secure state-based popular control and consent over national public policies.

The first national constitution between the states—the Articles of Confederation—reaffirmed the states' sovereignty while delegating certain powers to the United States. Article II stipulates that "[e]ach State retains its sovereignty, freedom and independence, and every Power, Jurisdiction and right, which is not by this confederation expressly delegated to the United States, in Congress assembled." Through the Articles of Confederation the states established a union from a self-defense posture not only against their former mother country, but against each other. Article III explains that

> The said States hereby severally enter into a firm league of friendship with each other, for their common defense, the security of their Liberties, and their mutual and general welfare, binding themselves to assist each other, against all force offered to, or attacks made upon them, on account of religion, sovereignty, trade, or any other pretence whatever.

The institutional structure of the national government, lacking separation of powers and checks and balances, and the fact that "[i]n determining questions in the United States, in Congress assembled, each State shall have one vote" (Article V), stem from the states' reluctance to delegate more than the bare minimum of their respective governing prerogatives to the national government. Nevertheless, by 1786 mounting dissatisfaction with the imbalance of power between the states and the national government resulted in an attempt to augment national power in order to improve commercial relations among the states. Five states convened in Annapolis, Maryland, during which time the delegates agreed to request that all the states send delegates to another convention in Philadelphia in 1787 to consider more substantive revisions to the Articles of Confederation. The states—some reluctantly and others with cautious optimism—responded. The end result was the ratification of the U.S. Constitution in 1789, a partly federal (states' rights) and partly national "plan of government."

By and large the Bill of Rights was added to the U.S. Constitution in 1791 as a concession by nationalists to advocates of states' rights. This is particularly the case with the Tenth Amendment, which maintains that "[t]he powers not delegated to the United States by the Constitution, nor prohibited by it to the States, are reserved to the States respectively or to the people." This amendment did not confer states' rights on the states—rather, it reaffirmed that certain powers were reserved by the states for the states. However, the demarcation between delegated and reserved powers was variously understood. Nationalists preferred a demarcation that favored national government prerogatives, whereas those who favored local control supported a demarcation advantageous to states' rights.

The constitutional mechanisms for resolving a dispute over national versus state prerogatives had not been adumbrated in the Constitution. The first significant dispute arose when the Federalist administration passed the 1798 Alien and Sedition Acts. Kentucky and Virginia responded with two resolutions drafted by Thomas Jefferson and James Madison, respectively. These resolutions asserted that the acts usurped the reserved powers of the states, and that the states could interpose "to prevent the enforcement of oppressive laws" and, in the language of the Kentucky Resolutions, nullify the unconstitutional acts of Congress. The crisis passed, but the fundamental issue of states' rights versus national power did not.

The authority to determine boundaries between national and state governing prerogatives was incrementally arrogated by the U.S. Supreme Court, not simply by promulgating through case law which powers were retained and which delegated by the states, but also by the insistence upon national judicial supremacy over state courts. Several landmark U.S. Supreme Court cases adumbrate the handling of states' rights in U.S. case law.

In *McCulloch v. Maryland* (1819) the court expanded the scope of the delegated powers by deriving implied powers from the enumerated powers, and by establishing national legislative supremacy over the states. This expansion necessarily results in a contraction of state policy prerogatives in the subsequently broadly defined policy area of interstate commerce.

When Virginia attempted to assert its prerogatives through a form of state judicial interposition, the U.S. Supreme Court established national judicial supremacy in civil (*Martin v. Hunter's Lessee* [1816]) and criminal (*Cohens v. Virginia* [1821]) cases. In *Gibbons v. Ogden* (1824) the U.S. Supreme Court established that states may not interfere with the U.S. Congress's regulation of commerce,

once again broadly interpreted. From the case of *Charles River Bridge v. Warren Bridge* (1837), in which the court articulated a rule of construction favorable to states' rights, but nevertheless under the watchful eyes of the national government, to *Texas v. White* (1868), in which the court denied the right of state secession from the Union, but acknowledged the right to revolution, the substance of states' rights was contingent upon national prerogatives.

Twentieth-century policy developments such as the theory of selective incorporation of ballot rights into the Fourteenth Amendment, thereby applying them against the states (*Gitlow v. New York* [1925]), the New Deal (*United States v. Darby* [1941]), and the civil rights movement (*Heart of Atlanta Motel v. United States* [1964]) impacted states' rights. In each of these examples, state public policy prerogatives were curtailed. Chief Justice Taney explicated the difficult role of the court in adjudicating states' rights issues. Acknowledging that the end of the national and state governments is "to promote the happiness and prosperity of the community by which it is established," the court must utilize a rule of construction that does not detract from that constitutional mandate (*Charles River Bridge v. Warren Bridge* [1837]). However, in the event of a conflict between states' rights and national interests the U.S. Supreme Court, and not the states, is the final arbiter. On balance, national interests have prevailed. Nevertheless, offshoots of the original states' rights doctrine have survived, such as dual sovereignty and state sovereign immunity, and those offshoots do accord the states a dignity that is a remnant of their original status as sovereign entities (see *Federal Maritime Commission v. South Carolina State Ports Authority et al.* [2002]). But recent court decisions partial to state sovereign immunity and dual sovereignty are tenuous, usually split along the lines of the justices' ideological orientations.

The justices' ideological preferences are weak reeds upon which to rest the popular control and popular consent embodied in the framers' original understanding of states' rights. Justice Holmes was prescient when in reference to states' rights and its constitutional protection in the Tenth Amendment he insisted that "[w]e must consider what this country has become in deciding what this Amendment has reserved" (*Missouri v. Holland* [1920]). As national interests have historically determined the substance of states' rights, one can only surmise that subsequent national and international developments will continue to determine the fate of states' rights. Many treaties, international agreements, and protocols that the United States has signed seem to demand a uniformity of policy quite inconsistent with states' rights and the doctrines of popular control and consent to which the United States' framers were committed.

—MARSHALL DeROSA

Further Reading

Cheek, H. Lee. *Calhoun and Popular Rule: The Political Theory of the Disquisition and Discourse.* Columbia, Mo.: University of Missouri Press, 2001.

DeRosa, Marshall L. *The Ninth Amendment and the Politics of Creative Jurisprudence: Disparaging the Fundamental Right of Popular Control.* New Brunswick, N.J.: Transaction, 1996.

McClellan, James. *Liberty, Order, and Justice: An Introduction to the Constitutional Principles of American Government.* Indianapolis, Ind.: Liberty Fund, 2000.

McDonald, Forrest. *States' Rights and the Union: Imperium in Imperio, 1776–1876.* Lawrence, Kans.: University Press of Kansas, 2000.

See also: Bill of Rights; Bledsoe, Albert Taylor; Calhoun, John C.; Davis, Jefferson; federalism; localism; Southern conservatism; Taylor, John (of Caroline); Thurmond, Strom

Stephens, Alexander Hamilton (1812–83)

Alexander Stephens was one of the most prominent Southern politicians of the nineteenth century. Yet he was eccentric and inconsistent, and, like other Southern Whigs, struggled to reconcile sectional affinities with national ones. He began his career as a convinced nationalist and warmly embraced the Whig party at its inception. But during his service in the U.S. House of Representatives (1843–59), facing a series of troubling issues ranging from the Mexican War to the Kansas-Nebraska Act, Stephens became torn between his Whig political principles and his visceral loyalty to the South. By the time of the Civil War he had become a Democrat and sectionalist.

But even as a Southern partisan Stephens retained an independent mind. He forcefully opposed secession until it was an accomplished fact; and though he served as the Confederacy's vice president, his Whiggish distrust of executive authority led him to challenge many of Jefferson Davis's centralizing wartime measures, such as conscription. The South, he felt, should not repeat the sins of the North, even if that meant losing the war. After the war Stephens returned to politics, eventually returning to Congress in 1872. But his principal postwar achievement was a historical work, called *A Constitutional View of the Late War between the States* (1868–70), that presented the case for Southern secession. It became a locus classicus for the postbellum Southern contention that the Civil War was fought less over slavery than over the philosophical conflict between confederated government and centralized "consolidated" government.

—WILFRED M. McCLAY

Further Reading

Howe, Daniel Walker. *The Political Culture of the American Whigs.* Chicago: University of Chicago Press, 1979.

Von Abele, Rudolph. *Alexander H. Stephens.* New York: Knopf, 1946.

See also: Southern conservatism

Stigler, George J. (1911–91)

One of the leading free-market economists of the twentieth century, Stigler played a major role in the development of economic analysis in a conservative direction, although unlike his friend and colleague Milton Friedman he did not proselytize for conservative policies. Rather, he favored "hard-headed" economics and found that many liberal theories lacked merit. Stigler perhaps jokingly explained that economists tend to be conservative because the discipline of economics requires clear thinking and intelligence.

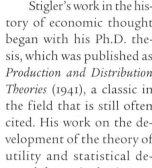

George J. Stigler

Stigler's major economic research was in four areas: his original field of interest, the history of economic thought; industrial organization; the economics of information, for which he received the Nobel Prize in 1982; and the economics of regulation. Most of his published work concentrates on the first two areas, but his ventures into the two latter areas created entire new fields in economics and changed the way economists and the public view the economy.

Stigler's life is recounted in a very pleasant autobiography, *Memoirs of an Unregulated Economist* (1988). He was born in Renton, Washington, and grew up in Seattle, graduated from the University of Washington in 1931, received a master's degree from Northwestern, and earned his Ph.D. at the University of Chicago. His dissertation on the history of economic thought was supervised by Frank H. Knight. He then taught briefly at Iowa State, Minnesota, and Brown, and for a decade at Columbia, before moving permanently to the University of Chicago in 1959. There he was a professor in both the economics department and the school of business. Along with Milton Friedman, he was the leader of the "Chicago school" of economic thinking in the 1960s and 1970s. In contrast to Friedman, who moved to the Hoover Institution at Stanford immediately upon retirement, Stigler stayed at Chicago, where he was actively involved in teaching and research until his death in 1991.

Stigler's work in the history of economic thought began with his Ph.D. thesis, which was published as *Production and Distribution Theories* (1941), a classic in the field that is still often cited. His work on the development of the theory of utility and statistical demand theory is also important. Stigler was particularly interested in Adam Smith's contributions and became known in the profession as "Adam Smith's best friend." He emphasized how microeconomic theory had developed over time in response to the *internal* needs of economic science.

Over many decades, Stigler contributed to the theory of industrial organization. His well-known textbook *The Theory of Price* (1966; original title, 1942, *The Theory of Competitive Price*) is a good example of his approach: that the careful and creative use of competitive price theory could explain most apparent paradoxes in industrial competition. This approach is in direct contrast to that of statist economists, who were much more likely to fall back on noncompetitive, monopoly, or noneconomic explanations. Through their work, Stigler and his colleagues and students at Chicago brought about a basic change in the view of competition in modern industry. Before their work, the dominant view had been that monopoly power was pervasive in the economy and a major threat. Over a generation, that view has changed to one in which the power of competition is seen as dominant in the economy. Regardless of industrial structure, firms with some market power quickly find competitors encroaching and their monopoly eroding. Many of Stigler's major articles on industrial competition are collected in *The Organization of Industry* (1988). He also completed two important monographs, *Capital and Rates of Return in Manufacturing Industries* (1963) and (with James K. Kindahl) *The Behavior of Industrial Prices* (1970).

Stigler's seminal contribution to the economics of information created a new approach to price theory. It is found in just two articles, which nicely show how Stigler extended price theoretic reasoning into new areas. Before Stigler, all economists agreed that people make decisions with incomplete information, but they had not found any practical way of including that fact in economic theory. In "The Economics of Information" (1961) and "Information in the Labor Market" (1962) Stigler provided a practical explanation of how people search for useful information. (These articles can be found in *The Organization of Industry* [1968].) Stigler showed how consumers search for low prices and workers search for jobs and high wages. The basic insight is that people know there is a distribution of high and low prices, and they compare the costs and benefits of searching for a low price. This approach integrated statistical theory with price theory and has revolutionized many fields of economics, where it is taken as a starting point that people must collect information to make decisions, and that they effectively use statistical principles in doing so. The "search" theory of unemployment, the "ra-

tional expectations" theory of macroeconomics, and the "option" theory of investments are all examples of the influence of Stigler's work on information.

Stigler's work on regulation, collected in *The Citizen and the State* (1975), was politically influential; it attacked the prevailing view that regulation was carried out in the "public interest." In contrast, Stigler emphasized the more cynical view that government acted for the benefit of politically powerful special interests. He showed empirically how to find the specific special interests that were obtaining the benefits. There is now a whole industry of economists building on Stigler's approach and analyzing regulations and laws to find the interested parties behind them. Their evidence has influenced public perceptions of government, and helped contribute to a more conservative tone in discussions of economic policy.

—Kenneth Koford

Further Reading

Stigler, George J. *The Essence of Stigler*. Edited by Kurt R. Leube and Thomas Gale Moore. Stanford, Calif.: Hoover Institution Press, 1986.

See also: Friedman, Milton; Knight, Frank H.

Storing, Herbert J. (1928–77)

For two decades before his death in 1977 at the age of 49, Storing taught political science at the University of Chicago, where his teaching and writings exerted a profound influence on the study of American government and politics, especially of the American founding, slavery and race issues, public administration and bureaucracy, and the presidency and statesmanship. Storing himself had been a graduate student at the University of Chicago in the early 1950s, where he had been influenced by three eminent political scientists: Leonard White, perhaps the nation's leading scholar of public administration; C. Herman Pritchett, a distinguished scholar of American constitutionalism; and Leo Strauss, whom some consider the foremost conservative political philosopher of the twentieth century.

Although Storing's teaching and scholarship focused more on the American political tradition than on contemporary policy issues, his 1969 essay "The Case against Civil Disobedience" stands as perhaps our most profound critique of Martin Luther King's defense of civil disobedience in his famous "Letter from a Birmingham Jail." In other essays on Frederick Douglass, Booker T. Washington, and W. E. B. Dubois, and in his influential collection of political writings by black Americans, *What Country Have I?* (1970), Storing sought to deepen the understanding of black leaders in their own tradition, to rehabilitate the importance of self-improvement and personal responsibility, and to instruct civil rights leaders in the difference between mere partisanship and a broader statesmanship. Similarly, in his important and widely reprinted essay "Slavery and the Moral Foundations of the American Republic," originally published in 1977, Storing defended the nation's founders against the charge that they did not understand the principle of human equality and equal rights as extending to blacks or other nonwhite races. Here Storing (and Martin Luther King) joined Thomas Jefferson and Abraham Lincoln against Senator Stephen Douglas, Chief Justice Roger Brooke Taney, and a growing number of contemporary academics and civil rights leaders.

No scholar of his era did more than Storing to recover the thought of the nation's founders and to instruct the American citizenry in their political principles. Foremost among Storing's scholarly contributions on the founding is his seven-volume work, *The Complete Anti-Federalist* (1981), the first complete collection ever compiled of the writings of those who opposed the ratification of the Constitution of 1787. Despite Storing's judgment that the most thoughtful of the Anti-Federalists had a deeper understanding than the Federalists of the need for republican government to rest on a foundation of sound morality, Storing concluded in the end that the Anti-Federalists "had the weaker argument." Thus, Storing took strong issue with modern conservatives who attributed the excesses of the modern welfare state to the original decision in 1787–89 to adopt a more energetic national government.

The central lesson that Storing derived from his study of the founders was the insufficiency of what he called "simplistic democracy": the notion that "the business of democratic government is simply to do whatever the people want it to do" (from his testimony before the U.S. Senate, given just weeks before he died, opposing a constitutional amendment to replace the electoral college with the direct election of presidents). Here Storing stood firmly against the populist tendencies of his age, whether from the left or the right. In so doing he stood with an older notion of republicanism that recognized the need to channel, moderate, and sometimes check public opinion in order to secure natural rights and the public good.

—Joseph M. Bessette

Further Reading

Storing, Herbert J. *Toward a More Perfect Union: Writings of Herbert J. Storing.* Edited by Joseph M. Bessette. Washington, D.C.: AEI Press, 1995.

———. *What the Anti-Federalists Were For.* Chicago: University of Chicago Press, 1981.

Bessette, Joseph M., Harry Clor, Ralph Rossum, Gary Schmitt, and Michael Zuckert. "A Symposium on Herbert J. Storing." *Political Science Reviewer* 29 (2000): 7–159.

Dry, Murray. "Herbert Storing: The American Founding and the American Regime." In *Leo Strauss, the Straussians, and the American*

Regime, edited by Kenneth L. Deutsch and John A. Murley. Lanham, Md.: Rowman & Littlefield, 1999.

See also: Anti-Federalists; Federalist Party

Strauss, Leo (1899–1973)

Leo Strauss is credited with reviving interest in classical political philosophy because he believed the study of the classics held the key to understanding the modern "crisis of the West." Through his classical scholarship, Strauss developed powerful critiques of behaviorism and "value-free" social science, historicism, and nihilism. Although Strauss espoused no original philosophy of his own and did not seek disciples, his students have come to be known as the "Straussian school" within academic political science.

Strauss was born in Germany in 1899 and was raised as an orthodox Jew. He studied at the universities of Marburg and Hamburg, and later at Freiburg with Husserl and Heidegger. Strauss left Germany in 1932, first for France and England, and finally for the United States in 1938. He held teaching posts at the New School for Social Research, the University of Chicago, Claremont Men's College, and St. Johns College in Annapolis, and he wrote more than a dozen books and scores of essays and reviews in scholarly journals.

Strauss is best known for working out an interpretation of the fundamental distinction between ancient and modern political philosophy. In this distinction, Strauss thought, lay the origin of the crisis of the West: "The most striking difference between classical political philosophy and present-day political science is that the latter is no longer concerned at all with what was the guiding question for the former: the question of the best political order." Classical political philosophy, especially that of Plato and Aristotle, was centrally concerned with the contemplation of the best regime according to nature. Hence the primacy, for the classics, of the idea of natural right, or "what is by nature right or just: is all right conventional (of human origin) or is there some right which is natural?" The contemplation of the best regime according to nature and the idea of natural right led to deliberation about ethics and individual virtue—the practical, political fruit of regimes guided by political philosophy. Classical philosophers understood that the actualization of the best regime was impossible or extremely improbable, but the contemplative nature of political philosophy generated standards by which to judge and improve actual regimes.

Leo Strauss

Strauss identified Machiavelli as the turning point in the history of political philosophy and political science: "Machiavelli appears to have broken with all preceding political philosophers." Strauss explained the Machiavellian turn in *Natural Right and History* (1950): Classical political philosophy had taken its bearings by how man ought to live; for Machiavelli the correct way of answering the question of the right order of society consisted in taking one's bearings from how men actually do live. Machiavelli's "realistic" revolt against tradition led to the substitution of patriotism or merely political virtue for human excellence or, more particularly, for moral virtue and the contemplative life. It entailed a deliberate lowering of the ultimate goal. The goal was lowered in order to increase the probability of its attainment.

This reorientation of the nature of political life, according to Strauss, opened the way for the development of modern natural right by Hobbes and Locke. This version of natural right is based chiefly on comfortable self-preservation. An important corollary of Machiavelli's—that fortune or chance can be conquered through force—opened the way for modern physical science as an instrumental means to progress, rather than as another subject of contemplation. From here it is a short step to Francis Bacon's promise of using science "for the relief of man's estate."

The modern understanding of natural right experienced several revisions at the hands of Rousseau, Kant, Hegel, and Nietzsche (among others). Rousseau turned the classical understanding of nature and civil society on its head. The classical philosophers thought imperfect human nature was improved through a well-constituted civil society; Rousseau taught that perfect or idyllic human nature was corrupted through civil society. Rousseau's teaching is the basis for modern totalitarian ideologies that seek a restoration of perfected human nature through force.

Strauss identified a second strand of modernity's rejection of classical natural right—historicism, or the view that all thought derives from changing historical circumstances. This part of Strauss's work has always been controversial among conservatives, since Strauss identified Edmund Burke as one of the progenitors of historicism:

> The historical school emerged in reaction to the French Revolution and to the [modern] natural right doctrines that had prepared that cataclysm. . . . The novel element in Burke's critique of reason reveals itself least ambigu-

ously in its most important practical consequence: he rejects the view that constitutions can be "made" in favor of the view that they must "grow"; he therefore rejects in particular the view that the best social order can be or ought to be the work of an individual, or a wise "legislator" or founder. . . . It is only a short step from this thought of Burke to the supersession of the distinction between good and bad by the distinction between the progressive and the retrograde, or between what is and what is not in harmony with the historical process. . . .

Strauss thought Burke's reaction to Rousseau opened the way for Hegelian historicism and the radical reactions to this historicism by Nietzsche and Heidegger.

In addition to the themes of natural right versus historicism, Strauss is known also for two other controversies, one wholly substantive and one partly methodological. The substantive controversy involves Strauss's ideas about the relationship of reason and revelation; the methodological controversy involves Strauss's interpretation of secret or esoteric writing.

Reacting to the monopolistic claim to truth on the part of modern science and the ostensible philosophic refutation of revealed religion beginning most conspicuously with Spinoza, Strauss held that neither modern science nor modern philosophy could refute the possibility of divine revelation. Although Strauss thought reason and revelation were incompatible, he thought that philosophy required a premise of faith equal to the premise of faith required by revealed religion. Strauss also thought that the tension between reason and revelation—between Athens and Jerusalem—was the secret of the vitality of the West. Moreover, modern science and modern philosophy attacked the common moral basis of both classical rationalism and revealed religion, which is why Strauss regarded the fate of both reason and revelation as so closely bound together.

Strauss's interpretive doctrine of secret or esoteric writing, first developed in his analysis of Moses Maimonides, holds that philosophers usually write carefully to conceal the key points of their ideas from general readers. This is done for two related reasons: to avoid persecution for impiety and to avoid directly challenging the political order or legitimacy of the society in which the philosophers live. Hence philosophers write "esoterically" so that only the most perceptive readers—usually other philosophers—will grasp the essence of their teachings. Employing this hermeneutic, Strauss and his students have produced idiosyncratic interpretations of most major philosophers, both ancient and modern.

Although Strauss's writing is usually detailed and sometimes dense, readers will find throughout his writings analyses of striking clarity and judgments of aphoristic quality. Strauss's criticism of "value-free" social science and behaviorism culminated in his famous analogy to Nero, that is, social science "fiddles while Rome burns. It is excused by two facts: it does not know that it fiddles, and it does not know that Rome burns." Another frequently recalled passage is Strauss's description of modern materialistic hedonism as "the joyless quest for joy."

Among Strauss's students are many accomplished conservative political scientists, including the late Allan Bloom, Harry Jaffa, Harvey Mansfield Jr., and Walter Berns.

—STEPHEN HAYWARD

Further Reading

Drury, Shadia B. *The Political Ideas of Leo Strauss.* New York: St. Martin's Press, 1988.

McAlister, Ted V. *Revolt against Modernity: Leo Strauss, Eric Voegelin, and the Search for a Postliberal Order.* Lawrence, Kans.: University Press of Kansas, 1996.

Strauss, Leo. *The City and Man.* New York: Rand McNally, 1964.

———. *Liberalism Ancient and Modern.* New York: Basic Books, 1968.

———. *On Tyranny.* 1963. New York: Free Press, 1991.

———. *Persecution and the Art of Writing.* New York: Free Press, 1952.

———. *The Rebirth of Classical Political Rationalism.* Chicago: University of Chicago Press, 1989.

———. *Spinoza's Critique of Religion.* New York: Schocken Books, 1965.

See also: émigré intellectuals; historicism; Jaffa, Harry V.; Mansfield, Harvey C.; modernity and postmodernity; natural law; Natural Right and History; Straussianism; tradition

Straussianism

Straussianism is the term used to denote the research methods, common concepts, theoretical presuppositions, central questions, and pedagogic style characteristic of the large number of conservatives who have been influenced by the thought and teaching of Leo Strauss (1899–1973). Straussianism is particularly influential among university professors of historical political theory, but it also sometimes serves as a common intellectual framework more generally among conservative activists, think tank professionals, and public intellectuals. Currently, Straussianism is associated in the public mind with neoconservatism, but the precise nature of this relationship is controversial.

Least controversially, Straussianism is defined by its method within the academic discipline of political theory. Straussians engage in a "close reading" of the "Great Books" of political thought; they strive to understand a thinker "as he understood himself"; they are unconcerned with questions about the historical context of, or historical influences on, a given author; they seek to be open to the possibility that in any given

Great Book from the past, one may come across something that is *the truth*, simply. Two things may at once be said about this approach, which resembles in important ways the old New Criticism in literary studies. First, the method is powerful, and the effort of intellectual discipline that it requires cultivates a particularly focused kind of discursive intelligence: Straussians, like the old New Critics, are often among the most penetrating readers of texts. Second, like the New Criticism, the Straussian method may be reproduced with relative facility. It does not require field research, extensive contextual historical investigations, technical skills such as paleography, or the acquisition of multiple foreign languages. All that is necessary is a properly trained mind and a Great Book. These two facts may help explain, on the one hand, the intellectual prestige of Straussians, and on the other hand, the widespread success of Straussianism as an academic "school."

There is a more controversial dimension to the Straussian method. Straussians make a strong distinction between works of political thought that rise to the level of Great Books and those that do not. Great Books are those written by authors—philosophers—of such sovereign critical self-knowledge and intellectual power that they can in no way be reduced to the general thought of their time and place. In fact, the great minds who write such books *create* the general thought of later times: books by lesser writers, no matter how important, are understood as epiphenomenal to the original insights of a thinker of the first rank. With respect to writers of the first rank, this premise leads to an intensity of hermeneutic engagement that is often described as Talmudic. Talmudic skills were, of course, developed in relationship to a divine text, one that could not err. In effect, the Straussian method encourages a like respect for the writings of true philosophers.

It is here that the possibility of "esoteric" writing is invoked. Given the example of Socrates' conviction and execution by Athens for the crimes of impiety and corrupting the youth, later philosophers, Straussians maintain, learned to write at two levels for two sorts of readers. On the surface, their teaching would strive to be unobjectionable to the authorities of their regime; their deepest insights—or their real opinions—would lie hidden, accessible only to those few with the intellectual penetration and patience to navigate the apparent lapses in argument, mistakes in citation, or peculiarities of presentation that had been made deliberately to draw the adept to the philosophical core of a work. While some Straussian writings can be marvels of hermeneutic display, the value of the resulting payoff is ambiguous. Thus, Machiavelli is shown by Straussians to be an immoralist: well, was that not the received interpretation of the readers of his time?

While there are students of Strauss who are not political conservatives, Straussianism is rightly recognized as an authentic form of conservatism. Strauss's approach to the Great Books was meant, in part, as a response to the historicist presuppositions of the mid-twentieth century, which read the history of political thought in a progressivist way, with past philosophies forever cut off from us in a superseded past. To be open to the possibility that Plato has hold of *the truth*—and that more recent thinkers are therefore wrong—is to reject the progressivist narrative radically. Moreover, one of Strauss's major themes concerned specifically the *problem* of modernity, and this has remained a perennial theme for his disciples. Modern political philosophers have been, Strauss argued, from the beginning engaged in a project to change the world rather than to understand it. Compared with the ancients (and the medievals), their project entails a "lowering of the sights" of political life—from the high end of virtue to the low end of commodious self-preservation. Something genuinely human is thereby in danger of being lost.

Modernity, moreover, progresses for Straussians in "waves" of deepening difficulty, each new crisis the handiwork of a philosopher-founder: Machiavelli, Rousseau, and Nietzsche. While these waves may be distinguished, they are also logically connected. Thus, the central political problem of the twentieth century—totalitarianism, whether national socialist or international communist—may be understood as a radicalized form of a more deep-rooted political and intellectual problematic within modernity as such. This analysis of the crisis of the twentieth century comported well with the spiritual stance of many other conservatives during the Cold War years—perhaps particularly with that of conservative Roman Catholics, who soon recognized in Strauss someone from outside their own faith community who nonetheless seemed to advance something very like a traditional Catholic critique of modern philosophy and the modern world.

From the beginning, Straussianism has been controversial. Being conservatives, and being devoted to the Great Books, they met with often fierce opposition within complacently progressive and scientistic political science departments and had difficulties finding academic positions. But the Straussians have been a subject of controversy among otherwise well-disposed conservatives as well. To make matters still more complex, some Straussians have turned against other Straussians. These changing attitudes are the result of the changing nature of Straussianism itself—or at least of its emphases and modes of presentation.

After Strauss's death, two prominent schools of Straussians evolved, usually described as East Coast and West Coast Straussians. The East Coast Straussians were in some sense led by Strauss's student Allan Bloom at the University of Chicago; the West Coast Straussians have been led by Strauss's student Harry Jaffa at Claremont McKenna College in California. Both schools have reflected deeply on Strauss's work in an effort to appropriate it more deeply; yet in so doing they have pushed elements of Strauss's thought in such a way as to create intellectual tensions with other varieties of American conservatism.

The East Coast Straussians have tended increasingly to emphasize philosophy as the one best way of life for man—and to emphasize that this way of life is not open to all. They have also interpreted Strauss's account of the relationship between reason and revelation, or Athens and Jerusalem, in such a way as to become dismissive of revealed religion.

In his own work, Strauss's attempt to revive the political science of Plato and Aristotle seemed to constitute a not unsympathetic rejoinder to modern liberal democracy, emphasizing instead natural hierarchies among human beings and the advantages of the "rule of the gentlemen," who are characterized by their moral virtues and their moderation. Natural inequalities and the importance of the virtues are clearly conservative themes. But East Coast Straussians have grown less political, less interested in correcting the modern regime. They are now more relativistic about many moral and civic virtues—which depend upon the regime and hence are conventional—while tending to restrict natural right (or natural justice) to the philosophical virtues and the philosophical life. What had been a hierarchy of soul-types has become more of a binary distinction between philosophers and nonphilosophers. What is more, the account of the philosophical life provided by a figure such as Allan Bloom has taken on certain overtones, with the most prominent place given to the act of skeptical unmasking or of penetrating to unsettling depths. It is difficult to find in such an account any room for a contemplative "delight in the truth," which others have taken to be the summit of the philosophical life. In fact, "truth" is not a prominent word in the lexicon of East Coast Straussianism.

Similarly, Strauss was careful and coy in his descriptions of the relationship between Athens and Jerusalem. Rhetorically, he treated them more or less as equals, each unable to refute the other dialectically and each founded on a kind of faith. In the context of his time, many readers understood him to be mounting a philosophical defense of the possibility of revelation—something quite remarkable in an age of scientific certainty and self-confidence. The East Coast Straussians, however, suggest that the respect with which Strauss treats revealed religion is an exoteric feature of his writing. Rather than a coequal, by nature Jerusalem is radically subordinate to Athens. Religion has dignity only within the limits of reason. And even if this is a doubtful interpretation of Strauss's position—there is some evidence to the contrary—what is certainly clear is that, for Strauss, the claims of Athens and Jerusalem can never be resolved into a "synthesis." Therefore, "Christian philosophy" is a misnomer, and the works of such thinkers as Augustine and Thomas Aquinas fall outside philosophy's Great Tradition.

Taken together, these features of the East Coast school have led some conservatives to view them as crypto-nihilists, sharing more with Nietzsche than with Plato. When such accusations are made, however, East Coast Straussians can recall that similar charges were raised against Socrates, and so they are in the best of company philosophically.

The West Coast Straussians are less philosophical and more political, concerned primarily with the American founding and America's liberal democratic regime. The West Coast school has produced excellent scholarship on the thought of the founding

generation and also on Abraham Lincoln. They are, however, accused by some conservatives of constructing an ideology out of the "self-evident" truths announced in the Declaration of Independence. "Truth" is very much a part of the West Coast lexicon—in particular, the truth that "all men are created equal."

In the face of the totalitarianisms of the twentieth century, Strauss deeply appreciated the moderation, security, and freedom of America. While generally critical of all modern regimes, he nonetheless treated America as the best regime under the circumstances. What was it about America that enabled this evidently—and perhaps preeminently—modern country to escape the ideological fanaticisms of the twentieth century? The answer given by the traditionalist Russell Kirk was that America was not as modern as its enthusiasts believed: in fact, a great deal of premodern tradition survived and flourished in the New World, both in custom and even in constitutional law. This Tocquevilleian perspective is not, however, the West Coast Straussian view. Rather, the West Coast school has held that it was America's foundation on universal natural rights that shielded it from the historicism that gave birth to the monsters of twentieth-century ideology. The natural rights of life, liberty, and the pursuit of happiness, and the government by consent that is the corollary of the truth of human equality, really do constitute natural justice. America is just insofar as it cleaves to those truths, and it errs only when it diverges from them—as has sometimes been the case, especially with slavery, and then after the Progressive Era. In his more immoderate statements, Harry Jaffa comes close to speaking of the American constitutional order (at least, as understood by Lincoln) as the Best Regime itself, the regime laid up in heaven come down to earth.

In the course of developing this position, at least two elements of Strauss's own thought have had to be modified. First, Strauss insisted on the irreconcilability of Athens and Jerusalem; the West Coast school claims that on the decisive point of equality, Athens and Jerusalem agree. Second, Strauss understood modernity in all its waves to participate in a general "lowering of the sights" of political life; America was no exception to that indictment. The West Coast school has tended to deny the modernity of America, at least in any negative sense. Consequently, whereas Strauss insisted on a strong distinction between ancient natural right, medieval natural law, and modern natural rights, the West Coast school tends to blur these distinctions.

The result of the West Coast school's efforts has been a well-developed theoretical defense of a conservatism closely identified with the Party of Lincoln. One feature of the position is its ready political utility: in effect, it provides a philosophical justification for patriotic pride in American exceptionalism. The work of the West Coast school has been influential among some California politicians and also, for example, in the jurisprudence of Clarence Thomas. The school's most heated arguments have been with traditionalist and often Southern conservatives, whom they accuse of unprincipled historicism. As recently as the 1980s, it was generally acknowledged that any possible American conservatism would have a disproportionately Southern complexion, the South being the most conservative region of the country. The West Coast school, however, has worked aggressively to render all forms of "Calhounianism" untenable within American conservatism.

This schematic account of Straussianism in two schools omits much. There are East Coast Straussians who have retained a genuinely political interest in correcting the one-sided partisanship of American liberal democracy. There are Europeans and Canadians who are deeply respectful of Strauss but who are in no way dogmatic, combining in fruitful ways what they have learned from Strauss with what they have learned from other great teachers. And there are by now indications of an emerging school of what might be called faith-based Straussians: those trained in Straussian methods and sympathetic to many Straussian concepts and lines of inquiry, but who consciously subordinate the more extreme Straussian presuppositions to revealed wisdom.

As America prepared for war against Iraq in response to the 9/11 terrorist attacks, a great deal of journalistic commentary, particularly in Europe, centered on the malignant influence of neoconservatives within the Bush administration—and of Straussians within neoconservatism. Numerous Straussians took to print to deny any connection between the neoconservative Bush Doctrine and the thought of Leo Strauss—and, in fact, most of the evidence adduced by the journalists leveling the charge was quite strained. The traces of Straussianism were said to be evident in (1) the Bush administration's view that liberal democracy is the "final" form of political order toward which all societies move in history, (2) the neoconservatives' approach to politics as a search for the right "enemy," and (3) the purported mendacity of the Bush administration concerning weapons of mass destruction. This is a peculiar bill of indictment. It was Alexandre Kojève, not Leo Strauss, who introduced the "end of history" thesis: Strauss argued at length against Kojève that the universal and homogeneous state could only be a tyranny. It was Carl Schmitt, not Leo Strauss, who introduced the *Freund/Feind* (friend/enemy) distinction at the core of "the political": Strauss had a critical dialogue with Schmitt as well. And the Platonic teaching concerning the "noble lie" certainly cannot be understood as providing blanket permission for opportunistic political dissembling.

However, one plausible link between

Straussianism and the neoconservatives who were prominent in advocating the Iraq War concerns the matter of "regime." The Greek word *politeia* had traditionally been translated into English as "constitution," but Strauss and his followers have always translated it as "regime." According to Aristotle, the regime is both the "arrangement of offices" in a city and the "way of life" of a city: politics and culture are deeply intertwined. Among some Straussians, particularly those engaged in intraconservative disputes with traditionalists, a vulgar view emerged which held that properly understood, regime analysis implies the straightforward *sovereignty* of politics over culture. In contrast, traditionalists have held, against the Marxists, that politics is deeper than economics, and culture deeper still than politics. It is possible that this Straussian certainty about the sovereignty of politics played a role in neoconservative expectations about the likely outcome of regime-change in Iraq.

—Mark C. Henrie

Further Reading

Deutsch, Kenneth L., ed. *The Crisis of Liberal Democracy: A Straussian Perspective*. Albany, N.Y.: State University of New York Press, 1987.

———, and John A. Murley, eds., *Leo Strauss, the Straussians, and the American Regime*. Lanham, Md.: Rowman & Littlefield, 1999.

Drury, Shadia. *The Political Ideas of Leo Strauss*. New York: St. Martin's, 1988.

See also: Bloom, Allan; Declaration of Independence; historicism; Iraq War; Jaffa, Harry V.; modernity and postmodernity; Natural Right and History; neoconservatism; Strauss, Leo

Students For America

The original Students For America (not to be confused with a later but ephemeral body by that name, headquartered in North Carolina) was the first nationwide conservative student organization in the United States. This organization grew out of the successful efforts of Bob Munger and some associates to wrest control of the student government at Los Angeles City College (a two-year institution) from the leftist faction that had dominated it. It was founded in late 1951, under the name National Collegiate MacArthur Clubs, by Munger, who had by then become a junior at George Pepperdine College (now University). A year after its founding, the National Collegiate MacArthur Clubs became Students For America, and General Douglas MacArthur accepted its honorary presidency.

Shortly after its establishment, the organization's membership in Southern California, where it began, exceeded that of the Young Democrats and the Young Republicans combined. By early 1953, it was represented on 106 campuses from coast to coast. Numerous well-known political figures endorsed Students For America, as did newspaper, radio, and television commentators and celebrities from the entertainment world. Distinguished scholars, such as Daniel S. Robinson, director of the School of Philosophy of the University of Southern California, and Kenneth W. Colegrove, head of the Department of Political Science at Northwestern University, served as faculty advisers to chapters.

Students For America's activities were varied but all dealt with the dissemination of conservative political and economic values and the struggle against leftist ideology, especially as embodied in Marxism. Among other things, it published a four-page monthly periodical, the *American Student*; circulated pamphlets from the Foundation for Economic Education, as well as other free-market and anticommunist literature; and produced research material and reports (e.g., on socialist bias in the National Students Association and Marxist influence at the University of Chicago). It also operated a student government election service and a speakers bureau.

Because its leadership was to a large extent composed of minors, legal control of the organization was vested in a small body of professed supporters, the Students For America Foundation. After Munger, Students For America's national director, entered military service, the foundation's officers, for reasons unknown, ceased to accept telephone calls or to answer letters from those who succeeded him. The body was paralyzed, even as requests for membership and information were flooding it.

By 1955, Students For America was effectively defunct. However, many notable contemporary conservatives and libertarians had already cut their political teeth in it, including historians Ralph Raico and Leonard Liggio, political scientist George W. Carey, economist George Reisman, social philosopher R. V. Andelson, jurist James D. Heiple, columnist Fulton Lewis III, and publicist Allan H. Ryskind. Munger went on to succeed in advertising, real estate investment, and film production.

—ROBERT V. ANDELSON

Sumner, William Graham (1840–1910)

William Graham Sumner, European-educated theologian and Anglican pastor, assumed a position as professor of political economy at Yale University in 1873, where he remained for the rest of his life. In his nearly forty years at Yale, Sumner migrated from his foundations in political economy to become one of America's premier sociologists. In *What Social Classes Owe to Each Other* (1883), *Folkways* (1906), and *Science of Society* (1927), and in countless articles and speeches, he countered the utopianism of progressives and socialists, skewering their arguments for

government-based melioration of existing social conditions with a penetrating, realistic logic. He offered a strong conservative intellectual response to utopian progressivism, emphasizing the profound importance of liberty, private property, and minimalist government to the human effort to win legitimate, hard-earned victories against a harsh, competitive natural order. The operation of the inexorable laws of this natural order, what he called the struggle for existence and the competition of life, could never be overcome but only offset by the continual acquisition and application of capital dedicated to advancing the arts and sciences. This scheme offered the only true means of societal advance within a given, limited territory.

Sumner battled the progressives from a foundation of assumptions held in common: original man was a brute transformed into a social, rational, and acquisitive being by some fortuitous accident of nature. Along with the progressives, he also rejected the concept of natural rights elaborated in the Declaration of Independence, arguing that it was a notion useful in the overthrow of feudal social organization, but beyond that devoid of substantive value and actually dangerous when used to justify utopian ideas. He rejected conceptions of universal human nature in favor of conventional social norms, but he also rejected assumptions regarding the infinite malleability of mankind directed by some extra-societal force toward perpetual advance and an improvement of the human condition. Mankind, rather, was limited in its ability to shape future social conditions by those unchanging social and economic laws, discoverable by science, which established the boundaries of legitimate political organization and action. The violation of laws such as supply and demand set in motion an inexorable decline toward man's original barbarism.

These philosophic (Sumner would say scientific) assertions informed his opposition to domestic and international policies favored by the progressives of his day. Government attempts at social melioration simply took from the productive elements of society those means by which they were able to promote the continued advance of the arts and sciences, giving those means instead to those who either could or would not make beneficial use of them. These views, combined with certain expressions in his phrasing, resulted in him being castigated as the leading social Darwinist of the age. Sumner also advocated resistance to the imperial impulse, as in the war with Spain, arguing that imperialism would undermine the favorable social and economic conditions that made republican government possible in the United States.

—LANCE ROBINSON

Further Reading

Curtis, Bruce. *William Graham Sumner*. Boston: Twayne, 1981.

Sumner, William Graham. *On Liberty, Society, and Politics: The Essential Essays of William Graham Sumner*. Edited by Robert C. Bannister. Indianapolis, Ind.: Liberty Fund, 1992.

See also: social Darwinism

supply-side economics

"Supply-side economics" is a term that describes a set of economic policies developed in the late 1970s as a counter to the then dominant Keynesian economics. Adopted in its main features by the Reagan administration, the principal element of supply-side economics was its advocacy of marginal tax-rate reductions as a means of stimulating economic growth.

Supply-side economics was not a fully-integrated school of economic thought, but rather a new way of presenting forgotten truths of classical economics. The main feature of classical economics, which began with Adam Smith, was its focus on the price system. Prices embodied all available knowledge about the supply and demand for goods and services and would instantly adjust to take account of new information. Thus, maintaining price flexibility through free markets was essential to allocate scarce resources efficiently and to maximize social welfare. Governments played no major role in the classical system, other than enforcing property rights and guaranteeing the value of the currency.

The depth and length of the Great Depression—marked by the oversupply of goods and labor—were thought to fundamentally contradict the classical view. Classical economists believed that prices would quickly fall and reestablish a new equilibrium, thus ending the depression. When this did not happen, the classical view was declared obsolete. John Maynard Keynes, a British economist, put forward a new view of economic policy in which governmental action would compensate for the free market's alleged failures. The main feature of Keynes's view was a reliance on deficit spending to stimulate aggregate demand in the economy; in other words, to provide purchasing power to allow consumers to buy goods, thereby stimulating additional production. The vast expansion of budget deficits and the apparent prosperity of World War II seemed to vindicate Keynes's theories. As a consequence, government macroeconomic policy increasingly adopted the Keynesian approach.

In fact, subsequent research indicates that governmental failure, rather than failure of the market system, was responsible for the Depression. In particular, the Smoot-Hawley Tariff caused world trade to collapse; Federal Reserve policy caused the money supply to shrink by one-third between 1929 and 1933; tax increases under both Presidents Hoover and Roosevelt sapped incentives; and government efforts to prevent prices from falling, through the National Recovery Act and other legislation, were the major causes of economic disintegration.

Ironically, the greatest success of Keynesian policy—the Kennedy tax cut of 1964—also proved to be the precursor of supply-side economics. In 1963, President John F. Kennedy accepted the recommendations of his Keynesian advisors, led by Walter Heller, to deliberately increase the budget deficit to stimulate economic growth. Although Kennedy's advisors favored an increase in government spending to raise the deficit, Kennedy proposed a tax cut instead. Moreover, he favored a tax-rate reduction to reduce the high World War II tax rates. Although not enacted until after his death, the Kennedy tax cut reduced the top income tax rate from 91 percent to 70 percent and the bottom rate from 20 percent to 14 percent.

In the 1970s, the Keynesian view came under attack. First, monetarists, led by Milton Friedman of the University of Chicago, argued that Keynesians paid insufficient attention to the role of the money supply in the economy, especially as the cause of inflation. Second, as budget deficits increased to record levels and the economy continued to stagnate, it became increasingly difficult to view deficits as stimulative. In fact, a growing number of economists began to view deficits as a drag on the economy.

Looking for a new method of stimulating growth, a number of people began to advocate tax-rate reductions in the late 1970s. Among them were Arthur Laffer, Robert Mundell, Paul Craig Roberts, and Norman Ture. Laffer had been chief economist at the Office of Management and Budget in the early 1970s and subsequently taught at the University of Chicago and the University of Southern California; Mundell also taught at Chicago and later at Columbia; Roberts worked on the congressional staff in the late 1970s and later became an assistant secretary of the treasury; Ture had worked on the Kennedy tax cut in the 1960s and was in the Reagan administration the undersecretary of the treasury for tax and economic affairs.

However, the most important converts to tax reduction were Congressman Jack Kemp (R-N.Y.) and the editors of the *Wall Street Journal*. Kemp began pushing across-the-board tax cuts in Congress, while the *Wall Street Journal* promoted the idea in its editorials, which were often written by Robert Bartley and Jude Wanniski. Wanniski wrote the first book explicitly devoted to supply-side economics, *The Way the World Works* (1978).

The gist of the emerging supply-side view was that inflation had sharply raised tax rates by pushing individuals into higher tax brackets and eroding the value of corporate depreciation allowances. These higher tax rates were gradually sapping the incentive to work, save, and invest, as the government took a higher and higher percentage of the return. A tax-rate reduction, therefore, would restore incentives and stimulate production. Indeed, it was hypothesized that growth might be so stimulated that there would be no loss of government revenue. This notion was popularized through the so-called Laffer curve, which showed that government revenue declines if tax rates are too high and rise if such rates are reduced.

The main vehicle for promoting supply-side economics was an individual tax-rate reduction proposed by Kemp and Senator William Roth (R-Del.), which would have cut the top tax rate from 70 percent to 50 percent and the bottom rate from 14 percent to 10 percent. It was thought that such a tax cut would roughly approximate the Kennedy tax cut. Another vehicle was the cut in capital-gains taxes sponsored by Congressman William Steiger (R-Wisc.).

The Carter administration strongly opposed both proposals. However, after passage of Proposition 13 in California in June 1978, support in Congress for some kind of tax cut became overwhelming. The Steiger proposal was ultimately enacted that year. Versions of the Kemp-Roth proposal passed both the House and Senate but were rejected in conference under strong pressure from the Carter administration.

In 1980, Ronald Reagan strongly endorsed the supply-side view. One of his first acts as president in 1981 was to propose a version of the Kemp-Roth bill. In August of that year, Reagan signed such a bill into law, reducing the top income tax rate from 70 percent to 50 percent. Subsequently, in 1986, the top rate was further reduced to 28 percent—its lowest level since the 1920s. These tax cuts are generally believed to have been a major factor in the growth and prosperity of the 1980s, in contrast to the inflation and stagnation of the 1970s.

In the 1990s, it became fashionable to deny the significance of supply-side economics. It was said that continuing budget deficits proved the fallacy of the Laffer curve. In fact, the Reagan administration's tax proposal never indicated that any revenues would be recouped, although subsequent research by Professor Lawrence Lindsey of Harvard has shown that a considerable amount of revenue was recovered through growth.

Although discussion of supply-side economics diminished after the 1980s, this is largely an indication of its success, rather than its failure. The fact is that the views of supply-side economics were almost entirely incorporated into economic policy and economic theory. Thus, there is no longer a meaningful distinction between the supply-side view and the mainstream view. The differences that remain between supply-side economists and mainstream economists are, to a large extent, differences of emphasis and degree, rather than arguments about fundamentals.

—BRUCE BARTLETT

Further Reading

Bartlett, Bruce. *Reaganomics: Supply-Side Economics in Action.* New Rochelle, N.Y.: Arlington House, 1981.

Bartlett, Bruce, and Timothy P. Roth, eds. *The Supply-Side Solution.* Chatham, N.J.: Chatham House, 1983.

Canto, Victor, Douglas H. Joines, and Arthur B. Laffer. *Foundations of Supply-Side Economics.* New York: Academic Press, 1983.

Gilder, George. *Wealth and Poverty.* New York: Basic Books, 1981.

Lindsey, Lawrence B. *The Growth Experiment.* New York: Basic Books, 1990.

Roberts, Paul. *The Supply-Side Revolution.* Cambridge, Mass.: Harvard University Press, 1984.

See also: Kemp, Jack F.; Keynesian economics; Laffer curve; Reagan, Ronald; Wall Street Journal

Supreme Court

The Supreme Court has been a source of particular concern for conservatives at least since the 1950s. But whereas many observers attempt to portray this concern as being rooted in conservatives' discontent with a specific set of decisions to have emerged from the Court during these years, it is closer to the truth to see the conservative criticism of the Court as rooted in an attachment to traditional American forms of self-government. George Carey, for example, has argued that the Constitution must be read in light of a "constitutional morality" governing its interpretation. This constitutional morality dictates that important political actors show self-restraint in order to maintain the separation of powers at the heart of our system of government.

Despite the numerous "auxiliary precautions" built into the Constitution, that document cannot, on its own, prevent the usurpation of inappropriate powers by any single branch of the national government. No political structure, no constitution, no matter how well constructed, can itself provide or maintain ordered liberty. Nor can any one person or institution—court, legislature, or executive—be trusted to protect that liberty on its own. In the system of government put together by the founders, the Supreme Court's limited though important role was that of enforcing preexisting common, statutory, and constitutional law within the given circumstances of the time. To do less would be to allow anarchy. To do more would be to move toward tyranny. Unfortunately, the Court has chosen to do more. And the resulting usurpation of legislative and executive powers by the Supreme Court over the course of the twentieth century, with its roots in significant earlier usurpations, has undermined America's original constitutional morality to the point of near irrelevance, while at the same time it has enshrined a new morality of judicial supremacy inimical to the local self-government conservatives find at the heart of the American tradition—and of good government in general.

The object of great fear on the part of the Constitution's Anti-Federalist opponents, the Supreme Court was presented by Alexander Hamilton in *The Federalist* as the "least dangerous branch," an institution possessing the powers neither of purse nor sword, and dependent on the executive even for the enforcement of its decisions. Early decisions, particularly under the leadership of Chief Justice John Marshall, served to solidify the position of the Court as the interpreter of the Constitution and the national government as the supreme government of the United States. *Marbury v. Madison* (1803) established the practice of judicial review, largely based on the logic of constitutionalism outlined by Hamilton, according to which a court must defer to and enforce the constitution (the law of the people) when it conflicts with lesser laws (passed by the people's representatives). *Fletcher v. Peck* (1810)

defined the Constitution's contracts clause (Article 1) broadly, allowing the Court to define limits to states' power to breach preexisting agreements. *Dartmouth College v. Woodward* (1819) barred states from rescinding or modifying private charters even as it left local, municipal charters open to unilateral revocation.

Despite Marshall's aggressive leadership, the Court by and large abided by the original constitutional morality of institutional restraint through the early part of the nineteenth century. After *Marbury* it did not overturn a single piece of federal legislation until its infamous decision in the Dred Scott case (*Scott v. Sanford*, 1857). Here the Court ruled (1) that Congress had no power to legislate regarding slavery in the United States territories (thus striking down the Missouri Compromise of 1820); (2) that Americans of African descent were incapable of being federal citizens; and (3) that slaveowners had a substantive right to enjoyment of their (slave) property, a right guaranteed by the due process clause of the Fifth Amendment. Thus, according to the Court, the federal government had a duty to protect the right to own slaves. This decision helped spark the Civil War. It also read into the text of the Constitution a doctrine ("substantive due process") according to which the Court itself would decide who had what rights, and how they were to be vindicated.

There is significant disagreement among conservatives regarding the legitimacy of the Court's decisions under the substantive due process doctrine, viz., whether the doctrine applied directly to federal laws or, as is more commonly thought, applied to state laws through the mechanism of an expansive reading of the Fourteenth Amendment. Some writers, particularly libertarians, see the Court's post–Civil War decisions on economic matters as imposing an appropriate set of rights against state and federal action. A wave of cases cresting with *Lochner v. New*

York (1905) struck down laws regulating various economic relationships. *Lochner,* for example, struck down a state law limiting the maximum number of hours a baker could work, on the grounds that the law improperly interfered with a substantive constitutional right to freedom of contract. The "Lochner Doctrine" required laws to have a real and substantial relationship to a legitimate state end, and interference with a substantive due process right was not a legitimate end. This line of economic due process cases was repudiated in *West Coast Hotel v. Parrish* (1937), on the grounds that it interfered with the rights of state legislatures. But another line of cases that has found substantive *civil* rights has come to dominate judicial discourse and, arguably, American public life.

A series of decisions culminating in *Roe v. Wade* (1973) found an increasingly wide "right to privacy," which included the right to abort a child ready to be born and a right to engage in homosexual sodomy, in the "emanations from penumbras" supposedly existing in the Constitution. It is this line of cases to which conservatives object most vehemently, and which shows the inherent bias of substantive due process jurisprudence toward judicial supremacy. For in these cases, as in those dealing with economic rights, the Court has purported to find rights in the Constitution that have no basis in the text; and it has further asserted a right to vindicate those rights by actively striking down longstanding laws, regulations, and customs, even ordering the other two branches of government—and the people at large—to act in accordance with its will.

Beginning in earnest in the 1950s, the Court has taken on powers properly belonging to the legislature and the executive branches or to the states. For example, in the follow-up to the school desegregation case *Brown v. Board of Education* (1954) known as *Brown II* (1955), the Court ordered the states to begin desegregating "with all deliberate speed." This in turn led to a series of decisions by which judges ordered the forced busing of students to schools far from their homes to meet predetermined racial quotas, to the judicial redrawing of district maps, and to the minute administration of school districts by judges, who went so far as to order the raising of taxes to achieve their own numerical goals.

In other areas as well, including the makeup of electoral districts and the awarding of broadcasting licenses, the courts have taken unto themselves the power to dictate social, economic, and political policies in direct opposition to the other branches of government, and with no basis in the text of the Constitution. The Court has turned the right to political speech into the right of nude dancers to ply their trade. It has turned the right to be free from a federally established religion into the right of atheists to prevent schools and municipalities from allowing prayer on their property and the right of judges to determine how Christmas displays are to be arranged.

The role of courts from time immemorial until the 1950s was that of deciding particular cases so as to vindicate settled rights in light of specific circumstances. Today, however, the Supreme Court, not to mention lower courts, engages in the wholesale rearrangement of political, social, and even religious institutions (e.g., marriage) to meet judges' subjective views of what is right. This transformation has undermined self-government. The Court has usurped for itself the right to define what a right is. Moreover, it has concentrated power in itself, first as the sole arbiter of the Constitution's meaning (thus freeing it from the trouble of justifying its textual contortions), and second, as the sole branch able to exercise judicial, legislative, and executive functions. Concentration of all three of these powers in one branch of government was defined by the founders as the very definition of tyranny. It leaves the people without defense or recourse against those in power who may choose to act oppressively or in direct opposition to their longstanding beliefs and traditions.

In the name of abstract rights that it itself defines, the Supreme Court has stamped out crucial, historically rooted rights of association and local participation, rights that once fostered—as they were reinforced by—those institutions of local life which made virtuous self-government possible. It has all but eliminated the people's ability to act meaningfully together to shape their common lives in their towns, schools, local associations, and even states. Thus, the Supreme Court has been a major player in the undermining of America's constitutional morality, and in the undermining of common Americans' attempts to pursue an entire range of individual and communal moral goods.

—BRUCE FROHNEN

Further Reading

Berger, Raoul. *Government by Judiciary: The Transformation of the Fourteenth Amendment.* Indianapolis, Ind.: Liberty Fund, 1999.

Carey, George W. *In Defense of the Constitution.* Indianapolis, Ind.: Liberty Fund, 1995.

Muncy, Mitchell S., ed. *The End of Democracy? The Celebrated "First Things" Debate, with Arguments Pro and Con, and "The Anatomy of a Controversy," by Richard John Neuhaus.* Dallas: Spence Publishing, 1997.

Presser, Stephen B. *Recapturing the Constitution.* Washington, D.C.: Regnery, 1994.

See also: abortion; Berger, Raoul; Bill of Rights; Bork, Robert H.; Brown v. Board of Education; *church and state; civil rights; Constitution, interpretations of; due process; education, public; equal protection; family; incorporation doctrine; judicial activism; Marshall, John; quotas; Rehnquist, William H.; rule of law; Scalia, Antonin; separation of powers; speech, freedom of; states' rights; Thomas, Clarence*

T

Taft, Robert A. (1889–1953)

The son of President William Howard Taft, Robert Taft was elected to the United States Senate in 1938, where he served until his death in 1953. Dubbed "Mr. Republican," Taft represented a noninterventionist and domestically combative wing of the Republican Party that would suffer an eclipse in the years following his death.

Taft was an outspoken opponent of Franklin Roosevelt's New Deal, and an opponent of the expansion of federal power. However, he was by no means uncompromising, favoring, for example, federal housing subsidies. Among his best-known legislative achievements was the so-called Taft-Hartley Act of 1947, an antiunion measure that enjoyed popular support at a time when public opinion had begun to swing away from labor unions. Taft-Hartley did not repeal the provisions of the Wagner Act of 1935 that had coercively imposed collective bargaining; instead, it added further regulations of its own, outlawing the closed shop and authorizing the president to seek court injunctions against strikes he believed threatened the national interest.

Although in the end he generally voted for many of the U.S. government's early Cold War measures, Taft and a number of other congressional conservatives remained skeptical of the precise extent of the Soviet threat and the utility and advisability of the global response that the Democrats and some internationalist Republicans were proposing. He condemned President Harry Truman's decision not to seek a congressional declaration of war against Korea in 1950, relying instead on authority allegedly invested in him by the United Nations. Some polls found Americans in favor of Truman's action by a margin of nine to one, but Taft was, as even his political enemies readily conceded, a man of principle.

Indeed, the intrepid Taft was in typical form when in 1946 he sharply criticized the Nuremberg trials of German war criminals. That the accused were evil and despicable Taft did not dispute, but he criticized the legal irregularities of the trials as mockeries of the rule of law and as bad omens for American constitutionalism at home. A young John Kennedy would devote a section of *Profiles in Courage* (1956) to Taft's stand on the issue, noting in particular that the Ohio senator had addressed the matter even though it had not been an issue that campaign season.

Taft lost the 1952 Republican presidential nomination to Dwight Eisenhower, whose posture was more internationalist and

Robert A. Taft

in domestic policy less hostile toward the legacy of the New and Fair Deals than Taft's own. Still, Taft campaigned for the general in the November elections.

Taft died on July 31, 1953, after a brief illness. Biographer William S. White, who was not sympathetic to the senator's views, remarked in 1954 that "it could almost be said that with him died one kind of Republican Party." Herbert Hoover, in a final tribute, called Taft "more nearly the irreplaceable man in American life than any we have seen in three generations."

—THOMAS E. WOODS JR.

Further Reading

Kirk, Russell, and James McClellan. *The Political Principles of Robert A. Taft.* New York: Fleet Press, 1967.

Patterson, James T. *Mr. Republican: A Biography of Robert A. Taft.* Boston, Houghton Mifflin, 1972.

See also: isolationism; McClellan, James; movement conservatism; paleoconservatism; right-to-work movement; Taft-Hartley Act

Taft, William Howard (1857–1930)

The only person to serve as both president of the United States and chief justice of the Supreme Court, William Howard Taft was conservative by temperament if not always in policy. Known as a defender of property rights who categorically condemned socialism, Taft was the forefather of a prominent Ohio Republican family influential to this day. He began his career as a lawyer and soon joined the Ohio Superior Court, where he was known as an injunction judge for repeatedly ordering labor groups to call off strikes.

Taft rose to national prominence at age thirty-three when President Benjamin Harrison appointed him solicitor general. Despite personal opposition to annexation of the Philippines, in 1900 Taft accepted President William McKinley's call to administer the islands and prepare the Filipinos for self-government.

He returned to America in 1904 to serve as secretary of war under President Theodore Roosevelt, who handpicked Taft to be his successor. In the 1908 presidential election, Taft ran as a reformer and once in office furthered progressive policies. Aggressive in continued enforcement of the Sherman Antitrust Act, Taft "busted" both the Standard Oil and the American Tobacco trusts during his tenure. He created the Department of Labor and supported employers' liability laws. He favored a graduated inheritance tax and fulfilled a campaign promise to initiate a federal income tax by supporting the Sixteenth Amendment, which was ratified in 1913.

Despite these moves, Taft angered Progressives by increasingly displaying conservative inclinations. Although he had pledged to reduce tariffs, Taft supported the unpopular and protectionist Payne-Aldrich Bill. He strongly opposed the recall of judges, even vetoing Arizona's statehood because it permitted the practice.

Taft's resistance to change alienated Republican Party insurgents and provoked Roosevelt to challenge his renomination. Roosevelt's personal popularity could not overcome the party machinery's support of Taft, so the former president ran as a third-party candidate, splitting the Republican vote and ensuring the election of Democrat Woodrow Wilson. After the loss Taft returned to his alma mater Yale University as a professor and during World War I served on the National Labor Board.

In 1921, President Warren Harding appointed him chief justice of the Supreme Court, thereby allowing Taft to realize a lifelong goal. His career on the bench proved him a capable administrator and strict constructionist of the Constitution.

—LILA ARZUA

Further Reading

Anderson, Judith Icke. *William Howard Taft: An Intimate History.* New York: W. W. Norton, 1981.

Duffy, Herbert S. *William Howard Taft.* New York: Minton, Balch and Company, 1930.

Hicks, Frederick C. *William Howard Taft: Yale Professor of Law and New Haven Citizen.* New Haven, Conn.: Yale University Press, 1945.

Pringle, Henry F. *The Life and Times of William Howard Taft.* 2 vols. New York: Farrar & Rinehart, 1939.

See also: Butler, Nicholas Murray; Root, Elihu

Taft-Hartley Act

A legislative measure that restricted union activity, the Taft-Hartley Act of 1947 proved to be a turning point against the growing union power in the tumultuous political climate of the post–World War II United States. Taft-Hartley, so called for its primary sponsors, Senator Robert A. Taft (R-Ohio) and Representative Fred Hartley (R-N.J.), is officially known as the Federal Labor-Management Relations Act of 1947.

The Taft-Hartley Act was a substantive and important amendment to the National Labor Relations (Wagner) Act of 1935 and nullified some aspects of the Federal Anti-Injunction (Norris-LaGuardia) Act of 1932. While Taft-Hartley retained guarantees from the Wagner Act for workers' rights, it outlawed some union tactics and introduced a broader definition of unfair labor practices. Under the new terms, unfair labor practices could be attributed to the practices of labor unions. The use of discrimination or force against individuals for union organizing purposes was strictly banned. The act also forbade the use of union dues for political contributions in national elections. Other tactics, such as jurisdictional strikes, secondary boycotts, and sympathy strikes, were similarly proscribed. (Jurisdictional strikes pertain to conflicts between rival unions over the right to work on a certain job. Secondary boycotts are union attempts to intimidate or incapacitate an employer by pressuring a third party to refrain from doing business with that employer. Sympathy strikes occur when one union calls a strike to show support for another union striking against a common employer.)

The act also enabled the federal government to demand that unions file financial statements and constitutions. Another provision of Taft-Harley enabled the president to delay those strikes, for up to eighty days, which he judges to have the potential to incite a national emergency. It also outlawed the closed shop and gave states the power to restrict the union shop. (The term "closed shop" describes the practice of offering employment only to union members. Similarly restrictive, the "union shop" allows the hiring of nonunion members but requires them to join the union once hired.) Groups on the far left saw the Taft-Hartley act as the outcome of pressure from corporate interests and referred to it as a "worker's nightmare." Unions branded the act a "slave labor law," and worked tirelessly to amend or repeal it. But in both the House and Senate the bill received strong bipartisan support. In the decade prior to Taft-Hartley, union membership had more than tripled from 4 million to 15 million. After World War II, simultaneous strikes among auto, steel, oil, and electrical workers, among others, had caused much turmoil and threatened the national economy with a general strike in basic industry. The prevalence of strikes convinced the nation's legislators that unions had grown too powerful.

The Taft bill, adopted by the Senate on May 13, 1947, was the most important among more than 200 antiunion bills pending in Congress at the time. The bill passed with a Senate vote of 68 to 21, with Democrats split evenly 21 for and 21 against. Although union pressure convinced President Truman to veto the bill at the last minute, both the House and Senate voted to override his veto.

—RICH HALVORSON

Further Reading

Epstein, Richard A. "A Common Law for Labor Relations: A Critique of the New Deal Labor Legislation," *Yale Law Journal* 92, no. 8 (July 1983): 1357-1408.

Kelly, George A. *Primer on the Taft-Hartley Act: A Moral Analysis.* Rochester, N.Y.: Christopher Press, 1948.

Lee, R. Alton. *Truman and Taft-Hartley.* Lexington, Ky.: University of Kentucky Press, 1966.

See also: right-to-work movement; Taft, Robert A.; unionism

Tansill, Charles (1890–1964)

A prominent and controversial revisionist historian holding Ph.D.'s from the Catholic University of America and Johns Hopkins University, Charles Tansill taught history at the Catholic University of America (1915-16), American University (1919-37), Fordham University (1939-44), and Georgetown University (1944-57). He wrote several works of diplomatic history, including *The Canadian Reciprocity Treaty of 1854* (1922), *The Purchase of the Danish West Indies* (1932), and *Major Issues in Canadian-American Relations* (1943). Attributing America's entry into World War I partly to lucrative economic ties to the Allies and the sympathy of President Woodrow Wilson's advisor Colonel Edward House and Secretary of State Robert Lansing for Britain, his massive, carefully documented *America Goes to War* (1938) won acclaim from fellow historians.

Back Door to War (1952), Tansill's voluminous critical history of President Franklin Roosevelt's 1933-41 foreign policy, was a major revisionist challenge to the mainstream account of World War II. Since 1900, Tansill asserted, America's foreign policy had mainly sought to preserve the British empire. He blamed America's involvement in the war partly on Henry Stimson's belligerence toward Japan since 1932. But mostly Tansill faulted Roosevelt, accusing him of pressuring Neville Chamberlain to fight Hitler; of increasingly involving America in Britain's war effort; of trying to provoke Hitler into attacking American warships in the Atlantic; and, by escalating economic and diplomatic pressure, of maneuvering the Japanese into attacking Pearl Harbor. Well documented, polemical, and Anglophobic, *Back Door to War* received mixed reviews. Tansill subsequently wrote for the John Birch Society's *American Opinion*.

—JOHN ATTARIAN

Further Reading

Tansill, Charles. *America and the Fight for Irish Freedom, 1866–1922: An Old Story Based upon New Data.* New York: Devin-Adair, 1957.

See also: Cold War revisionism; John Birch Society

Tate, Allen (1899–1979)

Poet, critic, biographer, editor, and social theorist, Allen Tate was one of America's leading men of letters for much of the twentieth century. Despite embracing institutions and ideas that were becoming increasingly unpopular among the academic and cultural elites of his day, Tate was a widely respected public intellectual. Like his friend T. S. Eliot, Tate synthesized a modernist literary aesthetic with a deep commitment to traditional religious and cultural principles.

Born in the Kentucky bluegrass country, Tate entered Vanderbilt University in Nashville in 1918. He quickly impressed one of his freshman professors, John Crowe Ransom, who invited Tate in his senior year to join a literary group known as the Fugitives. With Ransom, Donald Davidson, and others he entered into an intense period of literary and cultural reflection about the history and plight of the American South. In the poetry of Eliot, Tate found a sensibility much like the one he had arrived at in his own way. Both poets embraced a difficult elliptical style, interested not merely in private emotional life but in the broader historical and cultural issues shaping the modern world. Tate's poem "Ode to the Confederate Dead" exemplifies this sensibility. He would also later write a single novel, *The Fathers* (1938), which explored his central preoccupations with Southern history and culture.

Tate would go on to become a central figure in the New Criticism, an approach to literature that stressed close reading of texts rather than the importation of biographical, sociological, or other criteria into the act of interpretation. His association with fellow New Critics Cleanth Brooks and Robert Penn Warren led to a series of influential literary activities, including editorial posts such as the *Sewanee Review* (1944-47) and a role in editing several widely used literary anthologies (e.g., *The House of Fiction,* 1950).

With the Fugitives, Tate set himself the task of understanding the virtues and vices of the American South. Aside from a book of poems, his first two works were biographies of Stonewall Jackson (1928) and Jefferson Davis (1929). In 1930, the Fugitives transformed into the Southern Agrarians with the publication of *I'll Take My Stand,* a collection of essays defending the agricultural communities and culture of the South as a bulwark against the atomizing effects

Allen Tate

of modern industrial capitalism. Tate's contribution to the volume, "Remarks on the Southern Religion," demonstrated a concern for certain intellectual weaknesses in his patrimony—weaknesses that he would eventually, in 1950, seek to rectify by converting to the Roman Catholic Church.

Tate's interest in philosophy and theology informed both his friendships and his critical thought. He developed close relationships with some of the leading Catholic thinkers of the time, including the Thomist philosopher Jacques Maritain and the Trappist monk and writer, Thomas Merton. Some of his most influential essays, including "The Angelic Imagination" and "The Symbolic Imagination," exemplified a Christian critique of secularism, which Tate saw as devolving into alienation and solipsism.

T. S. Eliot summed up his friend's achievement: "Allen Tate is a good poet and a good literary critic who is distinguished for the sagacity of his social judgment and the consistency with which he has maintained the least popular of political attitudes—that of the sage. He believes in reason rather than enthusiasm, in wisdom rather than system; and he knows that many problems are insoluble and that in politics no solution is final."

Tate's personal life was legendarily tumultuous. His marriage to the novelist Caroline Gordon ended in 1959 and was followed by two other marriages before his death in Nashville in 1979.

—GREGORY WOLFE

Further Reading

Malvasi. Mark G. *The Unregenerate South: The Agrarian Thought of John Crowe Ransom, Allen Tate, and Donald Davidson*. Baton Rouge, La.: Louisiana State University Press, 1997.

Squires, Radcliffe. *Allen Tate: A Literary Biography*. New York: Pegasus, 1971.

Sullivan, Walter. *Allen Tate: A Recollection*. Baton Rouge, La.: Louisiana State University Press, 1988.

Tate, Allen. *Essays of Four Decades*. 3rd ed. Wilmington, Del.: Intercollegiate Studies Institute, 1999.

Underwood, Thomas A. *Allen Tate: Orphan of the South*. Princeton, N.J.: Princeton University Press, 2000.

See also: Agar, Herbert; agrarianism; Criterion; Davidson, Donald G.; Eliot, T. S.; I'll Take My Stand; New Criticism; Ransom, John Crowe; Sewanee Review; Southern Agrarians

Taylor, John (of Caroline) (1753–1824)

Planter, agricultural reformer, legislator, and U.S. Senator, John Taylor of Caroline was the premier political theorist behind Jeffersonian conservatism. A critic of Alexander Hamilton's financial plans, Taylor authored some of the earliest American attacks on central banking, paper currency, and federal debt during the 1790s.

John Taylor of Caroline

In 1798, faced with the choice between Virginia seceding from the Union or surrendering to what he considered Federalist tyranny, Taylor persuaded Thomas Jefferson and James Madison to pursue state interposition, or nullification, of unconstitutional federal laws. With Madison's assistance, Taylor secured passage of the Virginia Resolutions of 1798 and explained their purposes in the Virginia Report of 1800. The Principles of '98, as these ideas came to be known, served as the foundation for states' rights in the American South.

Unlike advocates who used states' rights to protect minority interests or as a means of perpetuating sectional conflict, Taylor believed states' rights were essential in diffusing political power nationally and conserving local majorities. Only by limiting political decisions to places where homogenous majorities could form, Taylor thought, could political order and liberty be protected.

Taylor's agrarian manifesto, *Arator* (1813), not only defended the virtues inculcated by farming, but his encouragement of agricultural reforms illustrated that Taylor had little fear that scientific and commercial progress would erode communal life. As he noted in his magnum opus, *An Inquiry into the Principles and Policy of the Government of the United States* (1794), the greatest danger to political liberty came from small factions, who, under the cover of partisan coalitions, used political power to further their own interests over those of the majority.

Taylor's work influenced generations of conservatives—both within and outside the South—well into the twentieth century, the literary critic and American founding scholar M. E. Bradford, who brought out a new edition of *Arator* in 1977, prominent among them.

—CAREY ROBERTS

Further Reading

Shalhope, Robert E. *John Taylor of Caroline: Pastoral Republican*. Columbia, S.C.: University of South Carolina Press, 1980.

Taylor, John. *Construction Construed and Constitutions Vindicated*. Reprint. New York: Da Capo Press, 1970.

———. *An Inquiry into the Principles and Policy of the Government of the United States*. New Haven, Conn.: Yale University Press, 1950.

See also: agrarianism; Southern conservatism

technology

Technology is a problem because we cannot do without it, and our use of it clearly makes us both better and worse. Human beings are—among other things—technological or tool-making animals. We use our brains and our freedom to transform nature, and in doing so transform ourselves. We also have a perverse capacity to make ourselves unhappy and take a singular pride in our misery. We are both proud of and wish to free ourselves from the burdens of our technological success. So we find it almost impossible to judge how much and what kind of technology would be best for us. In principle, we should be free to accept or reject various technological developments. Technology, after all, is supposed to be a means for the pursuit of whatever ends we choose. But in truth it might be our destiny to be moved along by impersonal and unlimited technological progress.

From a purely natural view at least, we do not know why human beings alone among the species are technological animals. Only we human beings can freely negate nature to satisfy our desires; only we human beings can create new and harder to satisfy needs through our technological success. One of the best pieces of evidence of our fundamental difference from the chimps and the dolphins is that we can so easily control them if that is what we want to do, but they cannot give orders to us. We do not know why we have the capability and the desire to threaten the very existence of all life on our planet. It is almost impossible to call what we have achieved through technological success—from a natural point of view—progress.

Technological change really is progress from another view. It is the index of our increasing power to control or manipulate nature. The general rule is that societies that encourage or are open to such change overwhelm those that are not. That is why the modern West has exerted its control over the whole world, and why the Europeans almost eliminated the Native Americans in our country. But this control, of course, is quite ambiguous. Technology is characteristically the imposition of human will over nature; we comprehend nature insofar as we control it. But our control and our comprehension are always far from complete.

Another reason we are not free to relinquish control once we have achieved it is that we cannot dispose of technological knowledge once we have acquired it. Surely we regret, on balance, our invention of nuclear weapons. But it would be the height of imprudence for America to destroy its nuclear weapons or even to stop trying to produce better ones. The knowledge of how to build them is everywhere, and otherwise insignificant powers such as North Korea and even transnational terrorists groups are going to find it progressively easier to use that knowledge.

The example of nuclear weapons reminds us that the progress of technology is in many ways not simply good for human life. Technological development often causes massive human displacement, imposing on many an urban misery that can resemble a living death. Indeed, we can say that any rapid technological advance always causes human disorientation, and its initial effect is to cause at least almost as much misery as it alleviates. Such change seems to become on balance beneficial only after it has become routinized, only after it assumes a place in a relatively settled way of life. Technological change would become an increasingly unambiguous evil were it to become too rapid for we habit- and tradition-dependent beings to live with it well.

According to Martin Heidegger, technology is what defines all of modern life. In other words, we moderns assume that what is real is what can be comprehended by reason; the real is what can be calculated or predicted or manipulated. Anything that cannot be objectively known—known as an object—by reason is not real. For Heidegger, this technological way of thinking is above all *nihilistic*; everything noble and beautiful that gives human life its seriousness or dignity is regarded, literally, as nothing. The modern view, on the other hand, is that technological thinking frees us from the irrational illusion of indebtedness. Technology can be put at the service of what we now call "free choice" because we have no knowledge of any purposes or ends or limits that are simply given. Unconstrained human choice or willfulness depends on a debt-negating or nihilistic foundation.

A contemporary critic of technology, Wendell Berry, explains that our dogma or "conventional prejudice" today is the uncritical acceptance of the goodness of technological liberation. Our intellectuals and educators mean to prejudice us "against old people, history, parental authority, religious faith, sexual discipline, manual work, rural people and rural life, anything that is local or small or inexpensive." We are prejudiced against all that is required to acquire moral virtue, to what we must have to subordinate technical means to human ends. We are prejudiced against "settled communities," against anything that has not been uprooted by the impersonal universalism of technological thinking. But it is only in the routinized and moralized context of such communities that any technology might be viewed as good, as not merely displacing or disorienting human beings for no particular purpose.

Berry agrees with Heidegger that in a technological age those who are best at manipulating others as objects will rule without restraint. Technological democracy tends to bring into existence a new sort of tyrannical ruling class composed of clever and liberated or communally irresponsible merito-crats who employ technology to impose a humanly destructive uniformity on those they rule. These meritocrats—believing maybe more than any prior ruling class that they *deserve* to rule—are full of contempt for those they control. And they themselves don't realize the extent to which they are controlled by technological thinking, by a way of thinking that has devalued all standards except wealth and power.

Heidegger and Berry, not without evidence, tend to view America as a sort of technological tyranny in which the unlimited pursuit of money and power that is the result of technological thinking has led the few to lay waste to the communal and moral world inhabited by the many. Technological progress tends to make true or communal democracy almost impossible, as even Tocqueville showed. Berry explains that we Americans characteristically "behave violently" toward the land and particular places because from the beginning we "belonged to no place." We have regarded the land or nature as an alien or hostile force to be conquered, not as our home. For Berry, what we modern Americans regard as the natural human propensities for wandering and violence are not really so natural at all. Our anxious dissatisfaction can at least be checked by our natural tendency to be bound by habit and familiarity. As even Heidegger says, the existential view that the truth is that we human beings alone have no natural place in particular is not shared by people who have the experience of belonging "deeply and intricately" to some place.

That human beings have to be some *place* to live and that technology erodes all particular human attachments is true. Beings with bodies have to be somewhere, and all human experience of the universal truth comes through reflection that occurs in the context of particular communities. But it is unclear to what extent that place has to literally be a piece of land; American Indian communities, for example, were often really bands of wanderers. And to some extent or other so too is any Christian community, any community composed of human beings who believe that they are really pilgrims or wayfarers in this world. According to one of the very first modern thinkers, Blaise Pascal, the truth is that human beings exist nowhere in particular. They are miserably contingent and displaced accidents. The truth, in fact, makes us so miserable that we spend most of our lives diverting ourselves from it. The only real remedy for our natural misery, according to Pascal, is believing in a God hidden from natural view. From this perspective, the disorientation we experience in this high-tech world is actually closer to the truth about what we are by nature than is the experience of the Old World peasant.

For Berry, Pascal is simply wrong. Berry seems to believe that we can live well according to nature by becoming deeply rooted in a particular place; we are not wanderers by nature. There is much human experience that supports such a view. But Berry is not simply right; we are different from the birds because most of us self-conscious beings do not accept our deaths serenely. It seems natural for us to fight and to hope to overcome our natural, mortal limits. It seems even noble for us to do so. Our longing for a personal God, winning our liberty by dying courageously, and resisting via technology the nature that is out to kill us all seem to be natural or authentic responses. The truth, surely, is somewhere between Berry and Pascal.

Yet the advent of the new biotechnology—our capacity to give orders to our genes—presents a new challenge to both the defenders and the critics of technology. The biotechnological project attempts to reduce radically the places of contingency and vulnerability in our lives. The aim is to eliminate genetically based diseases and to extend our lives indefinitely through regenerative medicine. We will soon be able to consciously and willfully design better human beings, ones that are smarter, healthier, more productive, and happier.

Biotechnology threatens to overcome the natural limits to the technological regulation of all of human life. Conservatives realize that our technologists are blind to the fact that if biotechnological development is unlimited, personal control will necessarily give way to impersonal or statist control over the most intimate human experiences and choices. Some fear that parents will assume tyrannical or technological control over their children by being able to design them according to their whims. But in our technological republic today we do not let parents—Christian Scientists or snake-handlers, for instance—choose against the health and safety of their children. Soon enough, government will make available and require that everyone employ the latest biotechnological means to have children in a way that maximizes each child's health and safety. That the state may come to control the means of reproduction and may force women to submit to therapeutic abortions are not far-fetched scenarios.

Leon Kass, chair of President Bush's Council on Bioethics, worries that Americans are now so dominated by technological thinking that they are not much bothered by the effects of our embryonic stem-cell research on us. The debate on such research, he writes, has largely ignored the consequences for human dignity of "coming to look upon nascent human life as a natural resource to be mined, exploited, commodified." Similarly, our main objection to human cloning is that it will be unsafe, not that it abolishes the distinction between procreating and manufacturing human beings. A world in which children are manufactured and sex and procreation are totally disconnected would surely be one without much love, one where one manufactured being would have little natural or real connection to other manufactured beings. Only through contemplating the extreme possibilities biotechnology opens for us can we see with neon clarity how the excessive attention given to the perpetuation of individual life characteristic of the modern technological project is destructive of the natural goods given to rational, social beings. The challenges posed by biotechnology—which are only extreme versions of the challenges posed by modern technology generally—may lead us to rediscover the relationships among birth, sex, marriage, the family, openness to the truth, God, and death that constitute human dignity.

—PETER AUGUSTINE LAWLER

Further Reading

Berry, Wendell. *The Art of the Commonplace: The Agrarian Essays of Wendell Berry.* Edited by Norman Wirzba. Washington, D.C.: Counterpoint, 2002.

Guardini, Romano. *Letters from Lake Como: Explorations in Technology and the Human Race.* Translated by Geoffrey W. Bromiley. Grand Rapids, Mich.: W. B. Eerdmans, 1994.

Heidegger, Martin. *The Question Concerning Technology, and Other Essays.* New York: Harper & Row, 1977.

Lawler, Peter Augustine. *Aliens in America: The Strange Truth about Our Souls.* Wilmington, Del.: ISI Books, 2002.

Postman, Neil. *Technopoly: The Surrender of Culture to Technology.* New York: Knopf, 1992.

See also: agrarianism; Boorstin, Daniel J.; environmentalism; Gilder, George; Ideas Have Consequences; *Lukacs, John; Percy, Walker; progressivism; Schindler, David L.; Senior, John*

Teller, Edward (1908–2003)

Edward Teller was the father of the hydrogen bomb and a key figure in persuading President Ronald Reagan to support building a space-based nuclear missile defense system.

Born in Hungary and educated in Germany, Teller left Germany for the United States after Adolf Hitler came to power; he became an American citizen in 1941. Although Teller became a strong and uncompromising anticommunist, he had not been in his youth. Immersed in science, he took little interest in politics but leaned to the Left, believing that communism provided greater justice for its people than did capitalism. His view changed in 1939 when a friend who had worked in the Soviet Union told him the truth about communism and described how Teller's mentor, a Russian physicist named Lev Landau, had been jailed and physically broken. Teller became an enemy of totalitarians of all types and strove to ensure that the United States would have the most powerful weapons in its arsenal.

In 1943 Teller moved to New Mexico and joined the atomic bomb project, later called the "Manhattan Project," and went on to play a key role in its development. Following the bomb's successful trial and use at Hiroshima and Nagasaki, Teller was one of the few atomic scientists to push for continued nuclear weapons research, calling for the rapid development of the hydrogen bomb following the Soviets' detonation of their own atomic bomb in 1949. Working with mathematician Stanislaw Ulam (a fact Teller overlooks in his autobiography), he developed the design for the hydrogen bomb in 1951; it was successfully tested in 1954.

The low point in Teller's career came during the 1954 hearings on whether or not to revoke renowned physicist Robert Oppenheimer's security clearance. Oppenheimer had advised the government against supporting Teller's crash program to build the H-bomb, and Teller testified that this had been bad advice and that he believed the government should no longer consult Oppenheimer. When Oppenheimer lost his clearance, Teller became a pariah to most of the nuclear physicists with whom he had worked. It is important to note that Andrei Sakharov, the Soviet physicist who won the Nobel Peace Prize in recognition of his work for human rights, wrote in his *Memoirs* (1990) that Teller was correct and Oppenheimer wrong in their analyses of the Soviet threat and intention to build the H-bomb regardless of what the United States did. Since Teller acted from principle in testifying against Oppenheimer, Sakharov wrote, he should not have been condemned by his colleagues.

Teller became a leading advocate for the peaceful use of nuclear energy, supported the continued development of weapons systems, and vigorously opposed test-ban negotiations. He was the model for Dr. Strangelove in Stanley Kubrick's film of that name. In the early 1980s, Teller gave the strategic defense initiative ("Star Wars") his strong support, helping to persuade Reagan of its feasibility, and he was involved in research to make it a reality.

—ROBERT WATERS

Further Reading

Blumberg, Stanley A., and Luis G. Panos. *Edward Teller: Giant of the Golden Age of Physics: A Biography*. New York: Scribner's, 1990.

Teller, Edward. *Memoirs: A Twentieth-Century Journey in Science and Politics*. Cambridge, Mass.: Perseus, 2001.

———. *The Legacy of Hiroshima*. Westport, Conn.: Greenwood Press, 1975.

See also: missile defense, national

Terror, War on

The "War on Terror" now being undertaken by the United States in order to eliminate incidents of attacks against civilians—particularly, but not exclusively, Americans—is difficult to define precisely because it is so broad and far-reaching. Its name was coined in the immediate aftermath of the terrorist attacks of September 11, 2001, by a Bush White House seeking to rally Americans behind a global effort to punish and render harmless the forces that had perpetrated (and continued to plan) such assaults.

Military strategists such as William Lind have suggested that the conflict with terrorist groups would be better described as "Fourth Generation Warfare." The first three generations of modern strategy, according to Lind, arrived with the technical and tactical advances that accompanied, respectively, the Thirty Years' War, the American Civil War, and World War I. As the technical power of each individual soldier has systematically increased (first to rifled muskets, then to machine guns, then to bazookas, TOW missiles, and "suitcase" nuclear devices), the importance of tightly massed men in formal units has steadily declined. The guerrilla, the infiltrator, the saboteur—even the terrorist—has moved to center stage.

Unlike the Cold War, which was waged against a particular enemy with a particular territory, civilian leadership, flag, and army, the War on Terror as now conceived is directed against a *tactic*—and a tactic, moreover, that has been employed by many nationalist movements throughout history, transforming "terrorists" such as Eamon de Valera, Menachem Begin, and Nelson Mandela into statesmen. The difference between guerrilla movements (which target military and police forces) and terrorist groups (which attack civilians) has tended to disappear in the current conflict. Military historian Caleb Carr has insisted on the distinction, grouping together punitive acts against civilians—by governments and guerilla movements alike—under the single label "terror." In *The Lessons of Terror* (2003), Carr points to the long history of anticivilian violence—from the murder of hostages in ancient Rome to the terror-bombing of London and Dresden during World War II to the 9/11 attacks—and argues that it is nearly always counterproductive. In contrast to disciplined military or guerilla actions aimed at combat units, anticivilian terror tends quickly to unite the population against its perpetrators, Carr concludes.

Because of the conceptual confusions attending its definition, some observers have said that the War on Terror ought not to be compared with previous military conflicts, but rather with the Reagan administration's "War on Drugs" or the Johnson administration's "War on Poverty." To these critics, the current "war" is a policy slogan rather than a constitutionally declared military engagement, although military and covert operations form a major component in its prosecution. Indeed, Senator John Kerry proposed during his failed presidential campaign that crime-fighting provided a better model for suppressing terrorist groups than an inchoate, borderless "war." However, the Bush administration's military metaphor proved more popular with voters, and it continues to shape American policy.

Others have noted that although the U.S. is primarily concerned with those terrorist groups which rely on Islamist ideology, it has been reluctant to name its enemies for fear of rallying Muslims worldwide around the militants in their midst. Instead, the U.S. and its allies have sought to divide Islamic opinion between moderates and fundamentalists, looking to the former for help in suppressing the violent rhetoric and actions of their radical coreligionists. Critics of Islam such as Srdja Trifkovic and Robert Spencer argue that the "radical/moderate" distinction is essentially spurious, and that the West should admit that what it really seeks to contain is, in fact, Islam itself; the policies they propose center on restricting immigration from Islamic countries and maintaining strict surveillance on Muslims

living in the West, if necessary through the dreaded tactic of "profiling." Opinion in nations such as the Netherlands has swung in favor of such policies after high-profile acts of extremism by Islamic residents.

An alternative label for U.S. policy was floated in summer 2005, when Bush spokesmen began to speak of the "struggle against violent extremism." However, the term had little traction and led some to suggest that the U.S. was somehow retrenching, so the older rhetoric returned with a new twist: President Bush began to echo the term employed by hawkish commentators in the blogosphere, who refer to the grandiose, theocratic fantasies of al-Qaeda and its allies by the invented epithet "Islamo-Fascism." Scholars both of the Islamic faith and of World War II remain skeptical of the term, which lumps together stateless, internationalist religious extremists and narrowly chauvinistic radical nationalists. These groups' only common features seem to be brutal illiberalism, disdain for civilian life, and anti-Semitism. Indeed, the role of Osama bin Laden as a roving inciter of revolutionary violence around the world recalls to some the career of Leon Trotsky more than that of any European dictator.

The War on Terror in practice encompasses many initiatives both foreign and domestic. Abroad, it began with the partly successful invasion of Afghanistan—a "failed state" that harbored Islamist terrorists who had received their first training and support from the American C.I.A. in their guerrilla war against Soviet occupiers. American forces aided tribal forces and regional militias, which by January 2002 had largely overthrown the radical Taliban regime, but failed to capture Osama bin Laden or many of his subordinates. Al-Qaeda then transformed itself from a centrally directed organization to a viral network of independent anti-Western terrorists akin to the "leaderless resistance" once invoked (though thankfully hardly practiced) by neo-Nazi groups in the 1970s. Affiliates and sympathizers of al-Qaeda have continued to perpetrate attacks in nations as far-flung as Britain, Spain, and Indonesia; governments from Russia to Uzbekistan attempting to suppress insurgencies by Islamic populations have lumped together all resistance by those populations as "terrorism" and linked such movements, accurately or not, with al-Qaeda.

Hundreds of suspected members of al-Qaeda and soldiers who fought for the (internationally unrecognized) Taliban regime have been interned at U.S. military bases such as Guantanamo Bay, out of the reach of U.S. courts' jurisdiction and unprotected by the Geneva Convention (which the Taliban never signed). At home, shortly after 9/11 the U.S. Congress created a new Department of "Homeland Security," the purpose of which is to protect the soil of the United States from attack—leaving some to wonder what had been the purpose of the existing Department of Defense. Congress also enacted and renewed the "PATRIOT Act," which (among many other extensions of federal power) enabled the FBI to undertake wiretaps of U.S. citizens with relative ease and to subpoena hitherto private documents. Most disturbing to many conservatives and libertarians was President Bush's invocation of the concept of "enemy combatant" to justify the arrest and indefinite detention without charge or legal recourse of U.S. citizens—a power which they compared to the ancien régime's infamous lettres de cachet. This power, upheld so far by federal courts and extended indefinitely into the future until the unforeseeable end of the undeclared War on Terror, is susceptible to enormous abuse, civil-liberties activists complained, amounting to a repeal not so much of the U.S. Constitution as of the Magna Carta.

Perhaps the centerpiece of the War on Terror has been the Bush administration's April 2003 invasion of Iraq—a nation which had links to Palestinian terror groups, but apparently few or none to al-Qaeda and other organizations involved in attacks on the U.S. However, administration claims to the contrary—combined with the fear that the brutal Iraqi leader Saddam Hussein was pursuing "weapons of mass destruction" that might someday be shared with terrorists—rallied public support behind this invasion and occupation, which continues as of publication. So do guerilla assaults on Anglo-American occupation forces and terrorist acts against Iraqis working with the newly constituted government. Threats of attacks on civilians on U.S. soil by agents of Iraqi insurgents and by "free-lance" terrorists inspired and even trained (via the Internet) by al-Qaeda, suggest that this "war" will continue for generations—as will, many traditional conservatives fear, the agglomeration of governmental authority required to constrain it. This phenomenon, the synergistic relationship between security "crises" and increasing federal power, has been noted by economic historian Robert Higgs. Advocates of limited government and U.S. disengagement from foreign wars find their warnings met (and so far, deflected) by charges of "appeasement," "defeatism," and even "unpatriotic" sentiments. The conservative movement is currently torn between its traditional commitment to ordered liberty and a potent strain of aggressive nationalism. It is unclear whether one will prevail or the movement will permanently split.

—John Zmirak

Further Reading

Anonymous. *Imperial Hubris*. Dulles, Va.: Brassey's, 2004.

Higgs, Robert. *Crisis and Leviathan*. New York: Oxford University Press, 1987.

Horowitz, David. *Unholy Alliance*. Washington, D.C.: Regnery Publishing, 2004.

Spencer, Robert. *The Politically Incorrect Guide to Islam (and the Crusades)*. Washington, D.C.:

Regnery Publishing, 2005.

Trifkovic, Srdja, *The Sword of the Prophet*. Salisbury, Mass.: Regina Orthodox Press, 2002.

See also: Bush, George W.; Cato Institute; Helprin, Mark; Iraq War

Thatcher, Margaret (1925–)

Margaret Thatcher was the second most important prime minister of the United Kingdom in the twentieth century. Ruling from 1979 until 1990, she dedicated her career to the expansion of freedom and achieved notable success toward this goal in her fights against the dead weight of socialism on the British economy and the iron hand of Soviet communism in Europe.

She was an unlikely prime minister. Born Margaret Roberts on October 13, 1925, in the town of Grantham in the north of England to a family of grocers, she attended Oxford University on scholarship and studied chemistry. After leaving Oxford she ran for Parliament in 1950 and 1951; though she lost both times, she gained publicity as the youngest woman candidate then standing for election. Thatcher used the rest of the 1950s to read for the bar and start a family with local businessman Denis Thatcher. By the end of the decade she was ready to enter the ring of politics again. In 1959 she won a seat in Parliament representing Finchley (a north London constituency), which she would represent for more than thirty years.

Upon her ascension to Parliament, Margaret Thatcher quickly established herself in the circles of the Conservative Party's leadership. Within two years she was holding a junior office in Prime Minister Harold Macmillan's administration. Starting in 1964, when the Conservatives were in the opposition, she served as a shadow minister, and then in 1970 when the Conservatives returned to office under Edward Heath, she became the education secretary. She was reviled for her job in that position. Education in Great Britain, as elsewhere, was at a low point, and Thatcher's term as education secretary made her infamous. When the government abolished the entitlement of free milk for elementary school students, she became known as "Thatcher, Milk Snatcher."

Thatcher was rescued from the dead end of education politics by the Heath administration's disastrous rule. Promising economic revival through free-market reforms, Heath did just the opposite and further extended the government's numbing reach into the economy. He was defeated at the polls in 1974 and Thatcher was freed for greater things. In 1975 she ran against Heath for leadership of the Conservative Party and, riding a crest of Tory dissatisfaction with the seemingly inexorable leftward drift of the party and government, won. The United Kingdom had its first female leader of a political party. In 1979 it had its first female prime minister.

The challenges facing Thatcher in her first term were immense. What in America was called economic malaise was called in the United Kingdom "the British Disease"—and it was much worse. The combination of zero employment growth and high inflation had crippled the British economy. Thatcher's economic reforms had the quality of a shot in the arm: the painful effects were felt immediately, but the benefits would take time. Taxes were cut, the budget was balanced, and interest rates shot up to bring inflation under control. The end of Thatcher's first term (1983) saw unemployment at more than three million as one inefficient manufacturing industry after another contracted severely. The high tide of unemployment would only start to recede in 1986.

But the ebbing of the worldwide recession of the early 1980s revealed Thatcher's determination to master the economy. In the 1970s inflation was thought to be endemic to democracies. Thatcher checked inflation and showed that she intended to keep it under control. Ending the expectation of unremitting inflation and instead creating the hope of price stability opened the field for private economic investment to bloom. Thatcher showed that modern democracies could have sound economic policy—they had not had it to that point not because of its impossibility, but because of a lack of will among the political class. This was a revolution in thought.

The modest signs of recovery in the British economy furthered the likelihood of Thatcher's reelection, but her prospects were sealed when she successfully prosecuted the Falklands War against Argentina in 1982. Argentina had disputed the United Kingdom's control of the Falkland Islands for over 150 years, but it was not until the Argentinean military junta then in power decided that a war would distract the populace from its increasingly desperate economic situation that the dispute resorted to arms. With support from President Reagan, who thought America's "special relationship" with the United Kingdom was more important than technical adherence to the Monroe Doctrine, Thatcher routed the ragtag Argentinean army that had invaded the Falklands in just 72 days of fighting, and this rout precipitated the return of civilian rule to Argentina. Her success in the war proved her determination to defend the United Kingdom's interests abroad.

Thatcher's second term started in 1983. The main economic task now was to rid the British economy of the choking weeds of state-owned corporations and militant trade unionism. The resistance of labor to Thatcher's economic reforms led to the

Margaret Thatcher

miners' union strike of 1984–85. The strike was among the longer and more violent strikes in British history, but in the end the miner's union was defeated and Thatcher's gains in trade union legislation were secured. Even the Labor Party pledged not to undo its key provisions. As the economy improved, Thatcher moved to privatize state assets, which constituted more than 20 percent of the economy in 1979. Companies such as British Airways and British Steel made the transition from drains of the public treasury to efficient and profitable private ventures. Her efforts to privatize state-owned industries would be the model for similar efforts by more than fifty other countries.

In her second term Thatcher also faced a new chance to flex the United Kingdom's muscles in foreign affairs, but this time the enemy was not a third-world junta, but a first-rate superpower—the Soviet Union. During the early 1980s the Soviet Union had built up a substantial arsenal of intermediate range nuclear missiles targeted at Western Europe. Negotiations to remove the missiles failed and the NATO alliance decided that they could counter this threat only by deploying Pershing II missiles throughout Western Europe. The reaction from the "nuclear freeze" movement was fierce and demonstrations were held in nearly all the major cities of NATO countries. Ignoring the massive protests, Margaret Thatcher, President Reagan, and Helmut Kohl of Germany persisted and deployed the missiles. When the Soviet Union got a new leader in Mikhail Gorbachev, the Soviets returned to the bargaining table and both sides removed their missiles. More importantly, Margaret Thatcher, along with Ronald Reagan, realized (before their conservative critics) that Gorbachev was someone they could work with. And while Reagan watched the Berlin Wall fall as he sat in retirement, Thatcher helped guide the beginning of the true end of the Cold War.

Thatcher's third term began in 1987 and was cut short in 1990. She was damaged first by her attempted implementation of the Community Charge, a poll tax that both shifted the burden of taxes and was exploited by local governments to implement tax increases that were then (wrongly) blamed on Thatcher's government. Taxpayers simply refused to comply with the new system, and it was abandoned in 1991. But the proximate cause that precipitated Thatcher's downfall was the United Kingdom's relationship to the project of European integration. Conservatives had traditionally been the party of European integration, but Thatcher saw that integration would not be used to further market reforms but to suffocate the member states in regulations from Brussels. She moved to oppose further integration, the party split, her leadership was challenged, and eventually she had to resign because her government lacked sufficient support. Left undone at her departure were reforms to the National Health Service and education. These issues continue to vex the British political establishment today.

Because of her leadership, "Thatcherism" became a political philosophy associated with free markets, monetarist economic policy, privatization of state-owned companies, low taxation, and opposition to the welfare state. Yet Margaret Thatcher fought not just for economic reforms at home, but to end the domination of one half of Europe by a totalitarian regime. Her economic reforms went further than President Reagan's and were an inspiration to her American allies. And her support for the Western cause in the Cold War was crucial to providing the united front needed to stare down commu-

nism. In all of this, we catch glimpses of what was perhaps the most important of Margaret Thatcher's fundamental beliefs, that the individual should never be sacrificed to the faceless collective.

—TIMOTHY WEBSTER

Further Reading

Campbell, John. *The Grocer's Daughter*. London: Jonathan Cape, 2000.

———. *The Iron Lady*. London: Jonathan Cape, 2003.

Freedman, Lawrence, and Virginia Gamba-Stonehouse. *Signals of War: The Falklands Conflict of 1982*. Princeton, N.J.: Princeton University Press, 1991.

Lawson, Nigel. *The View from No. 11*. New York: Doubleday, 1992.

Kavanagh, Dennis, and Anthony Seldon, eds. *The Thatcher Effect: A Decade of Change*. New York: Oxford University Press, 1989.

Sharp, Paul. *Thatcher's Diplomacy: The Revival of British Foreign Policy*. New York: St. Martin's Press, 1997.

Thatcher, Margaret. *The Downing Street Years*. New York: HarperCollins, 1993.

———. *The Path to Power*. New York: HarperCollins, 1995.

See also: anticommunism; Cold War; privatization; Reagan Doctrine; Reagan, Ronald

therapeutic state

The rise of the therapeutic state has recently become a subject of study for scholars who have attempted to clarify how what Philip Rieff originally called "the triumph of the therapeutic" has altered not only the normative structure but also the institutional structure of the state in advanced postindustrial societies. Most social commentators emphasize that the rise of a therapeutic worldview, grounded in psychological approaches to private and public life, redefined the understanding and conduct of political life during the last half of the twentieth century. For conservatives concerned with the growth and power of the state, the implications of therapeutic culture are especially important because the justifications and uses of state power have increasingly become therapeutic—the treatment or melioration of pathologies and assurance of citizens' sense of well-being—rather than the protection of rights and liberties or the provision of support for conventional moral constraints and democratic conceptions of citizenship.

The groundwork for the rise of the therapeutic state was probably laid in the United States during the Progressive Era and later expanded during the New Deal with the rise of a federal welfare state, which saw the expansion of human services under policies such as the Social Security Act. Although some scholars tend to equate the welfare state with the therapeutic state, a good case can be made for the rise of therapeutic states in Western Europe and the United States during the post–World War II era, insofar as conventional ideals of moral responsibility have gradually become subordinate to therapeutic ideals. Under what Jürgen Habermas has called a "therapeutocracy," the state has intervened in and challenged the autonomy of civil society, with the consequence that professional expertise, rather than financial aid, has become the more significant mode of state intervention.

During World War II, the role of psychological experts in the United States dramatically increased as such experts obtained a variety of policy positions charged with duties ranging from waging psychological warfare to protecting the mental health of military personnel. After 1945, the influence of psychological expertise in public policy continued to grow in the field of national security, by means of the Veterans Administration, and in new directions on the domestic front as symbolized by the passage of the National Mental Health Act of 1946, which supported research, professional training, and grants to states for mental health facilities. Generally, the political fortunes of psychology improved in the postwar decades with every state accepting the licensing of psychologists from 1946 to 1977, and most states recognizing psychologists as expert witnesses during the 1960s, 1970s, and 1980s.

The 1960s were a watershed for the growth of the therapeutic state, with the advance of the Great Society and such developments as the expansion of the definition of emotional injury in personal injury law and the rise of the "values clarification" movement in public education.

But the 1990s may have signaled a broader acceptance of therapeutic assumptions. Values clarification, for example, preceded the more successful "self-esteem" movement that gained widespread acceptance in education even among some conservatives by the 1990s. Similarly, therapeutic approaches to criminal justice—pioneered under the 1972 federal program known as Treatment Alternatives to Street Crime—expanded during the 1990s with such efforts as the popular Drug Court Movement. In short, by the end of the twentieth century the therapeutic state appeared to be well-enough established that opposition to the welfare state did not necessarily translate into a rejection of therapeutic efforts to reform the very definition of welfare itself.

—ALAN WOOLFOLK

Further Reading

Herman, Ellen. *The Romance of American Psychology: Political Culture in the Age of Experts.* Berkeley, Calif.: University of California Press, 1995.

Nolin, James, Jr. *The Therapeutic State: Justifying Government at Century's End.* New York: New York University Press, 1998.

Polsky, Andrew. *The Rise of the Therapeutic State.*

Princeton, N.J.: Princeton University Press, 1991.

Rieff, Philip. *The Triumph of the Therapeutic: Uses of Faith after Freud.* 2nd ed. Chicago: University of Chicago Press, 1987.

Wolfe, Alan. *Whose Keeper? Social Science and Moral Obligation.* Berkeley, Calif.: University of California Press, 1989.

See also: Lasch, Christopher; Rieff, Philip; welfare state

Thernstrom, Abigail (1936–)

A major critic of affirmative action and other race-based preferences, Abigail Thernstrom took her Ph.D. from Harvard University's Department of Government in 1975 and was subsequently a lecturer at Harvard (1988–89) and Boston College (1990). Thernstrom became a senior fellow at the Manhattan Institute in 1993.

In *Whose Votes Count? Affirmative Action and Minority Voting Rights* (1987), Thernstrom explained how the 1965 Voting Rights Act, originally intended to enable Southern blacks to vote, was amended to create racially gerrymandered voting districts so as to increase minority membership in legislatures. This, she argued, was a form of affirmative action with several drawbacks, most importantly the potential to inhibit interracial political coalition building.

With husband Stephan Thernstrom, she coauthored *America in Black and White: One Nation, Indivisible* (1997), which, grounded in an "optimistic premise" of "the potential for racial decency in most Americans," presented a comprehensive history of American black-white race relations from the post–Civil War, Jim Crow South to the present. The Thernstroms cited a variety of data on trends in crime, politics, the economic condition of blacks, and racial attitudes to argue that America has made great progress in race relations and that blacks have made substan-

tial gains. Criticizing racial preferences for their divisiveness, for promising more than they deliver, and for intensifying rather than lessening color consciousness, the Thernstroms recommended "color-blind public policies."

Although often characterized as a convert to conservatism, Thernstrom insists that her ideal has always been color blindness, which the Left in her view has forsaken for color consciousness.

—JOHN ATTARIAN

Further Reading

Thernstrom, Abigail, and Stephan Thernstrom, eds. *Beyond the Color Line: New Perspectives on Race and Ethnicity in America.* Stanford, Calif.: Hoover Institution Press, 2002.

———. *No Excuses: Closing the Racial Gap in Learning.* New York: Simon & Schuster, 2003.

See also: affirmative action; quotas

think tanks, conservative

Conservative think tanks have provided many of the key ideas that have animated the conservative revolution since the presidency of Ronald Reagan. Because universities have frequently been inhospitable to scholars on the right, conservative think tanks have played an essential role in providing them employment and seeing that their ideas receive a hearing.

Think tanks are nonprofit public policy research organizations that are either independent or affiliated with universities. Lynn Hellebust has identified 1,212 think tanks, of which 587 are nonacademic; the Heartland Institute, itself a conservative think tank, lists on its Internet Web site approximately 300 think tanks devoted to reducing the size and cost of government. The primary role that think tanks play is to provide credible research and analysis for those engaged in public policy debates. The need for conservative think tanks to produce high-quality scholarly output is especially great, because the policy and media establishments traditionally have looked skeptically at conservatives' work.

Traditionally, think tanks have provided scholars a sinecure from which they can research and write monographs, and they have been places where scholars and public officials can meet to discuss ideas. The liberal Brookings Institute was an early model for this sort of think tank, a sort of university without students. This model was later adopted by the American Enterprise Institute for Public Policy Research. Founded in 1943 to provide the public and government with information about business and its position on legislative issues, AEI's impact, supported by a tiny staff and little money, was negligible. On the verge of shutting down in 1954, its board decided to hire William Baroody and W. Glenn Campbell from the U.S. Chamber of Commerce in a last ditch effort to turn around the organization. Although Campbell ultimately left to lead the Hoover Institution on War, Revolution, and Peace, Baroody continued to lead AEI until 1978. He was known as an "intellectual entrepreneur" because of his ability to raise money and sell ideas. Baroody was one of the first to extend fundraising beyond rich individuals and corporations to include conservative foundations like Earhart and Sloan, explaining to their boards that conservative ideas concerning free markets and limited government were excluded from public policy debate, and that AEI could, if properly financed, inject these ideas into the public policy mainstream. In the early 1960s, Baroody cultivated conservative Arizona senator Barry Goldwater and became his chief adviser during the 1964 presidential campaign.

While AEI steadily grew in wealth and influence throughout the Baroody years, it was during the presidency of Richard Nixon that AEI became a Washington power. Nixon administration officials gave AEI their stamp of approval, working closely with the institute and playing a significant role in its fundraising efforts. In 1970, AEI had an eighteen-person staff and an annual budget of one million dollars. By the early 1980s, a $13 million budget supported a 150-person staff. Despite the turmoil that followed Baroody's departure, AEI remains moderately conservative and continues to be an important force in Washington's idea wars.

The archetypical conservative "university without students" is the Hoover Institution, located on the Stanford University campus in Palo Alto, California. Founded by Herbert Hoover in 1919 to focus on the causes and consequences of World War I, the Hoover Institution has grown into the world's most important archive and library on political, economic, and social change in the twentieth century. In the late 1940s, the institution began recruiting scholars who believed in individualism, economic and political freedom, and representative government to make use of the archives and to publish and disseminate their ideas. Herbert Hoover's personal hiring of W. Glenn Campbell from AEI brought a leader who was a skilled fundraiser and absolutely devoted to the former president's ideals. California governor Ronald Reagan had close ties to the institution while governor of California and maintained those ties after his election as president. Indeed, so many Hoover fellows were brought into his administration and so many policies that it had supported and collected in a book called *The United States in the 1980s* (1980) were put into practice that Mikhail Gorbachev bitterly complained to Secretary of State George Schulz (a Hoover alumnus) and Speaker of the House Tip O'Neill that the Reagan administration had been captured by "right-wing forces."

In a sort of reversal of the "university without students" paradigm, the Intercollegiate Studies Institute (the publisher of this book) is a quasi-think tank devoted to changing the intellectual climate on American college and university campuses. Founded by libertarian journalist Frank Chodorov in 1953, ISI's focus was American college campuses; its purpose, "to inform nonconformists that they have company." ISI began by providing students with free books on libertarian and conservative subjects, adding the free scholarly journal *Intercollegiate Review* in 1965 and the national conservative student newspaper *CAMPUS* in 1990. To assist "alternative" campus newspapers—independent, conservative, or libertarian student newspapers created as alternatives to the politically correct university-sponsored student press—ISI administers the Collegiate Network, which is dedicated to exposing the politicization of campus life, curricula, and classrooms. ISI also publishes *Modern Age* and the *Political Science Reviewer,* and the last few years have seen steady growth in its book imprint, ISI Books.

The late 1970s saw the Baroody and Campbell style of "intellectual entrepreneurship" taken to a new level by Edwin Feulner and Philip Truluck of the Heritage Foundation. Founded in 1973 with a budget of $250,000 by conservative activist Paul Weyrich, Heritage proved to be a marginal player at a time when Watergate had put Republicans into severe decline. The foundation was struggling when Feulner was brought in as president and Truluck as executive vice president in 1977. They shifted the organization's focus from the traditional think tank approach of holding conferences and publishing academic-style papers to a new style of rapid deployment as issues arose. For example, prior to a congressional hearing or markup session, Heritage began to act in a coordinated way to issue newspaper opinion columns, one- or two-page papers with briefing bullets for policymakers, and

longer, more substantive versions of the papers for staff and interest groups. Feulner and Truluck also moved Heritage away from more controversial social issues, like abortion and school prayer, to focus on economics and foreign policy. After just two years under Feulner and Truluck, Heritage had become well known and respected, with a budget of $2.8 million. By 2002, the budget had increased to $28 million, which supported a staff of 185.

Ronald Reagan's election to the presidency found Heritage ready with lists of potential staffers for sub-cabinet positions and a book, *Mandate for Leadership* (1981), which provided many of the ideas that proved central to Reagan's mission. Among the issues in which Heritage took the lead were supply-side economics, urban enterprise zones that provided tax breaks to businesses located in economically depressed urban areas, and strategic defense against nuclear missiles. Heritage's marketing strategies have been picked up by other think tanks Left and Right, including more traditional organizations like Brookings, AEI, and Hoover.

Think tanks have played a vital role in the growth of conservatism by laying the intellectual groundwork for the Reagan Revolution, training the public policy cadres needed for congressional and executive staffs, serving as policy goads through Heritage-style blitzkriegs, and changing the climate of opinion through conferences, articles and monographs. In a political culture such as Washington, where political advantage and gamesmanship often become the major purpose of political struggles, think tanks and their alumni help to keep debate grounded on the issues and larger philosophical questions—or to bring it back to these issues when it goes astray. Besides the aforementioned organizations, any list of the most significant conservative think tanks today would also have to include the Ethics and Public Policy Center, the Family Research Council, the Howard Center for Family, Religion, and Society, and the Manhattan Institute, among many others. The most influential libertarian think tank is the Cato Institute.

—ROBERT WATERS

Further Reading

Ricci, David M.. *The Transformation of American Politics: The New Washington and the Rise of Think Tanks*. New Haven, Conn.: Yale University Press, 1993.

Smith, James Allen. *The Idea Brokers: Think Tanks and the Rise of the New Policy Elite*. New York: Free Press, 1991.

See also: American Enterprise Institute; Cato Institute; Ethics and Public Policy Center; Family Research Council; Foreign Policy Research Institute; Heritage Foundation; Hoover Institution on War, Revolution and Peace; Howard Center for Family, Religion, and Society; Hudson Institute; Independent Institute; Intercollegiate Studies Institute; Manhattan Institute; Property and Environment Research Center; Rockford Institute

Thomas, Cal (1940–)

A prominent conservative evangelical Christian and America's most widely syndicated newspaper opinion columnist, Cal Thomas was raised in the Disciples of Christ and was educated at American University. In early adulthood he worked in television journalism and eventually became a Presybterian. He has written that, after being fired from his job in television, he "made a commitment to Jesus Christ and began to study the Bible." He voted for Jimmy Carter in 1976, but was increasingly troubled by Carter's unwillingness to confront such moral issues as abortion on demand. In 1980, hearing of Thomas's unhappiness with his career and his growing disaffection with the nation's political leadership, Jerry Falwell invited him to join the Moral Majority, which he, Howard Phillips, and Paul Weyrich had founded to involve conservative people of faith in politics.

Thomas accepted and became the Moral Majority's vice president for communications. In that capacity he wrote *Book Burning* (1983), a rebuttal to the secular humanist depiction of conservative Christians as intolerant book-burners. Such charges, Thomas showed, were exaggerated; the secularists, in fact, were the real censors, using public libraries and school curricula to present their points of view while suppressing Christian perspectives. Moreover, Thomas charged, many book reviewers refused to review Christian books, some editors and reporters refused to cover the Moral Majority, and Christian books were often kept out of bookstores and libraries.

The Los Angeles Times Syndicate offered Thomas a syndicated opinion column in 1984. The next year he left the Moral Majority to devote himself to writing. The number of newspapers carrying his column grew steadily and now exceeds 400.

Besides his column, Thomas has continued to write books. In *The Things that Matter Most* (1994) Thomas argued that the 1960s had promised liberation from the family; unfettered self-expression; enlightenment through drugs; sexual liberation; spiritual progress through "the death of God"; the elimination of poverty by a paternalistic government; the exaltation of youth; and progressive education. All of these promises failed, resulting in the social ills of the 1980s and 1990s. The things that matter most are spiritual, Thomas argued, and only spiritual renewal can reverse America's social decline.

Once confident that the political process could bring about a society and culture closer to that which conservative Christians desired, Thomas has become disillusioned with that strategy. In *Blinded by Might* (1999), which he coauthored with Baptist pastor Edward Dobson, he admitted that conservative Christians had been seduced by the temptation of power. Unfortunately, their political involvement gained them nothing: "a crisis of moral authority will not be solved by an appeal to political power," he argued. Moreover, associating the church too closely with politics and the state has led to compromising the gospel in order to gain access to the powerful and has brought humiliation on the church. Since only God can touch and move souls, Thomas now argues, Christians should deemphasize politics and focus their efforts on living the Christian life.

—JOHN ATTARIAN

Further Reading

Thomas, Cal. *The Wit and Wisdom of Cal Thomas.* Uhrichsville, Ohio: Promise Press, 2001.

See also: Protestantism, evangelical; Schaeffer, Francis A.

Thomas, Clarence (1948–)

Appointed to the United States Supreme Court as its 106th justice in 1991 by President George H. W. Bush, Clarence Thomas is one of the youngest judges ever to be nominated (he sat on the United States Court of Appeals for the District of Columbia Circuit for less than two years before his nomination to the higher court), and, as of the beginning of President George W. Bush's second term in office, was one of the Court's two most reliable conservatives. Indeed, when then governor Bush was campaigning for the presidency in 2000, he promised to appoint judges who would share the philosophy of Supreme Court associate justices Thomas and Scalia as a way of signaling to his conservative supporters that their wishes would be heeded with regard to the federal courts. Thomas was also only the second African-American ever to be nominated as an associate justice.

Thomas's nomination to the Court of Appeals encountered almost no objections, but once he was proposed for the Supreme Court, a crescendo of opposition arose against him. Some of Thomas's speeches and articles, produced during the time he was head of the Equal Employment Opportunity Commission or before, when he was an official in the Department of Education, indicated that he was a firm believer in interpreting the Constitution according to its original understanding and also that he was profoundly influenced by theories of natural law. Fearing that Thomas might provide a crucial vote in overruling many of the activist decisions of the Warren and Burger courts, his critics sought to argue that his judicial philosophy was out of the "mainstream." This effort did not seem to be gaining sufficient headway to defeat Thomas in the Senate, but then Thomas's nomination encountered unanticipated trouble when Anita Hill charged that he had made some unsavory suggestions to her when Hill had worked for him as a young staff aide, first when he was assistant secretary for civil rights at the Department of Education, and later when Thomas was chairman of the Equal Employment Opportunity Commission. Ms. Hill's charges were vehemently denied by Thomas in the unusual televised Senate proceedings that Thomas characterized as a "high-tech lynching." Hill's charges were never proven, and Thomas's nomination passed the Senate by a narrow vote of 52 to 48.

What may have been trumped-up charges of sexual harassment brought by Ms. Hill and her supporters against Thomas were a last-ditch effort to prevent a person with Thomas's jurisprudential views from ascending to a position on the only court in the land capable of overturning the Court's prior constitutional constructions. In particular, proponents of *Roe v. Wade*, the 1973 decision that found a constitutional right to secure an abortion, were alarmed that Thomas might represent the fifth vote needed to overturn that decision.

These fears were not realized: in the *Planned Parenthood v. Casey* decision of 1992, the Court reaffirmed *Roe v. Wade*, with Thomas in dissent. Nevertheless, while on the Court, Thomas, along with Scalia, has been a reliable and careful proponent of the view that the only valid means of constitutional interpretation is that of seeking to find the "original understanding" of constitutional provisions. He has also been a staunch proponent of restricting the power of the federal government to the limited role the Constitution's framers intended, a foe of race-based preferences in law, and an opponent of efforts to remove religion from the public square.

When the first President Bush offered Thomas's nomination, he declared that after a substantial search he had decided that Thomas was the "best person" for the job. This was generally ridiculed by pundits and legal academics because Thomas, who had written few opinions as a judge on the Court of Appeals, and who theretofore had relatively modest achievements in the executive branch, was thought to be in fact simply the best minority candidate a Republican president could find to take the seat of the nation's first African American justice, the extremely liberal Thurgood Marshall. A careful reader of Thomas's speeches, publications, and opinions before he was nominated for the Supreme Court, however, would have revealed that his was the mind of a thoughtful traditionalist conservative, and as time passes, the truth of the first President Bush's remarks about Thomas's suitability for the job becomes more evident.

—STEPHEN B. PRESSER

Further Reading

Gerber, Scott Douglas. *First Principles: The Jurisprudence of Clarence Thomas.* New York: New York University Press, 1999.

Presser, Stephen B. *Recapturing the Constitution: Race, Religion, and Abortion Reconsidered.* Washington, D.C.: Regnery, 1994.

See also: Brown v. Board of Education; *equal protection; natural law; separation of powers; Supreme Court*

Thornwell, James Henley (1812–62)

The antebellum South's leading Presbyterian educator and a man admired nationwide for his learning, James Henley Thornwell contributed prominently to shaping the South's religious outlook and intellectual life. Educated at the Cheraw Academy and the College of South Carolina, Henley became a Presbyterian and opted for the ministry. He attended the Andover (Massachusetts) Theological Seminary but found its theology too liberal and departed.

Licensed to preach in 1834, Thornwell served as pastor for several South Carolina churches. He became a professor of metaphysics at the College of South Carolina in 1837 and the president of the college in 1851 before leaving in 1855 to teach at the Presbyterian Theological Seminary in Columbia, South Carolina. In 1847 he founded the *Southern Presbyterian Review*, the South's foremost religious periodical. A vigorous, sometimes strident, controversialist, Thornwell upheld orthodox Calvinism against both the liberal, rationalist "New School" faction of Presbyterianism and the growing threat to Christianity from science and industrialization. His theology tried to blend reason and faith while clearly subordinating reason to scripture. Thornwell's social philosophy was that of a Burkean conservative. He disbelieved in man's natural goodness, was skeptical of universal philanthropy, and stressed the need to preserve order and implement reform only gradually.

Thornwell addressed public issues only in his last years. Although he loved the Union, loyalty to South Carolina led Thornwell to support her secession and the

Confederacy. His essay "The State of the Country" (1861) pleaded the South's cause. Seeking to arouse the enthusiasm of Confederate soldiers, "Our Danger and Our Duty" (1862) warned that Northern victory would mean the devastation of the South.

—JOHN ATTARIAN

Further Reading

Farmer, James Oscar, Jr. *The Metaphysical Confederacy: James Henley Thornwell and the Synthesis of Southern Values.* Macon, Ga.: Mercer University Press, 1986.

Palmer, B. M. *The Life and Letters of James Henley Thornwell.* New York: Arno Press, 1969.

Thornwell, James Henley. *The Collected Writings of James Henley Thornwell.* 2 vols. Edited by John B. Adger. Richmond, Va.: Presbyterian Committee of Publication, 1871.

See also: Southern conservatism

Thurmond, Strom (1902–2003)

One of the most enduring figures in American political history, Strom Thurmond was an influential spokesman for Southern conservatism throughout the post–World War II era. He rose to national prominence as a stalwart champion of segregation and states' rights. While he would later significantly modify his racial views, Thurmond never abandoned the core conservative values he harbored from the start of his legendary political career.

Born in South Carolina in 1902, Thurmond served as a Democratic state senator and judge during the early phase of his public life. South Carolinians elected him governor in 1946. In 1948, the Democratic National Convention nominated Harry Truman for president and included a civil rights plank in its platform over the loud objections of Thurmond and other segregationists. An infuriated Thurmond bolted the party and ran for president himself as the nominee of the States' Rights Democratic, or "Dixiecrat" Party. This right-wing defection, contemporaneous with the desertion of left-wing Democrats led by Henry Wallace, appeared to doom Truman's prospects for a second term. Thurmond captured four Deep South states and thirty-nine electoral votes, but Truman won a surprise victory over Republican Tom Dewey.

With the GOP then virtually nonexistent in the South, Thurmond had no choice but to return to the Democratic fold. In 1950 he unsuccessfully sought a U.S. Senate seat. When another Senate vacancy materialized in 1954, the South Carolina State Democratic Committee blocked Thurmond's nomination. But Thurmond ran as a write-in candidate and won, the only senator in history to be so elected. In 1956, the maverick in Thurmond surfaced again: fulfilling a campaign promise, he resigned his Senate seat and ran again for his own job, without the advantage of incumbency. He won without opposition, as he did in 1960.

Thurmond's Senate voting record reflected his staunch conservatism and regional origins. He was militantly anticommunist and hawkish on defense issues, yet he favored considerably less governmental activism on most domestic matters. Above all, Thurmond defended segregationist policies against the demands for federal legislation to support the emerging civil rights movement.

Among the Senate segregationists of this time, Thurmond probably acquired the most notoriety. He was the leading force behind the drafting of the "Southern Manifesto" (1956), a statement of opposition to the Supreme Court's *Brown v. Topeka Board of Education* (1954) decision declaring segregated public schools unconstitutional. Most of the Southern congressional delegation—nineteen senators and eighty-one representatives—signed the document. In 1957,

Thurmond personally filibustered against a mild civil rights bill by holding the floor with a speech lasting twenty-four hours and eighteen minutes—a record.

Thurmond's militancy continued into the early 1960s. He frequently sparred with Attorney General Robert Kennedy on issues involving integration and the proper balance between federal enforcement powers and states' rights. Thurmond strenuously opposed the Civil Rights Act of 1964, and even when its final passage was assured he sought to weaken its impact by introducing some thirty-six restrictive amendments, all of which were rejected.

On the subject of communism, Thurmond was equally contentious. He frequently criticized President John Kennedy's administration for not being resolute enough in the Cold War conflict with the USSR. In 1962 Thurmond accused the State and Defense departments of censoring, or "muzzling" as he called it, the speeches of hard-line anticommunist military officers. A Senate investigation into these charges uncovered no great scandal but did lead to some new procedural guidelines for government bureaucrats responsible for the review and clearance of military speeches. Thurmond also objected to Kennedy's policy toward communist Cuba, which the senator regarded as insufficiently tough. Even in late December 1962, two months after the Missile Crisis, Thurmond came out "in full favor of an invasion if it were necessary to clear the Communists out" of Cuba. When Kennedy unveiled the Nuclear Test-Ban Treaty (1963), Thurmond unsuccessfully fought against its ratification in the Senate.

Like many other conservative Democrats, Thurmond became increasingly estranged from his party as it grew steadily more liberal during the 1960s. But in 1964 Thurmond took a step that few Southern politicians, no matter how conservative, had ever dared: declaring that the Democratic Party was turning America into a "socialistic dictatorship," he announced that he was joining the Republicans. Thurmond campaigned hard for the GOP's hard-line conservative presidential nominee, Senator Barry Goldwater. Although Goldwater lost in a landslide to Lyndon Johnson, his campaign planted the seeds of a generation of Republican triumphs to follow. Goldwater won only six states, but all were in the Deep South. At last, the "Solid South," the Democratic Party's most reliable constituency since the Civil War, had been broken. For countless "yellow dog" Southern Democrats, voting Republican had to have been an agonizing political step— but one made easier by Thurmond's having led the way.

Strom Thurmond

In 1968, Thurmond once again played an important role in the presidential sweepstakes. His unwavering support for Richard Nixon's nomination during the GOP convention helped keep many Southern conservatives from straying toward their ideological favorite, Governor Ronald Reagan. In the general election, Nixon followed a "Southern Strategy" of contesting for votes in Dixie, notwithstanding the third-party bid of Alabama Governor George Wallace. With help from Thurmond and others, Nixon made impressive inroads in the South that year, and the GOP would build upon that success in future presidential campaigns.

In the Senate, Thurmond kept up a brisk work pace despite his advancing years. Taking care never to lose touch with the folks of his home state, he routinely won reelection every six years. When the GOP controlled the Senate from 1981 to 1986, Thurmond's seniority entitled him to the largely honorific post of president pro tempore of the Senate. He also took over as chairman of the Judiciary Committee. His main activities included promoting the expanded use of the death penalty and overseeing the confirmation of virtually all of President Reagan's conservative appointments to the federal judiciary. Also a member of the Senate Armed Services Committee, Thurmond enthusiastically supported Reagan's defense buildup and tougher posture toward the Soviet Union.

On race relations, Thurmond began mending fences with blacks soon after the great civil rights battles of the mid-to-late 1960s. He appointed a number of African Americans to his staff, came out in favor of making Martin Luther King's birthday a national holiday, supported the extension of the Voting Rights Act, supported statehood for the District of Columbia (which would guarantee the election of two African Americans to the U.S. Senate), and saw to it that his office's constituent-service operations, reportedly one of the best in Congress, gave equal treatment to black South Carolinians.

When Democrats regained the Senate in 1987, Thurmond became the ranking minority member of the Judiciary Committee. In this capacity he participated in the acrimonious Supreme Court confirmation battles involving Robert Bork and Clarence Thomas. Thurmond, now well into his eighties, conducted himself with commendable restraint, courtesy, and dignity during these spectacles.

In his latter years his health and attention span waned significantly. The press at times sought to embarrass him on this account, but it had become clear to most that his determination not to give up power had kept him in office long past his time. He had become the oldest person ever to have served in Congress before he finally retired from the Senate in January 2003. He died in June of that year, at the age of 100.

—GEORGE SIRGIOVANNI

Further Reading

Cohodas, Nadine. *Strom Thurmond and the Politics of Southern Change*. New York: Simon & Schuster, 1993.

Garson, Robert. *The Democratic Party and the Politics of Sectionalism, 1941–1948*. Baton Rouge, La.: Louisiana State University Press, 1974.

Lachicotte, Alberta. *Rebel Senator: Strom Thurmond of South Carolina*. New York: Devin-Adair Co., 1967.

See also: anticommunism; Brown v. Board of Education; *civil rights*; Goldwater, Barry M.

Tocqueville, Alexis de (1805–59)

Among conservatives and liberals alike, the French aristocrat Alexis de Tocqueville is perhaps the most often quoted political theorists of democracy. In the words of Harvey Mansfield and Delba Winthrop, Tocqueville's two-volume work *Democracy in America* (1835) remains "at once the best book ever written on democracy and the best book ever written on America." Touching on themes and conditions that have in some cases only become apparent to Americans themselves more than a century and a half after his 1830–31 visit to the United States, Tocqueville argued that democracy was a "providential" new political arrangement of modernity, a regime legitimated not only by the official activities of voting and representation but more importantly, a radically new social arrangement based upon "equality of conditions" that transformed every aspect of human life and from which all of democracy's unique virtues and vices flowed.

In using the phrase "equality of conditions" Tocqueville did not refer to the literal material equality of all American citizens, but rather the universal assumption that no *significance* was to be accorded any apparent differences—material, social, or personal. This assumption led to suspicion and the ultimate demise of aristocratic claims to excellence. Since every person's judgment is to be regarded as equal to one's own, the sole basis of determining the legitimacy of public issues is by means of majority rule. Regarded by Tocqueville as the "dogma of the sovereignty of the people," this form of rule—founded on the apparently benign principle of equality—in fact leads to the belief that the opinion of the majority on any specific issue is unassailable and must be followed. While Tocqueville knew that in America the actual physical repression of a dissenting minority was rare (though not unheard of), the result of such equality in mass democratic society is the ever-present potential for a "tyr-

Alexis de Tocqueville

anny of the majority," which bases its claim to rule upon numbers, not upon rightness or excellence. The fear of such a tyranny results in a new form of internalized psychological control, an anticipation of disapproval by majorities and a concomitant attempt to avoid public commitment on any issue. In such a context, the best means of avoiding public indignity is to retreat to the private dignity afforded by one's intimate family circle.

For Tocqueville, fear of "tyranny of the majority" leads to the rise of "individualism," a sense of personal significance that results from interaction in one's "little society." This sense of personal potency, which paradoxically stems from a loss of actual influence in political life, forces democratic man to retreat constantly before the potential indignities of public life in order to support his belief in his personal private significance. Democratic man is marked by an anxiety that this sense of individual potency might be lost at any time, which in turn creates universal democratic "restlessness," a form of mobility and crass materialism intended to add to each person's sense of individual significance. In fact, this "restlessness" becomes a perpetual state of motion and discontent, a grasping search for something better that cannot be satisfied. The attempt to find dignity in private life, both by means of an increasingly narrow circle of acquaintances and by engaging in an unending pursuit of trivial material pleasures, has the ironic effect of only increasing democratic man's felt sense of indignity and weakness.

In such a condition, the great danger for democracy, according to Tocqueville, is the rise of "democratic despotism," a benign form of social control by a centralized bureaucratic state supported by a weakened and isolated citizenry. Unable to turn to their wider circle of acquaintances and fellow citizens for assistance during hard times, democratic citizens turn instead to the state, "an immense tutelary power" that "takes charge of assuring their enjoyments and watches over their fate." The rule of such a state is "mild" and "does not tyrannize," but rather "hinders, compromises, enervates, extinguishes, dazes, and finally reduces each nation to being nothing more than a herd of timid and industrious animals of which the government is the shepherd." Tocqueville feared that the price of equality was the willing loss of liberty, and he therefore admonished democracies to guard against this deceptively gentle form of democratic tyranny.

Tocqueville recommended two strategies for democratic citizens who would resist isolation and weakness and attempt to maintain or regain their personal and political dignity. He recommended active participation in associations within civil society, by means of which one could find others who held similar views—even as one's own views might be enlarged—and thereby resist the psychological fear of the tyranny of the majority. And he further argued that democracy ultimately required firm religious commitments, which would curb individualism's worst excesses by instilling in persons a sense of dignity and humility. By identifying and attempting to ameliorate democracy's paradoxical excesses toward conformity and individualism, Tocqueville sought to make democracy safe for liberty and to promote an ennobled, rather than a debased, form of equality.

—PATRICK J. DENEEN

Further Reading

Jardin, André. *Tocqueville: A Biography.* Translated by Lydia Davis with Robert Hemenway. New York: Farrar Straus Giroux, 1988.

Lawler, Peter Augustine. *The Restless Mind: Alexis de Tocqueville on the Origin and Perpetuation of Human Liberty.* Lanham, Md.: Rowman & Littlefield, 1993.

Manent, Pierre. *Tocqueville and the Nature of Democracy.* Translated by John Waggoner. Lanham, Md.: Rowman & Littlefield, 1996.

See also: *community; culture wars; custom; democracy; Dietze, Gottfried; equality; individualism; Mansfield, Harvey C.; mediating structures; Nisbet, Robert A.*

Toledano, Ralph de (1916–)

A conservative investigative journalist and leftist-turned-Cold Warrior, Ralph de Toledano covered the travails of Alger Hiss for *Newsweek* in the late 1940s. Despite his prolific writing—as a reporter, author of several books, syndicated columnist, poet, and noted music critic—he will probably best be remembered for being one of Whittaker Chambers's friends and confidantes. Toledano got to know Chambers during the Hiss-Chambers imbroglio and developed a close friendship with him that lasted until Chambers's death in 1961.

The two corresponded frequently, often writing letters despairing about a host of cultural and political issues. The pessimism about the West's prospects Chambers exhibited in his bestselling book *Witness* is on abundant display in the Chambers-Toledano correspondence, which was published as *Notes from the Underground* in 1997.

In a lengthy journalistic career Toledano has authored nearly two dozen books, most notably the bestseller *Seeds of Treason: The True Story of the Hiss-Chambers Tragedy* (1950), which he coauthored with Victor Lasky. *Seeds of Treason* was the first major account of the Hiss-Chambers case and helped demonstrate to the American public the undeniability of Hiss's guilt. Other Toledano books profiled J. Edgar Hoover, Richard Nixon, and Ralph Nader. Toledano has also published widely on music, writing regularly on the topic for *National Review.* He was editor of *The Frontiers of Jazz* (1947), a compilation of writings investigating the roots of that musical art form.

—MAX SCHULZ

Further Reading

Toledano, Ralph de. *Let Our Cities Burn.* New Rochelle, N.Y.: Arlington House.

———. *Poems, You and I.* Gretna, La.: Pelican, 1978.

See also: *Chambers, Whittaker; Hiss-Chambers trial; Levine, Isaac Don*

Tonsor, Stephen J. (1923–)

Born in Jerseyville, Illinois, Stephen Tonsor served in the U.S. Army Signal Corps (1943–46) as a cryptographer in New Guinea and the Philippines. After the war, Tonsor received an A.B. (1948) and Ph.D. (1955) in European intellectual history from the University of Illinois. Working under the guidance of Professor Joseph Ward Swain, he wrote a dissertation on Lord Acton's mentor Ignaz von Dollinger. Tonsor then studied and taught at the Universities of Zurich (1948–49) and Munich (1953–54) until becoming an instructor in history at the University of Michigan, where he was tenured and taught until his retirement in 1992.

As a scholar of European intellectual history, education critic, and self-conscious conservative, Tonsor has published three books and hundreds of articles and book reviews over the course of his academic career, publishing often in such venues as *National Review* and *Modern Age,* for which latter journal Tonsor has served as an associate editor since 1970. He was a close friend of Henry Regnery, with whom he had a fruitful correspondence that further reveals the humanist nature of Tonsor's conservatism.

Tonsor is not an especially well-known conservative intellectual. For one thing, he has been eclipsed by the political trajectory of the conservative movement, and while he was a contemporary of Russell Kirk, Richard Weaver, and William F. Buckley Jr., men rightly credited for their influence on the development of conservatism, Tonsor never gained the recognition within the movement he truly deserved, at least not outside of a small circle of scholars at places like Liberty

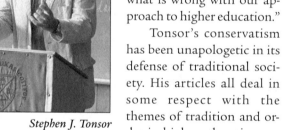

Stephen J. Tonsor

Fund, the Intercollegiate Studies Institute, and the Philadelphia Society.

As befits an intellectual historian, Tonsor's interests are eclectic. He is an expert on many topics, including German youth, Lord Acton, Edmund Burke, myth, and architecture. But it was in his capacity as cultural critic that he first gained national attention. In April 1969 he spoke before the National Association of Manufacturers on the topic "Alienation and Relevance in Higher Education." The article was reprinted in the *Chronicle of Higher Education* and attracted the interest of President Richard Nixon, who had the article circulated among the White House staff. Nixon praised Tonsor and endorsed the traditional views expressed in the speech, saying "it is the most significant and perceptive analysis of what is wrong with our approach to higher education."

Tonsor's conservatism has been unapologetic in its defense of traditional society. His articles all deal in some respect with the themes of tradition and order in higher education, religion, and the contemporary world. Tonsor gained notoriety at the April 1986 meeting of the Philadelphia Society when, for abandoning their principls, he excoriated his fellow conservatives—and neoconservatives in particular—in a witty, scathing, and highly controversial speech.

A charter member of the Philadelphia Society and member of the Mont Pelerin Society, Tonsor, who once wrote that he was "proud that most of his views are reactionary," has held many research fellowships and remains an active scholar.

—GREGORY L. SCHNEIDER

Further Reading

Tonsor, Stephen J. *Equality, Decadence, and Modernity. The Collected Essays of Stephen J. Tonsor.* Wilmington, Del.: ISI Books, 2005.

———. *National Socialism: Conservative Reaction or Nihilist Revolt? Source Problems in Western Civilization.* New York: Holt, Rinehart & Winston, 1959.

———. *Tradition and Reform in Education.* La Salle, Ill.: Open Court, 1974.

See also: French Revolution; paleoconservatism; Philadelphia Society; progress

Tories, American (Loyalists)

The Loyalists or, as the Patriots labeled them, "Tories," were colonists who maintained their allegiance to Great Britain during the American Revolution. Stubbornly faithful to the established government, Loyalists decried instability, mob rule, and what they saw as a "slow creep toward disorder." For this reason some thinkers have attempted to designate the Loyalists as the genesis of American conservatism (or at least hypothesized that the great purge of Loyalists during the Revolutionary Era explains the dormancy of American conservatism during the nineteenth century). Conservatives generally reject this interpretation. While some scholars have argued that Loyalists were the true law-abiding subjects of the British crown (or the "good Americans," as one historian hailed them), virtually no American political party or movement, old or new, has ever claimed the Loyalists. Conservatism claims the legacy of the founding fathers, and the debate over the connection between the Loyalists and modern conservatives, such as it is, essentially boils down to a debate over the Revolution and the founding impulse: Was it a liberal or conservative moment?

Preliminary distinctions between Loyalists and Patriots emerged as early as the Stamp Act Crisis of 1765. The Radicals labeled the Loyalists "Tories," conjuring a pejorative association with the diehard Royalists in England who had been discredited during the seventeenth and eighteenth centuries. These American Tories should not be confused with the subsequent revival of Toryism in England during the early nineteenth century. The revitalized English Tories, who evolved into the modern Conservative Party in the United Kingdom, emerged in response to the revulsion inspired by the French Revolution (which began in 1789). In truth, the Loyalists in America shared the same traditions of English liberty as the Radicals, but both parties swept aside this kinship as their division widened and the propaganda war escalated during the 1770s. The Tory predicament grew precarious after Radicals reinstated the nonimportation agreements following the Tea Act and the Intolerable Acts. Those who did not comply with the boycott customarily faced "tar and feathering" or other forms of mob violence at the hands of Radical vigilance committees. The agitation culminated in a complete schism during the spring of 1775 after Great Britain and the colonists exchanged the first shots of the War for Independence. Drawing a clear and irrevocable line between Loyalist and Patriot, the Second Continental Congress called for a general enlistment in the Continental Army. As British authority collapsed in the colonies during the spring of 1776, thousands of American subjects who remained loyal to the King, fearing physical violence and facing confiscation of their property, hastily evacuated mainland North America en masse.

Hard numbers reflecting the colonial division of opinion do not exist; therefore, scholars can only approximate the ratio of Loyalists to Patriots at any given time. Many historians concur with the famous prewar assessment of John Adams, who speculated that approximately one-third of the American population were Loyalist, one-third Patriot, and one-third undecided. Roughly 19,000 Americans served under British command and fought against the Continental Army. Although Loyalists came from all regions and all walks of life, some sectors of colonial society remained faithful to the Crown in greater numbers. Almost all royal officials maintained their loyalty to the king, as did most of the Anglican clergy. Concentrated in the seaports, many merchants refused to join the ranks of the Rebels. Well-to-do planters in the South were almost evenly divided, but backcountry farmers were likely to be Loyalists.

For British tacticians, purported Loyalist strength provided a key consideration in war planning. In 1777, British forces moved on and successfully captured Philadelphia, but the expected Tory support in the Pennsylvania backcountry failed to materialize. After the devastating defeat later that same year at Saratoga, the British switched to a defensive position in the North and attempted to isolate the more lucrative plantation colonies to the South. British high command, and King George himself, assumed that the inhabitants of Georgia and South Carolina were in large part steadfastly loyal to the Crown and stood ready to support and consolidate English military advances. After a series of impressive victories beginning in 1778, the British discovered that again they had overestimated Loyalist fervor in the backcountry.

British missteps in marshalling Loyalist sentiment in the southern colonies ultimately proved disastrous. Mixed signals regarding slavery hampered the British cause. Part of the multifaceted "Southern Strategy" included enlisting the aid of Loyalists to defeat the Rebels. At the same time, the British hoped to undermine Rebel resolve by sowing discord and encouraging revolt among the slave population and temporarily destabilizing the slave-based economy. How-

ever, the invaders found it impossible to destabilize the slave system of the Rebels while leaving that of the Loyalists undisturbed. Moreover, the British presence itself changed the tenor of the struggle. The invasion and occupation of the South resulted in what one scholar called a "milieu of chaos," in which the order and stability so favored by Loyalists became the first casualty of war. For most Southerners, the attack on the Rebels in the South seemed indiscriminate, and eventually the war came to be viewed as simply an attack on the community as a whole. As a result, Loyalist sentiment withered and proved incapable of sustaining British regulars against a ferocious and increasingly effective indigenous guerilla counterattack, which ultimately led to the British debacle at Yorktown.

Historians estimate that as many as 100,000 Loyalists fled the colonies during the early days of the American Revolution (approximately 3 percent of the population). The Tories who remained in the newly designated United States suffered ostracism, some incidents of violent reprisals (including lynchings), and the wholesale confiscation of their property during the war. After the Continental Army's victory at Yorktown, the status of this property emerged as an issue during the peace negotiations between the Rebels and the Mother Country. The American negotiators agreed to "earnestly recommend" to the states reinstatement of Loyalist rights, liberty, and all property confiscated during the preceding conflict. By 1787 all of the American states had rescinded discriminatory laws against the former Tories, but the promise of property restoration was never realized. For many years following the Peace of Paris, claimants petitioned American courts for restitution; they rarely succeeded. Great Britain exploited Loyalist difficulties in the new nation as a pretext for maintaining a string of forts along the Canadian border well into the late 1790s. However, violence against Tories during the Revolution and afterward was mild in comparison to the bloody French Revolution of the 1790s or to twentieth-century revolutions. After the war, the process of incorporating Loyalists into the new American culture proceeded smoothly. For the most part, the new republic embraced erstwhile Tories, reconfirmed their political rights, and reintegrated them into the community with very little lingering animosity.

—ASHLEY CRUSETURNER

Further Reading

Bakeless, John. *Turncoats, Traitors, and Heroes.* New York: Da Capo Press, 1998.

Callahan, North. *Flight from the Republic: The Tories of the American Revolution.* Indianapolis, Bobbs-Merrill, 1967.

See also: American Revolution

totalitarianism

"Totalitarianism," in its adjectival form, "totalitarian," originated in 1923 among opponents of Italian fascism, who used it as a term of abuse in describing the policies of the dictator Benito Mussolini. Quite quickly, however, the fascists embraced the word as a fitting description of the true goal and value of their regime. "Everything in the state, nothing outside the state, nothing against the state," Mussolini proclaimed in a 1925 speech—and he might have added, "everything *for* the state." Among other things, if nothing could stand outside the state, then there could be no free market or free corporations, no free families, no free churches, and of course, no free political parties. Totalitarianism therefore emerged as a term to describe a novel form of political regime in which a party or movement captured the apparatus of the state and—usually through means of terror—sought to mobilize *every*

energy of society for the use of the party-state, leaving *nothing* alone. Insofar as liberal societies boast of providing a maximum of freedom to individuals and their associations, totalitarianism could be understood as existing at the opposite pole from liberalism. Throughout the Cold War period, American conservatives usually understood themselves to be engaged in an immense effort to save "the free society" from the unique threat of totalitarianism.

Following the Second World War, as political thinkers sought to understand the recent calamity, at least two broad narratives were available. Communists and their socialist and left-liberal fellow travelers interpreted the war as one which pitted "progressive" international forces against extremist "reactionary" regimes (which, for communists at least, were the necessary outcome of capitalism in its late imperialist phase). World War II had been an "anti-fascist" war, which was to say, a war against dictatorships of the nationalist Right. Such a leftist interpretation tended to group Hitler's Germany, Mussolini's Italy, Franco's Spain—and later, many military regimes in Latin America—under the genus "fascism." Such an interpretation also identified the Soviet Union, and communist and socialist regimes more generally, as forces for "progress." The other available narrative centered on totalitarianism as the ideological foe in the war. But if this were so, then America's wartime alliance with the Soviet Union—an evidently totalitarian regime—was merely a transient phenomenon, dependent upon the circumstances. Moreover, given an adequately rigorous understanding of totalitarianism, it might be possible to recognize Franco's Spain, for example, as falling into a separate genus, that of more or less traditional authoritarianism.

Hannah Arendt's 1951 book *The Origins of Totalitarianism* was a major event, doing much to convince most sectors of American opinion of the continuity between National Socialism and Soviet communism, thus clearing the intellectual path toward the Cold War. The particular value of her work lay in its account of the origin of totalitarianism in the late-nineteenth-century transformation of the classes into the masses, with its immediate precondition being the alienation, isolation, and anomie of mass man. For conservatives, this meant that the defense of the free society against the totalitarian temptation would necessarily involve a critique of modern mass society with its atomizing popular culture and demotic rejection of traditional forms and institutions. Other writers who contributed to the early postwar literature on totalitarianism included Zbigniew Brzezinski and Carl Friedrich at Harvard.

Totalitarianism returned to the forefront of political debate in the late 1970s with Jeane Kirkpatrick's seminal *Commentary* article (and later book) titled *Dictatorships and Double Standards* (1982). The liberal moralist foreign policy of the Carter administration sought to pressure right-wing dictatorships allied with America on human rights grounds while seeking rapprochement with revolutionary regimes in the Third World. The left-liberal rationale for this policy stance was the view that while right-wing dictatorships were simple tyrannies, revolutionary regimes in the Third World were leftist-humanitarian and egalitarian—"progressive"—in intention, whether or not they were so in fact. They might therefore be open to an appeal, provided America could burnish its image as a progressive force in the world. Carter hoped to transcend the frozen divisions of the Cold War, at least in the Third World.

Kirkpatrick argued that America should properly follow precisely the opposite policy—and not merely for the old reason given with respect to the right-wing dictators: "He may be a son of a bitch, but at least he's *our* son of a bitch." Rather, Kirkpatrick argued that any policy must be based on a clear theoretical distinction between totalitarian and traditional authoritarian regimes. Traditional authoritarians were nonideological and did not presume to control all spheres of social life: families, churches, schools, and corporations were largely left to their own devices in such regimes, even if political parties and the press were subject to sometimes violent episodes of repression. Totalitarian regimes, on the other hand, operated from an ideological imperative to bring all social spheres under strict party control.

Kirkpatrick's distinction had an important implication. The intact and independent social worlds within an authoritarian regime created a basis for opposition that might eventually displace the dictatorship and bring about a free society. But a totalitarian party, once in power, systematically eliminated, through terror and propaganda, any possibility of an internal challenge to its rule. In light of the larger Cold War against Soviet communism, therefore, America's support for right-wing authoritarians (primarily in Latin America) and simultaneous denunciation of communist regimes worldwide did not constitute hypocrisy but was instead a principled stance. Kirkpatrick became U.S. ambassador to the United Nations under Reagan, and her views were fundamental to the foreign policies pursued by Reagan's administration.

Soviet totalitarianism did at last come to an end, though not without concerted American pressure during the culminating decade of the Cold War. And it is no accident that the communist collapse began in Poland, a country that, by historical accident, had retained a relatively independent church—in other words, a country that was not, quite, entirely totalitarian.

—MARK C. HENRIE

Further Reading

Abbott Gleason. *Totalitarianism: The Inner History of the Cold War.* Oxford University Press, 1995

Friedrich, Carl J., and Zbigniew K. Brzezinski. *Totalitarian Dictatorship and Autocracy.* New York: Praeger 1956.

Vetterli, Richard, and William E. Fort Jr. *The Essence of Totalitarianism.* Lanham, Md.: University Press of America, 1996.

See also: anticommunism; fascism; Kirkpatrick, Jeane J.; Marxism; Voegelin, Eric

Touchstone: A Journal of Mere Christianity

Touchstone began in 1986 as the newsletter of a Chicago-area Christian fellowship composed mainly of disaffected evangelicals seeking to ground their faith in the "Great Tradition" of the ancient church. By the early 1990s, the newsletter had expanded into a quarterly journal with a national readership. *Touchstone*'s ecumenical-yet-orthodox focus appealed to conservative mainline Protestants concerned about the increasing liberalism of their churches, as well as evangelicals interested in exploring the traditions of Catholicism and Eastern Orthodoxy. The journal's guiding lights included C. S. Lewis, G. K. Chesterton, and Russell Kirk. (In 1990, Kirk himself helped secure a grant to support the fledgling quarterly.)

Under the leadership of editor James Kushiner (an Orthodox convert), *Touchstone* assembled an editorial board consisting of James Hitchcock (Catholic), Leon Podles (Catholic), S. M. Hutchens (Protestant), Patrick Henry Reardon (Orthodox convert), and David Mills (Episcopalian, later a Catholic convert). This core group established the vision and tone of the journal, which remained consistent as it grew from a quarterly into a monthly by the year 2000.

Throughout its history, *Touchstone* has remained decidedly conservative and unabashedly patriarchal. Articles and editorials have frequently opposed women's ordination, "inclusive language" translations of the Bible, feminism, abortion, and homosexual activism. Beginning with a special extended-length issue in 1999, *Touchstone* took up the cause of "Intelligent Design," a movement among scientists opposed to materialism and naturalism. In 2001, anti-Darwinian author Phillip E. Johnson (Presbyterian) joined the magazine as a contributing editor and regular columnist.

In 2003, political philosopher Robert P. George (Catholic) joined the editorial board and spearheaded a widely publicized special issue on the secularization of the Democratic party—a relatively rare foray into partisan politics for the journal.

Two books have been compiled from *Touchstone*'s pages. *Signs of Intelligence: Understanding Intelligent Design* (2001) consists mainly of articles from the 1999 Intelligent Design issue. *Creed and Culture: A* Touchstone *Reader* (2003) collects the best essays from the journal's first ten years.

—SAM TORODE

tradition

In political argument, one of the leading methods of justification used on the right—though available to all parts of the political spectrum—has been the appeal to *tradition*. Proposed political innovations are resisted if they conflict with the traditional institutions and social patterns of a particular state. While related to it, a conservative's deference to tradition must be distinguished from simple piety—the preference for the old as old. After all, the ability of the pious to justify their opinions has been challenged in the Western tradition at least since Socrates' encounter with Cephalus in Plato's *Republic*. While conservatives certainly applaud a habit of piety, they have also sought to give a reasoned account of how tradition can be understood as normative. Still, the status of the appeal to tradition has remained problematic in conservative theory; an added difficulty in America is a dispute over the nature of the American tradition that is to be conserved.

Edmund Burke's seminal *Reflections on the Revolution in France* (1790) marks the beginning of conservative reflection on tradition. Burke counseled Englishmen to cleave to their inherited, traditional rights against the innovative natural-rights teaching of the Jacobins, which he saw as hopelessly abstract and ungrounded in historical practice. Burke maintained that he did not oppose all change, and in fact held that "a state without the means of some change is without the means of its conservation." But after centuries of human civilization, he doubted that any great discoveries could be made that would change the government of mankind markedly for the better. If the possibility of *revolutionary* progress in human affairs is doubted, an attachment to the ancestral is a rational position. For Burke, tradition constituted the unbroken development of the basic "wisdom" or "genius" of a people. This wisdom Burke placed in opposition to an individual's "own private stock of reason," which he believed to be small compared to "the general bank and capital of nations and ages."

In a famous formulation, Burke claimed that "society is indeed a contract . . . but between those who are living, those who are dead, and those who are to be born." In this we can see a forward-looking element in Burke's thought, for he maintained that "people will not look forward to posterity, who never look backward to their ancestors." Still, throughout his *Reflections*, Burke focused on "prescription." That which is prescribed by past practice can only be received and not made by a living generation. In Burke's thought, the hand of the past remains vital and *limiting* to the sovereignty of the living. He insists on this limitation because in the ideas of the Enlightenment, given political form in the French Revolution, Burke saw an essentially destructive egoism (a "selfish temper") and a temporal parochialism ("confined views"). These two great failings of the new philosophy could best be combated by awakening a people to the rationality inherent in a received tradition.

A problem with the appeal to tradition was evident from the very outset: what to do in the actual situation of France, a society that had by then experienced an obvious break with the wisdom of the past. Given the historical fact of the Revolution, it would seem that the ideas of the *philosophes* had entered into the French "tradition." Certainly any retreat to prerevolutionary institutions would itself require "revolutionary" change: any "restoration" would have to be by way of revolution. This predicament, never fully resolved, perhaps accounts for the peculiar element of willfulness that appears in the works of continental reactionaries such as Joseph de Maistre and Louis Bonald.

As with France, in America the status of tradition depends on the meaning of our revolution. One attitude toward the American experience holds that ours is a fundamentally liberal country. We had no feudal order to overcome; our history begins with a literal state of nature; our institutions are the implementation of Lockean ideas. Our "tradition" *is* liberalism. This perspective was dominant in the 1950s and early 1960s among elite scholars, notably Louis Hartz and Clinton Rossiter. In their reading of American history, "conservative liberals" serve to consolidate progressive liberal advances that bring the country ever closer to its philosophical ideal of maximal freedom and equality under the law. From this perspective, the gradual enlargement of constitutional rights in recent Supreme Court decisions fulfills the American tradition. While much of the postwar conservative intellectual movement sought to challenge the view that America's tradition is uniformly liberal, neoconservatives have revived and popularized this interpretation.

A second approach, that of traditionalist conservatism and, notably, Russell Kirk, has been to argue that the American Revolution was no revolution at all. In his *Reflections*, Edmund Burke both attacked the idea of revolution and defended the particular English settlement of the Glorious Revolution of 1688. He accomplished this feat by arguing that 1688 marked "a revolution not made but prevented." Kirk argued identically with respect to 1776 in America. This "war of independence," he maintained, was fought by the colonists to protect the "rights of Englishmen" against the encroachment of a centralizing and usurping Parliament. Early America was not a state of nature but a settlement of Englishmen; there is little evidence that our founding generation even read Locke's political works, and certain "liberal" drafts of the Bill of Rights (e.g., a right of "conscience") were consciously rejected in favor of historical English rights. A commitment to abstract liberal doctrines is therefore revealed as a deviation from our actually more complex tradition of aristocratic English political prudence.

Others have also argued that 1776 marked no revolutionary change, but they have offered different interpretations of the preexisting tradition. M. E. Bradford has pointed both to the religious beliefs of the founding generation and to the Roman references throughout this period to argue for an American *republican* tradition. This view is argued in greater depth by Willmoore Kendall and George Carey in *The Basic Symbols of the American Political Tradition* (1970). For Kendall and Carey, the authentic American tradition derives from Puritan, not aristocratic, England. They see the Mayflower Compact as our founding statement, reading subsequent public documents as continuous with this first social covenant. Thus Kendall and Carey see a tradition informed by the experience of an essentially homogeneous "virtuous people" governing themselves under God's ultimate authority by their "deliberate sense." The American tradition might best be described not as liberal democracy but as "Protestant republicanism." These arguments for a "traditionalist" American past are partially supported by historians such as J. G. A. Pocock and Gordon Wood, who have brought to light a tradition of civic republicanism in both England and America in the eighteenth century.

The third perspective on tradition evident on the American Right is more problematic than the first two and is related to the position of the continental reactionaries. In this view, the eighteenth-century liberal revolutions are merely a consequence of a larger historical movement that marks the true break in the great tradition of the West. For holders of this view, an ill-defined "modernity" is the source of a current "crisis," and modernity had begun its work long before the American founding. Political, social, and moral health could be restored by finding a way back behind or around modernity. The formulations of this view are many. Conservative Roman Catholic thinkers have pointed to the subjectivist individualism of the Reformation as the decisive break. Richard Weaver saw the turning point for the West in the triumph of Ockhamite nominalism over logical realism in the fourteenth century. For the students of Leo Strauss, the revolution in political philosophy begins with Machiavelli. Following Strauss, even George Will entertained such views when he argued in *Statecraft as Soulcraft* (1983) that liberal democratic societies are "ill founded." Will sought to inject an Aristotelian concern for virtue into our politics.

With some justice, Will claimed for his opinions the mantle of "the Oxford Movement, circa 1842." The greatest thinker of that movement, John Henry Newman, sought in his *Essay on the Development of Christian Doctrine* (1846) to show that the theology and ecclesiology of the Church of England was a logically continuous development within the Catholic Christian tradition. But Newman was driven by his research to reject the foundations of Anglicanism. His historical study uncovered principles of legitimate development in tradition, and the English Church failed to meet these criteria. To be faithful to the great tradition of Catholic Christianity, Newman would have to reject the traditions of his own, and deeply loved, Church of England. In Newman's dilemma we can see the radicalism to which the appeal to tradition can lead. Those conservatives who come to conclusions similar to Newman's can find themselves with at best an ambivalent relationship to the "American proposition" and indeed to the modern world. Newman could repeal the centuries and reconnect to what he believed was the true tradition by entering the Roman Catholic Church, which he did. For the conservative who concludes that modernity itself is deeply flawed, it is not clear by what revolution one could effect a "recovery of tradition."

—MARK C. HENRIE

Further Reading

Bradford, M. E. "A Teaching for Republicans: Roman History and the Nation's First Identity." In *A Better Guide than Reason: Studies in the American Revolution*. La Salle, Ill.: Sherwood Sugden, 1979.

Kirk, Russell. "A Revolution Not Made but Prevented." *Modern Age* 29 (1985): 295–303.

Strauss, Leo. *Natural Right and History*. Chicago: University of Chicago Press, 1953.

Weaver, Richard M. *Ideas Have Consequences*. Chicago: University of Chicago Press, 1984.

Wood, Gordon S. *The Creation of the American Republic, 1776–1787*. New York: Norton, 1969.

See also: Bradford, M. E.; Burke, Edmund; Burkean conservatism; Carey, George W.; Chesterton, G. K.; community; Conservative Mind, The; *education, public; fusionism; Kendall, Willmoore; Kirk, Russell; liberalism; Newman, John Henry; Parry, Stanley J.; progressivism;* Reflections on the Revolution in France; *Southern Agrarians; Strauss, Leo; traditionalism; Voegelin, Eric*

traditionalism

In the years following the Second World War, a group of writers emerged who became known as America's "New Conservatives," prominently including Richard M. Weaver, Peter Viereck, Robert Nisbet, and Russell Kirk. The New Conservatives articulated ideas and concepts that were virtually unprecedented in American intellectual history; with Kirk as their leader, in the context of the American conservative movement their position eventually became known as traditionalism, appropriately enough, since their writings were redolent with sometimes sweeping doubts about the "progress" of the modern project—and about the individualism at the heart of modern liberalism's liberty.

Central to the conservatism of the 1930s had been intransigent opposition to the "socialism" of Roosevelt's New Deal on the part of various Republican-leaning social groups. Among intellectuals, articulate conservatism in the 1930s had been represented by such men as H. L. Mencken, George Santayana, Irving Babbitt, and Albert Jay Nock. With the partial exception of Santayana, each may be said to have subscribed to a version of classical liberalism or libertarianism, emphasizing something resembling Mill's individuality as against social conformity. Without exception, their worldviews were markedly elitist and sharpened by religious skepticism. In other words, these prewar conservatives connected not at all with the lived traditions of the vast majority of the American people, except on the single point of the tradition of individualism, whether rugged or not.

While Kirk himself was influenced by some of the currents of thought in the 1930s, and while *The Conservative Mind* (1953) purported to be a "recovery" of a preexisting Burkean tradition in American political and social thought, it is difficult to deny that there was also a large element of invention in Kirk's account of the conservative tradition. Kirk's "canons" of conservatism begin with an orientation to "transcendent order" or "natural law," a view that political problems are at bottom religious and moral problems rather than the other way around: whereas the libertarian conservatives of the 1930s usually understood themselves as heirs of various Enlightenment dissenters from Europe's Christian civilization, Kirk is a dissenter from dissent, striving to learn from the sidelined champions of orthodox religion. Kirk therefore rejects rationalism, utilitarianism, and egalitarianism. He ties freedom to property-holding, but there is no discussion of the "magic of the marketplace" or interest in economic efficiency. He is hostile to the experimentalism of the social scientific mind, and he defends the latent reasonableness of evolved social forms. The three evils that emerge as antagonists throughout *The Conservative Mind* are the French Revolution, the industrial revolution, and the bureaucratic-managerial revolution of the first half of the twentieth century. Communism is mentioned hardly at all.

Focusing on the French Revolution, Kirk states emphatically that the overarching evil of the age is "ideology," and he claims that conservatism properly understood is "the negation of ideology." As such, conservatism prescribes a "politics of prudence," a cautious statesmanship founded upon a sensitive understanding of the complexities of human nature, the limitations of human history, and the capaciousness of the human good. Of course, liberalism's ancient boast has always been that it founds itself upon, and best adequates to, human nature—once that nature is shorn of illusions and superstition. To the liberal mind, one might even say that if ideology is defined as a project to achieve a utopian intellectual abstraction, then it is liberalism that is the negation of ideology.

From Kirk's perspective, there is a partial truth in liberalism's claims: liberty is a genuine element of the human good, and individual human beings are worthy of a respect which is roughly, imperfectly realized in a doctrine of rights. But to Kirk and to the American traditionalists he inspired, liberals ultimately fail to understand the partiality of their core principle. Their account of human nature excludes too much of what can be known, and is known, about the human good. The homogenization of the whole of the human world on the basis of the contract theory, thought Kirk and his traditionalist allies, is the dehumanizing threat we ultimately face, made all the more dangerous by the fact that America's political discourse has lacked any terms which would enable us to recognize the ideological or dogmatic character of liberalism.

Kirk's traditionalism quickly met with, and has long labored under, the accusation that it is, in effect, "un-American." The American tradition of political thought has always proceeded within the terms of the Constitution and the *Federalist Papers*—evidently liberal documents. As Louis Hartz so famously argued, America is the Lockean country par excellence, with an aboriginal condition (or original position) closely resembling Locke's state of nature, and a founding compact reflecting Lockean principles. Consequently, there never has been, nor ever could be, a genuinely conservative party—in the European sense—in American life.

But Kirk was actually quite close to the values and aspirations of common Americans untutored in political theory. Today's traditionalist conservatives continue to be closer to average Americans on religious and moral matters—and on what we might call the "national question"—than are either libertarians or neoconservatives. Traditionalists can be understood as "un-American" only when America is understood definitively as the abstract embodiment of liberal theory.

The traditionalist conservative's first feeling, the intuition that constitutes his moral source, is the sense of *loss*, and hence, of *nostalgia*. Those who are secure in the enjoyment of their own are often progressives of a sort, so confident in the solidity of their estate that they do not shrink from experimenting with new modes and orders. The conservative spirit, as such, arises only when loss is at hand, or, probably more frequently, when loss has occurred. Consequently, there is always a "reactionary" dimension to such conservatism; the conservative typically arrives "too late" for mere conservation.

While in possession, we take our good for granted and, so, often fail to recognize it. But in the face of loss, the human good is vividly revealed to us. We lament the loss of goods, not the loss of evils, which is why lament *illuminates*. While it may be true that nostalgia views the past through "rose-colored glasses," such a criticism misses the point. To see the good while blinkered against evils is, nevertheless, *to see the good*. This is a source of knowledge, as well as a moral source. And here we may begin to glimpse facets of the human good beyond mere utility, beyond all our theorizing.

So drenched in the progressive spirit is American political discourse that the backward glance is usually rejected out of hand, and with the most facile of arguments. Ever since Burke's solicitous phrases about "Gothick" and "monkish" traditions, traditionalist conservatives have notably looked to the Middle Ages as a source of inspiration. In doing so, one is met with a rejoinder

of the sort, "But would you really want to live in an age before modern dentistry?" Southern traditionalists who speak well of the antebellum South almost always stand accused of being racist defenders of slavery. But why should such rejoinders count as definitive when the modern project, which is usually understood to have begun in the Renaissance, took as an inspiring model *Athens*—a society which had no access to modern dentistry and a society built on a foundation of slave labor?

Traditionalists do *not* wish to "turn back the clock" to premodern dentistry, any more than the lovers of Periclean Athens wish to restore a slave economy. Polis-envy in the Renaissance and among some of our contemporaries serves as an indicator that a thinker is attracted to an ideal of political participation, as well as literary and philosophical originality, and perhaps, of leisure, that he believes is unavailable or frustrated in the present. Likewise, the traditional conservative's kind words about medievalism indicate that he is attracted to forms of communal solidarity, loyalty and friendship, leisure, honor and nobility, and religious "enchantment" that seem to be presently unavailable. As Tocqueville helps us to understand, this list is not idiosyncratic, but rather corresponds in its particulars to the deficits universally engendered by the modern regime. There are permanent features to the world remade by Enlightenment, and conservative "medievalism" is a catalog of the *loss* brought on by the achievement of the modern regime. Wherever there is a sense of loss, the conservative knows that there lies an indicator of some dimension of the human good.

From this discussion we can discover something else about the traditionalist's "method." The *philosophes* cast doubt on the universal applicability of Christian "morals" in light of the diverse folkways of "natural men" whom European explorers had discovered (or claimed to have discovered) in their voyages. A common trope of the French Enlightenment was to question even the incest taboo as an unscientific "prejudice" of Christian civilization. But the Enlightened builders of the liberal regime were quite certain that they had discovered principles of political right that *were* universally applicable—and which in time might be applied beyond politics to the sphere of morals. Burke in contrast was guided by a kind of certainty in (traditional) morals, by an immediate intuition of the human good, while he viewed with the deepest skepticism speculative theories of political right. Whereas the Enlightenment "builds down" from politics to morals, the conservative "builds up" from morals to politics. Perhaps it would be fair to say that the liberal tradition even today has not yet generated a credible account of moral life. Perhaps it would be similarly fair to say that the conservative tradition has not yet generated a credible account of political life.

Viewed in this way, it might be said that traditionalist conservatism is *not yet* a political theory, but rather, a tradition of social criticism which is working its way to a political philosophy adequate to its deepest moral intuitions. There is nothing extraordinary in such a view when we remember that the liberal tradition first reached something like a comprehensive theoretical articulation only in Locke, nearly two centuries after its moral rudiments came to light in the Renaissance and Reformation. We are only little more than two centuries on from conservatism's birth in the reaction to the French Revolution. Thus, the specifically *political* teaching of traditional conservatism remains provisional.

One might describe the traditionalist conservative's political project as one of "containing liberalism," of "boxing in" liberal justice. As the conservative movement in America crystalized in the 1950s and 1960s, a large, rather impressive, and decidedly un-

derstudied body of literature developed on the question of "tradition." In retrospect, we can now see that "tradition" was a word deployed to indicate those moral contents of life which are eroded under liberalism; these studies were undertaken in an effort to understand the prerequisites for the persistence of those moral contents, so that policies and jurisprudential concepts could be developed to safeguard those social structures in which the moral contents of life naturally arise. Emphasis was placed on "society"—but not on what we know as "civil society." That is, emphasis was placed on elements of *Gemeinschaft* (organic community) rather than *Gesellschaft* (contractual society). Conservatives have sought to "make room," both conceptually and practically, for the flourishing of *Gemeinschaft*. Hence, the frequent invocation of Burke's "little platoons," as against the modern "grid" which reduces everything to the superintendence of the equal-protection state and the free market. Put another way, the political goal of traditional conservatism might be to keep the "public" realm small—but not in the liberal way, which makes the private, i.e. *individual*, realm large. What is wanted is a large and authoritative "social" realm.

Today, we often find that practical political advocacy reflecting a traditionalist perspective takes place in institutions with the word "family" in their titles. The liberal contract tradition's reduction of human beings to autonomous individuals fosters a self-conception that destabilizes the marriage bond; the welfare state then lubricates exit from marriage with various substituting benefits. Love, it has been said, is the willingness to belong to another. There is little place for such love in a world of autonomous individuals bristling with rights—the world which liberalism understands as "natural." The popularity of a therapeutic language of "fulfillment" in contemporary America only exacerbates the weak institutional support that liberal jurisprudence provides for marriage. Traditional religious marriage ceremonies often included a prominent discussion of *sacrifice*, not a concept with ready appeal to autonomous individuals.

It is no accident that when liberalism attempts to think about marriage it characteristically neglects the children. Rather than a universal fact of human nature, the reproduction and rearing of children is considered an irritating anomaly in the social contract. Consequently, children are effectively relegated to an externality or assimilated to adult autonomy. What else is liberalism to do with such creatures—naturally dependent, naturally unequal, and naturally only potentially rational human beings, who naturally belong to their parents, who in turn naturally belong to them?

The weakness of liberalism's educational doctrine cannot easily be remedied, however, for liberalism's boast is that it chastely denies to itself any thick theory of the Good, and thus uniquely does not need to indoctrinate its citizens with controversial orthodoxies. But when the liberal state appropriated to itself the business of education with the advent of the "common school," it seized the responsibility of soulcraft—without really admitting to that fact. Education is in its nature value-laden. Liberalism's principled refusal to speak in teleological terms of a summum bonum therefore renders it a much-abashed patron of the schools: for as every parent knows, children ask *Why?*—and continue to ask *Why?*—until they come to the end of the matter. A consistently liberal schooling must always stop short of that end, satisfying no one. For most of American history, the common schools surreptitiously reflected shared local values, and the central organs of government looked the other way, a reasonable strategy for muddling through a theoretical inconsistency. Lately, however, courts have insisted on en-

forcing liberal norms on the schools, engendering a demoralization of society from the roots up. If in the past the schools stood in loco parentis, reflecting the values and exercising the discipline of parents in the domestic sphere, today the schools represent an ever-earlier exposure of children to the rights-bearing and market-choosing of the public sphere.

The traditionalist response has been to encourage experiments in alternatives of all kinds that might allow schools to reflect comprehensive conceptions of the good. A tuition tax credit was long the conservative goal, fostering the growth of an alternative, fully "private" (or, more properly, "social" or "domestic") system. Vouchers now seem a more politically feasible goal—though vouchers also raise anxieties, since nothing yet has escaped the *control* that accompanies state "help." Traditionalists furthermore take hope from the burgeoning growth of homeschooling in our time, hoping that as we absorb in our social imagination the fact of widespread homeschooling, we will begin to recognize something that was obscured by the progressive ideology of the common school—namely, that a public school is not an arrangement between the state and students, but rather between the state and parents: schools are best understood as providing one way (and not the only way) to serve, or even merely to supplement, the primarily *parental* office—simultaneously an obligation and a right—of educating one's own children.

Besides the family, we might consider here one other area of inquiry in which the approach of traditionalist conservatives has differed from others allied with them in the American conservative movement: economics. Traditionalists typically have taken private property, market exchange, and the price mechanism all as something more or less natural. But they have advanced no particular doctrinal commitments, and they are sensitive to the artificial abstractions of modern corporate capitalism. During the second half of the twentieth century, traditional conservatives did oppose socialism, the growth of the welfare state, and most government regulation of the economy—but they did not necessarily do so for reasons of classical liberal political economy. Their primary concern was with the *culture* of socialism or of welfarism. In a similar way, many traditional conservatives today have begun to voice reservations about the *culture* of globalizing capitalism.

The economic theorist with the greatest appeal to the traditionalists has been Wilhelm Röpke. A German-Swiss Protestant, Röpke's work proceeded in dialogue with the Catholic social thought tradition, especially the papal encyclicals *Rerum Novarum* (1891) and *Quadragesimo Anno* (1931). While fundamentally a defender of the free market, Röpke nonetheless embraced talk of a "third way" between socialism and capitalism. He warned of a kind of consumer materialism and social anomie arising from the totalizing reach of market "logic." He thus emphasized the need to embed the market amidst strong social institutions and structures—boxing in liberalism in its economic dimension. Withal, traditionalist conservatives have often written in favor of a widespread *distribution* of productive capital, and in favor of smaller units of economic production. The question is not whether markets will be regulated; the question is what values shall structure that regulation.

The national narratives of most European peoples celebrate their moment of settlement into a particular place, an end to nomadic wandering and the taking up of agriculture (and Christianity). It is striking that Americans celebrate not our settlement, but rather our movement—setting off for the frontier. The liberal narrative of America as a "universal nation" corresponds to this unsettledness: to be a "universal" nation is precisely *not* to be a nation, a *gens*. Traditionalists have been endeavoring to *settle* America, to celebrate our arrival and not our departure, our actuality and not our potentiality, to bring Americans to see their national experience both as more particular than universal (which is to say, ideological) and as more in continuity with European precedents than in discontinuity.

—Mark C. Henrie

Further Reading

Carey, George W., ed. *Freedom and Virtue: The Conservative-Libertarian Debate.* Wilmington, Del.: ISI Books, 1998.

Crunden, Robert, ed. *The Superfluous Men: Critics of American Culture, 1900–1945.* 2nd ed. Wilmington, Del.: ISI Books, 1999.

Frohnen, Bruce. *Virtue and the Promise of Conservatism: the Legacy of Burke and Tocqueville.* Lawrence, Kan.: University Press of Kansas, 1993.

Nisbet, Robert. *The Quest for Community: A Study in the Ethics of Order and Freedom.* New York: Oxford University Press, 1953.

Voegelin, Eric. *Order and History.* 5 vols. Baton Rouge, La.: Louisiana State University Press, 1956.

Weaver, Richard. *Ideas Have Consequences.* Chicago: University of Chicago Press, 1948.

See also: Burke, Edmund; community; Conservative Mind, The; *family; fusionism; homeschooling; individualism; Kirk, Russell; liberalism; Meyer, Frank S.; Nisbet, Robert A.; Röpke, Wilhelm;* Quest for Community, The; *tradition; Voegelin, Eric; Weaver, Richard M., Jr.*

Triumph

L. Brent Bozell founded *Triumph* in 1966 as a journal for conservative American Roman Catholics. Bozell was a lawyer and author of *The Warren Revolution* (1966), a critical study of the activist Supreme Court under Chief

Justice Earl Warren. He was also the brother-in-law of William F. Buckley Jr., with whom he had worked on *National Review* for the eleven years previous to founding *Triumph*. Bozell was dismayed by the changes sweeping through the Catholic Church in the aftermath of the Second Vatican Council (1962–65), especially because they coincided with the social upheavals of the sixties and the sexual revolution in America.

Bozell and his fellow editors Frederick Wilhelmsen, Michael Lawrence, Gary Potter, and John Wisner opposed the tendency of Catholics (politically on the Right and on the Left) to pick and choose among doctrines and Church teachings. They believed the purpose of the Council had been to *strengthen* orthodoxy, not to dilute it. They hoped the Church would continue to act as though it alone was the avenue to salvation, would continue to seek converts, and would continue to condemn all other religions as well as other forms of Christianity. They disliked the switch from Latin to the vernacular languages but, placing loyalty to the pope above all other virtues, grudgingly accepted it when the time came. Enamored of Spanish Catholicism (the Bozells and Wilhelmsen had spent years living in Spain), they held classes at the Escorial Palace near Madrid every summer. Wilhelmsen pointed out that Spain alone had defeated Christendom's two greatest enemies: Islam in the Reconquista, and communism during the Civil War. In Washington, D.C., a group of *Triumph*-led activists, the "Sons of Thunder," staged America's first pro-life demonstration (1970). They mystified onlookers by wearing the red berets of the Carlist militia and chanting Spanish slogans ("Viva Cristo Rey!").

Buckley's *National Review* had always been ecumenical, had always been willing to take Church teaching with a pinch of salt ("Mater sí, Magistra no!" it had once proclaimed in response to John XXIII's encyclical *Mater et Magistra*), and had even preached agnosticism on the abortion question in 1965. When *Triumph* began raising doubts about America's role in Vietnam and its consonance with Catholic just-war theory, the relationship between Buckley and Bozell became strained. Bozell declared that good Catholics, far from standing wholeheartedly in support of the nation, must estrange themselves from the United States because of its violation of religious and political principles on which compromise was impossible. The Catholic "tribe," *Triumph* argued in the early 1970s, was adrift in a sea of heresy and paganism.

Many readers who had accepted the rigorous *Triumph* line on religion balked when the magazine's writers spoke out against patriotism; neither did readers appreciate the fact that *Triumph* was almost as strident in its condemnation of libertarian capitalism as it was in its anticommunism. Circulation dropped off precipitously in the early 1970s. Appearing infrequently after 1972, the magazine closed down altogether in 1975, by which time its editor was suffering from bipolar disorder. In its heyday, however, *Triumph* had run vigorous articles by Wilhelmsen, brilliantly scathing editorials by Bozell himself, and thought-provoking columns by the likes of Jeffrey Hart, John Lukacs, and Thomas Molnar.

—Patrick Allitt

Further Reading

Allitt, Patrick. *Catholic Intellectuals and Conservative Politics in America, 1950–1985.* Ithaca, N.Y.: Cornell University Press, 1993.

Bozell, L. Brent. *Mustard Seeds: A Conservative Becomes a Catholic: Collected Essays.* Front Royal, Va.: Christendom Press, 2001.

Lawrence, E. Michael, ed. *The Best of Triumph.* Front Royal, Va.: Christendom Press, 2001.

See also: Bozell, L. Brent; Catholic social teaching; Wilhelmsen, Frederick

Tucker, St. George (1752–1827)

Prominent Virginia jurist, man of letters, stepfather of John Randolph of Roanoke, and founder of a long line of famous Virginia law professors, St. George Tucker was born near Port Royal, Bermuda, and educated at the College of William and Mary. During the Revolutionary War he commanded militia at Guilford Court House and Yorktown.

Appointed a judge of the general court of Virginia in 1788, Tucker shunned partisan politics, though he privately favored the Jeffersonians over the Federalists, opposed the Alien and Sedition Acts, and supported the Louisiana Purchase. Tucker taught law at the College of William and Mary from 1790 to 1803. Loathing slavery but seeking a prudent balance between the slaves' right to freedom, justice for slave owners, and social harmony, he proposed in his *Dissertation on Slavery* (1796) the gradual emancipation of female slaves and their children, compensation for slave owners, and encouragement of the freed blacks to resettle in the West.

In 1807, Tucker published the first American edition of Sir William Blackstone's great treatise on the common law, *Commentaries on the Laws of England*, adding appendices on state and federal law, civil liberty, equity courts, slavery, and other special topics to facilitate application of Blackstone to American experience. Tucker's Blackstone was America's dominant legal reference work for decades and helped impart Blackstone's natural law perspective to American jurisprudence.

Tucker served on the Virginia Court of Appeals from 1803 to 1811. President James Madison appointed him judge of the federal court for the Virginia district in 1813. He retired in 1825.

—John Attarian

Further Reading
Cullen, Charles T. *St. George Tucker and Law in Virginia, 1772–1804.* New York: Garland, 1987.

Hamilton, Phillip. *The Making and Unmaking of a Revolutionary Family: The Tuckers of Virginia, 1752–1830.* Charlottesville, Va.: University of Virginia Press, 2003.

See also: common law

Tullock, Gordon (1922–)

In opposing socialism, conservatives have often relied on theoretical arguments that free markets allocate resources efficiently. However, theoretical economics also has identified various "market failures," situations in which markets will fail to attain this ideal of economic efficiency, providing a possible justification for government intervention. The development of the study of *public choice* provided a counterargument against the interventionists, pointing out that politics was also an arena for the pursuit of self-interest, leading to possible "government failures." Gordon Tullock played a major role in the emergence of this field of study.

Tullock and James Buchanan are the authors of the classic *The Calculus of Consent* (1962), which focused on the rational choice of rules for making collective decisions. In 1967, Tullock made another seminal contribution to economics with his theory of *rent seeking*. Economists had previously measured inefficiencies of monopoly from reduced output. Tullock pointed out that these measures of inefficiency ignored the additional waste of resources used to influence government to protect monopolies.

In more than 140 articles and fifteen books, Tullock's research contributed much more to our knowledge of public choice. As one of the founders of the Public Choice Society and as the founding editor of its journal, *Public Choice*, Tullock has also fostered similar research by many others.

—John H. Beck

Further Reading

Brady, Gordon L., and Robert D. Tollison, eds. *On the Trail of Homo Economicus: Essays by Gordon Tullock*. Fairfax, Va.: George Mason University Press, 1994.

Fishback, Price, Gary Libecap, and Edward Zajac, eds. *Public Choice Essays in Honor of a Maverick Scholar*. Boston: Kluwer Academic, 2000.

Tullock, Gordon. *Economics of Income Redistribution*. 2nd ed. Boston : Kluwer Academic, 1997.

_____. "The Welfare Costs of Tariffs, Monopolies and Theft." *Western Economic Journal* 5 (1967): 224–32.

See also: Buchanan, James M.; public choice economics

Tyrrell, R. Emmett, Jr. (1943–)

The founding editor in chief of the *American Spectator*, as a graduate student at Indiana University in 1967 R. Emmett Tyrrell Jr. started the journal in a Bloomington farmhouse to combat leftists at the university.

Tyrrell looked to the 1920s literary and political culture of the *American Mercury* and the *New Yorker* for the magazine's inspiration, adopting an editorial style of "amused skepticism." Originally called the *Alternative*, his magazine evolved from an antiradical campus publication into a national conservative political and cultural monthly noted for its irreverence and wit.

Tyrrell is well known both as an editor and as a conservative cultural critic. He coined the word "Kultursmog" to describe the left-wing political ideology of America's intellectuals that had pervaded the country since the 1970s. In *The Conservative Crack-Up* (1992), Tyrrell blamed conservatives for not transforming American institutions when they had the opportunity in the 1980s, arguing that they lacked the imagination and flair for drama in public life that makes liberals successful. He dated the conservative crack-up to the failed Supreme Court nomination of Robert Bork.

Tyrrell received his B.A. and M.A. in history from Indiana University. Tyrrell's political thought was formed by Aristotle's *Politics* and *The Federalist*, with special admiration for James Madison. He credits his college swimming coach with encouraging his appreciation for reading, education, and opera. Other influences on Tyrrell include Luigi Barzini, George Jean Nathan, Sidney Hook, Malcolm Muggeridge, and Irving Kristol. Tyrrell's books include *The Impeachment of William Jefferson Clinton* (1997), *Boy Clinton: The Political Biography* (1996), *The Liberal Crack-Up* (1984), *Public Nuisances* (1979), and *The Future That Doesn't Work: Social Democracy's Failure in Britain* (1977).

Under Tyrrell's editorial guidance, the influence and circulation of the *American Spectator* skyrocketed in the 1990s, largely because the magazine relentlessly pursued investigative journalism stories intended to reveal the corruption and nefariousness of the Clintons and their people. In this it achieved some success, but it also brought on severe financial difficulties that led to the sale of the magazine to George Gilder in 2000 and the removal of Tyrrell from his post. However, Tyrrell returned in 2003 and is today the resurgent magazine's editor once again.

—William F. Meehan III

Further Reading

Tyrrell, R. Emmett. With Mark W. Davis. *Madame Hillary: The Dark Road to the White House*. Washington, D.C.: Regnery, 2004.

York, Byron. "The Life and Death of the *American Spectator*." *Atlantic Monthly,* November 2001, 91–105.

See also: American Spectator

U

unionism

The major determinant of the form and structure of unionism in the United States is the National Labor Relations Act (NLRA), which was enacted in 1935 (the Wagner Act) and substantively amended in 1947 (the Taft-Hartley Act). The ostensible purpose of the NLRA is to promote equality of bargaining power between employers and employees. Unionists present the history of unionism as a long and bitter struggle of employees as underdogs against employers as their exploitative masters. Students of the competitive market process, on the other hand, see that history as a battle of some employees (those who wanted to cartelize) against other employees (those who wished to remain independent). The unionist view of history triumphed during the New Deal. The Wagner Act was explicitly pro-union, anti–independent worker, and anti-employer. Although the Taft-Hartley Act restored some balance, the NLRA is still strongly biased in favor of unions and against independent workers and employers. Conservatives historically have been opposed to ideological unionism on the grounds that unions interfere with private contracts, often use the power of the state to enforce their will, and often have had close ties with various left-wing movements of socialist or communist leanings. Ronald Reagan (who won the endorsement of the Teamsters Union for his presidential campaign) was instrumental in bringing many union members into the conservative political fold. But divisions rooted in economic and political positions remain. Libertarians in particular have three principal areas of concern regarding American unionism: exclusive representation, union security, and the right to strike.

Under Section 9 of the NLRA, a union penetrates a hitherto union-free firm by seeking the signatures of at least 30 percent of the workers it is seeking to organize on authorization cards. The authorization cards amount to a petition for an election. If the union organizers are successful, the National Labor Relations Board (NLRB) conducts a secret ballot representation, or certification, election among the target workers. Once one union has secured the signatures of at least 30 percent of the workers, other unions may get on the ballot by getting as few as 5 percent of the workers to sign additional authorization cards. A "no union" choice is also included on the ballot.

The winner is that choice on the ballot that gets a majority of the votes cast. If no choice gets a clear majority, there is a run-off election between the two choices that received the most votes. If a union is the winner it becomes the exclusive bargaining agent for all of the workers who were eligible to vote. The winning union gets to represent the workers who voted for it, but it also gets to represent workers who voted for some other union, workers who voted for no union, and workers who didn't vote.

Unionists defend this winner-take-all election procedure by analogy with governmental elections. A member of the House of Representatives is the exclusive representative of all the people in his or her congressional district. Voters who voted for someone else and voters who did not vote must accept the representation services of the winning candidate.

But the unionists' analogy is inapt. Democracy is a principle that applies to government. Libertarians believe that it is improper to force people to conform to the will of a majority in the private sphere of human action. We don't vote to determine what clothes to wear or which tax accountant to hire; that is left to individual free choice. Yet, under the NLRA, when it comes to deciding whether to have a union represent us in the sale of our labor services, individual free choice is replaced by mandatory submission to the will of the majority. Moreover, a member of the House of Representatives must stand for reelection every two years. In contrast, a union that is certified as an exclusive bargaining agent in one election is presumed to continue to have majority support among the workers it represents indefinitely. There are no regularly scheduled recertification elections. The only way workers can get rid of an unwanted exclusive bargaining agent is to circulate a petition for a decertification election. If at least 30 percent of the workers sign it, the NLRB will conduct a secret ballot election for that purpose.

Ever since the Wagner Act imposed exclusive representation on employees, unions have argued that because the law requires a certified bargaining agent to represent all the workers who were eligible to vote in the certification election as well as all new employees in its "bargaining unit," all such workers should be forced either to become members of the certified union or at least to pay union dues as a condition of continued employment. This arrangement is euphemistically called "union security."

The Wagner Act permitted four forms of union security: the closed shop, the union shop, the agency shop, and maintenance of membership. The Taft-Hartley Act elimi-

nated the closed shop, but it still permits the latter three.

In a closed shop a prospective employee must already be a union member to be hired. In a union shop, an employee does not have to be a member when hired, but in order to continue employment must become a union member after a probationary period on the job (usually thirty days). In an agency shop a nonunion employee is not required to join the union, but must pay union dues and fees in order to keep his job. Under maintenance of membership no one is forced to join or pay dues, but if a worker voluntarily joins the union that employee may not resign membership as long as an existing collective bargaining contract between the union and the employer is in effect.

Unionists defend such arrangements through a "free rider" argument. Since all workers in a union's bargaining unit receive the benefits of the union's bargaining, it is only fair, unionists argue, that all of the workers should contribute to the union's support. A worker who did not would be a "free rider" or a "freeloader."

But unions could avoid free riders very easily if they bargained for their voluntary members and for no one else. In other words, if unions want to get rid of free riders they should advocate amending the NLRA to replace exclusive representation with proportional representation. Second, while unions may indeed capture some free riders by union security arrangements, they are just as likely to victimize "forced riders." A forced rider is a worker who, as far as the worker is concerned, receives net harms from a union's activities, but is nevertheless forced to support the union. For example, a young worker may want higher current pay rather than improvements in the employee pension plan. An older worker might have the opposite priorities. If, during collective bargaining, a union sacrifices current pay increases in exchange for a better employee pension plan, the young worker is made worse off by what the union does. If he or she is forced to pay the union for such disservice, the union will have captured a forced rider.

In 1988 the U.S. Supreme Court, in *Communications Workers v. Beck*, limited the amount of money that unions can conscript from dissenting workers under the NLRA to the amount that is necessary to pay for the costs of collective bargaining, contract administration, and the processing of grievances. No money exacted from unwilling workers can be used to pay for such things as partisan political or ideological activities, general union organizing expenses, and litigation not directly related to collective bargaining.

Sections 7 and 13 of the NLRA create an unambiguous legal right to strike. However, proponents of individual liberty question whether there is a moral right to strike. It all depends on the definition of a strike. If a strike is merely a collective withholding of labor services by workers who regard the terms and conditions of employment offered by an employer as unacceptable, and if these workers have not previously promised not to do so, then there is a moral right to strike. An individual worker owns his or her labor services, and if the worker does not like the wage offer of an employer the worker may refuse to do the work—i.e., refuse to accept the employer's employment offer or refuse to continue an existing employment relationship.

However, a strike is usually a collective withholding of labor services plus a shutting-out of others who wish to do business with the struck firm. In effect, strikers assert that they own the jobs that they are refusing to perform, and they have a right to prevent the struck firm from carrying on without them. The chief instrument of shutting-out is the picket line. While people who wish to withhold their own labor services have a moral right to do so, free-market proponents argue that no person has a moral right to withhold the labor services of another person or to deny the struck firm access to customers and deliveries of material and supplies.

Section 2(3) of the NLRA asserts that "The term 'employee' . . . shall include any individual whose work has ceased as a consequence of, or in connection with, any current labor dispute. . . ." In other words, a striker has a property right to the job he refuses to perform. But to a proponent of personal liberty the employment relationship is one of contract: a willing employee agrees to perform labor services for a willing employer on mutually acceptable terms. Absent this willingness, there is no employment relationship. In the voluntary exchange process, when a would-be seller rejects the terms offered by a would-be buyer (or vice versa), both parties are free to seek better terms from other people.

—Charles W. Baird

Further Reading

Baird, Charles W. *The Permissible Uses of Forced Union Dues: From Hanson to Beck*. Cato Policy Analysis No. 174. Washington, D.C.: Cato Institute, 1992.

———. "Toward Equality and Justice in Labor Markets." *Journal of Social, Political and Economic Studies* 20 (1995): 163–86.

Dickman, Howard. *Industrial Democracy in America: Ideological Origins of National Labor Relations Policy*. LaSalle, Ill.: Open Court, 1987.

Haggard, Thomas R. *Compulsory Unionism, The NLRB, and the Courts: A Legal Analysis of Union Security Agreements*. Philadelphia, Pa.: Wharton School, Industrial Research Unit, 1977.

Hutt, W. H. *The Strike-Threat System: The Economic Consequences of Collective Bargaining*. New Rochelle, N.Y.: Arlington House, 1973.

See also: Haberler, Gottfried; Hutt, William H.; New Deal; right-to-work movement; Taft-Hartley Act

United Nations

In the latter days of World War II, President Franklin D. Roosevelt persuaded the principal allies of the United States to agree to the resurrection of Woodrow Wilson's dream of an international organization that would promote world peace, progress, and human rights, but with a more effective structure than that of the failed League of Nations, as well as a more inclusive membership.

Under the United Nations Charter, the structure is three-fold: a General Assembly in which each member nation exercises one vote; a Security Council with fifteen members—five permanent members representing the great powers (United States, United Kingdom, France, Russia, and China), with each possessing veto power and the rest elected from the General Assembly and serving on a rotating basis; and finally, the Secretariat, a permanent bureaucracy headed by a Secretary General. Additionally, subsidiary organizations that deal with special problems also function under the umbrella of the United Nations, such as the International Court of Justice, the International Labor Organization, and the United Nations Educational, Scientific, and Cultural Organization (UNESCO).

From the very beginning of the United Nations project there has been conservative opposition. While the radical Right in America warned of a conspiracy to found a wold government, mainstream American conservatives have concentrated on several undesirable aspects of the United Nations. First, conservatives were inherently skeptical of the utopian vision that seemed to motivate some of the founders and supporters of this international organization, and they also pointed to the role of the League of Nations in propagating false hopes that international law would replace force and the balance of power in maintaining the peace and securing the rights of nations, which

ultimately ended in the tragedy of World War II. Conservatives also warned that commitments to the U.N. Charter might be used to undermine the constitutional order in the United States, even diminishing American sovereignty.

The Korean War heightened conservative opposition to the United Nations despite this organization's commitment of troops against communist aggression by North Korea. Since only the temporary absence of Soviet representatives from the Security Council permitted U.N. intervention in Korea, conservatives pointed out that the possession of the veto by the Soviet Union made it virtually certain that the United Nations would be of no use in the Cold War, the greatest ongoing crisis of the postwar world. In addition, President Harry S. Truman sent U.S. troops to Korea without congressional approval, citing the U.N. Charter as the source of his authority to do so. The Korean War ended in a prolonged and bloody stalemate.

In the decades since the founding of the United Nations, conservatives have come to see this organization as less of a serious threat and more of an expensive and inefficient nuisance. The General Assembly has come to be dominated by large numbers of former colonies of Western nations, which are typically underdeveloped, viscerally anti-Western, and ruled by corrupt and despotic regimes. The Secretariat, meanwhile, seems wasteful of resources, corrupt, and hostile to American interests.

In more recent years, many leading conservative politicians and intellectuals have concentrated not so much on ending U.S. membership in the United Nations as on obtaining a thoroughgoing reform of the structure and procedures of the United Nations. By withholding and then reducing its share of U.N. dues, Congress has forced some financial reforms. The United States' Reagan-era withdrawal from UNESCO effected enough change that Congress voted to re-join in 2003, despite some dissent. Until the presidency of George W. Bush, at least, through aggressive rhetorical responses, deft diplomacy, and by threatening reductions in aid to Third World nations, the United States had achieved some success in reducing the reflexive anti-Americanism so often in evidence at the United Nations.

Many problems borne of the U.N.'s large and unwieldy bureaucracy still trouble contemporary conservatives. The 2004 oil-for-food scandal (the program allegedly enriched Saddam Hussein personally as well as many of the permanent members of the Security Council) was named by many hawks and neoconservatives as the reason for the U.N.'s failure to pass a resolution against Iraq immediately prior to the Iraq war. Other conservatives regard this scandal—and others—as the inevitable outcome of this type of governing body and therefore advocate greater accountability.

To some conservatives, other flaws in the United Nations have also become more evident as it ages. The organization's goals of "[saving] succeeding generations from the scourge of war . . . [reaffirming] faith in the fundamental human rights . . . [establishing] conditions under which justice and respect for obligations can be made," and "[promoting] social progress and better standards of life" have remained only imperfectly met. The diversity of the member nations and their interests has, in many cases, weakened this body to the point of impotence. Furthermore, the presence of Sudan, Cuba, and China on the Human Rights Commission reveals a paralyzing conflict of interest.
—PATRICK M. O'NEIL

Further Reading

Buckley, William F., Jr. *United Nations Journal: A Delegate's Odyssey*. New York: Putnam, 1974.

Moynihan, Daniel P. *A Dangerous Place*. Boston: Little, Brown, 1978.

———. *Pandaemonium: Ethnicity in International Politics*. New York: Oxford University Press, 1993.

Roberts, Adam, and Benedict Kingsbury. *United Nations, Divided World: The UN's Roles in International Relations*. New York: Oxford University Press, 1994.

Meisler, Stanley. *United Nations: The First Fifty Years*. New York: Atlantic Monthly Press, 1997.

O'Neill, John T. *United Nations Peacekeeping in the Post-Cold War Era*. Oxford: Frank Cass Publishers, 2005.

Snow, Al, Sr. *Exceptional Profile of Courage: The United Nations vs. American Liberty*. Agreka Books, 2002.

See also: isolationism; Judd, Walter H.

University Bookman

Founded by Russell Kirk in 1960 as "A Quarterly Review of Educational Materials," the *University Bookman* went on to become a leading academic journal of books and opinion. The oldest continuously published conservative book journal in the United States, its aim has been to "restore and improve the standards of higher education in America," in the words of Kirk's opening editorial. From its inception until 1990, the *Bookman*, capitalizing on Kirk's relationship with William F. Buckley Jr. and his *National Review*, was distributed free of charge to the subscribers of that venerable organ of conservative thought. In addition to its *National Review* readers, the *Bookman* also maintained its own paid subscriber base, and it has continued to thrive and exert some influence on bookish corners principally through the generosity of its loyal readers. Until 2005, when Gerald Russello became editor, the editorship of the journal had remained a family affair, beginning with Russell Kirk, then extending to his wife Annette, and later to their son-in-law Jeffrey O. Nelson.

Now in its fifth decade, the *Bookman* continues to publish a wide range of essays, reviews, and poems from an impressive array of contributors, including, in the last few years, James Schall, Peter Augustine Lawler, Allan Carlson, John Lukacs, and George Nash. Special symposia have considered the legacy of communism; "town and country"; and modernity. Among the perennial themes of the journal have been the defense of traditional Western norms and institutions; concern for the state and quality of education in America; advocacy of localism and limited government and an economics subservient to ethical considerations; and a healthy antipathy to ideology of all stripes.

—CORY ANDREWS

Further Reading

Edwards, Lee. *Educating for Liberty: The First Half-Century of the Intercollegiate Studies Institute.* Washington, D.C.: Regnery, 2003.

See also: Kirk, Russell

Utley, Freda (1898–1978)

A prominent ex-communist, Freda Utley became one of America's leading anticommunist intellectuals in the decades after World War II. She was born in London in the closing years of the nineteenth century. After graduate study at the London School of Economics, Utley joined the British Communist Party in 1928. She met and married a Soviet citizen working in London, and in 1930 they moved to the Soviet Union. This set Utley apart from the many pro-Stalin Western intellectuals who hopelessly romanticized the Soviet Union without any real first-hand knowledge of life under the hammer and sickle. Utley wrote in her book, *Odyssey of a Liberal: Memoirs* (1970), that she possessed "the mentality which pursues beliefs and theories to their logical conclusion," and it did not take long for her to discern that Marx's doctrines were no panacea for mankind's ills. The arrest and disappearance of her husband in a 1936 purge reinforced her disillusion, to say the least, and she returned to London. As a journalist (Utley was a war correspondent in China in 1938 and again in 1945–46) and as author of books such as *The Dream We Lost* (1940) and *Last Chance in China* (1947) Utley became identified as a vociferous critic of Soviet and Chinese communism. In 1950, she became a naturalized citizen of the United States, where she would live until her death in 1978. With William F. Buckley Jr., John Chamberlain, Frank Meyer, James Burnham, Whittaker Chambers, and others, Utley helped shape and inform the nascent conservative political and intellectual movement throughout the 1950s and '60s.

—MAX SCHULZ

Further Reading

Utley, Freda. *Lost Illusion.* Philadelphia: Fireside Press, 1948.

———. *Will the Middle East Go West?* Chicago: Regnery, 1957.

See also: anticommunism; isolationism

V

van den Haag, Ernest (1915–2002)

One of several scholars who emigrated to the United States during the post–World War II era and helped to reinvigorate the conservative spirit among American intellectuals and policymakers, Ernest van den Haag was a forceful voice in the field of public policy. Van den Haag was educated at the Universities of Paris, Florence, and Naples and earned a doctorate from New York University.

The author of several influential books including *The Death Penalty: A Debate* (1983), *Political Violence and Civil Disobedience* (1972), and *Passion and Social Constraint* (1963), van den Haag contributed to dozens of anthologies, academic journals, newspapers, and magazines, including especially *National Review*, where he became a regular contributor in 1957. Van den Haag's most important works concern the death penalty and the moral implications of state-sanctioned executions. An ardent supporter of capital punishment, he was involved with several ongoing debates concerning life issues such as abortion and when life begins, irritating fellow conservatives by arguing that abortion should be allowed during the first trimester and that suicide was not morally problematic. Van den Haag was

Ernest van den Haag

a public agnostic. Nor did he believe in the natural law. However, at the end of his life he requested and received a Catholic funeral.

A fellow of both the Guggenheim Foundation and the National Endowment for the Humanities, van den Haag held various positions at research institutes nationwide. He taught at the Universities of Nevada, Minnesota, and Colorado, as well as at Vassar College and the School of Criminal Justice at SUNY-Albany. For six years he was the John M. Olin Professor of Jurisprudence and Public Policy at Fordham University, and in the 1980s he became a distinguished scholar of the Heritage Foundation.

—Glen Sproviero

Further Reading

Nash, George. *The Conservative Intellectual Movement in America since 1945*. Wilmington, Del.: Intercollegiate Studies Institute, 1996.

van den Haag, Ernest. *Education as an Industry.* New York: A. M. Kelley, 1956.

_____, ed. *Capitalism: Sources of Hostility.* New Rochelle, N.Y.: Epoch Books, 1979.

See also: abortion; capital punishment; émigré intellectuals; National Review

Van Til, Cornelius (1895–1987)

One of modern America's greatest Calvinist theologians, Cornelius Van Til was born at Grootegast, the Netherlands, and came to America in 1905. He received his A.B. at Calvin College (1922), theology degrees at Princeton Theological Seminary (1924, 1925), and a Ph.D. at Princeton University (1927). Ordained in 1927, Van Til was pastor at the Christian Reformed Church in Spring Lake, Michigan, before returning to Princeton Theological Seminary in 1928 to teach. When the seminary acquired a theologically liberal board of directors, he and other conservative Reformed theologians left to create the Westminster Theological Seminary in Philadelphia. Van Til taught apologetics there from 1929 until his retirement in 1972.

Cornelius Van Til

Van Til was the leading American follower of the Calvinist theologian Abraham Kuyper, who criticized the idea of man as autonomous—independent from God, with self-sufficient reason, acknowledging no higher authority, and so, a law unto himself. One cannot, Kuyper argued, maintain simultaneous belief in both man's autonomy and God's sovereignty.

Van Til attacked autonomous man on epistemological grounds. Anti-theists contend that unbelieving man can know reality as a Christian believer knows it, merely differing about God's existence. But if God is creator and sovereign, Van Til argued, then he is the ultimate reality, and no fact exists or is intelligible apart from him. Therefore (and this is Van Til's central point), "nothing whatever can be known unless God can be and is known." Christianity, then, is necessarily true.

Unbelievers possess practical knowledge for daily living, but it is stolen knowledge. Since believers and unbelievers cannot know reality in the same way, natural law philosophy—which assumes that they can and argues from self-evident facts—is untenable.

Van Til's position is known as presuppositionalism, because it presupposes God's existence and the truth of scripture. Any other starting point, he argued, entails "surrendering the sovereignty of God." Moreover, the proof of Christianity's truth is that "unless its truth is presupposed, there is no possibility of 'proving' anything at all."

Some Reformed theologians, such as Gordon H. Clark, criticized Van Til's apologetics, but others, e.g., Rousas J. Rushdoony, embraced them. Sharing Van Til's rejection of natural law, Rushdoony recognized the need for an alternative. Accordingly, he wrote the seminal works of Christian Reconstruction, which deems the Bible the final authority, argues that Old Testament law remains valid and should guide individuals and governments, and endorses capitalism and a minimal state. Rushdoony's son-in-law, libertarian economist and investment advisor Gary North, is a leading Christian Recon-structionist. Van Til privately described himself as "concerned" about Rushdoony's politics and North's views of the applicability of Old Testament law and hoped that Reconstructionists would not "claim that such views are inherent in the principles I hold."

One of the most important of Van Til's many books, *The Defense of the Faith* (1955), presents his apologetics, compares and contrasts them with Roman Catholic, evangelical, and other views, and engages his critics in lucid but very rigorous prose. Rushdoony's *Van Til* (1960) is a good introduction to Van Til's thought.

—JOHN ATTARIAN

Further Reading

Frame, John M. *Cornelius Van Til: An Analysis of His Thought.* Phillipsburg, N.J.: P&R, 1995.

Van Til, Cornelius. *Christian Apologetics.* 2nd ed. Edited by William Edgar. Phillipsburg, N.J.: P&R, 2003.

———. *A Christian Theory of Knowledge.* Philadelphia: P&R, 1969.

White, William, Jr. *Van Til, Defender of the Faith: An Authorized Biography.* Nashville, Tenn.: T. Nelson Publishers, 1979.

See also: Christian Reconstruction; Kuyper, Abraham; Rushdoony, Rousas John

Viereck, Peter (1916–)

The major voice of the post–World War II strain of politically moderate, historically minded thought that was at the time called the "New Conservatism," Peter Viereck outlined the ideas of this movement in his most important work, *Conservatism Revisited*, which was published in 1949. Viereck's new conservatism was criticized by many other conservative intellectuals, however, and his stance on certain key political issues made him a controversial presence in the conservative intellectual community. After 1964, Viereck settled into a long silence on conservative issues and withdrew from intellectual influence in the conservative movement.

Viereck was born in New York City, the son of German propagandist and Nazi agent George Sylvester Viereck. He earned his doctorate at Harvard University and published his dissertation in 1941 as *Metapolitics: The Roots of the Nazi Mind.* In 1949, he won the Pulitzer Prize for poetry. Viereck had a long teaching career at Mount Holyoke College

and published other significant books, including *Shame and Glory of the Intellectuals* (1953) and *The Unadjusted Man* (1956).

Viereck's first book, *Metapolitics*, outlines an important theme in his conservatism that grew out of his research on the Nazi phenomenon. As he studied Germany at the time of the Nazi ascendancy, Viereck explored the nation's intellectual heritage. He identified two divergent cultural influences: the classical and Christian heritages, more common to all of Europe, and the pagan Saxon tribalism with its cult of war, reinforced later by the antirationalism of romanticism. In his book, therefore, Viereck poses the stabilizing and traditionalist influences that he wants to see underscore conservatism against the cults of irrationalism and primitivism that were always for him dangerous and destabilizing undercurrents in Western culture.

When Viereck wrote *Conservatism Revisited* he was able to draw this outline with contemporary references. The recent experiences of communism and fascism, and the upheaval of war, illustrated for Viereck the cultural hemorrhage the West had experienced. Viereck decried mass society, with its deference to low tastes and standards, and he blamed the long influence of romanticism, with its faith in the innate goodness of man, for democracy's mindless worship of the common people and fascism's worship of the *Volk.* He lamented the loss of classical standards in the arts and denounced the fashionable assault on tradition. He called for a recovery of humanism, especially one based on permanent moral values that it was the business of education to instill. (To this extent, Viereck could call himself "a value-conserving classical humanist.") And he looked to religion to provide the needed institutional counterinfluence to materialism and social disorder.

Viereck became controversial among other conservatives when he applied his way of thinking to American politics. Insisting that any nation must be true to the best principles of its history, Viereck accepted the progressive tradition of the United States and gave a qualified approval to the New Deal programs of the 1930s. His favorite American politician was Adlai Stevenson. Viereck also broke with conservatives in his criticism of Senator Joseph McCarthy and his campaign against domestic communism. To Viereck, McCarthy represented the kind of anti-intellectual populism that was, he felt, one of the most dangerous products of democratic culture. In 1964, Viereck refused to endorse the presidential candidacy of Barry Goldwater, breaking defiantly with Goldwater defenders such as Russell Kirk.

Viereck stood in the tradition of classical conservatism as interpreted by Irving Babbitt. His conservatism was humanistic, literary, moral, and, above all, aristocratic in spirit. It supported democracy but only to the extent that democracy could be saved from its vices and excesses by locating the stabilizing forces and preserving influences that linked past and present.

—J. DAVID HOEVELER JR.

Further Reading

Lora, Ronald. *Conservative Minds in America*. Chicago: Rand-McNally, 1971.

Ryn, Claes. "Peter Viereck: Unadjusted Man of Ideas." *Political Science Reviewer* 7 (1977): 326–66.

Viereck, Peter. *Conservatism: From John Adams to Churchill*. Princeton, N.J.: Van Nostrand, 1956.

———. *Tide and Continuities: Last and First Poems, 1995–1938*. Fayetteville, Ark.: University of Arkansas Press, 1995.

See also: Babbitt, Irving

Vietnam War

Few events in American history have been more controversial or more misunderstood than the Vietnam War. After nearly a century of French colonial rule, French Indochina was occupied by Japanese forces during World War II. After the war, the United States initially pressured the French to grant independence to a nationalist regime, but Mao's victory in China, the 1950 invasion of South Korea, and the realization that communist Ho Chi Minh had seized control of the Viet Minh independence movement, led the United States to support the French—all the while continuing to press for concessions to genuine nationalism. Trained in Moscow, for three decades Ho Chi Minh had served as an agent of the Communist International (COMINTERN), but he gained broad support among many Vietnamese nationalists by concealing his Leninist past, advocating independence from France, and even quoting Thomas Jefferson in his 1945 Declaration of Independence. To ensure communist control of the resistance, Ho "invited" the French to return to Vietnam in 1946 and joined forces with them in military operations to crush, as "enemies of the peace," those nationalist opposition groups who had refused to "welcome" the French back. Having consolidated his leadership of the resistance by eliminating much of the noncommunist leadership, Ho then turned his forces on France and rallied much of the population under the banner of national independence. The Viet Minh carefully concealed its Leninist control from the people.

After the French withdrew in 1954, French Indochina was divided into Cambodia, Laos, and North and South Vietnam—with Ho's Viet Minh in control of the Democratic Republic of Vietnam above the 17th parallel and a noncommunist Republic of Vietnam supported by the United States in the south. Both the United States and South Vietnam demanded United Nations supervision of any future reunification elections and refused to join in the Geneva Agreements in July 1954 when communist delegations insisted on inadequate supervision. In May 1959 the Vietnam Workers' (i.e., Communist) Party in Hanoi decided to "liberate" South Vietnam and then opened the Ho Chi Minh Trail through Laos and Cambodia and began sending troops and supplies to South Vietnam. To deceive the West, the party set up a bogus "National Liberation Front" in South Vietnam the following year.

President Kennedy responded in 1961 by sending American military advisers to help the South. Following at least one August 1964 North Vietnamese attack on a U.S. warship in international waters in the Gulf of Tonkin, Congress overwhelmingly (unanimously in the House and by a vote of 88-2 in the Senate) authorized President Lyndon B. Johnson to use armed force to defend South Vietnam. During the Senate debate, Foreign Relations Chairman J. William Fulbright (D-Ark.) was asked whether the resolution would authorize the president to go to "war" in Vietnam; he replied, "That is the way I would interpret it." Congress tripled the president's request for funds for the conflict, and Johnson's public approval rating shot from 42 to 72 percent in one month. Both congressional votes and public opinion polls for years thereafter belie the common myth that neither Congress nor the public supported the U.S.'s initial commitment to the war.

As good Leninists, North Vietnam relied heavily on a political warfare campaign, using "peace movements" around the world to pressure the American Congress to legislate an end to the war. A clever campaign of half-truths and lies—asserting that Washington had opposed "nationalism" in Vietnam, blocked "free" elections, and supported a corrupt "dictator" in the South against Vietnam's "George Washington," Ho Chi Minh—quickly swelled the ranks of protesters from Berkeley and Washington to Stockholm. In the meantime, Defense Secretary Robert McNamara ignored the recommendations of the Joint Chiefs of Staff and the CIA to fight the war effectively, electing instead to pursue an indecisive policy of "gradualism" that many experts believe actually encouraged communist aggression.

At the end of January 1968, communist forces in South Vietnam launched the Tet Offensive—attacking cities and towns across the country during a holiday truce. The attacks contributed further to American misunderstanding of the conflict. Misreported by the press as a sign of communist military superiority and evidence of government and military "lies" about the progress of the war, in reality the Tet Offensive decimated the indigenous "Viet Cong" and across the country produced devastating defeats for communist forces. During the month-long struggle, U.S. and South Vietnamese forces lost about 6,000 soldiers, while communist fatalities totaled roughly ten times that sum. Throughout South Vietnam, the so-called "Viet Cong Infrastructure" of intelligence agents and secret leaders surfaced only to face the option of being killed or arrested as South Vietnamese military forces quickly seized control, or else abandoned their homes and fled into the jungle.

Weeks into the Tet Offensive, antiwar candidate Eugene McCarthy's strong challenge to President Johnson in the New Hampshire Democratic primary furthered the impression that the American people had turned against the war and supported withdrawal. In reality, antiwar votes for McCarthy were outnumbered by angry protest votes from people who wanted a more decisive response to North Vietnam—so-called superhawks. Long after LBJ announced that he would not seek reelection, exit poll information showed that a plurality of McCarthy voters in the New Hampshire primary had switched their support by the November election to third-party conservatives George Wallace and retired Strategic Air Command leader General Curtis ("Bomb Hanoi back to the Stone Age") LeMay. But the conventional wisdom was that McCarthy's success in New Hampshire was proof that the American people wanted the United States to abandon South Vietnam.

President Nixon pursued a policy of "Vietnamization"—withdrawing U.S. forces more quickly than LBJ had sent them to war while at the same time increasing support and training for South Vietnamese forces and removing many of the constraints on U.S. airpower. In 1970, after years of permitting North Vietnamese and Viet Cong guerrilla forces to operate out of neighboring Cambodian territory without risk of attack, South Vietnamese and American forces attacked these sanctuaries and further damaged communist forces, capturing vast quantities of arms and equipment. Like the Tet Offensive, however, the militarily successful and lawful Cambodian intervention turned still more Americans against the conflict. Violent student protests against the war led to the tragic shooting on May 4, 1970, of thirteen people (four of whom were killed) at Kent State University by Ohio National Guard troops. While some of the guardsmen were students themselves and others had no doubt joined to avoid the risk of service in Vietnam, the shootings were portrayed as a symbol of Nixon administration repression.

When the communists walked away from the Paris Peace Talks on the eve of the 1972 U.S. elections, President Nixon responded by approving the implementation of war plans the military had been advocating for years, including mining North Vietnamese harbors and bombing military targets in the key cities of Hanoi and Haiphong. In the meantime, North Vietnamese forces fighting in South Vietnam were facing repeated setbacks. By the end of 1972, many experts believed that the war had been essentially won and a demoralized Hanoi—

having exhausted its supply of surface-to-air missiles and totally vulnerable to continued American air attacks—returned to the Paris Talks and signed a peace agreement.

Unfortunately, the antiwar protest movement had taken its toll in Washington. In May, Congress enacted new legislation making it unlawful for the president to spend appropriated funds on combat operations in Indochina, in the words of former Director of Central Intelligence William Colby virtually "snatching defeat from the jaws of victory." Freed from the fear of American military action and facing a South Vietnamese army largely crippled by massive congressional cuts in U.S. assistance, in 1975 Hanoi sent almost its entire army outside its borders and conquered Laos, Cambodia, and South Vietnam by conventional invasions. In the three years that followed, communist bloodbaths in Indochina claimed more lives than had been lost on all sides during the previous fourteen years of war, and other Stalinist measures ranked the new "Socialist Republic of Vietnam" among the world's dozen worst human rights abusers. Millions of innocent people lost their lives, and tens of millions lost any chance at freedom. For decades thereafter, cries of "no more Vietnams" undermined U.S. efforts to promote peace from Angola and Central America to Central Europe and the Middle East.

—ROBERT F. TURNER

Further Reading

Lind, Michael. *Vietnam: The Necessary War: A Reinterpretation of America's Most Disastrous Military Conflict.* New York: Free Press, 2002.

Sorley, Lewis. *A Better War: The Unexamined Victories and Final Tragedy of America's Last Years in Vietnam.* New York: Harcourt Brace, 1999.

See also: anticommunism; Cold War; Cold War revisionism; containment; McCarthy, Eugene

Viguerie, Richard (1933–)

Of all the conservative activists who have toiled in the fields of politics over the last few decades, perhaps none has had as profound an impact as Richard Viguerie. A firebrand conservative who came to Washington from his native Texas in the 1960s, Viguerie helped establish the modern age of political fundraising through pioneering direct mail campaigns. He was among the first to grasp the possibilities of applying emerging computerized technologies to politics, and it is not much of an exaggeration to say that Viguerie "invented" the direct mail style of political campaigning so widely practiced today. Through an intensive cultivation of personal information, buoyed by the buying and selling of mailing lists and databases, Viguerie proved remarkably successful at raising both money and awareness of issues and candidates. These tactics energized conservative politics in the late 1960s and '70s by enabling candidates to make an end run around a mass media not favorably disposed to their points of view.

As a reward, Viguerie has been targeted as one of the Left's chief bogeymen, on the order of Jesse Helms and Pat Robertson. Throughout a lengthy career Viguerie has been associated with many conservative organizations, including Young Americans for Freedom, the Moral Majority, and the American Conservative Union. He backed Phil Crane against Ronald Reagan in the 1980 Republican primary and even ran unsuccessfully for lieutenant governor in Virginia in 1985. One of his latest ventures focuses on the Internet, where Viguerie recently started a right-wing clearinghouse called ConservativeHQ.com with the idea of applying many of the same direct marketing strategies to cyberspace that he brought to the mail nearly four decades ago.

—MAX SCHULZ

Further Reading
Viguerie, Richard A., and David Franke. *America's Right Turn: How Conservatives Used New and Alternative Media to Take Power.* Chicago: Bonus Books, 2004.

Villard, Henry (1835–1900)

Born in Speyer, Bavaria, Henry Villard changed his name from Ferdinand Hilgard when he came to New York in 1853. He wrote for the *Staats Zeitung*, covering the Lincoln-Douglas debates in 1858. Reporting the Civil War battles made him a pacifist. In 1866 Villard married Fanny Garrison, only daughter of William Lloyd Garrison. After the Panic of 1873 he represented German holders of American railroad bonds, eventually becoming the president of the Northern Pacific Railroad. In 1881 he purchased the *New York Evening Post* and the weekly *Nation* (founded in 1865 by Edwin L. Godkin). Godkin's deputy editor continued to be Wendell Philips Garrison, brother-in-law of Villard.

Villard was a disciple of Manchester liberalism and admired Richard Cobden, John Bright, J. S. Mill, Spencer, and William Graham Sumner. Villard held with William Lloyd Garrison: to be anti-tariff was the same as to be antislavery; slavery violated property rights, as each person had a right to the product of his own labor. He was an organizer of the American Free Trade League (1869). In opposition to "state socialism," such as the Interstate Commerce Act, Villard wished to limit the government's role in the economy to the collection and publication of statistics.

Villard's liberalism made him a supporter of Moral Money—the Gold Standard. In 1884 Villard and the liberals who supported Grover Cleveland were called Mugwumps (an Algonquin word for chieftain). Henry Villard died November 12, 1900, at his estate in Dobbs Ferry, New York.

—LEONARD LIGGIO

891

Further Reading

Villard, Henry. *Memoirs of Henry Villard: Journalist and Financier*. New York: Da Capo Press, 1969.

See also: Nation; *Villard, Oswald Garrison*

Villard, Oswald Garrison (1872–1949)

Born in Wiesbaden, Germany, the "aristocrat of liberalism" Oswald Garrison Villard, son of Henry Villard, taught history at Harvard in the mid-1890s. He joined the *New York Post* in 1897. A founder of the Anti-Imperialism League and the National Association for the Advancement of Colored People, he was also active in the American Free Trade League as a disciple of Frederic Bastiat.

Villard became editor of the *Nation* during the First World War. He opposed Woodrow Wilson's globalism and in September 1918 the *Nation* was banned from the mails by the U.S. Post Office censor for "pacifism and highbrowism." The offending editorial had been written by Albert Jay Nock. The *Nation* opposed ratification of the Versailles Treaty and supported independence for Ireland and India.

Villard sold the *Nation* in 1935 but continued as a columnist. He had been fully awakened to Stalinism by the Purge Trials of 1934–35. The *Nation*'s editorials criticized Villard's columns, especially his opposition to Roosevelt's 1937 plan to pack the U.S. Supreme Court. Villard's final column appeared June 29, 1940, after opposing the *Nation*'s support for conscription. Villard's articles then appeared in *Christian Century*, *Harper's*, and *Human Events*. In August 1940 he joined William H. Regnery, John T. Flynn, Potter Stewart, Gerald Ford, R. Sargent Shriver, and John F. Kennedy in founding the America First Committee. Villard died in New York City, October 1, 1949.

—LEONARD LIGGIO

Further Reading

Humes, D. Joy. *Oswald Garrison Villard: Liberal of the 1920's*. Syracuse, N.Y.: Syracuse University Press, 1960.

Kauffman, Bill. *America First! Its History, Culture, and Politics*. Amherst, N.Y.: Prometheus Books, 1995.

Villard, Oswald Garrison. *Fighting Years: Memoirs of a Liberal Editor*. New York: Harcourt Brace, 1939.

Wreszin, Michael. *Oswald Garrison Villard, Pacifist at War*. Bloomington, Ind.: Indiana University Press, 1965.

See also: America First Committee; Human Events; Nation; *Nock, Albert Jay; Villard, Henry*

Vivas, Eliseo (1901–93)

Eliseo Vivas was born of Venezuelan parents in Pamolona, Colombia. He came to the United States in 1915, entered the Brooklyn Polytechnic Institute and, after taking a class from Joseph Wood Krutch, switched majors from engineering to philosophy. He received his B.A. and Ph.D. from the University of Wisconsin, where he first began teaching philosophy in 1935. He later taught at the University of Chicago and at Ohio State University prior to accepting the John Evans Chair of Moral and Intellectual Philosophy at Northwestern University in 1951, where he remained until his retirement in 1969. Over the years, Vivas presented his philosophical position in eight books and in more than 240 book reviews, critiques, and articles in professional journals and magazines. Three of his books have been translated into foreign languages.

Vivas was a breaker of molds. He was a philosopher who took poets seriously, and a metaphysician who abandoned naturalism at the height of its popularity, thereby incurring the wrath of former colleagues who took his desertion personally. Vivas vigorously defended the objectivity of values in an age that he said betrayed an "instinct for the hatred of values." He called his position "axiological realism."

Vivas's conservatism, which always centered on this defense of axiological realism, was coupled with his tragic conviction that the cosmos is "flawed" and that evil is an inescapable fact of human existence. He was one of very few American philosophers to address himself to the crisis of our age, our "hatred of values" together with the loss of our sense of mystery, our reduction of spirit to matter, our idolatry of technology, and our blind adoration of the idol "Progress."

Vivas's attack on liberal socialism echoed the cries of Nietzsche and Dostoyevsky and drew inspiration from Freud's analysis of the human psyche. It assumed its most vivid expression in his book *Contra Marcuse*, published in 1971. In that book, Vivas attacked Marcuse's "dystopian view" of our world, which regarded human suffering as eradicable through social engineering. As Vivas saw it, evil is one of the ineluctable conditions of human existence; consequently, he called for the affirmation of life as we find it. He argued against Marcuse's rejection of this world, his hopeless delusions that promise a less-than-human life without pain. We are confronted here with a fundamental difference in the *Weltanschauung* that separates liberals and conservatives: conservatives view evil as part of the fabric of human existence, while liberals hold that evil can, at least theoretically, be eliminated through human effort.

In a profound observation made almost in passing, Vivas noted that "Marcuse's total rejection of almost everything that is . . .

Eliseo Vivas

is a condition of adolescence which the negative thinker never outgrows." Such a position, as Vivas saw it, is little more than an expression of immature outrage. Marcuse overlooked the joy and beauty of human existence that make life valuable.

Vivas's major asset as a philosopher was that he never lost sight of the problem at hand. The subject matter of his inquiry was always kept sharply in focus. Unlike so many of his fellow theorists, he resisted the temptation to languish on the soft bed of argument-for-its-own-sake: he did not get lost in what John Dewey called the "dialectic of concepts." As a critic, Vivas approached a work of literature with profound reverence: no one was more alive to the subtleties of the poet's imagination, not even the poet himself.

The importance of Vivas as a philosopher cannot be estimated by his influence within restricted philosophical circles. He never tried to be "fashionable." Vivas's importance must be measured by the scope of his mind, a powerful prose style that "stings and celebrates," and the relevance of his theories to the immense complexities of human experience. In these terms, he was a philosopher of considerable importance.

—HUGH MERCER CURTLER

Further Reading

Curtler, Hugh Mercer. *A Theory of Art, Tragedy and Literature: The Philosophy of Eliseo Vivas*. New York: Haven Publishing, 1981.

Regnery, Henry, ed. *Viva Vivas!* Indianapolis, Ind.: Liberty Press, 1976.

Vivas, Eliseo. *The Artistic Transaction and Essays on the Theory of Literature*. Columbus, Ohio: Ohio State University Press, 1963.

———. *The Moral Life and the Ethical Life*. Chicago: University of Chicago Press, 1950.

Voegelin, Eric (1901–85)

A seminal political theorist, Eric Voegelin wrote on a variety of topics, including the history of political ideas, the philosophy of order and history, and the philosophy of consciousness. Voegelin's five-volume *Order and History* (1956) and his *New Science of Politics* (1952) are among his best-known works.

Voegelin was born in Cologne, Germany, and moved to Vienna, Austria, at the age of nine. Receiving his Ph.D. from the University of Vienna in 1922, he was investigated by the Nazis after the *Anschluss* and escaped to the United States in 1938 via Switzerland. He became an American citizen in 1944 and held academic appointments at Harvard, Bennington College, and the University of Alabama before accepting a position at Louisiana State University, where he remained for sixteen years. In 1958 he was named the director of the Institute for Political Science at the University of Munich, but he returned to the United States in 1969 as a Henry Salvatori Distinguished Scholar at the Hoover Institute.

Voegelin's connection to conservatism is ambivalent. He insisted on rejecting all ideologies and "ismic" constructions, including conservatism. He classified conservatism as a "secondary ideology," by which he meant that it was created in reaction to radical ideologies like National Socialism, Marxism, even liberal progressivism. Radical ideologies destroy traditions, customs, and laws that conservatives believe are vital to the good society. To counteract the destructive effects of radical and revolutionary movements, conservatives try to preserve the wisdom of the past by defending tradition as if it were the same as truth itself. In doing so, Voegelin argued, truth becomes reified and separated from its engendering experience.

Voegelin considered the moral skeptic David Hume to be a representative of conservatism, but he had very little to say about Edmund Burke. Hume he criticized for being philosophically shallow because he relied on tradition and common sense. To gain philosophical insight, argued Voegelin, it is necessary to go beyond mere tradition and penetrate to the core experiences of order by recalling them to consciousness. Following Plato, Voegelin called this process of recollection *anamnesis*. He also disparaged the contribution of Cicero to political theory in his posthumously published *History of Political Ideas* (1997). Cicero, an important figure to conservatives, was criticized by Voegelin for thinking too highly of Roman institutions— for addressing the complex philosophical problems associated with political order by professing the majesty of Rome. Cicero's political theory is too concrete. Plato, in Voegelin's estimation, was a far superior thinker because he understood that true philosophers are more satisfied by questions than institutional answers. Political institutions always fall short of representing the true, the good, and the beautiful. They are not the source of philosophical wisdom. And philosophers ought never to be satisfied with particular representations of the good. The philosophical quest ends only in death.

Many aspects of Voegelin's political theory are consistent with conservatism, however. He influenced greatly such conservative thinkers as Russell Kirk, Gerhart Niemeyer, and Ellis Sandoz. (Voegelin's influence on Kirk is especially evident in Kirk's *Enemies of the Permanent Things* (1969).) Conservatives have found Voegelin's work appealing for several reasons. First, he was a severe critic of left-wing ideologies and political movements. He was especially critical of progressivism, positivism, Marxism, and liberalism. Voegelin also contributed to the recrudescence of scholarship in the classical and Judeo-Christian philosophical traditions, drawing on the political theory of thinkers like Plato, Aristotle, Augustine, and Thomas Aquinas. Finally, Voegelin made insightful theoretical connections between liberalism and totalitarianism.

Nevertheless, Voegelin has been criticized by some Christian conservatives for his treatment of Christianity. They claim that Voegelin did not appreciate fully the contribution of Christianity to history and Western civilization. They point to the fact that in the fourth volume of *Order and History* (*The Ecumenic Age*), Voegelin connected St. Paul and other Christian figures to modern gnosticism and modern political movements. These Christian critics charge that Voegelin seems to have underestimated the positive contributions of Christianity. Other conservatives have criticized Voegelin's conception of transcendence for being too abstract and distant from politics. Like Plato, Voegelin tended to recoil from concrete representations of the good in political life.

Voegelin was a fierce and consistent opponent of totalitarianism in all its forms. In 1933, he published two books on the race problem (*Race and State* [English translation, 1997] and *The History of the Race Idea* (English translation, 1998]) and his opposition to communism is evident in many of his books and essays. Voegelin's review of Hannah Arendt's *The Origins of Totalitarianism* (1951) reveals his disdain for totalitarianism as well as his impatience with critics of the Left and Right who failed to identify the spiritual causes of totalitarianism and the philosophical roots it shared with liberalism. His lectures on Hitler at the University of Munich in 1964, published in English as *Hitler and*

Eric Voegelin

the Germans (1999), are representative of this aspect of his work.

The core of Voegelin's political theory is the insight that ideas and language symbols are secondary to historical experience. Human understanding of reality develops from experience with transcendence. Transcendent experience is articulated by spiritually sensitive individuals (e.g., Homer, Plato, Augustine) who create language symbols to convey the meaning of reality. These symbols make it possible for others to imaginatively relive the experiences of order and in turn order their souls. In this way historical experience becomes a living force that is capable of resisting disorder. The common ordering element in all historical experience with transcendence is the *parousia* or the "indelible presence of the divine." In different civilizations at different times in history, a common reality is discovered that is recognizable to those who are capable of achieving a similar level of transcendent consciousness. Restoring these experiences and keeping them vibrant was Voegelin's life project.

The crisis of Western civilization was caused by the loss of consciousness of these experiences. Consequently, the restoration of Western political and social order depended on the reawaking of Western consciousness to the truth of existence embodied in the formative historical experiences of Western civilization. Voegelin insisted that dogma and doctrine obscure the truth of reality by reifying it. Dogmatizing truth obscures reality by separating experience and symbols. Voegelin believed that the modern crisis was due in large part to the fact that the symbols of transcendence had become obscure because of ideological doctrinization.

Voegelin determined that human understanding of truth varied in terms of its "compactness" or "differentiation." Advances or differentiations, however, do not guarantee parallel progress in political and social order. In fact, Voegelin believed that differentiation can have a socially and politically destabilizing affect.

—MICHAEL P. FEDERICI

Further Reading

Cooper, Barry. *Eric Voegelin and the Foundations of Modern Political Science*. Columbia, Mo.: University of Missouri Press, 1999.

Federici, Michael P. *Eric Voegelin: The Restoration of Order*. Wilmington, Del.: ISI Books, 2002.

McAllister, Ted V. *Revolt against Modernity: Leo Strauss, Eric Voegelin, and the Search for a Postliberal Order*. Lawrence, Kan.: University Press of Kansas, 1996.

Voegelin, Eric. *Autobiographical Reflections*. Edited by Ellis Sandoz. Baton Rouge, La.: Louisiana State University Press, 1989.

———. *Science, Politics and Gnosticism*. 3rd ed. Wilmington, Del.: Intercollegiate Studies Institute, 2004.

See also: community; custom; émigré intellectuals; Gnosticism; historicism; Marxism; New Science of Politics, The

Wade, John Donald (1892–1963)

Planter, writer, editor, biographer, teacher, civic leader, and social and literary critic, John Donald Wade exemplified the rural way of life he promoted along with his fellow Southern Agrarians in the 1930s. Throughout his life Wade used history, especially Southern history and experience, to highlight conservative traditions and themes in literature and their role in a rapidly changing world. His major publications include biographies of Augustus Baldwin Longstreet and John Wesley (as well as an unfinished autobiography); contributions to the two Agrarian symposia of the 1930s: *I'll Take My Stand* (1930) and *Who Owns America?* (1936); and numerous articles and essays in major journals, including the *Georgia Review*, which he founded in 1947, and to which he contributed until his death in 1963. Wade's home in Marshallville, Georgia, was the center of his life and in an unstable world served as a retreat for friends and colleagues, including the Donald Davidson family.

Born in Marshallville in 1892, Wade was a descendant of Georgia's first governor. He received degrees from the University of Georgia (A.B., 1910), Harvard (M.A., 1915), and Columbia (Ph.D., 1924) and served as an army second lieutenant in World War I. After teaching at the University of Georgia for seven years, Wade went to Britain on a Guggenheim Fellowship to research his biography of John Wesley. He returned to teach at Vanderbilt University and contributed to the literary and scholarly environment that produced the renowned Fugitive and Agrarian groups, whose members included John Crowe Ransom, Allen Tate, Robert Penn Warren, and Wade's lifelong friend, Donald Davidson. Wade returned to the University of Georgia in 1934 and was a respected, popular, and influential faculty member until his retirement in 1950. He spent his last thirteen years in his beloved Marshallville, where he led efforts to ensure that the small rural town remained vital through beautification projects and a privately funded historical foundation. Wade's firm belief in the traditional Southern loyalty to community and individual responsibility is evident in both his life and his writings.

Wade's first book, *Augustus Baldwin Longstreet: A Study of the Development of Culture in the South* (1924), was a landmark study that set a new standard for literary biography. It also helped fuel and call attention to the Southern renaissance in literature by strengthening the historical foundation for Southern culture and philosophy. Wade invested his narrative with drama, wit, and a deft treatment of the diverse professional, intellectual, and political pursuits of the author-judge-statesman-educator Longstreet. In this biography, as in his future works, Wade looked to the past for guidance and support in contemporary matters of principle and aesthetics. His other biographical studies include insightful essays on Henry Grady, Joel Chandler Harris, Thomas Watson, and more than a hundred entries in the *Dictionary of American Biography*, which he briefly edited in the late 1920s.

Perhaps Wade's greatest contribution to conservatism during the Depression era was his participation in both Agrarian symposia. The first and most influential of these, *I'll Take My Stand*, included Wade's narrative, "The Life and Death of Cousin Lucius," which was based on the life of his own Uncle Walter, a teacher and community leader in rural Georgia. This story is the best brief illustration of Wade's style and his view of the good life: the intellectual Lucius exemplifies the best conservative qualities by choosing to teach in his community over more financially rewarding offers elsewhere. He also helps to temper the cries for radical change by the proponents of a New South, and to shape a future based on the soundest values of the past. Wade's understated yet touching narrative is often ironic, at times satiric, and is ultimately provocative as he dares the reader to doubt Lucius's very real contributions to society.

In 1947 Wade helped edit *Masterworks of American Literature*, a standard college text for many years. That same year in Athens he founded the *Georgia Review*, which was highly acclaimed as a forum for literary, historical, social, and academic topics. While the emphasis was placed on works with regional and Agrarian themes, conservative writers like Russell Kirk were also frequently featured.

—JOEL STANCLIFF

Further Reading

Davidson, Donald. "The Gardens of John Donald Wade." Introduction to *Selected Essays and Other Writings of John Donald Wade*. Athens, Ga.: University of Georgia Press, 1966.

Wade, John Donald. *Selected Essays and Other Writings of John Donald Wade*. Athens, Ga.: University of Georgia Press, 1966.

See also: I'll Take My Stand; Southern Agrarians

Wall Street Journal

The largest financial newspaper in the world and the second largest daily in the United States, the *Wall Street Journal* has been a major conservative media voice throughout the twentieth century. Its prominence has expanded greatly in the last several decades. At one time, there were several other conservative influences in the major American press, such as the *Chicago Tribune* and the now defunct *New York Herald Tribune*, and arguably even the *New York Times* in the 1930s and 1940s when Henry Hazlitt was an editorial writer. By the 1960s, however, the *Chicago Tribune* had abandoned its aggressive conservatism, the *Herald Tribune* had suspended publication, and the *Times* had adopted liberal editorial positions on virtually every issue.

The *WSJ*'s reputation as a leading conservative paper was strengthened during the editorship of Vermont Royster (1914–96), who ran the editorial side of the paper from 1958 to 1971. A Pulitzer Prize–winning journalist, Royster continued to write a regular column until 1986. The newspaper's conservative editorial thrust became even sharper when Robert Bartley replaced Royster and began a thirty-year reign in 1972, first as editor of the editorial page and then as editor. A son of a midwestern veterinarian, Bartley joined the *WSJ* in 1962. As editor, he championed supply-side economics, promoting tax reductions such as the Kemp-Roth tax bill (which included large reductions in marginal tax rates), and the Steiger (capital gains) amendment. Under Bartley, supply-siders like Jude Wanniski, Alan Reynolds, Paul Craig Roberts, Bruce Bartlett, and others used the *WSJ*'s editorial page to provide the intellectual firepower for the cornerstone of the Reagan revolution, the 1981 tax cut.

In the 1990s, the *WSJ* became less of a lonely voice on the right, as new conservative newspapers (e.g., the *Washington Times*), network television (e.g., Fox News), and a host of Web sites and talk radio commentators became prominent. While continuing to argue for smaller government, the *WSJ* took up new crusades, exposing the corruption surrounding President Bill Clinton, as well as prosecutorial excesses in criminal proceedings. To the consternation of paleoconservatives, the pro-business WSJ has remained committed to free trade and open borders.

As columnist Brent Bozell has pointed out, "If the *Journal* editorial page was important during the Reagan era, it was indispensable during the Clinton years." Day after day for years, the *Wall Street Journal* was filled with stories on the financial scandals, cover-ups, sexual escapades, and other transgressions that marred the Clinton presidency. Ultimately, the output filled five volumes.

In August 2001, the *WSJ* announced that Paul Gigot would replace Bartley as editor. A *Journal* columnist for thirteen years and a regular on Jim Lehrer's PBS *News Hour*, Gigot is known for his incisive political analysis, wit, and unquestioned conservatism. Gigot took over in 2001.

The *Journal's* editorial page staff operates separately from the news gathering operation, which has no conservative or libertarian orientation to speak of. Yet the news staff is known for its objective, fair-minded, and generally balanced reporting. Moreover, the newspaper's editorial pages frequently contain opinion pieces written by non-conservatives, including regular liberal columnist Al Hunt. Owned by parent company Dow Jones, the *Wall Street Journal* has a circulation of about 1.8 million and successful editions are published in both Asia and Europe. The parent company, closely controlled by members of the Bancroft family, also produces the conservative *Barron's*, a weekly investors' magazine.

—Richard Vedder

Further Reading

Bartley, Robert L. *The Seven Fat Years, and How To Do It Again: With a 1995 Introduction: Resuming the Revolution.* 2nd ed. New York: Free Press, 1995.

Royster, Vermont. *My Own, My Country's Time: A Journalist's Journey.* Chapel Hill, N.C.: Algonquin Books, 1983.

See also: Bartley, Robert L.; media, conservative; Royster, Vermont C.; supply-side economics

Wallace, George C. (1919–98)

Forever engraved in historical memory as the Alabama governor who physically blocked the entry of black students to the University of Alabama in Birmingham, George Corley Wallace was always more complicated than his critics allowed. Born in rural Alabama in 1919, he descended from tenant farmers and himself tilled soil while in his early twenties. Wallace studied law and became licensed to practice in 1942; first, however, he joined the Army Air Force, in which he served, in Europe, until 1945. He got himself elected state district judge in Alabama in 1952 and attracted attention in 1956 when he refused to comply with a federal court order to produce voting records. Wallace's pugilistic advocacy of segregation (he boxed bantam-weight in high school) made him notorious as governor, an office that he held intermittently from 1962 through 1987. (The interregna were taken up by his wife Lurleen—his political surrogate—when state law barred him from serving a consecutive term.)

Analysts believe that Wallace's participation in the 1968 presidential election, as the candidate of his own American Independent Party, threw the election to Richard Nixon by attracting Democrat voters in the South away from the liberal favorite Hubert Humphrey. When Wallace essayed a second presidential run in 1972, he fell victim, while campaigning in Maryland, to a would-be assassin's bullet. The trauma shackled him to a wheelchair, in chronic pain, for the rest of his life. He nevertheless resumed the governorship, serving his last term after the death of his wife, which had been the second great blow to his body and soul.

In later years, Wallace experienced a genuine conversion, bringing Alabama blacks into his administration and publicly repudiating his earlier pro-segregation position; only large-scale black support could have sent him back to the statehouse. Prominent figures from the civil rights movement guaranteed his sincerity. While Wallace's early advocacy of racial discrimination now seems like the last hurrah of a morally retrograde attitude, his warnings about the self-aggrandizing tendency of the federal government have proven uncanny in their foresight. He was a Ninth and Tenth Amendment man before his time. In other respects (his welfare programs for rural Alabama), he behaved as something other than a conservative. He bears no little resemblance to another southern governor, Huey Long. When Wallace died in 1998, President Clinton eulogized him in a speech.

—THOMAS BERTONNEAU

Further Reading

Lesher, Stephan. *George Wallace: American Populist.* Reading, Mass.: Addison-Wesley, 1994.

Rohler, Lloyd. *George Wallace: Conservative Populist.* Westport, Conn.: Praeger Publishers, 2004.

See also: Democratic Party; LeMay, General Curtis E.; Thurmond, Strom; Vietnam War

Washington, George (1732–99)

Commander in chief of the Continental Army and first president of the United States, George Washington was born Febru-
ary 22, 1732, in Westmoreland County in the English colony of Virginia, son of Augustine Washington, an ambitious planter. Though Washington was deprived at age 11, by his father's death, of the chance of English schooling (which had been given his elder half brothers), the young man's early life was spent ascending the established ladders of success. He worked as a surveyor for rich in-laws, served as an officer in the colonial militia, and fought with distinction in the French and Indian War (his exploits were noted in London newspapers and by King George II). In his twenties, he married Martha Custis, a rich widow, won a seat in the colonial legislature, and inherited the main family estate of Mt. Vernon, named for a British admiral. Only a commission in the regular British army had been denied him.

Britain's efforts to tighten control over its North American colonies, however, pulled him steadily in the direction of disaffection. "Parliament," he wrote a loyalist stepbrother in 1774, "hath no more right to put their hands into my pocket, without my consent, than I have to put my hands into yours for money." That year, Virginia sent him as a delegate to the first Continental Congress; he attended the second Continental Congress in 1775 in his old uniform, showing his willingness to fight, and was picked to command the colonial forces besieging Boston.

From 1775 to 1783, Washington oversaw a war that stretched from Savannah, Georgia, to Quebec. He had to deal with untrained troops, unpaid officers, and inadequate supplies; he lost more battles than he won. But he mastered the principles of warfare in North America (military historian John Keegan ranks him as a strategist with Ulysses S. Grant). Equally important, he kept his often unhappy army obedient to civilian control.

In 1783, victorious, he surrendered his commission to Congress and retired to Mount Vernon.

In 1787 he returned to public life to attend the Constitutional Convention in Philadelphia; his fellow delegates unanimously chose him to preside. The war-time structure of government could not deal with the wartime debts the new country had accumulated, and anxious reformers like Alexander Hamilton and James Madison called for change. But it was Washington's presence at the Convention that reconciled skeptics to its work. He had held more power than any other man in the country, and he had given it up; if he approved the new Constitution, they reasoned, then it could not be a power grab.

The office of the presidency had been created with Washington in mind, and he was unanimously elected to be its first occupant in 1789. But as he took "the chair of government," he wrote that he felt like "a culprit . . . going to the place of his execution." He was mindful of the risks of failure, and though his first cabinet was brilliant—including Hamilton (treasury secretary), Thomas Jefferson (secretary of state), and Henry Knox (secretary of war)—and his first term prosperous and peaceful, by the time of his 1793 reelection (which was also unanimous), the country was drifting toward conflict. The western frontier was filled with angry, often violent, tax protesters who resented the whiskey excise; the French Revolution had plunged Europe into ideological upheaval and an Anglo-French world war. In 1794 Washington sent an army over the Alleghenies to suppress the Whiskey Rebellion: if "a minority . . . is to dictate to the majority," he wrote, "there is an end put at one stroke to republican government." In 1795, he signed a treaty settling outstanding

George Washington

differences with Great Britain, over the protests of Francophiles such as Jefferson, now in opposition.

Washington's final political act was to decline to seek a third term, which he would certainly have won. His Farewell Address (1796), stressing national unity and an independent foreign policy, was his political testament. He died, of a sore throat, at Mount Vernon on December 14, 1799.

The American Revolution, first of the modern revolutions, was one of the few that did not end in anarchy or despotism. Washington, who was at the center of events for twenty-four years, was the man most responsible for its success. His colleague and critic Thomas Jefferson admitted as much. Washington had "the singular destiny and merit," Jefferson wrote in 1814, "of scrupulously obeying the laws through the whole of his career, civil and military, of which the history of the world furnishes no other example."

—RICHARD BROOKHISER

Further Reading

Brookhiser, Richard. *Founding Father: Rediscovering George Washington.* New York: Free Press, 1996.

Ellis, Joseph J. *His Excellence: George Washington.* New York: Alfred A. Knopf, 2004.

Washington, George. *Writings.* Selected by John Rhodehamel. New York: Library of America, 1997.

See also: Adams, John; American Revolution; Bradford, M. E.; education, public; Enlightenment; Federalist Party; Hamilton, Alexander; Marshall, John; McDonald, Forrest; Rutledge, John

Washington Legal Foundation

The Washington Legal Foundation (WLF) is one of the nation's most influential non-profit public interest law centers. Founded in 1977 by former White House legal aide Dan Popeo, who continues to serve as the organization's chairman and general counsel, WLF is the prototype of conservative public interest law groups, the right-wing answer to the array of left-wing public interest groups that dominate Washington, D.C. With a small but dedicated staff, WLF refuses to seek or accept government funding; it also has a policy not to accept court-awarded taxpayer-funded fees (quite unlike the American Civil Liberties Union). The pro bono support it receives from prestigious law firms helps to keep costs down.

Its strong commitment to a market economy has made WLF the nation's premier legal advocate of economic liberty and limited government. But it is also friend to the underrepresented—namely, ordinary working Americans, men and women whose interests are frequently overlooked, if not trampled upon, by public interest groups on the left. To be specific, WLF is one of the few forces at work today defending the rights of crime victims. In this regard, the Crime Victim Impact Statement developed by WLF must be ranked among its most visible contributions: it is used in many states throughout the country.

The litigation department of WLF is the backbone of the organization. WLF litigates in state and federal courts, bringing its expertise to bear on business, environmental, criminal, administrative, and constitutional law. Scholarship is another area of interest to WLF. The legal studies division publishes a plethora of works aimed at a highly select policymaking audience as well as the media and influential legal scholars. Through its "Legal Backgrounders," "Working Papers," and "Monographs" series, WLF brings its authority to bear on federal and state judges, members of Congress, and key administration officials. It has published backgrounders on subjects ranging from affirmative action to judicial activism; working papers have covered everything from the ACLU's economic views to the Racketeer Influenced and Corrupt Organizations Act (RICO); and monographs have appeared on such diverse subjects as capital punishment and corporate criminal liability.

The media presence of WLF spokesmen is another significant achievement. WLF attorneys give hundreds of major television, radio, and newspaper interviews each year. In addition, WLF's legal policy advisory board lists more than fifty distinguished attorneys and legal scholars, all of whom bring WLF's message to the classroom as well as to the media.

—William A. Donohue

See also: Federalist Society; law and order

Washington Times

The *Washington Times* provides an important outlet for conservative commentary and investigative reporting—both to the Washington metro area and to the nation as a whole through its Internet and "National Weekly" editions.

The Rev. Sun Myung Moon, an exile from communist North Korea, founded the newspaper in 1982. True to its founder's staunch anticommunist beliefs, the *Times* has earned a reputation for its extensive coverage of far-Left regimes around the world. During the final years of the Cold War, the paper took a hawkish anti-Soviet editorial position. Today, the *Times*'s Bill Gertz, author of *Betrayal* (1999), is widely regarded as the media's leading expert on Red China. The paper's editorial pages also rail against the likes of Fidel Castro and

North Korean dictator Kim Il-sung on a regular basis.

In its domestic reporting, the *Times* enjoys a reputation for having inside access to conservatives on Capitol Hill and throughout Washington's policy community. Edited by Wesley Pruden, the paper also boasts a lineup of conservative reporters that is without peer at any other major general interest newspaper in America. Bill Sammon, for instance, rose to prominence for documenting the efforts of Al Gore's campaign staffers to hijack the 2000 presidential vote. His reporting later became the foundation of *At Any Cost: How Al Gore Tried To Steal the Election* (2001)—one of the earliest and most authoritative works on the disputed vote.

In addition to the investigative reporting of Sammon and others, the *Times*'s editorial pages offer a highly visible platform for conservative pundits and policymakers, and it is not unusual for politicians to rally support for their domestic policy initiatives by pleading their cases there.

This reputation for conservative reporting and editorial judgment has proven both an asset and a liability to the paper. Certainly the *Times* enjoys a prominence that extends well beyond the reach of most other metro papers its size. Yet the *Times* often has been criticized for covering global and national issues at the expense of its metro reporting. The paper's editorial position also places it squarely in opposition to the opinions of its target audience in the D.C. area, which is largely left-of-center. Liberal critics also view the *Times*'s conservatism as a hindrance to its journalistic responsibility to report objectively and without bias. These problems have compounded to leave the *Times* in the red since its inception, reportedly losing more than $1 billion since 1982.

Still, the paper serves a missionary purpose of sorts. Circulation and profitability remain secondary to its goal of bringing conservative news and opinion to a large, general audience. Indeed common consensus holds that the *Times* serves as a valuable conservative counterpoint to the left-leaning *New York Times* and *Washington Post*.

—SCOTT RUBUSH

See also: media, conservative

Wattenberg, Ben J. (1933–)

A self-described "Scoop Jackson" Democrat, Ben Wattenberg argued during the Cold War for an assertive foreign policy, especially with respect to human rights, and potent military forces to deter Soviet power. With the fall of the Soviet Union, Wattenberg has maintained that America has a right to be an unrivaled political, cultural, and military superpower, or what he calls, the "first universal nation." Domestically, he supports the intentions and defends the outcomes of the Lyndon B. Johnson administration's Great Society programs, programs he helped formulate as an LBJ speechwriter.

Wattenberg gained public recognition in the mid-1970s as an author and public-television commentator known for defending America against the popular view that the nation had failed the needy and minorities at home and was the aggressor abroad. Against such arguments, Wattenberg presented mountains of data showing that virtually all Americans were better off materially than they had ever been. He also defended the goals, if not the execution, of America's involvement in Vietnam. For Wattenberg, America is the greatest success story in history—and he has the numbers to prove it. His ability to bring dry demographic data to life and use such data to make a political point made him a widely respected spokesman for optimism.

Wattenberg believes that his party's capture by the McGovern wing put it permanently at odds with the American people, who want a social safety net but reject the social permissiveness of the Left. With the end of the Cold War, Wattenberg became increasingly concerned with the impact this permissiveness had had on American culture. This concern, however, continued to be modulated by his aggressive optimism, which is founded on the idea that history is the story of human progress.

—JEFFREY SALMON

Further Reading

Wattenberg, Ben J. *Fewer: How the New Demography of Depopulation Will Shape Our Future.* Chicago: Ivan R. Dee, 2004.

———. *The First Universal Nation.* New York: Free Press, 1991.

———. *The Good News Is the Bad News Is Wrong.* New York: Simon & Schuster, 1984.

———. *Values Matter Most.* New York: Free Press, 1995.

See also: neoconservatism

Weaver, Richard M., Jr. (1910–63)

Intellectual historian, rhetorician, and political philosopher, Richard Malcolm Weaver Jr. was born in Asheville, Buncombe County, North Carolina. He was the son of Richard Malcolm Weaver Sr. and of Carolyn Embry Weaver, originally of Fayette County, Kentucky. Professor Weaver was also the great-grandson of the Reverend Jacob Weaver of Reem's Creek, who was the patriarch of the Weaver family in western North Carolina and whose descendants continue to gather at Weaverville each summer.

Weaver was educated in the public schools of Asheville and of Lexington, Kentucky, where his immediate family resettled in the years following his father's untimely death. In 1932, Weaver earned his B.A. degree at the University of Kentucky, where he was a member of Phi Beta Kappa. In 1933, Weaver enrolled at Vanderbilt University and earned an M.A. in English the following year, but he left Vanderbilt in 1936 without completing the terminal degree. Three years of teaching at Texas A&M strengthened his determination to finish his professional education and round out the sequence of studies he had begun in Nashville with instruction from John Crowe Ransom and Donald Davidson. Therefore, in 1940 Weaver entered the Ph.D. program in the Department of English at Louisiana State University, where, under the direction of Cleanth Brooks, he completed his dissertation, "The Confederate South, 1865-1910: A Study in the Survival of a Mind and a Culture," in 1943. In this work, Weaver laid the groundwork for his entire career. Upon his departure from LSU in 1944 he joined the faculty of the University of Chicago, where he remained for the rest of his life.

Weaver began publishing while still in Baton Rouge, but once he had relocated in the North he published even more frequently. In his 1950 essay, "Agrarianism in Exile," Weaver described his situation at Robert Hutchins's university (and that of a number of his mentors among the Southern Agrarians) as a "strategic withdrawal," an effort to gain an audience he knew, at that time, was not available to Southern intellectuals—so long as they spoke from within the *patria.* Having begun his research with a close consideration of Southern intellectual history, he turned to examine the larger context of radical change within which the struggles of his own people had their most lasting significance. In 1932, Weaver had been a socialist. By the time of his arrival in Chicago, he had become a principled advocate of traditionalist conservatism. With the 1948 publication of his first important book, *Ideas Have Consequences,* he emerged as a major figure in the postwar revival of intellectual conservatism in America. His policy had been to divest the vision of life that he had inherited from his North Carolina forebears of its fortuitous regional overtones in idiom and preoccupation.

Soon Weaver became an advisory editor of *Modern Age,* a trustee of the Intercollegiate Society of Individualists, and a regular contributor to William F. Buckley Jr.'s new magazine, *National Review.* His work covered a wide range of subjects. But his next book reflected his growing competence in a new area of specialization. In *The Ethics of Rhetoric* (1953), Weaver became a leading figure in the restoration of the ancient discipline of rhetoric to its proper place as a basic component of a liberal education. His main argument in these studies was that corruption in the use of language has been a major source of the confusion concerning the hierarchy of human values so characteristic of our time. How a thing is said and what it means, he insisted, are inseparable. Some of his best work in the field of rhetoric concerned the operation of concealed pleading in the diction of social scientists and politicians and in the structures of famous debates. Weaver wrote a rhetoric textbook. He also composed distinguished commentaries on the rhetorical design of famous texts from Plato and Milton. A posthumous collection of his rhetorical papers, *Language Is Sermonic* (1970), contains further confirmation of Weaver's authority in this field.

In the last decade of his life, Weaver did a good deal of public speaking and produced some powerful commentary on the besetting political questions of the day. As an editor of *National Review,* Weaver was especially concerned by egalitarian attacks on his native culture, "the regime of the South." Philo-

Richard M. Weaver Jr.

sophically this preoccupation resulted in his most important work in political theory, *Visions of Order* (1964), and in the collection *Life without Prejudice and Other Essays* (1965), a defense of the prescriptive approach to social questions and an attack on the utopianism of liberal schemes. But throughout the Chicago years Weaver had kept ready for the press the book he had made out of his dissertation. This study, *The Southern Tradition at Bay: A History of Postbellum Thought,* finally appeared in 1968. To this opus he planned to add an American Plutarch, a set of brief intellectual biographies matching figures from North and South. But there was not time remaining to complete this final return to the intellectual interests with which he had begun his research.

In these last years, Weaver returned to North Carolina and Weaverville at every opportunity, to reassuring places, friends, and the magic circle of the blood. Furthermore, at the end of his life he was planning to leave Chicago to accept an appointment to the faculty of Vanderbilt University, where the odyssey of his mature intellectual life had begun. In moving to succeed Donald Davidson at Vanderbilt, he had completed the pattern and was, at the time of his death, one of the most significant Southern thinkers and conservative voices in the nation. His public life was the solitary life of the mind. Yet a passion for dialectics was not the source of his achievements. During a 1950 family reunion, Weaver spoke of the necessity of knowing who you are and where you are from. Concerning these home truths he was not confused. Weaver died in Chicago. He is buried at Weaverville.

—M. E. BRADFORD

Further Reading

Bradford, M. E. "The Agrarianism of Richard Weaver: Beginnings and Completions." *Modern Age* 14 (1970): 249–56.

Kendall, Willmoore. "How to Read Richard Weaver: Philosopher of 'We the (Virtuous) People.'" *Intercollegiate Review* 2 (1965): 77–86.

Smith, Ted J., III, ed. *Steps Toward Restoration: The Consequences of Richard Weaver's Ideas.* Wilmington, Del.: Intercollegiate Studies Institute, 1998.

Weaver, Richard. *In Defense of Tradition: Collected Shorter Writings of Richard M. Weaver, 1929–1963.* Edited with an introduction by Ted J. Smith III. Indianapolis, Ind.: Liberty Fund, 2000.

See also: agrarianism; fusionism; Ideas Have Consequences; individualism; Lincoln, Abraham; localism; Scopes trial; Southern Agrarians; Southern conservatism; tradition

Webster, Daniel (1782–1852)

Regarded as the foremost constitutional lawyer, orator, and statesman of his day, Daniel Webster was a four-term member of the House of Representatives (1812–27), elected four times to the United States Senate (1827–50), and served as secretary of state in the administrations of Presidents Harrison, Tyler, and Fillmore. Landmark cases argued by Webster before the Supreme Court included *Dartmouth College v. Woodward* (1819), *McCulloch v. Maryland* (1819), *Ogden v. Saunders* (1827), and *The Charles River Bridge Case* (1837). As secretary of state in the Fillmore administration, Webster negotiated the Webster-Ashburton Treaty, which settled the long-standing Maine boundary dispute between the United States and England and provided for the searching of ships off the coast of Africa to interdict the outlawed international slave trade.

Too young to have any part in the founding of the republic, Webster sought his highest aspirations in the defense and preservation of the Constitution and the Union. In his 1825 "Address Delivered at the Laying of the Corner Stone of the Bunker Hill Monument," Webster set forth the theme that would guide his public life:

> We can win no laurels in a war for independence. Heartier and worthier hands have gathered them all. Nor are there places for us by the side of Solon, and Alfred, and other founders of states. Our fathers have filled them. But there remains to us a great duty of defense and preservation. . . . Let our object be, OUR COUNTRY, OUR WHOLE COUNTRY, AND NOTHING BUT OUR COUNTRY.

Webster's defense of the Constitution and the Union was dramatized in 1830 during the Senate debate on Foot's Resolution. The confrontation between Webster and Robert Y. Hayne of South Carolina arose when Samuel A. Foot of Connecticut requested an inquiry into the wisdom of suspending surveys of unsold public lands. Hayne, recognized as the spokesman for John C. Calhoun's doctrine of nullification, used the occasion to attack the New England states as part of a corrupt consolidated government's attempt to check the growth of the West and to impoverish the South.

In his "First Speech on Foot's Resolution," Webster expounded on the good that had been accomplished by the federal government's public land policy. Far from being the tool of a corrupt consolidated government, the public lands belonged to all, "a common fund, . . . a common trust to be used for the common benefit." He denied that the prosperity of the states carved out of the Northwest Territory was the result of any attempt by the government to impoverish the South. Rather, Webster argued, the prosperity of those states, guided by the public land policy of the Northwest Ordinance of 1787, was rooted in the freedom made possible by the ordinance, which "fixed forever the character of the population in the vast regions northwest of Ohio by excluding from them involuntary servitude" and "impressed on the soil itself . . . an incapacity to sustain any other than freemen."

Webster's arguments stung Hayne and Calhoun to the quick. The following day, with John C. Calhoun presiding over the Senate, Hayne offered a full exposition and defense of nullification, a doctrine which was used to justify Southern resistance to any attempt by Congress to use its constitutional authority to regulate slavery in the territories. In reply, Webster made his "Second Speech on Foot's Resolution" known ever since, as the "Second Reply to Hayne." Speaking for more than three hours to a packed gallery, he traced the fifty-year history of the Constitution and the benefits derived from the Union. Webster denied the central tenet of nullification, which was that the Constitution was the creature of the states in that it was a compact between sovereign states. Webster responded that: "It is, sir, the people's Constitution, the people's government, made for the people, made by the people, and answerable to the people." The people of the entire country, Webster maintained, had made "the Constitution the supreme law of the land." To those who clung to the "delusion and folly of Liberty first and Union afterwards," Webster responded with the political teaching that always guided his public life, "Liberty and Union, now and for ever, one and inseparable." Webster's replies to Hayne earned him the title "Defender of the Constitution."

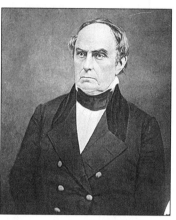

Daniel Webster

In 1832, after the reelection of Andrew Jackson, South Carolina passed under Calhoun's guidance an ordinance that affirmed the right of a state to secede from the Union and pledged if necessary "to repel force by force." Again it was Webster who rose in defense of the Union and the sovereignty of the Constitution. His speech "The Constitution Not a Compact Between Sovereign States" offered, in response to Calhoun's theories of confederation and nullification, a historical and theoretical rebuttal. The Articles of Confederation, Webster conceded, may have created a league or confederation. Even so the Union had existed for some national purposes as early as 1774. Upon ratifying the Constitution, however, the people had abandoned the Articles to form "a more perfect union" headed by a sovereign national government with the Constitution as its fundamental law. Not the states but "we the people" had, by their consent, "ordained and established" a government, not a league or confederation. Whatever role nullification (the power of veto by a single state) had had under the Articles of Confederation, Webster regarded such an understanding as the antithesis of republican government, having no place under the Constitution.

Having long feared that slavery would spread into any territory acquired by the United States, Webster opposed both the annexation of Texas and the resulting war with Mexico. By 1850, however, the status of slavery in the territories again threatened the Union. Northern abolitionists, under the banner "no Union with slave holders," were demanding the breakup of the Union and denouncing the Constitution as "a covenant with death and a league with hell."

Meanwhile, leaders of the slave states were preparing the groundwork for secession and the creation of a Southern slaveholding confederacy.

On March 7, 1850, with both antislavery and proslavery forces willing to destroy the Union, Webster rose to support the compromise measures of 1850 and "to beat down both Northern and Southern follies." He wished "to speak not as a Massachusetts man, nor as a Northern man but as an American . . . to speak today for the preservation of the Union."

From his earliest moments in public life Webster regarded slavery as "a great moral, social, and political evil." He had opposed the admission of Missouri as a slave state in 1819 and voted repeatedly in favor of the Wilmot Proviso, which barred slavery from the lands acquired from Mexico. But although Webster considered slavery a great evil, he believed it was not so great an evil as the destruction of the Union. Webster recognized the authority of Congress to exclude slavery from the territories, and after Texas was admitted to the Union he believed that there was no territory left to which slavery could go. "[T]here is not at this moment," said Webster, "within the United States, or any territory of the United States, a single foot of land, the character of which in regard to its being free territory or slave territory is not fixed by some law." If the Union could be maintained in the face of this latest threat of disunion occasioned by the impending applications for statehood by California and New Mexico, Webster believed slavery no longer would be a divisive issue and ultimately would be eliminated. Yet the Union existed by virtue of the agreements and obligations found in the Constitution, which now were being repudiated in both the North and the South.

In his "Seventh of March Speech" Webster reminded the South that its opinion of slavery had changed over the years. In the beginning, Webster recalled, everyone had viewed slavery as an evil. But now the South regarded slavery as a positive good. The South's interests had changed, and as a result Southerners had changed their opinion of slavery. Webster denied the South's claim to constitutional protections for slavery; slavery existed not by virtue of the Constitution but only by local state law. He urged the South to stop their threats of secession and warned that there could be no such thing "as peaceable secession."

Webster reminded the North, on the other hand, of the constitutional agreements that included not only the power to prohibit importation of slaves but also the Fugitive Slave clause. He urged the North to support all the guarantees found in the Constitution, no matter how despised, as part of the original constitutional bargain. Though abolitionists savaged Webster for his support of the hated fugitive slave laws, his "Seventh of March Speech" was well received and widely recognized for its political courage. The Compromise Measures of 1850 were accepted and the threats both of secession and of civil war receded for another decade.

Webster's orations on the floor of the United States Senate in support of the Compromise of 1850, and his earlier replies to Calhoun and Hayne, did not prevent the Civil War but they were not futile. His defense of the Union provided the time and the understanding necessary to form public opinion and to strengthen the political will necessary to preserve the Union.

—JOHN A. MURLEY

Further Reading

Baxter, Maurice G. *One and Inseparable: Daniel Webster and the Union*. Cambridge, Mass.: Harvard University Press, 1984.

Lodge, Henry Cabot. *Daniel Webster*. Boston: Houghton, Mifflin, 1883.

Peterson, Merrill D. *The Great Triumvirate*. New York: Oxford University Press, 1987.

Remini, Robert V. *Daniel Webster.* New York: Norton, 1997.

See also: Calhoun, John C.; Clay, Henry; Constitution, interpretations of

Wedemeyer, General Albert C. (1896–1989)

A career army officer, General Albert C. Wedemeyer came to prominence in the era of World War II as a strategic planner on the War Department General Staff and as a soldier-diplomat in the Far East. A native of Omaha, Nebraska, he graduated from the United States Military Academy in 1919 and subsequently attended the army's Command and General Staff School at Fort Leavenworth, Kansas, and the German War College in Berlin.

As a member of the general staff in Washington in 1941, Wedemeyer authored key portions of the famed Victory Plan—a broad concept for mobilizing and employing American power for all-out war with the Axis powers. After serving in the Anglo-American Southeast Asia Command (1943–44), he succeeded General Joseph W. Stilwell as commander of U.S. forces in China and as chief of staff to Generalissimo Chiang Kai-shek. In these latter capacities he developed effective working relations with the Chinese government, improved the efficiency of the Chinese armed forces, and helped contain a major Japanese land offensive in China.

While accepting the expediency of a wartime alliance with the Soviet Union, Wedemeyer viewed communism as a totalitarian menace that differed little from the fascism the Western democracies had fought to defeat. He accordingly opposed the postwar advance of communism in East Asia and urged the continued support of America's wartime ally, the Nationalist government of China, in its ongoing struggles against the

Chinese communists. Long after the communists emerged victorious on the mainland in 1949, the question of "who lost China" remained a bitterly divisive issue in U.S. domestic politics. Wedemeyer never abandoned his conviction that the Korean War of the early 1950s and the long agonies of Vietnam in the 1960s and 1970s would not have occurred had China remained in hands friendly to the West.

After retiring from the army in 1951, Wedemeyer assumed leadership of the Citizens for Taft organization during the presidential campaign of 1952. He later played an active role in Barry Goldwater's bid for the presidency and in the campaigns of other conservative candidates. In 1958 he published a memoir, *Wedemeyer Reports!* (1958), which sharply criticized allied policies and leadership in World War II. Distressed by war's human and material costs, he long expounded an integrated concept of national strategy and encouraged a search for more effective methods of public policymaking.

In his later years, Wedemeyer's concerns turned increasingly toward the disintegration he observed in American social life. From the sidelines of officialdom, he devoted much of his energy to the support of such conservative causes as limited government, ordered individual freedom, and private enterprise, as well as to the strengthening of the basic institutions of home, church, and school. President Reagan awarded him the Medal of Freedom in 1985.

—KEITH E. EILER

Further Reading

Eiler, Keith E., ed. *Wedemeyer on War and Peace.* Stanford, Calif.: Hoover Institution Press, 1987.

Stueck, William. *The Wedemeyer Mission: American Politics and Foreign Policy during the Cold War.* Athens, Ga.: University of Georgia Press, 1984.

See also: anticommunism; Chamberlain, John

Weekly Standard

Journalist Fred Barnes, neoconservative intellectual William Kristol, and former Ronald Reagan speechwriter John Podhoretz launched the *Weekly Standard* magazine in 1995. The *Standard* was conceived in response to the 1994 political realignment in which Republicans reclaimed the majority in both houses of Congress. To this end, the *Standard* initially sought "to speak for, interpret and guide this realignment," explained opinion editor David Tell in the magazine's first issue.

Despite its Republican Party roots, the *Standard* has fiercely asserted its intellectual independence. Its staff of political theory and public policy experts has commented on issues ranging from national defense to human cloning, often resulting in open criticism of Republican presidential and congressional initiatives. The magazine in recent years has gained recognition for being the leading organ of aggressive neoconservative foreign policy ideas. Its editors have also espoused a kind of conservative approach to policy matters that they have characterized as motivated by the ideal of "national greatness." Furthermore, in its book reviews and editorials, the magazine has been certain to dissociate itself from those strands of conservatism that bring modernity itself into question. The *Standard* is more interested in promoting conservative policies and principles that have a realistic chance of being influential in today's Washington.

The *Standard* is financed by media magnate Rupert Murdoch, whose News Corporation also owns the *New York Post*, *TV Guide*, and the Fox Broadcasting Company. Thus, the magazine is comfortably situated to influence and interpret, rather than justify, public policy.

While its circulation of 65,000 is significantly smaller than either its left-wing rival, the *New Republic*, or its major counterpart within the conservative movement, *National Review*, the *Standard* benefits from, as it also enhances, the visibility of its editors—Fred Barnes and William Kristol. Both men appear frequently on television news and commentary programs to discuss policy issues under consideration in Washington, D.C. The result is a kind of synergy between editors and magazine.

—SARA HENARY

See also: Brooks, David; Iraq War; Kristol, William; media, conservative; neoconservatism

Weigel, George (1951–)

Often grouped with other Roman Catholic neoconservatives of the 1990s (sometimes called "theocons"), George Weigel combines an affirmation of the free market, a concern for the quality of culture, and the imperative for political freedom with a robust commitment to Christian doctrinal orthodoxy. He received his B.A. from Saint Mary's Seminary and University, Baltimore, and his M.A. from the University of Saint Michael's College, Toronto. He is best described as a public intellectual; presently, he is a senior fellow of the Ethics and Public Policy Center and the author of a dozen or so books, including *Idealism without Illusions: U.S. Foreign Policy in the 1990s* (1994), *Soul of the World: Notes on the Future of Public Catholicism* (1996), and *Witness to Hope: The Biography of John Paul II* (1999).

In his role as a public intellectual, Weigel has consistently sounded three themes. The first is the nature of the relationship of Christianity, particularly Catholicism, to public life. In discussing this theme, Weigel often invokes the centrality of fostering a Christian humanism, which he sometimes calls "incarnational humanism," and exposits and applies modern Catholic social teaching to the American political context. His second theme is the role such Christian humanism played in the endgame of the Cold War. Weigel is certain that, more than economic or political reasons, a spiritual renewal precipitated the revolutions that in 1989 brought an end to communist regimes in Eastern Europe. Weigel's third theme—and perhaps the source of his most significant contribution—is the pontificate of John Paul II; Weigel's 1999 biography of the pope, the fruit of unprecedented access to the Holy See, describes not only the character of the pope's spiritual journey and the contours of his pontificate but also John Paul's important role as a bridge between the Cold War and the post–Cold War worlds, as well as between modern and postmodern thought.

Weigel began his career in theology by teaching at the St. Thomas Seminary School in Washington state in 1975. From 1977 to 1984, he was scholar in residence at the World Without War Council of Seattle. He spent the following year as a fellow at the Woodrow Wilson International Center for Scholars in Washington, D.C., and in 1986 became the founding president of the James Madison Foundation. He then served as president of the Ethics and Public Policy Center from 1989 until 1996, when he took up his current position as a senior fellow at the center.

—GREGORY DUNN

Further Reading

Weigel, George. *Catholicism and the Renewal of American Democracy.* New York: Paulist Press, 1989.

———. *The Courage To Be Catholic: Crisis, Reform, and the Future of the Church.* New York: Basic Books, 2002.

———. *Letters To a Young Catholic.* New York: Basic Books, 2004.

See also: Ethics and Public Policy Center; John Paul II, Pope; Novak, Michael; Neuhaus, Richard John

welfare policy

President George W. Bush's chief political advisor Karl Rove drew the ire of liberals several years ago when he defined compassionate conservatism as "Ronald Reagan Meets Bobby Kennedy." Rove was referring to Reagan's conservative demands for personal responsibility coupled with Kennedy's progressive call for societal responsibility to the poor. However one judges Mr. Rove's interpretation of political history, no policies better exhibit the place where compassion meets conservatism than do the welfare reform packages of the 1990s. Following mounting dissatisfaction with the welfare state's massive expenditures, which yielded increased poverty, decreased employment, and rapidly eroding family structures, a national consensus finally formed during these years that indicted Great Society welfare policies for their unintentional consequences.

In both his 1987 and 1988 State of the Union addresses, President Ronald Reagan invited states to succeed where the federal government had failed. Pointing to a long neglected provision in the Social Security Act enabling states to seek federal waivers from the Aid to Families with Dependent Children (AFDC) program, Reagan challenged the governors to reform the welfare system from the bottom up. The states were quick to accept the invitation. More than three dozen states administered myriad waiver demonstration projects as antecedents to the systematic changes eventually wrought by the 1996 welfare law.

Most of the waiver programs reversed the work disincentives inherent in AFDC. Requiring stricter work activities for more of their caseload, allowing these new workers to keep more of their earnings, and widening the supportive services necessary to sustain productive employment were among the states' most popular requests. Rigorous evaluation criteria and cost neutrality were the federal conditions that accompanied the privilege of state flexibility.

This federal-state bargain helped produce the twin objectives that defined welfare reform in the 1990s: higher expectations for personal responsibility on the part of recipients joined to a heightened emphasis on improved public performance by welfare agencies and their service providers.

The growing success of state welfare reform efforts stimulated the debate that led to adoption of the 1996 welfare law upending sixty years of entitlement welfare. The new law replaced AFDC with the Temporary Assistance to Needy Families (TANF) program, which contains three features that have completely redefined American welfare policy:

(1) *Work requirements.* States are obligated by the federal law to engage more than half of their welfare caseload in work activities as a condition of receiving public assistance. This traded the "something for nothing" culture of AFDC to one of mutual obligation. It also prepared the poor for the only sure route out of poverty: sustainable private sector employment.

(2) *Time limits.* The new law caps the receipt of welfare to five years over a person's lifetime. States are granted permission to impose even stricter time limits. This sent the very clear message that welfare support was to be a temporary way-station—not a way of life. The welfare bureaucracy was affected, too, for now there is a real sense of urgency to its labors.

(3) *Block grants.* States are given unprecedented spending and policymaking authority through a block grant funding structure that caps spending over a five-year period but carries far fewer spending restraints than AFDC's rigid reimbursement formula.

Three prominent Clinton officials resigned in protest of the 1996 law, citing an Urban Institute study predicting two million families would be added to the poverty rolls as a result. Happily, those predictions have proven to be inaccurate. In the first five years after the new law came into force the national welfare caseload had been cut in half, down to 1972 levels. In addition, five million fewer people lived in poverty and the poverty rate for black children reached its lowest level ever.

Even amid these unprecedented successes, welfare policy cannot be maintained at the status quo. Many families remaining on assistance or seeking new help today face severe barriers to employment. The TANF program and other workforce development services are continually being adapted to better meet these challenges. Among the leading strategies are generous wage supplements (e.g., the Earned Income Tax Credit) and necessary support services, such as childcare and medical assistance.

The compassionate conservative welfare policies also acknowledge that government alone cannot meet all the needs of low-income families, nor are their needs merely economic. Thus, the TANF program contains a "charitable choice" provision that opens the door wider to government partnerships with the faith community. In addition, efforts are being made to strengthen families by encouraging two-parent families and preventing teen pregnancy.

—Jay Hein

Further Reading

Besharov, Douglas J., ed. *Family and Child Well-Being after Welfare Reform.* New Brunswick, N.J.: Transaction, 2003.

Murray, Charles A. *Losing Ground: American Social Policy, 1950–1980.* 2nd ed. New York, Basic, 1994.

Olasky, Marvin. *The Tragedy of American Compassion.* Washington, D.C.: Regnery, 1992.

See also: Anderson, Martin; Friedman, Milton; Hudson Institute; liberalism; Manhattan Institute; Murray, Charles; neoconservatism; New Deal; poverty; Reagan Democrats; welfare state

welfare state

Twentieth-century American conservatism can hardly be understood without placing it against the backdrop of the rise of the welfare state. A welfare state is a centralized government that creates and manages services of many domestic varieties aimed at securing basic citizen well-being. Typically, these services were once administered under local public and private institutions. Welfare states grew out of nineteenth- and twentieth-century policies that attempted to maintain a base-level standard of living for citizens through income subsidies, health insurance, retirement income, housing assistance, and educational and vocational training.

The rise of the welfare state represents two monumental shifts in government practice that conservatives have long deplored. The first shift was from subsidiarity in government—in which the many layers of family, congregation, voluntary association, community, county, and state separated the individual from the national government—to a centralized regime that has a direct relationship with individual citizens. A welfare state taxes individuals directly, assigns them unique identifiers such as Social Security numbers, and provides them with services *as* individuals (e.g., direct income subsidies). Conservatives, contrariwise, have long defended the importance of the institutions of civil society that mediate between the large institutions of public life and individual citizens.

The second shift was from a federal government that concerned itself with a common defense, commerce, and foreign relations to a government that centralized services (and the decisions that go with them) in nearly every domestic category imaginable. The welfare state is a service-providing state. Conservatives have long maintained that individual liberty is better preserved, and government decision-making better executed, when domestic concerns remain decentralized as much as possible in the communities in which citizens reside.

The beginning of the modern American welfare state is often attributed to President Franklin D. Roosevelt's New Deal (1933–39), which, among other things, initiated hallmarks of welfare policy such as Social Security and welfare payments to poor families. The welfare state's genesis, however, takes us back a bit further. The late nineteenth century witnessed a trend of consolidation and growth among the Western political powers that ultimately made welfare states possible. The United States decidedly became a union after the Civil War (1861–65), joining an international trend toward increasingly stronger centralized regimes; Otto von Bismarck consolidated the thirty-nine states of the German Confederation into a unified empire during approximately the same period (1866-1871); during this time Britain's Second Empire expanded its power and created governmental bureaucrats; and France's Third Republic built a vast system of secular public schools in the 1880s, expanded its empire around the world, and eventually disestablished the church.

As consolidation and expansion began to characterize the Western world, "progressivism" as a political philosophy began working its way into the American political mainstream with the 1909 publication of Herbert Croly's *The Promise of American Life*. Croly and progressives argued that national programs, headquartered in the nation's capital, were the key to future American success. Progressives believed in the ability of the national government to take responsibility for improving the lives of individuals.

This required money. In 1913, with revenues of $714 million, the federal government began taxing the incomes of individuals, and by 1919, its receipts reached $5.1 billion. Thus, in just six years, federal revenues had more than quintupled, and the federal government had established a direct fiscal relationship with every American household. Mediating institutions became less important as caretakers of communities, and a centralized capacity for service delivery by the federal government began to be achieved.

By the time of FDR's New Deal, the federal government was equipped to become a welfare state. It began offering a previously unparalleled array of services to individuals and families. In 1943, the federal government imposed a withholding tax on wages, and federal revenues jumped from $24 billion to $43.7 billion in just one year; ten years later, revenues reached $69.6 billion.

Because very few checks were installed to curb government growth, welfare state programs had exploded by the time of Lyndon Johnson's Great Society initiative in the 1960s. Many have continued to expand. What began as a cash assistance program for widows with children under the New Deal, for instance, grew into a welfare program for unwed single mothers in the Great Society. What began as policies based on a belief that the truly needy should not be allowed to fall into abject poverty grew into policies that offered poor Americans a range of services, from housing to job training to money for their children's school lunches to family planning education. The Great Society was the culmination of the idea that experts could come together to formulate national solutions to social problems, even though those problems are always manifested locally. In 1964 President Johnson said, "We are going to assemble the best thought and broadest knowledge from all over the world to find . . . answers" to pressing social problems. He created numerous task forces to analyze problems and propose massive-scale solutions. Great Society policies created Medicare, Medicaid, Head Start, food stamps, the Department of Housing and Urban Development, the Model Cities program, and much more.

By 2002, the U.S. Catalogue of Federal Domestic Assistance had grown to include more than 1,500 programs. The budget of the Department of Health and Human Services ($460 billion), the largest of all the federal agencies committed to social welfare (but not the only one focused on social welfare), is approximately 75 percent of the size of the entire nonprofit sector ($620 billion) in the United States.

Reforms in the last two decades of the twentieth century, advanced mainly by conservatives, have addressed the second of the two governmental shifts cited earlier. Welfare reform policies, for instance, have devolved funding and decision-making to the state and local levels. The large share of federal domestic spending that goes to welfare programs is now made through block grants and other means of entering more local control into the federal spending equation. However, the first shift—the welfare state's establishment of a direct relationship with citizens through services and taxation—has remained largely unaffected by recent reforms and is a dominant characteristic in early-twenty-first-century welfare states.

—RYAN STREETER

Further Reading

Beito, David T. *From Mutual Aid to the Welfare State: Fraternal Societies and Social Services, 1890–1967.* Chapel Hill, N.C.: University of North Carolina Press, 2000.

Schmidtz, David, and Robert E. Goodin. *Social Welfare and Individual Responsibility.* Cambridge: Cambridge University Press, 1998.

See also: centralization; entitlements; envy; Friedman, Milton; fusionism; Hazlitt, Henry; Kirkpatrick, Jeane J.; Lasch, Christopher; liberalism; movement conservatism; neoconservatism; New Deal; Old Right; paleoconservatism; privatization; progressivism; therapeutic state; welfare policy

West (the)

Conservatism is distinguished from other modern political movements in that it is primarily defensive rather than progressive. The conservative seeks to hold fast to that which is good—and *experienced* as such—whereas other political movements, tendencies, and ideologies reach for a posited good, one that is not yet possessed. Characteristically, the imagined goods of progressive ideologies are conceived to be "universal" values (such as liberty, equality, and fraternity), whereas the goods and values defended by conservatives are more readily understood as particulars. There does not appear to be a single substance knowable as Tradition, but rather many historical traditions, great and small, each making its claim for conservation on its own particular terms. As a result, there may be a Socialist International or a Communist International—one may even speak of a Liberal International—but there has never been a Conservative International.

There is, however, a "quasi-universal" that conservatives of many nations, and American conservatives among them, have understood themselves to be conserving: *the West*. Obviously, the very word indicates that this good or value is not universal—it excludes, at least, the East. On the other hand, insofar as the term denotes a civilization transcending in space any particular Western state, transcending in time the history of any particular Western nation, and transcending in intellectual scope or catholicity any particular Western philosophy or theoretical doctrine, "the West" appears to stretch toward a kind of universality. To speak of the West is to speak of something cosmopolitan, and yet not deracinated. If it is not an eternal essence, then perhaps at least it is something sempiternal. The defense of the West is close to the heart of what it means to be a conservative in the modern world—yet the definition of the West is also a deep source of conflict among conservatives of various sorts.

As a practical matter, and for evident geopolitical reasons, "the West" has been a term most often employed with respect to matters of international conflict. By invoking loyalty to the West as a whole, one may make "one's own" the political concerns of other peoples who are not immediately evidently one's own. In other words, the West is a basis or rationale for "natural" alliance in time of war. Thus, the British during the First World War were eager for that conflict to be seen by their potential allies as one pitting the liberal and civilized traditions of Western Europe against invading hordes from the East, "the Hun." In this way, isolationist America and unenthusiastic Commonwealth countries could be brought into the conflict as allies in the common defense of (Western) civilization itself—rather than in the defense of British imperial interests. The inclusion of the Soviet Union among the Allies of the Second World War obstructed recourse to the language of the West, but even still, both Churchill and de Gaulle in their wartime speeches spoke of the defense of "liberal and Christian civilization," a good short description of the meaning of the West. With the Nazi defeat and the advent of the Cold War with the Soviet Union, the defense of the West could once more serve as the basis for the NATO alliance against the totalitarianism of the East Bloc.

It was in the context of the Cold War that the West became an especially important concept for American conservatives. Given that context, the term carried in the first instance both geostrategic and economic connotations—mirroring the fact that our communist adversaries understood economics to be at the "base" of all political, cultural, and spiritual life. Thus, despite its cultural dissimilarity, Japan could be understood to stand among the Western nations, since it was a free-market democracy and a U.S. ally, while Spain under Franco might be understood to stand outside the West, since it was not (yet) a NATO member, nor a democracy.

Yet throughout the Cold War period, conservative thinkers worked to reach a deeper level of analysis of the crisis of the twentieth century. Many, following Eric Voegelin, concluded that Soviet communism was an extreme instance of "Gnostic revolt"—in effect, a characteristic *heresy* within the Western experience, rather than something arising from outside the West. If the "armed doctrine" threatening the West was itself a bastard child of the West's own traditions, however, then the defense of the West began not on the tense military frontier dividing the two Germanies; rather, the defense of the West must begin with an effort to educate Western publics about the *orthodox* strains of the Western heritage. But what exactly *were* the "orthodox" traditions of the West?

That last question became urgent after the fall of communism in 1989–91. No longer facing an Eastern Bloc, the contours and boundaries of the West were thrown into doubt. Just as the various strains of American conservatism found themselves in growing tension absent the unifying "glue" of communism, so the various strains of the Western tradition jostled for preeminence in our civilizational self-understanding. The standard nineteenth-century accounts of Western civilization understood the West to have four roots. Athens stood emblematically as the source of the West's philosophical traditions. Jerusalem was the source of the West's religious traditions. Rome was the source of the West's legal traditions. And Germany—the German forests, in which had dwelt the Gothic tribes—was the source of the peculiarly Western spirit of liberty and contract. In such an account, the West was merely an alternative term for "Western Christendom." Christianity, after all, had absorbed ancient philosophy; the Church had displaced the Roman empire as a uni-

versal jurisdiction; and the Goths were converted. In such an account, Christianity is the primary "marker" of the West, and so Rome, the eternal city, might be understood as the main taproot among the other, lesser roots. Such an account had, and continues to have, a particular appeal for traditionalist conservatives: the West they seek to defend is Christendom.

The first challenge to this standard nineteenth-century account of the West occurred during the First World War: for the purposes of that war, Germany had to be located outside the West, and so a rich literature on the Gothic dimensions of the Western experience was lost. As a result, we would in time no longer be able to understand what Montesquieu, for example, meant when he praised England for having retained its Gothic constitution; Western liberty would have to be extracted from other and perhaps less adequate sources.

In Protestant-dominated America, moreover, a Jerusalem-Athens-Rome account of the West was generally thought unsatisfactory, since it conferred primacy to Roman Catholicism as the synthesis of Athens and Jerusalem—something non-Catholics were not prepared to do. Many American conservatives were therefore attracted to Leo Strauss's articulation of the West's tradition as one of Jerusalem and Athens in irresolvable tension. This account had something to offer everyone. Catholics could read Strauss and supply Rome as the arena in which this tension had been worked out in history. Jews could appreciate an account of the West in which the religion of the Old Testament was understood to have priority over the New. Post-Kierkegaardian Protestants could resonate with the either-or existential choice between Athens and Jerusalem that Strauss posited as the fate of every thinking man. For all of that, Strauss's own choice was for Athens, not Jerusalem: Athens is the taproot in this account of the West. For the neoconservative followers of Strauss, therefore, Socratic enlightenment is the primary "marker" of the West. The West they seek to defend is not Christendom, but rather the civilization that enlightenment built and in which universal reason has its home: in other words, the civilization of liberalism.

Of course, enlightenment reason is not a "quasi-universal" to be defended on its own particular terms. It is a universal, simply. The neoconservative champions of an America understood not as the youngest daughter of the West but rather as "the first universal nation" are therefore engaged in a project that more closely resembles the other progressive ideologies which have characterized the modern age than it resembles traditional conservatism. Consequently, it is noteworthy that in the current "war on terror," in which Western societies confront the ancient threat from the East—Islam—we nevertheless hear little from prominent neoconservatives about the defense of the West.

—MARK C. HENRIE

Further Reading

Dawson, Christopher. *Religion and the Rise of Western Culture*. New York: Sheed & Ward, 1950.

Evans, M. Stanton. *The Theme Is Freedom: Religion, Politics, and the American Tradition*. Washington, D.C.: Regnery, 1996.

Gress, David. *From Plato to NATO: The Idea of the West and Its Opponents*. New York: Free Press, 1998.

Huntington, Samuel P. *The Clash of Civilizations and the Remaking of World Order*. New York: Simon & Schuster, 1996.

Spengler, Oswald. *The Decline of the West*. New York: Knopf, 1926.

See also: anticommunism; Burnham, James; Chambers, Whittaker; Cold War; conservatism; fusionism; Kennan, George; liberalism, classical; Strauss, Leo; tradition; Witness

West, American

It is curious but true that the folklore and symbolism of the American West play a central role in American conservative thought and politics. It is not for nothing that such conservative icons as Barry Goldwater and Ronald Reagan so often sought to be photographed in cowboy hats. Their doing so tapped into some of the deepest features of the American soul, and in so doing nicely illustrated some of the chief differences between the American and European varieties of conservatism. Where European conservatism has always tended to stress the value of hereditary institutions and a settled hierarchical social order, American conservatism has instead tended to exalt the rugged, independent, and self-reliant individual, treating with great suspicion any use of state or society to foster greater cohesion and equity. Modern American conservatism has both populist and elitist elements in it, and imagery of the West serves as a particularly powerful rallying point for the former.

The centrality of the West in the American imagination, however, goes back much further, back to the nation's very beginnings. America was understood by the earliest European settlers as a land of renewal, and that theme runs consistently through all its subsequent history. The Puritans thought of New England as a New Zion. Thomas Jefferson saw the western lands as the key to the preservation of the nation's virtuous "naturalness." Mid-nineteenth-century romantics such as Walt Whitman saw the West as an avenue of escape from the past, and the staging ground for a "newer, mightier world." Historian Frederick Jackson Turner's famed "frontier thesis," which argued that the existence of a western frontier had decisively shaped the American national character, was only the most famous expression of a widely held belief that the West was the most American of the sections, precisely because of its distance, physical and intellectual, from Europe. This is why westerner Mark Twain, rather than easterner William Dean Howells or expatriate Henry James, came to be seen as the greatest and most quintessentially American of nineteenth-century novelists.

This last example perhaps explains why, in the twentieth century, a kind of prairie-populist, wildcatting romance of the western frontier has managed to become so closely associated with American conservatism. That this image is based more on the West's symbolic meaning than its reality does nothing to alter its power. To wear a ten-gallon hat was not only an assertion of personal expansiveness, but an act of American patriotism, defiantly affirming the distinctive worth of a manly and independent American way of life. It was also a way of shoring up an independent social ideal that was being steadily eroded and undermined by the corporatism and statism of an increasingly organized world. It was, in short, a way of affirming individual liberty in the most radical sense, a sense that has become as central to American conservatism as the symbolism of the soaring bald eagle.

And just as important, Ronald Reagan's jaunty cowboy hats were an implicit rebuke to the gloom of historical revisionism, which found in the history of the United States nothing but a dismal swamp of genocide, racism, imperialism, and greed, evils all perpetrated by white male European settlers. Reagan wanted no part of such exercises in national self-loathing, and the conservative movement, as well as the national electorate of the 1980s, was pleased to follow his lead. So too was George W. Bush, who chose to downplay his preppy, Ivy League pedigree in favor of an enthusiastically embraced identity as a drawling, folksy, ranch-owning, brush-clearing, cowboy-hat-wearing Texan, and moreover a guy who really didn't much care what other people thought of him.

Bush's many detractors, domestic and foreign, seemed not to realize that in disparaging him as a "cowboy," they were helping his cause, not their own, by reinforcing the connection between Bush's persona and the endlessly fertile symbolism of the American West.

—WILFRED M. McCLAY

Further Reading

Athearn, Robert. *The Mythic West in Twentieth-Century America*. Lawrence, Kan.: University Press of Kansas, 1986.

Goetzmann, William H., and William N. Goetzmann. *The West of the Imagination*. New York: Norton, 1986.

Turner, Frederick Jackson. "The Significance of the Frontier in American History." In *The Frontier in American History*. New York: Henry Holt, 1920.

See also: Bush, George W.; Clay, Henry; Goldwater, Barry M.; Hayes, Carlton J. H.; Parkman, Francis; Reagan, Ronald; Wister, Owen

West, E. G. (Edwin George) (1922–2001)

Writing from a classical liberal or Whig perspective, E. G. West made major contributions to conservative economic thought. Born in Yorkshire, England, in 1922, West obtained a bachelor of science degree in economics at University College, Exeter, in 1948, a master's degree in economics from the University of London in 1959, and a doctorate in economics from the University of London in 1964. He taught at the University of Newcastle upon Tyne (1962–65) and at the University of Kent at Canterbury (1966–70) before migrating to Canada to take up a chair in economics at Carleton University, where he spent the remainder of an extremely productive career. He was elected to membership in the Mont Pelerin Society in 1964.

Edwin West's major scholarship is to be found in his contributions to public finance and public choice (most notably with respect to education policy) and in his many works on Adam Smith. His seminal book, *Education and the State* (1965), challenged the conventional wisdom in favor of universal, compulsory, and free state provision of education by demonstrating that private education provision in England prior to 1870 had provided very high levels of literacy. In light of his historical research, West suggested that education in Britain should be returned to private ownership, that all government subsidies should be withdrawn, and that parents should be free to choose whether and how much to educate their children. His works on Adam Smith played a major role in carrying the free-market insights of the maestro through the troubled second half of the twentieth century.

West wrote ten major books, dozens of monographs and in excess of 170 articles in leading journals of economics, public finance, and public choice.

—CHARLES K. ROWLEY

Further Reading

West, E. G. *Adam Smith.* New Rochelle, N.Y.: Arlington House, 1969.

———. *Education and the Industrial Revolution.* 2nd ed., rev. and expanded. Indianapolis, Ind.: Liberty Fund, 2001.

See also: education, public; public choice economics; Smith, Adam

Weyrich, Paul M. (1942–)

A leading social conservative for more than three decades, Paul Michael Weyrich was born in Racine, Wisconsin, on October 7, 1942. Currently the president of the Free Congress Research and Education Foundation and national chairman of Coalitions for America, Weyrich began his professional career working in local radio in Wisconsin and then as a reporter for the *Milwaukee Sentinel* in the early 1960s. He came to Washington in 1967 as press secretary to U.S. Senator Gordon Allott (R-Colo.).

In 1973, the young Weyrich helped found three separate institutions: the American Legislative Exchange Council (ALEC), the Republican Study Committee, and The Heritage Foundation. Each of these continues to play a major role in American politics today. ALEC is now the nation's largest nonpartisan, individual membership association of state legislators. Weyrich served as ALEC's director from 1975 to 1978. He organized the Republican Study Committee with Edwin J. Feulner and Congressman Philip Crane to advance a conservative agenda in the House of Representatives.

Weyrich served as the founding president of the Heritage Foundation, which was the fruit of another collaboration with Feulner while both were still working on the Hill. They were motivated by the lack of independent conservative research on issues before the Congress, and with the financial backing of Joseph Coors they set about to remedy the problem. Always an activist at heart, Weyrich resigned as president of Heritage in 1974 to work on the fall congressional elections. Because of the crisis surrounding the Nixon presidency, he had concluded that the Republican Party was headed for disaster. He responded by starting the Committee for the Survival of a Free Congress, which would evolve into the Free Congress Foundation and the Free Congress PAC.

Weyrich's influence in the early Reagan years is reflected in his association with major figures of the Religious Right such as Jerry Falwell, who named his organization the Moral Majority at Weyrich's suggestion. Weyrich was voted one of the three "most popular conservatives in America not in

Congress" by readers of *Conservative Digest* in 1981, 1982, and 1983.

A lifelong lover of trains, Weyrich has been involved in transportation issues since his days as a Senate staffer. He was a member of the National Railroad Passenger Corporation (AMTRAK) from 1987 until 1993. Later he was a member of the Amtrak Reform Council, receiving a five-year appointment from the Senate majority leader in 1998. He was elected vice chairman of that council in 1998 and again in 2000.

The health of the larger culture, however, remained Weyrich's primary concern, even as his own religious faith remained prominent in his personal life (he was ordained a deacon in the Melkite Rite of the Catholic Church in 1990). Thus, frustrated by the fact that conservative political gains had done little to arrest his nation's cultural and moral decline, in 1999 Weyrich ignited a firestorm within the conservative movement when he wrote an open letter to conservatives proclaiming the ultimate failure of conservative electoral victories over the last thirty years. He urged his fellow religious conservatives to "turn off, tune out, and drop out" of the popular culture and its influences. And he argued that nonpolitical tactics had to be employed in a new strategy for restoring traditional values and culture.

—CHRISTOPHER THACKER

See also: Free Congress Foundation; Heritage Foundation; political action committees; think tanks, conservative

Wilbur Foundation

Established in 1975, the Marguerite Eyer Wilbur Foundation is known today simply as the Wilbur Foundation and remains located in Santa Barbara, California, where it was incorporated. Its unique residential educational program, however, has since 1979

been conducted in Mecosta, Michigan, at the ancestral home of Russell Kirk (1918–94). Indeed, Kirk was asked by Marguerite Eyer Wilbur to assume the presidency of her foundation in 1979.

By all accounts, Mrs. Wilbur was a remarkable woman. She was born in 1889 in Illinois. A lawyer's daughter and a Stanford graduate she married Van Rensselaer Wilbur in 1919 a year after completing a master's degree at the University of Southern California. At that point she began an active career advancing the fine arts and the craft of writing. She edited five books and translated nine others, including two by Dumas and several about the exploits of Spanish buccaneers and missionaries in early California. She also authored several books, among them a study of the East India Company and biographies of Francis Drake, Phillip II, and Thomas Jefferson. Chief among Mrs. Wilbur's ambitions was to create a program for assisting writers of promise, a colony for serious thinkers and artists. She was a conservative and a great admirer of Kirk's writings, so late in life when she established her foundation she asked Kirk to be an integral part of it. Mrs. Wilbur wanted to establish a little platoon that would endure, but California is an expensive place to engage in such a property-based endeavor. It was in this context that the California-Michigan connection was made. Mrs. Wilbur had the pockets, Kirk had the property, and both shared a vision. As Kirk put it upon accepting the Wilbur presidency: "It seems to me that the work of this foundation is the nurturing of the moral imagination among those who write and read." And so the Wilbur Foundation has done ever since.

The program they developed to extend that mission is the Wilbur Fellowship Program, an academic community centered about the household of Russell and Annette Kirk. Each year undergraduate and graduate students apply for a residential research and study grant. The awardees come to live and work at Piety Hill, the name of the Kirk homestead. This community of writers comprises six buildings and centers on Kirk's Dutch-barn library and his ancestral house. Kirk was the founding editor of the book review quarterly, the *University Bookman*, and fellows often served an editorial apprenticeship on that publication or assisted Kirk in the preparation of his various books and writings. To this day, young students come there to reside, study, and write at what is now the Russell Kirk Center for Cultural Renewal, founded after Kirk's death to institutionalize this unique literary community. Upon Mrs. Wilbur's death, her lawyer, Gary Ricks, assumed a leadership role in this cultural endeavor—or the "Mecosta Mission," as the *Salisbury Review* called it. After Kirk's passing in 1994, Ricks became president of the foundation and has been a faithful steward of Mrs. Wilbur and Kirk's original pact. Annette Kirk took her husband's place on the board, extending the family connection into another generation.

The Wilbur Foundation's fellowship program at Piety Hill and the Russell Kirk Center has been in continuous operation for more than twenty-five years. It counts among its numbers hundreds of alumni currently teaching at secondary and university levels, as well as publishers and editors, officers in the services, business and legal professionals, and religious leaders.

—Jeffrey O. Nelson

See also: Kirk, Russell; University Bookman

Wilhelmsen, Frederick D. (1923–96)

Frederick Daniel Wilhelmsen was a multidimensional and interdisciplinary voice for a philosophically realist, historical, literary, and Catholic vision of conservatism. Born in Detroit, he attended the Jesuit University of Detroit from 1941 to 1943, when his academic pursuits were interrupted by World War II, in which he served as a medic. After the war, he finished his undergraduate degree at the University of San Francisco (1947) and received his M.A. from Notre Dame the following year under the guidance of the prominent neo-Thomists Yves Simon and Gerald Phelan. He was named professor of philosophy at the University of Santa Clara in 1950, a post he held for ten years. At Santa Clara, he led a high-profile protest in response to the U.S. government's failure to aid the Hungarian freedom fighters in 1956. During this time he completed his doctoral dissertation on Jacques Maritain (1958) at the University of Madrid (Complutense) under the tutelage of the Spanish political theorist Rafael Calvo Serar.

While at Santa Clara Wilhelmsen penned several books and numerous essays, emerging as a prominent figure in two great twentieth-century movements—"neo-Scholastism" and the "new conservatism." In 1960 he left Santa Clara for a one-year teaching position at Al-Hikma University in Baghdad, Iraq. The following year he relocated to Spain to become professor of philosophy at the University of Navarra in Pamplona. He was invited to return to America to take part in the re-creation of the University of Dallas by its new president, Donald Cowen. Along with Willmoore Kendall, he anchored Dallas's innovative and influential graduate Institute for Philosophic Studies, the creation, largely, of the educator/literary critic Louise Cowan. Wilhelmsen held a dual appointment as professor of philosophy and politics until his death.

Patrick Allitt has written that among the conservatives of his generation, Wilhelmsen was distinguished by a "brilliantly acute intellect" and powerful rhetorical style. More than any other postwar American public intellectual, he carried forward the banner of a resurgent Catholicism with confidence, vigor, and a romantic swagger. Though he was greatly influenced by modern writers such as G. K. Chesterton, Hilaire Belloc, Etienne Gilson, Gabriel Marcel, and Christopher Dawson, no one exerted a greater influence on Wilhelmsen's thought than St. Thomas Aquinas. Wilhelmsen earned a high place among the vanguard of new Thomists, elucidating his own brand of existential Thomism and metaphysical realism in opposition to modern idealist philosophies in five books, most notably *Man's Knowledge of Reality* (1956) and *The Paradoxical Structure of Existence* (1970). Wilhelmsen was an implacable adversary to any notion that faith and reason were incompatible or contradictory. Rather, he argued philosophically and historically for their essential harmony. Wilhelmsen was considered by many of his contemporaries to be one of the finest Christian philosophers of his day.

Frederick D. Wilhelmsen

In his book *Christianity and Political Philosophy* (1978), Wilhelmsen applied his Thomist philosophy of existence to the political order with profoundly original meditations on the importance of a society's "public orthodoxy" and the nature of and distinction between authority and power. An unrelenting critique of modernity, Wilhelmsen's "Incarnational politics" attempted to retrieve a workable ideal of a sacral, as opposed to secular, society. A proponent of the moral natural law tradition, Wilhelmsen held that the family was the fundamental unit of society. He therefore favored monarchy as the best political regime, believing that it was the best political representation and defense of the significance of the family. Wilhelmsen saw both liberal individualism and Nazi- or Soviet-style collectivism as related manifestations rooted in the same heresy: the rejection of God and the consequent depersonalization of society. This was the foundation for his traditionalist brand of conservatism, one that "defines the modern temper by opposition and contrast." He respected liberalism's role in shaping the social conscience of our time, but dissented from its vision: science liberated from traditional life, the state freed from the religious convictions of the people, and art separated from a living culture, all of which, he argued, had fashioned an age characterized by "abstraction and violence."

Like most of his coreligionists and fellow conservatives, Wilhelmsen fiercely opposed "atheistic" communism. But he was an equally strong opponent of unfettered capitalism: "It would be an abuse of language to label as conservative or Rightist attempts to defend the vestiges of the nineteenth-century laissez-faire order," he contended. Wilhelmsen instead embraced the "distributism" of Chesterton and Belloc, incorporating their belief that capitalism was spawned by the Protestant revolution. By extension and unlike many other conservatives, Wilhelmsen located the ultimate source of the problems plaguing modern society in the Protestant Reformation. He argued that the "Incarnational" core of Catholicism made it a philosophy of "being," as opposed to Protestantism's "eschatological" orientation, which made it (and its descendant, liberalism) a philosophy of "becoming" and transformation. For Wilhelmsen, this shift had led to the contemporary "technologized" society, which he argued sinned against the human spirit by requiring it to conform to the "rhythm of the machine" and its alienating economic scale. These insights led him to understand earlier than most the pioneering importance of the Canadian media philosopher Marshall McLuhan, with whom he began a friendship and correspondence in the mid-1950s. Wilhelmsen also published two works (with Jane Bret) on the social problems raised by modern technology.

Besides his books, Wilhelmsen's philosophical and historical ideas were disseminated through *Triumph* (1966-75), a magazine he cofounded with his friend L. Brent Bozell. In essence, *Triumph* was an implicit statement of dissent from the *National Review* template of modern American conservatism. If in the minds of *Triumph*'s editors *National Review* proposed a contradictory yoking of conservatism to an older variety of liberalism, *Triumph* was a thoroughgoing—if at times self-consciously eccentric—attempt to provide a deeply traditional and Catholic vision of conservatism in America. In Wilhelmsen's first book, a careful reading of Belloc subtitled *No Alienated Man* (1953), he had worked out a view of the historical and sacral character of Christian culture, which he believed was the normative culture of the West (its high point being the Middle Ages). *Triumph* was an attempt to connect America to that cultural norm.

In 1970, with Bozell and other *Triumph* editors, Wilhelmsen led an "Action for Life" or "rescue" mission at an abortion clinic in Washington, D.C.—the first of its kind in America. In the pages of *Triumph*, Wilhelmsen combated Church innovations championed by the architects of Vatican II, for as he put it succinctly, "Catholicism is right—so why change it?" (Wilhelmsen's *Triumph* articles and essays are collected in his 1979 book, *Citizen of Rome*.) In retrospect, *Triumph* was ahead of its time in charting the contours of the coming culture wars in

America, while unrealistic and quixotic in its application of European political forms and traditionalism to the American political cal order (Wilhelmsen was an advocate of the Carlist cause, an antiliberal dynastic claimant to the throne of Spain). Over and against the bland homogenization of modern mass culture, Wilhelmsen raised the colorful flag of Christendom. He is that rarity in any society: a sign of contradiction and, in his particular case, a philosopher with a historian's imagination and a poet's soul.

—JEFFREY O. NELSON

Further Reading

Allitt, Patrick. *Catholic Intellectuals and Conservative Politics in America: 1950–1985.* Ithaca, N.Y.: Cornell University Press, 1993.

Herrera, R. A., James Lehrberger, O. Cist., and M. E. Bradford, eds. *Saints, Sovereigns and Scholars: Studies in Honor of Frederick D. Wilhelmsen.* New York: P. Lang, 1993.

Lehrberger, James, O. Cist.. "Christendom's Troubadour: Frederick D. Wilhelmsen." *Intercollegiate Review* 32, no. 2 (Spring 1997): 52-55.

See also: abortion; Bozell, L. Brent; Catholic social teaching; distributism; Roman Catholicism; Triumph

Will, George F. (1941–)

Syndicated columnist and television commentator, George Will proclaims his mission to be the reconstitution of American conservatism. According to Will, what passes for conservatism in America is little more than libertarianism, or the alchemical belief that private indulgences, checked and balanced, can be transmuted into public virtues. In his view, civic virtue—character manifested in conduct—has to be taught and the state must play a leading educational role. It cannot, in fact, do otherwise, for statecraft is inevitably soulcraft. Will advanced this argument in the Godwin Lectures he delivered at Harvard in 1981, and he has returned to it repeatedly in his columns. Indeed, the cultivation of character may be said to be his controlling theme. Small wonder, then, that he often looks to the ancients for inspiration. It was Aristotle who wrote that the polis "must devote itself to the end of encouraging goodness."

One of the ways in which the Greeks pursued that end was to promote sports. Athletic excellence, Will maintains, is most praiseworthy "when the activity demands virtues of the spirit—of character—as well as physical prowess." Baseball is such an activity and Will writes about the game with unoppressive seriousness. In *Men at Work: The Craft of Baseball* (1990), he emphasized the discipline and dedication required of today's successful managers and players; the Greeks, he thinks, would be loyal fans.

Will comes by his devotion to classical ideals—including classical republicanism—honestly. The son of a philosophy professor, he earned a Ph.D. at Princeton and for a brief interval taught political philosophy at Michigan State and the University of Toronto. From 1970 to 1972, he served on Republican senator Gordon Allott's staff and contributed to *National Review*, for which he subsequently worked. During the Watergate crisis, however, he added his voice to the chorus calling for Richard Nixon's resignation; the beleaguered president, he concluded, lacked the moral vertebrae that support great leaders.

It was Will's independence and erudition that gained him entrée to the *Washington Post*'s editorial page. Since arriving there, he has provoked the Left by savaging its hostility to America, sympathy for totalitarian regimes, and endless talk of "rights." But he has also, at times, incensed the Right by affecting an air of intellectual superiority and championing the welfare state as "an embodiment of a wholesome ethic of common provision"—as a means, that is, of strengthening character.

Will has not concealed the reason for his preoccupation with character. An "almost obsessive student" of the Third Reich, he thinks that its history teaches important, if unwelcome, truths: that no evil is unthinkable and that any nation, the United States included, can sink into barbarism. His fear of moral decline at home has not been allayed by the collapse of communist governments abroad. In fact, the national pathologies that he diagnoses with clinical precision would seem to pose a difficulty for his oft-repeated contention that America is mankind's crowning achievement.

—LEE CONGDON

Further Reading

Chappell, Larry W. *George F. Will*. New York: Twayne Publishers, 1997.

Hirsch, Alan. *Talking Heads: Political Talk Shows and Their Star Pundits*. New York: St. Martin's Press, 1991.

Will, George F. *Statecraft as Soulcraft: What Government Does*. New York: Touchstone, 1983.

———. *The Woven Figure: Conservatism and America's Fabric, 1994-1997*. New York: Scribner, 1997.

———. *With a Happy Eye but—America and the World, 1997-2002*. New York: Free Press, 2002.

See also: Enlightenment; movement conservatism; tradition

Williams, Walter E. (1936–)

Professor of economics, nationally syndicated columnist, and public commentator, Walter Williams has spent his entire career, as an academic and as a public figure, challenging the beliefs of contemporary liberalism. Williams is best known to the public for two reasons: his work as a guest host for Rush Limbaugh's syndicated radio show, and the nationally syndicated column he began writing in 1980.

In his syndicated column, carried in approximately 140 newspapers nationwide, Williams uses basic economic principles to comment on a wide range of topics, including education, gun control, free trade, the minimum wage, corporate welfare, environmental regulations, and tobacco litigation. Four collections of his commentary have been published: *America: A Minority Viewpoint* (1982), *All It Takes Is Guts: A Minority View* (1987), *Do the Right Thing: The People's Economist Speaks* (1995), and *More Liberty Means Less Government: Our Founders Knew This Well* (1999). An uncompromising defender of personal liberty and limited government, Williams argued in these books that the only legitimate and moral role for government is to protect the inalienable right to life, liberty, and property as set forth in the Declaration of Independence and Constitution. The common theme in his essays is that we have moved away from these constitutional principles, to the detriment of our social, moral, and economic well-being.

In addition to his public commentary, Williams is a distinguished academic, publishing in respected economic journals such as the *American Economic Review* and *Economic Inquiry*. Williams's most important academic work is his 1982 book *The State against Blacks*, which was later made into the PBS documentary *Good Intentions*. In this book, Williams argued that, contrary to public opinion, racial bigotry and discrimination on the part of whites in America is not a satisfactory explanation of economic differences between blacks and whites. Using economic theory, historical examples, and empirical data, Williams concluded that government, through the passage of laws that may be well-intentioned (e.g., occupational licensure, minimum wage laws), limits the economic opportunities available to most blacks in the United States.

Born in Philadelphia, Williams earned his bachelor's degree in economics from California State University. He then went on to receive his master's and doctoral degrees in economics from the University of California at Los Angeles, the latter awarded in 1972. After teaching at several colleges and universities, including Los Angeles City College, California State University, and Temple University, Williams joined the faculty at George Mason University in 1980, where he is currently the John M. Olin Distinguished Professor of Economics.

—Joshua Hall

Further Reading

Williams, Walter E. *South Africa's War against Capitalism.* New York: Praeger, 1989.

See also: Limbaugh, Rush; Olin Foundation; Reason

Williamson, René de Visme (1908–98)

A Harvard Ph.D., René de Visme Williamson held faculty positions at Princeton University, Davidson and Beloit Colleges, the University of Tennessee, and Louisiana State University, whose department of political science he chaired from 1955 to 1963 and from 1965 to 1968. He also taught at the University of Michigan, Vanderbilt University, Johns Hopkins University, and Duke University. He served as editor of the *Journal of Politics* from 1949 to 1953 and was a member of the executive council of the American Political Science Association from 1959 to 1961. In 1959 he was elected president of the Southern Political Science Association. Williamson was regarded as a marvelous professor who believed that the teacher must have a strong commitment to his subject matter as well as to his role as mentor.

Williamson was one of the leading political theorists of his generation, particularly in the field of political theology. Indeed, his lifelong fidelity to the reformed Calvinist tradition informed his devotion to family and church, and it became the foundation for his political thought. As he wrote in a 1974 lecture prepared for faculty and students at Davidson College (later cited extensively by Russell Kirk in a 1976 issue of *Imprimis*): "It is my contention that reverence is the root of obedience to and respect for constituted authority, of decent and civilized dissent, of being a member of an opposition which is loyal and constructive instead of destructive or subversive, of regarding nature as God's handiwork to be tended and preserved rather than something to be exploited and desecrated."

—CECIL EUBANKS

Further Reading

Williamson, René de Visme. *Independence and Involvement: A Christian Re-Orientation in Political Science*. Baton Rouge, La.: Louisiana State University Press, 1964.

———. *Politics and Protestant Theology: An Interpretation of Tillich, Barth, Bonhoeffer, and Brunner*. Baton Rouge, La.: Louisiana State University Press, 1976.

See also: authority

Wills, Garry (1934–)

Prize-winning author, journalist, and professor, Garry Wills, a prominent and often brilliant columnist for the conservative *National Review* in the 1960s, had broken with the conservative movement by the 1970s. Wills, a longtime contributor to the *New York Review of Books*, writes frequently for publications such as *Esquire, New York Magazine*, the *New York Times Magazine*, and *Playboy*. He teaches American history at Northwestern University and has lectured at numerous others.

Raised a Roman Catholic, Wills entered a Jesuit seminary in 1951, where he began to question his faith. After six years Wills left and went on to earn a Ph.D. in classics from Yale (1961). While there, Wills finished a study of G. K. Chesterton (*Chesterton: Man and Mask,* 1961). He also, throughout his career, has written on Augustine (e.g., *Saint Augustine,* 1999).

Wills began his journalism career in 1957 as a protégé of William F. Buckley Jr. at *National Review*, criticizing Ayn Rand's objectivism as merely a variation of liberal utopianism, and even contributing "The Convenient State" to Frank Meyer's collection of essays titled *What Is Conservatism?* (1964). But he had a falling out with Buckley; a falling out Wills has attributed to his own opposition to the Vietnam War. He joined *Esquire* in 1966 and began to write for the *New York Review of Books*. He drew liberal acclaim for dismantling Richard Nixon in *Nixon Agonistes* (1970).

Wills went on to deconstruct American founders such as Jefferson and Madison and to sharply critique Ronald Reagan and John Wayne. He won the Pulitzer Prize for *Lincoln at Gettysburg* (1992), in which he credited Lincoln for orienting America towards the Declaration of Independence and equality as its founding principle. Wills's *A Necessary Evil* (1999) attacked anti-government sentiment and argued against a constitutional right to gun ownership. He also authored the fictional thriller *At Buttons* (1979).

A frequent commentator on Catholicism, Wills is an ardent and highly visible dissenter from official Church teaching on a number of sexual and moral issues. From *Bare Ruined Choirs* (1972) to *Papal Sin* (2000), Wills has argued that Church authority resides in the lay Catholic community rather than in what he has deemed the deceitful magisterial hierarchy. He advocates radical changes in church practice and discipline, including the ordination of women.

—MATTHEW BOWMAN

Further Reading

Wills, Garry. *Inventing America: Jefferson's Declaration of Independence.* Boston: Houghton Mifflin, 2002.

———. *James Madison.* New York: Times Books, 2002.

———. *Reagan's America.* New York: Penguin, 2000.

See also: National Review; *Newman, John Henry*

Wilson, Francis Graham (1901–76)

A distinguished political scientist, Francis Graham Wilson was a central figure in the postwar American conservative intellectual movement. Born near Junction, Texas, Wilson graduated from the University of Texas, earned his doctorate at Stanford, and began teaching at the University of Washington. He also served as a member of the executive committee of the American Political Science Association (1937–40). During this period he was awarded a Social Science Research Council fellowship to study international labor relations, a continuation of his dissertation research eventually published as *Labor in the League System* in 1934. His *Elements of Modern Politics*, a theoretical introduction to the study of government directed against the pursuit of "political authoritarianism," appeared two years later.

In 1939 Wilson accepted a position at the University of Illinois, where he remained until 1967. During his tenure at Illinois, Wilson assumed a significant role in promoting the study of political philosophy and humane learning while mentoring many students, including Willmoore Kendall. This was the period of his most significant schol-

Francis Graham Wilson

arship. In his textbook *The American Political Mind* (1949), Wilson articulated many of his central arguments about the nature of the American regime. Two years before Russell Kirk's *Conservative Mind* (1953), Wilson's *Case for Conservatism* (1951) defended a conservatism grounded in tradition rather than ideology. His *Theory of Public Opinion* (1962) was a major critique of the limits of behaviorist methodologies in political science, while *Political Thought in National Spain* (1967) was dedicated to reclaiming the enduring insights contained in the Spanish political tradition. Wilson also wrote two hundred scholarly articles and book reviews.

After his retirement from the University of Illinois in 1967, Wilson taught at Long Island University from 1967 to 1970 before moving to Washington, D.C. In Washington, he became more devoted to political activism, serving as president of Accuracy in Media and the Committee on Constitutional Integrity and as chairman of the Catholic Commission on Intellectual and Cultural Affairs. He left an unpublished manuscript, *An Anchor in the Latin Mind*, portions of which have been published posthumously.

—H. LEE CHEEK JR.

Further Reading

Wilson, Francis Graham. *Order and Legitimacy: Political Thought in National Spain.* Edited by H. Lee Cheek Jr., M. Susan Power, Kathy B. Cheek, and Thomas Metallo. New Brunswick, N.J.: Transaction Publishers, 2004.

———. *Political Philosophy and Cultural Renewal: Collected Essays.* Edited by H. Lee Cheek Jr., M. Susan Power, and Kathy B. Cheek. New Brunswick, N.J.: Transaction Publishers, 2001.

See also: *Kendall, Willmoore; Roman Catholicism; tradition*

Wilson, James Q. (1931–)

Sociologist, author, and professor, James Quinn Wilson's cross-disciplinary analyses of crime incorporating the insights of psychology, economics, and sociobiology have shaped much of the debate about how society should reduce criminal behavior. Wilson taught at Harvard from 1961 to 1987 and is currently the James Collins Professor of Management at UCLA.

Wilson was born in 1931 in Denver, Colorado. He received his Ph.D. from the University of Chicago in 1959. His books addressing crime and urban affairs were influential from the beginning. One commentator acclaimed his *Varieties of Police Behavior* (1968) as "the finest book on the American police ever written." And his 1982 *Atlantic Monthly* article with George L. Kelling introduced the "Broken Windows" theory of crime, which holds that seemingly insignificant but visible crime and disorder (e.g., one broken window) is conducive to the generation of more serious criminal activity in a neighborhood if it is not prosecuted. Mayor Rudolph Guiliani of New York City, a believer in the theory, achieved dramatic reductions in crime from 1994 to 2000 by bringing its insights to bear on the city's police practice.

In *Thinking About Crime* (1975), Wilson called for effective crime deterrence as an alternative to the liberal method of focusing on environmental causes of criminal behavior. In his *Crime and Human Nature* (1985), coauthored with Richard J. Herrnstein, Wilson argued that deterrence was more effective at restraining the natural disposition of people (particularly young males) to choose instant gratification through criminal activity over hard work and thrift. The book did much to put on the defensive those sociological theorists who argued that environmental factors were decisive in generating criminal behavior. At the same time, Wilson maintained that a lack of formative moral training was nonetheless a primary cause of crime. Like Herrnstein's later work with Charles Murray, *The Bell Curve* (1996), Wilson was tarred by the Left as a biological determinist—a simplistic and unfair reading of his work.

Wilson's *The Moral Sense* (1993) more fully extolled each person's individual choice to resist or succumb to natural criminal tendencies, as well as the importance of family life in building character. He attempted to establish through anthropological and sociobiological arguments (rather than religious or philosophical ones) the natural existence of basic universal virtues and obligations like fairness and duty.

—Matthew Bowman

Further Reading

Wilson, James Q. *On Character: Essays.* Expanded ed. Washington, D.C.: AEI Press, 1995.

———. *The Marriage Problem: How Our Culture Has Weakened Families.* New York: HarperCollins, 2002.

See also: *law and order; sociobiology*

Wister, Owen (1860–1939)

Author of *The Virginian: A Horseman of the Plains* (1902), the archetypal novel of the American West, Owen Wister was a securely Philadelphian patrician. When the Harvard graduate (1882) developed health problems he was advised to travel west. Wister returned east to graduate from Harvard Law School (1888) and sporadically practiced law in Philadelphia, but the 1885 trip west had changed his life. During that and many subsequent western journeys, Wister recorded observations that became the basis for several collections of western tales.

Wister is associated primarily with his western fiction, but James Butler has noted that the author should be considered a novelist of manners for whom "character [was] the real issue." The hero of Wister's most famous novel, which the author dedicated to his lifelong friend Theodore Roosevelt, possessed unpolished manners but was the true democratic aristocrat of merit and character. In *Lady Baltimore* (1906), Wister focused on South Carolina society. An unfinished Philadelphia novel would have completed a regional trilogy critiquing the nation's changing moral values.

An active reformer, Wister urged America to participate in World War I in order to aid England in preserving civilization (*The Pentecost of Calamity*, 1915). The author continued to reflect on the meaning of the war in two more books (*A Straight Deal, or The Ancient Grudge*, 1920; *Neighbors Henceforth*, 1922). Wister also penned short biographies of three presidents he admired: *Ulysses S. Grant* (1900), *The Seven Ages of Washington* (1907), and *Roosevelt: The Story of a Friendship, 1880–1919* (1930), the last of which is partly autobiographical.

—ANNE KRULIKOWSKI

Further Reading

Butler, James A. "Introduction." In Romney: *And Other New Works about Philadelphia*. University Park, Pa.: Pennsylvania State University Press, 2001.

Cobbs, John L. *Owen Wister*. Boston: Twayne Publishers, 1984

Payne, Darwin. *Owen Wister: Chronicler of the West, Gentleman of the East.* Dallas: Southern Methodist University Press, 1985.

White, G. Edward. *The Eastern Establishment and the Western Experience: The West of Frederic Remington, Theodore Roosevelt, and Owen Wister.* New Haven, Conn.: Yale University Press, 1968.

See also: West, American

Witherspoon, John (1723–94)

Throughout his career as Presbyterian minister, university president, revolutionary, and statesman, John Witherspoon demonstrated an intellect and strength of spirit that recalled his maternal relationship to John Knox. His life provides an enduring model of the relationship between religion and public life at the time of the American founding.

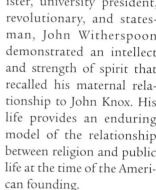

John Witherspoon

In 1768, after more than twenty years of ministry in the Scottish pulpit, the man who would be called "Scotch Granite" accepted the invitation to serve as president of the College of New Jersey (later Princeton University) and emigrated from Scotland to the New World. Witherspoon brought with him a revolutionary spirit and the Scottish commonsense realism for which Princeton would become known.

Witherspoon's career as an American statesman, often forgotten by the heirs of the Revolution, did not escape the notice of his British contemporaries: He was often publicly vilified alongside George Washington, Benjamin Franklin, and John Adams. As a member of the Second Continental Congress, Witherspoon was the only clergyman to sign the Declaration of Independence. He continued in public service as a signer of the Articles of Confederation and as a member of the New Jersey general assembly.

Significant though his political labors

were, perhaps Witherspoon's most significant contribution to the new republic came not in his role as statesman but rather as educator. Though the students under his tutelage numbered only 478, history finds among them a United States president (James Madison) and vice president (Aaron Burr), three U.S. Supreme Court justices, seventy-seven members of the United States Congress, and nineteen presidents of institutions of higher education.

—Douglas Minson

Further Reading

Stohlman, Martha Lou Lemmon. *John Witherspoon: Parson, Politician, Patriot.* Philadelphia: Westminster Press, 1976.

Tait, L. Gordon. *The Piety of John Witherspoon: Pew, Pulpit, and Public Forum.* Louisville, Ky.: Geneva Press, 2001.

Witherspoon, John. *The Selected Writings of John Witherspoon.* Edited by Thomas Miller. Carbondale, Ill.: Southern Illinois University Press, 1990.

See also: American Revolution; Declaration of Independence

Witness

On one level the autobiography of Whittaker Chambers, *Witness* is far more than simply a detailed account of one man's spiritual odyssey from a difficult Long Island childhood to committed, believing, and active membership in the Communist Party to—finally—deep religious faith and complete rejection of communism. The book also explains why people chose to abandon Western democracy for communism during the 1920s and 1930s, provides an account of Communist activity in and around the United States government that had an extent far beyond that which many were willing to believe, and offers a philosophical analysis of the spiritual crisis of the twentieth century, a crisis Chambers believed was epitomized by the conflict between the communist world and the West. This theme seemed to evoke the strongest reaction from many readers.

First published in 1952, *Witness* came on the heels of the McCarthy hearings and the notorious Hiss case in which Chambers was the principal accuser of and witness against Alger Hiss, a high-ranking State Department official. The book was immediately caught up in the ongoing public debate over whether Hiss was in fact a communist guilty of treason and espionage, and also in the debate over communism itself, what it was and how to deal with it. There was already a body of what one reviewer called "the literature of counter-communism," which included works by Arthur Koestler (*Darkness at Noon,* 1940), Ignazio Silone, Andre Malraux, and James Burnham. Chambers's book, however, had a greater impact than the works of these authors for several reasons.

First, Chambers was already well known as the government and society outsider who had accused the "insider" Hiss of treason, a charge many refused to believe despite the evidence Chambers detailed in his book. Second, Chambers gave details about the Communist Party in the United States, its cells, its apparatus, its spies and underground activities, and named highly placed government officials besides Hiss who were communists or communist sympathizers. At a time when many believed the communist threat to the United States was greatly exaggerated, Chambers provided detailed accounts of the sometimes ineffective and sometimes effective labors by communists to undermine the West. Third, and more controversially, Chambers attacked liberalism, arguing that it was, in effect, a weaker form of communism, or a stage on the way to it, and that liberals were intellectually incapable of comprehending the dangers of communism. His attacks on the New Deal were particularly resented by those who argued that the New Deal showed precisely the strength of Western capitalist societies, which had thereby proved that they could reform themselves from within on the basis of moderation or pragmatism.

Fourth, Chambers starkly analyzed the human situation in terms of evil versus good, communism versus belief in God, or what he called "the two irreconcilable faiths of our time—Communism and Freedom." He saw the world in terms of this categorical opposition, for which he was accused of being an absolutist who had merely converted from one extreme to another, insisting rigidly on an absolute religious faith rather than taking a more moderate position on the basis of humane values not religiously based (Chambers had become a nondogmatic Quaker). Chambers's view challenged both those who believed the basic impulse of communism was, although unfortunately perverted, a good that could still be striven for through various socialist and collectivist policies, and those who believed that the foundations of Western freedom and institutions were inherently secular and even atheistic—that morality, a good and well-ordered society, and human happiness could be achieved through secular strategies and policies. Chambers, on the other hand, directly connected real freedom with God and the soul's striving for God, stating "without the soul there is no justification for freedom." To Chambers this meant "every sincere break with Communism is a religious experience."

Fifth, Chambers was, at the time he abandoned communism, as pessimistic about the eventual demise of the West as a believing communist would have been optimistic. Many of those who became communists believed in the inevitable triumph of what they saw as communism's humanitarian ideals over the decadent and corrupt bourgeois world. They preferred to be on the winning side. Chambers, after seeing the true anti-humanitarian nature of communism emerge with particular clarity in the 1930s, came to the conclusion that communism was essentially evil and that he could no longer serve such a cause, even though he himself believed that he was "leaving the winning world for the losing world." When penning *Witness* in the early 1950s, Chambers still believed this to be a correct assessment.

Fundamentally, Chambers's book is an intensely written autobiography of a soul, a soul struggling in darkness to find the light. Some have compared *Witness* to Augustine's *Confessions*. Chambers meant his title in every sense of the word: he had served as a witness against Hiss in court but, even more importantly, he was serving as a witness in the religious sense—a witness to and martyr for the truth. This latter mission gave his book much greater impact than would have come from a mere description of the external events of his life. Despite its occasional flaws, inaccuracies, and omissions, *Witness* was a major contribution to the conservative counterattack against communism and socialism, reinforcing the belief that communism was in fact a significant danger and arguing that a fundamental spiritual weakness undermined the West's power to resist.

—MICHAEL HENRY

Further Reading

Swan, Patrick, ed. *Alger Hiss, Whittaker Chambers, and the Schism in the American Soul.* Wilmington, Del.: ISI Books, 2003

Tanenhaus, Sam. *Whittaker Chambers: A Biography.* New York: Random House, 1997.

See also: anticommunism; Chambers, Whittaker; fusionism; Hiss-Chambers trial

Wittfogel, Karl A. (1896–1988)

Sinologist and political scientist, Karl August Wittfogel is best remembered for his 1957 book *Oriental Despotism*. Born in Woltersdorf, Germany, Wittfogel first studied sinology at Leipzig. He became a youthful Marxist, joined the German Communist Party in 1920, and wrote a number of propagandistic plays that were widely produced. At Frankfurt's famous Institute of Social Research, which he joined in 1924, Wittfogel first developed his theory of "hydraulic bureaucracy." He took as his starting point Marx's notion of an "Asiatic Mode of Production," distinct and different from all four of the modes (primitive communism, slave society, feudalism, capitalism) through which European societies passed in Marx's theory of historical development. Wittfogel argued that in regions of uncertain rainfall, the need for huge water-management projects drove social development toward a form that could mobilize masses of labor under central direction. This led to a static, atomized "hydraulic society" lacking significant private property or constitutional development and made up of politically inert peasant communes farmed by a huge bureaucratic apparatus.

Briefly interned by the Nazis in 1933–34, Wittfogel fled to New York, becoming a U.S. citizen in 1939. From 1947 he taught at the University of Washington, where he wrote *Oriental Despotism*. By that time he had become a committed anticommunist, seeing the twentieth-century communist empires as modern counterparts of the preindustrial hydraulic despotisms. Whatever one may think of his "hydraulic" theories, *Oriental Despotism* provides a gripping and very detailed survey of unfree societies across a great swathe of history and geography.

—JOHN DERBYSHIRE

Further Reading

Ulmen, G. L., ed. *Society and History: Essays in Honor of Karl August Wittfogel.* The Hague: Mouton, 1978.

Wittfogel, Karl A. *Agriculture: A Key to the Understanding of Chinese Society, Past and Present.* Canberra: Australian National University Press, 1970.

See also: Davidson, Eugene A.; equality; managerial revolution

Wolfe, Tom (1931–)

Tom Wolfe might reasonably be called the "agent provocateur" of contemporary American letters. Since the early 1960s he has produced a steady stream of literary journalism and fiction that has combined sharp social observation, a rambunctious prose style, and a sly, indirect moralism to create a large and controversial body of work. His omnivorous appetite for information and documentary writing has led him to cover everything from hippies and stock car racers to astronauts and intellectuals. He has coined phrases that have become staples of American English. His aesthetics and his tendency to frequently turn his satiric gaze on left-of-center elites have earned him a reputation for conservatism, though he has demonstrated little interest in the institutional world of the conservative political movement.

Born and raised in Richmond, Virginia, Wolfe earned his B.A. from Washington and Lee College and his Ph.D. in American Studies from Yale University. Despite his academic credentials, he was drawn to journalism and became a reporter for a series of newspapers, including the *Washington Post* and the *New York Herald Tribune*.

In 1963 he rocketed to national prominence as the author of essays in the nascent style of writing known as the New Journalism. While he did not invent the style, which was already associated with such writers as Jimmy Breslin, Hunter S. Thompson, and Gay Talese, he certainly became its most public champion. Wolfe once defined the New Journalism as "the use by people writing nonfiction of techniques which heretofore had been thought of as confined to the novel or the short story, to create in one form both the kind of objective reality of journalism and the subjective reality that people have always gone to the novel for."

The essays collected in his first book, *The Kandy-Kolored Tangerine-Flake Streamline Baby* (1965) demonstrate his lifelong fascination with pop culture. In *The Electric Kool-Aid Acid Test* (1968) he renders the world of Ken Kesey and the Merry Pranksters as they head out "on the bus" to spread the good news of liberation and psychedelic drugs. *Radical Chic and Mau-Mauing the Flak Catchers* includes the famous essay in which Wolfe recounted an elegant party at the apartment of composer Leonard Bernstein where the wealthy elite of New York happily signed checks for the Black Panthers. His best-known book may be *The Right Stuff* (later made into a film), which chronicles the early years of the U.S. space program.

Another one of Wolfe's abiding interests is that of modern art, which he generally detests. In *The Painted Word* he attacks both the insularity of the art world and the way he believes that modern art since Picasso has abdicated its role of rendering justice to the visible world. *From Bauhaus to Our House* (1981) does much the same for architecture. And in a long essay originally published in *Harper's*, "Stalking the Billion-Footed Beast," Wolfe takes contemporary fiction to task for similarly avoiding the tradition of social realism he believes reached its apex in the works of Charles Dickens and Emile Zola. (It should be noted that many conservative critics do not share Wolfe's reactionary aesthetic.)

In the mid-1980s, Wolfe's writing took a new turn as he shifted to fiction. *The Bonfire of the Vanities* (1987) was originally written as a serial in *Rolling Stone*. It chronicles the tribulations of Sherman McCoy, a rising Wall Street star, who is implicated in a hit-and-run accident that kills an African-American. The ensuing melodrama encompasses the politics, ideology, and cultural life of New York City in the 1980s. Several other novels followed, most recently *I Am Charlotte Simmons* (2004), a "campus novel" of the early-twenty-first century that details the amoral life of American youth and describes a debauched educational system.

Even Wolfe's clothing is provocative: his trademark white suit and white homburg hat have been the subject of much derision, but in characteristic style Wolfe calls his dress "a harmless form of aggression."

—GREGORY WOLFE

Further Reading

McKeen, William. *Tom Wolfe*. New York: Twayne Publishers, 1995.

Scura, Dorothy M., ed. *Conversations with Tom Wolfe*. Jackson, Miss.: University Press of Mississippi, 1990.

See also: diversity; Mencken, H. L.

Woodson, Robert (1937–)

One of America's leading advocates of black self-help through neighborhood organizations, Robert Woodson received a master's degree in social work from the University of Pennsylvania and became an adjunct professor at the New School for Social Research and Policy Analysis. From 1972 to 1978 he headed the National Urban League's Administration of Justice Department. He was an American Enterprise Institute resident fellow and the director of AEI's Neighborhood Revitalization Project.

Woodson edited several volumes stressing the need to involve blacks in tackling their community's problems: *Black Perspectives on Crime and the Criminal Justice System* (1977), a symposium of black criminologists; *Youth Crime and Urban Policy* (1981), a forum of neighborhood organizations helping delinquent youths; and *On the Road to Economic Freedom* (1987), which recommended utilizing black entrepreneurial skills and the strengths of black families.

Believing that local efforts would outperform welfare state approaches that generate dependency, Woodson founded the National Center for Neighborhood Enterprise in 1981. NCNE seeks out and supports low-income community organizations and trains community leaders. Its Violence Free Zone project combats gang violence in major cities.

Woodson's *The Triumphs of Joseph* (1998) argued that politicians, civil rights leaders, and social welfare bureaucrats, having an interest in perpetuating an image of blacks as hapless victims, have suppressed a history of black entrepreneurship that reveals blacks' capacity for self-help, and that black grassroots organizations are reclaiming their neighborhoods from drugs, crime, and dependency and could do better if helped by business leaders who would supply needed resources and receive spiritual renewal in turn.

—JOHN ATTARIAN

Further Reading

Woodson, Robert L. *A Summons to Life: Mediating Structures and the Prevention of Youth Crime.* Cambridge, Mass.: Ballinger, 1981.

See also: enterprise zones; poverty; welfare policy

XYZ

Young America's Foundation

Founded in 1969 at Vanderbilt University by a group of students, including Charles Stowe, Young America's Foundation is one of the principal outreach organizations of the conservative movement. Headquartered in Sterling, Virginia, since 1974 and led by Young Americans for Freedom alumni Jerry Norton, Frank Donatelli, and, since 1979, Ron Robinson, Young America's Foundation is a spin-off of the older conservative student group. Over the years the foundation has developed a comprehensive national program of lectures, conferences, and publications that aim to foster the principles of individual freedom, limited government, free markets, and traditional values.

Among the foundation's most popular programs is its conference series that serves thousands of students each year as an entry point to the conservative movement. YAF sponsors numerous regional conferences as well as, since 1979, an annual National Conservative Student Conference and, since 1997, a National High School Leadership Conference. At these conferences, students are energized by hearing some of the nation's best-known and most eloquent supporters of conservative causes. They are also provided with the training necessary to become agents of change. In addition to the conferences, YAF sponsors a very successful speakers series, bringing conservative speakers to schools across the country. Another well-respected program sponsored by the foundation is the Sarah T. Hermann Intern Scholars Program.

In 1998, the foundation took a major step in preserving a site with exceptional importance to conservatives. By purchasing Ronald Reagan's ranch in Santa Barbara, California, the foundation has opened an important page of history to hundreds of students each year.

—Craig T. Cobane

See also: Young Americans for Freedom

Young Americans for Freedom

Young Americans for Freedom (YAF) is a national youth organization created in 1960 to give young people an independent conservative voice and a means of organizing for political action. It was one of the largest student organizations of the 1960s, with only the radical Students for a Democratic Society (SDS) and the Student Non-Violent Coordinating Committee (SNCC) of comparable size.

YAF began as an outgrowth of the 1960 fight for the Republican Party presidential nomination. Students and young conservative professionals had been instrumental in organizing and serving as foot soldiers in the effort to win Senator Barry Goldwater the presidential nomination. Following Vice President Richard Nixon's nomination for president, a band of young conservatives began to organize, led by *National Review* magazine publisher William F. Buckley Jr. and conservative public relations man Marvin Liebman. Liebman, who played behind-the-scenes roles for numerous conservative organizations and initiatives, set to work in his firm's office, calling his numerous contacts for money and support. Over the weekend of September 9–11, 1960, almost one hundred young conservatives met at Great Elm, Buckley's home in Sharon, Connecticut, and founded YAF. M. Stanton Evans, the twenty-seven-year-old editor of the *Indianapolis News*, wrote the group's founding document, known thereafter as the Sharon Statement. The Sharon Statement was a concise explication of *National Review* editor Frank Meyer's "fusionism," which combined vigorous anti-communism, support for the Constitution as "the best arrangement yet devised for empowering government to fulfill its proper role, while restraining it from concentration of power," traditional conservatives' belief in a God-given moral order and human free will, and the libertarian doctrine of limited government and unfettered free enterprise. Debate broke out over whether to include "God" in the document, with approval by a narrow 44 to 40 vote. Although the debate was friendly, it foreshadowed a deeper divide between traditionalists and libertarians that would ultimately tear YAF apart.

YAF found its base on college campuses, with chapters quickly organized across the country. Like many conservative groups founded during this period, YAF struggled with factionalism. Supporters of Nelson Rockefeller, the liberal Republican governor of New York, and members of the conspiratorially minded John Birch Society each tried to take over, as did those who would make the organization an arm of the Republican Party, not to mention the nakedly ambitious. Conservatives and libertarians maintained a fragile alliance against such efforts. Purges and lawsuits followed. In the end, *National Review*–style conservatives won out, pushing their brand of "fusion." The leadership eventually purged the Birchers in 1965, fearing that their extremism would destroy the group's effectiveness.

YAF's early years were devoted to opposing the Kennedy and Johnson administrations, accusing them of dangerously expanding federal power at home and failing to stand up to communism abroad. During the first year, the logistics and methods for this opposition were often overseen by Liebman, the public relations guru. Liebman had once been a communist, and he brought to YAF the sort of organizing tactics perfected by the Left, including high-profile rallies, the use of front groups like the "Committee for an Effective Peace Corps," pickets, counter-pickets, and petitions signed by prominent public figures. YAFers became adept at organizing and carrying out these activities. Despite his financial and organizational efforts, Liebman became a victim of factional disputes, and his firm quit working for YAF in January 1962.

YAF's most important cause was organizing for Barry Goldwater's expected run for the presidency in 1964. The Goldwater campaign served as a breeding ground for YAF members and a training camp for the group's leaders, many of whom would go on to political careers. A YAF-organized rally for Goldwater held at Madison Square Garden was attended by a raucous crowd of 18,500. "Barry Goldwater made YAF, but YAF also made Barry Goldwater," wrote Lee Edwards, a former editor of *New Guard*, YAF's magazine, and later a prominent Republican campaign consultant. A month before the election, Buckley spoke to YAFers at a New York City rally presumptively held to motivate them for the campaign's final push. Instead, Buckley told a tear-stricken audience that Goldwater was doomed but they had to stay united after their defeat and organize for the future when Americans would be ready for their message.

Although YAF was never a leader in the civil rights movement because of its belief in the right of free association and fears of encroaching federal power, the *New Guard* published a few articles on the subject, which always attacked those who would deny equal rights to blacks. YAF's most important confrontation with racism came at its first national meeting, held in Florida. When their hotel refused to give a room to a black delegate, almost 500 YAFers gathered in the lobby and demanded that the hotel change its policy or they would leave. The hotel backed down, allowed all black delegates to have rooms, and ended its segregationist policies.

Following the Goldwater campaign, YAF organized "Stop Red Trade" boycotts against such companies as Firestone Tire and Rubber, American Motors Company, IBM, and Mack Truck, which sought to trade with communist countries. YAF successfully pushed Firestone to break a contract with the government of Romania when it threatened to distribute 500,000 flyers at the Indianapolis 500 auto race and send a small plane over the speedway towing a banner that read "The Vietcong ride on Firestone," mimicking the tag line from Firestone's commercials. AMC also broke a contract with the Soviet bloc in the face of YAF pressure.

Local elections were also important causes for YAF, with Ronald Reagan's 1966 campaign for governor among the most important. California chapters experienced tremendous growth in the wake of Reagan's successful campaign. YAF would go on to endorse Reagan for president in 1968 against Richard Nixon—at a time when other conservatives like *National Review* and the American Conservative Union equivocated—in 1976 against Gerald Ford, and in 1980 and 1984. Another electoral success in which YAF played a central role was the 1970 campaign of James Buckley, brother of William F. Buckley Jr., who won election to the United States Senate from New York while running as the candidate of the tiny Conservative Party. New York's YAF more than doubled in size as a result of the campaign.

Vietnam, social protest, and the rise of the New Left in the late 1960s and early 1970s produced the period of YAF's greatest growth. Its slogan became "We have not been heard because we were studying. Now we must be heard!" YAF successfully sued universities for breach of contract when they suspended classes during antiwar moratoria, demonstrated against leftist speakers, and counterdemonstrated against leftist demonstrations. "Sock It to the Left" was the slogan for the group's August 1969 national convention in St. Louis. Instead, YAF self-destructed, splitting between its libertarian and traditionalist wings.

As a means to increase membership on college campuses, YAF had often focused its message on opposition to the draft and calls for repeal of marijuana laws. When the issues were put to a vote in St. Louis, a bitter split emerged. Traditionalists either supported the draft or called for its gradual abolition, while libertarians called for active resistance by legal or illegal means. Traditionalists won and added a clause to the resolution condemning draft resistance and the burning of draft cards. In reply, obscene chants against the draft broke out and a libertarian grabbed a microphone in the middle of the hall, violently condemned the resolution, and symbolically burned his YAF card. Shoving and punches followed. Conservatives chanted, "Kill the Commies!" Most libertarians resigned and others were purged. They organized a new group, the Society for Individual Liberty, which evolved into the Libertarian Party.

Internecine warfare, the end of the draft, and the decline of the New Left badly hurt YAF, taking away the issues that had spurred its growth. Apathy on college campuses became the norm. Watergate deepened the crisis, shaking the faith even of true believers. By 1974, the organization was broke and in sharp decline. Nationally, YAF was a shell: a national headquarters with a mailing list and a board of directors most of whom were not even college students. The growth of the national conservative movement in the late 1970s did little to help: the Young Republicans had become as conservative as YAF had been, young people joined increasingly successful conservative political campaigns, and new organizations like the Moral Majority siphoned off young conservative talent. YAF was also hurt because it was not a tax-exempt organization, which damaged fundraising. YAF had become irrelevant.

YAF still survives today, with chapters on a few college campuses. A YAF spin-off, the tax-exempt Young America's Foundation, is much more successful, providing assistance to conservative campus organizations.

—ROBERT WATERS

Further Reading

Andrew, John A., III. *The Other Side of the Sixties: Young Americans for Freedom and the Rise of Conservative Politics.* New Brunswick, N.J.: Rutgers University Press, 1997.

Klatch, Rebecca. *A Generation Divided: The New Left, the New Right, and the 1960s.* Berkeley, Calif.: University of California Press, 1999.

Schneider, Gregory L. *Cadres for Conservatism: Young Americans for Freedom and the Rise of the Contemporary Right.* New York: New York University Press, 1999.

See also: Evans, M. Stanton; Fusionism; Goldwater, Barry M.; Libertarian Party; Liebman, Marvin; Meyer, Frank S.; Young America's Foundation

Zoll, Donald Atwell (1927–)

A political science professor—and self-described "sentimental monarchist" and Tory—Donald Atwell Zoll was a significant, provocative, and productive conservative writer until scandal cut short his career.

From 1966 to 1970 Zoll taught philosophy and political science at the University of Saskatchewan, and beginning about 1972 he taught at Arizona State University. Zoll's volume of essays, *The Twentieth-Century Mind* (1967), maintained that the social underpinnings of American democracy, such as the idea of personal responsibility, were ominously weakening, and that the sixties' widespread "civil disobedience" revealed a rising extremism and rejection of reasoned discourse and accommodation.

From 1969 to 1976 Zoll published frequently in *Modern Age, National Review,* and other conservative periodicals. In a famous exchange with Frank Meyer, Zoll's *National Review* essay "Shall We Let America Die?" (1969) argued that liberal paralysis in the face of New Left radicalism threatened society's existence and that conservatives should assign priority to the preservation of order and resist, "uninhibited by . . . liberal proprieties as to method." Zoll, Meyer retorted, wanted an authoritarian regime and was hostile to America's "tradition of freedom under law and ordered civility." Zoll later attacked Meyer's fusionism as "expedient eclecticism."

Unfortunately, it eventually emerged that Zoll did not, as he claimed, actually hold a doctorate. This led to his dismissal from his teaching post in 1989. He has ceased writing on conservatism, and has apparently made a new career in elephant training. With Alan Roocroft, he coauthored *Managing Elephants: An Introduction to Their Training and Management* (1994), a leading book in its field.

—JOHN ATTARIAN

Further Reading

Zoll, Donald Atwell. *Reason and Rebellion: An Informal History of Political Ideas.* Englewood Cliffs, N.J.: Prentice-Hall, 1963.

———. *Twentieth-Century Political Philosophy.* Englewood Cliffs, N.J.: Prentice-Hall, 1974.

ABOUT THE CONTRIBUTORS

M. D. Aeschliman is professor of education at Boston University.

Patrick Allitt is professor of United States history at Emory University School of Law.

Ralph E. Ancil is the former president of the Roepke Institute and associate professor of business, accounting, and management at Geneva College.

Robert V. Andelson (1931–2003) was professor emeritus of philosophy at Auburn University and a distinguished research fellow at the American Institute for Economic Research.

Cory Andrews was editor in chief of the *Florida Law Review* in 2004–5 and is currently law clerk to the Hon. Steven Merryday, U.S. District Court, Middle District of Florida.

Glenn C. Arbery is the author of *Why Literature Matters* (2001).

Larry Arnhart is professor of political science at Northern Illinois University.

Lila Arzua is staff writer for the *Washington Post*.

John Attarian (1956–2004) was an editorial advisor to *Modern Age*, associate editor of the *Social Critic*, and a contributing editor to *Religion and Liberty*.

Andrew J. Bacevich is director of the Center for International Relations and professor of international relations at Boston University.

Charles W. Baird is professor of economics and director of the Smith Center for Private Enterprise Studies at California State University, Hayward.

John Baker is professor of law at Louisiana State University.

Stephen Balch is the founder and president of the National Association of Scholars.

Laura Barrosse-Antle is a former ISI honors fellow.

Bruce Bartlett is senior fellow at the National Center for Policy Analysis.

John H. Beck is professor of economics at Gonzaga University.

Jeremy Beer is the editor in chief of ISI Books.

Herman Belz is professor of history at the University of Maryland.

Barry Bercier is lecturer in theology at Assumption College.

Herb Berkowitz is managing director of Proactive Solutions.

Bracy Bersnak is adjunct professor of political science at Christendom College.

Thomas Bertonneau is visiting assistant professor of English at the State University of New York at Oswego.

Joseph M. Bessette is professor of government and ethics and associate director of the Salvatori Center at Claremont McKenna College.

Bradley J. Birzer is associate professor of history and director of American studies at Hillsdale College.

Morton Blackwell is founder and president of the Leadership Institute.

David Boaz is executive vice president of the Cato Institute.

Lee Bockhorn is an alumnus of the Collegiate Network.

Peter Boettke is professor of economics at George Mason University and deputy director of the James M. Buchanan Center for Political Economy.

Matthew Bowman, a graduate of the Ave Maria School of Law, currently serves as law clerk to Federal Appeals Court Judge Samuel Alito.

Douglas E. Bradford is an attorney in Dallas, Texas.

M. E. Bradford (1934–93) was professor of English at the University of Dallas. His best-known work is *A Better Guide than Reason: Studies in the American Revolution.*

William M. Brailsford is coeditor of *A Free Society Reader: Principles for the New Millennium* (2000).

Richard Brookhiser is senior editor at *National Review.*

Cicero Bruce is assistant professor of English at McMurry University.

Sean R. Busick is assistant professor of history at Kentucky Wesleyan College.

Gregory S. Butler is associate professor of government at New Mexico State University

William Campbell is secretary of the Philadelphia Society.

Nicholas Capaldi holds the Legendre-Soule Distinguished Chair in Business Ethics at Loyola University.

George W. Carey is professor of government at Georgetown University.

Allan Carlson is president of the Howard Center for Family, Religion, and Society, director of the Family in America Studies Center, and editor of *The Family in America.*

H. Lee Cheek Jr. is chair of the social and behavioral sciences division and professor of political science at Brewton-Parker College.

Alexandria Chiasson graduated with a degree in history from Christendom College.

Bryce J. Christensen is assistant professor of English and director of the English Language Study Center at Southern Utah University.

Craig T. Cobane is assistant professor of political science at Culver-Stockton College.

Eric Cohen is director of the Biotechnology and American Democracy program at the Ethics and Public Policy Center and editor of the *New Atlantis.*

James Como is professor of rhetoric and speech communication at York College of the City University of New York and founder of the New York C. S. Lewis Society.

Lee Congdon is professor of history at James Madison University.

Richard Cornelius is professor emeritus of English at Bryan College.

N. Alan Cornett is a Church of Christ clergyman in Wilsonville, Alabama.

Kenneth R. Craycraft Jr. is the author of *The American Myth of Religious Freedom* (1999).

Alan R. Crippen II is the founder and president of the John Jay Institute for Faith, Law, and Society.

Michael Cromartie is vice president of the Ethics and Public Policy Center.

Ian Crowe is a senior fellow at the Russell Kirk Center.

Ashley Cruseturner is an instructor in the department of history at McLennan Community College.

Hugh Mercer Curtler is professor of philosophy at Southwest Minnesota State University.

Katherine Dalton is a contributing editor to *Chronicles*.

Patrick J. Deneen is the Markos and Eleni Tsakopoulos-Kounalakis Associate Professor of Government at Georgetown University.

Charles Denison is an attorney in Washington, D.C.

William C. Dennis is a writer and consultant on philanthropic giving.

John Derbyshire is a contributing editor to *National Review*.

Marshall DeRosa is professor of political science at Florida Atlantic University.

Thomas J. DiLorenzo is professor of economics at Loyola College and senior fellow at the Ludwig von Mises Institute.

Justus D. Doenecke is professor of history at the New College of Florida.

Brian Domitrovic is assistant professor of history at Sam Houston State University.

William A. Donohue is president of the Catholic League for Religious and Civil Rights.

Andrew J. Dowdle is professor of political science at the University of Arkansas.

Gregory Dunn is an adjunct fellow at the John M. Ashbrook Center for Public Affairs.

Michelle Easton is founder and president of the Clare Boothe Luce Policy Institute.

Henry T. Edmondson III is professor of political science and public administration at Georgia College and State University.

Lee Edwards is adjunct professor of politics at Catholic University of America and distinguished fellow of conservative thought at the Heritage Foundation.

John Ehrman is a foreign affairs analyst for the federal government.

Keith E. Eiler is a research fellow at the Hoover Institution.

Edward E. Ericson Jr. is professor emeritus of English at Calvin College.

Edward J. Erler is professor of political science at California State University San Bernardino and senior fellow of the Claremont Institute.

Cecil Eubanks is Alumni Professor of Political Science at Louisiana State University.

William Edmund Fahey is assistant professor and chairman of classical and early Christian studies at Christendom College.

J. Rufus Fears is David Ross Boyd Professor of Classics at the University of Oklahoma, where he holds the G. T. and Libby Blankenship Chair in the History of Liberty.

Michael P. Federici is professor of political science at Mercyhurst College and director of the Center for Constitutional Studies at the National Humanities Institute.

Fred Foldvary is lecturer in economics at Santa Clara University.

Burton W. Folsom Jr. is professor of history at Hillsdale College.

Elizabeth Fox-Genovese is professor of history at Emory University.

Samuel T. Francis (1947–2005) was the author of *Beautiful Losers: Essays on the Failure of American Conservatism* (1993).

Murray Friedman (1926–2005) was professor of history and director of the Myer and Rosaline Feinstein Center for American Jewish History at Temple University and the Middle Atlantic States director of the American Jewish Committee.

Bruce Frohnen is associate professor of law at Ave Maria School of Law.

Timothy Fuller is professor of political philosophy at Colorado College.

William Funderburk is a high school teacher in Oxford, Mississippi.

Arlan Gilbert is college historian at Hillsdale College.

Alexandra Gilman, former senior editor of *Choosing the Right College,* is a graduate student in Boston.

Gary Glenn is professor of political science at Northern Illinois University.

Timothy Goodman is assistant director of global policy at Pfizer.

Paul Gottfried is professor of humanities at Elizabethtown College.

Lino A. Graglia is professor at the University of Texas at Austin School of Law.

Kenneth Grasso is professor of political science at Texas State University–San Marcos.

Gary L. Gregg is chair in leadership and director of the McConnell Center for the Study of Leadership at the University of Louisville.

Ingrid Gregg is president of Earhart Foundation.

Samuel Gregg is director of academic research at the Acton Institute.

André Gushurst-Moore is a fellow with the Russell Kirk Center for Cultural Renewal.

James Gwartney is professor of economics and director of the Stavros Center for the Advancement of Free Enterprise and Economic Education at Florida State University.

Joshua Hall is senior fellow in education policy at the Buckeye Institute.

Rich Halvorson took his B.A. from Harvard University.

Charles Scott Hamel is president of the Foundation for American Education.

J. Daniel Hammond is professor of economics at Wake Forest University.

A. G. Harmon is a writer and writing instructor at Catholic University of America Columbus School of Law.

Darryl G. Hart is director of the American Universities and the Principles of Liberty Program and scholar-in-residence at the Intercollegiate Studies Institute.

William Anthony Hay is assistant professor of history at Mississippi State University and senior research fellow at the Foreign Policy Research Institute's Center for the Study of America and the West.

Steven Hayward is senior fellow at the Pacific Research Institute for Public Policy and fellow at the American Enterprise Institute.

Jay Hein is the founding president of the Sagamore Institute for Policy Research.

Sara Henary is a graduate student in the department of politics at the University of Virginia.

Mark C. Henrie is senior editor for journals at the Intercollegiate Studies Institute and editor of the *Intercollegiate Review*.

Michael Henry is professor of philosophy at St. John's University.

James Hitchcock is professor of history at St. Louis University.

Russell Hittinger is research professor of law and professor of Catholic Studies at the University of Tulsa School of Law and academic fellow at the American Enterprise Institute.

Christopher H. Hoebeke is systems librarian at the University of Virginia.

David A. Hoefer is an independent poet.

J. David Hoeveler Jr. is professor of history at the University of Wisconsin-Milwaukee.

Michael Jordan is professor and chair of English at Hillsdale College.

Bill Kauffman is an essayist and novelist and associate editor of *The Family in America*.

Daniel Kelly is retired from teaching modern European history at New York University's Washington Square College and York College of the City University of New York.

Russell Kirk (1918–94) was an independent man of letters whose most important book was *The Conservative Mind: From Burke to Eliot* (1953).

Morgan N. Knull teaches philosophy at Northern Virginia Community College.

Kenneth Koford (1949–2004) was professor of economics, political science, and legal studies at the University of Delaware.

E. Christian Kopff is professor of classics and director of the honors program at the University of Colorado at Boulder.

Joseph W. Koterski, S.J., is associate professor and chair of philosophy, chaplain, and tutor at Fordham University.

Stephen M. Krason is professor of political science at Fransican University of Steubenville.

Anne Krulikowski teaches history at West Chester University.

Peter Augustine Lawler is professor and chair of government and international studies at Berry College.

Robert Lawson is professor of economics at Capital University.

Catesby Leigh is an independent architecture and fine art critic.

Leonard Liggio is senior scholar at the Institute for Humane Studies, professor at George Mason University School of Law, and executive vice president of the Atlas Economic Research Foundation.

William Lind is director of the Center for Cultural Conservatism for the Free Congress Foundation.

Damon Linker is the former editor of *First Things*.

William Luckey is chair and professor of political science and economics at Christendom College.

Tibor R. Machan is research fellow at the Hoover Institution at Stanford University and professor of business ethics and free enterprise at the Argyros School of Business and Economics, Chapman University.

Doug MacKenzie has a Ph.D. in economics from George Mason University and teaches economics at Kean University.

Daniel J. Mahoney is professor of politics at Assumption College.

Mark G. Malvasi is professor of history at Randolph-Macon College.

Ken Masugi is director of the Center for Local Government at the Claremont Institute.

Nancy Maveety is professor and chair of political science at Tulane University.

Wilfred M. McClay is professor of history and chair of humanities at the University of Tennessee at Chattanooga and senior scholar at the Woodrow Wilson International Center for Scholars.

James McClellan (1937–2005) was lastly James Bryce Visiting Fellow at the Institute of United States Studies at the University of London.

Forrest McDonald is professor emeritus of history at the University of Alabama.

W. Wesley McDonald is professor of political science at Elizabethtown College.

Brian McGuire is a journalist in Washington, D.C.

William F. Meehan III is the editor of *William F. Buckley Jr.: A Bibliography* (2002).

George Michos is a former Weaver and Salvatori Fellow at the Intercollegiate Studies Institute.

John J. Miller is national political reporter for *National Review*.

Douglas Minson is associate rector of the Witherspoon Fellowship at the Family Research Council.

Mark C. Molesky is assistant professor of history at Seton Hall University.

Glenn Moots is assistant professor of philosophy and economics at Northwood University.

Larry Morahan is a senior staff writer at Cybercast News Service.

John A. Murley is chair and professor of political science at the Rochester Institute of Technology.

George H. Nash is an independent scholar, historian, lecturer, and author of *The Conservative Intellectual Movement in America since 1945* (rev. ed., 1996).

Jeffrey O. Nelson is senior vice president at the Intercollegiate Studies Institute and the publisher of ISI Books.

Jacob Neusner is professor of theology and senior fellow at the Institute of Advanced Theology at Bard College.

Gerhart Niemeyer's (1907–97) last post was professor of government at the University of Notre Dame.

P. Bradley Nutting is professor of history Framingham State College.

Patrick O'Neil is professor of politics and government at the University of Puget Sound and academic fellow at the Foundation for the Defense of Democracies.

William L. O'Neill is professor of history at Rutgers State University of New Jersey.

Edmund Opitz is a senior staff member at the Foundation for Economic Education.

E. C. Pasour Jr. is professor emeritus of agricultural and resource economics at North Carolina State University.

James E. Person Jr. is editorial manager for the Gale Group.

Rorin M. Platt is professor of history at Campbell University.

James Pontuso is professor of political science at Hampden-Sydney College.

Robert W. Poole Jr. is director of transportation studies at, and founder of, the Reason Foundation.

Stephen B. Presser is professor of legal history and law at Northwestern University.

George L. Priest is professor of law and economics at Yale University.

Frank Palmer Purcell, a contributing editor to *Choosing the Right College,* wrote his dissertation on the American philosopher Charles Sanders Peirce.

Ralph Raico is professor of European history at the State University College at Buffalo.

Salim Rashid is professor of economics at the University of Illinois at Urbana-Champaign.

Charles J. Reid Jr. is professor of law at the University of St. Thomas.

Charles E. Rice is professor emeritus of law at the University of Notre Dame Law School

John Richardson is vice president of programs at the Landmark Legal Foundation.

Daniel E. Ritchie is professor of English at Bethel University.

Carey Roberts is professor of history at Arkansas Tech University.

Llewellyn H. Rockwell Jr. is founder and president of the Ludwig von Mises Institute and vice president of the Center for Libertarian Studies.

John P. Rossi is professor of history at La Salle University.

Murray N. Rothbard (1926–95) was professor of economics at the University of Nevada, Las Vegas, and vice president for academic affairs at the Ludwig von Mises Institute.

Tracey Rowland is associate professor and dean of the John Paul II Institute for Marriage and Family in Melbourne, Australia.

Charles K. Rowley is professor of economics at George Mason University and general director of the Locke Institute.

Robert Royal is president of the Faith and Reason Institute.

Scott Rubush is a grant writer at the Intercollegiate Studies Institute.

Gerald J. Russello is an attorney and editor of *Christianity and European Culture: Selections from the Work of Christopher Dawson.*

Claes G. Ryn is professor of politics at the Catholic University of America.

Sean Salai is an alumnus of the Collegiate Network and a Jesuit novice.

Joseph T. Salerno is senior fellow at the Ludwig von Mises Institute, professor of economics at Pace University, and editor of the *Quarterly Journal of Austrian Economics.*

Jeffrey Salmon is senior policy advisor for the Office of Science at the U.S. Department of Energy.

Steven Alan Samson is professor of government and chairman of the Helms School of Government at Liberty University.

Andrew Savchenko teaches in the history, philosophy, and social sciences department at Rhode Island School of Design.

James V. Schall, S.J., is professor of government at Georgetown University.

Gregory L. Schneider is associate professor of history at Emporia State University.

Roger Schultz is professor and chair of the history department at Liberty University.

Max Schulz is editorial director of the Mackinac Center for Public Policy.

James Seaton is professor of English at Michigan State University.

Edward S. Shapiro is professor emeritus of history at Seton Hall University.

Kristen Sifert is the former director of admissions at Thomas More College.

George Sirgiovanni is chair and professor of history at the College of Saint Elizabeth.

Rev. Robert A. Sirico is president and co-founder of the Acton Institute for the Study of Religion and Liberty.

Daniel W. Skubik is professor of philosophy at California Baptist University.

Nicholas Slepko is an International Freedom Corps fellow.

Kevin Smant teaches history at Indiana University–South Bend.

Oran P. Smith is president of the Palmetto Family Council.

S. P. Smith is a lawer for the Department of Energy.

Elizabeth Spalding is assistant professor of government at Claremont McKenna College.

Glen Sproviero is a graduate student in politics at St. Andrew's University.

Peter J. Stanlis is professor emeritus of humanities at Rockford College.

Caleb Stegall is an attorney and editor of the *New Pantagruel.*

Brad Lowell Stone is professor of sociology at Oglethorpe University.

Ryan Streeter is special assistant to the president for domestic policy.

Joseph R. Stromberg is historian-in-residence at the Ludwig von Mises Institute and research fellow at the Independent Institute.

Patrick Swan is editor of *Alger Hiss, Whittaker Chambers, and the Schism in the American Soul* (2003).

Christopher Thacker practices law in Kentucky.

David J. Theroux is founder and president of the Independent Institute.

Ewa M. Thompson is professor of German and Slavic studies at Rice University and editor of the *Sarmatian Review.*

Stephen J. Tonsor is professor emeritus of history at the University of Michigan.

Sam Torode is co-compiler of *Aflame: Ancient Wisdom on Marriage* (2005).

Michael Toth is a graduate student at the University of Virginia School of Law.

Lee Trepanier is assistant professor of political science at Saginaw Valley State University.

Anthony C. Troncone teaches history at Dominican College.

Jeffrey Tucker is vice president of the Ludwig von Mises Institute.

Robert F. Turner is professor of law and director of the Center for National Security Law at the University of Virginia School of Law.

Joshua Vandiver is a graduate student in political philosophy at Princeton University.

Richard Vedder is distinguished professor of economics at Ohio University and senior fellow at the Independent Institute.

John M. Vella is the managing editor of *Modern Age*, the *Intercollegiate Review*, and the *Political Science Reviewer.*

Harry Veryser is chairman of the department of finance and economics at the Walsh College.

David Wagner is associate professor of law at Regent University School of Law.

Richard E. Wagner is the Harris Professor in Economics at George Mason University.

Robert Waters is associate professor of history at Southern University.

Carl Watner is editor of the *Voluntaryist*.

Timothy Webster holds degrees from Princeton and Cambridge and is now a doctoral candidate in political theory at the University of Notre Dame.

George Weigel is director of the Catholic Studies Center and senior fellow at the Ethics and Public Policy Center.

Robert Whaples is associate professor of economics at Wake Forest University.

John Wheldon is a doctoral student in philosophy in California.

Gleaves Whitney is director of the Hauenstein Center for Presidential Studies at Grand Valley State University.

Keith E. Whittington is professor of politics at Princeton University.

Mark Winchell is professor of American literature at Clemson University.

Gregory Wolfe is publisher and editor of *Image* and writer-in-residence and instructor of English at Seattle Pacific University.

Raymond Wolters is professor of history at the University of Delaware.

W. Kirk Wood is professor of history at Alabama State University.

Thomas E. Woods Jr. is assistant professor of history at Suffolk County Community College.

Alan Woolfolk is professor of sociology and director of the core curriculum at Oglethorpe University.

Jean Yarbrough is the Gary M. Pendy Professor in Social Sciences at Bowdoin College.

R. V. Young is professor of English at North Carolina State University and coeditor of the *John Donne Journal*.

Scot Zentner is professor of political science at California State University–San Bernardino.

John Zmirak is a contributing editor to the *American Conservative* and editor in chief of *Choosing the Right College*.

INDEX

Index